THE SCOUTING NOTEBOOK 2001

Produced by STATS, Inc.
(Sports Team Analysis and Tracking Systems, Inc.)

John Dewan, Editor
Tony Nistler, Associate Editor
Thom Henninger, Jim Henzler & Chuck Miller,
Assistant Editors

Statistics by STATS, Inc.

STATS INC.™
PUBLISHING

**This book is dedicated
to the members of the STATS Publishing Department,
whose talent and commitment to excellence
have been evident since our first volumes back in 1990.
More than that, you guys have always been a joy to work with.**

**—Don Zminda
STATS Director of Publications, 1990-2000**

The photographs which appear in *The Scouting Notebook 2001* were furnished individually by the 30 teams that comprise Major League Baseball. Their cooperation is gratefully acknowledged: Anaheim Angels, Baltimore Orioles/Jerry Wachter & Mort Tadder, Boston Red Sox, Chicago White Sox/Ron Vesely, Cleveland Indians, Detroit Tigers, Kansas City Royals, Minnesota Twins, New York Yankees, Oakland Athletics/Michael Zagaris, Seattle Mariners, Tampa Bay Devil Rays, Texas Rangers, Toronto Blue Jays, Arizona Diamondbacks, Atlanta Braves, Chicago Cubs, Cincinnati Reds, Colorado Rockies/Rick Clarkson and Associates, Florida Marlins, Houston Astros, Los Angeles Dodgers, Milwaukee Brewers, Montreal Expos, New York Mets, Philadelphia Phillies, Pittsburgh Pirates, St. Louis Cardinals, San Diego Padres and San Francisco Giants/Kuno. Thanks also to Mel Bailey, who provided our Ichiro Suzuki photo.

Cover by Ryan Balock, Marc Elman and Chuck Miller

Cover photos by David Durochick (Mike Piazza) and Scott Jordan Levy (Pedro Martinez)

First Edition: January, 2001

ISBN 1-884064-88-4

Acknowledgments

The largest and most labor-intensive annual published by STATS, Inc. is *The Scouting Notebook*. The countless hours invested during the fall months produce a volume of work of which we all are proud. Thanks to all who had a hand in our efforts.

The STATS team is successfully anchored by founder John Dewan and President Alan Leib, and lending invaluable assistance to the guys at the top is Jennifer Manicki. Bob Meyerhoff oversees our Research & Development efforts, while Sue Dewan oversees special projects. Jeff Smith leads the Technical Operations Department, which helps support every business unit.

Marc Elman oversees the Publications Department that produced this book and all of our other sports titles. Getting the numbers programmed appropriately fell into the hands of Tim Coletta, with help from Jim Henzler. Chuck Miller painstakingly manipulated the many columns and graphs that are key to the book's design. Tony Nistler and Thom Henninger oversaw editorial responsibilities, with help from Taylor Bechtold, Marc Carl and Norm DeNosaquo. Getting the word out about and fulfilling orders for *The Scouting Notebook* and other STATS publications requires the hard work of Ryan Balock, Mike Janosi, Antoinette Kelly and Mike Sarkis. Ryan designed this book's cover. Joe Sclafani oversees the department's historical data efforts.

We couldn't get the book out without our Data Collection Department. Managing the collection of all the numbers you'll find on these pages is Allan Spear. Special thanks to Jeff Chernow, who oversees the accuracy of our MLB data. Thanks also to the vast network of reporters who cover each and every major league game.

The efforts of our Commercial, Fantasy, Interactive and Sales departments help pay most of our bills at STATS. Steve Byrd heads up the Fantasy Department, while Robert Schur directs an active Interactive group. Jim Capuano heads Sales.

Keeping us in the game is the Financial/Administrative/Human Resources/Legal Department. Howard Lanin facilitates the financial and administrative concerns of the company. Tracy Lickton is in charge of human resources, while Carol Savier aids with legal matters.

Our Research Department for Fox Sports in Los Angeles is headed by Don Zminda, and his team of sports researchers and technical staff provide many of the stats that are broadcast daily from the Fox Sports studios, as well as remote game telecasts on Fox and Fox Sports Net.

—Tracy Lickton/Chuck Miller

Editor's Note

For 12 years, STATS has produced the most comprehensive major league baseball scouting annual in print. What began as *The Scouting Report* back in the '80s has evolved into *The Scouting Notebook* that you hold in your hands today. Besides the different title, however, the book has seen a number of other changes over the past dozen seasons, including some significant differences this year that I would like to take a moment to highlight.

First and foremost is a change that long-time readers surely will pick up on before they even turn a page. For the first time, Don Zminda's name does not appear on the front cover. Don, who co-edited this and all of STATS publications with me for more than a decade, took his talents out to Los Angeles in July to head up the recently-formed STATS research department that supports the numerous studio shows, remote live broadcasts and live game telecasts for Fox Sports. He now oversees the creation of a wealth of sports information that is broadcast into millions of homes each day, and he has done an outstanding job of helping to expand STATS' borders beyond our home offices in suburban Chicago.

During his tenure as Director of Publications, Don played an integral role, actually *the* integral role, in making *The Scouting Notebook* an industry standard. He coordinated all phases of production and built the network of writers without whom a work such as this would not be possible. He also brought three essential tools to the office with him every day: a wealth of baseball knowledge, a truly exceptional writer's pen and a demeanor that made him not only my co-editor, but continues to make him my good friend.

One of the more important things Don left behind was an editorial staff that has helped make this year's transition a smooth one for me, as well as for you, the reader. This latest edition contains the same exclusive, insightful and well-written analysis from our group of nationally-known writers—including ESPN's Peter Gammons and Fox' Tracy Ringolsby—that you have come to expect from *The Scouting Notebook*.

I would like to note the yoeman efforts of my associate editor Tony Nistler. Tony was given the challenging task of coordinating the writers, editors, programmers and stat-checkers for this edition. It was his job to make sure that all the pieces were in place before they got to me, and I greatly appreciate his efforts.

I would like to thank assistant editors Thom Henninger, Jim Henzler and Chuck Miller for their efforts. On top of fulfilling their editorial responsibilities, Tony and Chuck oversaw upgrades to both the hitter and pitcher charts that are a staple of this publication. We hope that you find the diagrams not only easier to read, but also more visually interesting.

I also would like to highlight Thom's efforts, as he and minor league analyst Josh Boyd diligently researched and wrote the prospects reports. Thanks also to Jim, who penned the "Others" section for all 30 teams.

Whether you use this book for work or for play, or both, I'm sure you'll join me in thanking Don for laying the groundwork for *The Scouting Notebook*. . . and then for leaving it in such capable hands.

—John Dewan

The Scouting Staff

The scouting reports on each team's ballpark, manager and significant players were written by the following people, in conjunction with our editors:

Anaheim Angels	Josh Boyd *STATS, Inc.*
Baltimore Orioles	Rick Wilton *STATS, Inc.*
Boston Red Sox	Peter Gammons *ESPN/Baseball America*
Chicago White Sox	Phil Rogers *Chicago Tribune/ Baseball America*
Cleveland Indians	Paul Hoynes *Cleveland Plain Dealer*
Detroit Tigers	Pat Caputo *Oakland (Mich.) Press/ Baseball America*
Kansas City Royals	Marc Bowman *STATS, Inc.*
Minnesota Twins	John Sickels *STATS, Inc.*
New York Yankees	Mike Morrissey *New York Post*
Oakland Athletics	Lawr Michaels *www.creativesports.com*
Seattle Mariners	Mat Olkin *Baseball Weekly*
Tampa Bay Devil Rays	Marc Topkin *St. Petersburg Times/ Baseball America*
Texas Rangers	Gerry Fraley *Dallas Morning News/ Baseball America*
Toronto Blue Jays	Mike Mittleman *STATS, Inc.*
Arizona Diamondbacks	Ed Price *Tribune Newspapers (Mesa, Ariz.)*
Atlanta Braves	Bill Ballew *Baseball America*
Chicago Cubs	Mat Olkin *Baseball Weekly*
Cincinnati Reds	Peter Pascarelli *ESPN*
Colorado Rockies	Tracy Ringolsby *Rocky Mountain News (Denver)/Baseball America*
Florida Marlins	Mike Berardino *The Sun-Sentinel (Fort Lauderdale)/Baseball America*
Houston Astros	David Rawnsley *Baseball America*
Los Angeles Dodgers	Don Hartack *STATS, Inc.*
Milwaukee Brewers	Mat Olkin *Baseball Weekly*
Montreal Expos	Mat Olkin *Baseball Weekly*
New York Mets	Bill Ballew *Baseball America*
Philadelphia Phillies	Tony Blengino *Diamond Library*
Pittsburgh Pirates	John Perrotto *Beaver County (Pa.) Times/ Baseball America*
St. Louis Cardinals	Peter Pascarelli *ESPN*
San Diego Padres	Mat Olkin *Baseball Weekly*
San Francisco Giants	David Rawnsley *Baseball America*

The minor league prospect reports were written by Thom Henninger (AL) and Josh Boyd (NL), and we'd like to thank the player-development personnel who were willing to discuss their teams' farm systems. *Baseball America's* Jim Callis was a big help at filling in some blanks. The "Other Anaheim Angels," etc., were written by Jim Henzler.

I'd also like to offer my personal thanks to Ryan Balock, Tim Coletta and Chuck Miller for the integral roles they played in helping to get this edition to print.

Finally, I would like to thank editor John Dewan, who, among other things, edited every single scouting report with an unwavering eye for detail—just as he has done for the past 11 editions.

—Tony Nistler

Table of Contents

Foreword

by Andy MacPhail
President and Chief Executive Officer, Chicago Cubs

It all comes down to scouting.

No matter how much the game of baseball changes, everything is still predicated on the production of your scouting department. Be it amateur scouting or professional scouting, the ability to uncover talent is the key ingredient in putting together a solid organization.

Scouts are our lifeblood. They're out there, trying to find the next Kirby Puckett or Greg Maddux. They have to look beyond the raw numbers—trying to project the direction each player's career is heading and trying to read what is in each player's heart and mind. Scouting is very important, probably as much an art as it is a science.

In turn, baseball personnel are poring over scouting reports literally every day of the year. It's always important to have as much information as you can, and that's where *The Scouting Notebook* comes in. *The Scouting Notebook* is an invaluable tool, as it helps reinforce the information we have, both on paper and what we've seen with our own eyes. It is a significant supplement in our day-to-day operations.

The Scouting Notebook, along with the STATS, Inc. annual red/green/blue book trilogy of the *Major League Handbook*, *Minor League Handbook* and *Player Profiles*, can always be found around the ballpark. These books are tremendously useful for members of the baseball industry—including broadcasters and beat writers—and are greatly utilized by general managers and their staffs.

I hope you find *The Scouting Notebook* as useful as I do.

Introduction

Welcome to the seventh edition of *The Scouting Notebook*. This is the 12th annual book of scouting reports that STATS, Inc. has created. We get several prominent baseball analysts and have them give us detailed reports on every major league player who saw significant action last season. Our scouting staff features some of the top baseball minds around, including Peter Gammons, Peter Pascarelli, David Rawnsley, Tracy Ringolsby and Phil Rogers. Marc Bowman, Paul Hoynes and John Perrotto have contributed to all 12 books.

This is an encyclopedia of contemporary major league baseball. We tell you about the strengths and weaknesses of hundreds of players. Our analysis extends beyond major league players, too, covering each club's top minor league prospects. We study the statistics and we talk to the scouts. We look for the true ability that may have been exaggerated or obscured by the hype.

The Ballparks

We report on each club's ballpark. We detail how each stadium affects hitters, pitchers and fielders in general, as well as which players it helps and hurts the most. We also project what the park will do to rookies and other newcomers in 2001. We provide vital statistics for each park, such as its dimensions, capacity, elevation, playing surface and the amount of foul territory.

We also present our trademark park indexes, with which readers of our *Major League Handbook* are familiar. In a variety of statistical categories, we show how the home team and its opponents performed at the park and on the road. Interleague games aren't included. By comparing the overall totals at the park and on the road, we get a measure of the stadium's impact. We divide the home totals by the road totals and multiply by 100 to get the park index. An index of greater than 100 shows that the park favors a particular statistic, while an index of less than 100 means the opposite.

Most of the indexes are calculated on a per at-bat basis. Runs, hits, errors and infield errors are figured on a per-game basis. For most parks, we present data for both 2000 and the last three years overall. If the park's configuration has changed since the end of the 1998 season, we present the data for the different setups separately.

Most of the abbreviations are common, with these exceptions:

E-Infield: Infield errors.

LHB-Avg: Batting average by lefthanded hitters.

LHB-HR: Home runs by lefthanded hitters.

RHB-Avg: Batting average by righthanded hitters.

RHB-HR: Home runs by righthanded hitters.

We also list any indexes in which the park ranked in the top or bottom three in its league in 2000.

The Managers

On these pages, we analyze each manager's strengths and weaknesses, style and strategy, and outlook for 2001. We present his 2000 and career managerial record, and we also show how often he used starting pitchers on various days of rest. We compare his use and the performance of his starters to the league average.

We also provide statistical breakdowns detailing his handling of his pitching staff and his use of strategies like the sacrifice, the hit-and-run and defensive substitutions. To qualify for the rankings, a manager had to have his team for at least 100 games in 2000. Some of the terms listed in the statistics and rankings sections may be unfamiliar. They include:

Hit & Run Success %: The percentage of hit-and-runs resulting in baserunner advancement with no double play.

Platoon Pct.: Frequency that the manager gets his hitters the platoon advantage (lefty vs. righty and vice versa). Switch-hitters always are considered to have the advantage.

Defensive Subs: The number of straight defensive substitutions with the team leading by four runs or fewer.

High-Pitch Outings: The number of times a manager's starting pitchers threw more than 120 pitches in a ballgame.

Quick/Slow Hooks: A Quick Hook occurs when a pitcher is removed after having pitched less than six innings and given up three runs or fewer. A Slow Hook occurs when a pitcher works more than nine innings, allows seven or more runs, or his total innings and runs equal 13 or more.

First-Batter Platoon Percentage: The percentage of times the managers' relievers had a platoon advantage over the first hitter they faced (lefty vs. lefty, righty vs. righty).

Mid-Inning Changes: The number of times the manager changed pitchers in the middle of an inning.

Pitchouts with a Runner Moving: The number of times the opposition was running when the manager called a pitchout.

Sacrifice Bunt Percentage: The percentage of bunts resulting in sacrifices or hits with runners on.

Starting Lineups Used: Based on batting order, 1-8 for National Leaguers, 1-9 for American Leaguers.

2+ Pitching Changes in Low-Scoring Games: The number of times a manager used at least three pitchers in a game in which his team allowed two runs or fewer.

The Players

For each major league team, we give extensive reports on 22 players. Twelve of them get a full page of scouting information, while 10 receive half-page reports. Because we like to get this book into your hands as soon as possible, players are listed with their 2000 clubs. We keep abreast of postseason transactions, and all player moves that took place through December 19, 2000 are noted. If you can't find a particular player, check the detailed index in the back.

Pages for primary players have two columns. The left column provides an in-depth report by an analyst. The right column contains statistical information:

Position: The first position shown is the player's most common position in 2000. Positions at which he played 10 or more games also are shown. For pitchers, SP stands for starting pitcher and RP for relief pitcher.

Bats and Throws: L stands for lefthanded, R stands for righthanded, and B stands for both (switch-hitter).

Ht: Height.

Wt: Weight.

Opening Day Age: This is the player's age on April 1, 2001.

Born: Birthdate and birthplace.

ML Seasons: This number indicates the number of different major league seasons in which the player has appeared. For example, if a player was called up to play in September in each of the last three seasons, the number shown would be 3. This is different from major league service, which is used to determine arbitration and free-agency eligibility.

Overall Statistics: These are traditional major league statistics for the player's 2000 season and his career. The one non-traditional stat that appears here is ratio, which is the number of baserunners allowed by a pitcher per inning:
((hits + walks)/IP).

Where He Hits The Ball

For every major league game in 2000, STATS reporters entered into our computers every ball hit into play. They kept track of the type of batted balls—grounders, flyballs, popups, line drives and bunts—as well as the distance each ball traveled. Direction was tracked by dividing the field into 26 "wedges" projecting out from home plate. Distance was measured in 10-foot increments outward from home plate.

Below are the hitting diagrams for lefthanded-hitting Warren Morris of the Pittsburgh Pirates. The chart on the left shows where Morris hit the ball against lefthanders, while the chart on the right shows what he did against righties.

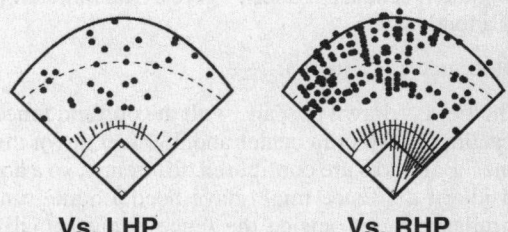

Vs. LHP   **Vs. RHP**

In the diagrams, groundballs and short line drives are shown by the lines of various lengths in the

infield. The longer the line, the more groundballs and line drives were hit in that direction. As you can see from the charts on page 3, Morris didn't face lefthanded pitching often during 2000. When he played, he obviously sprayed the ball all over the field. As a rookie in 1999, Morris had some success turning on inside fastballs. Clearly he turned on many pitches that he hit through the infield against righthanded pitching in 2000.

Last summer, however, as his essay on page 605 states, "Morris was fed a steady diet of fastballs and breaking pitches on the outside corner, and he spent most of the season lifting weak flyballs to the opposite field." That adjustment pitchers made to Morris, who had a much better season in 1999, is apparent in his hitting chart. That's a steady stream of mid-outfield dots running from the left-field line into right-center.

A lot of experimentation went into producing the hitting diagrams. When we first started, we tried to show every single batted ball that was put into play by each player. We found that the charts became very cluttered for everyday players, so we began experimenting with trying to show only the most meaningful information. When all was said and done, here's what we ended up with:

a. Popups and bunts are excluded. We excluded popups because 95 percent of these are caught regardless of how fielders are positioned. We excluded bunts because defensing a bunt is an entirely different strategy primarily used against a select number of players or in specific situations.

b. For groundballs and short line drives, we include all batted balls.

c. For balls hit to the outfield, we excluded isolated points only if the chart contains more than 125 batted balls to the outfield. In such cases, if a player hits only one ball to a given area and had no other batted balls in the vicinity all season, we exclude it because it doesn't give a true indication of a tendency.

Other notes of interest:

The field is drawn to scale, with the outfield fence reaching 400 feet in center and 330 feet down the lines. Ballparks are configured differently, so a dot inside of the fence might have been a home run. Similarly, a dot outside the fence might actually have been in play.

Line drives under 170 feet are part of the infield.

We give responsibility for short liners to the infielders.

No distinction is made between hits and outs.

How Often He Throws Strikes

Our STATS reporters also tracked every pitch thrown in a major league game in 2000. The pitching graphs show how often the hurler throws strikes in different situations. Our data shows most pitchers will toss a strike between 40 and 80 percent of the time. Therefore we've constructed the chart to represent the 40-80 percent range.

The strike count includes swinging strikes, taken strikes, foul balls and balls put in play. Though not all batted balls come on pitches thrown within the strike zone, our theory is that most are and the ones that aren't would be difficult to judge. Our charts reflect these assumptions.

The charts are broken into four categories. *All Pitches* is straightforward, as is *First Pitch*. We define *Ahead* as counts with more strikes than balls. *Behind* includes counts with more balls than strikes. The appropriate league average is shown in each chart.

Below are the 2000 league averages. The National League threw a slightly higher percentage of strikes than the American League, as it has in all 12 years we have tracked this.

Strike Percentage by League — 2000		
	American	National
All Pitches	61.3%	61.6%
First Pitch	56.3%	56.3%
Ahead in the Count	59.0%	60.3%
Behind in the Count	66.2%	65.8%

2000 Situational Stats

There are eight situational breakdowns for every primary player. *Home* and *Road* show performance in his home ballpark and on the road. *First Half* and *Scnd Half* show performance before and after the 2000 All-Star break. For hitters, *LHP* and *RHP* show how the player hit against lefthanders and righthanders. For pitchers, *LHB* and *RHB* show how the opposition lefthanders and righthanders hit against the pitcher. *Sc Pos* shows batting or pitching performance with runners in scoring position. *Clutch* shows batting or pitching performance in clutch situations, defined as the seventh inning or later with the batting team ahead by one run, tied or with the tying run on base, at bat or on deck. Our definition is consistent with save situations.

2000 Rankings

This section shows how the player ranked in his league and among his teammates. Because of space considerations, we omitted some of the less interesting rankings when a player placed high in numerous categories.

We include many less traditional categories. The Definitions and Qualifications section below provides details for these statistics.

Definitions and Qualifications

The following are definitions and qualifications for the Major League Leaders and Rankings.

Definitions:

Times on Base — Hits plus walks plus hit-by-pitch.

Groundball-Flyball Ratio — Groundballs hit divided by the total of flyballs and popups hit. Bunts and line drives are excluded.

Runs/Times on Base — Runs scored divided by times on base.

Clutch — A player's batting average in the late innings of close games, defined as the seventh inning or later with the batting team ahead by one run, tied or with the tying run on base, at bat or on deck.

Bases Loaded — A player's batting average in bases-loaded situations.

GDP per GDP situation — Groundball double plays divided by groundball double-play situations, defined as a man on first base with less than two out.

Percentage of Pitches Taken — The percentage of pitches a player lets go by without swinging.

Percentage Swings Put In Play — The percentage of swings resulting in a batted ball into fair territory or a foul-ball out.

Run Support per Nine Innings — The number of runs scored for a pitcher while he was pitching, scaled to a nine-inning figure.

Baserunners per Nine Innings — The total of hits, walks and hit batsmen allowed per nine innings.

Strikeout-Walk Ratio — Strikeouts divided by walks.

Stolen-Base Percentage Allowed — Stolen bases divided by stolen-base attempts.

Save Percentage — Saves divided by save opportunities. Save opportunities include saves plus blown saves.

Blown Saves — A blown save is charged any time a pitcher enters a game in a save situation and loses the lead. A save situation is defined as any time a reliever enters the game with a lead, isn't the pitcher of record and either a) pitches at least one inning with a lead of no more than three runs; b) enters the game with the potential tying run on base, at bat or on deck; or c) pitches effectively for at least three innings.

Holds — A hold is given to a pitcher when he enters a game in a save situation and is removed before the end of the game while maintaining his team's lead. The pitcher must retire at least one batter to get a hold.

Percentage of Inherited Runners Scored — Percentage of runners already on base when a pitcher enters a game that he allows to score.

First Batter Efficiency — The batting average allowed by a reliever to the first batter he faces in a game.

Qualifications:

In order to be ranked, a player had to qualify with a minimum number of opportunities, as follows:

Batters

Batting average, slugging percentage, on-base percentage, home run frequency, groundball-flyball ratio, runs scored per time reached base and pitches seen per plate appearance — 3.1 plate appearances per team game

Percentage of pitches taken, lowest percentage of swings that missed and percentage of swings put into play — 9.26 pitches seen per team game

Percentage of extra bases taken as a runner — .09 opportunities to advance per team game

Stolen-base percentage — .12 stolen-base attempts per team game

Runners in scoring position — .62 plate appearances with runners in scoring position per team game

Clutch — .31 plate appearances in the clutch per team game

Bases loaded — .06 plate appearances with the bases loaded per team game

GDP per GDP situation — .31 plate appearances in GDP situations per team game

BA vs. LHP — .77 plate appearances against lefthanders per team game

BA vs. RHP — 2.33 plate appearances against righthanders per team game

BA at home — 1.55 plate appearances at home per team game

BA on the road — 1.55 plate appearances on the road per team game

Leadoff on-base percentage — .93 plate appearances in the No. 1 lineup spot per team game

Cleanup slugging percentage — .93 plate appearances in the No. 4 lineup spot per team game

BA on 3-1 count — .06 plate appearances with a 3-1 count per team game

BA with 2 strikes — .62 plate appearances with two strikes per team game

BA on 0-2 count — .12 plate appearances with an 0-2 count per team game

BA on 3-2 count — .12 plate appearances with a 3-2 count per team game

Pitchers

Earned run average, run support per nine innings, baserunners per nine innings, batting average allowed, slugging percentage allowed, on-base percentage allowed, home runs per nine innings, strikeouts per nine innings, strikeout-walk ratio, stolen-base percentage allowed, GDPs per nine innings, pitches thrown per batter and groundball-flyball ratio against — one inning per team game

Winning percentage — .09 decisions per team game

GDPs induced per GDP situation — .19 batters faced in GDP situations per team game

BA allowed, runners in scoring position — .77 batters faced with runners in scoring position per team game

ERA at home — .5 innings at home per team game

ERA on the road — .5 innings on the road per team game

BA vs. LHB — .77 lefthanders faced per team game

BA vs. RHB — 1.39 righthanders faced per team game

Relievers

ERA, batting average allowed, baserunners per nine innings, strikeouts per nine innings — .31 relief innings per team game

Save percentage — .12 save opportunities per team game

Percentage of inherited runners scoring — .19 inherited runners per team game

First batter efficiency — .25 games in relief per team game

Fielders

Percentage caught stealing by catchers — .43 stolen-base attempts per team game

Fielding percentage — .62 games at a position per team game (.19 chances per team game for pitchers)

Other Players

Some players didn't play enough to merit a full- or half-page essay, and aren't young enough or good enough to deserve a prospect report. But they did play in the majors last year, so we give them a brief evaluation. Following the half-page reports for each team, you'll find a page devoted to these part-timers under the heading "Other Anaheim Angels," etc. Each player gets a short summary and his 2001 Outlook is graded as follows:

A — Should be an important contributor.

B — Should play most of the season in the majors and contribute.

C — Unlikely to play much in the majors or contribute much if he does.

D — Unlikely to play in the majors.

Minor League Prospects

We present two pages of minor league prospects for each team. Thom Henninger and Josh Boyd spoke directly to player-development personnel with each major league team and also looked beyond athletic tools by analyzing statistics. Each club has seven or eight featured prospects. We try to include most of the top phenoms, but our primary emphasis is on advanced players with the best chance of contributing in the majors in 2001.

For featured prospects who are hitters and played in Double-A or Triple-A in 2000, we include major league equivalencies. Developed by Bill James, the MLE translates minor league statistics into major league numbers. It does this by making a series of adjustments for a player's home ballpark, his league, his level of competition and his future major league home park.

We also include an organizational overview for each team, which gives you a glimpse into the current state of each club's minor league system. In addition, we summarize a few more notable prospects per team in a section called "Others to Watch."

Where we mention that managers voted a player as the best in a specific category in his league, our source is *Baseball America*.

Major League Leaders

After the team sections, we provide a complete listing of Major League Leaders. The top three players in each category are shown for the American and National Leagues. You'll notice a STATS flavor to these leaders. Not only do we show the leaders for the common categories such as batting average, home runs and ERA, but you'll also find less traditional categories like steals of third and total pitches thrown.

Stars, Bums and Sleepers

This section tells you what to expect from each player in 2001: whether he'll improve, decline, remain consistent or emerge and surprise.

STATS' Top 50 Prospects

The book closes with STATS' ranking of the top 50 prospects in the game, based on the individual lists of Josh Boyd and members of the Publications Department. All players who haven't exceeded the rookie limits of 130 at-bats or 50 innings pitched in the major leagues are eligible.

American League Players

Edison International Field

Offense

While scoring has increased at Edison Field since reconstructing the Big A in 1998, it remains a fairly neutral park. Anaheim simply has put better offenses on the field, with four 100-plus RBI men and five 25-plus home-run men in the everyday lineup last year. The presence of the 18-foot wall ranging from right to center field effectively closes the gap and reduces triples to doubles. The fans can come into play on balls hit high off the wall, making for tough umpire judgment calls.

Defense

Despite losing perennial Gold Glover Jim Edmonds, the Angels were able to boast one of the best defensive outfields in the league. The park's asymmetrical configuration can present challenges with tricky caroms in right field, but Tim Salmon and Garret Anderson are reliable, and Darin Erstad is in a class by himself defensively. Only Texas committed more errors than the Angels last year, thanks in large part to Anaheim's youth around the horn and the absence of Gary DiSarcina's stabilizing influence.

Who It Helps the Most

Lefthanded hitters enjoy playing pepper with the 18-foot wall in right field. Adam Kennedy took advantage of the home dimensions last year, posting a slugging percentage of .472 at Edison, compared to just .334 on the road. Darin Erstad could hit in Yosemite Park, but he also feasted on home cooking.

Who It Hurts the Most

The righthanded power tandem of Troy Glaus and Tim Salmon saw its production suffer slightly at home. Also, Anaheim's corps of young righthanders will have to learn to adjust to the friendly dimensions in right.

Rookies & Newcomers

The Angels had an influx of promising young talent last year. The development process will continue for pitchers Ramon Ortiz, Jarrod Washburn and Scott Schoeneweis, as well as for Adam Kennedy and Ben Molina. The Disneyesque ballpark shouldn't hamper or boost their performance.

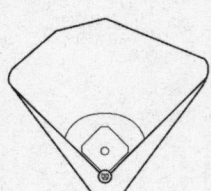

Dimensions: LF-330, LCF-396, CF-408, RCF-370, RF-330

Capacity: 45,050

Elevation: 160 feet

Surface: Grass

Foul Territory: Average

Park Factors

	2000 Season						
	Home Games			Away Games			
	Angels	Opp	Total	Angels	Opp	Total	Index
G	72	72	144	72	72	144	—
Avg	.279	.279	.279	.274	.275	.275	102
AB	2418	2542	4960	2566	2445	5011	99
R	378	382	760	377	409	786	97
H	675	709	1384	704	673	1377	101
2B	123	126	249	143	119	262	96
3B	10	6	16	20	11	31	52
HR	115	99	214	93	102	195	111
BB	271	285	556	270	308	578	97
SO	424	375	799	471	363	834	97
E	64	42	106	58	35	93	114
E-Infield	57	33	90	49	27	76	118
LHB-Avg	.287	.266	.278	.269	.282	.274	101
LHB-HR	57	36	93	52	48	100	95
RHB-Avg	.269	.288	.280	.282	.270	.275	102
RHB-HR	58	63	121	41	54	95	127

	1998-2000						
	Home Games			Away Games			
	Angels	Opp	Total	Angels	Opp	Total	Index
G	217	217	434	217	217	434	—
Avg	.265	.268	.267	.271	.272	.272	98
AB	7220	7563	14783	7718	7243	14961	99
R	1019	1121	2140	1089	1105	2194	98
H	1915	2030	3945	2095	1969	4064	97
2B	352	403	755	425	392	817	94
3B	40	26	66	35	37	72	93
HR	233	271	504	248	231	479	106
BB	729	865	1594	722	871	1593	101
SO	1311	1296	2607	1418	1213	2631	100
E	162	140	302	146	141	287	105
E-Infield	140	116	256	130	114	244	105
LHB-Avg	.280	.263	.272	.274	.273	.273	100
LHB-HR	119	112	231	134	97	231	101
RHB-Avg	.249	.272	.262	.269	.271	.270	97
RHB-HR	114	159	273	114	134	248	112

2000 Rankings (American League)
- Second-highest RHB home-run factor
- Third-highest infield-error factor
- Second-lowest triple factor

Mike Scioscia

2000 Season

As a rookie manager, Mike Scioscia stepped up to the task of restoring order in a clubhouse that had long been in disarray. His laid-back approach matched the club's personality better than that of his fiery predecessor, Terry Collins. With their young staff, the Angels were forced to come from behind early and often, and they displayed resiliency that was nowhere to be found in the past. Scioscia kept the Angels in the wild-card hunt into September, but injuries eventually took their toll.

Offense

One of Scioscia's first objectives was to improve the team's plate discipline. While Anaheim showed marked improvement in on-base percentage from 1999, Garret Anderson, Adam Kennedy and Ben Molina are three of the most aggressive hitters in the league. The Angels' bats came alive after a dismal '99, making Scioscia look prophetic when he referred to the offense as a "sleeping giant." They finished third in home runs and first in slugging percentage. He didn't have a lot of speed to work with, but he employs an aggressive style.

Pitching & Defense

The absence of Gary DiSarcina took its toll on the defense. Scioscia did his best with a rookie still learning to play second base and a revolving door of journeymen at shortstop. The pitching staff has become the same old song and dance; it is inexperienced and often injured. With Tim Belcher on the disabled list and Kent Bottenfield shipped to Philadelphia, Scioscia was forced to use his young hurlers. After Scott Schoeneweis' fast start, nobody stepped in to replace longtime ace Chuck Finley. While the young staff showed poise and promise, they were overworked and worn down.

2001 Outlook

The future looks bright in Anaheim. Acquiring pitching is once again the No. 1 priority. It will be interesting to see how GM Bill Stoneman approaches his second offseason, after trading an MVP-caliber player like Jim Edmonds in his first. Scioscia has made the Dodgers look foolish for not keeping him in their family, as he has emerged as one of the premier young managers.

Born: 11/27/58 in Upper Darby, PA

Playing Experience: 1980-1992, LA

Managerial Experience: 1 season

Manager Statistics

Year	Team, Lg	W	L	Pct	GB	Finish
2000	Anaheim, AL	82	80	.506	9.5	3rd West
1 Season		82	80	.506	—	—

2000 Starting Pitchers by Days Rest

	<=3	4	5	6+
Angels Starts	0	99	28	20
Angels ERA	—	5.79	5.63	5.24
AL Avg Starts	2	88	40	22
AL ERA	4.87	5.03	5.03	5.28

2000 Situational Stats

	Mike Scioscia	AL Average
Hit & Run Success %	37.0	35.1
Stolen Base Success %	64.1	68.8
Platoon Pct.	61.5	57.8
Defensive Subs	4	23
High-Pitch Outings	6	13
Quick/Slow Hooks	27/21	18/19
Sacrifice Attempts	63	55

2000 Rankings (American League)

- 1st in squeeze plays (9) and hit-and-run attempts (100)
- 2nd in pitchouts (40), pitchouts with a runner moving (13) and first-batter platoon percentage (66.9)
- 3rd in intentional walks (32), quick hooks (27) and relief appearances (441)

Garret Anderson

2000 Season

For the fifth straight season, Garret Anderson proved to be one of the few constants in Anaheim's oft-injured lineup. With Jim Edmonds gone, Anderson also stepped up into a run-producing role. Last year was far from typical. Usually good for a .300 average, 15-20 home runs and 80 RBI, Anderson crushed 30 homers in the first four months alone. His power output tailed off down the stretch, but he finished with career-highs in home runs, RBI and slugging percentage.

Hitting

One thing that didn't change was Anderson's aggressive approach at the plate. Only four American League regulars saw fewer pitches per plate appearance than his 3.29 figure. However, his .307 on-base percentage was low, even by his standards. The smooth-swinging lefty loves to drive the first pitch he sees and usually has great success doing so. He always has hit southpaws as well or better than righthanders, and last year was no exception. He is a bad-ball hitter, putting the wood on high pitches, punching outside stuff the other way and waiting back on offspeed offerings.

Baserunning & Defense

Anderson's value has increased the past three years as he has filled voids at all three outfield positions. He may not make the highlight reel catches that Edmonds regularly does, but Anderson displays plenty of range in center field. His arm has proven to be strong and accurate enough to play right field as well, although his assists have tapered off in each of the last four years. He has average speed.

2001 Outlook

Anderson has survived myriad trade rumors and become one of Anaheim's most consistent performers. He picked up the slack left in Edmonds' wake by muscling up with his first-half power surge. However, Anderson was so different between the first and second halves that no one knows which player will show up this season. He's in his prime, and an improvement in pitch selection could truly elevate his status as a legitimate run producer. Until then, his 35 bombs most likely were a fluke.

Position: CF/RF/DH
Bats: L **Throws:** L
Ht: 6' 3" **Wt:** 220

Opening Day Age: 28
Born: 6/30/72 in Los Angeles, CA
ML Seasons: 7

Overall Statistics

	G	AB	R	H	D	T	HR	RBI	SB	BB	SO	Avg	OBP	Slg
2000	159	647	92	185	40	3	35	117	7	24	87	.286	.307	.519
Career	887	3507	447	1043	205	18	107	510	41	163	469	.297	.327	.458

Where He Hits the Ball

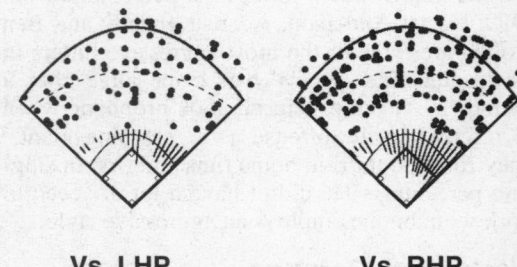

Vs. LHP   Vs. RHP

2000 Situational Stats

	AB	H	HR	RBI	Avg		AB	H	HR	RBI	Avg
Home	322	89	20	63	.276	LHP	189	63	15	42	.333
Road	325	96	15	54	.295	RHP	458	122	20	75	.266
First Half	354	87	26	65	.246	Sc Pos	179	52	9	85	.291
Scnd Half	293	98	9	52	.334	Clutch	103	22	0	7	.214

2000 Rankings (American League)

- 1st in lowest on-base percentage vs. righthanded pitchers (.290)
- 3rd in at-bats, slugging percentage vs. lefthanded pitchers (.661) and lowest percentage of pitches taken (44.6)
- 4th in fielding percentage in center field (.992)
- 5th in games played and fewest pitches seen per plate appearance (3.29)
- 6th in total bases (336) and GDPs (21)
- 7th in lowest on-base percentage
- Led the Angels in doubles, RBI, sacrifice flies (9) and GDPs (21)
- Led AL center fielders in home runs, at-bats, hits, doubles, total bases (336), sacrifice flies (9) and GDPs (21)

Darin Erstad

2000 Season

Darin Erstad took a look at himself after his abominable 1999 campaign and admitted that he "stunk." Known for his intensity on the field, he applied his passion off the field and spent the winter breaking down every plate appearance. The result was a complete turnaround from his dismal '99 season, as Erstad mustered an offensive assault on the record books. His 240 hits were more than anyone since Wade Boggs in 1985, and he collected his 200th hit by August 29.

Hitting

The top of the lineup isn't the ideal place for Erstad's bat. However, after five years in the organization, he has adapted to the role and evolved into one of the game's most dynamic leadoff hitters. A middle-of-the-order presence, Erstad ignites the offense. He established a major league record for most RBI by a leadoff hitter while posting a career-best .541 slugging percentage. In 1999, pitchers continuously put him away with a steady diet of outside sinkers. Last year, he cut down his swing and narrowed the strike zone, rejuvenating the line-drive stroke that fans had grown accustomed to in his young career.

Baserunning & Defense

Erstad is one of the most electrifying players on the bases and in the field. He runs down drives in the gaps with reckless abandon and hustles around the bases like he was shot out of a cannon. Despite his maniacal appearance when in motion, Erstad remains under control, stealing bases with a high rate of success. He's developed into a Gold Glover in left field.

2001 Outlook

The Angels expressed their confidence in Erstad after his poor '99 performance by not entertaining any trade inquiries, and their patience was rewarded. Nothing is holding back the 26-year-old now. It will be tough to improve upon last season, but given his work ethic, Erstad certainly will try. A 30-30 season or an AL batting title could be on the immediate horizon.

Position: LF/CF/DH
Bats: L **Throws:** L
Ht: 6' 2" **Wt:** 212

Opening Day Age: 26
Born: 6/4/74 in Jamestown, ND
ML Seasons: 5

Overall Statistics

	G	AB	R	H	D	T	HR	RBI	SB	BB	SO	Avg	OBP	Slg
2000	157	676	121	240	39	6	25	100	28	64	82	.355	.409	.541
Career	628	2545	422	767	139	19	77	332	87	222	375	.301	.358	.462

Where He Hits the Ball

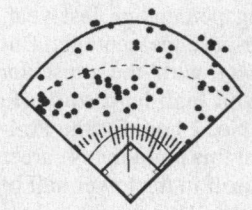 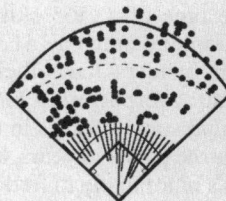

Vs. LHP   **Vs. RHP**

2000 Situational Stats

	AB	H	HR	RBI	Avg		AB	H	HR	RBI	Avg
Home	348	135	11	58	.388	LHP	210	71	9	34	.338
Road	328	105	14	42	.320	RHP	466	169	16	66	.363
First Half	375	144	17	66	.384	Sc Pos	136	47	3	70	.346
Scnd Half	301	96	8	34	.319	Clutch	101	31	5	19	.307

2000 Rankings (American League)

- 1st in at-bats, hits, singles, plate appearances (747), on-base percentage for a leadoff hitter (.409), batting average at home and highest percentage of extra bases taken as a runner (70.3)
- 2nd in batting average, total bases (366) and batting average vs. righthanded pitchers
- 3rd in runs scored and fielding percentage in left field (.990)
- Led the Angels in batting average, at-bats, runs scored, hits, singles, total bases (366), stolen bases, times on base (305), plate appearances (747), on-base percentage, highest ground-ball/flyball ratio (1.6), stolen-base percentage (77.8) and batting average with runners in scoring position

Ron Gant

Position: LF/DH
Bats: R   **Throws:** R
Ht: 6' 0"   **Wt:** 196

Opening Day Age: 36
Born: 3/2/65 in Victoria, TX
ML Seasons: 13

2000 Season

After years of swirling trade rumors that surrounded Jim Edmonds, the Angels dealt their longtime center fielder to St. Louis for Adam Kennedy and Kent Bottenfield last March. But four months into the season, Anaheim gave up on Bottenfield, sending the veteran righthander to Philadelphia for the power-hitting Ron Gant. The 35-year-old played sparingly for the Angels, splitting time between left field and designated hitter. Still, Gant managed to top the 20-homer mark for the seventh time in his career.

Hitting

No longer an everyday threat, Gant has become a platoon player. He crushed lefthanded pitchers to the tune of a .565 slugging percentage last year, complementing a .412 on-base percentage. But righthanders have their way with the muscular Gant, overpowering him with high hard stuff. He found some success in the No. 2 hole for the Phillies the past two years, but at this point in his career he's more likely to find himself in the lower half of the order; he batted a meager .136 in 103 at-bats with runners in scoring position last season.

Baserunning & Defense

Gant also is no longer the basestealer that he once was. He was successful on only half of his 12 attempts last year. He plays hard, however, and his veteran experience helps him on the bases. He looks lost in left field at times, has trouble reading flyballs and his arm doesn't put fear into the hearts of opposing baserunners.

2001 Outlook

Gant will be on the move for the third time in three years. After his brief debut in the American League in 2000, he returns to the National League by signing a one-year, $1.5 million deal with the Rockies. It's likely that Gant will share left field with Todd Hollandsworth in Colorado, where Gant has batted .384-5-14 in 23 games at Coors Field. The high altitude may spur on Gant, whose 26 bombs last year brought him within eight of 300 for his career.

Overall Statistics

	G	AB	R	H	D	T	HR	RBI	SB	BB	SO	Avg	OBP	Slg
2000	123	425	69	106	19	3	26	54	6	56	91	.249	.335	.492
Career	1620	5847	972	1499	275	46	292	910	234	697	1263	.256	.336	.469

Where He Hits the Ball

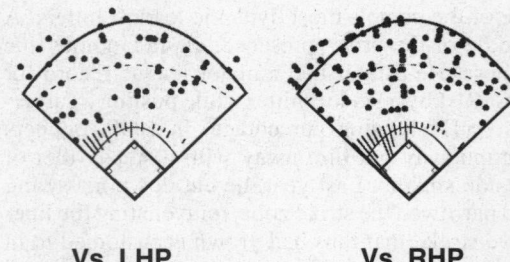

Vs. LHP   **Vs. RHP**

2000 Situational Stats

	AB	H	HR	RBI	Avg		AB	H	HR	RBI	Avg
Home	188	49	14	27	.261	LHP	124	39	7	14	.315
Road	237	57	12	27	.241	RHP	301	67	19	40	.223
First Half	297	74	14	27	.249	Sc Pos	103	14	1	22	.136
Scnd Half	128	32	12	27	.250	Clutch	76	19	7	13	.250

2000 Rankings (American League)
- Did not rank near the top or bottom in any category

Troy Glaus

2000 Season

Nobody could have predicted the improvement Troy Glaus made from 1999 to 2000. He began last season in torrid fashion, batting .330 with 16 homers through the first two months. Pitchers adjusted to the rising superstar, causing him to hit just .222 in June and July. But in a testament to his maturity, Glaus was able to make adjustments and finish with a flourish. On the way to breaking Al Rosen's 46-year-old American League record for home runs by a third baseman, Glaus also shattered Reggie Jackson's franchise record by becoming the first Angel to surpass 40 longballs in a season.

Hitting

Capable of walloping mammoth home runs, Glaus hammers fastballs that are out over the plate. He's only beginning to use the whole field and is an absolute terror against lefthanders. He exhibited advanced strike-zone judgment by drawing 112 walks in his second full big league season. Despite striking out 163 times, he is a patient hitter who will work the count and wait for a pitcher to make a mistake he can mash.

Baserunning & Defense

Although he led the league with 33 errors, Glaus shows the tools to become an outstanding third baseman. He displays impressive athletic range and lateral mobility for someone his size and showcases a cannon arm. His throws can get wild and sail on him, something that's expected to improve with experience. Glaus charges slow rollers aggressively and already is adept at the barehanded scoop and fire. He showed the surprising ability to swipe a base last year, although he wasn't successful enough to be a factor. As he learns to pick his spots, he could add that extra dimension to his burgeoning game.

2001 Outlook

Glaus has arrived. His ability to make adjustments as a 23-year-old is a terrifying sign for the rest of the American League. Tim Salmon, Anaheim's all-time home-run leader, predicts 50-plus home-run seasons on the horizon for Glaus. Anaheim would be wise to lock him up, as the Angels did with most of their homegrown players in the 1990s.

Position: 3B
Bats: R **Throws:** R
Ht: 6' 5" **Wt:** 229

Opening Day Age: 24
Born: 8/3/76 in Tarzana, CA
ML Seasons: 3
Pronunciation: GLOSS

Overall Statistics

	G	AB	R	H	D	T	HR	RBI	SB	BB	SO	Avg	OBP	Slg
2000	159	563	120	160	37	1	47	102	14	112	163	.284	.404	.604
Career	361	1279	224	328	75	1	77	204	20	198	357	.256	.358	.497

Where He Hits the Ball

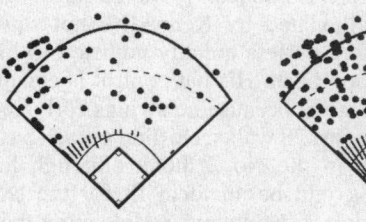

Vs. LHP   **Vs. RHP**

2000 Situational Stats

	AB	H	HR	RBI	Avg		AB	H	HR	RBI	Avg
Home	271	72	24	54	.266	LHP	130	48	17	32	.369
Road	292	88	23	48	.301	RHP	433	112	30	70	.259
First Half	300	88	25	60	.293	Sc Pos	146	39	10	60	.267
Scnd Half	263	72	22	42	.274	Clutch	98	31	10	15	.316

2000 Rankings (American League)

- 1st in home runs, batting average on a 3-1 count (.769), slugging percentage vs. lefthanded pitchers (.854), on-base percentage vs. lefthanded pitchers (.500) and errors at third base (33)
- 2nd in lowest stolen-base percentage (56.0)
- 3rd in strikeouts, pitches seen (2,843), HR frequency (12.0 ABs per HR) and lowest fielding percentage at third base (.933)
- Led the Angels in home runs, caught stealing (11), walks, pitches seen (2,843), slugging percentage, HR frequency (12.0 ABs per HR), most pitches seen per plate appearance (4.19), batting average vs. lefthanded pitchers, batting average on a 3-1 count (.769) and slugging percentage vs. lefthanded pitchers (.854)

Adam Kennedy

2000 Season

Adam Kennedy entered last year on the inside track for the Cardinals' second-base job. That plan was altered after St. Louis acquired Fernando Vina, and Kennedy was packaged with Kent Bottenfield to the Angels in a deal for Jim Edmonds. Kennedy immediately assumed the starting keystone duties in Anaheim, and the rookie got off to a blistering start. He provided the Angels with consistent production and stability that they hadn't seen at the position since Johnny Ray in the 1980s.

Hitting

A lot was hinging on Kennedy's performance in order to justify swapping him for an MVP-caliber center fielder like Edmonds. While some of the pressure was alleviated by Kennedy's hot start, American League hurlers quickly adjusted to his free-swinging approach. His bat control is exceptional, which is good because he swings early and often—drawing just 28 walks. He didn't reach base enough to stay in the No. 2 hole, although his contact hitting could be an ideal fit for the slot should he develop some patience. He's more than just a slap-hitter, however. He can yank balls into the gaps, as evidenced by his 33 doubles and 11 triples.

Baserunning & Defense

The Cardinals drafted Kennedy as a shortstop with their first-round pick in 1997, but he didn't possess the necessary range or arm strength to stay at the position. While he's still in the adjustment period, especially on the pivot, he's adapted fairly well to second base. He isn't a speed-burner, though he's aggressive on the basepaths. He uses his quickness and intelligence to read pitchers, get good jumps and steal bases.

2001 Outlook

For the first month of 2000, Darin Erstad and Kennedy formed a very productive one-two punch atop the order. Mike Scioscia would love to count on the tablesetting tandem again, but that will be determined by Kennedy's willingness to take a pitch. His bat is his ticket, and the Angels hope to see more of the pure hitting he showcased prior to the All-Star break last year.

Position: 2B
Bats: L **Throws:** R
Ht: 6' 1" **Wt:** 180

Opening Day Age: 25
Born: 1/10/76 in Riverside, CA
ML Seasons: 2

Overall Statistics

	G	AB	R	H	D	T	HR	RBI	SB	BB	SO	Avg	OBP	Slg
2000	156	598	82	159	33	11	9	72	22	28	73	.266	.300	.403
Career	189	700	94	185	43	12	10	88	22	31	81	.264	.298	.403

Where He Hits the Ball

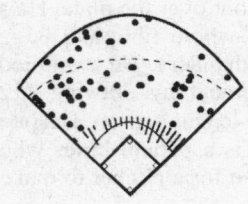 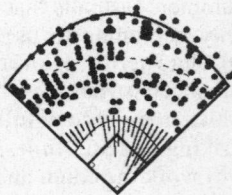

Vs. LHP   **Vs. RHP**

2000 Situational Stats

	AB	H	HR	RBI	Avg		AB	H	HR	RBI	Avg
Home	299	90	7	38	.301	LHP	142	39	0	16	.275
Road	299	69	2	34	.231	RHP	456	120	9	56	.263
First Half	335	95	6	40	.284	Sc Pos	154	42	3	59	.273
Scnd Half	263	64	3	32	.243	Clutch	97	27	1	13	.278

2000 Rankings (American League)

- 1st in errors at second base (19) and lowest fielding percentage at second base (.976)
- 2nd in triples
- 3rd in lowest on-base percentage and lowest on-base percentage vs. righthanded pitchers (.296)
- 4th in highest percentage of extra bases taken as a runner (67.3)
- 6th in batting average on an 0-2 count (.314) and lowest slugging percentage vs. lefthanded pitchers (.345)
- Led the Angels in triples and steals of third (3)
- Led AL second basemen in triples, intentional walks (5), fewest GDPs per GDP situation (7.9%), highest percentage of extra bases taken as a runner (67.3) and games played (156)

Ben Molina

Position: C
Bats: R **Throws:** R
Ht: 5'11" **Wt:** 207

Opening Day Age: 26
Born: 7/20/74 in Rio Piedras, Puerto Rico
ML Seasons: 3

2000 Season

One of the most pleasant surprises of last season, Ben Molina quickly established himself as an American League Rookie of the Year candidate. A .297 career hitter over seven nondescript minor league campaigns, Molina's performance never suggested he would hit enough to garner full-time catching duties in the big leagues. But a monstrous month of May, in which the Puerto Rico native hit .461, marked his arrival as a legitimate major league receiver.

Hitting

Molina emerged from relative obscurity to handle a position that has proven to be troublesome since Bob Boone's tenure with the Angels ended more than a decade ago. Hitting out of a slight crouch, Molina sprays hits from line to line and puts his bat on nearly everything thrown. To underscore his aggressive approach, only Nomar Garciaparra saw fewer pitches per plate appearance. Molina also led the league by swinging at the first pitch almost half of the time. He had never clubbed more than 10 dingers in a season, but he connected for 14 homers last year. He was at his best in the clutch, hitting .360 in close & late situations.

Baserunning & Defense

A former shortstop, Molina's quickness behind the dish complements his sound fundamentals. He is adept at blocking pitches in the dirt, improving over the course of the season as he learned his pitching staff. A former big league backstop himself, Mike Scioscia stresses the importance of interaction between the signal caller and pitcher, another facet of the game where Molina progressed. His quick reflexes behind the plate don't translate into any kind of running speed, however.

2001 Outlook

Molina exceeded expectations with his bat and was rock-solid behind the plate during his breakthrough rookie campaign. He helped secure the starting receiving duties by throwing out 33 percent of would-be basestealers. The Angels have a track record of tying up their young, homegrown players early, and Molina looks like a long-term answer at a key position.

Overall Statistics

	G	AB	R	H	D	T	HR	RBI	SB	BB	SO	Avg	OBP	Slg
2000	130	473	59	133	20	2	14	71	1	23	33	.281	.318	.421
Career	163	575	67	159	25	2	15	81	1	29	39	.277	.317	.405

Where He Hits the Ball

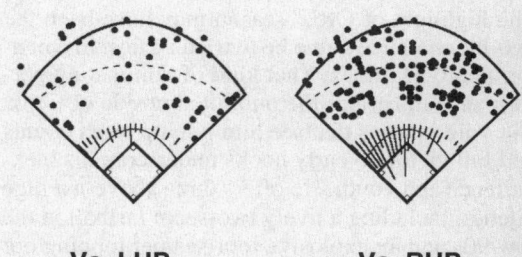

Vs. LHP   **Vs. RHP**

2000 Situational Stats

	AB	H	HR	RBI	Avg		AB	H	HR	RBI	Avg
Home	240	66	11	37	.275	LHP	123	36	8	28	.293
Road	233	67	3	34	.288	RHP	350	97	6	43	.277
First Half	251	77	11	42	.307	Sc Pos	137	36	2	53	.263
Scnd Half	222	56	3	29	.252	Clutch	86	31	1	14	.360

2000 Rankings (American League)

- 1st in lowest percentage of pitches taken (42.9) and highest percentage of swings on the first pitch (44.6)
- 2nd in highest percentage of runners caught stealing as a catcher (32.7) and fewest pitches seen per plate appearance (3.13)
- Led the Angels in batting average in the clutch and lowest percentage of swings that missed (10.4)
- Led AL catchers in sacrifice flies (7), batting average vs. righthanded pitchers, slugging percentage vs. lefthanded pitchers (.537), batting average on a 3-2 count (.438), batting average on the road and batting average with two strikes (.277)

Ramon Ortiz

Position: SP
Bats: R **Throws:** R
Ht: 6' 0" **Wt:** 175

Opening Day Age: 25
Born: 3/23/76 in Las Matas Cotui, Dominican Republic
ML Seasons: 2
Pronunciation: or-TEEZ

2000 Season

Last season began rather inauspiciously for Ramon Ortiz with the news that his throwing shoulder had a slightly torn labrum. While the injury cost him a shot at joining the Opening Day rotation, he avoided the knife and spent the majority of the season in the Angels' rotation. His ERA was over twice as high away from Edison International Field, but he did seem to show overall progress in the season's second half. Though Ortiz can be tough to hit, he puts himself into too many early-inning binds. It's a problem that could be curbed if the animated youngster learns to channel his energy.

Pitching

The highlight of Ortiz' season may have been the two-hit complete game he twirled against his mentor, Pedro Martinez. That kind of dominating performance illustrates the unlimited upside of Ortiz. But wild outings that see him pile up pitch counts and fall victim to early hooks underscore his inexperience and youth. He offers three above-average pitches, including a lively two-seam fastball in the low 90s and an explosive four-seamer topping out in the mid-90s. He is aggressive with his sinking changeup and isn't afraid to use it as an out pitch or when behind in the count. His hard slider shows flashes of being a third pitch that can send hitters back to the dugout.

Defense

A bundle of energy on the mound, the 6-foot, 175-pounder plays his position like a fifth infielder, leaping off the rubber with cat-like quickness. Ortiz hasn't committed an error in two years. Baserunners usually can't get big leads against him because of a quick move to first, an effective slide step and the presence of Ben Molina behind the plate.

2001 Outlook

Ortiz is one of the only young Anaheim starters with overpowering velocity. He needs to work on little things like maintaining a consistent arm slot and repeating his delivery if he wants to emerge as a frontline presence in the rotation. He signed a one-year deal with Anaheim in late November.

Overall Statistics

	W	L	Pct.	ERA	G	GS	Sv	IP	H	BB	SO	HR	Ratio
2000	8	6	.571	5.09	18	18	0	111.1	96	55	73	18	1.36
Career	10	9	.526	5.52	27	27	0	159.2	146	80	117	25	1.42

How Often He Throws Strikes

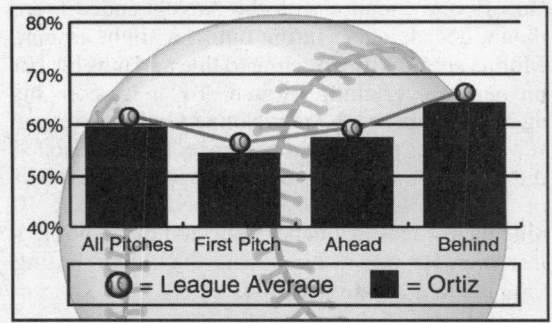

= League Average   ■ = Ortiz

2000 Situational Stats

	W	L	ERA	Sv	IP		AB	H	HR	RBI	Avg
Home	6	3	3.58	0	65.1	LHB	220	55	11	34	.250
Road	2	3	7.24	0	46.0	RHB	187	41	7	25	.219
First Half	3	2	6.16	0	38.0	Sc Pos	81	23	4	40	.284
Scnd Half	5	4	4.54	0	73.1	Clutch	20	0	0	0	.000

2000 Rankings (American League)

- 2nd in balks (4)
- Led the Angels in complete games (2), wild pitches (7), balks (4) and lowest batting average allowed vs. lefthanded batters

Troy Percival

2000 Season

For the fifth consecutive year, Troy Percival was the hammer in the Angels pen. However, injuries to the fireballing righthander have taken their toll and caused him to struggle for stretches over the past two seasons. Last year he blew a league-leading 10 saves and watched his ERA rise for the sixth straight campaign. He also fanned fewer than one batter per inning for the first time in his career.

Pitching

Percival's squinting stare to the catcher is part of his intimidation game. But it's his explosive fastball, usually pumped in at 93-96 MPH, that pays his bills. While he is primarily a two-pitch, fastball-curveball pitcher, he has started to mix in a cutter. His latest experiment with a changeup could yield some promising results if he refines the rarely-used offering. He may have returned too early from his offseason surgery in 1999 on his right shoulder. As a result, he was forced to make slight alterations to his mechanics.

Defense

While Percival lacks a quick move to first and generally disregards baserunners, not many attempt to steal against him. Those who do are successful the majority of the time, though the presence of Ben Molina behind the plate helps keep thieves at bay. Percival can appear awkward getting off the mound to make plays after exuding maximum effort on each pitch, but the former catcher hasn't made an error in more than two years.

2001 Outlook

With nagging injuries taking their toll, Percival could be at a pivotal point in his career. Not many closers throughout history have held up as long and effectively as Percival. He has led the Angels in saves every season since 1996, averaging more than 33 per year. He has shown resiliency and will anchor the Anaheim bullpen once again in 2001.

Position: RP
Bats: R **Throws:** R
Ht: 6' 3" **Wt:** 236

Opening Day Age: 31
Born: 8/9/69 in Fontana, CA
ML Seasons: 6
Nickname: Percy

Overall Statistics

	W	L	Pct.	ERA	G	GS	Sv	IP	H	BB	SO	HR	Ratio
2000	5	5	.500	4.50	54	0	32	50.0	42	30	49	7	1.44
Career	19	27	.413	3.16	360	0	171	373.2	240	168	460	41	1.09

How Often He Throws Strikes

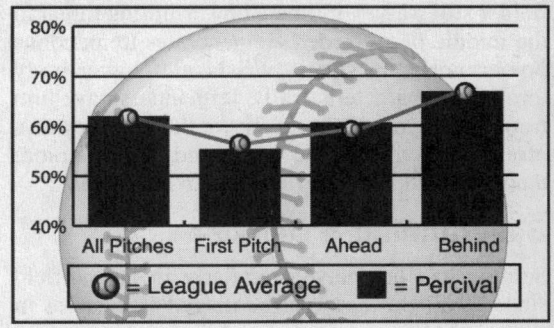

2000 Situational Stats

	W	L	ERA	Sv	IP		AB	H	HR	RBI	Avg
Home	3	2	4.01	14	24.2	LHB	93	22	3	13	.237
Road	2	3	4.97	18	25.1	RHB	91	20	4	15	.220
First Half	4	4	4.25	20	29.2	Sc Pos	42	12	1	16	.286
Scnd Half	1	1	4.87	12	20.1	Clutch	151	40	6	26	.265

2000 Rankings (American League)

- 1st in blown saves (10)
- 4th in save opportunities (42) and lowest save percentage (76.2)
- 9th in first batter efficiency (.208) and saves
- Led the Angels in saves, games finished (45), save opportunities (42), save percentage (76.2), blown saves (10), lowest batting average allowed in relief (.228) and most strikeouts per nine innings in relief (8.8)

Tim Salmon

2000 Season

The past couple of years have been frustrating ones for Tim Salmon. Injuries and last-place finishes marred his campaigns. But after one of his typical slow starts last year, Salmon returned to form following the All-Star break and finished with a flourish. In his ninth season, he broke Brian Downing's franchise record for career home runs. He also tied a personal best with 34 dingers, the fifth time in his career that he's reached 30.

Hitting

Foot and wrist injuries hindered Salmon's production for two years. But a relatively injury-free 2000 season was all it took to prove the 32-year-old right fielder still was a legitimate power-hitting threat in the middle of the order. He generates tremendous power with his strong wrists and lower-body torque. Uncharacteristically, lefthanders gave him trouble last year. Salmon shows the qualities of a professional disciplined hitter, and he drew more than 100 walks for the first time in his career.

Baserunning & Defense

Salmon had not played regularly in the outfield since 1997. But last year he played 124 games in right and demonstrated the ability to go aggressively after balls in any direction. He is particularly adept at coming in on short flies and gets rid of the ball in a hurry. He tied for second among AL right fielders in assists and was fourth in the junior circuit in total chances in right. His strong and accurate throwing arm is a weapon that accounts for his assist total. Salmon didn't steal a base last year and has been successful on just four of eight attempts in the last three years.

2001 Outlook

Despite his accomplishments, the lifelong Angel was mysteriously omitted from the all-time Angels team that adorned the outfield walls at Edison Field last year. The Rangers have openly expressed interest in the perennial Texas-killer. Offseason surgeries on his left shoulder and right foot should have him healthy as he heads into spring training, and he should go quietly about producing his steady .290-30-100 season no matter which cap he wears.

Position: RF/DH
Bats: R **Throws:** R
Ht: 6' 3" **Wt:** 231

Opening Day Age: 32
Born: 8/24/68 in Long Beach, CA
ML Seasons: 9
Pronunciation: SAM-men

Overall Statistics

	G	AB	R	H	D	T	HR	RBI	SB	BB	SO	Avg	OBP	Slg
2000	158	568	108	165	36	2	34	97	0	104	139	.290	.404	.540
Career	1113	4051	716	1180	231	16	230	757	29	683	959	.291	.394	.527

Where He Hits the Ball

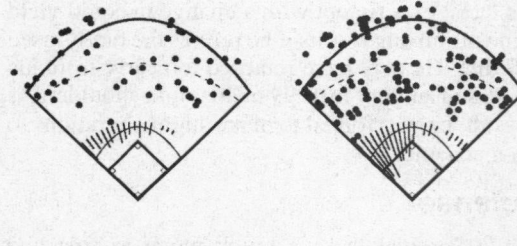

Vs. LHP　　　　**Vs. RHP**

2000 Situational Stats

	AB	H	HR	RBI	Avg		AB	H	HR	RBI	Avg
Home	268	73	17	47	.272	LHP	155	35	12	22	.226
Road	300	92	17	50	.307	RHP	413	130	22	75	.315
First Half	309	82	18	48	.265	Sc Pos	145	41	9	63	.283
Scnd Half	259	83	16	49	.320	Clutch	85	24	8	19	.282

2000 Rankings (American League)

- 3rd in errors in right field (6) and lowest fielding percentage in right field (.980)
- 6th in strikeouts and lowest percentage of swings put into play (34.9)
- 7th in walks and on-base percentage vs. righthanded pitchers (.422)
- Led the Angels in cleanup slugging percentage (.540)
- Led AL right fielders in runs scored, walks, times on base (275), strikeouts, pitches seen (2,765), plate appearances (680) and games played (158)

Scott Schoeneweis

2000 Season

Scott Schoeneweis entered last year with a renewed attitude on the heels of a bitter end to his 1999 season. He started the 2000 campaign on a positive note, apologizing to his teammates during spring training for his immature behavior. His spring success carried over into the first month of the regular season, as he got off to a 4-0 start with a 3.15 ERA. But he managed to win just three of his final 22 starts while posting a 6.04 ERA after April. A strained ribcage muscle in June contributed to his derailment.

Pitching

When Schoeneweis was sharp in the early part of the year, he was spotting his pitches with precision. The southpaw conjured up comparisons to Tom Glavine's finesse-lefty standard. Schoeneweis proved to be durable, working at least six innings in 21 of his starts. His fastball, thrown between 89-91 MPH, is best when he works it in and out to make more effective use of its sinking action. The pitch helped him lead the league in inducing groundballs and double plays. He completes his repertoire by mixing in a sweeping slider and a well-developed changeup.

Defense

Schoeneweis doesn't do a good job of holding runners. Even with the strong-armed Ben Molina on duty, basestealers ran wild on Schoeneweis. If he simply learns to vary his moves, he could help curtail the thieves. A good athlete, he gets off the mound in fine shape and is an above-average fielder.

2001 Outlook

Due to a strained lower back, Schoeneweis limped across the finish line last year with three poor starts. Overall though, his first full season in the rotation was encouraging enough to secure a spot this year. The lefty showed the early makings of being a workhorse-style pitcher, along with the attitude to fit the mold. His control needs refinement, however, as he posted the worst strikeout-walk ratio among American League starters.

Position: SP
Bats: L **Throws:** L
Ht: 6' 0" **Wt:** 186

Opening Day Age: 27
Born: 10/2/73 in Long Branch, NJ
ML Seasons: 2
Pronunciation: SHOW-en-wice

Overall Statistics

	W	L	Pct.	ERA	G	GS	Sv	IP	H	BB	SO	HR	Ratio
2000	7	10	.412	5.45	27	27	0	170.0	183	67	78	21	1.47
Career	8	11	.421	5.46	58	27	0	209.1	230	81	100	25	1.49

How Often He Throws Strikes

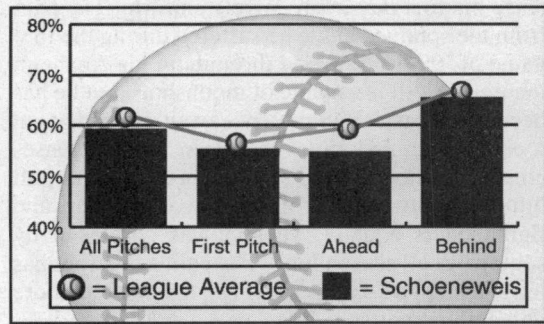

= League Average   ■ = Schoeneweis

2000 Situational Stats

	W	L	ERA	Sv	IP		AB	H	HR	RBI	Avg
Home	4	3	5.11	0	68.2	LHB	153	45	4	24	.294
Road	3	7	5.68	0	101.1	RHB	509	138	17	72	.271
First Half	5	5	5.08	0	90.1	Sc Pos	164	49	3	69	.299
Scnd Half	2	5	5.87	0	79.2	Clutch	62	15	4	8	.242

2000 Rankings (American League)

- 1st in GDPs induced (30), highest groundball/flyball ratio allowed (2.4), most GDPs induced per nine innings (1.6), lowest strikeout/walk ratio (1.2) and fewest strikeouts per nine innings (4.1)
- 2nd in fewest pitches thrown per batter (3.47)
- 3rd in balks (3), highest ERA and highest ERA on the road
- Led the Angels in ERA, losses, games started, innings pitched, hits allowed, batters faced (742), walks allowed, hit batsmen (6), strikeouts, pitches thrown (2,572), stolen bases allowed (20), GDPs induced (30), highest strikeout/walk ratio (1.2), lowest batting average allowed (.276) and lowest slugging percentage allowed (.437)

Mo Vaughn

2000 Season

When the Angels signed Mo Vaughn to a six-year, $80 million deal after the 1998 season, he was coming off five straight years where he batted better than .300 while averaging 37 homers and 112 RBI. The 1995 American League MVP was promoted as the key to the Angels' turnaround, and he was renowned as a clubhouse leader. Nobody wants to win more than Vaughn, but his first two years in Anaheim have to be considered disappointing. Last year his slugging percentage dipped under .500 for the first time since 1992.

Hitting

In fairness to Vaughn, injuries have hampered him since his first day in an Angels uniform. The pain from the sprained ankle he suffered during the first game of '99 has lingered throughout his Anaheim tenure. He still is capable of moonshots, but he has become an easier victim to put away. He struck out a career-high 181 times last year. Most defenses employ a heavy infield shift against the dead-pull hitter. Usually capable of handling lefthanders and righthanders equally, Vaughn was perplexed by southpaws all season long. The pain in his foot has led to a lot of off-balance swings, making him more vulnerable to offspeed pitches.

Baserunning & Defense

Vaughn may be the slowest runner in baseball. He feels pain every time he plants his foot and is nothing more than a station-to-station runner. After spending nearly half of '99 as the DH, he was back at first base on a regular basis last year. He's starting to look like a DH in the field, though, displaying little mobility on grounders. While his soft hands help him scoop low throws, he doesn't help his infielders much on many errant tosses.

2001 Outlook

Vaughn's production disappeared in the second half last year. Much of that probably can be attributed to the pain he played through, but he hasn't provided the type of offense expected. He still possesses tremendous power, however. If the Angels can find a suitor, they might entertain the thought of trading Vaughn and the remaining four years on his contract.

Position: 1B/DH
Bats: L **Throws:** R
Ht: 6' 1" **Wt:** 268

Opening Day Age: 33
Born: 12/15/67 in Norwalk, CT
ML Seasons: 10
Nickname: The Hit Dog

Overall Statistics

	G	AB	R	H	D	T	HR	RBI	SB	BB	SO	Avg	OBP	Slg
2000	161	614	93	167	31	0	36	117	2	79	181	.272	.365	.498
Career	1346	4966	784	1479	250	10	299	977	30	652	1262	.298	.387	.533

Where He Hits the Ball

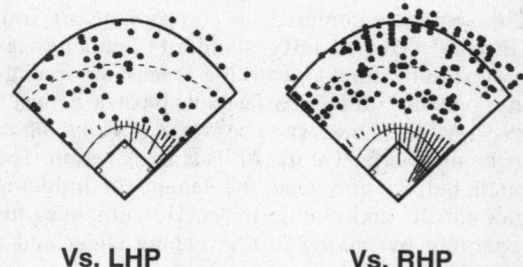

Vs. LHP   **Vs. RHP**

2000 Situational Stats

	AB	H	HR	RBI	Avg		AB	H	HR	RBI	Avg
Home	300	84	18	62	.280	LHP	191	39	6	22	.204
Road	314	83	18	55	.264	RHP	423	128	30	95	.303
First Half	348	105	23	68	.302	Sc Pos	172	51	11	85	.297
Scnd Half	266	62	13	49	.233	Clutch	93	27	4	17	.290

2000 Rankings (American League)

- 1st in strikeouts, errors at first base (14) and lowest fielding percentage at first base (.990)
- 2nd in highest percentage of swings that missed (30.8) and lowest percentage of swings put into play (33.2)
- 3rd in hit by pitch (14), games played, lowest batting average vs. lefthanded pitchers and lowest percentage of extra bases taken as a runner (26.9)
- 5th in intentional walks (11) and plate appearances (712)
- Led the Angels in RBI, intentional walks (11), hit by pitch (14), strikeouts, slugging percentage vs. righthanded pitchers (.560) and games played
- Led AL first basemen in strikeouts

Jarrod Washburn

2000 Season

Just when it seems like Jarrod Washburn is on the verge of realizing his potential, an ill-timed injury jumps up and bites him. Shoulder stiffness forced the southpaw to exit in the sixth inning of a no-hitter last May 29. He eventually landed on the shelf with a strained left biceps. Upon his return from the disabled list, Washburn suffered a fractured shoulder blade and missed the rest of the year. Regardless, he posted his best hits-innings ratio and surrendering a stingy .215 batting average.

Pitching

When he's healthy, Washburn flashes the type of great stuff that could help fill Chuck Finley's shoes. Washburn can be dominant at times, using a fastball between 88-92 MPH that possesses good life in the strike zone. He also throws an effective offspeed attack consisting of a slider, curveball and changeup. He was particularly tough away from Edison International Field, fashioning a 2.13 ERA and .162 batting average allowed on the road. His command still needs sharpening and his pitch counts tend to add up quickly, leading to early exits. Only once in 14 starts did he work into the eighth inning last season.

Defense

Washburn is a fairly athletic pitcher and does a good job handling plays around the mound. In parts of three seasons in the majors, he hasn't committed an error. The lefthander doesn't own a particularly good pickoff move, but only five of 10 basestealers were successful against him last year.

2001 Outlook

Washburn's performance in Instructional League was encouraging enough to put him right back in line for a job in the rotation. His strikeout-walk ratio has declined in each of his first three years, albeit in small sample sizes. Nevertheless, aside from Ramon Ortiz, Washburn possesses the best pure stuff of any of Anaheim's recent influx of young guns. He has the arm to help anchor the staff with some additional fine-tuning.

Position: SP
Bats: L **Throws:** L
Ht: 6' 1" **Wt:** 198

Opening Day Age: 26
Born: 8/13/74 in LaCrosse, WI
ML Seasons: 3

Overall Statistics

	W	L	Pct.	ERA	G	GS	Sv	IP	H	BB	SO	HR	Ratio
2000	7	2	.778	3.74	14	14	0	84.1	64	37	49	16	1.20
Career	17	10	.630	4.46	45	35	0	220.0	195	90	136	33	1.30

How Often He Throws Strikes

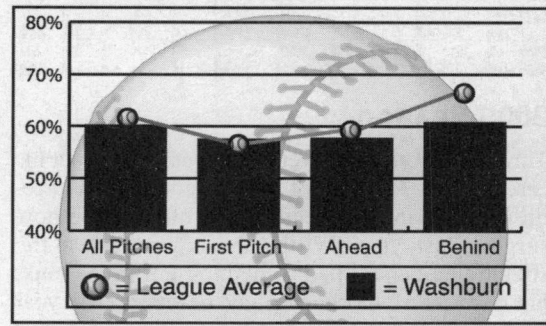

○ = League Average   ■ = Washburn

2000 Situational Stats

	W	L	ERA	Sv	IP		AB	H	HR	RBI	Avg
Home	5	2	5.05	0	46.1	LHB	65	14	4	8	.215
Road	2	0	2.13	0	38.0	RHB	233	50	12	28	.215
First Half	5	2	3.90	0	67.0	Sc Pos	39	11	1	18	.282
Scnd Half	2	0	3.12	0	17.1	Clutch	12	2	0	0	.167

2000 Rankings (American League)

- 5th in lowest batting average allowed vs. righthanded batters

Tim Belcher

Position: SP
Bats: R **Throws:** R
Ht: 6' 3" **Wt:** 235
Opening Day Age: 39
Born: 10/19/61 in Sparta, OH
ML Seasons: 14

Overall Statistics

	W	L	Pct.	ERA	G	GS	Sv	IP	H	BB	SO	HR	Ratio
2000	4	5	.444	6.86	9	9	0	40.2	45	22	22	8	1.65
Career	146	140	.510	4.16	394	373	5	2442.2	2423	860	1519	264	1.34

2000 Situational Stats

	W	L	ERA	Sv	IP		AB	H	HR	RBI	Avg
Home	2	2	9.00	0	16.0	LHB	74	23	2	11	.311
Road	2	3	5.47	0	24.2	RHB	86	22	6	16	.256
First Half	2	2	9.69	0	13.0	Sc Pos	39	11	1	15	.282
Scnd Half	2	3	5.53	0	27.2	Clutch	11	2	0	0	.182

2000 Season

Tim Belcher has been very resilient throughout his career. Now 39 years of age, he contemplated retirement during his rehab from offseason elbow surgery last year. While he showed down the stretch that he still had something left in the tank, his days as a workhorse may be over. Last year marked the first time since his rookie season that he didn't amass at least 132 innings.

Pitching & Defense

Belcher has made the transition from young power pitcher to a guy who relies on savvy to outsmart hitters. It's a recipe that has proven successful when he's been healthy. He works a cut fastball off of his high-80s fastball, which he speeds up by mixing in a slider, splitter and change. He always has been a reliable fifth infielder and does an effective job of keeping basestealers at bay.

2001 Outlook

The Angels declined the $5.1 million option on Belcher's contract, but they are bringing him back on a minor league contract this spring. Although he had some decent outings last September, he'll have to use every ounce of guile to outpitch Anaheim's young arms.

Brian Cooper

Position: SP
Bats: R **Throws:** R
Ht: 6' 1" **Wt:** 185
Opening Day Age: 26
Born: 8/19/74 in Hollywood, CA
ML Seasons: 2

Overall Statistics

	W	L	Pct.	ERA	G	GS	Sv	IP	H	BB	SO	HR	Ratio
2000	4	8	.333	5.90	15	15	0	87.0	105	35	36	18	1.61
Career	5	9	.357	5.65	20	20	0	114.2	128	53	51	21	1.58

2000 Situational Stats

	W	L	ERA	Sv	IP		AB	H	HR	RBI	Avg
Home	1	4	6.12	0	42.2	LHB	152	46	7	26	.303
Road	3	4	5.68	0	44.1	RHB	198	59	11	33	.298
First Half	3	3	4.14	0	58.2	Sc Pos	89	23	4	38	.258
Scnd Half	1	5	9.53	0	28.1	Clutch	12	6	0	1	.500

2000 Season

Brian Cooper was drafted in the fourth round in 1995 and his progression through the minors has been tedious and not particularly encouraging at times. He repeated Class-A and Double-A, showing marked improvement the second time around at each level. He's had impressive flashes since his 1999 major league debut, including his first major league shutout on June 30 against Oakland.

Pitching & Defense

Cooper's strength is his command. Even when he was getting knocked around in the minors, he displayed precise control of his stuff, boasting a strikeout-walk ratio of better than three-to-one. His control too often deserted him in his limited time in the majors. His fastball registers in the mid- to upper 80s. But he needs his best stuff—a sharp-breaking slider and deceiving changeup—to keep hitters guessing. He is working on being consistent with his mechanics and is beginning to realize the importance of location and changing speeds.

2001 Outlook

Cooper was knocked out before the fifth inning in five of his final seven starts for Anaheim. He lost five straight decisions before a demotion to Triple-A. Still, he looked masterful in some games, giving the Angels hope that he'll contribute this year.

Gary DiSarcina

Position: SS
Bats: R **Throws:** R
Ht: 6' 2" **Wt:** 195
Opening Day Age: 33
Born: 11/19/67 in Malden, MA
ML Seasons: 12
Pronunciation: dee-sar-SEE-nuh

Overall Statistics

	G	AB	R	H	D	T	HR	RBI	SB	BB	SO	Avg	OBP	Slg
2000	12	38	6	15	2	0	1	11	0	1	3	.395	.425	.526
Career	1086	3744	444	966	186	20	28	355	47	154	306	.258	.292	.341

2000 Situational Stats

	AB	H	HR	RBI	Avg		AB	H	HR	RBI	Avg
Home	36	13	1	11	.361	LHP	4	1	0	0	.250
Road	2	2	0	0	1.000	RHP	34	14	1	11	.412
First Half	38	15	1	11	.395	Sc Pos	9	6	0	10	.667
Scnd Half	0	0	0	0	-	Clutch	5	1	0	0	.200

2000 Season

Just 12 games into last season, an MRI revealed a torn rotator cuff for Gary DiSarcina. The competitive clubhouse leader tried to play through the pain, but he could put nothing on his throws and season-ending surgery became inevitable. He now has missed 231 games the past two years.

Hitting, Baserunning & Defense

DiSarcina is an aggressive hitter with excellent bat control, which enables him to hit behind runners, hit-and-run and bunt well. It remains to be seen how his forearm and shoulder injuries will affect his ability to drive balls into the gaps. DiSarcina's instincts take over in the field and on the bases. Defense is his strength, as he displays above-average range, soft hands and an accurate arm.

2001 Outlook

The Angels declined DiSarcina's $3.45 million option, but they are keeping the 13-year relationship intact by virtue of a minor league contract. Doctors give him an 80 percent chance of a full recovery. He's never been counted on for production with his bat. The Angels received almost nothing offensively from their shortstops last year, so DiSarcina's steady glovework and leadership skills will be welcomed back. His rehab work may carry over into the start of the season.

Seth Etherton

Traded To REDS

Position: SP
Bats: R **Throws:** R
Ht: 6' 1" **Wt:** 200
Opening Day Age: 24
Born: 10/17/76 in Laguna Beach, CA
ML Seasons: 1

Overall Statistics

	W	L	Pct.	ERA	G	GS	Sv	IP	H	BB	SO	HR	Ratio
2000	5	1	.833	5.52	11	11	0	60.1	68	22	32	16	1.49
Career	5	1	.833	5.52	11	11	0	60.1	68	22	32	16	1.49

2000 Situational Stats

	W	L	ERA	Sv	IP		AB	H	HR	RBI	Avg
Home	2	0	3.33	0	27.0	LHB	124	35	10	18	.282
Road	3	1	7.29	0	33.1	RHB	121	33	6	15	.273
First Half	3	1	4.98	0	34.1	Sc Pos	57	9	1	10	.158
Scnd Half	2	0	6.23	0	26.0	Clutch	5	1	0	0	.200

2000 Season

Anaheim has a checkered draft history, but recent first-rounders Darin Erstad and Troy Glaus have developed into franchise players. After Anaheim selected Seth Etherton with the 18th overall pick in 1998, his rapid ascent landed him in the majors after only two years.

Pitching & Defense

Etherton's not overpowering, but he's smart enough to succeed by changing speeds. He has an advantage over most young pitchers in that he already has a good idea of what he is trying to do on the mound. His fastball is sneaky, in the range of 86-90 MPH. But the key for Etherton is mixing in an excellent changeup, curve and palmball. In limited chances, Etherton was perfect in the field but allowed five of eight basestealers to advance successfully.

2001 Outlook

Shoulder tendinitis shelved Etherton for last season's final two months. The soreness was a culmination of year-round pitching since coming out of college. The Angels thus shut him down for the winter. But his five-game winning streak, coupled with impressive poise and a polished arsenal, encouraged the Reds to deal for him during the off-season.

Mike Fyhrie

Position: RP
Bats: R **Throws:** R
Ht: 6' 2" **Wt:** 203

Opening Day Age: 31
Born: 12/9/69 in Long Beach, CA
ML Seasons: 3
Pronunciation: FEAR-ee

Overall Statistics

	W	L	Pct.	ERA	G	GS	Sv	IP	H	BB	SO	HR	Ratio
2000	0	0	-	2.39	32	0	0	52.2	54	15	43	4	1.31
Career	0	5	.000	3.97	50	7	0	106.2	119	39	69	12	1.48

2000 Situational Stats

	W	L	ERA	Sv	IP		AB	H	HR	RBI	Avg
Home	0	0	2.22	0	28.1	LHB	81	18	0	6	.222
Road	0	0	2.59	0	24.1	RHB	120	36	4	15	.300
First Half	0	0	2.45	0	29.1	Sc Pos	59	14	0	16	.237
Scnd Half	0	0	2.31	0	23.1	Clutch	9	1	0	0	.111

2000 Season

After toiling in the minors for 10 years, Mike Fyhrie finally established a role in the majors as an effective middle reliever. His minor league tenure included stops in two organizations and in the Japanese Pacific League before he joined Anaheim as a free agent after the 1998 season. A starter throughout his pro career, Fyhrie filled a vital role in the Angels' bullpen.

Pitching & Defense

Fyhrie displayed outstanding command of a polished repertoire last season. The 31-year-old righthander issued only 15 walks in 52.2 innings and painted the corners with his fastball. He can change speeds effectively by mixing in a cutter, slider and changeup. He comes off the mound squarely, in good fielding position, and has been flawless on his first 13 career chances. Fyhrie keeps potential thieves close to the bag and few even consider running on him.

2001 Outlook

The Angels would like to increase Fyhrie's workload in the same bullpen role this year. He provides a reliable bridge to Shigetoshi Hasegawa and Troy Percival in the late innings and probably could fill a rotation spot in a pinch.

Shigetoshi Hasegawa

Position: RP
Bats: R **Throws:** R
Ht: 5'11" **Wt:** 178

Opening Day Age: 32
Born: 8/1/68 in Kobe, Japan
ML Seasons: 4
Pronunciation:
shig-eh-TOE-shee
hos-eh-GAH-wa
Nickname: Shiggy

Overall Statistics

	W	L	Pct.	ERA	G	GS	Sv	IP	H	BB	SO	HR	Ratio
2000	10	5	.667	3.48	66	0	9	95.2	100	38	59	11	1.44
Career	25	21	.543	3.82	241	8	16	386.2	384	150	259	53	1.38

2000 Situational Stats

	W	L	ERA	Sv	IP		AB	H	HR	RBI	Avg
Home	6	2	2.83	5	47.2	LHB	171	42	5	28	.246
Road	4	3	4.13	4	48.0	RHB	199	58	6	25	.291
First Half	6	2	4.88	2	51.2	Sc Pos	111	32	2	44	.288
Scnd Half	4	3	1.84	7	44.0	Clutch	245	59	6	35	.241

2000 Season

Shigetoshi Hasegawa has proven to be durable, reliable and versatile. He can shoulder a heavy workload, averaging just over 60 games and 96 innings per season since 1997 without any signs of wear and tear. Last year he allowed only one run from July 15 to the end of August.

Pitching & Defense

Not many pitchers change speeds and hit their spots better than Hasegawa. He doesn't present an imposing figure on the mound and his stuff isn't overpowering. What he does possess is impeccable command of a well developed bag of tricks, which includes a sneaky-fast fastball that sinks and runs. His "shuto" (Japanese for forkball) serves as his changeup and his good slider helps keep hitters guessing. Hasegawa does a good job of thwarting basestealers and his sound fielding skills have kept him error-free since his rookie season.

2001 Outlook

Hasegawa's importance to the Angels shouldn't be underestimated. The Angels acknowledged his value when they exercised Hasegawa's $1.15 million option in October. Mike Scioscia's 2000 MVP admirably fills every role asked of him and he even slammed the door on four of five games while Troy Percival was disabled last year.

Mike Holtz

Position: RP
Bats: L **Throws:** L
Ht: 5' 9" **Wt:** 188

Opening Day Age: 28
Born: 10/10/72 in
Arlington, VA
ML Seasons: 5

Orlando Palmeiro

Position: LF/RF/DH
Bats: L **Throws:** L
Ht: 5'11" **Wt:** 175

Opening Day Age: 32
Born: 1/19/69 in
Hoboken, NJ
ML Seasons: 6
Pronunciation:
pall-MARE-oh

Overall Statistics

	W	L	Pct.	ERA	G	GS	Sv	IP	H	BB	SO	HR	Ratio
2000	3	4	.429	5.05	61	0	0	41.0	37	18	40	4	1.34
Career	13	16	.448	4.49	238	0	3	166.1	160	82	157	15	1.45

2000 Situational Stats

	W	L	ERA	Sv	IP		AB	H	HR	RBI	Avg
Home	2	0	5.30	0	18.2	LHB	89	19	2	12	.213
Road	1	4	4.84	0	22.1	RHB	60	18	2	8	.300
First Half	0	1	4.42	0	18.1	Sc Pos	50	10	0	14	.200
Scnd Half	3	3	5.56	0	22.2	Clutch	47	14	1	6	.298

Overall Statistics

	G	AB	R	H	D	T	HR	RBI	SB	BB	SO	Avg	OBP	Slg
2000	108	243	38	73	20	2	0	25	4	38	20	.300	.395	.399
Career	431	966	140	275	47	8	1	84	16	123	86	.285	.369	.353

2000 Situational Stats

	AB	H	HR	RBI	Avg		AB	H	HR	RBI	Avg
Home	110	27	0	10	.245	LHP	31	8	0	3	.258
Road	133	46	0	15	.346	RHP	212	65	0	22	.307
First Half	117	35	0	10	.299	Sc Pos	52	15	0	21	.288
Scnd Half	126	38	0	15	.302	Clutch	42	11	0	6	.262

2000 Season

Coming off a pair of subpar seasons, Mike Holtz re-established himself as the Angels go-to lefthanded specialist last year. It looked as though he had carved his niche while appearing in 66 games in 1997, but he worked just 52.2 innings over the next two years. After a bout with control problems, he regained the feel for his bread-and-butter pitch and stepped in to replace Mike Magnante last year.

Pitching & Defense

The key to Holtz' success is a big, slow, sweeping curveball that baffles hitters with its low-70s velocity. His fastball is only average but has good action in the strike zone, and he provides a deceptive look to lefthanded batters. Righthanders get a better look at Holtz' stuff and batted .300 against him for the third straight year. A former high school outfielder, he is athletic and makes the routine plays. His delivery isn't quick and runners can take advantage.

2001 Outlook

The Angels think Holtz can be more than a one-out reliever, although his track record versus righthanders doesn't necessarily support that belief. As long as he continues to get lefties out, however, the bullpen phone will continue to ring for him.

2000 Season

Orlando Palmeiro thrives as Anaheim's fourth outfielder. He understands and accepts the role and makes the most of it. Always at the ready when Mike Scioscia calls, Palmeiro's approach is tailored for the No. 2 slot, with his slashing, bunting and contact-style of hitting.

Hitting, Baserunning & Defense

A scrappy line-drive hitter, Palmeiro is a good tablesetter for the meat of the lineup. He posted a career-high 20 doubles. He'll shorten up to put the ball in play when he falls behind in the count, and his .340 average with two strikes topped the league. An intelligent baserunner, he'll swipe an occasional base, but his hustle pays off most often in the field and when taking extra bases. Palmeiro can fill in at all three outfield positions. Although he won't intimidate anyone with his arm, his throws are generally on the mark.

2001 Outlook

Scioscia will be more than happy to have Palmeiro back in the same capacity this year. Palmeiro gets little attention because he quietly goes about his business as one of the game's best outfield reserves, yet he never stirs up controversy about his playing time.

Scott Spiezio

Position: DH/1B/3B
Bats: B **Throws:** R
Ht: 6' 2" **Wt:** 225

Opening Day Age: 28
Born: 9/21/72 in Joliet, IL
ML Seasons: 5
Pronunciation: SPEE-zee-oh

Overall Statistics

	G	AB	R	H	D	T	HR	RBI	SB	BB	SO	Avg	OBP	Slg
2000	123	297	47	72	11	2	17	49	1	40	56	.242	.334	.465
Career	482	1517	196	377	84	7	50	205	11	161	227	.249	.321	.412

2000 Situational Stats

	AB	H	HR	RBI	Avg			AB	H	HR	RBI	Avg
Home	155	38	10	25	.245	LHP	56	14	2	6	.250
Road	142	34	7	24	.239	RHP	241	58	15	43	.241
First Half	197	47	8	25	.239	Sc Pos	78	19	4	30	.244
Scnd Half	100	25	9	24	.250	Clutch	62	17	3	14	.274

2000 Season

When the Athletics converted Scott Spiezio to second base, they envisioned developing a power-hitting middle infielder. But he hit just .249 in his first three seasons at the new position and Oakland let him go. Anaheim picked him up last year, and he was its leading second-base candidate until Adam Kennedy arrived. Spiezio was used primarily against righthanders as a designated hitter, but he provided versatility around the infield, too.

Hitting, Baserunning & Defense

Spiezio hit 17 home runs last year, a career high. Still, the switch-hitter wasn't very productive for a DH. But when he delivered, it seemed to be in the clutch. His newfound patience also was a bonus. Spiezio is a jack-of-all-trades for Anaheim. He is average at first, second and third base, and logged his first outfield experience last year. Slow feet and poor range also reduced him to just two games at second in 2000. A knee injury and some added bulk keep him from being a factor on the bases.

2001 Outlook

Spiezio should be able to handle a similar reserve role for the Angels this year, minus the regular DH duties. His switch-hitting bat and occasional pop can be a nice option off the bench for Mike Scioscia.

Matt Wise

Position: SP
Bats: R **Throws:** R
Ht: 6' 4" **Wt:** 190

Opening Day Age: 25
Born: 11/18/75 in Montclair, CA
ML Seasons: 1

Overall Statistics

	W	L	Pct.	ERA	G	GS	Sv	IP	H	BB	SO	HR	Ratio
2000	3	3	.500	5.54	8	6	0	37.1	40	13	20	7	1.42
Career	3	3	.500	5.54	8	6	0	37.1	40	13	20	7	1.42

2000 Situational Stats

	W	L	ERA	Sv	IP			AB	H	HR	RBI	Avg
Home	1	2	4.15	0	21.2	LHB	84	21	4	9	.250
Road	2	1	7.47	0	15.2	RHB	63	19	3	11	.302
First Half	0	0	-	0	0.0	Sc Pos	25	9	3	14	.360
Scnd Half	3	3	5.54	0	37.1	Clutch	8	2	0	0	.250

2000 Season

After a strained right elbow prematurely ended his 1999 season in Double-A, Matt Wise bounced back better than anyone could have expected last year. He pitched well in Triple-A before debuting with the Angels in August. He made six starts with Anaheim before fatigue caught up with his elbow. He was then shut down as a precautionary measure.

Pitching & Defense

A wiry righthander, Wise never has been an overpowering force on the mound. He relies on commanding both sides of the plate and keeping his pitches down in the zone. He works an excellent changeup off his fastball by using the same arm speed. He also mixes in a slurve. Wise keeps lefthanded hitters in check with his offspeed stuff. He holds runners well and looks like a capable fielder on comebackers.

2001 Outlook

The Angels were encouraged by Wise's debut. The long and lean righty is expected to spend more time trying to maintain his weight by hitting the weight room during the season. He has a history of dropping up to 15 pounds over the course of a campaign. Depending on his health and the Angels' activity in the free-agent market, Wise should compete for a job in the starting rotation.

Other Anaheim Angels

Juan Alvarez (Pos: LHP, **Age**: 27)

	W	L	Pct.	ERA	G	GS	Sv	IP	H	BB	SO	HR	Ratio
2000	0	0	-	13.50	11	0	0	6.0	14	7	2	3	3.50
Career	0	1	.000	10.00	19	0	0	9.0	15	11	6	3	2.89

Alvarez has been groomed as a situational lefthander virtually from the time he signed as a nondrafted free agent in 1995. But he allowed a .571 on-base percentage to lefties last year with Anaheim. 2001 Outlook: C

Justin Baughman (Pos: 2B, **Age**: 26, **Bats**: R)

	G	AB	R	H	D	T	HR	RBI	SB	BB	SO	Avg	OBP	Slg
2000	16	22	4	5	2	0	0	0	3	1	2	.227	.261	.318
Career	79	218	28	55	11	1	1	20	13	7	38	.252	.275	.326

Baughman's only superior offensive talent seems to be his ability to steal bases. While he can play either second base or shortstop, he needs to hit a little better. 2001 Outlook: C

Edgard Clemente (Pos: LF/RF/DH, **Age**: 25, **Bats**: R)

	G	AB	R	H	D	T	HR	RBI	SB	BB	SO	Avg	OBP	Slg
2000	46	78	4	17	2	0	0	5	0	0	27	.218	.228	.244
Career	114	257	30	64	12	3	8	32	0	9	81	.249	.276	.412

Clemente looked like a nice prospect when he reached Triple-A at age 21, but his career has grinded to a halt in recent years. It would help if he'd consider drawing a walk. 2001 Outlook: C

Jason Dickson (Pos: RHP, **Age**: 28)

	W	L	Pct.	ERA	G	GS	Sv	IP	H	BB	SO	HR	Ratio
2000	2	2	.500	6.11	6	6	0	28.0	39	7	18	5	1.64
Career	26	25	.510	4.99	73	63	0	397.0	474	122	214	60	1.50

Dickson was bothered by hip problems last year and underwent shoulder surgery for the second straight season. He signed a minor league deal with the Blue Jays after the campaign. 2001 Outlook: C

Trent Durrington (Pos: 2B, **Age**: 25, **Bats**: R)

	G	AB	R	H	D	T	HR	RBI	SB	BB	SO	Avg	OBP	Slg
2000	4	3	0	0	0	0	0	0	0	0	0	.000	.000	.000
Career	47	125	14	22	2	0	0	2	4	9	28	.176	.231	.192

The Angels did the logical thing with Durrington after he had hit .180 for Anaheim in 1999 and .219 at Triple-A last year. They released him. His speed simply doesn't compensate for his deficiencies. 2001 Outlook: C

Benji Gil (Pos: SS, **Age**: 28, **Bats**: R)

	G	AB	R	H	D	T	HR	RBI	SB	BB	SO	Avg	OBP	Slg
2000	110	301	28	72	14	1	6	23	10	30	59	.239	.317	.352
Career	377	1095	102	243	47	6	20	103	14	79	325	.222	.277	.331

Few players have displayed Gil's career course. He reached the majors at the age of 20 in 1993, but has played sporadically since. Injuries gave Gil a chance last year, though he didn't seize the moment. He re-signed with the Angels in mid-December. 2001 Outlook: C

Brett Hinchliffe (Pos: RHP, **Age**: 26)

	W	L	Pct.	ERA	G	GS	Sv	IP	H	BB	SO	HR	Ratio
2000	0	0	-	5.40	2	0	0	1.2	1	1	0	0	1.20
Career	0	4	.000	8.63	13	4	0	32.1	42	22	14	10	1.98

The Angels signed Hinchliffe after the Mariners had released him last January. Anaheim then traded him to the Cubs in July. He moved to the bullpen last year after previously working as a starter. He signed a minor league deal with the Mets in December. 2001 Outlook: C

Keith Johnson (Pos: 1B, **Age**: 29, **Bats**: R)

	G	AB	R	H	D	T	HR	RBI	SB	BB	SO	Avg	OBP	Slg
2000	6	4	2	2	0	0	0	0	0	2	0	.500	.667	.500
Career	6	4	2	2	0	0	0	0	0	2	0	.500	.667	.500

Johnson can play any infield position and has gap power. He doesn't walk a lot, but he would come off the bench hacking and could provide some versatility. 2001 Outlook: C

Scott Karl (Pos: LHP, **Age**: 29)

	W	L	Pct.	ERA	G	GS	Sv	IP	H	BB	SO	HR	Ratio
2000	4	5	.444	7.42	23	13	0	87.1	126	45	38	16	1.96
Career	54	56	.491	4.81	178	161	0	1002.0	1164	369	513	120	1.53

Karl has seemingly lived on the edge with his pedestrian stuff for years now, and last year it caught up to him. The Angels traded for him last August, but he signed with the Padres in December. 2001 Outlook: B

Al Levine (Pos: RHP, **Age**: 32)

	W	L	Pct.	ERA	G	GS	Sv	IP	H	BB	SO	HR	Ratio
2000	3	4	.429	3.87	51	5	2	95.1	98	49	42	10	1.54
Career	6	9	.400	4.25	172	6	2	284.0	299	117	132	34	1.46

Levine posted a fairly nice ERA last year despite striking out fewer men than he walked. He actually started four games in September, though he didn't last through the fifth inning in any of them. 2001 Outlook: B

Keith Luuloa (Pos: SS, **Age**: 26, **Bats**: R)

	G	AB	R	H	D	T	HR	RBI	SB	BB	SO	Avg	OBP	Slg
2000	6	18	3	6	0	0	0	0	0	1	1	.333	.368	.333
Career	6	18	3	6	0	0	0	0	0	1	1	.333	.368	.333

Luuloa joined Fred Kuhaulua as the only Hawaiians ever to have played for the Angels. Luuloa then was traded to the Cubs last July. He controls the strike zone though his hitting has usually been fair. He signed a minor league deal with the Padres in November. 2001 Outlook: C

Kent Mercker (Pos: LHP, **Age**: 33)

	W	L	Pct.	ERA	G	GS	Sv	IP	H	BB	SO	HR	Ratio
2000	1	3	.250	6.52	21	7	0	48.1	57	29	30	12	1.78
Career	63	61	.508	4.31	366	150	19	1069.1	1062	488	713	117	1.45

Mercker's season nearly turned tragic when he suffered a cerebral hemmorage last May. While he returned to the Angels in August, he was rarely effective and later became a free agent. 2001 Outlook: C

Mark Petkovsek (Pos: RHP, Age: 35)

	W	L	Pct.	ERA	G	GS	Sv	IP	H	BB	SO	HR	Ratio
2000	4	2	.667	4.22	64	1	2	81.0	86	23	31	8	1.35
Career	45	26	.634	4.49	335	41	5	633.1	694	194	316	68	1.40

Petkovsek won't knock your socks off with his stuff, but he's appeared in 64 games each of the past two years. His walk rate is low and he's a savvy hurler. He signed a two-year deal with Texas in December. 2001 Outlook: B

Lou Pote (Pos: RHP, Age: 29)

	W	L	Pct.	ERA	G	GS	Sv	IP	H	BB	SO	HR	Ratio
2000	1	1	.500	3.40	32	1	1	50.1	52	17	44	4	1.37
Career	2	2	.500	2.94	52	1	4	79.2	75	29	64	5	1.31

Pote hasn't done a bad job the last two years when called up to Anaheim. He became basically a full-time reliever last season and saved 12 games at Triple-A. 2001 Outlook: B

Kevin Stocker (Pos: SS, Age: 31, Bats: B)

	G	AB	R	H	D	T	HR	RBI	SB	BB	SO	Avg	OBP	Slg
2000	110	343	41	75	20	4	2	24	1	51	81	.219	.326	.318
Career	846	2773	340	703	124	28	23	248	45	313	541	.254	.338	.343

The Angels signed Stocker after Tampa Bay had released him in May. He hit less than .200 with no power for Anaheim and was bothered by knee problems for the second straight year. He declared free agency in late October. 2001 Outlook: C

Matt Walbeck (Pos: C, Age: 31, Bats: B)

	G	AB	R	H	D	T	HR	RBI	SB	BB	SO	Avg	OBP	Slg
2000	47	146	17	29	5	0	6	12	0	7	22	.199	.240	.356
Career	595	1885	200	447	73	4	27	199	13	127	303	.237	.287	.323

Walbeck's playing time shrunk last season with the emergence of Ben Molina. Walbeck's batting average shriveled below the Mendoza Line, as well. He declared free agency in November. 2001 Outlook: B

Bryan Ward (Pos: LHP, Age: 29)

	W	L	Pct.	ERA	G	GS	Sv	IP	H	BB	SO	HR	Ratio
2000	0	0	-	3.29	27	0	0	27.1	22	10	14	3	1.17
Career	1	3	.250	5.09	95	0	1	93.2	115	28	66	17	1.53

The Angels signed Ward in August soon after the Phillies had released him. Interestingly, the lefthander limited righthanded hitters to a .194 average last season, half the rate of the year before. He refused assignment and opted for free agency. 2001 Outlook: C

Eric Weaver (Pos: RHP, Age: 27)

	W	L	Pct.	ERA	G	GS	Sv	IP	H	BB	SO	HR	Ratio
2000	0	2	.000	6.87	17	0	0	18.1	20	16	8	5	1.96
Career	2	3	.400	6.27	32	0	0	37.1	39	30	27	8	1.85

Nothing on Weaver's resume would indicate that he'll ever compete for anything other than a middle relief role. He became a free agent for a second straight year after last season. 2001 Outlook: C

Ben Weber (Pos: RHP, Age: 31)

	W	L	Pct.	ERA	G	GS	Sv	IP	H	BB	SO	HR	Ratio
2000	1	1	.500	6.35	19	0	0	22.2	28	6	14	0	1.50
Career	1	1	.500	6.35	19	0	0	22.2	28	6	14	0	1.50

Weber pitched a couple years in Taiwan before returning to the mainland in 1999. The Angels grabbed him off waivers from the Giants last August. He didn't hurt his chances with his work the final month. 2001 Outlook: C

Shawn Wooten (Pos: C, Age: 28, Bats: R)

	G	AB	R	H	D	T	HR	RBI	SB	BB	SO	Avg	OBP	Slg
2000	7	9	2	5	1	0	0	1	0	0	0	.556	.556	.667
Career	7	9	2	5	1	0	0	1	0	0	0	.556	.556	.667

Wooten swings the bat with authority and can play catcher. He's otherwise a fringe prospect who has played only 73 games above Double-A. On the other hand, he's hit .360 in those games. 2001 Outlook: C

Anaheim Angels Minor League Prospects

Organization Overview:

Entering the 2000 season, a host of young pitchers—led by Ramon Ortiz, Seth Etherton, Brian Cooper and Matt Wise—represented most of the Angels' top talent in the high minors. It's possible that all but Etherton, who was traded to the Reds, will work in the Anaheim rotation this year. Otherwise, hardly anyone at the Double-A and Triple-A levels was especially productive in 2000. Luckily for the Angels, a new crop of talent emerged from the low minors last year. Guys like Alfredo Amezaga, Elpidio Guzman, Gary Johnson, John Lackey, Francisco Rodriguez, Brian Specht and Joe Torres are breathing new life into the system. Nurturing the young is a new regime headed by general manager Bill Stoneman. The job of rebuilding the Angels' farm system has begun.

Elpidio Guzman

Position: OF
Bats: L **Throws:** L
Ht: 6' 2" **Wt:** 165

Opening Day Age: 22
Born: 2/24/79 in Santo Domingo, DR

Recent Statistics

	G	AB	R	H	D	T	HR	RBI	SB	BB	SO	Avg
1999 A Cedar Rapds	130	526	74	144	26	13	4	48	52	41	84	.274
2000 A Lk Elsinore	135	532	96	150	20	16	9	72	53	61	116	.282

The jump to high-A ball at age 21 didn't slow Guzman, who solidified his status as a budding five-tool prospect in the California League last summer. Comparing his numbers at Lake Elsinore in 2000 to his Class-A Midwest League stats from 1999, Guzman got on base more frequently and provided more pop last season. He's a strong kid who sometimes turns pull-conscious, and the Angels want him to walk more, strike out less, and become a better bunter. While Guzman may have a few rough spots, he's an exciting player with excellent speed that produced 16 triples and 53 stolen bases at Lake Elsinore. He's also a very polished center fielder. Guzman, signed out of the Dominican Republic in 1995, should get his first taste of Double-A ball in the spring.

Nathan Haynes

Position: OF
Bats: L **Throws:** L
Ht: 5' 9" **Wt:** 170

Opening Day Age: 21
Born: 9/7/79 in Oakland, CA

Recent Statistics

	G	AB	R	H	D	T	HR	RBI	SB	BB	SO	Avg
1999 A Visalia	35	145	28	45	7	1	1	14	12	17	27	.310
1999 A Lk Elsinore	26	110	19	36	5	5	1	15	10	12	19	.327
1999 AA Erie	5	19	3	3	1	0	0	0	0	5	5	.158
2000 AA Erie	118	457	56	116	16	4	6	43	37	33	107	.254
2000 MLE	118	446	49	105	14	3	5	37	27	24	114	.235

During his best season as a pro in 1999, Haynes was acquired from Oakland in the Randy Velarde-Omar Olivares deal. To maximize his above-average speed, Haynes shortened his swing in '99, hit the ball on the ground more, and drew walks more frequently. Last summer, at the Double-A level, Haynes abandoned his plate patience and little ball skills in the early going, but the Angels were pleased with a second-half rebound in which he used his skills more wisely. Defensively, Haynes' speed and good instincts make him very effective in center. His arm is average. A supplemental first-round pick in 1997, Haynes is expected to return to Double-A ball for the start of his fifth pro season.

Gary Johnson

Position: OF
Bats: L **Throws:** L
Ht: 6' 3" **Wt:** 210

Opening Day Age: 25
Born: 10/29/75 in Monroe, CA

Recent Statistics

	G	AB	R	H	D	T	HR	RBI	SB	BB	SO	Avg
1999 A Boise	71	264	56	83	17	1	2	48	6	34	44	.314
2000 A Lk Elsinore	70	266	56	90	20	2	13	62	13	41	59	.338
2000 AA Erie	71	258	44	74	10	4	10	56	4	35	63	.287
2000 MLE	71	251	38	67	9	3	8	49	2	26	67	.267

Johnson's career was put on hold when he spent two years on a Mormon mission, but he's quickly climbed to the Double-A level since being drafted in 1999. The Angels love his tools, and they are pleased with his emergence as a run producer and clutch performer. With a sweet lefthanded swing that generates punch to all fields, Johnson engaged in a Triple Crown chase in the high Class-A California League before a midseason promotion. While he continued to hit well at Double-A Erie, his defensive game needs work. Balls hit over his head give him trouble, but Johnson is an above-average runner who put in lots of time refining his fielding and throwing. He works hard at his game.

John Lackey

Position: P
Bats: R **Throws:** R
Ht: 6' 5" **Wt:** 200

Opening Day Age: 22
Born: 10/23/78 in Abilene, TX

Recent Statistics

	W	L	ERA	G	GS	Sv	IP	H	R	BB	SO	HR
1999 A Boise	6	2	4.98	15	15	0	81.1	81	59	50	77	7
2000 A Cedar Rapds	3	2	2.08	5	5	0	30.1	20	7	5	21	1
2000 A Lk Elsinore	6	6	3.40	15	15	0	100.2	94	56	42	74	9
2000 AA Erie	6	1	3.30	8	8	0	57.1	58	23	9	43	6

After showing good stuff in his pro debut at short-season Boise in 1999, Lackey climbed all the way to Double-A Erie in his second season. The Angels like the upside of their 6-foot-5 righthander. Lackey throws a plus fastball that can put hitters away, and he has a good feel for an average curveball. He's also working on a changeup, but it's not as far along as his other two pitches. More than anything, though, the Angels like Lackey's smarts and competitive makeup. It's the whole package that has allowed this second-round pick from '99 to climb so high so quickly.

Scott Morgan

Position: OF
Bats: R **Throws:** R
Ht: 6' 7" **Wt:** 230

Opening Day Age: 27
Born: 7/19/73 in Westlake, CA

Recent Statistics

	G	AB	R	H	D	T	HR	RBI	SB	BB	SO	Avg
1999 AA Akron	88	344	72	97	26	2	26	70	6	38	96	.282
1999 AA Buffalo	48	171	32	44	9	0	8	31	2	18	38	.257
2000 AAA Buffalo	11	33	5	12	3	0	0	4	1	7	7	.364
2000 AAA Edmonton	90	320	53	79	25	2	9	54	8	32	74	.247
2000 MLE	101	340	45	78	23	1	7	45	5	31	84	.229

Morgan is a 6-foot-7, 230-pound power threat who draws comparisons to Richie Sexson. Both Morgan, a seventh-round pick in 1995, and Sexson came up in the Cleveland system, but the Tribe lost Morgan on a waiver claim in April. He's been slow to develop, and he didn't approach his .274-34-101 combined performance of 1999 at the Double- and Triple-A level last summer. But Morgan's 2000 season was hampered by a cyst on his wrist that made it painful to swing. He runs well for a big guy, but his defensive skills aren't the best and his arm is below average. Left field is his ticket as an outfielder.

Francisco Rodriguez

Position: P
Bats: R **Throws:** R
Ht: 6' 0" **Wt:** 165

Opening Day Age: 19
Born: 1/7/82 in Caracas, VZ

Recent Statistics

	W	L	ERA	G	GS	Sv	IP	H	R	BB	SO	HR
1999 R Butte	1	1	3.31	12	9	0	51.2	33	21	21	69	1
1999 A Boise	1	0	5.40	1	1	0	5.0	3	4	1	6	0
2000 A Lk Elsinore	4	4	2.81	13	12	0	64.0	43	29	32	79	2

The Angels were smart in outbidding several clubs and signing a 16-year-old Rodriguez for $900,000 in 1998. *Baseball America* named him the best prospect in the Pioneer League in 1999, and Rodriguez followed up with a strong showing in the high Class-A California League last summer at age 18. He already throws a mid-90s fastball and a nearly unhittable, sharp-breaking slurve, power pitches that are remarkable from a 165-pound teenager. During his fine season at Class-A Lake Elsinore, Rodriguez made real progress on his changeup, a pitch that will be at least major league average. He needs to become more consistent with his delivery, but the stuff is there to become a top-flight pitcher.

Scot Shields

Position: P
Bats: R **Throws:** R
Ht: 6' 1" **Wt:** 175

Opening Day Age: 25
Born: 7/22/75 in Fort Lauderdale, FL

Recent Statistics

	W	L	ERA	G	GS	Sv	IP	H	R	BB	SO	HR
1999 A Lk Elsinore	10	3	2.52	24	9	1	107.1	91	37	39	113	1
1999 AA Erie	4	4	2.89	10	10	0	74.2	57	26	26	81	10
2000 AAA Edmonton	7	13	5.41	27	27	0	163.0	158	114	82	156	16

After signing as a 38th-round pick and working strictly as a reliever in his first two pro seasons, Shields became a starter in 1999 and pitched remarkably well at Class-A

Lake Elsinore and Double-A Erie (14-7, 2.67). That success didn't carry over to his first Triple-A season at Edmonton in 2000, though he kept the ball down better late in the season. While Shield's fastball-slider combo isn't a power-pitch package, his hard-sinking, low-90s fastball and late-breaking slider have life. Although his stuff is good, he doesn't always trust it, and he went to instructional league in the fall to work on his changeup. After some fine-tuning at Triple-A, Shields could join the host of young pitchers in Anaheim.

Derrick Turnbow

Position: P
Bats: R **Throws:** R
Ht: 6' 3" **Wt:** 180

Opening Day Age: 23
Born: 1/25/78 in Union City, TN

Recent Statistics

	W	L	ERA	G	GS	Sv	IP	H	R	BB	SO	HR
2000 AL Anaheim	0	0	4.74	24	1	0	38.0	36	21	36	25	7

A fifth-round high school pick in 1997, Turnbow stayed with Anaheim for all of 2000 after being plucked away from the Phillies in the Rule 5 draft in December 1999. The 6-foot-3 righthander had pitched in low-A ball in '99, so it's not surprising that he struggled in the majors. But the Angels have to like his low-90s sinker, which has late movement, as well as the promise of a curveball with good depth and break. Work continues on his changeup, and he didn't use it as much with the Angels as he might have in a minor league context. While Turnbow pitched well in the Arizona Fall League, he's probably destined for more minor league seasoning in 2001.

Others to Watch

For his age, **Alfredo Amezaga** (23) is a polished player with impressive makeup, leadership skills and a good bat. He controls the strike zone and successfully took up switch-hitting in 2000. He also stole 73 bases at Class-A Lake Elsinore last summer. He has the range to play shortstop, but his small build and average arm make him a better candidate for second base. . . At the time he was acquired from Oakland in 1999, **Jeff DaVanon** (27) wasn't young or a top-tier prospect. But he was in the midst of a season in which he batted .338 and slugged .567 in the high minors. His battle for a reserve role with Anaheim in 2000 was sidetracked by a torn labrum, but he's back in the mix for 2001. . . The 10th overall pick in the 2000 draft, **Joe Torres** (18) went to the short-season Northwest League and showed his stuff as the youngest player in the circuit. He throws a 90-MPH fastball and shows decent command of a big curve and slider that are advanced pitches. Torres, may end up at or near the top of big league rotation. . . The hard-working and competitive **Phil Wilson** (20) reminds the Angels of Lackey. A third-round pick in 1999, Wilson debuted in the Midwest League in 2000 and finished the year with six solid starts for high Class-A Lake Elsinore. The righthander throws a moving fastball in the 88-92 MPH range and an exceptional changeup.

Oriole Park at Camden Yards

Offense

Mike Hargrove's decision to run more is one of the reasons Oriole Park at Camden Yards finished below the league average in home runs allowed. It's 318 feet down the right-field line, but the 373 feet to right-center field and the 25-foot wall don't help lefthanded hitters. Camden Yards is now the third-toughest ballpark on American League hitters for batting average. Righthanded batters are productive here, as the ball travels well to left field, especially at night in the warmer months. Still, Camden Yards yielded a much lower number of runs than the typical American League ballpark.

Defense

The Orioles continue to have the grass cut higher than most American League ballparks. This helped compensate for a defense that was steady, but isn't known to have a lot of range. Even though the ballpark is asymmetrical, it does not yield a high number of doubles or triples.

Who It Helps the Most

The team as a whole doesn't derive any particular benefit from playing at Camden Yards. Rookie Luis Matos and veteran Cal Ripken Jr. felt more comfortable at Camden than on the road. Ripken's batting average was markedly higher at home last season. The pitching staff benefits from the high infield grass.

Who It Hurts the Most

Delino DeShields rebounded after a poor first season with the Orioles, but his home ballpark can't be credited for his success. Youngsters Chris Richard and Jerry Hairston Jr. were much more productive away from Baltimore.

Rookies & Newcomers

Free-agent pickup Pat Hentgen is 4-1 (3.76) in seven lifetime appearances at Oriole Park. Calvin Pickering might end up in Baltimore at some point in the season, especially if Chris Richard struggles at first base. Pitching prospect Matt Riley was expected to arrive on the scene in 2001, but arm woes have set him back a year.

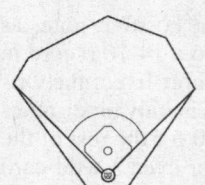

Dimensions: LF-333, LCF-364, CF-410, RCF-373, RF-318

Capacity: 48,876

Elevation: 20 feet

Surface: Grass

Foul Territory: Average

Baltimore

Park Factors

2000 Season

| | Home Games | | | Away Games | | | |
	Orioles	Opp	Total	Orioles	Opp	Total	Index
G	72	72	144	72	72	144	—
Avg	.270	.260	.265	.272	.291	.281	94
AB	2348	2515	4863	2583	2492	5075	96
R	345	371	716	373	443	816	88
H	634	655	1289	702	725	1427	90
2B	118	101	219	161	155	316	72
3B	8	13	21	14	20	34	64
HR	76	96	172	85	86	171	105
BB	278	292	570	223	308	531	112
SO	392	474	866	411	422	833	108
E	51	38	89	54	52	106	84
E-Infield	43	34	77	44	42	86	90
LHB-Avg	.264	.251	.257	.278	.295	.287	90
LHB-HR	29	36	65	40	32	72	98
RHB-Avg	.275	.268	.271	.267	.287	.277	98
RHB-HR	47	60	107	45	54	99	109

1998-2000

| | Home Games | | | Away Games | | | |
	Orioles	Opp	Total	Orioles	Opp	Total	Index
G	217	217	434	217	217	434	—
Avg	.274	.260	.267	.273	.283	.278	96
AB	7236	7544	14780	7713	7319	15032	98
R	1068	1059	2127	1148	1202	2350	91
H	1980	1964	3944	2105	2073	4178	94
2B	359	319	678	456	419	875	79
3B	22	36	58	29	51	80	74
HR	260	261	521	274	263	537	99
BB	804	805	1609	790	853	1643	100
SO	1166	1431	2597	1245	1303	2548	104
E	124	120	244	142	139	281	87
E-Infield	106	108	214	121	112	233	92
LHB-Avg	.271	.248	.259	.277	.290	.284	91
LHB-HR	112	98	210	135	111	246	89
RHB-Avg	.275	.271	.273	.270	.277	.273	100
RHB-HR	148	163	311	139	152	291	107

2000 Rankings (American League)

- Highest walk factor
- Second-highest strikeout factor
- Lowest double factor
- Second-lowest run factor
- Second-lowest LHB batting-average factor
- Third-lowest batting-average factor
- Third-lowest hit factor
- Third-lowest triple factor
- Third-lowest error factor

Mike Hargrove

2000 Season

The 2000 season opened on a positive note, as Mike Hargrove led Baltimore to a 14-10 record in April. But that optimism was short-lived; the Orioles slumped and struggled to win only nine games in May. They played under .500 for the rest of the season and never challenged for even a wild-card spot. On the positive side, Hargrove's team played hard, and the chemistry in the clubhouse was an improvement over Ray Miller's final season.

Offense

Hargrove was an aggressive manager from Opening Day, using the running game to ignite a stagnant offense. The Orioles led the circuit in stolen-base attempts and successful steals. Hargrove preferred to use the stolen base over the hit-and-run, even though Baltimore was just slightly below the league average in basestealing percentage. He also avoided the sacrifice bunt, attempting the second-lowest total in the American League. Hargrove prefers to go with a set lineup, and a relatively healthy Orioles team allowed him to do that often. Once the Orioles decided to go with the kids, Chris Richard, Melvin Mora, Luis Matos and Ryan Kohlmeier all got a long look.

Pitching & Defense

Unlike his days in Cleveland, Hargrove didn't have the luxury of a deep bullpen. So he tended to leave his starters in the game longer than any other manager. Once Kohlmeier showed he could do the job late in the season, Hargrove changed his style and relied on his closer more. In the past, he would stick with the same closer through tough times, but the struggles of Mike Timlin and Mike Trombley were too much for his patience. Hargrove was much more reluctant to issue a free pass than he did while he was managing in Cleveland. His teams play smart, sound defense.

2001 Outlook

The Orioles' season looks bleaker with Mike Mussina heading to New York. Now Hargrove must retool an already-thin pitching staff around Pat Hentgen, and his options are limited. The team clearly is rebuilding, and Baltimore again will be hard pressed to reach the .500 mark.

Born: 10/26/49 in Perryton, TX

Playing Experience: 1974-1985, Tex, Cle, SD

Managerial Experience: 10 seasons

Manager Statistics

Year	Team, Lg	W	L	Pct	GB	Finish
2000	Baltimore, AL	74	88	.457	13.5	4th East
10 Seasons		795	679	.539	—	—

2000 Starting Pitchers by Days Rest

	<=3	4	5	6+
Orioles Starts	1	81	45	24
Orioles ERA	9.53	5.47	4.78	5.40
AL Avg Starts	2	88	40	22
AL ERA	4.87	5.03	5.03	5.28

2000 Situational Stats

	Mike Hargrove	AL Average
Hit & Run Success %	28.4	35.1
Stolen Base Success %	66.0	68.8
Platoon Pct.	54.3	57.8
Defensive Subs	19	23
High-Pitch Outings	24	13
Quick/Slow Hooks	7/30	18/19
Sacrifice Attempts	36	55

2000 Rankings (American League)

- 1st in stolen base attempts (191) and slow hooks (30)
- 2nd in steals of third base (19), double steals (6) and starts with over 120 pitches (24)

Brady Anderson

2000 Season

Brady Anderson was able to play in 141 games in 2000, but a collection of sprains and strains reduced his effectiveness both in the field and at the plate. Hitting .278 at the end of May, Anderson's batting average took a dive during the middle months of the season, though he was able to sustain his ability to get on base. He finished strong with a .308 batting average and .477 on-base percentage in September.

Hitting

Anderson no longer hangs over the plate as he once did, and he was plunked by pitches only eight times last season, his lowest mark in nine years. He also no longer drives the ball with the authority that he did just a few seasons ago. He is pulling the ball a lot less as he gets older, preferring to use left field more often. Breaking pitches on the outside corner have become more of a problem, causing him to reach at times. Anderson still is able to catch up to inside fastballs, but he doesn't drive them with the same authority.

Baserunning & Defense

Anderson's speed from first to third is still good, although stealing bases has become a much more difficult task. His 16 stolen bases in 2000 were his lowest total in the past nine seasons. He's getting caught more often too, as Anderson posted the second-lowest success rate of his career. In the field, his range in center has decreased, and he spent more time in left and right than he has since 1995. While he gets a good jump on the ball, he's lost a step and isn't able to cover the gaps as he once did. His arm has weakened, and he registered only one assist all season.

2001 Outlook

There's been talk that Anderson might be moved to a corner position because of dwindling range in center, but a move to right actually may be necessitated by Albert Belle's degenerative hip condition. Anderson still has the ability to get on base, so he should continue in the leadoff spot for at least another campaign. It wouldn't be a surprise if both his home-run and stolen-base totals barely reach the mid-teens in 2001.

Position: CF/RF/LF
Bats: L **Throws:** L
Ht: 6' 1" **Wt:** 202

Opening Day Age: 37
Born: 1/18/64 in Silver Spring, MD
ML Seasons: 13

Overall Statistics

	G	AB	R	H	D	T	HR	RBI	SB	BB	SO	Avg	OBP	Slg
2000	141	506	89	130	26	0	19	50	16	92	103	.257	.375	.421
Career	1669	5989	1008	1561	322	64	201	711	299	882	1090	.261	.366	.436

Where He Hits the Ball

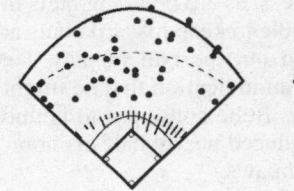
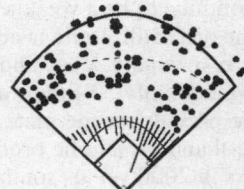

Vs. LHP   **Vs. RHP**

2000 Situational Stats

	AB	H	HR	RBI	Avg		AB	H	HR	RBI	Avg
Home	240	64	9	26	.267	LHP	146	38	3	14	.260
Road	266	66	10	24	.248	RHP	360	92	16	36	.256
First Half	297	74	11	30	.249	Sc Pos	90	19	1	26	.211
Scnd Half	209	56	8	20	.268	Clutch	56	8	2	3	.143

2000 Rankings (American League)

- 1st in lowest batting average in the clutch
- 4th in lowest stolen-base percentage (64.0)
- 5th in fewest GDPs per GDP situation (4.3%), on-base percentage for a leadoff hitter (.374) and lowest batting average with runners in scoring position
- Led the Orioles in runs scored, sacrifice bunts (5), walks, hit by pitch (8), strikeouts, pitches seen (2,510), on-base percentage, most pitches seen per plate appearance (4.06), fewest GDPs per GDP situation (4.3%), on-base percentage for a leadoff hitter (.374), slugging percentage vs. righthanded pitchers (.433), on-base percentage vs. righthanded pitchers (.372), bunts in play (8) and highest percentage of pitches taken (59.3)

Albert Belle

2000 Season

By the time the 2000 season ended, there were concerns that Albert Belle's degenerating left hip would either curtail his career or relegate him to full-time designated hitter duty. His hip condition surfaced in June, and Belle hit only five home runs after the All-Star break as he struggled to generate power. He surpassed 100 RBI for the ninth straight season, but his 103 represented his lowest output since the strike-shortened 1994 season.

Hitting

Belle's hip condition prevented him from driving the ball out of the ballpark late in the season. Before the injury, he was one of the American League's most feared power hitters. High fastballs continue to be a weakness, as are breaking balls in the dirt. Still, Belle is able to keep his strikeouts at a respectable level and put the ball in play. He walked only 52 times, an indication that he might be pressing at the plate. Belle continues to pound lefthanders, and he produced nearly half his homers in 2000 versus southpaws.

Baserunning & Defense

Belle always has been an opportunistic baserunner, as evidenced by his 17 stolen bases in 1999. However, his sore hip all but stopped his basestealing and severely limited his ability to go from first to third, relegating him to being a station-to-station baserunner. In the field, Belle became a liability after the All-Star break because his range in covering the right-center gap suffered dramatically. His arm remained strong, but he was unable to reach double digits in assists.

2001 Outlook

Cloudy at best describes Belle's immediate future. He will spend the entire offseason in a stringent rehab program to rebuild the strength in his left hip, but it is a condition that eventually will require surgery. The Orioles are not optimistic that he'll return to right field in 2001, so they are prepared to move him to the DH spot on a full-time basis. That move should take some pressure off the hip this year, but Belle's power numbers and production may continue their downward trend.

Position: RF/DH
Bats: R **Throws:** R
Ht: 6' 2" **Wt:** 225

Opening Day Age: 34
Born: 8/25/66 in Shreveport, LA
ML Seasons: 12

Overall Statistics

	G	AB	R	H	D	T	HR	RBI	SB	BB	SO	Avg	OBP	Slg
2000	141	559	71	157	37	1	23	103	0	52	68	.281	.342	.474
Career	1539	5853	974	1726	389	21	381	1239	88	683	961	.295	.369	.564

Where He Hits the Ball

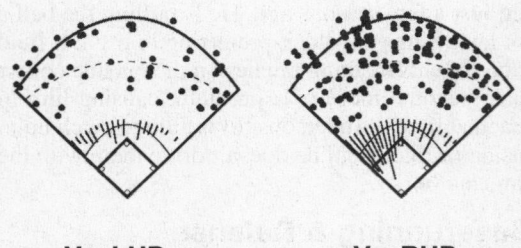

Vs. LHP   **Vs. RHP**

2000 Situational Stats

	AB	H	HR	RBI	Avg			AB	H	HR	RBI	Avg
Home	278	76	14	60	.273		LHP	137	47	10	33	.343
Road	281	81	9	43	.288		RHP	422	110	13	70	.261
First Half	335	99	18	68	.296		Sc Pos	156	46	9	81	.295
Scnd Half	224	58	5	35	.259		Clutch	78	18	1	10	.231

2000 Rankings (American League)

- 4th in batting average with the bases loaded (.625), slugging percentage vs. lefthanded pitchers (.650) and lowest cleanup slugging percentage (.474)
- 5th in intentional walks (11) and fielding percentage in right field (.986)
- Led the Orioles in home runs, total bases (265), RBI, intentional walks (11), GDPs (17), slugging percentage, HR frequency (24.3 ABs per HR), batting average with the bases loaded (.625), cleanup slugging percentage (.474), slugging percentage vs. lefthanded pitchers (.650) and on-base percentage vs. lefthanded pitchers (.424)
- Led AL right fielders in intentional walks (11) and batting average with the bases loaded (.625)

Delino DeShields

2000 Season

The 2000 edition of Delino DeShields was the version the Orioles expected when they inked him to a three-year deal before the start of the 1999 campaign. He was a highly productive hitter all season, collecting a career-best 82 RBI and posting a .369 on-base percentage, one of the highest of his 11-year career. On the bases, he returned to the form that made him a threat to steal every time he was aboard. A key ingredient to his solid 2000 season was DeShields' ability to stay healthy.

Hitting

DeShields has changed his approach versus lefthanders and now goes with the pitch, and this produced a career-best season versus southpaws in 2000. He makes consistent contact on all types of pitches and displays solid gap power. He was given the bulk of his at-bats in the No. 3 spot in the batting order for the first time in his career and adapted quickly to the role. DeShields improved his ability to hit with runners in scoring position after his move down in the batting order. Bunting was never his forte and he rarely attempts to lay one down any more, preferring to swing away.

Baserunning & Defense

A healthy season allowed DeShields to become a force on the basepaths again. Both his totals and success rate returned to pre-1999 levels. He occasionally can score from first when the ball is hit into the gap, and his ability to go from first to third remains among the best in the American League. The biggest change in his career is the move from second base to left field late in 1999. The decline in his lateral movement and the promise of prospect Jerry Hairston Jr. facilitated the move. His range in left is above average, and he displays an average throwing arm.

2001 Outlook

Deshields enters the last year of his three-year deal with the Orioles as the projected starting left fielder, though playing time in center also is a possibility. A healthy DeShields was a very productive player in 2000, and he should continue to adapt to a new position in the field and the No. 3 spot in the lineup.

Position: 2B/LF/DH
Bats: L **Throws:** R
Ht: 6' 1" **Wt:** 175

Opening Day Age: 32
Born: 1/15/69 in Seaford, DE
ML Seasons: 11
Pronunciation: duh-LINE-oh

Overall Statistics

	G	AB	R	H	D	T	HR	RBI	SB	BB	SO	Avg	OBP	Slg
2000	151	561	84	166	43	5	10	86	37	69	82	.296	.369	.444
Career	1422	5282	797	1438	221	68	72	514	430	674	946	.272	.354	.381

Where He Hits the Ball

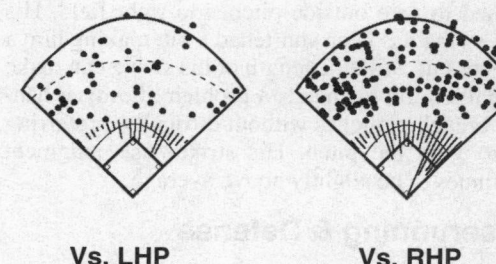

Vs. LHP   **Vs. RHP**

2000 Situational Stats

	AB	H	HR	RBI	Avg		AB	H	HR	RBI	Avg
Home	265	75	4	42	.283	LHP	154	53	2	24	.344
Road	296	91	6	44	.307	RHP	407	113	8	62	.278
First Half	292	85	3	36	.291	Sc Pos	130	45	3	70	.346
Scnd Half	269	81	7	50	.301	Clutch	76	21	0	11	.276

2000 Rankings (American League)

- 3rd in stolen bases and steals of third (6)
- 5th in caught stealing (10)
- 6th in highest percentage of extra bases taken as a runner (64.9)
- 7th in errors at second base (11)
- 8th in doubles
- 9th in batting average with runners in scoring position and batting average vs. lefthanded pitchers
- 10th in sacrifice flies (9), stolen-base percentage (78.7) and lowest HR frequency (56.1 ABs per HR)
- Led the Orioles in batting average, at-bats, hits, singles, doubles, triples, sacrifice flies (9), stolen bases and caught stealing (10)

Brook Fordyce

2000 Season

Brook Fordyce began the 2000 season entrenched as the White Sox' starting catcher after a solid 1999 campaign. But a broken left foot in spring training derailed his season until late May. Once he returned, he picked up where he left off at the plate. Surprisingly, the White Sox dealt him to Baltimore in a six-player deal in exchange for Charles Johnson at the end of July. Fordyce finished the season strong as the Orioles' No. 1 catcher.

Hitting

Fordyce posted career numbers across the board. Increased playing time at the major league level has helped him hone his skills at the plate. He is very effective versus southpaws because he has learned to take outside pitches to right field. His long swing has been shortened a bit, making him a tougher out. Still, the length of his swing can make fastballs in on his hands a problem. Fordyce handles breaking pitches without difficulty, preferring to go with the pitch. His strike-zone judgment continues to be slightly above average.

Baserunning & Defense

Fordyce's running ability is average for a catcher. He rarely goes from first to third unless the ball is hit deep into the gaps. His four career stolen bases are indicative of his lack of foot speed. His throwing arm is average and accurate, but his skills aren't strong enough to shut down an opponent's running game. Last season he threw out only 11 of 66 baserunners. Fordyce struggles at times to block pitches in the dirt.

2001 Outlook

The Orioles signed Fordyce to a three-year contract extension after the World Series. Baltimore believes he has the skills and handles pitchers well enough to be the team's everyday starting catcher. Fordyce never has caught more than 103 games at the major league level, so his stamina will be tested this season. If he gets 400-plus at-bats, he should surpass the career highs that he set in 2000. Behind the plate, the Orioles believe Fordyce can correct the mechanics that have reduced his throwing efficiency.

Position: C
Bats: R **Throws:** R
Ht: 6' 0" **Wt:** 190

Opening Day Age: 30
Born: 5/7/70 in New London, CT
ML Seasons: 6

Overall Statistics

	G	AB	R	H	D	T	HR	RBI	SB	BB	SO	Avg	OBP	Slg
2000	93	302	41	91	18	1	14	49	0	17	50	.301	.341	.507
Career	310	886	93	250	59	2	27	121	4	61	142	.282	.331	.445

Where He Hits the Ball

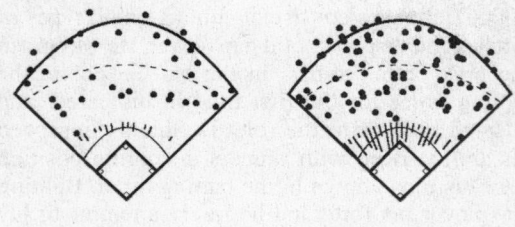

Vs. LHP　　　　**Vs. RHP**

2000 Situational Stats

	AB	H	HR	RBI	Avg		AB	H	HR	RBI	Avg
Home	150	37	8	21	.247	LHP	72	25	6	18	.347
Road	152	54	6	28	.355	RHP	230	66	8	31	.287
First Half	86	20	3	17	.233	Sc Pos	82	21	2	35	.256
Scnd Half	216	71	11	32	.329	Clutch	50	10	0	4	.200

2000 Rankings (American League)

- 2nd in fielding percentage at catcher (.993)
- 7th in lowest batting average in the clutch (.200)
- Led AL catchers in fewest GDPs per GDP situation (6.7%)

Ryan Kohlmeier

2000 Season

Ryan Kohlmeier was recalled at the end of July when the Orioles were shuffling their roster, which included sending closer Mike Timlin to the Cardinals. Kohlmeier made the most of his chance by recording 13 saves in 14 tries and posting a 2.39 ERA in 25 games. His rookie season was a surprise because Baltimore considered him a borderline prospect.

Pitching

Kohlmeier isn't overpowering and doesn't have a dominating pitch, but he does use what he has to the maximum of his ability. A nifty slider is more of a power pitch than his 89-90 MPH fastball, which tends to be straight. When the fastball has some movement, it's an effective pitch. Currently, Kohlmeier has better command of the slider than his four-seam fastball. Because he doesn't have a viable offspeed pitch, he needs to work in short relief to cover up that deficiency. Mentally, he challenges hitters, a quality that led the Orioles to try him in the closer role. Though he has a reputation of displaying good control, Kohlmeier nearly walked as many as he struck out in 2000, indicating he wasn't as dominant as some of his statistics suggest.

Defense

His defense around the mound is average, but he does have difficulty getting over to cover the first-base bag. That could change as he gets more comfortable with the major league team. He has an average move to first, which is typical of most righthanders.

2001 Outlook

Kohlmeier gave the Orioles mixed signals about his future. He wasn't as dominating as his 2.39 ERA and 13 saves suggest, since he yielded 30 hits and 15 walks in only 26.1 innings. Before he gets the stamp of approval, he needs a full trip around the American League to judge how well he'll react to hitters. If he passes that test and reduces the number of baserunners he allows, the Orioles may have found their closer for the present and future.

Position: RP
Bats: R **Throws:** R
Ht: 6' 2" **Wt:** 197

Opening Day Age: 23
Born: 6/25/77 in Salina, KS
ML Seasons: 1

Baltimore

Overall Statistics

	W	L	Pct.	ERA	G	GS	Sv	IP	H	BB	SO	HR	Ratio
2000	0	1	.000	2.39	25	0	13	26.1	30	15	17	1	1.71
Career	0	1	.000	2.39	25	0	13	26.1	30	15	17	1	1.71

How Often He Throws Strikes

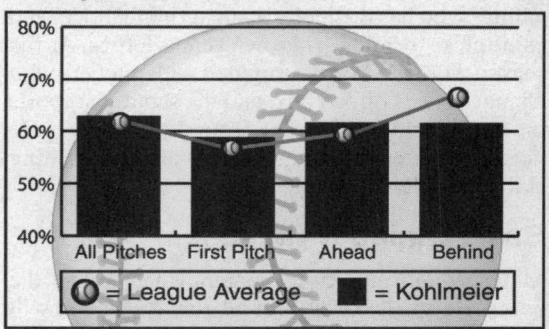

2000 Situational Stats

	W	L	ERA	Sv	IP		AB	H	HR	RBI	Avg
Home	0	0	1.23	6	14.2	LHB	54	18	1	7	.333
Road	0	1	3.86	7	11.2	RHB	49	12	0	4	.245
First Half	0	0	-	0	0.0	Sc Pos	31	6	0	8	.194
Scnd Half	0	1	2.39	13	26.1	Clutch	61	14	0	6	.230

2000 Rankings (American League)
- Led the Orioles in saves

37

Luis Matos

2000 Season

Luis Matos was recalled from the minors on June 19 and filled in both in center field and right field. He was brought up to get his feet wet while serving as a backup outfielder. After an 0-for-11 June, Matos rebounded to hit .297 in July, but fizzled in August and looked like an overmatched rookie the rest of the season. The one positive was his speed, as he stole 13 bases in 17 tries.

Hitting

Even though Matos is slightly built, he has deceptive strength that helps him generate gap power. That pop hasn't been apparent at the major league level yet. His first go-round in the majors revealed a hitter who has difficulty against righthanders and came close to holding his own versus lefties. As the season wore on, Matos struggled with pitchers who change speeds effectively, and the scouting reports on him quickly circulated around the league. He needs to better utilize his speed, and his bunting skills need development.

Baserunning & Defense

Matos' athletic ability is apparent when he runs the bases. He steals bases with his raw speed and will become even more productive once he learns to read pitchers. Matos can score from second on most hits to the outfield, and his ability to go from first to third is impressive. His range covering the gaps is good but not great. Part of his problem is that he doesn't get a great jump on the ball, a flaw that will improve with experience. His arm has been compared to Alex Ochoa's—strong but erratic.

2001 Outlook

Matos covers more ground in center than the incumbent Brady Anderson does. So Matos gets the first shot at center field while Anderson moves to right to replace Albert Belle. The Orioles will need to be patient because Matos is a talented but raw player with very few at-bats above Double-A. Baltimore hopes his speed and defensive range in center field will offset his troubles at the plate for now. The O's feel he's only two years away from being a force with the bat.

Position: CF/RF
Bats: R **Throws:** R
Ht: 6' 0" **Wt:** 179

Opening Day Age: 22
Born: 10/30/78 in Bayamon, Puerto Rico
ML Seasons: 1

Overall Statistics

	G	AB	R	H	D	T	HR	RBI	SB	BB	SO	Avg	OBP	Slg
2000	72	182	21	41	6	3	1	17	13	12	30	.225	.281	.308
Career	72	182	21	41	6	3	1	17	13	12	30	.225	.281	.308

Where He Hits the Ball

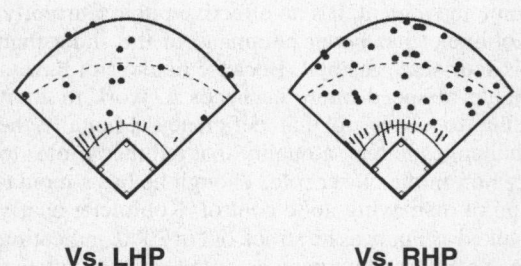

Vs. LHP   **Vs. RHP**

2000 Situational Stats

	AB	H	HR	RBI	Avg		AB	H	HR	RBI	Avg
Home	103	27	1	12	.262	LHP	58	15	1	7	.259
Road	79	14	0	5	.177	RHP	124	26	0	10	.210
First Half	23	4	0	0	.174	Sc Pos	41	8	1	17	.195
Scnd Half	159	37	1	17	.233	Clutch	26	5	0	4	.192

2000 Rankings (American League)

- Did not rank near the top or bottom in any category

Jose Mercedes

2000 Season

Opportunity is the word that best describes Jose Mercedes' 2000 season. When Scott Erickson went down with an elbow injury, the Orioles recalled Mercedes from Triple-A Rochester. He struggled in a starter's role in April and was moved to the bullpen in May and June. After a successful string of relief appearances, he earned another shot at starting in July. He responded with 11 quality starts and a career-high 14 wins.

Pitching

While Mercedes hasn't accumulated high innings totals because of injuries, he demonstrates maturity on the mound. His command and control are borderline for a major league pitcher, so he uses guile to get by at times. Because he doesn't have a dominating pitch, Mercedes uses a collection of pitches and changes speeds, moving his offerings around the strike zone to keep hitters off stride. His fastball rarely reaches 89-90 MPH, so he turns it over and cuts it to give it a different look. His breaking ball is average at best, but he's able to change speeds with it to help keep hitters off balance. Mercedes generates baserunners with high walk totals, so he spends most innings pitching with runners on base.

Defense

Mercedes gets off the mound fairly quickly but is erratic in fielding his position. His throws to other bases can be off the mark at times. He handles bunts equally well to his left and right, as well as charging ones in front of the plate. Mercedes' move to first is average, but baserunners have some trouble reading it. His pickoff move has improved during his short major league career.

2001 Outlook

The Orioles believe Mercedes has the ability to be an end-of-the-rotation starter. But there might be warning signs on the horizon. He doesn't have a dominating pitch and allows too many baserunners. His 14 wins last season were surprising until you realize that he received 6.7 runs per nine innings. Look for a dropoff in Mercedes' production this season.

Position: SP/RP
Bats: R **Throws:** R
Ht: 6' 1" **Wt:** 180

Opening Day Age: 30
Born: 3/5/71 in El Seibo, Dominican Republic
ML Seasons: 6
Pronunciation: mer-SAY-deez

Overall Statistics

	W	L	Pct.	ERA	G	GS	Sv	IP	H	BB	SO	HR	Ratio
2000	14	7	.667	4.02	36	20	0	145.2	150	64	70	15	1.47
Career	25	22	.532	4.34	107	48	0	391.2	392	155	184	55	1.40

How Often He Throws Strikes

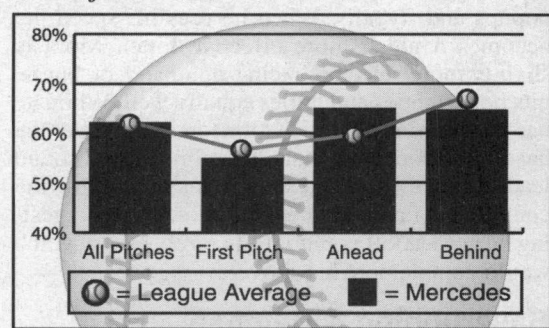

2000 Situational Stats

	W	L	ERA	Sv	IP		AB	H	HR	RBI	Avg
Home	7	4	3.94	0	80.0	LHB	265	77	8	30	.291
Road	7	3	4.11	0	65.2	RHB	290	73	7	41	.252
First Half	3	4	6.25	0	44.2	Sc Pos	137	33	3	55	.241
Scnd Half	11	3	3.03	0	101.0	Clutch	22	7	1	1	.318

2000 Rankings (American League)
- 7th in winning percentage
- Led the Orioles in wins, runners caught stealing (5), GDPs induced (20), most GDPs induced per GDP situation (16.5%), lowest batting average allowed vs. righthanded batters, lowest batting average allowed with runners in scoring position and winning percentage

Melvin Mora

Position: SS/CF/LF
Bats: R **Throws:** R
Ht: 5'10" **Wt:** 180

Opening Day Age: 29
Born: 2/2/72 in Agua
Negar, Venezuela
ML Seasons: 2

2000 Season

Melvin Mora began last season as a utility player for the New York Mets. When starting shortstop Rey Ordonez went down with a broken arm in late May, Mora had a great opportunity to fill the shortstop role. But he struggled, mainly in the field, so he was shipped off to Baltimore in a deal that sent Mike Bordick to the Mets. At the plate, Mora was slightly more productive with the Mets than he was in Baltimore.

Hitting

Mora is a line-drive hitter who tries to lift and pull the ball more than his physical talents will allow. The result is wasted at-bats that often produce popups and flyballs. When he uses his speed, he becomes a much more effective hitter. Mora is slightly more selective facing righthanders, but he hits both righties and lefties equally well. While he has the speed for batting at the top of the order, he hasn't developed the plate discipline to be a sound leadoff hitter. Mora did show signs of working the count to his favor for much of the season, suggesting he has leadoff potential. He rarely bunts, which would complement his above-average speed.

Baserunning & Defense

He stole 12 bases and was thrown out 11 times last season. With more experience, that percentage should improve. His speed pays off handsomely when he occasionally scores from first on balls hit into the gap. Mora goes from first to third as well as anyone on the team. In the field is where his major shortcomings are. Mora made 19 errors in part-time play at shortstop. While he can make the play in the hole, it's his inconsistency on the routine plays that frustrates his manager. He gets a quick release on throws, but his arm is average.

2001 Outlook

The Orioles seem determined to see if Mora can play short on a full-time basis, though he also may be shifted to the outfield if Luis Matos is not ready for full-time duty. Baltimore is likely to learn the same thing the Mets did last year; Mora is a utility player, not a starting shortstop. If he changes his approach at the plate, he can become a force at the top of the Baltimore lineup, but that's a big if.

Overall Statistics

	G	AB	R	H	D	T	HR	RBI	SB	BB	SO	Avg	OBP	Slg
2000	132	414	60	114	22	5	8	47	12	35	80	.275	.337	.411
Career	198	445	66	119	22	5	8	48	14	39	87	.267	.333	.393

Where He Hits the Ball

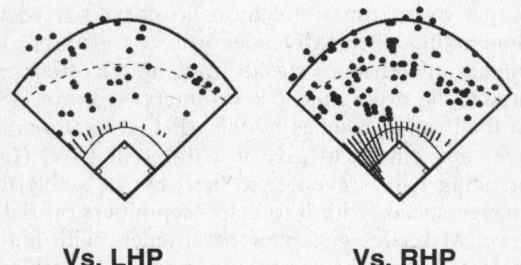

Vs. LHP   **Vs. RHP**

2000 Situational Stats

	AB	H	HR	RBI	Avg		AB	H	HR	RBI	Avg
Home	217	66	5	23	.304	LHP	93	26	3	13	.280
Road	197	48	3	24	.244	RHP	321	88	5	34	.274
First Half	174	49	5	26	.282	Sc Pos	90	23	1	33	.256
Scnd Half	240	65	3	21	.271	Clutch	67	13	1	11	.194

2000 Rankings (American League)

- Led the Orioles in bunts in play (8)

Mike Mussina

2000 Season

Mike Mussina avoided the slow start of the year before, and that set the tone for his season. While seldom a dominating force, he produced one of the more consistent seasons of his career under the cloud of his pending free agency. Mussina recorded the third-highest innings total of his career, pitching much better than his 11-15 record indicated. Weak run support (3.7 runs per nine innings) cost him wins.

Pitching

Mussina is able to get his two- and four-seam fastballs up to the plate in the 93-94 MPH range. His two-seamer continues to be an effective sinker. The four-seamer is used a little bit less now because it lacks some of the movement it once had. His high homers-allowed total in 2000 was an indicator that his pitching style needed to change. His knuckle-curve is a favorite pitch, though he throws it less than he used to. He has one of the best over-the-top curveballs that continues to freeze American League hitters. Righthanders showed marked improvement versus Mussina last summer, a problem that he corrected later with changes in pitch selection.

Defense

An annual Gold Glover on the mound, Mussina fields his position as well as anyone in the American League. Though he did not capture the award in 2000, his lone error was only his second in five seasons. Mussina, well known for his deep knee bend during his pitching motion, saw the stolen bases against him rise into double digits. Even with Charles Johnson, one of the best catchers in the majors at holding runners at bay, behind the plate for nearly two-thirds of Mussina's starts, AL runners still took liberties with Mussina on the mound.

2001 Outlook

One of the gems of the free-agent class of 2000, Mussina rejected a number of in-season contract offers from the Orioles before signing with the Yankees in November. Mussina, who secured a six-year, $88.5 million contract, will be paid well for being one of the better starters in the majors.

Position: SP
Bats: B **Throws:** R
Ht: 6' 2" **Wt:** 185

Opening Day Age: 32
Born: 12/8/68 in Williamsport, PA
ML Seasons: 10
Pronunciation: myoo-SEE-nuh
Nickname: Moose

Baltimore

Overall Statistics

	W	L	Pct.	ERA	G	GS	Sv	IP	H	BB	SO	HR	Ratio
2000	11	15	.423	3.79	34	34	0	237.2	236	46	210	28	1.19
Career	147	81	.645	3.53	288	288	0	2009.2	1895	467	1535	210	1.18

How Often He Throws Strikes

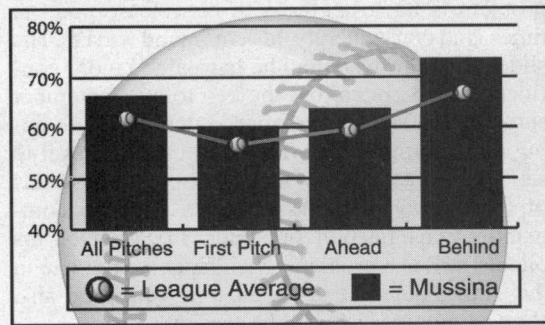

= League Average   = Mussina

2000 Situational Stats

	W	L	ERA	Sv	IP		AB	H	HR	RBI	Avg
Home	7	7	2.90	0	133.2	LHB	404	90	9	42	.223
Road	4	8	4.93	0	104.0	RHB	520	146	19	59	.281
First Half	6	7	3.68	0	134.2	Sc Pos	202	57	7	73	.282
Scnd Half	5	8	3.93	0	103.0	Clutch	110	32	1	11	.291

2000 Rankings (American League)

- 1st in innings pitched and least run support per nine innings (3.7)
- 2nd in losses, batters faced (987), pitches thrown (3,658), lowest on-base percentage allowed (.291) and lowest ERA at home
- 3rd in ERA, games started, complete games (6), strikeouts, highest strikeout/walk ratio (4.6) and fewest walks per nine innings (1.7)
- 5th in hits allowed
- Led the Orioles in ERA, losses, games started, complete games (6), innings pitched, hits allowed, batters faced (987), strikeouts, pitches thrown (3,658), highest strikeout/walk ratio (4.6), lowest batting average allowed (.255) and lowest slugging percentage allowed (.404)

Sidney Ponson

2000 Season

A quick review of Sidney Ponson's 2000 season might not show improvement from his first full season in the majors in 1999. He won only nine games last year, but other signs were there. He struck out 40 more batters and allowed five fewer home runs in 12 more innings. Plus, he shaved 24 points off the 1999 batting average he allowed. Ponson still took the O's on a roller-coaster ride from month to month. His best month was September, when he posted a 3.21 ERA in six starts.

Pitching

When Ponson's mechanics are in sync, his fastball is clocked at 95 MPH and can be dominating. The problem is he struggles with his release point at times, and consequently, his command wavers. His slider has improved, and he has gained more confidence in the pitch, but the key to his September surge in 2000 was his offspeed pitch. He's becoming more comfortable with the pitch and uses it to set up his fastball. In fact, Ponson turns to his offspeed stuff when he struggles with the command of his fastball or slider. Location of his pitches still is a problem when he gets tired late in the game, but that is an area in which he also showed progress later in the season.

Defense

Because of Ponson's stocky build, he does not move around the mound well. He has improved at covering first base, but he still is slow to cover the bag. Ponson will miss Charles Johnson more than any other pitcher because the catcher helped keep runners close to the bag. Ponson's move to first base is adequate at best, so he needs a solid backstop to help curtail his opponents' running game.

2001 Outlook

Conditioning—or the lack of it in Ponson's case—continues to be an issue with the Orioles. They believe a better-conditioned pitcher would be less prone to losing velocity and wearing down. Pat Hentgen takes over as the No. 1 starter for Mike Mussina, and Ponson comes to camp as the No. 2 man. A key to his 2001 season will be how hard he works in the offseason to get in better shape.

Position: SP
Bats: R **Throws:** R
Ht: 6' 1" **Wt:** 225

Opening Day Age: 24
Born: 11/2/76 in Noord, Aruba
ML Seasons: 3

Overall Statistics

	W	L	Pct.	ERA	G	GS	Sv	IP	H	BB	SO	HR	Ratio
2000	9	13	.409	4.82	32	32	0	222.0	223	83	152	30	1.38
Career	29	34	.460	4.89	95	84	1	567.0	607	205	349	84	1.43

How Often He Throws Strikes

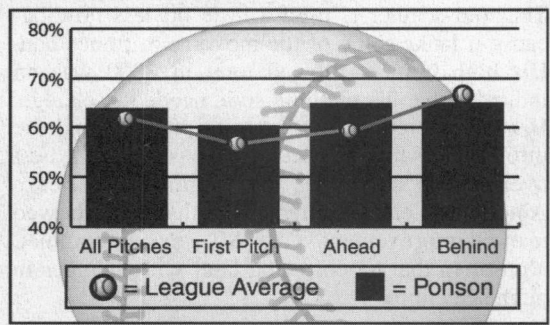

● = League Average   ■ = Ponson

2000 Situational Stats

	W	L	ERA	Sv	IP		AB	H	HR	RBI	Avg
Home	4	7	4.95	0	107.1	LHB	422	109	12	53	.258
Road	5	6	4.71	0	114.2	RHB	441	114	18	57	.259
First Half	5	4	5.17	0	118.1	Sc Pos	198	51	6	75	.258
Scnd Half	4	9	4.43	0	103.2	Clutch	91	22	4	12	.242

2000 Rankings (American League)

- 3rd in complete games (6)
- 5th in innings pitched
- Led the Orioles in complete games (6), home runs allowed, walks allowed, stolen bases allowed (17), runners caught stealing (5), fewest pitches thrown per batter (3.60) and lowest ERA on the road

Chris Richard

2000 Season

Chris Richard came to the Orioles from the Cardinals in the Mike Timlin deal on July 30. There was an opening at first base the next day when Will Clark also was dealt to St. Louis. The Orioles were pleased with Richard's first half-season in the majors, as he showed just enough power—14 doubles and 14 home runs in 215 at-bats—to be a regular at first.

Hitting

In his first major league season, Richard pulled the ball more against righthanders than the initial scouting reports suggested he would. He also improved at waiting on offspeed pitches as the season progressed. He was not overwhelmed by pitchers from either side of the rubber, but he clearly generates most of his production versus righthanders. His swing is smooth and not too long, suggesting he will learn to make better contact as he gains experience. Richard struggled to drive in runs or even make consistent contact with teammates in scoring position, which may have been caused by a lack of experience.

Baserunning & Defense

While Richard has only average speed and rarely steals a base, he's an intelligent baserunner who can take the extra sack if the opportunity arises. His range to the line is average, and he goes toward second base slightly better than the average first baseman. His glovework is adequate in scooping throws out of the dirt, and he displays a decent arm when throwing across the diamond. He has played the outfield on occasion, but he's much more comfortable at first.

2001 Outlook

The Orioles aren't sure if prospect Calvin Pickering is nimble enough to play first, so Richard will get a long look there as they rebuild the team. Richard has overcome rotator cuff surgery in 1998 and has regained all of the power in his swing. He never will be a major power hitter, but the Orioles are likely to get a Brian Daubach-type season out of him in 2001.

Position: 1B
Bats: L **Throws:** L
Ht: 6' 2" **Wt:** 190

Opening Day Age: 26
Born: 6/7/74 in San Diego, CA
ML Seasons: 1

Overall Statistics

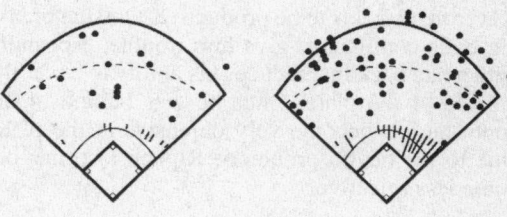

	G	AB	R	H	D	T	HR	RBI	SB	BB	SO	Avg	OBP	Slg
2000	62	215	39	57	14	2	14	37	7	17	40	.265	.326	.544
Career	62	215	39	57	14	2	14	37	7	17	40	.265	.326	.544

Where He Hits the Ball

Vs. LHP	Vs. RHP

2000 Situational Stats

	AB	H	HR	RBI	Avg		AB	H	HR	RBI	Avg
Home	107	27	4	11	.252	LHP	39	10	1	3	.256
Road	108	30	10	26	.278	RHP	176	47	13	34	.267
First Half	0	0	0	0	-	Sc Pos	51	9	3	21	.176
Scnd Half	215	57	14	37	.265	Clutch	30	10	1	2	.333

2000 Rankings (American League)

- 9th in errors at first base (5)
- Led the Orioles in batting average on a 3-1 count (.556)
- Led AL right fielders in batting average on a 3-2 count (.400)

Cal Ripken Jr.

2000 Season

In September 1999, Cal Ripken had back surgery on the scar tissue and nerve inflammation that have caused him pain for several years. Ripken, an off-season workout warrior, recovered in time for spring training, yet he was far from 100 percent. Ripken battled his ongoing back problems into late June before landing on the disabled list on June 28. He returned to the lineup just after Labor Day to hit .307 in 75 at-bats.

Hitting

Because he still was struggling with his back early in the season, Ripken used a slightly open stance to compensate for his physical woes and advancing age. Surprisingly, he was able to generate enough power to all fields to be productive. Outside breaking balls continue to give him trouble, especially with a bad back that reduces his ability to cover the outside of the plate. Once he gets behind in the count he has become very defensive at the plate. Due to his health problems, Ripken also has become less selective.

Baserunning & Defense

The loss of flexibility caused by his back condition has reduced his lateral movement in the field. This decreased range to his left forces the shortstop to lean a bit toward the hole to compensate for Ripken's lack of range. He makes the plays to his right on a regular basis, and his throws from the line are strong though not exceptional. He's no longer a basestealing threat, and he uses his veteran savvy to compensate for a lack of speed on the bases.

2001 Outlook

Ripken inked a one-year, $6.3 million deal, probably his last, early in November. Because of his back problems, there has been speculation that he'll see more time at first base and designated hitter in 2001. If Ryan Minor isn't productive at third in place of Ripken, it wouldn't be a surprise to see Ripken over at the hot corner on a semi-regular basis. He will continue to show power at the plate, but his days of 25 homers and 80 RBI are long gone. This future Hall of Famer will have a grand farewell tour.

Position: 3B/DH
Bats: R **Throws:** R
Ht: 6' 4" **Wt:** 220

Opening Day Age: 40
Born: 8/24/60 in Havre de Grace, MD
ML Seasons: 20
Nickname: Junior

Overall Statistics

	G	AB	R	H	D	T	HR	RBI	SB	BB	SO	Avg	OBP	Slg
2000	83	309	43	79	16	0	15	56	0	23	37	.256	.310	.453
Career	2873	11074	1604	3070	587	44	417	1627	36	1103	1242	.277	.343	.451

Where He Hits the Ball

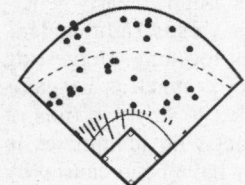
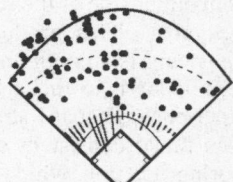

Vs. LHP **Vs. RHP**

2000 Situational Stats

	AB	H	HR	RBI	Avg		AB	H	HR	RBI	Avg
Home	123	35	8	25	.285	LHP	95	25	2	16	.263
Road	186	44	7	31	.237	RHP	214	54	13	40	.252
First Half	234	56	13	43	.239	Sc Pos	83	23	1	35	.277
Scnd Half	75	23	2	13	.307	Clutch	46	10	2	7	.217

2000 Rankings (American League)

- Led the Orioles in batting average on an 0-2 count (.250)

Jeff Conine

Position: 3B/1B/DH/RF
Bats: R **Throws:** R
Ht: 6' 1" **Wt:** 220

Opening Day Age: 34
Born: 6/27/66 in Tacoma, WA
ML Seasons: 10
Pronunciation: COH-nine

Overall Statistics

	G	AB	R	H	D	T	HR	RBI	SB	BB	SO	Avg	OBP	Slg
2000	119	409	53	116	20	2	13	46	4	36	53	.284	.341	.438
Career	1106	3804	487	1089	206	19	132	597	15	379	720	.286	.350	.455

2000 Situational Stats

	AB	H	HR	RBI	Avg		AB	H	HR	RBI	Avg
Home	179	51	6	19	.285	LHP	120	40	7	16	.333
Road	230	65	7	27	.283	RHP	289	76	6	30	.263
First Half	234	66	10	31	.282	Sc Pos	107	29	2	34	.271
Scnd Half	175	50	3	15	.286	Clutch	64	15	0	6	.234

2000 Season

Jeff Conine produced a solid season as an Orioles utility player, spending time at first, third, both corner outfield spots and the designated hitter slot. He opened and closed the season as one of Baltimore's top hitters and hit in every lineup spot except the first two.

Hitting, Baserunning & Defense

Early in his career Conine was a pull hitter, but in recent seasons he had become more of a hit-it-where-it-is-pitched hitter. Now he's back to being an almost dead-pull hitter, especially his home runs. Conine makes solid contact and has good plate discipline. On the bases, he's an intelligent baserunner who will take an extra base if the opportunity arises. When the Orioles needed help at third, Conine was there to assist and handled the position adequately. His range is average at first and third, and slightly below average in the outfield.

2001 Outlook

As the Orioles move to add younger players to the roster, Conine will see less playing time in the field and more at the DH spot, although Albert Belle's health may limit those opportunities for Conine. We shouldn't see a big dropoff in the quality of his play, but his playing time may slip.

Scott Erickson

Position: SP
Bats: R **Throws:** R
Ht: 6' 4" **Wt:** 230

Opening Day Age: 33
Born: 2/2/68 in Long Beach, CA
ML Seasons: 11

Overall Statistics

	W	L	Pct.	ERA	G	GS	Sv	IP	H	BB	SO	HR	Ratio
2000	5	8	.385	7.87	16	16	0	92.2	127	48	41	14	1.89
Career	135	116	.538	4.43	326	322	0	2106.1	2281	745	1152	191	1.44

2000 Situational Stats

	W	L	ERA	Sv	IP		AB	H	HR	RBI	Avg
Home	3	3	8.47	0	34.0	LHB	195	76	8	46	.390
Road	2	5	7.52	0	58.2	RHB	189	51	6	25	.270
First Half	4	6	7.22	0	77.1	Sc Pos	114	39	5	57	.342
Scnd Half	1	2	11.15	0	15.1	Clutch	8	4	0	0	.500

2000 Season

The wear and tear on Scott Erickson's right elbow finally caught up with him at the start of spring training. Elbow problems flared up from the first day of camp, and he finally succumbed to surgery to remove bone spurs on March 3. Erickson rushed back from the surgery in early May and pitched into July at less than 100 percent. The Orioles finally placed him on the disabled list at the end of July and his season was over.

Pitching & Defense

Erickson's out pitch, a sharp-breaking slider, was absent from his arsenal in 2000 because of his elbow problems. His fastball hasn't reached the 90-MPH level for several seasons, and he used it to set up other pitches. His curveball flattened out and he rarely threw it as the season wore on. He got by for several months on guile alone. Erickson's move to first and delivery to home are deliberate, and that puts extra pressure on his catcher to shut down the running game. He's slow to get off the mound and cover bunts and first base.

2001 Outlook

Erickson had Tommy John surgery in August and is expected to miss 12 months as he recovers. It's unlikely that he will make a significant contribution to the Orioles this season.

Buddy Groom

Position: RP
Bats: L **Throws:** L
Ht: 6' 2" **Wt:** 207

Opening Day Age: 35
Born: 7/10/65 in Dallas, TX
ML Seasons: 9

Overall Statistics

	W	L	Pct.	ERA	G	GS	Sv	IP	H	BB	SO	HR	Ratio
2000	6	3	.667	4.85	70	0	4	59.1	63	21	44	5	1.42
Career	21	21	.500	5.10	479	15	12	467.2	541	197	306	47	1.58

2000 Situational Stats

	W	L	ERA	Sv	IP		AB	H	HR	RBI	Avg
Home	3	0	3.18	1	28.1	LHB	88	17	2	10	.193
Road	3	3	6.39	3	31.0	RHB	141	46	3	30	.326
First Half	3	3	4.59	4	33.1	Sc Pos	72	21	4	37	.292
Scnd Half	3	0	5.19	0	26.0	Clutch	128	32	2	23	.250

2000 Season

The Orioles inked Buddy Groom to a two-year deal after the 1999 season to be their lefthanded specialist, and he turned in a successful season. He got into trouble, however, when he was asked to face righthanded hitters. Groom earned four saves and six wins, both career highs.

Pitching & Defense

Groom relies heavily on a sharp-breaking curveball to get lefthanders out. Righthanders get a better look at the pitch, and since he doesn't have another high quality offering, they can sit on the breaking ball. He has worked on an offspeed pitch and a cut fastball, but neither is that effective. His command and control continue to be solid but not exceptional. Groom has some trouble fielding to his left and committed two errors last season. His move to first is slightly above average and strong enough to keep most baserunners at bay.

2001 Outlook

Groom returns to complete the two-year deal he signed last winter. As long as he remains the lefthanded specialist, he should be effective. He and the Orioles run into trouble when they veer from that plan. With Baltimore lacking a veteran in the closer role, it won't be a surprise if Groom duplicates his 2000 save total.

Jerry Hairston Jr.

Position: 2B
Bats: R **Throws:** R
Ht: 5'10" **Wt:** 175

Opening Day Age: 24
Born: 5/29/76 in Naperville, IL
ML Seasons: 3

Overall Statistics

	G	AB	R	H	D	T	HR	RBI	SB	BB	SO	Avg	OBP	Slg
2000	49	180	27	46	5	0	5	19	8	21	22	.256	.353	.367
Career	105	362	55	93	17	1	9	36	17	32	47	.257	.333	.384

2000 Situational Stats

	AB	H	HR	RBI	Avg		AB	H	HR	RBI	Avg
Home	105	25	2	14	.238	LHP	45	11	1	6	.244
Road	75	21	3	5	.280	RHP	135	35	4	13	.259
First Half	0	0	0	0	-	Sc Pos	39	12	1	15	.308
Scnd Half	180	46	5	19	.256	Clutch	20	6	0	3	.300

2000 Season

Jerry Hairston Jr. began the season in the minors, hoping the Orioles would deal Delino DeShields to open the second-base job for him. It didn't happen, and Hairston spent most of the 2000 season at Triple-A Rochester. Baltimore decided to audition DeShields in left field, which gave Hairston the second-base job later in the season.

Hitting, Baserunning & Defense

Hairston already has the ability to work the count, looking for a pitch he can drive to the gaps. His swing is level and fairly compact, allowing him to make consistent contact. His ability to get on base will improve once he gets more at-bats at the major league level. The Orioles want him at second base because of his quickness and his ability to turn the double play. He covers more ground than DeShields, making him an asset in the middle of the infield. He's average when it comes to stealing a base, but very effective going from first to third, or scoring from second on a base hit to the outfield.

2001 Outlook

Hairston begins this season as the starter at second base, with DeShields in left. It would take a major collapse at the plate for Hairston to lose his job.

Jason Johnson

Position: SP/RP
Bats: R **Throws:** R
Ht: 6' 6" **Wt:** 235

Opening Day Age: 27
Born: 10/27/73 in Santa Barbara, CA
ML Seasons: 4

Overall Statistics

	W	L	Pct.	ERA	G	GS	Sv	IP	H	BB	SO	HR	Ratio
2000	1	10	.091	7.02	25	13	0	107.2	119	61	79	21	1.67
Career	11	22	.333	6.10	63	47	0	289.0	323	144	189	48	1.62

2000 Situational Stats

	W	L	ERA	Sv	IP		AB	H	HR	RBI	Avg
Home	0	6	7.32	0	51.2	LHB	195	52	11	39	.267
Road	1	4	6.75	0	56.0	RHB	233	67	10	46	.288
First Half	0	8	6.84	0	73.2	Sc Pos	124	40	9	69	.323
Scnd Half	1	2	7.41	0	34.0	Clutch	25	4	0	0	.160

2000 Season

Jason Johnson finished the 1999 season with a 3-0 record and 2.63 ERA in his final four starts. Baltimore penciled him into the rotation last winter and expected big things in 2000. While Johnson got out of the gates quickly with a 2.77 ERA in April, his season went downhill. By season's end, he was buried in the bullpen as a long reliever.

Pitching & Defense

Johnson struggles with his mechanics and from a lack of experience. His fastball, a four-seamer with very good movement, can be unhittable, although it flattens out when he loses his release point. His curveball is a roller rather than sharp-breaking, leaving it up in the zone for the hitter. His changeup still is below average with no signs of improving. The lanky Johnson has a slow move to both the plate and first base, making him vulnerable to baserunners. He fields his position in a very methodical manner.

2001 Outlook

The Orioles aren't ready to give up on Johnson because they see the raw talent and are hurting for quality starters. But he must string together a couple of decent months to establish himself. If he doesn't, he might get stuck in the bullpen again, or even find himself back in the minors.

Alan Mills

Position: RP
Bats: B **Throws:** R
Ht: 6' 1" **Wt:** 195

Opening Day Age: 34
Born: 10/18/66 in Lakeland, FL
ML Seasons: 11

Overall Statistics

	W	L	Pct.	ERA	G	GS	Sv	IP	H	BB	SO	HR	Ratio
2000	4	1	.800	5.29	41	0	2	49.1	56	35	36	9	1.84
Career	38	31	.551	3.99	459	5	15	622.0	557	384	447	77	1.51

2000 Situational Stats

	W	L	ERA	Sv	IP		AB	H	HR	RBI	Avg
Home	1	1	5.23	1	20.2	LHB	83	26	3	15	.313
Road	3	0	5.34	1	28.2	RHB	114	30	6	14	.263
First Half	3	1	4.81	2	39.1	Sc Pos	61	12	3	21	.197
Scnd Half	1	0	7.20	0	10.0	Clutch	48	9	1	4	.188

2000 Season

Alan Mills began the season as the setup man for Jeff Shaw in Los Angeles. He was dealt back to the Orioles in mid-June for reliever Al Reyes plus cash, and he pitched well through July. A bone spur in his pitching shoulder derailed his season early in August.

Pitching & Defense

Mills struggled to get his fastball up to 90 MPH most of the season, most likely because of his shoulder trouble. His slider has lost some of its bite and isn't an out pitch anymore. Mills always has generated most of his strikeouts via his split-finger pitch, but a lack of command has reduced its effectiveness. A loss of control at times also has contributed to his struggle to throw strikes. Mills' move to first base is deliberate, allowing baserunners to take advantage of him. He's slow off the mound to field his position and cover first base.

2001 Outlook

Mills' season ended in September when he complained of right shoulder pain. The Orioles hope rest, rehabilitation and several cortisone shots this offseason will help him recover and avoid surgery. If he doesn't respond by January, he's a candidate to go under the knife. So Mills could enter the 2001 season as a huge medical question mark.

Ryan Minor

Position: 3B
Bats: R **Throws:** R
Ht: 6' 7" **Wt:** 245

Opening Day Age: 27
Born: 1/5/74 in Canton, OH
ML Seasons: 3

Overall Statistics

	G	AB	R	H	D	T	HR	RBI	SB	BB	SO	Avg	OBP	Slg
2000	32	84	4	11	1	0	0	3	0	3	20	.131	.170	.143
Career	87	222	20	41	9	0	3	14	1	11	66	.185	.226	.266

2000 Situational Stats

	AB	H	HR	RBI	Avg		AB	H	HR	RBI	Avg
Home	47	5	0	2	.106	LHP	29	4	0	2	.138
Road	37	6	0	1	.162	RHP	55	7	0	1	.127
First Half	21	5	0	1	.238	Sc Pos	18	3	0	3	.167
Scnd Half	63	6	0	2	.095	Clutch	3	0	0	0	.000

2000 Season

Ryan Minor began the season at Triple-A Rochester, but when Cal Ripken went down with a bad back early in the season, Minor was recalled. He split playing time at third with several players and never took control of the job.

Hitting, Baserunning & Defense

Minor can generate power with his long swing, but he hasn't shown it at the major league level yet. He struggles with pitches up in the strike zone and breaking balls off the plate, and he needs to make adjustments to how pitchers are working him. His swing is long, and the Orioles have been reluctant to shorten it. Minor's athletic ability is apparent when he runs the bases, especially when he goes from first to third. At the hot corner, his arm is as strong as any third baseman in the AL. He has good footwork around the bag and does a good job of charging bunts and slowly-hit balls.

2001 Outlook

Minor is the player who replaced Cal Ripken at third base when his streak ended. He also was a basketball star at the University of Oklahoma who chose baseball as a career. Minor is now at the crossroads of his baseball career. He needs to show marked improvement at the plate this season, or he will end up as a career Triple-A player.

Pat Rapp

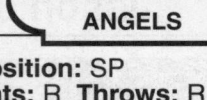

Signed By
ANGELS

Position: SP
Bats: R **Throws:** R
Ht: 6' 3" **Wt:** 215

Opening Day Age: 33
Born: 7/13/67 in Jennings, LA
ML Seasons: 9

Overall Statistics

	W	L	Pct.	ERA	G	GS	Sv	IP	H	BB	SO	HR	Ratio
2000	9	12	.429	5.90	31	30	0	174.0	203	83	106	18	1.64
Career	65	79	.451	4.67	228	211	0	1217.1	1299	612	743	113	1.57

2000 Situational Stats

	W	L	ERA	Sv	IP		AB	H	HR	RBI	Avg
Home	4	6	5.88	0	85.2	LHB	335	94	4	44	.281
Road	5	6	5.91	0	88.1	RHB	366	109	14	66	.298
First Half	5	6	5.63	0	96.0	Sc Pos	197	63	5	89	.320
Scnd Half	4	6	6.23	0	78.0	Clutch	25	6	0	5	.240

2000 Season

Pat Rapp had a golden opportunity when he signed on with the Orioles last winter. Baltimore needed a veteran starter to step up and fill a rotation spot. With the exception of the month of May, Rapp struggled to post even average numbers. He lost 12 times and recorded a career-worst ERA of 5.90.

Pitching & Defense

For most of his career, Rapp relied on a sharp-breaking curveball as his out pitch. Now his trademark curve tends to flatten out at times, making him vulnerable. He's reverted to throwing an assortment of cut fastballs and a four-seamer to set up his breaking ball. His control tends to desert him for innings at a time and he gets hit hard. Defensively, Rapp lumbers off the mound to field his position and isn't athletic enough to be an asset to his team. His pickoff move continues to be one of the best among righthanders in the American League.

2001 Outlook

Rapp's option was not picked up by the Orioles after the season ended, and the Angels signed him to a one-year deal in December. He'll hang around the majors for another year or two because of the shortage of starting pitchers, but his effectiveness is far from guaranteed.

B.J. Ryan

Position: RP
Bats: L **Throws:** L
Ht: 6' 6" **Wt:** 230

Opening Day Age: 25
Born: 12/28/75 in
Bossier City, LA
ML Seasons: 2

Overall Statistics

	W	L	Pct.	ERA	G	GS	Sv	IP	H	BB	SO	HR	Ratio
2000	2	3	.400	5.91	42	0	0	42.2	36	31	41	7	1.57
Career	3	3	.500	5.00	56	0	0	63.0	49	44	70	7	1.48

2000 Situational Stats

	W	L	ERA	Sv	IP		AB	H	HR	RBI	Avg
Home	2	0	5.49	0	19.2	LHB	57	10	1	8	.175
Road	0	3	6.26	0	23.0	RHB	103	26	6	25	.252
First Half	1	3	7.91	0	19.1	Sc Pos	51	12	3	27	.235
Scnd Half	1	0	4.24	0	23.1	Clutch	54	11	2	9	.204

2000 Season

B.J. Ryan, who came over from the Reds in 1999 in exchange for veteran Juan Guzman, began 2000 with the Orioles and was later sent to Triple-A Rochester. Upon his recall, he showed promise as a lefthanded specialist with Baltimore, but he also displayed some weaknesses. Ryan allowed seven home runs in only 42.2 innings.

Pitching & Defense

Ryan relies on a funky motion that makes it difficult to pick up his pitches. His fastball can get up to the plate in the 90-91 MPH range, and it has good movement. His slider has a sharp break to it, although Ryan has a tendency to throw it at speeds close to his fastball, thus reducing its effectiveness. He throws a curveball and change to help set up his other pitches. His control is above average, but his command needs to improve to be effective in the majors. He is an average fielder with a decent move to first.

2001 Outlook

Ryan enters this season behind Buddy Groom as a lefthanded relief specialist. Ryan is more talented than Groom, and only lacks the experience to stick in the majors. Once the command of his pitches improves, he should be effective as a major league reliever.

Mike Trombley

Position: RP
Bats: R **Throws:** R
Ht: 6' 2" **Wt:** 204

Opening Day Age: 33
Born: 4/14/67 in
Springfield, MA
ML Seasons: 9
Pronunciation:
TROM-blee

Overall Statistics

	W	L	Pct.	ERA	G	GS	Sv	IP	H	BB	SO	HR	Ratio
2000	4	5	.444	4.13	75	0	4	72.0	67	38	72	15	1.46
Career	34	38	.472	4.43	435	36	38	713.2	725	281	597	103	1.41

2000 Situational Stats

	W	L	ERA	Sv	IP		AB	H	HR	RBI	Avg
Home	3	2	3.38	2	37.1	LHB	108	26	5	13	.241
Road	1	3	4.93	2	34.2	RHB	163	41	10	30	.252
First Half	4	2	4.55	2	31.2	Sc Pos	93	16	3	27	.172
Scnd Half	0	3	3.79	2	40.1	Clutch	141	37	8	27	.262

2000 Season

Mike Trombley began last season as closer insurance in case Mike Timlin couldn't handle the job. When Timlin struggled as the Orioles' stopper, Trombley got his shot and he failed, saving only four of 11 games. Baltimore shipped Timlin to the Cardinals at the trading deadline in July, but Trombley had no save opportunities after August.

Pitching & Defense

Trombley's most effective pitch is a split-finger fastball that he uses to garner most of his strikeouts. When he keeps it low in the strike zone, he's almost unhittable. His problem is that command of the pitch deserts him from time to time. His curveball isn't as sharp as it used to be, and his fastball, which reaches 90 MPH occasionally, is too straight to be an out pitch. Trombley's move to first is below average, but his delivery to home is average and baserunners don't run wild on him. He fields well and hasn't made an error in five seasons.

2001 Outlook

Ryan Kohlmeier starts the 2001 season as the Orioles' closer after saving 13 games during the second half of the season. Trombley is slated to fill the setup role and back up Kohlmeier when needed. Based on previous trials, Trombley isn't likely to get another shot at closing full-time.

Other Baltimore Orioles

Rich Amaral (**Pos**: CF, **Age**: 38, **Bats**: R)

	G	AB	R	H	D	T	HR	RBI	SB	BB	SO	Avg	OBP	Slg
2000	30	60	10	13	1	1	0	6	6	7	8	.217	.299	.267
Career	727	1788	305	493	82	10	11	159	112	176	277	.276	.344	.351

At his age, Amaral value is somewhat dubious. He really struggled with the Orioles, batting .178 against lefties, before Baltimore released him. He later signed a minor league contract with Atlanta. 2001 Outlook: C

Carlos Casimiro (**Pos**: DH, **Age**: 24, **Bats**: R)

	G	AB	R	H	D	T	HR	RBI	SB	BB	SO	Avg	OBP	Slg
2000	2	8	0	1	1	0	0	3	0	0	2	.125	.125	.250
Career	2	8	0	1	1	0	0	3	0	0	2	.125	.125	.250

Casimiro, from San Pedro de Macoris, shifted from second base to third in 2000. Outside of an occasional home run, he doesn't offer much offensively, and Baltimore released him after the season. 2001 Outlook: C

Ivanon Coffie (**Pos**: 3B, **Age**: 23, **Bats**: L)

	G	AB	R	H	D	T	HR	RBI	SB	BB	SO	Avg	OBP	Slg
2000	23	60	6	13	4	1	0	6	1	5	11	.217	.284	.317
Career	23	60	6	13	4	1	0	6	1	5	11	.217	.284	.317

Coffie has a strong arm and can play either shortstop or third base. But he has very little experience, much less success, above Double-A. He's another Orioles prospect from the Netherlands Antilles. 2001 Outlook: C

Jesse Garcia (**Pos**: 2B, **Age**: 27, **Bats**: R)

	G	AB	R	H	D	T	HR	RBI	SB	BB	SO	Avg	OBP	Slg
2000	14	17	2	1	0	0	0	0	0	2	2	.059	.158	.059
Career	31	46	8	7	0	0	2	2	0	4	5	.152	.220	.283

The Orioles picked Garcia in the 26th round of the 1993 draft. He doesn't offer much except the ability to play either middle-infield position. He was traded to the Braves in mid-December for third baseman Steve Sisco. 2001 Outlook: C

Karim Garcia (**Pos**: RF, **Age**: 25, **Bats**: L)

	G	AB	R	H	D	T	HR	RBI	SB	BB	SO	Avg	OBP	Slg
2000	16	33	1	3	0	0	0	0	0	0	10	.091	.091	.091
Career	254	714	84	155	20	11	24	83	7	44	174	.217	.264	.377

While he knocks the cover off the ball in Triple-A, Garcia simply hasn't been able to establish himself against major league pitching. He still has time to find himself, though Baltimore released him in mid-October. 2001 Outlook: C

Trenidad Hubbard (**Pos**: LF/RF, **Age**: 34, **Bats**: R)

	G	AB	R	H	D	T	HR	RBI	SB	BB	SO	Avg	OBP	Slg
2000	92	108	18	20	2	2	1	6	4	11	23	.185	.267	.269
Career	372	605	104	162	27	6	15	63	23	65	133	.268	.342	.407

Hubbard was part of the B.J. Surhoff deal with Atlanta last July. Hubbard was nothing if not consistent, batting exactly .185 for both the Braves and Orioles. Baltimore released him after the season. 2001 Outlook: C

Gene Kingsale (**Pos**: CF, **Age**: 24, **Bats**: B)

	G	AB	R	H	D	T	HR	RBI	SB	BB	SO	Avg	OBP	Slg
2000	26	88	13	21	2	1	0	9	1	2	14	.239	.253	.284
Career	68	175	23	42	4	1	0	16	2	7	28	.240	.274	.274

Kingsale, from the Netherlands Antilles, has been playing professionally since age 17. While he plays center field, he provides very little extra-base power for a guy his size. 2001 Outlook: C

Mike Kinkade (**Pos**: DH, **Age**: 27, **Bats**: R)

	G	AB	R	H	D	T	HR	RBI	SB	BB	SO	Avg	OBP	Slg
2000	5	9	0	3	1	0	0	1	0	0	1	.333	.400	.444
Career	36	57	5	12	3	1	2	7	1	3	10	.211	.286	.404

Kinkade was part of the Mike Bordick swap last July. He played for Team USA in the Olympics, his biggest highlight since being named Texas League MVP in 1997. He also can serve as an emergency catcher. 2001 Outlook: C

Mark Lewis (**Pos**: 3B/2B/SS, **Age**: 31, **Bats**: R)

	G	AB	R	H	D	T	HR	RBI	SB	BB	SO	Avg	OBP	Slg
2000	82	182	20	46	18	0	2	24	7	13	34	.253	.305	.385
Career	896	2782	319	735	155	13	48	306	29	196	507	.264	.313	.381

The Orioles acquired Lewis off waivers from Cincinnati last April. He may never again get a shot at everyday duty and his on-base percentage likely won't be great, but he can play three infield positions. He became a free agent in November. 2001 Outlook: B

Fernando Lunar (**Pos**: C, **Age**: 23, **Bats**: R)

	G	AB	R	H	D	T	HR	RBI	SB	BB	SO	Avg	OBP	Slg
2000	31	70	5	12	1	0	0	6	0	3	19	.171	.247	.186
Career	31	70	5	12	1	0	0	6	0	3	19	.171	.247	.186

Lunar was a fine defensive catcher in the Atlanta system, but his bat never was going to challenge Javy Lopez. The Orioles got Lunar in the B.J. Surhoff swap last July. 2001 Outlook: C

Calvin Maduro (**Pos**: RHP, **Age**: 26)

	W	L	Pct.	ERA	G	GS	Sv	IP	H	BB	SO	HR	Ratio
2000	0	0	-	9.64	15	2	0	23.1	29	16	18	8	1.93
Career	3	8	.273	7.22	34	17	0	109.2	125	60	60	21	1.69

Maduro started a couple of games in April, got crushed, and wasn't much better after moving to the bullpen. He wound up missing most of the season with a strained elbow. 2001 Outlook: C

Chuck McElroy (**Pos**: LHP, **Age**: 33)

	W	L	Pct.	ERA	G	GS	Sv	IP	H	BB	SO	HR	Ratio
2000	3	0	1.000	4.69	43	2	0	63.1	60	34	50	6	1.48
Career	36	27	.571	3.74	605	2	17	664.1	637	316	557	52	1.43

McElroy helped the Orioles in his limited role—mostly in relief—last season. He held lefthanded batters to a .204 average and even compiled a 0.82 ERA in two starts. 2001 Outlook: B

Willie Morales (Pos: C, Age: 28, Bats: R)

	G	AB	R	H	D	T	HR	RBI	SB	BB	SO	Avg	OBP	Slg
2000	3	11	1	3	1	0	0	0	0	0	3	.273	.273	.364
Career	3	11	1	3	1	0	0	0	0	0	3	.273	.273	.364

After seven years in the Oakland system, Morales signed with Baltimore last season as a minor league free agent. He has struggled offensively above Double-A, though he has shown flashes of power. 2001 Outlook: C

Greg Myers (Pos: C, Age: 34, Bats: L)

	G	AB	R	H	D	T	HR	RBI	SB	BB	SO	Avg	OBP	Slg
2000	43	125	9	28	6	0	3	12	0	8	29	.224	.271	.344
Career	850	2378	243	602	121	7	55	290	3	181	403	.253	.304	.379

Myers' two-year contract with the Orioles runs through the 2001 campaign. He'll most likely serve the same role he always has as a backup catcher. This year it will be for Brook Fordyce. 2001 Outlook: B

Baltimore Orioles Minor League Prospects

Organization Overview:

While the Orioles are an aging major league club with few prospects ready to fill shoes, the organization isn't as barren of talent as it was a few years ago. Not many of the acquisitions made during the club's summer purge are top-flight pickups, but Chris Richard immediately secured a job and guys like Luis Rivera and Lesli Brea could join the pitching staff soon. While Tommy John surgery sidetracked top pitching prospect Matt Riley late in 2000, the Orioles saw a number of others—Ryan Kohlmeier, Ntema Ndungini, Ed Rogers and Richard Stahl among them—take major strides in their development in 2000. Plus, some key international signings have boosted the growing core of talent in the low minors. If only the youngsters could be developed quickly enough to fill the holes left by the old folks in Baltimore.

Ntema Ndungidi

Position: OF   **Opening Day Age:** 22
Bats: L **Throws:** R   **Born:** 3/15/79 in
Ht: 6' 2" **Wt:** 199   Kisangani, Zaire

Recent Statistics

	G	AB	R	H	D	T	HR	RBI	SB	BB	SO	Avg
1999 A Delmarva	64	217	33	42	8	2	0	24	18	49	54	.194
1999 A Frederick	60	192	40	51	10	3	0	18	4	39	43	.266
2000 A Frederick	90	313	53	89	16	4	10	59	16	60	83	.284
2000 AA Bowie	41	136	17	32	6	0	3	14	2	25	33	.235

Born in Zaire, which now is known as the Congo, Ndungidi grew up in the hockey hotbed of Montreal and discovered baseball. Blessed with a package of potential power and speed, he was very raw when the Orioles made him a supplemental first-round pick in 1997. His career started slowly, but he's quickly improved as he's played more baseball. Despite failing to hit a home run in 1999, Ndungidi made decent contact and drew walks during the second half at high Class-A Frederick. Then his power emerged in 2000 at Frederick and Double-A Bowie. Still quite raw, Ndungidi increasingly looks like a major league left fielder in the making. Some mental health issues arose during the Arizona Fall League. Hopefully they won't sidetrack a promising career.

Calvin Pickering

Position: 1B   **Opening Day Age:** 24
Bats: L **Throws:** L   **Born:** 9/29/76 in St.
Ht: 6' 5" **Wt:** 275   Thomas, Virgin Islands

Recent Statistics

	G	AB	R	H	D	T	HR	RBI	SB	BB	SO	Avg
1999 AAA Rochester	103	372	63	106	20	0	16	63	1	60	99	.285
1999 AL Baltimore	23	40	4	5	1	0	1	5	0	11	16	.125
2000 AAA Rochester	60	197	20	43	10	0	6	30	2	36	70	.218

After an MVP season at Double-A Bowie in 1998, during which he batted .309-31-114 with a .434 on-base percentage, Pickering didn't get a crack at the Orioles'

first-base job that next spring. The Orioles inked an unproductive Will Clark instead, and Pickering reportedly let his misfortune get in the way mentally of a productive '99 season at Triple-A Rochester. A chance to rebound in 2000 ended prematurely when Pickering tore a quadriceps muscle above his left knee in July. The guy can flat-out hit, but there always have been concerns about his work ethic and weight. Pickering went unclaimed on waivers in November en route to Rochester.

Keith Reed

Position: OF   **Opening Day Age:** 22
Bats: R **Throws:** R   **Born:** 10/8/78 in
Ht: 6' 4" **Wt:** 215   Yarmouth Port, MA

Recent Statistics

	G	AB	R	H	D	T	HR	RBI	SB	BB	SO	Avg
1999 R Bluefield	4	16	2	3	0	0	0	0	0	1	3	.188
1999 A Delmarva	61	240	36	62	14	3	4	25	3	22	53	.258
2000 A Delmarva	70	269	43	78	16	1	11	59	20	25	56	.290
2000 A Frederick	65	243	33	57	10	1	8	31	9	21	58	.235

A basketball player growing up in Massachusetts, Reed went to Providence College, where he was recruited to play baseball. Only after a big junior year in 1999 did the baseball world take notice. And now, less than two years after the Orioles made him a first-rounder in '99, Reed is rated the best prospect in the Baltimore system by *Baseball America*. He is a budding five-tool talent with an incredible arm. The power began to emerge in 2000, with Reed combining for 19 homers between Class-A Demarva and high Class-A Frederick. Harnessing his speed is further along, as Reed was caught just five times while stealing 29 bases last summer. Reed may return to Frederick for the start of the 2001 season.

Matt Riley

Position: P   **Opening Day Age:** 21
Bats: L **Throws:** L   **Born:** 8/2/79 in Antioch,
Ht: 6' 1" **Wt:** 205   CA

Recent Statistics

	W	L	ERA	G	GS	Sv	IP	H	R	BB	SO	HR
1999 A Frederick	3	2	2.61	8	8	0	51.2	34	19	14	58	5
1999 AA Bowie	10	6	3.22	20	20	0	125.2	113	53	42	131	13
1999 AL Baltimore	0	0	7.36	3	3	0	11.0	17	9	13	6	4
2000 AAA Rochester	0	2	14.14	2	2	0	7.0	15	12	4	8	3
2000 AA Bowie	5	7	6.08	19	14	1	74.0	74	56	49	66	9

Easily the Orioles' top prospect heading into 2000, Riley endured a summer that can only be described as a disaster. Appearing late for practices and an incident outside a Fort Lauderdale nightclub marred his spring training, quickly ending his bid for the fifth-starter spot. Then he was sidelined with a rotator cuff strain after just two Triple-A starts. In September, Riley underwent Tommy John surgery that will cost him all of the 2001 season. There's plenty of rehab ahead before Riley finds out if he can recapture the mid-90s fastball and curveball that made him the pride of the organization.

Luis Rivera

	Position: P	Opening Day Age: 22
	Bats: R Throws: R	Born: 6/21/78 in
	Ht: 6' 3" Wt: 163	Chihuahua, Mexico

Recent Statistics

	W	L	ERA	G	GS	Sv	IP	H	R	BB	SO	HR
2000 R Braves	0	0	0.00	3	3	0	4.0	2	0	1	2	0
2000 AAA Richmond	0	2	8.06	8	7	0	22.1	29	20	18	12	3
2000 AAA Rochester	0	1	3.38	3	3	0	8.0	11	5	5	4	0
2000 NL Atlanta	1	0	1.35	5	0	0	6.2	4	1	5	5	0
2000 AL Baltimore	0	0	0.00	1	0	0	0.2	1	0	1	0	0

The key to the O's B.J. Surhoff trade in July, Rivera has the highest ceiling among the 15 players acquired before the trade deadline. Injuries frequently have sidelined him, and in 2000, he was plagued by back spasms, a shoulder strain and blisters. When he's healthy, Rivera throws a mid-90s fastball that moves and a plus breaking pitch. The Orioles will get their first long look at Rivera this spring, as he was shut down with a tired arm shortly after his debut on September 20. A candidate for Triple-A Rochester, Rivera soon may be in the Orioles' rotation.

Rich Stahl

	Position: P	Opening Day Age: 19
	Bats: R Throws: L	Born: 4/11/81 in
	Ht: 6' 7" Wt: 185	Covington, GA

Recent Statistics

	W	L	ERA	G	GS	Sv	IP	H	R	BB	SO	HR
2000 A Delmarva	5	6	3.34	20	20	0	89.0	97	47	51	83	3

Comparisons to Randy Johnson—or even Ryan Anderson—aren't fair, but the 6-foot-7 lefthander has the loose delivery and mid-90s heat of a future No. 1 starter. Stahl has the best arm in the system, and he's fine-tuning a curveball that soon will rank with his impressive fastball. Getting his mechanics, pitches and game plan in sync will take some time, but he will blossom when the pieces come together. It's doubtful that Stahl will be rushed. Making his debut in 2000 after signing too late in '99, Stahl is targeted for high Class-A Frederick in 2001.

John Stephens

	Position: P	Opening Day Age: 21
	Bats: R Throws: R	Born: 11/15/79 in
	Ht: 6' 1" Wt: 200	Sydney, Australia

Recent Statistics

	W	L	ERA	G	GS	Sv	IP	H	R	BB	SO	HR
1999 A Delmarva	10	8	3.22	28	27	0	170.1	148	75	36	217	10
2000 A Frederick	7	6	3.05	20	20	0	118.0	119	45	22	121	5

An Australian signed in 1996, Stephens has stellar command of three pitches, but one is a fastball that tops out near 85 MPH. In the Class-A Sally League in 1998, Stephens suffered an injury similar to whiplash while diving for a bunt. When he returned in '99, Stephens' fastball had dropped from the high 80s to the low 80s, and he lost the break on his curve. That didn't keep him from dominating at Class-A Delmarva in '99, with just 36 walks and 217 strikeouts in 170.1 innings. In 2000,

with Stephens regaining a little velocity, he went 7-6 (3.05) and fanned 121 in 118 innings in the high Class-A Carolina League. The master of command, he uses the same motion and arm action on all of his pitches.

Others to Watch

Two spots are open in Baltimore's rotation. One candidate is lefthander **John Bale** (26), who was acquired from Toronto in exchange for catching prospect Jayson Werth in December. A 1996 draft pick, Bale worked as a starter until shoulder tendinitis struck in 1998. He succeeded in the bullpen with a good fastball and curve. Mixing in a changeup, Bale enjoyed a solid season at Triple-A Syracuse in 2000 in a swing role. . . The Orioles also traded for righthander **Lesli Brea** (22), who came in the Mike Bordick deal in July. Brea has been fanning better than a batter an inning as a reliever with a mid-90s fastball and a hard slider. Walks have been high and command has been an issue, but Brea gained better command of a changeup in the Arizona Fall League. He could end up a closer. . . First baseman-left fielder **Jay Gibbons** (24) was another pickup from Toronto, courtesy of December's Rule 5 draft. The stocky Gibbons has a short, quick swing that has allowed him to hit above .300 at four stops in three pro seasons. Gibbons batted .321-19-75 with 38 doubles, 61 walks and a .404 on-base percentage at Double-A Tennessee in 2000. Gibbons isn't fast, but he has a decent arm for left. . . Another rotation candidate is southpaw **John Parrish** (23), who throws his curveball and changeup for strikes and uses his fastball to set up those pitches. Last summer he got into trouble trying to be more of a power pitcher. Parrish had a few good outings with the O's in the second half. . . With his first-step quickness and speed, outfielder **Tim Raines Jr.** (21), son of the former major league star, stole 81 bases at high Class-A Frederick in 2000. Raines also draws walks, but a switch-hitting experiment of three years still leaves Raines struggling from his adopted left side. . . Blessed with five-tool potential, shortstop **Ed Rogers** (19) reached Double-A ball as a teenager last summer, batting .286 in 49 at-bats at Bowie. Rogers has the great arm, speed and impressive range of a star shortstop, and he's strong for his size and has handled the bat adequately with his 150-pound frame. . . The youngest player in pro ball in 1998, **Jacobo Sequea** (19) came to the O's in a 1999 trade deadline deal with Cincinnati. He handled high Class-A Frederick adaquately in 2000, and may reach Double-A Bowie as a teenager this summer. . . After a lackluster season at Frederick in 1999, **Jay Spurgeon** (24) climbed four levels from Frederick to the big club in 2000. He defeated Tampa Bay in his first pro start on August 27, but his future may be in the bullpen. . . Righthander **Joshua Towers** (24) walked just 21 batters and fanned 102 in 148 innings at Triple-A Rochester. He went 8-6 (3.47) by showing excellent command of his four-pitch arsenal. Both Towers and Spurgeon may win Opening Day jobs.

Fenway Park

Offense

By now, the cliche about Fenway being a home-run park should be dispelled, especially when compared to stadiums like Enron Field and Coors Field. Look back over the last three years and you'll find that there's barely any difference in the number of runs scored in non-interleague games at Fenway as opposed to on the road—2,148 at home, 2,066 on the road. It clearly is not a home-run haven, either—525 dingers on the road by both teams in non-interleague games, 418 at Fenway.

Defense

There are many spring and fall nights when the east wind kills anything in the air. Due to the space in center and right-center field, there is a lot of room for pitchers to get hitters out. A lack of foul territory, especially down the lines, hurts the defense.

Who It Helps the Most

Because of the drift over the last 25 years to using the whole field as the strike zone has moved down and away, Fenway is in most cases a lefthanded hitters' park. Ask Fred Lynn (.352 lifetime there), Carl Yastrzemski (.306 home, .264 road), Wade Boggs, Mike Greenwell or Mo Vaughn. Fenway is a good doubles park, a fact that Nomar Garciaparra and Jason Varitek take advantage of.

Who It Hurts the Most

Other than outdated clubhouses and the dank nature of the park, the biggest complaint is the playing surface. Fenway was built on landfill so it's like a lily pad, with water seeping up through the park after prolonged rain. If you wonder about Garciaparra's error numbers, consider Boston's non-interleague games over the last three years. During that time there were 276 infield errors made at Fenway overall, but just 202 such miscues on the road. That's the biggest home-road index in the majors.

Rookies & Newcomers

Manny Ramirez averaged roughly 38 doubles and 37 homers the past five seasons. In Boston, he may generate a few more doubles and a few less longballs. Dernell Stenson, one of Boston's top prospects, is a lefthanded hitter with power, which typically has been a good combination at Fenway.

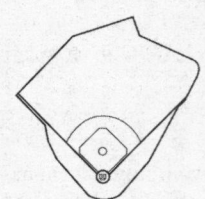

Dimensions: LF-310, LCF-379, CF-420, RCF-380, RF-302

Capacity: 33,871

Elevation: 21 feet

Surface: Grass

Foul Territory: Small

Park Factors

2000 Season

	Home Games Red Sox	Opp	Total	Away Games Red Sox	Opp	Total	Index
G	72	72	144	72	72	144	—
Avg	.274	.272	.273	.263	.244	.254	107
AB	2445	2573	5018	2579	2394	4973	101
R	354	349	703	371	322	693	101
H	671	699	1370	679	584	1263	108
2B	152	127	279	135	119	254	109
3B	17	16	33	12	10	22	149
HR	59	66	125	95	86	181	68
BB	268	205	473	274	239	513	91
SO	439	521	960	459	491	950	100
E	59	54	113	41	32	73	155
E-Infield	54	40	94	32	24	56	168
LHB-Avg	.269	.272	.270	.256	.242	.250	108
LHB-HR	36	26	62	57	36	93	69
RHB-Avg	.280	.271	.275	.271	.246	.258	107
RHB-HR	23	40	63	38	50	88	68

1998-2000

	Home Games Red Sox	Opp	Total	Away Games Red Sox	Opp	Total	Index
G	217	217	434	217	217	434	—
Avg	.286	.263	.274	.267	.246	.257	107
AB	7314	7643	14957	7713	7183	14896	100
R	1151	997	2148	1115	951	2066	104
H	2092	2012	4104	2060	1766	3826	107
2B	477	388	865	411	347	758	114
3B	53	32	85	46	25	71	119
HR	213	205	418	288	237	525	79
BB	790	631	1421	788	689	1477	96
SO	1305	1551	2856	1349	1416	2765	103
E	173	150	323	129	116	245	132
E-Infield	152	124	276	115	87	202	137
LHB-Avg	.288	.268	.278	.263	.255	.259	107
LHB-HR	110	72	182	158	108	266	70
RHB-Avg	.285	.259	.271	.271	.238	.255	106
RHB-HR	103	133	236	130	129	259	89

2000 Rankings (American League)

- Highest error factor
- Highest infield-error factor
- Second-highest batting-average factor
- Second-highest hit factor
- Second-highest RHB batting-average factor
- Third-highest triple factor
- Third-highest LHB batting-average factor
- Lowest LHB home-run factor
- Second-lowest home-run factor
- Second-lowest walk factor
- Second-lowest RHB home-run factor

Jimy Williams

2000 Season

Jimy Williams' strengths as a manager are many. First, he is a teacher, running and developing the Red Sox as if he were in the Florida State League. Second, he is a strong talent evaluator, as evidenced by the decisions he's made on players like Jason Varitek, Trot Nixon, Derek Lowe, Brian Daubach and others. Third, he gives his coaches respect and leeway. Fourth, in a tough media town, he accepts the heat, and what he has to say to players is said only to them in the privacy of his office. These qualities helped the BoSox to their third straight winning season, though they failed to make the playoffs for the first time since 1997.

Offense

In terms of running a game, Williams is quixotic. He used more lineups than any manager in baseball. At times he had Darren Lewis batting third or Andy Sheets as the DH. Although Williams likes to hit and run, he didn't run, which brought some second-guessing by players like Carl Everett and Nomar Garciaparra. He used more sacrifice bunts last year because the team struggled offensively, but he usually prefers the strategy with the game on the line in the late innings.

Pitching & Defense

With the help of Kerrigan and bullpen coach John Cumberland, Williams is protective of hurlers. Last season Boston starters were last in innings while the staff ranked first in ERA. Williams employed the fewest slow hooks and the most quick hooks last year, and the Red Sox have piled up 51 saves of more than one inning over the past three seasons. While Williams and Kerrigan don't believe in the slide step, they order all the pitchouts—114, 74 more than the next AL team. Because he loves defense, Williams often is near the top of AL managers in defensive substitutions.

2001 Outlook

At the end of last season, it appeared that Williams might not be back because of conflicts with GM Dan Duquette. They clashed over where to play Jose Offerman and how to deal with Everett. Still, after four seasons at the helm, Williams already ranks sixth in wins among Red Sox managers.

Born: 10/04/43 in Santa Maria, CA

Playing Experience: 1966-1967, StL

Managerial Experience: 8 seasons

Manager Statistics

Year	Team, Lg	W	L	Pct	GB	Finish
2000	Boston, AL	85	77	.525	2.5	2nd East
8 Seasons		630	540	.538	—	—

2000 Starting Pitchers by Days Rest

	<=3	4	5	6+
Red Sox Starts	1	75	50	24
Red Sox ERA	3.60	4.19	4.07	5.20
AL Avg Starts	2	88	40	22
AL ERA	4.87	5.03	5.03	5.28

2000 Situational Stats

	Jimy Williams	AL Average
Hit & Run Success %	38.1	35.1
Stolen Base Success %	58.9	68.8
Platoon Pct.	66.7	57.8
Defensive Subs	30	23
High-Pitch Outings	9	13
Quick/Slow Hooks	39/8	18/19
Sacrifice Attempts	49	55

2000 Rankings (American League)

- 1st in sacrifice-bunt percentage (89.8), pitchouts (114), pitchouts with a runner moving (34), starting lineups used (140) and quick hooks
- 2nd in saves with over 1 inning pitched (16)
- 3rd in fewest caught stealings of second base (27), hit-and-run success percentage, defensive substitutions and pinch-hitters used (158)

Boston

Rolando Arrojo

2000 Season

The Red Sox were so desperate for a starting pitcher at the July trading deadline that they were willing to assume Mike Lansing's 2001 contract, which costs them more than $7 million, in order to land Rolando Arrojo. Although Arrojo did go 5-2 for Boston, his 5.05 ERA was disappointing. And while he pitched brilliantly against Orlando Hernandez—his longtime playoff opponent in Cuba—Arrojo had games when he appeared as if his mind were back in his homeland.

Pitching

According to his Cuban baseball card, Arrojo will turn 37 this season. But his stuff is still very good. He throws four or five different pitches from every conceivable arm angle. His sidearm delivery is easier to pick up for lefthanded batters, and lefties slugged .545 against him. He has a good sinker, which has helped him produce a 1.47 career groundball-flyball ratio. But the rap on Arrojo has been his concentration. There were starts in which he crossed up his catchers on more than 20 pitches. And the fact that the league slugged .463 against him with his stuff makes some wonder where he's coming from on certain days. However, the start in Yankee Stadium underscored what the Red Sox believe—that he gets bored, and that in pressure situations he will pitch like El Duque, whom he used to beat in the playoffs back home. Several of the teams that pursued Arrojo last season thought he'd be better suited to a relief role.

Defense

Arrojo's long arm action and delivery make him a target for basestealers, but he allowed only 10 steals last season. Though he has an average move to first, he'll hold the ball, change his tempo to the plate and sometimes slide step, all geared to messing up runners' timing. He is an average fielder.

2001 Outlook

With a shortage of starting pitchers, the Red Sox plan to use Arrojo in that role. Pitching coach Joe Kerrigan believes that with a spring training, which would allow pitchers and catchers to work together and get to know each other better, Arrojo could have a far better season.

Position: SP
Bats: R **Throws:** R
Ht: 6' 4" **Wt:** 220

Opening Day Age: 32
Born: 7/18/68 in Havana, Cuba
ML Seasons: 3
Pronunciation: uh-ROH-ho

Overall Statistics

	W	L	Pct.	ERA	G	GS	Sv	IP	H	BB	SO	HR	Ratio
2000	10	11	.476	5.63	32	32	0	172.2	187	68	124	24	1.48
Career	31	35	.470	4.70	88	88	0	515.1	544	193	383	68	1.43

How Often He Throws Strikes

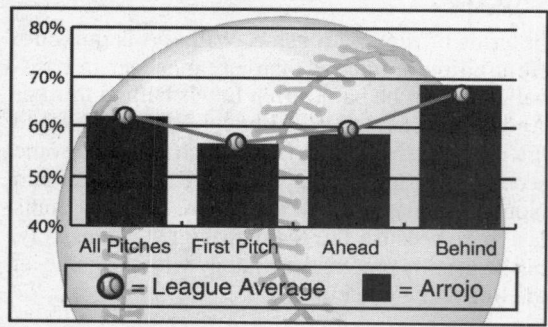

2000 Situational Stats

	W	L	ERA	Sv	IP		AB	H	HR	RBI	Avg
Home	5	5	6.98	0	80.0	LHB	332	99	17	62	.298
Road	5	6	4.47	0	92.2	RHB	344	88	7	48	.256
First Half	5	6	6.05	0	83.1	Sc Pos	163	45	7	84	.276
Scnd Half	5	5	5.24	0	89.1	Clutch	15	4	0	1	.267

2000 Rankings (American League)

- Did not rank near the top or bottom in any category

Dante Bichette

2000 Season

After seven monstrous seasons in Colorado, Dante Bichette moved on in 2000, first to the Reds, then to the Red Sox. Neither stop exactly worked out like a dream. The Riverfront outfield turf was a problem, and he hit 16 homers in 461 at-bats for Cincinnati. He was traded to Boston in late August, where he played 30 games, batted .289 and hit seven homers.

Hitting

Bichette still is a good RBI producer. He will catch the odd breaking ball and hit it across counties. But he's a situational hitter who fights off good fastballs and tries to put the ball in play in the alleys. While Colorado was the perfect park for Bichette, Fenway might also be good. He's hit .341 against flyball pitchers over the last five years, so he could tomahawk a few 85-MPH heaters into the screen.

Baserunning & Defense

At age 37, Bichette has slowed down from the days when he used to play center field. He can't throw as he once did, although getting off the turf could energize him and minimize his speed problems. On turf, he was sometimes given to misjudging plays. But that won't be a problem if he moves over to left in Fenway, or especially if he moves to DH. He always has been a decent, if not speedy, baserunner. He will steal in some situations and runs the bases hard. He'll have to get used to how little time there is to make a decision in Fenway on balls hit to left field; there's a tombstone every inch for baserunners without instinct and third-base coaches with indecision.

2001 Outlook

At this point in his career, Bichette is likely going to be a DH and part-time outfielder, unless the Red Sox make space for him to play left field. Bichette is a seasoned RBI man who shouldn't have a lot of pressure to produce now that the team has Manny Ramirez to drive in a bulk of its runs.

Position: RF/DH
Bats: R **Throws:** R
Ht: 6' 2" **Wt:** 235

Opening Day Age: 37
Born: 11/18/63 in West Palm Beach, FL
ML Seasons: 13
Pronunciation: DON-tay bih-SHET

Boston

Overall Statistics

	G	AB	R	H	D	T	HR	RBI	SB	BB	SO	Avg	OBP	Slg
2000	155	575	80	169	32	2	23	90	5	49	91	.294	.350	.477
Career	1597	5990	889	1794	371	26	262	1092	150	335	1002	.299	.337	.501

Where He Hits the Ball

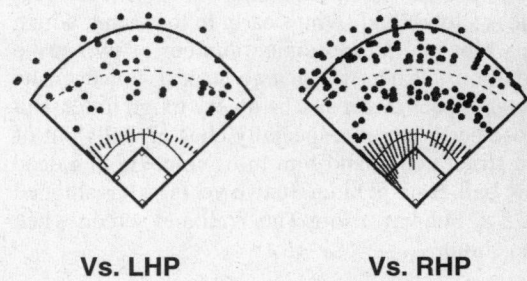

Vs. LHP   **Vs. RHP**

2000 Situational Stats

	AB	H	HR	RBI	Avg		AB	H	HR	RBI	Avg
Home	298	92	15	44	.309	LHP	127	37	8	26	.291
Road	277	77	8	46	.278	RHP	448	132	15	64	.295
First Half	295	87	13	46	.295	Sc Pos	158	42	6	65	.266
Scnd Half	280	82	10	44	.293	Clutch	94	28	2	15	.298

2000 Rankings (American League)

- Did not rank near the top or bottom in any category

Brian Daubach

2000 Season

When Brian Daubach beat the Mets with a ninth-inning double in the first game after the All-Star break, Todd Pratt said he "doesn't respect Daubach because he was a replacement player." The strike was five years ago, however, when Daubach was seemingly buried in the Mets organization. He got his shot with Boston at age 27 and seems to have carved out his niche with consecutive 21-homer, 70-plus RBI seasons.

Hitting

Daubach is a very streaky hitter. He batted .354 in April, .187 in June and .162 in September and October. When he struggles, his 130-44 strikeout-walk ratio in 495 at-bats speaks for itself. He produces a lot of bad swings early in the count, which gets him into an inordinate number of two-strike situations. When he has two strikes, however, he tends to bear down and be a very tough hitter. But those early lapses, especially chasing balls out of the strike zone, land him in trouble. He is a dead low-ball, fastball hitter. In two years he has slugged .525 at Fenway, using The Wall and screen when he is hot.

Baserunning & Defense

Typecast as a non-positional, slow player in the Mets and Marlins organizations, Daubach has made himself into an average first baseman. He is adept enough that when the Red Sox ran out of third basemen last summer, Jimy Williams actually worked him out at third base. Daubach has adequate hands, works hard on the throw to second and knows what he can and cannot chase on the ground. As a baserunner, he gets there when he can. His major league total of one steal and two caught stealings is not going to change appreciably in the next decade.

2001 Outlook

The Red Sox feel that Daubach is so strong, so willing and so diligent that if he generates a better game plan for every at-bat and avoids those two-strike holes, he can hit .280 with 30-35 home runs. At 29, this is the time, because with prospects Juan Diaz and Dernell Stenson on the horizon, Daubach has to do it now.

Position: 1B/DH
Bats: L **Throws:** R
Ht: 6' 1" **Wt:** 201

Opening Day Age: 29
Born: 2/11/72 in Belleville, IL
ML Seasons: 3
Pronunciation: DAW-back
Nickname: The Belleville Basher

Overall Statistics

	G	AB	R	H	D	T	HR	RBI	SB	BB	SO	Avg	OBP	Slg
2000	142	495	55	123	32	2	21	76	1	44	130	.248	.315	.448
Career	262	891	116	238	66	5	42	152	1	81	227	.267	.334	.494

Where He Hits the Ball

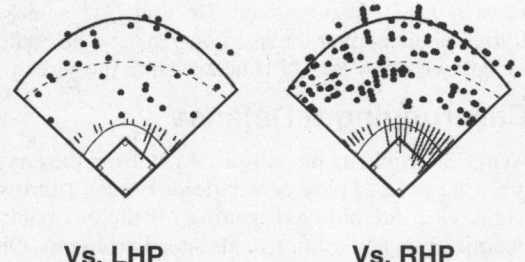

Vs. LHP	Vs. RHP

2000 Situational Stats

	AB	H	HR	RBI	Avg		AB	H	HR	RBI	Avg
Home	237	63	10	44	.266	LHP	102	22	3	11	.216
Road	258	60	11	32	.233	RHP	393	101	18	65	.257
First Half	268	74	14	52	.276	Sc Pos	132	35	7	57	.265
Scnd Half	227	49	7	24	.216	Clutch	81	18	3	18	.222

2000 Rankings (American League)

- 8th in strikeouts and lowest percentage of swings put into play (35.9)
- 10th in lowest batting average and lowest batting average on the road
- Led the Red Sox in strikeouts and games played
- Led designated hitters in hit by pitch (6), strikeouts, fewest GDPs per GDP situation (5.8%) and batting average on an 0-2 count (.250)

Carl Everett

2000 Season

Forget for a moment some of those Carl Everett controversies. He's a switch-hitter who hit 34 homers, knocked in 108 runs and had 70 extra-base hits in only 496 at-bats last season. Granted, after making the All-Star team his slugging percentage dropped 145 points in the second half, but much of that had to do with his loss of temper, suspension and eventual run-ins with writers, umpires, his manager and a teammate or two.

Hitting

From the left side, Everett is Junior Griffey: 30 homers, 85 RBI and a .613 slugging percentage. From the right side, as he steps out of the box and sets up over the inside corner, he looks like Gary Sheffield: less power but a .348 batting average. He's a dead lowball hitter batting lefthanded and a highball hitter righthanded. Everett is so strong that he can hit almost any fastball for power, driving the ball all over the field from both sides of the plate. He also performs well with runners on base (.308) and runners in scoring position (.306).

Baserunning & Defense

Everett plays an extremely shallow center field and likes to challenge hitters. He sometimes gets beaten on balls over his head, but he is a very smart player who plays percentages. Although he sometimes gets out of control going hard after balls in the gaps, he has one of the rare strong center-field throwing arms. One of his beefs with Jimy Williams was that Everett felt he and the entire team should run more and be more aggressive. While Everett himself is an average basestealer, he's a good baserunner.

2001 Outlook

The problem is that between injuries and Carl Everett moments, he has never had 500 at-bats in a season. At the end of last season, his relationship with his manager and, to a degree, some of his teammates, had deteriorated. If he curbs his anger and learns to cope with the Boston environment, Everett can be a Fenway star as part of a tremendously productive heart-of-the-order along with Manny Ramirez and Nomar Garciaparra.

Position: CF
Bats: B **Throws:** R
Ht: 6' 0" **Wt:** 215

Opening Day Age: 29
Born: 6/3/71 in Tampa, FL
ML Seasons: 8

Boston

Overall Statistics

	G	AB	R	H	D	T	HR	RBI	SB	BB	SO	Avg	OBP	Slg
2000	137	496	82	149	32	4	34	108	11	52	113	.300	.373	.587
Career	742	2421	382	682	149	16	103	425	82	242	555	.282	.353	.484

Where He Hits the Ball

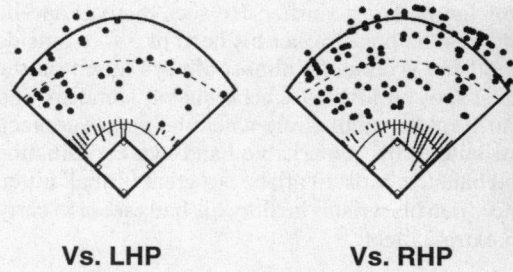

Vs. LHP   **Vs. RHP**

2000 Situational Stats

	AB	H	HR	RBI	Avg		AB	H	HR	RBI	Avg
Home	252	71	17	51	.282	LHP	132	46	4	23	.348
Road	244	78	17	57	.320	RHP	364	103	30	85	.283
First Half	289	95	24	69	.329	Sc Pos	134	41	10	74	.306
Scnd Half	207	54	10	39	.261	Clutch	75	21	4	15	.280

2000 Rankings (American League)

- 2nd in fewest GDPs per GDP situation (3.1%) and lowest fielding percentage in center field (.980)
- 3rd in errors in center field (6)
- 4th in slugging percentage vs. righthanded pitchers (.613)
- 5th in highest percentage of swings that missed (28.8)
- Led the Red Sox in home runs, RBI, stolen bases, hit by pitch (8), pitches seen (2,151), HR frequency (14.6 ABs per HR), fewest GDPs per GDP situation (3.1%), batting average on a 3-1 count (.588), slugging percentage vs. righthanded pitchers (.613), steals of third (2) and batting average on a 3-2 count (.320)

Nomar Garciaparra

2000 Season

Nomar Garciaparra, Boston's entry in the present-day Holy Trinity of shortstops, won another batting title, ranked fifth in the American League with a .434 on-base percentage and placed seventh with a .599 slugging percentage. What's remarkable is that Garciaparra played hurt much of last season. Though a wrist injury clearly affected his power, he probably would have reached 100 RBI had the top of the Red Sox lineup not struggled and had he not been intentionally walked a league-high 20 times. This just in—the man can hit.

Hitting

The 3.05 pitches he saw per plate appearance in 2000 (fewest in the majors) prove Garciaparra to be what he is—a slasher. He sees the ball and he hits it. Whether it's over his head or a foot outside or off the ground, he almost always hits it on the same spot on his bat. Check his bat someday and you'll find a small circle where he makes contact, a tribute to his remarkable hand-eye coordination and balance. Most of all, he is a great fastball hitter, and when his wrist is healthy his balls seem to carry an extra 25 feet.

Baserunning & Defense

Garciaparra's home infield has the largest error ratio in the major leagues, so his error totals can be deceptive. This past season was his best defensively, as his consistency was way up. He is unique in that he plays on the run, making plays in left field with the ability to throw strongly across his body while running in the opposite direction. At times last season he seemed frustrated by the Red Sox style of one base at a time. He likes to run, has above-average speed and is a daredevil. In every phase of his game, he has an X-Games style.

2001 Outlook

As long as he stays healthy, there is no reason that Garciaparra won't continue to improve. The big question entering 2001 was what were the Red Sox going to put around him in the batting order, and the answer came in the form of one of the best RBI men in baseball—Manny Ramirez. Ted Williams still believes Garciappara can bat .400.

Position: SS
Bats: R **Throws:** R
Ht: 6' 0" **Wt:** 180

Opening Day Age: 27
Born: 7/23/73 in Whittier, CA
ML Seasons: 5
Pronunciation: NO-mar gar-see-uh-PARR-uh

Overall Statistics

	G	AB	R	H	D	T	HR	RBI	SB	BB	SO	Avg	OBP	Slg
2000	140	529	104	197	51	3	21	96	5	61	50	.372	.434	.599
Career	595	2436	451	812	176	29	117	436	58	184	257	.333	.382	.573

Where He Hits the Ball

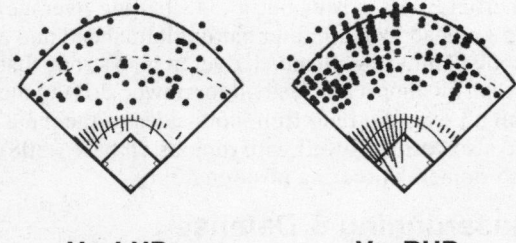

Vs. LHP　　　　**Vs. RHP**

2000 Situational Stats

	AB	H	HR	RBI	Avg		AB	H	HR	RBI	Avg
Home	259	97	7	51	.375	LHP	141	54	6	29	.383
Road	270	100	14	45	.370	RHP	388	143	15	67	.369
First Half	252	98	12	55	.389	Sc Pos	131	49	2	66	.374
Scnd Half	277	99	9	41	.357	Clutch	81	30	1	11	.370

2000 Rankings (American League)

- 1st in batting average, intentional walks (20), batting average vs. righthanded pitchers, batting average on the road and fewest pitches seen per plate appearance (3.05)
- 2nd in doubles, batting average vs. lefthanded pitchers, batting average at home and batting average with two strikes (.331)
- 3rd in cleanup slugging percentage (.610) and on-base percentage vs. lefthanded pitchers (.457)
- Led the Red Sox in batting average, at-bats, runs scored, hits, singles, doubles, total bases (317), sacrifice flies (7), intentional walks (20), times on base (260), plate appearances (599), slugging percentage, on-base percentage and batting average with runners in scoring position

Derek Lowe

2000 Season

Derek Lowe's selection to the All-Star team signaled his rise to the stature of one of the game's premier closers. He converted 42 of 47 save opportunities and held opponents to a .304 on-base percentage. Since being moved into the full-time closer role in August of 1999, Lowe has converted 52 of 60 save opportunities.

Pitching

Lowe is a classic sinkerballer. His hard, running, skittery sinker is a dominant pitch. It produced a 3.45 groundball-flyball ratio, which was better than any starter in baseball. His 2.56 ERA was a testament to his ability, considering the problems and injuries in the Red Sox infield behind him, not to mention the fact that Fenway has the highest groundball error factor in the American League. To complement the sinker, Lowe has a big breaking curveball that he can use away from righthanders and underneath the hands of lefthanders. He also has a changeup that comes out of his hand like a fastball and has screwball action, but as a reliever he doesn't get to use it too often. When he's pitching well, Lowe throws fewer than 12 pitches an inning, so Jimy Williams likes to bring him into games in the eighth inning if the situation dictates.

Defense

Because of his big leg kick, the fact that his sinker is hard to catch and his curveball has such a long arc, Lowe can be run on. Teams like to start runners against him to try to stay out of double plays. He only occasionally will slide step. He is an average fielder, though he has to be calmed down.

2001 Outlook

The Red Sox considered moving Lowe into the rotation if they could have found another closer last fall. But when their search went past December 1, Boston decided to keep him in the bullpen because there wasn't enough time to make the transition. Lowe went through two mediocre months last June and July, then made adjustments and finished strong. The Red Sox believe that his maturation and the development of his changeup will keep him in the elite class of relievers.

Position: RP
Bats: R **Throws:** R
Ht: 6' 6" **Wt:** 200

Opening Day Age: 27
Born: 6/1/73 in Dearborn, MI
ML Seasons: 4

Boston

Overall Statistics

	W	L	Pct.	ERA	G	GS	Sv	IP	H	BB	SO	HR	Ratio
2000	4	4	.500	2.56	74	0	42	91.1	90	22	79	6	1.23
Career	15	22	.405	3.67	231	19	61	392.2	374	112	288	29	1.24

How Often He Throws Strikes

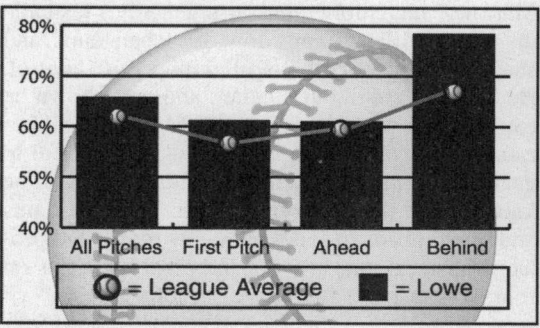

= League Average = Lowe

2000 Situational Stats

	W	L	ERA	Sv	IP		AB	H	HR	RBI	Avg
Home	4	3	3.48	16	41.1	LHB	164	44	3	16	.268
Road	0	1	1.80	26	50.0	RHB	186	46	3	17	.247
First Half	2	3	2.82	19	51.0	Sc Pos	97	19	1	26	.196
Scnd Half	2	1	2.23	23	40.1	Clutch	239	60	4	27	.251

2000 Rankings (American League)

- 1st in save opportunities (47), saves and games finished (64)
- 2nd in relief innings (91.1)
- 3rd in save percentage (89.4) and relief ERA (2.56)
- 5th in games pitched and worst first batter efficiency (.333)
- Led the Red Sox in games pitched, saves, games finished (64), save opportunities (47), save percentage (89.4), blown saves (5), most GDPs induced per GDP situation (17.9%), lowest batting average allowed in relief with runners on base (.207), relief innings (91.1) and relief ERA (2.56)

Pedro Martinez

Position: SP
Bats: R **Throws:** R
Ht: 5'11" **Wt:** 170

Opening Day Age: 29
Born: 10/25/71 in Manoguayabo, Dominican Republic
ML Seasons: 9

2000 Season

Just about the only category that Pedro Martinez didn't lead the American League in last year was wins, and that was primarily due to lack of run support. His ERA in August was 2.60, and that was his *worst* month. His overall ERA of 1.74 was 1.96 better than runner-up Roger Clemens. Martinez now leads all active starting pitchers in career winning percentage, earned run average, quality-start percentage, strikeout-walk ratio, hits allowed per nine innings, baserunners per nine innings and opponents batting average and slugging percentage.

Pitching

There isn't a pitcher in the game with better stuff. Martinez' incredibly quick arm generates fastballs up to 98 MPH, dumps low-80s changeups and snaps off nasty curveballs, all with precise control. He also can crank out a cutter, and he's shown he can succeed when he has an 88-MPH fastball because of his control and instincts. He's careful to get hitters off his plate, and he reads hitters as if he knows what they're trying to do. Jimy Williams and pitching coach Joe Kerrigan work hard to protect Martinez, and last year he made 14 starts on four days rest and 15 on five or more.

Defense

Martinez is a good fielder. He's quick off the mound and able to throw from any angle. Because of his instincts, he rarely makes mistakes in judgment throwing to the right base. He allowed 10 stolen bases, but Boston pitchers seldom slide step. He slows runners by holding the ball. He has a good move to first base because of his quick feet and arm. The way the Red Sox view it, they'd rather have Martinez strike out hitters than waste his time and energy throwing to bases.

2001 Outlook

With the addition of Manny Ramirez and the good health of several key players, there is every reason to believe that the Red Sox will provide Martinez with better run support this season. As long as he remains healthy, he should continue to get better because he's still learning. For every major league hitter not currently in a Boston uniform, that is a truly scary thought.

Overall Statistics

	W	L	Pct.	ERA	G	GS	Sv	IP	H	BB	SO	HR	Ratio
2000	18	6	.750	1.74	29	29	0	217.0	128	32	284	17	0.74
Career	125	56	.691	2.68	278	211	3	1576.1	1178	442	1818	124	1.03

How Often He Throws Strikes

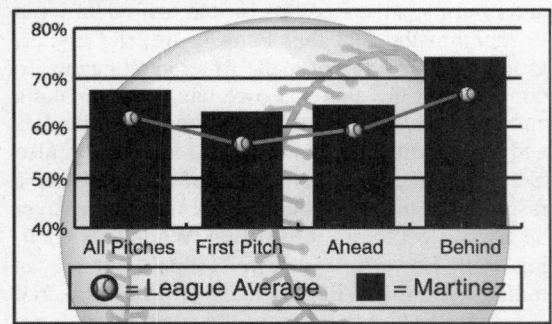

2000 Situational Stats

	W	L	ERA	Sv	IP		AB	H	HR	RBI	Avg
Home	6	5	1.84	0	98.0	LHB	399	60	5	19	.150
Road	12	1	1.66	0	119.0	RHB	369	68	12	22	.184
First Half	9	3	1.44	0	106.0	Sc Pos	128	17	2	24	.133
Scnd Half	9	3	2.03	0	111.0	Clutch	101	20	4	9	.198

2000 Rankings (American League)

- 1st in ERA, shutouts (4), strikeouts, highest strikeout/walk ratio (8.9), lowest batting average allowed (.167), lowest slugging percentage allowed (.259), lowest on-base percentage allowed (.213), fewest home runs allowed per nine innings (.71), most strikeouts per nine innings (11.8), lowest ERA at home, lowest ERA on the road, lowest batting average allowed vs. lefthanded batters, lowest batting average allowed vs. righthanded batters and lowest batting average allowed with runners in scoring position
- 2nd in complete games (7), hit batsmen (14), fewest walks per nine innings (1.3) and winning percentage
- 4th in wins

Trot Nixon

2000 Season

When Trot Nixon was 18 years old, he was the seventh pick in the nation with a swing so pretty that one Mets scout compared him to "a young Will Clark." Then came back and eyesight problems, as well as the intense pressure that he mounted on himself. But by last May, when he was hitting .321 with seven homers, the Red Sox were comparing him to Paul O'Neill, and writers argued that Nixon *never* should be traded for Sammy Sosa. However, by the end of the season Nixon had posted rather pedestrian totals.

Hitting

Nixon is will draw a walk and rarely will put the first pitch in play. When he does connect, he is a line-drive hitter who can rack up doubles in bunches, and he has the hustle to turn some of those drives into triples. One problem was that he injured a hamstring muscle in June and wasn't the same until the last few weeks of the 2000 campaign. But true to his makeup, he kept playing hard, though the leg never allowed him to drive the ball for power or to run normally. In addition, Jimy Williams insists on platooning Nixon, so he has only 99 career at-bats against lefthanded pitching.

Baserunning & Defense

Fenway's right field arguably is the most difficult outfield position in the American League with its space, angles and sunlight, and Nixon is the best the Red Sox have had there since Dwight Evans. Nixon runs good routes to balls, is very aggressive cutting balls off, has a good arm and works hard at getting his body in position to throw. He's an average runner, but since he plays so hard and has such good instincts, he is an above-average baserunner.

2001 Outlook

This may be Nixon's make-or-break season in terms of defining whether he can hit close to .300 with 25 home runs. The Red Sox believe he'll bust out, as do teams like the Indians, A's and others that tried to trade for him in the offseason. Rumors will continue to float since the Red Sox now have Manny Ramirez and Nixon is a valuable trade commodity. It's still unclear if Ramirez will displace Nixon in right or Troy O'Leary in left.

Position: RF
Bats: L **Throws:** L
Ht: 6' 2" **Wt:** 200

Opening Day Age: 26
Born: 4/11/74 in Durham, NC
ML Seasons: 4

Overall Statistics

	G	AB	R	H	D	T	HR	RBI	SB	BB	SO	Avg	OBP	Slg
2000	123	427	66	118	27	8	12	60	8	63	85	.276	.368	.461
Career	262	839	138	230	51	13	27	112	12	117	164	.274	.361	.462

Where He Hits the Ball

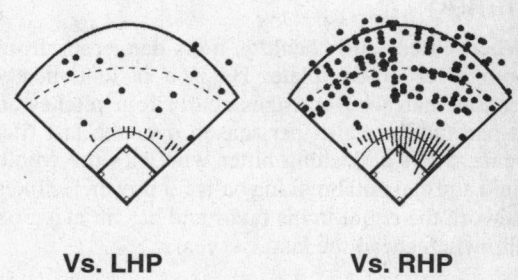

Vs. LHP **Vs. RHP**

2000 Situational Stats

	AB	H	HR	RBI	Avg		AB	H	HR	RBI	Avg
Home	192	50	4	20	.260	LHP	53	14	1	6	.264
Road	235	68	8	40	.289	RHP	374	104	11	54	.278
First Half	236	69	8	39	.292	Sc Pos	88	27	1	45	.307
Scnd Half	191	49	4	21	.257	Clutch	68	23	1	9	.338

2000 Rankings (American League)

- 2nd in on-base percentage for a leadoff hitter (.398)
- 3rd in lowest percentage of swings on the first pitch (13.3)
- 4th in fielding percentage in right field (.991)
- 5th in triples
- Led the Red Sox in triples, on-base percentage for a leadoff hitter (.398), highest percentage of pitches taken (63.6) and lowest percentage of swings on the first pitch (13.3)
- Led AL right fielders in triples, on-base percentage for a leadoff hitter (.398), highest percentage of pitches taken (63.6) and lowest percentage of swings on the first pitch (13.3)

Boston

Jose Offerman

2000 Season

Jose Offerman played the entire 2000 season hurt, which helped to cripple Boston's offense. In the previous two years, Offerman had averaged a .397 on-base percentage, 52 extra-base hits and 105 runs. But last year, playing with a bad knee that he never complained about, those numbers dropped to .354, 26 and 73, respectively. He also didn't steal a base. The hard-edged flair that had been so important to the '99 team was missing, and Jimy Williams kept bouncing him around from second to first base. That movement was a major bone of contention between Williams and Dan Duquette, who constantly pointed out that the club was 42-31 with Offerman starting at second.

Hitting

When Offerman is healthy, he is dangerous from both sides of the plate. He is a patient, heady leadoff man who averages nearly four pitches an at-bat and 74 walks per season over the last five years. He is a slashing hitter who uses the whole field and can pull breaking balls for power. He likes to work the count in his favor and has hit at a .368 clip when ahead the last five years.

Baserunning & Defense

As Offerman has bulked up and improved offensively over the years, his speed and basestealing have declined. He stole only 18 bases in '99 before going 0-for-8 with a bad knee in 2000. Remember, this is a guy who stole 45 bases in 1998. Defense never has been his forte, at least not the double play; he tends to be long and struggles turning the pivot. He is, however, one of the better second basemen at going into the outfield after balls hit in the air.

2001 Outlook

At the end of October, Offerman had his knee scoped and undertook a rehab program. He is a player who seemed to be coming into his own in 1999. Then came the injury and the bad year. If he's healthy and regains his confidence by not being moved around, there is no reason that Offerman shouldn't go back to being an offensive second baseman who produces a .400 on-base percentage, 50 extra-base hits and 100-plus runs.

Position: 2B/1B
Bats: B **Throws:** R
Ht: 6' 0" **Wt:** 190

Opening Day Age: 32
Born: 11/8/68 in San Pedro de Macoris, Dominican Republic
ML Seasons: 11

Overall Statistics

	G	AB	R	H	D	T	HR	RBI	SB	BB	SO	Avg	OBP	Slg
2000	116	451	73	115	14	3	9	41	0	70	70	.255	.354	.359
Career	1259	4596	683	1277	200	65	39	422	157	634	731	.278	.365	.375

Where He Hits the Ball

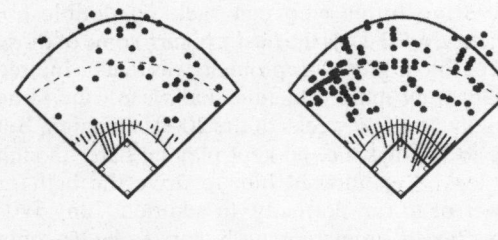

Vs. LHP   **Vs. RHP**

2000 Situational Stats

	AB	H	HR	RBI	Avg		AB	H	HR	RBI	Avg
Home	234	66	3	23	.282	LHP	134	39	4	16	.291
Road	217	49	6	18	.226	RHP	317	76	5	25	.240
First Half	267	69	5	25	.258	Sc Pos	87	20	0	31	.230
Scnd Half	184	46	4	16	.250	Clutch	54	16	0	10	.296

2000 Rankings (American League)

- 3rd in lowest slugging percentage and lowest slugging percentage vs. righthanded pitchers (.331)
- 5th in lowest on-base percentage for a leadoff hitter (.336)
- 7th in lowest batting average vs. righthanded pitchers
- Led the Red Sox in caught stealing (8), walks, highest groundball/flyball ratio (1.5), most pitches seen per plate appearance (3.93) and lowest percentage of swings that missed (12.5)
- Led AL second basemen in batting average in the clutch

Troy O'Leary

2000 Season

Heading into last season, it appeared that Troy O'Leary's career was on the upswing. Both his home-run and RBI totals had increased in each of the last two years. His defense also had improved steadily. Then came a disastrous 2000 campaign. He was distracted by personal problems and at one point even took a leave of absence from the club. His final offensive numbers were more suitable for defensive middle infielders.

Hitting

O'Leary was confused and aloof most of last year. He had become a dead Fenway hitter, staying back with his head still, taking fastballs to left-center and off The Wall and pulling breaking balls—especially balls down—for power to right field. But he was dreadful last season, by his own admission. He swung at bad pitches in bear-down situations; he knocked in only 13 runs in clutch opportunities despite hitting behind All-Stars Nomar Garciaparra and Carl Everett.

Baserunning & Defense

O'Leary has made himself a decent left fielder, especially in Fenway. He charges balls well and is very aggressive on his throws. He handles The Wall and makes up for a below-average arm by quickly cutting balls off. He is a prototypical Boston player, with average speed and only six stolen bases in 19 attempts over the last five seasons. To his credit, he almost always runs hard down the line, has decent instincts on the bases and can score from first on balls hit into the seams.

2001 Outlook

By the end of the season, the Red Sox were begging teams to take the last two years and more than $9 million on O'Leary's contract. As he approaches 32, he is at a turning point. Soon after Boston signed Manny Ramirez, talk of putting O'Leary on the trading block increased in order to make room for Ramirez in left field. After all, O'Leary is a left fielder who has knocked in 85 runs only once in his career and owns a career slugging percentage of only .460.

Position: LF
Bats: L **Throws:** L
Ht: 6' 0" **Wt:** 200

Opening Day Age: 31
Born: 8/4/69 in Compton, CA
ML Seasons: 8
Nickname: Yum-Yum

Overall Statistics

	G	AB	R	H	D	T	HR	RBI	SB	BB	SO	Avg	OBP	Slg
2000	138	513	68	134	30	4	13	70	0	44	76	.261	.320	.411
Career	904	3222	452	902	197	32	106	476	12	261	510	.280	.335	.460

Where He Hits the Ball

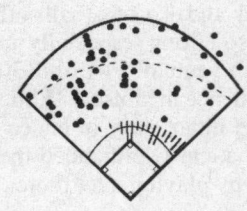 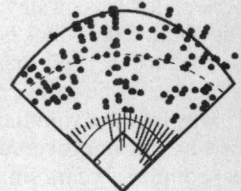

Vs. LHP   **Vs. RHP**

2000 Situational Stats

	AB	H	HR	RBI	Avg		AB	H	HR	RBI	Avg
Home	261	73	7	42	.280	LHP	147	37	3	23	.252
Road	252	61	6	28	.242	RHP	366	97	10	47	.265
First Half	233	53	7	23	.227	Sc Pos	151	43	5	57	.285
Scnd Half	280	81	6	47	.289	Clutch	75	19	2	13	.253

2000 Rankings (American League)
- 4th in errors in left field (3), fielding percentage in left field (.988) and lowest on-base percentage vs. lefthanded pitchers (.291)

Boston

Jason Varitek

2000 Season

After an impressive 1999, Jason Varitek hit a temporary wall last year. But there was a reason for his offensive slump. He hurt his wrist early in the season and wasn't right thereafter. Understand this about him: he arrives at the park every day worrying about his pitchers, and his focus is on making the staff better. For the second year in a row, the Red Sox led the American League in ERA.

Hitting

Sometimes Varitek struggles because he tries too hard at the plate. He gets into stretches when he chases too many bad pitches, especially offerings up and out of the strike zone. When patient, he's a good low breaking-ball hitter with power. Lefthanded, he can stay back and drive fastballs off The Wall. Many feel he's so strong, especially in his tree trunk legs, that he eventually will hit 30 home runs as he gains confidence in himself. While he was a better righthanded hitter early in his career, he has improved dramatically lefthanded the last couple of years simply by playing a lot more.

Baserunning & Defense

Varitek is one of the best catchers in the game. He is prepared, works hard, communicates with his staff and thinks like a pitcher. The Red Sox don't much worry about basestealers. Boston hurlers don't slide step much, but will instead throw over to first and pitch out more than any team. Because they aren't quick to the plate and because of his wrist problem, Varitek threw out only 34 of 172 would-be thieves last season. While he isn't fast, he runs the bases as hard as anyone and compensates with effort and instinct.

2001 Outlook

Granted, Varitek is 29, but this is the year that could determine just how good he is going to be. If healthy, the Red Sox believe he can hit .275 with 30 home runs. After all, last year was only his second major league season as a regular. Often, catchers don't climb into their own until they approach 30 if they take their primary receiving duties seriously. And Varitek most definitely does.

Position: C
Bats: B **Throws:** R
Ht: 6' 2" **Wt:** 220

Opening Day Age: 28
Born: 4/11/72 in Rochester, MI
ML Seasons: 4
Pronunciation: VARE-ih-tek

Overall Statistics

	G	AB	R	H	D	T	HR	RBI	SB	BB	SO	Avg	OBP	Slg
2000	139	448	55	111	31	1	10	65	1	60	84	.248	.342	.388
Career	370	1153	156	298	83	3	37	174	4	123	214	.258	.331	.432

Where He Hits the Ball

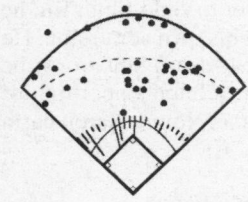 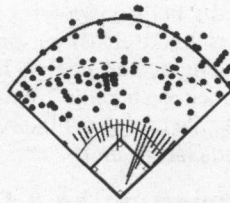

Vs. LHP **Vs. RHP**

2000 Situational Stats

	AB	H	HR	RBI	Avg		AB	H	HR	RBI	Avg
Home	218	63	2	32	.289	LHP	130	33	3	19	.254
Road	230	48	8	33	.209	RHP	318	78	7	46	.245
First Half	229	65	5	33	.284	Sc Pos	125	29	2	50	.232
Scnd Half	219	46	5	32	.210	Clutch	87	20	1	17	.230

2000 Rankings (American League)

- 2nd in lowest batting average on the road and lowest percentage of runners caught stealing as a catcher (18.8)
- 5th in errors at catcher (7)
- Led the Red Sox in GDPs (16)

Tim Wakefield

2000 Season

Tim Wakefield ended the 1999 season with hard feelings. After starting 17 games, saving 15 other contests when Tom Gordon went down and finishing as a swingman, Wakefield was taken off Boston's ALCS roster by Jimy Williams. Over the winter, Wakefield was told he would be a starter and prepared for that role last spring training. But just as the Red Sox left Florida, they signed Pete Schourek and Wakefield was dumped back into the bullpen. He went on to start 17 games and relieved in 34 in 2000, with only one save opportunity.

Pitching

Wakefield is the classic knuckleballer, although he occasionally will sneak in a fastball and slider. When he pitches regularly, he changes speeds on his primary pitch. Like most knuckleballers, he can get out of sync. There is debate within Boston circles as to whether Wakefield should start or relieve. But there is no debate over his value to a staff that hasn't had an 11-win starter other than Pedro Martinez since 1998. In the last four years, Wakefield has started on two and three days rest, closed games, worked the middle role and once last season was left out to save the staff and absorb the humiliation of a seven-run ninth inning.

Defense

Wakefield originally signed with the Pirates as an infielder, and it shows. He is a very good fielder with excellent balance on the mound. He slide steps and has a quick move to first. Throwing a knuckler makes him susceptible to basestealers, and they were 31-for-33 against him last season. But he has learned through the years to not let stolen bases rattle him.

2001 Outlook

Boston didn't pick up Wakefield's 2001 option last fall and allowed him to go to free agency before re-signing him in early December for two years and $6.5 million. There were a lot of teammates who were stunned that he returned, since he was unhappy with being yanked from the rotation. He will go into spring training with a chance to start, but Williams may again move him into his middle man/emergency starter role once the season opens.

Position: RP/SP
Bats: R **Throws:** R
Ht: 6' 2" **Wt:** 210

Opening Day Age: 34
Born: 8/2/66 in Melbourne, FL
ML Seasons: 8

Overall Statistics

	W	L	Pct.	ERA	G	GS	Sv	IP	H	BB	SO	HR	Ratio
2000	6	10	.375	5.48	51	17	0	159.1	170	65	102	31	1.47
Career	85	77	.525	4.47	267	188	15	1344.0	1342	571	872	181	1.42

How Often He Throws Strikes

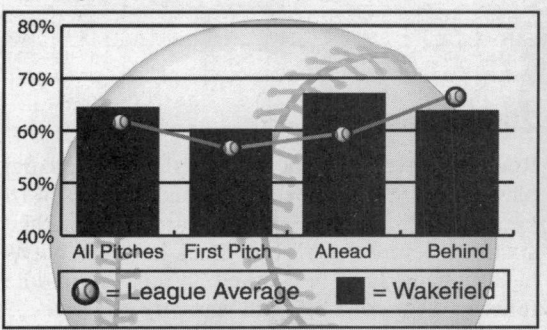

= League Average = Wakefield

2000 Situational Stats

	W	L	ERA	Sv	IP		AB	H	HR	RBI	Avg
Home	4	5	5.92	0	83.2	LHB	283	69	11	45	.244
Road	2	5	5.00	0	75.2	RHB	342	101	20	54	.295
First Half	5	5	4.98	0	81.1	Sc Pos	172	44	8	72	.256
Scnd Half	1	5	6.00	0	78.0	Clutch	84	19	3	4	.226

2000 Rankings (American League)

- 1st in stolen bases allowed (31) and highest ERA at home
- 5th in home runs allowed and lowest winning percentage
- 8th in lowest batting average allowed in relief with runners on base (.211)
- Led the Red Sox in losses, hits allowed, home runs allowed, stolen bases allowed (31) and lowest batting average allowed with runners in scoring position

Boston

Rod Beck

Position: RP
Bats: R **Throws:** R
Ht: 6' 1" **Wt:** 235

Opening Day Age: 32
Born: 8/3/68 in Burbank, CA
ML Seasons: 10
Nickname: Shooter

Overall Statistics

	W	L	Pct.	ERA	G	GS	Sv	IP	H	BB	SO	HR	Ratio
2000	3	0	1.000	3.10	34	0	0	40.2	34	12	35	2	1.13
Career	29	37	.439	3.20	574	0	260	628.0	574	143	534	70	1.14

2000 Situational Stats

	W	L	ERA	Sv	IP		AB	H	HR	RBI	Avg
Home	1	0	2.92	0	24.2	LHB	69	17	1	8	.246
Road	2	0	3.38	0	16.0	RHB	84	17	1	10	.202
First Half	0	0	1.50	0	6.0	Sc Pos	44	11	0	13	.250
Scnd Half	3	0	3.38	0	34.2	Clutch	64	16	2	9	.250

2000 Season

Rod Beck saved 51 games and got the Cubs into the playoffs in 1998. Since then he's had 10 saves in 18 opportunities and one arm operation. He pitched six times before the All-Star break last year, but as his arm came back he worked 28 times in middle relief in the second half and was very effective.

Pitching & Defense

There were times at the end of last season when Beck's velocity nudged up closer to 90 MPH than the 84 MPH he'd dropped down to when he was injured, which in turn brought better life to his splitter. He held opponents to a .307 slugging percentage, maintained a solid 1.56 groundball-flyball ratio and minimized damage against lefties. His fastball, slider and fork also were effective against righthanders. Beck struggled with a 4.91 ERA when used eight times in back-to-back games and he's better starting an inning with no one on base. He's not particularly agile around the mound, and if runners go, they usually succeed.

2001 Outlook

The Red Sox respect Beck so much they picked up his 2001 option for $4.5 million as a setup man for Derek Lowe. He goes into the season with the hope that his fastball will get back to 88-89 MPH and his splitter will regain its bite and angle.

Rico Brogna

Signed By
BRAVES

Position: 1B
Bats: L **Throws:** L
Ht: 6' 2" **Wt:** 203

Opening Day Age: 30
Born: 4/18/70 in Turners Falls, MA
ML Seasons: 8
Pronunciation: BRONE-yuh

Overall Statistics

	G	AB	R	H	D	T	HR	RBI	SB	BB	SO	Avg	OBP	Slg
2000	81	185	20	43	17	0	2	21	1	10	41	.232	.278	.357
Career	776	2752	364	744	167	13	103	437	29	213	609	.270	.321	.453

2000 Situational Stats

	AB	H	HR	RBI	Avg		AB	H	HR	RBI	Avg
Home	86	23	2	15	.267	LHP	38	4	1	6	.105
Road	99	20	0	6	.202	RHP	147	39	1	15	.265
First Half	114	28	1	12	.246	Sc Pos	50	12	1	19	.240
Scnd Half	71	15	1	9	.211	Clutch	42	14	1	11	.333

2000 Season

While Rico Brogna had recorded at least 20 homers and 100 RBI in each of the two seasons prior to 2000, a slow start and a broken wrist compromised his production. He was coming around, batting .310 in May, when a wayward pitch from Montreal's Matt Blank on May 10 sidelined him for two months. The Phillies waived Brogna in early August. The Red Sox picked him up, but he batted just .196 in 56 at-bats with them.

Hitting, Baserunning & Defense

Brogna has improved as a hitter by learning to be effective against lefthanders. His gains against lefties disappeared in 2000, when he batted .105 with 11 strikeouts in 38 at-bats. Brogna never has displayed much plate discipline, and he can be enticed with high fastballs and breaking pitches off the plate. Defensively, he ranks among the game's best first basemen. He's strong at getting to grounders and scooping bad throws, and he's particularly good at starting the 3-6-3 double play.

2001 Outlook

Brogna heads to Atlanta, where he figures to take over the everyday duties at first base from the departed Andres Galarraga after signing a one-year, $1.5 million deal in December. Playing for a contender may help Brogna rebound.

Rheal Cormier

Signed By
PHILLIES

Position: RP
Bats: L **Throws:** L
Ht: 5'10" **Wt:** 187

Opening Day Age: 33
Born: 4/23/67 in Moncton, Canada
ML Seasons: 9
Pronunciation: RAY-al KOR-mee-ay
Nickname: Frenchy

Overall Statistics

	W	L	Pct.	ERA	G	GS	Sv	IP	H	BB	SO	HR	Ratio
2000	3	3	.500	4.61	64	0	0	68.1	74	17	43	7	1.33
Career	43	42	.506	4.18	293	108	0	846.1	906	183	507	84	1.29

2000 Situational Stats

	W	L	ERA	Sv	IP		AB	H	HR	RBI	Avg
Home	1	2	5.97	0	31.2	LHB	87	23	1	8	.264
Road	2	1	3.44	0	36.2	RHB	182	51	6	23	.280
First Half	2	1	3.92	0	39.0	Sc Pos	66	19	1	23	.288
Scnd Half	1	2	5.52	0	29.1	Clutch	102	30	3	10	.294

2000 Season

When the Phillies signed the 34-year old Cormier to a three-year, $8.75 million contract in November of 2000, it proved that he had finalized his comeback. For a guy who appeared in one game in '97 and did not pitch in the big leagues in '98, last year's totals of 64 appearances and just 17 walks in 68.1 innings established him as a situational lefthanded reliever who is capable of long relief.

Pitching & Defense

Some of the credit for Cormier's comeback should go to manager Jimy Williams, as he didn't use Cormier too often. He throws a hard sinking fastball, a tight breaking ball and splitter that he can run on either side of the plate. He lost the breaking ball and split at times last season, and where lefties batted only .198 against him in 1999, that rose to .264 in 2000. Cormier is an aggressive fielder, and he works hard to hold runners on base. He will throw often to first base to measure intent and mess up timing; he only allowed six steals.

2001 Outlook

Cormier indicated that he would like to start. But because of the dearth of lefthanded relievers and the fact that the Phillies are loaded with lefthanded starters, they plan to use him in the role he developed in Boston.

Rich Garces

Position: RP
Bats: R **Throws:** R
Ht: 6'0" **Wt:** 215

Opening Day Age: 29
Born: 5/18/71 in Maracay, Venezuela
ML Seasons: 8
Pronunciation: GARR-suss
Nickname: El Guapo

Overall Statistics

	W	L	Pct.	ERA	G	GS	Sv	IP	H	BB	SO	HR	Ratio
2000	8	1	.889	3.25	64	0	1	74.2	64	23	69	7	1.17
Career	17	8	.680	3.38	199	0	6	253.0	214	127	229	22	1.35

2000 Situational Stats

	W	L	ERA	Sv	IP		AB	H	HR	RBI	Avg
Home	4	1	2.93	0	43.0	LHB	115	24	2	18	.209
Road	4	0	3.69	0	31.2	RHB	165	40	5	16	.242
First Half	3	0	2.74	1	46.0	Sc Pos	76	14	1	27	.184
Scnd Half	5	1	4.08	0	28.2	Clutch	114	27	3	15	.237

2000 Season

Rich Garces, nicknamed after the character in Three Amigos, has become such a cult hero that even behind opposing bullpens there are El Guapo Fan Club sightings. The fact he's 13-2 the last two seasons and has become a premier setup man certainly doesn't hurt his cult status.

Pitching & Defense

Garces throws in the low 90s with a hacksaw curveball, and he recently has added a nasty splitter. Due to his success against lefthanded hitters, Jimy Williams has the luxury of using him in situations where a lefthanded specialist might be required. Only 15 of 43 inherited runners scored against him in 2000, even though he often was called upon in rough situations. His body makes him appear as though he might field like Jackie Gleason, but Garces gets by. He has light feet and good instincts, getting to what he can and making plays. He has a quick move to first but runners were successful stealing on him 11 out of 13 times.

2001 Outlook

The concern about Garces is that he might break down, and he had arm trouble early in his career. The Red Sox feel that he will be more important this year with Rheal Cormier gone, as Garces may *have* to fill the lefthanded specialist role.

Boston

Tom Gordon

Position: RP
Bats: R **Throws:** R
Ht: 5' 9" **Wt:** 190

Opening Day Age: 33
Born: 11/18/67 in Sebring, FL
ML Seasons: 12
Nickname: Flash

Overall Statistics

	W	L	Pct.	ERA	G	GS	Sv	IP	H	BB	SO	HR	Ratio
2000						Did Not Play							
Career	104	96	.520	4.15	444	203	71	1645.0	1516	807	1431	133	1.41

2000 Situational Stats

	W	L	ERA	Sv	IP		AB	H	HR	RBI	Avg
Home	—	—	—	—	—	LHB	—	—	—	—	—
Road	—	—	—	—	—	RHB	—	—	—	—	—
First Half	—	—	—	—	—	Sc Pos	—	—	—	—	—
Scnd Half	—	—	—	—	—	Clutch	—	—	—	—	—

2000 Season

The 1999 season began with a tender elbow, and Tom Gordon was shut down in June. That December, he underwent Tommy John surgery and missed the entire 2000 campaign. Gordon rehabbed his elbow throughout 2000, and by the end of the year he threw for a number of teams who were interested in his services.

Pitching & Defense

Gordon's key weapon has been a nasty curveball that he snaps off with tremendous force. It's a pitch that will be a big test for his rebuilt elbow. He had such good command of the pitch, which may take time to re-establish. Gordon may have to call on his softer curve more frequently. His fastball moved up to the mid-90s when he left Boston's rotation for the bullpen in late 1997. The righthander was 57-for-60 in save opportunities before his elbow acted up in '99. An average fielder, Gordon tends to focus on the hitter much more than baserunners.

2001 Outlook

Several teams, including the Royals, Orioles, Red Sox and Cubs, pursued Gordon, who joins the Cubs after signing a two-year, $5 million deal that is loaded with incentives. His fastball was clocked closer to 90 MPH during his December workout, but he was impressive and has time to add velocity.

Scott Hatteberg

Position: C/DH
Bats: L **Throws:** R
Ht: 6' 1" **Wt:** 205

Opening Day Age: 31
Born: 12/14/69 in Salem, OR
ML Seasons: 6

Overall Statistics

	G	AB	R	H	D	T	HR	RBI	SB	BB	SO	Avg	OBP	Slg
2000	92	230	21	61	15	0	8	36	0	38	39	.265	.367	.435
Career	360	1032	129	282	67	2	31	134	0	142	183	.273	.363	.432

2000 Situational Stats

	AB	H	HR	RBI	Avg		AB	H	HR	RBI	Avg
Home	97	31	2	14	.320	LHP	37	7	0	4	.189
Road	133	30	6	22	.226	RHP	193	54	8	32	.280
First Half	100	25	4	20	.250	Sc Pos	66	19	4	31	.288
Scnd Half	130	36	4	16	.277	Clutch	51	18	1	5	.353

2000 Season

When Scott Hatteberg first hurt his elbow—actually, it was a crack from little league days—in 1999, he was platooning with Jason Varitek. With Hatteberg down, Varitek became the everyday guy. But Hatteberg still was a valuable player for Boston last year, hitting .265 with eight homers and 36 RBI in just 230 at-bats and continuing to be a very respected handler of pitchers.

Hitting, Baserunning & Defense

Hatteberg is a dead lowball, uppercut swinger, and he has enough power to hit 20 home runs if he got a regular shot. He's also a patient hitter who saw 4.22 pitches per plate appearance last year. He hits righthanders, and he is strong enough and in such good shape that he easily could hold up for an entire season. He's only had 180 career at-bats against lefties, so no one knows if he can do the job at the plate everyday. The defensive knock on Hatteberg is his throwing, as he nabbed only 13 of 68 runners last season. Though his arm strength has come back, he hasn't recovered his mechanics.

2001 Outlook

Hatteberg needs an opportunity to catch 100-120 games. His game-calling instincts, power and the respect he commands in clubhouses outweigh what throwing difficulties he's endured.

Darren Lewis

Position: CF/RF/LF
Bats: R **Throws:** R
Ht: 6' 0" **Wt:** 190

Opening Day Age: 33
Born: 8/28/67 in Berkeley, CA
ML Seasons: 11

Overall Statistics

	G	AB	R	H	D	T	HR	RBI	SB	BB	SO	Avg	OBP	Slg
2000	97	270	44	65	12	0	2	17	10	22	34	.241	.305	.307
Career	1214	3838	582	956	125	35	26	323	241	388	478	.249	.323	.320

2000 Situational Stats

	AB	H	HR	RBI	Avg			AB	H	HR	RBI	Avg
Home	143	33	0	10	.231	LHP		112	31	1	8	.277
Road	127	32	2	7	.252	RHP		158	34	1	9	.215
First Half	122	31	1	6	.254	Sc Pos		53	13	0	13	.245
Scnd Half	148	34	1	11	.230	Clutch		35	7	0	1	.200

2000 Season

Darren Lewis is a manager's player. Dusty Baker named his son after Lewis. Jimy Williams believes that Darren is one of the most important players on the Red Sox, even though he's a reserve outfielder who knocked in just 17 runs in 270 at-bats.

Hitting, Baserunning & Defense

Lewis is a situational outfielder best suited to the Nos. 2 or 9 holes in the order. He chokes up and tries to punch the ball into play, and most of his extra-base hits are poked down the right-field line. His .307 slugging percentage indicates his power, but his .305 on base percentage indicates he is not a leadoff man. He will give himself up, he can bunt and he can lift the ball in the air with a runner on third. There are few more consistent outfielders. He glides to balls and runs excellent routes. His arm is below average, which is a problem in Fenway's right field. He is an excellent baserunner and occasional basestealer—one of the few Red Sox who actually will steal a base.

2001 Outlook

With the addition of Manny Ramirez in right field and the injury history of Carl Everett, Lewis likely will keep an important role on the Red Sox. He is a tremendous person whose presence and character are vital to the team concept Williams tries to build.

Ramon Martinez

Position: SP
Bats: B **Throws:** R
Ht: 6' 4" **Wt:** 184

Opening Day Age: 33
Born: 3/22/68 in Santo Domingo, Dominican Republic
ML Seasons: 13

Overall Statistics

	W	L	Pct.	ERA	G	GS	Sv	IP	H	BB	SO	HR	Ratio
2000	10	8	.556	6.13	27	27	0	127.2	143	67	89	16	1.64
Career	135	86	.611	3.62	297	293	0	1880.0	1675	779	1418	166	1.31

2000 Situational Stats

	W	L	ERA	Sv	IP			AB	H	HR	RBI	Avg
Home	6	5	5.11	0	79.1	LHB		255	70	8	40	.275
Road	4	3	7.82	0	48.1	RHB		250	73	8	38	.292
First Half	6	5	5.79	0	82.1	Sc Pos		122	37	8	67	.303
Scnd Half	4	3	6.75	0	45.1	Clutch		6	4	0	0	.667

2000 Season

Ramon Martinez made 27 starts and was second only to brother Pedro on the Red Sox in starts and wins. But to get there, Ramon barely struggled to five innings per start, his ERA was 6.13 and he managed just seven quality starts. At season's end, the club declined his $8 million option for 2001.

Pitching & Defense

It was Martinez' first full season since undergoing shoulder surgery in 1998. But he never seemed to regain the loose, free arm action he once enjoyed. He had problems warming up, often throwing several pitches up and out of the strike zone in the first inning, then struggling to maintain any consistent arm angle. The result was inconsistent command, and he averaged 18.3 pitches per inning. Martinez' elongated delivery and slower arm action make him susceptible to stolen bases, although his quick feet and baseball acumen help keep runners at bay. He is smart about holding the ball and forcing runners to stop. He is a good fielder with a relaxed demeanor in fielding situations.

2001 Outlook

Some believe that another year could get Ramon another 3-4 MPH and better command. If that happens, he will win, because this man has a giant heart and a unique understanding of pitching.

Boston

Tomokazu Ohka

Position: SP
Bats: R **Throws:** R
Ht: 6' 1" **Wt:** 179

Opening Day Age: 25
Born: 3/18/76 in Kyoto, Japan
ML Seasons: 2

Overall Statistics

	W	L	Pct.	ERA	G	GS	Sv	IP	H	BB	SO	HR	Ratio
2000	3	6	.333	3.12	13	12	0	69.1	70	26	40	7	1.38
Career	4	8	.333	3.61	21	14	0	82.1	91	32	48	9	1.49

2000 Situational Stats

	W	L	ERA	Sv	IP			AB	H	HR	RBI	Avg
Home	2	4	2.34	0	42.1	LHB		159	44	5	15	.277
Road	1	2	4.33	0	27.0	RHB		107	26	2	10	.243
First Half	0	0	-	0	0.0	Sc Pos		61	11	1	17	.180
Scnd Half	3	6	3.12	0	69.1	Clutch		11	7	2	3	.636

2000 Season

Tomokazu Ohka enjoyed a solid season at Triple-A Pawtucket, going 9-6 (2.96) while allowing just 137 baserunners in 130.2 innings. He pitched a nine-inning perfect game against Charlotte on June 1, then fired six perfect innings en route to a two-hit shutout of Syracuse on July 3. Still, his chance to help the Red Sox didn't come until late July, and Ohka allowed two runs or less in 10 of his 12 starts.

Pitching & Defense

While the righthander went 15-0 in 1999, he was a better pitcher in 2000 because of the gains he made in locating his pitches. Ohka is not overpowering, which explains Boston's slowness in promoting him, but he is very effective at keeping hitters off balance and spotting his offspeed stuff—a split-finger pitch and changeup. Ohka also throws a 90-MPH fastball with late sink. He hasn't been tested much as a major league fielder, but Ohka made one error in 15 chances in 2000. Five of 12 basestealers were nabbed on his watch last year.

2001 Outlook

There are plenty of questions about the Boston rotation heading into spring training, but Ohka can quickly answer one of them if he displays the feel for pitching and stuff that he showed in 2000. The more starts he made, the better he looked.

John Valentin

Position: 3B
Bats: R **Throws:** R
Ht: 6' 0" **Wt:** 185

Opening Day Age: 34
Born: 2/18/67 in Mineola, NY
ML Seasons: 9
Pronunciation: VAL-en-tin
Nickname: Val

Overall Statistics

	G	AB	R	H	D	T	HR	RBI	SB	BB	SO	Avg	OBP	Slg
2000	10	35	6	9	1	0	2	2	0	2	5	.257	.297	.457
Career	971	3649	588	1031	264	17	120	523	47	432	479	.283	.362	.463

2000 Situational Stats

	AB	H	HR	RBI	Avg		AB	H	HR	RBI	Avg
Home	16	3	0	0	.188	LHP	5	2	0	0	.400
Road	19	6	2	2	.316	RHP	30	7	2	2	.233
First Half	35	9	2	2	.257	Sc Pos	12	1	0	0	.083
Scnd Half	0	0	0	0	-	Clutch	5	0	0	0	.000

2000 Season

John Valentin struggled with knee problems for most of 1999. Then, after a strong postseason that year, he had surgery only to collapse in a heap in his 10th game back in 2000. The collapse required another complicated knee operation that put the rest of his 2000 campaign on hold and now puts his 2001 season—and career—in jeopardy.

Hitting, Baserunning & Defense

When healthy, Valentin is a good Fenway hitter who stands right up on the plate. He can get to and loft the fastball or take the fastball away and either send it into the Fenway spaces of right-center or hook it off The Wall. How quick he is with the bat after the layoff remains to be seen. There are few better defensive third basemen when his knee is healthy. Valentin has good hands, a strong arm and he charges the ball well. On the bases, he's not much of a thief, but he has good instincts and effectively moves from first to third.

2001 Outlook

The Red Sox traded for Chris Stynes in November because they are uncertain whether Valentin will be ready for the start of the 2001 season. If Valentin makes it back, he could rekindle his career in the midst of a powerful lineup, hitting from a spot in the order that should be fastball heaven.

Other Boston Red Sox

Israel Alcantara (Pos: RF, Age: 27, Bats: R)

	G	AB	R	H	D	T	HR	RBI	SB	BB	SO	Avg	OBP	Slg
2000	21	45	9	13	1	0	4	7	0	3	7	.289	.333	.578
Career	21	45	9	13	1	0	4	7	0	3	7	.289	.333	.578

Alcantara strikes out an awful lot, but he'll also smash his share of homers. He's a little old to be a prospect and his best position may be designated hitter. 2001 Outlook: C

Manny Alexander (Pos: 3B/SS, Age: 30, Bats: R)

	G	AB	R	H	D	T	HR	RBI	SB	BB	SO	Avg	OBP	Slg
2000	101	194	30	41	4	3	4	19	2	13	41	.211	.261	.325
Career	541	1198	161	280	46	11	15	108	37	81	259	.234	.285	.328

Acquired from the Cubs in a trade last offseason, Alexander played 63 games at third base for the Red Sox. That would appear to have been a misallocation of resources, considering his weak hitting. 2001 Outlook: C

Sean Berry (Pos: 3B, Age: 35, Bats: R)

	G	AB	R	H	D	T	HR	RBI	SB	BB	SO	Avg	OBP	Slg
2000	33	50	1	7	2	0	1	2	0	4	15	.140	.204	.240
Career	860	2413	310	657	153	10	81	369	47	206	438	.272	.334	.445

Berry was released by the Brewers in June and the Red Sox in August before signing a minor league deal with Cleveland. He's just 10-for-64 (.156) as a pinch-hitter over the past two seasons. 2001 Outlook: C

Morgan Burkhart (Pos: DH, Age: 29, Bats: B)

	G	AB	R	H	D	T	HR	RBI	SB	BB	SO	Avg	OBP	Slg
2000	25	73	16	21	3	0	4	18	0	17	25	.288	.442	.493
Career	25	73	16	21	3	0	4	18	0	17	25	.288	.442	.493

Burkhart spent four years in an independent league before hooking on with the Red Sox after the 1998 season. Though he does almost nothing but hit, he wasn't overmatched in his trials with Boston. 2001 Outlook: C

Hector Carrasco (Pos: RHP, Age: 31)

	W	L	Pct.	ERA	G	GS	Sv	IP	H	BB	SO	HR	Ratio
2000	5	4	.556	4.69	69	1	1	78.2	90	38	64	8	1.63
Career	24	33	.421	4.10	402	1	14	493.1	479	249	385	32	1.48

The Red Sox parted with minor league outfielder Lew Ford in order to rent Carrasco for the final three weeks last year. His 69 appearances were a career high. He's now a free agent. 2001 Outlook: B

Rick Croushore (Pos: RHP, Age: 30)

	W	L	Pct.	ERA	G	GS	Sv	IP	H	BB	SO	HR	Ratio
2000	2	1	.667	7.88	11	0	0	16.0	19	11	14	1	1.88
Career	5	11	.313	4.88	111	0	11	142.0	131	83	149	16	1.51

After appearing in 59 games with St. Louis in 1999, Croushore was traded to Colorado and then Boston. His screwball-type action helps him be more effective against lefthanders than righties. 2001 Outlook: C

Midre Cummings (Pos: RF/DH, Age: 29, Bats: L)

	G	AB	R	H	D	T	HR	RBI	SB	BB	SO	Avg	OBP	Slg
2000	98	206	29	57	10	0	4	24	0	17	28	.277	.341	.383
Career	416	1037	125	265	55	8	20	116	8	89	183	.256	.317	.382

After releasing Cummings just before the '99 campaign, the Red Sox traded for him last August. He then delivered no extra-base hits in 25 at-bats and signed a one-year deal with Arizona in mid-December. 2001 Outlook: C

Jeff Fassero (Pos: LHP, Age: 38)

	W	L	Pct.	ERA	G	GS	Sv	IP	H	BB	SO	HR	Ratio
2000	8	8	.500	4.78	38	23	0	130.0	153	50	97	16	1.56
Career	100	91	.524	3.89	404	217	10	1595.1	1592	557	1326	162	1.35

Afer blowing up in 1999, Fassero pitched better last year. He worked exclusively in relief in September, when he fashioned a 1.20 ERA. He signed a two-year, $5.1 million deal with the Cubs in early December, giving Chicago another lefthanded option in the bullpen in 2001. 2001 Outlook: A

Bryce Florie (Pos: RHP, Age: 30)

	W	L	Pct.	ERA	G	GS	Sv	IP	H	BB	SO	HR	Ratio
2000	0	4	.000	4.56	29	0	1	49.1	57	19	34	5	1.54
Career	20	23	.465	4.34	254	29	2	485.0	488	236	388	45	1.49

Florie suffered one of the most horrific injuries in recent memory when his orbital socket was shattered by a line drive last September. It's unclear whether he'll be able to return from the injury. 2001 Outlook: C

Gary Gaetti (Pos: DH, Age: 42, Bats: R)

	G	AB	R	H	D	T	HR	RBI	SB	BB	SO	Avg	OBP	Slg
2000	5	10	0	0	0	0	0	1	0	0	3	.000	.000	.000
Career	2507	8951	1130	2280	443	39	360	1341	96	634	1602	.255	.308	.434

After batting .204 in 1999, Gaetti lasted until April 14 before retiring this past season. He finished with the fourth-lowest lifetime average among the 59 players with 350 or more home runs. 2001 Outlook: D

Bernard Gilkey (Pos: RF, Age: 34, Bats: R)

	G	AB	R	H	D	T	HR	RBI	SB	BB	SO	Avg	OBP	Slg
2000	74	164	17	29	6	1	3	15	0	17	28	.177	.265	.280
Career	1170	3955	598	1086	238	24	116	532	115	455	677	.275	.352	.435

Gilkey was hitting just .110 when Arizona released him last June. While he recovered a little bit with the Red Sox, the question is whether he's truly slipped that much. Remember, he hit .294 in 1999. 2001 Outlook: B

Mike Lansing (Pos: 2B, Age: 32, Bats: R)

	G	AB	R	H	D	T	HR	RBI	SB	BB	SO	Avg	OBP	Slg
2000	139	504	72	121	18	6	11	60	8	38	75	.240	.292	.365
Career	1004	3798	509	1036	231	17	76	406	116	277	520	.273	.327	.403

The injuries have piled up and the production has fallen. Third base is open, but Lansing doesn't reach base enough and isn't the defender he used to be. He made a poor first impression in Boston. 2001 Outlook: C

Boston

Lou Merloni (**Pos**: 3B, **Age**: 29, **Bats**: R)

	G	AB	R	H	D	T	HR	RBI	SB	BB	SO	Avg	OBP	Slg
2000	40	128	10	41	11	2	0	18	1	4	22	.320	.341	.438
Career	122	350	38	100	24	2	2	46	2	19	58	.286	.329	.383

Merloni left his Japanese team last July to return to the Red Sox. Although limited talent-wise, he can play any infield position and certainly won't hurt a club if he can hit .320. 2001 Outlook: B

Steve Ontiveros (**Pos**: RHP, **Age**: 40)

	W	L	Pct.	ERA	G	GS	Sv	IP	H	BB	SO	HR	Ratio
2000	1	1	.500	10.13	3	1	0	5.1	9	4	1	1	2.44
Career	34	31	.523	3.67	207	73	19	661.2	622	207	382	60	1.25

Ontivares, one of the greatest injury risks in baseball, pitched in an independent league last season before making it back to the majors for the first time since 1995. He declared his free agency at the end of October. 2001 Outlook: D

Jesus Pena (**Pos**: LHP, **Age**: 26)

	W	L	Pct.	ERA	G	GS	Sv	IP	H	BB	SO	HR	Ratio
2000	2	1	.667	5.13	22	0	1	26.1	28	19	20	7	1.78
Career	2	1	.667	5.21	48	0	1	46.2	49	42	40	10	1.95

Despite his promise, Pena went from the White Sox to the Red Sox in late September for a player to be named later. He's experienced problems with his control during his tenure in the majors. 2001 Outlook: C

Juan Pena (**Pos**: RHP, **Age**: 23)

	W	L	Pct.	ERA	G	GS	Sv	IP	H	BB	SO	HR	Ratio
2000							Did Not Play						
Career	2	0	1.000	0.69	2	2	0	13.0	9	3	15	0	0.92

Pena's problem is that he keeps getting hurt. In 1999, it was shoulder woes. Last year, he had a chance for a rotation spot until being lost for the season with a bum elbow. 2001 Outlook: C

Hipolito Pichardo (**Pos**: RHP, **Age**: 31)

	W	L	Pct.	ERA	G	GS	Sv	IP	H	BB	SO	HR	Ratio
2000	6	3	.667	3.46	38	1	1	65.0	63	26	37	1	1.37
Career	48	42	.533	4.39	319	68	20	734.2	793	275	377	51	1.45

Pichardo missed time in 1998 and '99 with elbow problems, but he showed enough last year that Boston picked up his 2001 option at $1.66 million. He only allowed a .322 slugging percentage last year. 2001 Outlook: B

Curtis Pride (**Pos**: LF, **Age**: 32, **Bats**: L)

	G	AB	R	H	D	T	HR	RBI	SB	BB	SO	Avg	OBP	Slg
2000	9	20	4	5	1	0	0	0	0	1	7	.250	.286	.300
Career	313	630	110	162	30	11	17	67	25	70	164	.257	.334	.421

Pride injured his wrist and was released by Kansas City before the 1999 season even opened. He returned to play for three Triple-A teams last year, finishing up in the Dodgers' organization. 2001 Outlook: C

Bret Saberhagen (**Pos**: RHP, **Age**: 36)

	W	L	Pct.	ERA	G	GS	Sv	IP	H	BB	SO	HR	Ratio
2000							Did Not Play						
Career	166	115	.591	3.33	396	368	1	2547.2	2433	471	1705	215	1.14

There were three stints on the DL in 1999, when Saberhagen went 10-6 (2.95). But his injury-riddled 2000 season, troubled by shoulder and groin woes, may mark the end of his career. 2001 Outlook: C

Donnie Sadler (**Pos**: SS/2B/CF, **Age**: 25, **Bats**: R)

	G	AB	R	H	D	T	HR	RBI	SB	BB	SO	Avg	OBP	Slg
2000	49	99	14	22	5	0	1	10	3	5	18	.222	.262	.303
Career	156	330	53	80	14	5	4	29	9	16	66	.242	.283	.352

Although Sadler is a versatile and valuable defensive performer with terrific speed, he simply hasn't hit enough. Boston included him in a trade with the Reds for Chris Stynes this past November. 2001 Outlook: C

Pete Schourek (**Pos**: LHP, **Age**: 31)

	W	L	Pct.	ERA	G	GS	Sv	IP	H	BB	SO	HR	Ratio
2000	3	10	.231	5.11	21	21	0	107.1	116	38	63	17	1.43
Career	65	72	.474	4.59	255	176	2	1118.2	1163	405	793	136	1.40

Schourek always seems to be a health risk, and last year he had shoulder and elbow woes. He hasn't been a .500 pitcher since 1995, the year he finished second in the National League Cy Young voting. The Red Sox bought out his $2.25 million option for 2001, then re-signed him to a minor league deal. 2001 Outlook: C

Andy Sheets (**Pos**: SS, **Age**: 29, **Bats**: R)

	G	AB	R	H	D	T	HR	RBI	SB	BB	SO	Avg	OBP	Slg
2000	12	21	1	2	0	0	0	1	0	0	3	.095	.095	.095
Career	266	658	90	140	26	3	14	77	12	52	199	.213	.269	.325

Sheets spent most of last season at Triple-A, where he continued to display a weak batting average and limited power. Tampa Bay nevertheless signed him to a minor league contract after the campaign. 2001 Outlook: C

Dan Smith (**Pos**: RHP, **Age**: 25)

	W	L	Pct.	ERA	G	GS	Sv	IP	H	BB	SO	HR	Ratio
2000	0	0	-	8.10	2	0	0	3.1	2	1	0	1	1.50
Career	4	9	.308	6.10	22	17	0	93.0	106	42	73	12	1.59

Smith went 4-9 for Montreal in 1999 but spent most of last season in Triple-A after signing with Boston. Though fairly young, he's on the move again, having signed a minor league deal with Cleveland. 2001 Outlook: C

Rob Stanifer (**Pos**: RHP, **Age**: 29)

	W	L	Pct.	ERA	G	GS	Sv	IP	H	BB	SO	HR	Ratio
2000	0	0	-	7.62	8	0	0	13.0	22	4	3	3	2.00
Career	3	6	.333	5.43	82	0	2	106.0	119	42	61	17	1.52

Stanifer saved 16 games with a sub-2.00 ERA at Triple-A last year. But his role, if he's fortunate enough to work in the majors, will almost certainly be in middle or long relief. Stanifer signed a minor league contract with the Cubs in December. 2001 Outlook: C

Tim Young (**Pos**: LHP, **Age**: 27)

	W	L	Pct.	ERA	G	GS	Sv	IP	H	BB	SO	HR	Ratio
2000	0	0	-	6.43	8	0	0	7.0	7	2	6	3	1.29
Career	0	0	-	6.23	18	0	0	13.0	13	6	13	3	1.46

Young is a little southpaw drafted in the 19th round in 1996 by Montreal. He won't find his niche if he allows three homers every 11 at-bats to lefthanders, as he did with Boston. 2001 Outlook: C

Boston Red Sox Minor League Prospects

Organization Overview:

Over the last three years, the Red Sox have dealt the likes of Tony Armas Jr., Michael Coleman, Adam Everett, Matt Kinney, Cole Liniak, Greg Miller, Carl Pavano, Robert Ramsay, Chris Reitsma, Brian Rose, Donnie Sadler and Dennis Tankersley to acquire veterans Rod Beck, Dante Bichette, Carl Everett, Butch Huskey, Mike Lansing, Pedro Martinez, Ed Sprague, Mike Stanley, Chris Stynes and Greg Swindell. While many of these deals had a payoff, chasing the New York Yankees has been costly to the farm system. In recent years, only Trot Nixon has come out of the system to be a productive player. While the talent level clearly is better than it was before GM Dan Duquette took over in 1994, it's not as good as it was just a few short years ago.

Jin Ho Cho

Position: P **Opening Day Age:** 25
Bats: R **Throws:** R **Born:** 8/16/75 in Jun Ju
Ht: 6' 3" **Wt:** 220 City, South Korea

Recent Statistics

	W	L	ERA	G	GS	Sv	IP	H	R	BB	SO	HR
1999 AAA Pawtucket	9	3	3.45	17	17	0	109.2	99	46	29	80	12
2000 A Sarasota	1	1	2.40	3	3	0	15.0	13	5	0	15	1
2000 AA Trenton	3	5	5.83	10	10	0	58.2	76	45	8	32	8
2000 AAA Pawtucket	4	3	4.65	13	9	0	71.2	77	37	13	37	9

After signing in March 1998, Cho impressed immediately, showing remarkable control and reaching Boston during his debut season. Cho continued his climb by fanning 15 in a Triple-A win in April 1999, and by June he was back in Boston. He turned in just two quality starts there, but completed a solid 9-3 season at Triple-A Pawtucket. Cho throws a low-90s fastball, splitter, slider and changeup. He exhibits great control, but his major league troubles show that he needs to be finer within the strike zone. His rapid rise slowed in 2000, when Cho suffered a back problem that affected him for much of the summer. After pitching in the Arizona Fall League, Cho is in line to join the Boston rotation this spring.

Paxton Crawford

Position: P **Opening Day Age:** 23
Bats: R **Throws:** R **Born:** 8/4/77 in Little
Ht: 6' 3" **Wt:** 205 Rock, AR

Recent Statistics

	W	L	ERA	G	GS	Sv	IP	H	R	BB	SO	HR
2000 AA Trenton	2	3	3.10	9	9	0	52.1	50	20	6	54	3
2000 AAA Pawtucket	7	4	4.55	12	11	0	61.1	47	32	22	47	6
2000 AL Boston	2	1	3.41	7	4	0	29.0	25	15	13	17	0

There have been many more highly regarded pitching prospects in the Boston system since he was drafted in the ninth round in 1995. Yet it was Crawford who started 2000 at Double-A Trenton and posted his first major league win on July 6, holding Minnesota to one run over seven innings. He threw a Triple-A no-hitter later in the month and returned to Boston in September. While none of his pitches are special, his best may be his changeup. His fastball has good sink, and all of his pitches are aided by an unusual delivery that makes his stuff hard to pick up. Crawford looks like an end-of-the-rotation guy, and that may be his role this spring.

Juan Diaz

Position: 1B **Opening Day Age:** 25
Bats: R **Throws:** R **Born:** 2/19/76 in San
Ht: 6' 2" **Wt:** 228 Jose De Las Lajas, Cuba

Recent Statistics

	G	AB	R	H	D	T	HR	RBI	SB	BB	SO	Avg
1999 AA San Antonio	66	254	42	77	21	1	9	52	0	26	77	.303
2000 A Sarasota	14	51	7	14	2	1	4	12	0	4	15	.275
2000 AA Trenton	50	198	36	62	14	1	17	53	0	10	56	.313
2000 AAA Pawtucket	13	43	11	12	0	0	7	17	1	6	9	.279
2000 MLE	63	232	36	65	13	0	18	54	0	10	68	.280

One of the Cuban free agents signed illegally by the Dodgers, Diaz inked a $400,000 minor league deal with the Red Sox last March. His power is what makes him a prospect to watch, and Diaz combined for 30 homers between high Class-A Vero Beach and Double-A San Antonio in 1998. Still, hardly anyone took notice until he hit .301-28-82 in just 292 at-bats between high Class-A Sarasota, Double-A Trenton and Triple-A Pawtucket last summer. He hit seven homers in his first 12 games at Pawtucket, but Diaz' breakout season ended prematurely in late July, when he fractured and dislocated his right ankle on an awkward slide at second base. He doesn't offer much defensively, but Diaz, with his impressive bat speed and quick stroke, is a legitimate power prospect.

Sun-Woo Kim

Position: P **Opening Day Age:** 23
Bats: R **Throws:** R **Born:** 9/4/77 in Inchon,
Ht: 6' 2" **Wt:** 180 South Korea

Recent Statistics

	W	L	ERA	G	GS	Sv	IP	H	R	BB	SO	HR
1999 AA Trenton	9	8	4.89	26	26	0	149.0	160	86	44	130	16
2000 AAA Pawtucket	11	7	6.03	26	25	0	134.1	170	98	42	116	17

One of the first Asian prospects to sign with Boston in 1997, Kim has taken time to develop. After pitching at Double-A Trenton in 1999, Kim emerged with a strong showing in the Arizona Fall League. In 2000 he was at Triple-A Pawtucket, where he may be best remembered for an inseason altercation with fellow Boston prospect Tomokazu Ohka, over who was the better prospect. Ohka is farther along right now, but Kim throws harder and has the higher ceiling. He has a moving, mid-90s fastball that he can pinpoint for strikes, plus a breaking pitch and changeup that are shaping up as solid offerings. Keeping the ball down and targeting his pitches better within the strike zone are critical to reaching Boston.

Sang-Hoon Lee

Position: P
Bats: L **Throws:** L
Ht: 6' 1" **Wt:** 190

Opening Day Age: 30
Born: 3/11/71 in Seoul, South Korea

Recent Statistics

	W	L	ERA	G	GS	Sv	IP	H	R	BB	SO	HR
2000 AAA Pawtucket	5	2	2.03	45	1	2	71.0	51	23	24	73	5
2000 AL Boston	0	0	3.09	9	0	0	11.2	11	4	5	6	2

A seasoned pro, Lee was a big winner as a starter in South Korea during the mid-1990s before a back injury sparked a move to the bullpen. He led his league in saves in 1997, moved on to play in Japan, and then signed a two-year major league deal in December 1999. Lee was effective in relief at Triple-A Pawtucket in 2000, allowing just 76 baserunners to reach and fanning 73 in 71 innings. He works with a low-90s fastball and a solid changeup—pitches that are enhanced by his deceptive arm angle—and he mixes in a curve and slider. Lee could be used as a starter or reliever, but he got his feet wet and held his own in the Boston bullpen in September.

Steve Lomasney

Position: C
Bats: R **Throws:** R
Ht: 6' 0" **Wt:** 195

Opening Day Age: 23
Born: 8/29/77 in Melrose, MA

Recent Statistics

	G	AB	R	H	D	THR	RBI	SB	BB	SO	Avg
1999 A Sarasota	55	189	35	51	10	0	8	28	5	26	57	.270
1999 AA Trenton	47	151	24	37	6	0	12	31	7	31	44	.245
1999 AL Boston	1	2	0	0	0	0	0	0	0	0	2	.000
2000 AA Trenton	66	233	30	57	16	1	8	27	5	24	81	.245
2000 R Red Sox	6	15	2	4	2	0	0	1	0	4	6	.267
2000 MLE	66	227	23	51	15	0	6	21	2	16	86	.225

There's been little doubt about Lomasney's catching skills since he was drafted in 1995. He has the body, the strength and durability, the solid catching fundamentals and the strong arm. Initial concerns focused on his bat, but Lomasney staved them off when he started driving the ball better at Class-A Michigan in 1997. Breaking stuff has given him trouble, and it did again in his second go-round at Double-A Trenton in 2000. While he's a career .236 hitter, Lomasney draws walks and has a .350 on-base percentage in six pro seasons. That plate discipline didn't leave him when he started poorly last season.

Dernell Stenson

Position: 1B
Bats: L **Throws:** L
Ht: 6' 1" **Wt:** 230

Opening Day Age: 22
Born: 6/17/78 in La Grange, GA

Recent Statistics

	G	AB	R	H	D	THR	RBI	SB	BB	SO	Avg
1999 R Red Sox	6	23	2	5	0	0	2	7	0	3	5	.217
1999 AA Pawtucket	121	440	64	119	28	2	18	82	2	55	119	.270
2000 AAA Pawtucket	98	380	59	102	14	0	23	71	0	45	99	.268
2000 MLE	98	368	47	90	13	0	16	56	0	35	103	.245

Boston added a big bat by signing Manny Ramirez, but the Red Sox may have a potent run producer in Stenson.

With his quick bat and short stroke, Stenson looks like a professional hitter. He may have two Triple-A seasons under his belt, but he's still just 22 and oozing with power potential. He excels at recognizing pitches, but lefties give him trouble. His key weakness is his defense. Stenson has bulked up and put on weight, which forced a move from the outfield to first base in 1999. His 34 errors at first base were the worst in the minors that season, although Stenson's error total dropped to 12 while playing first and some left field in 2000.

Wilton Veras

Position: 3B
Bats: R **Throws:** R
Ht: 6' 2" **Wt:** 198

Opening Day Age: 23
Born: 1/19/78 in Montecristy, DR

Recent Statistics

	G	AB	R	H	D	THR	RBI	SB	BB	SO	Avg
2000 AAA Pawtucket	60	218	18	46	9	0	3	25	0	12	18	.211
2000 AL Boston	49	164	21	40	7	1	0	14	0	7	20	.244
2000 MLE	60	213	14	41	8	0	2	19	0	9	18	.192

After signing in 1995, Veras quickly established himself as Boston's third baseman of the future. He has shown flashes of his impressive power potential, an ability to make contact and a strong arm while steadily climbing through the system. The power seems to evaporate when the Red Sox call, and in 2000 Veras didn't fare well at the plate (no hitting percentage above .300) or in the field (13 errors in 49 games) when he subbed for the injured John Valentin. Veras' free-swinging ways are key to his struggles, and his poor season continued at Triple-A Pawtucket after he was demoted in June. His lack of plate discipline compromises even his best minor league seasons, and it could doom his major league career.

Others to Watch

A 1999 supplemental first-round pick, righthander **Brad Baker** (20) already looks like the best pitching prospect in the system. He went 12-7 (3.07) at Class-A Augusta, throwing two solid pitches, a low-90s fastball and a curve. . . Teenage third baseman **Tony Blanco** (19) has a lightning-quick bat, and he hit .384 and tied a Gulf Coast League record with 13 homers in 2000. He also has an incredible arm. The Dominican native won't be rushed, but he could be a good one. . . Another supplemental first-round pick in '99, lefthander **Casey Fossum** (23) will start 2001 at Double-A Trenton after a solid performance (9-10, 3.44) in his first full season at high Class-A Sarasota. He has good command of a low-90s fastball and hard slider, and could see Fenway Park before the year's out. . . Another impressive southpaw is Mexican native **Mauricio Lara** (21). Signed in 1998, Lara throws a low-90s fastball and a solid curveball. He posted a 1.92 ERA between short-season Lowell and Class-A Augusta in his first exposure to North American ball, walking 34 and fanning 116 in 117 innings.

Comiskey Park

Offense

Despite its reputation as a pitchers' haven, Comiskey Park played more like a hitters' paradise last summer—partially because of slightly higher temperatures during 2000 home games and higher velocity readings when the wind blew out compared to the previous three seasons. Now the fences come in for 2001, with the biggest changes down the lines. The effect on scoring will have to be studied over several years, but the expectation is that the smaller dimensions will have minimal impact for all but pull hitters. Comiskey still will have deep power alleys.

Defense

Comiskey also will have shorter outfield fences next season. The White Sox are cutting the height of the fences from nine feet to eight. They also are adding seats in what has previously been a moat between the fence and the bleachers, so fans will be able to get in the action like they do at Camden Yards. The infield is one of the best in the majors.

Who It Helps the Most

While the White Sox had an identical 4.66 ERA at home and on the road last year, Comiskey remained a great place for veteran pitchers to work. Lefties Mike Sirotka and Jim Parque know how to milk those big outfield dimensions, getting outs on long flyballs. Parque's ERA was more than one run lower at home than on the road in 2000. Sirotka's career ERA is more than a half a run lower at Comiskey. Rookie lefty Kelly Wunsch also pitched much better at Comiskey.

Who It Hurts the Most

Frank Thomas once said that Comiskey had cost him 100 homers over the years, but the numbers don't back that up. He hit 30 of his 43 homers at Comiskey last year and has hit 26 more at home than on the road over his career. Ray Durham always has hit for more power on the road.

Rookies & Newcomers

The park still should be a good place to break in young pitchers. Mark Buehrle, Lorenzo Barcelo, Jon Garland, Matt Ginter and Jon Rauch are among those who may work there this year.

Dimensions: LF-330, LCF-377, CF-400, RCF-372, RF-335

Capacity: 46,321

Elevation: 595 feet

Surface: Grass

Foul Territory: Average

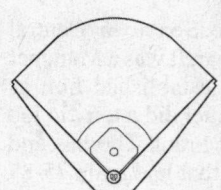

Park Factors

2000 Season							
	Home Games			Away Games			
	White Sox	Opp	Total	White Sox	Opp	Total	Index
G	72	72	144	72	72	144	—
Avg	.289	.269	.279	.280	.273	.277	101
AB	2416	2503	4919	2579	2444	5023	98
R	456	375	831	400	357	757	110
H	699	673	1372	722	667	1389	99
2B	138	119	257	146	117	263	100
3B	18	14	32	11	17	28	117
HR	110	88	198	77	78	155	130
BB	283	246	529	237	288	525	103
SO	383	485	868	457	412	869	102
E	51	42	93	67	60	127	73
E-Infield	50	37	87	59	53	112	78
LHB-Avg	.271	.276	.274	.254	.277	.266	103
LHB-HR	22	39	61	26	36	62	100
RHB-Avg	.298	.264	.282	.294	.270	.283	100
RHB-HR	88	49	137	51	42	93	151

1998-2000							
	Home Games			Away Games			
	White Sox	Opp	Total	White Sox	Opp	Total	Index
G	218	218	436	217	217	434	—
Avg	.281	.274	.278	.273	.280	.276	100
AB	7256	7680	14936	7737	7399	15136	98
R	1184	1161	2345	1140	1158	2298	102
H	2041	2105	4146	2114	2069	4183	99
2B	396	382	778	420	377	797	99
3B	52	31	83	43	41	84	100
HR	276	267	543	236	271	507	109
BB	762	756	1518	701	824	1525	101
SO	1080	1313	2393	1290	1240	2530	96
E	166	148	314	194	182	376	83
E-Infield	148	125	273	169	156	325	84
LHB-Avg	.266	.281	.274	.266	.290	.278	98
LHB-HR	67	123	190	77	119	196	100
RHB-Avg	.291	.269	.280	.278	.272	.275	102
RHB-HR	209	144	353	159	152	311	113

2000 Rankings (American League)
- Highest RHB home-run factor
- Second-highest home-run factor
- Lowest error factor
- Lowest infield-error factor

Chicago (AL)

Jerry Manuel

2000 Season

Jerry Manuel took the White Sox to a Central Division title in just his third year. It was a Manager of the Year performance that established him as more than just a nice guy. Manuel did a terrific job in spring training, confronting Frank Thomas and building confidence in a team that had gone 75-87 a year earlier. Manuel pushed his players to build a big lead while they were white-hot in the first half. After the team opened a big lead, Manuel kept his players focused on the task ahead. The only downside to Manuel's season was Seattle's sweep in the Division Series. Manuel consistently was a step behind Lou Piniella. Count on him to learn from his experiences.

Offense

Manuel has molded the White Sox into the kind of team he wants—one that can manufacture runs when it isn't mashing homers. Left fielder Carlos Lee embodies what Manuel wants—hitters with power who have enough speed to run and can make contact at the plate with runners in motion. While the Sox set a club record with 216 home runs, they also were among American League leaders in sacrifice bunts and stolen bases.

Pitching & Defense

Fielding has been a chronic weakness, as the Sox' defense ranked 12th in the league last year and 13th the previous two seasons. Those figures are likely to improve a bit in 2001 with the trade for Royce Clayton, who will take over for Jose Valentin at short. Manuel does a good job handling his pitching staff. He leaned on his bullpen, leading the American League with 466 pitching changes. He isn't afraid of putting young pitchers in big situations. That's a good thing, because the Sox have a lot of young pitchers and more are on the way.

2001 Outlook

With success arriving ahead of schedule, Manuel will be challenged to keep his players on track. Many believe Manuel has a budding dynasty on his hands, but the Cleveland Indians will have much to say about that. The entire Central Division should be improved in 2001.

Born: 12/23/53 in Hahira, Georgia

Playing Experience: 1975-1982, Det, Mon, SD

Managerial Experience: 3 seasons

Manager Statistics

Year	Team, Lg	W	L	Pct	GB	Finish
2000	Chicago, AL	95	67	.586	—	1st Central
3 Seasons		250	235	.513	—	—

2000 Starting Pitchers by Days Rest

	<=3	4	5	6+
White Sox Starts	1	82	46	20
White Sox ERA	1.80	4.73	4.85	4.30
AL Avg Starts	2	88	40	22
AL ERA	4.87	5.03	5.03	5.28

2000 Situational Stats

	Jerry Manuel	AL Average
Hit & Run Success %	33.8	35.1
Stolen Base Success %	73.9	68.8
Platoon Pct.	52.9	57.8
Defensive Subs	20	23
High-Pitch Outings	8	13
Quick/Slow Hooks	30/18	18/19
Sacrifice Attempts	75	55

2000 Rankings (American League)

- 1st in sacrifice bunt attempts (75), relief appearances (466), saves with over 1 inning pitched (18) and one-batter pitcher appearances (44)
- 2nd in steals of second base (108) and quick hooks (30)
- 3rd in stolen base attempts (161), stolen-base percentage (73.9%) and hit-and-run attempts (77)

James Baldwin

2000 Season

This was a breakout season for the middle-aged James Baldwin. He made his first All-Star team, was named the American League Player of the Month in May and won twice as many games as he lost. Yet, the season did not end with Baldwin's star on the rise. In his first eight starts of the season, he went 7-0 with a 2.51 ERA. After May 20, he was 7-7 with a 5.67 ERA. Twice Baldwin was sidelined with shoulder problems late in the season, and his injury woes probably contributed to his sluggish second half.

Pitching

When Baldwin was at his best last season, he assumed a commanding presence on the mound. He stood tall, worked fast—practically throwing his next pitch as soon as he got the return throw from the catcher—and threw strikes. But when he didn't get ahead of hitters, or when runners cluttered the bases, he appeared indecisive and uncertain. His fastball can reach 94 MPH when he's healthy, but was rarely over 90 MPH late in the season. His best pitch is a curveball, which he can throw with either sweeping action or a sharp break. He also has learned to change speeds effectively.

Defense

There's no nice way to say this: Baldwin is a brutal fielder. He gets off the mound slowly and is easily rattled when multiple runners are in motion. He did end a long streak in 2000, however, participating in the first two double plays of his career. He is average when it comes to holding on runners.

2001 Outlook

Baldwin presents a dilemma. His salary continues to climb, and it's tough to invest long-term in a guy whose career ERA a year from now probably will be the highest among all pitchers who have thrown 1,000 innings. Plus, his sore shoulder led to offseason surgery to remove a bone chip and make some minor repairs. Baldwin may start slow in 2001, further complicating the issue of a long-term contract.

Position: SP
Bats: R **Throws:** R
Ht: 6' 3" **Wt:** 210

Opening Day Age: 29
Born: 7/15/71 in Southern Pines, NC
ML Seasons: 6

Overall Statistics

	W	L	Pct.	ERA	G	GS	Sv	IP	H	BB	SO	HR	Ratio
2000	14	7	.667	4.65	29	28	0	178.0	185	59	116	34	1.37
Career	62	48	.564	5.09	167	149	0	920.0	985	349	624	135	1.45

How Often He Throws Strikes

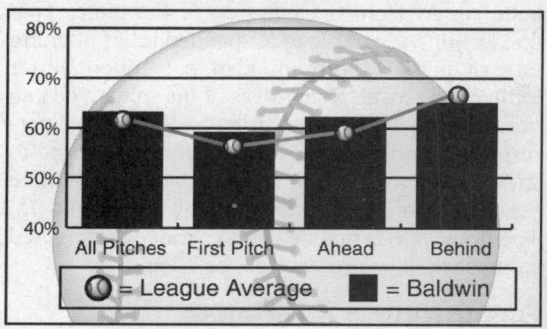

◉ = League Average   ■ = Baldwin

2000 Situational Stats

	W	L	ERA	Sv	IP		AB	H	HR	RBI	Avg
Home	5	5	6.08	0	80.0	LHB	362	101	17	42	.279
Road	9	2	3.49	0	98.0	RHB	318	84	17	41	.264
First Half	11	4	4.28	0	111.1	Sc Pos	132	34	10	54	.258
Scnd Half	3	3	5.27	0	66.2	Clutch	34	7	0	1	.206

2000 Rankings (American League)

- 1st in most home runs allowed per nine innings (1.72)
- 3rd in home runs allowed
- 5th in highest slugging percentage allowed (.471)
- 6th in lowest ERA on the road
- 7th in winning percentage
- 8th in runners caught stealing (8), lowest stolen-base percentage allowed (50.0) and most GDPs induced per nine innings (1.0)
- 9th in most run support per nine innings (6.4)
- Led the White Sox in complete games (2), home runs allowed, runners caught stealing (8), highest strikeout/walk ratio (2.0), fewest pitches thrown per batter (3.63), most strikeouts per nine innings (5.9) and fewest walks per nine innings (3.0)

Chicago (AL)

Ray Durham

Position: 2B
Bats: B **Throws:** R
Ht: 5' 8" **Wt:** 170

Opening Day Age: 29
Born: 11/30/71 in Charlotte, NC
ML Seasons: 6

2000 Season

The White Sox seem to follow the lead of second baseman Ray Durham. The switch-hitting leadoff man was a catalyst in the truest sense of the word. When he and fellow table-setter Jose Valentin created opportunities, the middle of the batting order feasted. Not only did Durham rank third in the American League with 121 runs scored, but his team also was a whopping 61-22 (.735) when he scored at least one run in a game. He earned a second trip to the All-Star Game.

Hitting

After hitting .301 batting righthanded in 1999, Durham reverted to his old ways and was a much better hitter from the left side of the plate. That makes him vulnerable to lefthanded relief pitching late in games. Durham also has much better lefthanded power. Regardless of his splits, you can pretty much count on getting a .280-16-65 performance from him. He has somehow managed to strike out exactly 105 times in each of the last three years, with his walk totals reading 73, 73 and 75. The downside is that he can experience protracted slumps when he does not get on base.

Baserunning & Defense

With Valentin hitting behind Durham, Jerry Manuel did not have his second sacker running as much in 2000. Still, there's no reason Durham shouldn't return to the 30-steal club this year. Durham is among the reasons the White Sox' fielding has been substandard of late. He had a respectable .980 fielding percentage last year, but he failed to make too many plays, including one that was critical to the Sox' 2-1 loss in the last game of the Division Series against Seattle.

2001 Outlook

Durham is halfway through his four-year, $20 million contract. His performance this season could determine if the White Sox will seek to sign him to a long-term extension or consider trading him. The lack of both quality second basemen and leadoff hitters make Durham a valuable commodity on the market. For the moment, though, Durham's job is to lead the Sox back into the playoffs—and perhaps even to a World Series.

Overall Statistics

	G	AB	R	H	D	T	HR	RBI	SB	BB	SO	Avg	OBP	Slg
2000	151	614	121	172	35	9	17	75	25	75	105	.280	.361	.450
Career	898	3523	609	980	187	41	77	371	176	371	589	.278	.351	.420

Where He Hits the Ball

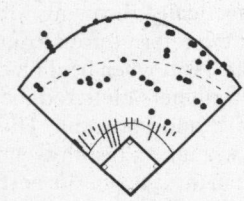 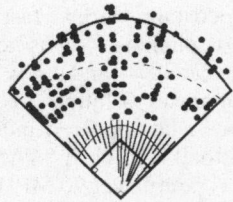

Vs. LHP **Vs. RHP**

2000 Situational Stats

	AB	H	HR	RBI	Avg		AB	H	HR	RBI	Avg
Home	288	86	5	33	.299	LHP	129	32	4	16	.248
Road	326	86	12	42	.264	RHP	485	140	13	59	.289
First Half	353	99	13	48	.280	Sc Pos	133	36	3	54	.271
Scnd Half	261	73	4	27	.280	Clutch	72	15	3	11	.208

2000 Rankings (American League)

- 2nd in caught stealing (13) and errors at second base (15)
- 3rd in runs scored and lowest fielding percentage at second base (.980)
- 4th in triples
- 5th in lowest stolen-base percentage (65.8)
- Led the White Sox in at-bats, runs scored, triples, stolen bases, caught stealing (13), plate appearances (709), highest groundball/flyball ratio (1.6), batting average vs. lefthanded pitchers, batting average on an 0-2 count (.255), on-base percentage for a leadoff hitter (.361), slugging percentage vs. lefthanded pitchers (.419), on-base percentage vs. lefthanded pitchers (.305) and steals of third (4)

Keith Foulke

2000 Season

No longer one of baseball's best-kept secrets, Keith Foulke continued on his upwardly mobile path by taking over the closer's role. After two years as a setup man for Bob Howry, they essentially swapped roles. Foulke finished with 34 saves, converting 15 of his last 16 chances. Not all of his chances were of the one-inning variety, either, as he worked more than an inning 14 times for saves and two innings five times. He suffered a five-stitch cut below his left eye in a brawl with Detroit on April 22 and later had to serve a three-game suspension for the incident.

Pitching

A starter during his minor league career, Foulke has more pitches than most closers but generally he relies on a low-90s fastball and a seldom-telegraphed changeup. The change often has screwball action on it, running inside on righthanded hitters. He also throws breaking pitches to righthanded hitters, who batted only .192 off him last year. He is almost as effective against lefthanded batters. He will struggle when he loses the feel for his changeup. That happened last June, when he gave up 21 hits and 15 earned runs in 12.2 innings.

Defense

Foulke could use a little work on comebackers— too many go past him up the middle. But generally he is an average fielder. He does a good job holding runners on base and has allowed a total of nine stolen bases over the past three years.

2001 Outlook

Foulke's durability makes him a good fit for the bullpen, but he would like to get another chance as a starting pitcher. That could happen down the line, but not until somebody like Lorenzo Barcelo, Matt Ginter or even Howry shows that he is ready to do a good job in Foulke's place. It's a safe bet to pencil in the arbitration-eligible Foulke for 30-plus saves again in 2001, and forty is not out of the question.

Position: RP
Bats: R   **Throws:** R
Ht: 6' 0"   **Wt:** 200

Opening Day Age: 28
Born: 10/19/72 in Ellsworth AFB, SD
ML Seasons: 4
Pronunciation: FOLK

Overall Statistics

	W	L	Pct.	ERA	G	GS	Sv	IP	H	BB	SO	HR	Ratio
2000	3	1	.750	2.97	72	0	34	88.0	66	22	91	9	1.00
Career	13	11	.542	3.71	220	8	47	332.0	277	86	325	42	1.09

How Often He Throws Strikes

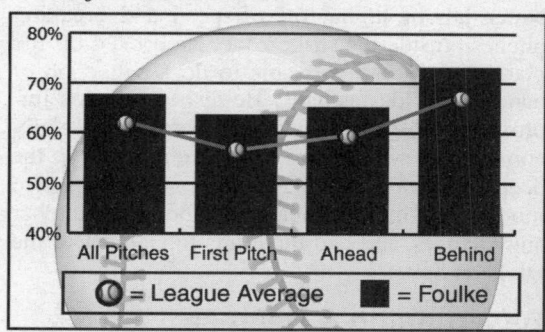

2000 Situational Stats

	W	L	ERA	Sv	IP		AB	H	HR	RBI	Avg
Home	1	1	4.85	12	42.2	LHB	163	36	7	23	.221
Road	2	0	1.19	22	45.1	RHB	156	30	2	10	.192
First Half	1	0	3.21	16	53.1	Sc Pos	76	17	2	23	.224
Scnd Half	2	1	2.60	18	34.2	Clutch	198	42	7	21	.212

2000 Rankings (American League)

- 1st in fewest baserunners allowed per nine innings in relief (9.2)
- 3rd in relief innings (88.0)
- 4th in lowest batting average allowed in relief (.207)
- 5th in saves, save percentage (87.2) and games finished (58)
- Led the White Sox in saves, games finished (58), save opportunities (39), save percentage (87.2), blown saves (5), relief innings (88.0), lowest batting average allowed in relief (.207), most strikeouts per nine innings in relief (9.3) and fewest baserunners allowed per nine innings in relief (9.2)

Charles Johnson

2000 Season

Like a rolling stone, Charles Johnson just keeps on moving. He was traded from Baltimore to the White Sox on July 29, giving him four teams over the last three seasons. While Johnson was dealt because of his impending free agency, the mystery to this trade was why Baltimore couldn't get more than Brook Fordyce, fringe prospect Juan Figueroa and two other minor leaguers for him. He had a career year with 31 home runs between the Orioles and White Sox, while remaining in the top tier of catchers defensively.

Hitting

Selectivity was a major key for Johnson, who did a better job of laying off offspeed and breaking pitches outside the strike zone. He backed off the plate slightly and was able to do a better job of handling inside fastballs. He also was much improved against righthanders. He seemed especially comfortable when placed in the ninth spot in the deep White Sox order. He hit .326 in his two months in Chicago, including .366 in September and October, and had three hits in Game 1 of the Division Series.

Baserunning & Defense

Johnson is a four-time Gold Glove winner. His big body provides a great target and he does a good job of framing pitches. He uses his body well to block pitches in the dirt. He does not have an Ivan Rodriguez-like cannon but has a quick release and a track record for accuracy. His throwing numbers were down last year—when he caught only 27 percent of runners trying to steal—but until further notice, the blame for that drop will fall to Baltimore's pitching staff.

2001 Outlook

While Johnson did a great job with the White Sox, he was strictly a rent-a-player. The South Florida native returned home to his original club, the Marlins, by dropping his asking price and signing a five-year, $35 million deal. He should do a solid job, although he's not a good bet to repeat his success at the plate, especially in the power department.

Position: C
Bats: R **Throws:** R
Ht: 6' 2" **Wt:** 220

Opening Day Age: 29
Born: 7/20/71 in Fort Pierce, FL
ML Seasons: 7

Overall Statistics

	G	AB	R	H	D	T	HR	RBI	SB	BB	SO	Avg	OBP	Slg
2000	128	421	76	128	24	0	31	91	2	52	106	.304	.379	.582
Career	741	2434	300	607	116	4	110	346	3	299	617	.249	.333	.436

Where He Hits the Ball

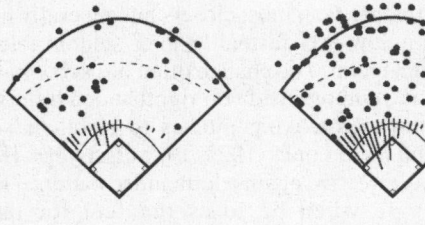

Vs. LHP   **Vs. RHP**

2000 Situational Stats

	AB	H	HR	RBI	Avg		AB	H	HR	RBI	Avg
Home	201	64	19	55	.318	LHP	115	29	6	21	.252
Road	220	64	12	36	.291	RHP	306	99	25	70	.324
First Half	240	74	20	47	.308	Sc Pos	116	35	6	57	.302
Scnd Half	181	54	11	44	.298	Clutch	72	20	7	16	.278

2000 Rankings (American League)

- 4th in highest percentage of runners caught stealing as a catcher (27.0) and highest percentage of swings that missed (29.8)
- Led AL catchers in home runs (31) and RBI (91)

Paul Konerko

2000 Season

The White Sox couldn't have asked for much more from Paul Konerko in his second full season in the big leagues. He showed the ability to adjust to pitchers who had figured out that he's a tough man to sneak a fastball past. He was on his way to a 100-RBI season before Harold Baines arrived in the Charles Johnson trade on July 30. Konerko's playing time slipped in August, which allowed him to rest a hand injury he suffered when he was hit by a pitch.

Hitting

A tough out at any time, Kornerko has a short swing for a big man, and he has bought into hitting coach Von Joshua's philosophy of hitting the ball the other way. He no longer simply looks to jerk something down the left-field line, as he tried to do when he was with Los Angeles and Cincinnati. He does most of his damage on pitches left up in the strike zone, but he also does a decent job of fighting off nasty breaking pitches down. He doesn't bail against tough righthanders, and is developing a solid idea about controlling the strike zone.

Baserunning & Defense

Konerko spent much of spring training working at third base. The Sox expected to play him there with Thomas at first, but abandoned that plan early because of Thomas' nagging ankle injury. Konerko wound up playing a career-high 122 games at first. There's a perception that he's much better than Thomas, but it's mostly myth. Konerko has as little range as Thomas and committed 10 errors. He is the slowest runner on his team, though he somehow made it around the bags on an inside-the-park homer at Tampa Bay.

2001 Outlook

Despite Konerko's consistent production, the White Sox might use him as bait to land a veteran starter. His fate could be tied to a decision on Jeff Liefer, a lefthanded-hitting first baseman who was second in the International League with 32 homers. If the Sox did trade Konerko, he would be missed in the clubhouse and by the local media. He's popular with his teammates and probably the most quoted member of the club.

Position: 1B
Bats: R **Throws:** R
Ht: 6' 3" **Wt:** 211

Opening Day Age: 25
Born: 3/5/76 in Providence, RI
ML Seasons: 4
Pronunciation: kuh-NER-koh

Overall Statistics

	G	AB	R	H	D	T	HR	RBI	SB	BB	SO	Avg	OBP	Slg
2000	143	524	84	156	31	1	21	97	1	47	72	.298	.363	.481
Career	366	1261	176	355	66	5	52	207	2	109	182	.282	.343	.466

Where He Hits the Ball

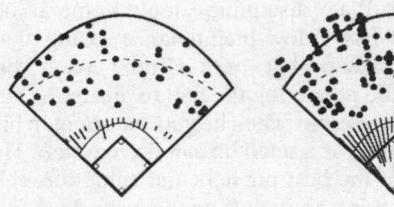

Vs. LHP	Vs. RHP

2000 Situational Stats

	AB	H	HR	RBI	Avg		AB	H	HR	RBI	Avg
Home	258	75	10	48	.291	LHP	96	29	2	20	.302
Road	266	81	11	49	.305	RHP	428	127	19	77	.297
First Half	294	88	12	55	.299	Sc Pos	163	49	4	74	.301
Scnd Half	230	68	9	42	.296	Clutch	72	19	2	6	.264

2000 Rankings (American League)

- 2nd in lowest fielding percentage at first base (.991)
- 3rd in errors at first base (10)
- 5th in GDPs (22)
- 7th in hit by pitch (10)
- Led the White Sox in hit by pitch (10) and highest percentage of swings put into play (49.6)
- Led AL first basemen in highest percentage of extra bases taken as a runner (51.6)

Carlos Lee

2000 Season

In just his second big league season, Carlos Lee established himself as a future All-Star. The powerfully built Panamanian was the White Sox' regular left fielder and held his own in one of the most productive lineups in the major leagues. Manager Jerry Manuel batted him seventh at the start of the season, trying to keep him from feeling too much pressure, but Lee looked at home in the No. 5 spot at year's end. His power dropped off a bit late in the season, but overall he was a consistent, reliable performer who fell just eight RBI short of the century mark.

Hitting

Lee loves to hit, but he could stand to be a little more patient. Plate discipline should come as he matures. He has a low-maintenance swing that generates impressive bat speed. Hitting coach Von Joshua has Lee peppering the ball to all fields, but Lee is most dangerous when he gets the count in his favor and looks for a pitch he can drive to left. He isn't afraid of the best pitchers and came through with a game-tying homer off countryman Mariano Rivera on June 23.

Baserunning & Defense

A third baseman until 1999, Lee is beginning to look more comfortable in left field. He has decent range to either side, but struggles to read balls that are hit hard directly at him. Opponents run on his arm, but he has quickened his release and can make them pay. He had 10 assists and only three errors in 2000—numbers the Sox find encouraging. Lee can play the infield corners in a pinch. He has good speed on the bases for a big man, and a 20-stolen base season is not out of the question.

2001 Outlook

Look for even bigger and better things from this guy. If he's healthy, Lee should be good for at least 25 homers and 100 RBI in the middle of Jerry Manuel's order. There should be no more talk about moving him to first base or designated hitter. He's not only an adequate outfielder, but he's also on his way to joining teammate Magglio Ordonez on the All-Star team.

Position: LF
Bats: R **Throws:** R
Ht: 6' 2" **Wt:** 220

Opening Day Age: 24
Born: 6/20/76 in Aguadulce, Panama
ML Seasons: 2

Overall Statistics

	G	AB	R	H	D	T	HR	RBI	SB	BB	SO	Avg	OBP	Slg
2000	152	572	107	172	29	2	24	92	13	38	94	.301	.345	.484
Career	279	1064	173	316	61	4	40	176	17	51	166	.297	.330	.475

Where He Hits the Ball

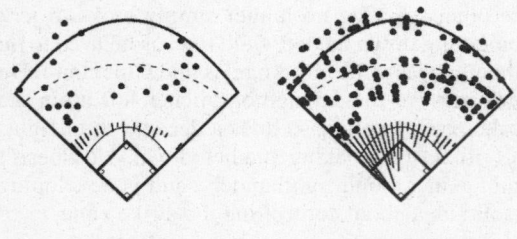

Vs. LHP   Vs. RHP

2000 Situational Stats

	AB	H	HR	RBI	Avg		AB	H	HR	RBI	Avg
Home	277	75	12	43	.271	LHP	98	32	4	18	.327
Road	295	97	12	49	.329	RHP	474	140	20	74	.295
First Half	309	93	17	62	.301	Sc Pos	162	46	6	70	.284
Scnd Half	263	79	7	30	.300	Clutch	68	21	3	10	.309

2000 Rankings (American League)

- 2nd in fielding percentage in left field (.990)
- 4th in errors in left field (3)
- Led the White Sox in singles and batting average on the road

Magglio Ordonez

2000 Season

For the second-year in a row, the White Sox' most pleasant surprise, Magglio Ordonez, had an All-Star season while hitting in the cleanup spot. The young right fielder joined Frank Thomas to form the most dangerous 1-2 combination in franchise history. They hit back-to-back home runs six times while combining for 269 RBI, breaking the standard set by Zeke Bonura and Luke Appling in 1936. Ordonez was suspended for five games for his part in an April brawl with the Detroit Tigers, but that was about the only mark on another wire-to-wire performance.

Hitting

Ordonez has a backward lean in his stance, but he gets all the parts moving in the right direction when the pitch is on the way. He has a short, quick swing and tremendous eyesight, allowing him to recognize pitches quicker than many hitters. He seldom seems to get fooled. Ordonez hits the ball to all fields, taking what pitchers give him. Jerry Manuel was briefly worried about Ordonez's approach during the spring, when he set a Sox record with eight homers, but this is not a guy who too often swings for the fences.

Baserunning & Defense

Ordonez is not flashy, but he's solid in every way. His range in right field is average, but he has a great knack for making running catches. He is especially good running into the right-field corner. Ordonez' arm is good but not exceptional. His 12 assists in 2000 were more proof of his unusual accuracy than his arm strength. He runs well and is learning to get good jumps. He stole a career-high 18 bases in 2000 but isn't likely to become a 30-30 man.

2001 Outlook

The Venezuelan native enters his arbitration years and is likely to get a long-term contract at top dollar. He should just be coming into his own at 27. It's hard to imagine that no team invested $50,000 in Ordonez when the Sox left him off the 40-man roster after his Double-A season in 1996, but the White Sox are glad no one did.

Position: RF
Bats: R **Throws:** R
Ht: 6' 0" **Wt:** 200

Opening Day Age: 27
Born: 1/28/74 in Caracas, Venezuela
ML Seasons: 4
Pronunciation: or-DOAN-yez

Overall Statistics

	G	AB	R	H	D	T	HR	RBI	SB	BB	SO	Avg	OBP	Slg
2000	153	588	102	185	34	3	32	126	18	60	64	.315	.371	.546
Career	476	1816	284	546	99	8	80	319	41	137	189	.301	.349	.496

Where He Hits the Ball

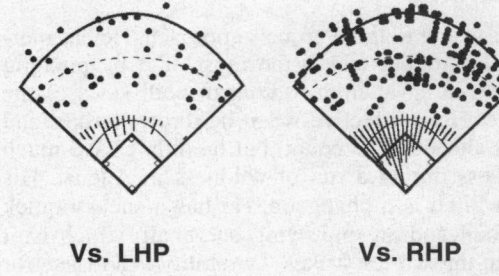

Vs. LHP   **Vs. RHP**

2000 Situational Stats

	AB	H	HR	RBI	Avg		AB	H	HR	RBI	Avg
Home	283	93	21	65	.329	LHP	98	33	6	27	.337
Road	305	92	11	61	.302	RHP	490	152	26	99	.310
First Half	306	101	21	74	.330	Sc Pos	171	57	8	96	.333
Scnd Half	282	84	11	52	.298	Clutch	77	25	3	14	.325

2000 Rankings (American League)

- 1st in sacrifice flies (15)
- 2nd in GDPs (28)
- 4th in errors in right field (5) and lowest fielding percentage in right field (.983)
- 5th in stolen-base percentage (81.8) and most GDPs per GDP situation (18.7%)
- Led the White Sox in sacrifice flies (15), GDPs (28), batting average in the clutch, cleanup slugging percentage (.547) and batting average with two strikes (.267)
- Led AL right fielders in RBI, sacrifice flies (15), GDPs (28), stolen-base percentage (81.8) and highest percentage of extra bases taken as a runner (54.7)

Jim Parque

2000 Season

Jim Parque was comfortable enough in his third big league season to attempt a higher calling: moonlighting as a sportswriter for the *Chicago Sun-Times*. He was a candid columnist who criticized official scoring and the size of bonuses paid to high school and college players, but Parque shelved his weekly gig after an unproductive stretch of pitching in midseason. What would he have said about his season? That he was lucky at times when he wasn't good. He won seven more games than he lost, but he relied on some generous run support to finish with that record. He probably deserved some good fortune after ending 1999 in a nine-game losing streak.

Pitching

You've got to like Parque's approach. He has marginal stuff but makes the most of it by pitching inside in an attempt to control both sides of the plate. He is effective when he throws strikes and gets ahead in the count, but he didn't have much success during a run of wildness in August. His best pitch is a changeup. He has a sneaky-quick fastball and an improving curveball, which isn't often thrown for strikes. Durability is an issue for the diminutive Parque. He never got more than 22 outs in a start, averaging only 5.2 innings.

Defense

Parque, like most of the Sox' pitchers, is a below-average fielder. He moves fairly well on the mound, getting to a lot of comebackers, but is prone to forcing the action when he should concede a hit. He has an excellent pickoff move, which he used to get five outs last year.

2001 Outlook

Along with Mike Sirotka, Parque gives the White Sox an excellent 1-2 combination of lefthanders. He doesn't have to think about anything except his pitching, as he signed a three-year deal in 2000. This could be the year he becomes as reliable as Sirotka. The first step would be getting deeper into more games, and 200 innings should remain a goal. With no overpowering pitch, Parque may never be more than a No. 3 or 4 starter.

Position: SP
Bats: L **Throws:** L
Ht: 5'11" **Wt:** 165

Opening Day Age: 25
Born: 2/8/76 in Norwalk, CA
ML Seasons: 3
Pronunciation: par-KAY

Overall Statistics

	W	L	Pct.	ERA	G	GS	Sv	IP	H	BB	SO	HR	Ratio
2000	13	6	.684	4.28	33	32	0	187.0	208	71	111	21	1.49
Career	29	26	.527	4.79	85	83	0	473.2	553	199	299	58	1.59

How Often He Throws Strikes

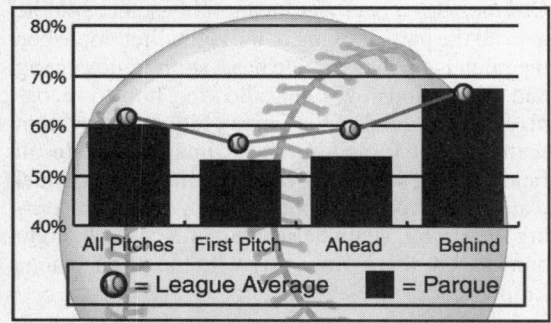

○ = League Average ■ = Parque

2000 Situational Stats

	W	L	ERA	Sv	IP		AB	H	HR	RBI	Avg
Home	7	3	3.66	0	93.1	LHB	187	59	5	26	.316
Road	6	3	4.90	0	93.2	RHB	549	149	16	60	.271
First Half	8	2	3.81	0	101.2	Sc Pos	184	46	3	57	.250
Scnd Half	5	4	4.85	0	85.1	Clutch	17	9	1	3	.529

2000 Rankings (American League)

- 1st in balks (5)
- 3rd in lowest fielding percentage at pitcher (.900)
- 4th in hit batsmen (11) and pickoff throws (156)
- 5th in most run support per nine innings (6.8), errors at pitcher (3) and winning percentage
- Led the White Sox in games started, hits allowed, walks allowed, hit batsmen (11), balks (5), pitches thrown (3,208), highest groundball/fly-ball ratio allowed (1.7), lowest stolen-base percentage allowed (50.0), most run support per nine innings (6.8), fewest home runs allowed per nine innings (1.01), lowest batting average allowed with runners in scoring position and winning percentage

Chris Singleton

2000 Season

To no one's surprise, Chris Singleton was unable to maintain the same level of play he had during his outstanding, out-of-nowhere rookie year in 1999. It didn't help that his hands were banged up almost all year. He was hitting .279 when he dislocated his right index finger sliding into second base on May 14. He didn't go on the disabled list, but clearly was affected at the plate. He also struggled in the Division Series against Seattle, when he went hit-less after a second-inning triple in Game 1.

Hitting

Pitchers found the holes in Singleton's swing, and he spent the season trying to make his own adjustments. Lefthanded pitchers were largely responsible for the difference in his hitting. After batting .408 against lefties as a rookie, his average against them dropped to .206 in 2000. Singleton can turn on inside pitches, but struggles to do much on the outside part of the plate. He is a skilled bunter who doesn't often try to bunt for hits.

Baserunning & Defense

Singleton is an excellent center fielder. He cheats in at Comiskey Park and rarely gets burned on balls over his head. He has the ability to cover ground going both ways, which comes in handy with Carlos Lee playing left field. Singleton's arm is considered average, but it is accurate enough to foil guys who take the extra base on him. He has good speed and could steal 30-plus bases if he could find a way to get aboard more often.

2001 Outlook

There's room for a defensive specialist in the White Sox' hitter-heavy lineup, and Singleton is it. Still, his playing time may be cut back with the arrival of Royce Clayton. One option for the Sox is to play Jose Valentin or Ray Durham in center, which would push Singleton to the bench. The long-term solution in center, however, may be top 2000 draft pick Joe Borchard. If he can play there—and the jury still is out—Borchard may reach the majors in a hurry. No matter who mans center in 2001, the long-term picture for Singleton isn't particularly bright.

Position: CF/LF
Bats: L **Throws:** L
Ht: 6' 2" **Wt:** 195

Opening Day Age: 28
Born: 8/15/72 in Martinez, CA
ML Seasons: 2

Overall Statistics

	G	AB	R	H	D	T	HR	RBI	SB	BB	SO	Avg	OBP	Slg
2000	147	511	83	130	22	5	11	62	22	35	85	.254	.301	.382
Career	280	1007	155	279	53	11	28	134	42	57	130	.277	.314	.435

Where He Hits the Ball

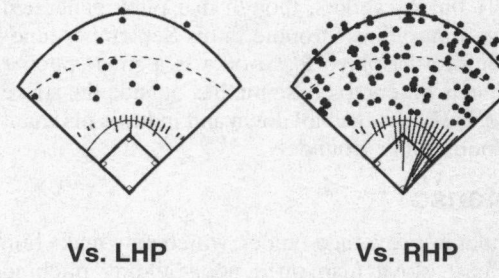

Vs. LHP   Vs. RHP

2000 Situational Stats

	AB	H	HR	RBI	Avg		AB	H	HR	RBI	Avg
Home	241	70	5	37	.290	LHP	68	14	0	7	.206
Road	270	60	6	25	.222	RHP	443	116	11	55	.262
First Half	305	78	6	36	.256	Sc Pos	126	36	3	50	.286
Scnd Half	206	52	5	26	.252	Clutch	65	15	1	3	.231

2000 Rankings (American League)

- 3rd in fielding percentage in center field (.992) and highest percentage of extra bases taken as a runner (68.0)
- 4th in sacrifice bunts (12) and highest percentage of swings on the first pitch (42.2)
- 5th in bunts in play (24), lowest on-base percentage, lowest on-base percentage vs. righthanded pitchers (.306) and lowest batting average on the road
- 7th in batting average with the bases loaded (.600)
- Led the White Sox in fewest GDPs per GDP situation (5.7%), batting average with the bases loaded (.600) and highest percentage of extra bases taken as a runner (68.0)

Mike Sirotka

Position: SP
Bats: L **Throws:** L
Ht: 6' 1" **Wt:** 200

Opening Day Age: 29
Born: 5/13/71 in
Chicago, IL
ML Seasons: 6
Pronunciation:
sir-ROT-kuh

2000 Season

Mike Sirotka has everything except a high profile. There haven't been many better lefthanded pitchers in the American League the last two years, and he just keeps getting better. While Sirotka was bypassed for the All-Star team in each of the last two summers, he won a career-high 15 games in 2000 and cut his earned run average for the second year in a row. His ERA was the best among AL lefties, and that's after he was hit hard in April. He went 13-7 with a 3.40 ERA in his last 26 outings.

Pitching

Sirotka is a classic three-pitch lefty who changes speeds and generally does a good job locating his pitches. He has a good curveball and changeup. He rarely throws sliders, though that pitch generated some minor elbow trouble in his September tune-up before the playoffs. Sirotka is a smart pitcher who gets hitters to chase pitches outside the strike zone. He keeps the ball down and induces his share of double-play grounders.

Defense

Sirotka is an average fielder, which may make him the best glove man on a poor-fielding pitching staff. He can start double plays on comebackers and has good enough instincts not to force the action on tough plays. He does a good job holding on runners, yielding just eight stolen bases in 197.0 innings.

2001 Outlook

The White Sox have to be a little concerned about Sirotka. He experienced minor arm problems in March, April and again in September. His workload fell below 200 innings for the first time in his three full big league seasons. None of the injuries seemed serious, however, so the Sox should be able to put him down for 32 starts and at least 200 frames. If there's such a thing as justice, another fast first half will be rewarded with a trip to Seattle for the All-Star Game.

Overall Statistics

	W	L	Pct.	ERA	G	GS	Sv	IP	H	BB	SO	HR	Ratio
2000	15	10	.600	3.79	32	32	0	197.0	203	69	128	23	1.38
Career	45	42	.517	4.31	125	111	0	710.1	803	207	435	86	1.42

How Often He Throws Strikes

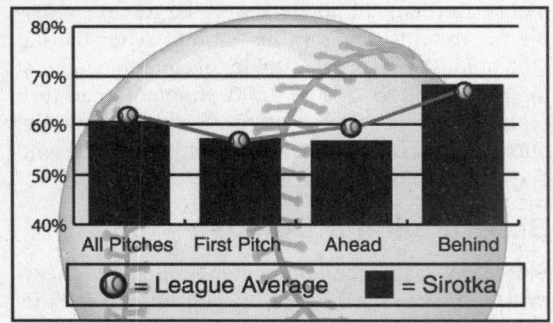

○ = League Average   ■ = Sirotka

2000 Situational Stats

	W	L	ERA	Sv	IP		AB	H	HR	RBI	Avg
Home	8	5	3.56	0	108.2	LHB	177	55	7	28	.311
Road	7	5	4.08	0	88.1	RHB	578	148	16	60	.256
First Half	8	6	3.73	0	103.2	Sc Pos	161	48	5	63	.298
Scnd Half	7	4	3.86	0	93.1	Clutch	34	6	0	1	.176

2000 Rankings (American League)

- 2nd in pickoff throws (162)
- 4th in ERA
- 5th in GDPs induced (25) and most GDPs induced per nine innings (1.1)
- 6th in balks (2) and lowest ERA at home
- 8th in lowest ERA on the road
- 9th in wins
- 10th in lowest slugging percentage allowed (.405) and most pitches thrown per batter (3.80)
- Led the White Sox in ERA, wins, losses, games started, innings pitched, batters faced (832), strikeouts, wild pitches (8), pickoff throws (162), GDPs induced (25), lowest batting average allowed (.269) and lowest slugging percentage allowed (.405)

Frank Thomas

2000 Season

The 1993 and '94 American League MVP reclaimed his position among the league's toughest hitters. Frank Thomas' big year followed a spring training clash with manager Jerry Manuel, which seemed to have a cathartic effect on both Thomas and his teammates. The Big Hurt was the front man for the Sox's stunning march to 95 victories and a first-ever title in the Central. He set career highs in both home runs and RBI while playing through some injuries. The only minus was an 0-for-9 performance in Seattle's postseason sweep.

Hitting

Following back-to-back subpar seasons, Thomas re-examined both his mental and physical approach. He met former hitting coach Walt Hriniak in Arizona for a pre-spring hitting tutorial, searching for an adjustment that would make him less vulnerable to being busted inside. Thomas came out crushing the ball to all fields, but he still wasn't getting much elevation on his drives. He adopted an open hitting stance in late May after watching Andres Galarraga on television, and balls started flying out of the park. Plus, his strike-zone judgment returned. He was less prone to taking strikes and swinging at balls, a problem the previous two seasons.

Baserunning & Defense

Thomas worked hard in the field during the spring. It showed in his fielding at first, which was much improved. He wound up playing only 30 games there, partly because of an ankle injury suffered early in the season. Infielders like his large target at first base. The downside to his fielding remains his arm, which causes him to be reluctant to make throws. Thomas runs like the big man he is.

2001 Outlook

Thomas is only 32 and there's no reason he can't remain one of the AL's most productive hitters now that he's got his groove back. The White Sox hope so, because he has six years and about $60 million remaining in the deal that he signed in 1997. If he slumps again, however, his contract has an out clause that allows the Sox to defer all but $250,000 per year after 2001. That shouldn't happen.

Position: DH/1B
Bats: R **Throws:** R
Ht: 6' 5" **Wt:** 270

Opening Day Age: 32
Born: 5/27/68 in Columbus, GA
ML Seasons: 11
Nickname: Big Hurt

Overall Statistics

	G	AB	R	H	D	T	HR	RBI	SB	BB	SO	Avg	OBP	Slg
2000	159	582	115	191	44	0	43	143	1	112	94	.328	.436	.625
Career	1530	5474	1083	1755	361	10	344	1183	29	1188	835	.321	.440	.579

Where He Hits the Ball

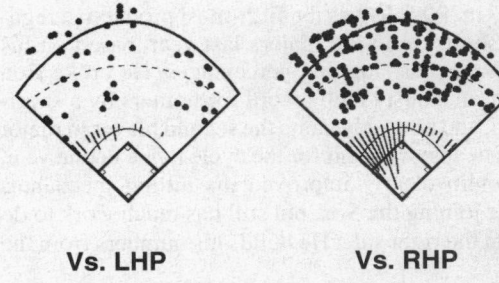

Vs. LHP   **Vs. RHP**

2000 Situational Stats

	AB	H	HR	RBI	Avg		AB	H	HR	RBI	Avg
Home	291	101	30	86	.347	LHP	91	37	10	32	.407
Road	291	90	13	57	.309	RHP	491	154	33	111	.314
First Half	312	104	26	75	.333	Sc Pos	159	60	17	108	.377
Scnd Half	270	87	17	68	.322	Clutch	71	19	1	9	.268

2000 Rankings (American League)

- 2nd in home runs and intentional walks (18)
- 3rd in total bases (364), RBI, times on base (308) and batting average with runners in scoring position
- 4th in walks, slugging percentage and on-base percentage
- 5th in doubles, pitches seen (2,806) and games played
- Led the White Sox in batting average, home runs, hits, doubles, total bases (364), RBI, walks, intentional walks (18), times on base (308), pitches seen (2,806), slugging percentage, on-base percentage, HR frequency (13.5 ABs per HR), most pitches seen per plate appearance (3.97) and batting average with runners in scoring position

Chicago (AL)

Jose Valentin

2000 Season

While Frank Thomas was the MVP candidate in the American League, some believe Jose Valentin was more valuable to the Central Division champions. Then-general manager Ron Schueler made the deal of the year when he stole Valentin and Cal Eldred from Milwaukee for Jaime Navarro and Jon Snyder. Valentin quickly turned shortstop from a major weakness on the South Side into a strength. Along with Thomas' hitting, a career year from Valentin was the biggest difference between the White Sox team that won 75 games in 1999 and the one that won 95 in 2000.

Hitting

What happened to the guy who hit .224 in 1998 and .227 in '99? He was the fifth-most productive regular shortstop in the majors last year, based on his on-base plus slugging percentages. He broke Ron Hansen's dusty club record for homers by a shortstop, and almost became the second player in major league history to hit for the cycle twice in one year. Valentin clearly improved his hitting mechanics after joining the Sox, but still has much work to do from the right side. He builds his numbers from the left.

Baserunning & Defense

Valentin is a defensive conundrum. He makes tons of errors yet also helps pitchers escape jams with big plays and double plays. The belief is his concentration wanders when the game is not close. He has both a strong arm and a quick release, making him ideal on the double-play pivot. He doesn't shy away from contact, either. Valentin isn't the fastest baserunner but has outstanding instincts. He takes chances but rarely gets thrown out.

2001 Outlook

Valentin's role in winning a division title obviously made an impression on the White Sox, who signed him to a three-year, $15 million deal in November. With Royce Clayton coming over from Texas, Valentin is likely to move to third base. Another scenario has Valentin moving to center field. Or the Sox may consider moving Valentin to second and Durham to center.

Position: SS
Bats: B **Throws:** R
Ht: 5'10" **Wt:** 173

Opening Day Age: 31
Born: 10/12/69 in Manati, Puerto Rico
ML Seasons: 9
Pronunciation: VAL-en-teen

Overall Statistics

	G	AB	R	H	D	T	HR	RBI	SB	BB	SO	Avg	OBP	Slg
2000	144	568	107	155	37	6	25	92	19	59	106	.273	.343	.491
Career	906	2977	485	732	169	24	115	435	97	357	691	.246	.327	.435

Where He Hits the Ball

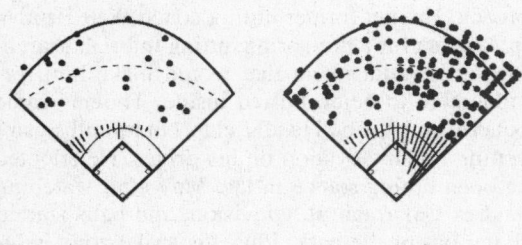

Vs. LHP　　　　　**Vs. RHP**

2000 Situational Stats

	AB	H	HR	RBI	Avg		AB	H	HR	RBI	Avg
Home	262	79	16	56	.302	LHP	79	17	1	10	.215
Road	306	76	9	36	.248	RHP	489	138	24	82	.282
First Half	325	86	13	46	.265	Sc Pos	133	43	4	62	.323
Scnd Half	243	69	12	46	.284	Clutch	67	18	2	11	.269

2000 Rankings (American League)

- 1st in errors at shortstop (36) and lowest fielding percentage at shortstop (.950)
- 2nd in sacrifice bunts (13), stolen-base percentage (90.5) and bunts in play (25)
- 3rd in lowest groundball/flyball ratio (0.7)
- 8th in triples
- Led the White Sox in sacrifice bunts (13), strikeouts, stolen-base percentage (90.5) and bunts in play (25)
- Led AL shortstops in stolen-base percentage (90.5) and batting average with the bases loaded (.429)

Harold Baines

Position: DH
Bats: L **Throws:** L
Ht: 6' 2" **Wt:** 195

Opening Day Age: 42
Born: 3/15/59 in St. Michaels, MD
ML Seasons: 21

Overall Statistics

	G	AB	R	H	D	T	HR	RBI	SB	BB	SO	Avg	OBP	Slg
2000	96	283	26	72	13	0	11	39	0	36	50	.254	.338	.417
Career	2798	9824	1296	2855	487	49	384	1622	34	1054	1425	.291	.357	.467

2000 Situational Stats

	AB	H	HR	RBI	Avg		AB	H	HR	RBI	Avg
Home	142	32	4	16	.225	LHP	26	5	0	3	.192
Road	141	40	7	23	.284	RHP	257	67	11	36	.261
First Half	188	46	9	26	.245	Sc Pos	78	18	2	26	.231
Scnd Half	95	26	2	13	.274	Clutch	55	14	0	3	.255

2000 Season

Harold Baines was reduced to part-time status with Baltimore and the White Sox. He finished the season with only 72 hits, leaving him 145 shy of 3,000. Baines got off to a slow start with the Orioles, hitting .233 through the end of May. Dealt to the Sox in the Charles Johnson trade on July 29, Baines was a bad fit on a team with an already deep lineup. He hit only .213 in 24 games after the trade.

Hitting, Baserunning & Defense

Baines' mission in life is to hit quality pitching, though his bat has slowed down. He still hangs in against lefthanders but rarely gets the chance to face them anymore. Give him credit for keeping himself in good shape, despite being limited to designated hitter duties almost exclusively since 1986. He runs as well as he did when he was younger, but he was never fast. He has played only one game in the field since '92.

2001 Outlook

Baines is a career .291 hitter who drove in 103 runs as recently as 1999. He wants to continue playing and has been promised a job with the White Sox. Unless they trade Paul Konerko, it's hard to see how they can get enough at-bats to justify keeping Baines on the roster, let alone enough at-bats to allow him to reach 3,000 hits.

Lorenzo Barcelo

Position: RP
Bats: R **Throws:** R
Ht: 6' 4" **Wt:** 220

Opening Day Age: 23
Born: 8/10/77 in San Pedro de Macoris, Dominican Republic
ML Seasons: 1

Overall Statistics

	W	L	Pct.	ERA	G	GS	Sv	IP	H	BB	SO	HR	Ratio
2000	4	2	.667	3.69	22	1	0	39.0	34	9	26	5	1.10
Career	4	2	.667	3.69	22	1	0	39.0	34	9	26	5	1.10

2000 Situational Stats

	W	L	ERA	Sv	IP		AB	H	HR	RBI	Avg
Home	2	0	4.35	0	20.2	LHB	66	13	3	10	.197
Road	2	2	2.95	0	18.1	RHB	81	21	2	9	.259
First Half	0	0	-	0	0.0	Sc Pos	39	11	2	16	.282
Scnd Half	4	2	3.69	0	39.0	Clutch	28	4	1	4	.143

2000 Season

In his first full season back from Tommy John surgery, Lorenzo Barcelo delivered on the potential that made him one of the main pieces in the controversial White Flag trade with the Giants in 1997. He rewarded the White Sox by pitching well out of the bullpen after a midseason promotion from Triple-A Charlotte.

Pitching & Defense

Barcelo already has an intimidating presence on the mound. He also throws 94-95 MPH, which still is not as hard as before his 1998 surgery. His velocity increased when he was moved to the bullpen, and the Sox believe it will jump again this year. But he is not a one-pitch fireballer. He has a sharp-breaking curveball and a good changeup, and he has amazing command of all his offerings. He is a poor fielder with slow reactions who finished with just one total chance last year. His move to first is slow but he didn't allow a stolen base.

2001 Outlook

Look for Barcelo to remain in a long-relief role when the season begins, but he should get some chances to serve as the setup man and probably will get some save opportunities. His stuff is better than Keith Foulke's, and eventually Barcelo could supplant him as the Sox' closer. But not this year.

Chicago (AL)

Mark Buehrle

Position: RP
Bats: L **Throws:** L
Ht: 6' 2" **Wt:** 200

Opening Day Age: 22
Born: 3/23/79 in St. Charles, MO
ML Seasons: 1

Overall Statistics

	W	L	Pct.	ERA	G	GS	Sv	IP	H	BB	SO	HR	Ratio
2000	4	1	.800	4.21	28	3	0	51.1	55	19	37	5	1.44
Career	4	1	.800	4.21	28	3	0	51.1	55	19	37	5	1.44

2000 Situational Stats

	W	L	ERA	Sv	IP		AB	H	HR	RBI	Avg
Home	0	1	3.14	0	28.2	LHB	73	19	2	12	.260
Road	4	0	5.56	0	22.2	RHB	129	36	3	21	.279
First Half	0	0	-	0	0.0	Sc Pos	61	18	1	26	.295
Scnd Half	4	1	4.21	0	51.1	Clutch	24	7	1	2	.292

2000 Season

In his first full season as a pro, Mark Buehrle reached the big leagues and also struck out Alex Rodriguez in the playoffs. Buehrle was a Double-A All-Star before joining the Sox on July 16, and he showed amazing polish for a kid with barely 200 innings in the minors. He got three starts for the Sox, but was best as the second lefty in the bullpen.

Pitching & Defense

Buehrle's biggest asset is his otherworldly poise on the mound. He almost always works ahead in the count and isn't afraid to throw inside. He has command of as many as five pitches. His fastball rarely tops 91-92 MPH, but he keeps hitters guessing with two sliders, a curveball and an improving changeup. His confidence in his changeup has improved to the point where he can use it in fastball counts. His move to first thoroughly flummoxed baserunners in the Southern League, where he picked off 20 runners last year. He did have one error with the Sox but countered that with a pair of double plays.

2001 Outlook

Buehrle's future is in the starting rotation. He reminds some scouts of a young Tom Glavine. He probably will remain in the pen in the spring before joining the rotation near midseason.

Cal Eldred

Position: SP
Bats: R **Throws:** R
Ht: 6' 4" **Wt:** 237

Opening Day Age: 33
Born: 11/24/67 in Cedar Rapids, IA
ML Seasons: 10

Overall Statistics

	W	L	Pct.	ERA	G	GS	Sv	IP	H	BB	SO	HR	Ratio
2000	10	2	.833	4.58	20	20	0	112.0	103	59	97	12	1.45
Career	74	67	.525	4.52	194	189	0	1190.2	1160	507	783	149	1.40

2000 Situational Stats

	W	L	ERA	Sv	IP		AB	H	HR	RBI	Avg
Home	4	0	3.38	0	40.0	LHB	209	49	7	28	.234
Road	6	2	5.25	0	72.0	RHB	214	54	5	22	.252
First Half	10	2	4.76	0	104.0	Sc Pos	106	29	3	39	.274
Scnd Half	0	0	2.25	0	8.0	Clutch	9	2	0	0	.222

2000 Season

Cal Eldred rebounded from back-to-back seasons plagued by injuries to have a terrific first half, then got hurt again. His 10-2 run played a big role in the White Sox' Central Division championship, but Eldred wasn't able to enjoy the success. He was sidelined with elbow problems after the All-Star break. He did everything he could to pitch—even having a five-inch screw placed in his elbow—but couldn't throw in the playoffs.

Pitching & Defense

When the White Sox traded for Eldred, they did so based on scouting reports that said he was throwing 87-88 MPH. They were happily shocked when he arrived in Arizona with gas. He was throwing 93-94 MPH in June, when he was in the middle of an eight-game winning streak. Eldred also had more movement on his curveball than he had in years, and he has a good changeup. Control can be a problem. Eldred is a good athlete who fields his position well, but struggles holding baserunners.

2001 Outlook

Eldred was diagnosed with first neuritis in his right elbow and then a stress fracture below his elbow. He hopes to be fine by spring training, where he will prepare to re-join the Sox' rotation after signing a one-year, $1 million deal.

Tony Graffanino

Position: 2B/SS/3B
Bats: R **Throws:** R
Ht: 6' 1" **Wt:** 195

Opening Day Age: 28
Born: 6/6/72 in
Amityville, NY
ML Seasons: 5
Pronunciation:
graf-a-NEEN-oh

Overall Statistics

	G	AB	R	H	D	T	HR	RBI	SB	BB	SO	Avg	OBP	Slg
2000	70	168	33	46	6	1	2	17	7	22	27	.274	.363	.357
Career	340	819	125	204	39	8	17	80	17	85	176	.249	.322	.379

2000 Situational Stats

	AB	H	HR	RBI	Avg		AB	H	HR	RBI	Avg
Home	79	21	1	9	.266	LHP	58	13	2	8	.224
Road	89	25	1	8	.281	RHP	110	33	0	9	.300
First Half	67	23	0	7	.343	Sc Pos	43	12	1	16	.279
Scnd Half	101	23	2	10	.228	Clutch	16	4	0	1	.250

2000 Season

Like Herbert Perry, Tony Graffanino wound up in the playoffs with the White Sox after being discarded by Tampa Bay. Graffanino was acquired in a May trade for reliever Tanyon Sturtze and filled the Sox' need for a utility infielder. He served as a backup for shortstop Jose Valentin and also started games at second base and third.

Hitting, Baserunning & Defense

Graffanino has hit well in a reserve role throughout his career. He can drive mistake pitches and has improved his ability to make contact. He's also more disciplined at the dish. In 2000, he struck out only five more times than he walked. Graffanino is a smart fielder with good hands, but his range and his arm are below average. He has a quick release that helps him on the double-play pivot. He is a good baserunner with average speed, and he has a knack for breaking up double plays.

2001 Outlook

Graffanino, who is arbitration eligible, has to be careful about not pricing himself out of Chicago's plans. His experience is a plus, but the deep stable of young talent in the organization—especially pitching—could make it tough to keep Graffanino on the 40-man roster. If he does stick around, it's hard to see him getting more than 200 at-bats.

Bob Howry

Tough on Lefties

Position: RP
Bats: L **Throws:** R
Ht: 6' 5" **Wt:** 215

Opening Day Age: 27
Born: 8/4/73 in
Phoenix, AZ
ML Seasons: 3

Overall Statistics

	W	L	Pct.	ERA	G	GS	Sv	IP	H	BB	SO	HR	Ratio
2000	2	4	.333	3.17	65	0	7	71.0	54	29	60	6	1.17
Career	7	10	.412	3.31	178	0	44	193.0	149	86	191	21	1.22

2000 Situational Stats

	W	L	ERA	Sv	IP		AB	H	HR	RBI	Avg
Home	0	2	4.45	3	28.1	LHB	121	21	2	7	.174
Road	2	2	2.32	4	42.2	RHB	129	33	4	24	.256
First Half	1	1	3.20	4	39.1	Sc Pos	67	14	2	27	.209
Scnd Half	1	3	3.13	3	31.2	Clutch	134	29	2	20	.216

2000 Season

Bob Howry produced another solid year. He switched roles with Foulke during a shaky April, and made only ninth-inning cameos the rest of the season. Yet Howry actually lowered his ERA from 1999, when he had 28 saves. He finished with a career-high 71 innings in 2000 and earned seven saves along the way, but he wasn't going strong at season's end and had shoulder surgery a week after the campaign ended.

Pitching & Defense

In the spring, Howry tried to pick up a changeup from Foulke—with little success. Howry remains mostly a one-pitch pitcher, challenging hitters with a fastball that reaches 94 MPH. While he'll throw a curve when he's ahead in the count, he isn't the type to trick hitters. Still, he's effective against both lefthanded and righthanded batsmen. He moves well for a big man and does a good job fielding his position. His delivery to the plate can be slow, giving runners a chance to get a good jump.

2001 Outlook

Howry's surgery was not considered too serious. He should return for a fourth season in the White Sox' bullpen, probably as Foulke's setup man. If Foulke falters, the Sox enjoy the luxury of having two relievers with a closer's mentality.

Chicago (AL)

Mark Johnson

Position: C
Bats: L **Throws:** R
Ht: 6' 0" **Wt:** 185

Opening Day Age: 25
Born: 9/12/75 in Wheat Ridge, CO
ML Seasons: 3

Overall Statistics

	G	AB	R	H	D	T	HR	RBI	SB	BB	SO	Avg	OBP	Slg
2000	75	213	29	48	11	0	3	23	3	27	40	.225	.315	.319
Career	155	443	58	97	22	2	7	40	6	64	106	.219	.320	.325

2000 Situational Stats

	AB	H	HR	RBI	Avg		AB	H	HR	RBI	Avg
Home	109	22	2	15	.202	LHP	23	4	0	3	.174
Road	104	26	1	8	.250	RHP	190	44	3	20	.232
First Half	148	33	3	18	.223	Sc Pos	64	13	2	21	.203
Scnd Half	65	15	0	5	.231	Clutch	24	6	0	3	.250

2000 Season

For the second year in a row, Mark Johnson served as the White Sox' backup catcher. He platooned with Brook Fordyce and Josh Paul early in the season, but saw his playing time dwindle after Charles Johnson was acquired. He nearly duplicated his 1999 numbers, performing well behind the plate while doing the little things as a hitter.

Hitting, Baserunning & Defense

Johnson is a .219 career hitter, but seldom is an easy out because he has terrific strike-zone judgment. His career on-base percentage is a respectable .320. He sees very few lefthanded pitchers and has trouble against them. He is a good bunter and a good athlete who runs well for a catcher. Pitchers like throwing to Johnson. He is an old-style receiver who works to get the best out of his battery-mates. He has an average arm but has developed a quick release, throwing out 33.3 percent of runners last year.

2001 Outlook

Johnson was dropped from the playoff roster before Game 1 against Seattle in favor of a more versatile Josh Paul, yet the White Sox are going to count on Johnson to help them return to the playoffs. He won't be the starter, though, as the Sox signed Sandy Alomar to be the starting catcher.

Herbert Perry

Position: 3B
Bats: R **Throws:** R
Ht: 6' 2" **Wt:** 220

Opening Day Age: 31
Born: 9/15/69 in Live Oak, FL
ML Seasons: 5

Overall Statistics

	G	AB	R	H	D	T	HR	RBI	SB	BB	SO	Avg	OBP	Slg
2000	116	411	71	124	30	1	12	62	4	24	75	.302	.350	.467
Career	245	803	125	230	54	3	21	118	6	57	148	.286	.347	.440

2000 Situational Stats

	AB	H	HR	RBI	Avg		AB	H	HR	RBI	Avg
Home	210	71	7	31	.338	LHP	81	24	1	10	.296
Road	201	53	5	31	.264	RHP	330	100	11	52	.303
First Half	174	53	6	23	.305	Sc Pos	117	39	3	48	.333
Scnd Half	237	71	6	39	.300	Clutch	53	12	3	8	.226

2000 Season

Perry spent almost a full season in the major leagues for the first time, albeit with two teams. A strong spring and an injury to Vinny Castilla led to a job on the Opening Day roster, but he later was put on waivers by Tampa Bay. He landed on his feet with the White Sox and emerged as the regular third baseman. Though he was slowed by injuries late in the year, Perry provided more than his share of clutch hits and played a solid third base.

Hitting, Baserunning & Defense

Perry was at his best in big situations last year. He is a smart hitter who doesn't swing at many bad pitches. He hits the ball all over the field and has a quick swing that makes him a threat even against fireballers. He crowds the plate and isn't intimidated by inside pitches. Perry is considered an excellent defensive first baseman but lacks range at third. He makes the plays on balls hit to him and has an accurate arm. A series of knee injuries has robbed him of his speed.

2001 Outlook

Perry's playing time is likely to fall off if he remains in Chicago. Joe Crede could come out of spring training as the Sox' regular third sacker. If Crede starts at Triple-A Charlotte, he's unlikely to stay there beyond midseason.

Bill Simas

Position: RP
Bats: L **Throws:** R
Ht: 6' 3" **Wt:** 235

Opening Day Age: 29
Born: 11/28/71 in
Hanford, CA
ML Seasons: 6
Pronunciation:
SEE-muss
Nickname: Steamer

Overall Statistics

	W	L	Pct.	ERA	G	GS	Sv	IP	H	BB	SO	HR	Ratio
2000	2	3	.400	3.46	60	0	0	67.2	69	22	49	9	1.34
Career	18	19	.486	3.83	308	0	23	338.1	332	149	265	39	1.42

2000 Situational Stats

	W	L	ERA	Sv	IP		AB	H	HR	RBI	Avg
Home	0	1	3.18	0	34.0	LHB	94	27	5	16	.287
Road	2	2	3.74	0	33.2	RHB	156	42	4	21	.269
First Half	1	2	3.45	0	44.1	Sc Pos	60	13	3	30	.217
Scnd Half	1	1	3.47	0	23.1	Clutch	78	24	0	11	.308

2000 Season

Bill Simas has been a reliable reliever for the White Sox throughout his six-year major league career. He's never pitched better than he did last season, however, finishing with a career-low 3.46 ERA. It was his first year since his inaugural campaign without a save, yet he did well as a middle man. He got a lot of tough outs, but seldom pitched after the seventh inning.

Pitching & Defense

There's nothing tricky about Simas. He is a fast-ball-sinkerball pitcher who isn't afraid to challenge hitters. He gets hurt when he leaves pitches up in the strike zone and gives up too many home runs. In 2000, Simas did a better job of getting ahead in the count, which allowed him to work the corners of the plate rather than have to fire fastballs over the middle. Simas is a good fielder who knocks down a lot of comebackers. He has a slow move to first base, but his slide step was so effective he didn't allow a single stolen base.

2001 Outlook

With one year left on his two-year contract, Simas will add depth to someone's bullpen. The White Sox' pen is becoming a crowded house so a trade is possible. Wherever he is, Simas will do the dirty work without complaint. It's all he's ever done.

Kelly Wunsch

Tough on Lefties

Position: RP
Bats: L **Throws:** L
Ht: 6' 5" **Wt:** 192

Opening Day Age: 28
Born: 7/12/72 in
Houston, TX
ML Seasons: 1

Overall Statistics

	W	L	Pct.	ERA	G	GS	Sv	IP	H	BB	SO	HR	Ratio
2000	6	3	.667	2.93	83	0	1	61.1	50	29	51	4	1.29
Career	6	3	.667	2.93	83	0	1	61.1	50	29	51	4	1.29

2000 Situational Stats

	W	L	ERA	Sv	IP		AB	H	HR	RBI	Avg
Home	5	2	1.78	1	35.1	LHB	106	17	1	12	.160
Road	1	1	4.50	0	26.0	RHB	120	33	3	18	.275
First Half	3	2	2.48	0	36.1	Sc Pos	62	13	0	22	.210
Scnd Half	3	1	3.60	1	25.0	Clutch	102	29	1	14	.284

2000 Season

Kelly Wunsch came from nowhere to fill the White Sox' annual void in the left side of the bullpen. He won a job with Chicago in spring training, and went on to lead the American League with 83 appearances. That's an impressive performance for a rookie who never had pitched in more than 38 games a year as a pro.

Pitching & Defense

Wunsch succeeds with a sidearm motion rarely seen from a lefthander. It not only made him nasty against lefthanded hitters, who hit .160 against him in 2000, but also gave him deception that kept righthanded hitters off balance. He throws in the high 80s and has a sweeping curveball and a changeup. But in his specialty role, Wunsch rarely needs more than his fastball. His unusual delivery causes him to fall off the mound, which limits his ability on comebackers. He has a good move to first base and did an excellent job of controlling the running game last season.

2001 Outlook

For the first time in years, the Sox enter a campaign with a lefty reliever whom they are counting on. Wunsch should approach his rookie numbers, but he'll have to make some adjustments against lefthanded hitters who saw him a lot last year.

Other Chicago White Sox

Jeff Abbott (**Pos**: CF/LF/RF, **Age**: 28, **Bats**: R)

	G	AB	R	H	D	T	HR	RBI	SB	BB	SO	Avg	OBP	Slg
2000	80	215	31	59	15	1	3	29	2	21	38	.274	.343	.395
Career	205	554	77	146	30	2	18	78	6	35	84	.264	.306	.422

Abbott will likely never be a regular, but he can play any outfield position and isn't a bad hitter. He handled righthanders better than southpaws last year. Abbott was dealt to Florida in December. 2001 Outlook: B

Kevin Beirne (**Pos**: RHP, **Age**: 27)

	W	L	Pct.	ERA	G	GS	Sv	IP	H	BB	SO	HR	Ratio
2000	1	3	.250	6.70	29	1	0	49.2	50	20	41	9	1.41
Career	1	3	.250	6.70	29	1	0	49.2	50	20	41	9	1.41

The White Sox have a lot of pitching prospects in their system, so it may be tough for Beirne to avoid getting passed over. His best chance will likely have to be in the bullpen. 2001 Outlook: C

Rocky Biddle (**Pos**: RHP, **Age**: 24)

	W	L	Pct.	ERA	G	GS	Sv	IP	H	BB	SO	HR	Ratio
2000	1	2	.333	8.34	4	4	0	22.2	31	8	7	5	1.72
Career	1	2	.333	8.34	4	4	0	22.2	31	8	7	5	1.72

Biddle missed all of 1999 due to injury, but made a successful recovery in Double-A last year. He has no experience above that level besides his brief time in the majors. 2001 Outlook: C

Chad Bradford (**Pos**: RHP, **Age**: 26)

	W	L	Pct.	ERA	G	GS	Sv	IP	H	BB	SO	HR	Ratio
2000	1	0	1.000	1.98	12	0	0	13.2	13	1	9	0	1.02
Career	3	1	.750	4.13	44	0	1	48.0	49	13	20	1	1.29

Bradford hadn't allowed an ERA above 2.11 in his last three minor league seasons, so last year's effort with the White Sox wasn't out of character. Still, he was traded to Oakland in December. 2001 Outlook: C

McKay Christensen (**Pos**: CF, **Age**: 25, **Bats**: L)

	G	AB	R	H	D	T	HR	RBI	SB	BB	SO	Avg	OBP	Slg
2000	32	19	4	2	0	0	0	1	1	2	6	.105	.227	.105
Career	60	72	14	14	1	0	1	7	3	6	13	.194	.259	.250

A former first-round pick of the Angels, Christensen is a fine defensive outfielder and has the speed to steal bases. He just doesn't make enough hard contact to be an offensive plus. 2001 Outlook: C

Scott Eyre (**Pos**: LHP, **Age**: 28)

	W	L	Pct.	ERA	G	GS	Sv	IP	H	BB	SO	HR	Ratio
2000	1	1	.500	6.63	13	1	0	19.0	29	12	16	3	2.16
Career	9	14	.391	5.66	78	29	0	211.2	243	122	142	44	1.72

No longer in the White Sox' plans as a starter, Eyre saved some games while posting more strikeouts than hits allowed at Triple-A last year. He was traded to Toronto in November. 2001 Outlook: C

Ken Hill (**Pos**: RHP, **Age**: 35)

	W	L	Pct.	ERA	G	GS	Sv	IP	H	BB	SO	HR	Ratio
2000	5	8	.385	7.16	18	17	0	81.2	107	59	50	16	2.03
Career	117	108	.520	4.03	327	315	0	1965.2	1928	847	1179	158	1.41

The Angels and White Sox both released Hill last year and he may be near the end of the line. It's unclear whether he would accept a bullpen role if he can't start somewhere. 2001 Outlook: C

Jeff Liefer (**Pos**: RF, **Age**: 26, **Bats**: L)

	G	AB	R	H	D	T	HR	RBI	SB	BB	SO	Avg	OBP	Slg
2000	5	11	0	2	0	0	0	0	0	0	4	.182	.182	.182
Career	50	124	8	30	7	1	0	14	2	8	32	.242	.286	.315

Liefer slugged over 30 homers at Triple-A last season. He is up for a reserve role, as the Sox are set at the positions he plays best, first base and the outfield. 2001 Outlook: B

Sean Lowe (**Pos**: RHP, **Age**: 30)

	W	L	Pct.	ERA	G	GS	Sv	IP	H	BB	SO	HR	Ratio
2000	4	1	.800	5.48	50	5	0	70.2	78	39	53	10	1.66
Career	8	7	.533	5.19	124	10	0	189.0	206	100	125	23	1.62

After being used exclusively in relief in 1999, Lowe had some shoulder problems and saw his ERA rise by almost two runs last season. He was actually a little more effective in his five starts. 2001 Outlook: B

Greg Norton (**Pos**: 3B/1B, **Age**: 28, **Bats**: B)

	G	AB	R	H	D	T	HR	RBI	SB	BB	SO	Avg	OBP	Slg
2000	71	201	25	49	6	1	6	28	1	26	47	.244	.333	.373
Career	337	993	134	245	51	5	33	118	8	127	231	.247	.334	.408

After serving as the White Sox' primary third baseman in 1999, Norton lost the job to Herbert Perry last year. Joe Crede is also in Chicago's future there, so Norton now may be stuck on the bench. 2001 Outlook: B

Craig Wilson (**Pos**: 3B, **Age**: 30, **Bats**: R)

	G	AB	R	H	D	T	HR	RBI	SB	BB	SO	Avg	OBP	Slg
2000	28	73	12	19	3	0	0	4	1	5	11	.260	.316	.301
Career	139	372	54	101	16	1	7	40	3	31	39	.272	.328	.376

Wilson had back problems and the White Sox had better infield options, so he saw most of his action at Triple-A last year. Despite batting .370 there, Chicago released him in November, and he signed a minor league deal with the Royals. 2001 Outlook: C

Chicago White Sox Minor League Prospects

Organization Overview:

The White Sox already had Jim Parque, Lorenzo Barcelo, Mark Buehrle, Jon Garland, Aaron Myette and Kip Wells in the system prior to the 1999 draft. That June they added Matt Ginter, Jon Rauch, Jason Stumm and Dan Wright. Those '99 draft choices will contribute to a promising future for the White Sox. Yet, little did the Sox brass know when they drafted in 1999 that the first taste of the future would come as soon as 2000. With homegrown products of the 1990s leading the way—from Frank Thomas and Ray Durham to more recent arrivals Mike Sirotka, Magglio Ordonez, Carlos Lee and Parque—the Sox put an end to Cleveland's reign over the American League Central. The key long term questions facing Chicago involve catching, third base, center field and the starting rotation. Josh Paul, Joe Crede, last summer's first-round pick Joe Borchard, and more than a half-dozen homegrown hurlers may provide answers.

Joe Borchard

Position: OF   **Opening Day Age:** 22
Bats: B **Throws:** R   **Born:** 11/25/78 in
Ht: 6' 5" **Wt:** 220   Panorama City, CA

Recent Statistics

	G	AB	R	H	D	T	HR	RBI	SB	BB	SO	Avg
2000 R White Sox	7	29	3	12	4	0	0	8	0	4	4	.414
2000 A Winston-Sal	14	52	7	15	3	0	2	7	0	6	9	.288
2000 AA Birmingham	6	22	3	5	0	1	0	3	0	3	8	.227

After going 12th overall and signing for a stunning $5.3 million last summer, Borchard split time between the White Sox' Rookie-level team in Arizona and high Class-A Winston-Salem before finishing the season at Double-A Birmingham. If not for signing with the White Sox, he probably would be quarterbacking the Stanford football squad this fall. The athletic Borchard has terrific tools; he comes equipped with power potential from both sides of the plate, solid skills in right field and an excellent arm. This spring he will work with minor league outfield instructor Gary Pettis to see if he can handle center field, where eventually he would work between young studs Carlos Lee and Magglio Ordonez.

Joe Crede

Position: 3B   **Opening Day Age:** 22
Bats: R **Throws:** R   **Born:** 4/26/78 in
Ht: 6' 3" **Wt:** 195   Jefferson City, MO

Recent Statistics

	G	AB	R	H	D	T	HR	RBI	SB	BB	SO	Avg
2000 AA Birmingham	138	533	84	163	35	0	21	94	3	56	111	.306
2000 AL Chicago	7	14	2	5	1	0	0	3	0	0	3	.357
2000 MLE	138	528	82	158	34	0	20	92	2	46	117	.299

Drafted in the fifth round in 1996, Crede had a breakout season in the high Class-A Carolina League in 1998, nearly claiming Triple Crown honors despite a painful bone spur in his right big toe. The injury lingered into 1999, and the pain forced season-ending surgery that July. Crede returned to his '98 form last summer at Double-A Birmingham, hitting for both average and power, which should carry over to the majors. Defensively, Crede has come along nicely, though he's still working on his lateral-movement footwork at third. If he doesn't unseat Herbert Perry at third this spring, look for Crede to play at Triple-A Charlotte.

Jon Garland

Position: P   **Opening Day Age:** 21
Bats: R **Throws:** R   **Born:** 9/27/79 in
Ht: 6' 6" **Wt:** 205   Valencia, CA

Recent Statistics

	W	L	ERA	G	GS	Sv	IP	H	R	BB	SO	HR
2000 AAA Charlotte	9	2	2.26	16	16	0	103.2	99	28	32	63	3
2000 AA Birmingham	0	0	0.00	1	1	0	6.0	4	0	1	10	0
2000 AL Chicago	4	8	6.46	15	13	0	69.2	82	55	40	42	10

A first-round pick of the Cubs in 1997, Garland was dealt to the White Sox for Matt Karchner in a 1998 trade that may haunt the North Side team for years. Garland has developed quickly with the help of a devastating low-90s sinker that has been compared to Kevin Brown's. His curveball also is advanced, and work continues on a slider he added in 1999. Garland opened the 2000 season by dominating the Triple-A International League before debuting with the Sox on July 4. He turned in a quality start in his second major league game against Milwaukee, but mostly struggled the rest of the way. Sox GM Ken Williams believes the key to Garland's success is learning to trust his stuff within the strike zone.

Matt Ginter

Position: P   **Opening Day Age:** 23
Bats: R **Throws:** R   **Born:** 12/24/77 in
Ht: 6' 1" **Wt:** 215   Lexington, KY

Recent Statistics

	W	L	ERA	G	GS	Sv	IP	H	R	BB	SO	HR
2000 AA Birmingham	11	8	2.25	27	26	0	179.2	153	72	60	126	6
2000 AL Chicago	1	0	13.50	7	0	0	9.1	18	14	7	6	5

The Sox' first-round pick in 1999, Ginter missed his chance to join Jon Rauch on the 2000 Olympic team when he was promoted to Chicago in September. He didn't fare well in seven relief appearances. By the time Ginter had arrived, however, he had far exceeded his highest single-season innings total and tired considerably, which especially hurt his slider. During the Double-A season, Ginter had made outstanding progress on all of his pitches. He throws a mid-90s fastball and a nasty slider. He also improved upon a changeup that will serve him well if he continues to start, but with his power pitches and the riches of the White Sox' system, closing may be his calling.

Josh Paul

Position: C	**Opening Day Age:** 25	
Bats: R **Throws:** R	**Born:** 5/19/75 in	
Ht: 6' 1" **Wt:** 185	Evanston, IL	

Recent Statistics

	G	AB	R	H	D	T	HR	RBI	SB	BB	SO	Avg
2000 AAA Charlotte	51	168	28	40	5	1	4	19	6	13	38	.238
2000 AL Chicago	36	71	15	20	3	2	1	8	1	5	17	.282

Paul's development as a hitter may have been slowed when he broke the hamate bone in his right wrist in 1997. Still, he's an athletic catcher with advanced receiving and leadership skills. A second-round pick in '96, he made the team last spring after starting catcher Brook Fordyce broke his foot in March. Paul spent the first six weeks of the season and all of September with the Sox, and hit better with the big club than he did at Triple-A Charlotte. Sox GM Ken Williams figures that Paul must turn it up a notch, becoming a more tenacious hitter. The Sox still expect him to emerge offensively, and with his arm, quickness and solid makeup behind the plate, he should be in the mix for 2001.

Jon Rauch

Position: P	**Opening Day Age:** 22	
Bats: R **Throws:** R	**Born:** 9/27/78 in	
Ht: 6' 10" **Wt:** 230	Louisville, KY	

Recent Statistics

	W	L	ERA	G	GS	Sv	IP	H	R	BB	SO	HR
1999 R Bristol	4	4	4.45	14	9	2	56.2	65	44	16	66	4
1999 A Winston-Sal	0	0	3.00	1	1	0	6.0	4	3	3	7	1
2000 A Winston-Sal	11	3	2.86	18	18	0	110.0	102	49	33	124	10
2000 AA Birmingham	5	1	2.25	8	8	0	56.0	36	18	16	63	4

After a decent debut in the rookie-level Appy League in 1999, the 6-foot-10 Rauch took his 94-MPH fastball to the high Class-A Carolina League and dominated. For someone his size, he showed a remarkable mix of power and control. He has a very good arm and superb mechanics. He moved on to Double-A Birmingham in July, and went 5-1 (2.25) while allowing a miniscule .179 batting average. He might have reached Chicago by September, but instead pitched on the gold-medal Olympic team, for which he fanned 21 batters in 13 innings against South Africa and Cuba. After Rauch's stunning emergence in his second pro season, *Baseball America* named him the Minor League Player of the Year.

Aaron Rowand

Position: OF	**Opening Day Age:** 23	
Bats: R **Throws:** R	**Born:** 8/29/77 in	
Ht: 6' 1" **Wt:** 200	Portland, OR	

Recent Statistics

	G	AB	R	H	D	T	HR	RBI	SB	BB	SO	Avg
1999 A Winston-Sal	133	512	96	143	37	3	24	88	15	33	94	.279
2000 AA Birmingham	139	532	80	137	26	5	20	98	22	38	117	.258
2000 MLE	139	528	78	133	25	4	19	96	17	31	124	.252

Drafted in 1998, Rowand has excelled as a run producer in his three minor league seasons. In 2000, he batted .258-20-98 and led the Double-A Southern League in RBI. Rowand also is a solid right fielder with good range. His strongest tool is an outfield arm that managers rated the best in the Southern League, according to *Baseball America*. While Rowand's quick bat is a big plus, the Sox would like him to pull less and go to right field more. He also needs to be more selective at the plate and reduce the difference between his strikeouts and walks. Rowand is nearly ready for Chicago, but he's blocked from regular duty by Magglio Ordonez and Carlos Lee.

Kip Wells

Position: P	**Opening Day Age:** 23	
Bats: R **Throws:** R	**Born:** 4/21/77 in	
Ht: 6' 3" **Wt:** 196	Houston, TX	

Recent Statistics

	W	L	ERA	G	GS	Sv	IP	H	R	BB	SO	HR
2000 AAA Charlotte	5	3	5.37	12	12	0	62.0	67	38	27	38	10
2000 AL Chicago	6	9	6.02	20	20	0	98.2	126	76	58	71	15

Chicago's first-round pick in 1998, Wells waited until that December to sign, but was with the White Sox eight months later. A deceptive delivery makes his low-90s fastball difficult to pick up, and his sharp-breaking curve gives hitters even more trouble. Wells was impressive in winning four of seven starts with the Sox late in 1999, but the solid command of his pitches that he had in his debut all but deserted him for long stretches last summer. He made the Opening Day roster, but executed just four quality starts in 15 outings before a demotion to Triple-A Charlotte on July 1. Wells made some adjustments to smooth out his delivery late last season, and the Sox are hoping his command will be back on track in 2001.

Others to Watch

Righthander **Josh Fogg** (24) continues to pitch well at each level since being drafted by the Sox in 1998. He was 11-7 (2.57) at Double-A Birmingham in 2000, moving four average pitches around the strike zone effectively. He has a great feel for pitching. . . Acquired from Oakland in December in exchange for pitcher Chad Bradford, catcher **Miguel Olivo** (22) has a throwing arm that is compared to Ivan Rodriguez'. The rest of his catching game isn't as far along, but he continues to progress. A broken hook of the hamate bone in 2000 has slowed his progress, but eventually he should hit for average and power. . . The Sox also traded for **Julio Ramirez** (23) in December. Ramirez is a tools-rich prospect who came from the Marlins in exchange for Jeff Abbott. The two are opposites. Abbott has few tools but can hit, while Ramirez hasn't converted his tools into enough useful skills in six pro seasons. Plate discipline is a critical shortcoming for Ramirez. . . A second-round pick in 1999, **Dan Wright** (23) reaches the high 90s with his fastball and he mixes in a hard knuckle-curve with good depth. His changeup has improved enough that he throws it when he's behind in the count. The Sox like how he goes after hitters, which sparked his quick rise to Double-A.

Jacobs Field

Offense

In their seven years at Jacobs Field, the Indians are 325-202 (.617) and have averaged a .294 batting average. Last year they increased their hits, doubles and homers at home, but won just one more game compared to 1999. Lefthanded power hitters have an edge because the measurements in right field are basically the same as left, but the wall is eight feet tall compared to 19 feet in left. Hitters are at a disadvantage in day games, especially against tall lefthanders, because the ball gets lost against a light-colored parking garage behind center field.

Defense

The Indians had the best defense in the American League last year, but still made 42 of their 72 errors at home. The ball gets through the infield grass quickly, and there is an occasional bad hop on the infield dirt. The rubberized warning track gets slippery in wet and cold weather and can trip unsuspecting outfielders. Flyballs don't take true bounces where the left-center and center-field walls merge.

Who It Helps the Most

Russell Branyan, taking advantage of the prevailing wind to right field, hit 13 of his 16 homers at home. He hit .314 at home and .170 on the road. Groundball pitchers Chuck Finley (10-3), Dave Burba (9-3) and Bob Wickman (1-1, eight saves) took advantage of the three Gold Glove winners in the Tribe infield.

Who It Hurts the Most

After hitting .359 at the Jake in 1999, Omar Vizquel dropped to .254 last year. He hit .319 on the road. Catcher Einar Diaz hit .252 at home compared to .287 on the road, though he did hit .326 at Jacobs Field in 1999, so the jury still is out.

Rookies & Newcomers

If rookie pitchers C.C. Sabathia and Danys Baez get called up, they'll have to get used to pitching in front of large crowds in a hitters' ballpark. Steve Woodard will face the same scrutiny should he earn a rotation spot. Free agent Ellis Burks will have to contend with the aforementioned high left-field wall when he's at the plate.

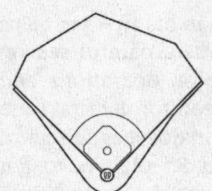

Dimensions: LF-325, LCF-370, CF-405, RCF-375, RF-325

Capacity: 42,865

Elevation: 660 feet

Surface: Grass

Foul Territory: Small

Park Factors

2000 Season

	Home Games			Away Games			
	Indians	Opp	Total	Indians	Opp	Total	Index
G	72	72	144	72	72	144	—
Avg	.297	.272	.284	.286	.274	.280	101
AB	2488	2572	5060	2590	2402	4992	101
R	439	366	805	417	372	789	102
H	738	700	1438	741	658	1399	103
2B	132	146	278	148	123	271	101
3B	15	18	33	13	10	23	142
HR	106	71	177	84	79	163	107
BB	304	291	595	297	302	599	98
SO	439	545	984	480	538	1018	95
E	36	62	98	27	57	84	117
E-Infield	30	51	81	22	47	69	117
LHB-Avg	.303	.258	.281	.270	.283	.276	102
LHB-HR	62	36	98	40	34	74	127
RHB-Avg	.290	.284	.287	.301	.267	.284	101
RHB-HR	44	35	79	44	45	89	90

1998-2000

	Home Games			Away Games			
	Indians	Opp	Total	Indians	Opp	Total	Index
G	217	217	434	217	217	434	—
Avg	.293	.279	.286	.274	.265	.270	106
AB	7397	7794	15191	7719	7273	14992	101
R	1300	1151	2451	1233	1069	2302	106
H	2170	2174	4344	2117	1930	4047	107
2B	404	456	860	456	371	827	103
3B	45	42	87	40	42	82	105
HR	294	243	537	258	239	497	107
BB	917	846	1763	906	815	1721	101
SO	1338	1573	2911	1504	1447	2951	97
E	152	172	324	106	158	264	123
E-Infield	121	138	259	86	129	215	120
LHB-Avg	.298	.276	.287	.271	.267	.269	107
LHB-HR	141	126	267	121	109	230	114
RHB-Avg	.289	.282	.285	.278	.264	.271	105
RHB-HR	153	117	270	137	130	267	100

2000 Rankings (American League)

- Third-highest error factor
- Third-highest LHB home-run factor

Cleveland

Charlie Manuel

2000 Season

Charlie Manuel won 90 games in his first year as a big league manager. Still, it was a painful season because he underwent two colon operations and the Indians missed the postseason for the first time in six years. Manuel needed a major league record 32 pitchers and a club record 55 players to get through an injury-marred season. He clashed with Roberto Alomar twice because Alomar didn't feel he was protected after being hit by pitches. In the second half, however, Manuel led the Indians to the best record in the American League at 46-30, missing the American League wild-card by one game.

Offense

Manuel likes a wide-open offense. Kenny Lofton, Omar Vizquel and Robbie Alomar always have the green light to steal, and he lets most of his power hitters swing on 3-0 counts. He used a set lineup when players were healthy and seldom went to his bench, especially in the last two months of the season when the season seemed to ride on each and every game. He made average use of the sacrifice bunt, didn't call one squeeze play and registered the second most intentional walks in the league.

Pitching & Defense

When he managed in the minors, Manuel tried to show patience with starting pitchers. While he was patient in certain instances last year, he used a quick hook in the last two months of the season with the playoffs at stake. He had the second busiest bullpen in the league and down the stretch consistently used Paul Shuey, Steve Karsay and Bob Wickman in the final two or three innings. Manuel had the good fortune to manage the best defense in the league, a unit that featured three Gold Glove infielders.

2001 Outlook

If Manuel's health holds, he'll be a better manager this year. But will the Indians be a better team? They lost cleanup hitter Manny Ramirez to Boston and catcher Sandy Alomar Jr. to the rival White Sox. Manuel may have gotten his big break at the wrong time. After dominating the AL Central for five years, the division—or at the very least the White Sox—has caught up to the Indians.

Born: 1/04/44 in Northfork, WV

Playing Experience: 1969-1975, Min, LA

Managerial Experience: 1 season

Manager Statistics

Year	Team, Lg	W	L	Pct	GB	Finish
2000	Cleveland, AL	90	72	.556	5.0	2nd Central
1 Season		90	72	.556	—	—

2000 Starting Pitchers by Days Rest

	<=3	4	5	6+
Indians Starts	4	85	36	27
Indians ERA	3.98	4.93	5.06	6.11
AL Avg Starts	2	88	40	22
AL ERA	4.87	5.03	5.03	5.28

2000 Situational Stats

	Charlie Manuel	AL Average
Hit & Run Success %	37.0	35.1
Stolen Base Success %	76.9	68.8
Platoon Pct.	64.2	57.8
Defensive Subs	26	23
High-Pitch Outings	20	13
Quick/Slow Hooks	21/12	18/19
Sacrifice Attempts	59	55

2000 Rankings (American League)

- 1st in steals of third base (26) and steals of home plate (2)
- 2nd in stolen-base percentage (76.9%), double steals (6), intentional walks (38), starts on three days rest (4) and relief appearances (462)
- 3rd in starts with over 120 pitches (20) and mid-inning pitching changes (219)

Roberto Alomar

2000 Season

Roberto Alomar had two seasons in one. Bothered by ankle, wrist and shoulder problems, and not seeing eye-to-eye with manager Charlie Manuel, Alomar slumped to .260 on July 17. He rebounded to hit .379 over his last 65 games, including .421 in September, to fuel the Tribe's stretch drive and save his season. He made his 11th trip to the All-Star Game, won his ninth Gold Glove, pocketed his fourth Silver Slugger and had hitting streaks of 17 and 18 games.

Hitting

Alomar is a line-drive hitter who uses the whole field. He has 20-homer power and will change his stance from pitch to pitch to take advantage of certain hurlers, but he will chase fastballs out of the strike zone. Throughout his career, he's hit for a higher average lefthanded than righthanded, but for the second straight campaign he had a higher average from the right side. The majority of his power comes from the left side. He's a good bunter and two-strike hitter. After hitting .392 with runners in scoring position in 1999, his average dropped to .276.

Baserunning & Defense

One of the best basestealers in the game, Alomar finished second in the AL in steals and had the best percentage in the league. He likes to dive into first base on infield grounders and is not afraid to score from first on doubles to right. Alomar's defense remains breathtaking, but he made 15 errors, his most since 1991. He has good range to his left and right and the majority of his errors came on throws. He has a strong arm, especially on relays from the outfield.

2001 Outlook

The Indians need a complete season from Alomar. They need him to be in good health and in a good frame of mind from Opening Day. That means he and Manuel will have to be on the same page, and that may be asking a lot. Their dispute arose when Alomar didn't think Manuel defended him after he'd been hit by pitches.

Position: 2B
Bats: B **Throws:** R
Ht: 6' 0" **Wt:** 185

Opening Day Age: 33
Born: 2/5/68 in Ponce, Puerto Rico
ML Seasons: 13
Pronunciation: AL-uh-mar
Nickname: Robby

Overall Statistics

	G	AB	R	H	D	T	HR	RBI	SB	BB	SO	Avg	OBP	Slg
2000	155	610	111	189	40	2	19	89	39	64	82	.310	.378	.475
Career	1877	7221	1228	2196	412	60	170	918	416	822	878	.304	.375	.448

Where He Hits the Ball

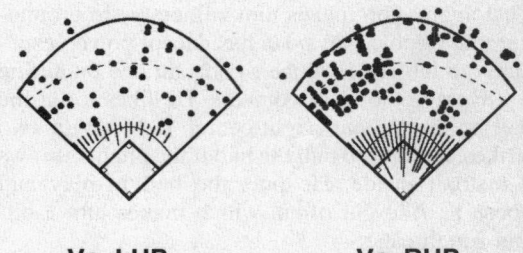

Vs. LHP   **Vs. RHP**

2000 Situational Stats

	AB	H	HR	RBI	Avg		AB	H	HR	RBI	Avg
Home	303	95	8	36	.314	LHP	151	48	3	17	.318
Road	307	94	11	53	.306	RHP	459	141	16	72	.307
First Half	329	88	9	39	.267	Sc Pos	163	45	1	61	.276
Scnd Half	281	101	10	50	.359	Clutch	74	19	3	11	.257

2000 Rankings (American League)

- 1st in stolen-base percentage (90.7) and steals of third (12)
- 2nd in stolen bases and errors at second base (15)
- 4th in lowest fielding percentage at second base (.980)
- Led the Indians in runs scored, hits, doubles, sacrifice bunts (11), stolen bases, GDPs (18), highest groundball/flyball ratio (1.5), stolen-base percentage (90.7), batting average vs. lefthanded pitchers, slugging percentage vs. lefthanded pitchers (.464), steals of third (12) and batting average with two strikes (.274)
- Led AL second basemen in batting average, home runs, hits, singles, total bases (290), RBI, stolen bases, times on base (259) and GDPs (18)

Cleveland

Sandy Alomar Jr.

Position: C
Bats: R **Throws:** R
Ht: 6' 5" **Wt:** 220

Opening Day Age: 34
Born: 6/18/66 in Salinas, Puerto Rico
ML Seasons: 13
Pronunciation: AL-uh-mar

2000 Season

After playing just 37 games in 1999 because of knee surgery, Sandy Alomar Jr. appeared in 97 games last year to complete his 11th season in Cleveland. On the final day of the 2000 campaign, he hit his seventh homer of the year to give him a club-record 91 as a catcher. Alomar went on the disabled list from April 19 to May 8 with a strained right hamstring. He also shared time with Einar Diaz. But in the last three weeks of the season, with the wild-card at stake, he was the regular backstop and hit .288.

Hitting

Alomar is a first-pitch hitter, batting .348 (23-for-66) last year when he put the first offering in play. That aggression makes him vulnerable to grounding into double plays. He has decent power, especially to left field, but he's concentrated on hitting for average the last two years. He likes to hit the ball to center and right-center field. With two strikes, he'll try to pull the ball if the pitcher throws a fastball inside. He puts the ball in play and doesn't strike out often, which makes him a hit-and-run threat.

Baserunning & Defense

Eight knee operations, including seven on his left knee, have taken the spring out of Alomar's step. He still runs hard to first base and will beat out the odd infield hit. He showed his ability to work with a variety of pitchers last year, as the Indians used 32 different hurlers. His game-calling ability is a strength, and he's exceptional when it comes to blocking balls in the dirt. The knee injuries also have hurt his throwing. He was 21-for-96 (22 percent) throwing out baserunners last year.

2001 Outlook

Cleveland traded for Reds catcher Eddie Taubensee in mid-November, and the Tribe also wants to give Diaz more playing time. That spelled the end for Alomar, who wanted to spend the rest of his career with the Indians. The veteran catcher signed a two-year, $5.4 million deal with Cleveland's Central Division rival, the White Sox. Alomar had been a team leader since joining Cleveland in 1990 and will be missed.

Overall Statistics

	G	AB	R	H	D	T	HR	RBI	SB	BB	SO	Avg	OBP	Slg
2000	97	356	44	103	16	2	7	42	2	16	41	.289	.324	.404
Career	993	3429	417	948	195	8	93	459	24	168	390	.276	.315	.419

Where He Hits the Ball

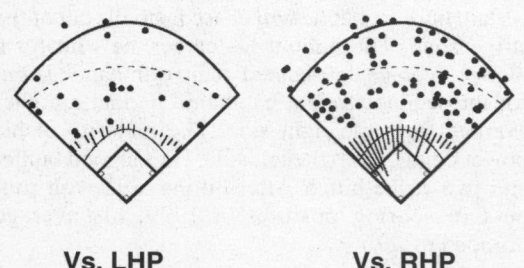

Vs. LHP   Vs. RHP

2000 Situational Stats

	AB	H	HR	RBI	Avg		AB	H	HR	RBI	Avg
Home	196	61	5	21	.311	LHP	74	26	1	8	.351
Road	160	42	2	21	.263	RHP	282	77	6	34	.273
First Half	166	51	3	18	.307	Sc Pos	87	27	2	35	.310
Scnd Half	190	52	4	24	.274	Clutch	39	10	0	3	.256

2000 Rankings (American League)

- 2nd in errors at catcher (8) and lowest fielding percentage at catcher (.989)

Dave Burba

2000 Season

Dave Burba keeps getting better. After consecutive 15-win seasons, he won 16 games last year. He started and finished strong, going 7-1 in his first 12 starts and 8-2 after the All-Star break. The Indians were worried about Burba after he developed forearm and elbow problems late in the 1999 season, but he made 32 starts, reaching the sixth inning 25 times.

Pitching

Burba isn't a pure power pitcher, but he gets a lot of strikeouts because of his 80-84 MPH split-finger fastball. He complements the splitter with a 88-94 MPH fastball, curveball and changeup. Burba's splitter is effective because he throws it with the same downhill style as his fastball. Hitters think it's a fastball when it leaves his hand, but then it sinks below their bats. He gets into trouble when he throws too many splitters and forgets his fastball. He's vulnerable early in the game because he pitches with so much emotion that he overthrows his fastball. He's more effective when he throws 88 MPH instead of 92. In spring training, Burba talked about not throwing his curveball because of his elbow and forearm problems, but he threw it with no problem.

Defense

Burba is an average fielder. If the ball is hit to him, he'll catch it and throw to the right base. He hustles to first base. In the past he has done a good job of holding runners, but last year basestealers were extremely successful going 23-for-27 when he was on the mound.

2001 Outlook

The Indians will be counting on Burba to be their most consistent starter, especially with the uncertain status of starters Charles Nagy and Jaret Wright because of injuries. He's become a solid six- to seven-inning starter. Look for the Indians to follow the schedule they set up for him last year. They limited his work *between* starts—Burba was constantly working on his mechanics—to keep his arm strong, and he responded with career marks in strikeouts and victories.

Position: SP
Bats: R **Throws:** R
Ht: 6' 4" **Wt:** 240

Opening Day Age: 34
Born: 7/7/66 in Dayton, OH
ML Seasons: 11

Overall Statistics

	W	L	Pct.	ERA	G	GS	Sv	IP	H	BB	SO	HR	Ratio
2000	16	6	.727	4.47	32	32	0	191.1	199	91	180	19	1.52
Career	95	70	.576	4.26	376	184	1	1361.1	1322	606	1100	157	1.42

How Often He Throws Strikes

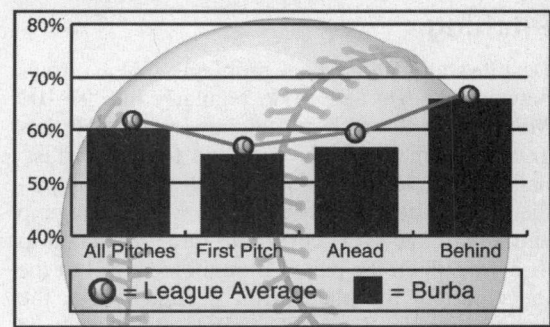

= League Average   = Burba

2000 Situational Stats

	W	L	ERA	Sv	IP		AB	H	HR	RBI	Avg
Home	9	3	5.04	0	110.2	LHB	351	91	8	39	.259
Road	7	3	3.68	0	80.2	RHB	394	108	11	47	.274
First Half	8	4	5.63	0	102.1	Sc Pos	191	45	2	60	.236
Scnd Half	8	2	3.13	0	89.0	Clutch	22	7	0	1	.318

2000 Rankings (American League)

- 3rd in winning percentage
- 4th in stolen bases allowed (23), most strikeouts per nine innings (8.5) and highest stolen-base percentage allowed (85.2)
- 5th in fewest home runs allowed per nine innings (.89), most pitches thrown per batter (3.90) and highest walks per nine innings (4.3)
- 6th in wins, walks allowed, fewest GDPs induced per nine innings (0.5) and highest ERA at home
- 7th in strikeouts
- 8th in most run support per nine innings (6.4)
- Led the Indians in wins, pickoff throws (110), stolen bases allowed (23), most run support per nine innings (6.4), fewest home runs allowed per nine innings (.89) and winning percentage

Bartolo Colon

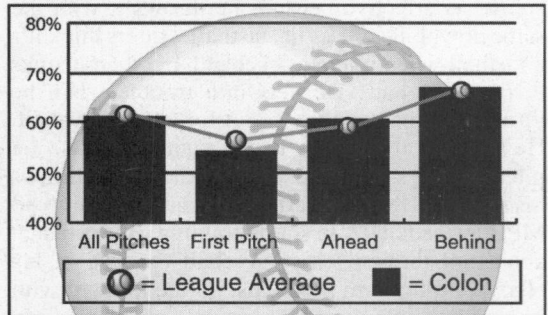

Cy Young Stuff

2000 Season

Bartolo Colon's season began with him rolling into spring training overweight for the second straight year. It ended with him winning three of his last four starts—including a one-hit shutout of the Yankees—in dominating fashion following a meeting with manager Charlie Manuel. In the meeting, Manuel told Colon he wanted him to pitch like a No. 1 starter. After a sluggish first half in which he went on the disabled list with a strained left oblique muscle, he went 6-0 with a 3.05 ERA in 12 starts after August 1. He finished second in the American League with 212 strikeouts to become the first Indian since Dennis Eckersley in 1976 to strike out 200 or more batters in a season.

Pitching

Despite shoulder and knee problems, Colon throws between 95-100 MPH. He regularly hits 97-100 MPH in the seventh and eighth innings. He has great movement on his two- and four-seam fastballs, which he's learning to control. He complements his fastball with an 79-82 MPH changeup and a hard, 82-MPH curveball. Often reluctant to throw inside in the past, Colon took control of the inner part of the plate in the second half at the urging of pitching coach Dick Pole. Before that, he had spent most of his time working hitters away with his fastball.

Defense

Colon's weight hurts his defense. He gets off the mound quickly, but has 10 errors in four seasons. He has taken control of the running game over the last two years, using a slide step and a quick move to the plate to stop baserunners.

2001 Outlook

The Indians will open next season with Colon as their No. 1 starter. If he ever believed he was as good as they think he is, the Indians could have their first 20-game winner since Gaylord Perry in 1974. Colon will send an important signal to management if he accepts that role and comes to spring training in shape and ready to pitch.

Position: SP
Bats: R **Throws:** R
Ht: 6' 0" **Wt:** 230

Opening Day Age: 25
Born: 5/24/75 in Altamira, Dominican Republic
ML Seasons: 4
Pronunciation: bar-TOE-loh ko-LONE

Overall Statistics

	W	L	Pct.	ERA	G	GS	Sv	IP	H	BB	SO	HR	Ratio
2000	15	8	.652	3.88	30	30	0	188.0	163	98	212	21	1.39
Career	51	29	.638	4.09	112	110	0	691.0	660	298	597	72	1.39

How Often He Throws Strikes

2000 Situational Stats

	W	L	ERA	Sv	IP		AB	H	HR	RBI	Avg
Home	6	2	4.34	0	87.0	LHB	335	81	12	35	.242
Road	9	6	3.48	0	101.0	RHB	365	82	9	39	.225
First Half	9	5	4.28	0	88.1	Sc Pos	161	33	3	47	.205
Scnd Half	6	3	3.52	0	99.2	Clutch	43	12	2	6	.279

2000 Rankings (American League)

- 1st in most pitches thrown per batter (4.01)
- 2nd in strikeouts, lowest slugging percentage allowed (.371), most strikeouts per nine innings (10.1) and highest walks per nine innings (4.7)
- 3rd in lowest batting average allowed (.233)
- 4th in walks allowed
- 5th in ERA, lowest stolen-base percentage allowed (42.9), lowest ERA on the road and lowest batting average allowed with runners in scoring position
- Led the Indians in ERA, hit batsmen (4), strikeouts, highest strikeout/walk ratio (2.2), lowest batting average allowed (.233), lowest slugging percentage allowed (.371) and lowest on-base percentage allowed (.329)

Chuck Finley

2000 Season

Chuck Finley signed a three-year, $27 million contract with the Indians in December of 1999 thinking he was guaranteed to make the postseason for the first time since 1986. Cleveland missed by one game, but Finley went 6-1 in September, starting and winning twice on three days rest in his last three starts. He made the All-Star team for the fifth time, and his 16 wins were his most since 1993.

Pitching

The durable Finley throws a fastball, splitter and curveball. His out pitch is the splitter, but he has to concentrate on his 90-92 MPH fastball for his other two pitches to be effective. He changes his pitch patterns well, but usually is at his best when he can throw his fastball for strikes in the early innings and use his offspeed stuff late. He's big and strong and threw over 200 innings for the ninth time in his career. Right after the All-Star break, Finley seemed to have one bad inning in every start. By the time he'd reclaim the strike zone, often the game was over or he was on his way to the showers.

Defense

Finley has a smooth, over the top delivery, but falls off hard to the third-base side of the mound. That and trying to harness his large body led to him leading Tribe pitchers with four errors. He did a nice job holding basestealers, with nine of 22 would-be thieves thrown out on his watch. Teams like to make him field the ball because they know he's never going to win a Gold Glove.

2001 Outlook

Last year was Finley's first in 14 years that he wasn't wearing an Angels uniform. He seemed homesick, and when he struggled after the All-Star break, there were questions about whether he could pitch in pressure situations for a contender. He answered those questions with a strong September. The Indians think their lefthanded ace will feel more comfortable this year, and hopefully won't put so much pressure on himself.

Position: SP
Bats: L **Throws:** L
Ht: 6' 6" **Wt:** 225

Opening Day Age: 38
Born: 11/26/62 in
Monroe, LA
ML Seasons: 15

Overall Statistics

	W	L	Pct.	ERA	G	GS	Sv	IP	H	BB	SO	HR	Ratio
2000	16	11	.593	4.17	34	34	0	218.0	211	101	189	23	1.43
Career	181	151	.545	3.76	470	413	0	2893.0	2755	1219	2340	277	1.37

How Often He Throws Strikes

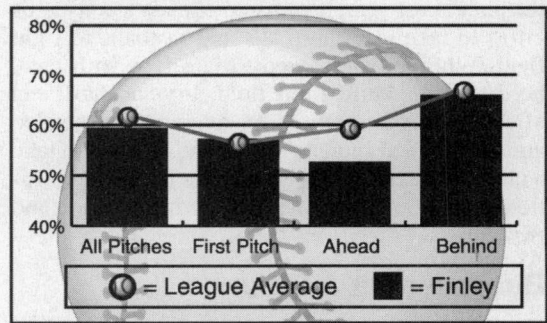

| = League Average | = Finley |

2000 Situational Stats

	W	L	ERA	Sv	IP		AB	H	HR	RBI	Avg
Home	10	3	3.20	0	107.0	LHB	175	42	4	18	.240
Road	6	8	5.11	0	111.0	RHB	649	169	19	72	.260
First Half	7	6	3.73	0	123.0	Sc Pos	170	43	4	61	.253
Scnd Half	9	5	4.74	0	95.0	Clutch	47	12	1	6	.255

2000 Rankings (American League)

- 1st in lowest fielding percentage at pitcher (.886)
- 2nd in walks allowed and errors at pitcher (4)
- 3rd in games started, pitches thrown (3,645), highest groundball/flyball ratio allowed (1.8) and lowest ERA at home
- 4th in strikeouts
- 5th in runners caught stealing (9) and lowest slugging percentage allowed (.392)
- Led the Indians in wins, losses, games started, complete games (3), innings pitched, hits allowed, batters faced (936), home runs allowed, walks allowed, wild pitches (9), pitches thrown (3,645), runners caught stealing (9), GDPs induced (22) and highest groundball/flyball ratio allowed (1.8)

Cleveland

Travis Fryman

Position: 3B
Bats: R **Throws:** R
Ht: 6' 1" **Wt:** 205

Opening Day Age: 32
Born: 3/25/69 in
Lexington, KY
ML Seasons: 11

2000 Season

Travis Fryman had his best overall season last year. He set career highs in batting average, hits and RBI. He won a Gold Glove at third base and went to his fifth All-Star Game, making his first start for injured Cal Ripken. Fryman's performance was gratifying because he played just 85 games in 1999 thanks to a significant injury to his right knee.

Hitting

Fryman had the most consistent offensive season of any Cleveland batsman, hitting .321 in the first half and .321 in the second half. He's always been one of the best high fastball hitters in baseball but can be fooled by pitchers who work both sides of the plate. Last year, however, he made a conscious effort to take breaking balls and fastballs to right field. When pitchers tried to jam him with heat, he'd pull the ball to left field. Fryman has been afraid to sacrifice power for average, but nestled amidst a loaded Indians' lineup, he decided to take a chance. He hit .335 with runners in scoring position, and .345 with runners in scoring position and two out.

Baserunning & Defense

On the bases, Fryman runs hard and goes into second with a purpose when breaking up double plays. He stole 10 bases in 1998, but stole only one last year. He led major league third basemen with a .978 fielding percentage and had a 61-game errorless streak. Fryman has a strong, accurate arm and can make clean throws even when he's going toward the line. The knee injury may have robbed him of some range to his left, but he still comes in on bunts well.

2001 Outlook

With Sandy Alomar Jr. and Manny Ramirez departing as free agents, Fryman's influence on the club will have to grow. He's quiet and unemotional on the field, but if someone isn't playing the game right, he'll let them know it. Good health is a must, too. The Indians need Fryman in the lineup on a daily basis.

Overall Statistics

	G	AB	R	H	D	T	HR	RBI	SB	BB	SO	Avg	OBP	Slg
2000	155	574	93	184	38	4	22	106	1	73	111	.321	.392	.516
Career	1482	5750	819	1602	316	37	209	929	71	532	1224	.279	.339	.455

Where He Hits the Ball

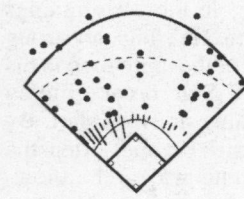

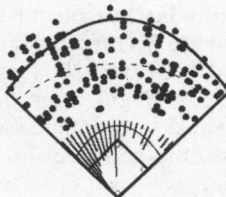

Vs. LHP   Vs. RHP

2000 Situational Stats

	AB	H	HR	RBI	Avg		AB	H	HR	RBI	Avg
Home	293	91	9	50	.311	LHP	118	35	4	17	.297
Road	281	93	13	56	.331	RHP	456	149	18	89	.327
First Half	287	92	14	48	.321	Sc Pos	170	57	4	81	.335
Scnd Half	287	92	8	58	.321	Clutch	77	21	1	7	.273

2000 Rankings (American League)

- 1st in fielding percentage at third base (.978)
- 6th in sacrifice flies (10) and batting average on a 3-1 count (.600)
- 7th in batting average vs. righthanded pitchers
- 8th in on-base percentage vs. lefthanded pitchers (.422) and batting average on the road
- 10th in singles
- Led the Indians in sacrifice flies (10) and on-base percentage vs. lefthanded pitchers (.422)
- Led AL third basemen in batting average, doubles, triples, sacrifice flies (10), batting average vs. righthanded pitchers and batting average on the road

Kenny Lofton

2000 Season

Doctors said Kenny Lofton wouldn't be back in the lineup until late June or the All-Star break following surgery to repair a tear in the rotator cuff in his left shoulder. Driven partly because he was in his option year, Lofton made the Opening Day lineup, but he probably should have waited. Unable to throw or swing at full strength, he struggled so badly in the first half that some baseball people thought he was finished. In the second half, with his shoulder healing, Lofton hit .294 with 41 of his career-high 73 RBI to restore his reputation as a quality leadoff hitter.

Hitting

Lofton found salvation in left field after the break. Pitchers were working him away with fastballs and breaking balls because they knew he'd try to pull everything. When he started hitting those pitches to left, he turned his season around. Too patient in the first half, Lofton started swinging early in the count in the second half. Lefthanders have given him problems the last two years, but he's still a career .299 hitter against them. He remains a good bunter but too often forgets that part of his game.

Baserunning & Defense

Lofton stole 30 bases last year, but his shoulder prevented him from stealing more. Doctors didn't want him sliding head first into second or third for fear of re-injury. When he got the green light at midseason, he was still hesitant. Lofton no longer is a Gold Glove center fielder, but he still has outstanding speed. He has good hops and will steal one or two homers at year at the fence.

2001 Outlook

Lofton is back after the Indians picked up his $8 million option in mid-November. They had talked about negotiating a multiyear pact, but they liked the hunger he showed in the final two months of last season on what amounted to a one-year deal. The one question Lofton must answer is if he can steal a base with the game on the line. He looked hesitant last year.

Position: CF
Bats: L **Throws:** L
Ht: 6' 0" **Wt:** 190

Opening Day Age: 33
Born: 5/31/67 in East Chicago, IN
ML Seasons: 10

Overall Statistics

	G	AB	R	H	D	T	HR	RBI	SB	BB	SO	Avg	OBP	Slg
2000	137	543	107	151	23	5	15	73	30	79	72	.278	.369	.422
Career	1233	4922	959	1507	235	65	78	485	463	616	662	.306	.383	.428

Where He Hits the Ball

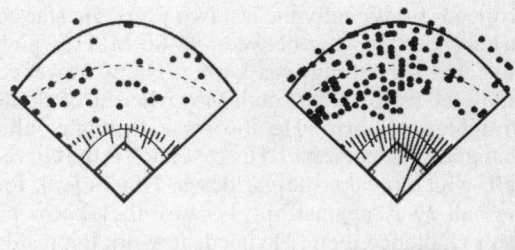

Vs. LHP   **Vs. RHP**

2000 Situational Stats

	AB	H	HR	RBI	Avg		AB	H	HR	RBI	Avg
Home	265	84	10	47	.317	LHP	123	32	2	20	.260
Road	278	67	5	26	.241	RHP	420	119	13	53	.283
First Half	247	64	7	32	.259	Sc Pos	114	38	3	56	.333
Scnd Half	296	87	8	41	.294	Clutch	56	20	3	14	.357

2000 Rankings (American League)

- 3rd in lowest percentage of swings that missed (9.5)
- 5th in stolen bases, fielding percentage in center field (.989) and highest percentage of extra bases taken as a runner (65.5)
- 6th in stolen-base percentage (81.1) and steals of third (4)
- Led the Indians in triples, on-base percentage for a leadoff hitter (.357) and highest percentage of extra bases taken as a runner (65.5)
- Led AL center fielders in stolen bases, stolen-base percentage (81.1), batting average at home, lowest percentage of swings that missed (9.5) and steals of third (4)

Cleveland

Charles Nagy

2000 Season

Charles Nagy will remember 2000 by one word: pain. He came to spring training with his right arm hurting and made eight starts to open the season before undergoing surgery to remove cartilage from his right elbow. The surgery ended his streaks of 192 consecutive starts and four straight seasons with over 200 innings pitched. He rushed his comeback, re-injured the elbow and didn't return to the rotation until September 14. Far from 100 percent, Nagy lost three straight starts before being shut down for good.

Pitching

Nagy is a finesse pitcher who is most effective when he throws 87-88 MPH. His velocity has dropped significantly the last two years. He started last season throwing between 84-86 MPH, which indicated something was wrong. Nagy, however, didn't tell team trainers until May when he couldn't straighten his arm. He throws a fastball, split, changeup and curveball. His best pitch is the curveball, which breaks straight down. Hitters look for the ball away against him because they know he can't challenge them. He needs to work the inside part of the plate with his fastball to get the best out of his breaking pitches.

Defense

Well-conditioned and quick off the mound, Nagy is Cleveland's best fielding pitcher. He's made just 11 errors in 11 seasons. He covers first base well, but he has never focused on stopping the running game. Only 15 of 54 (27.7 percent) basestealers have been caught on his watch over the past three years.

2001 Outlook

The Indians don't know if Nagy will be ready for spring training. By rushing his comeback last year, he did more damage to the elbow and probably shouldn't have been allowed to pitch when he did rejoin the rotation in September. Initial tests in the offseason indicated additional surgery was not needed, but the Indians aren't counting on Nagy to be ready for Opening Day. He has two years left on a four-year, $24 million contract.

Position: SP
Bats: L **Throws:** R
Ht: 6' 3" **Wt:** 200

Opening Day Age: 33
Born: 5/5/67 in Fairfield, CT
ML Seasons: 11
Pronunciation: NAG-ee

Overall Statistics

	W	L	Pct.	ERA	G	GS	Sv	IP	H	BB	SO	HR	Ratio
2000	2	7	.222	8.21	11	11	0	57.0	71	21	41	15	1.61
Career	123	93	.569	4.32	279	277	0	1823.1	1995	550	1184	197	1.40

How Often He Throws Strikes

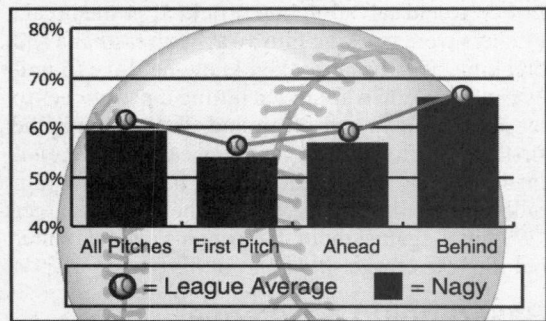

2000 Situational Stats

	W	L	ERA	Sv	IP		AB	H	HR	RBI	Avg
Home	1	3	5.79	0	23.1	LHB	132	40	7	18	.303
Road	1	4	9.89	0	33.2	RHB	105	31	8	29	.295
First Half	2	4	7.19	0	46.1	Sc Pos	57	20	5	33	.351
Scnd Half	0	3	12.66	0	10.2	Clutch	3	1	1	1	.333

2000 Rankings (American League)
- 3rd in fewest GDPs induced per GDP situation (0.0%)

Manny Ramirez

Position: RF/DH
Bats: R **Throws:** R
Ht: 6' 0" **Wt:** 205

Opening Day Age: 28
Born: 5/30/72 in Santo Domingo, Dominican Republic
ML Seasons: 8

2000 Season

Despite missing 44 games with a left hamstring injury, Manny Ramirez hit .351 and drove in 122 runs in 118 games. In the last two seasons, Ramirez has amassed 287 RBI in 265 games. He missed 39 games with his hamstring, and the Indians went 19-20 and fell out of the American League Central race. When he returned to the cleanup spot after the break, the Tribe went 46-30. In Ted Williams-like fashion, Ramirez hit a 452-foot homer in his final at-bat as an Indian.

Hitting

No one makes better contact on a greater variety of pitches than Ramirez. He can do it all with the bat, hitting for average, power and production. He is particularly effective against lefthanders. High fastballs and hard sliders away give him problems, but he hits just about everything else. The thing about Ramirez is that he hits the ball to all field with authority. He has a tension-free swing. Hitting coaches call it "slow feet and quick hands."

Baserunning & Defense

People think Ramirez is a one-dimensional player, but he's a solid right fielder with a good, accurate arm. He has a deceiving stride that makes it look like he's not running hard, but he can track balls down in the gap and make plays going towards the line. He's improved on the bases, but it was hard to tell that last year because he spent most of his time running with a limp.

2001 Outlook

After the season, Ramirez filed for free agency and rejected a seven-year, $119 million offer from the Indians. Soon after the Indians signed right fielder Ellis Burks away from the Giants in late November, Ramirez inked an eight-year, $160 million pact with Boston. Can he deal with the added media attention that will follow? He rarely talked to reporters in Cleveland, but that act won't wash in a major market. If there is one danger sign, it's how long it took him to recover from last year's hamstring injury. If that malady becomes chronic, his numbers will suffer.

Overall Statistics

	G	AB	R	H	D	T	HR	RBI	SB	BB	SO	Avg	OBP	Slg
2000	118	439	92	154	34	2	38	122	1	86	117	.351	.457	.697
Career	967	3470	665	1086	237	11	236	804	28	541	780	.313	.407	.592

Where He Hits the Ball

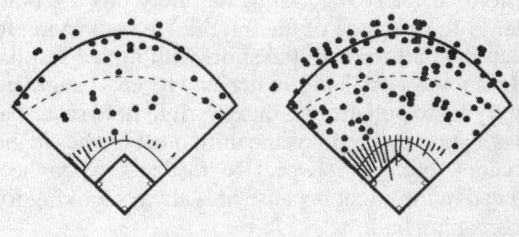

Vs. LHP   **Vs. RHP**

2000 Situational Stats

	AB	H	HR	RBI	Avg		AB	H	HR	RBI	Avg
Home	213	76	22	69	.357	LHP	91	36	7	25	.396
Road	226	78	16	53	.345	RHP	348	118	31	97	.339
First Half	183	59	13	47	.322	Sc Pos	147	52	11	79	.354
Scnd Half	256	95	25	75	.371	Clutch	54	24	3	12	.444

2000 Rankings (American League)

- 1st in slugging percentage, HR frequency (11.6 ABs per HR), most pitches seen per plate appearance (4.27), batting average in the clutch and cleanup slugging percentage (.697)
- 3rd in batting average, on-base percentage, batting average on a 3-1 count (.667), slugging percentage vs. righthanded pitchers (.684), on-base percentage vs. righthanded pitchers (.437) and lowest batting average on an 0-2 count (.042) 237
- Led the Indians in batting average, home runs, total bases (306), RBI, intentional walks (9), slugging percentage, on-base percentage, HR frequency (11.6 ABs per HR) and most pitches seen per plate appearance (4.27)

Cleveland

Jim Thome

2000 Season

It was a season of change for Jim Thome. He regularly faced infield shifts and lost playing time at first base when David Segui was acquired on July 28. The shift probably cost him between 20-25 hits, and he batted only .235 at DH. What Thome didn't lose was power. His 37 homers gave him five straight seasons with 30 or more longballs. He tied his club record for strikeouts with 171 for the second straight year, and drew the third most walks in the league. Thome gored his average by going 6-for-63 from September 7-23.

Hitting

Teams loaded the right side of the infield against Thome because they know he rarely hits a grounder to the left side of the infield. He kept trying to slap the ball through the shift, with mixed results. He's always had a big swing, and he gets caught up in trying to pull the ball into the right field seats. He has a good eye and saw the third most pitches in the majors, but he's suspect to fastballs when he's ahead in the count because he's always looking for a breaking ball.

Baserunning & Defense

Thome is a large man who runs well for his size. Defensively, he had a decent year. He lost 10 pounds during the offseason and that helped his quickness going to his right. He still doesn't look comfortable scooping low throws, but he has a decent arm.

2001 Outlook

The Indians want Thome to stop being so pull crazy. They feel if he concentrates on hitting the ball to left-center and center field—his natural swing—his average and home runs will increase. He also has to deal with the shift. He's going to have to learn to hit a double down the third-base line once in a while to make the opposition play him straight. It looks like he'll be back at first base as Segui headed to Baltimore via free agency. Thome's power will be counted on to help ease the blow of Manny Ramirez' departure.

Position: 1B/DH
Bats: L **Throws:** R
Ht: 6' 4" **Wt:** 240

Opening Day Age: 30
Born: 8/27/70 in Peoria, IL
ML Seasons: 10
Pronunciation: TOE-mee

Overall Statistics

	G	AB	R	H	D	T	HR	RBI	SB	BB	SO	Avg	OBP	Slg
2000	158	557	106	150	33	1	37	106	1	118	171	.269	.398	.531
Career	1074	3634	715	1033	214	17	233	685	17	764	1053	.284	.410	.545

Where He Hits the Ball

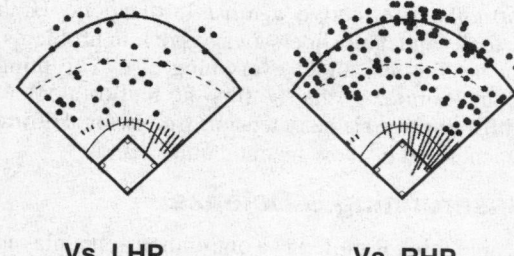

Vs. LHP   **Vs. RHP**

2000 Situational Stats

	AB	H	HR	RBI	Avg		AB	H	HR	RBI	Avg
Home	275	85	21	71	.309	LHP	152	38	6	19	.250
Road	282	65	16	35	.230	RHP	405	112	31	87	.277
First Half	296	78	23	56	.264	Sc Pos	163	43	7	71	.264
Scnd Half	261	72	14	50	.276	Clutch	67	16	5	15	.239

2000 Rankings (American League)

- 1st in highest percentage of swings that missed (32.5) and lowest percentage of swings put into play (31.3)
- 2nd in strikeouts and pitches seen (2,869)
- 3rd in walks and most pitches seen per plate appearance (4.19)
- 5th in fielding percentage at first base (.995)
- Led the Indians in walks, times on base (272), strikeouts, pitches seen (2,869), fewest GDPs per GDP situation (5.6%) and games played
- Led AL first basemen in most pitches seen per plate appearance (4.19)

Omar Vizquel

2000 Season

Once again, Omar Vizquel provided stunning defense and consistent offense at shortstop. He won his eighth straight Gold Glove after making just three errors all season. He had a 95-game errorless streak from September 26, 1999 to July 21, 2000. After a quiet first-half offensively, he hit .314 in his last 97 games. On September 20 against Boston, he made the first straight steal of home by an Indian since Kenny Lofton turned the trick back on April 26, 1992.

Hitting

Vizquel had a career year in 1999, and he paid the price last year. A good fastball hitter, Vizquel was being pitched like a power hitter. He saw change-ups and curveballs in fastball counts. It didn't help that leadoff hitter Kenny Lofton, No. 3 hitter Robbie Alomar and No. 4 man Manny Ramirez battled injuries most of the first half. It was one of the reasons the switch-hitter struggled against lefties. After hitting .333 against southpaws in 1999, he hit .218 last year. When Lofton, Alomar and Ramirez got healthy in the second half, Vizquel saw a lot more fastballs in the No. 2 spot and reaped the benefits.

Baserunning & Defense

A daring baserunner, Vizquel's steals dropped from 42 to 22 last year. He was thrown out 10 times, but managed to steal third seven times. Defensively, few can compare. He makes the routine play and the flashy barehanded play. He can go into the hole or make a diving stop behind second. He doesn't have a great arm, but he compensates with a quick release and is nimble turning two.

2001 Outlook

The Indians will take a carbon copy of Vizquel's 1999 season with few questions asked. Apparently inexhaustible, he has become a solid two-way player. He's a great defender who has hit .287 or better for the past five years. Cleveland would like to see Vizquel, Lofton and Robbie Alomar bunt down the first-base line more often, as opposing third basemen play in on them to take the bunt away. But when that is the chief complaint about your game, well. . .

Position: SS
Bats: B **Throws:** R
Ht: 5' 9" **Wt:** 185

Opening Day Age: 33
Born: 4/24/67 in Caracas, Venezuela
ML Seasons: 12
Pronunciation: viz-KELL

Overall Statistics

	G	AB	R	H	D	T	HR	RBI	SB	BB	SO	Avg	OBP	Slg
2000	156	613	101	176	27	3	7	66	22	87	72	.287	.377	.375
Career	1620	5809	835	1605	250	36	41	515	260	582	576	.276	.342	.353

Where He Hits the Ball

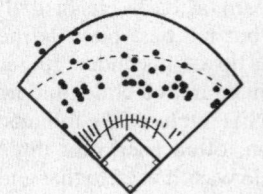
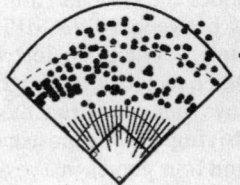

Vs. LHP　　　　**Vs. RHP**

2000 Situational Stats

	AB	H	HR	RBI	Avg		AB	H	HR	RBI	Avg
Home	303	77	1	28	.254	LHP	156	34	1	16	.218
Road	310	99	6	38	.319	RHP	457	142	6	50	.311
First Half	324	89	5	37	.275	Sc Pos	151	41	1	53	.272
Scnd Half	289	87	2	29	.301	Clutch	70	14	0	1	.200

2000 Rankings (American League)

- 1st in fielding percentage at shortstop (.995), highest percentage of swings put into play (54.9) and lowest slugging percentage vs. lefthanded pitchers (.282)
- 2nd in bunts in play (25), lowest percentage of swings that missed (9.4) and steals of third (7)
- 3rd in plate appearances (717)
- 4th in lowest HR frequency (87.6 ABs per HR)
- 5th in singles, caught stealing (10) and lowest batting average vs. lefthanded pitchers
- Led the Indians in at-bats, singles, caught stealing (10), plate appearances (717), bunts in play (25), highest percentage of pitches taken (63.3) and lowest percentage of swings that missed (9.4)

Bob Wickman

2000 Season

The day before Milwaukee held Bob Wickman Night, they traded him to the Indians. Wickman's wife, mother and grandmother still went to County Stadium to collect their Bob Wickman posters, while he became the Indians' closer. He hated to leave his home in Wisconsin but loved being part of the Indians' futile, but thrilling, wild-card chase. He converted 30 of 37 save opportunities, going 14-for-17 with the Indians and 16-for-20 with the Brewers.

Pitching

Wickman wore a Green Bay Packers T-shirt under his uniform, and he looks like he could have played guard for Vince Lombardi. He throws a sinker, slider and two- and four-seam fastballs. His fastball is between 90-93 MPH, but his best pitch is the sinker. Wickman lost the tip of his index finger when he stuck his finger in a fan as a child, and he says that put extra sink on his pitches. The Indians, driving for the postseason, often used him three and four games in a row. He wasn't used to that and it took him a while to adjust. When he struggled, he usually was done in by walks and cheap hits. He allowed just one homer in 72.2 innings.

Defense

Wickman looks more like a bulldozer than a ballerina when he fields his position, but he gets the job done. He didn't commit a single error last year, though he piled up four miscues with Milwaukee in '99. He does not hold baserunners well, but he was rarely tested after the Indians acquired him.

2001 Outlook

Wickman will go into the season as the closer. The Indians like the bullpen much better with him at the end because it allows Paul Shuey and Steve Karsay to fill the vital setup roles. Karsay, however, may push for the closer's role in spring training. Wickman fits the salary range of a Tribe closer; he's signed through this year at $2.4 million. The Indians have never paid big money to a closer.

Position: RP
Bats: R   **Throws:** R
Ht: 6' 1"   **Wt:** 234

Opening Day Age: 32
Born: 2/6/69 in Green Bay, WI
ML Seasons: 9

Overall Statistics

	W	L	Pct.	ERA	G	GS	Sv	IP	H	BB	SO	HR	Ratio
2000	3	5	.375	3.10	69	0	30	72.2	64	32	55	1	1.32
Career	53	42	.558	3.76	521	28	104	761.0	751	343	537	54	1.44

How Often He Throws Strikes

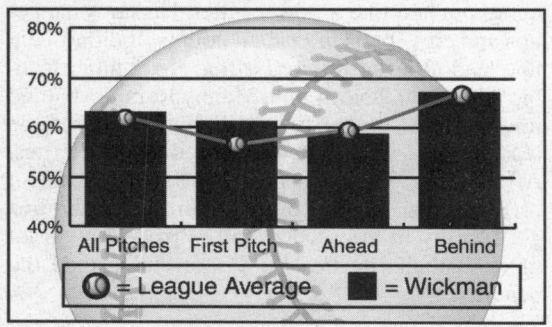

O = League Average   ■ = Wickman

2000 Situational Stats

	W	L	ERA	Sv	IP		AB	H	HR	RBI	Avg
Home	2	2	2.13	16	38.0	LHB	132	34	0	15	.258
Road	1	3	4.15	14	34.2	RHB	140	30	1	15	.214
First Half	2	2	3.07	13	41.0	Sc Pos	74	17	0	28	.230
Scnd Half	1	3	3.13	17	31.2	Clutch	163	39	0	21	.239

2000 Rankings (American League)

- Did not rank near the top or bottom in any category

Jason Bere

Position: SP
Bats: R **Throws:** R
Ht: 6' 3" **Wt:** 215

Opening Day Age: 29
Born: 5/26/71 in Cambridge, MA
ML Seasons: 8
Pronunciation: burr-AY

Overall Statistics

	W	L	Pct.	ERA	G	GS	Sv	IP	H	BB	SO	HR	Ratio
2000	12	10	.545	5.47	31	31	0	169.1	180	89	142	25	1.59
Career	59	44	.573	5.28	161	153	0	830.2	821	519	679	108	1.61

2000 Situational Stats

	W	L	ERA	Sv	IP		AB	H	HR	RBI	Avg
Home	7	5	5.62	0	83.1	LHB	281	75	7	35	.267
Road	5	5	5.34	0	86.0	RHB	374	105	18	58	.281
First Half	6	6	4.82	0	104.2	Sc Pos	144	36	8	67	.250
Scnd Half	6	4	6.54	0	64.2	Clutch	9	1	1	1	.111

2000 Season

After the Indians acquired Jason Bere from Milwaukee on July 28, he either was very good or very bad. He went 6-7 with the Brewers and 6-3 with the Tribe. He won his first two starts for Cleveland, lost his next two and won his next two. It's been his pattern since he underwent elbow surgery in 1996.

Pitching & Defense

Bere is still re-learning how to pitch following surgery. There were times last year when he threw a fastball between 90-95 MPH with a good curveball and splitter. He no longer can consistently throw high heat past people, however, and is much more effective when he keeps the ball down. One encouraging sign is that Bere once again was able to throw his curveball. It was a good pitch for him with the White Sox in the early 1990s. A six-inning starter at best, he is a good fielder who did well holding runners in 2000.

2001 Outlook

The Indians felt Bere was asking for too much money as a free agent, but the Cubs gave him a two-year deal worth $4.5 million. He showed flashes last year that his two best pitches, the fastball and curve, were coming back. He's worth a gamble, but the Cubs better be ready for his Jekyll & Hyde results.

Wil Cordero

Position: LF
Bats: R **Throws:** R
Ht: 6' 2" **Wt:** 200

Opening Day Age: 29
Born: 10/3/71 in Mayaguez, Puerto Rico
ML Seasons: 9
Pronunciation: cor-DAIR-oh

Overall Statistics

	G	AB	R	H	D	T	HR	RBI	SB	BB	SO	Avg	OBP	Slg
2000	127	496	64	137	35	5	16	68	1	32	76	.276	.328	.464
Career	900	3329	470	928	209	18	95	436	45	231	573	.279	.332	.438

2000 Situational Stats

	AB	H	HR	RBI	Avg		AB	H	HR	RBI	Avg
Home	261	75	8	27	.287	LHP	127	41	5	24	.323
Road	235	62	8	41	.264	RHP	369	96	11	44	.260
First Half	291	83	13	43	.285	Sc Pos	142	44	2	49	.310
Scnd Half	205	54	3	25	.263	Clutch	78	20	3	12	.256

2000 Season

Every time Wil Cordero puts on an Indians uniform, he hurts his hand. He had a promising 1999 season derailed when he broke his left wrist making a diving catch in left field. This year the Indians re-acquired him in a July 28 trade with Pittsburgh, but he suffered a broken bone in his right hand September 9 after being hit by a pitch.

Hitting, Baserunning & Defense

The Indians re-acquired Cordero because they needed a high-contact, low-strikeout hitter. He made contact, but he went homerless in 38 games after hitting 16 with the Pirates. What he does well is hit lefthanders and good pitchers late in the game. He is no threat as a baserunner and is an average outfielder with a poor arm. He played left field for the Indians, but he would be well served if someone made him a designated hitter.

2001 Outlook

Cordero could be the Indians' starting left fielder. However, he'll probably be in a platoon situation with Russell Branyan or Jacob Cruz if he's not traded. Cleveland let Cordero walk at the end of '99 and snickered when Pittsburgh signed him to a three-year, $9 million deal. Then the Indians brought him back, contract and all. The question now is who will have the last laugh.

Cleveland

Einar Diaz

Position: C
Bats: R **Throws:** R
Ht: 5'10" **Wt:** 185

Opening Day Age: 28
Born: 12/28/72 in
Chiriqui, Panama
ML Seasons: 5

Overall Statistics

	G	AB	R	H	D	T	HR	RBI	SB	BB	SO	Avg	OBP	Slg
2000	75	250	29	68	14	2	4	25	4	11	29	.272	.323	.392
Career	220	698	81	190	37	3	9	67	15	37	74	.272	.321	.372

2000 Situational Stats

	AB	H	HR	RBI	Avg		AB	H	HR	RBI	Avg
Home	107	27	2	6	.252	LHP	57	15	0	5	.263
Road	143	41	2	19	.287	RHP	193	53	4	20	.275
First Half	152	42	3	16	.276	Sc Pos	61	13	1	19	.213
Scnd Half	98	26	1	9	.265	Clutch	36	8	0	4	.222

2000 Season

Einar Diaz again backed up catcher Sandy Alomar Jr. Diaz caught just 74 games last year, compared to '99 when he caught 119 games because of Alomar's knee problems. He did become Bartolo Colon's personal caddy, catching 20 of his 30 starts. The high point of Diaz' season may have been his five-hit effort against Toronto on May 5.

Hitting, Baserunning & Defense

Diaz is a fastball hitter who will chase low breaking balls away and high fastballs. If he gets regular playing time, he could develop into a guy who hits between .280-.300 with 10-15 homers. Diaz has a strong arm and threw out 33.3 percent (17-for-51) of the basestealers he faced. Diaz' game-calling skills are improving, but he still doesn't block balls or move his body well. He has good speed for a catcher and appeared at third base in one game.

2001 Outlook

Indications at the end of the season were that Diaz would get a chance to start in 2001. Alomar, 35, filed for free agency and eventually departed for Chicago. But in mid-November, Cleveland acquired catcher Eddie Taubensee, so Diaz still may not be handed the everyday job. One of Diaz' biggest challenges will be gaining the respect of the Tribe's veteran pitchers.

Steve Karsay

Position: RP
Bats: R **Throws:** R
Ht: 6' 3" **Wt:** 215

Opening Day Age: 29
Born: 3/24/72 in
Flushing, NY
ML Seasons: 6
Pronunciation:
CAR-say

Overall Statistics

	W	L	Pct.	ERA	G	GS	Sv	IP	H	BB	SO	HR	Ratio
2000	5	9	.357	3.76	72	0	20	76.2	79	25	66	5	1.36
Career	22	29	.431	4.37	169	40	21	389.1	422	132	287	39	1.42

2000 Situational Stats

	W	L	ERA	Sv	IP		AB	H	HR	RBI	Avg
Home	3	5	3.16	9	42.2	LHB	139	31	2	19	.223
Road	2	4	4.50	11	34.0	RHB	158	48	3	23	.304
First Half	1	5	3.54	17	40.2	Sc Pos	80	27	0	33	.338
Scnd Half	4	4	4.00	3	36.0	Clutch	174	51	4	34	.293

2000 Season

Steve Karsay won the closer's job in early April and lost it when the Indians acquired Bob Wickman from Milwaukee on July 28. That sent him into a 20-game tailspin in which he went 2-3 with 7.27 ERA while Cleveland was trying to make the postseason. Karsay was 19-for-24 as a closer.

Pitching & Defense

Karsay has a great arm. As a reliever, he'll throw a 96-97 MPH fastball and also come at hitters with a sharp breaking curveball between 76-82 MPH. As a starter, he'll add a changeup and splitter. Despite a history of elbow problems, he made 72 relief appearances and led Tribe relievers with 76.2 innings. Fatigue and disappointment over losing the closer's job led to his late-season slump. He's a good fielder with great range coming off the mound.

2001 Outlook

Karsay wants to either start or close this year. He feels his talents are being wasted in the setup role and that middle relief would hurt his chances of getting a big contract. He was eligible for arbitration last winter, and likely will file for free agency after 2001 if the Indians don't give him a shot at one of his two desired roles.

Steve Reed

Position: RP
Bats: R **Throws:** R
Ht: 6' 2" **Wt:** 212

Opening Day Age: 35
Born: 3/11/66 in Los Angeles, CA
ML Seasons: 9

Overall Statistics

	W	L	Pct.	ERA	G	GS	Sv	IP	H	BB	SO	HR	Ratio
2000	2	0	1.000	4.34	57	0	0	56.0	58	21	39	7	1.41
Career	35	23	.603	3.69	537	0	16	583.1	531	194	442	78	1.24

2000 Situational Stats

	W	L	ERA	Sv	IP		AB	H	HR	RBI	Avg
Home	2	0	4.99	0	30.2	LHB	59	16	3	11	.271
Road	0	0	3.55	0	25.1	RHB	157	42	4	18	.268
First Half	1	0	6.04	0	28.1	Sc Pos	69	20	2	23	.290
Scnd Half	1	0	2.60	0	27.2	Clutch	43	14	0	4	.326

2000 Season

Steve Reed made *only* 57 appearances last year, after seven consecutive seasons of making 60 or more. He weathered a first half in which he had a 6.04 ERA in 31 appearances and fell into disfavor, and became a valuable setup man for the Tribe's second-half run. He did not allow a run in his last eight appearances, covering 8.2 innings. He had a stretch in July where he retired 18 straight batters.

Pitching & Defense

Reed lowered his three-quarter delivery to more of a submarine delivery last year. He throws a sinking fastball between 85-86 MPH, a slider and changeup. He was used mostly against righthanders and had success throwing inside fastballs against them. He throws changeups and sinkers away to lefties. Reed is a solid fielder with a quick move to the plate. Four of the five runners who tried to steal against him were thrown out.

2001 Outlook

The Indians used a record 32 pitchers last year and Reed seemed to live on the bubble. He showed he could get righthanders out late in the game in the second half, and he should fill that role again this season unless the Indians find an upgrade. About the only definitive thing to say about his future as of presstime is that he's signed through 2001.

David Segui

Position: 1B/DH
Bats: B **Throws:** L
Ht: 6' 1" **Wt:** 202

Opening Day Age: 34
Born: 7/19/66 in Kansas City, KS
ML Seasons: 11
Pronunciation: suh-GHEE

Overall Statistics

	G	AB	R	H	D	T	HR	RBI	SB	BB	SO	Avg	OBP	Slg
2000	150	574	93	192	42	1	19	103	0	53	84	.334	.388	.510
Career	1263	4177	591	1220	249	14	121	590	15	433	544	.292	.357	.445

2000 Situational Stats

	AB	H	HR	RBI	Avg		AB	H	HR	RBI	Avg
Home	314	106	8	49	.338	LHP	155	48	4	23	.310
Road	260	86	11	54	.331	RHP	419	144	15	80	.344
First Half	306	105	9	52	.343	Sc Pos	167	53	4	81	.317
Scnd Half	268	87	10	51	.325	Clutch	79	26	1	14	.329

2000 Season

David Segui set career highs in batting average, hits, runs and RBI last year. He started the season with Texas before the Indians acquired him on July 28 for the stretch run. Playing almost every day at first base, DH or right field, Segui hit .332 with eight homers and 46 RBI for the Tribe.

Hitting, Baserunning & Defense

Segui is an intense hitter, breaking bats and screaming when he makes outs. He has unexpected power but mostly goes with the pitch. He has more power lefthanded, driving inside fastballs and breaking balls. Batting righthanded, he likes to slap offspeed pitches the opposite way. He hit safely in 45 of the 57 games with the Indians and came to bat 20 times with the bases loaded, going 8-for-20 (.400) in those situations. Segui is a slick defender, playing 74 errorless games at first, with a good arm. He played last year with a broken metal plate in his left foot, which made him ineffective running the bases or playing right field.

2001 Outlook

The talented, but much-traveled Segui filed for free agency and signed a four-year deal with Baltimore. He underwent surgery on his left foot and left knee after the season, but was expected to be all right for spring training.

Cleveland

115

Paul Shuey

Position: RP
Bats: R **Throws:** R
Ht: 6' 3" **Wt:** 215

Opening Day Age: 30
Born: 9/16/70 in Lima, OH
ML Seasons: 7
Pronunciation: SHOO-ey

Overall Statistics

	W	L	Pct.	ERA	G	GS	Sv	IP	H	BB	SO	HR	Ratio
2000	4	2	.667	3.39	57	0	0	63.2	51	30	69	4	1.27
Career	26	18	.591	3.88	275	0	19	313.0	279	166	341	30	1.42

2000 Situational Stats

	W	L	ERA	Sv	IP		AB	H	HR	RBI	Avg
Home	2	1	3.03	0	35.2	LHB	118	24	2	18	.203
Road	2	1	3.86	0	28.0	RHB	115	27	2	16	.235
First Half	3	1	2.42	0	26.0	Sc Pos	73	17	1	30	.233
Scnd Half	1	1	4.06	0	37.2	Clutch	154	40	4	28	.260

2000 Season

Paul Shuey and Steve Karsay competed for the closer's job in the spring. Shuey didn't pitch well and opened the season as a setup man. Despite missing five weeks with a torn labrum in his right hip, he made 57 appearances. It was Shuey's eighth trip to the disabled list with leg problems. He's had more strikeouts than innings for four straight years.

Pitching & Defense

The Indians have had three different pitching coaches in as many years and they all say Shuey has the best combination of pitches they've ever seen. He throws a 94-97 MPH fastball, 92-MPH splitter and a 78-82 MPH curveball. He has a tendency to throw the splitter too much, but last year he kept it in the dirt and wasn't hurt by the home run. Even with all his leg problems, Shuey has made only one error in his career, but baserunners are 23-for-30 against him over the past three years.

2001 Outlook

Cleveland would like to see Shuey become a closer. His inability to throw strikes consistently and a lack of confidence have hurt him. The Indians believe he could be a late-bloomer such as Mike Jackson or Jose Mesa. If not, they're happy with him in the setup role, and proved it by exercising his $2 million option for 2001.

Justin Speier

Position: RP
Bats: R **Throws:** R
Ht: 6' 4" **Wt:** 205

Opening Day Age: 27
Born: 11/6/73 in Walnut Creek, CA
ML Seasons: 3

Overall Statistics

	W	L	Pct.	ERA	G	GS	Sv	IP	H	BB	SO	HR	Ratio
2000	5	2	.714	3.29	47	0	0	68.1	57	28	69	9	1.24
Career	5	5	.500	4.82	85	0	0	117.2	112	54	108	24	1.41

2000 Situational Stats

	W	L	ERA	Sv	IP		AB	H	HR	RBI	Avg
Home	3	1	4.04	0	35.2	LHB	117	20	4	14	.171
Road	2	1	2.48	0	32.2	RHB	135	37	5	17	.274
First Half	1	1	2.00	0	27.0	Sc Pos	61	15	3	25	.246
Scnd Half	4	1	4.14	0	41.1	Clutch	49	18	4	14	.367

2000 Season

Justin Speier started the season as a closer at Triple-A Buffalo before getting promoted on May 25. Pitching long and short relief, Speier notched 68.1 innings, second most in the bullpen. He went 3-0 in August and rebounded from a second-half slump allowing just one earned run in his last six appearances. His best game came June 18 when he struck out seven in 3.2 innings against Detroit.

Pitching & Defense

Speier throws a fastball, slider and forkball. He works the gun between 90-93 MPH and his out pitch is the forkball, which sometimes moves like a knuckleball. He may have found his niche as a middle reliever, but he needs to curb his aggression when behind in the count. He challenged hitters too many times, giving up nine homers. He's an average fielder who pays no attention to the running game. Basestealers went 13-for-13 against Speier as he drove his catchers to distraction.

2001 Outlook

Speier made the most of his opportunity in 2000 and should be able to help the Cleveland pen this year, as well. The son of former big leaguer Chris Speier still is learning how to pitch in the majors, but he took a big step last year.

Steve Woodard

Position: SP/RP
Bats: L **Throws:** R
Ht: 6' 4" **Wt:** 217

Opening Day Age: 25
Born: 5/15/75 in Hartselle, AL
ML Seasons: 4

Overall Statistics

	W	L	Pct.	ERA	G	GS	Sv	IP	H	BB	SO	HR	Ratio
2000	4	10	.286	5.85	40	22	0	147.2	182	44	100	26	1.53
Career	28	33	.459	4.83	112	84	0	535.0	610	119	386	73	1.36

2000 Situational Stats

	W	L	ERA	Sv	IP		AB	H	HR	RBI	Avg
Home	1	5	6.17	0	77.1	LHB	272	78	11	55	.287
Road	3	5	5.50	0	70.1	RHB	325	104	15	50	.320
First Half	1	6	6.22	0	85.1	Sc Pos	140	50	8	78	.357
Scnd Half	3	4	5.34	0	62.1	Clutch	48	13	1	3	.271

2000 Season

Steve Woodard was Milwaukee's Opening Day starter and then disappeared. He was traded to the Indians in late July and became a hero. With the Indians trying to win the AL wild-card, Woodard beat Pedro Martinez and David Wells in the last 12 days of the season. Cleveland had never beaten Martinez and was 8-14 lifetime in games in which Wells had started. After going 1-7 with the Brewers, Woodard went 3-3 with the Tribe.

Pitching & Defense

Woodard relies on the movement and control of his 88-89 MPH fastball. When those two keys are not present when he unloads his two- or four-seamer, he gets hit hard and leaves games quickly. He uses a changeup as his out pitch, and he also throws a curveball. He can start or relieve and showed the Indians durability when he pitched 8.2 innings in a three-day span. Woodard is a good fielder.

2001 Outlook

The Indians aren't sure what they have in Woodard, but he should get a chance to be the fourth or fifth starter because of questions surrounding the health of Jaret Wright (shoulder) and Charles Nagy (elbow). At 25, Woodard gives the Indians youth and versatility. If he doesn't make the club as a starter, he could be a long man and spot starter.

Jaret Wright

Position: SP
Bats: R **Throws:** R
Ht: 6' 2" **Wt:** 230

Opening Day Age: 25
Born: 12/29/75 in Anaheim, CA
ML Seasons: 4

Overall Statistics

	W	L	Pct.	ERA	G	GS	Sv	IP	H	BB	SO	HR	Ratio
2000	3	4	.429	4.70	9	9	0	51.2	44	28	36	6	1.39
Career	31	27	.534	5.03	83	83	0	468.1	476	227	330	55	1.50

2000 Situational Stats

	W	L	ERA	Sv	IP		AB	H	HR	RBI	Avg
Home	1	2	3.38	0	18.2	LHB	88	26	5	13	.295
Road	2	2	5.45	0	33.0	RHB	99	18	1	10	.182
First Half	3	4	4.70	0	51.2	Sc Pos	38	10	1	15	.263
Scnd Half	0	0	-	0	0.0	Clutch	9	2	1	2	.222

2000 Season

The hard-throwing Jaret Wright, who started the seventh game of the World Series as a rookie, underwent surgery on the labrum in his right shoulder last year. After a disappointing 1999 effort, he worked hard in the offseason. He kicked off 2000 with two straight wins, but left his seventh start with tightness in his shoulder and was placed on the disabled list. He'd make only two more starts.

Pitching & Defense

Wright throws between 95-97 MPH with a two- and four-seam fastball. He throws a hard curveball at 85 MPH, a changeup and also was making progress on becoming more of a pitcher than a thrower when he went on the DL. Mechanically, Wright has been through numerous changes, but last year he seemed comfortable with his no-windup delivery. Wright's fielding improved last year, but he needs to continue to work on holding baserunners.

2001 Outlook

Wright is expected to come to spring training ready to pitch. Because of his desire to try to avoid surgery, he didn't have the operation until August 17. That meant he couldn't start throwing until December, but team officials were optimistic that he could begin to compete for a job in the rotation sometime in March.

Cleveland

Other Cleveland Indians

Jamie Brewington (Pos: RHP, Age: 29)

	W	L	Pct.	ERA	G	GS	Sv	IP	H	BB	SO	HR	Ratio
2000	3	0	1.000	5.36	26	0	0	45.1	56	19	34	3	1.65
Career	9	4	.692	4.85	39	13	0	120.2	124	64	79	11	1.56

Brewington made it back to the majors last season, five years after debuting with the Giants. He rarely pitched down the stretch, however, and the Indians released him in October. 2001 Outlook: C

Jim Brower (Pos: RHP, Age: 28)

	W	L	Pct.	ERA	G	GS	Sv	IP	H	BB	SO	HR	Ratio
2000	2	3	.400	6.24	17	11	0	62.0	80	31	32	11	1.79
Career	5	4	.556	5.75	26	13	0	87.2	107	41	50	19	1.69

Brower was included in the November deal with Cincinnati that brought Eddie Taubensee back to Cleveland. Brower isn't a strikeout sort. The Reds may choose to shift him to the bullpen. 2001 Outlook: C

Jolbert Cabrera (Pos: OF/2B, Age: 28, Bats: R)

	G	AB	R	H	D	T	HR	RBI	SB	BB	SO	Avg	OBP	Slg
2000	100	175	27	44	3	1	2	15	6	8	15	.251	.290	.314
Career	131	214	33	51	4	1	2	15	9	9	24	.238	.278	.294

Colbert was a significant part of Cleveland's roster last year, serving as a defensive sub. He played five positions, including center field, shortstop and second base, a coveted combination. 2001 Outlook: B

Cam Cairncross (Pos: LHP, Age: 28)

	W	L	Pct.	ERA	G	GS	Sv	IP	H	BB	SO	HR	Ratio
2000	1	0	1.000	3.86	15	0	0	9.1	11	3	8	1	1.50
Career	1	0	1.000	3.86	15	0	0	9.1	11	3	8	1	1.50

Cairncross is from Australia and has missed three full seasons since beginning his professional career in 1991. As you can tell from his games-innings ratio, he's a situational lefty. 2001 Outlook: C

Chris Haney (Pos: LHP, Age: 32)

	W	L	Pct.	ERA	G	GS	Sv	IP	H	BB	SO	HR	Ratio
2000	0	0	-	9.00	1	0	0	1.0	1	1	0	0	2.00
Career	38	52	.422	5.11	172	125	0	794.2	892	276	427	92	1.47

Haney underwent elbow surgery last spring but returned to fashion a fine ERA at Triple-A. Nevertheless, the Indians released him after the season. 2001 Outlook: C

Andrew Lorraine (Pos: LHP, Age: 28)

	W	L	Pct.	ERA	G	GS	Sv	IP	H	BB	SO	HR	Ratio
2000	1	2	.333	5.88	18	5	0	41.1	44	23	30	6	1.62
Career	6	10	.375	6.18	54	25	0	163.0	196	77	103	24	1.67

The Cubs found Lorraine lacking and let him go last May. The Indians then tried him for a spell, thus keeping intact his streak of pitching for a new major league team for a sixth straight season. He became a free agent at the conclusion of the year. 2001 Outlook: C

Tom Martin (Pos: LHP, Age: 30)

	W	L	Pct.	ERA	G	GS	Sv	IP	H	BB	SO	HR	Ratio
2000	1	0	1.000	4.05	31	0	0	33.1	32	15	21	3	1.41
Career	7	5	.583	4.61	106	0	2	113.1	126	53	74	10	1.58

Martin struggled with shoulder tendinitis last year, but wasn't a disaster in his 31 appearances with the Tribe. His roster spot may depend on the health of Ricky Rincon. 2001 Outlook: C

Willie Martinez (Pos: RHP, Age: 23)

	W	L	Pct.	ERA	G	GS	Sv	IP	H	BB	SO	HR	Ratio
2000	0	0	-	3.00	1	0	0	3.0	1	1	1	0	0.67
Career	0	0	-	3.00	1	0	0	3.0	1	1	1	0	0.67

Once a prized prospect with the Indians, Martinez was acquired off waivers by Minnesota after last season. He's still quite young. His promise could re-emerge with the change of scenery. 2001 Outlook: C

John McDonald (Pos: SS, Age: 26, Bats: R)

	G	AB	R	H	D	T	HR	RBI	SB	BB	SO	Avg	OBP	Slg
2000	9	9	0	4	0	0	0	0	0	0	1	.444	.444	.444
Career	27	30	2	11	0	0	0	0	0	0	4	.367	.367	.367

McDonald is an impressive defensive infielder with the range to play shortstop. His offensive skills aren't on the same level, but his fielding prowess may be enough to help him land a utility role. 2001 Outlook: C

Mike Mohler (Pos: LHP, Age: 32)

	W	L	Pct.	ERA	G	GS	Sv	IP	H	BB	SO	HR	Ratio
2000	1	2	.333	9.00	24	0	0	20.0	27	15	10	2	2.10
Career	14	27	.341	4.91	334	20	10	403.1	414	223	274	42	1.58

After failing his lefty reliever role with St. Louis, Mohler signed with the Indians in June, before finishing the year in the Oakland system. If he can't retire lefthanded hitters, he isn't of much use. 2001 Outlook: C

Jaime Navarro (Pos: RHP, Age: 33)

	W	L	Pct.	ERA	G	GS	Sv	IP	H	BB	SO	HR	Ratio
2000	0	6	.000	10.53	12	7	0	33.1	54	23	16	9	2.31
Career	116	126	.479	4.72	361	309	2	2055.1	2313	690	1113	214	1.46

Navarro's ugly stats the past four seasons make it curious that three organizations would try him out for size last year. He's now 25-49 with a 6.32 ERA since 1997, but Toronto is giving him another chance. 2001 Outlook: C

Alan Newman (Pos: LHP, Age: 31)

	W	L	Pct.	ERA	G	GS	Sv	IP	H	BB	SO	HR	Ratio
2000	0	0	-	20.25	1	0	0	1.1	6	1	0	1	5.25
Career	2	2	.500	7.94	19	0	0	17.0	28	10	20	3	2.24

A three-year veteran of an independent league, Newman signed with Cleveland last season after getting released by Tampa Bay. He's big, throws hard, has improved his control with age and is a free agent. 2001 Outlook: C

Chris Nichting (**Pos**: RHP, **Age**: 34)

	W	L	Pct.	ERA	G	GS	Sv	IP	H	BB	SO	HR	Ratio
2000	0	0	-	7.00	7	0	0	9.0	13	5	7	0	2.00
Career	0	0	-	7.02	20	0	0	33.1	49	18	13	1	2.01

Nichting, an eight-year veteran of Triple-A, became a closer at age 34 last season and enjoyed some success. He throws strikes, but it's hard to see him in any team's plans. 2001 Outlook: C

Chan Perry (**Pos**: RF, **Age**: 28, **Bats**: R)

	G	AB	R	H	D	T	HR	RBI	SB	BB	SO	Avg	OBP	Slg
2000	13	14	1	1	0	0	0	0	0	0	5	.071	.071	.071
Career	13	14	1	1	0	0	0	0	0	0	5	.071	.071	.071

Perry makes contact and can drive the ball, but he doesn't excel in any particular phase. In 14 at-bats with the Indians, he hit only two balls out of the infield. Atlanta signed him in November. 2001 Outlook: C

Ricky Rincon (**Pos**: LHP, **Age**: 30)

	W	L	Pct.	ERA	G	GS	Sv	IP	H	BB	SO	HR	Ratio
2000	2	0	1.000	2.70	35	0	0	20.0	17	13	20	1	1.50
Career	8	13	.381	3.42	216	0	18	189.2	159	90	185	18	1.31

Rincon may go down as the player the Indians acquired for Brian Giles. Rincon underwent elbow surgery last June but returned in August. Cleveland was satisfied enough to exercise an option for 2002. 2001 Outlook: A

Dave Roberts (**Pos**: LF, **Age**: 28, **Bats**: L)

	G	AB	R	H	D	T	HR	RBI	SB	BB	SO	Avg	OBP	Slg
2000	19	10	1	2	0	0	0	0	1	2	2	.200	.333	.200
Career	60	153	27	36	4	0	2	12	12	11	18	.235	.285	.301

Roberts' fate was sealed last season by the early return of Kenny Lofton from injury. Roberts is an adequate defensive outfielder with leadoff skills, but he's probably confined to a reserve role. 2001 Outlook: C

Bill Selby (**Pos**: 2B, **Age**: 30, **Bats**: L)

	G	AB	R	H	D	T	HR	RBI	SB	BB	SO	Avg	OBP	Slg
2000	30	46	8	11	1	0	0	4	0	1	9	.239	.271	.261
Career	70	141	20	37	5	0	3	10	1	10	20	.262	.316	.362

Selby is a jack-of-all-trades who packs a bit of a wallop for someone his size. He's not the most talented guy around, but he might be a useful player off the bench. The Reds signed him to a minor league deal. 2001 Outlook: C

Mark Watson (**Pos**: LHP, **Age**: 27)

	W	L	Pct.	ERA	G	GS	Sv	IP	H	BB	SO	HR	Ratio
2000	0	1	.000	8.53	6	0	0	6.1	12	2	4	0	2.21
Career	0	1	.000	8.53	6	0	0	6.1	12	2	4	0	2.21

Watson was claimed by Seattle when the Indians waived him last June. He became a full-time reliever in 2000 and finally reached Triple-A at age 26. 2001 Outlook: C

Mark Whiten (**Pos**: CF, **Age**: 34, **Bats**: B)

	G	AB	R	H	D	T	HR	RBI	SB	BB	SO	Avg	OBP	Slg
2000	6	7	2	2	1	0	0	1	0	3	2	.286	.500	.429
Career	940	3104	465	804	129	20	105	423	78	378	712	.259	.341	.415

Whiten spent a considerable amount of time in Triple-A for the second consecutive season. He doesn't offer a whole lot outside of his magnificent throwing arm. 2001 Outlook: C

Brian Williams (**Pos**: RHP, **Age**: 32)

	W	L	Pct.	ERA	G	GS	Sv	IP	H	BB	SO	HR	Ratio
2000	1	1	.500	7.23	29	0	1	42.1	51	31	20	6	1.94
Career	26	38	.406	5.37	256	59	6	595.1	655	332	397	62	1.66

The Indians signed Williams last June after he had blown up in the Cubs' bullpen. He throws hard but continually struggles with command. He's now a free agent. 2001 Outlook: C

Bobby Witt (**Pos**: RHP, **Age**: 36)

	W	L	Pct.	ERA	G	GS	Sv	IP	H	BB	SO	HR	Ratio
2000	0	1	.000	7.63	7	2	0	15.1	28	6	6	4	2.22
Career	138	156	.469	4.84	416	390	0	2421.2	2457	1350	1924	246	1.57

After making 32 starts for Tampa Bay in 1999, Witt was hammered in his seven games with Cleveland last year. The Indians released him in May, and he didn't pitch competitively the rest of the season. 2001 Outlook: D

Cleveland Indians Minor League Prospects

Organization Overview:

The organization that produced Albert Belle, Sean Casey, Bartolo Colon, Brian Giles, Danny Graves, Charles Nagy, Manny Ramirez and Jim Thome during the 1990s isn't as deep in prospects now as it was a few years ago. Also gone are guys still on the rise, including Steve Kline, Paul Rigdon, Richie Sexson and Enrique Wilson. The loss of talent has been the cost of staying competitive for most of the last decade. While C.C. Sabathia, Danys Baez and Russell Branyan are the only players in the high minors destined for Cleveland, a new international effort and the amateur draft provide hope in the lower reaches of the system. The Tribe's growing international presence has inked Baez, who defected from Cuba in 1999, Dominican outfielder Willy Taveras and Venezuelans Maicer Izturis and Alex Requena. The key draft picks of late to watch include last summer's first-rounder Corey Smith, lefthanders Brian Tallet and Derek Thompson, and power prospects Sean Swedlow and Mark Folsom.

Danys Baez

Position: P **Opening Day Age:** 23
Bats: R **Throws:** R **Born:** 9/10/77 in Pinar
Ht: 6' 4" **Wt:** 225 Del Rio, Cuba

Recent Statistics

	W	L	ERA	G	GS	Sv	IP	H	R	BB	SO	HR
2000 A Kinston	2	2	4.71	9	9	0	49.2	45	29	20	56	5
2000 AA Akron	4	9	3.68	18	18	0	102.2	98	46	32	77	6

Baez, who in 1999 defected from Cuba during the Pan American Games in Winnipeg, signed a four-year major league contract for $14.5 million. While Cleveland may have been disappointed that his mechanics were a mess and he wasn't as far along developmentally as anticipated, Baez throws a live mid-90s fastball and a curveball that will be a terrific big league pitch with a little more tightening. He showed flashes of the major league pitcher he will be during his stint at Double-A Akron in 2000, but he still needs to refine a changeup and smooth out his mechanics. He's fairly polished and has a great deal of desire, and the Indians had to be encouraged by his strong showing in the Arizona Fall League.

Russ Branyan

Position: 3B **Opening Day Age:** 25
Bats: L **Throws:** R **Born:** 12/19/75 in
Ht: 6' 3" **Wt:** 195 Warner Robins, GA

Recent Statistics

	G	AB	R	H	D	THR	RBI	SB	BB	SO	Avg
2000 AAA Buffalo	64	229	46	56	9	2 21	60	1	28	93	.245
2000 AL Cleveland	67	193	32	46	7	2 16	38	0	22	76	.238
2000 MLE	64	227	42	54	8	1 19	55	0	26	97	.238

The home runs and strikeouts go hand in hand with Branyan, a seventh-round pick in 1994 who has fanned

280 times in 624 at-bats at Triple-A Buffalo the last two seasons. While he continued that strikeout pace with Cleveland last summer, Branyan also stroked 16 homers in just 193 at-bats and drew walks at a decent clip. There's no denying Branyan's remarkable power potential, and his athleticism and hard work have helped him become a consistent third baseman with a strong arm. Pitch recognition is an ongoing learning experience for Branyan, and his plate discipline has been a plus. If Branyan continues to close the gap between his walk and strikeout totals, the loss of Richie Sexson at the trade deadline in July will not be a costly one.

Jamie Brown

Position: P **Opening Day Age:** 24
Bats: R **Throws:** R **Born:** 3/31/77 in
Ht: 6' 2" **Wt:** 205 Meridian, MS

Recent Statistics

	W	L	ERA	G	GS	Sv	IP	H	R	BB	SO	HR
1999 AA Akron	5	9	4.57	23	23	0	138.0	140	72	39	98	11
1999 AAA Buffalo	1	0	5.40	1	0	0	5.0	8	4	1	2	0
2000 AA Akron	7	6	4.38	17	17	0	96.2	95	49	26	57	12

After going 22-11 in his first two pro seasons, Brown hasn't been able to master Double-A ball in two summers at Akron. His stuff is good enough that Brown suddenly could find himself pitching in Cleveland. He works with a fastball-changeup combination that is above average, but his slider needs work. Command of all of his pitches wavered at times. Back problems in 2000 may have affected his delivery, compromising his ability to produce consistent results, so a breakout season remains a possibility. A 21st-round pick in 1996, Brown may return to the Akron rotation to open the 2001 campaign, or the Indians may bump him up to Triple-A Buffalo.

Jacob Cruz

Position: OF **Opening Day Age:** 28
Bats: L **Throws:** L **Born:** 1/28/73 in Oxnard,
Ht: 6' 0" **Wt:** 179 CA

Recent Statistics

	G	AB	R	H	D	THR	RBI	SB	BB	SO	Avg
2000 AL Cleveland	11	29	3	7	3	0 0	5	1	5	4	.241

Cruz was a good pickup by the Tribe in a July 1998 trade that shipped Jose Mesa, Shawon Dunston and Alvin Morman to San Francisco for Steve Reed and the lefthanded outfielder. Cruz looked like he finally would get a chance to play in 2000, but he tore the ACL in his left knee at the end of April and his season was over. Capable of handling all three outfield positions with a solid arm, Cruz also hits for average and has gap power. Wil Cordero, Russ Branyan and Cruz will battle for playing time in left field in 2001. With a platoon possible, it works against Cruz that he and Branyan bat lefthanded. Cruz clearly is the best defender in the group.

Sean DePaula

Position: P
Bats: R **Throws:** R
Ht: 6' 4" **Wt:** 215
Opening Day Age: 27
Born: 11/7/73 in Newton, MA

Recent Statistics

	W	L	ERA	G	GS	Sv	IP	H	R	BB	SO	HR
2000 AA Akron	0	0	1.80	4	0	0	5.0	1	1	2	4	0
2000 AAA Buffalo	1	0	5.54	9	0	1	13.0	16	10	7	11	1
2000 AL Cleveland	0	0	5.94	13	0	0	16.2	20	11	14	16	3

A ninth-round pick in 1996, DePaula wasn't on the 40-man roster at the start of 1999, but he pitched at four levels and performed well for Cleveland in the postseason. He looked like a sure thing to assume setup duties last spring, but elbow tendinitis sidelined him in midseason and he didn't pitch again in 2000. When he's healthy, his fastball, slider and splitter are major league offerings. DePaula must re-establish his command and the confidence he showed in his pitches in '99. It may take a brief stay at Triple-A Buffalo to get DePaula back on track, but he has the mental toughness to pitch in any bullpen role.

Tim Drew

Position: P
Bats: R **Throws:** R
Ht: 6' 1" **Wt:** 195
Opening Day Age: 22
Born: 8/31/78 in Valdosta, GA

Recent Statistics

	W	L	ERA	G	GS	Sv	IP	H	R	BB	SO	HR
2000 AA Akron	3	2	2.42	9	9	0	52.0	41	19	15	22	1
2000 AAA Buffalo	7	8	5.87	16	16	0	95.0	122	69	31	53	12
2000 AL Cleveland	1	0	10.00	3	3	0	9.0	17	12	8	5	1

Drew joined brother J.D. as a first-round pick in 1997, and Tim reached high Class-A Kinston in '98. He returned to Kinston in 1999 and went 13-5 (3.73) to lead the Carolina League in wins. Drew pitched well at Double-A Akron to open 2000, but wasn't ready to debut for an injury-riddled Cleveland staff in May. The Indians didn't have much choice, and he didn't fare well. He then went to Triple-A Buffalo, where the going was rough. He needs to work on the command of his 90-MPH fastball. While his changeup is his out pitch, setting up hitters more effectively will improve his fastball-changeup combo. He's smart and mentally tough, and both qualities will be critical to his success at higher levels.

C.C. Sabathia

Position: P
Bats: L **Throws:** L
Ht: 6' 7" **Wt:** 235
Opening Day Age: 20
Born: 7/21/80 in Vallejo, CA

Recent Statistics

	W	L	ERA	G	GS	Sv	IP	H	R	BB	SO	HR
1999 A Mahoning Vy	0	0	1.83	6	6	0	19.2	9	5	12	27	0
1999 A Columbus	2	0	1.08	3	3	0	16.2	8	2	5	20	1
1999 A Kinston	3	3	5.34	7	7	0	32.0	30	22	19	29	3
2000 A Kinston	3	2	3.54	10	10	0	56.0	48	23	24	69	4
2000 AA Akron	3	7	3.59	17	17	0	90.1	75	41	48	90	6

There's little not to like about the big lefthander, who has the arm and size to be a dominant major league pitcher. Sabathia is a power pitcher with an excellent fastball that regularly hits the high 90s, and he mixes in a solid curveball and changeup. He has a great feel for pitching and effectively changes speeds, and those assets helped him reach Double-A Akron two months before his 20th birthday last July. Sabathia has been kept on a strict pitch count, so it's hard to treat his 3-7 record at Akron seriously. His inning totals also have been watched carefully, and Sabathia surpassed 100 innings in a season for the first time in 2000. He handled 146 innings of work without any trouble, a good sign for a future No. 1 starter.

Jake Westbrook

Position: P
Bats: R **Throws:** R
Ht: 6' 3" **Wt:** 185
Opening Day Age: 23
Born: 9/29/77 in Athens, GA

Recent Statistics

	W	L	ERA	G	GS	Sv	IP	H	R	BB	SO	HR
2000 AAA Columbus	5	7	4.65	16	15	0	89.0	94	53	38	61	3
2000 AL New York	0	2	13.50	3	2	0	6.2	15	10	4	1	1

A Colorado first-round pick in 1996, Westbrook and two other minor leaguers were dealt to Montreal for Mike Lansing in '97. Since posting double-digit wins in three straight seasons in the Montreal system, Westbrook has been on the move. He was traded to the Yankees in the Hideki Irabu deal in December 1999, then moved to Cleveland in the David Justice trade last July. Westbrook throws a 90-MPH sinker and mixes in a slider and changeup. With three average offerings, Westbrook hasn't been able to dominate hitters at higher levels. What can help put him over the top are his smarts and his feel for mixing his pitches. Westbrook will make his debut in the Cleveland organization this spring, as he arrived from New York while nursing a broken rib.

Others to Watch

Acquired in the David Justice trade with New York, **Zach Day** (22) impressed with a strong return from rotator cuff surgery in 1999. The 6-foot-4 righthander started the 2000 season with New York's Class-A Greensboro and advanced all the way to Double-A Akron. He fanned 180 batters in 165.2 innings, using a solid low-90s sinker and changeup. . . There's nothing he can't do as a shortstop, thanks to his soft hands, great range and strong arm, but **Macier Izturis** (20) has missed a lot of time because of shoulder surgery (1999) and elbow problems (2000). He's well-rounded as a hitter, too, and could become a top prospect if he gets a full season in this year. . . Southpaw **Roy Padilla** (25) was signed by Boston out of Panama in 1992, became a position player in 1996, but returned to pitching in '99. He's raw and looks destined for the Double-A Akron pen, but his fastball reaches the high 90s. . . A first-round pick in 1996, **Danny Peoples** (26) has struggled with injuries and strikeouts. He has enticing bat speed and raw power. He hit .260-21-74 at Triple-A Buffalo in 2000, but his best chance may come after the 2001 trade deadline, when Cleveland might package him in a pennant-drive deal.

Comerica Park

Offense

Comerica Park is great for line-drive, gap hitters. But it's a nightmare for righthanded power hitters because it is 398 feet to the left-center field gap and the wall goes out quickly from the foul line. Right field is slightly more reasonable. The park is like Coors Field in that there is so much room that many bloop hits and flyballs drop in. The difference is that Detroit doesn't sit a mile high above sea level. The Tigers hit .283 as a team at home and .268 on the road during the 2000 season. Conversely, they hit 69 home runs at home and 108 on the road.

Defense

There is a lot of room in the outfield, so there is a need for outfielders who can cover ground. It helps to have infielders with strong throwing arms because a lot of balls get into the outfield gaps, causing the need for relay throws. The infield is quicker than it was at Tiger Stadium, where it was particularly slow. The wind tends to swirl because the stadium is not completely enclosed.

Who It Helps the Most

Pitchers such as Brian Moehler, who give up a lot of deep flyballs, benefit the most. Lefthanded hitting Bobby Higginson didn't try to pull the ball as much at Comerica Park and became a better all-around hitter as a result. The new park is the reason a gap hitter such as Deivi Cruz had more doubles.

Who It Hurts the Most

The Tigers wanted a National League-style team by the time they moved into Comerica Park. Instead they featured a bunch of righthanded power hitters last season. Juan Gonzalez, in particular, struggled there. Dean Palmer is not hurt as much as Gonzalez due to his ability to hit to right.

Rookies & Newcomers

The Tigers' best prospects should be OK in the new stadium. First baseman Eric Munson is a lefthanded hitter who can find the gaps. Catcher Brandon Inge has grooved his righthanded stroke to hit the ball inside-out, ideal for Comerica Park. The Tigers are trying to groom speedy center fielder Andres Torres for the future. He will be at Double-A Erie this season, and may be the answer.

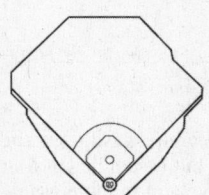

Dimensions: LF-345, LCF-398, CF-420, RCF-380, RF-330

Capacity: 40,000

Elevation: 585 feet

Surface: Grass

Foul Territory: Average

Park Factors

2000 Season

	Home Games			Away Games			
	Tigers	Opp	Total	Tigers	Opp	Total	Index
G	72	72	144	72	72	144	—
Avg	.280	.281	.280	.275	.281	.278	101
AB	2445	2572	5017	2573	2430	5003	100
R	350	358	708	396	401	797	89
H	684	723	1407	708	682	1390	101
2B	136	143	279	134	126	260	107
3B	20	19	39	16	21	37	105
HR	64	58	122	102	98	200	61
BB	273	203	476	233	250	483	98
SO	388	413	801	476	434	910	88
E	50	57	107	46	49	95	113
E-Infield	39	46	85	38	41	79	108
LHB-Avg	.291	.272	.280	.260	.261	.261	107
LHB-HR	27	37	64	33	56	89	72
RHB-Avg	.273	.289	.281	.282	.300	.290	97
RHB-HR	37	21	58	69	42	111	52

1998-1999 (Tiger Stadium)

	Home Games			Away Games			
	Tigers	Opp	Total	Tigers	Opp	Total	Index
G	145	145	290	144	144	288	—
Avg	.261	.270	.265	.265	.286	.275	96
AB	4857	5087	9944	5085	4849	9934	99
R	673	784	1457	633	798	1431	101
H	1268	1372	2640	1348	1387	2735	96
2B	230	251	481	309	256	565	85
3B	30	27	57	26	31	57	100
HR	185	208	393	142	155	297	132
BB	418	536	954	389	515	904	105
SO	925	877	1802	938	810	1748	103
E	94	120	214	107	83	190	112
E-Infield	74	103	177	84	68	152	116
LHB-Avg	.260	.271	.266	.275	.295	.286	93
LHB-HR	83	94	177	66	88	154	116
RHB-Avg	.262	.269	.265	.258	.278	.267	99
RHB-HR	102	114	216	76	67	143	150

2000 Rankings (American League)

- Lowest home-run factor
- Lowest strikeout factor
- Lowest RHB home-run factor
- Second-lowest LHB home-run factor
- Third-lowest run factor
- Third-lowest RHB batting-average factor

Phil Garner

2000 Season

Phil Garner's cool-under-fire attitude really bene-fited his team last season. After a 9-23 start, the Tigers recovered nicely. They moved to over .500 at one point in September and got onto the fringe of the American League wild-card race. Garner never panicked. He found ways to get the most out of his team despite numerous injuries and a disap-pointing season by Juan Gonzalez.

Offense

Garner plays with the hand he is dealt. He doesn't try to force his team into one style of play over another, rather letting the situation dictate what he's going to do. He won't bunt players such as Juan Gonzalez and Dean Palmer, nor will he expect somebody such as Shane Halter to hit a three-run homer. Garner doesn't stick to one set lineup card, either. He moves his players all over the batting order, and he is not afraid to call upon a pinch-hit-ter.

Pitching & Defense

Garner milks his pitching staff. He will use a starter between starts if he didn't pitch many innings in his previous outing or is skipping a day or two because of an off day. He generally doesn't stick with his starters when they get in trouble, however. He makes good use of his middle relievers and expects them to eat up innings when called upon early. In terms of defense, his challenge will be to figure out how best to cover the new dimensions of Comerica Park. He will continue to make liberal use of defen-sive substitutions.

2001 Outlook

Garner hasn't managed a winning team since his first season at Milwaukee in 1992. He is tired of just getting a lot out of below-average teams, something he did again last season. That's why he prefers older, veteran players and resists putting young prospects into the everyday lineup. To Gar-ner, the future is now. He is looking to win games, not develop prospects.

Born: 4/30/49 in Jefferson City, TN

Playing Experience: 1973-1988, Oak, Pit, Hou, LA, SF

Managerial Experience: 9 seasons

Manager Statistics

Year	Team, Lg	W	L	Pct	GB	Finish
2000	Detroit, AL	79	83	.488	16.0	3rd Central
9 Seasons		642	700	.478	—	—

2000 Starting Pitchers by Days Rest

	<=3	4	5	6+
Tigers Starts	3	90	39	20
Tigers ERA	9.45	4.70	4.92	5.24
AL Avg Starts	2	88	40	22
AL ERA	4.87	5.03	5.03	5.28

2000 Situational Stats

	Phil Garner	AL Average
Hit & Run Success %	33.9	35.1
Stolen Base Success %	68.6	68.8
Platoon Pct.	53.1	57.8
Defensive Subs	25	23
High-Pitch Outings	8	13
Quick/Slow Hooks	18/18	18/19
Sacrifice Attempts	58	55

2000 Rankings (American League)
- 2nd in mid-inning pitching changes (228)
- 3rd in one-batter pitcher appearances (41)

Detroit

Brad Ausmus

2000 Season

There was little rest for Brad Ausmus last season. He caught 150 games, 140 of them in a starting role, when he'd never appeared in more than 130 games before in his eight-year major league career. But if Ausmus wore down, it wasn't noticeable. He hit for a higher average during the second half of the season than during the first, while maintaining his typically high defensive standards.

Hitting

Ausmus is at his best when he tries to stay inside the ball and drive it up the middle or toward the opposite field. He doesn't have a particularly quick bat and doesn't generate enough bat speed to hit with a lot of power or to pull the ball with authority. He's never hit more than nine home runs in a season nor produced more than 25 doubles. In 523 at-bats last season, he had just 35 extra-base hits. He was a much better hitter versus lefthanded pitching last season than in the past, when he tended to struggle against southpaws.

Baserunning & Defense

Ausmus is athletic. He moves quickly behind the plate. He is smart, thinks on his feet, frames pitches well and calls a good game. The pitchers like and respect him. His arm strength is above average, he gets rid of the ball quickly and throws accurately. Ausmus also has above-average speed—well above average for a catcher. He's reached double figures in stolen bases five times in his career, including each of the past four seasons. He had 11 steals in 16 attempts last season and is a heady baserunner.

2001 Outlook

After two seasons in Detroit, Ausmus returned to the Astros in a six-player deal executed in December. The Tigers shipped Ausmus and pitchers Doug Brocail and Nelson Cruz to Houston for catcher Mitch Meluskey, outfielder Roger Cedeno and pitcher Chris Holt. Switch-hitting Meluskey replaces Ausmus in the Tiger lineup, while Ausmus assumes starter duties in Houston. Ausmus should continue to provide a timely hit now and then, as well as be an excellent deterrent to would-be basestealers.

Position: C
Bats: R **Throws:** R
Ht: 5'11" **Wt:** 195

Opening Day Age: 31
Born: 4/14/69 in New Haven, CT
ML Seasons: 8
Pronunciation: AHHS-muss

Overall Statistics

	G	AB	R	H	D	T	HR	RBI	SB	BB	SO	Avg	OBP	Slg
2000	150	523	75	139	25	3	7	51	11	69	79	.266	.357	.365
Career	913	3008	397	791	137	20	48	299	74	317	507	.263	.338	.370

Where He Hits the Ball

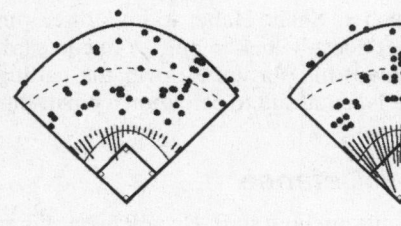

Vs. LHP   **Vs. RHP**

2000 Situational Stats

	AB	H	HR	RBI	Avg		AB	H	HR	RBI	Avg
Home	254	73	3	33	.287	LHP	137	44	3	15	.321
Road	269	66	4	18	.245	RHP	386	95	4	36	.246
First Half	291	69	5	27	.237	Sc Pos	131	30	1	42	.229
Scnd Half	232	70	2	24	.302	Clutch	68	18	1	10	.265

2000 Rankings (American League)

- 1st in batting average on an 0-2 count (.333) and highest percentage of runners caught stealing as a catcher (43.2)
- 2nd in errors at catcher (8)
- 4th in lowest slugging percentage and lowest slugging percentage vs. righthanded pitchers (.342)
- Led the Tigers in caught stealing (5), most pitches seen per plate appearance (4.00), batting average on an 0-2 count (.333), on-base percentage vs. lefthanded pitchers (.422), batting average on a 3-2 count (.369) and batting average with two strikes (.237)
- Led AL catchers in at-bats, singles, stolen bases, caught stealing (5) and GDPs (19)

Tony Clark

2000 Season

An injury that had plagued Tony Clark in the past returned last season at the worst possible time. After getting off to his traditional slow start (.115 batting average in April), Clark was on a hot streak when he came down with back problems. He had surgery on his back in 1991 when he was in the minor leagues and it forced him to stop playing college basketball. Clark finished with just 208 at-bats for the season, with only 46 of those coming after the All-Star break.

Hitting

Clark is a switch-hitter, but he has the same strengths and weaknesses from both sides. He likes low fastballs out over the plate, and pitchers have success tying him up high and inside. He doesn't take well to breaking balls, either. When he slumps, it's because his stroke has become so long that he can't catch up with even mediocre fastballs. He gets in situations where he has a hair trigger, making it even more difficult for him to adjust to offspeed offerings. When he makes consistent contact, his power is exceptional, but he's streaky, and the cold streaks often outlast the hot ones.

Baserunning & Defense

Clark is not fluid fielding groundballs and his throwing arm is poor. He does not turn the 3-6-3 double play well. He is a good receiver, however, saving many an error for infielders by picking balls out of the dirt. A converted outfielder, he plays popups surprisingly well. Clark is uncommonly slow on the bases and does not display good instincts on the basepaths. He slides awkwardly, a task he should avoid given his size and history of back trouble.

2001 Outlook

It was deemed unnecessary for Clark to undergo back surgery following the season, but his health is an obvious concern. He has a live bat, is hard working and is confident even in the worst of times. Yet his slow starts the past three seasons have killed the Tigers. In 1998 and 1999, the team was out of the race before he even got going. One way or the other, he needs to exorcise the slow-start demon.

Position: 1B
Bats: B **Throws:** R
Ht: 6' 7"   **Wt:** 245

Opening Day Age: 28
Born: 6/15/72 in Newton, KS
ML Seasons: 6

Overall Statistics

	G	AB	R	H	D	T	HR	RBI	SB	BB	SO	Avg	OBP	Slg
2000	60	208	32	57	14	0	13	37	0	24	51	.274	.349	.529
Career	646	2403	361	660	127	4	140	439	6	281	613	.275	.351	.506

Where He Hits the Ball

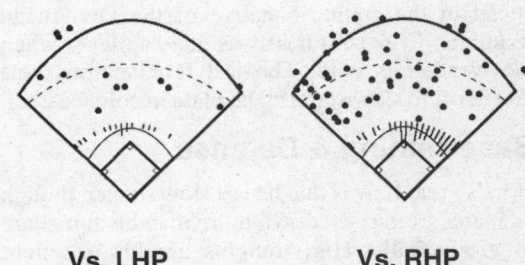

Vs. LHP   **Vs. RHP**

2000 Situational Stats

	AB	H	HR	RBI	Avg		AB	H	HR	RBI	Avg
Home	94	25	6	14	.266	LHP	39	12	3	9	.308
Road	114	32	7	23	.281	RHP	169	45	10	28	.266
First Half	162	42	12	31	.259	Sc Pos	57	14	3	22	.246
Scnd Half	46	15	1	6	.326	Clutch	29	10	0	5	.345

2000 Rankings (American League)
- 3rd in most GDPs per GDP situation (18.9%)

Deivi Cruz

Position: SS
Bats: R **Throws:** R
Ht: 6' 0" **Wt:** 184

Opening Day Age: 25
Born: 11/6/75 in Nizao de Bani, Dominican Republic
ML Seasons: 4
Pronunciation: DAY-vee

2000 Season

Deivi Cruz continued to show dramatic improvement as a hitter, reaching career highs in most major offensive categories. He also managed to stay injury-free for the second straight season, and he closed strongly, hitting .323 after the All-Star break and .349 from September 1 on.

Hitting

Cruz has never met a pitch he didn't like. He rarely walks and rarely strikes out. He has excellent hand-eye coordination, but he does get himself out at times by swinging at bad pitches. He loves fastballs out over the plate, with many of his doubles coming in the form of line drives pounded up the left-center field gap off fastballs after he's gotten ahead in the count. A native of the Dominican Republic, Cruz isn't nearly as good a player when the weather is cold. The last four seasons he's gotten off to slow starts at the plate in cold weather.

Baserunning & Defense

Cruz's great flaw is that he is a slow runner, though he manages to track down more than his fair share of groundballs. His strengths are his excellent hands, his ability to make the routine play and his exceptional arm strength. He positions himself well, and that helps compensate for his lack of range. Cruz lacks speed, runs himself into outs and doesn't cut the corners well when rounding bases. In four major league seasons, he has just eight stolen bases in 26 attempts.

2001 Outlook

By the end of last season, Phil Garner didn't hesitate to hit Cruz in the fifth or sixth position because of his increased power production. In his first three seasons, Cruz rarely hit above ninth in the order. Because of his strides at the plate, his good hands and his arm strength, there has been speculation that Cruz eventually might be moved to third base. That move is unlikely to happen in 2001, however.

Overall Statistics

	G	AB	R	H	D	T	HR	RBI	SB	BB	SO	Avg	OBP	Slg
2000	156	583	68	176	46	5	10	82	1	13	43	.302	.318	.449
Career	593	1991	219	546	129	8	30	225	8	52	210	.274	.294	.392

Where He Hits the Ball

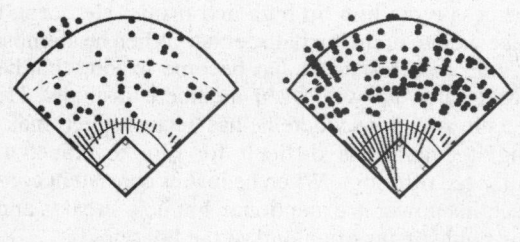

Vs. LHP **Vs. RHP**

2000 Situational Stats

	AB	H	HR	RBI	Avg		AB	H	HR	RBI	Avg
Home	287	88	1	32	.307	LHP	139	48	5	27	.345
Road	296	88	9	50	.297	RHP	444	128	5	55	.288
First Half	286	80	5	36	.280	Sc Pos	163	50	3	67	.307
Scnd Half	297	96	5	46	.323	Clutch	85	21	2	10	.247

2000 Rankings (American League)

- 2nd in highest percentage of swings put into play (54.1) and most GDPs per GDP situation (20.5%)
- 3rd in doubles, GDPs (25) and fewest pitches seen per plate appearance (3.16)
- 4th in fielding percentage at shortstop (.982) and lowest on-base percentage vs. righthanded pitchers (.304)
- 8th in batting average vs. lefthanded pitchers and lowest percentage of swings that missed (12.0)
- 9th in batting average on an 0-2 count (.286) and lowest HR frequency (58.3 ABs per HR)
- 10th in lowest percentage of pitches taken (47.6)
- Led the Tigers in batting average, singles, doubles, GDPs (25) and batting average with runners in scoring position

Damion Easley

2000 Season

Damion Easley has declined as a hitter since setting his career standard with 27 home runs and 100 RBI in 1998, and his .259 batting average was his lowest since being acquired by Detroit late in the '96 season. A strained ribcage muscle suffered during the opening weeks of the season was followed shortly thereafter by a hairline fracture of his right wrist. Both injuries put Easley on the disabled list and did not help his cause.

Hitting

Easley loves a good fastball over the heart of the plate and will drive that pitch extraordinary distances for a middle infielder. He has a strong, compact body, a short stroke and good balance in his stance. But he never really mastered the art of hitting a good breaking ball—or laying off one when need be—especially with runners in scoring position. Easley spent a fair amount of time in the leadoff spot last season, but that was more out of necessity than fitting his skills. He has done his best work hitting second, where he sees a lot of fastballs.

Baserunning & Defense

Easley turns the double play exceptionally well and rarely boots a routine grounder. He has a strong, accurate arm and above-average range. He is talented enough to play shortstop but has balked at the idea of changing positions. Where Easley often fails in the clutch at the plate, he rarely does in the field. He makes good defensive plays in key situations. He used to have above-average speed, but that's no longer the case. Still, he's a smart baserunner who can steal a base when the situation dictates.

2001 Outlook

Easley had an excellent spring and was primed to have a big year when injuries got to him early last season. He's 31 years old, so he's no longer a kid who is part of a rebuilding program. Easley is expected to carry a heavy load on a winning team, not only in terms of production on the field, but as a quiet leader in the clubhouse.

Position: 2B
Bats: R **Throws:** R
Ht: 5'11" **Wt:** 185

Opening Day Age: 31
Born: 11/11/69 in New York, NY
ML Seasons: 9

Overall Statistics

	G	AB	R	H	D	T	HR	RBI	SB	BB	SO	Avg	OBP	Slg
2000	126	464	76	120	27	2	14	58	13	55	79	.259	.350	.416
Career	952	3300	477	852	182	13	100	411	94	320	598	.258	.336	.412

Where He Hits the Ball

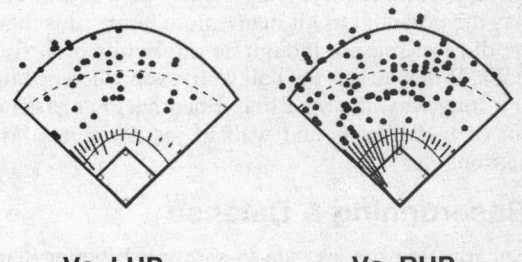

Vs. LHP   **Vs. RHP**

2000 Situational Stats

	AB	H	HR	RBI	Avg		AB	H	HR	RBI	Avg
Home	213	65	5	32	.305	LHP	125	35	3	13	.280
Road	251	55	9	26	.219	RHP	339	85	11	45	.251
First Half	192	46	6	19	.240	Sc Pos	122	30	1	41	.246
Scnd Half	272	74	8	39	.272	Clutch	63	15	2	6	.238

2000 Rankings (American League)

- 1st in fielding percentage at second base (.990) and lowest batting average with the bases loaded (.000)
- 4th in lowest batting average on the road
- 6th in hit by pitch (11) and on-base percentage for a leadoff hitter (.373)
- Led the Tigers in hit by pitch (11), batting average on a 3-1 count (.545), on-base percentage for a leadoff hitter (.373) and highest percentage of pitches taken (59.8)
- Led AL second basemen in hit by pitch (11), batting average on a 3-1 count (.545) and on-base percentage for a leadoff hitter (.373)

Detroit

Juan Encarnacion

2000 Season

Juan Encarnacion changed positions last season, moving from left field, where he mainly played in 1999, to center. While not a candidate to win a Gold Glove, he did play the position adequately. Offensively, he did not make the expected progress. His batting average rose 34 points, but he had fewer home runs, RBI and stolen bases than he did in 1999, his first full season in the majors.

Hitting

When he first came to the majors, Encarnacion held his bat high above his head in his stance and sometimes had trouble catching up with a good inside fastball. He's dropped his bat down and is making contact more consistently as a result. He has the potential to hit many more home runs than he did last season, though he rarely hits high fly-balls. When he hits the ball well, even when he hits it a long way, it's on a line. Encarnacion chases a lot of bad pitches and walked just 29 times last season.

Baserunning & Defense

Encarnacion moves side-to-side much better than he moves straight back. Therefore, the organization was hesitant to move him to center field. He became more consistent last season at making the routine play after dropping numerous flyballs in 1999. Encarnacion has above-average arm strength and threw the ball consistently well last season despite registering only three assists. He also has above-average speed. He didn't steal that much last season, but he was successful 80 percent of the time when he attempted.

2001 Outlook

Ideally, the Tigers would like to move Encarnacion back to a corner outfield spot because he struggles at times with balls hit directly over his head. That now is likely with the acquisition of Roger Cedeno in a December deal with Houston. Offensively, Encarnacion needs to sting the ball more consistently if he is going to be the five-tool star many are projecting him to become. His power production last season was disappointing.

Position: CF
Bats: R **Throws:** R
Ht: 6' 3" **Wt:** 187

Opening Day Age: 25
Born: 3/8/76 in Las Matas de Faran, Dominican Republic
ML Seasons: 4
Pronunciation: en-car-NAH-see-own

Overall Statistics

	G	AB	R	H	D	T	HR	RBI	SB	BB	SO	Avg	OBP	Slg
2000	141	547	75	158	25	6	14	72	16	29	90	.289	.330	.433
Career	324	1253	170	349	65	17	41	172	59	53	246	.279	.316	.456

Where He Hits the Ball

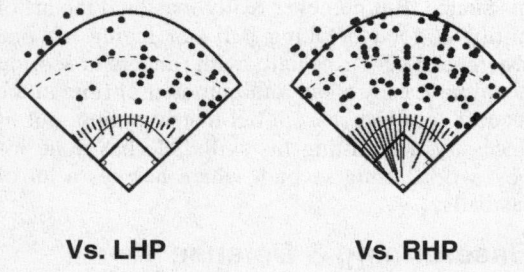

Vs. LHP   **Vs. RHP**

2000 Situational Stats

	AB	H	HR	RBI	Avg		AB	H	HR	RBI	Avg
Home	256	68	4	28	.266	LHP	140	44	7	27	.314
Road	291	90	10	44	.309	RHP	407	114	7	45	.280
First Half	279	84	7	30	.301	Sc Pos	130	38	4	58	.292
Scnd Half	268	74	7	42	.276	Clutch	64	20	1	6	.313

2000 Rankings (American League)

- 5th in lowest fielding percentage in center field (.987)
- Led the Tigers in triples, stolen bases, highest groundball/flyball ratio (1.7), stolen-base percentage (80.0), batting average with the bases loaded (.364), batting average on the road and highest percentage of extra bases taken as a runner (60.0)

Juan Gonzalez

2000 Season

Acquired in a nine-player trade from Texas before last season, Juan Gonzalez had his worst year since the strike-shortened 1994 campaign. The Tigers expected more than 22 home runs and 67 RBI from the two-time American League MVP. He was limited to 115 games because of foot, ankle and back injuries. He also complained loudly about the distance to the fence in left-center at Comerica Park and left the team with two days remaining in the season while sidelined with a herniated disk.

Hitting

Despite his subpar statistics, Gonzalez showed just enough last season to serve notice that he remains a formidable hitter. When he's on, he has exceptional plate coverage and is capable of driving any type of pitch out of the park. His biggest weakness remains chasing outside breaking balls. His slugging percentage last season on the road was .545, not far below his career mark of .566. It was at home where Gonzalez struggled the most, hitting just eight home runs—one inside-the-park—in 217 at-bats. He slugged just .461 at home.

Baserunning & Defense

Gonzalez isn't going to crash into walls trying to make spectacular plays. It's rare when he makes a diving effort, still he's a solid right fielder. Though he has only average speed, he gets a good jump on the ball, and his hands are sure. He throws well and usually to the right base. Gonzalez is not particularly fast, but he's a smart baserunner. He makes good decisions about when to take the extra base and when to hold up. He rarely attempts to steal.

2001 Outlook

Although he's been around for more than a decade and his trophy case is full, Gonzalez is only 31 years old. He's coming off a poor season, but it's not necessarily because his physical tools are fading—the move from Texas to Detroit proved to be a difficult adjustment for him. His back is a concern, however, and the extent of that injury could play a key role in determining whether he stays in Detroit or finds another team willing to buck up big free-agent dollars to take a chance that he'll return to form.

Position: RF/DH
Bats: R **Throws:** R
Ht: 6' 3" **Wt:** 220

Opening Day Age: 31
Born: 10/16/69 in Vega Baja, Puerto Rico
ML Seasons: 12
Nickname: Igor

Overall Statistics

	G	AB	R	H	D	T	HR	RBI	SB	BB	SO	Avg	OBP	Slg
2000	115	461	69	133	30	2	22	67	1	32	84	.289	.337	.505
Career	1363	5292	860	1554	312	21	362	1142	22	376	1031	.294	.343	.566

Where He Hits the Ball

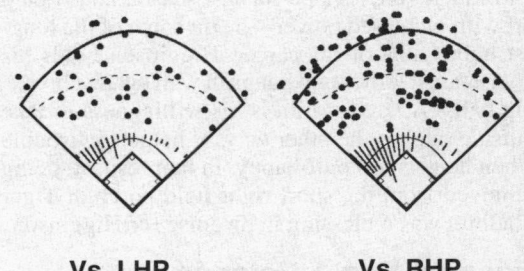

Vs. LHP   Vs. RHP

2000 Situational Stats

	AB	H	HR	RBI	Avg		AB	H	HR	RBI	Avg
Home	217	58	8	31	.267	LHP	114	41	6	17	.360
Road	244	75	14	36	.307	RHP	347	92	16	50	.265
First Half	266	73	13	33	.274	Sc Pos	129	31	5	43	.240
Scnd Half	195	60	9	34	.308	Clutch	61	16	4	9	.262

2000 Rankings (American League)

- 5th in lowest cleanup slugging percentage (.507)
- Led the Tigers in cleanup slugging percentage (.507)
- Led designated hitters in highest percentage of extra bases taken as a runner (48.8)

Detroit

Bobby Higginson

2000 Season

Bobby Higginson bounced back from a disappointing 1999 campaign and posted solid numbers across the board in 2000. He was on the trading block during spring training, but several teams passed on him. It turned out to be an addition by no subtraction for the Tigers. Higginson reached the 30-home run mark for the first time in his career, topped 100-RBI for the second time and reached the .300 mark for the second time.

Hitting

Higginson is a classic lefthanded pull hitter. He loves the low, inside fastball and hits many of his home runs off that pitch. Higginson got himself into much better shape for last season and it paid off with increased power—he hit some of the longest home runs of his career. Higginson holds his own against lefties and hangs in well against breaking balls. A key for him is his willingness to take outside pitches the other way, as he gets in trouble when he gets too pull-happy. In that respect, being removed from the short right-field porch at Tiger Stadium was a blessing in disguise for Higginson.

Baserunning & Defense

There were concerns that Higginson, who has below-average speed, would have trouble covering the extra ground at Comerica Park. They proved to be unfounded. Higginson was brilliant defensively last season, showing excellent range and making several outstanding catches. His arm always has been a plus, and he led the American League in outfield assists (19) for the third time. Higginson doesn't have a powerful arm, but it's exceptionally accurate, and he gets rid of the ball quickly. Higginson stole a career-best 15 bases last season. He's a smart baserunner who runs and slides hard.

2001 Outlook

Trade rumors won't haunt Higginson this offseason. He quelled the thought that he was beginning the backside of his career with his performance last season. He will be in the middle of the Detroit lineup every day against all types of pitching and will continue to prowl left field. At 30, he's in his prime and set to produce at a level similar to last season.

Position: LF/DH
Bats: L **Throws:** R
Ht: 5'11" **Wt:** 195

Opening Day Age: 30
Born: 8/18/70 in Philadelphia, PA
ML Seasons: 6

Overall Statistics

	G	AB	R	H	D	T	HR	RBI	SB	BB	SO	Avg	OBP	Slg
2000	154	597	104	179	44	4	30	102	15	74	99	.300	.377	.538
Career	825	2982	477	839	181	18	134	458	46	398	524	.281	.367	.489

Where He Hits the Ball

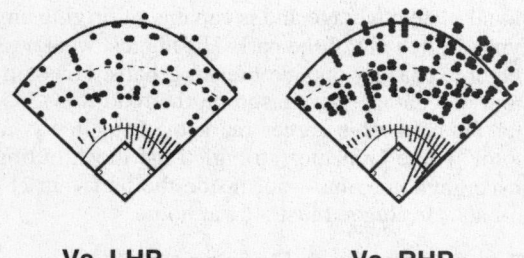

Vs. LHP   Vs. RHP

2000 Situational Stats

	AB	H	HR	RBI	Avg		AB	H	HR	RBI	Avg
Home	288	96	12	56	.333	LHP	182	48	4	19	.264
Road	309	83	18	46	.269	RHP	415	131	26	83	.316
First Half	295	84	17	52	.285	Sc Pos	158	47	9	68	.297
Scnd Half	302	95	13	50	.315	Clutch	81	27	3	13	.333

2000 Rankings (American League)

- 1st in errors in left field (7) and lowest fielding percentage in left field (.979)
- 2nd in lowest groundball/flyball ratio (0.7)
- 4th in fewest GDPs per GDP situation (3.4%)
- 5th in doubles
- Led the Tigers in home runs, at-bats, runs scored, hits, total bases (321), RBI, walks, intentional walks (6), times on base (255), pitches seen (2,710), plate appearances (679), slugging percentage, on-base percentage, fewest GDPs per GDP situation (3.4%), batting average in the clutch, batting average vs. righthanded pitchers, slugging percentage vs. righthanded pitchers (.600), on-base percentage vs. righthanded pitchers (.394) and batting average at home

Todd Jones

2000 Season

Todd Jones had his best season in 2000, saving a career-high 42 games and tying Boston's Derek Lowe for the American League lead in that category. He blew just four opportunities. Jones was stronger during the first half of the season, as he seemed to wear down near the end. His ERA in September was 5.73, and he was unavailable for a couple days because of a tired arm.

Pitching

Jones has a deceptive motion in which his arm flies out first with his body following behind. His delivery makes his fastball difficult for hitters to time. Although he gets up to 95 MPH, Jones usually sits at about 93 MPH. His fastball has good sinking action on it, too. He has developed a good slider, which was a key to his success early last season. His changeup is improving, though he rarely throws it. Normally when he goes to a breaking ball, it's a sloppy, roundhouse curveball. It's an effective pitch only because his fastball is so good, and because Jones gets it over the plate consistently.

Defense

Jones rarely is involved defensively. He doesn't field many groundballs, although he does cover first base adequately. He is not a great athlete but does give maximum effort. He's been around long enough and is enough of a team player to have acquired the fundamentals he needs to get by in the field. He does not have a good pickoff move and is somewhat slow to the plate, but will keep runners close when necessary. He only allowed one stolen base in three attempts in 2000.

2001 Outlook

There was a time when Jones seemed too emotional to ever become a star-caliber closer, but he has turned those emotions into a strength. He has the veteran savvy to bounce back from rough outings, and there's no reason to think last season was a fluke. Improving his changeup and developing a slider has helped. He also has better command of his fastball and isn't putting himself in as many dangerous situations, so another 40-save effort is not out of the question.

Position: RP
Bats: L **Throws:** R
Ht: 6' 3" **Wt:** 230

Opening Day Age: 32
Born: 4/24/68 in Marietta, GA
ML Seasons: 8

Overall Statistics

	W	L	Pct.	ERA	G	GS	Sv	IP	H	BB	SO	HR	Ratio
2000	2	4	.333	3.52	67	0	42	64.0	67	25	67	6	1.44
Career	30	28	.517	3.54	459	0	170	530.2	479	256	486	43	1.39

How Often He Throws Strikes

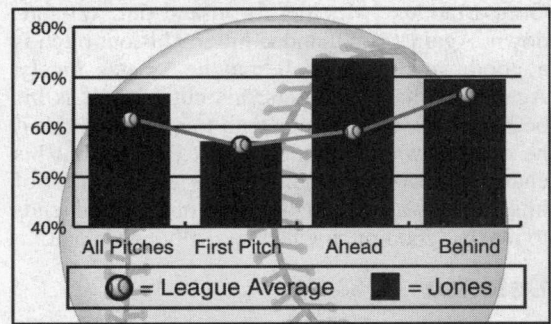

= League Average   = Jones

2000 Situational Stats

	W	L	ERA	Sv	IP		AB	H	HR	RBI	Avg
Home	2	1	3.00	21	33.0	LHB	126	37	3	17	.294
Road	0	3	4.06	21	31.0	RHB	117	30	3	17	.256
First Half	0	1	2.53	24	32.0	Sc Pos	90	24	4	32	.267
Scnd Half	2	3	4.50	18	32.0	Clutch	184	50	2	25	.272

2000 Rankings (American League)

- 1st in saves
- 2nd in save opportunities (46) and save percentage (91.3)
- 4th in games finished (60)
- 7th in most strikeouts per nine innings in relief (9.4) and worst first batter efficiency (.333)
- Led the Tigers in saves, games finished (60), save opportunities (46), save percentage (91.3) and most strikeouts per nine innings in relief (9.4)

Brian Moehler

2000 Season

Nobody benefited more from the Tigers' move to spacious Comerica Park than Brian Moehler. He was 12-9 for a career-best .571 winning percentage last season, including a 9-3 mark with a 4.17 ERA at Comerica Park. In 1999, Moehler was 6-10 with a 5.46 ERA at home. His 12 wins in 2000 came despite the fact that he missed more than a month following an emergency appendectomy in April.

Pitching

Moehler did surprise club officials by hitting 94 MPH once or twice last season, but throwing that hard is counterproductive to what he tries to accomplish on the mound. The pitcher he emulates is Greg Maddux. Moehler is in-and-out, up-and-down. Against righthanded hitters, his out pitch is a good, sinking fastball that he locates nicely. Against lefthanded hitters, his cut fastball is his best pitch. Both offerings tend to straighten out if he overthrows. His slider is just average but his changeup has improved. He does give up a lot of hits, but he walked just 40 in 178 innings and tends to make a good pitch when he really needs one.

Defense

Moehler is a bad fielder; his reactions are not good and he took numerous well-struck grounders off his legs as a result. He hasn't made an error in two seasons, but he doesn't cover a lot of ground on bunts or balls tapped out in front of the plate. He does cover first base adequately, however. He doesn't hold runners particularly well, though opposing baserunners attempted just seven steals on his watch last year.

2001 Outlook

On a really good pitching staff, Moehler would be the ideal third or fourth starter. On the Tigers, his role has had to be more than that. He's a bulldog, the guy who takes the ball no matter what, and he delivers superior effort if not always excellent results. As such, he will have a long major league career. His won-lost record will be tied to how well his team plays behind him in the field and how much run support he receives.

Position: SP
Bats: R **Throws:** R
Ht: 6' 3" **Wt:** 235

Opening Day Age: 29
Born: 12/31/71 in Rockingham, NC
ML Seasons: 5
Pronunciation: MOE-lur

Overall Statistics

	W	L	Pct.	ERA	G	GS	Sv	IP	H	BB	SO	HR	Ratio
2000	12	9	.571	4.50	29	29	0	178.0	222	40	103	20	1.47
Career	47	51	.480	4.50	127	127	0	781.1	880	224	431	95	1.41

How Often He Throws Strikes

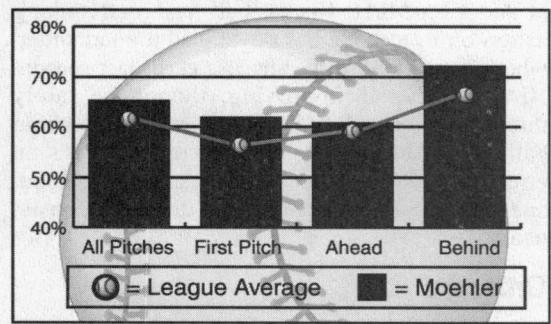

= League Average   = Moehler

2000 Situational Stats

	W	L	ERA	Sv	IP		AB	H	HR	RBI	Avg
Home	9	3	4.17	0	101.1	LHB	351	100	13	40	.285
Road	3	6	4.93	0	76.2	RHB	376	122	7	46	.324
First Half	5	5	3.79	0	80.2	Sc Pos	175	46	4	63	.263
Scnd Half	7	4	5.09	0	97.1	Clutch	21	6	1	2	.286

2000 Rankings (American League)

- 2nd in highest batting average allowed (.305)
- 3rd in fewest pitches thrown per batter (3.49), highest stolen-base percentage allowed (85.7) and highest batting average allowed vs. righthanded batters
- 4th in highest groundball/flyball ratio allowed (1.8)
- 5th in fewest walks per nine innings (2.0)
- Led the Tigers in wins, complete games (2), hits allowed, pickoff throws (107), highest groundball/flyball ratio allowed (1.8), fewest pitches thrown per batter (3.49), most run support per nine innings (5.8), fewest home runs allowed per nine innings (1.01) and most GDPs induced per nine innings (1.0)

Hideo Nomo

2000 Season

Hideo Nomo was the victim of poor run support many times during the 2000 season, but even when the Tigers' bats cooperated, he often labored. He struck out 181 hitters in 190 innings and allowed 191 hits, certainly good ratios. His downfall was that he allowed 31 longballs despite pitching in a home stadium that ranked as the most homer-*unfriendly* park in the majors last year. He also walked a hitter nearly every two innings.

Pitching

Nomo pitches much better when he's got a big lead. That's when he attacks hitters and racks up a lot of strikeouts. His approach changes in tight games, where he starts to nibble at the corners, tends to fall behind in the count and comes in with fat fastballs that often leave the park. Despite his strikeout totals, Nomo doesn't throw very hard, topping out at about 90 MPH. The deception created by his slow, back-bending windup makes his fastball appear quicker than it actually is, however. He has one of the best split-finger pitches in the game and also gets many of his strikeouts using that pitch.

Defense

Because of the length of his delivery, Nomo is easier than most pitchers to steal on. He does, however, work on delivering the ball toward home plate quicker from the stretch position. He will make the effort to hold runners close to the base, though it's often futile once he goes into his motion. Nomo is not athletic and his delivery doesn't put him in good fielding position. He makes remarkably few plays afield.

2001 Outlook

The Tigers declined to pick up Nomo's $5.5 million option for 2001. He is not the same pitcher he was when he arrived in the major leagues from Japan in 1995, but he still is effective enough to be a starter on most pitching staffs. Nomo will join the Boston rotation in the spring after signing a one-year, $4.5 million contract in December.

Position: SP
Bats: R **Throws:** R
Ht: 6' 2" **Wt:** 200

Opening Day Age: 32
Born: 8/31/68 in Osaka, Japan
ML Seasons: 6
Pronunciation: hih-DAY-oh NO-mo

Overall Statistics

	W	L	Pct.	ERA	G	GS	Sv	IP	H	BB	SO	HR	Ratio
2000	8	12	.400	4.74	32	31	0	190.0	191	89	181	31	1.47
Career	69	61	.531	3.97	183	181	0	1150.2	991	516	1212	137	1.31

How Often He Throws Strikes

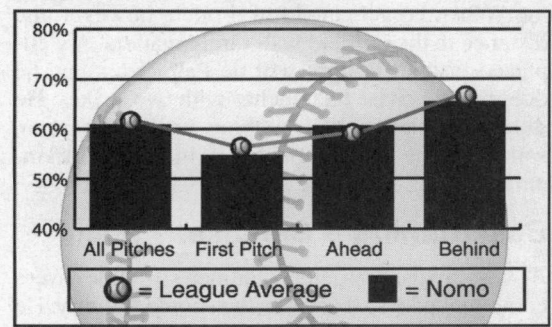

◐ = League Average   ■ = Nomo

2000 Situational Stats

	W	L	ERA	Sv	IP		AB	H	HR	RBI	Avg
Home	3	5	4.37	0	90.2	LHB	357	86	16	43	.241
Road	5	7	5.07	0	99.1	RHB	370	105	15	44	.284
First Half	3	7	4.74	0	117.2	Sc Pos	171	41	4	52	.240
Scnd Half	5	5	4.73	0	72.1	Clutch	25	8	0	2	.320

2000 Rankings (American League)

- 1st in runners caught stealing (14)
- 2nd in wild pitches (16)
- 3rd in most strikeouts per nine innings (8.6)
- 4th in lowest groundball/flyball ratio allowed (0.9)
- 5th in home runs allowed
- Led the Tigers in games started, home runs allowed, walks allowed, strikeouts, wild pitches (16), stolen bases allowed (16), runners caught stealing (14), lowest batting average allowed (.263), most strikeouts per nine innings (8.6), lowest batting average allowed vs. lefthanded batters and lowest batting average allowed with runners in scoring position

Detroit

Dean Palmer

2000 Season

That he played in 145 games despite a painful injury to his right shoulder is a testament to Dean Palmer's toughness. He also missed eight games in May after being suspended for charging the mound and setting off a nasty brawl with the White Sox. He still managed to drive in 100 runs for the third straight season, and for the fourth time in five years.

Hitting

Palmer was more effective hitting breaking balls last season. The dimensions of Comerica Park do not hinder him severely, as he poked several home runs to right field where the stadium is more forgiving. When he gets ahold of a pitch, however, the distance to the outfield wall rarely matters. A well-placed fastball in tight will tie Palmer up, and he does tend to chase bad pitches with two strikes. He did not hit lefthanded pitching well last season, something he did do effectively in previous campaigns.

Baserunning & Defense

Always a suspect fielder, Palmer's troubles were compounded last season by the shoulder injury. He made 23 errors in 115 games at third base and posted five two-error games. His range, hands and arm now are below average. When he played first base, he looked like a third baseman playing out of position. Even if he fully recovers from the shoulder injury, his future might be as a designated hitter. Palmer is not a fast runner and wisely plays it station-to-station on the bases.

2001 Outlook

Palmer remains a productive power hitter who can bat fifth or sixth on any team in baseball. He's a good leader because he plays hard, regardless of the situation. He's shown a willingness to play with pain and the ability to perform reasonably well when not at full health. It remains to be seen whether his future is at third, first or DH, though his flaws defensively are less obvious at first base than at third.

Position: 3B/1B/DH
Bats: R **Throws:** R
Ht: 6' 1" **Wt:** 210

Opening Day Age: 32
Born: 12/27/68 in Tallahassee, FL
ML Seasons: 11

Overall Statistics

	G	AB	R	H	D	T	HR	RBI	SB	BB	SO	Avg	OBP	Slg
2000	145	524	73	134	22	2	29	102	4	66	146	.256	.338	.471
Career	1270	4588	697	1169	218	15	264	803	44	465	1240	.255	.327	.481

Where He Hits the Ball

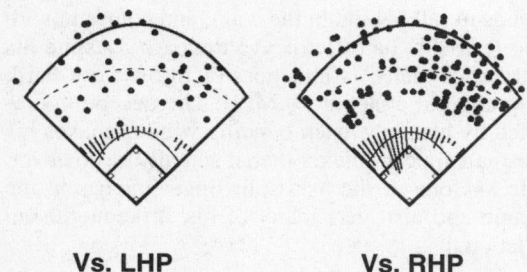

Vs. LHP   **Vs. RHP**

2000 Situational Stats

	AB	H	HR	RBI	Avg		AB	H	HR	RBI	Avg
Home	251	66	15	54	.263	LHP	123	28	6	20	.228
Road	273	68	14	48	.249	RHP	401	106	23	82	.264
First Half	266	69	18	45	.259	Sc Pos	143	40	8	73	.280
Scnd Half	258	65	11	57	.252	Clutch	66	14	1	9	.212

2000 Rankings (American League)

- 1st in lowest cleanup slugging percentage (.387)
- 2nd in lowest fielding percentage at third base (.914)
- 3rd in errors at third base (23)
- 5th in strikeouts
- 6th in sacrifice flies (10)
- 7th in lowest percentage of swings put into play (35.3)
- 8th in lowest groundball/flyball ratio (0.8), lowest batting average vs. lefthanded pitchers and highest percentage of swings that missed (27.9)
- Led the Tigers in RBI, sacrifice flies (10), strikeouts and HR frequency (18.1 ABs per HR)

Jeff Weaver

2000 Season

Although his record was below .500, Jeff Weaver showed the type of consistency last season which was lacking during his rookie year in 1999. Weaver, who struggles with his temper, held it together through the tough periods better than he did the previous campaign. He won two of his last three decisions and worked seven innings or more in his final five starts. He made 30 starts, pitched 200 innings and made the expected strides.

Pitching

Weaver throws from a variety of arm angles, making him difficult on righthanded hitters, but relatively easy for lefthanded hitters to center the ball. He throws hard, up to 96 MPH. His breaking ball is either excellent or awful, depending upon whether he keeps his hand on top of the ball at the release point. He tends to get his hand underneath the ball, and then it just rolls up to the plate on a flat plane. That's usually when lefthanded batsmen feast on him. Weaver has good command and is extremely competitive, which is both a strength and weakness because sometimes he gets out of hand in the form of tantrums on the mound.

Defense

Weaver is an excellent athlete. He's quick, runs well and has good hands. He fields his position well, though he did make his first error in the bigs last year. Sometimes he loses focus and doesn't hold runners as well as he should, though he benefitted last year by having the best throwing backstop in the league. It's a shame he's in the American League because he's an exceptional hitter for a pitcher.

2001 Outlook

Weaver has the potential to become one of the top starting pitchers in baseball. In order to reach that potential, he has to stay on top of his breaking ball and locate his fastball more consistently, especially against lefthanded hitters. He also has to keep his emotions in check, as his outbursts on the mound are making him unpopular with umpires. The Tigers see Weaver as their ace of the future, but he's got some rungs to climb before he can claim the top spot.

Position: SP
Bats: R **Throws:** R
Ht: 6' 5" **Wt:** 210

Opening Day Age: 24
Born: 8/22/76 in Northridge, CA
ML Seasons: 2

Overall Statistics

	W	L	Pct.	ERA	G	GS	Sv	IP	H	BB	SO	HR	Ratio
2000	11	15	.423	4.32	31	30	0	200.0	205	52	136	26	1.29
Career	20	27	.426	4.88	61	59	0	363.2	381	108	250	53	1.34

How Often He Throws Strikes

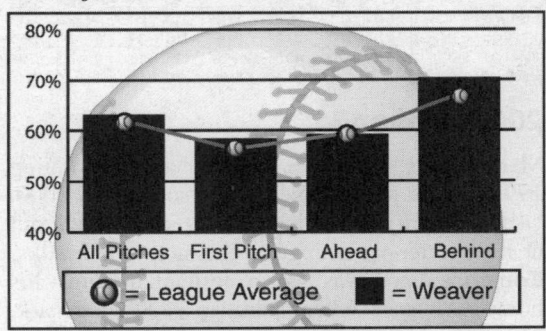

● = League Average ■ = Weaver

2000 Situational Stats

	W	L	ERA	Sv	IP		AB	H	HR	RBI	Avg
Home	5	9	4.12	0	107.0	LHB	402	108	19	59	.269
Road	6	6	4.55	0	93.0	RHB	367	97	7	34	.264
First Half	5	7	4.62	0	101.1	Sc Pos	146	41	4	57	.281
Scnd Half	6	8	4.01	0	98.2	Clutch	74	20	0	1	.270

2000 Rankings (American League)

- 1st in hit batsmen (15) and lowest stolen-base percentage allowed (26.7)
- 2nd in losses
- 3rd in runners caught stealing (11) and fewest GDPs induced per nine innings (0.5)
- 4th in least run support per nine innings (4.2)
- Led the Tigers in ERA, losses, complete games (2), innings pitched, batters faced (849), hit batsmen (15), balks (2), pitches thrown (3,170), highest strikeout/walk ratio (2.6), lowest slugging percentage allowed (.432), lowest on-base percentage allowed (.322), lowest stolen-base percentage allowed (26.7), lowest ERA at home, lowest ERA on the road and lowest batting average allowed vs. righthanded batters

Matt Anderson

Position: RP
Bats: R **Throws:** R
Ht: 6' 4" **Wt:** 200

Opening Day Age: 24
Born: 8/17/76 in
Louisville, KY
ML Seasons: 3

Overall Statistics

	W	L	Pct.	ERA	G	GS	Sv	IP	H	BB	SO	HR	Ratio
2000	3	2	.600	4.72	69	0	1	74.1	61	45	71	8	1.43
Career	10	4	.714	4.55	148	0	1	156.1	132	111	147	19	1.55

2000 Situational Stats

	W	L	ERA	Sv	IP		AB	H	HR	RBI	Avg
Home	1	1	6.63	1	36.2	LHB	110	22	4	22	.200
Road	2	1	2.87	0	37.2	RHB	158	39	4	24	.247
First Half	3	1	4.05	0	40.0	Sc Pos	75	18	4	40	.240
Scnd Half	0	1	5.50	1	34.1	Clutch	70	14	1	7	.200

2000 Season

Matt Anderson came back from a disappointing 1999 season and enjoyed some success in 2000. Used primarily as a middle reliever, he struck out nearly a hitter per inning and cut back on his walks. Comerica Park was not beneficial to him—his home ERA was 6.63 compared to a 2.87 road mark.

Pitching & Defense

There were times last season when Anderson hit triple digits on the radar gun, but he didn't throw that hard consistently. It was by design. He still was throwing 95 MPH regularly, but with better command. He also improved his breaking ball. He's at his best when his pitches are down, as he gets better movement then. When Anderson misses, it's usually high. He wasn't effective as a setup man when Doug Brocail was hurt late last season. Anderson has a lot of footspeed and quick reflexes. He is an excellent fielder, but he doesn't hold runners particularly well.

2001 Outlook

The first overall selection in the 1997 draft, Anderson has been labeled as the Tigers' closer of the future since the day he signed. But the future is not now, not with Todd Jones in the fold. It's a good thing for Anderson, too, because he's not yet polished enough to close.

Doug Brocail

Position: RP
Bats: L **Throws:** R
Ht: 6' 5" **Wt:** 235

Opening Day Age: 33
Born: 5/16/67 in
Clearfield, PA
ML Seasons: 9
Pronunciation:
broh-KALE

Overall Statistics

	W	L	Pct.	ERA	G	GS	Sv	IP	H	BB	SO	HR	Ratio
2000	5	4	.556	4.09	49	0	0	50.2	57	14	41	5	1.40
Career	28	36	.438	3.87	338	42	5	563.0	564	190	403	60	1.34

2000 Situational Stats

	W	L	ERA	Sv	IP		AB	H	HR	RBI	Avg
Home	4	3	4.32	0	25.0	LHB	110	27	5	17	.245
Road	1	1	3.86	0	25.2	RHB	90	30	0	10	.333
First Half	4	3	4.62	0	39.0	Sc Pos	67	18	2	22	.269
Scnd Half	1	1	2.31	0	11.2	Clutch	137	38	3	22	.277

2000 Season

After the two best seasons of his major league career, Doug Brocail was limited to 49 games last year because of an inflamed right elbow. He was having a typically strong campaign before the ailment forced him to miss most of August and September. The elbow began bothering Brocail regularly in early July, though he did post a 2.38 ERA in 11 appearances during the month.

Pitching & Defense

Brocail consistently throws 92-95 MPH fastballs with a lot of sink. His breaking ball is a knuckle-curve—a devastating pitch when he gets it over the plate. He has improved from his days in the National League because he locates his pitches better. He rarely throws a fat pitch down the middle, even if he falls behind in the count, which isn't very often. Brocail holds runners exceptionally well, and boasts a variety of pickoff moves. He is a fast runner and an outstanding fielder.

2001 Outlook

Brocail is the consummate veteran pitcher, and the elbow injury is not expected to be a lingering issue. He's a fiery sort and a good team leader. He joins the Astros after Detroit moved him in a six-player deal in December.

Shane Halter

Position: 3B/1B/SS/2B
Bats: R **Throws:** R
Ht: 6' 0" **Wt:** 180

Opening Day Age: 31
Born: 11/8/69 in LaPlata, MD
ML Seasons: 4

Overall Statistics

	G	AB	R	H	D	T	HR	RBI	SB	BB	SO	Avg	OBP	Slg
2000	105	238	26	62	12	2	3	27	5	14	49	.261	.302	.366
Career	272	565	59	141	29	3	7	50	11	36	115	.250	.297	.349

2000 Situational Stats

	AB	H	HR	RBI	Avg		AB	H	HR	RBI	Avg
Home	98	22	0	10	.224	LHP	91	26	3	14	.286
Road	140	40	3	17	.286	RHP	147	36	0	13	.245
First Half	117	33	1	6	.282	Sc Pos	63	13	0	23	.206
Scnd Half	121	29	2	21	.240	Clutch	27	10	0	4	.370

2000 Season

Shane Halter filled in adequately at several different positions because of injuries, but he also produced clutch hits and made some surprisingly good plays defensively. Halter tied or set career bests in nearly every offensive category and managed to log time at every position, including pitcher.

Hitting, Baserunning & Defense

Halter too often pulls the ball and hits flyballs for someone without much power. He also seems to be extremely reluctant to earn a free pass. He can lay down a bunt, however, and is a smart baserunner, though he has little feel for the art of thievery. Halter is exceptionally versatile in the field. He made 10 or more appearances at each infield spot last season, playing mostly third base and first base because of injuries to Dean Palmer and Tony Clark. Halter came up as a middle infielder. He's not a regular there because he has below-average speed and range and does not turn the double play well. First base is his best position defensively.

2001 Outlook

Halter is the perfect 25th man on the roster in the American League, where there is less need for pinch-hitters during the late innings. If someone goes out for a few days, he can plug the gap and perform satisfactorily at any position.

Jose Macias

Position: 2B/3B
Bats: B **Throws:** R
Ht: 5'10" **Wt:** 173

Opening Day Age: 27
Born: 1/25/74 in Panama City, Panama
ML Seasons: 2

Overall Statistics

	G	AB	R	H	D	T	HR	RBI	SB	BB	SO	Avg	OBP	Slg
2000	73	173	25	44	3	5	2	24	2	18	24	.254	.328	.364
Career	78	177	27	45	3	5	3	26	2	18	25	.254	.327	.379

2000 Situational Stats

	AB	H	HR	RBI	Avg		AB	H	HR	RBI	Avg
Home	96	24	2	13	.250	LHP	40	14	1	10	.350
Road	77	20	0	11	.260	RHP	133	30	1	14	.226
First Half	74	20	0	7	.270	Sc Pos	54	17	1	22	.315
Scnd Half	99	24	2	17	.242	Clutch	26	6	1	5	.231

2000 Season

When Detroit's regular second baseman Damion Easley was injured early in the season, Jose Macias came up from Triple-A Toledo and opened some eyes. He hit .290 in May while playing second base regularly. When asked to play third later in the season to spell Dean Palmer, Macias held his own defensively.

Hitting, Baserunning & Defense

That the switch-hitting Macias hit .350 against lefthanders and just .226 against righties last season is telling. He doesn't hit for much power and mostly is a slap hitter who uses all fields. He doesn't have that one tool that sets him apart from other players. He's an adequate runner, his arm strength is below average and his range at second base is ordinary. He does turn the double play well, and he's versatile. Macias plays center field as well as he plays second base, although the Tigers used him only once in center last season.

2001 Outlook

For a lightly regarded prospect, Macias made a good impression last season. His chances of ever becoming an everyday major leaguer are slim, but he does have value as a utility man, especially given he can play both the infield and the outfield.

Detroit

Wendell Magee

Position: RF/LF
Bats: R **Throws:** R
Ht: 6' 0" **Wt:** 220

Opening Day Age: 28
Born: 8/3/72 in
Hattiesburg, MS
ML Seasons: 5
Pronunciation:
muh-GHEE

Overall Statistics

	G	AB	R	H	D	T	HR	RBI	SB	BB	SO	Avg	OBP	Slg
2000	91	186	31	51	4	2	7	31	1	10	28	.274	.310	.430
Career	199	532	60	130	22	3	13	70	2	36	96	.244	.291	.370

2000 Situational Stats

	AB	H	HR	RBI	Avg		AB	H	HR	RBI	Avg
Home	91	25	2	11	.275	LHP	132	36	2	17	.273
Road	95	26	5	20	.274	RHP	54	15	5	14	.278
First Half	76	22	5	15	.289	Sc Pos	48	16	2	23	.333
Scnd Half	110	29	2	16	.264	Clutch	35	9	2	4	.257

2000 Season

There were concerns that Wendell Magee would not be able to perform in a backup role, but those concerns proved unfounded last season. Magee batted .385 as a pinch-hitter and hit .274 overall while playing sparingly. He displayed good power during his first full season in the major leagues, where he turned 28 in August.

Hitting, Baserunning & Defense

Magee has a long swing and when he gets his arms extended, he drives the ball with good power. But like virtually all hitters with a long stroke, he gets tied up by inside fastballs. He is not a particularly good breaking ball hitter, either. Magee will chase bad pitches and he doesn't take many walks. Surprisingly, he hit righthanders better than lefties last season, as he had carried a reputation for being more effective against lefthanders. Magee has average speed and average arm strength, but he runs the bases well. He's an adequate outfielder.

2001 Outlook

Magee is an ideal bench player. His work ethic and attitude are outstanding, and he prepares himself even on the days he doesn't play. He is efficient enough defensively that he can be used as a late-inning replacement, and he proved last season that he can be an effective pinch-hitter, as well.

Billy McMillon

Position: DH/RF
Bats: L **Throws:** L
Ht: 5'11" **Wt:** 179

Opening Day Age: 29
Born: 11/17/71 in
Otero, NM
ML Seasons: 3

Overall Statistics

	G	AB	R	H	D	T	HR	RBI	SB	BB	SO	Avg	OBP	Slg
2000	46	123	20	37	7	1	4	24	1	19	19	.301	.388	.472
Career	111	264	34	71	12	2	6	42	3	30	57	.269	.338	.398

2000 Situational Stats

	AB	H	HR	RBI	Avg		AB	H	HR	RBI	Avg
Home	74	25	3	14	.338	LHP	15	4	0	4	.267
Road	49	12	1	10	.245	RHP	108	33	4	20	.306
First Half	0	0	0	0	-	Sc Pos	33	13	1	21	.394
Scnd Half	123	37	4	24	.301	Clutch	17	9	0	3	.529

2000 Season

Billy McMillon hit .345 with 13 home runs and 50 RBI at Triple-A Toledo, but it was his .446 on-base percentage that caught the collective eye of club officials and earned him the call to the major leagues on July 31. He was playing regularly at the end of the season because of injuries to Juan Gonzalez and hit .301 for the parent club.

Hitting, Baserunning & Defense

McMillon has good knowledge of the strike zone and doesn't swing at a lot of bad pitches. He is willing to take a walk, which was appreciated on a Detroit club that finished ninth in the American League with a .343 on-base percentage. He had 12 extra-base hits in 123 at-bats last season, but he isn't exactly a slugger. What kept McMillon from becoming a major leaguer is a lack of speed. He does not run well and has the label of being a liability on the bases and in the outfield.

2001 Outlook

McMillon has made enough strides as a hitter that his lack of footspeed is starting to be overlooked. But he has to hit for average and show decent power to have any value to a club. He will have to earn a paycheck with his bat because his value as an extra man is limited to what he can do at the plate.

Dave Mlicki

Position: SP
Bats: R **Throws:** R
Ht: 6' 4" **Wt:** 205

Opening Day Age: 32
Born: 6/8/68 in Cleveland, OH
ML Seasons: 8
Pronunciation: mah-LICK-ee

Overall Statistics

	W	L	Pct.	ERA	G	GS	Sv	IP	H	BB	SO	HR	Ratio
2000	6	11	.353	5.58	24	21	0	119.1	143	44	57	17	1.57
Career	51	59	.464	4.41	206	148	1	979.0	1033	364	680	123	1.43

2000 Situational Stats

	W	L	ERA	Sv	IP		AB	H	HR	RBI	Avg
Home	3	8	5.50	0	70.1	LHB	235	66	9	36	.281
Road	3	3	5.69	0	49.0	RHB	256	77	8	29	.301
First Half	3	9	5.72	0	83.1	Sc Pos	109	29	4	45	.266
Scnd Half	3	2	5.25	0	36.0	Clutch	22	6	0	0	.273

2000 Season

After posting the best year of his career in 1999, Dave Mlicki floundered in 2000. Mlicki lost his first five starts and never recovered. A sinus condition which caused him severe headaches and required surgery in early August was largely to blame. The discomfort kept him off the mound until September 7.

Pitching & Defense

Mlicki's best pitch is a 90-MPH fastball. His heater has some tailing action to it, and he can sink the ball effectively when necessary. He has a serviceable curveball and a good changeup, both of which he can throw for strikes. He doesn't strike out a lot of hitters, however. When Mlicki gets hurt, it's usually because his pitches are up—he doesn't have enough velocity to pitch high in the zone. A below-average fielder in the past, Mlicki was better in that area last season. He uses the slide-step and holds runners well.

2001 Outlook

Mlicki is in the second-year of a three-year contract and will be used as a starter. He won eight straight outings during a span of the 1999 season, a campaign that saw him win 14 games. Last season, his control wasn't quite what it had been the previous year. That holds the key to his success.

C.J. Nitkowski

Position: RP/SP
Bats: L **Throws:** L
Ht: 6' 3" **Wt:** 205

Opening Day Age: 28
Born: 3/9/73 in Suffern, NY
ML Seasons: 5

Overall Statistics

	W	L	Pct.	ERA	G	GS	Sv	IP	H	BB	SO	HR	Ratio
2000	4	9	.308	5.25	67	11	0	109.2	124	49	81	13	1.58
Career	15	27	.357	5.42	209	44	3	368.1	392	190	258	46	1.58

2000 Situational Stats

	W	L	ERA	Sv	IP		AB	H	HR	RBI	Avg
Home	2	1	3.77	0	45.1	LHB	147	32	5	34	.218
Road	2	8	6.30	0	64.1	RHB	286	92	8	41	.322
First Half	4	7	5.83	0	71.0	Sc Pos	123	43	4	64	.350
Scnd Half	0	2	4.19	0	38.2	Clutch	71	18	3	14	.254

2000 Season

C.J. Nitkowski began the season as the only lefthander in Detroit's starting rotation. The results were not good. He was 2-7 with a 7.30 ERA in 11 starts. Moved back to the bullpen, he was much more effective, going 2-2 with a 3.34 ERA in 56 relief appearances.

Pitching & Defense

Nitkowski has found his niche as a middle reliever. He's more than just a situational southpaw, although lefthanded hitters batted .218 off him compared to a .322 by righties. Most of that damage by righthanded hitters was done when he was in the starting rotation. His fastball is good, running up to 94 MPH, and his breaking ball is sharp. He can get a strikeout when he needs it. He is durable and bounces back well, showing the stamina to work on consecutive days. Nitkowski is not athletic and is a poor fielder. He has a good lefthanded move to first base, but he doesn't concentrate on holding baserunners.

2001 Outlook

Nitkowski will be back where he belongs—in middle relief. He's capable of putting together a good inning or two to keep his team in games. Therein lies his long-term value, and as long as he understands that, he will have a lengthy career.

Detroit

Danny Patterson

Position: RP
Bats: R **Throws:** R
Ht: 6' 0" **Wt:** 225

Opening Day Age: 30
Born: 2/17/71 in San Gabriel, CA
ML Seasons: 5

Overall Statistics

	W	L	Pct.	ERA	G	GS	Sv	IP	H	BB	SO	HR	Ratio
2000	5	1	.833	3.97	58	0	0	56.2	69	14	29	4	1.46
Career	19	12	.613	4.20	228	0	3	257.1	290	78	179	23	1.43

2000 Situational Stats

	W	L	ERA	Sv	IP		AB	H	HR	RBI	Avg
Home	2	1	5.08	0	28.1	LHB	96	28	2	10	.292
Road	3	0	2.86	0	28.1	RHB	127	41	2	16	.323
First Half	3	1	3.06	0	35.1	Sc Pos	68	17	0	21	.250
Scnd Half	2	0	5.48	0	21.1	Clutch	106	34	0	9	.321

2000 Season

Danny Patterson gave the Tigers an inning in the middle of games, held things together and in the process came away with five victories. He was more effective during the first half than the second because he was hindered by an inflamed elbow that put him on the disabled list in July.

Pitching & Defense

Patterson primarily throws two pitches: a fastball and a split-finger fastball. His fastball usually reaches 90 MPH, and it tails inward and sinks down on righthanded hitters. His split-finger pitch is more like a changeup than a traditional forkball. The velocity on his splitter is much slower than his fastball. He wants to let hitters put the ball in play, and the more they do so on the ground, the better for him. He always has been steady afield, and his good righthanded pickoff move and quick delivery combine to keep runners on first base.

2001 Outlook

When healthy, Patterson will give his team an inning when they need it. But he can't pitch much more than twice a week and by no means will he eat up innings. Durability remains a question mark, as he has had a shoulder injury that required surgery in the past to go along with last season's elbow troubles. If overused, he will break down.

Steve Sparks (Knuckleballer)

Position: SP
Bats: R **Throws:** R
Ht: 6' 0" **Wt:** 180

Opening Day Age: 35
Born: 7/2/65 in Tulsa, OK
ML Seasons: 5
Nickname: Sparky

Overall Statistics

	W	L	Pct.	ERA	G	GS	Sv	IP	H	BB	SO	HR	Ratio
2000	7	5	.583	4.07	20	15	1	104.0	108	29	53	7	1.32
Career	34	38	.472	4.92	123	101	1	671.0	716	307	333	78	1.52

2000 Situational Stats

	W	L	ERA	Sv	IP		AB	H	HR	RBI	Avg
Home	4	2	4.01	1	58.1	LHB	216	57	5	27	.264
Road	3	3	4.14	0	45.2	RHB	195	51	2	18	.262
First Half	0	1	8.44	1	10.2	Sc Pos	93	25	2	31	.269
Scnd Half	7	4	3.57	0	93.1	Clutch	10	3	0	0	.300

2000 Season

After a slow start following his callup in June, Steve Sparks gave the Tigers such a shot in the arm that he thrust the club into American League wild-card contention. From August 5 to September 1, Sparks won six straight starts and posted a 2.05 ERA. His 4.07 ERA for the year was tops on Detroit among staffers with at least one start.

Pitching & Defense

Sparks is a knuckleballer who either is really good or really bad. His knuckleball flutters, though it doesn't have a sharp breaking action. He varies the speed of his primary offering and commands it well, as he walked just 29 hitters in 104 innings last season. As is the case with most knucklers, he does throw a token 82-MPH fastball that comes in very straight. Sparks will mix in a slider now and then, but the offering doesn't possess much break. He uses the slide-step method and holds baserunners exceptionally well. He's quick and agile, so his move to first is strong and his fielding is excellent.

2001 Outlook

Sparks did for the Tigers last season what he did for the Angels in 1998. He came out of nowhere to provide a huge lift. He tends to fade in and out of the picture, however. The Tigers have their fingers crossed that last season wasn't a mirage.

Dusty Allen (Pos: 1B, **Age**: 28, **Bats**: R)

	G	AB	R	H	D	T	HR	RBI	SB	BB	SO	Avg	OBP	Slg
2000	27	28	5	7	2	0	2	2	0	4	12	.250	.344	.536
Career	27	28	5	7	2	0	2	2	0	4	12	.250	.344	.536

Allen came to the Tigers in a deal with the Padres last July. He doesn't have super power but can draw walks and serve a utility role. 2001 Outlook: C

Rich Becker (Pos: RF/LF/CF, **Age**: 29, **Bats**: L)

	G	AB	R	H	D	T	HR	RBI	SB	BB	SO	Avg	OBP	Slg
2000	115	285	59	69	14	0	8	39	2	67	87	.242	.384	.375
Career	789	2227	345	570	100	12	45	243	66	350	616	.256	.358	.372

Becker can play any outfield spot and draws walks, but he's helpless against lefties. 2001 Outlook: B

Willie Blair (Pos: RHP, **Age**: 35)

	W	L	Pct.	ERA	G	GS	Sv	IP	H	BB	SO	HR	Ratio
2000	10	6	.625	4.88	47	17	0	156.2	185	35	74	20	1.40
Career	59	82	.418	4.93	409	135	4	1250.0	1400	404	744	167	1.44

Blair is 29-25 as a Tiger, 30-57 as something else. He is a finesse pitcher who relies on control and savvy. His greatest value may be as a swingman. 2001 Outlook: B

Dave Borkowski (Pos: RHP, **Age**: 24)

	W	L	Pct.	ERA	G	GS	Sv	IP	H	BB	SO	HR	Ratio
2000	0	1	.000	21.94	2	1	0	5.1	11	7	1	2	3.38
Career	2	7	.222	7.13	19	13	0	82.0	97	47	51	12	1.76

Borkowski appeared to be overmatched when he pitched in 17 games for the Tigers at the age of 22 in 1999. But last year he was overwhelmed. 2001 Outlook: C

Nelson Cruz (Pos: RHP, **Age**: 28)

	W	L	Pct.	ERA	G	GS	Sv	IP	H	BB	SO	HR	Ratio
2000	5	2	.714	3.07	27	0	0	41.0	39	13	34	4	1.27
Career	7	9	.438	5.04	75	6	0	134.0	142	45	103	21	1.40

Cruz has demonstrated an ability to retire lefties as well as righties. He will battle for a job in Houston after being dealt in December. 2001 Outlook: C

Erik Hiljus (Pos: RHP, **Age**: 28)

	W	L	Pct.	ERA	G	GS	Sv	IP	H	BB	SO	HR	Ratio
2000	0	0	-	7.36	3	0	0	3.2	5	1	2	1	1.64
Career	0	0	-	5.84	9	0	0	12.1	12	6	3	4	1.46

Hiljus has posted great strikeout-walk ratios in the minors the past couple seasons. The A's signed him to a minor league deal in December. 2001 Outlook: C

Gregg Jefferies (Pos: 1B/2B, **Age**: 33, **Bats**: B)

	G	AB	R	H	D	T	HR	RBI	SB	BB	SO	Avg	OBP	Slg
2000	41	142	18	39	8	0	2	14	0	16	10	.275	.344	.373
Career	1465	5520	761	1593	300	27	126	663	196	472	348	.289	.344	.421

Jefferies didn't play after May due to a pulled hamstring last year. Rather than face a reserve role in 2001, he decided to retire. 2001 Outlook: D

Mark Johnson (Pos: RHP, **Age**: 25)

	W	L	Pct.	ERA	G	GS	Sv	IP	H	BB	SO	HR	Ratio
2000	0	1	.000	7.50	9	3	0	24.0	25	16	11	3	1.71
Career	0	1	.000	7.50	9	3	0	24.0	25	16	11	3	1.71

The Tigers picked up Johnson in the Rule 5 draft in December 1999. He had never before pitched above Double-A. As bad as he was with Detroit last year, he was arguably worse at Triple-A. 2001 Outlook: C

Masao Kida (Pos: RHP, **Age**: 32)

	W	L	Pct.	ERA	G	GS	Sv	IP	H	BB	SO	HR	Ratio
2000	0	0	-	10.13	2	0	0	2.2	5	0	0	1	1.88
Career	1	0	1.000	6.42	51	0	1	67.1	78	30	50	7	1.60

After 10 years in Japan, Kida signed with the Tigers following the 1998 campaign. A disappointment in Detroit, he returned to Japan last June. 2001 Outlook: D

Rod Lindsey (Pos: CF, **Age**: 25, **Bats**: R)

	G	AB	R	H	D	T	HR	RBI	SB	BB	SO	Avg	OBP	Slg
2000	11	3	6	1	1	0	0	0	2	0	1	.333	.500	.667
Career	11	3	6	1	1	0	0	0	2	0	1	.333	.500	.667

Lindsey may be the fastest runner and best defensive outfielder in the Tigers' minor league system. His offense was dreadful at Triple-A last year. 2001 Outlook: C

Allen McDill (Pos: LHP, **Age**: 29)

	W	L	Pct.	ERA	G	GS	Sv	IP	H	BB	SO	HR	Ratio
2000	0	0	-	7.20	13	0	0	10.0	13	1	7	2	1.40
Career	0	0	-	9.45	23	0	0	20.0	25	11	12	6	1.80

McDill refused a minor league assignment when the Tigers tried to send him down last June. He later pitched for the Cardinals' Triple-A affiliate. He'll be hoping to stick somewhere as a situational lefty. 2001 Outlook: C

Hal Morris (Pos: 1B, **Age**: 35, **Bats**: L)

	G	AB	R	H	D	T	HR	RBI	SB	BB	SO	Avg	OBP	Slg
2000	99	169	24	47	9	1	3	14	0	31	26	.278	.391	.396
Career	1246	3998	535	1216	246	21	76	513	45	356	548	.304	.361	.433

The Tigers acquired Morris from the Reds last July. If he continues to hit .325 as a pinch-hitter, as he did last year, he can keep a job somewhere. 2001 Outlook: B

Sean Runyan (Pos: LHP, **Age**: 26)

	W	L	Pct.	ERA	G	GS	Sv	IP	H	BB	SO	HR	Ratio
2000	0	0	-	6.00	3	0	0	3.0	2	2	1	0	1.33
Career	1	5	.167	3.66	103	0	1	64.0	58	33	46	9	1.42

After leading the AL in appearances in '98, Runyan had shoulder surgery and was back in the minors last year. He re-signed with Detroit in October. 2001 Outlook: C

Kevin Tolar (Pos: LHP, **Age**: 30)

	W	L	Pct.	ERA	G	GS	Sv	IP	H	BB	SO	HR	Ratio
2000	0	0	-	3.00	5	0	0	3.0	1	1	3	0	0.67
Career	0	0	-	3.00	5	0	0	3.0	1	1	3	0	0.67

Tolar persists, having worked for 15 minor league teams and eight organizations in his career. Not overly talented, his nomadic ways may continue. 2001 Outlook: C

Brandon Villafuerte (Pos: RHP, **Age**: 25)

	W	L	Pct.	ERA	G	GS	Sv	IP	H	BB	SO	HR	Ratio
2000	0	0	-	10.38	3	0	0	4.1	4	4	1	0	1.85
Career	0	0	-	10.38	3	0	0	4.1	4	4	1	0	1.85

A 66th-round pick of the Mets in 1994, Villafuerte was traded from the Marlins to the Tigers in 1999 for former first-round choice Mike Drumright. Villafuerte was dealt to Texas in December. 2001 Outlook: C

Detroit

Detroit Tigers Minor League Prospects

Organization Overview:

The Tigers' farm system hasn't been much of an asset for years, dating back nearly a dozen years to a time when the Tigers frequently contended and traded prospects to stay near the top. Player development became a higher priority when Randy Smith took over as general manager in late 1995. Matt Anderson and Jeff Weaver are key picks early in the Smith regime, but in the high minors at the close of the 2000 season, only Eric Munson and Brandon Inge were ranked by *Baseball America* as being among the top 20 prospects in their respective leagues. Still, Munson and Robert Fick should bring some extra power to the club, and the Tigers are working to develop a promising crop of young arms that includes Nate Cornejo, Shane Loux, Adam Pettyjohn, Fernando Rodney, Calvin Chipperfield and Victor Santos.

Adam Bernero

Position: P
Bats: R **Throws:** R
Ht: 6' 4" **Wt:** 205
Opening Day Age: 24
Born: 11/28/76 in San Jose, CA

Recent Statistics

	W	L	ERA	G	GS	Sv	IP	H	R	BB	SO	HR
2000 AA Jacksnville	2	5	2.79	10	10	0	61.1	54	26	24	46	6
2000 AAA Toledo	3	1	2.47	7	7	0	47.1	34	16	10	37	5
2000 AL Detroit	0	1	4.19	12	4	0	34.1	33	18	13	20	3

A polished pitcher from Armstrong Atlantic (GA) State, Bernero was a fifth-year senior who went undrafted but signed with Detroit in 1999. Though he was a bit old for the league, he pitched well in the Class-A Midwest League in '99. He made it all the way to Detroit in 2000 after solid stints at the Double-A and Triple-A levels. Bernero pitched respectably in three of his four Tiger starts, using four pitches, including a fastball with excellent sinking action and a very good changeup. He also throws a slider and split-finger pitch. Bernero pitched into the seventh only once with Detroit, and the Tigers want him to increase his strength and durability. That would help Bernero in the majors, where every pitch takes a little more out of a pitcher.

Javier Cardona

Position: C
Bats: R **Throws:** R
Ht: 6' 1" **Wt:** 185
Opening Day Age: 25
Born: 9/15/75 in Santurce, PR

Recent Statistics

	G	AB	R	H	D	T	HR	RBI	SB	BB	SO	Avg
2000 AAA Toledo	56	218	29	60	10	0	11	43	0	15	33	.275
2000 AL Detroit	26	40	1	7	1	0	1	2	0	0	9	.175
2000 MLE	56	209	22	51	9	0	7	33	0	11	34	.244

Neither his hitting nor his catching skills have been viewed as a sure ticket to the majors, but Cardona, drafted in 1994, has developed into an adequate defensive catcher. He moves well behind the plate and throws decently with good accuracy. His bat has needed extra time at most minor league levels, especially in the high minors. Developing some power would boost his big league chances, and Cardona broke through in 1999. He filled out physically, started turning on more balls, and shattered his single-season home-run total with 26 at Double-A Jacksonville. He might have built on his '99 success as a regular at Triple-A Toledo, but he spent too much time on the Tiger bench after Gregg Zaun was traded and Robert Fick was lost to injury.

Jermaine Clark

Position: 2B
Bats: L **Throws:** R
Ht: 5' 10" **Wt:** 175
Opening Day Age: 24
Born: 9/29/76 in Berkeley, CA

Recent Statistics

	G	AB	R	H	D	T	HR	RBI	SB	BB	SO	Avg
1999 A Lancasnville	126	502	112	158	27	8	6	61	33	58	80	.315
2000 AA New Haven	133	447	80	131	23	9	2	44	38	87	69	.293
2000 MLE	133	438	80	122	21	7	2	44	30	75	75	.279

A three-time All-America infielder at the University of San Francisco, Clark hit .322 in his first three pro campaigns. Only in 2000 did he drop below the .300 mark, batting .293 in his first exposure to Double-A ball. Clark employs an unorthodox uppercut swing, but he regularly makes contact, hits ropes and draws lots of walks. He's also speedy and maximizes that tool with his ability to bunt. Southpaws give him trouble, though: over the last two seasons at two classifications, he has batted .330 against righties and .223 against lefties. He's still fine-tuning his defensive game. Clark joins the Tigers in 2001, courtesy of the Rule 5 draft.

Robert Fick

Position: DH-1B
Bats: L **Throws:** R
Ht: 6' 1" **Wt:** 189
Opening Day Age: 27
Born: 3/15/74 in Torrance, CA

Recent Statistics

	G	AB	R	H	D	T	HR	RBI	SB	BB	SO	Avg
2000 AAA Toledo	17	68	5	10	5	0	1	7	1	6	13	.147
2000 AL Detroit	66	163	18	41	7	2	3	22	2	22	39	.252

Fick was drafted by the Tigers in 1996 for one reason—he could hit. He can handle fastballs or breaking stuff, and he's capable of turning on pitches or going the other way. Fick also can draw walks and doesn't strike out much. What he *can't* do is stay healthy. After two successful seasons in the minors in 1997 and '98, Fick missed nearly all of 1999 after dislocating his left shoulder in spring training. Last season with Detroit, he missed two months after separating his right shoulder in an early-July collision at first base. The lost time has slowed his progress as a hitter. He's adequate defensively with soft hands. If the Tigers ever deal Tony Clark, Fick would battle Eric Munson for his job.

Brandon Inge

Position: C
Bats: B **Throws:** R
Ht: 5' 11" **Wt:** 185

Opening Day Age: 23
Born: 5/19/77 in Lynchburg, VA

Recent Statistics

	G	AB	R	H	D	T	HR	RBI	SB	BB	SO	Avg
1999 A W Michigan	100	352	54	86	25	2	9	46	15	39	87	.244
2000 AA Jacksnville	78	298	39	77	25	1	6	53	10	26	73	.258
2000 AAA Toledo	55	190	24	42	9	3	5	20	2	15	51	.221
2000 MLE	133	474	51	105	31	2	7	59	8	29	128	.222

Drafted as a college shortstop, Inge moved behind the plate and adjusted remarkably well. He's quick and athletic, with a strong arm and sound throwing mechanics. The mental and physical grind of catching and learning the position may have hurt him offensively. Inge doesn't draw walks, his swing tends to grow long, and so far he hasn't hit for average or power. After winning the batting title in the California Fall League a year ago, he skipped the high Class-A level. The Tigers believe he will hit, and Inge finished 2000 as one of the Arizona Fall League's top prospects. His athleticism, makeup and leadership skills make him an organizational bright spot.

Eric Munson

Position: 1B
Bats: L **Throws:** R
Ht: 6' 3" **Wt:** 220

Opening Day Age: 23
Born: 10/3/77 in San Diego, CA

Recent Statistics

	G	AB	R	H	D	T	HR	RBI	SB	BB	SO	Avg
2000 AA Jacksnville	98	365	52	92	21	4	15	68	5	39	96	.252
2000 AL Detroit	3	5	0	0	0	0	0	1	0	0	1	.000
2000 MLE	98	355	44	82	19	3	11	57	3	28	101	.231

The third overall pick in 1999, Munson was moved from catcher to first base because of a shoulder injury and Detroit's catching depth. His defensive work needs polishing, but it's Munson's power that will propel him to the majors. His bat is exceptionally quick, capable of pulling nearly any fastball. The Tigers jumped Munson from low-A to Double-A ball for his first full pro season in 2000, and he adjusted well, but a stress fracture in his back sidelined him and slowed his progress. At times Munson was too pull-oriented at Jacksonville—the Tigers want him to use the whole field more. Munson also must learn to make better contact against lefties. When he connects he demonstrates above-average power.

Adam Pettyjohn

Position: P
Bats: R **Throws:** L
Ht: 6' 3" **Wt:** 190

Opening Day Age: 23
Born: 6/11/77 in Phoenix, AZ

Recent Statistics

	W	L	ERA	G	GS	Sv	IP	H	R	BB	SO	HR
1999 A Lakeland	3	4	3.77	9	9	0	59.2	62	35	11	51	2
1999 AA Jacksnville	9	5	4.69	20	20	0	126.2	134	75	35	92	13
2000 AA Jacksnville	2	2	3.40	8	8	0	50.1	43	20	12	45	4
2000 AAA Toledo	0	4	6.69	7	7	0	39.0	45	34	22	23	5

The Tigers selected Fresno State teammates Jeff Weaver and Pettyjohn in the first two rounds of the 1998 draft, and Pettyjohn isn't far behind Weaver developmentally. Pettyjohn's best pitches are his curveball and a high-80s fastball, both thrown from a three-quarters delivery. The arm angle makes his curve more of a slurve, and the fastball tails away from righthanded hitters. Pettyjohn has good command of both offerings. Because he doesn't throw hard, his changeup will be critical. Pettyjohn experienced minor shoulder troubles early in 2000, which hurt his velocity a bit, but he is ready for Triple-A Toledo.

Ramon Santiago

Position: SS
Bats: B **Throws:** R
Ht: 5' 11" **Wt:** 150

Opening Day Age: 19
Born: 8/31/81 in Las Matas De Farfan, DR

Recent Statistics

	G	AB	R	H	D	T	HR	RBI	SB	BB	SO	Avg
1999 R Tigers	35	134	25	43	9	2	0	11	20	9	17	.321
1999 A Oneonta	12	50	9	17	1	2	1	8	5	2	12	.340
2000 A W Michigan	98	379	69	103	15	1	1	42	39	34	60	.272

Santiago debuted in '99 and played in the Class-A Midwest League in his second pro season. He was much younger than the competition, yet Santiago was more polished defensively at short than his peers, demonstrating soft hands, quick feet and very strong throws. Detroit scouting director Greg Smith says Santiago's overall instincts for the game maximize his defensive skills—and also aid his bat. He bunts well and can steal a base, but Santiago must draw more walks. The Tigers like his approach at the plate, but he must get stronger. He made just eight errors in 81 games before labrum surgery in July ended his season. He may DH early in the 2001 season while he continues his rehab work.

Others to Watch

Righthander **Calvin Chipperfield** (23) went 12-3 (2.13) and led the Midwest League in ERA. Throwing an above-average curve and average fastball, the Australian native shows good command and an ability to set up hitters. . . Barely two years after graduating from a Kansas high school, righthander **Nate Cornejo** (21) reached Double-A Jacksonville near midseason in 2000. He has shown good command of an 89-92 MPH sinker and mixes in a curveball that is a major league-plus pitch at times. Both pitches have good life, but work on his changeup is ongoing. . . Righthander **Shane Loux** (21) turned a corner in 2000, pitching successfully at Double-A Jacksonville with a low-90s sinker that he commands well. Not only are his offspeed pitches coming along, Loux also exhibits a nice feel for pitching. . . **Fernando Rodney** (20) has an explosive fastball that reaches 98 MPH, but his slider, changeup and mechanics need lots of work. Still, the young righty handled the Midwest League well in 2000. . . The Tigers acquired **Andy Van Hekken** (21) from Seattle in 1999 and he epitomizes the phrase "crafty lefthander." He works intelligently with a high-80s fastball, curve and change. Going 16-6 (2.45), he tied for the Midwest League lead in wins in 2000.

Ewing M. Kauffman Stadium

Offense

Since the fences came in 10 feet in 1996, Kauffman Stadium has been among the best hitters' parks in the American League, promoting both homers and batting average. Sight lines are good, further reducing strikeout totals and improving batting averages. As the park is symmetrical, all hitters are enhanced equally. When the weather is hot, as it usually is during the summer months, the ball carries very well, further promoting the longball. Because the outfield expanse is relatively large, fleet-footed outfield trios are necessary to prevent a large number of extra-base hits. Only doubles have been hampered by this park.

Defense

The Kauffman grounds crew has a reputation for excellence, and it is well earned, as the grass always is in perfect condition. The slight angles of the outfield walls at the foul poles can spell trouble for corner outfielders if they fail to cut balls off. Those hits can hug the wall as it curves around to the bullpen, permitting baserunners extra bases.

Who It Helps the Most

Power hitters thrive at "The K." Mike Sweeney, Jermaine Dye and Mark Quinn all have benefited from the park's short fences. The good sight lines have helped Johnny Damon's batting average at home. Finesse pitchers who keep the ball down will have better success than their counterparts; Jeff Suppan, Chris Fussell and Chad Durbin all had better results in Kauffman than in other parks.

Who It Hurts the Most

Power pitchers and pitchers who work up in the strike zone suffer the most at Kauffman Stadium. They have to keep the ball down and in the park to survive here. Blake Stein and Brian Meadows allowed more homers at home than on the road.

Rookies & Newcomers

Hector Ortiz had good success at Kauffman Stadium, as did Durbin. Dee Brown should enjoy swinging for Kauffman's fences, and Chris George's control style of pitching is a good fit, too. Jeff Austin may have more difficulty in the park than George.

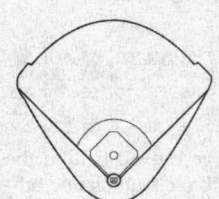

Dimensions: LF-330, LCF-375, CF-400, RCF-375, RF-330

Capacity: 40,625

Elevation: 750 feet

Surface: Grass

Foul Territory: Average

Park Factors

2000 Season

| | Home Games | | | Away Games | | | |
	Royals	Opp	Total	Royals	Opp	Total	Index
G	72	72	144	72	72	144	—
Avg	.304	.292	.298	.273	.272	.273	109
AB	2496	2602	5098	2559	2381	4940	103
R	408	442	850	373	392	765	111
H	758	760	1518	699	648	1347	113
2B	124	145	269	123	128	251	104
3B	17	14	31	9	11	20	150
HR	77	106	183	53	108	161	110
BB	212	305	517	229	321	550	91
SO	330	424	754	403	385	788	93
E	46	61	107	43	71	114	94
E-Infield	36	51	87	33	63	96	91
LHB-Avg	.302	.285	.291	.253	.275	.267	109
LHB-HR	15	53	68	9	50	59	108
RHB-Avg	.304	.300	.303	.281	.269	.277	109
RHB-HR	62	53	115	44	58	102	112

1998-2000

| | Home Games | | | Away Games | | | |
	Royals	Opp	Total	Royals	Opp	Total	Index
G	215	215	430	217	217	434	—
Avg	.283	.288	.286	.271	.276	.273	104
AB	7352	7735	15087	7659	7254	14913	102
R	1109	1262	2371	1065	1189	2254	106
H	2079	2230	4309	2074	2004	4078	107
2B	346	382	728	403	373	776	93
3B	68	44	112	36	31	67	165
HR	212	288	500	171	284	455	109
BB	677	820	1497	668	889	1557	95
SO	1133	1213	2346	1293	1213	2506	93
E	154	174	328	156	186	342	97
E-Infield	128	142	270	130	160	290	94
LHB-Avg	.284	.288	.286	.269	.271	.270	106
LHB-HR	46	121	167	37	122	159	102
RHB-Avg	.282	.288	.285	.272	.280	.275	103
RHB-HR	166	167	333	134	162	296	113

2000 Rankings (American League)

- Highest batting-average factor
- Highest hit factor
- Highest LHB batting-average factor
- Highest RHB batting-average factor
- Second-highest triple factor
- Third-highest run factor
- Lowest walk factor
- Third-lowest strikeout factor

Tony Muser

2000 Season

Following a 1999 season that featured the worst record in club history, expectations for manager Tony Muser were low. But with virtually the same players from the previous year, Muser led the Royals to 13 more wins in 2000. Once again the team's strength was its offense—Kansas City improved upon several club records set in 1999. And once again, the Royals' biggest problem was pitching, specifically the bullpen. The pen's failure aside, Muser dealt successfully with an unusual personnel situation when Carlos Beltran was suspended after refusing a minor league rehabilitation assignment. The manager shifted other outfielders into Beltran's spot, and the offense never missed a beat.

Offense

Muser sets his lineup according to the talents of his players. He primarily works from a set lineup but will shift reserves into the lineup periodically to give regulars a rest. The Royals run the bases aggressively and successfully, as Muser uses both the bunt and the hit-and-run liberally. Pinch-hitters usually don't appear until the last inning. Muser likes leadoff men who hit for a high average. Consecutive outstanding rookie performances by Carlos Beltran and Mark Quinn attest to Muser's commitment to developing young position players.

Pitching & Defense

Muser would like to establish well-defined relief roles, but due to the failures of his egregious bullpen, he didn't have that luxury last year. The Royals also have lacked lefthanded relievers, so Muser hasn't always been able to gain a platoon advantage. He likes offensive players and will choose offense over a defensive specialist, with the notable exception of first base, his old position. Muser was an excellent defensive first baseman in his day.

2001 Outlook

The Royals are a young and improving team with a solid, set lineup and a starting staff with great potential. The biggest challenge for Muser's Royals is an on-going dilemma from previous seasons: their awful bullpen. Fixing it could mean another 13-game jump in the standings but might require an expenditure of cash the small-market club lacks.

Born: 8/01/47 in Van Nuys, California

Playing Experience: 1969-1978, Bos, CWS, Bal, Mil

Managerial Experience: 4 seasons

Manager Statistics

Year	Team, Lg	W	L	Pct	GB	Finish
2000	Kansas City, AL	77	85	.475	18.0	4th Central
4 Seasons		244	319	.433	—	—

2000 Starting Pitchers by Days Rest

	<=3	4	5	6+
Royals Starts	1	92	42	16
Royals ERA	5.40	5.14	5.19	5.92
AL Avg Starts	2	88	40	22
AL ERA	4.87	5.03	5.03	5.28

2000 Situational Stats

	Tony Muser	AL Average
Hit & Run Success %	33.8	35.1
Stolen Base Success %	77.6	68.8
Platoon Pct.	46.9	57.8
Defensive Subs	14	23
High-Pitch Outings	19	13
Quick/Slow Hooks	12/12	18/19
Sacrifice Attempts	72	55

2000 Rankings (American League)

- 1st in stolen-base percentage (77.6) and steals of second base (112)
- 2nd in fewest caught stealings of second base (26), squeeze plays (6) and hit-and-run attempts (80)
- 3rd in sacrifice-bunt percentage (87.5)

Carlos Beltran

2000 Season

After an outstanding rookie campaign in 1999, Carlos Beltran suffered through such a tumultuous second season that he made Kansas City fans forget Bob Hamelin's failures. Beltran hit poorly from the outset and was dropped to the fifth spot in the batting order, then eventually to sixth and seventh. After he missed nearly all of July with a deep bone bruise, he shook up the baseball community by refusing a rehabilitation assignment to Florida. He was suspended by the Royals until late August, then spent two weeks on minor league rehab before finishing the year with the parent club.

Hitting

Beltran is an aggressive hitter with a smooth swing that generates surprising power. Although he usually is able to make good contact, Beltran gets himself into trouble by trying to pull pitches too often and by not being selective. A switch-hitter, Beltran doesn't have much platoon differential. He thrives on fastballs and can be carved up by sharp breaking pitches. In 2000, Beltran was a confused hitter who gave away a lot of at-bats. To succeed, he must return to that easy batting stroke that led to so much success in 1999.

Baserunning & Defense

Beltran is a good center fielder, capable of running down flies to all parts of the park, racing in to take away shallow flyballs or leaping at the fence to deny a home run. All too often in 2000, however, Beltran appeared to give up on flies that would fall close in front of him for hits. His arm is fairly strong and accurate. Beltran has above-average speed and runs the bases intelligently. He is an accomplished base thief.

2001 Outlook

The Royals' organization clearly is disappointed with Beltran, as much for his refusal to accept a rehab assignment as for his unexpectedly poor sophomore season. He was not a regular player when he returned last September and will enter the spring having to re-establish himself. It is a crowded and productive outfield, and Beltran will have to show most of his five tools again before he will be assured of a regular job.

Position: CF
Bats: B **Throws:** R
Ht: 6' 1" **Wt:** 190

Opening Day Age: 23
Born: 4/24/77 in Manati, Puerto Rico
ML Seasons: 3

Overall Statistics

	G	AB	R	H	D	T	HR	RBI	SB	BB	SO	Avg	OBP	Slg
2000	98	372	49	92	15	4	7	44	13	35	69	.247	.309	.366
Career	268	1093	173	302	47	14	29	159	43	84	204	.276	.327	.425

Where He Hits the Ball

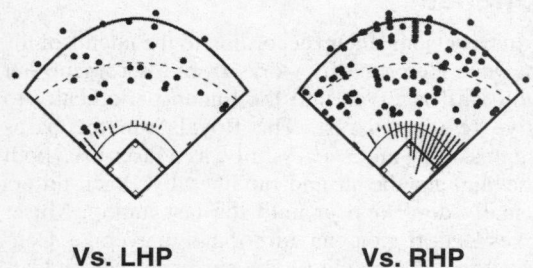

Vs. LHP   **Vs. RHP**

2000 Situational Stats

	AB	H	HR	RBI	Avg		AB	H	HR	RBI	Avg
Home	184	51	4	29	.277	LHP	71	22	4	12	.310
Road	188	41	3	15	.218	RHP	301	70	3	32	.233
First Half	296	73	6	32	.247	Sc Pos	102	23	1	36	.225
Scnd Half	76	19	1	12	.250	Clutch	73	17	0	9	.233

2000 Rankings (American League)

- 3rd in errors in center field (6)
- 7th in lowest batting average with two strikes (.139)
- 9th in lowest batting average with runners in scoring position and lowest batting average on an 0-2 count (.069)

Johnny Damon

2000 Season

As it was in 1999, Johnny Damon started slowly in 2000, carrying a Mendoza-line batting average into the last few days of April. Just as in past seasons, though, Damon warmed with the weather. In the second half, he had no equal in the majors, leading baseball in hits and batting average after the All-Star break. Damon continued to improve as a hitter, added a stolen-base crown to his resume and set a new Royals club record for runs scored.

Hitting

With his short batting stroke, Damon is able to wait until the last possible moment before pulling the trigger, helping him make excellent contact. His smooth, easy swing belies moderate power, and he can pull the ball to the fence in right or drive doubles and triples down either line. Improved patience has helped make Damon a good leadoff hitter. He also showed considerable improvement against lefties, who sometimes made him look foolish in past years. Hard-throwing righthanders succeed against Damon by pitching him inside. He handles low pitches especially well and thrives against finesse pitchers.

Baserunning & Defense

With his great speed, Damon has few peers on the basepaths or in running down flyballs. He runs effortlessly and is an intelligent, aggressive baserunner who always looks to take an extra base. His 85-percent steal rate over the last two years is one of the best in the game. Although improving, Damon's ability to read flyballs off the bat is below average, but a poor throwing arm is his biggest flaw, which is exposed in center field.

2001 Outlook

Damon is an All-Star caliber player, capable of contributing offensively in every way except with power. Signing him for the long term is a Royals priority over the winter, but he prefers to wait to see the Royals' level of commitment to winning right away. Damon's combination of speed and batting average is a catalyst for a high-average offense like the Royals', although their glut of outfielders and his caution about re-signing make it tempting to trade him before spring training.

Position: CF/LF/DH
Bats: L **Throws:** L
Ht: 6' 2" **Wt:** 190

Opening Day Age: 27
Born: 11/5/73 in Fort Riley, KS
ML Seasons: 6
Pronunciation: DAY-mun

Overall Statistics

	G	AB	R	H	D	T	HR	RBI	SB	BB	SO	Avg	OBP	Slg
2000	159	655	136	214	42	10	16	88	46	65	60	.327	.382	.495
Career	803	3057	504	894	156	47	65	352	156	275	350	.292	.351	.438

Where He Hits the Ball

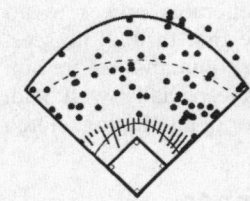 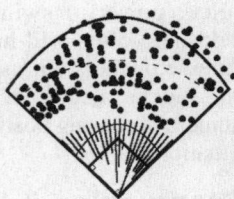

Vs. LHP   **Vs. RHP**

2000 Situational Stats

	AB	H	HR	RBI	Avg		AB	H	HR	RBI	Avg
Home	330	119	10	45	.361	LHP	171	61	4	33	.357
Road	325	95	6	43	.292	RHP	484	153	12	55	.316
First Half	326	87	8	36	.267	Sc Pos	120	41	3	65	.342
Scnd Half	329	127	8	52	.386	Clutch	89	25	1	16	.281

2000 Rankings (American League)

- 1st in runs scored and stolen bases
- 2nd in at-bats, hits, plate appearances (741) and batting average with the bases loaded (.667)
- 3rd in triples, sacrifice flies (12) and batting average at home
- Led the Royals in at-bats, runs scored, hits, doubles, triples, stolen bases, caught stealing (9), plate appearances (741), stolen-base percentage (83.6), fewest GDPs per GDP situation (5.3%), batting average with the bases loaded (.667), batting average on an 0-2 count (.217), on-base percentage for a leadoff hitter (.381), batting average at home, steals of third (5), lowest percentage of swings on the first pitch (21.0) and games played

Jermaine Dye

2000 Season

A repeat of his 1999 breakout season was all the Royals wanted when they gave Dye a two-year, $6.1 million contract before the 2000 season. They got that and more, as Dye improved in nearly every offensive category while serving as their cleanup hitter. Dye responded well to his new contract, slugging .847 with 11 homers in April on his way to his first All-Star berth.

Hitting

An aggressive, intelligent hitter who adjusts to both location and situation, Dye hits lefties and righties equally well. He hits off the fastball, trying to adjust down to breaking pitches, and can handle even the best heater from hard throwers. Dye's quick, powerful swing generates power to all fields. He often will hit the first fastball he sees. Finesse pitchers with sharp command can tie him up, and he also hasn't hit especially well with runners in scoring position or in late-inning, clutch situations.

Baserunning & Defense

Although he has some speed, Dye is a below-average baserunner, relegated to station-to-station advances. He rarely gets a good jump when trying to steal. His speed is better displayed once he gets his long legs churning, which helps him cover a lot of ground in the outfield. He also reads flyballs very well. Dye has an outstanding arm—both strong and accurate; it is one of the best guns in the game. While his fielding percentage and range were down a bit in 2000, Dye is one of the game's best right fielders, and he was rewarded with his first Gold Glove.

2001 Outlook

Signed for another year, Dye will remain the Royals' cleanup hitter in 2001. As with Mike Sweeney, Dye's success depends largely upon his teammates. He feeds off the ability of the top-of-the-order hitters to get on base. There has been some discussion of shifting Dye to first base in order to ease the glut of outfielders, but that would be a waste of his defensive prowess. He is an All-Star caliber outfielder who is entering his prime years.

Position: RF/DH
Bats: R **Throws:** R
Ht: 6' 5" **Wt:** 220

Opening Day Age: 27
Born: 1/28/74 in Vacaville, CA
ML Seasons: 5

Overall Statistics

	G	AB	R	H	D	T	HR	RBI	SB	BB	SO	Avg	OBP	Slg
2000	157	601	107	193	41	2	33	118	0	69	99	.321	.390	.561
Career	548	1978	285	566	120	11	84	319	7	163	382	.286	.340	.485

Where He Hits the Ball

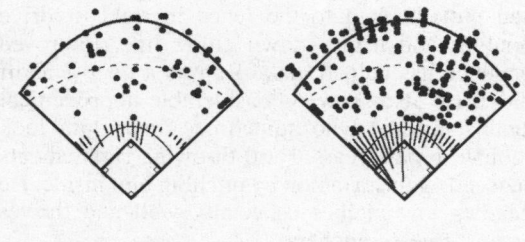

Vs. LHP　　　　　**Vs. RHP**

2000 Situational Stats

	AB	H	HR	RBI	Avg		AB	H	HR	RBI	Avg
Home	305	104	15	57	.341	LHP	133	43	7	25	.323
Road	296	89	18	61	.301	RHP	468	150	26	93	.321
First Half	307	98	22	65	.319	Sc Pos	174	47	5	72	.270
Scnd Half	294	95	11	53	.323	Clutch	101	27	3	19	.267

2000 Rankings (American League)

- 1st in errors in right field (7) and lowest fielding percentage in right field (.976)
- 5th in total bases (337) and cleanup slugging percentage (.560)
- 7th in hits
- 8th in slugging percentage vs. lefthanded pitchers (.579) and batting average at home
- Led the Royals in home runs, total bases (337), intentional walks (6), strikeouts, pitches seen (2,644), slugging percentage, HR frequency (18.2 ABs per HR), most pitches seen per plate appearance (3.89), cleanup slugging percentage (.560) and slugging percentage vs. righthanded pitchers (.556)
- Led AL right fielders in hits and total bases (337)

Carlos Febles

2000 Season

As he did in his rookie season, Carlos Febles lost a significant portion of the season due to a pair of injuries. This time around, his maladies included his wrist, left shoulder and right ankle. Febles hit well early in the season, then began to struggle in the No. 2 spot in the order. When he returned from his first rehabilitation assignment after the All-Star break, Febles hit ninth with modestly better results.

Hitting

Febles has a short stroke and generates a bit of power. He doesn't make consistent contact, although he has learned to better control his free-swinging habits. He tries to hit the ball on the ground to take advantage of his speed. He usually will pull grounders to the left side, while his fly-balls are spread around the park but more often go to the opposite field. Febles has power to left field only. An outstanding bunter, he collected several bunt singles while leading the Royals in sacrifices for the second straight season in 2000.

Baserunning & Defense

Playing deep helps Febles display decent range, especially going to his left. He turns the double play well enough and is getting better. He occasionally fails to put the ball in his pocket, making throwing errors on impossible plays. He is capable of making an error and immediately following it with a breath-taking play. Febles has great speed, although he still is learning how to steal bases. He runs the bases aggressively.

2001 Outlook

As long as he flashes spectacular defense, Febles will play regularly. The Royals would like him to make some progress as a hitter, but it's equally important to them that he remain healthy. He is seen as a top-of-the-order hitter and one of the young players around whom the team is building. Although Kansas City has been pleased with what it has seen from Febles, it would like him to take a step forward in 2001 and become the kind of player his talent says he can be.

Position: 2B
Bats: R **Throws:** R
Ht: 5'11" **Wt:** 185

Opening Day Age: 24
Born: 5/24/76 in El Seybo, Dominican Republic
ML Seasons: 3
Pronunciation: FAY-bless

Overall Statistics

	G	AB	R	H	D	T	HR	RBI	SB	BB	SO	Avg	OBP	Slg
2000	100	339	59	87	12	1	2	29	17	36	48	.257	.345	.316
Career	234	817	135	213	35	12	12	84	39	87	146	.261	.344	.377

Where He Hits the Ball

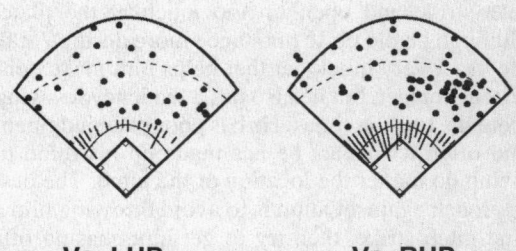

Vs. LHP   **Vs. RHP**

2000 Situational Stats

	AB	H	HR	RBI	Avg		AB	H	HR	RBI	Avg
Home	174	47	2	18	.270	LHP	92	25	0	12	.272
Road	165	40	0	11	.242	RHP	247	62	2	17	.251
First Half	196	53	2	16	.270	Sc Pos	89	26	1	26	.292
Scnd Half	143	34	0	13	.238	Clutch	50	12	1	5	.240

2000 Rankings (American League)

- 2nd in sacrifice bunts (13) and bunts in play (25)
- 7th in hit by pitch (10)
- 8th in errors at second base (10)
- Led the Royals in sacrifice bunts (13), bunts in play (25) and highest percentage of pitches taken (58.5)
- Led AL second basemen in sacrifice bunts (13) and bunts in play (25)

Mark Quinn

2000 Season

Expected to battle for a part-time outfield or designated hitter job in 2000, Mark Quinn had a topsy-turvy first half in which he alternated extra-base hits with strikeouts. After a brief June demotion to Triple-A Omaha, Quinn came back to a regular left-field job that opened when Johnny Damon moved to center to replace Carlos Beltran. Quinn was a wrecking crew after the All-Star break, hitting for average and power while also showing improvement as an outfielder. His second-half *tour de force* placed him squarely at the head of the American League rookie class.

Hitting

Quinn's is not a picture-perfect swing. He tends to over-stride and open up too much at the plate, although he did close his stance more during 2000. He has a very quick bat that helps him make consistent contact, but he also has a tendency to swing from the heels at times. He has poor plate judgment and often it appears he has made up his mind to swing no matter the location of the pitch. The best approach against Quinn is to avoid throwing him a first-pitch strike, then try to get him chasing off-speed stuff.

Baserunning & Defense

Quinn has displayed a strong arm on occasion, although his throws haven't been as accurate as desired. He has looked lost in the outfield all too often, misplaying flyballs into hits or permitting extra bases by not cutting off hits to the outfield. Quinn is not a good baserunner. He has some speed but doesn't know how to use it, and he doesn't show good baserunning judgment.

2001 Outlook

Even though he has proven capable of playing regularly, Quinn faces a crowded outfield picture in Kansas City. A trade would open up more playing time, but barring that, he may wind up in a DH role. He is a surprising young hitter with a lot of upside potential. Should he learn a little plate discipline, Quinn could contend for a batting title. At the very least, he should be a high-average hitter with moderate power.

Position: LF/DH
Bats: R **Throws:** R
Ht: 6' 1" **Wt:** 195

Opening Day Age: 26
Born: 5/21/74 in La Miranda, CA
ML Seasons: 2

Overall Statistics

	G	AB	R	H	D	T	HR	RBI	SB	BB	SO	Avg	OBP	Slg
2000	135	500	76	147	33	2	20	78	5	35	91	.294	.342	.488
Career	152	560	87	167	37	3	26	96	6	39	102	.298	.347	.514

Where He Hits the Ball

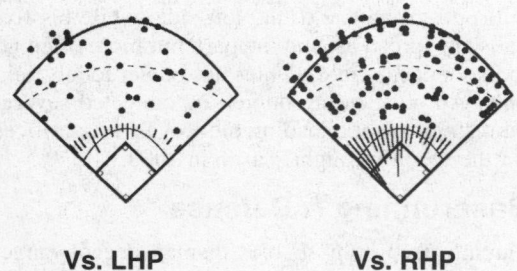

Vs. LHP   **Vs. RHP**

2000 Situational Stats

	AB	H	HR	RBI	Avg		AB	H	HR	RBI	Avg
Home	247	76	12	41	.308	LHP	103	37	6	19	.359
Road	253	71	8	37	.281	RHP	397	110	14	59	.277
First Half	229	61	11	38	.266	Sc Pos	141	42	2	53	.298
Scnd Half	271	86	9	40	.317	Clutch	86	23	3	12	.267

2000 Rankings (American League)

- 7th in highest percentage of swings on the first pitch (39.0)
- Led designated hitters in sacrifice bunts (3) and stolen bases

Joe Randa

2000 Season

Hitting over .300 for the fourth time in five seasons, Joe Randa enjoyed a 2000 season that was similar to his '99 campaign. He did establish a personal best by reaching the 100-RBI plateau for the first time in his career. Considering Randa's low home-run total, his RBI count speaks volumes about the on-base percentages of hitters in front of him—specifically Mike Sweeney and Jermaine Dye. It also says a lot about Randa's clutch hitting; he had the second-lowest slugging percentage among the 53 hitters who reached 100 RBI in 2000.

Hitting

An aggressive hitter, Randa has become even more aggressive in recent years. He'll swing at the first hittable offering and looks to pull pitches early in the count. He adjusts later in the count, instead trying more to go with the pitch. He's a line-drive hitter to all fields with extra-base power to left. Pitchers who work against Randa's early-count tendencies will have more success than those who try to challenge him with fastballs. Impatience has sometimes put Randa in a hole, giving pitchers an advantage.

Baserunning & Defense

Randa has the range and quickness necessary for the hot corner and the arm for any infield spot. He excels at chasing popups in foul ground. Randa has been plagued by streaky fielding, making errors in bunches for a few games, then none for long periods. Despite average speed, he has some basestealing ability, though his steals usually are generated by smarts more than foot speed. He doesn't run into unnecessary outs, but he doesn't take many chances, either.

2001 Outlook

For 2001. . . more of the same. Randa's nearing the end of his prime years as a high-average, low-power run producer. He'll never be a star since he lacks raw power, but he clearly fits the budget-conscious Royals well. Because it's likely that he's peaked as a hitter, he needs to curb his free-swinging tendencies to remain productive.

Position: 3B
Bats: R **Throws:** R
Ht: 5'11" **Wt:** 190

Opening Day Age: 31
Born: 12/18/69 in Milwaukee, WI
ML Seasons: 6
Nickname: The Joker

Overall Statistics

	G	AB	R	H	D	T	HR	RBI	SB	BB	SO	Avg	OBP	Slg
2000	158	612	88	186	29	4	15	106	6	36	66	.304	.343	.438
Career	722	2550	336	748	139	24	54	352	36	200	344	.293	.347	.430

Where He Hits the Ball

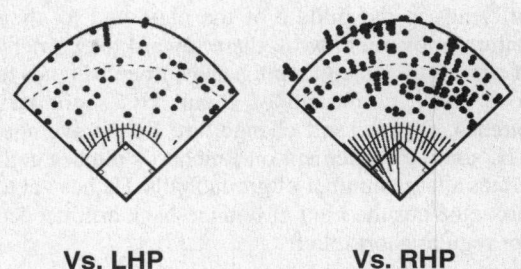

Vs. LHP   **Vs. RHP**

2000 Situational Stats

	AB	H	HR	RBI	Avg		AB	H	HR	RBI	Avg
Home	303	100	9	61	.330	LHP	126	39	0	24	.310
Road	309	86	6	45	.278	RHP	486	147	15	82	.302
First Half	316	100	9	55	.316	Sc Pos	176	61	6	93	.347
Scnd Half	296	86	6	51	.291	Clutch	92	36	2	18	.391

2000 Rankings (American League)

- 4th in batting average in the clutch and errors at third base (19)
- 5th in lowest fielding percentage at third base (.957)
- 6th in singles and sacrifice flies (10)
- Led the Royals in GDPs (19)
- Led AL third basemen in hits, singles, triples, sacrifice flies (10), GDPs (19), batting average with runners in scoring position, batting average in the clutch, batting average at home and highest percentage of swings put into play (50.4)

Dan Reichert

2000 Season

Used in a dual role, Dan Reichert had modest success. Early in the season, he helped keep a tattered Royals bullpen together until Ricky Bottalico demonstrated some effectiveness. Inserted into the starting rotation at the end of June, Reichert became one of the club's most effective pitchers, winning five straight decisions at one point.

Pitching

Reichert works primarily with two hard pitches: a sinking fastball and slider. His low-90s fastball is particularly effective because it has a lot of movement. When both pitches are working for Reichert, he can be very hard to hit, as he can throw both offerings at the middle of the plate and let their natural movement work them toward the corners. If he tries to aim either pitch at a corner, he tends to lose sharp command of them. His secondary pitches, a curve and change, are below average. The sinking movement on Reichert's pitches generates a large number of groundballs. He has yet to prove he has the kind of bounce-back arm needed for regular short relief.

Defense

A fine athlete who is quick on his feet, Reichert is an above-average fielder. He handles bunts and grounders well and throws well to the bases. He has yet to commit a major league fielding error. With just an average pickoff move, he has trouble holding runners close. Runners also are aided by the movement on his pitches, which can give his catcher trouble.

2001 Outlook

Another of the young, hard-throwing hurlers expected to populate the Royals' rotation, Reichert is seen as a potential No. 2 starter. A small refinement in his command could bring outstanding results. Because he has the kind of stuff to be successful as a closer, the Royals may be tempted to force him into that role should they continue to suffer significant bullpen woes. In either case, as starter or reliever, Reichert will serve an important role on the Royals' staff.

Position: RP/SP
Bats: R **Throws:** R
Ht: 6' 3" **Wt:** 175

Opening Day Age: 24
Born: 7/12/76 in Monterey, CA
ML Seasons: 2

Overall Statistics

	W	L	Pct.	ERA	G	GS	Sv	IP	H	BB	SO	HR	Ratio
2000	8	10	.444	4.70	44	18	2	153.1	157	91	94	15	1.62
Career	10	12	.455	5.54	52	26	2	190.0	205	123	114	17	1.73

How Often He Throws Strikes

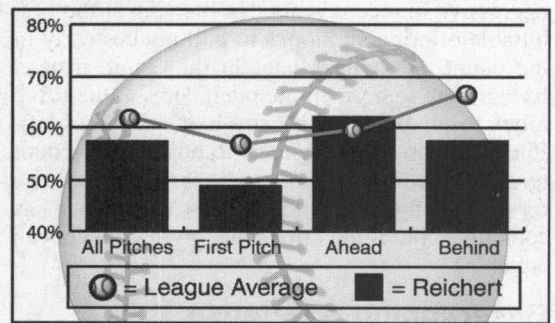

○ = League Average   ■ = Reichert

2000 Situational Stats

	W	L	ERA	Sv	IP		AB	H	HR	RBI	Avg
Home	4	5	4.78	0	64.0	LHB	295	81	5	37	.275
Road	4	5	4.63	2	89.1	RHB	285	76	10	40	.267
First Half	3	5	4.16	2	62.2	Sc Pos	153	43	4	59	.281
Scnd Half	5	5	5.06	0	90.2	Clutch	107	28	4	19	.262

2000 Rankings (American League)

- 1st in wild pitches (18)
- 4th in GDPs induced (28)
- 6th in walks allowed
- Led the Royals in losses, hit batsmen (7), wild pitches (18), GDPs induced (28) and lowest ERA on the road

Rey Sanchez

2000 Season

Steady defense was expected from the Royals' on-field leader, and that's primarily what Rey Sanchez provided. Although he largely goes unnoticed among the ranks of American League shortstops, Sanchez turned in one of the most consistent performances ever, committing just four errors all year. Struggling through an ineffective season at the plate, he was inserted into the second spot in the batting order at midseason and did an about-face, hitting better than .300 over the last half of the season.

Hitting

Using a short stroke, Sanchez tries to punch grounders through holes in the infield. He's an extremely impatient hitter, often swinging at the first hittable pitch. While his short stroke further exacerbates his lack of power, Sanchez manages to contribute in little ways, such as hitting behind runners. He is a fairly good bunter, too. The best way to handle Sanchez is to challenge him with high heat and get him to hit the ball in the air.

Baserunning & Defense

Sanchez doesn't have an especially strong arm, but it is strong enough for his position and highly accurate. He doesn't have great range, although he can go deep into the hole for grounders. Overall, Sanchez is an above-average shortstop who makes all the routine plays and is adept at the double-play pivot. He has average speed. He's not a very good basestealer despite his modest record of success the last two years.

2001 Outlook

With another year left on his two-year, $4.6 million contract, Sanchez will be the Royals' starting shortstop in 2001. What they expect from him is what he gave them the last two years: steady defense and occasional production with the bat. While Sanchez is in decline as a hitter, his defense never has been better. The Royals hope he will mentor second baseman Carlos Febles in the finer points of middle-infield defense.

Position: SS
Bats: R **Throws:** R
Ht: 5' 9" **Wt:** 175

Opening Day Age: 33
Born: 10/5/67 in Rio Piedras, Puerto Rico
ML Seasons: 10
Pronunciation: RAY SAN-chezz

Overall Statistics

	G	AB	R	H	D	T	HR	RBI	SB	BB	SO	Avg	OBP	Slg
2000	143	509	68	139	18	2	1	38	7	28	55	.273	.314	.322
Career	1018	3277	384	894	140	18	12	263	40	167	358	.273	.312	.338

Where He Hits the Ball

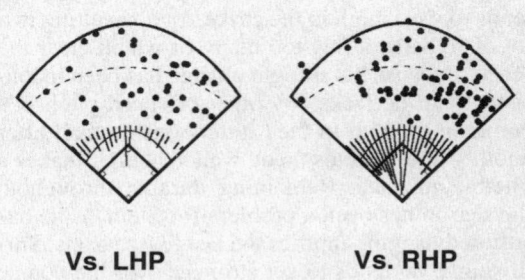

Vs. LHP　　　　**Vs. RHP**

2000 Situational Stats

	AB	H	HR	RBI	Avg		AB	H	HR	RBI	Avg
Home	251	73	1	19	.291	LHP	131	38	0	7	.290
Road	258	66	0	19	.256	RHP	378	101	1	31	.267
First Half	263	63	1	19	.240	Sc Pos	127	32	1	36	.252
Scnd Half	246	76	0	19	.309	Clutch	78	23	1	11	.295

2000 Rankings (American League)

- 1st in highest groundball/flyball ratio (3.3) and lowest HR frequency (509.0 ABs per HR)
- 2nd in fielding percentage at shortstop (.994), lowest slugging percentage and lowest slugging percentage vs. righthanded pitchers (.323)
- 3rd in highest percentage of swings put into play (54.0)
- Led the Royals in highest groundball/flyball ratio (3.3), lowest percentage of swings that missed (10.3), highest percentage of swings put into play (54.0) and highest percentage of extra bases taken as a runner (62.3)
- Led AL shortstops in highest groundball/flyball ratio (3.3)

Blake Stein

2000 Season

After spending the first half of the season on the disabled list with a fractured right forearm, Stein was recalled at midseason and started slowly. He gradually worked his way into the rotation and won seven of his last nine decisions while posting a 3.69 ERA and holding opponents to a .231 batting average over the last two months. Stein tied for the second most wins among Royals starters and was the team's best pitcher in the second half of the season.

Pitching

Stein is a big guy who throws hard, working mostly with two- and four-seam fastballs that he throws in the low 90s. His slider also comes in very hard. He tends to work high in the strike zone, resulting in a lot of flyballs, a few too many of which clear the fence. Because his straight change has been inconsistent and he lacks any other offspeed pitch, it's common for him to feed hitters one fastball after another until he fans them, walks them or makes a hittable mistake. Remaining durable throughout the season has been a problem for Stein, as he has suffered nagging injuries the last few seasons. Surprisingly, he tends to get stronger over the course of a start.

Defense

Although he is persistent in chasing baserunners back to first and has a good pickoff move, Stein takes a while to unwind in his delivery, giving baserunners a chance to steal. He also has trouble getting into proper fielding position for grounders back through the box. Otherwise, Stein is a capable defender.

2001 Outlook

Stein has the stuff to pitch at the top of the rotation. He needs to have better command to succeed, of course, and durability over the course of the season remains a question mark. For 2001, the Royals would like to see him take a regular turn in the rotation for the whole season and reduce the number of walks he allows. With just a slight improvement in his control, he would become a solid starting pitcher.

Position: SP
Bats: R **Throws:** R
Ht: 6' 7" **Wt:** 240

Opening Day Age: 27
Born: 8/3/73 in McComb, MS
ML Seasons: 3

Overall Statistics

	W	L	Pct.	ERA	G	GS	Sv	IP	H	BB	SO	HR	Ratio
2000	8	5	.615	4.68	17	17	0	107.2	98	57	78	19	1.44
Career	14	16	.467	5.32	54	49	0	298.0	280	175	214	52	1.53

How Often He Throws Strikes

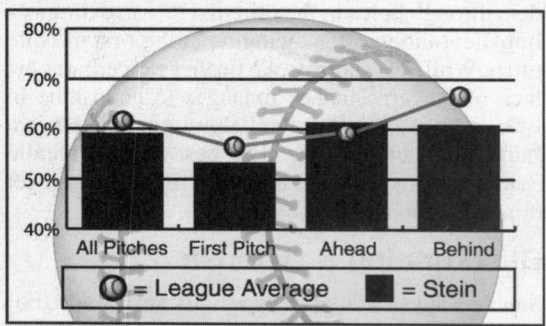

◉ = League Average   ■ = Stein

2000 Situational Stats

	W	L	ERA	Sv	IP		AB	H	HR	RBI	Avg
Home	5	3	5.83	0	54.0	LHB	184	40	8	20	.217
Road	3	2	3.52	0	53.2	RHB	213	58	11	34	.272
First Half	0	1	10.80	0	5.0	Sc Pos	87	21	6	37	.241
Scnd Half	8	4	4.38	0	102.2	Clutch	25	4	1	2	.160

2000 Rankings (American League)

- Led the Royals in runners caught stealing (6) and lowest batting average allowed vs. lefthanded batters

Jeff Suppan

Position: SP
Bats: R **Throws:** R
Ht: 6' 2" **Wt:** 210

Opening Day Age: 26
Born: 1/2/75 in Oklahoma City, OK
ML Seasons: 6
Pronunciation: soo-PAWN

2000 Season

As the only Royal to reach double-digit wins in each of the last two seasons, Jeff Suppan was the club's most successful pitcher. He started slowly and was hit hard before a brief bullpen stint at midseason, but then he turned things around. Suppan ended the year on a high note, winning eight of his last eleven decisions, including consecutive complete games to finish the season.

Pitching

Suppan succeeds by setting up hitters with a well-placed fastball, then getting them to chase his plus-curveball. He also will throw a slider and changeup, although both pitches rarely are up to the quality of his sharp-breaking curve. Because he doesn't throw very hard, barely reaching the low 90s with his fastball, he has to work the corners. When he gets too much of the plate he becomes prone to the gopher ball. The first pitch from Suppan is critical. If he can get ahead in the count, he can work with his offspeed stuff. Although he's very durable over the course of the season, Suppan does tend to wear down once he reaches the late innings; his curve loses its sharpness and opponents are able to drive the pitch for extra bases.

Defense

Opponents have had especially good success running against Suppan, although they don't run as much now as they have in the past due to his tendency to surrender home runs. He has a slow delivery and relies upon an offspeed repertoire, so he has been unable to hold runners close with his merely average move to first base. At times, Suppan has looked unsteady with the glove and unsure of where to throw the ball as a fielder.

2001 Outlook

Because he lacks an overpowering fastball, Suppan is best suited for a lower rotation spot. His durability and steady performance make him a good candidate for double-digit wins each season, although he'll never be a big winner. Suppan is the veteran, steadying influence on the Royals' young pitching staff, and will be counted on to provide regular quality starts.

Overall Statistics

	W	L	Pct.	ERA	G	GS	Sv	IP	H	BB	SO	HR	Ratio
2000	10	9	.526	4.94	35	33	0	217.0	240	84	128	36	1.49
Career	30	34	.469	5.15	123	108	0	662.0	751	222	381	96	1.47

How Often He Throws Strikes

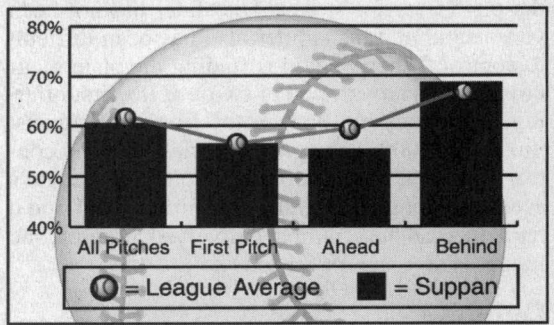

◯ = League Average   ■ = Suppan

2000 Situational Stats

	W	L	ERA	Sv	IP		AB	H	HR	RBI	Avg
Home	8	3	4.33	0	108.0	LHB	457	130	15	42	.284
Road	2	6	5.53	0	109.0	RHB	389	110	21	64	.283
First Half	2	6	5.84	0	111.0	Sc Pos	174	45	6	63	.259
Scnd Half	8	3	3.99	0	106.0	Clutch	66	15	0	5	.227

2000 Rankings (American League)

- 1st in home runs allowed
- 2nd in highest slugging percentage allowed (.489)
- Led the Royals in wins, games started, complete games (3), innings pitched, hits allowed, batters faced (948), home runs allowed, hit batsmen (7), pitches thrown (3,584), highest strikeout/walk ratio (1.5), highest groundball/flyball ratio allowed (1.4), lowest stolen-base percentage allowed (69.2), most run support per nine innings (4.8), most GDPs induced per nine innings (1.0), fewest walks per nine innings (3.5) and lowest ERA at home

Makoto Suzuki

2000 Season

Makoto Suzuki found the plate more regularly in 2000 and enjoyed his best season ever. He was the club's top starter through July and led the starting staff in ERA for the season. Despite some outstanding starts, Suzuki had trouble winning games at home, as the Royals failed to give him enough run support. The only downside to Suzuki's fourth big league campaign was his won-lost record.

Pitching

A prototypical power pitcher, Suzuki regularly hits 95 MPH with his fastball. He has had inconsistent control of his heater, however, and often suffers through one inning each start when he just can't get the pitch over for strikes. His slider has not been very useful and his splitter also has been difficult to control. When Suzuki is finding the plate regularly, batters are advised to swing at the first offering; opponents hit .353 on the first pitch against Suzuki in 2000. When he struggles with his control, however, hitters should exhibit patience. He's especially tough on righthanded hitters, who find it hard to read his flailing delivery. Durability no longer is an issue for Suzuki.

Defense

Suzuki has improved as a fielder. He's now less tentative in his approach to grounders but occasionally is forgetful about covering first base. His throws to the bases have improved. Suzuki's move to first is poor and he sometimes will ignore baserunners entirely. Opponents stole 27 times in 28 tries against Suzuki in 2000.

2001 Outlook

Now that he has learned to harness his unruly fastball, Suzuki needs to work on some of the finer points of the game, such as holding baserunners. He has the stuff to be a top-of-the-rotation starter, but he must become more consistent from first pitch to last within each start to become a No. 1 man. Another option being considered is grooming him to be a closer. Suzuki underwent arthroscopic shoulder surgery following the 2000 season, and while he is expected to be ready for spring training, a slow start isn't out of the question.

Position: SP
Bats: R **Throws:** R
Ht: 6' 3" **Wt:** 205

Opening Day Age: 25
Born: 5/31/75 in Kobe, Japan
ML Seasons: 4

Overall Statistics

	W	L	Pct.	ERA	G	GS	Sv	IP	H	BB	SO	HR	Ratio
2000	8	10	.444	4.34	32	29	0	188.2	195	94	135	26	1.53
Career	11	17	.393	5.46	77	47	0	326.1	355	175	223	45	1.62

How Often He Throws Strikes

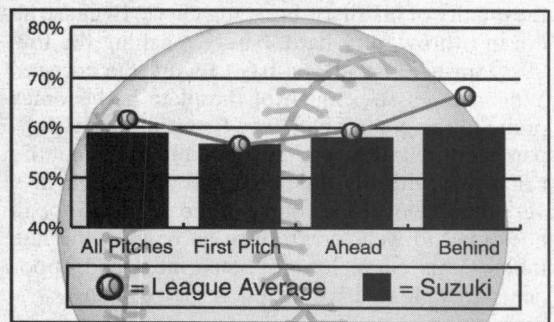

2000 Situational Stats

	W	L	ERA	Sv	IP		AB	H	HR	RBI	Avg
Home	2	7	4.80	0	110.2	LHB	400	109	18	51	.273
Road	6	3	3.69	0	78.0	RHB	337	86	8	39	.255
First Half	4	3	3.59	0	95.1	Sc Pos	183	36	3	57	.197
Scnd Half	4	7	5.11	0	93.1	Clutch	40	12	4	10	.300

2000 Rankings (American League)

- 1st in highest stolen-base percentage allowed (96.4)
- 2nd in stolen bases allowed (27)
- 3rd in lowest batting average allowed with runners in scoring position and highest walks per nine innings (4.5)
- Led the Royals in ERA, losses, walks allowed, strikeouts, pickoff throws (141), stolen bases allowed (27), lowest batting average allowed (.265), lowest slugging percentage allowed (.429), lowest on-base percentage allowed (.349), fewest pitches thrown per batter (3.70), fewest home runs allowed per nine innings (1.24) and most strikeouts per nine innings (6.4)

Mike Sweeney

Position: 1B/DH
Bats: R **Throws:** R
Ht: 6' 3"   **Wt:** 225

Opening Day Age: 27
Born: 7/22/73 in
Orange, CA
ML Seasons: 6

2000 Season

Shifted to third in the batting order to supplant struggling Carlos Beltran, Mike Sweeney thrived as the most productive RBI man in Royals history. In nearly every offensive category, Sweeney took a step up from his breakthrough season of 1999. He was consistent throughout the year and deadly in the clutch, and his intensity with runners in scoring position earned Sweeney accolades from opposing managers and his first All-Star berth.

Hitting

Formerly an aggressive, first-ball free-swinger, Sweeney has transformed into a more patient hitter who strokes line drives to all parts of the park. He has good power when he's able to turn on a pitch. Pitchers can bust Sweeney in on the hands, and he's susceptible to swinging at high fastballs. He becomes more aggressive when ahead in the count, extending his arms and getting a bigger rip, or shortening his swing in order to make contact when behind. His batting eye has improved, and he now swings at fewer bad balls.

Baserunning & Defense

Sweeney has average wheels, at best. He can look awkward and plodding on the bases and will often run into outs. Despite his recent hitting success, it's Sweeney's first-base defense that has shown the most improvement over the last year. He's far from smooth, but he no longer resembles Frankenstein with the glove. He has worked hard to learn the position and it shows. Sweeney has adequate range and has improved on scooping low throws.

2001 Outlook

One of the best RBI threats in baseball, Sweeney is a productive, high-average hitter whose success depends greatly upon his surroundings. As a part of a high-average offense, replete with baserunners, Sweeney can challenge for an RBI crown without hitting 30 homers. Because he's such a consistent hitter, it's unlikely Sweeney will experience much of a dropoff from his current level and is capable of again reaching new bests.

Overall Statistics

	G	AB	R	H	D	T	HR	RBI	SB	BB	SO	Avg	OBP	Slg
2000	159	618	105	206	30	0	29	144	8	71	67	.333	.407	.523
Career	539	1884	292	569	110	2	70	336	20	184	207	.302	.371	.474

Where He Hits the Ball

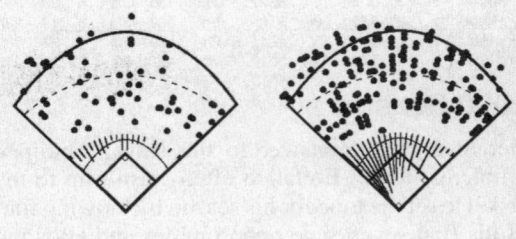

Vs. LHP   **Vs. RHP**

2000 Situational Stats

	AB	H	HR	RBI	Avg		AB	H	HR	RBI	Avg
Home	309	95	17	73	.307	LHP	131	49	6	29	.374
Road	309	111	12	71	.359	RHP	487	157	23	115	.322
First Half	339	122	15	78	.360	Sc Pos	205	79	10	119	.385
Scnd Half	279	84	14	66	.301	Clutch	108	38	4	32	.352

2000 Rankings (American League)

- 1st in hit by pitch (15), batting average with runners in scoring position and batting average on a 3-2 count (.439)
- 2nd in RBI, sacrifice flies (13) and batting average on the road
- 3rd in hits, singles, plate appearances (717) and batting average vs. lefthanded pitchers
- Led the Royals in batting average, singles, RBI, sacrifice flies (13), walks, hit by pitch (15), times on base (292), on-base percentage, batting average with runners in scoring position, batting average vs. lefthanded pitchers, batting average vs. righthanded pitchers, slugging percentage vs. lefthanded pitchers (.580) and on-base percentage vs. lefthanded pitchers (.443)

Ricky Bottalico

Position: RP
Bats: L **Throws:** R
Ht: 6' 1" **Wt:** 215

Opening Day Age: 31
Born: 8/26/69 in New Britain, CT
ML Seasons: 7
Pronunciation: buh-TAL-ih-co

Overall Statistics

	W	L	Pct.	ERA	G	GS	Sv	IP	H	BB	SO	HR	Ratio
2000	9	6	.600	4.83	62	0	16	72.2	65	41	56	12	1.46
Career	24	31	.436	4.01	364	0	111	421.2	370	223	402	47	1.41

2000 Situational Stats

	W	L	ERA	Sv	IP			AB	H	HR	RBI	Avg
Home	8	3	3.18	8	39.2	LHB		133	32	6	20	.241
Road	1	3	6.82	8	33.0	RHB		139	33	6	17	.237
First Half	7	2	4.68	5	42.1	Sc Pos		89	16	3	24	.180
Scnd Half	2	4	5.04	11	30.1	Clutch		152	36	8	25	.237

2000 Season

Heralded as the answer to the Royals' bullpen problems, Ricky Bottalico often wasn't up to the task. He set the tone for his season by blowing four of his first seven save opportunities and allowing runs to score in eight of his 18 appearances in April and May. Bottalico had more success over the last four months of the season and blew just one save after July 1. Still, in the second half, he was plagued by the longball and too many walks.

Pitching & Defense

Usually capable of throwing his fastball in the low to mid-90s, Bottalico also works with a changeup and a curve. When all three pitches are working, he can be difficult to hit. Bottalico tends to go through periodic wild streaks, getting behind hitters, then having to groove his fastball. By varying his delivery, Bottalico does an excellent job of controlling the running game. He has a tendency to lose focus when locked in a tight game and sometimes forgets his role as a fielder once the pitch is delivered.

2001 Outlook

Bottalico's career as a closer is in jeopardy after blowing 15 saves over the last two seasons. He gets another chance to compete for closer duties when he signed a one-year deal with Philadelphia in December.

Todd Dunwoody

Position: CF/LF/DH
Bats: L **Throws:** L
Ht: 6' 1" **Wt:** 205

Opening Day Age: 25
Born: 4/11/75 in Lafayette, IN
ML Seasons: 4

Overall Statistics

	G	AB	R	H	D	T	HR	RBI	SB	BB	SO	Avg	OBP	Slg
2000	61	178	12	37	9	0	1	23	3	8	42	.208	.238	.275
Career	260	848	92	200	44	12	10	78	13	48	217	.236	.280	.351

2000 Situational Stats

	AB	H	HR	RBI	Avg		AB	H	HR	RBI	Avg
Home	84	22	1	14	.262	LHP	17	3	0	3	.176
Road	94	15	0	9	.160	RHP	161	34	1	20	.211
First Half	45	9	1	3	.200	Sc Pos	45	9	0	21	.200
Scnd Half	133	28	0	20	.211	Clutch	33	5	0	0	.152

2000 Season

Acquired a year ago in an offseason trade with the Marlins, Todd Dunwoody spent the first two months of 2000 on the disabled list with a right ankle injury. Once recalled, he played sporadically and hit poorly, fanning more often than he hit safely. When Carlos Beltran returned in September, Dunwoody was a forgotten man.

Hitting, Baserunning & Defense

Poor strike-zone judgment continues to be an impairment to Dunwoody's development as a hitter. He will chase high stuff out of the strike zone, and he cannot make consistent contact with breaking pitches. When he does make contact, Dunwoody has power to the gaps and to right field. He has not succeeded in a bench role, hitting poorly as a pinch-hitter tand in situational at-bats against righthanded pitchers. He has decent speed, but he takes a while to get going, preventing him from stealing many bases. Dunwoody owns a plus-arm and enough speed to play center field.

2001 Outlook

Dunwoody has done little over the last two years to regain a full-time role. He'll enter the 2001 season as a reserve outfielder and lefty bat off the bench. It would take an unexpected rebound by Dunwoody to even win a platoon starting role.

Chris Fussell

Position: RP
Bats: R **Throws:** R
Ht: 6' 2" **Wt:** 200

Opening Day Age: 24
Born: 5/19/76 in
Oregon, OH
ML Seasons: 3
Pronunciation:
FUSS-sul

Overall Statistics

	W	L	Pct.	ERA	G	GS	Sv	IP	H	BB	SO	HR	Ratio
2000	5	3	.625	6.30	20	9	0	70.0	76	44	46	18	1.71
Career	5	9	.357	6.90	40	19	2	135.2	159	89	91	28	1.83

2000 Situational Stats

	W	L	ERA	Sv	IP		AB	H	HR	RBI	Avg
Home	3	1	5.40	0	33.1	LHB	138	36	9	23	.261
Road	2	2	7.12	0	36.2	RHB	128	40	9	23	.313
First Half	4	2	6.28	0	53.0	Sc Pos	60	15	2	25	.250
Scnd Half	1	1	6.35	0	17.0	Clutch	12	6	1	1	.500

2000 Season

Although Chris Fussell collected the first victories of his big league career in 2000, it was not a successful season. An injury to Jose Rosado forced Fussell into the starting rotation, where he had a few good starts but otherwise was hit hard. Sandwiched around his rotation duty and two trips to Triple-A were ineffective appearances in relief. He was scored upon in eight of 11 bullpen outings.

Pitching & Defense

Fussell has decent stuff, featuring a good low-90s fastball, curveball, slider and changeup. He runs into problems by trying to be too fine around the edges of the strike zone. He gets behind many hitters, then grooves a fastball and gets hammered. Because he won't go right after hitters, Fussell often runs up high pitch counts. Developing a slide step has helped him reduce baserunners' leads, although his pickoff move is still below average. A career .857 fielding average is indicative of Fussell's shaky fielding skills.

2001 Outlook

He needs more confidence to challenge hitters, and for the time being, Fussell remains a fringe major leaguer who will be used for spot starting duty or as a fifth starter. Making the Royals' staff in 2001 is not a given.

Dave McCarty

Position: 1B
Bats: R **Throws:** L
Ht: 6' 5" **Wt:** 215

Opening Day Age: 31
Born: 11/23/69 in
Houston, TX
ML Seasons: 6

Overall Statistics

	G	AB	R	H	D	T	HR	RBI	SB	BB	SO	Avg	OBP	Slg
2000	103	270	34	75	14	2	12	53	0	22	68	.278	.329	.478
Career	381	1019	119	244	44	7	22	118	8	77	249	.239	.297	.361

2000 Situational Stats

	AB	H	HR	RBI	Avg		AB	H	HR	RBI	Avg
Home	133	38	6	25	.286	LHP	104	38	5	24	.365
Road	137	37	6	28	.270	RHP	166	37	7	29	.223
First Half	116	37	8	26	.319	Sc Pos	76	26	3	38	.342
Scnd Half	154	38	4	27	.247	Clutch	58	15	2	12	.259

2000 Season

Acquired from Oakland during spring training to offer the Royals another option at the plate, Dave McCarty emerged as the team's top hitter off the bench, batting .381 as a pinch-hitter while also filling in at first base and occasionally in the outfield. After hitting .300 over the first half of the season, McCarty began to see more regular playing time and his performance suffered. Still, McCarty's season was a pleasant surprise.

Hitting, Baserunning & Defense

McCarty hits from an upright stance with a long swing that generates some power, mostly to left field. He looks fastball and has trouble adjusting to breaking pitches, leaving him prone to strikeouts. He is an adept fielder around the base at first, making scoops on low throws and fielding his position well. McCarty also handled himself well in the outfield despite very limited experience there. A station-to-station baserunner, McCarty doesn't steal and rarely takes chances on the bases.

2001 Outlook

It would be a stretch to expect the same kind of season from McCarty in 2001. Kept in a reserve role, he can be a productive bench player. Forcing him into the regular starting lineup would decrease his productivity.

Brian Meadows

Position: SP
Bats: R **Throws:** R
Ht: 6' 4" **Wt:** 220

Opening Day Age: 25
Born: 11/21/75 in Montgomery, AL
ML Seasons: 3

Overall Statistics

	W	L	Pct.	ERA	G	GS	Sv	IP	H	BB	SO	HR	Ratio
2000	13	10	.565	5.13	33	32	0	196.1	234	64	79	32	1.52
Career	35	38	.479	5.31	95	94	0	549.0	670	167	239	83	1.52

2000 Situational Stats

	W	L	ERA	Sv	IP		AB	H	HR	RBI	Avg
Home	6	6	4.69	0	101.2	LHB	395	122	19	57	.309
Road	7	4	5.61	0	94.2	RHB	390	112	13	51	.287
First Half	7	6	5.13	0	98.1	Sc Pos	187	50	5	71	.267
Scnd Half	6	4	5.14	0	98.0	Clutch	56	15	1	7	.268

2000 Season

Acquired from the Padres in a July deadline deal, Brian Meadows was a revelation for the Royals' staff, winning six of 10 starts. In four months with San Diego, Meadows was inconsistent, never posting more than two straight quality starts.

Pitching & Defense

To succeed, Meadows has to have very fine command. His fastball barely touches 90 MPH, so he has to hit spots effectively with it. He also must pinpoint his slider and curveball. The slider is especially effective when it is working, while his curve is merely average. Durability is not an issue for Meadows; he has made at least 31 starts in each of his three major league seasons. He tends to tire early in a game, though, and his pitches flatten out. Meadows is not a good fielder. His deliberate delivery and below-average move to first give baserunners a distinct advantage.

2001 Outlook

Meadows has a mediocre track record as a starting pitcher. He cannot succeed near the top of the rotation, but will do fine in the fourth or fifth slot. For a stronger team, Meadows would be relegated to a middle-innings job. With a weaker team he might be pressed into a more important starting spot, a role beyond his limited capabilities.

Hector Ortiz

Position: C
Bats: R **Throws:** R
Ht: 6' 0" **Wt:** 205

Opening Day Age: 31
Born: 10/14/69 in Rio Piedras, Puerto Rico
ML Seasons: 2

Overall Statistics

	G	AB	R	H	D	T	HR	RBI	SB	BB	SO	Avg	OBP	Slg
2000	26	88	15	34	6	0	0	5	0	8	8	.386	.443	.455
Career	30	92	16	34	6	0	0	5	0	8	8	.370	.426	.435

2000 Situational Stats

	AB	H	HR	RBI	Avg		AB	H	HR	RBI	Avg
Home	40	17	0	2	.425	LHP	43	14	0	4	.326
Road	48	17	0	3	.354	RHP	45	20	0	1	.444
First Half	0	0	0	0	-	Sc Pos	13	8	0	5	.615
Scnd Half	88	34	0	5	.386	Clutch	11	6	0	1	.545

2000 Season

Hector Ortiz began the year as Triple-A Omaha's primary catcher. He hit .322 there to earn a recall to Kansas City just after the All-Star break. He maintained his high-average hitting style, collecting more than one hit in 12 of his 25 starts. It was a fine season overall for Ortiz.

Hitting, Baserunning & Defense

Ortiz hits the ball where it is pitched, content to protect the plate and serve the ball to the outfield instead of trying to muscle it to left field. His approach detracts from any power he might generate, leaving Ortiz as strictly a singles hitter. He is not an especially adept handler of pitchers, and his other defensive skills are merely average. He throws well enough but hasn't had success against the running game. Ortiz has below-average speed, befitting a veteran catcher.

2001 Outlook

Ortiz has earned a longer look and should challenge for a big league platoon role. Because he is not a great defensive catcher and has little power, he'll have to hit for a high average to keep a regular job. Ortiz has a long history as a minor league journeyman catcher, so it remains to be seen if last year was a true breakthrough or merely a fluke.

Jose Rosado

Position: SP
Bats: L **Throws:** L
Ht: 6' 0" **Wt:** 185

Opening Day Age: 26
Born: 11/9/74 in Jersey City, NJ
ML Seasons: 5
Pronunciation: ro-SAH-doh

Overall Statistics

	W	L	Pct.	ERA	G	GS	Sv	IP	H	BB	SO	HR	Ratio
2000	2	2	.500	5.86	5	5	0	27.2	29	9	15	4	1.37
Career	37	45	.451	4.27	125	112	1	720.1	715	237	484	86	1.32

2000 Situational Stats

	W	L	ERA	Sv	IP		AB	H	HR	RBI	Avg
Home	1	0	3.86	0	11.2	LHB	17	5	0	3	.294
Road	1	2	7.31	0	16.0	RHB	90	24	4	13	.267
First Half	2	2	5.86	0	27.2	Sc Pos	23	5	1	11	.217
Scnd Half	0	0	-	0	0.0	Clutch	1	1	0	1	1.000

2000 Season

After five starts, Opening Day starter Jose Rosado was sidelined with shoulder tendinitis. The problem worsened, and he eventually was lost for the season. The injury left the Royals without a single lefthanded pitcher on their staff, and robbed them of their most experienced pitcher.

Pitching & Defense

Rosado works off a low-90s fastball, using an above-average changeup as an out pitch. He also will throw a cut fastball to lefties and uses a curveball merely for show. His pitches lack movement, so he must rely on changing speeds to be effective. Pitching deep into the game often causes Rosado to lose effectiveness on his curve and weakens his fastball. Working slowly with runners on has helped him limit stolen bases, but also has a detrimental effect on the fielders behind him. His own fielding is below average. Rosado often is out of position to field grounders or back up throws.

2001 Outlook

Expected to be fully healed for 2001, Rosado will reclaim a spot near the top of the Royals' rotation. Before the injury, he was among the American League's better lefthanded starters. Now backed by a more potent Kansas City offense, Rosado is poised for the best season of his career.

Jose Santiago

Position: RP
Bats: R **Throws:** R
Ht: 6' 3"   **Wt:** 215

Opening Day Age: 26
Born: 11/5/74 in Fajardo, Puerto Rico
ML Seasons: 4

Overall Statistics

	W	L	Pct.	ERA	G	GS	Sv	IP	H	BB	SO	HR	Ratio
2000	8	6	.571	3.91	45	0	2	69.0	70	26	44	7	1.39
Career	11	10	.524	3.73	85	0	4	123.0	127	42	62	14	1.37

2000 Situational Stats

	W	L	ERA	Sv	IP		AB	H	HR	RBI	Avg
Home	3	3	4.73	1	32.1	LHB	147	33	2	25	.224
Road	5	3	3.19	1	36.2	RHB	122	37	5	25	.303
First Half	6	3	3.99	1	47.1	Sc Pos	81	25	2	43	.309
Scnd Half	2	3	3.74	1	21.2	Clutch	107	30	4	25	.280

2000 Season

Jose Santiago had an awful year. When given a chance to close games, Santiago blew six of eight opportunities and permitted 21 of 33 inherited runners to score. His midseason ineffectiveness resulted in a one-month stint at Triple-A Omaha, and he wasn't much better upon his return.

Pitching & Defense

Santiago works almost exclusively with a 94-MPH fastball, though he also throws an inconsistent slider. When pitching with his normal windup, Santiago gets natural sinking motion on his heater and has no trouble locating the strike zone. Having to work from the stretch interrupts his delivery, and his pitches come in much flatter and far more hittable. When he has adjusted his delivery from the stretch, Santiago has had bouts of wildness. He has not displayed the kind of day-to-day durability expected from an ace reliever. Baserunners haven't had a lot of success running against Santiago, although few try. He is an average fielder.

2001 Outlook

If he somehow learns to pitch the same with runners on base as he does with the bases clear, Santiago could become a valuable short reliever. Until then he will be limited to middle-innings duty.

Kris Wilson

Position: RP
Bats: R **Throws:** R
Ht: 6' 4" **Wt:** 225

Opening Day Age: 24
Born: 8/6/76 in Washington, DC
ML Seasons: 1

Overall Statistics

	W	L	Pct.	ERA	G	GS	Sv	IP	H	BB	SO	HR	Ratio
2000	0	1	.000	4.19	20	0	0	34.1	38	11	17	3	1.43
Career	0	1	.000	4.19	20	0	0	34.1	38	11	17	3	1.43

2000 Situational Stats

	W	L	ERA	Sv	IP		AB	H	HR	RBI	Avg
Home	0	0	2.42	0	22.1	LHB	72	22	2	10	.306
Road	0	1	7.50	0	12.0	RHB	60	16	1	8	.267
First Half	0	0	-	0	0.0	Sc Pos	40	9	1	14	.225
Scnd Half	0	1	4.19	0	34.1	Clutch	34	11	1	4	.324

2000 Season

After spending the bulk of the season in the Double-A Wichita starting rotation, Kris Wilson was given his first taste of the majors when he was called up at the end of July. Wilson immediately became an important part of the Royals' bullpen, working successfully in both long and short relief roles. By season's end, he was one of the club's most reliable setup men.

Pitching & Defense

Wilson sets up his low-90s fastball with average offspeed stuff that includes a curve and change. He has been a starter for most of his four years in the minors but worked strictly in relief for Kansas City. Wilson adjusted easily to the changing role. His stuff isn't particularly overpowering, but he has very good command and location. He stays away from hitters' zones and makes them swing at pitches that are not to their liking. Wilson has a decent pickoff move and a quick delivery that keeps runners close to the base. He's still somewhat inexperienced with the glove.

2001 Outlook

The Royals need a reliable short reliever, and Wilson will be given every chance to fill the role. If he's incapable of pitching short relief regularly, he could return to the rotation or fill a long-relief role.

Gregg Zaun

Position: C
Bats: B **Throws:** R
Ht: 5'10" **Wt:** 190

Opening Day Age: 29
Born: 4/14/71 in Glendale, CA
ML Seasons: 6

Overall Statistics

	G	AB	R	H	D	T	HR	RBI	SB	BB	SO	Avg	OBP	Slg
2000	83	234	36	64	11	0	7	33	7	43	34	.274	.390	.410
Career	390	1011	126	247	49	6	20	123	16	144	145	.244	.341	.364

2000 Situational Stats

	AB	H	HR	RBI	Avg		AB	H	HR	RBI	Avg
Home	103	27	2	8	.262	LHP	34	11	2	3	.324
Road	131	37	5	25	.282	RHP	200	53	5	30	.265
First Half	92	22	3	13	.239	Sc Pos	70	22	0	24	.314
Scnd Half	142	42	4	20	.296	Clutch	45	18	1	7	.400

2000 Season

Acquired prior to the season from Detroit, Zaun had his most successful summer, playing surprisingly adequate defense and contributing several dramatic hits in the middle part of the year. Despite losing much of the first two months to a partial tear of his medial ligament in his right elbow, he set new career bests in most offensive categories while earning a share of the Royals' catching duties.

Hitting, Baserunning & Defense

A patient hitter, Zaun hits out of a hunched stance, usually looking to pull the ball. Zaun has a keen sense of game situations. He'll go to bat specifically to work the pitcher for a walk when his team needs a baserunner, or to pull the ball for extra bases if they need a homer. Zaun doesn't control the running game; he throws accurately, but his late release gives baserunners an advantage. Zaun runs well and has some basestealing speed. He tends to be reckless on the basepaths, however, and will run into some outs.

2001 Outlook

A journeyman catcher whose skills aren't good enough for regular duty, Zaun can serve a club successfully in a reserve role. Wherever he ends up, he should provide a useful bat and adequate defense behind the plate.

Other Kansas City Royals

Miguel Batista (Pos: RHP, **Age**: 30)

	W	L	Pct.	ERA	G	GS	Sv	IP	H	BB	SO	HR	Ratio
2000	2	7	.222	8.54	18	9	0	65.1	85	37	37	19	1.87
Career	13	24	.351	5.24	134	45	1	384.2	421	194	258	46	1.60

The Royals acquired Batista from Montreal last April in exchange for Brad Rigby. Batista surrendered a ton of homers before being banished to Triple-A. He signed a minor league deal with Arizona. 2001 Outlook: C

Doug Bochtler (Pos: RHP, **Age**: 30)

	W	L	Pct.	ERA	G	GS	Sv	IP	H	BB	SO	HR	Ratio
2000	0	2	.000	6.48	6	0	0	8.1	13	10	4	2	2.76
Career	9	18	.333	4.57	220	0	6	260.0	231	166	215	36	1.53

The Royals signed Bochtler to a minor league contract following the 1999 season. He battled control problems last year and declared free agency in October. 2001 Outlook: C

Tim Byrdak (Pos: LHP, **Age**: 27)

	W	L	Pct.	ERA	G	GS	Sv	IP	H	BB	SO	HR	Ratio
2000	0	1	.000	11.37	12	0	0	6.1	11	4	8	3	2.37
Career	0	4	.000	8.27	48	0	1	32.2	48	24	26	9	2.20

Byrdak is a small lefthander who has pitched much better at Triple-A than in the majors the last three seasons. His control sometimes escapes him. 2001 Outlook: C

Jeff D'Amico (Pos: RHP, **Age**: 26)

	W	L	Pct.	ERA	G	GS	Sv	IP	H	BB	SO	HR	Ratio
2000	0	1	.000	9.22	7	1	0	13.2	19	15	9	2	2.49
Career	0	1	.000	9.22	7	1	0	13.2	19	15	9	2	2.49

This is the smaller Jeff D'Amico, the one the Royals received as part of the Kevin Appier swap in 1999. D'Amico was Oakland's second-round pick in 1993 and has some talent, despite last year's record. 2001 Outlook: C

Wilson Delgado (Pos: 2B/SS, **Age**: 25, **Bats**: B)

	G	AB	R	H	D	T	HR	RBI	SB	BB	SO	Avg	OBP	Slg
2000	64	128	21	33	2	0	1	11	4	11	26	.258	.312	.297
Career	123	240	33	62	6	1	1	17	4	18	45	.258	.316	.304

The Royals acquired Delgado from the Yankees last August in exchange for minor league shortstop Nick Ortiz. Delgado has shown a pretty good stick in the past, and at age 25 he may surprise. 2001 Outlook: B

Jorge Fabregas (Pos: C, **Age**: 31, **Bats**: L)

	G	AB	R	H	D	T	HR	RBI	SB	BB	SO	Avg	OBP	Slg
2000	43	142	13	40	4	0	3	17	1	8	11	.282	.320	.373
Career	528	1524	131	380	48	3	18	173	4	103	189	.249	.296	.320

Fabregas has been with five organizations the past three seasons. He didn't play poorly with the Royals last year, though he endured some injury problems. Fabregas signed with Anaheim in November. 2001 Outlook: B

Ray Holbert (Pos: SS, **Age**: 30, **Bats**: R)

	G	AB	R	H	D	T	HR	RBI	SB	BB	SO	Avg	OBP	Slg
2000	3	4	0	1	0	0	0	0	0	0	2	.250	.250	.250
Career	115	202	28	45	5	1	2	11	11	18	51	.223	.290	.287

Holbert spent his 13th season in the minors last year after closing 1999 by batting .304 over 17 September games with Kansas City. He signed a minor league contract with Tampa Bay in November. 2001 Outlook: C

Brian Johnson (Pos: C, **Age**: 33, **Bats**: R)

	G	AB	R	H	D	T	HR	RBI	SB	BB	SO	Avg	OBP	Slg
2000	37	125	9	26	6	0	4	18	0	4	28	.208	.229	.352
Career	468	1411	132	350	60	6	49	195	1	80	267	.248	.291	.403

Johnson opened last year as Kansas City's starting catcher, but then batted .185 in April. The Royals released him in June, and St. Louis signed him in July, but he did not make it back to the major leagues. 2001 Outlook: C

Andy Larkin (Pos: RHP, **Age**: 26)

	W	L	Pct.	ERA	G	GS	Sv	IP	H	BB	SO	HR	Ratio
2000	0	3	.000	7.96	21	0	1	26.0	35	16	24	6	1.96
Career	3	11	.214	8.86	39	15	1	105.2	139	75	69	18	2.03

Larkin passed from the Cubs to the Reds to the Royals' organization last year. He did little to improve his career record and ERA, and he inked a minor league contract with Colorado in December. 2001 Outlook: C

Brett Laxton (Pos: RHP, **Age**: 27)

	W	L	Pct.	ERA	G	GS	Sv	IP	H	BB	SO	HR	Ratio
2000	0	1	.000	8.10	6	1	0	16.2	23	10	14	0	1.98
Career	0	2	.000	7.86	9	3	0	26.1	35	17	23	1	1.97

The Royals traded Jeremy Giambi in order to acquire Laxton last February. Laxton walked too many batters last year, though he does a good job limiting the damage by allowing few home runs. 2001 Outlook: C

Scott Mullen (Pos: LHP, **Age**: 26)

	W	L	Pct.	ERA	G	GS	Sv	IP	H	BB	SO	HR	Ratio
2000	0	0	-	4.35	11	0	0	10.1	10	3	7	2	1.26
Career	0	0	-	4.35	11	0	0	10.1	10	3	7	2	1.26

Mullen switched to relief last year and thrived in the role. Throw out his final appearance with the Royals, and he compiled a 0.96 ERA over his first 10 games of major league exposure. 2001 Outlook: C

Dan Murray (Pos: RHP, **Age**: 27)

	W	L	Pct.	ERA	G	GS	Sv	IP	H	BB	SO	HR	Ratio
2000	0	0	-	4.66	10	0	0	19.1	20	10	16	7	1.55
Career	0	0	-	5.76	15	0	0	29.2	33	16	25	11	1.65

Murray has posted a winning record each of the past five minor league seasons. The Royals got him in exchange for Glendon Rusch in September 1999. 2001 Outlook: C

Luis Ordaz (**Pos**: SS/2B, **Age**: 25, **Bats**: R)

	G	AB	R	H	D	T	HR	RBI	SB	BB	SO	Avg	OBP	Slg
2000	65	104	17	23	2	0	0	11	4	5	10	.221	.257	.240
Career	144	288	32	61	8	0	0	22	10	19	32	.212	.260	.240

Ordaz spent last season as a spare middle infielder after the Royals picked him up off waivers from Arizona. What you saw last year is probably what you can expect to get from him. 2001 Outlook: B

Scott Pose (**Pos**: RF, **Age**: 34, **Bats**: L)

	G	AB	R	H	D	T	HR	RBI	SB	BB	SO	Avg	OBP	Slg
2000	47	48	6	9	0	0	0	1	0	6	13	.188	.278	.188
Career	202	313	52	75	7	1	0	21	9	38	50	.240	.321	.268

Remember when Pose was Florida's leadoff hitter in its inaugural game of 1993? Of course Orestes Destrade was the Marlins' cleanup hitter that day, and we haven't heard from him in seven years. 2001 Outlook: D

Jason Rakers (**Pos**: RHP, **Age**: 27)

	W	L	Pct.	ERA	G	GS	Sv	IP	H	BB	SO	HR	Ratio
2000	2	0	1.000	9.14	11	0	0	21.2	33	7	16	5	1.85
Career	2	0	1.000	8.76	13	0	0	24.2	35	11	16	6	1.86

The Royals converted Rakers into primarily a reliever after acquiring him off waivers from Cleveland last off-season. He remains very hittable. 2001 Outlook: C

Jeff Reboulet (**Pos**: 2B/3B, **Age**: 36, **Bats**: R)

	G	AB	R	H	D	T	HR	RBI	SB	BB	SO	Avg	OBP	Slg
2000	66	182	29	44	7	0	0	14	3	23	32	.242	.325	.280
Career	793	1706	235	406	72	2	14	153	20	226	293	.238	.330	.307

Reboulet has fashioned a nine-year career out of being a backup. Sooner or later, though, someone's going to figure out he's slugged just .238 over the past two seasons. He's now a free agent. 2001 Outlook: C

Paul Spoljaric (**Pos**: LHP, **Age**: 30)

	W	L	Pct.	ERA	G	GS	Sv	IP	H	BB	SO	HR	Ratio
2000	0	0	-	6.52	13	0	0	9.2	9	5	6	4	1.45
Career	8	17	.320	5.52	195	12	4	277.1	275	163	278	41	1.58

Spoljaric pitched so poorly last spring that the Cardinals released him. The Royals rescued him and he pitched well in Triple-A, but his major league ERA has been in the sixes the past three years. He signed a minor league contract with Tampa Bay in November. 2001 Outlook: C

Kansas City Royals Minor League Prospects

Organization Overview:

The Royals have succeeded at converting draft picks into major league regulars, from Johnny Damon and Mike Sweeney to recent arrivals Carlos Beltran, Carlos Febles and Mark Quinn. Dee Brown looks like the next everyday player to reach Kansas City, and plenty of young arms will follow. Two 1998 selections, Royals top pitching prospect Chris George and Jeff Austin, aren't far away, and 1996 pick Chad Durbin will be in the mix in 2001. Plus, three other promising prospects—Junior Guerrero, Mike MacDougal and Corey Thurman—will open the season at Double-A Wichita. And if that isn't enough pitching on the horizon, it's noteworthy that MacDougal is one of six pitchers the Royals selected in the first two rounds of the 1999 draft. Few organizations are as rich in pitching talent as the Royals' system.

Jeff Austin

Position: P **Opening Day Age:** 24
Bats: R **Throws:** R **Born:** 10/19/76 in San
Ht: 6' 0" **Wt:** 185 Bernardino, CA

Recent Statistics

	W	L	ERA	G	GS	Sv	IP	H	R	BB	SO	HR
1999 A Wilmington	7	2	3.77	18	18	0	112.1	108	52	39	97	10
1999 AA Wichita	3	1	4.46	6	6	0	34.1	40	19	11	21	1
2000 AA Wichita	2	2	2.93	6	6	0	43.0	33	16	4	31	3
2000 AAA Omaha	7	9	4.48	23	19	0	126.2	150	85	35	57	16

After being named *Baseball America*'s College Player of the Year in 1998, Austin reached the Double-A level in his first pro season in '99. Armed with the desire and work ethic to succeed, Austin finished his second year in the Triple-A Omaha rotation. His best pitch is a curveball, and he complements it with a low-90s fastball and changeup. Austin also started working on a slider last summer. He tends to keep the ball down and limit the number of home-run balls he serves up, but he more than doubled his career home runs allowed in his 126.2 innings worked in the Pacific Coast League in 2000. After some Triple-A duty to tighten his command, Austin will get his chance to crack the Kansas City rotation.

Dee Brown

Position: OF **Opening Day Age:** 23
Bats: L **Throws:** R **Born:** 3/27/78 in Bronx,
Ht: 6' 0" **Wt:** 215 NY

Recent Statistics

	G	AB	R	H	D	T	HR	RBI	SB	BB	SO	Avg
2000 AAA Omaha	125	479	76	129	25	6	23	70	20	37	112	.269
2000 AL Kansas City	15	25	4	4	1	0	0	4	0	3	9	.160
2000 MLE	125	469	65	119	22	6	19	60	14	31	112	.254

Brown has the bat speed, power and foot speed to do it all offensively. He did just that in 1999, tearing up the Class-A Carolina League and Double-A Texas League to the tune of 24 doubles, 25 homers, 30 stolen bases, a .331

average and .436 on-base percentage. Brown got off to a slow start at Triple-A Omaha in 2000—and the final numbers weren't as impressive—but he finished strong. While Brown needs to work at making better contact, and his walk rate was down substantially at Omaha, it's worth remembering that Brown was just 22 years old last summer. Defensively, he is ready to man a major league outfield, and that could happen on Opening Day if the Royals part with Johnny Damon.

Chad Durbin

Position: P **Opening Day Age:** 23
Bats: R **Throws:** R **Born:** 12/3/77 in Spring
Ht: 6' 2" **Wt:** 200 Valley, IL

Recent Statistics

	W	L	ERA	G	GS	Sv	IP	H	R	BB	SO	HR
2000 AAA Omaha	4	4	4.46	12	12	0	72.2	75	37	22	53	10
2000 AL Kansas City	2	5	8.21	16	16	0	72.1	91	71	43	37	14

A third-round pick in 1996, Durbin made the Opening Day roster last spring, and showed flashes of what he may do with a little more seasoning. He debuted with six innings of one-hit ball in a victory over Toronto, but that promising beginning was one of just five quality starts that Durbin registered in 16 outings for the Royals. He split the 2000 campaign between Kansas City and his first exposure to Triple-A. Durbin throws a remarkable changeup that makes his low-90s fastball that much better. He's been working on a hard curveball, but spotting it effectively needs work. Command of his fastball was an issue in 2000, particularly in the majors, when Durbin was prone to overthrowing. He's in the mix to stick with the Royals in 2001.

Mark Ellis

Position: SS **Opening Day Age:** 23
Bats: R **Throws:** R **Born:** 6/6/77 in Rapid
Ht: 5' 11" **Wt:** 180 City, SD

Recent Statistics

	G	AB	R	H	D	T	HR	RBI	SB	BB	SO	Avg
1999 A Spokane	71	281	67	92	14	0	7	47	21	47	40	.327
2000 A Wilmington	132	484	83	146	27	4	6	62	25	78	72	.302
2000 AA Wichita	7	22	4	7	1	0	0	4	1	5	5	.318

Ellis, a ninth-round pick in 1999, has already demonstrated that defensively he is dependable and surehanded as a shortstop. On top of that, his bat has been just as impressive. En route to a brief stint at Double-A Wichita late in the 2000 season, Ellis has batted well above .300, shown some gap power and an ability to draw walks, and has a career on-base percentage of .412. Still, his greatest assets may be his smarts and his desire. He's a classic overachiever whose abilities have continued to develop through hard work. While Ellis is a polished player with a strong arm and a good glove, his opportunity in the majors is likely to come at second base.

Chris George

Position: P
Bats: L **Throws:** L
Ht: 6' 1" **Wt:** 165

Opening Day Age: 21
Born: 9/16/79 in Houston, TX

Recent Statistics

	W	L	ERA	G	GS	Sv	IP	H	R	BB	SO	HR
1999 A Wilmington	9	7	3.60	27	27	0	145.0	142	65	53	142	8
2000 AA Wichita	8	5	3.14	18	18	0	97.1	92	41	51	80	5
2000 AAA Omaha	3	2	4.84	8	8	0	44.2	47	29	20	27	8

Drafted as a high school pitcher in 1998, George vaulted over two levels in '99 and reached Triple-A Omaha in less than three seasons. His success earned him a spot on the U.S. Olympic team, to which he contributed 3.2 innings of scoreless relief en route to gold. The key to his meteoric rise has been his combination of skill and polish. He exhibits a wide range of velocity and movement with an extremely effective fastball-changeup package, and his curveball and slider are at least major league average. His fastball will touch 94 MPH, but its normal range is 89-91. His walk rate was high in 2000. To reach the majors, George must fine-tune his control and focus on keeping the ball down in the strike zone.

Junior Guerrero

Position: P
Bats: R **Throws:** R
Ht: 6' 2" **Wt:** 175

Opening Day Age: 21
Born: 8/21/79 in Santo Domingo, DR

Recent Statistics

	W	L	ERA	G	GS	Sv	IP	H	R	BB	SO	HR
1999 A Chston-WV	7	3	2.76	19	19	0	104.1	90	39	45	113	6
1999 A Wilmington	4	2	1.40	9	9	0	51.1	30	10	26	68	2
2000 AA Wichita	4	10	5.70	28	24	0	131.0	153	93	69	79	25

In his first two pro seasons, Guerrero simply overpowered hitters. His mid-90s fastball was all he needed to post impressive numbers in the Rookie-level Gulf Coast League in '98, and he was even more dominating in Class-A ball in '99. Pitching at Charleston in the Sally League and Wilmington in the high Class-A Carolina League, Guerrero ranked among minor league leaders with a stunning 2.31 ERA and 181 strikeouts—good for an average of 10.46 whiffs per nine. Then he took his one-pitch arsenal to Double-A Wichita and learned he needed to diversify. He mostly worked on a splitter, which is coming along fairly well. Because he must continue working on new pitches, Guerrero is likely to return to Wichita for the start of the 2001 campaign.

Mike MacDougal

Position: P
Bats: B **Throws:** R
Ht: 6' 4" **Wt:** 195

Opening Day Age: 24
Born: 3/5/77 in Las Vegas, NV

Recent Statistics

	W	L	ERA	G	GS	Sv	IP	H	R	BB	SO	HR
1999 A Spokane	2	2	4.47	11	11	0	46.1	43	25	17	57	3
2000 A Wilmington	9	7	3.92	26	25	1	144.2	115	79	76	129	5
2000 AA Wichita	0	1	7.71	2	2	0	11.2	16	10	7	9	0

MacDougal was part of the bumper crop of impressive young arms that joined the Royals courtesy of the 1999 draft. He quickly capitalized on his heater, riding it through the Royals' system all the way to Double-A Wichita in 2000. This lanky righthander throws a mid-90s fastball that has tremendous movement and sink. While *Baseball America* concluded that MacDougal had the best fastball in the Carolina League in 2000, because of its life, pinpointing it precisely in the strike zone has been difficult. In fact, MacDougal went to instructional league in the fall to work on its location. He has great stuff, and demonstrated marked improvement with his hard slider and changeup last summer, as well.

Corey Thurman

Position: P
Bats: R **Throws:** R
Ht: 6' 1" **Wt:** 215

Opening Day Age: 22
Born: 11/5/78 in Augusta, GA

Recent Statistics

	W	L	ERA	G	GS	Sv	IP	H	R	BB	SO	HR
1999 A Wilmington	8	11	4.88	27	27	0	149.1	160	89	64	131	11
2000 A Wilmington	10	5	2.26	19	19	0	115.2	97	33	46	96	6
2000 AA Wichita	4	5	4.83	9	9	0	50.1	46	34	24	47	10

Drafted in 1996, Thurman had a less-than-stellar 1999 at Class-A Wilmington, in which he was 8-11 (4.88) and allowed 160 hits and 64 walks in 149.1 innings, Thurman turned it around at Wilmington in 2000. He went 10-5 (2.26) in 19 starts before moving up to Double-A Wichita for his first taste of the high minors. He throws a fastball that approaches 90 MPH, a curve and an above-average changeup. He isn't going to dominate hitters, and the Royals aren't going to rush his development. Look for him to return to Wichita when camp breaks in the spring.

Others to Watch

Signed out of the Dominican Republic in 1997, **Alexis Gomez** (20) played in the high Class-A Carolina League as a teenager in 2000. Facing many pitchers with college experience, he held his own with the bat and used his speed to play a solid center field. If his 6-foot-2 frame fills out, he could be a nice blend of power and speed. . . With a mid-90s fastball and a quality slider, **Orber Moreno** (23) was on the fast track to possibly replace Jeff Montgomery as the Royals' closer. A strained flexor tendon during spring training in 2000 eventually required Tommy John surgery in late June. Moreno is expected back early in 2001. . . Another of the Royals' six young pitchers selected early in the 1999 draft, righthander **Brian Sanches** (22) fanned 51 batters in 34 innings in his pro debut at short-season Spokane before jumping over the Sally League for a spot in the Wilmington rotation in the high Class-A Carolina League in 2000. He wasn't overmatched throwing a low-90s fastball and a curve that is among the best in the organization. . . The Royals' first-round pick in 1999, righthander **Kyle Snyder** (23) came with a mid-90s fastball, solid secondary pitches and great makeup. He had Tommy John surgery last year, but the Royals are convinced that Snyder's makeup will spearhead his return in 2002.

Hubert H. Humphrey Metrodome

Offense

The Metrodome no longer deserves the Homerdome label it earned in its early days. The park actually is negative for home runs overall over the past three seasons. Lefthanded hitters can shoot for the short porch in right field, but righthanded sluggers find the fairly deep power alley in left field to be annoying. The venue is good for batting average and offense in general. The spongy artificial turf increases doubles substantially and triples occur more frequently than in most parks.

Defense

While the artificial turf is fast, hops are true and fewer errors generally are committed in the Metrodome. On the other hand, the infamous white roof makes finding high popups and long flyballs difficult for fielders, especially in day games. It's not uncommon for opposing players to lose the ball in the roof, and it even happens to the Twins themselves on occasion.

Who It Helps the Most

Players who have good speed and hit the ball in the gaps, like Matt Lawton, Cristian Guzman, Torii Hunter and Jacque Jones, are very dangerous in the Metrodome. Lefthanded hitters David Ortiz and Corey Koskie have yet to take full advantage of the short porch in right field.

Who It Hurts the Most

Righthanded hitters like Ron Coomer and Matt LeCroy have a hard time showing their natural power here. Eric Milton often struggles in the dome, and young pitchers usually take time to adjust to the quirks of the facility. Any fielder new to the dome will have a hard time catching a flyball initially.

Rookies & Newcomers

The Twins will continue their youth movement in 2001. Matt Kinney likely will enter the starting rotation and will have to improve on the 9.69 ERA he posted at home in three starts in 2000. Young hitters like Ortiz, Koskie and LeCroy must hit for more power if the Twins are to improve their anemic offense. Luis Rivas, a gap hitter with good speed and doubles power, should do well here.

Dimensions: LF-343, LCF-385, CF-408, RCF-367, RF-327

Capacity: 48,678

Elevation: 815 feet

Surface: Turf

Foul Territory: Small

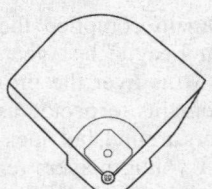

Minnesota

Park Factors

2000 Season

	Home Games Twins	Opp	Total	Away Games Twins	Opp	Total	Index
G	72	72	144	72	72	144	—
Avg	.280	.293	.286	.264	.283	.273	105
AB	2479	2639	5118	2540	2431	4971	103
R	374	419	793	312	379	691	115
H	693	773	1466	671	687	1358	108
2B	161	150	311	136	132	268	113
3B	30	15	45	14	14	28	156
HR	47	97	144	56	94	150	93
BB	254	217	471	239	245	484	95
SO	425	512	937	478	406	884	103
E	39	53	92	55	62	117	79
E-Infield	35	48	83	48	54	102	81
LHB-Avg	.303	.297	.300	.268	.289	.277	108
LHB-HR	29	41	70	32	32	64	109
RHB-Avg	.250	.291	.274	.259	.278	.270	102
RHB-HR	18	56	74	24	62	86	82

1998-2000

	Home Games Twins	Opp	Total	Away Games Twins	Opp	Total	Index
G	217	217	434	217	217	434	—
Avg	.273	.286	.280	.258	.283	.270	104
AB	7420	7924	15344	7578	7331	14909	103
R	1026	1194	2220	928	1104	2032	109
H	2029	2265	4294	1954	2076	4030	107
2B	442	471	913	370	387	757	117
3B	67	51	118	35	47	82	140
HR	133	280	413	166	259	425	94
BB	731	682	1413	675	635	1310	105
SO	1278	1398	2676	1303	1207	2510	104
E	136	163	299	145	178	323	93
E-Infield	114	143	257	118	162	280	92
LHB-Avg	.285	.286	.285	.260	.288	.272	105
LHB-HR	70	141	211	84	90	174	117
RHB-Avg	.261	.285	.275	.256	.279	.269	102
RHB-HR	63	139	202	82	169	251	79

2000 Rankings (American League)

- Highest run factor
- Highest triple factor
- Second-highest double factor
- Second-highest LHB batting-average factor
- Third-highest batting-average factor
- Third-highest hit factor
- Third-highest strikeout factor
- Second-lowest error factor
- Second-lowest infield-error factor
- Third-lowest walk factor

Tom Kelly

2000 Season

The Minnesota Twins once again compiled the worst record in the American League last year, though they improved by six wins over the previous campaign. Tom Kelly remains respected as one of the best in-game managers around, but questions regarding his handling of young players resurfaced, especially after the exile of Todd Walker to the minor leagues in early May. Several players felt Kelly lacks patience and is too quick to publicly criticize youngsters. Others were supportive of their manager, and it's true that Kelly has been remarkably patient with players such as LaTroy Hawkins and Matt Lawton.

Offense

To put it bluntly, the Twins' offense stinks. The club ranked 13th in the league in runs scored, thanks to a dearth of both power and on-base percentage. Minnesota cleanup hitters slugged a putrid .378. Kelly doesn't like to bunt much, but will call the hit-and-run and wants players to be very aggressive on the bases. He prefers contact hitters and is critical of players with long swings who strike out often. He usually keeps his reserves involved in the game and will bench his best players for a day or two if they make too many mistakes.

Pitching & Defense

A player with a mediocre glove but a good bat has a hard time finding a spot in a Kelly lineup. The emphasis on defense helps the Twins maintain a decent pitching staff despite the small budget. Minnesota has the nucleus of a very good starting rotation, and Kelly always has been able to piece a bullpen together. He keeps his pitchers healthy and avoids pushing them beyond their limits.

2001 Outlook

There were rumors at the end of last season that Kelly's job was on the line, but he signed a one-year contract in October. He has a strong relationship with owner Carl Pohlad, though others in the organization are quietly critical of Kelly's approach. The Twins enter 2001 the same way they entered 2000: rebuilding with youth, but needing more hitters in the lineup without hurting the defense that Kelly loves.

Born: 8/15/50 in Graceville, MN

Playing Experience: 1975, Min

Managerial Experience: 15 seasons

Manager Statistics

Year	Team, Lg	W	L	Pct	GB	Finish
2000	Minnesota, AL	69	93	.426	26.0	5th Central
15 Seasons		1055	1167	.475	—	—

2000 Starting Pitchers by Days Rest

	<=3	4	5	6+
Twins Starts	5	91	36	20
Twins ERA	3.90	5.59	5.00	6.64
AL Avg Starts	2	88	40	22
AL ERA	4.87	5.03	5.03	5.28

2000 Situational Stats

	Tom Kelly	AL Average
Hit & Run Success %	36.1	35.1
Stolen Base Success %	66.7	68.8
Platoon Pct.	68.2	57.8
Defensive Subs	11	23
High-Pitch Outings	9	13
Quick/Slow Hooks	8/20	18/19
Sacrifice Attempts	37	55

2000 Rankings (American League)

- 1st in pinch-hitters used (182) and starts on three days rest (5)
- 3rd in squeeze plays (5) and starting lineups used (131)

Ron Coomer

2000 Season

Every year, the Twins talk about reducing Ron Coomer's role in favor of younger hitters. It never seems to happen. Coomer's defense and work ethic endear him to manager Tom Kelly, who sticks with the veteran through thick and thin. Coomer remained in the lineup most days last year until nagging ankle, elbow and shoulder injuries wore him down. He hit .283 or higher each month from May through August, before stumbling to a .155 average in September.

Hitting

Although Coomer is very strong, he does not possess a power swing. While he makes good contact and does not strike out excessively, his home-run power is at best sporadic by contemporary standards. The Metrodome is a difficult park for Coomer, since most of his power is to the deepest part of the dome. Not surprisingly, he blasted only three of his 16 dingers at home last season. He hits the ball hard and on the ground, which makes him vulnerable to the double play. Coomer shows little patience at the plate, resulting in a weak on-base percentage. He is not a legitimate cleanup hitter, and would be more effective in a platoon role.

Baserunning & Defense

At his best, Coomer is very slow. When his ankles and knees are acting up, he's downright immobile. While he has decent baserunning instincts, he just can't run fast. When healthy, Coomer is a very good defensive player, with soft hands, good field presence at first base and a strong throwing arm. In an emergency, he can handle third base without killing the defense.

2001 Outlook

Coomer is miscast as a regular, and would be better suited for bench and platoon duties for a contending team. While Tom Kelly loves him, the Twins are unsure they want to meet Coomer's likely arbitration demands. They may let him go in the offseason to free up financial resources for their younger players.

Position: 1B
Bats: R **Throws:** R
Ht: 5'11" **Wt:** 206

Opening Day Age: 34
Born: 11/18/66 in Chicago, IL
ML Seasons: 6

Minnesota

Overall Statistics

	G	AB	R	H	D	T	HR	RBI	SB	BB	SO	Avg	OBP	Slg
2000	140	544	64	147	29	1	16	82	2	36	50	.270	.317	.415
Career	676	2397	283	667	121	7	77	364	13	132	317	.278	.315	.431

Where He Hits the Ball

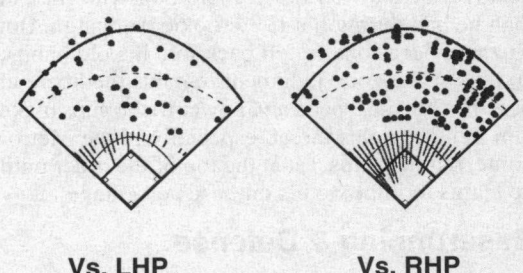

Vs. LHP   **Vs. RHP**

2000 Situational Stats

	AB	H	HR	RBI	Avg		AB	H	HR	RBI	Avg
Home	287	75	3	41	.261	LHP	125	32	5	16	.256
Road	257	72	13	41	.280	RHP	419	115	11	66	.274
First Half	318	88	11	55	.277	Sc Pos	171	49	5	68	.287
Scnd Half	226	59	5	27	.261	Clutch	78	20	1	11	.256

2000 Rankings (American League)

- 1st in most GDPs per GDP situation (21.9%) and lowest percentage of extra bases taken as a runner (20.4)
- 2nd in fielding percentage at first base (.995) and lowest cleanup slugging percentage (.395)
- 3rd in GDPs (25)
- Led the Twins in GDPs (25), cleanup slugging percentage (.395), slugging percentage vs. lefthanded pitchers (.456), highest percentage of swings put into play (50.9) and lowest percentage of swings on the first pitch (28.9)
- Led AL first basemen in GDPs (25) and highest percentage of swings put into play (50.9)

Cristian Guzman

2000 Season

Cristian Guzman opened last season by batting .290 in April, courtesy of a new approach at the plate. He connected for four home runs in May, however, and returned to bad habits. Guzman rebounded to hit well in July and August, and was rewarded with a long-term contract worth up to $9 million. Although he played very poorly after signing the new deal, the Twins generally were happy with his development.

Hitting

Guzman adopted a new hitting style in spring training, reducing his movement at the plate to provide better balance for his swing. The results were very positive: he showed much more pop with the bat than he had during his 1999 rookie campaign. But Guzman occasionally fell back into his old habits, and his strike-zone judgment remains mediocre at best. His blazing speed and power to the gaps make him a huge triples threat, especially in the Metrodome, but he is miscast at the top of the order until he learns to improve his on-base percentage.

Baserunning & Defense

Guzman is the fastest man on the club, and improved his ability to read pitchers and steal bases in 2000. Scouts think he could swipe 40 bases a year as he gains experience and learns to obtain better jumps. Guzman is a gifted athlete, and he displays his talent on defense. He possesses decent range and a very strong arm, but lacks concentration on routine plays and commits too many sloppy mistakes.

2001 Outlook

At age 23 and with two major league seasons under his belt, Guzman has just scratched the surface of his ability. He was benched a few times for lack of hustle last year, but the Twins are committed to him long-term. Whether he becomes a star or just another player depends on how hard he works and on whether he learns to control the strike zone better.

Position: SS
Bats: B **Throws:** R
Ht: 6' 0" **Wt:** 195

Opening Day Age: 23
Born: 3/21/78 in Santo Domingo, Dominican Republic
ML Seasons: 2
Pronunciation: GOOZ-mahn

Overall Statistics

	G	AB	R	H	D	T	HR	RBI	SB	BB	SO	Avg	OBP	Slg
2000	156	631	89	156	25	20	8	54	28	46	101	.247	.299	.388
Career	287	1051	136	251	37	23	9	80	37	68	191	.239	.286	.343

Where He Hits the Ball

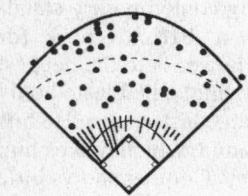
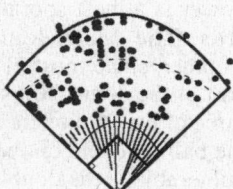

Vs. LHP   **Vs. RHP**

2000 Situational Stats

	AB	H	HR	RBI	Avg		AB	H	HR	RBI	Avg
Home	328	95	3	33	.290	LHP	172	36	4	19	.209
Road	303	61	5	21	.201	RHP	459	120	4	35	.261
First Half	347	90	6	33	.259	Sc Pos	149	34	0	42	.228
Scnd Half	284	66	2	21	.232	Clutch	78	23	3	14	.295

2000 Rankings (American League)

- 1st in triples, lowest on-base percentage, lowest on-base percentage vs. lefthanded pitchers (.225) and lowest batting average on the road
- 2nd in lowest on-base percentage for a leadoff hitter (.301)
- 3rd in errors at shortstop (22)
- Led the Twins in at-bats, runs scored, triples, sacrifice bunts (7), stolen bases, caught stealing (10), plate appearances (690), on-base percentage for a leadoff hitter (.301), bunts in play (22), highest percentage of extra bases taken as a runner (62.7) and games played
- Led AL shortstops in at-bats, triples, stolen bases, caught stealing (10) and fewest GDPs per GDP situation (4.3%)

LaTroy Hawkins

2000 Season

After three dismal seasons as a starter, LaTroy Hawkins entered 2000 with an ugly career ERA of 6.16. The Twins didn't know what else to do with him, and he began the year as a mopup man in their bullpen. Hawkins started slowly, but then took to the bullpen like a fish to water, easing into a larger share of the closer-by-committee plan. By the end of the year, he was the main option in late-game situations, successfully converting all 14 of his save opportunities.

Pitching

Hawkins pumps his fastball as high as 95 MPH, but because the heater lacked movement he was routinely blasted when he started games. Working out of the bullpen, he displayed better control within the strike zone on all of his pitches. Another problem as a starter was a repertoire that was too diverse. While he threw a slider, curve, splitter and changeup, he couldn't use any of them consistently. Toiling as a reliever, Hawkins concentrated on improving the slider while placing his other offerings on the backburner in most games. He showed good confidence in pressure situations and had no trouble adjusting to the bullpen routine or workload. He's never had a hint of significant arm trouble.

Defense

Hawkins is an excellent athlete and is very mobile for someone 6-foot-5. Still, he does make occasional mistakes and isn't likely to win any gold gloves. His move to first has improved since he entered the league, and runners have to be careful against him.

2001 Outlook

Three Twins saved at least nine games each last season, but unless he completely bombs in spring training, Hawkins should be the Minnesota closer in 2001. The Twins were patient with him for a long time, and they believe they finally have found a role in which he can thrive.

Position: RP
Bats: R **Throws:** R
Ht: 6' 5" **Wt:** 204

Opening Day Age: 28
Born: 12/21/72 in Gary, IN
ML Seasons: 6

Overall Statistics

	W	L	Pct.	ERA	G	GS	Sv	IP	H	BB	SO	HR	Ratio
2000	2	5	.286	3.39	66	0	14	87.2	85	32	59	7	1.33
Career	28	49	.364	5.76	165	98	14	609.0	765	221	358	93	1.62

How Often He Throws Strikes

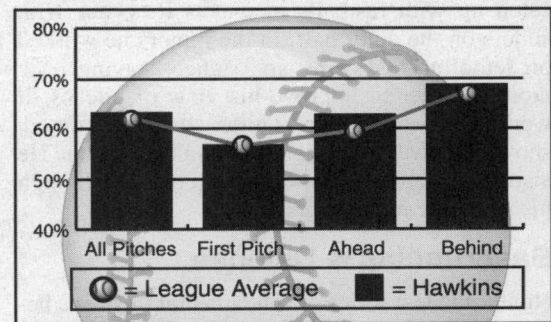

= League Average   ■ = Hawkins

2000 Situational Stats

	W	L	ERA	Sv	IP		AB	H	HR	RBI	Avg
Home	1	1	3.81	6	49.2	LHB	128	31	4	16	.242
Road	1	4	2.84	8	38.0	RHB	204	54	3	19	.265
First Half	2	2	3.98	4	54.1	Sc Pos	92	20	2	28	.217
Scnd Half	0	3	2.43	10	33.1	Clutch	130	36	2	12	.277

2000 Rankings (American League)

- 4th in relief innings (87.2)
- 5th in lowest percentage of inherited runners scored (18.2)
- Led the Twins in saves, games finished (38), lowest percentage of inherited runners scored (18.2), relief innings (87.2) and relief ERA (3.39)

Torii Hunter

2000 Season

After platooning for most of 1999, Torii Hunter opened 2000 as the Twins' regular center fielder. But he played so poorly that he was demoted to the minors on May 25. He proceeded to tear up Triple-A, hitting .368 with 18 homers in just 55 games. He rejoined the Twins in late July and batted .332 the rest of the way, providing a glimpse of the talent that had made him a first-round pick in the 1993 draft.

Hitting

Hunter always has possessed good natural strength and bat speed, but he had trouble maintaining a consistent swing. Before his demotion, he couldn't catch up with fastballs in on his fists, nor with sliders on the outer half. In the minors he worked on retooling his swing and stance, staying back more in order to improve his view of pitches. It worked; he was a different hitter when he returned, showing power to all fields and quicker hands. He also displayed better strike-zone judgment, though his walk rate remains poor.

Baserunning & Defense

Hunter made a series of fundamental mistakes before his demotion, but the overall quality of his play was much better upon his return. While he is fast on the bases he is not adept at stealing, one area he still needs to improve. With the glove, Hunter is excellent. He's a pure center fielder with outstanding range and a strong and accurate arm. Twins officials think he is one of the best defensive outfielders in the American League.

2001 Outlook

Hunter did a lot to improve his standing in 2000, and once again will open a new season as Minnesota's regular center fielder. He must maintain his progress at the plate, which means continuing to improve his batting eye. The Twins value his glove, and if he keeps hitting, they'll have a complete player to aid their rebuilding efforts.

Position: CF
Bats: R **Throws:** R
Ht: 6' 2" **Wt:** 205

Opening Day Age: 25
Born: 7/18/75 in Pine Bluff, AR
ML Seasons: 4

Overall Statistics

	G	AB	R	H	D	T	HR	RBI	SB	BB	SO	Avg	OBP	Slg
2000	99	336	44	94	14	7	5	44	4	18	68	.280	.318	.408
Career	241	737	96	196	32	9	14	81	14	46	146	.266	.313	.391

Where He Hits the Ball

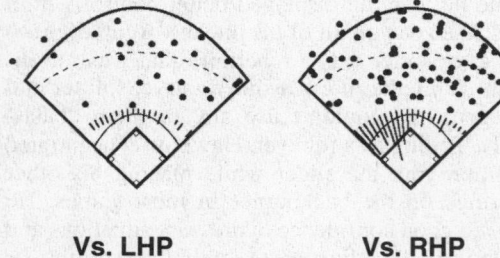

Vs. LHP   **Vs. RHP**

2000 Situational Stats

	AB	H	HR	RBI	Avg		AB	H	HR	RBI	Avg
Home	164	47	4	22	.287	LHP	83	20	2	10	.241
Road	172	47	1	22	.273	RHP	253	74	3	34	.292
First Half	140	29	0	9	.207	Sc Pos	102	30	2	39	.294
Scnd Half	196	65	5	35	.332	Clutch	51	16	0	7	.314

2000 Rankings (American League)

- 6th in most GDPs per GDP situation (18.1%)
- 7th in triples
- 9th in errors in center field (3)
- Led the Twins in batting average with two strikes (.258)
- Led AL center fielders in triples, batting average on a 3-2 count (.571) and batting average with two strikes (.258)

Jacque Jones

2000 Season

Jacque Jones began 2000 in fine form, hitting over .300 in April and May, and slugging over .500 in June. He slumped in August because he lost control of the strike zone: he didn't draw a walk all month. By September he had regained his patience and was again one of Minnesota's best hitters, batting .310 for the month and ensuring his starting job for next year.

Hitting

Jones has excellent bat speed, thanks to very quick wrists. Most of his power is to left-center and center field, and he gets in trouble when he tries to pull too much. His main flaw as a hitter is over-aggressiveness; he swings at the first pitch too frequently and draws few free passes. He lunges at pitches outside the strike zone and has a bad habit of diving across the plate when he's in a slump. He seems more comfortable batting lower in the order, which may be for the best as long as his on-base percentage remains mediocre.

Baserunning & Defense

Although Jones has some speed on the bases, he isn't much of a stealer at this point in his career since he doesn't read pitchers well. He has the speed to swipe 20 bases a year if he improves his technique. He split time between left and center field, and performs solidly at either position. His range is well above average, and his arm is fairly strong and usually very accurate. He makes few errors and has learned to deal with the tricky Metrodome roof when landing flyballs.

2001 Outlook

As it stands, Jones is a good player, one of the few power threats in the Twins' lineup. If he gains more patience at the plate, he could develop into a consistent .300, 20-homer threat. He'll be in the lineup nearly every day once again in 2001, so he'll have the opportunity to reach both plateaus.

Position: LF/CF
Bats: L **Throws:** L
Ht: 5'10" **Wt:** 176

Opening Day Age: 25
Born: 4/25/75 in San Diego, CA
ML Seasons: 2

Overall Statistics

	G	AB	R	H	D	T	HR	RBI	SB	BB	SO	Avg	OBP	Slg
2000	154	523	66	149	26	5	19	76	7	26	111	.285	.319	.463
Career	249	845	120	242	50	7	28	120	10	43	174	.286	.323	.462

Where He Hits the Ball

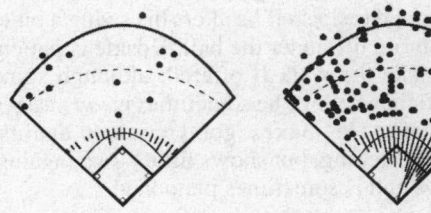

Vs. LHP   **Vs. RHP**

2000 Situational Stats

	AB	H	HR	RBI	Avg		AB	H	HR	RBI	Avg
Home	257	73	11	45	.284	LHP	74	17	1	8	.230
Road	266	76	8	31	.286	RHP	449	132	18	68	.294
First Half	298	87	13	44	.292	Sc Pos	138	39	5	57	.283
Scnd Half	225	62	6	32	.276	Clutch	77	24	2	9	.312

2000 Rankings (American League)

- 2nd in lowest percentage of pitches taken (44.1)
- 3rd in highest groundball/flyball ratio (2.1) and highest percentage of swings on the first pitch (43.0)
- 9th in fewest pitches seen per plate appearance (3.45)
- 10th in batting average on a 3-2 count (.333)
- Led the Twins in home runs, strikeouts, slugging percentage, HR frequency (27.5 ABs per HR), highest groundball/flyball ratio (2.1) and batting average with the bases loaded (.455)
- Led AL left fielders in highest groundball/flyball ratio (2.1)

Corey Koskie

2000 Season

Corey Koskie started slowly last year, perhaps distracted by the impending birth of his first child. He got hot after the baby was born in June, hitting .366 for the month and .315 in July. While he didn't show the power the Twins expected, he has now hit .300 or better in both of his years as a regular, confirming his status as a key component on the everyday Minnesota roster.

Hitting

While Koskie is strong, he has more of a line-drive approach at the plate. He can put a charge in a ball if he pulls it, but is often content to hit balls the opposite way or into the gaps. The Twins would like him to hit for more power, and he certainly is strong enough to do so if he alters his swing a bit to generate more lift under the ball. Koskie is patient and will take the walk if offered, although some Twins officials believe he sometimes is *too* passive at the plate. He makes good contact against lefthanded pitching, but shows little power against southpaws and is sometimes platooned.

Baserunning & Defense

Although Koskie is not a fast runner, he has good instincts on the bases and is very aggressive about moving up on flyballs and challenging the defense. Koskie has made great strides with the glove. He sometimes has trouble fielding bunts. But he has a strong arm, is reliable on the routine play and has improved his footwork, especially on the double play. He made just 12 errors in 139 games at third.

2001 Outlook

The Twins think that Koskie has 20-25 home run potential, and given his size that's easy to understand. The Twins need his strong on-base percentage in the lineup even if his power doesn't develop as hoped. So expect him to remain a regular as long as they can afford his salary. Since he turns 28 in June, a power spike is a decent bet for 2001.

Position: 3B
Bats: L **Throws:** R
Ht: 6' 3" **Wt:** 217

Opening Day Age: 27
Born: 6/28/73 in Anola, BC, Canada
ML Seasons: 3
Pronunciation: KOSS-kee

Overall Statistics

	G	AB	R	H	D	T	HR	RBI	SB	BB	SO	Avg	OBP	Slg
2000	146	474	79	142	32	4	9	65	5	77	104	.300	.400	.441
Career	274	845	123	252	53	4	21	125	9	119	186	.298	.388	.445

Where He Hits the Ball

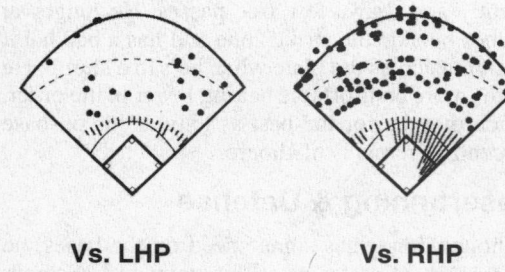

Vs. LHP / Vs. RHP

2000 Situational Stats

	AB	H	HR	RBI	Avg		AB	H	HR	RBI	Avg
Home	211	59	1	27	.280	LHP	90	30	0	12	.333
Road	263	83	8	38	.316	RHP	384	112	9	53	.292
First Half	254	79	6	40	.311	Sc Pos	135	36	1	51	.267
Scnd Half	220	63	3	25	.286	Clutch	63	11	0	6	.175

2000 Rankings (American League)

- 3rd in lowest batting average in the clutch
- 4th in fielding percentage at third base (.966)
- 8th in batting average on a 3-2 count (.348)
- Led the Twins in batting average on a 3-2 count (.348) and batting average on the road
- Led AL third basemen in triples, highest groundball/flyball ratio (1.5), on-base percentage vs. righthanded pitchers (.395) and highest percentage of extra bases taken as a runner (60.0)

Matt Lawton

2000 Season

Matt Lawton hoped 2000 would erase the disappointment of his poor 1999 season. He far exceeded that goal, in the process proving he was far past the beaning that marred the previous campaign. Lawton was especially hot early in the year, hitting .330 before the All-Star break. He played well in every month except September, when he was bothered by a severe case of turf toe that inhibited his running and defense.

Hitting

Lawton made mental and physical adjustments hoping to recover from the 1999 setback. He improved his hitting mechanics by lowering his hands at the plate, and hired a personal trainer to develop his positive thinking. Both changes worked. A very patient hitter with gap power to all fields, Lawton is effective against both lefthanded and righthanded pitching and is increasingly confident in the clutch. He usually bats third in the order, but his high on-base percentage would be perfect in the leadoff spot, should the Twins find a way to improve their power core. He makes good contact and is reliable in hit-and-run situations.

Baserunning & Defense

Lawton has above-average speed, and is excellent at getting good jumps and reading pitchers for steals. The injured toe reduced his ability to run in the second half of the season, but that isn't expected to be a long-term problem. He split the season between left and right field, and can play center in an emergency. Lawton's speed gives him acceptable range. While his arm strength is average, it is very accurate, and the Twins are comfortable playing him in right.

2001 Outlook

In 2000, Lawton emerged not only as a solid player, but also as a team leader. He has matured into a strong clubhouse presence, and the anemic Twins desperately need his bat. Lawton is willing to stay in Minnesota long-term, and the Twins will try to fit his increasing salary into their tight payroll structure.

Position: RF/LF
Bats: L **Throws:** R
Ht: 5'10" **Wt:** 186

Opening Day Age: 29
Born: 11/3/71 in Gulfport, MS
ML Seasons: 6

Overall Statistics

	G	AB	R	H	D	T	HR	RBI	SB	BB	SO	Avg	OBP	Slg
2000	156	561	84	171	44	2	13	88	23	91	63	.305	.405	.460
Career	668	2296	352	629	138	13	62	333	77	345	289	.274	.377	.426

Where He Hits the Ball

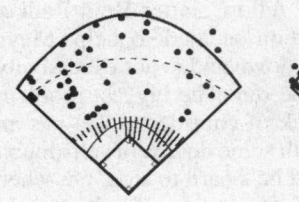 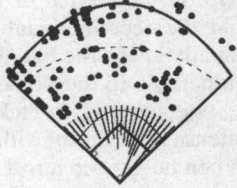

Vs. LHP   **Vs. RHP**

2000 Situational Stats

	AB	H	HR	RBI	Avg		AB	H	HR	RBI	Avg
Home	290	94	8	56	.324	LHP	163	48	2	28	.294
Road	271	77	5	32	.284	RHP	398	123	11	60	.309
First Half	330	109	6	57	.330	Sc Pos	159	49	3	71	.308
Scnd Half	231	62	7	31	.268	Clutch	93	35	4	17	.376

2000 Rankings (American League)

- 5th in doubles, batting average in the clutch and on-base percentage vs. righthanded pitchers (.424)
- Led the Twins in batting average, hits, singles, doubles, total bases (258), RBI, walks, intentional walks (8), hit by pitch (7), times on base (269), pitches seen (2,459), on-base percentage, stolen-base percentage (76.7), most pitches seen per plate appearance (3.70), batting average with runners in scoring position, batting average in the clutch, batting average vs. lefthanded pitchers, batting average vs. righthanded pitchers, batting average on an 0-2 count (.259), slugging percentage vs. righthanded pitchers (.490) and on-base percentage vs. righthanded pitchers (.424)

Joe Mays

2000 Season

Sophomore Joe Mays opened last year in the rotation. He pitched poorly in April, but did well in May and June before slumping in July, losing confidence in himself. Control artists have to possess some self-assurance, so Mays wound up back in the minors in August. The refresher course helped, and he pitched very well in September, with a 2.79 ERA and no walks in three late-season starts.

Pitching

Relying on command and control to get hitters out, Mays uses an 89-90 MPH fastball, a curveball and a changeup as the main weapons in his arsenal. The changeup was his best pitch as a rookie, but he struggled with it last year. He eventually altered his grip on the advice of fellow starter Brad Radke, and the recommendation seemed to help. Mays usually keeps the ball down and is not excessively vulnerable to the home run. The biggest problem he encounters is a lack of confidence. He has an intense personality with some degree of self-doubt. When he gets on a roll he's hard to stop, but when he slumps he gets down on himself, which only makes the problem worse.

Defense

Mays isn't the best athlete in the world and is not a polished fielder. He is smart, but needs more situational experience, especially since he is a ground-ball pitcher. He committed a pair of errors but also was involved in a pair of double plays. His move to first base is adequate, which is good enough when he is in rhythm and working quickly.

2001 Outlook

Mays was a victim of poor run support last season. He struggles when he tries to be too perfect, so more runs on the scoreboard would help him relax a bit. His strong September performance ensures a roster spot in 2001, probably as Minnesota's No. 4 starter.

Position: SP
Bats: B **Throws:** R
Ht: 6' 1" **Wt:** 185

Opening Day Age: 25
Born: 12/10/75 in Flint, MI
ML Seasons: 2

Overall Statistics

	W	L	Pct.	ERA	G	GS	Sv	IP	H	BB	SO	HR	Ratio
2000	7	15	.318	5.56	31	28	0	160.1	193	67	102	20	1.62
Career	13	26	.333	4.94	80	48	0	331.1	372	134	217	44	1.53

How Often He Throws Strikes

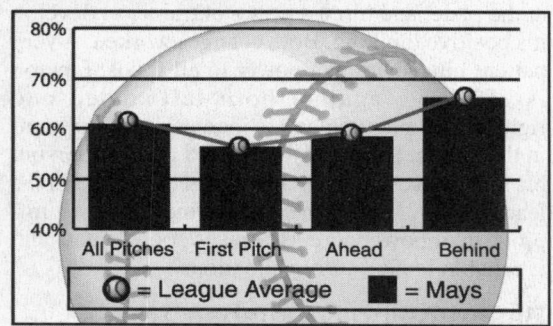

= League Average   = Mays

2000 Situational Stats

	W	L	ERA	Sv	IP		AB	H	HR	RBI	Avg
Home	4	7	6.01	0	79.1	LHB	310	93	10	44	.300
Road	3	8	5.11	0	81.0	RHB	336	100	10	43	.298
First Half	4	10	5.70	0	107.1	Sc Pos	150	42	5	69	.280
Scnd Half	3	5	5.26	0	53.0	Clutch	35	10	0	2	.286

2000 Rankings (American League)

- 2nd in losses and lowest winning percentage
- 5th in wild pitches (11)
- 8th in highest ERA on the road
- 9th in highest batting average allowed vs. righthanded batters
- 10th in lowest fielding percentage at pitcher (.943)
- Led the Twins in walks allowed and GDPs induced (18)

Eric Milton

2000 Season

After his strong effort in the second half of 1999, many observers expected Eric Milton to emerge as one of the American League's best pitchers in 2000. It didn't quite happen, due in part to inconsistency. He pitched very well in June (3.47 ERA) and August (3.00), was adequate in April and July, but struggled in both May (6.26) and September (7.09). Although dogged by a nagging knee injury as well as occasional fatigue, he nevertheless ranked fifth in the league in fewest baserunners allowed per nine innings.

Pitching

Milton was timed at 96 MPH on one occasion last year, although 91-93 is his usual range. His fastball has good movement, and he can nail the corners with it when he's going well. His curveball has improved greatly over the last two years, and his changeup remains an effective complement. Milton's biggest problem is throwing too many pitches high in the strike zone. He is an extreme flyball pitcher and gets tattooed with homers if his control isn't sharp. He's lowered his walk rate over the last two years, which has helped to contain the damage from the gopherballs. Milton's workload must be monitored carefully; he has bouts of shoulder and elbow soreness, and the Twins don't want to risk his future.

Defense

While Milton possesses good athletic ability, he can be a bit error-prone. Though he has improved his infield fundamentals, there is more work to do. He recorded just 15 assists in 200 innings in 2000. Milton *does* control the running game well, as he surrendered just four stolen bases in those 200 frames.

2001 Outlook

Although Milton's ERA was just around league average, he improved his strikeout-walk ratio, which is often the best indicator of future success. He got some run support last year and won 13 games. If he remains healthy and the Twins' hitting attack improves, he could win 15-18 games in 2001.

Position: SP
Bats: L   **Throws:** L
Ht: 6' 3"   **Wt:** 220

Opening Day Age: 25
Born: 8/4/75 in State College, PA
ML Seasons: 3

Overall Statistics

	W	L	Pct.	ERA	G	GS	Sv	IP	H	BB	SO	HR	Ratio
2000	13	10	.565	4.86	33	33	0	200.0	205	44	160	35	1.25
Career	28	35	.444	4.96	99	99	0	578.2	590	177	430	88	1.33

How Often He Throws Strikes

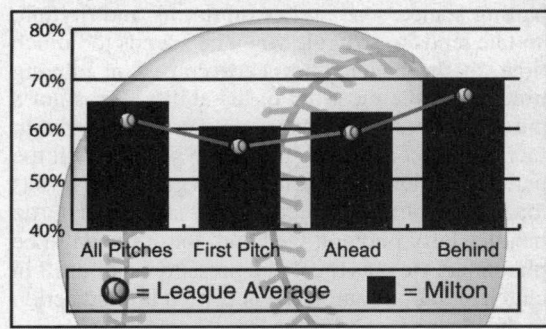

◯ = League Average   ■ = Milton

2000 Situational Stats

	W	L	ERA	Sv	IP		AB	H	HR	RBI	Avg
Home	4	6	5.64	0	97.1	LHB	149	36	7	21	.242
Road	9	4	4.12	0	102.2	RHB	638	169	28	82	.265
First Half	8	4	5.22	0	112.0	Sc Pos	160	44	4	58	.275
Scnd Half	5	6	4.40	0	88.0	Clutch	38	5	2	2	.132

2000 Rankings (American League)

- 2nd in home runs allowed, lowest groundball/flyball ratio allowed (0.6) and most home runs allowed per nine innings (1.58)
- 3rd in fewest GDPs induced per nine innings (0.5)
- Led the Twins in wins, home runs allowed, hit batsmen (7), strikeouts, highest strikeout/walk ratio (3.6), lowest batting average allowed (.260), lowest slugging percentage allowed (.455), lowest on-base percentage allowed (.303), lowest stolen-base percentage allowed (66.7), most run support per nine innings (5.7), most strikeouts per nine innings (7.2), fewest walks per nine innings (2.0), lowest ERA on the road and lowest batting average allowed vs. righthanded batters

David Ortiz

2000 Season

David Ortiz began last year on the bench because manager Tom Kelly didn't like Ortiz' defense at first base and felt compelled to play free-agent acquisition Butch Huskey in the DH slot. Ortiz didn't see consistent action until mid-June, but he quickly made up for lost time and was particularly hot in July, batting .421 for the month. He cooled down the stretch, and while his final numbers were a bit disappointing, he was one of the few offensive threats in a weak lineup.

Hitting

While Ortiz is very strong, he hasn't fully developed his power. With a high leg kick and a coiled batting stance, Ortiz relies on timing and rhythm, and he tends to struggle when he spends too much time on the bench—he needs consistent playing time to get the most out of his ability. He is not a pure pull hitter, but flashes power to all fields. In fact, Twins coaches would like to see him pull the ball more often. His batting eye is good, and he has made great strides in reducing his strikeouts. Ortiz handles lefty pitching well and doesn't need to be platooned. He puts too much pressure on himself in clutch situations and fared poorly in limited action in the cleanup spot last year.

Baserunning & Defense

Ortiz is very slow and never will steal more than a handful of bases. His instincts on the basepaths aren't very good either, and the Twins would like him to improve his fundamentals across the board. Though he made just one error in 27 games at first base, his range is limited and he tends to make mental mistakes that don't show up in the box scores. Kelly does everything he can to keep Ortiz off the field.

2001 Outlook

Minnesota was disappointed that Ortiz clubbed just 10 home runs last year. However, the 36 doubles promise more power to come, and he's still just 25. His strike-zone judgment greatly improved in 2000, and Ortiz should see everyday action as the designated hitter this season. The Twins should expect gradual but steady improvement from this developing youngster.

Position: DH/1B
Bats: L **Throws:** L
Ht: 6' 4" **Wt:** 230

Opening Day Age: 25
Born: 11/18/75 in Santo Domingo, Dominican Republic
ML Seasons: 4
Pronunciation: or-TEEZ

Overall Statistics

	G	AB	R	H	D	T	HR	RBI	SB	BB	SO	Avg	OBP	Slg
2000	130	415	59	117	36	1	10	63	1	57	81	.282	.364	.446
Career	241	762	117	210	59	1	20	115	2	103	184	.276	.361	.434

Where He Hits the Ball

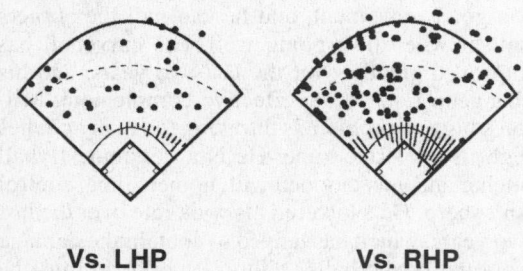

Vs. LHP   **Vs. RHP**

2000 Situational Stats

	AB	H	HR	RBI	Avg		AB	H	HR	RBI	Avg
Home	227	71	7	41	.313	LHP	78	33	1	13	.423
Road	188	46	3	22	.245	RHP	337	84	9	50	.249
First Half	163	43	5	28	.264	Sc Pos	126	29	2	51	.230
Scnd Half	252	74	5	35	.294	Clutch	65	19	0	9	.292

2000 Rankings (American League)

- 9th in batting average on a 3-2 count (.345)
- 10th in lowest batting average vs. righthanded pitchers
- Led the Twins in sacrifice flies (6)

Brad Radke

2000 Season

Uncertainty surrounded Brad Radke at the beginning of 2000. Could the Twins sign their staff anchor to a long-term contract? Would he be traded? The questions didn't seem to distract Radke, however, and he wound up signing a new deal in early July. He pitched poorly in August due to fatigue and a possible mechanical hitch, but was otherwise his steady self, posting better-than-league ERAs in five of six months. Radke is one of only nine pitchers in baseball to win at least 11 games in each of the past six seasons.

Pitching

Radke does not have a blazing fastball. His heater comes in at a steady 89-91 MPH, but often looks faster than it is due to his command of breaking pitches and his ability to change speeds. His changeup is one of the best in baseball, and he also can hit spots with his curve and slider. Radke was overstriding during his August slump (6.39 ERA), but solved the problem and posted a decent 4.29 mark in September. His mechanics usually are excellent, and they're the main reason he's remained so durable throughout his career. He gives up hits, but holds up well in pressure situations and is regarded as the leader of the staff.

Defense

Radke made an error last year, only the second of his career. He is quick off the mound and a solid fielder in every respect. He works fast, which helps him control runners despite an average move to first base. Radke has allowed fewer than 15 stolen bases in each of the last two seasons.

2001 Outlook

Poor run support led to Radke's 12-16 record; he usually works against the opposition's ace starters, which is a tough assignment for the punchless Twins. Give this guy some runs, and he'll win 15 games a year. As usual, his ERA was considerably better than league average, and there is no reason for that to change in 2001.

Position: SP
Bats: R **Throws:** R
Ht: 6' 2" **Wt:** 188

Opening Day Age: 28
Born: 10/27/72 in Eau Claire, WI
ML Seasons: 6

Overall Statistics

	W	L	Pct.	ERA	G	GS	Sv	IP	H	BB	SO	HR	Ratio
2000	12	16	.429	4.45	34	34	0	226.2	261	51	141	27	1.38
Career	78	84	.481	4.32	198	197	0	1311.2	1402	290	805	178	1.29

How Often He Throws Strikes

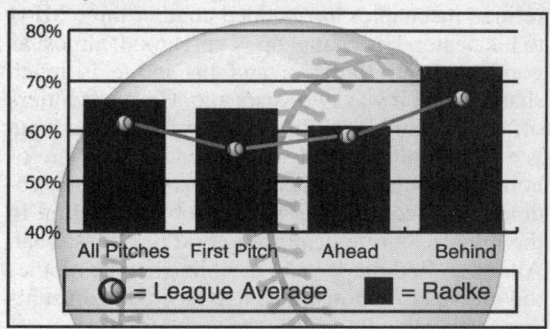

2000 Situational Stats

	W	L	ERA	Sv	IP		AB	H	HR	RBI	Avg
Home	7	7	3.94	0	123.1	LHB	499	148	16	63	.297
Road	5	9	5.05	0	103.1	RHB	412	113	11	45	.274
First Half	5	10	4.28	0	132.1	Sc Pos	215	56	8	74	.260
Scnd Half	7	6	4.67	0	94.1	Clutch	95	30	2	10	.316

2000 Rankings (American League)

- 1st in losses
- 2nd in hits allowed
- 3rd in games started, batters faced (978) and least run support per nine innings (4.2)
- Led the Twins in ERA, losses, games started, complete games (4), innings pitched, hits allowed, batters faced (978), pitches thrown (3,524), pickoff throws (50), stolen bases allowed (14), runners caught stealing (6), highest groundball/flyball ratio allowed (1.3), fewest pitches thrown per batter (3.60), fewest home runs allowed per nine innings (1.07), most GDPs induced per nine innings (0.6), lowest ERA at home and lowest batting average allowed vs. lefthanded batters

Mark Redman

2000 Season

A first-round pick from the University of Oklahoma in 1995, Mark Redman had an inconsistent minor league career, especially after reaching Triple-A. He earned a spot in the Twins' bullpen with a strong performance in spring training last year, before moving into the rotation in May. He pitched well enough to earn some consideration for Rookie of the Year before his season ended early due to a bruised left knee.

Pitching

Redman uses three pitches: a fastball, curve and changeup. His fastball was just 87 MPH when he was drafted, but increased physical strength and refined mechanics have added another three MPH to his heater. His changeup is very good, almost as good as Brad Radke's, and his curve is much sharper than it was two years ago. He keeps hitters off balance and is willing to throw inside. Redman is a flyball pitcher and will surrender his share of homers, though he adjusted quickly to the Metrodome. Self-confidence was a problem for him in the minors, but he displayed good poise last year. Although Redman gets in trouble when he nibbles too much, he demonstrated that he could adjust his approach when things start to go poorly.

Defense

Redman is an average fielder who won't get to a high number of groundballs back up the box. But he does have a good move to first base and can control the running game. Opponents were successful on only two of eight stolen-base attempts with Redman on the mound last year.

2001 Outlook

The Twins have Redman penciled in as their No. 3 starter for 2001, giving them a solid 1-2-3 rotation punch with Brad Radke, Eric Milton and Redman. There is always the chance Redman could backslide, but he pitched well enough last year that the Twins are confident in his abilities.

Position: SP
Bats: L **Throws:** L
Ht: 6' 5" **Wt:** 220

Opening Day Age: 27
Born: 1/5/74 in San Diego, CA
ML Seasons: 2

Overall Statistics

	W	L	Pct.	ERA	G	GS	Sv	IP	H	BB	SO	HR	Ratio
2000	12	9	.571	4.76	32	24	0	151.1	168	45	117	22	1.41
Career	13	9	.591	5.05	37	25	0	164.0	185	52	128	25	1.45

How Often He Throws Strikes

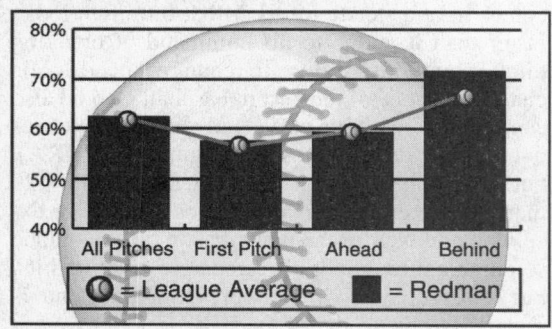

= League Average   = Redman

2000 Situational Stats

	W	L	ERA	Sv	IP		AB	H	HR	RBI	Avg
Home	7	5	4.14	0	76.0	LHB	149	42	5	20	.282
Road	5	4	5.38	0	75.1	RHB	449	126	17	63	.281
First Half	6	4	4.81	0	86.0	Sc Pos	146	42	5	56	.288
Scnd Half	6	5	4.68	0	65.1	Clutch	28	5	3	5	.179

2000 Rankings (American League)

- Led the Twins in runners caught stealing (6) and winning percentage

Jay Canizaro

Position: 2B
Bats: R **Throws:** R
Ht: 5' 9" **Wt:** 178

Opening Day Age: 27
Born: 7/4/73 in Beaumont, TX
ML Seasons: 3

Overall Statistics

	G	AB	R	H	D	T	HR	RBI	SB	BB	SO	Avg	OBP	Slg
2000	102	346	43	93	21	1	7	40	4	24	57	.269	.318	.396
Career	157	484	59	125	27	2	10	57	5	34	97	.258	.309	.384

2000 Situational Stats

	AB	H	HR	RBI	Avg		AB	H	HR	RBI	Avg
Home	158	43	2	24	.272	LHP	93	25	2	15	.269
Road	188	50	5	16	.266	RHP	253	68	5	25	.269
First Half	189	52	4	19	.275	Sc Pos	83	25	2	30	.301
Scnd Half	157	41	3	21	.261	Clutch	43	11	1	6	.256

2000 Season

After being stuck for years in the Giants' farm system, Jay Canizaro finally got an extended opportunity in the majors in 2000, getting called up to play second base after the Twins dumped Todd Walker. Canizaro showed steady if unspectacular offense and handled the keystone defensive chores decently. He played poorly in September, however, and ended the year on the bench.

Hitting, Baserunning & Defense

Canizaro has some pop in his bat and could hit 10-12 homers in a full season of play. He can handle a fastball but will look bad on sliders and good curves. Canizaro's speed is average, and he is not a stealing threat. He has quick hands and appears smoother on the double play than Walker did, but his range is fairly limited—especially on artificial turf—and his reliability is average.

2001 Outlook

The Twins are going to take a long look at prospect Luis Rivas in spring training, leaving Canizaro with a bench job at best. He doesn't have the range for shortstop, which limits his use as a utility infielder. His main chance for playing time will be if Rivas falters.

Eddie Guardado

Position: RP
Bats: R **Throws:** L
Ht: 6' 0" **Wt:** 194

Opening Day Age: 30
Born: 10/2/70 in Stockton, CA
ML Seasons: 8
Pronunciation: gwar-DAH-doe

Overall Statistics

	W	L	Pct.	ERA	G	GS	Sv	IP	H	BB	SO	HR	Ratio
2000	7	4	.636	3.94	70	0	9	61.2	55	25	52	14	1.30
Career	25	38	.397	5.06	438	25	18	498.0	512	213	408	78	1.46

2000 Situational Stats

	W	L	ERA	Sv	IP		AB	H	HR	RBI	Avg
Home	4	2	5.40	3	25.0	LHB	87	25	5	19	.287
Road	3	2	2.95	6	36.2	RHB	144	30	9	17	.208
First Half	4	2	3.38	4	34.2	Sc Pos	64	19	3	23	.297
Scnd Half	3	2	4.67	5	27.0	Clutch	119	28	7	17	.235

2000 Season

The Twins used a closer-by-committee approach making "Everyday Eddie" Guardado's role even more important than usual last season. Aside from a rough patch in April (8.31 ERA), his effectiveness again made Guardado an integral part of the staff. He converted nine of 11 save opportunities.

Pitching & Defense

Guardado uses a fastball clocked around 92 MPH. He owns a sharp curve that is especially effective against lefthanded hitters, although he struggled more than usual against them in 2000. His biggest weakness is a tendency to hang the curve; when that happens, he gives up long home runs. Guardado is used to pressure situations and did fine when he got a chance to close games. His quick delivery to the plate and compact motion make it difficult for runners to steal. He's made just two errors in eight years.

2001 Outlook

If LaTroy Hawkins takes over the closer role full-time in 2001, Guardado will return to his familiar short relief job. Either way, he's a valued member of the staff. Every summer the Twins fend off trade requests from contending teams looking to Guardado for bullpen reinforcement. He's signed through 2002 with an option for 2003.

Denny Hocking

Position:
2B/CF/RF/3B/LF/SS/1B
Bats: B **Throws:** R
Ht: 5'10" **Wt:** 183

Opening Day Age: 30
Born: 4/2/70 in
Torrance, CA
ML Seasons: 8

Overall Statistics

	G	AB	R	H	D	T	HR	RBI	SB	BB	SO	Avg	OBP	Slg
2000	134	373	52	111	24	4	4	47	7	48	77	.298	.373	.416
Career	579	1429	189	364	70	13	17	143	30	120	264	.255	.311	.358

2000 Situational Stats

	AB	H	HR	RBI	Avg		AB	H	HR	RBI	Avg
Home	174	55	1	17	.316	LHP	111	31	2	20	.279
Road	199	56	3	30	.281	RHP	262	80	2	27	.305
First Half	192	53	2	28	.276	Sc Pos	88	23	1	39	.261
Scnd Half	181	58	2	19	.320	Clutch	71	18	1	9	.254

2000 Season

Denny Hocking owes his roster spot to versatility and hard-nosed play. Last year he added hitting to the mix, setting career highs in runs, hits, RBI, on-base percentage and slugging percentage. As usual, he saw action at nearly every defensive position, moving in and out of the lineup as required. He was especially hot in the second half, hitting .320 after the break.

Hitting, Baserunning & Defense

Hocking is a line-drive hitter who became more dangerous last year by improving his patience. Better plate discipline helped him select pitches to drive into the gaps, making him a menace in the Metrodome. He has good running speed, though he doesn't steal many bases. He can bunt if needed and is adept at little ball. Hocking has the range, arm and reliability to play anywhere on the field. His best positions are second base and shortstop, but he can handle both infield corners as well as the outfield without trouble.

2001 Outlook

Hocking is locked in with a 2001 contract, and will return in his super-utility role. If he continues to be patient at the plate, he'll again be one of the best bench players in the American League.

Matt LeCroy

Position: C
Bats: R **Throws:** R
Ht: 6' 2" **Wt:** 225

Opening Day Age: 25
Born: 12/13/75 in
Belton, SC
ML Seasons: 1

Overall Statistics

	G	AB	R	H	D	T	HR	RBI	SB	BB	SO	Avg	OBP	Slg
2000	56	167	18	29	10	0	5	17	0	17	38	.174	.254	.323
Career	56	167	18	29	10	0	5	17	0	17	38	.174	.254	.323

2000 Situational Stats

	AB	H	HR	RBI	Avg		AB	H	HR	RBI	Avg
Home	84	12	2	9	.143	LHP	59	10	1	2	.169
Road	83	17	3	8	.205	RHP	108	19	4	15	.176
First Half	147	25	5	16	.170	Sc Pos	49	6	0	11	.122
Scnd Half	20	4	0	1	.200	Clutch	22	3	1	4	.136

2000 Season

The power-hungry Twins inserted rookie Matt Le-Croy in the lineup coming out of spring training, despite the fact that he had played only 32 games above Class-A. Not surprisingly, he struggled. Le-Croy showed power, but struck out too much and couldn't hit for average, earning a ticket back to the minors in mid-June.

Hitting, Baserunning & Defense

LeCroy was a masher in the minors due to his natural strength and powerful stroke. He demonstrated he could hit the ball a long way in the majors, but had trouble making consistent contact and lost confidence in himself. Scouts still expect him to be a 30-homer threat once he adjusts. LeCroy has typical catcher speed; he's stolen a meager two bases his entire pro career. He displays a strong arm, but his release is inconsistent and he still needs to improve his footwork. Twins pitchers generally were pleased with his work, but he played a few games at first base in September to improve his versatility.

2001 Outlook

Although the Twins still love LeCroy's offensive potential, they're no longer certain they want him behind the plate. He'll be in the catcher/first base/DH mix going into spring training.

Jason Maxwell

Position: 2B/3B
Bats: R **Throws:** R
Ht: 6' 1" **Wt:** 180

Opening Day Age: 29
Born: 3/26/72 in Lewisburg, TN
ML Seasons: 2

Overall Statistics

	G	AB	R	H	D	T	HR	RBI	SB	BB	SO	Avg	OBP	Slg
2000	64	111	14	27	6	0	1	11	2	9	32	.243	.298	.324
Career	71	114	16	28	6	0	2	13	2	9	34	.246	.299	.351

2000 Situational Stats

	AB	H	HR	RBI	Avg		AB	H	HR	RBI	Avg
Home	59	16	1	8	.271	LHP	72	16	0	7	.222
Road	52	11	0	3	.212	RHP	39	11	1	4	.282
First Half	73	19	1	8	.260	Sc Pos	30	8	0	10	.267
Scnd Half	38	8	0	3	.211	Clutch	16	4	0	1	.250

2000 Season

Jason Maxwell, a 74th-round draft pick in 1993, finally got a major league job last year after several successful seasons in the high minors. He opened in a partial platoon with Todd Walker, but Denny Hocking and Jay Canizaro eventually took over most of the second-base duties, leaving Maxwell as the roster's little-used 25th man.

Hitting, Baserunning & Defense

In the minors, Maxwell displayed good patience and above-average pop with the bat. Neither was evident in the majors last year. He had trouble making contact against good pitching and showed little punch, though his sporadic playing time didn't give him much time to adjust. Maxwell has decent speed but is not especially dangerous as a stealer. His best defensive position is second base. His arm is marginal for third, and he doesn't have enough range to play shortstop regularly.

2001 Outlook

Despite Maxwell's scrappy style and good work ethic, manager Tom Kelly hasn't seemed to warm to him. The Twins probably will leave Maxwell off the 40-man roster, making him a free agent in search of another chance.

Travis Miller

Position: RP
Bats: R **Throws:** L
Ht: 6' 3" **Wt:** 215

Opening Day Age: 28
Born: 11/2/72 in Dayton, OH
ML Seasons: 5

Overall Statistics

	W	L	Pct.	ERA	G	GS	Sv	IP	H	BB	SO	HR	Ratio
2000	2	3	.400	3.90	67	0	1	67.0	83	32	62	4	1.72
Career	6	14	.300	5.11	153	14	1	214.2	272	91	166	22	1.69

2000 Situational Stats

	W	L	ERA	Sv	IP		AB	H	HR	RBI	Avg
Home	0	2	5.40	1	31.2	LHB	105	26	1	10	.248
Road	2	1	2.55	0	35.1	RHB	174	57	3	27	.328
First Half	1	2	3.21	1	42.0	Sc Pos	98	29	3	35	.296
Scnd Half	1	1	5.04	0	25.0	Clutch	52	20	2	15	.385

2000 Season

With the Twins using Eddie Guardado as a co-closer in 2000, Travis Miller moved into Guardado's old role as the main lefthanded setup man. He performed decently; he earned 10 holds and proved effective against lefthanded hitters. However, he blew three of four save chances, ensuring that he will get few opportunities to earn saves in the future.

Pitching & Defense

Miller's fastball hits 89-90 MPH. He complements it with a pretty good slider and an occasional changeup. He handcuffs lefthanded hitters, limiting them to a .333 slugging percentage last year. Still, righthanders find him very hittable, which precludes his use as even a part-time closer. His control is adequate, but sometimes he nibbles too much and gets tentative. Miller is a decent fielder about the mound, and as a southpaw he does a good job holding runners.

2001 Outlook

Miller will remain in middle relief for the foreseeable future. He's not spectacular, but he gets the job done against lefthanded hitters, which is more than enough to earn a big league pension.

Chad Moeller

Position: C
Bats: R **Throws:** R
Ht: 6' 3" **Wt:** 210

Opening Day Age: 26
Born: 2/18/75 in
Upland, CA
ML Seasons: 1

Overall Statistics

	G	AB	R	H	D	T	HR	RBI	SB	BB	SO	Avg	OBP	Slg
2000	48	128	13	27	3	1	1	9	1	9	33	.211	.261	.273
Career	48	128	13	27	3	1	1	9	1	9	33	.211	.261	.273

2000 Situational Stats

	AB	H	HR	RBI	Avg		AB	H	HR	RBI	Avg
Home	54	11	1	6	.204	LHP	45	9	0	3	.200
Road	74	16	0	3	.216	RHP	83	18	1	6	.217
First Half	42	10	0	2	.238	Sc Pos	47	6	1	8	.128
Scnd Half	86	17	1	7	.198	Clutch	16	4	1	4	.250

2000 Season

Chad Moeller was the Twins' seventh-round pick in 1996 out of USC. He made gradual progress through their system and finally got a chance in the majors last year when Minnesota pulled the plug on Matt LeCroy. Moeller was the regular catcher from late June to early August before being disabled with torn knee cartilage. He returned in September but hit just .160.

Hitting, Baserunning & Defense

Moeller's track record in the minors was inconsistent, and he showed little offensive ability in the majors. He was impatient and had trouble making contact against good fastballs. He hits the ball on the ground a lot and never will be a power hitter. Moeller won't steal many bases, though he ran well for a catcher before the injury. The Twins like his defense. His arm strength is average, but he has a quick release. Tom Kelly was impressed with Moeller's ability to handle pitchers.

2001 Outlook

Assuming his knees are OK, Moeller will be in the catching mix for 2001. He doesn't hit enough to play regularly, at least for a decent club, and his likely role is as a backup.

A.J. Pierzynski

Position: C
Bats: L **Throws:** R
Ht: 6' 3" **Wt:** 220

Opening Day Age: 24
Born: 12/30/76 in
Bridgehampton, NY
ML Seasons: 3
Pronunciation:
PEER-zin-skee

Overall Statistics

	G	AB	R	H	D	T	HR	RBI	SB	BB	SO	Avg	OBP	Slg
2000	33	88	12	27	5	1	2	11	1	5	14	.307	.354	.455
Career	49	120	16	36	7	1	2	15	1	7	20	.300	.353	.425

2000 Situational Stats

	AB	H	HR	RBI	Avg		AB	H	HR	RBI	Avg
Home	48	16	1	8	.333	LHP	4	0	0	1	.000
Road	40	11	1	3	.275	RHP	84	27	2	10	.321
First Half	0	0	0	0	-	Sc Pos	25	6	1	9	.240
Scnd Half	88	27	2	11	.307	Clutch	12	5	1	3	.417

2000 Season

A.J. Pierzynski was promoted to the majors last August after Chad Moeller went down with a knee injury. Pierzynski quickly laid claim to the regular catching job, playing especially well in September, when he hit .333. He was one of the bright spots in a mostly disappointing Twins season.

Hitting, Baserunning & Defense

Despite his impressive stats, scouts say Pierzynski has a slow bat and is unlikely to be a great offensive performer. He offers decent power from the left side, but his main weakness in the minors was strike-zone judgment—even when he was going well last year, he often swung at pitches off the plate. That will hurt him in the long run. Like most catchers, Pierzynski is slow and isn't a baserunning threat. His arm is average in strength but accurate. He is very reliable behind the plate and works well with pitchers, although he needs more situational experience.

2001 Outlook

While Pierzynski has made progress with the bat, don't expect him to develop into a consistent .300 hitter unless he learns to lay off a few more pitches that are out of the strike zone. The Twins like his glove, and he'll have a chance to see significant action in 2001.

J.C. Romero

Position: SP
Bats: B **Throws:** L
Ht: 5'11" **Wt:** 195

Opening Day Age: 24
Born: 6/4/76 in Rio
Piedras, Puerto Rico
ML Seasons: 2

Overall Statistics

	W	L	Pct.	ERA	G	GS	Sv	IP	H	BB	SO	HR	Ratio
2000	2	7	.222	7.02	12	11	0	57.2	72	30	50	8	1.77
Career	2	7	.222	6.55	17	11	0	67.1	85	30	54	8	1.71

2000 Situational Stats

	W	L	ERA	Sv	IP		AB	H	HR	RBI	Avg
Home	1	3	5.40	0	30.0	LHB	57	16	1	10	.281
Road	1	4	8.78	0	27.2	RHB	174	56	7	33	.322
First Half	0	0	-	0	0.0	Sc Pos	58	21	2	32	.362
Scnd Half	2	7	7.02	0	57.2	Clutch	3	0	0	0	.000

2000 Season

J.C. Romero was in contention for a bullpen spot in spring training, but shoulder soreness forced him to begin the season on the disabled list. During his rehab in the minors, the Twins decided to convert him to a starter. He pitched well enough to earn a recall in late July. Effective in August, he pitched poorly in September, leaving his immediate future in doubt.

Pitching & Defense

Romero has a live arm, owning a 90-92 MPH fastball with good movement. His second pitch is a sharp slider that is effective against lefthanded hitters. He added a changeup when he moved to the rotation, though it still needs some work. His shaky command was the main reason he struggled last year. While Romero is a good athlete and fielded his position without making any errors, he still needs work on fundamentals.

2001 Outlook

Although Tom Kelly questioned whether Romero was emotionally ready for the majors at the end of last season, Romero will be in the mix for 2001. It would surprise no one if he returned to the bullpen, however.

Bob Wells

Position: RP
Bats: R **Throws:** R
Ht: 6' 0" **Wt:** 200

Opening Day Age: 34
Born: 11/1/66 in
Yakima, WA
ML Seasons: 7

Overall Statistics

	W	L	Pct.	ERA	G	GS	Sv	IP	H	BB	SO	HR	Ratio
2000	0	7	.000	3.65	76	0	10	86.1	80	15	76	14	1.10
Career	30	22	.577	4.92	301	21	13	509.0	538	166	338	81	1.38

2000 Situational Stats

	W	L	ERA	Sv	IP		AB	H	HR	RBI	Avg
Home	0	4	2.55	5	53.0	LHB	120	28	1	10	.233
Road	0	3	5.40	5	33.1	RHB	204	52	13	41	.255
First Half	0	6	3.80	6	45.0	Sc Pos	99	21	4	39	.212
Scnd Half	0	1	3.48	4	41.1	Clutch	168	44	11	31	.262

2000 Season

It was a season of contrasts for Bob Wells. On the one hand, there was nothing wrong with his fine 3.65 ERA or his excellent 76-15 strikeout-walk ratio. By those measures, it was the best year of his career. On the other hand, he went winless in seven decisions while blowing half of his save opportunities.

Pitching & Defense

Though Wells has average stuff, he's learned the art of control and how to help hitters get themselves out. He can throw his fastball on the fists, then use a breaking pitch or changeup on the outside corner. As a flyball pitcher, Wells is vulnerable to the home run, especially against righthanded hitters. He is not a great athlete, doesn't show much range around the infield and commits his share of errors.

2001 Outlook

The Twins attribute Wells' 2000 record and poor save conversion rate more to bad luck than genuine ineffectiveness. Still, LaTroy Hawkins has a good chance to be the full-time closer in 2001, which would relegate Wells to middle relief.

Other Minnesota Twins

Chad Allen (**Pos**: RF, **Age**: 26, **Bats**: R)

	G	AB	R	H	D	T	HR	RBI	SB	BB	SO	Avg	OBP	Slg
2000	15	50	2	15	3	0	0	7	0	3	14	.300	.345	.360
Career	152	531	71	148	24	3	10	53	14	40	103	.279	.331	.392

Allen illustrates the Twins' unconventional theories about player development, having him go from Double-A to the majors to Triple-A in successive years. Whether he recovers is uncertain. 2001 Outlook: B

Danny Ardoin (**Pos**: C, **Age**: 26, **Bats**: R)

	G	AB	R	H	D	T	HR	RBI	SB	BB	SO	Avg	OBP	Slg
2000	15	32	4	4	1	0	1	5	0	8	10	.125	.300	.250
Career	15	32	4	4	1	0	1	5	0	8	10	.125	.300	.250

The Twins acquired Ardoin from Oakland in July and kept him on their roster for most of August. He's a solid receiver with a keen batting eye and some power, but he's not a youngster. 2001 Outlook: C

Sean Bergman (**Pos**: RHP, **Age**: 30)

	W	L	Pct.	ERA	G	GS	Sv	IP	H	BB	SO	HR	Ratio
2000	4	5	.444	9.66	15	14	0	68.0	111	33	35	18	2.12
Career	39	47	.453	5.28	196	117	0	750.1	912	272	455	99	1.58

Bergman absolutely self-destructed last season, surrendering an alarming .374 batting average and tons of home runs. The Twins released him in June, but Tampa Bay signed him over the winter. 2001 Outlook: C

Casey Blake (**Pos**: 3B, **Age**: 27, **Bats**: R)

	G	AB	R	H	D	T	HR	RBI	SB	BB	SO	Avg	OBP	Slg
2000	7	16	1	3	2	0	0	1	0	3	7	.188	.333	.313
Career	21	55	7	13	4	0	1	2	0	5	14	.236	.306	.364

Blake hit well at Triple-A after being waived by Toronto, but at age 27 he's certainly not a true prospect. He could serve a useful role coming off the bench, however. 2001 Outlook: C

Brian Buchanan (**Pos**: RF, **Age**: 27, **Bats**: R)

	G	AB	R	H	D	T	HR	RBI	SB	BB	SO	Avg	OBP	Slg
2000	30	82	10	19	3	0	1	8	0	8	22	.232	.301	.305
Career	30	82	10	19	3	0	1	8	0	8	22	.232	.301	.305

The former first-round draft pick of the Yankees in 1994 is well past his gruesome ankle injury in 1995, but can't seem to make it past Triple-A. His power surged in his third year there last season. 2001 Outlook: C

Jack Cressend (**Pos**: RHP, **Age**: 25)

	W	L	Pct.	ERA	G	GS	Sv	IP	H	BB	SO	HR	Ratio
2000	0	0	-	5.27	11	0	0	13.2	20	6	6	0	1.90
Career	0	0	-	5.27	11	0	0	13.2	20	6	6	0	1.90

After the Red Sox waived Cressend in April 1999, the Twins claimed him and converted him into a reliever. Though not a flamethrower, he throws strikes and normally keeps the ball in the park. 2001 Outlook: C

Marcus Jensen (**Pos**: C, **Age**: 28, **Bats**: B)

	G	AB	R	H	D	T	HR	RBI	SB	BB	SO	Avg	OBP	Slg
2000	52	139	16	29	7	1	3	14	0	24	36	.209	.325	.338
Career	117	279	31	54	15	1	5	23	0	46	85	.194	.308	.308

The gold medal Jensen helped the United States win in Sydney will likely be the highlight of his career. He can be useful to some team as a backup catcher, but the Twins have younger options and he became a free agent. 2001 Outlook: B

Mike Lincoln (**Pos**: RHP, **Age**: 25)

	W	L	Pct.	ERA	G	GS	Sv	IP	H	BB	SO	HR	Ratio
2000	0	3	.000	10.89	8	4	0	20.2	36	13	15	10	2.37
Career	3	13	.188	7.70	26	19	0	97.0	138	39	42	21	1.82

Always a big winner in the minors, Lincoln has simply been overwhelmed in the majors, surrendering a .755 slugging percentage last year. His reconstructive elbow surgery puts his career in jeopardy. 2001 Outlook: D

Doug Mientkiewicz (**Pos**: 1B, **Age**: 26, **Bats**: L)

	G	AB	R	H	D	T	HR	RBI	SB	BB	SO	Avg	OBP	Slg
2000	3	14	0	6	0	0	0	4	0	2	3	.429	.400	.429
Career	129	366	35	86	22	3	2	38	2	47	54	.235	.326	.328

Mientkiewicz went from a surprise starter in 1999, to a demotion to Triple-A in 2000, to a gold-medal winner. He hit well at Salt Lake, and David Ortiz still hasn't commandeered the first base job. 2001 Outlook: B

Danny Mota (**Pos**: RHP, **Age**: 25)

	W	L	Pct.	ERA	G	GS	Sv	IP	H	BB	SO	HR	Ratio
2000	0	0	-	8.44	4	0	0	5.1	10	1	3	1	2.06
Career	0	0	-	8.44	4	0	0	5.1	10	1	3	1	2.06

Another player acquired in the Chuck Knoblauch trade prior to the '98 campaign, Mota pitched well in his return from elbow surgery, working at four different levels last year. 2001 Outlook: C

Johan Santana (**Pos**: LHP, **Age**: 22)

	W	L	Pct.	ERA	G	GS	Sv	IP	H	BB	SO	HR	Ratio
2000	2	3	.400	6.49	30	5	0	86.0	102	54	64	11	1.81
Career	2	3	.400	6.49	30	5	0	86.0	102	54	64	11	1.81

Florida acquired Santana in the Rule 5 draft and then traded him to the Twins, who gave him a decent amount of work last year. Since he had never pitched above Class-A before, he may now be sent down to gain more experience. 2001 Outlook: D

Minnesota Twins Minor League Prospects

Organization Overview:

If you're a Twins prospect, can you spell *opportunity*? Sixteen different rookies made it to Minnesota during the 2000 season. The next wave of kids may come from the Twins' solid crop of picks in 1997: Michael Cuddyer, Matthew LeCroy, Mike Restovich and J.C. Romero. LeCroy may begin the new season as the starting catcher, and Romero will battle for a rotation spot. Also look for 21-year-old Luis Rivas at second base on Opening Day. Because the Twins draft well, the wave of kids will continue. They have decent prospects scattered throughout the minors, and *Baseball America* rated four Minnesota farmhands—Rafael Boitel, Rob Bowen, Justin Morneau and Jeff Randazzo—as being among the 20 best in their rookie-ball leagues in 2000.

John Barnes

Position: OF   **Opening Day Age:** 24
Bats: R **Throws:** R   **Born:** 4/24/76 in San
Ht: 6' 2" **Wt:** 205   Diego, CA

Recent Statistics

	G	AB	R	H	D	T	HR	RBI	SB	BB	SO	Avg
2000 AAA Salt Lake	120	441	107	161	37	6	13	87	7	57	48	.365
2000 AL Minnesota	11	37	5	13	4	0	0	2	0	2	6	.351
2000 MLE	120	409	71	129	31	4	8	57	4	38	51	.315

Drafted by Boston in 1996, Barnes was acquired in 1998 at the trade deadline. In 2000 the Twins received a payoff on that deal. Barnes went to spring training facing duty as a fourth outfielder at Triple-A Salt Lake, but played so well that he started, led all full-season minor leaguers in batting average and reached Minnesota in September. His tools don't wreak of prospect status, but Barnes is a gap, line-drive hitter who puts the ball in play successfully. He has an accurate arm and can play center field, but he is better suited for right. His baserunning needs work, but that shouldn't keep him from getting a look in Minnesota before long.

Michael Cuddyer

Position: 3B   **Opening Day Age:** 22
Bats: R **Throws:** R   **Born:** 3/27/79 in Norfolk,
Ht: 6' 2" **Wt:** 202   VA

Recent Statistics

	G	AB	R	H	D	T	HR	RBI	SB	BB	SO	Avg
1999 A Fort Myers	130	466	87	139	24	4	16	82	14	76	91	.298
2000 AA New Britain	138	490	72	129	30	8	6	61	5	55	93	.263
2000 MLE	138	475	57	114	27	6	4	49	3	38	101	.240

A 1997 first-round pick, Cuddyer made a fairly smooth transition from shortstop to third base in 1999 while playing in the high Class-A Florida State League. His numbers at the plate didn't suffer while making the change in '99, but they did drop off at Double-A New Britain in 2000. Still, he drives the ball to all fields with a short, quick swing, and he has shown an aptitude to hit

offspeed pitches and draw walks. No one in pro ball matched his 61 errors as a shortstop in 1998, though his total fell to 28 at third in '99. He committed 34 last season, but their frequency dropped off significantly as the year wore on. The Twins not only like his advanced hitting skills and power potential, they like his enthusiasm and makeup just as much.

Bobby Kielty

Position: OF   **Opening Day Age:** 24
Bats: B **Throws:** R   **Born:** 8/5/76 in Fontana,
Ht: 6' 1" **Wt:** 215   CA

Recent Statistics

	G	AB	R	H	D	T	HR	RBI	SB	BB	SO	Avg
1999 A Quad City	69	245	52	72	13	1	13	43	12	43	56	.294
2000 AA New Britain	129	451	79	118	30	3	14	65	6	98	109	.262
2000 AAA Salt Lake	9	33	8	8	4	0	0	2	0	7	10	.242
2000 MLE	138	468	68	110	31	2	11	53	4	72	130	.235

Because of injuries, few scouts saw Kielty play in college and he went undrafted. After leading the Cape Cod League in hitting in 1998, he received a $500,000 bonus to sign. His first pro season at Class-A Quad City in 1999 was cut short by an allergic reaction to airborne oak pollen, which affected his use of contact lenses. After Kielty underwent laser surgery and abandoned contacts, he showed enough at Double-A New Britain to suggest he has the size, strength and tools to be a complete player. A switch-hitter, he has shown power from both sides of the plate, solid outfield skills and an average arm. He's still raw, but his power potential may lead to a corner outfield role in the majors.

Matt Kinney

Position: P   **Opening Day Age:** 24
Bats: R **Throws:** R   **Born:** 12/16/76 in
Ht: 6' 5" **Wt:** 220   Bangor, ME

Recent Statistics

	W	L	ERA	G	GS	Sv	IP	H	R	BB	SO	HR
2000 AA New Britain	6	1	2.71	15	15	0	86.1	74	31	35	93	7
2000 AAA Salt Lake	5	2	4.25	9	9	0	55.0	42	26	26	59	5
2000 AL Minnesota	2	2	5.10	8	8	0	42.1	41	26	25	24	7

The hardest thrower in the system, Kinney arrived with John Barnes in a 1998 trade with Boston. After elbow surgery for a bone chip in '99, Kinney rebounded with a dominating start at Double-A New Britain in 2000. He went 6-1 (2.71) before moving on to Triple-A Salt Lake and Minnesota, where he exhibited both promise (five quality starts) and inconsistency in eight late-season outings. Kinney throws four quality pitches—fastball, slider, curveball and changeup—and with a smooth, effortless delivery he throws his low-90s fastball to all reaches of the strike zone. His poorer outings were troubled by deep counts at a time when he already had set a career high for innings and tired easily. Kinney is a strong candidate for the fifth-starter spot this spring.

Mike Restovich

Position: OF
Bats: R **Throws:** R
Ht: 6' 4" **Wt:** 233

Opening Day Age: 22
Born: 1/3/79 in Rochester, MN

Recent Statistics

	G	AB	R	H	D	T	HR	RBI	SB	BB	SO	Avg
1999 A Quad City	131	493	91	154	30	6	19	107	7	74	100	.312
2000 A Fort Myers	135	475	73	125	27	9	8	64	19	61	100	.263

Like Cuddyer, Restovich is a 1997 pick with great promise who has endured a positional move—from first base to the outfield. His size may slow his launch to full speed, but in 2000 he improved significantly at taking better routes to balls and releasing good throws. Restovich started slowly at the plate, but by year's end he was demonstrating the plate discipline and two-strike approach that make him such an advanced hitter for his age. Pitched inside all summer, he also made some progress at pulling pitches with authority. Restovich has hit for both average and power, and a more consistent power game should develop as he matures.

Juan Rincon

Position: P
Bats: R **Throws:** R
Ht: 5' 11" **Wt:** 187

Opening Day Age: 22
Born: 1/23/79 in Maracaibo, VZ

Recent Statistics

	W	L	ERA	G	GS	Sv	IP	H	R	BB	SO	HR
1999 A Quad City	14	8	2.92	28	28	0	163.1	146	67	66	153	8
2000 A Fort Myers	5	3	2.12	13	13	0	76.1	67	26	23	55	3
2000 AA New Britain	3	9	4.65	15	15	0	89.0	96	55	39	79	9

Since signing as a free agent in 1996, Rincon has relied on a 91-92 MPH fastball and hard curveball to dominate hitters. Blowing hitters away in the Midwest League was more difficult in 1998, but in '99, the Venezuelan native returned, sharpened the break on his curve and led the circuit in strikeouts. Rincon's success continued in the first half of 2000, when he posted a 2.12 ERA in 13 starts in the high Class-A Florida State League. A midseason promotion to Double-A New Britain revealed that his changeup remains a work in progress, and his location must be better with all three of his pitches. Still, his ceiling is as high as any Twins pitching prospect, and he's learned a great deal about setting up hitters by facing major leaguers in winter ball in his homeland.

Luis Rivas

Position: 2B
Bats: R **Throws:** R
Ht: 5' 11" **Wt:** 175

Opening Day Age: 21
Born: 8/30/79 in La Guaira, VZ

Recent Statistics

	G	AB	R	H	D	T	HR	RBI	SB	BB	SO	Avg
2000 AA New Britain	82	328	56	82	23	6	3	40	11	36	41	.250
2000 AAA Salt Lake	41	157	33	50	14	1	3	25	7	13	21	.318
2000 AL Minnesota	16	58	8	18	4	1	0	6	2	2	4	.310
2000 MLE	123	466	66	113	32	4	3	48	11	32	66	.242

Rivas signed as a 16-year-old free agent in 1995, and a year later was named the Gulf Coast League's top prospect by *Baseball America*. Playing in the Pacific Coast League last summer, he continued his annual tradition of being one of the youngest players in his league. A solid defender with a strong arm and impressive speed and range, Rivas made the move from shortstop to second base at Triple-A Salt Lake. He's a gifted athlete with quick hands and feet, which helped him learn to make the pivot at second. While his offensive game has lagged behind his defense, Rivas made better contact and improved his plate discipline in 2000—welcome trends for a speedster who can steal a base. He may claim the Twins' second-base job with a decent spring.

Jason Ryan

Position: P
Bats: B **Throws:** R
Ht: 6' 3" **Wt:** 195

Opening Day Age: 25
Born: 1/23/76 in Long Branch, NJ

Recent Statistics

	W	L	ERA	G	GS	Sv	IP	H	R	BB	SO	HR
2000 AAA Salt Lake	9	2	4.38	17	17	0	96.2	94	52	31	66	16
2000 AL Minnesota	0	1	7.62	16	1	0	26.0	37	24	10	19	8

A 1994 draft pick by the Cubs, Ryan pitched so well in his debut season that he reached Double-A that year as an 18-year-old. He continued to progress at Class-A Daytona in 1995 before slumping for three straight seasons. He was prone to the home-run ball during his struggles, but finally rebounded in 1999 before being dealt to Minnesota for Rick Aguilera. He can throw strikes with four pitches—an 88-MPH fastball, curveball, slider and changeup—but he can't hit the middle of the plate with them. Because none of his offerings are exceptional, Ryan must have perfect control and command to succeed in the majors. When he is effective, he is changing speeds adeptly and his breaking balls are key pitches for him. His curve is an out pitch.

Others to Watch

Twins 1999 first-round pick **B.J. Garbe** (20) is a great athlete with good bat speed, a strong arm and excellent outfield range. He struggled in the Midwest League, but he was playing with guys a few years older. He only lacks power to become a five-tool prospect. . . Last summer's first-rounder, righthander **Adam Johnson** (21), left Cal State Fullerton as the school's strikeout king before fanning 92 batters in 69.1 innings at high Class-A Fort Myers. He throws 92-93 MPH, pitches inside and has a decent change. He may be the 2000 pick who is closest to the majors. . . A 1999 pick, Canadian **Justin Morneau** (19) is adjusting to a move behind the plate. That didn't stop the lefthanded hitter from batting .402 in the Gulf Coast League in 2000. . . Coming off a Player of the Year season in the Appy League in 1999, second baseman **Ruben Salazar** (23) didn't show as much power or patience at Class-A Fort Myers. Still, the pint-sized infielder hit .311 and slugged at a .427 clip.

Yankee Stadium

Offense

It's called the House That Ruth Built for a reason. The cozy right-field porch has been a haven for lefthanded home-run hitters for years, and remained so in 2000. With a 314-foot foul pole in right field, that was about the only place where a team could score a cheap run or three. Otherwise, the ballpark favors pitchers. A spacious outfield and slow infield ensure that.

Defense

With high grass that is grown all the way to the foul lines, the infield is a pitcher's friend. The extremely soft area around home plate often causes hard-hit balls to die or curve away from foul territory. Playing left field is extremely difficult because of Death Valley, where the left-field dimension of 314 extends to 399 in left-center. The most defensively-challenged outfielder should be stuck in right.

Who It Helps the Most

Lefthanded pull hitters are the biggest beneficiary. Tino Martinez hit 12 of his 14 homers here last summer. David Justice should have huge numbers this season. Justice hit 14 of his 20 Yankee homers at home and batted 12 points better at the Stadium. Both righthanded and lefthanded pitchers can excel in the Bronx. Andy Pettitte was 9-2 with a 3.93 ERA in New York and 10-7 with a 4.72 away from home. Roger Clemens had a better record at home but a higher ERA.

Who It Hurts the Most

Righthanded power hitters are at a disadvantage. Scott Brosius, a weaker righthanded hitter, batted .214 at home but .247 on the road. Righty Orlando Hernandez was 4-8 with a 5.57 ERA at home and 8-5 with a 3.73 ERA on the road.

Rookies & Newcomers

There seem to be few rookies on the horizon, but Alfonso Soriano and D'Angelo Jimenez may man utility-infield slots in 2001. New York struck gold in the winter free-agent market with the signing of Mike Mussina, who is 2-4 with a 3.51 ERA in nine starts at Yankee Stadium.

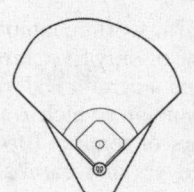

Dimensions: LF-318, LCF-399, CF-408, RCF-385, RF-314

Capacity: 57,545

Elevation: 55 feet

Surface: Grass

Foul Territory: Average

Park Factors

2000 Season

	Home Games Yankees	Opp	Total	Away Games Yankees	Opp	Total	Index
G	72	72	144	72	72	144	—
Avg	.280	.261	.270	.272	.271	.272	99
AB	2421	2526	4947	2536	2427	4963	100
R	400	361	761	373	369	742	103
H	677	660	1337	691	658	1349	99
2B	128	132	260	137	135	272	96
3B	11	9	20	12	15	27	74
HR	105	78	183	79	76	155	118
BB	303	246	549	252	283	535	103
SO	421	506	927	469	435	904	103
E	48	44	92	50	55	105	88
E-Infield	41	33	74	44	45	89	83
LHB-Avg	.271	.267	.269	.281	.271	.276	97
LHB-HR	57	36	93	36	32	68	134
RHB-Avg	.288	.256	.271	.265	.271	.268	101
RHB-HR	48	42	90	43	44	87	106

1998-2000

	Home Games Yankees	Opp	Total	Away Games Yankees	Opp	Total	Index
G	216	216	432	218	218	436	—
Avg	.283	.247	.265	.283	.268	.275	96
AB	7249	7497	14746	7778	7319	15097	99
R	1184	925	2109	1255	1043	2298	93
H	2052	1850	3902	2200	1959	4159	95
2B	387	366	753	417	372	789	98
3B	34	25	59	49	42	91	66
HR	264	205	469	275	231	506	95
BB	915	691	1606	858	771	1629	101
SO	1297	1531	2828	1396	1370	2766	105
E	146	137	283	137	165	302	95
E-Infield	121	115	236	115	137	252	95
LHB-Avg	.273	.256	.265	.287	.271	.279	95
LHB-HR	135	107	242	141	109	250	99
RHB-Avg	.291	.239	.265	.280	.265	.272	97
RHB-HR	129	98	227	134	122	256	91

2000 Rankings (American League)

- Second-highest LHB home-run factor
- Third-highest home-run factor
- Third-lowest infield-error factor

New York (AL)

Joe Torre

2000 Season

Manager Joe Torre won his fourth world championship last season, becoming one of only five skippers to accomplish the feat. He is a certain Hall of Famer based on this accomplishment, which was done in a remarkable five years of tenure. Torre gains the utmost respect of players and baseball people alike because of his solid playing career and a fair but no-nonsense approach. While the Yankees won only 87 games during the regular season, they came on strong in the postseason.

Offense

No manager in baseball sacrificed less often than Torre last season, for good reason. The Yankees traditionally have been so strong at inducing walks and extending innings due to patience that there's been no need to give up something for nothing. Torre has confidence in his regulars and is on the low end among American League managers in pinch-hitting. But he's also not afraid to shake up his lineup, which he did during the postseason. Torre used 112 different lineups last summer, which was in the middle of the pack among AL skippers.

Pitching & Defense

Few managers have as much patience as Torre, who let his starters throw at least 120 pitches a major league-leading 27 times in 2000. He stands somewhere in the middle in terms of slow hooks and quick hooks with his starters. Of course, he has the horses to stand by. He also is a big believer in allowing his closer, Mariano Rivera, to go more than one inning. Defensively, Torre substituted for the shaky Chuck Knoblauch late in games.

2001 Outlook

The bottom line is Torre relies more on people than "the book," which is a key reason why players respect him. Early last season when the team struggled, there were rumors that he would step down after the 2000 season. Reinvigorated by his team's gutsy run to a world title, Torre shed tears as his players carried him off the field. He is signed through 2001 and plans to manage a stronger team—at least from a pitching standpoint—this season.

Born: 7/18/40 in Brooklyn, NY

Playing Experience: 1960-1977, Atl, StL, NYM

Managerial Experience: 19 seasons

Manager Statistics

Year	Team, Lg	W	L	Pct	GB	Finish
2000	New York, AL	87	74	.540	—	1st East
19 Seasons		1360	1310	.509	—	—

2000 Starting Pitchers by Days Rest

	<=3	4	5	6+
Yankees Starts		91	34	22
Yankees ERA	3.25	4.91	4.86	4.63
AL Avg Starts	2	88	40	22
AL ERA	4.87	5.03	5.03	5.28

2000 Situational Stats

	Joe Torre	AL Average
Hit & Run Success %	46.6	35.1
Stolen Base Success %	67.3	68.8
Platoon Pct.	63.4	57.8
Defensive Subs	27	23
High-Pitch Outings	27	13
Quick/Slow Hooks	13/21	18/19
Sacrifice Attempts	22	55

2000 Rankings (American League)

- 1st in fewest caught stealings of third base (2), starts with over 120 pitches (27) and 2+ pitching changes in low-scoring games (30)
- 2nd in hit-and-run success percentage (46.6), starts on three days rest (4) and saves with over 1 inning pitched (16)

Roger Clemens

2000 Season

After a 4-6 start, a strained right groin muscle had Roger Clemens on the disabled list from mid-June to early July. Then a beaning of Mike Piazza on July 8 sullied his reputation. But the Rocket took off in the second half. He went 15 straight starts without a loss after his stint on the DL, winning nine straight. Clemens then shook off a rep as a poor October pitcher by tossing the first complete-game one-hitter in LCS history and beating the Mets in the World Series. Still, many will remember his bat-throwing incident with Piazza more.

Pitching

Clemens will deny it, but he pitches best when he's intimidated. It's no coincidence he came back strong after being challenged by owner George Steinbrenner while on the DL. He has a line-backer's mentality. He topped 97 MPH during his ALCS one-hitter, proving he still has remarkable stamina and power. Clemens throws a nearly unhittable forkball to complement a four-seam fastball. He also calls on a slider. He won't strike out 250-plus hitters anymore, but his postseason efforts prove he can overwhelm even the best hitters.

Defense

Clemens almost seems uncomfortable throwing to first or fielding, and he isn't particularly agile. Probably the best thing you can say is that he is always ready to field because of his proper throwing mechanics. Clemens throws to first often, but he's not too effective at slowing runners. Basestealers were 17 of 22 against him last year.

2001 Outlook

Clemens seemed to have regained some things he had lost in 1999: confidence and his ability to intimidate. In mid-August he signed a three-year, $30.9 million deal that also includes an option for 2004, ensuring that he'll be in New York for as long as he cares to pitch. He has sent mixed messages on the subject of going for 300 wins, but he will move ever closer to that vaunted mark on a team that now features four legitimate No. 1 starters. If Clemens can weather the bad publicity generated by the bat-throwing incident, he's made it clear he can last a while longer in this game.

Position: SP
Bats: R **Throws:** R
Ht: 6' 4" **Wt:** 238

Opening Day Age: 38
Born: 8/4/62 in Dayton, OH
ML Seasons: 17
Nickname: Rocket

Overall Statistics

	W	L	Pct.	ERA	G	GS	Sv	IP	H	BB	SO	HR	Ratio
2000	13	8	.619	3.70	32	32	0	204.1	184	84	188	26	1.31
Career	260	142	.647	3.07	512	511	0	3666.2	3101	1186	3504	260	1.17

How Often He Throws Strikes

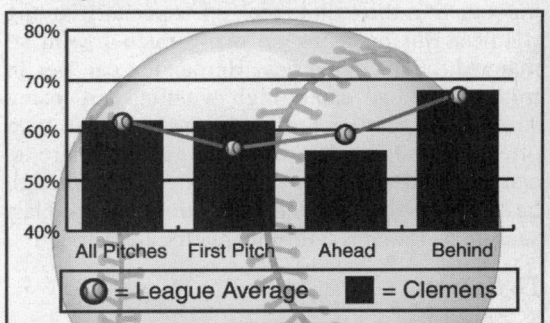

○ = League Average ■ = Clemens

2000 Situational Stats

	W	L	ERA	Sv	IP		AB	H	HR	RBI	Avg
Home	8	4	3.86	0	126.0	LHB	407	84	11	30	.206
Road	5	4	3.45	0	78.1	RHB	374	100	15	60	.267
First Half	6	6	4.33	0	95.2	Sc Pos	195	40	6	63	.205
Scnd Half	7	2	3.15	0	108.2	Clutch	55	13	2	6	.236

2000 Rankings (American League)

- 2nd in ERA
- 4th in lowest batting average allowed (.236), lowest slugging percentage allowed (.384) and most pitches thrown per batter (3.91)
- 5th in strikeouts and most strikeouts per nine innings (8.3)
- Led the Yankees in ERA, games started, walks allowed, hit batsmen (10), strikeouts, pickoff throws (144), stolen bases allowed (17), lowest batting average allowed (.236), lowest slugging percentage allowed (.384), most strikeouts per nine innings (8.3), lowest ERA at home, lowest batting average allowed vs. lefthanded batters and lowest batting average allowed with runners in scoring position

New York (AL)

Orlando Hernandez

2000 Season

For the first time in this country, Orlando "El Duque" Hernandez struggled through a mediocre season. Hernandez' stuff remained good, as he was among the league leaders in opposition batting average and runners allowed per nine innings. But his 12-13 record was a major disappointment, especially his work at Yankee Stadium. He had right elbow discomfort and mild back spasms that forced him onto the disabled list in July.

Pitching

A power pitcher with great command, El Duque can throw everything but the kitchen sink at hitters. He has a wicked slider and curve, and his fastball's movement is difficult to pick up, especially among righties. But by using so many pitches with so many different deliveries, Hernandez can get in trouble. He had career-high winning and losing streaks last season. Still, he is a workhorse who often demands to stay deep into games, where he can maintain his velocity in the mid-90s. Although he saw his postseason unbeaten streak snapped last season, he remains a formidable foe in October.

Defense

A few years ago, after a comebacker got stuck in his glove, El Duque tossed both ball and glove to first to record an out. That speaks of his cat-like reactions and understanding of the importance of playing the position. He is a good athlete who someday could conceivably win the Gold Glove. He holds runners on fairly well, as only 12 of 19 baserunners stole off him in 2000.

2001 Outlook

Hernandez found himself in the organizational doghouse last July, when he accused an unnamed coach of saying he was faking his injury. Clearly, he proved to be a warrior in the postseason and is a very proud man. But he needs to step up and keep quiet in the manner of his teammates. He needs to fare better at home, because like just about every other Yankees starter, he could win 20 games and the Cy Young Award if he remains healthy and consistent.

Position: SP
Bats: R **Throws:** R
Ht: 6' 2" **Wt:** 220

Opening Day Age: 31
Born: 10/11/69 in Villa Clara, Cuba
ML Seasons: 3
Pronunciation: her-NAN-dezz
Nickname: El Duque

Overall Statistics

	W	L	Pct.	ERA	G	GS	Sv	IP	H	BB	SO	HR	Ratio
2000	12	13	.480	4.51	29	29	0	195.2	186	51	141	34	1.21
Career	41	26	.612	4.00	83	83	0	551.0	486	190	429	69	1.23

How Often He Throws Strikes

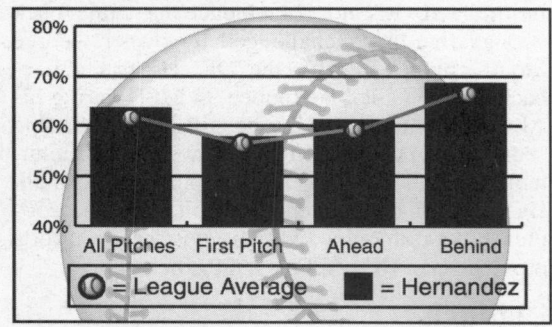

	All Pitches	First Pitch	Ahead	Behind

= League Average   = Hernandez

2000 Situational Stats

	W	L	ERA	Sv	IP			AB	H	HR	RBI	Avg
Home	4	8	5.57	0	82.1	LHB		397	111	20	55	.280
Road	8	5	3.73	0	113.1	RHB		357	75	14	41	.210
First Half	8	6	4.22	0	106.2	Sc Pos		152	39	6	55	.257
Scnd Half	4	7	4.85	0	89.0	Clutch		51	13	1	4	.255

2000 Rankings (American League)

- 1st in fewest GDPs induced per nine innings (0.3)
- 3rd in home runs allowed, lowest on-base percentage allowed (.298), lowest groundball/flyball ratio allowed (0.7) and most home runs allowed per nine innings (1.56)
- 4th in lowest batting average allowed vs. righthanded batters
- 5th in least run support per nine innings (4.4) and highest ERA at home
- Led the Yankees in complete games (3), home runs allowed, runners caught stealing (7), highest strikeout/walk ratio (2.8), lowest on-base percentage allowed (.298), fewest pitches thrown per batter (3.74), fewest walks per nine innings (2.3) and lowest ERA on the road

Derek Jeter

2000 Season

Nobody better exemplifies the current Yankees than Derek Jeter, who perhaps had his best season ever in New York. He won MVP honors for both the All-Star Game and the World Series. The Yankees' shortstop may not have the power of Nomar Garciaparra or the fielding slickness of Alex Rodriguez, as he hit his fewest homers since 1997 and committed 24 errors. But Jeter's day-to-day steadiness and all-around ability have people thinking he'll be a league MVP someday soon.

Hitting

Jeter probably is best suited for the second spot in the order, which is where he batted for most of last season. He also is a very competent leadoff hitter, though he often pounces on the first pitch and generally is not the most patient of the Yankees' hitters. When he sees a mistake, he jumps on it, as he did in Game 4 of the World Series for a leadoff homer. He destroys lefthanded pitching and handles flyball pitchers the best. He can be jammed inside with hard stuff and went through a prolonged slump in September without an extra-base hit. Jeter doesn't hit many homers in this dinger-crazy era, but he is likely to hit them on a more consistent basis as he matures.

Baserunning & Defense

Jeter is not only a fast baserunner, but also a savvy navigator who runs hard. He can leg out infield hits and stretch gappers into doubles. He is capable of stealing 30 bases per season, but the team and the state of the game don't demand it. Defensively, Jeter can improve. He is a solid shortstop, although there are better fielders at the position in both leagues. His arm is strong and he can make plays on the run, both in the hole and up the middle.

2001 Outlook

Someday Jeter will be one of the game's highest-paid players, and the organization made a huge mistake not locking him up long-term as Boston did with Nomar Garciaparra a few seasons back. It could be a $50 million mistake. As other Yankees get older or move on, Jeter will play a bigger role in the clubhouse. He also will get better, though he already is one of the top players in the game today.

Position: SS
Bats: R **Throws:** R
Ht: 6' 3" **Wt:** 195

Opening Day Age: 26
Born: 6/26/74 in Pequannock, NJ
ML Seasons: 6
Pronunciation: JEE-ter

New York (AL)

Overall Statistics

	G	AB	R	H	D	T	HR	RBI	SB	BB	SO	Avg	OBP	Slg
2000	148	593	119	201	31	4	15	73	22	68	99	.339	.416	.481
Career	786	3130	605	1008	153	35	78	414	108	341	572	.322	.394	.468

Where He Hits the Ball

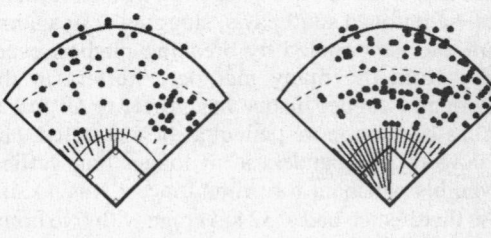

Vs. LHP   **Vs. RHP**

2000 Situational Stats

	AB	H	HR	RBI	Avg		AB	H	HR	RBI	Avg
Home	299	101	8	36	.338	LHP	147	58	4	17	.395
Road	294	100	7	37	.340	RHP	446	143	11	56	.321
First Half	301	97	9	37	.322	Sc Pos	130	41	3	54	.315
Scnd Half	292	104	6	36	.356	Clutch	66	23	1	7	.348

2000 Rankings (American League)

- 1st in batting average vs. lefthanded pitchers
- 2nd in singles, highest groundball/flyball ratio (2.1), on-base percentage vs. lefthanded pitchers (.461), errors at shortstop (24) and lowest fielding percentage at shortstop (.961)
- 3rd in stolen-base percentage (84.6) and batting average with two strikes (.312)
- 4th in hits
- 5th in batting average and hit by pitch (12)
- Led the Yankees in batting average, at-bats, runs scored, hits, singles, sacrifice bunts (3), stolen bases, hit by pitch (12), times on base (281), pitches seen (2,608), plate appearances (679), highest groundball/flyball ratio (2.1), stolen-base percentage (84.6) and steals of third (3)

David Justice

Position: LF/RF/DH
Bats: L **Throws:** L
Ht: 6' 3" **Wt:** 200

Opening Day Age: 34
Born: 4/14/66 in
Cincinnati, OH
ML Seasons: 12

2000 Season

Many people thought David Justice was the team's MVP after he was acquired from Cleveland on June 29 for Ricky Ledee and two minor leaguers. Justice slugged 20 homers for the Bombers and was a dangerous bat in the middle of the lineup. In the postseason, he may have had two of New York's biggest hits—a double in Game 2 and a monstrous homer in Game 6 of the ALCS. Justice seems to love the spotlight, and he thus far has excelled under the bright lights of New York.

Hitting

Justice stroked a career-high 41 homers despite adjusting to a new team midway through the season. After a dismal 1999 showing against lefthanders, he tattooed southpaws, slugging .716 against them. He isn't fooled by breaking pitches, especially from the many mediocre hurlers in the American League. Justice has power to all fields. He has become more patient as he's matured, and he'll work righthanders a bit longer than lefties. Given his penchant for prime time, it was no surprise that Justice had a .324 average with five home runs in 74 close-and-late at-bats last season.

Baserunning & Defense

Justice has been bothered by knee problems for a few seasons and eventually will become a full-time DH. Hence, he doesn't run the bases harder than he has to, nor does he stretch base hits the way he would 10 years ago. But he is fairly swift afield, getting to almost every ball hit to him. He's better coming in on the ball, and he has a deceptively strong and accurate arm that produced eight assists in 2000.

2001 Outlook

Signed through 2002 with a club option for 2003, Justice is one of the few position players who the organization won't have to worry about for at least the next couple of seasons. After a subpar '99 campaign, Justice rebounded and had a career year in 2000. That shouldn't be expected from him again, but he should be an everyday factor either in left field, right field or as a DH. With some of the other Yankees getting older, Justice will become more prominent, both this season and next.

Overall Statistics

	G	AB	R	H	D	T	HR	RBI	SB	BB	SO	Avg	OBP	Slg
2000	146	524	89	150	31	1	41	118	2	77	91	.286	.377	.584
Career	1381	4846	817	1373	246	20	276	917	48	779	850	.283	.381	.513

Where He Hits the Ball

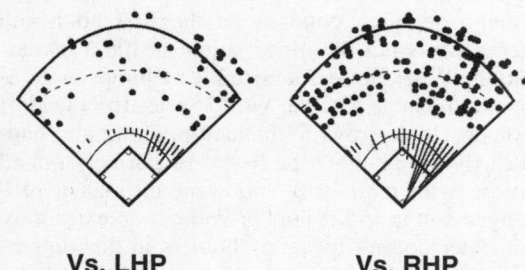

Vs. LHP   **Vs. RHP**

2000 Situational Stats

	AB	H	HR	RBI	Avg		AB	H	HR	RBI	Avg
Home	268	78	24	67	.291	LHP	134	41	15	36	.306
Road	256	72	17	51	.281	RHP	390	109	26	82	.279
First Half	275	70	22	61	.255	Sc Pos	157	45	8	72	.287
Scnd Half	249	80	19	57	.321	Clutch	74	24	5	17	.324

2000 Rankings (American League)

- 2nd in slugging percentage vs. lefthanded pitchers (.716)
- 3rd in batting average on an 0-2 count (.333)
- 4th in home runs (41) and HR frequency (12.8 ABs per HR)
- 9th in slugging percentage (.584)
- Led AL left fielders in home runs (41), RBI (118), slugging percentage (.584), HR frequency (12.8 ABs per HR), batting average on an 0-2 count (.333) and slugging percentage vs. lefthanded pitchers (.716)

Chuck Knoblauch

2000 Season

Fans new to the sport will have a hard time believing Chuck Knoblauch was once a Gold Glove second baseman. Sadly, Knoblauch's throwing woes, exacerbated by a bum elbow last season, overshadowed every other aspect of his game. He missed 24 games while on the disabled list with right elbow tendinitis and struggled at the plate throughout the season. After hitting a career-high 18 homers in 1999, his total dipped to five last year. Still, he is a productive leadoff hitter.

Hitting

Knoblauch may have one of the most unique stances in the game. He crouches down, crowds the plate and holds his bat nearly parallel to the ground. This enables a lightning-quick stroke, and he's certainly the prototypical leadoff man for today's game. When Knoblauch struggles, he often chases high fastballs and hits way too many flyballs. He mainly is a gap hitter who actually enjoys going the other way with a pitch.

Baserunning & Defense

Because of a mental block with his throwing, Knoblauch is simply one of the worst second baseman in the game. He doesn't know if the ball will end up in the stands or Tino Martinez' glove. Statistically, his range is among the worst as well. To his credit, he has worked on his throwing problem, but it comes and goes mysteriously. Manager Joe Torre would not play him in the field during the World Series, and often replaced him in the late innings of regular-season games. Knoblauch is quick and runs the bases well, although he won't steal the 40-60 bases he once did.

2001 Outlook

It's hard to say how Knoblauch fits in if his throwing problems continue. The Yankees have two middle-infield prospects in Alfonso Soriano and D'Angelo Jimenez, although neither appears ready to unseat Knoblauch entering 2001. The DH spot will become more crowded as other Yankees get older and break down. New York would trade Knoblauch if it could get value in return, but a large contract precludes that. The best scenario would be for Knoblauch to conquer his throwing woes.

Position: 2B/DH
Bats: R **Throws:** R
Ht: 5' 9" **Wt:** 175

Opening Day Age: 32
Born: 7/7/68 in Houston, TX
ML Seasons: 10
Pronunciation: NOB-lock
Nickname: Knobby

Overall Statistics

	G	AB	R	H	D	T	HR	RBI	SB	BB	SO	Avg	OBP	Slg
2000	102	400	75	113	22	2	5	26	15	46	45	.283	.366	.385
Career	1415	5545	1025	1646	293	61	83	549	350	718	625	.297	.386	.417

Where He Hits the Ball

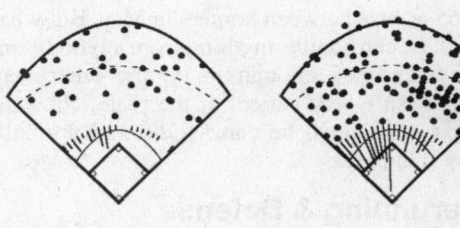

Vs. LHP   **Vs. RHP**

2000 Situational Stats

	AB	H	HR	RBI	Avg		AB	H	HR	RBI	Avg
Home	181	58	5	16	.320	LHP	100	21	2	5	.210
Road	219	55	0	10	.251	RHP	300	92	3	21	.307
First Half	264	77	4	18	.292	Sc Pos	74	19	2	23	.257
Scnd Half	136	36	1	8	.265	Clutch	43	12	0	3	.279

2000 Rankings (American League)

- 1st in lowest percentage of swings that missed (7.6)
- 2nd in errors at second base (15)
- 4th in batting average on an 0-2 count (.321)
- 6th in highest percentage of swings put into play (51.5)
- 7th in on-base percentage for a leadoff hitter (.367) and lowest stolen-base percentage (68.2)
- Led the Yankees in batting average on an 0-2 count (.321), on-base percentage for a leadoff hitter (.367), lowest percentage of swings that missed (7.6), highest percentage of swings put into play (51.5) and highest percentage of extra bases taken as a runner (55.4)

Tino Martinez

Position: 1B
Bats: L **Throws:** R
Ht: 6' 2" **Wt:** 210

Opening Day Age: 33
Born: 12/7/67 in Tampa, FL
ML Seasons: 11

2000 Season

It was a miserable regular season for Tino Martinez, who had as many double plays as home runs last year. Like his team, he redeemed himself with a masterful Division Series and ALCS, finishing strong when it counted. Martinez' numbers dropped in most categories, leading many to believe he's on his last leg. But his solid defensive play and quiet leadership have been a cornerstone of the team for five years.

Hitting

Martinez no longer can be considered a power hitter per se. Breaking balls gave him trouble last season, especially those down and away. A classic streak hitter, he went 0-for-28 in September and went 65 at-bats between homers in May. But when he's hot, he can handle anything from anybody, and he is disciplined enough to go the other way. Martinez isn't very patient at the plate, choosing the first good pitch he can handle and normally putting it in play.

Baserunning & Defense

The slowest afoot of the Yankees, Martinez won't stretch too many gappers. He hits into his share of double plays and doesn't steal at all. But he's also a savvy baserunner who knows when to go and when to stay. Statistically, Martinez is an average first baseman, but he has a good arm to go along with fair range. He has helped Chuck Knoblauch limit his errors with some acrobatic moves over the past few seasons, and he digs the ball well.

2001 Outlook

Many fans were disappointed with Martinez, whose 2001 option was exercised by the Yankees last March. He'll never be Lou Gehrig, but highly-touted prospect Nick Johnson was injured last season. So for the time being, the first-base job is Martinez' unless the Yanks import a superstar or sign a free agent. Martinez is a stand-up player, which the New York media certainly appreciate. He would like to finish his career with the Yankees, although his long-term future is cloudy and his days of 20-plus homers and 100-plus RBI might be over.

Overall Statistics

	G	AB	R	H	D	T	HR	RBI	SB	BB	SO	Avg	OBP	Slg
2000	155	569	69	147	37	4	16	91	4	52	74	.258	.328	.422
Career	1312	4774	684	1303	262	15	229	889	17	523	712	.273	.345	.478

Where He Hits the Ball

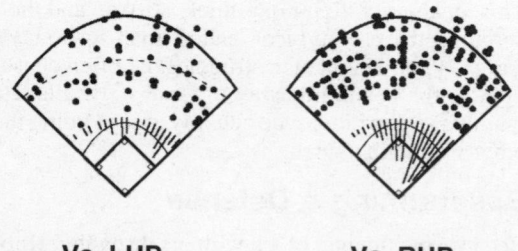

Vs. LHP   **Vs. RHP**

2000 Situational Stats

	AB	H	HR	RBI	Avg		AB	H	HR	RBI	Avg
Home	282	70	12	48	.248	LHP	171	48	3	28	.281
Road	287	77	4	43	.268	RHP	398	99	13	63	.249
First Half	306	80	8	49	.261	Sc Pos	160	47	3	72	.294
Scnd Half	263	67	8	42	.255	Clutch	68	20	3	20	.294

2000 Rankings (American League)

- 6th in errors at first base (7) and fielding percentage at first base (.994)
- Led the Yankees in doubles, lowest percentage of swings on the first pitch (18.4) and games played
- Led AL first basemen in triples

Denny Neagle

Position: SP
Bats: L **Throws:** L
Ht: 6' 3" **Wt:** 225

Opening Day Age: 32
Born: 9/13/68 in Gambrills, MD
ML Seasons: 10
Pronunciation: NAY-gull

2000 Season

The Yankees acquired Denny Neagle from the Reds on July 12 for four prospects. At the time, the deal looked great, as Neagle was 8-2 with Cincinnati. He began his Yankees career strong, with seven wins in his first 12 starts. But he faltered down the stretch, losing his final three starts of the regular season and two more in the postseason. Although he pitched fairly well in his only World Series start, manager Joe Torre yanked him after 4.2 innings, much to Neagle's chagrin.

Pitching

Neagle is a classic finesse lefthander. He'll never blow you away, although his good fastball can register 90 MPH. Neagle's top-shelf pitches are his changeup, which is one of the best in the league, and his sinking fastball. He also throws a cutter, and like most pitchers, he is most effective when he can work it inside. Once in a while you'll see an old-school, over-the-top curveball from him, but it's more for show than anything else. He has excellent control but sometimes gives hitters too good of a look on the first pitch.

Defense

Neagle is a good athlete who fields his position well because of good mechanics, and he seems comfortable fielding bunts and covering first base. He doesn't have a great pickoff move, but he is adept at holding runners on. A career National Leaguer for the most part, Neagle can bunt when asked to.

2001 Outlook

Neagle signed a five-year, $51.5 million deal with the Rockies just days after the Yankees nabbed Mike Mussina. Neagle was disappointed to be pulled from his last start in the World Series, and it was no surprise to see him leave New York for a more comfortable fit. He pitched more than 200 innings and made 33 starts last year, winning a solid 15 games. He is a proud man who now has accomplished almost everything in the game, from a 20-win season to a World Championship, and he will join Mike Hampton, Pedro Astacio, Brain Bohanon and Ron Villone in what has become a solid Colorado rotation.

Overall Statistics

	W	L	Pct.	ERA	G	GS	Sv	IP	H	BB	SO	HR	Ratio
2000	15	9	.625	4.52	34	33	0	209.0	210	81	146	31	1.39
Career	105	69	.603	3.92	320	221	3	1520.0	1478	459	1144	183	1.27

How Often He Throws Strikes

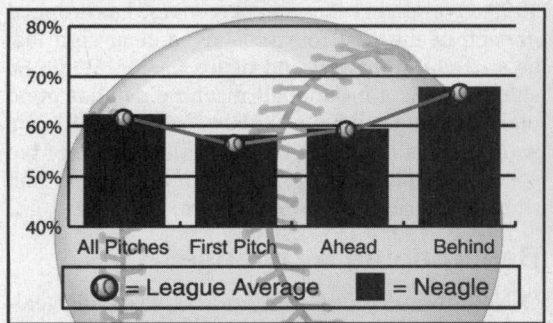

2000 Situational Stats

	W	L	ERA	Sv	IP		AB	H	HR	RBI	Avg
Home	10	5	4.35	0	132.1	LHB	200	59	9	16	.295
Road	5	4	4.81	0	76.2	RHB	606	151	22	84	.249
First Half	8	2	3.52	0	117.2	Sc Pos	191	48	8	71	.251
Scnd Half	7	7	5.81	0	91.1	Clutch	41	9	1	2	.220

2000 Rankings (American League)

- Did not rank near the top or bottom in any category

New York (AL)

Paul O'Neill

2000 Season

Paul O'Neill had an up-and-down season by almost any measuring stick. He became only the fourth Yankees outfielder ever with four straight 100-RBI seasons, yet he struggled mightily with only 10 extra-base hits from August 1 on. O'Neill was pinch-hit for in the ALCS twice, but he came back with a blistering World Series. The .474 average in the Fall Classic doesn't tell the whole story; O'Neill is simply the heart and soul of this Yankees group.

Hitting

O'Neill improved considerably against lefthanders last season after batting .190 against southpaws in 1999. Overall, his slugging percentage has dropped in each of the past four seasons, a clear sign that he's reaching the tail end of his career. When he slumps, he is a groundball machine. He has good plate coverage, which explains why he still is a solid contact hitter. He may have lost a tick of bat speed, depending on how much a hip pointer and ribcage injuries have affected him.

Baserunning & Defense

O'Neill moves pretty well for a 37-year-old, stealing 14 bases in 23 attempts last season. Even in the World Series he showed the ability to leg out doubles and triples a man 10 years his junior would have had trouble doing. He is a conscientious baserunner, even if he's lost a step. As a right fielder, O'Neill has decent range when healthy. He made only two errors afield, although only five assists. People long ago stopped running on him, but injuries seemed to hamper his throwing last season.

2001 Outlook

After the Yankees won their third straight championship, the first thing the club did was re-sign O'Neill to a one-year, $6.5 million contract. That was the prudent thing to do, although he may be more effective down in the lineup instead of in the third spot. He may see more time in left field this season, depending on how often David Justice and others can play the position, and depending on who the Yankees sign during the offseason.

Position: RF
Bats: L **Throws:** L
Ht: 6' 4"   **Wt:** 215

Opening Day Age: 38
Born: 2/25/63 in Columbus, OH
ML Seasons: 16

Overall Statistics

	G	AB	R	H	D	T	HR	RBI	SB	BB	SO	Avg	OBP	Slg
2000	142	566	79	160	26	0	18	100	14	51	90	.283	.336	.424
Career	1916	6808	964	1969	418	20	260	1199	119	844	1107	.289	.365	.471

Where He Hits the Ball

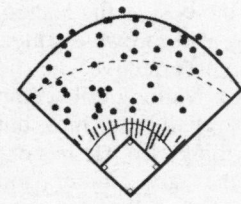   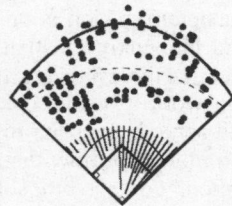

Vs. LHP   **Vs. RHP**

2000 Situational Stats

	AB	H	HR	RBI	Avg		AB	H	HR	RBI	Avg
Home	279	80	10	51	.287	LHP	156	54	3	28	.346
Road	287	80	8	49	.279	RHP	410	106	15	72	.259
First Half	326	95	10	53	.291	Sc Pos	177	52	4	77	.294
Scnd Half	240	65	8	47	.271	Clutch	66	16	1	16	.242

2000 Rankings (American League)

- 2nd in fielding percentage in right field (.993)
- 3rd in lowest stolen-base percentage (60.9)
- 4th in sacrifice flies (11)
- 6th in highest groundball/flyball ratio (1.8)
- 7th in batting average vs. lefthanded pitchers
- 8th in caught stealing (9)
- Led the Yankees in sacrifice flies (11), caught stealing (9) and GDPs (17)
- Led AL right fielders in caught stealing (9), highest groundball/flyball ratio (1.8) and batting average vs. lefthanded pitchers

Andy Pettitte

2000 Season

On many staffs, Andy Pettitte would be the un-qualified No. 1 starter. On the Yankees, he's often considered a comfortable middle-of-the-rotation guy who can rise to Cy Young level when pitching on the biggest stage. But he was the best, most consistent starter on the team last year. He ran a postseason winning streak to five games after going 19-9 in the regular season. He finished with two impressive no-decisions in the World Series.

Pitching

Pettitte can be summed up in one word: workhorse. He has started at least 26 games every season, and he eats as many innings as any pitcher in baseball. He also has averaged 105 pitches per start over the last five years. He seemed to regain some lost velocity in 2000, especially in the postseason when he hit 93 MPH. He earned his reputation in the league with a cut fastball that handcuffs righties, but he now throws it less often. Pettitte has an above-average changeup and a sinker that makes him a very effective groundball pitcher.

Defense

Pettitte has one of the best pickoff moves in baseball, although he ranked among the league leaders with three balks last summer. Somewhat surprisingly, he's allowed 64 stolen bases in the past five years. He sped up from the stretch, however, and allowed only five steals last year. For a 6-foot-5 pitcher, he fields well, but he committed an uncharacteristic four errors last season after having only eight in his career prior to 2000. He is diligent in covering first base and can field bunts successfully.

2001 Outlook

Only two pitchers have won more games than Pettitte's 88 over the past five seasons: Greg Maddux and Pedro Martinez. The best may be yet to come for the 28-year-old lefty, who signed to a three-year, $25.5 million contract with a club option before last season, so he'll be in pinstripes for years to come. Amazingly, he might be the No. 3 or 4 starter on a staff that now boasts Mike Mussina, Roger Clemens and Orlando Hernandez. Still, as long as Pettitte stays healthy, there's no telling the type of career numbers that he can accumulate.

Position: SP
Bats: L **Throws:** L
Ht: 6' 5" **Wt:** 225

Opening Day Age: 28
Born: 6/15/72 in Baton Rouge, LA
ML Seasons: 6
Pronunciation: PET-it

New York (AL)

Overall Statistics

	W	L	Pct.	ERA	G	GS	Sv	IP	H	BB	SO	HR	Ratio
2000	19	9	.679	4.35	32	32	0	204.2	219	80	125	17	1.46
Career	100	55	.645	3.99	197	190	0	1249.0	1306	456	834	102	1.41

How Often He Throws Strikes

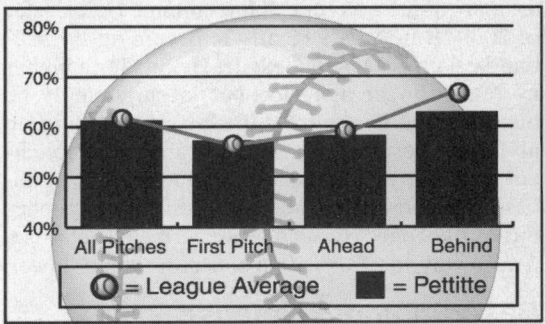

= League Average   = Pettitte

2000 Situational Stats

	W	L	ERA	Sv	IP		AB	H	HR	RBI	Avg
Home	9	2	3.93	0	94.0	LHB	176	45	1	16	.256
Road	10	7	4.72	0	110.2	RHB	632	174	16	73	.275
First Half	9	5	4.38	0	100.2	Sc Pos	202	51	2	65	.252
Scnd Half	10	4	4.33	0	104.0	Clutch	40	13	0	5	.325

2000 Rankings (American League)

- 1st in most run support per nine innings (7.6)
- 2nd in errors at pitcher (4)
- 3rd in wins, balks (3) and fewest home runs allowed per nine innings (.75)
- 6th in GDPs induced (24), highest ground-ball/flyball ratio allowed (1.7) and winning percentage
- 7th in complete games (3), pitches thrown (3,435), lowest slugging percentage allowed (.402), most GDPs induced per nine innings (1.1) and lowest fielding percentage at pitcher (.926)
- 10th in batters faced (903)
- Led the Yankees in wins, games started, complete games (3), innings pitched, hits allowed, batters faced (903), balks (3) and pitches thrown (3,435)

Jorge Posada

Position: C/1B
Bats: B **Throws:** R
Ht: 6' 2" **Wt:** 200

Opening Day Age: 29
Born: 8/17/71 in
Santurce, Puerto Rico
ML Seasons: 6
Pronunciation:
HOR-hay poh-SOD-uh

2000 Season

In his first season as a full-time catcher, Jorge Posada made nearly every Yankees fan forget Joe Giradi. He proved he had the ability to hit and the capacity to work seamlessly with one of the best pitching staffs in baseball. The first-time All-Star spent the first half of last season carrying a struggling Yankees offense, and after slumping somewhat in the second half, he handled the difficult task of catching every playoff game with aplomb.

Hitting

Posada is a rare breed at catcher: he's a switch-hitter who gets on base a lot and slugs. Casual fans might be surprised to know that he had nearly twice as many homers as superstar teammate Derek Jeter in 2000. But Posada clearly is becoming the second-best catcher in the league. He hits for a higher average from the right side, but not surprisingly, he hits for more power from the left. He can turn on all but the best fastballs, and hits groundball pitchers well. He was one of the league leaders in on-base percentage, but he chases too many pitches out of the zone. His staggering strikeout total is a reason why Joe Torre often bats him sixth or lower.

Baserunning & Defense

Posada runs fairly well for a catcher, as he is a good athlete and hasn't endured the wear and tear of many major league seasons behind the plate. He cut down on his number of passed balls from the 1999 season. A converted infielder, he finally seemed comfortable and competent behind the plate. Posada has a strong arm, but he threw out only 30 percent of baserunners in 2000.

2001 Outlook

Posada has been signed on a year-by-year basis throughout his career and should cash in at some point soon. Whether the Yankees pay him commensurate with what the top backstops in baseball are making is another story. The organization should be happy that Posada rebounded last season after a shaky 1999 effort. New York inked backup catcher Joe Oliver from the Mariners during the offseason, but that was a precautionary move. Posada has answered the question as to whether he can be a long-term solution behind the plate.

Overall Statistics

	G	AB	R	H	D	T	HR	RBI	SB	BB	SO	Avg	OBP	Slg
2000	151	505	92	145	35	1	28	86	2	107	151	.287	.417	.527
Career	443	1444	228	382	89	3	63	231	4	238	373	.265	.371	.461

Where He Hits the Ball

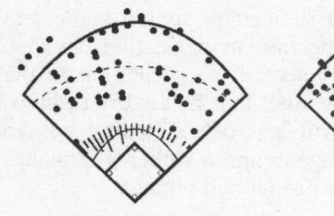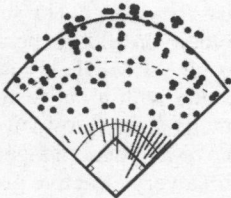

Vs. LHP   **Vs. RHP**

2000 Situational Stats

	AB	H	HR	RBI	Avg		AB	H	HR	RBI	Avg
Home	250	79	18	56	.316	LHP	159	51	6	28	.321
Road	255	66	10	30	.259	RHP	346	94	22	58	.272
First Half	256	79	14	41	.309	Sc Pos	118	31	6	49	.263
Scnd Half	249	66	14	45	.265	Clutch	67	23	7	13	.343

2000 Rankings (American League)

- 3rd in fielding percentage at catcher (.993)
- Led the Yankees in walks, strikeouts, on-base percentage, most pitches seen per plate appearance (3.92), batting average on a 3-1 count (.583), on-base percentage vs. righthanded pitchers (.421) and highest percentage of pitches taken (62.7)
- Led AL catchers in batting average, runs scored, hits, doubles, total bases (266), walks, intentional walks (10), hit by pitch (8), times on base (260), strikeouts, pitches seen (2,446), plate appearances (624), slugging percentage, on-base percentage, HR frequency (18.0 ABs per HR) and slugging percentage vs. righthanded pitchers (.523)

Mariano Rivera

2000 Season

Funny how the postseason can wipe away a so-so regular season. Although Yankees closer Mariano Rivera had another stellar season in pinstripes, his numbers weren't as spectacular as they were in 1999. His ERA rose from 1.83 to 2.85 and his saves shrunk from 45 to 36. But he was indispensable during the Yankees' run to a 26th world championship, as manager Joe Torre often used him for as much as two innings. He may be showing signs of age, but he is the best closer in baseball because of his makeup.

Pitching

Rivera throws as hard as 97 MPH despite being slight of frame and having a compact delivery. Hitters, especially young ones, have no idea how to handle his cut fastball, which can move as much as eight or nine inches and can shatter bats. It's the best in baseball. Rivera goes right after batters and never nibbles, although he has good enough command to paint the corners. He came up through the Yankees' system as a starter, and his arm easily can accommodate more than one inning an appearance. Rivera always wants the ball, even after pitching on consecutive days.

Defense

Like many other Yankees, Rivera is a good athlete who handles his position well. He can snag grounders and handle bunts as well as any pitcher. Only four runners stole on Rivera in 75.2 innings in 2000, but he isn't the most diligent of pitchers in terms of holding men on. He needs to remind himself to cover first base, but that's a concern that will be addressed.

2001 Outlook

Whether Rivera has a strong 2001 season depends in large part on what kind of setup help the Yankees get him. Free agent Jeff Nelson was signed by Seattle in December and Rivera, 31, can't keep pitching two innings at a time as he did in October. If Ramiro Mendoza bounces back and becomes that setup guy, Rivera will shine once more. He is one of the cornerstones of a pitching staff that has more cornerstones than corners, and as long as he remains in form, the Yankees will contend.

Position: RP
Bats: R **Throws:** R
Ht: 6' 2" **Wt:** 185

Opening Day Age: 31
Born: 11/29/69 in Panama City, Panama
ML Seasons: 6

Overall Statistics

	W	L	Pct.	ERA	G	GS	Sv	IP	H	BB	SO	HR	Ratio
2000	7	4	.636	2.85	66	0	36	75.2	58	25	58	4	1.10
Career	33	17	.660	2.63	332	10	165	452.1	358	144	395	26	1.11

How Often He Throws Strikes

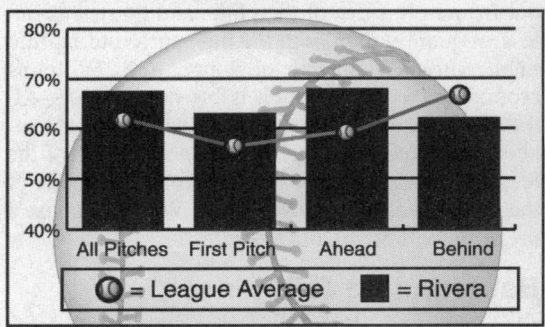

⊙ = League Average   ■ = Rivera

2000 Situational Stats

	W	L	ERA	Sv	IP		AB	H	HR	RBI	Avg
Home	4	2	3.41	14	34.1	LHB	143	30	1	19	.210
Road	3	2	2.40	22	41.1	RHB	136	28	3	16	.206
First Half	2	3	2.95	21	39.2	Sc Pos	78	23	3	34	.295
Scnd Half	5	1	2.75	15	36.0	Clutch	199	47	4	31	.236

2000 Rankings (American League)

- 2nd in first batter efficiency (.177) and fewest baserunners allowed per nine innings in relief (9.9)
- 3rd in games finished (61)
- 4th in saves and save percentage (87.8)
- 5th in save opportunities (41) and lowest batting average allowed in relief (.208)
- 6th in relief ERA (2.85)
- 8th in relief wins (7)
- Led the Yankees in saves, games finished (61), save opportunities (41), save percentage (87.8), blown saves (5) and fewest baserunners allowed per nine innings in relief (9.9)

New York (AL)

Bernie Williams

2000 Season

One of these days, a Yankee will win the MVP award. It very well could be Bernie Williams, who was the most consistent player on his team last season. Williams set career highs with 30 home runs and 121 RBI, outstanding numbers for a player who broke in as a leadoff hitter. After winning his fourth world title in the last five years, Williams was awarded his fourth straight Gold Glove. He is a perennial All-Star who remains a quiet contributor to his team.

Hitting

Williams combines the best aspects of a power hitter and a contact hitter. He is an extremely tough out from both sides of the plate, and he strikes out less frequently than both the men surrounding him in the order. Managers no longer turn Williams around to the right, which is his natural side. Although he learned how to hit lefthanded as a Yankees farmhand back in 1989, he now is one of the league's most dangerous hitters from either side of the plate. Occasionally you'll see Williams chase a breaking ball down, but it's rare.

Baserunning & Defense

Maybe the most overrated aspect of Williams' game is his defense. He doesn't usually get good breaks on the ball and doesn't have a strong arm, even for a center fielder. He didn't make an error last season, but statistically his range is in the middle of the pack. Like most center fielders, Williams is fast and his long strides usually cut down balls in the gaps. On the bases, he is hardly the best Yankee baserunner, but he can glide from first to third with no problem.

2001 Outlook

The Yankees went out on a limb after the 1998 season by signing Williams to a seven-year, $87.5 million contract. The move looks better every day. Williams likely will finish the contract—and his career—in pinstripes, becoming one of the most beloved of all the players to wear the uniform. As long as he shows the desire to improve and hunger for world titles, he'll get better offensively and stay solid in the field.

Position: CF
Bats: B **Throws:** R
Ht: 6' 2"   **Wt:** 205

Opening Day Age: 32
Born: 9/13/68 in San Juan, Puerto Rico
ML Seasons: 10

Overall Statistics

	G	AB	R	H	D	T	HR	RBI	SB	BB	SO	Avg	OBP	Slg
2000	141	537	108	165	37	6	30	121	13	71	84	.307	.391	.566
Career	1237	4806	862	1463	278	50	181	802	119	666	763	.304	.389	.496

Where He Hits the Ball

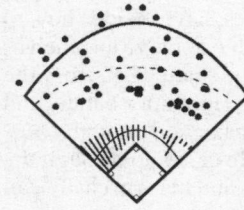
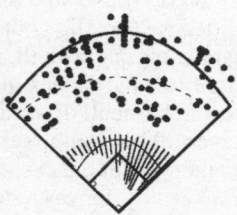

Vs. LHP   **Vs. RHP**

2000 Situational Stats

	AB	H	HR	RBI	Avg		AB	H	HR	RBI	Avg
Home	239	74	15	62	.310	LHP	166	48	9	43	.289
Road	298	91	15	59	.305	RHP	371	117	21	78	.315
First Half	331	109	19	80	.329	Sc Pos	172	55	12	94	.320
Scnd Half	206	56	11	41	.272	Clutch	68	25	8	25	.368

2000 Rankings (American League)

- 1st in batting average with the bases loaded (.692)
- 4th in cleanup slugging percentage (.590)
- 5th in intentional walks (11) and highest ground-ball/flyball ratio (1.8)
- 7th in batting average in the clutch and slugging percentage vs. righthanded pitchers (.598)
- 8th in triples
- 9th in RBI
- 10th in runs scored
- Led the Yankees in home runs, doubles, triples, total bases (304), RBI, intentional walks (11), slugging percentage, HR frequency (17.9 ABs per HR), batting average with runners in scoring position and batting average in the clutch

Scott Brosius

Position: 3B
Bats: R **Throws:** R
Ht: 6' 1" **Wt:** 202

Opening Day Age: 34
Born: 8/15/66 in Hillsboro, OR
ML Seasons: 10
Pronunciation: BRO-shus

Overall Statistics

	G	AB	R	H	D	T	HR	RBI	SB	BB	SO	Avg	OBP	Slg
2000	135	470	57	108	20	0	16	64	0	45	73	.230	.299	.374
Career	1026	3461	487	878	175	6	128	482	54	314	616	.254	.320	.419

2000 Situational Stats

	AB	H	HR	RBI	Avg		AB	H	HR	RBI	Avg
Home	243	52	7	31	.214	LHP	104	27	6	20	.260
Road	227	56	9	33	.247	RHP	366	81	10	44	.221
First Half	227	57	8	36	.251	Sc Pos	131	31	8	51	.237
Scnd Half	243	51	8	28	.210	Clutch	65	12	3	10	.185

2000 Season

Scott Brosius had a subpar year that included time on the disabled list in April. He hit .308 in the World Series, but his regular-season batting average slipped for the second straight campaign. His power numbers were nonexistent for a corner infielder. Despite his trials at the plate, he remained a Gold Glove-caliber defensive player and a steady teammate.

Hitting, Baserunning & Defense

Brosius still can hit even the best fastballs. He is susceptible to breaking stuff, particularly sliders, and he is virtually an automatic out when he falls behind in the count. Brosius is one of the slowest Yankees and seldom takes the extra base. Defensively, he has outstanding range on both sides. He has a very accurate arm and is great on slowly-hit grounders. It's extremely tough to bunt for a base hit when he is manning third.

2001 Outlook

It's hard to say how many more years the Yankees will need Brosius, whose contract ends after the 2001 season. Infield prospects D'Angelo Jimenez and Alfonso Soriano appear no more than a season away from everyday status. For now, though, Brosius will continue to give the Yankees above-average defense, even if his hitting is slipping.

Jose Canseco

Position: DH
Bats: R **Throws:** R
Ht: 6' 4" **Wt:** 240

Opening Day Age: 36
Born: 7/2/64 in Havana, Cuba
ML Seasons: 16
Pronunciation: can-SAY-co

Overall Statistics

	G	AB	R	H	D	T	HR	RBI	SB	BB	SO	Avg	OBP	Slg
2000	98	329	47	83	18	0	15	49	2	64	102	.252	.377	.444
Career	1811	6801	1140	1811	332	14	446	1358	198	861	1867	.266	.352	.516

2000 Situational Stats

	AB	H	HR	RBI	Avg		AB	H	HR	RBI	Avg
Home	124	25	6	24	.202	LHP	77	22	6	17	.286
Road	205	58	9	25	.283	RHP	252	61	9	32	.242
First Half	157	41	7	20	.261	Sc Pos	89	18	5	32	.202
Scnd Half	172	42	8	29	.244	Clutch	55	14	1	6	.255

2000 Season

The Yankees grabbed Jose Canseco on a waiver claim from Tampa Bay in August as a preventive measure. It was a wasted move, as Canseco virtually filled the same role as Glenallen Hill, who was red-hot after his arrival from Chicago. Still, Canseco was able to ride the wave and win his second world title.

Hitting, Baserunning & Defense

Canseco is a classic power hitter with as many holes as hot zones. He loves the inside pitch, and sits on top of the plate in order to get it. Conversely, he often strikes out looking at good fastballs on the outside half, and is prone to high heaters. Canseco used to be good for 30-40 stolen bases, but numerous back and foot injuries have robbed him of his desire, if not his speed. He is a major liability defensively and would rather not play the outfield.

2001 Outlook

Canseco claims he was running 4.3 40-yard dashes in September and expects to have a huge season in 2001. It won't be with New York, as the Yankees elected to buy out his $4 million option. Canseco wants to play until he hits 500 homers, and he's only 54 away. Look for him to land with an American League team so that he may DH full-time.

New York (AL)

David Cone

Position: SP
Bats: L **Throws:** R
Ht: 6' 1" **Wt:** 200

Opening Day Age: 38
Born: 1/2/63 in Kansas City, MO
ML Seasons: 15

Overall Statistics

	W	L	Pct.	ERA	G	GS	Sv	IP	H	BB	SO	HR	Ratio
2000	4	14	.222	6.91	30	29	0	155.0	192	82	120	25	1.77
Career	184	116	.613	3.40	420	390	1	2745.0	2336	1067	2540	237	1.24

2000 Situational Stats

	W	L	ERA	Sv	IP		AB	H	HR	RBI	Avg
Home	2	6	5.33	0	77.2	LHB	318	96	11	59	.302
Road	2	8	8.50	0	77.1	RHB	310	96	14	49	.310
First Half	1	7	6.40	0	90.0	Sc Pos	191	53	9	82	.277
Scnd Half	3	7	7.62	0	65.0	Clutch	11	5	1	1	.455

2000 Season

The Yankees thought giving David Cone a two-year contract last offseason was a huge gamble, and unfortunately, they were right. Cone settled for a one-year, $12 million deal, and the season ended with his pitching future in doubt. A bright spot was his last two outings in relief in the postseason, after he separated his left shoulder in September.

Pitching & Defense

Some say Cone has too many pitches, but last season he didn't have enough good ones. His out pitch, the slider, was flat and very hittable almost the entire year. Cone also throws a sinker, cut fastball and two different curves. He used to change speeds better than anyone, although his fastball has lost enough life that hitters sit on the other stuff. Cone rushes too much when fielding, and he rarely bothers with holding runners on.

2001 Outlook

There's no telling what the future holds for Cone, who could be a solid setup man if he could bear the day-to-day work. He also could fit in as a fifth starter, but his opportunities would be very limited in that role. A proud veteran, Cone wants to pitch again. The Yankees probably would re-sign him to a minor league deal, although he'll be 38 next year. Other teams should show interest as well.

Dwight Gooden

Position: SP/RP
Bats: R **Throws:** R
Ht: 6' 3" **Wt:** 210

Opening Day Age: 36
Born: 11/16/64 in Tampa, FL
ML Seasons: 16
Nickname: Doc, Dr. K

Overall Statistics

	W	L	Pct.	ERA	G	GS	Sv	IP	H	BB	SO	HR	Ratio
2000	6	5	.545	4.71	27	14	2	105.0	119	44	55	23	1.55
Career	194	112	.634	3.51	430	410	3	2800.2	2564	954	2293	210	1.26

2000 Situational Stats

	W	L	ERA	Sv	IP		AB	H	HR	RBI	Avg
Home	1	4	6.26	0	46.0	LHB	184	50	10	35	.272
Road	5	1	3.51	2	59.0	RHB	230	69	13	26	.300
First Half	3	3	6.50	0	45.2	Sc Pos	111	25	3	33	.225
Scnd Half	3	2	3.34	2	59.1	Clutch	23	5	0	1	.217

2000 Season

If David Cone is looking for a role model, Dwight Gooden may be able to offer some advice. Gooden literally came back from the dead after being discarded by three teams in a span of seven months. Doc worked with roving pitching instructor Billy Connors after getting released by Tampa Bay in May, revamped his delivery and approach, and had a decent season.

Pitching & Defense

Gooden used to work off two pitches: his devastating fastball and drop-off-the-table curve. Those pitches are long gone, and he now must work the corners far more than he ever did as a youth. Connors helped him refine the mental aspects of pitching, and the righthander does a good job at mixing up his stuff. While no great shakes defensively, Gooden can make the plays he needs to make. He isn't very adept at holding runners and doesn't have a great pickoff move.

2001 Outlook

While it was nice to see Doc respond well after getting another chance in New York, the decision to bring him back was by no means unanimous. Still, Gooden returns in the spring after signing a minor league deal. He'll battle for a bullpen job.

Jason Grimsley

Position: RP
Bats: R **Throws:** R
Ht: 6' 3" **Wt:** 205

Opening Day Age: 33
Born: 8/7/67 in
Cleveland, TX
ML Seasons: 9

Overall Statistics

	W	L	Pct.	ERA	G	GS	Sv	IP	H	BB	SO	HR	Ratio
2000	3	2	.600	5.04	63	4	1	96.1	100	42	53	10	1.47
Career	28	29	.491	5.11	219	72	3	597.1	616	345	385	52	1.61

2000 Situational Stats

	W	L	ERA	Sv	IP			AB	H	HR	RBI	Avg
Home	1	0	5.88	1	56.2	LHB		162	37	5	31	.228
Road	2	2	3.86	0	39.2	RHB		211	63	5	30	.299
First Half	3	2	4.09	0	61.2	Sc Pos		121	31	3	53	.256
Scnd Half	0	0	6.75	1	34.2	Clutch		35	7	0	3	.200

2000 Season

Jason Grimsley had a season that was quite simply uncomfortable. He pitched through forearm and elbow pain in his right arm all season, but finally was shut down on September 30 and underwent arthroscopic surgery in November. Still, he was able to fill both starting and relieving roles for the Yankees last year.

Pitching & Defense

The problem isn't with Grimsley's stuff; it's with his command. He throws a fastball in the mid-90s and possesses a great sinker, but he often can't get either pitch over for a strike. Grimsley might need to take something off both pitches in order to be more effective. He doesn't do a good job of keeping baserunners honest, as eight of nine thieves have been successful against him over the past two years. He is only a mediocre fielder.

2001 Outlook

Grimsley was released by the Yankees in November and became a free agent. He showed a lot of guts pitching through pain as long as he did, but it remains to be seen if another club will reward his bravado. In light of his decent showing in New York in 1999, the 33-year-old righthander should have no problem catching on somewhere because of his above-average stuff.

Glenallen Hill

Position: LF/DH
Bats: R **Throws:** R
Ht: 6' 3" **Wt:** 230

Opening Day Age: 36
Born: 3/22/65 in Santa
Cruz, CA
ML Seasons: 12

Overall Statistics

	G	AB	R	H	D	T	HR	RBI	SB	BB	SO	Avg	OBP	Slg
2000	104	300	45	88	9	1	27	58	0	19	76	.293	.336	.600
Career	1146	3649	524	996	187	21	185	584	96	270	825	.273	.324	.488

2000 Situational Stats

	AB	H	HR	RBI	Avg		AB	H	HR	RBI	Avg
Home	157	53	17	36	.338	LHP	140	43	13	30	.307
Road	143	35	10	22	.245	RHP	160	45	14	28	.281
First Half	138	34	9	23	.246	Sc Pos	78	19	4	28	.244
Scnd Half	162	54	18	35	.333	Clutch	60	11	4	10	.183

2000 Season

One of the last pieces to the Yankees' championship puzzle, Glenallen Hill provided punch off the bench down the stretch. Hill was acquired from the Cubs on July 21 and hit 16 homers in 132 at-bats with New York. He didn't fare well in the playoffs, although the Yankees were happy to have him as a threat. Hill did not play much outfield for New York and has become a prototypical DH.

Hitting, Baserunning & Defense

A dead-red hitter, Hill has power to all fields and can hit mistakes into next week. He is vulnerable to good sliders and doesn't do much after falling behind in the count. He is particularly adept at pinch-hitting. Hill didn't steal any bases last season, but he isn't downright slow. He probably shouldn't play much in the field unless it's the smallest corner outfield spot. Hill actually has a nice arm, although he's a liability because he doesn't read flyballs well.

2001 Outlook

New York exercised Hill's 2001 option for $1.5 million, and he will resume his role as a pinch-hitter and part-time DH. He is tied for second among active players since 1990 with 13 pinch-hit home runs, and even though he'll be 36 next season, his bat speed remains good.

New York (AL)

Ramiro Mendoza

Position: SP
Bats: R **Throws:** R
Ht: 6' 2" **Wt:** 195

Opening Day Age: 28
Born: 6/15/72 in Los Santos, Panama
ML Seasons: 5

Overall Statistics

	W	L	Pct.	ERA	G	GS	Sv	IP	H	BB	SO	HR	Ratio
2000	7	4	.636	4.25	14	9	0	65.2	66	20	30	9	1.31
Career	38	26	.594	4.27	159	55	6	506.1	575	115	282	51	1.36

2000 Situational Stats

	W	L	ERA	Sv	IP		AB	H	HR	RBI	Avg
Home	1	2	4.50	0	28.0	LHB	127	38	5	18	.299
Road	6	2	4.06	0	37.2	RHB	127	28	4	13	.220
First Half	7	3	3.72	0	65.1	Sc Pos	49	11	1	20	.224
Scnd Half	0	1	108.00	0	0.1	Clutch	13	5	2	6	.385

2000 Season

Anybody who questioned the value of Ramiro Mendoza now realizes that the Yankees nearly didn't get out of the first round of the playoffs because they couldn't call upon this versatile pitcher. Shoulder tendinitis hampered him beginning in late June and put him on the shelf from August on.

Pitching & Defense

Mendoza began the season as a reliever, moved to the rotation and ended the year as an observer. A groundball pitcher, he is the only major leaguer to record wins as both a starter and a reliever in each of the past five years. He throws the heavy ball, a.k.a. the sinker, to great effect. Mendoza also has a serviceable change and a fastball in the low 90s. He is a good athlete who holds runners fairly well.

2001 Outlook

Mendoza prefers to start but has much better numbers in relief. He had arthroscopic surgery to repair a torn labrum in his right shoulder on September 21, but he should be healthy by the start of the 2001 season. The Yankees obviously have a wealth of starters, and since setup man Jeff Nelson left via free agency, look for Mendoza's role to be that of New York's primary seventh- and eighth-inning specialist.

Jeff Nelson

Position: RP
Bats: R **Throws:** R
Ht: 6' 8" **Wt:** 235

Opening Day Age: 34
Born: 11/17/66 in Baltimore, MD
ML Seasons: 9

Overall Statistics

	W	L	Pct.	ERA	G	GS	Sv	IP	H	BB	SO	HR	Ratio
2000	8	4	.667	2.45	73	0	0	69.2	44	45	71	2	1.28
Career	35	32	.522	3.29	534	0	17	555.1	464	287	560	37	1.35

2000 Situational Stats

	W	L	ERA	Sv	IP		AB	H	HR	RBI	Avg
Home	7	1	2.54	0	39.0	LHB	82	19	1	10	.232
Road	1	3	2.35	0	30.2	RHB	159	25	1	14	.157
First Half	6	2	1.69	0	48.0	Sc Pos	75	13	1	22	.173
Scnd Half	2	2	4.15	0	21.2	Clutch	106	19	1	19	.179

2000 Season

Jeff Nelson arguably was the best setup man in baseball for most of 2000. He was sensational before the All-Star break, posting six wins and a 1.69 ERA. While shakier in the second half, he was tough in the postseason. The loss of Ramiro Mendoza affected Nelson more than anybody, and he often had to enter games earlier than usual.

Pitching & Defense

Nelson has one of the nastier sliders in the game, and the righty makes it all the more devastating by dropping down to throw it. It is a bona fide strike-out pitch, and it's no wonder righthanders can't hit it, as the pitch often breaks entirely out of the strike zone. Nelson doesn't have the zip on his fastball that he did before elbow problems, but he should throw it more than he does. He needs to work on holding runners better because stealing on him is a piece of cake. Defensively, Nelson is adequate.

2001 Outlook

Christmas came three weeks early for Nelson when he signed a three-year, $10.65 million deal with the Mariners. He broke into the majors in 1992 with Seattle and spent four years there before joining the Yankees. He professes no desire to be the closer, is enjoying his best years, and should be Kazuhiro Sasaki's primary righthanded setup man.

Luis Sojo

Position: 3B/2B
Bats: R **Throws:** R
Ht: 5'11" **Wt:** 185

Opening Day Age: 35
Born: 1/3/66 in
Barquisimeto, Venezuela
ML Seasons: 11
Pronunciation: SO-ho

Overall Statistics

	G	AB	R	H	D	T	HR	RBI	SB	BB	SO	Avg	OBP	Slg
2000	95	301	33	86	18	1	7	37	2	17	22	.286	.325	.422
Career	806	2488	295	658	101	12	36	252	27	120	186	.264	.300	.358

2000 Situational Stats

	AB	H	HR	RBI	Avg		AB	H	HR	RBI	Avg
Home	172	43	4	20	.250	LHP	84	20	2	11	.238
Road	129	43	3	17	.333	RHP	217	66	5	26	.304
First Half	169	46	5	20	.272	Sc Pos	77	23	1	26	.299
Scnd Half	132	40	2	17	.303	Clutch	49	11	0	3	.224

2000 Season

If it wasn't for Luis Sojo, the Yankees might not be celebrating a fourth championship in five years. Sojo was a catalyst throughout the postseason for New York after becoming the last addition through a trade with Pittsburgh on August 7. He became the club's regular second baseman in October when Chuck Knoblauch's fielding became a liability.

Hitting, Baserunning & Defense

Sojo is a contact hitter who has virtually zero power. He tied a career high with seven homers, although only two came with the Yankees. He is a pesky hitter who never gives away an at-bat and often goes the other way. He is not in great shape and is believed to be older than his listed age of 34. Yet he's not a bad baserunner. Sojo has good instincts defensively and was a very good double-play partner for Derek Jeter. What he lacks in range he makes up for in savvy.

2001 Outlook

Sojo makes too much money to justify keeping, especially with prospects D'Angelo Jimenez and Alfonso Soriano able to play the same positions. But the Yankees did lose Jose Vizcaino, so the cash-rich club re-signed its World Series hero to a one-year, $500,000 deal.

Mike Stanton

Position: RP
Bats: L **Throws:** L
Ht: 6' 1" **Wt:** 215

Opening Day Age: 33
Born: 6/2/67 in
Houston, TX
ML Seasons: 12

Overall Statistics

	W	L	Pct.	ERA	G	GS	Sv	IP	H	BB	SO	HR	Ratio
2000	2	3	.400	4.10	69	0	0	68.0	68	24	75	5	1.35
Career	37	32	.536	4.00	680	1	65	665.1	632	251	566	62	1.33

2000 Situational Stats

	W	L	ERA	Sv	IP		AB	H	HR	RBI	Avg
Home	2	2	3.58	0	37.2	LHB	118	40	3	19	.339
Road	0	1	4.75	0	30.1	RHB	141	28	2	13	.199
First Half	2	1	2.89	0	43.2	Sc Pos	76	15	2	26	.197
Scnd Half	0	2	6.29	0	24.1	Clutch	101	32	4	22	.317

2000 Season

Mike Stanton had a mediocre season because he wasn't very good at getting lefthanders out. After signing a three-year, $7.35 million deal after the 1999 campaign, Stanton responded with a streaky effort in 2000. He seemed to regain velocity in the playoffs and finished with a stellar World Series.

Pitching & Defense

Stanton has a full complement of pitches, and he was throwing as hard, or harder, than 93 MPH in the Fall Classic. His command of his curveball, slider and changeup is so-so, although he doesn't walk many batters. More often than not, Stanton will leave something out over the plate. He's not afraid to challenge hitters with his good fastball, even throwing it high in the strike zone effectively. He doesn't let poor stretches get to him. He doesn't allow many stolen bases and is an average fielder.

2001 Outlook

When Jeff Nelson signed with the Mariners, Stanton's role with the Yankees immediately grew in importance. Whether Stanton emerges as the primary setup man in New York this season depends on the team's spending habits, though the signing of Mike Mussina probably was a good omen. Stanton obviously sees his outstanding effort in the 2000 postseason as a springboard to a larger role.

Other New York Yankees

Clay Bellinger (**Pos**: CF/2B/3B/LF, **Age**: 32, **Bats**: R)

	G	AB	R	H	D	T	HR	RBI	SB	BB	SO	Avg	OBP	Slg
2000	98	184	33	38	8	2	6	21	5	17	48	.207	.288	.370
Career	130	229	45	47	10	2	7	23	6	18	58	.205	.276	.358

Bellinger saw action at seven positions last year, including 20 starts in center field. But he didn't solidify his status by excelling with the bat. 2001 Outlook: C

Randy Choate (**Pos**: LHP, **Age**: 25)

	W	L	Pct.	ERA	G	GS	Sv	IP	H	BB	SO	HR	Ratio
2000	0	1	.000	4.76	22	0	0	17.0	14	8	12	3	1.29
Career	0	1	.000	4.76	22	0	0	17.0	14	8	12	3	1.29

Choate, a fifth-round pick in 1997, is used exclusively in relief. Based on last year's debut with the Yankees, he could be around for a while. 2001 Outlook: C

Craig Dingman (**Pos**: RHP, **Age**: 27)

	W	L	Pct.	ERA	G	GS	Sv	IP	H	BB	SO	HR	Ratio
2000	0	0	-	6.55	10	0	0	11.0	18	3	8	1	1.91
Career	0	0	-	6.55	10	0	0	11.0	18	3	8	1	1.91

Dingman, a 36th-round pick by the Yankees in 1993, has enjoyed success in the minors the past three years and is a candidate for middle relief. 2001 Outlook: C

Darrell Einertson (**Pos**: RHP, **Age**: 28)

	W	L	Pct.	ERA	G	GS	Sv	IP	H	BB	SO	HR	Ratio
2000	0	0	-	3.55	11	0	0	12.2	16	4	3	1	1.58
Career	0	0	-	3.55	11	0	0	12.2	16	4	3	1	1.58

An 11th-round pick in 1995, Einertson reached Triple-A at age 27 last year. Despite mediocre numbers there, the Yankees promoted him several times. 2001 Outlook: C

Ben Ford (**Pos**: RHP, **Age**: 25)

	W	L	Pct.	ERA	G	GS	Sv	IP	H	BB	SO	HR	Ratio
2000	0	1	.000	9.00	4	2	0	11.0	14	7	5	1	1.91
Career	0	1	.000	9.43	12	2	0	21.0	27	10	10	3	1.76

The Yankees traded Ford to the Cubs in the Glenallen Hill deal, with less than encouraging results. The Cubs released him in November. 2001 Outlook: C

Lance Johnson (**Pos**: DH, **Age**: 37, **Bats**: L)

	G	AB	R	H	D	T	HR	RBI	SB	BB	SO	Avg	OBP	Slg
2000	18	30	6	9	1	0	0	2	2	0	7	.300	.300	.333
Career	1448	5379	767	1565	175	117	34	486	327	352	384	.291	.334	.386

Johnson didn't make it past June without getting released for the third time in eight months. 2001 Outlook: C

Felix Jose (**Pos**: RF, **Age**: 35, **Bats**: B)

	G	AB	R	H	D	T	HR	RBI	SB	BB	SO	Avg	OBP	Slg
2000	20	29	4	7	0	0	1	5	0	2	9	.241	.281	.345
Career	716	2490	316	697	134	14	51	314	102	193	496	.280	.332	.406

Since last playing in the majors in 1995, Jose toiled in Mexico and Korea. 2001 Outlook: C

Roberto Kelly (**Pos**: LF, **Age**: 36, **Bats**: R)

	G	AB	R	H	D	T	HR	RBI	SB	BB	SO	Avg	OBP	Slg
2000	10	25	4	3	1	0	1	1	0	1	6	.120	.185	.280
Career	1337	4797	687	1390	241	30	124	585	235	317	862	.290	.337	.430

Kelly suffered a sprained right elbow last April and ultimately underwent reconstructive surgery. If healthy, he may resurface, since he's a .344 hitter versus lefthanders over the last five years. 2001 Outlook: C

Luis Polonia (**Pos**: DH/LF/RF, **Age**: 36, **Bats**: L)

	G	AB	R	H	D	T	HR	RBI	SB	BB	SO	Avg	OBP	Slg
2000	117	344	48	95	14	5	7	30	12	29	32	.276	.329	.407
Career	1379	4840	728	1417	189	70	36	405	321	369	543	.293	.342	.383

The Yankees signed Polonia after the Tigers released him last August. His offensive value is limited if he doesn't hit .300 and he's not a defensive asset. 2001 Outlook: C

Shane Spencer (**Pos**: LF/DH, **Age**: 29, **Bats**: R)

	G	AB	R	H	D	T	HR	RBI	SB	BB	SO	Avg	OBP	Slg
2000	73	248	33	70	11	3	9	40	1	19	45	.282	.330	.460
Career	171	520	76	143	25	3	27	87	1	42	108	.275	.329	.490

Spencer was headed for a productive season before tearing an ACL in July and missing the rest of the campaign. He's a .335 career hitter versus lefties. 2001 Outlook: B

Jay Tessmer (**Pos**: RHP, **Age**: 29)

	W	L	Pct.	ERA	G	GS	Sv	IP	H	BB	SO	HR	Ratio
2000	0	0	-	6.75	7	0	0	6.2	9	1	5	3	1.50
Career	1	0	1.000	7.77	20	0	0	22.0	29	9	14	5	1.73

Despite a boatload of saves in the minor leagues, Tessmer is a long way from becoming the next Dan Quisenberry. The sidearmer may have to look elsewhere in order to land a bullpen role. 2001 Outlook: C

Ryan Thompson (**Pos**: LF, **Age**: 33, **Bats**: R)

	G	AB	R	H	D	T	HR	RBI	SB	BB	SO	Avg	OBP	Slg
2000	33	50	12	13	3	0	3	14	0	5	12	.260	.339	.500
Career	336	1089	143	262	57	4	44	150	8	82	301	.241	.302	.421

Thompson clubbed 26 homers between New York and Triple-A last year. He still strikes out too much. He signed on with Toronto. 2001 Outlook: C

Chris Turner (**Pos**: C, **Age**: 32, **Bats**: R)

	G	AB	R	H	D	T	HR	RBI	SB	BB	SO	Avg	OBP	Slg
2000	37	89	9	21	3	1	1	7	0	10	21	.236	.320	.303
Career	158	379	49	90	16	2	4	36	5	36	89	.237	.307	.322

The Yankees used Turner as Jorge Posada's backup catcher for most of last season. Joe Oliver will assume that role this year. 2001 Outlook: C

Jose Vizcaino (**Pos**: 2B/3B/SS, **Age**: 33, **Bats**: B)

	G	AB	R	H	D	T	HR	RBI	SB	BB	SO	Avg	OBP	Slg
2000	113	267	32	67	10	2	0	14	6	22	43	.251	.308	.303
Career	1181	3841	460	1035	133	34	21	339	65	279	541	.269	.319	.338

Vizcaino helped the Yanks with his infield versatility. In November he signed a $1.5 million deal with the Astros. 2001 Outlook: B

Allen Watson (**Pos**: LHP, **Age**: 30)

	W	L	Pct.	ERA	G	GS	Sv	IP	H	BB	SO	HR	Ratio
2000	0	0	-	10.23	17	0	0	22.0	30	18	20	6	2.18
Career	51	55	.481	5.03	206	137	1	892.0	979	351	589	139	1.49

Watson was dreadful in his limited action between three stints on the disabled list last season. His contract runs for another year with the Yankees. 2001 Outlook: C

New York Yankees Minor League Prospects

Organization Overview:

Most of the competitive teams of the last decade have seen a decline in their farm systems, by virtue of trading away kids for veterans. The Yankees have been key players in moving prospects, yet they may have as much minor league talent as any team in baseball. When the Yankees are looking to fill a hole next July and August, they have an excess of young shortstops—Alfonso Soriano, D'Angelo Jimenez, Erick Almonte and 17-year-old Deivi Mendez—a few budding position players led by Nick Johnson, and lots of promising arms in the low minors. It's true the Yanks have surrendered some terrific talent in the last year, including Drew Henson, Jackson Melian and Ed Yarnall. Still, New York added pitching prospects Ted Lilly and Christian Parker from Montreal in the Hideki Irabu trade, and they soon will compete for big league jobs with Randy Keisler, Adrian Hernandez and southpaw Alex Graman.

Erick Almonte

Position: SS
Bats: R **Throws:** R
Ht: 6' 2" **Wt:** 180
Opening Day Age: 23
Born: 2/1/78 in Santo Domingo, DR

Recent Statistics

	G	AB	R	H	D	THR	RBI	SB	BB	SO	Avg
1999 R Yankees	9	30	5	9	2	0	2	9	1	3	10	.300
1999 A Tampa	61	230	36	59	8	2	5	25	3	18	49	.257
2000 AA Norwich	131	454	56	123	18	4	15	77	12	35	129	.271
2000 MLE	131	442	48	111	16	2	12	66	8	25	138	.251

Almonte joins the stable of Yankee shortstop prospects. Signed out of the Dominican Republic in 1996, Almonte ranked among the top prospects in the Rookie-level Gulf Coast League in '97. He struggled with making contact and plate discipline for the next two seasons, but he hit for power last summer. While his strikeout-walk ratio in 2000 still reflects some trouble with strike-zone judgment, Almonte batted .297 over the final three months of the season. He runs and throws well, and he mostly needs to work on his free-swinging ways. Almonte's tendency to boot the routine grounder suggests he needs more time to refine his defensive game, but he has matured into a decent prospect.

Adrian Hernandez

Position: P
Bats: R **Throws:** R
Ht: 6' 1" **Wt:** 180
Opening Day Age: 26
Born: 3/2/75 in Cuba

Recent Statistics

	W	L	ERA	G	GS	Sv	IP	H	R	BB	SO	HR
2000 A Tampa	1	0	1.35	1	1	0	6.2	3	1	1	13	0
2000 A Norwich	5	1	4.04	6	6	0	35.2	34	17	18	44	1
2000 AAA Columbus	2	1	4.40	5	5	0	30.2	24	18	18	29	2

A Cuban defector who signed a four-year, $4 million contract with the Yankees last April, Hernandez starts the 2001 campaign as the Yankees' best pitching prospect. He's in line to battle for a rotation spot in New York this spring. As a pitcher, Hernandez is strikingly similar to Yankee teammate Orlando Hernandez, and for that Adrian has been dubbed "El Duquecito." His pitches—two fastballs (sinker and cutter), curve, slider and changeup—come from several arm angles at varying speeds. His offerings are enhanced by good movement, and his delivery adds to the deception. A little fine-tuning with the changeup should help keep lefties at bay, and that will quicken his rise to the majors. A sprained knee ligament ended his 2000 season prematurely, but he should be ready to go.

D'Angelo Jimenez

Position: 2B
Bats: B **Throws:** R
Ht: 6' 0" **Wt:** 194
Opening Day Age: 23
Born: 12/21/77 in Santo Domingo, DR

Recent Statistics

	G	AB	R	H	D	THR	RBI	SB	BB	SO	Avg
1999 AAA Columbus	126	526	97	172	32	5	15	88	26	59	75	.327
1999 AL Yankees	7	20	3	8	2	0	0	4	0	3	4	.400
2000 R Yankees	4	10	2	1	0	0	0	0	0	5	1	.100
2000 A Tampa	12	41	8	8	1	1	1	2	0	8	7	.195
2000 AAA Columbus	21	73	11	17	3	1	1	5	2	7	12	.233

One of the best minor league shortstops in the business in 1999, Jimenez was more major league-ready than Alfonso Soriano when the '99 season came to a close. His opportunity to join the Yankees as a utility player in 2000 ended, however, when he broke his neck in an auto accident in the Dominican Republic last January. The Dominican native, signed by the Yankees in 1994, is a polished defender who does most things well. He could become the Yankees' second baseman, and refining his double-play pivot is his only defensive weakness of note. Jimenez excels at making contact and displaying good strike-zone judgment. While he doesn't have Soriano's power potential, Jimenez generates surprising gap power with his wiry frame.

Nick Johnson

Position: 1B
Bats: L **Throws:** L
Ht: 6' 3" **Wt:** 224
Opening Day Age: 22
Born: 9/19/78 in Sacramento, CA

Recent Statistics

	G	AB	R	H	D	THR	RBI	SB	BB	SO	Avg
1999 AA Norwich	132	420	114	145	33	5	14	87	8	123	88	.345

A checked swing during spring training last March resulted in a season-ending hand injury for Johnson, who was expected to replace Tino Martinez at first base in 2001 before he was hurt. When Johnson last played in 1999, the lefthanded first baseman was wrapping up a Double-A Eastern League hitting title (.345) and ranked first throughout the minors in walks (123) and on-base percentage (.525). Already Johnson hits for average and

demonstrates good plate discipline, and he should develop above-average power. While a year of development time was lost, Johnson worked on hitting drills in Tampa this winter. The Yankees gave him another year to develop by picking up Martinez' option for 2001. So look for Johnson, one of the game's top young hitters, to fine-tune his bat and a defensive tendency to get caught between hops at Triple-A Columbus.

Randy Keisler

Position: P
Bats: L **Throws:** L
Ht: 6' 3" **Wt:** 190

Opening Day Age: 25
Born: 2/24/76 in Richards, TX

Recent Statistics

	W	L	ERA	G	GS	Sv	IP	H	R	BB	SO	HR
2000 AA Norwich	6	2	2.60	11	11	0	72.2	63	29	34	70	4
2000 AAA Columbus	8	3	3.02	17	17	0	113.1	104	44	42	86	9
2000 AL New York	1	0	11.81	4	1	0	10.2	16	14	8	6	1

Drafted out of Louisiana State in 1998, Keisler reached Double-A Norwich late in his first full season in pro ball. That's a remarkable climb for a pitcher who endured Tommy John surgery during his college years. Keisler's rapid emergence can be attributed to a 90-92 MPH fastball and a decent curveball. He also has refined a changeup that could prove to be above average at the major league level. His second stint at Norwich in 2000 didn't last long. After going 6-2 (2.60) in 11 starts, Keisler moved up to Triple-A Columbus and succeeded there, as well. The power-pitching southpaw beat the Red Sox in his debut on September 10, but later showed the need to tighten his command. Keisler will battle for a rotation spot in New York this spring.

Ted Lilly

Position: P
Bats: L **Throws:** L
Ht: 6' 0" **Wt:** 185

Opening Day Age: 25
Born: 1/4/76 in Lemeta, CA

Recent Statistics

	W	L	ERA	G	GS	Sv	IP	H	R	BB	SO	HR
2000 A Tampa	0	0	1.35	1	1	0	6.2	5	3	1	6	0
2000 AAA Columbus	8	11	4.19	22	22	0	137.1	157	77	48	127	14
2000 AL New York	0	0	5.63	7	0	0	8.0	8	6	5	11	1

This promising lefty was a steal in the 23rd round of the 1996 draft, but the Dodgers under interim GM Tommy Lasorda gave him away in a July 1998 trade with Montreal. The Expos then shipped Lilly and two other prospects to the Yankees for Hideki Irabu before the start of the 2000 season. That offseason also included surgery to remove bone chips from his elbow, but Lilly looks like he could help the Yankees as soon as 2001. He throws a curveball that ranks among the best in the minors, and he complements it with a low-90s four-seam fastball and a decent changeup. While Lilly struggled in his first big league stint in 1999, he was impressive in five of his seven relief appearances with the Yankees last summer.

Alfonso Soriano

Position: SS-2B
Bats: R **Throws:** R
Ht: 6' 1" **Wt:** 180

Opening Day Age: 23
Born: 1/7/78 in San Pedro De Marcois, DR

Recent Statistics

	G	AB	R	H	D	T	HR	RBI	SB	BB	SO	Avg
2000 AAA Columbus	111	459	90	133	32	6	12	66	14	25	85	.290
2000 AL New York	22	50	5	9	3	0	2	3	2	1	15	.180
2000 MLE	111	440	70	114	27	4	9	51	10	19	89	.259

A Dominican native who played three seasons in Japan before signing with the Yankees as a free agent in 1998, Soriano is all tools with poor instincts for the game. He has a very quick bat that generates some power. His success at the plate, though, is compromised by his free-swinging approach. He seldom takes a walk and strikes out frequently. Soriano has the speed and the arm to be a solid defender at short, but he remains inconsistent in the field. His stint with the Yankees in 2000 illustrated how Soriano hasn't converted his gifts into useful skills. He not only must master the strike zone, he needs to smooth out his defensive inconsistencies before he can handle a shift to second base, third or the outfield with the Yankees.

Others to Watch

Southpaw **Alex Graman** (23) reached Double-A in his first full season as a pro, using a polished four-pitch arsenal that includes a low-90s fastball, changeup, curve and splitter. He probably starts at Double-A Norwich, but could come on quickly. . . The baby of the shortstop prospects is **Deivi Mendez** (17), but he does it all defensively. His tools at short far exceed his elders'. He debuted in the Rookie-level Gulf Coast League at 16, and batted .300 in 210 at-bats. He also stroked 20 doubles and drew 26 walks for an OBP of .382. The Dominican native will move slowly. . . Shoulder troubles slowed hard-throwing righthander **Todd Noel** (22) in 2000. He eventually had arthroscopic surgery to clean up his labrum. He throws in the mid-90s, and his fastball, curve, slider and change all benefit from a smooth delivery. Noel should be ready in the spring. He has the stuff to succeed. . . The organization's five-tool prospect is **Willy Mo Pena** (19). He wasn't ready for a full-season league last summer as an 18-year-old. Still, his future is bright. . . New York's right fielder of the future is shaping up to be **Juan Rivera** (22). He batted .276-14-69 at high Class-A Tampa, although he must work on his plate discipline and defensive game. . . The Yanks signed their first Taiwanese player, righthander **Chien-Ming Wang** (21). He went 4-4 (2.48) for the Staten Island Yankees, the champions of the short-season Class-A New York-Penn League. The SI rotation also included prospects **Danny Borrell** (22), **Matt Smith** (22), **Andy Beal** (22) and **Jason Anderson** (21). Smith (5-4, 2.38) and Anderson (6-5, 4.03) are righthanded, Borrell (4-2, 3.20) and Beal (9-3, 2.34) are southpaws.

Network Associates Coliseum

Offense

Network Associates Coliseum is as symmetrical as a park can get. It does take a good poke to put it over the wall in center, but since enclosing the park a few years back to increase football attendance, the ball carries a bit better. The Net has the most foul territory of any major league park. Foul balls that would be harmless in most venues will inhibit batting averages and assist ERAs in Oakland. Over the last three years, no American League park has quelled runs per game or batting averages to a greater degree than the Coliseum.

Defense

The afternoon sun, which falls across the mound and into right field after the All-Star break, can kill the unsuspecting fielder. The grass is thick, cropped and well maintained, helping groundball pitchers. There is not a lot of room between the foul lines and the stands in left and right. The bullpen mounds are adjacent to each line, sometimes making an interesting obstacle for defenders.

Who It Helps the Most

Tied for the second-best home record in the American League last year, the Athletics clearly love playing before the home crowd. Tim Hudson was 12-1 with a 3.63 ERA at home and 8-5 with a 4.83 ERA on the road. Likewise, Kevin Appier was a schizophrenic 6-6 3.84 at home, but 9-5, 5.30 away.

Who It Hurts the Most

Most of the Oakland hitters play the patience game, and that makes for some consistent hitting no matter where they play. But in general most hitters on the team fared slightly better on the road than they did at home. The big exception was Ryan Christensen, who hit .303 away but just .170 at home.

Rookies & Newcomers

The club already is very young, but watch for Adam Piatt to excel in right field and for Mark Mulder to step up during his second pro season. Jose Ortiz, who had a Jose Vidro-type season (.351-24-108) at Triple-A last year, may earn a starting job at second base now that Randy Velarde has moved on to Texas.

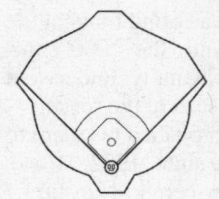

Dimensions: LF-330, LCF-362, CF-400, RCF-362, RF-330

Capacity: 43,012

Elevation: 25 feet

Surface: Grass

Foul Territory: Large

Park Factors

2000 Season

	Home Games			Away Games			
	Athletics	Opp	Total	Athletics	Opp	Total	Index
G	72	72	144	71	71	142	—
Avg	.264	.257	.260	.278	.287	.282	92
AB	2381	2521	4902	2565	2434	4999	97
R	417	324	741	437	379	816	90
H	628	648	1276	713	699	1412	89
2B	106	133	239	139	139	278	88
3B	11	12	23	11	11	22	107
HR	109	56	165	101	76	177	95
BB	336	256	592	332	294	626	96
SO	493	449	942	539	401	940	102
E	56	42	98	56	48	104	93
E-Infield	41	34	75	44	40	84	88
LHB-Avg	.271	.258	.265	.287	.294	.290	91
LHB-HR	65	24	89	67	37	104	84
RHB-Avg	.254	.257	.256	.268	.282	.276	93
RHB-HR	44	32	76	34	39	73	110

1998-2000

	Home Games			Away Games			
	Athletics	Opp	Total	Athletics	Opp	Total	Index
G	217	217	434	216	216	432	—
Avg	.260	.262	.261	.267	.289	.278	94
AB	7135	7617	14752	7676	7411	15087	97
R	1143	1021	2164	1228	1220	2448	88
H	1852	1992	3844	2050	2140	4190	91
2B	349	408	757	419	438	857	90
3B	31	36	67	22	49	71	97
HR	265	195	460	286	242	528	89
BB	927	727	1654	986	805	1791	94
SO	1405	1300	2705	1621	1215	2836	98
E	171	159	330	178	160	338	97
E-Infield	137	136	273	147	133	280	97
LHB-Avg	.272	.268	.270	.280	.284	.282	96
LHB-HR	154	87	241	174	102	276	86
RHB-Avg	.246	.256	.252	.255	.292	.274	92
RHB-HR	111	108	219	112	140	252	92

2000 Rankings (American League)
- Second-lowest batting-average factor
- Second-lowest hit factor
- Second-lowest RHB batting-average factor
- Third-lowest double factor
- Third-lowest LHB batting-average factor
- Third-lowest LHB home-run factor

Oakland

Art Howe

2000 Season

Perhaps the rest of the world was blind to what the Athletics possessed heading into the 2000 campaign. But Art Howe—who actually underwent LASIK surgery just before the start of the season—clearly saw what lay ahead and pushed his team to its first postseason appearance since 1992. Howe, who surrounds himself with a cerebral group of coaches, is known for his calm demeanor. Yet his team always knows who's in charge. Guiding a roster that featured a number of regulars who were 25 or younger, Howe and his young squad came within one bad inning of knocking the Yankees out of the playoffs.

Offense

The statistics tell it all: 750 walks, 239 home runs and 40 steals. This is a team founded on patience at the plate. It's a philosophy that breeds success. It isn't so much that Howe tries to play Earl Weaver baseball, although three-run homers aren't a bad thing. It's more than that. Oakland attempts to work the pitcher, forcing opposing hurlers to make a lot of pitches. The Athletics also try to mitigate how many strikes and outs they concede.

Pitching & Defense

Howe relied mostly on his young pitchers, and they delivered the goods. He was able to squeeze out just a few complete games from his arms, and only three teams in the majors summoned their bullpens more often than the Athletics. In the field, the team still makes the mistakes that a young team sometimes will, but it is stocked with quick learners, and it is rare for his players to make the same mistake twice. Still, Howe did not hesitate to make defensive substitutions last season.

2001 Outlook

While Oakland surprised last year, the American League was served notice that a new generation of Athletics is ready to step forward and try to claim a World Championship. Howe, with his firm and focused manner, will be the man to guide them there. However, anything less than a postseason appearance could mark the end of his Oakland tenure.

Born: 12/15/46 in Pittsburgh, PA

Playing Experience: 1974-1985, Pit, Hou, StL

Managerial Experience: 10 seasons

Manager Statistics

Year	Team, Lg	W	L	Pct	GB	Finish
2000	Oakland, AL	91	70	.565	—	1st West
10 Seasons		787	832	.486	—	—

2000 Starting Pitchers by Days Rest

	<=3	4	5	6+
Athletics Starts	0	78	55	19
Athletics ERA	—	4.19	4.82	5.89
AL Avg Starts	2	88	40	22
AL ERA	4.87	5.03	5.03	5.28

2000 Situational Stats

	Art Howe	AL Average
Hit & Run Success %	15.6	35.1
Stolen Base Success %	72.7	68.8
Platoon Pct.	58.5	57.8
Defensive Subs	39	23
High-Pitch Outings	9	13
Quick/Slow Hooks	14/17	18/19
Sacrifice Attempts	40	55

2000 Rankings (American League)

- 1st in steals of home plate (2), fewest caught stealings of second base (12), fewest caught stealings of third base (2), intentional walks (45) and starts with over 140 pitches (1)
- 2nd in defensive substitutions (39) and pinch-hitters used (162)
- 3rd in pitchouts (38), pitchouts with a runner moving (11) and 2+ pitching changes in low-scoring games (24)

Kevin Appier

Position: SP
Bats: R **Throws:** R
Ht: 6' 2" **Wt:** 200

Opening Day Age: 33
Born: 12/6/67 in Lancaster, CA
ML Seasons: 12
Pronunciation: APE-ee-er

2000 Season

If Kevin Appier had pitched only during day games at Network Associates Coliseum, against only righthanded hitters, he may have captured a Cy Young Award. Of course, sometimes things don't work out as desired. Oakland expected the veteran hurler to take the No. 1 job and lead the starting corps in 2000. Though Appier pitched well, especially down the stretch, his season was viewed largely as a disappointment. While he did win 15 games, he also led the American League in walks allowed.

Pitching

Not one to back down, Appier continued to pitch aggressively last year. However, his command has been slipping. His fastball now settles in the high 80s, though Appier augments it with a good splitter, slider and two- and four-seam fastballs. He again proved durable, pitching nearly 200 innings last season. He also lasted at least five innings in 28 of his 31 starts. But Appier's overall effectiveness just wasn't there, as his home runs allowed, hit batsmen and walks totals would indicate.

Defense

A solid athlete, Appier fields his position well, though he is quite slow off the mound. That means he doesn't always get to balls topped in front of him and has trouble covering first. He improved a lot at holding baserunners last season, allowing just nine successful swipes out of the 16 attempted against him.

2001 Outlook

The A's weren't inclined to shell out the $6 million that Appier commanded in 2000. The Mets were, however, and Appier signed a four-year, $42 million deal with them in December. Appier has totaled at least 15 wins and nearly 200 innings in each of the last two seasons. He'll be paid a lot more to approach those numbers in 2001, as well as help New York compensate for the loss of Mike Hampton.

Overall Statistics

	W	L	Pct.	ERA	G	GS	Sv	IP	H	BB	SO	HR	Ratio
2000	15	11	.577	4.52	31	31	0	195.1	200	102	129	23	1.55
Career	136	105	.564	3.63	324	312	0	2084.2	1926	759	1633	166	1.29

How Often He Throws Strikes

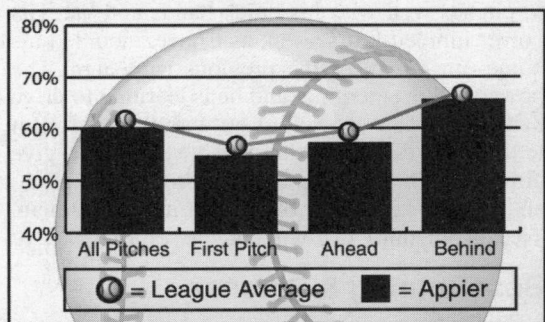

= League Average   = Appier

2000 Situational Stats

	W	L	ERA	Sv	IP		AB	H	HR	RBI	Avg
Home	6	6	3.84	0	105.1	LHB	405	120	13	57	.296
Road	9	5	5.30	0	90.0	RHB	357	80	10	36	.224
First Half	8	5	4.37	0	101.0	Sc Pos	180	42	3	63	.233
Scnd Half	7	6	4.67	0	94.1	Clutch	30	12	1	3	.400

2000 Rankings (American League)

- 1st in walks allowed and highest walks per nine innings (4.7)
- 3rd in lowest strikeout/walk ratio (1.3)
- 4th in most run support per nine innings (7.1)
- 5th in pickoff throws (154), highest on-base percentage allowed (.354) and highest ERA on the road
- Led the Athletics in losses, batters faced (884), walks allowed, hit batsmen (9), pitches thrown (3,314), pickoff throws (154), runners caught stealing (7), lowest stolen-base percentage allowed (56.3), fewest home runs allowed per nine innings (1.06) and lowest batting average allowed with runners in scoring position

Oakland

Eric Chavez

2000 Season

After a solid spring, Eric Chavez was hot out of the blocks to begin the 2000 season. His bat stalled in May, and it appeared he might have to return to a platoon role at third base with Olmedo Saenz. But injuries to Saenz forced the hand of manager Art Howe, and Chavez worked through the rugged month (.188 batting average) to produce a big June. From there he was steady, registering career highs across the board.

Hitting

Chavez possesses one of the prettiest swings around. His pure hitting talent helped make him the 10th overall selection in the 1996 draft. He reacts to pitches well with his quick hands and bat. His power jumped last season, as Chavez doubled his home-run output of the previous campaign. The power still is emerging, and he is learning to drive balls to the gaps as well as go with the pitch. But lefthanders, especially those who work inside, give him grief. Though he can hit, he still allows pitchers to work him more often than he works them. That's something that will change soon.

Baserunning & Defense

Chavez has good speed, especially for a corner infielder. Still, he isn't much of a base thief. But since his team doesn't steal much, it doesn't really matter. He does run the bases well and is developing better reactions at third base, in the style of Carney Lansford. Chavez has a strong arm and can play shortstop in a pinch.

2001 Outlook

Chavez' periodic struggles over his first couple of campaigns are understandable. After all, he just turned 23 this past offseason. He is on the verge of becoming one of the dominant third basemen in the game. Watch for an increase in batting average and on-base percentage, although the power numbers will stay roughly the same as he hones his craft. A batting title looms in the future.

Position: 3B
Bats: L **Throws:** R
Ht: 6' 0" **Wt:** 204

Opening Day Age: 23
Born: 12/7/77 in Los Angeles, CA
ML Seasons: 3

Overall Statistics

	G	AB	R	H	D	T	HR	RBI	SB	BB	SO	Avg	OBP	Slg
2000	153	501	89	139	23	4	26	86	2	62	94	.277	.355	.495
Career	284	902	142	241	48	7	39	142	4	111	155	.267	.346	.466

Where He Hits the Ball

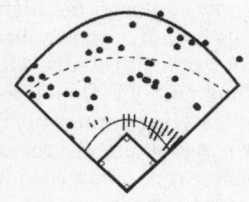
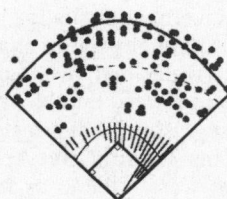

Vs. LHP   Vs. RHP

2000 Situational Stats

	AB	H	HR	RBI	Avg		AB	H	HR	RBI	Avg
Home	236	65	15	41	.275	LHP	122	24	3	16	.197
Road	265	74	11	45	.279	RHP	379	115	23	70	.303
First Half	261	71	13	42	.272	Sc Pos	121	32	3	56	.264
Scnd Half	240	68	13	44	.283	Clutch	65	10	0	4	.154

2000 Rankings (American League)

- 1st in lowest batting average vs. lefthanded pitchers
- 2nd in lowest batting average in the clutch and lowest on-base percentage vs. lefthanded pitchers (.244)
- 3rd in lowest slugging percentage vs. lefthanded pitchers (.320)
- 4th in lowest fielding percentage at third base (.951)
- 5th in errors at third base (18)
- Led the Athletics in intentional walks (8) and batting average on an 0-2 count (.250)
- Led AL third basemen in triples, intentional walks (8) and batting average on an 0-2 count (.250)

Jason Giambi

2000 Season

What more can you say? Jason Giambi's 1999 campaign, when he hit .315 with 33 homers and 123 RBI, was certainly solid. Still, last year he brought the notion of "Can you top this?" to a whole new level. Giambi not only emerged as the Athletics' clear leader on the field, but he also led the team in virtually every offensive category. He helped carry Oakland to the American League West pennant, setting a single-season Oakland record with 137 RBI. The total represented the most for any Athletic since Jimmie Foxx plated 163 for the Philadelphia A's in 1933. The net result was Giambi's first AL MVP Award.

Hitting

While it certainly will be hard to improve upon his 2000 totals, Giambi is a player who takes his performance seriously. He uses the entire field, and his quick wrists and knowledge of opposing pitchers allow him to take advantage of any hurler. He hit a spectacular .636 with the bases loaded last year, but it was his performance against lefties that perhaps was most indicative of his maturation at the plate. In 1998, he hit just .257 off southpaws, but last year he tagged lefties at a .324 clip.

Baserunning & Defense

Giambi works hard at all aspects of his game and has evolved into a solid first baseman. By his own admission, Giambi doesn't possess a lot of speed. He does get the most out of his abilities, stealing two bases last year without getting caught. He scored more than 100 runs for the second straight season, though it certainly helps when you reach base more than 300 times, as Giambi did last year.

2001 Outlook

Giambi is going into the final year of his contract, and he could fare very well in the free-agent market. But he loves playing in the Bay Area and Billy Beane has made extending his first sacker's tenure at The Net a primary goal during the offseason. Giambi should continue to produce solid totals and be a team leader on and off the field for a number of years.

Position: 1B/DH
Bats: L **Throws:** R
Ht: 6' 3" **Wt:** 235

Opening Day Age: 30
Born: 1/8/71 in West Covina, CA
ML Seasons: 6
Pronunciation: gee-AHM-bee

Overall Statistics

	G	AB	R	H	D	T	HR	RBI	SB	BB	SO	Avg	OBP	Slg
2000	152	510	108	170	29	1	43	137	2	137	96	.333	.476	.647
Career	799	2878	492	870	181	5	149	555	7	457	519	.302	.399	.524

Where He Hits the Ball

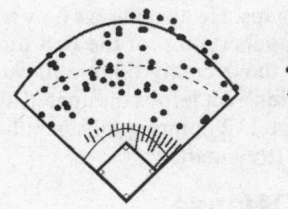 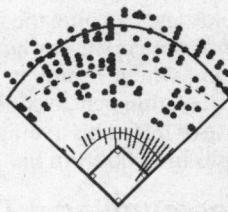

Vs. LHP   **Vs. RHP**

2000 Situational Stats

	AB	H	HR	RBI	Avg		AB	H	HR	RBI	Avg
Home	252	88	23	75	.349	LHP	176	57	7	36	.324
Road	258	82	20	62	.318	RHP	334	113	36	101	.338
First Half	290	97	22	78	.334	Sc Pos	118	42	13	88	.356
Scnd Half	220	73	21	59	.332	Clutch	58	20	4	14	.345

2000 Rankings (American League)

- 1st in walks, on-base percentage and on-base percentage vs. righthanded pitchers (.499)
- 2nd in home runs, times on base (316), HR frequency (11.9 ABs per HR), batting average on a 3-1 count (.667) and slugging percentage vs. righthanded pitchers (.719)
- 3rd in slugging percentage, batting average with the bases loaded (.636) and highest percentage of pitches taken (64.5)
- Led the Athletics in batting average, home runs, runs scored, hits, total bases (330), RBI, sacrifice flies (8), walks, hit by pitch (9), times on base (316), pitches seen (2,748), slugging percentage, on-base percentage and HR frequency (11.9 ABs per HR)

Oakland

Ben Grieve

2000 Season

Although Ben Grieve turned in a solid year in 2000, there's some concern mixed in among the numbers. While he broke the century mark in ribbies for the first time and enjoyed a more consistent season at the plate than he did in 1999, Grieve still hasn't shown the command he displayed as a rookie. He also led the American League in grounding into double plays. Still, he hit well in pressure situations while improving his ability to battle lefthanders.

Hitting

Grieve has such a sweet swing that he sometimes makes it look too easy, so it is hard to understand why he struggles. He's able to generate power to all fields and can plug the gaps. He also knows how to work the count, but he gets on top of the ball too often, which results in those costly double plays. Speculation that he couldn't hit lefties dissipated as Grieve raised his average 112 points against southpaws in 2000 from his 1999 mark.

Baserunning & Defense

Grieve is just 24, but based upon his defense and baserunning ability, he was born to be a designated hitter. To be fair, he knows his limitations and doesn't make mistakes. But slow feet on the basepaths and in the field are his enemy. Grieve's glove is adequate, but those feet seem to keep him from getting any sort of good jump on the ball. He did throw out six baserunners for the second straight season.

2001 Outlook

Grieve signed a four-year, $13 million deal just as the 2000 season was about to begin, so he could be patrolling left field in Oakland for a while. With experience, he should be able to improve his numbers, and he is more than capable of a .300-30-100 season. The Oakland farm system is deep in outfield prospects and Grieve is another lefthanded hitter on a club with many. At some point his solid trade value may be considered if the Athletics want to fill a need or two.

Position: LF/DH
Bats: L **Throws:** R
Ht: 6' 4" **Wt:** 230

Opening Day Age: 24
Born: 5/4/76 in Arlington, TX
ML Seasons: 4
Pronunciation: GREEVE

Overall Statistics

	G	AB	R	H	D	T	HR	RBI	SB	BB	SO	Avg	OBP	Slg
2000	158	594	92	166	40	1	27	104	3	73	130	.279	.359	.487
Career	485	1756	278	492	108	3	76	303	9	234	386	.280	.370	.475

Where He Hits the Ball

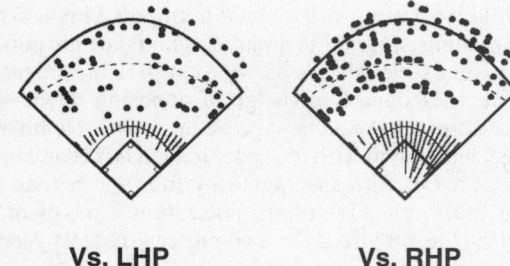

Vs. LHP   **Vs. RHP**

2000 Situational Stats

	AB	H	HR	RBI	Avg		AB	H	HR	RBI	Avg
Home	293	75	13	46	.256	LHP	190	51	8	38	.268
Road	301	91	14	58	.302	RHP	404	115	19	66	.285
First Half	333	100	16	65	.300	Sc Pos	165	52	8	80	.315
Scnd Half	261	66	11	39	.253	Clutch	79	21	3	11	.266

2000 Rankings (American League)

- 1st in GDPs (32)
- 3rd in lowest fielding percentage in left field (.988)
- 4th in errors in left field (3)
- Led the Athletics in doubles, strikeouts, GDPs (32), highest groundball/flyball ratio (1.5) and cleanup slugging percentage (.554)
- Led AL left fielders in strikeouts, GDPs (32) and cleanup slugging percentage (.554)

Gil Heredia

2000 Season

No longer a journeyman, Gil Heredia was a mainstay of the Athletics' rotation last year from the very first pitch of spring training. During the exhibition season, manager Art Howe had suggested that the only difference between the old "Dr. Gil" and the new version was that Heredia could now throw strikes whenever he wanted. The results included a career-high 15 wins and an ERA that was among the best in the American League through most of the 2000 campaign.

Pitching

Heredia needs to stay around the plate, since his fastball only registers in the high 80s on his best day. He does vary the pitch, however, tossing both two- and four-seamers, along with split-finger and cut versions that complement a slider. He doesn't hide much and must move the ball around, and patient hitters can be rewarded. Heredia tends to lose effectiveness in pressure situations and often has trouble in the first inning, as evidenced by his poor performance in Game 5 of last year's Division Series. Once he survives those early innings, he generally lasts a good six frames. He made it into the sixth inning in 26 of his 32 starts last year.

Defense

Heredia features a compact delivery that allows him to defend adequately, though he could be quicker covering first base. His glove is both good and consistent. Runners have some success off him—12 of 19 were successful last year—but Heredia takes care of his defensive duties well.

2001 Outlook

General manager Billy Beane exercised the $3.3 million option on Heredia for the 2001 season, and he can be expected to again be a steadying presence every fifth game. In a rotation containing some live young arms, Heredia, who now has two full seasons as a regular in the rotation, may improve his game even further.

Position: SP
Bats: R **Throws:** R
Ht: 6' 1" **Wt:** 221

Opening Day Age: 35
Born: 10/26/65 in Nogales, AZ
ML Seasons: 9
Pronunciation: her-RAY-dee-uh

Overall Statistics

	W	L	Pct.	ERA	G	GS	Sv	IP	H	BB	SO	HR	Ratio
2000	15	11	.577	4.12	32	32	0	198.2	214	66	101	24	1.41
Career	50	43	.538	4.32	243	110	4	844.1	935	192	499	88	1.33

How Often He Throws Strikes

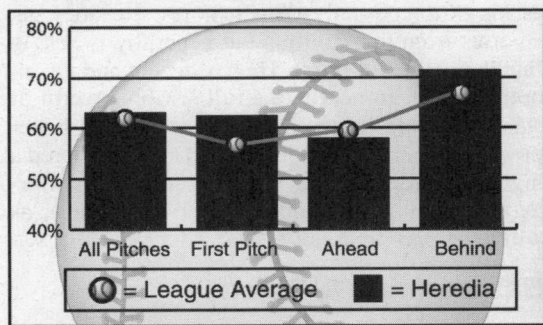

◉ = League Average   ■ = Heredia

2000 Situational Stats

	W	L	ERA	Sv	IP		AB	H	HR	RBI	Avg
Home	4	9	4.70	0	107.1	LHB	395	101	11	40	.256
Road	11	2	3.45	0	91.1	RHB	385	113	13	50	.294
First Half	9	7	3.99	0	112.2	Sc Pos	176	43	5	60	.244
Scnd Half	6	4	4.29	0	86.0	Clutch	32	10	1	3	.313

2000 Rankings (American League)
- 2nd in fewest strikeouts per nine innings (4.6)
- 4th in fewest pitches thrown per batter (3.50) and lowest ERA on the road
- 6th in pickoff throws (153)
- 7th in ERA
- 8th in fewest GDPs induced per nine innings (0.6)
- 9th in wins and highest groundball/flyball ratio allowed (1.6)
- 10th in runners caught stealing (7)
- Led the Athletics in ERA, losses, games started, complete games (2), hits allowed, home runs allowed, runners caught stealing (7), fewest pitches thrown per batter (3.50), fewest walks per nine innings (3.0) and lowest ERA on the road

Ramon Hernandez

2000 Season

After blowing past prospects Danny Ardoin and A.J. Hinch in 1999, Ramon Hernandez endured a rough start to the 2000 campaign. Hernandez hit .164 in April before finally heating up with a .321 average in May. While he finished with a .241 average overall, the 24-year-old provided a steady and improving bat. He was terrific behind the plate, guiding a young staff to a division title and setting a single-season record for Athletics backstops by catching in 142 games. His total broke Ray Fosse's old mark of 139.

Hitting

As a backstop, Hernandez knows the strike zone, as his hitting usually demonstrates. He does get anxious from time to time but generally is able to line the ball to all fields. He has decent and developing power. In nearly one full season's worth of stats at the big league level, he's produced better power numbers against lefties and also registered a higher on-base percentage versus southpaws. Hernandez' hitting will improve with experience, as will his home-run totals.

Baserunning & Defense

Hernandez possesses only moderate speed, but then he is a catcher. Once on base, he knows what to do and stays out of trouble. Behind the plate he is good and improving, although he was able to throw out just 19 of 87 basestealers (21.8 percent). His ability to handle pitchers and call a game improved dramatically over the course of last season.

2001 Outlook

Entering the '99 campaign, Hinch found himself in a similar position to Hernandez. He was 24 and coming off a year in which he had established himself as Oakland's primary receiver. But he subsequently played himself out of the job. Now it's Hernandez who's the veteran catcher, hoping to hold his spot. He probably can look forward to a better season behind the plate, and his offensive totals, especially his batting average and on-base percentage, should increase. A .280 batting average and 20 homers are well within reach in 2001.

Position: C
Bats: R **Throws:** R
Ht: 6' 0" **Wt:** 227

Opening Day Age: 24
Born: 5/20/76 in Caracas, Venezuela
ML Seasons: 2

Overall Statistics

	G	AB	R	H	D	T	HR	RBI	SB	BB	SO	Avg	OBP	Slg
2000	143	419	52	101	19	0	14	62	1	38	64	.241	.311	.387
Career	183	555	65	139	26	0	17	83	2	56	75	.250	.324	.389

Where He Hits the Ball

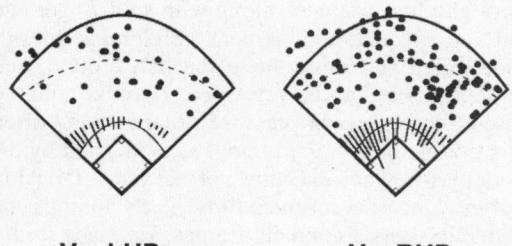

Vs. LHP   **Vs. RHP**

2000 Situational Stats

	AB	H	HR	RBI	Avg		AB	H	HR	RBI	Avg
Home	217	50	7	34	.230	LHP	107	26	4	17	.243
Road	202	51	7	28	.252	RHP	312	75	10	45	.240
First Half	216	53	8	31	.245	Sc Pos	111	31	5	49	.279
Scnd Half	203	48	6	31	.236	Clutch	56	19	3	10	.339

2000 Rankings (American League)

- 1st in errors at catcher (13) and lowest fielding percentage at catcher (.984)
- Led the Athletics in sacrifice bunts (10) and bunts in play (15)
- Led AL catchers in batting average with the bases loaded (.500) and bunts in play (15)

Tim Hudson

2000 Season

After his surprising debut in 1999, big expectations and crossed fingers awaited Tim Hudson last season. But no one expected a 20-game winner and staff ace to emerge so quickly. He did experience some adjustments in April, as teams tried to exert patience, and then had back-to-back rough months in July and August. But Hudson was the best pitcher in the majors during the month of September, when he went 5-0 with a 1.69 ERA and a complete-game shutout against Tampa Bay.

Pitching

Though Hudson brings a fastball in the low 90s, his splitter and heavy sinker keep hitters off balance and lunging at the ball. Factor in a curve, as well as a great delivery that generates a similar release point and rotation for all of his pitches, and it's amazing that hitters fare as well as they do against him. In addition to his strong repertoire, Hudson also brings a headiness to his game that lends an air of invincibility. Hitters are most successful against him when they stand back on his breaking pitches, but that is not as easy as it sounds.

Defense

If there is a flaw within Hudson's game, it's that his motion is slow and deliberate. Opposing runners chewed him up last year, stealing successfully on 24 of 27 attempts. Similarly, his defense can be suspect. Although he is fairly quick off the mound, he can be slow to get to first base.

2001 Outlook

Hudson might be the anchor of a championship rotation. He and teammate Barry Zito could be the next Maddux/Glavine combo, leading their team to repeated postseason play. Winning 20 games again will be a tough chore, but look for Hudson to provide another 200 innings while improving his command, reducing his walks-innings ratio and cutting down on his wild pitches.

Position: SP
Bats: R **Throws:** R
Ht: 6' 0" **Wt:** 160

Opening Day Age: 25
Born: 7/14/75 in Columbus, GA
ML Seasons: 2

Overall Statistics

	W	L	Pct.	ERA	G	GS	Sv	IP	H	BB	SO	HR	Ratio
2000	20	6	.769	4.14	32	32	0	202.1	169	82	169	24	1.24
Career	31	8	.795	3.77	53	53	0	338.2	290	144	301	32	1.28

How Often He Throws Strikes

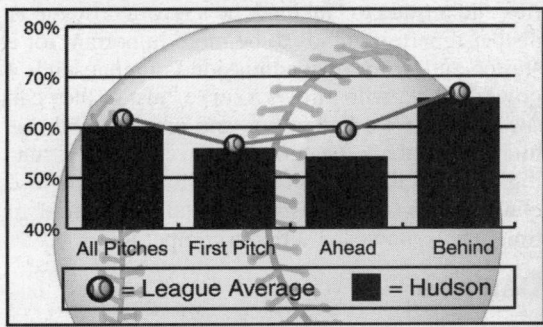

◉ = League Average ■ = Hudson

2000 Situational Stats

	W	L	ERA	Sv	IP		AB	H	HR	RBI	Avg
Home	12	1	3.63	0	116.2	LHB	420	97	17	54	.231
Road	8	5	4.83	0	85.2	RHB	326	72	7	34	.221
First Half	10	2	4.27	0	109.2	Sc Pos	141	36	5	65	.255
Scnd Half	10	4	3.98	0	92.2	Clutch	36	8	2	3	.222

2000 Rankings (American League)

- 1st in wins and winning percentage
- 2nd in shutouts (2), lowest batting average allowed (.227), highest groundball/flyball ratio allowed (2.0), most run support per nine innings (7.3), errors at pitcher (4), highest stolen-base percentage allowed (88.9) and lowest fielding percentage at pitcher (.897)
- 3rd in stolen bases allowed (24) and lowest slugging percentage allowed (.374)
- Led the Athletics in wins, games started, complete games (2), shutouts (2), innings pitched, home runs allowed, strikeouts, wild pitches (7), stolen bases allowed (24), highest strikeout/walk ratio (2.1), lowest batting average allowed (.227) and lowest slugging percentage allowed (.374)

Oakland

Jason Isringhausen

2000 Season

Jason Isringhausen picked up last season right where he left off at the end of 1999, when he successfully converted eight straight save opportunities. He established himself as Oakland's closer, a job he held for most of last year. There were rough periods, especially in May and August, but for the final three weeks of the season Isringhausen converted seven chances to wind up with over 30 saves in his first full year in the bullpen.

Pitching

Isringhausen had looked like a rotation anchor when he first arrived in the big leagues with the Mets back in 1995. After shoulder and elbow injuries and a trade to Oakland, he's now a reliever. A deeper repertoire tends to be more important for a starter, and by his own admission Isringhausen is a power pitcher who throws a curve "just so they can see it." It isn't a bad curve, and coupled with his high-90s fastball, the combination can be devastating. In general, Izzy is effective, though he can lose concentration and then command from time to time. He is, however, a fierce competitor.

Defense

Isringhausen throws hard and has a closer's mentality, so he generally doesn't concern himself with baserunners. That partly explains why all eight stolen-base attempts against him were successful last year. He isn't a lot of help with the glove, either. But if he is on his game, he's striking hitters out, which means that most of the team's leather—including his own—can rest.

2001 Outlook

Last season was a relatively new experience for Isringhausen. It was his first full season as a closer, his first full year in Oakland, and he was working for a contender. With a year under his belt, he should settle in and improve his numbers as confidence and experience enhance his natural ability. While he finished last season as a free agent, he was expected to sign a new deal.

Position: RP
Bats: R **Throws:** R
Ht: 6' 3" **Wt:** 210

Opening Day Age: 28
Born: 9/7/72 in Brighton, IL
ML Seasons: 5
Pronunciation: IS-ring-how-zin
Nickname: Izzy

Overall Statistics

	W	L	Pct.	ERA	G	GS	Sv	IP	H	BB	SO	HR	Ratio
2000	6	4	.600	3.78	66	0	33	69.0	67	32	57	6	1.43
Career	24	26	.480	4.37	146	52	42	428.0	449	192	302	37	1.50

How Often He Throws Strikes

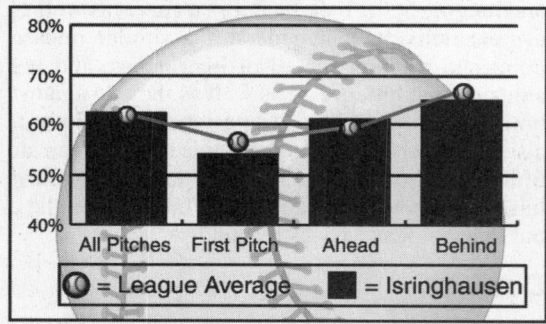

= League Average   = Isringhausen

2000 Situational Stats

	W	L	ERA	Sv	IP		AB	H	HR	RBI	Avg
Home	4	0	2.19	17	37.0	LHB	153	37	4	19	.242
Road	2	4	5.63	16	32.0	RHB	113	30	2	15	.265
First Half	4	2	2.79	19	38.2	Sc Pos	75	18	1	26	.240
Scnd Half	2	2	5.04	14	30.1	Clutch	170	40	5	26	.235

2000 Rankings (American League)

- 6th in save opportunities (40)
- 7th in saves and save percentage (82.5)
- Led the Athletics in saves, games finished (57), save opportunities (40), save percentage (82.5), blown saves (7), relief wins (6), lowest batting average allowed in relief (.252) and most strikeouts per nine innings in relief (7.4)

Terrence Long

2000 Season

Plucked by Billy Beane (with hurler Leoner Vasquez) in a terrific swap for Kenny Rogers at the 1999 trade deadline, Terrence Long enjoyed a solid spring but was optioned out at the start of last season. Suffering at the leadoff spot, Oakland recalled Long following a strong April at Triple-A Sacramento in which he batted .400 with 15 RBI. The Athletics promptly installed him in the top spot in their order. Despite missing that first month of the season, he finished among the rookie leaders in homers, and his presence helped to kick-start a potent offense.

Hitting

Long came to Oakland with good credentials and excellent tools, but for a young player thrown into a pennant race as a rookie, he handled the adjustment to the big leagues well. He does get anxious, swinging at bad pitches more often than he should, but Long seems to learn from his experiences. He has good power, setting a professional high in homers during his first major league season. He hangs in well versus righthanders, but he needs to improve against southpaws. He struggled some at the dish last year after breaking his cheek in batting practice.

Baserunning & Defense

Considering his great speed, it's surprising that Long attempted only five steals last year; he had stolen as many as 32 bases in a season in the minor leagues. He also scored over 100 runs for the Athletics despite the incomplete year, a testimony to both his swiftness and his ability to take advantage of opposing arms and situations. His defense needs work, as balls have a tendency to turn Long inside out. He possesses an average arm.

2001 Outlook

Yet another young Oakland player with a full season stashed away, Long learned as much from last year's pennant race as anyone. His lapses fueled some of Art Howe's strongest tirades, but Long rebounded a better player. Handling any adversity during his sophomore season will prove to be another challenge, but he should be up to it.

Position: CF
Bats: L **Throws:** L
Ht: 6' 1" **Wt:** 190

Opening Day Age: 25
Born: 2/29/76 in Montgomery, AL
ML Seasons: 2

Overall Statistics

	G	AB	R	H	D	T	HR	RBI	SB	BB	SO	Avg	OBP	Slg
2000	138	584	104	168	34	4	18	80	5	43	77	.288	.336	.452
Career	141	587	104	168	34	4	18	80	5	43	79	.286	.334	.450

Where He Hits the Ball

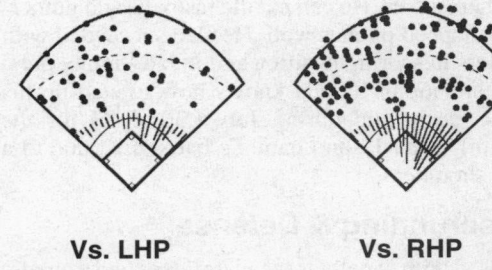

Vs. LHP   **Vs. RHP**

2000 Situational Stats

	AB	H	HR	RBI	Avg		AB	H	HR	RBI	Avg
Home	276	77	9	37	.279	LHP	171	45	1	11	.263
Road	308	91	9	43	.295	RHP	413	123	17	69	.298
First Half	258	70	9	37	.271	Sc Pos	111	41	3	58	.369
Scnd Half	326	98	9	43	.301	Clutch	69	17	0	11	.246

2000 Rankings (American League)

- 1st in errors in center field (10) and lowest fielding percentage in center field (.971)
- 4th in lowest on-base percentage for a leadoff hitter (.333)
- 5th in batting average with runners in scoring position and lowest percentage of swings on the first pitch (14.4)
- 6th in batting average with the bases loaded (.611)
- 7th in lowest on-base percentage vs. lefthanded pitchers (.302)
- Led the Athletics in singles, batting average with runners in scoring position, on-base percentage for a leadoff hitter (.333) and lowest percentage of swings that missed (14.5)

Miguel Tejada

2000 Season

It is sad that so few fans outside of Oakland were aware of Miguel Tejada's stellar 2000 campaign. Even in the Bay Area, few realized that the Athletics' shortstop actually delivered more RBI than cross-bay left fielder Barry Bonds. But that he did, as he topped both 100 RBI and 30 homers for the first of what promises to be many times. Both figures represented records for an Oakland shortstop. Tejada's name is not far from being mentioned in the same sentence with the likes of Nomar Garciaparra, Derek Jeter and Alex Rodriguez.

Hitting

Not naturally gifted with plate discipline, Tejada has learned how to take a pitch. The results speak for themselves. He can handle fastballs and numerous offspeed pitches well. He also succeeded with runners in scoring position and in late-inning pressure situations. Tejada knows how to step up his game, as he did during July (.305-8-23 for the month) when Jason Giambi's bat stalled due to a sore shoulder.

Baserunning & Defense

Blessed with excellent speed, reflexes and a terrific arm, Tejada is one of those players who can turn in an acrobatic play that drops jaws. He tends to make the occasional bad decision in the field, though playing with veteran second baseman Randy Velarde has helped quell that habit. Tejada is capable of 20 steals, but since that isn't Oakland's game, he doesn't run that often. Still, he was successful on all six of his stolen-base attempts last season, a marked improvement over his 8-for-15 ledger of 1999.

2001 Outlook

Right after last season began, the Athletics secured Tejada's signature on a new four-year, $11.3 million deal. He responded with a career year. He will be just 24 years of age when Opening Day arrives this season, yet he already possesses significant skills and the experience of a veteran. Expect his defense and baserunning numbers to improve right along with his batting average as he solidifies his place among the top shortstops in the game.

Position: SS
Bats: R **Throws:** R
Ht: 5' 9" **Wt:** 188

Opening Day Age: 24
Born: 5/25/76 in Bani, Dominican Republic
ML Seasons: 4
Pronunciation: mee-GHEL teh-HAH-duh

Overall Statistics

	G	AB	R	H	D	T	HR	RBI	SB	BB	SO	Avg	OBP	Slg
2000	160	607	105	167	32	1	30	115	6	66	102	.275	.349	.479
Career	450	1664	261	421	88	8	64	254	21	153	304	.253	.323	.431

Where He Hits the Ball

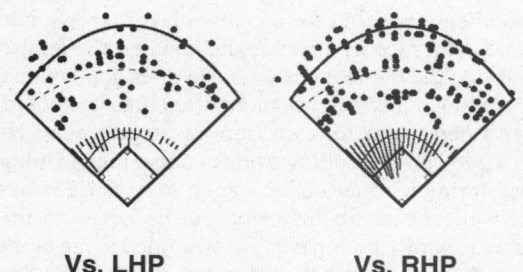

Vs. LHP	Vs. RHP

2000 Situational Stats

	AB	H	HR	RBI	Avg		AB	H	HR	RBI	Avg
Home	297	80	16	57	.269	LHP	168	37	10	26	.220
Road	310	87	14	58	.281	RHP	439	130	20	89	.296
First Half	332	83	15	63	.250	Sc Pos	167	47	7	78	.281
Scnd Half	275	84	15	52	.305	Clutch	66	24	8	16	.364

2000 Rankings (American League)

- 4th in errors at shortstop (21) and games played
- 6th in lowest batting average vs. lefthanded pitchers and lowest fielding percentage at shortstop (.972)
- 8th in batting average in the clutch
- Led the Athletics in at-bats, plate appearances (681), batting average in the clutch, highest percentage of extra bases taken as a runner (62.0) and games played
- Led AL shortstops in batting average on a 3-1 count (.545) and games played (160)

Randy Velarde

Traded To
RANGERS

2000 Season

Even under perfect circumstances, Randy Velarde would have had a hard time topping his 200-hit, 105-run campaign of 1999. Sure enough, the injury bug that has plagued him for most of his career once again materialized as camp broke, and he was placed on the disabled list with a strained knee. Once he returned, he never really got into a groove. Still, Velarde did provide solid numbers offensively. Perhaps more importantly, he lent a veteran's perspective and presence to the charging Athletics.

Hitting

As with all aspects of his game, Velarde conducts his hitting with a very businesslike approach. He has developed good patience at the plate and is able to drive balls to all fields. His power has increased over the years, and he's reached double figures in home runs in each of the last three seasons in which he was able to play 100 games. Velarde can handle inside pitches and has continued to improve his hitting against righthanded pitchers. His slugging percentage did drop last year, though it was primarily due to the dip in his average.

Baserunning & Defense

A focused player, Velarde came within 23 tallies of tying his 1999 runs scored total despite 146 fewer at-bats. Though he has good speed, injuries, particularly leg woes, reduced his steal attempts last year. At age 38, it's a trend that should continue. Velarde is solid in the field, and his steadying hand helped settle shortstop Miguel Tejada.

2001 Outlook

Signed through the coming season, Velarde was dealt to Texas in mid-November for minor league pitchers Aaron Harang and Ryan Cullen. Velarde will take the reigns as a stopgap at second base for the Rangers, provided his body obliges. While his totals likely will be closer to those of last year than his 1999 effort, he still is a productive and valued member of any infield.

Position: 2B
Bats: R **Throws:** R
Ht: 6' 0" **Wt:** 200

Opening Day Age: 38
Born: 11/24/62 in Midland, TX
ML Seasons: 14
Pronunciation: vuh-LARR-dee

Overall Statistics

	G	AB	R	H	D	T	HR	RBI	SB	BB	SO	Avg	OBP	Slg
2000	122	485	82	135	23	0	12	41	9	54	95	.278	.354	.400
Career	1124	3769	561	1046	187	21	89	405	69	414	735	.278	.353	.409

Where He Hits the Ball

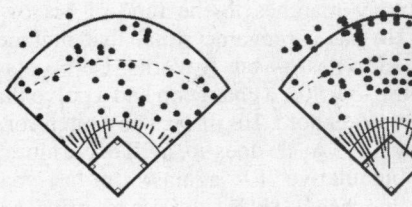

Vs. LHP   **Vs. RHP**

2000 Situational Stats

	AB	H	HR	RBI	Avg		AB	H	HR	RBI	Avg
Home	260	73	11	24	.281	LHP	145	38	3	9	.262
Road	225	62	1	17	.276	RHP	340	97	9	32	.285
First Half	208	62	7	23	.298	Sc Pos	91	19	3	29	.209
Scnd Half	277	73	5	18	.264	Clutch	54	15	3	11	.278

2000 Rankings (American League)
- 1st in lowest percentage of swings on the first pitch (12.0)
- 4th in fielding percentage at second base (.982) and lowest batting average with runners in scoring position
- Led the Athletics in stolen bases, steals of third (3) and lowest percentage of swings on the first pitch (12.0)
- Led AL second basemen in lowest percentage of swings on the first pitch (12.0)

Oakland

Barry Zito

2000 Season

From out of nowhere, and just when the Athletics needed him most, Barry Zito arrived on the scene to team with Tim Hudson and provide Oakland a devastating 1-2 punch of youthful starters. Zito had been a polished collegiate hurler whom the Athletics drafted in the first round in 1999. He swept through the minors and won his first big league start despite some control issues. He proceeded to dominate hitters over the final two months of the season, going 5-1 with a 1.73 ERA in September. He capped the year with a brilliant five-plus inning performance against the Yankees en route to his first postseason win.

Pitching

Zito absolutely marches to the tune of his own drummer. He has a pregame ritual that includes yoga and teddy bears—but it works. He boasts a fastball in the low 90s, a changeup and a curve that is something to behold. He throws any pitch for a strike at any time. As he does so, he'll leave hitters, who hit a cumulative .195 against him last year, scratching their heads. He is calm yet assertive, and he is poised to take on the league over the course of a full season.

Defense

Zito is a smart player who concentrates and makes few mistakes, especially for someone so young. He is quick off the mound and good at covering first base. Similarly, his move to first is quick. That makes runners, who were caught four out of seven times, wary.

2001 Outlook

Hudson may be the soul of the Oakland pitching staff, but Zito is the one with the dynamite stuff. That makes the pair more than complementary, and anyone who thinks that Zito's 2000 numbers were an aberration should be served notice: he is a Cy Young Award waiting to happen. That honor may not come in 2001, but then again, who knows?

Position: SP
Bats: L **Throws:** L
Ht: 6' 4" **Wt:** 205

Opening Day Age: 22
Born: 5/13/78 in Las Vegas, NV
ML Seasons: 1

Overall Statistics

	W	L	Pct.	ERA	G	GS	Sv	IP	H	BB	SO	HR	Ratio
2000	7	4	.636	2.72	14	14	0	92.2	64	45	78	6	1.18
Career	7	4	.636	2.72	14	14	0	92.2	64	45	78	6	1.18

How Often He Throws Strikes

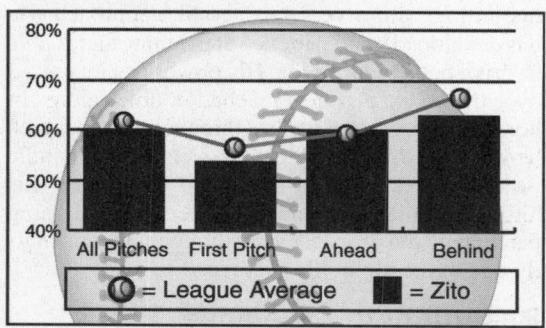

2000 Situational Stats

	W	L	ERA	Sv	IP		AB	H	HR	RBI	Avg
Home	4	2	2.87	0	53.1	LHB	72	14	0	2	.194
Road	3	2	2.52	0	39.1	RHB	256	50	6	26	.195
First Half	0	0	-	0	0.0	Sc Pos	73	14	2	21	.192
Scnd Half	7	4	2.72	0	92.2	Clutch	10	2	0	1	.200

2000 Rankings (American League)

- 2nd in lowest batting average allowed vs. righthanded batters

Ryan Christenson

Position: LF/CF/RF
Bats: R **Throws:** R
Ht: 6' 0" **Wt:** 191

Opening Day Age: 27
Born: 3/28/74 in Redlands, CA
ML Seasons: 3

Overall Statistics

	G	AB	R	H	D	T	HR	RBI	SB	BB	SO	Avg	OBP	Slg
2000	121	129	31	32	2	2	4	18	1	19	33	.248	.349	.388
Career	344	767	128	183	36	5	13	82	13	93	197	.239	.320	.349

2000 Situational Stats

	AB	H	HR	RBI	Avg		AB	H	HR	RBI	Avg
Home	53	9	3	9	.170	LHP	54	9	2	9	.167
Road	76	23	1	9	.303	RHP	75	23	2	9	.307
First Half	78	22	3	10	.282	Sc Pos	38	10	1	13	.263
Scnd Half	51	10	1	8	.196	Clutch	17	6	1	1	.353

2000 Season

"If all players were like Ryan Christenson," one Athletics coach remarked just prior to the end of the 2000 season, "the world would be a better place." Christenson, a selfless player, opened last season as part of a center-field platoon. He then found a spot as the fourth outfielder following the promotion of Terrence Long. When he saw action, Christenson played hard and produced career highs in several offensive categories.

Hitting, Baserunning & Defense

Christenson made strides last season in improving his patience at the plate and his ability to hit righthanders. Unfortunately, his numbers against lefties tumbled. While he can generate decent power and take the extra base with his speed, he needs to develop consistency against all pitchers on a daily basis. His arm is fine and his glove is sensational, making him a logical late-inning replacement for Ben Grieve.

2001 Outlook

Christenson will enter 2001 as a reserve outfielder. With a full season of major league experience, he should be able to raise his production a bit. But finding a starting job on this team, rich with starters and prospects, will be a tough chore.

Jeremy Giambi

Position: RF/DH/1B
Bats: L **Throws:** L
Ht: 6' 0" **Wt:** 200

Opening Day Age: 26
Born: 9/30/74 in San Jose, CA
ML Seasons: 3
Pronunciation: gee-AHM-bee

Overall Statistics

	G	AB	R	H	D	T	HR	RBI	SB	BB	SO	Avg	OBP	Slg
2000	104	260	42	66	10	2	10	50	0	32	61	.254	.338	.423
Career	212	606	82	161	27	3	15	92	0	83	137	.266	.355	.394

2000 Situational Stats

	AB	H	HR	RBI	Avg		AB	H	HR	RBI	Avg
Home	142	31	3	23	.218	LHP	64	17	5	17	.266
Road	118	35	7	27	.297	RHP	196	49	5	33	.250
First Half	150	42	7	35	.280	Sc Pos	84	25	4	42	.298
Scnd Half	110	24	3	15	.218	Clutch	49	12	2	12	.245

2000 Season

Jeremy Giambi, or "Little G," was acquired just before spring training last year from Kansas City in exchange for pitcher Brett Laxton. Giambi first faced a challenge just earning a spot amongst the crush of Oakland outfielders. He then worked through several minor injuries. His two September homers—he hit .368 that month—came at moments that helped energize the team.

Hitting, Baserunning & Defense

A smart hitter, Giambi actually produced a higher average and better power totals than his brother Jason did in the minors. He possesses the same genetically quick bat, learns what pitchers throw and remembers accordingly. Jeremy can generate power to all fields. He doesn't boast a lot of speed and his glove at first base and in the outfield is adequate at best.

2001 Outlook

Giambi likely will enter spring training as part of a right-field platoon with Adam Piatt. Giambi performed well as a pinch-hitter and can handle a spot role. But he also has the talent and makeup to perform very well as a starter. He just needs 450 at-bats, something that may be tough to come by in Oakland.

John Jaha

Position: DH
Bats: R **Throws:** R
Ht: 6' 1" **Wt:** 224

Opening Day Age: 34
Born: 5/27/66 in Portland, OR
ML Seasons: 9
Pronunciation: JAH-hah

Overall Statistics

	G	AB	R	H	D	T	HR	RBI	SB	BB	SO	Avg	OBP	Slg
2000	33	97	14	17	1	0	1	5	1	33	38	.175	.398	.216
Career	814	2730	468	726	123	5	141	482	36	424	671	.266	.372	.470

2000 Situational Stats

	AB	H	HR	RBI	Avg		AB	H	HR	RBI	Avg
Home	55	9	0	3	.164	LHP	34	8	0	1	.235
Road	42	8	1	2	.190	RHP	63	9	1	4	.143
First Half	97	17	1	5	.175	Sc Pos	29	2	0	4	.069
Scnd Half	0	0	0	0	-	Clutch	14	2	0	1	.143

2000 Season

John Jaha got to share in none of the excitement associated with Oakland's title run last season. He injured his shoulder during the spring and never really got untracked. His 33 games, 97 at-bats and .175 batting average all were career lows.

Hitting, Baserunning & Defense

A key to the Athletics' success is their ability to work pitchers, and Jaha is perhaps the prime example. He drew 33 walks in the same number of games last season. His batting eye allowed him to post a lofty .398 on-base percentage despite his puny batting average. When he is right, he drives the ball to all fields, especially right-center. He is a plodder on the bases and rarely tries to steal. His glove is adequate, though injuries and prospects have limited Jaha to a DH role.

2001 Outlook

Trying to keep the essence of their contending club intact, the Athletics signed Jaha for two years following his resurgent 1999 effort. If he is healthy, his approach to hitting is harmonious with Oakland's overall style. A trade is unlikely because Oakland probably would have to bear the brunt of his salary.

Jim Mecir

Position: RP
Bats: B **Throws:** R
Ht: 6' 1" **Wt:** 210

Opening Day Age: 30
Born: 5/16/70 in Queens, NY
ML Seasons: 6
Pronunciation: meh-SEER

Overall Statistics

	W	L	Pct.	ERA	G	GS	Sv	IP	H	BB	SO	HR	Ratio
2000	10	3	.769	2.96	63	0	5	85.0	70	36	70	4	1.25
Career	18	11	.621	3.62	201	0	5	268.1	236	118	228	21	1.32

2000 Situational Stats

	W	L	ERA	Sv	IP		AB	H	HR	RBI	Avg
Home	8	2	3.19	0	48.0	LHB	152	31	1	13	.204
Road	2	1	2.68	5	37.0	RHB	159	39	3	22	.245
First Half	6	1	2.18	1	41.1	Sc Pos	102	19	2	31	.186
Scnd Half	4	2	3.71	4	43.2	Clutch	188	44	4	31	.234

2000 Season

General manager Billy Beane recognized that his bullpen was getting tired last summer, so he dealt minor league phenom Jesus Colome to Tampa Bay in exchange for Jim Mecir just before the trading deadline. Mecir filled in well, appearing in 25 games and functioning as Oakland's closer in late August and early September when Jason Isringhausen faltered. Mecir was especially effective in September, going 2-0 with three saves and a 1.53 ERA over 17.2 innings.

Pitching & Defense

While Mecir delivers a fastball in the high 80s, his big pitch is a screwball that makes him effective against lefthanded hitters, who managed a meager .204 average against him in 2000. He owns a solid glove, as evidenced by the fact that in 201 major league games and 61 chances he has yet to commit an error. On the other hand, runners can go wild on him. Basestealers succeeded on 13 of 15 attempts last season.

2001 Outlook

Oakland's front office didn't surrender a top pitching prospect for Mecir just to let him walk away. The Athletics will try to re-sign him for the 2001 campaign and use him to augment Jeff Tam and even Isringhausen as necessary.

Mark Mulder

Position: SP
Bats: L **Throws:** L
Ht: 6' 6" **Wt:** 200

Opening Day Age: 23
Born: 8/5/77 in South Holland, IL
ML Seasons: 1

Overall Statistics

	W	L	Pct.	ERA	G	GS	Sv	IP	H	BB	SO	HR	Ratio
2000	9	10	.474	5.44	27	27	0	154.0	191	69	88	22	1.69
Career	9	10	.474	5.44	27	27	0	154.0	191	69	88	22	1.69

2000 Situational Stats

	W	L	ERA	Sv	IP		AB	H	HR	RBI	Avg
Home	6	3	3.94	0	75.1	LHB	155	57	4	21	.368
Road	3	7	6.86	0	78.2	RHB	466	134	18	74	.288
First Half	5	4	5.07	0	87.0	Sc Pos	146	50	3	65	.342
Scnd Half	4	6	5.91	0	67.0	Clutch	19	4	0	0	.211

2000 Season

Mark Mulder was the second overall pick in the 1998 draft. After a credible first full season at Triple-A in 1999, he began 2000 as a member of Oakland's starting rotation. He was spotty, alternating regularly between a couple of rough outings and one good one. Just when he seemed to get into a groove in mid-September, he suffered a disk injury that ended his erratic yet promising rookie year.

Pitching & Defense

Mulder owns a fastball in the low 90s, a cut fastball, a changeup and an above-average curve. Command shouldn't be a problem, but he often finds himself behind in the count. Improved knowledge of the strike zone, coupled with the aggressiveness that comes with experience, will be big aids to Mulder in his sophomore campaign. His defense needs improvement, though the lanky lefty has a solid move to first.

2001 Outlook

While Mulder now works in the middle of the rotation, his skills and command suggest he could be a No. 1 guy on a few other teams. A year of experience and reduced individual pressure should add up to an improved 2001, starting him on an uphill curve of major league success.

Omar Olivares

Position: SP
Bats: R **Throws:** R
Ht: 6' 1" **Wt:** 205

Opening Day Age: 33
Born: 7/6/67 in Mayaguez, Puerto Rico
ML Seasons: 11
Pronunciation: oh-lih-VARE-es

Overall Statistics

	W	L	Pct.	ERA	G	GS	Sv	IP	H	BB	SO	HR	Ratio
2000	4	8	.333	6.75	21	16	0	108.0	134	60	57	10	1.80
Career	71	77	.480	4.53	304	217	3	1481.2	1555	643	784	142	1.48

2000 Situational Stats

	W	L	ERA	Sv	IP		AB	H	HR	RBI	Avg
Home	1	5	6.45	0	51.2	LHB	195	59	6	31	.303
Road	3	3	7.03	0	56.1	RHB	239	75	4	42	.314
First Half	3	8	6.64	0	80.0	Sc Pos	125	35	3	57	.280
Scnd Half	1	0	7.07	0	28.0	Clutch	12	4	0	3	.333

2000 Season

Fresh off a career season, Omar Olivares signed a two-year deal with Oakland and proceeded to struggle with his control last year. He also spent nearly two months on the disabled list with a sore shoulder. He did make two starts near the end of the regular season to help the Athletics secure the American League West title.

Pitching & Defense

Olivares lives and dies by his fastball, primarily by changing speeds between the low 70s and low 90s. While he relies on the sharp break of his fastball to get groundouts, his actual outs are fairly well split between those in the air and on the ground. He holds runners well and has an excellent move to first, though his defense is suspect; he has piled up 19 errors in 11 big league seasons.

2001 Outlook

Oakland bought the services of Olivares for the upcoming season and he'll probably be a member of its starting rotation, at least heading into spring training. Not overpowering, he might fit in well between hard throwers Tim Hudson and lefthander Barry Zito. But if Olivares is ineffective, which he has been more often than not, don't expect Art Howe to keep him in the rotation.

Oakland

Adam Piatt

Position: RF/3B/DH
Bats: R **Throws:** R
Ht: 6' 2" **Wt:** 195

Opening Day Age: 25
Born: 2/8/76 in
Chicago, IL
ML Seasons: 1

Overall Statistics

	G	AB	R	H	D	T	HR	RBI	SB	BB	SO	Avg	OBP	Slg
2000	60	157	24	47	5	5	5	23	0	23	44	.299	.392	.490
Career	60	157	24	47	5	5	5	23	0	23	44	.299	.392	.490

2000 Situational Stats

	AB	H	HR	RBI	Avg		AB	H	HR	RBI	Avg
Home	57	18	3	8	.316	LHP	84	31	5	17	.369
Road	100	29	2	15	.290	RHP	73	16	0	6	.219
First Half	33	10	2	8	.303	Sc Pos	48	15	2	18	.313
Scnd Half	124	37	3	15	.298	Clutch	23	8	0	4	.348

2000 Season

Third baseman Adam Piatt had assembled a pair of unbelievable minor league seasons, including a Texas League Triple Crown in 1999. But where would he play? The struggles of Matt Stairs and the injury to Olmedo Saenz provided a solution. Piatt registered good numbers while learning to play right field on the fly.

Hitting, Baserunning & Defense

Piatt belted 80 minor league homers over three-plus seasons. He has power but is also quite disciplined. He did have some trouble with righthanded pitchers at the major league level, but Piatt has belted lefties at every step of the way. While he possesses excellent speed, stealing is not a strength. He plays a solid third base, though his immediate future lies in the outfield, where he needs some improvement.

2001 Outlook

Piatt played winter ball during the offseason to get more time in the outfield. The Athletics traded Stairs to the Cubs in late November, a sign that Piatt will play right field this season, platooning with Jeremy Giambi. Eventually Piatt should evolve into a full-time player. He is another Athletic capable of a .300-30-100 season.

Olmedo Saenz

Position: DH/3B/1B
Bats: R **Throws:** R
Ht: 6' 0" **Wt:** 185

Opening Day Age: 30
Born: 10/8/70 in Chitre
Herrera, Panama
ML Seasons: 3
Pronunciation: SIGNS

Overall Statistics

	G	AB	R	H	D	T	HR	RBI	SB	BB	SO	Avg	OBP	Slg
2000	76	214	40	67	12	2	9	33	1	25	40	.313	.401	.514
Career	178	483	83	139	30	3	20	74	2	47	92	.288	.374	.487

2000 Situational Stats

	AB	H	HR	RBI	Avg		AB	H	HR	RBI	Avg
Home	91	29	3	9	.319	LHP	94	30	2	10	.319
Road	123	38	6	24	.309	RHP	120	37	7	23	.308
First Half	163	49	6	22	.301	Sc Pos	67	21	1	24	.313
Scnd Half	51	18	3	11	.353	Clutch	33	12	1	7	.364

2000 Season

In 1999, Olmedo Saenz and his timely bat provided a solid righthanded complement to rookie lefty Eric Chavez at third base. With Chavez entrenched at the hot corner in 2000, Saenz expected to see most of his playing time at DH. Instead, he spent considerable time on the DL, as leg injuries hampered him for most of the year. Even so, Saenz provided a spark when healthy and enjoyed his most successful offensive season to date in the big leagues.

Hitting, Baserunning & Defense

Saenz truly is the type of hitter who can be in a deep freeze for long stretches yet still get a hit in his first swing after the thaw. He knows the strike zone and his power is developing. He has good speed and can take an extra base, though stealing is not his forte. In the field, Saenz is passable as a backup, but not much more.

2001 Outlook

A free agent at the end of last season, the Athletics would like to retain the services of Saenz. He projects to be a Geronimo Berroa type of player: a solid hitter who can deliver .290-25-90 totals if given a full-time opportunity. If nothing else, the departure of Matt Stairs could present Saenz with some additional DH opportunities.

Matt Stairs

Traded To CUBS

Position: RF/DH
Bats: L **Throws:** R
Ht: 5' 9" **Wt:** 217

Opening Day Age: 33
Born: 2/27/68 in Saint John, NB, Canada
ML Seasons: 8

Overall Statistics

	G	AB	R	H	D	T	HR	RBI	SB	BB	SO	Avg	OBP	Slg
2000	143	476	74	108	26	0	21	81	5	78	122	.227	.333	.414
Career	690	2145	350	573	119	6	123	409	19	306	444	.267	.360	.500

2000 Situational Stats

	AB	H	HR	RBI	Avg		AB	H	HR	RBI	Avg
Home	243	56	9	42	.230	LHP	114	23	5	23	.202
Road	233	52	12	39	.223	RHP	362	85	16	58	.235
First Half	275	60	14	47	.218	Sc Pos	135	30	7	64	.222
Scnd Half	201	48	7	34	.239	Clutch	63	16	3	14	.254

2000 Season

After a pair of strong seasons that helped point the Athletics in the right direction, Matt Stairs' numbers fell off the map even as his team rushed to a division title. Trade rumors swirled and he was dogged by little aches for nearly the entire season. The drops in batting average and on-base percentage were disconcerting, and his 21 homers were his lowest total since 1996. He did hit well down the stretch, batting .297 over the final month.

Hitting, Baserunning & Defense

Stairs lives—or thinks he does—by the power he can generate. The reality is that when he is taking pitches and making contact, he can hit for both average and power. He is a smart baserunner with deceptive speed considering his squat build. He is a good defender with a decent arm in right field.

2001 Outlook

His subpar season, coupled with the presence of young hitters Adam Piatt and Jeremy Giambi, may have led the Athletics to deal Stairs to the Cubs in mid-November for minor league pitcher Eric Ireland. The Cubs quickly signed Stairs to a one-year, $3.2 million deal, and the team could use him at first base or for spot duty in the outfield. His sagging power numbers could get a boost from the friendly confines of Wrigley Field.

Jeff Tam

Position: RP
Bats: R **Throws:** R
Ht: 6' 1" **Wt:** 202

Opening Day Age: 30
Born: 8/19/70 in Fullerton, CA
ML Seasons: 3

Overall Statistics

	W	L	Pct.	ERA	G	GS	Sv	IP	H	BB	SO	HR	Ratio
2000	3	3	.500	2.63	72	0	3	85.2	86	23	46	3	1.27
Career	4	4	.500	3.39	97	0	3	111.2	107	31	62	8	1.24

2000 Situational Stats

	W	L	ERA	Sv	IP		AB	H	HR	RBI	Avg
Home	2	2	2.81	0	41.2	LHB	125	45	2	18	.360
Road	1	1	2.45	3	44.0	RHB	196	41	1	14	.209
First Half	3	2	2.40	2	60.0	Sc Pos	99	21	0	27	.212
Scnd Half	0	1	3.16	1	25.2	Clutch	144	39	0	17	.271

2000 Season

Tam was a non-roster invitee to spring training last year. Formerly of the Mets and Indians, he signed with Oakland during the offseason and surprisingly made the Athletics' Opening Day roster. The surprises didn't end there, either, as Tam earned the setup job for the bulk of the campaign and was the team leader in pitching appearances and relief innings.

Pitching & Defense

Although Tam relies on good control to induce groundouts, he can register a whiff when needed. His out pitch is a good sinker, and while his fastball is usually in the high 80s, he can crack 90 MPH when required. He is a better pitcher in the daylight than at night and quells righties a lot better than lefthanders. He is quick off the mound and fields his position well. Tam also is adept at holding baserunners, and only one successful steal was lodged against him last year.

2001 Outlook

A return to the bullpen, sharing setup duties with Jim Mecir, likely will reduce Tam's innings a little but should improve his effectiveness. Last year's 85.2 innings were the second most of his career, and he may be better served by a little less exposure.

Oakland

Other Oakland Athletics

Mark Bellhorn (Pos: 2B, Age: 26, Bats: B)

	G	AB	R	H	D	T	HR	RBI	SB	BB	SO	Avg	OBP	Slg
2000	9	13	2	2	0	0	0	0	0	2	6	.154	.267	.154
Career	88	249	36	54	10	1	6	20	9	37	80	.217	.321	.337

Bellhorn has versatility, fine plate discipline, decent power and he can steal a base. 2001 Outlook: B

Sal Fasano (Pos: C, Age: 29, Bats: R)

	G	AB	R	H	D	T	HR	RBI	SB	BB	SO	Avg	OBP	Slg
2000	52	126	21	27	6	0	7	19	0	14	47	.214	.306	.429
Career	213	583	77	127	22	0	27	86	2	46	157	.218	.304	.395

Fasano came to Oakland from Kansas City last March. It appears he'll linger as a backup catcher who will knock the occasional home run. 2001 Outlook: B

A.J. Hinch (Pos: C, Age: 26, Bats: R)

	G	AB	R	H	D	T	HR	RBI	SB	BB	SO	Avg	OBP	Slg
2000	6	8	1	2	0	0	0	0	0	1	1	.250	.333	.250
Career	202	550	61	124	14	1	16	59	9	42	131	.225	.284	.342

Hinch will have a hard time regaining the starting catcher's job in Oakland. But he has the smarts to be a useful roster component. 2001 Outlook: C

Doug Jones (Pos: RHP, Age: 43)

	W	L	Pct.	ERA	G	GS	Sv	IP	H	BB	SO	HR	Ratio
2000	4	2	.667	3.93	54	0	2	73.1	86	18	54	6	1.42
Career	69	79	.466	3.30	846	4	303	1128.1	1155	247	909	86	1.24

He pitched well in 73.1 innings last year, but Jones retired this offseason. 2001 Outlook: D

Marcus Jones (Pos: RHP, Age: 26)

	W	L	Pct.	ERA	G	GS	Sv	IP	H	BB	SO	HR	Ratio
2000	0	0	-	15.43	1	1	0	2.1	5	3	1	1	3.43
Career	0	0	-	15.43	1	1	0	2.1	5	3	1	1	3.43

Jones is a big guy, but his strikeout rate dipped last year in the minors. He's been primarily a starter since being drafted in the third round in 1997. 2001 Outlook: C

Mike Magnante (Pos: LHP, Age: 35)

	W	L	Pct.	ERA	G	GS	Sv	IP	H	BB	SO	HR	Ratio
2000	1	1	.500	4.31	55	0	0	39.2	50	19	17	3	1.74
Career	23	29	.442	4.11	387	19	3	533.2	578	210	313	36	1.48

Magnante's role is to retire lefthanded hitters, but they managed a .288 average against him last year. It had been .211 over the previous three seasons. 2001 Outlook: B.

T.J. Mathews (Pos: RHP, Age: 31)

	W	L	Pct.	ERA	G	GS	Sv	IP	H	BB	SO	HR	Ratio
2000	2	3	.400	6.03	50	0	0	59.2	73	25	42	10	1.64
Career	31	25	.554	3.80	320	0	15	379.1	348	147	315	43	1.30

Mathews worked at least 50 games each of the past five seasons. Last year his ERA rose by over two runs and he suffered shoulder and elbow problems. 2001 Outlook: B

Frank Menechino (Pos: 2B, Age: 30, Bats: R)

	G	AB	R	H	D	T	HR	RBI	SB	BB	SO	Avg	OBP	Slg
2000	66	145	31	37	9	1	6	26	1	20	45	.255	.345	.455
Career	75	154	31	39	9	1	6	26	1	20	49	.253	.339	.442

Menechino has always had great strike zone judgement and has yet to produce an on-base percentage lower than .391 in eight minor league seasons. He may now be seizing a big league utility job. 2001 Outlook: B

Bo Porter (Pos: RF, Age: 28, Bats: R)

	G	AB	R	H	D	T	HR	RBI	SB	BB	SO	Avg	OBP	Slg
2000	17	13	3	2	0	0	1	2	0	2	5	.154	.267	.385
Career	41	39	5	7	1	0	1	2	0	4	18	.179	.256	.282

The Athletics waived Porter after the season and Texas picked him up. He has impressive tools and he's also willing to take a walk. 2001 Outlook: C

Ariel Prieto (Pos: RHP, Age: 31)

	W	L	Pct.	ERA	G	GS	Sv	IP	H	BB	SO	HR	Ratio
2000	1	2	.333	5.12	8	6	0	31.2	42	13	19	3	1.74
Career	15	24	.385	4.88	67	60	0	348.2	401	174	229	34	1.65

Prieto returned from 1999 elbow surgery to pitch most of last season at Triple-A. If he's really 31 years old, he may still have some life in him. 2001 Outlook: C

Jon Ratliff (Pos: RHP, Age: 29)

	W	L	Pct.	ERA	G	GS	Sv	IP	H	BB	SO	HR	Ratio
2000	0	0	-	0.00	1	0	0	1.0	0	0	0	0	0.00
Career	0	0	-	0.00	1	0	0	1.0	0	0	0	0	0.00

Ratliff was a first-round pick of the Cubs in 1993. He reached the majors with Oakland after passing through the Tigers and Braves organizations. 2001 Outlook: C

Rich Sauveur (Pos: LHP, Age: 37)

	W	L	Pct.	ERA	G	GS	Sv	IP	H	BB	SO	HR	Ratio
2000	0	0	-	4.35	10	0	0	10.1	13	1	7	3	1.35
Career	0	1	.000	6.07	34	3	0	46.0	58	24	28	10	1.78

Sauveur's been at this game for 18 years, with rarely a sniff of the major leagues. He became a free agent after last season. 2001 Outlook: C

Scott Service (Pos: RHP, Age: 34)

	W	L	Pct.	ERA	G	GS	Sv	IP	H	BB	SO	HR	Ratio
2000	1	2	.333	6.38	20	0	1	36.2	45	19	35	5	1.75
Career	19	19	.500	4.90	284	1	15	361.2	373	164	361	47	1.48

Service split time between Oakland and Triple-A last year. But he's posted major league ERAs in the sixes for three of the past four years. 2001 Outlook: C

Mike Stanley (Pos: 1B/DH, Age: 37, Bats: R)

	G	AB	R	H	D	T	HR	RBI	SB	BB	SO	Avg	OBP	Slg
2000	90	282	33	67	12	0	14	46	0	44	65	.238	.339	.429
Career	1467	4222	625	1138	220	7	187	702	13	652	929	.270	.370	.458

The Athletics signed Stanley last August after the Red Sox had released him. Oakland left him off its postseason roster and he later declared his free agency. He hit .301 against lefthanders last year. 2001 Outlook: C

Luis Vizcaino (Pos: RHP, Age: 23)

	W	L	Pct.	ERA	G	GS	Sv	IP	H	BB	SO	HR	Ratio
2000	0	1	.000	7.45	12	0	0	19.1	25	11	18	2	1.86
Career	0	1	.000	7.15	13	0	0	22.2	28	14	20	3	1.85

Vizcaino looked like an up-and-comer in 1998 when he blew away Double-A. He's stagnated a bit since then but is still relatively young and still has a terrific arm. 2001 Outlook: B

Oakland Athletics Minor League Prospects

Organization Overview:

Oakland continues to stock its team through the draft. The A's developed their stud hitter, Jason Giambi, their anchor at short, Miguel Tejada, budding stars Eric Chavez, Ben Grieve and Ramon Hernandez, and three promising youngsters in the rotation—Tim Hudson, Barry Zito and Mark Mulder. In 2000, the pieces came together and the A's won the American League West with one of the game's lowest payrolls. This offseason, the A's dealt Randy Velarde to make room for rookie Jose Ortiz, and a host of unproven talent will battle for outfield spots. Plus, Justin Miller and Todd Belitz may grab jobs on the pitching staff. It's no accident that *Baseball America* regularly ranks the A's among the best organizations in baseball.

Todd Belitz

Position: P
Bats: L **Throws:** L
Ht: 6' 3" **Wt:** 200
Opening Day Age: 25
Born: 10/23/75 in Des Moines, IA

Recent Statistics

	W	L	ERA	G	GS	Sv	IP	H	R	BB	SO	HR
2000 AAA Durham	1	1	3.83	43	0	2	47.0	33	24	28	46	1
2000 AAA Sacramento	0	1	4.38	12	0	1	12.1	12	6	5	10	2
2000 AL Oakland	0	0	2.70	5	0	0	3.1	4	2	4	3	0

A fourth-round pick by the Devils Rays in 1997, Belitz was acquired in a July trade. Belitz made a smooth transition from starter to reliever last spring with Triple-A Durham, and he capped his successful conversion with five bullpen appearances for Oakland in September. Belitz throws a low-90s fastball that is above average at times. Because he is not afraid to come inside with it—and because his slider can be worked down and in effectively against righthanders—Belitz can face both lefties and righties and be a 1-2 inning guy for the A's. His bulldog mentality and fastball-slider combination work for him. He has a changeup he would call on more if he was starting.

Eric Byrnes

Position: OF
Bats: R **Throws:** R
Ht: 6' 2" **Wt:** 205
Opening Day Age: 25
Born: 2/16/76 in Redwood City, CA

Recent Statistics

	G	AB	R	H	D	T	HR	RBI	SB	BB	SO	Avg
2000 AA Midland	67	259	49	78	25	2	5	37	21	43	38	.301
2000 AAA Sacramento	67	243	55	81	23	1	9	47	12	31	30	.333
2000 AL Oakland	10	10	5	3	0	0	0	0	2	0	1	.300
2000 MLE	134	478	80	135	40	1	10	65	22	49	69	.282

Byrnes hasn't demonstrated much power since his eighth-round selection in 1998, but he shows a makeup to succeed and a work ethic seldom seen. After winning the Class-A California League batting title with a .337 mark in 1999, Byrnes batted .301 at Double-A Midland

and .333 at Triple-A Sacramento this past summer. He homered more frequently at Sacramento, suggesting he may be developing a little power to go with his decent contact skills and speed. Byrnes' swing isn't picture-perfect and his defense needs fine-tuning, but it's hard to expect failure from a guy whom Oakland farm director Keith Lieppman describes as a "relentless player."

Mario Encarnacion

Position: OF
Bats: R **Throws:** R
Ht: 6' 2" **Wt:** 205
Opening Day Age: 23
Born: 9/24/77 in Bani, DR

Recent Statistics

	G	AB	R	H	D	T	HR	RBI	SB	BB	SO	Avg
1999 AA Midland	94	353	69	109	21	4	18	71	9	47	86	.309
1999 AAA Vancouver	39	145	18	35	5	0	3	17	5	6	44	.241
2000 A Modesto	5	15	1	3	0	0	0	1	0	1	4	.200
2000 AAA Sacramento	81	301	51	81	16	3	13	61	15	36	95	.269
2000 MLE	81	290	42	70	14	2	10	50	11	28	97	.241

A 1994 free agent from Oakland's Dominican academy, Encarnacion has required a second season at a classification before dominating at that level. Still, he has the best all-around tools in the organization. His second Triple-A stint in 2000 was hampered by a pesky wrist injury, which sidelined him for six weeks, and a recurring hamstring problem. He'll probably open the 2001 season in Triple-A, where he needs to make consistent contact, be less aggressive on pitches out of the strike zone, and get more wood on the pitch he can drive. Encarnacion should hit consistently for both average and power as his strike-zone judgment improves. Defensively, he features solid center-field skills and a right fielder's arm.

Jason Hart

Position: 1B
Bats: R **Throws:** R
Ht: 6' 3" **Wt:** 225
Opening Day Age: 23
Born: 9/5/77 in Walnut Creek, CA

Recent Statistics

	G	AB	R	H	D	T	HR	RBI	SB	BB	SO	Avg
1999 A Modesto	135	550	96	168	48	2	19	123	2	56	105	.305
2000 AA Midland	135	546	98	178	44	3	30	121	4	67	112	.326
2000 AAA Sacramento	5	18	4	5	1	0	1	4	0	3	7	.278
2000 MLE	140	531	74	150	36	2	21	91	2	42	124	.282

After leading the high Class-A California League in doubles and RBI in 1999, this 1998 fifth-round pick enjoyed an even better season in Double-A in 2000. Hart ranked first among all minor leaguers in hits, extra-base hits and total bases, and he nearly won the Texas league Triple Crown. Despite the reputation of Midland's Christensen Stadium, Hart hit half of his 30 homers on the road, and his slugging percentage on the road was nearly identical to his home mark. Hart hit his 31st homer in Triple-A at season's end, and the big first baseman is likely to start 2001 there. Also known as a hard worker, Hart used two instructional leagues and the last offseason to make himself into a solid first sacker with soft hands.

Oakland

Chad Harville

Position: P   **Opening Day Age:** 24
Bats: R **Throws:** R   **Born:** 9/16/76 in Selmer,
Ht: 5' 9" **Wt:** 180   TN

Recent Statistics

	W	L	ERA	G	GS	Sv	IP	H	R	BB	SO	HR
1999 AA Midland	2	0	2.01	17	0	7	22.1	13	6	9	35	1
1999 AAA Vancouver	1	0	1.75	22	0	11	25.2	24	5	11	36	0
2000 AAA Sacramento	5	3	4.50	53	0	9	64.0	53	35	35	77	8

A second-round pick in 1997, Harville throws a high-90s fastball and a slider, which makes him a closer in training. While he continues to pile up strikeouts at a rate much higher than one per inning, Harville was touched for far more homers at Triple-A Sacramento (8) in 2000 than he had been in his three other minor league seasons combined (3). The surge in homers is a warning that Harville needs more movement on his fastball, which is a little too straight. He's working on a sinker, but it lacks depth and his control of it wavers. Working more effectively in the bottom half of the strike zone with all of his pitches will help him get to Oakland faster.

Justin Miller

Position: P   **Opening Day Age:** 23
Bats: R **Throws:** R   **Born:** 8/27/77 in
Ht: 6' 2" **Wt:** 195   Torrance, CA

Recent Statistics

	W	L	ERA	G	GS	Sv	IP	H	R	BB	SO	HR
1999 A Salem	1	2	4.14	8	8	0	37.0	35	18	11	35	3
2000 AA Midland	5	4	4.55	18	18	0	87.0	74	49	41	82	8
2000 AAA Sacramento	4	1	2.47	9	9	0	54.2	42	18	13	34	3

Coming off a 1999 season in which elbow tendinitis limited him to eight starts, Miller was dealt by Colorado to Oakland last winter. Miller responded with a solid season, surviving hitter-friendly Double-A Midland before posting a 4-1 record and 2.47 ERA in nine starts for Triple-A Sacramento. Miller utilizes four pitches, including a sinking fastball with good life, a splitter that is his put-away pitch, a slider and changeup. He worked hard on the changeup and was able to take it to Triple-A and succeed. Drafted by Colorado in 1997, Miller will battle to join Barry Zito and Mark Mulder in the rotation.

Jose Ortiz

Position: 2B-SS   **Opening Day Age:** 23
Bats: R **Throws:** R   **Born:** 6/13/77 in Santo
Ht: 5' 9" **Wt:** 177   Domingo, DR

Recent Statistics

	G	AB	R	H	D	THR	RBI	SB	BB	SO	Avg
2000 AAA Sacramento	131	518	107	182	34	5	24	108	22	47	64	.351
2000 AL Oakland	7	11	4	2	0	0	0	1	0	2	3	.182
2000 MLE	131	495	88	159	30	3	19	89	16	37	65	.321

Ortiz has quickly climbed the developmental ladder and exploded offensively in his second season in the Pacific Coast League. While he has a typically small build for a middle infielder, Ortiz packs a wallop and drills the ball to all fields. He enjoyed a breakout season at Triple-A Sacramento in which his .351-24-108 numbers were all career highs. Oakland farm director Keith Lieppman credits Ortiz' improved selectivity at the plate for his consistent display of power in 2000. With Miguel Tejada entrenched at shortstop in Oakland, Ortiz has moved to second base, where he actually is better suited. With Randy Velarde dealt to Texas during the offseason, Ortiz is in line for the second-base job.

Mario Valdez

Position: 1B-DH   **Opening Day Age:** 26
Bats: L **Throws:** R   **Born:** 11/19/74 in
Ht: 6' 1" **Wt:** 210   Obregon, Mexico

Recent Statistics

	G	AB	R	H	D	THR	RBI	SB	BB	SO	Avg
2000 AAA Salt Lake	88	317	76	116	24	1	18	85	1	57	46	.366
2000 A Visalia	1	2	0	1	0	0	0	0	0	1	1	.500
2000 AAA Sacramento	17	61	11	14	3	0	2	11	0	9	13	.230
2000 AL Oakland	5	12	0	0	0	0	0	0	0	0	3	.000
2000 MLE	105	354	59	106	22	0	13	65	0	45	62	.299

A 48th round draft pick by the White Sox in 1993, Valdez has shown he can hit for average with some power—and draw walks to boot. Yet, he hasn't been given a chance in three organizations over the last three seasons. He was stuck behind Frank Thomas and Paul Konerko in 1999, and now he has Jason Giambi in front of him. David Ortiz began to blossom in Minnesota in the weeks leading up to Valdez' trade to Oakland last July. Valdez has learned to play the outfield adequately, so he may hook on as a fourth or fifth outfielder.

Others to Watch

Shortstop **Angel Berroa** (21), has the speed, range and power arm to be a flashy fielder. So far, he's been an effective bad-ball hitter, but he needs to work on his strike zone. This fall he showed some power in instructional league that hadn't been seen before. . . The A's second-round pick in 2000, shortstop **Freddie Bynum** (21), has a great arm and a very high ceiling defensively. The lefthanded hitter held his own against both lefties and righties in the short-season Northwest League, and *Baseball America* ranked him the top prospect in the circuit. . . The A's also have second sacker **Esteban German** (22), a 1996 signee from the Dominican who once again made contact, drew walks and ran wild (78 SB) in his second season in the high Class-A California League. . . An impressive outfielder with big-time power potential, **Ryan Ludwick** (22) initially swung for the fences and struggled at high Class-A Modesto in 2000. He later tapped into his power (.264-29-102) when he began stroking the ball to all fields. The A's want him to be a more complete hitter. . . A fourth-round pick in 1999, **Keith Surkont** (23) was much more dominant in his second pro season at high Class-A Visalia (8-7, 2.72), thanks to an excellent curveball and solid changeup. His command of all of his pitches is coming along nicely, and his composure and intensity climb a notch when he gets in trouble.

Safeco Field

Offense

The Mariners' switch to the retractable-roof, grass-surfaced Safeco Field midway through the 1999 season was no minor adjustment. Safeco played as a pitchers' park in '99 and nothing changed last year. A season and a half usually is too short a time frame to make any definitive statements about a park's effects, but in this case it's clear: Safeco is as much a pitchers' haven as the Kingdome was a hitters' park. Open to the cool, heavy Pacific air, Safeco cuts batting averages significantly and limits its homers and extra-base hits, and a new hitters' background did little to boost batting averages last year. It's said the ball carries better with the roof closed. The ball also seems to carry better to right field than it does to left. Another apparent disadvantage for hitters is the glare from the sun and the shadows in day games.

Defense

The park's most dominant feature is its deep power alleys and enormous outfield. As such, it requires a fleet center fielder—even more so than most parks with artificial surfaces. The infield surface seems to produce true hops and prevent infield errors. The eight-foot-high outfield walls allow outfielders occasionally to take away potential home runs.

Who It Helps the Most

The pitchers, almost without exception, are the ones who take best advantage of Safeco, especially those who induce flyballs. Among the pitchers who have been with the Mariners since the park opened, Gil Meche and Paul Abbott have the widest home-road splits so far. Newcomers Kazuhiro Sasaki and Brett Tomko pitched very well at Safeco last year.

Who It Hurts the Most

Conversely, it's hard to find a Mariners hitter who doesn't suffer at Safeco. David Bell, Mike Cameron, John Olerud and Alex Rodriguez have been hit the hardest, losing power and average.

Rookies & Newcomers

Al Martin hit poorly in limited time here last year and isn't a good bet to reach his customary levels this year. The expectations for Carlos Guillen now climb a bit, but he could come up short.

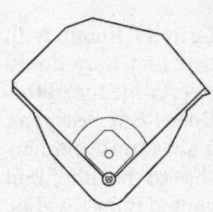

Dimensions: LF-331, LCF-390, CF-405, RCF-386, RF-326

Capacity: 47,145

Elevation: -2 feet

Surface: Grass

Foul Territory: Average

Park Factors

2000 Season

	Home Games			Away Games			
	Mariners	Opp	Total	Mariners	Opp	Total	Index
G	72	72	144	72	72	144	—
Avg	.249	.249	.249	.292	.279	.286	87
AB	2341	2511	4852	2573	2400	4973	98
R	375	321	696	453	396	849	82
H	583	624	1207	751	670	1421	85
2B	109	135	244	160	139	299	84
3B	10	4	14	13	16	29	49
HR	83	66	149	100	90	190	80
BB	367	282	649	321	287	608	109
SO	499	483	982	463	382	845	119
E	43	44	87	46	52	98	89
E-Infield	34	36	70	40	41	81	86
LHB-Avg	.232	.252	.243	.292	.281	.286	85
LHB-HR	23	25	48	15	45	60	85
RHB-Avg	.259	.246	.252	.292	.278	.286	88
RHB-HR	60	41	101	85	45	130	78

1999-2000 (post All-Star 1999)

	Home Games			Away Games			
	Mariners	Opp	Total	Mariners	Opp	Total	Index
G	108	108	216	105	105	210	—
Avg	.247	.248	.248	.280	.282	.281	88
AB	3496	3735	7231	3717	3519	7236	97
R	534	480	1014	599	568	1167	84
H	864	926	1790	1040	993	2033	86
2B	154	192	346	216	206	422	82
3B	13	9	22	17	26	43	51
HR	124	108	232	146	118	264	88
BB	509	413	922	440	426	866	107
SO	754	725	1479	726	560	1286	115
E	64	64	128	73	75	148	84
E-Infield	51	53	104	62	62	124	82
LHB-Avg	.238	.240	.239	.279	.285	.282	85
LHB-HR	43	38	81	27	60	87	97
RHB-Avg	.252	.254	.253	.280	.280	.280	90
RHB-HR	81	70	151	119	58	177	84

2000 Rankings (American League)

- Highest strikeout factor
- Second-highest walk factor
- Lowest batting-average factor
- Lowest run factor
- Lowest hit factor
- Lowest triple factor
- Lowest LHB batting-average factor
- Lowest RHB batting-average factor
- Second-lowest double factor
- Third-lowest home-run factor
- Third-lowest RHB home-run factor

Seattle

Lou Piniella

2000 Season

For years, Piniella loaded the Mariners' lineup with top-to-bottom bashers and hoped that they could blast enough balls into orbit to overcome the club's shaky pitching and woeful bullpen. But last year, as the M's spent their first full season in pitcher-friendly Safeco Field, Piniella shot to the other end of the spectrum. Suddenly, he wanted bunts, walks, steals and various long-ignored National League-style plays. And just as suddenly, he had starting pitching and even a bullpen, which he ran like a manager who'd actually had one before. So who knows what he prefers? But the team won, and he probably liked that best of all.

Offense

Could it be that what we thought were Piniella's natural tendencies were, in actuality, his understandable reactions to the Kingdome? It was clear from the first day of spring training last year that Piniella had completely shifted his emphasis from the longball to little ball. New hitting coach Gerald Perry emphasized working the count; every hitter—even John Olerud, for heaven's sake—was required to practice bunting. . . daily. When the regular-season bell rang, Piniella called for plenty of hit-and-runs, squeezes, sacrifices and steals.

Pitching & Defense

As for Piniella's supposed inability to handle young pitchers, perhaps that was just the Kingdome too. Last year, his best starters were youngsters Freddy Garcia and Gil Meche, and he found the proper roles for Robert Ramsay and Brett Tomko. Having a good bullpen helped to make him much more careful with pitchers' arms. His new emphasis on defense over hitting was illustrated by shifting David Bell to third base replacing the departed all-hit, no-glove Russ Davis.

2001 Outlook

The departure of Alex Rodriguez could make Piniella a significantly "dumber" manager this year. He faces, at best, an uphill battle to remain in contention, and at worst, a full-blown rebuilding project.

Born: 8/28/43 in Tampa, FL

Playing Experience: 1964-1984, Bal, Cle, KC, NYY

Managerial Experience: 14 seasons

Manager Statistics

Year	Team, Lg	W	L	Pct	GB	Finish
2000	Seattle, AL	91	71	.562	0.5	2nd West
14 Seasons		1110	1020	.521	—	—

2000 Starting Pitchers by Days Rest

	<=3	4	5	6+
Mariners Starts	1	97	36	19
Mariners ERA	10.38	4.79	4.17	4.78
AL Avg Starts	2	88	40	22
AL ERA	4.87	5.03	5.03	5.28

2000 Situational Stats

	Lou Piniella	AL Average
Hit & Run Success %	30.8	35.1
Stolen Base Success %	68.5	68.8
Platoon Pct.	50.4	57.8
Defensive Subs	52	23
High-Pitch Outings	1	13
Quick/Slow Hooks	25/12	18/19
Sacrifice Attempts	73	55

2000 Rankings (American League)

- 1st in double steals (7) and defensive substitutions (52)
- 2nd in stolen base attempts (178), steals of second base (108), sacrifice bunt attempts (73), sacrifice-bunt percentage (87.7) and 2+ pitching changes in low-scoring games (26)
- 3rd in steals of third base (14) and intentional walks (32)

David Bell

Position: 3B/2B
Bats: R **Throws:** R
Ht: 5'10" **Wt:** 190

Opening Day Age: 28
Born: 9/14/72 in
Cincinnati, OH
ML Seasons: 6

2000 Season

Coming off his fine season in 1999, David Bell had a big letdown in 2000. The team's regular second baseman in '99, Bell got off to a slow start and was moved from second to third, where he spent most of the rest of the year and continued to field well. He struggled at the plate all season before recovering in September.

Hitting

Perhaps Bell's dropoff could have been foreseen. Last year, the M's midseason move out of the Kingdome—where Bell always had hit well—into Safeco Field sent Bell into a two-month tailspin. He didn't hit well at all at Safeco in 1999, and nothing changed last year. Bell, a flyball hitter who needs to pull the ball to drive it, found Safeco's left-field fence harder to reach; the enormous outfield routinely swallowed up his flies. He did learn to take outside pitches from southpaws the other way, and he hit well against them after having had little success against them in the past.

Baserunning & Defense

Bell's switch from second to third was a reflection of his versatility, not his inadequacy at the keystone. He continued to make appearances at second, where he showed decent range, a strong arm and a good pivot. At third, the same virtues made him the team's best defensive third baseman. He has average speed and runs conservatively.

2001 Outlook

With the return of Mark McLemore to Seattle guaranteed for 2001, Bell likely will find himself at third again this year. He probably will remain a regular, and could improve his numbers as he continues to adjust to his new home field. He probably won't match his impressive 1999 figures again unless he winds up in a more favorable park.

Overall Statistics

	G	AB	R	H	D	T	HR	RBI	SB	BB	SO	Avg	OBP	Slg
2000	133	454	57	112	24	2	11	47	2	42	66	.247	.316	.381
Career	591	1913	231	486	105	10	46	214	12	151	296	.254	.310	.392

Where He Hits the Ball

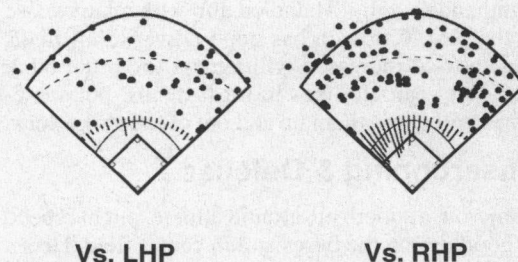

Vs. LHP   **Vs. RHP**

2000 Situational Stats

	AB	H	HR	RBI	Avg		AB	H	HR	RBI	Avg
Home	225	55	4	20	.244	LHP	108	31	4	15	.287
Road	229	57	7	27	.249	RHP	346	81	7	32	.234
First Half	277	64	6	31	.231	Sc Pos	128	31	2	36	.242
Scnd Half	177	48	5	16	.271	Clutch	61	13	1	3	.213

2000 Rankings (American League)

- 3rd in lowest batting average vs. righthanded pitchers
- 6th in lowest slugging percentage vs. righthanded pitchers (.358)
- 7th in lowest batting average and lowest batting average at home
- 8th in lowest slugging percentage and lowest on-base percentage vs. righthanded pitchers (.312)
- 9th in errors at third base (12)
- 10th in lowest groundball/flyball ratio (0.9)
- Led the Mariners in batting average on a 3-1 count (.500)

Mike Cameron

2000 Season

Talk about having big shoes to fill. Mike Cameron came over from Cincinnati in the Ken Griffey Jr. trade and drew the unenviable assignment of replacing the Seattle icon in center field. To the surprise of the Mariners—and their fans—he proved to be just as gifted a fielder, and his hitting was quite respectable. Under the most difficult circumstances, Cameron rose to the challenge and put together his best season.

Hitting

Safeco Field masked Cameron's growth as a hitter last year; in another park he might have hit over .300 and approached 30 home runs. His most significant improvement was his performance against righthanders, who'd handled him with relative ease in the past. Cameron has good power to all fields and showed increased willingness to go the other way last year. He likes to hit fastballs, but sometimes will chase them up and out of the strike zone.

Baserunning & Defense

Cameron, a superb all-around athlete, put his speed to good use on the bases and in center field. He's a daring baserunner and high-percentage basestealer, though he rarely runs on lefties. He's also an excellent outfielder who gets terrific jumps and outruns plenty of long flies. His leaping catches to take away homers last year were—dare we say?—Griffeyesque. His arm is strong enough for the position.

2001 Outlook

Cameron hit all over the batting order last year, and what he must do now is find an offensive role. He doesn't have quite enough power to be an RBI man, although he gets on base just enough to consider wasting his power at the top of the lineup. A little growth in either direction could determine the eventual path he takes. Either way, he'll likely keep producing, especially with Griffey's shadow one year removed.

Position: CF
Bats: R **Throws:** R
Ht: 6' 2" **Wt:** 190

Opening Day Age: 28
Born: 1/8/73 in LaGrange, GA
ML Seasons: 6

Overall Statistics

	G	AB	R	H	D	T	HR	RBI	SB	BB	SO	Avg	OBP	Slg
2000	155	543	96	145	28	4	19	78	24	78	133	.267	.365	.438
Career	597	1909	310	473	98	21	63	244	112	254	502	.248	.341	.420

Where He Hits the Ball

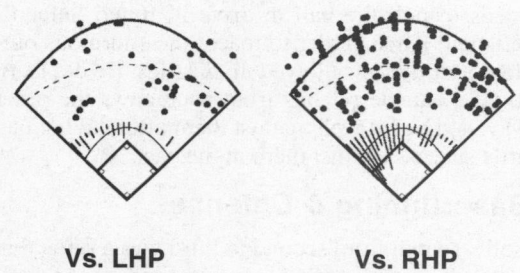

Vs. LHP   **Vs. RHP**

2000 Situational Stats

	AB	H	HR	RBI	Avg		AB	H	HR	RBI	Avg
Home	255	56	5	29	.220	LHP	110	30	3	14	.273
Road	288	89	14	49	.309	RHP	433	115	16	64	.266
First Half	288	75	11	40	.260	Sc Pos	136	36	3	56	.265
Scnd Half	255	70	8	38	.275	Clutch	62	18	5	15	.290

2000 Rankings (American League)

- 1st in lowest batting average on an 0-2 count (.033)
- 2nd in lowest batting average at home
- 3rd in errors in center field (6)
- 4th in lowest fielding percentage in center field (.985)
- 5th in most pitches seen per plate appearance (4.16)
- 7th in strikeouts
- Led the Mariners in hit by pitch (9), strikeouts, batting average vs. lefthanded pitchers, slugging percentage vs. lefthanded pitchers (.427) and highest percentage of extra bases taken as a runner (63.8)

Freddy Garcia

2000 Season

A hairline fracture in his right leg prevented righthander Freddie Garcia from improving upon his fine rookie season in 2000. He suffered the injury in late April and was out until July. After returning in July, he pitched as well as he had in 1999, becoming the Mariners' best second-half starter and quickly re-established himself as their future ace.

Pitching

Garcia has good stuff, and unlike many pitchers his age, he knows how to use it. He changes speeds very well, hitting his spots with a low-90s fastball and a terrific changeup that he's come to rely upon more heavily. He also has good movement on his curveball and sinking two-seamer. For some reason, he's more effective from the stretch—an attribute that helps him pitch out of trouble when he needs to. As a big, strong guy with nice, loose arm action, he maintains his stuff well into the late innings. Garcia still occasionally loses focus at key moments, but he is maturing, as he demonstrated with several strong performances in the postseason.

Defense

Garcia concentrates more on getting the out at the plate than holding runners, and is easy to run on. He did ring up a pair of pickoffs last season, however. He's also prone to occasional concentration lapses in the field. He's a good athlete, so there's no reason his fielding can't improve.

2001 Outlook

One positive aspect of his two-month layoff last year is that it prevented him from being overworked. That was a particular concern after he threw a high number of innings in 1999. His arm should be fresher than ever this year, and he could be in line for his best season. Few pitchers are better bets to improve their numbers in 2001.

Position: SP
Bats: R **Throws:** R
Ht: 6' 4" **Wt:** 235

Opening Day Age: 24
Born: 10/6/76 in Caracas, Venezuela
ML Seasons: 2

Overall Statistics

	W	L	Pct.	ERA	G	GS	Sv	IP	H	BB	SO	HR	Ratio
2000	9	5	.643	3.91	21	20	0	124.1	112	64	79	16	1.42
Career	26	13	.667	4.01	54	53	0	325.2	317	154	249	34	1.45

How Often He Throws Strikes

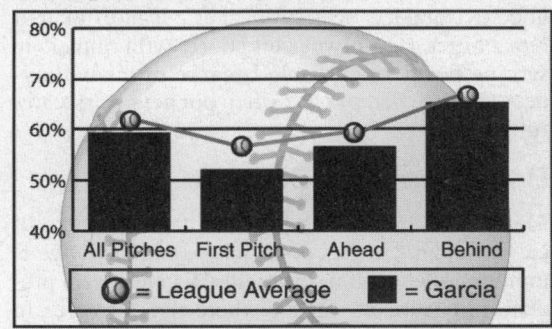

= League Average   = Garcia

2000 Situational Stats

	W	L	ERA	Sv	IP		AB	H	HR	RBI	Avg
Home	4	4	4.43	0	63.0	LHB	246	67	12	37	.272
Road	5	1	3.38	0	61.1	RHB	219	45	4	14	.205
First Half	2	1	6.00	0	24.0	Sc Pos	124	28	3	37	.226
Scnd Half	7	4	3.41	0	100.1	Clutch	35	11	3	3	.314

2000 Rankings (American League)

- 3rd in lowest batting average allowed vs. righthanded batters
- 5th in errors at pitcher (3)
- 6th in balks (2)
- 8th in lowest batting average allowed with runners in scoring position
- Led the Mariners in balks (2)

Seattle

Al Martin

2000 Season

One of Seattle's few moves that backfired last year was the deadline trade with San Diego for Al Martin. The M's took on Martin—and his not inconsiderable contract—to give them outfield depth down the stretch, but Martin faded badly and did very little for Seattle after hitting well for the Padres earlier in the year.

Hitting

Martin's principal weakness at the plate is continued inability to hit lefties, as he is essentially a platoon player. A pull hitter with good power who feasts on fastballs, Martin is vulnerable to breaking balls and offspeed pitches. He doesn't have a very good eye and has been miscast as a leadoff man or No. 2 hitter. He's always hit poorly with runners in scoring position, probably because of his willingness to chase bad pitches when pitchers work carefully to him.

Baserunning & Defense

Martin has above-average speed but isn't much of an outfielder. He gets poor jumps, and his range is unimpressive even in left field. His weak arm prevents him from playing anywhere else, however. In the past, he's put his speed to better use on the basepaths, but a knee injury bothered him last year and he was thrown out on nine of 19 stolen-base attempts.

2001 Outlook

Martin is under contract for $5 million for this year, which virtually guarantees two things: the M's won't be able to deal him without eating a good portion of his salary, and wherever he ends up, he won't be left to rot on the bench. Seattle did not pick up Rickey Henderson's 2001 option, so the team may be able to use Martin in left field. But he will need a platoon partner, and his stats could continue to suffer in Safeco Field.

Position: LF
Bats: L **Throws:** L
Ht: 6' 2" **Wt:** 214

Opening Day Age: 33
Born: 11/24/67 in West Covina, CA
ML Seasons: 9

Overall Statistics

	G	AB	R	H	D	T	HR	RBI	SB	BB	SO	Avg	OBP	Slg
2000	135	480	81	137	15	10	15	36	10	36	85	.285	.338	.452
Career	1032	3721	604	1044	193	44	122	417	162	336	769	.281	.341	.454

Where He Hits the Ball

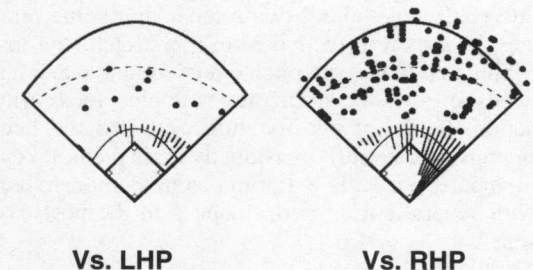

Vs. LHP　　　　**Vs. RHP**

2000 Situational Stats

	AB	H	HR	RBI	Avg		AB	H	HR	RBI	Avg
Home	218	62	10	21	.284	LHP	77	12	0	3	.156
Road	262	75	5	15	.286	RHP	403	125	15	33	.310
First Half	292	88	10	22	.301	Sc Pos	95	16	1	18	.168
Scnd Half	188	49	5	14	.261	Clutch	60	14	0	1	.233

2000 Rankings (American League)

- Did not rank near the top or bottom in any category

Edgar Martinez

2000 Season

All things considered, last year might have been Edgar Martinez' best season. Though his numbers—with the exception of his RBI count—weren't all that much better than what he'd done in the past, they meant much more this time around. For one thing, Seattle was playing its first full season in pitcher-friendly Safeco Field, where each run meant a lot more than it did back in the Kingdome. The M's, adjusting to their new park, no longer featured a lineup of top-to-bottom sluggers, and they relied more heavily than ever on Martinez' run-producing abilities. Martinez, who lifted weights all winter and came to camp stronger than ever, was up to the challenge.

Hitting

With excellent power to all fields, a terrific batting eye and a line-drive bat, Martinez has few weaknesses at the plate. Pitchers try to feed him hard stuff in on his hands, but even this approach can be dangerous when a pitch strays too far toward the plate. A selective, studious hitter, Martinez is the master of waiting for a particular pitch and jumping on it when he gets it. He's not only a terrific RBI man, but also creates RBI opportunities for the hitters behind him, annually placing among the league leaders in on-base percentage.

Baserunning & Defense

Martinez, a former third baseman who was moved to DH to preserve his health, plays only a handful of games a year in the field (as required in interleague contests), always at first base. He has survived these forays uninjured, which is the main objective. He doesn't run well but is fairly aggressive for a player of his age. He knows his limits when it comes to basestealing, however.

2001 Outlook

The Mariners picked up Martinez' 2001 option for a cool $5.5 million, and were happy to pay that sum. Even as he enters his late 30s, Martinez has shown no signs of slowing down, and Seattle expects him to continue to anchor its lineup, especially with Alex Rodriguez' departure to Texas.

Position: DH
Bats: R **Throws:** R
Ht: 5'11" **Wt:** 200

Opening Day Age: 38
Born: 1/2/63 in New York, NY
ML Seasons: 14

Overall Statistics

	G	AB	R	H	D	T	HR	RBI	SB	BB	SO	Avg	OBP	Slg
2000	153	556	100	180	31	0	37	145	3	96	95	.324	.423	.579
Career	1540	5432	980	1738	403	14	235	925	43	973	841	.320	.426	.529

Where He Hits the Ball

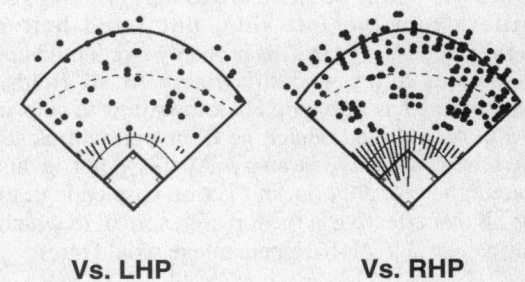

Vs. LHP   **Vs. RHP**

2000 Situational Stats

	AB	H	HR	RBI	Avg		AB	H	HR	RBI	Avg
Home	263	80	19	70	.304	LHP	92	33	9	34	.359
Road	293	100	18	75	.341	RHP	464	147	28	111	.317
First Half	285	101	23	87	.354	Sc Pos	171	55	11	102	.322
Scnd Half	271	79	14	58	.292	Clutch	68	22	3	11	.324

2000 Rankings (American League)

- 1st in RBI
- 2nd in lowest percentage of swings on the first pitch (12.1) and lowest percentage of extra bases taken as a runner (22.0)
- 5th in highest percentage of pitches taken (64.0)
- Led the Mariners in batting average, hits, singles, RBI, on-base percentage, batting average with runners in scoring position, batting average in the clutch, batting average vs. righthanded pitchers, cleanup slugging percentage (.553), on-base percentage vs. righthanded pitchers (.417), batting average at home and lowest percentage of swings on the first pitch (12.1)
- Led designated hitters in RBI, sacrifice flies (8) and most pitches seen per plate appearance (4.03)

Mark McLemore

2000 Season

Mark McLemore was signed by the Mariners to get on base at the top of their batting order. He ultimately failed in that respect, but he ended up making important contributions anyhow. He began the season in left field before being moved back to his natural position, second base. His slow start—perhaps related to his offseason knee surgery—prompted the club to sign Rickey Henderson. Dropped to the bottom of the order, McLemore finished strongly and set a career high with 30 steals. His fine play at second base was an asset all year long.

Hitting

The switch-hitting McLemore usually is a stronger hitter from the left side, but fared better righthanded last year. This probably won't hold up. A patient hitter who hits liners to all fields, McLemore has little pop but knows how to coax a walk. As a skilled bunter, he fit in well with Seattle's new offensive strategy. At this point in his career, he probably doesn't get on base enough to be all that effective at the top of the order, to which his career .346 on-base percentage would attest.

Baserunning & Defense

Age and persistent knee problems have cut into McLemore's range afield, but he still is a reliable defender with a strong arm and an excellent double-play pivot. He's also an underrated outfielder who gets to the ball quickly. McLemore also runs the bases aggressively and is something of a stolen-base threat against righthanded pitchers.

2001 Outlook

In light of the loss of free-agent shortstop Alex Rodriguez, the Mariners are probably just as happy that McLemore earned his self-vesting option for 2001 at the bargain-basement price of $2 million. His glove and his legs should be enough to keep him in the lineup unless his bat completely collapses.

Position: 2B/LF
Bats: B **Throws:** R
Ht: 5'11" **Wt:** 207

Opening Day Age: 36
Born: 10/4/64 in San Diego, CA
ML Seasons: 15

Overall Statistics

	G	AB	R	H	D	T	HR	RBI	SB	BB	SO	Avg	OBP	Slg
2000	138	481	72	118	23	1	3	46	30	81	78	.245	.353	.316
Career	1427	4887	748	1260	193	34	37	459	210	666	732	.258	.346	.334

Where He Hits the Ball

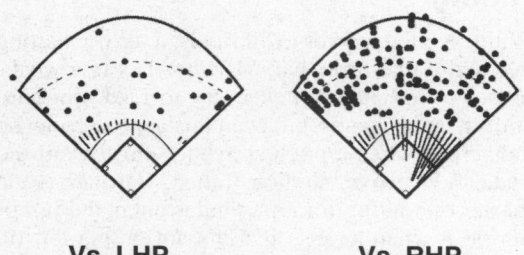

Vs. LHP   **Vs. RHP**

2000 Situational Stats

	AB	H	HR	RBI	Avg		AB	H	HR	RBI	Avg
Home	227	50	2	21	.220	LHP	75	22	1	6	.293
Road	254	68	1	25	.268	RHP	406	96	2	40	.236
First Half	274	64	1	23	.234	Sc Pos	112	29	0	39	.259
Scnd Half	207	54	2	23	.261	Clutch	61	16	0	5	.262

2000 Rankings (American League)

- 1st in caught stealing (14), lowest slugging percentage, lowest on-base percentage for a leadoff hitter (.292) and lowest slugging percentage vs. righthanded pitchers (.305)
- 2nd in fielding percentage at second base (.987), highest percentage of pitches taken (64.6) and lowest HR frequency (160.3 ABs per HR)
- 3rd in lowest batting average with the bases loaded (.000) and lowest batting average at home
- Led the Mariners in sacrifice bunts (11), caught stealing (14), highest groundball/flyball ratio (1.5), bunts in play (17), highest percentage of pitches taken (64.6) and highest percentage of swings put into play (50.4)

John Olerud

2000 Season

The 2000 season was a quiet one for John Olerud, as most are. After signing a three-year, free-agent contract with Seattle over the winter, he ran hot and cold over the course of the season but finished with fairly typical numbers. He didn't hit very well in Safeco Field, but he wasn't alone in that regard and fared well overall at the plate. As he always does, he hit for a good average with plenty of doubles, drew walks, drove in runs and played superb defense.

Hitting

Olerud's effortless swings send liners all over the diamond. He's a patient, disciplined hitter who collects doubles by placing the ball into the gaps and down the left field line. He has enough power to reach the fences when he pulls the ball. Olerud long ago shook off his platoon label, but he hasn't hit well against lefties the last two years. He's strongest on low pitches and covers the entire plate well.

Baserunning & Defense

Olerud plays Gold Glove defense without the flash and finally pocketed his first career award in 2000. He has quick reactions and great hands, routinely scoops difficult throws and is very good at running down popups down the line. He led American League first basemen in fielding percentage and had 41 more assists than any other AL first sacker. He doesn't have an ounce of speed, however.

2001 Outlook

Of all the hitters in the major leagues, Olerud is perhaps the best bet to stay healthy and post good numbers in any given season. Whenever he has his first major injury or off year, it will come as a shock to everyone. The only thing that might change for Olerud this year is that he might move up to the third spot in the lineup now that Alex Rodriguez has moved on.

Position: 1B
Bats: L **Throws:** L
Ht: 6' 5" **Wt:** 220

Opening Day Age: 32
Born: 8/5/68 in Seattle, WA
ML Seasons: 12
Pronunciation: OAL-uh-rude

Overall Statistics

	G	AB	R	H	D	T	HR	RBI	SB	BB	SO	Avg	OBP	Slg
2000	159	565	84	161	45	0	14	103	0	102	96	.285	.392	.439
Career	1555	5330	836	1595	367	11	186	865	8	922	732	.299	.404	.477

Where He Hits the Ball

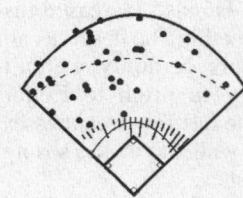 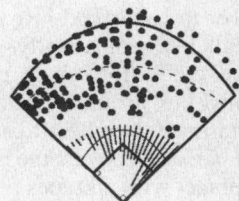

Vs. LHP   **Vs. RHP**

2000 Situational Stats

	AB	H	HR	RBI	Avg		AB	H	HR	RBI	Avg
Home	284	71	8	52	.250	LHP	124	30	0	23	.242
Road	281	90	6	51	.320	RHP	441	131	14	80	.297
First Half	307	94	8	60	.306	Sc Pos	155	46	5	90	.297
Scnd Half	258	67	6	43	.260	Clutch	64	16	1	9	.250

2000 Rankings (American League)

- 1st in fielding percentage at first base (.996)
- 2nd in lowest slugging percentage vs. lefthanded pitchers (.315)
- 4th in doubles
- 5th in intentional walks (11) and games played
- 6th in sacrifice flies (10) and lowest cleanup slugging percentage (.525)
- 9th in walks and errors at first base (5)
- 10th in highest percentage of pitches taken (63.2) and lowest batting average at home
- Led the Mariners in at-bats, doubles, walks, intentional walks (11), GDPs (16), plate appearances (683), on-base percentage vs. lefthanded pitchers (.354) and games played

Seattle

Alex Rodriguez

2000 Season

Alex Rodriguez had his best season last year, but no one knew it. Safeco Field dulled his numbers, preventing him from making a run at the Triple Crown. He had the best road numbers in the American League, with a league-high 28 homers and 81 RBI, and a .356 average, third-best in the circuit. He did all this while showing a vastly improved batting eye, nearly doubling his walk total. No one even thought to ask if he felt any pressure filling the departed Ken Griffey Jr.'s third spot in the batting order.

Hitting

Rodriguez' power always has extended from foul pole to foul pole, but he showed more strength than ever to right field last year. He also increased his walk rate dramatically—something he deserves all the credit for, since pitchers certainly weren't working around Rodriguez to pitch to Edgar Martinez. Needless to say, he has few weaknesses at bat, as he covers the plate well and makes strong contact with all types of pitches.

Baserunning & Defense

In an effort to conserve his strength over the course of the summer, and as a natural result of dropping from the second to the third spot in the order, Rodriguez ran less often last year. He remained an excellent percentage basestealer but did almost all of his running against righthanded pitchers. He also had his best year in the field, committing only 10 errors and leading major league shortstops with 123 double plays. His strong arm is his biggest asset, but he also has good hands and positions himself well.

2001 Outlook

In a deal that sent shockwaves through the baseball establishment, Rodriguez left Seattle for Texas by agreeing to a 10-year, $252 million contract. If he doesn't get bogged down in the pressure generated by his megadeal, Rodriguez should find his new ballpark—unlike Safeco Field—very beneficial to his righthanded bat. He joins a potent Texas lineup that also includes Rafael Palmeiro, Ivan Rodriguez, Andres Galarraga, Ken Caminiti, Rusty Greer and Gabe Kapler.

Position: SS
Bats: R **Throws:** R
Ht: 6' 3" **Wt:** 210

Opening Day Age: 25
Born: 7/27/75 in New York, NY
ML Seasons: 7
Nickname: A-Rod

Overall Statistics

	G	AB	R	H	D	T	HR	RBI	SB	BB	SO	Avg	OBP	Slg
2000	148	554	134	175	34	2	41	132	15	100	121	.316	.420	.606
Career	790	3126	627	966	194	13	189	595	133	310	616	.309	.374	.561

Where He Hits the Ball

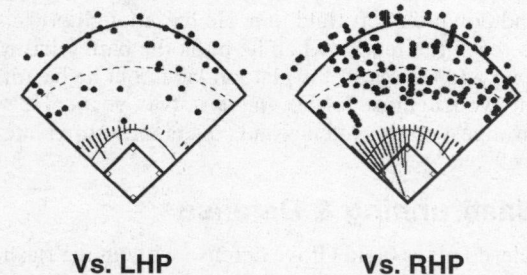

Vs. LHP   **Vs. RHP**

2000 Situational Stats

	AB	H	HR	RBI	Avg		AB	H	HR	RBI	Avg
Home	265	72	13	51	.272	LHP	93	34	11	29	.366
Road	289	103	28	81	.356	RHP	461	141	30	103	.306
First Half	316	109	24	78	.345	Sc Pos	149	44	11	87	.295
Scnd Half	238	66	17	54	.277	Clutch	59	12	5	12	.203

2000 Rankings (American League)

- 2nd in runs scored and most pitches seen per plate appearance (4.23)
- 3rd in batting average on the road and fielding percentage at shortstop (.986)
- 4th in home runs, sacrifice flies (11) and pitches seen (2,842)
- 5th in slugging percentage and HR frequency (13.5 ABs per HR)
- Led the Mariners in home runs, runs scored, total bases (336), sacrifice flies (11), times on base (282), pitches seen (2,842), slugging percentage, HR frequency (13.5 ABs per HR), most pitches seen per plate appearance (4.23), fewest GDPs per GDP situation (6.5%) and slugging percentage vs. righthanded pitchers (.573)

Kazuhiro Sasaki

2000 Season

When Kazuhiro Sasaki signed with the Mariners over the winter, few knew what to expect. Though he was introduced as the best reliever in Japanese League history, some wondered if he was past his prime or could adapt to American baseball. Plus, he was coming off elbow surgery. His early performance only reinforced the doubts. Though he won the closer's job from Jose Mesa in spring training, his first month in the majors was rocky, as he allowed five homers in his first 12 appearances. He steadily gained velocity and effectiveness as the season wore on, however, and was one of the game's top closers in the second half. Overall, it was a fine season—more than good enough to win the American League Rookie of the Year Award.

Pitching

Sasaki's signature pitch is a diving forkball, reminiscent of Hideo Nomo's in his prime. Sasaki throws harder than Nomo ever did, however, routinely reaching the mid-90s after his arm strength fully returned. Hitters usually can't distinguish between his forkball and his heater until it's too late. He gives up an occasional homer when a hitter guesses right on a high fastball, but is very tough to hit overall.

Defense

As a strikeout/flyball pitcher, Sasaki rarely has to flag down comebackers or cover first base but does the job when necessary, remaining error free thus far in the major leagues. His heavy splitter makes it tough for catchers to get off good throws, and all eight stolen-base attempts against him were successful.

2001 Outlook

It looks like the Mariners have uncovered a gem in Sasaki, and don't think they don't know it. In early November, the team exercised a $5 million option on its stopper for the 2002 season. There should be no fears that he'll lose his effectiveness once the novelty wears off, as Nomo did. Nomo relied more on his unique delivery and began to slip during the second half of his very first season; Sasaki, on the other hand, succeeds with pure stuff and was even more effective his second time around.

Position: RP
Bats: R **Throws:** R
Ht: 6' 4" **Wt:** 209

Opening Day Age: 33
Born: 2/22/68 in Sendai, Japan
ML Seasons: 1
Nickname: Daimajin

Overall Statistics

	W	L	Pct.	ERA	G	GS	Sv	IP	H	BB	SO	HR	Ratio
2000	2	5	.286	3.16	63	0	37	62.2	42	31	78	10	1.16
Career	2	5	.286	3.16	63	0	37	62.2	42	31	78	10	1.16

How Often He Throws Strikes

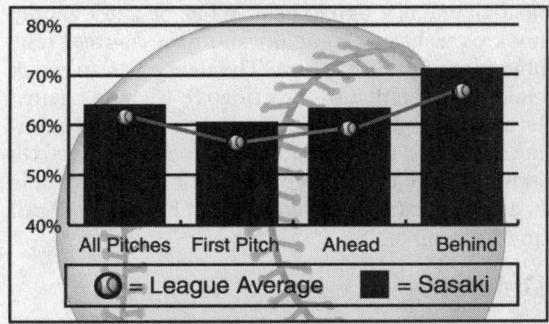

= League Average ◯ ■ = Sasaki

2000 Situational Stats

	W	L	ERA	Sv	IP		AB	H	HR	RBI	Avg
Home	2	1	1.60	18	33.2	LHB	116	23	8	20	.198
Road	0	4	4.97	19	29.0	RHB	112	19	2	9	.170
First Half	1	5	3.48	19	33.2	Sc Pos	75	13	3	20	.173
Scnd Half	1	0	2.79	18	29.0	Clutch	149	22	4	20	.148

2000 Rankings (American League)

- 1st in save percentage (92.5), lowest batting average allowed in relief with runners on base (.168) and most strikeouts per nine innings in relief (11.2)
- 2nd in lowest batting average allowed in relief (.184)
- 3rd in saves and lowest batting average allowed in relief with runners in scoring position (.173)
- Led the Mariners in saves, games finished (58), save opportunities (40), save percentage (92.5), first batter efficiency (.218), lowest batting average allowed in relief with runners on base (.168), lowest batting average allowed in relief with runners in scoring position (.173) and relief ERA (3.16)

Seattle

Aaron Sele

2000 Season

It looks like Aaron Sele got the last laugh on the Orioles. Sele, a free agent, signed with Baltimore over the winter, but the O's voided the deal when they didn't like the results of his physical. Undaunted, Sele signed with Seattle and didn't miss a single start. He won 17 games to help the Mariners reach the playoffs, while the Orioles sunk like a stone.

Pitching

Sele's effectiveness depends largely upon his command of a superb overhand curve. When he's able to spot it close enough to the strike zone to make hitters chase it, he mixes it with his upper-80s fastball and is tough to beat. When he can't get the hook over, however, he doesn't have another reliable pitch to fall back on. The deuce has so much sinking action that it's an effective weapon against lefties and righties alike. He's shown decent stamina in the past but often ran out of gas after the sixth inning last year. A native of Washington state, Sele is a cold-weather pitcher who's at his best in April and September.

Defense

Sele has a below-average pickoff move and isn't especially quick to the plate, but he cuts off the running game well for a righthander by varying his delivery enough to keep runners off balance. As a fielder, he's mobile enough but can be scatter-armed at times.

2001 Outlook

Regardless of what the Orioles' medical staff think they saw on Sele's X-rays, he's earned the right to be called a durable, reliable starter. He's been blessed with good run support over the last few years and could just as easily win 13 games as 17, but he'll likely approach 200 innings again and pitch well enough to keep winning. . . and to keep the O's ruing their decision, especially since Baltimore ace Mike Mussina left for the Yankees in late November.

Position: SP
Bats: R **Throws:** R
Ht: 6' 5" **Wt:** 215

Opening Day Age: 30
Born: 6/25/70 in Golden Valley, MN
ML Seasons: 8
Pronunciation: SEE-lee

Overall Statistics

	W	L	Pct.	ERA	G	GS	Sv	IP	H	BB	SO	HR	Ratio
2000	17	10	.630	4.51	34	34	0	211.2	221	74	137	17	1.39
Career	92	63	.594	4.46	208	208	0	1251.1	1364	497	968	112	1.49

How Often He Throws Strikes

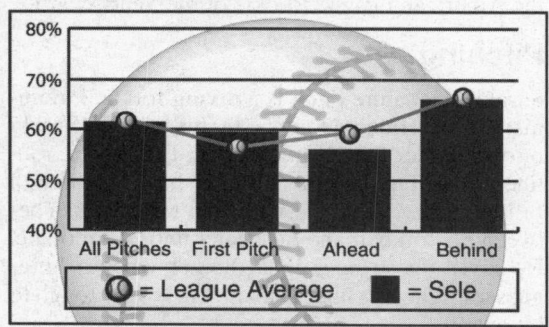

○ = League Average   ■ = Sele

2000 Situational Stats

	W	L	ERA	Sv	IP		AB	H	HR	RBI	Avg
Home	9	5	4.03	0	109.1	LHB	443	122	10	49	.275
Road	8	5	5.01	0	102.1	RHB	373	99	7	46	.265
First Half	11	3	3.95	0	114.0	Sc Pos	172	54	5	77	.314
Scnd Half	6	7	5.16	0	97.2	Clutch	17	9	0	5	.529

2000 Rankings (American League)

- 2nd in shutouts (2) and fewest home runs allowed per nine innings (.72)
- 3rd in games started
- 4th in runners caught stealing (10)
- 5th in wins and errors at pitcher (3)
- Led the Mariners in wins, losses, games started, complete games (2), shutouts (2), innings pitched, hits allowed, batters faced (908), strikeouts, wild pitches (5), pitches thrown (3,395), stolen bases allowed (14), runners caught stealing (10), GDPs induced (23), highest strikeout/walk ratio (1.9), lowest slugging percentage allowed (.397), highest groundball/flyball ratio allowed (1.3), most run support per nine innings (6.6) and most strikeouts per nine innings (5.8)

Ichiro Suzuki

2000 Season

Ichiro Suzuki has been regarded as the best player in Japan, and he has the numbers to back it up. Last year he won his seventh straight batting title with a .387 average, and no one in the Japanese Leagues was within 40 points of him. It was the second-highest single-season average in Japanese League history, bettering his own mark of .385 set in 1994. At the end of the year, the Mariners won an auction for the rights to Suzuki with a sealed bid of $13.1 million, and they ultimately signed him to a three-year deal worth at least $15 million. He will be the first Japanese position player to play in the American major leagues.

Hitting

Ichiro, a lefthanded line-drive hitter who uses the whole field, has been compared to Tony Gwynn. Like Gwynn, he makes excellent contact and rarely strikes out, though he puts the ball in play so often that he doesn't draw very many walks, either. He's reputed to have better power than Gwynn, and should be good for at least a dozen homers. The Mariners intend to bat him leadoff, but he's said to be strong enough to make a good No. 3 hitter.

Baserunning & Defense

Suzuki, a natural center fielder with excellent speed, will move to right in deference to Mike Cameron's defensive prowess. Suzuki should be one of the top-fielding players at that position; scouts say his arm is as accurate as any American outfielder's. He has tremendous quickness and has ranked among the league's stolen-base leaders in the past, although he hasn't run as often over the last three years.

2001 Outlook

Suzuki faces a big adjustment in learning the nuances of American baseball, as well as American culture. But this challenge mustn't be overstated; he trained with the Mariners in spring training in 1999, which should help him feel more comfortable. His friend, Kazuhiro Sasaki, also will be there to help him settle in. At age 27, Suzuki is at the top of his game and should be able to prove that baseball superstardom can transcend national boundaries.

Position: RF
Bats: L **Throws:** R
Ht: 6' 0" **Wt:** 156

Opening Day Age: 27
Born: 10/22/73 in Kasagai, Aichi prefecture, Japan
ML Seasons: 0
Pronunciation: ee-chee-row

Career Statistics (Orix Blue Wave-Japan)

	G	AB	R	H	D	T	HR	RBI	SB	BB	SO	Avg	OBP	Slg
1992	40	95	9	24	5	0	0	5	3	3	11	.253	.276	.305
1993	43	64	4	12	2	0	1	3	0	2	7	.188	.212	.266
1994	130	546	111	210	41	5	13	54	29	51	53	.385	.445	.549
1995	130	524	104	179	23	4	25	80	49	68	52	.342	.432	.544
1996	130	542	104	193	24	4	16	84	35	56	52	.356	.422	.504
1997	135	536	94	185	31	4	17	91	39	62	36	.345	.414	.513
1998	135	506	79	181	36	3	13	71	11	43	35	.358	.414	.518
1999	103	411	80	141	27	2	21	68	12	45	46	.343	.412	.572
2000	105	395	73	153	22	1	12	54	21	54	36	.387	.460	.539
Career	951	3619	658	1278	211	23	118	510	199	384	328	.353	.421	.522

Career Highlights (Japan)

- 2000—Became the first Japanese-born position player to sign with a major league team. Won a Gold Glove Award. Led the Pacific League in batting average and on-base percentage.
- 1999—Won a Gold Glove Award. Led the Pacific League in batting average and on-base percentage.
- 1998—Won a Gold Glove Award. Led the Pacific League in batting average.
- 1997—Won a Gold Glove Award. Led the Pacific League in batting average. Set Japanese baseball record by going 216 consecutive plate appearances without striking out (April 16 through June 25).
- 1996—Won the Pacific League Most Valuable Player Award and a Gold Glove Award. Led the Pacific League in batting average and on-base percentage.
- 1995—Won the Pacific League Most Valuable Player Award and a Gold Glove Award. Led the Pacific League in batting average, on-base percentage, stolen bases and RBI.
- 1994—Won the Pacific League Most Valuable Player Award and a Gold Glove Award. Led the Pacific League in batting average and on-base percentage. Set Japanese baseball record with 210 base hits.

Dan Wilson

2000 Season

Dan Wilson inked a new three-year contract with the Mariners, and promptly went out and had his worst season in years. He hit so poorly in spring training that manager Lou Piniella—usually a Wilson supporter—threatened to bench him in favor of Tom Lampkin. Wilson played, but never really got going and missed time with a pulled oblique muscle in June. Meanwhile, the club picked up journeyman Joe Oliver, who took on an increasing share of the catching chores as the campaign wore on. The late-season acquisition of Chris Widger was a clear vote of no-confidence for Wilson.

Hitting

Wilson caught a lot of games in 1996 and '97 and hasn't been nearly as durable or productive ever since. Plus, the move from the Kingdome to Safeco Field seems to have pushed the fences beyond the reach of most of his drives. It may be a matter of losing bat speed; he seems to struggle to catch up to good heaters. He used to hit lefties well, but hasn't even done that over the last two years. He remains an excellent bunter, which at least allows him to contribute something to the club's new little-ball approach.

Baserunning & Defense

Wilson still is a good thrower from his backstop position, although his release is not as quick as it once was. His ability to block balls and his mobility behind the plate are valued, especially with a staff full of breaking-ball pitchers. He has decent speed but isn't a basestealer.

2001 Outlook

Right now, the only thing that gives Wilson a semblance of job security is his contract. Joe Oliver clearly outplayed him last year, Lampkin is expected to return at some point and Widger still is on the roster. Clearly, Wilson will need to rebound at the plate in order to grab back the bulk of the catching chores.

Position: C
Bats: R **Throws:** R
Ht: 6' 3" **Wt:** 202

Opening Day Age: 32
Born: 3/25/69 in Barrington, IL
ML Seasons: 9

Overall Statistics

	G	AB	R	H	D	T	HR	RBI	SB	BB	SO	Avg	OBP	Slg
2000	90	268	31	63	12	0	5	27	1	22	51	.235	.291	.336
Career	851	2788	305	730	147	9	66	355	19	201	494	.262	.313	.392

Where He Hits the Ball

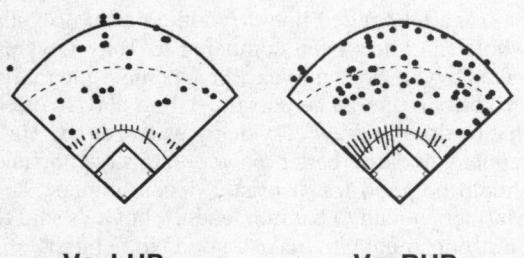

Vs. LHP   **Vs. RHP**

2000 Situational Stats

	AB	H	HR	RBI	Avg		AB	H	HR	RBI	Avg
Home	129	29	2	10	.225	LHP	64	15	2	8	.234
Road	139	34	3	17	.245	RHP	204	48	3	19	.235
First Half	147	36	3	13	.245	Sc Pos	72	17	2	23	.236
Scnd Half	121	27	2	14	.223	Clutch	31	4	1	1	.129

2000 Rankings (American League)

- 7th in sacrifice bunts (11)
- Led the Mariners in sacrifice bunts (11)
- Led AL catchers in sacrifice bunts (11)

Paul Abbott

Position: SP
Bats: R **Throws:** R
Ht: 6' 3" **Wt:** 195

Opening Day Age: 33
Born: 9/15/67 in Van Nuys, CA
ML Seasons: 7

Overall Statistics

	W	L	Pct.	ERA	G	GS	Sv	IP	H	BB	SO	HR	Ratio
2000	9	7	.563	4.22	35	27	0	179.0	164	80	100	23	1.36
Career	21	17	.553	4.29	97	53	0	387.2	344	202	278	45	1.41

2000 Situational Stats

	W	L	ERA	Sv	IP		AB	H	HR	RBI	Avg
Home	4	4	3.40	0	90.0	LHB	370	96	9	42	.259
Road	5	3	5.06	0	89.0	RHB	306	68	14	40	.222
First Half	5	3	4.25	0	84.2	Sc Pos	158	42	10	65	.266
Scnd Half	4	4	4.20	0	94.1	Clutch	23	5	1	1	.217

2000 Season

Paul Abbott debuted with the Minnesota Twins in 1990, and it took him the better part of the next decade to nail down a spot in a major league starting rotation. He began the year in long relief for Seattle, moving into the rotation shortly after Freddy Garcia was injured in April. Abbot made his first start on May 9, and for the rest of the season he was one of the club's most effective starters, posting a 3.98 ERA in 27 starts.

Pitching & Defense

Abbott's out pitch is a terrific changeup that he'll throw at any point in the count. He has good command and mixes in a low-90s fastball and a hard slider. His reliance on the change makes him tough on lefties as well as righties. He works mainly off the outside corner. He has a weak pickoff move but his compact delivery makes him tough to run on.

2001 Outlook

For the first time in his career, Abbott could get a chance to spend an entire season in a major league starting rotation. He probably won't throw enough innings to win more than a dozen games, but he projects to pitch decently and be a creditable third starter.

Jay Buhner

Position: RF
Bats: R **Throws:** R
Ht: 6' 3" **Wt:** 210

Opening Day Age: 36
Born: 8/13/64 in Louisville, KY
ML Seasons: 14
Pronunciation: BYEW-ner
Nickname: Bone

Overall Statistics

	G	AB	R	H	D	T	HR	RBI	SB	BB	SO	Avg	OBP	Slg
2000	112	364	50	92	20	0	26	82	0	59	98	.253	.361	.522
Career	1453	4968	794	1263	231	19	308	960	6	784	1397	.254	.359	.494

2000 Situational Stats

	AB	H	HR	RBI	Avg		AB	H	HR	RBI	Avg
Home	194	44	15	42	.227	LHP	90	25	6	19	.278
Road	170	48	11	40	.282	RHP	274	67	20	63	.245
First Half	213	54	15	54	.254	Sc Pos	102	30	15	62	.294
Scnd Half	151	38	11	28	.252	Clutch	42	8	3	7	.190

2000 Season

After enduring two injury-marred seasons, Jay Buhner was re-signed to a one-year deal with the mutual understanding that he frequently would be rested. The plan worked, as Buhner provided good production in a limited role. Playing right field four or five times a week, he hit well until he injured his wrist in August. He returned in September and played in pain for the rest of the year.

Hitting, Baserunning & Defense

Buhner, a flyball hitter with power to all fields, hits southpaws very well. Last year, he also proved he was still productive against righthanders. A patient hitters who isn't afraid to strike out, Buhner has lost a little bat speed and sometimes has trouble getting to high fastballs. He never was fleet afoot and hamstring problems have made him more tentative and immobile in the outfield. He still catches what he can get to and throws acceptably, though he registered just four assists in 104 games in right. He hasn't swiped a bag in seven years.

2001 Outlook

Buhner signed a one-year, $1.85 million deal with Seattle in December. He'll likely be used to spell newly signed Ichiro Suzuki in right field. He'll also see time in left field, log a handful of games at first base and be used as a backup DH.

Seattle

Carlos Guillen

Position: 3B/SS
Bats: B **Throws:** R
Ht: 6' 1" **Wt:** 180

Opening Day Age: 25
Born: 9/30/75 in
Maracay, Venezuela
ML Seasons: 3
Pronunciation:
GHEE-un

Overall Statistics

	G	AB	R	H	D	T	HR	RBI	SB	BB	SO	Avg	OBP	Slg
2000	90	288	45	74	15	2	7	42	1	28	53	.257	.324	.396
Career	105	346	56	90	16	3	8	50	3	32	68	.260	.324	.393

2000 Situational Stats

	AB	H	HR	RBI	Avg		AB	H	HR	RBI	Avg
Home	133	34	3	18	.256	LHP	50	16	1	7	.320
Road	155	40	4	24	.258	RHP	238	58	6	35	.244
First Half	75	11	0	6	.147	Sc Pos	71	23	3	37	.324
Scnd Half	213	63	7	36	.296	Clutch	28	7	0	1	.250

2000 Season

Carlos Guillen, whose 1999 season was wiped out by a torn knee ligament, returned with much less fanfare last year. He hit poorly in April and May as a backup infielder and was sent down in June. Recalled in July to sub for injured shortstop Alex Rodriguez, Guillen suddenly began to hit, and he continued to see plenty of time at third after Rodriguez returned. He was unsteady at the new position but hit well enough to maintain his status as a future regular in the club's eyes.

Hitting, Baserunning & Defense

The switch-hitting Guillen has decent power on inside pitches from the left side of the plate. His righthanded stroke is more unproven. In the field, he has a very strong arm, as well as the hands and range to play shortstop. His inexperience at third showed last year. He can play second if needed. Despite decent speed, he's been an ineffectual basestealer in both the high minors and the majors.

2001 Outlook

With Alex Rodriguez heading to the Lone Star State, Guillen is the overwhelming favorite to replace Seattle's departed superstar at short. His progress in 2000 suggests he's capable of playing every day and posting respectable numbers.

John Halama

Position: SP
Bats: L **Throws:** L
Ht: 6' 5" **Wt:** 210

Opening Day Age: 29
Born: 2/22/72 in
Brooklyn, NY
ML Seasons: 3
Pronunciation:
huh-LAH-muh

Overall Statistics

	W	L	Pct.	ERA	G	GS	Sv	IP	H	BB	SO	HR	Ratio
2000	14	9	.609	5.08	30	30	0	166.2	206	56	87	19	1.57
Career	26	20	.565	4.74	74	60	0	378.0	436	125	213	39	1.48

2000 Situational Stats

	W	L	ERA	Sv	IP		AB	H	HR	RBI	Avg
Home	9	4	4.35	0	97.1	LHB	166	57	4	26	.343
Road	5	5	6.10	0	69.1	RHB	502	149	15	63	.297
First Half	8	4	4.86	0	87.0	Sc Pos	148	50	5	68	.338
Scnd Half	6	5	5.31	0	79.2	Clutch	26	7	1	1	.269

2000 Season

Like Jamie Moyer, John Halama is the type of pitcher who looks much better in the box score than on the mound. Despite his decent success last year, he often seemed to be on the verge of losing his rotation spot. Consistently average and rarely brilliant, he filled an important role by staying healthy and giving six decent innings every five days.

Pitching & Defense

Halama works both sides of the plate with sinkers, changeups and big, slow curves; by the time he comes with his batting-practice fastball, he usually has the hitter too off-balance to do anything with it. His curve is not an important enough weapon to give him an edge against lefthanded hitters, who've hit him better than righthanded batters in each of the last two years. He's durable and never gets hurt, but he routinely runs out of steam around 90 pitches. Halama has an embarrassingly good pickoff move—he led the American League with 10 pickoffs in 2000.

2001 Outlook

Halama gets the absolute most out of his ability and probably can't do much better than he's done the last two years. On the other hand, he's a low injury risk and is an excellent bet to remain a decent back-of-the-rotation starter.

Rickey Henderson (Hall of Famer)

Position: LF
Bats: R **Throws:** L
Ht: 5'10" **Wt:** 190

Opening Day Age: 42
Born: 12/25/58 in Chicago, IL
ML Seasons: 22

Overall Statistics

	G	AB	R	H	D	T	HR	RBI	SB	BB	SO	Avg	OBP	Slg
2000	123	420	75	98	14	2	4	32	36	88	75	.233	.368	.305
Career	2856	10331	2178	2914	486	62	282	1052	1370	2060	1547	.282	.404	.423

2000 Situational Stats

	AB	H	HR	RBI	Avg		AB	H	HR	RBI	Avg
Home	199	47	2	19	.236	LHP	90	18	0	7	.200
Road	221	51	2	13	.231	RHP	330	80	4	25	.242
First Half	241	55	4	17	.228	Sc Pos	89	23	0	28	.258
Scnd Half	179	43	0	15	.240	Clutch	51	9	0	4	.176

2000 Season

After enjoying a fine comeback year with the Mets in 1999, Rickey Henderson complained from the start of the 2000 season, played poorly and earned his release in May. He landed on his feet, signing with Seattle three days later. As the Mariners' left fielder and leadoff man, he hit poorly but did a decent job getting on base and scoring runs before slumping in September.

Hitting, Baserunning & Defense

Henderson's sole remaining offensive skill is his ability to get on base, mostly via bases on balls. He has trouble getting to the high fastball and what little power he has left seemed to evaporate last year. At this point, he's a liability in left—a tentative defender with a weak arm. He still can steal, however, and swiped 36 bases last year, easily a record for a player his age.

2001 Outlook

Henderson was useful last year, but not useful enough to induce the Mariners to pick up his $3.01 million option, as the club instead gave him a $260,000 buyout. Henderson still has some personal goals to chase—he's 86 hits shy of 3,000 and just 67 runs short of Ty Cobb's mark—so he may try to stick with another club. He's been able to bounce back from poor seasons in the past.

Stan Javier

Position: LF/RF/CF
Bats: B **Throws:** R
Ht: 6' 0" **Wt:** 200

Opening Day Age: 37
Born: 1/9/64 in San Francisco de Macoris, Dominican Republic
ML Seasons: 16
Pronunciation: HAH-vee-air

Overall Statistics

	G	AB	R	H	D	T	HR	RBI	SB	BB	SO	Avg	OBP	Slg
2000	105	342	61	94	18	5	5	40	4	42	64	.275	.351	.401
Career	1674	4766	737	1276	211	39	53	470	235	542	792	.268	.343	.362

2000 Situational Stats

	AB	H	HR	RBI	Avg		AB	H	HR	RBI	Avg
Home	165	41	5	22	.248	LHP	55	16	0	7	.291
Road	177	53	0	18	.299	RHP	287	78	5	33	.272
First Half	194	52	3	19	.268	Sc Pos	83	26	2	35	.313
Scnd Half	148	42	2	21	.284	Clutch	52	12	0	7	.231

2000 Season

Stan Javier was signed as free agent before the 2000 season to be the Mariners' fourth outfielder and did exactly what he was expected to. Javier played all three outfield positions, frequently spelling Jay Buhner in right and Rickey Henderson in left. As always, he hit for decent average and gave the bench good flexibility.

Hitting, Baserunning & Defense

Javier is a true switch-hitter, spraying line drives all over the field with equal skill from either side of the plate. He rarely reaches the fences but can do the little things like work a walk, lay down a sacrifice and hit behind the runner. Bothered by a minor foot problem and a groin injury last year, he didn't run as often. He's slowed down a bit and now has average speed, but he makes up for it in the outfield by positioning himself well and getting good jumps. Javier has enough range for center field and is above-average in left and right field. His arm is accurate but not very strong.

2001 Outlook

The Mariners exercised their $1.5 million option on Javier for 2001 in early November. One of the most consistent hitters in the league from season to season, Javier also should remain one of the better fourth outfielders around.

Gil Meche

Position: SP
Bats: R **Throws:** R
Ht: 6' 3" **Wt:** 200

Opening Day Age: 22
Born: 9/8/78 in Lafayette, LA
ML Seasons: 2
Pronunciation: MESH

Overall Statistics

	W	L	Pct.	ERA	G	GS	Sv	IP	H	BB	SO	HR	Ratio
2000	4	4	.500	3.78	15	15	0	85.2	75	40	60	7	1.34
Career	12	8	.600	4.25	31	30	0	171.1	148	97	107	16	1.43

2000 Situational Stats

	W	L	ERA	Sv	IP		AB	H	HR	RBI	Avg
Home	2	1	3.06	0	35.1	LHB	178	42	6	17	.236
Road	2	3	4.29	0	50.1	RHB	135	33	1	11	.244
First Half	4	4	3.78	0	85.2	Sc Pos	63	13	0	18	.206
Scnd Half	0	0	-	0	0.0	Clutch	4	1	0	0	.250

2000 Season

Gil Meche's impressive stuff and uncommon poise was evident during the first half, but a mysterious arm problem put him out of commission in the second half. A spring training shoulder strain healed, recurred in May and ultimately shelved him in July. He tried to rehab in the second half, without success. Doctors, finding no structural problems with his shoulder, were baffled and simply ordered him not to throw until December.

Pitching & Defense

As a 20-year-old rookie in 1999, Meche sometimes hit the high 90s. He wasn't quite as fast last year, but still showed a good fastball in the low to mid-90s. With a sharp breaking ball and decent changeup, he works up in the strike zone and makes life tough on lefties and righties alike. He controls the running game very well for a young pitcher, shortening up and getting the ball home quickly. Only four basestealers ran on him last year, and two of those runners were caught.

2001 Outlook

Meche could be the next Freddy Garcia, or the next Roger Salkeld. He threw 175.2 innings in 1999, so last year's shoulder troubles are especially worrisome. His health this spring may be the only clue to the kind of season he will have.

Jamie Moyer

Position: SP
Bats: L **Throws:** L
Ht: 6' 0" **Wt:** 175

Opening Day Age: 38
Born: 11/18/62 in Sellersville, PA
ML Seasons: 14

Overall Statistics

	W	L	Pct.	ERA	G	GS	Sv	IP	H	BB	SO	HR	Ratio
2000	13	10	.565	5.49	26	26	0	154.0	173	53	98	22	1.47
Career	131	111	.541	4.30	372	320	0	2082.1	2201	620	1262	243	1.35

2000 Situational Stats

	W	L	ERA	Sv	IP		AB	H	HR	RBI	Avg
Home	6	5	4.76	0	81.1	LHB	160	46	5	23	.288
Road	7	5	6.32	0	72.2	RHB	456	127	17	72	.279
First Half	8	3	4.21	0	68.1	Sc Pos	146	49	7	71	.336
Scnd Half	5	7	6.51	0	85.2	Clutch	14	5	0	3	.357

2000 Season

Jamie Moyer went on the disabled list in April with a strained shoulder and there were whispers later that the injury never fully healed. He was activated in early June and reeled off nine wins in 11 decisions, but he suffered through a horrible slump in August. His postseason was ended by a broken kneecap during the Division Series.

Pitching & Defense

Moyer relies more on changing speeds than any pitcher in the majors. He has excellent command, throws a mid-80s fastball, an excellent changeup and a slow curve, and he will change speeds on all three pitches. He's just as tough on righthanded hitters as he is on lefties. His problems last year came almost entirely when he was pitching from the stretch position. Moyer often lost his stuff completely after the 75-pitch mark last year. He has a below-average pickoff move for a lefty but is an active fielder who makes a lot of plays.

2001 Outlook

Moyer goes into the final year of his contract this season needing to prove he can be the quality pitcher he's been in the past. If his problems last year were health-related, and if his knee injury doesn't cause him to miss significant time in the spring, then there's no reason he can't bounce back.

Jose Paniagua

Position: RP
Bats: R **Throws:** R
Ht: 6' 2" **Wt:** 190

Opening Day Age: 27
Born: 8/20/73 in San
Jose de Ocoa,
Dominican Republic
ML Seasons: 5
Pronunciation:
pahn-ee-AH-gwah

Overall Statistics

	W	L	Pct.	ERA	G	GS	Sv	IP	H	BB	SO	HR	Ratio
2000	3	0	1.000	3.47	69	0	5	80.1	68	38	71	6	1.32
Career	14	17	.452	4.16	168	14	9	249.0	242	134	196	23	1.51

2000 Situational Stats

	W	L	ERA	Sv	IP		AB	H	HR	RBI	Avg
Home	1	0	2.97	2	39.1	LHB	126	26	1	16	.206
Road	2	0	3.95	3	41.0	RHB	165	42	5	28	.255
First Half	1	0	3.86	1	44.1	Sc Pos	84	19	2	39	.226
Scnd Half	2	0	3.00	4	36.0	Clutch	76	13	0	7	.171

2000 Season

To Jose Paniagua, a fraction of an inch made all the difference in the world. In late May, the slumping reliever took his troubles to Tampa Bay closer Roberto Hernandez, who suggested that Paniagua spread out the grip on his fastball for better control. The tip produced immediate and lasting dividends, as Paniagua pitched very well for the rest of the year and emerged as Seattle's primary righthanded setup man.

Pitching & Defense

Until last year, Paniagua's velocity kept him in the big leagues, and his control kept him from consistently succeeding. Now he uses a mid-90s fastball and good forkball to operate on lefties and righties alike, working in a sinker and slider. With the ability to pitch several days in a row, he's perfectly suited to short relief. He paid better attention to basestealers last year. Sure-handed afield, he has only one career error.

2001 Outlook

It looks like Paniagua has matured into the type of pitcher who can be an asset in the bullpen for years to come. With his stuff and newfound command, he'll likely keep rolling in a park that has proven quite favorable to keeping ERAs down.

Arthur Rhodes

Position: RP
Bats: L **Throws:** L
Ht: 6' 2" **Wt:** 205

Opening Day Age: 31
Born: 10/24/69 in
Waco, TX
ML Seasons: 10

Overall Statistics

	W	L	Pct.	ERA	G	GS	Sv	IP	H	BB	SO	HR	Ratio
2000	5	8	.385	4.28	72	0	0	69.1	51	29	77	6	1.15
Career	48	44	.522	4.80	310	61	9	691.2	626	345	656	85	1.40

2000 Situational Stats

	W	L	ERA	Sv	IP		AB	H	HR	RBI	Avg
Home	2	5	4.54	0	37.2	LHB	109	24	2	17	.220
Road	3	3	3.98	0	31.2	RHB	140	27	4	18	.193
First Half	2	3	2.68	0	40.1	Sc Pos	70	20	2	29	.286
Scnd Half	3	5	6.52	0	29.0	Clutch	154	35	3	24	.227

2000 Season

Southpaw Arthur Rhodes signed a four-year deal with Seattle before the 2000 season and immediately became an important member of the bullpen. As the Mariners' primary lefthanded short man, he worked often, putting together a great first half before slumping in August.

Pitching & Defense

Rhodes is a power pitcher but brings more than just 95-MPH heat. He also has a good curveball, a slider and a changeup, and varies the speeds of his breaking pitches. Lefthanded hitters tend to pound his breaking pitches into the ground, while righthanded hitters produce more air outs off his high heat, but he's effective against both. With Baltimore, he had been more of a two-inning pitcher who rarely worked on consecutive days, but last year Rhodes pitched on consecutive days 17 times with no apparent problems. He has a poor move to first but allowed only one stolen base last year. He fields his position adequately.

2001 Outlook

As long as Rhodes' arm bounces back from last year's more frequent workload, he should remain a top lefthanded setup man. And as long as such usage agrees with him, there's no reason he couldn't be a good closer as well if needed.

Other Seattle Mariners

Charles Gipson (**Pos**: RF/LF, **Age**: 28, **Bats**: R)

	G	AB	R	H	D	T	HR	RBI	SB	BB	SO	Avg	OBP	Slg
2000	59	29	7	9	1	1	0	3	2	4	9	.310	.394	.414
Career	158	160	34	39	7	3	0	14	7	15	31	.244	.316	.325

Gipson has beaten the odds, reaching the majors after being drafted in the 63rd round of 1991. His versatility and speed are his greatest assets. 2001 Outlook: C

Carlos Hernandez (**Pos**: 3B, **Age**: 25, **Bats**: R)

	G	AB	R	H	D	T	HR	RBI	SB	BB	SO	Avg	OBP	Slg
2000	2	1	0	0	0	0	0	0	0	0	1	.000	.000	.000
Career	18	15	4	2	0	0	0	1	3	0	1	.133	.133	.133

The M's traded minor league catcher Carlos Maldonado to Houston last March for Hernandez. He moved back to second last year after a season at short. 2001 Outlook: B.

Kevin Hodges (**Pos**: RHP, **Age**: 27)

	W	L	Pct.	ERA	G	GS	Sv	IP	H	BB	SO	HR	Ratio
2000	0	0	-	5.19	13	0	0	17.1	18	12	7	4	1.73
Career	0	0	-	5.19	13	0	0	17.1	18	12	7	4	1.73

Houston traded Hodges to the Mariners in 1999. Hodges is a mature pitcher who split time between starting and relief at Triple-A last year. 2001 Outlook: C

Raul Ibanez (**Pos**: RF/LF, **Age**: 28, **Bats**: L)

	G	AB	R	H	D	T	HR	RBI	SB	BB	SO	Avg	OBP	Slg
2000	92	140	21	32	8	0	2	15	2	14	25	.229	.301	.329
Career	231	478	59	115	22	2	14	58	7	36	86	.241	.295	.383

Ibanez can play either corner outfield position but doesn't have the type of power usually desired there. He's also been a weak hitter off the bench, going 7-for-48 as a pinch-hitter in his career. 2001 Outlook: B

Tom Lampkin (**Pos**: C, **Age**: 37, **Bats**: L)

	G	AB	R	H	D	T	HR	RBI	SB	BB	SO	Avg	OBP	Slg
2000	36	103	15	26	6	1	7	23	0	9	17	.252	.325	.534
Career	594	1311	164	315	58	7	41	177	18	137	186	.240	.322	.389

Lampkin tore a ligament in a knee last year and later required surgery on his throwing elbow. When healthy, he's not a bad-hitting catcher, but he'll be 37 years old this season and is a free agent. 2001 Outlook: C

Brian Lesher (**Pos**: 1B, **Age**: 30, **Bats**: R)

	G	AB	R	H	D	T	HR	RBI	SB	BB	SO	Avg	OBP	Slg
2000	5	5	1	4	1	1	0	3	1	1	0	.800	.833	1.400
Career	84	225	29	54	9	2	9	36	5	15	50	.240	.287	.418

Lesher signed with the Mariners last year after eight seasons in the Oakland system. He has a good batting eye and a touch of power, but the Mariners released him in mid-November. 2001 Outlook: C

Robert Machado (**Pos**: C, **Age**: 27, **Bats**: R)

	G	AB	R	H	D	T	HR	RBI	SB	BB	SO	Avg	OBP	Slg
2000	8	14	2	3	0	0	1	1	0	1	4	.214	.267	.429
Career	73	168	21	37	8	1	4	20	0	11	38	.220	.268	.351

Machado actually hit .300 in the minors last year, his highest mark since 1993. But he would seem to be strictly a backup at best in the majors. He signed a minor league deal with the Cubs. 2001 Outlook: C

Jose Mesa (**Pos**: RHP, **Age**: 34)

	W	L	Pct.	ERA	G	GS	Sv	IP	H	BB	SO	HR	Ratio
2000	4	6	.400	5.36	66	0	1	80.2	89	41	84	11	1.61
Career	58	75	.436	4.42	556	95	138	1096.2	1163	454	728	104	1.47

Mesa became a setup man in Seattle after losing the closer duties. He signed a two-year deal with Philadelphia in November and could contend for the closer's job there. 2001 Outlook: B

Joe Oliver (**Pos**: C, **Age**: 35, **Bats**: R)

	G	AB	R	H	D	T	HR	RBI	SB	BB	SO	Avg	OBP	Slg
2000	69	200	33	53	13	1	10	35	2	14	38	.265	.313	.490
Career	1059	3319	316	819	172	3	101	473	13	246	622	.247	.299	.392

Oliver is winding down his career by bouncing from team to team. He signed a one-year contract with the Yankees in November. 2001 Outlook: B

Rob Ramsay (**Pos**: LHP, **Age**: 27)

	W	L	Pct.	ERA	G	GS	Sv	IP	H	BB	SO	HR	Ratio
2000	1	1	.500	3.40	37	1	0	50.1	43	40	32	3	1.65
Career	1	3	.250	4.19	43	4	0	68.2	66	49	43	6	1.67

Ramsay is a big lefthander drafted in 1996. He struggled with his control in Seattle last season, but he has a chance to help as a situational southpaw. 2001 Outlook: B

Frank Rodriguez (**Pos**: RHP, **Age**: 28)

	W	L	Pct.	ERA	G	GS	Sv	IP	H	BB	SO	HR	Ratio
2000	2	1	.667	6.27	23	0	0	47.1	60	22	19	8	1.73
Career	29	39	.426	5.45	177	82	5	645.1	721	277	362	75	1.55

Rodriguez' major league production has rarely matched the talent he supposedly possessed when originally drafted. But he'll probably get another chance if his shoulder is healthy. 2001 Outlook: B

Anthony Sanders (**Pos**: RF, **Age**: 27, **Bats**: R)

	G	AB	R	H	D	T	HR	RBI	SB	BB	SO	Avg	OBP	Slg
2000	1	1	1	1	0	0	0	0	0	0	0	1.000	1.000	1.000
Career	4	8	2	3	1	0	0	2	0	0	2	.375	.375	.500

Sanders is a good athlete and improved his batting average in Triple-A last year, but he still strikes out a lot. 2001 Outlook: C

Brett Tomko (**Pos**: RHP, **Age**: 27)

	W	L	Pct.	ERA	G	GS	Sv	IP	H	BB	SO	HR	Ratio
2000	7	5	.583	4.68	32	8	1	92.1	92	40	59	12	1.43
Career	36	31	.537	4.40	121	87	1	601.0	571	211	448	79	1.30

Tomko pitched well in 24 relief appearances posting a 3.99 ERA, but injuries marred his 2000 campaign. If healthy, he might enjoy the 15-win season people have been expecting from him. 2001 Outlook: A

Chris Widger (**Pos**: C, **Age**: 29, **Bats**: R)

	G	AB	R	H	D	T	HR	RBI	SB	BB	SO	Avg	OBP	Slg
2000	96	292	32	68	17	2	13	35	1	30	63	.233	.306	.438
Career	467	1426	143	342	78	7	50	183	10	112	309	.240	.298	.410

Originally drafted by the Mariners, Widger returned to Seattle in a waiver deal with Montreal last August. The Mariners rarely used him, though he would seem to be more than just a backup. 2001 Outlook: A

Seattle Mariners Minor League Prospects

Organization Overview:

Constant change has been the norm for Seattle of late. General manager Woody Woodward gave way to Pat Gillick in 1999, and unhappy superstars Randy Johnson and Ken Griffey Jr. were dealt for youngsters Mike Cameron, Freddy Garcia, John Halama, Brett Tomko, Carlos Guillen and Antonio Perez. While free agents have replenished the Mariners at key positions, the trade acquisitions and minor league system provide hope for the future. Bolstering that hope is a decent 1999 draft, which included Willie Bloomquist, Ryan Christianson, Jeff Heaverlo and Clint Nageotte. The M's also signed promising Australians Chris Snelling and Craig Anderson in '99 after inking Korean teenager Cha Baek in '98. Seattle's growing presence in the Pacific Rim has added to a wealth of talent in the low minors.

Ryan Anderson

Position: P   **Opening Day Age:** 21
Bats: L **Throws:** L   **Born:** 7/12/79 in
Ht: 6' 10" **Wt:** 215   Southfield, MI

Recent Statistics

	W	L	ERA	G	GS	Sv	IP	H	R	BB	SO	HR
1999 AA New Haven	9	13	4.50	24	24	0	134.0	131	77	86	162	9
2000 AAA Tacoma	5	8	3.98	20	20	0	104.0	83	51	55	146	8

A first-round pick in 1997, Anderson held his own against older, more experienced hitters in the Pacific Coast League. For a second straight season, he led his entire classification in Ks per nine innings (12.63). It's hard to ignore the live mid-90s fastball and gaudy strikeout totals, but Anderson also throws a decent changeup and a curveball that is devastating when he controls it. Command is an issue, and he tended to get a little too fine with his location during a midseason slump in 2000. He rebounded before being shut down with mild shoulder tendinitis. A bit more time at Triple-A Tacoma may be in the cards, but he has the stuff to anchor a big league staff.

Willie Bloomquist

Position: 2B   **Opening Day Age:** 23
Bats: R **Throws:** R   **Born:** 11/27/77 in
Ht: 5' 11" **Wt:** 180   Bremerton, WA

Recent Statistics

	G	AB	R	H	D	T	HR	RBI	SB	BB	SO	Avg
1999 A Everett	42	178	35	51	10	3	2	27	17	22	25	.287
2000 A Lancaster	64	256	63	97	19	6	2	51	22	37	27	.379
2000 AAA Tacoma	51	191	17	43	5	1	1	23	5	7	28	.225

It's a testament to Bloomquist's willpower and hard work that he reached Triple-A in his first full season as a pro. A star shortstop at Arizona State, he didn't let a move to second base slow his progress. He jumped to high Class-A Lancaster last spring and performed admirably as a No. 2 hitter and second baseman. The tools may not be overwhelming, but Bloomquist's makeup, work ethic and focus on fundamentals make him a legitimate prospect. While batting .379 at Lancaster, he worked hard at his new position, improving dramatically at hanging in on the pivot and turning double plays. In July he moved up to Tacoma, where better breaking pitches gave him trouble. The Mariners believe he'll be fine when he learns to make more frequent adjustments to pitchers who can pinpoint their better pitching in the high minors.

Jason Grabowski

Position: 3B   **Opening Day Age:** 24
Bats: L **Throws:** R   **Born:** 5/24/76 in New
Ht: 6' 3" **Wt:** 200   Haven, CT

Recent Statistics

	G	AB	R	H	D	T	HR	RBI	SB	BB	SO	Avg
1999 A Charlotte	123	434	68	136	31	6	12	87	13	65	66	.313
1999 AA Tulsa	2	6	1	1	0	0	0	0	0	2	2	.167
2000 AA Tulsa	135	493	93	135	33	5	19	90	8	88	106	.274
2000 MLE	135	483	79	125	30	4	17	76	5	63	112	.259

A second-round pick by Texas in 1997, Grabowski moved out from behind the plate to third base for the 1999 season. Despite the move, Grabowski hit .313-12-87 with a .407 on-base percentage for high Class-A Charlotte that season. Though he has some raw power, Grabowski is more of a gap-to-gap hitter right now. He continues to work counts and draw walks frequently, and he has the bat speed to eventually turn on pitches. Defensively he is solid with an above-average arm. Only his footwork at third needs a little work, which would iron out his occasionally inaccurate throws. Seattle claimed Grabowski off waivers in December.

Jeff Heaverlo

Position: P   **Opening Day Age:** 23
Bats: R **Throws:** R   **Born:** 1/13/78 in Palo
Ht: 6' 1" **Wt:** 215   Alto, CA

Recent Statistics

	W	L	ERA	G	GS	Sv	IP	H	R	BB	SO	HR
1999 A Everett	1	0	2.08	3	0	0	8.2	5	5	2	9	1
1999 A Wisconsin	1	0	2.55	3	3	0	17.2	15	6	7	24	1
2000 AAA Tacoma	0	1	4.85	2	2	0	13.0	14	7	6	4	2
2000 A Lancaster	14	6	4.22	27	27	0	155.2	170	84	52	159	18

A mature and polished pitcher out of the University of Washington, Heaverlo has come on quickly since the M's drafted him in '99. He arrived with a wicked slider and started his second pro season in the high Class-A California League. The only negative spin on Heaverlo's 14-6 season at Lancaster was his tendency to rely on his slider, a habit that began in college, where pitching away from hitters is the norm because of aluminum bats. Seattle believes he has enough movement and velocity on his fastball, and that he made great strides with both his fastball and changeup in 2000. He learned to trust his fastball as the season wore on, and more confidence in it will go a long way as he moves to the high minors.

Antonio Perez

Position: SS
Bats: R **Throws:** R
Ht: 5' 11" **Wt:** 175

Opening Day Age: 19
Born: 7/26/81 in Bani, DR

Recent Statistics

	G	AB	R	H	D	THR	RBI	SB	BB	SO	Avg
1999 A Rockford	119	385	69	111	20	3	7	41	35	43	80	.288
2000 A Lancaster	98	395	90	109	36	6	17	63	28	58	99	.276

Signed by the Reds in 1998, Perez escaped a crowded middle-infield picture when he was dealt to Seattle in last winter's Ken Griffey Jr. trade. Despite a move from second base to short, Perez took the high Class-A California League by storm in 2000, delivering 59 extra-base hits in just 395 at-bats. A quick, short stroke generates pop that one wouldn't expect from a slight middle infielder who turned 19 on July 26, and Perez may fill out and develop a bit more power. He also shows good command of the strike zone, which only enhances the value of his speed. His defensive game features his quickness, good hands and a strong arm.

Joel Pineiro

Position: P
Bats: R **Throws:** R
Ht: 6' 1" **Wt:** 180

Opening Day Age: 22
Born: 9/25/78 in Rio Pedres, PR

Recent Statistics

	W	L	ERA	G	GS	Sv	IP	H	R	BB	SO	HR
2000 AA New Haven	2	1	4.13	9	9	0	52.1	42	25	12	43	6
2000 AAA Tacoma	7	1	2.80	10	9	0	61.0	53	20	22	41	3
2000 AL Seattle	1	0	5.59	8	1	0	19.1	25	13	13	10	3

After going 16-6 in his first two pro campaigns and pitching well in winter ball prior to the 1999 season, Pineiro led the Double-A Eastern League with 15 losses in '99. His winter work may have taken its toll, as Pineiro's fastball dropped from the low 90s to the high 80s. In 2000 he returned to New Haven, his velocity bounced back, he exhibited better command and kept his pitches low in the strike zone. After nine Double-A starts, Pineiro went 7-1 (2.80) at Triple-A Tacoma, leading to his first trip to the majors. He debuted with six strong innings and beat the White Sox on August 8, but then went to the bullpen and didn't do as well. His curveball has been his best pitch, but his changeup has improved and his fastball has good movement.

Juan Silvestre

Position: OF
Bats: R **Throws:** R
Ht: 5' 11" **Wt:** 180

Opening Day Age: 23
Born: 1/10/78 in Hato, DR

Recent Statistics

	G	AB	R	H	D	THR	RBI	SB	BB	SO	Avg
1999 A Wisconsin	137	534	89	154	34	4	21	107	5	47	124	.288
2000 A Lancaster	127	506	104	154	15	3	30	137	9	60	126	.304

Signed in 1994 at the age of 16, Silvestre's power blossomed in his second of two seasons in the Class-A Midwest League in 1999. He already was 21 when he recorded 34 doubles, 21 homers and 107 RBI, and he wasn't really young for the California League last summer, but it's hard to ignore his 137 RBI in 127 games. While he was aided by the winds at his home park at Lancaster, Silvestre is a smart hitter who can do the little things with the bat. He often drives the ball the other way with power, much like current Mariner Edgar Martinez, and Silvestre will take that power stroke to Double-A New Haven in 2001. His strikeout numbers are high, which isn't likely to change, and his defensive game needs work, but he may be worth watching.

Greg Wooten

Position: P
Bats: R **Throws:** R
Ht: 6' 7" **Wt:** 210

Opening Day Age: 26
Born: 3/30/74 in Eugene, OR

Recent Statistics

	W	L	ERA	G	GS	Sv	IP	H	R	BB	SO	HR
1999 A Lancaster	10	4	4.33	17	17	0	114.1	123	62	30	72	13
2000 AA New Haven	17	3	2.31	26	26	0	179.1	166	50	15	115	9

After going in the third round of the 1995 draft, Wooten had a promising pro debut, going 15-5 between Class-A clubs at Wisconsin and Lancaster in 1996. He made the jump to Double-A Memphis in '97, but a strained elbow ligament cost him most of 1998. He returned to Lancaster in '99 and pitched well enough—going 10-4 with a 4.33 ERA—but he suffered through a drop-off in velocity before regaining his arm strength and command. Relying on a fastball, slider and split-finger pitch, Wooten re-emerged as a candidate for the Seattle rotation with a 17-3 season at Double-A New Haven in 2000. While he doesn't overpower hitters, Wooten allowed just nine homers and 15 walks in 179.1 innings by mixing his pitches well and working the strike zone effectively.

Others to Watch

Australian lefty **Craig Anderson** (20) locates an average fastball and keeps hitters off balance when he adds his slider and change. He held his own against older hitters in the Midwest League in 2000, finishing 11-8 (3.71). . . Promising Korean import **Cha Baek** (20) saw his low-90s fastball dip into the mid-80s when he hid an elbow problem from the M's, but his velocity later returned. He showed a late-breaking slider and added a two-seam fastball that gives him five pitches he mixes well. . . Despite average pitches, a herky-jerky motion and late movement on his fastball have allowed lefthander **Brian Fuentes** (25) to average well more than a strikeout per inning in five minor league seasons. He returned to Double-A New Haven after a lackluster 1999 and turned in his best season since '97. . . Aussie outfielder **Chris Snelling** (19) ranked among the top prospects in his league for a second straight season in 2000, showing some pop, drawing walks, flashing some range and playing solid defense. After batting .305-9-56 at Class-A Wisconsin, the teenager looks headed for high Class-A Lancaster in 2001.

Tropicana Field

Offense

After three years and several adjustments, Tropicana Field still hasn't proven to be the good hitters' park everyone thought it would be. Unfortunately for the Devil Rays, it certainly didn't give them much of an advantage when they were at the plate. For the third straight year, the Rays were outhit, outhomered and outscored by significant margins at home. Unlike 1999, there were no appreciable differences for righthanders or lefthanders in 2000.

Defense

The Rays switched to a new artifical surface called FieldTurf (an artifical surface that plays more like grass) in 2000, and there were few complaints and no significant problems. The infield configuration of all-dirt basepaths around a turf infield continued to cause a few grumbles and a number of miscues. Because of the off-white ceiling and stadium catwalks, there also are a handful of flyballs lost every season. The Tropicana Field outfield is large, and when the Devil Rays finally get a trio of speedy outfielders they will do a better job of defending their turf.

Who It Helps the Most

Greg Vaughn liked hitting at the dome, but more for average (.308-.212) than for power (13 home homers/15 road). There were also appreciable differences in the home/road averages of Steve Cox, John Flaherty and Aubrey Huff.

Who It Hurts the Most

On the other hand, Fred McGriff, who was much better at home in 1999, had better numbers away from Tropicana in 2000—a .309 average and 17 homers on the road, .243 and 10 homers at home. Roberto Hernandez has trouble pitching in the dome, posting six of his losses and a 4.06 ERA at home, compared to a 1.86 ERA on the road.

Rookies & Newcomers

Travis Harper struggled mightily in his three home starts. If rookie catcher Toby Hall makes the squad, he will need to spend extra time working on foul popups, since they tend to get lost in the ceiling and catwalks.

Dimensions: LF-315, LCF-370, CF-404, RCF-370, RF-322

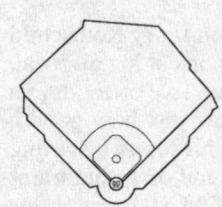

Capacity: 44,397

Elevation: 15 feet

Surface: Turf

Foul Territory: Average

Park Factors

	2000 Season						
	Home Games			Away Games			
	Devil Rays	Opp	Total	Devil Rays	Opp	Total	Index
G	71	71	142	72	72	144	—
Avg	.250	.276	.263	.260	.281	.271	97
AB	2372	2575	4947	2511	2400	4911	102
R	306	385	691	330	368	698	100
H	592	710	1302	654	675	1329	99
2B	115	138	253	97	134	231	109
3B	9	17	26	7	15	22	117
HR	68	98	166	77	79	156	106
BB	261	226	487	219	245	464	104
SO	426	453	879	474	380	854	102
E	59	44	103	46	45	91	115
E-Infield	52	41	93	38	38	76	124
LHB-Avg	.255	.273	.266	.270	.305	.291	91
LHB-HR	20	42	62	22	36	58	106
RHB-Avg	.247	.278	.261	.256	.257	.256	102
RHB-HR	48	56	104	55	43	98	106

	1999 Season						
	Home Games			Away Games			
	Devil Rays	Opp	Total	Devil Rays	Opp	Total	Index
G	72	72	144	72	72	144	—
Avg	.270	.286	.278	.281	.279	.280	99
AB	2381	2543	4924	2567	2400	4967	99
R	331	403	734	367	380	747	98
H	642	727	1369	721	670	1391	98
2B	110	160	270	137	122	259	105
3B	10	17	27	14	11	25	109
HR	55	81	136	74	73	147	93
BB	244	290	534	239	320	559	96
SO	456	494	950	463	438	901	106
E	55	43	98	60	50	110	89
E-Infield	48	38	86	50	40	90	96
LHB-Avg	.290	.296	.293	.276	.276	.276	106
LHB-HR	25	38	63	24	37	61	109
RHB-Avg	.257	.278	.267	.284	.282	.283	94
RHB-HR	30	43	73	50	36	86	83

2000 Rankings (American League)
- Second-highest infield-error factor

Tampa Bay

Larry Rothschild

2000 Season

There may yet be a season when Larry Rothschild has a full complement of weapons at his disposal, gets to use the same basic lineup five or six days a week and has a chance to show just how good a manager he is. Rothschild lost his top two starting pitchers for the season by the end of spring training, and he saw three of the four sluggers in the middle of his lineup spend time on the DL. The Rays were buried after a 16-34 start, meaning few people even noticed they were an impressive 43-40 during the middle three months of the season.

Offense

Rothschild prefers an aggressive offense, but he had little choice due to the construction of the roster except to sit back and wait for home runs that rarely came. Ideally, he would like to have speed at the top and bottom of the order, with the power in the middle. That would allow him to use what is more of the National League-style game he prefers, putting runners in motion and calling for bunts and hit-and-runs. The Rays showed some of that little-ball game toward the end of the 2000 season when they had some of their younger and more versatile players in the lineup.

Pitching & Defense

A former pitching coach, Rothschild tends to be cautious—perhaps even over-protective—of the young arms on his staff. He ranks near the top of the league in quick hooks. With closer Roberto Hernandez at the back of the bullpen, Rothschild likes to get the other relievers slotted into roles. He prefers to use Hernandez for only one inning at a time, and likes him to start the inning. Rothschild likes a quick and aggressive defense, and the addition of center fielder Gerald Williams was a huge step in that direction.

2001 Outlook

There was speculation that Rothschild would be fired after the 2000 season, but GM Chuck LaMar said he couldn't blame his manager for the team's woes. The team definitely has some holes, as well as some potential. It would be interesting to see what Rothschild could do if he at least had a healthy squad to work with for the full season.

Born: 3/12/54 in Chicago, IL

Playing Experience: 1981-1982, Det

Managerial Experience: 3 seasons

Manager Statistics

Year	Team, Lg	W	L	Pct	GB	Finish
2000	Tampa Bay, AL	69	92	.429	18.0	5th East
3 Seasons		201	284	.414	—	—

2000 Starting Pitchers by Days Rest

	<=3	4	5	6+
Devil Rays Starts	1	85	42	22
Devil Rays ERA	5.14	5.19	6.17	3.45
AL Avg Starts	2	88	40	22
AL ERA	4.87	5.03	5.03	5.28

2000 Situational Stats

	Larry Rothschild	AL Average
Hit & Run Success %	36.4	35.1
Stolen Base Success %	66.2	68.8
Platoon Pct.	49.2	57.8
Defensive Subs	28	23
High-Pitch Outings	7	13
Quick/Slow Hooks	21/21	18/19
Sacrifice Attempts	73	55

2000 Rankings (American League)

- 2nd in sacrifice bunt attempts (73) and starting lineups used (138)

Miguel Cairo

2000 Season

Miguel Cairo's troubles started in the second game of the season. He made a ninth-inning error that cost the Rays the game, and everything seemed to be downhill from there. After starting 52 of the first 60 games, he lost his job when Bobby Smith was promoted from Triple-A in June and Cairo never seemed to regain the confidence of the coaching staff. His batting average also dropped more than 30 points from 1999.

Hitting

Cairo does a good job of getting the bat on the ball, consistently ranking among the tougher American League batters to strike out. But he needs to do a better job once he makes contact. Cairo tends to hit the ball in the air too much, especially for a player with good speed. He experimented in 1999 with an extremely wide grip that was designed to force him to hit the ball on the ground more, but went back to more of a conventional grip in 2000. Cairo doesn't have much power or much patience at the plate, so his success is going to come with slapping the ball around and running hard.

Baserunning & Defense

Once Cairo does get on base, he does an excellent job of moving along. Finally free of the hamstring injuries that plagued him in 1998 and '99, Cairo stole a team-record 28 bases in 2000. Even though Cairo made the same number of errors as the previous season (nine), there was a general sense of disappointment with his fielding in 2000. While Cairo can be flashy and is capable of making some extraordinary plays, he is too inconsistent on the routine plays and his range is limited.

2001 Outlook

The Rays released Cairo in November, at which time GM Chuck LaMar cited his disappointment in Cairo for his failure to do the "little things" like taking pitches and drawing walks, moving runners over and maintaining his focus on routine defensive plays. Cairo also stood to triple his salary via arbitration. So with cheaper alternatives on the roster, he is a free agent looking for work.

Position: 2B
Bats: R **Throws:** R
Ht: 6' 1" **Wt:** 200

Opening Day Age: 26
Born: 5/4/74 in Anaco, Venezuela
ML Seasons: 5
Pronunciation: KY-roh

Overall Statistics

	G	AB	R	H	D	T	HR	RBI	SB	BB	SO	Avg	OBP	Slg
2000	119	375	49	98	18	2	1	34	28	29	34	.261	.314	.328
Career	414	1411	171	386	62	12	9	118	69	81	136	.274	.318	.354

Where He Hits the Ball

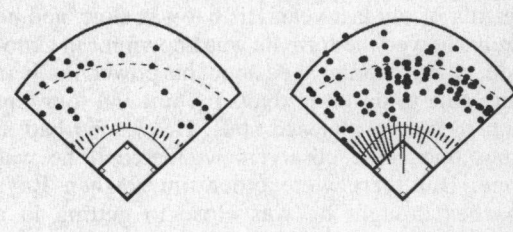

Vs. LHP   **Vs. RHP**

2000 Situational Stats

	AB	H	HR	RBI	Avg		AB	H	HR	RBI	Avg
Home	167	34	0	11	.204	LHP	74	20	0	5	.270
Road	208	64	1	23	.308	RHP	301	78	1	29	.259
First Half	227	60	0	19	.264	Sc Pos	66	26	1	33	.394
Scnd Half	148	38	1	15	.257	Clutch	67	19	0	10	.284

2000 Rankings (American League)

- 1st in lowest batting average on a 3-1 count (.000)
- 3rd in fielding percentage at second base (.983)
- 6th in steals of third (4)
- Led the Devil Rays in stolen bases, stolen-base percentage (80.0), batting average on an 0-2 count (.185), steals of third (4) and batting average with two strikes (.200)

Tampa Bay

257

Vinny Castilla

Position: 3B
Bats: R **Throws:** R
Ht: 6' 1" **Wt:** 205

Opening Day Age: 33
Born: 7/4/67 in Oaxaca, Mexico
ML Seasons: 10
Pronunciation: cas-TEE-yah

2000 Season

Having arrived in Tampa Bay via trade with a reputation for durability, Vinny Castilla pulled an oblique muscle halfway through spring training and never seemed to get on track. When he was feeling good, he wasn't swinging well. As soon as he started looking like he was getting comfortable at the plate, he would get hurt again. By the end of what was easily the worst season of his career, Castilla had landed on the disabled list three times.

Hitting

Castilla once was considered one of the best fastball hitters in the game. But whether it was the injuries, the shift to the American League or advancing age, he didn't look anything like the Vinny Castilla of old last year. His bat was slow, and he rarely showed the form he was known for in Colorado, where people raved about his power. Pitchers were able to throw fastballs by him and fool him with mediocre offspeed stuff. He was so bad at times that some observers wondered if he was done. But there were other times when Rays coaches thought he was close to getting in a groove.

Baserunning & Defense

Running never has been a key part of Castilla's game and that's not going to change. While his speed is limited and he doesn't steal bases, he can score from second on most base hits. If his sore back doesn't create limitations, he's an excellent defensive player. Castilla charges balls very well. He may not be that quick, but he positions himself well and has an extremely strong arm, which allows him to cheat a bit.

2001 Outlook

Towards the end of last season, Castilla told reporters he would be the Comeback Player of the Year in 2001. Unless someone takes him off their hands, the Rays can only hope he's right. His injuries gave Tampa Bay a chance to look at prospect Aubrey Huff, and the team liked what it saw. The best scenario would be for him to come back strong, allowing Huff more time to develop and the Rays time to make a July deal involving Castilla.

Overall Statistics

	G	AB	R	H	D	T	HR	RBI	SB	BB	SO	Avg	OBP	Slg
2000	85	331	22	73	9	1	6	42	1	14	41	.221	.254	.308
Career	1041	3847	540	1122	175	18	209	653	23	237	562	.292	.334	.509

Where He Hits the Ball

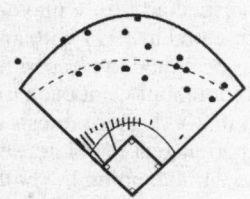
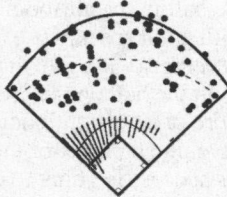

Vs. LHP   **Vs. RHP**

2000 Situational Stats

	AB	H	HR	RBI	Avg		AB	H	HR	RBI	Avg
Home	150	31	2	14	.207	LHP	69	14	1	7	.203
Road	181	42	4	28	.232	RHP	262	59	5	35	.225
First Half	243	54	6	34	.222	Sc Pos	89	22	1	34	.247
Scnd Half	88	19	0	8	.216	Clutch	56	12	0	7	.214

2000 Rankings (American League)
- Did not rank near the top or bottom in any category

Steve Cox

2000 Season

Steve Cox hit his way into the Devil Rays' lineup, forcing them to find a place to play him. A November 1997 expansion draft pick who blossomed in 1999 at Triple-A Durham, Cox turned out to be one of the Rays' most productive hitters. With Fred McGriff entrenched at first base, and the DH slot filled by Jose Canseco and Greg Vaughn, Cox usually found himself in the outfield but didn't let his unfamiliarity with the position affect his hitting.

Hitting

Cox may not have the most technically correct swing, but teammates call him "The Natural" because of the results he gets. He has a good eye, a quick bat and enough power that he probably could hit 20 homers over a full season. That may not match the production of a classic first baseman, but the Rays will take it given Cox' consistency. He usually hits the ball on the ground or drives it into the gaps, and he doesn't give away many at-bats. He is a smart hitter who rarely is fooled by the same pitch twice and doesn't fall into protracted slumps. He also was an effective pinch-hitter, which is unusual for an inexperienced player.

Baserunning & Defense

Cox never is going to be known for his speed, but he is a fundamentally sound runner who does a decent job getting around the diamond. He is a very smooth fielding first baseman, quick and nimble around the bag. In 1999 he was named the top defensive first baseman in the International League. While he got more comfortable in the outfield as the season went on, it became clear that he did not have the speed or arm strength to succeed in right field for an extended period of time.

2001 Outlook

The Rays are going to find a way to get Cox in the starting lineup for more than the 87 games they did in 2000. With GM Chuck LaMar saying his top offseason priority was to find a right fielder, Cox likely will split his time between first base and DH, alternating to some degree with Fred McGriff. Eventually, Cox will be the full-time first baseman.

Position: RF/LF/1B/DH
Bats: L **Throws:** L
Ht: 6' 4" **Wt:** 222

Opening Day Age: 26
Born: 10/31/74 in Delano, CA
ML Seasons: 2

Overall Statistics

	G	AB	R	H	D	T	HR	RBI	SB	BB	SO	Avg	OBP	Slg
2000	116	318	44	90	19	1	11	35	1	46	47	.283	.379	.453
Career	122	337	44	94	20	1	11	35	1	46	49	.279	.371	.442

Where He Hits the Ball

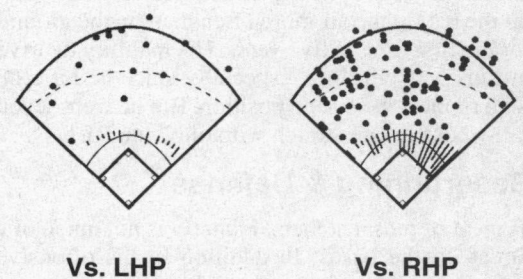

Vs. LHP   **Vs. RHP**

2000 Situational Stats

	AB	H	HR	RBI	Avg		AB	H	HR	RBI	Avg
Home	174	53	7	18	.305	LHP	53	13	3	7	.245
Road	144	37	4	17	.257	RHP	265	77	8	28	.291
First Half	100	30	4	13	.300	Sc Pos	69	14	2	22	.203
Scnd Half	218	60	7	22	.275	Clutch	51	15	2	7	.294

2000 Rankings (American League)
- 3rd in errors in left field (4)

John Flaherty

2000 Season

John Flaherty followed one of his most productive major league seasons with a mediocre one, and there was no apparent reason for the drop-off. Usually a slow starter, he posted a hot April last year but began to struggle in May and never really recovered. He ultimately hit for a lower average, produced barely half as many runs and threw out considerably fewer runners than he had in 1999.

Hitting

Flaherty is best when he hits the ball where it's pitched and sprays line drives around the park. He got away from that approach at times last season as he struggled to compensate for a lack of production and made a series of adjustments to his stance. He hit the ball in the air more often than on the ground for the first time in five years. His inability to drive in runs was puzzling, especially since he hit .268 with runners in scoring position. But he went seven full weeks in one stretch with only one RBI.

Baserunning & Defense

Typical of most catchers, Flaherty is not much of a threat on the bases. In addition to his offensive struggles, his performance behind the plate was disappointing. After ranking second in the majors in '99 by throwing out nearly 40 percent of attempted basestealers, he nailed just 25 percent last year. His arm appeared to be just as strong, so the decline may have been the product of poor footwork or fundamentals.

2001 Outlook

Unless the Devil Rays are forced to trade Flaherty as part of an effort to dump salary, he'll return as their starting catcher with the chance to prove that his 2000 slump was an aberration. He most likely will start about five days a week, with Mike DiFelice also picking up spot duty. The Rays didn't rehire bullpen coach Orlando Gomez, who was in charge of catchers, so Flaherty will have a new position coach this season.

Position: C
Bats: R **Throws:** R
Ht: 6' 1" **Wt:** 200

Opening Day Age: 33
Born: 10/21/67 in New York, NY
ML Seasons: 9
Nickname: Flash

Overall Statistics

	G	AB	R	H	D	T	HR	RBI	SB	BB	SO	Avg	OBP	Slg
2000	109	394	36	103	15	0	10	39	0	20	57	.261	.296	.376
Career	759	2484	235	636	117	2	60	292	7	135	361	.256	.295	.377

Where He Hits the Ball

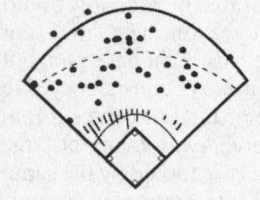
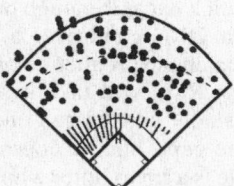

Vs. LHP   **Vs. RHP**

2000 Situational Stats

	AB	H	HR	RBI	Avg		AB	H	HR	RBI	Avg
Home	191	52	7	22	.272	LHP	89	24	2	9	.270
Road	203	51	3	17	.251	RHP	305	79	8	30	.259
First Half	221	61	4	21	.276	Sc Pos	97	26	4	31	.268
Scnd Half	173	42	6	18	.243	Clutch	66	14	2	6	.212

2000 Rankings (American League)

- 4th in fielding percentage at catcher (.993)
- Led the Devil Rays in batting average with two strikes (.200)

Jose Guillen

2000 Season

Jose Guillen had his chance to establish himself as the Devil Rays' everyday right fielder but didn't take advantage of it. After opening the season on the disabled list and then at Triple-A Durham, Guillen joined the Rays on May 12 and started 43 of his first 50 games. He proceeded to display the same inconsistencies and inadequacies that have dogged him throughout his career. As a result, he spent most of the second half on the bench and finished with a .253 batting average for the second straight year.

Hitting

Guillen is neither a very patient nor disciplined hitter. He swings at most everything, illustrated by his mere 18 walks in 349 plate appearances in 2000. Guillen has a relatively quick bat and some decent power, so when he does hit the ball, he can drive it into the gaps and over the fence. At times he tries to pull the ball too much and gets caught up in trying to hit home runs. His performance with runners in scoring position and in the clutch was brutal, forcing Tampa Bay to hit him down in the order.

Baserunning & Defense

Guillen seems to have good speed when he hits the ball into the gap, but he doesn't do much when he is on base. His most impressive tool is his arm strength. He throws so well that teams will alter their approach if he is in right field, refusing to take even the slightest chance. Guillen, however, tends to show off his arm too much, frequently missing cutoff men and making unnecessary throws.

2001 Outlook

Just as he did in Pittsburgh, Guillen seems to have played his way out of the Rays' plans. They had hopes he would man right field for the next decade, but GM Chuck LaMar said his primary offseason goal was to obtain a right fielder. That means Guillen could either make the team as a reserve (which doesn't seem likely), head back to Triple-A for yet another year of seasoning, or be on his way to a third team before turning 25.

Position: RF
Bats: R **Throws:** R
Ht: 5'11" **Wt:** 195

Opening Day Age: 24
Born: 5/17/76 in San Cristobal, Dominican Republic
ML Seasons: 4
Pronunciation: GHEE-un

Overall Statistics

	G	AB	R	H	D	T	HR	RBI	SB	BB	SO	Avg	OBP	Slg
2000	105	316	40	80	16	5	10	41	3	18	65	.253	.320	.430
Career	488	1675	200	439	90	12	41	226	8	76	310	.262	.306	.404

Where He Hits the Ball

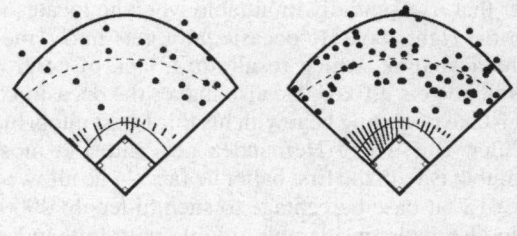

Vs. LHP   **Vs. RHP**

2000 Situational Stats

	AB	H	HR	RBI	Avg		AB	H	HR	RBI	Avg
Home	187	44	5	23	.235	LHP	87	17	5	14	.195
Road	129	36	5	18	.279	RHP	229	63	5	27	.275
First Half	168	42	7	21	.250	Sc Pos	77	17	2	29	.221
Scnd Half	148	38	3	20	.257	Clutch	54	11	1	6	.204

2000 Rankings (American League)

- 4th in hit by pitch (13)
- 5th in errors in right field (4)
- 9th in lowest batting average in the clutch
- Led the Devil Rays in triples and hit by pitch (13)
- Led AL right fielders in hit by pitch (13)

Roberto Hernandez

2000 Season

To have 32 saves and four victories for a team that won only 69 games was not a bad year's work for Roberto Hernandez. But unfortunately, he also blew eight saves, lost seven times, yielded a .272 batting average and surrendered nine home runs. Hernandez' biggest problem was inconsistency. He blew four of his first six save opportunities, converted 29 of his next 31 (including 14 straight), and finished by squandering two of his final three chances.

Pitching

Hernandez still is one of the most dominating closers around, pushing the radar guns to 100 MPH with a blistering fastball. He mixes in a nasty splitter that is essentially unhittable when he locates it in the right spot. He occasionally gets into a mechanical funk, which results in a lack of control until he gets it fixed. He also makes the occasional mistake of getting beat with his third-best pitch, his slider. But where Hernandez gets into the most trouble is with the first batter he faces—he allowed a .412 on-base percentage to such hitters in 2000. He also had considerable trouble with lefthanded batters last season, allowing a .328 batting average.

Defense

Hernandez can move pretty well for a big man, but he tends to get a little too excited on bunt plays and can make some unforced errors. He also has a somewhat dangerous habit of trying to grab bouncing balls with his bare hand. He usually doesn't pay much attention to baserunners, allowing six stolen bases in eight chances.

2001 Outlook

While Hernandez didn't have that poor of a season in 2000, the Devil Rays know he can do better based on his awesome showing in 1999. They'd probably settle for something in the middle for 2001, with the hope that the team's overall improvement makes Hernandez' job all the more interesting.

Position: RP
Bats: R **Throws:** R
Ht: 6' 4" **Wt:** 250

Opening Day Age: 36
Born: 11/11/64 in Santurce, Puerto Rico
ML Seasons: 10
Pronunciation: her-NAN-dezz

Overall Statistics

	W	L	Pct.	ERA	G	GS	Sv	IP	H	BB	SO	HR	Ratio
2000	4	7	.364	3.19	68	0	32	73.1	76	23	61	9	1.35
Career	42	42	.500	3.04	580	3	266	655.1	567	267	631	49	1.27

How Often He Throws Strikes

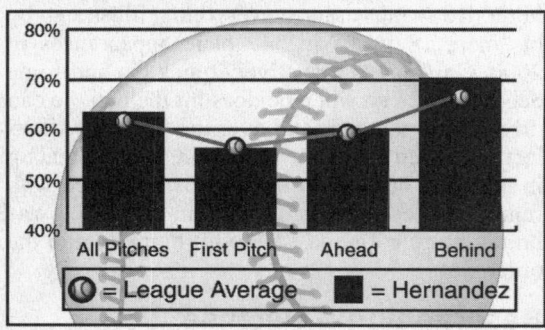

= League Average   = Hernandez

2000 Situational Stats

	W	L	ERA	Sv	IP		AB	H	HR	RBI	Avg
Home	2	6	4.06	16	44.1	LHB	131	43	4	23	.328
Road	2	1	1.86	16	29.0	RHB	148	33	5	15	.223
First Half	2	3	4.20	12	40.2	Sc Pos	84	23	1	27	.274
Scnd Half	2	4	1.93	20	32.2	Clutch	203	54	6	31	.266

2000 Rankings (American League)

- 3rd in relief losses (7) and worst first batter efficiency (.344)
- 5th in games finished (58)
- 6th in save opportunities (40), blown saves (8) and lowest save percentage (80.0)
- Led the Devil Rays in games pitched, saves, games finished (58), save opportunities (40), save percentage (80.0), blown saves (8), relief losses (7), relief innings (73.1) and relief ERA (3.19)

Albie Lopez

2000 Season

Though the move was made almost out of desperation at the time, the decision to shift Albie Lopez from the bullpen to the starting rotation in late May proved to be a good one. Though he had been a decent setup man for two years, he quickly established himself as the Devil Rays' top starter, going 9-9 with a 3.88 ERA, including a stretch where he won eight of 12. He earned an American League Player of the Week award, a selection to the post-season All-Star team that toured Japan and, in the minds of some teammates, the right to be this year's Opening Day starter.

Pitching

Lopez keeps it simple. He throws hard, keeps the ball down, works fast and lets his defense do its job. He throws a low to mid-90s fastball, a curve and a changeup. The three-pitch assortment usually was plenty when he worked one or two innings at a time. But the addition of a cut fastball, which acts like a slider, has made a huge difference, allowing him to offer different looks and patterns as he goes through a lineup for the second and third times. As his repertoire has improved, so has his confidence. Lopez was a starter early in his career with Cleveland, and he doesn't plan on returning to the bullpen anytime soon.

Defense

Lopez does a good job defensively. He makes all the routine plays and is not shy about throwing the ball around. However, he doesn't hold runners well, allowing 15 of 18 to steal successfully. He's a smart player who always is learning by watching.

2001 Outlook

By virtue of his strong performance in 2000, Lopez earned the right to open this season in the rotation. He struggled toward the end of last year and will have to show that he can be consistent over the course of an entire season to truly be considered a top-notch starter. With Wilson Alvarez, Juan Guzman and Ryan Rupe all coming back from injuries, Lopez is the closest the Rays have to a sure thing.

Position: SP/RP
Bats: R **Throws:** R
Ht: 6' 2" **Wt:** 240

Opening Day Age: 29
Born: 8/18/71 in Mesa, AZ
ML Seasons: 8
Pronunciation: LOE-pezz

Overall Statistics

	W	L	Pct.	ERA	G	GS	Sv	IP	H	BB	SO	HR	Ratio
2000	11	13	.458	4.13	45	24	2	185.1	199	70	96	24	1.45
Career	33	33	.500	4.73	219	55	4	557.1	605	233	368	78	1.50

How Often He Throws Strikes

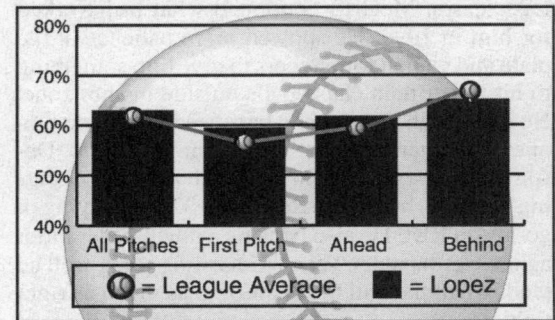

◉ = League Average   ■ = Lopez

2000 Situational Stats

	W	L	ERA	Sv	IP		AB	H	HR	RBI	Avg
Home	7	5	3.31	1	103.1	LHB	363	111	10	45	.306
Road	4	8	5.16	1	82.0	RHB	355	88	14	47	.248
First Half	5	6	4.32	2	75.0	Sc Pos	177	48	5	67	.271
Scnd Half	6	7	4.00	0	110.1	Clutch	114	28	4	15	.246

2000 Rankings (American League)

- 2nd in GDPs induced (29), most GDPs induced per nine innings (1.4) and least run support per nine innings (4.0)
- 3rd in fewest strikeouts per nine innings (4.7)
- 4th in lowest ERA at home and lowest fielding percentage at pitcher (.906)
- 5th in complete games (4), highest ground-ball/flyball ratio allowed (1.8) and errors at pitcher (3)
- Led the Devil Rays in ERA, wins, losses, complete games (4), innings pitched, batters faced (798), walks allowed, pitches thrown (2,835), stolen bases allowed (15), GDPs induced (29), lowest batting average allowed (.277) and lowest slugging percentage allowed (.439)

Tampa Bay

Fred McGriff

2000 Season

Having signed a contract extension at the end of the 1999 campaign, Fred McGriff showed he was still a big-time player and delivered his typical season—quiet and productive. He set a team record with 106 RBI, falling one shy of his career best and giving him consecutive 100-plus RBI campaigns for the first time since 1992-93. He netted his 400th career homer and 2,000th hit during the same June weekend series. Leg problems that bothered him in '99 were non-existent due to extra conditioning work he began in spring training and an extensive stretching routine.

Hitting

Last season McGriff continued what had worked for him in 1999. He showed more patience at the plate and waited for pitchers to give him something to hit rather than chase balls outside his hot zone. He still has the power and bat speed that made him one of the game's most consistent producers. Despite hitting a pedestrian .280 with runners in scoring position, he led the Rays with 32 game-tying or go-ahead RBI. He also became a much better hitter against lefthanders. When McGriff is going well he tends to hit the ball to center field as much as right field.

Baserunning & Defense

McGriff never has been fast and his casual manner on the bases makes him look even slower than he is, occasionally drawing boos from fans who perceive a lack of hustle. He has slipped a bit defensively, but he committed fewer errors in 2000 (10) than he did in '99 (13) despite handling more chances at first.

2001 Outlook

McGriff, who has a no-trade clause, will remain in the center of the Rays' lineup. But there may be a gradual process of shifting him off of first base and into the DH role on more of a full-time basis in order to make room for Steve Cox. How McGriff adjusts to that could be interesting to watch. Over the last three years, he has hit .278 as a DH and .292 as a first baseman.

Position: 1B/DH
Bats: L **Throws:** L
Ht: 6' 3" **Wt:** 215

Opening Day Age: 37
Born: 10/31/63 in Tampa, FL
ML Seasons: 15
Nickname: Crime Dog

Overall Statistics

	G	AB	R	H	D	T	HR	RBI	SB	BB	SO	Avg	OBP	Slg
2000	158	566	82	157	18	0	27	106	2	91	120	.277	.373	.452
Career	2055	7352	1176	2103	372	20	417	1298	70	1136	1592	.286	.381	.512

Where He Hits the Ball

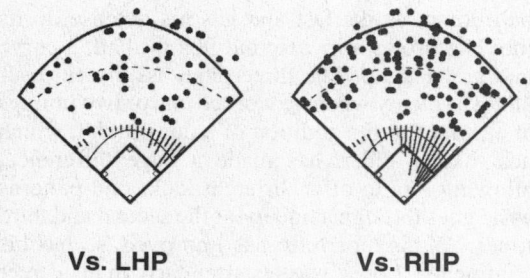

Vs. LHP **Vs. RHP**

2000 Situational Stats

	AB	H	HR	RBI	Avg		AB	H	HR	RBI	Avg
Home	268	65	10	46	.243	LHP	161	44	10	43	.273
Road	298	92	17	60	.309	RHP	405	113	17	63	.279
First Half	316	89	18	62	.282	Sc Pos	157	44	8	78	.280
Scnd Half	250	68	9	44	.272	Clutch	90	25	6	15	.278

2000 Rankings (American League)

- 3rd in errors at first base (10) and lowest cleanup slugging percentage (.448)
- 5th in batting average with the bases loaded (.615) and lowest fielding percentage at first base (.993)
- 6th in lowest batting average at home and highest percentage of swings on the first pitch (40.4)
- Led the Devil Rays in batting average, RBI, sacrifice flies (7), walks, intentional walks (10), times on base (248), GDPs (16), pitches seen (2,508), on-base percentage, highest ground-ball/flyball ratio (1.2), batting average with the bases loaded (.615), batting average vs. lefthanded pitchers and batting average vs. righthanded pitchers

Ryan Rupe

2000 Season

As much of a pleasant surprise as Ryan Rupe was for the Devil Rays in his 1999 rookie season, he was a frustrating disappointment in 2000. Rupe struggled early in the season, was sent down to Triple-A Durham, was on the disabled list there after experiencing shoulder stiffness, then came back in July and pitched well in spurts. He had his season come to a traumatic end in early September when a blood clot was discovered in his right arm, requiring hospitalization and a surgical procedure.

Pitching

Rupe has a free and easy motion that allows him to throw a mid-90s fastball with movement, as well as a slider that can be flat-out nasty when he can keep it down and bury it. But his best pitch is a changeup that just frustrates hitters. He was leaving the ball up and over the plate too much during the 2000 season, giving up 121 hits in 91 innings. Rupe is a fierce competitor and is not afraid to go right at hitters and work aggressively. But the Rays felt he was trying to do too much early in the season and his struggles led to a lack of confidence.

Defense

Rupe is something of a classic power pitcher—big, tall and gangly, and thus not a very polished fielder. However, he can make all the standard plays, though he sometimes gets so worked up on the mound that he appears to be a bit out of control. He does not do a very good job holding runners on, as 10 of 12 thieves were successful against him last year.

2001 Outlook

The Rays are hoping Rupe is healthy for a full season. He said at the end of the summer that he was relieved that doctors found the blood clot because he knew something wasn't right. Now he had some peace of mind going into the offseason. He is expected to be at full speed by the start of spring training, and Tampa Bay will be looking for him to assume a spot, but not the top spot, in its rotation.

Position: SP
Bats: R **Throws:** R
Ht: 6' 5" **Wt:** 230

Opening Day Age: 25
Born: 3/31/75 in Houston, TX
ML Seasons: 2
Pronunciation: ROOP

Overall Statistics

	W	L	Pct.	ERA	G	GS	Sv	IP	H	BB	SO	HR	Ratio
2000	5	6	.455	6.92	18	18	0	91.0	121	31	61	19	1.67
Career	13	15	.464	5.48	42	42	0	233.1	257	88	158	36	1.48

How Often He Throws Strikes

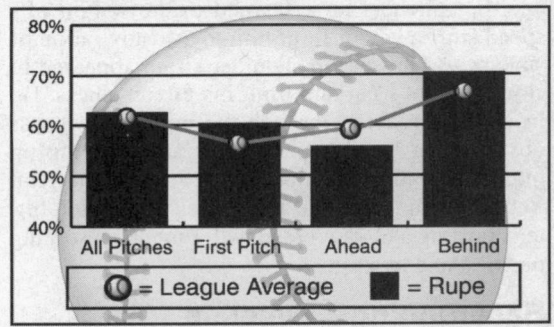

2000 Situational Stats

	W	L	ERA	Sv	IP		AB	H	HR	RBI	Avg
Home	2	3	8.21	0	34.0	LHB	201	63	9	33	.313
Road	3	3	6.16	0	57.0	RHB	176	58	10	36	.330
First Half	0	4	9.99	0	33.1	Sc Pos	99	29	5	51	.293
Scnd Half	5	2	5.15	0	57.2	Clutch	3	0	0	0	.000

2000 Rankings (American League)

- 8th in hit batsmen (9) and highest batting average allowed vs. lefthanded batters

Greg Vaughn

2000 Season

When healthy, Greg Vaughn was everything the Devil Rays expected when they signed him to a four-year, $34-million contract. He hit home runs, delivered in the clutch, hustled constantly and provided much-needed clubhouse leadership. Unfortunately, a series of injuries limited his contributions. Still, Vaughn led the team with 28 homers and ranked third with 74 RBI despite making just 124 starts.

Hitting

Vaughn is an excellent fastball hitter, often waiting for an inside heater that he can pull with his short but powerful swing. It's beautiful when he gets one, but pitchers have learned to throw him off-speed stuff away or limit him to a steady ration of sinkers. A late-season shoulder strain appeared to slow Vaughn's bat and limit his effectiveness. He insisted on playing through the injury, but it was obvious that he was fouling off and popping up pitches he had been hammering earlier in the year. Yet he remained one of the game's top clutch hitters, posting a .348 average with runners in scoring position and two outs.

Baserunning & Defense

Vaughn is underrated on the bases and in the field. He's actually an excellent baserunner and knows when to pick his spots, going 8-for-9 in steals despite hamstring troubles. He's even more valuable beating out infield hits, going from first to third and taking an extra base. He doesn't have tremendous range in the outfield, but manages to catch everything he gets to and enhances his average arm with hustle and anticipation.

2001 Outlook

The shoulder strain limited Vaughn to DH duties for much of the second half of last season, but the Rays are hoping a winter of rest and strengthening exercises will allow him to return to left field on a full-time basis. They have seen the impact he can have and would like nothing more than to pencil him into the No. 3 spot in the order for 155 or so games.

Position: LF/DH
Bats: R **Throws:** R
Ht: 6' 0" **Wt:** 202

Opening Day Age: 35
Born: 7/3/65 in Sacramento, CA
ML Seasons: 12

Overall Statistics

	G	AB	R	H	D	T	HR	RBI	SB	BB	SO	Avg	OBP	Slg
2000	127	461	83	117	27	1	28	74	8	80	128	.254	.365	.499
Career	1504	5330	907	1314	246	21	320	956	107	745	1288	.247	.340	.481

Where He Hits the Ball

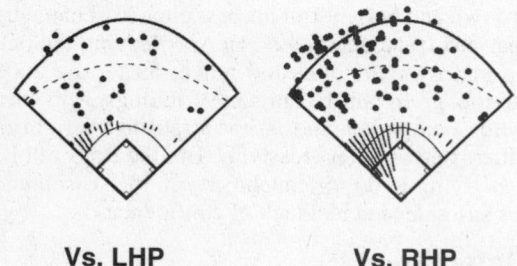

Vs. LHP   **Vs. RHP**

2000 Situational Stats

	AB	H	HR	RBI	Avg		AB	H	HR	RBI	Avg
Home	201	62	13	33	.308	LHP	87	23	4	11	.264
Road	260	55	15	41	.212	RHP	374	94	24	63	.251
First Half	218	64	14	37	.294	Sc Pos	106	30	7	45	.283
Scnd Half	243	53	14	37	.218	Clutch	77	25	7	15	.325

2000 Rankings (American League)

- 3rd in lowest batting average on the road
- 5th in lowest percentage of swings put into play (34.5)
- 6th in highest percentage of swings that missed (28.6)
- Led the Devil Rays in home runs, strikeouts, slugging percentage, HR frequency (16.5 ABs per HR), most pitches seen per plate appearance (4.01), batting average in the clutch, slugging percentage vs. righthanded pitchers (.505), highest percentage of pitches taken (55.7) and lowest percentage of swings on the first pitch (36.4)
- Led AL left fielders in walks and most pitches seen per plate appearance (4.01)

Gerald Williams

2000 Season

Gerald Williams seemed almost like an after-thought when the Devil Rays signed him as a free agent, but he turned out to be their most valuable player last year. He established himself as the club's leadoff hitter and center fielder and quickly became the top performer the Rays have ever had at either position. He set career highs in home runs and RBI while playing good defense.

Hitting

Williams is hardly the prototypical leadoff hitter, not with three times as many strikeouts as walks, a .312 on-base percentage and a tendency to get himself out with a weak swing at balls outside the strike zone. But he got the job done. Overcoming previous problems against righthanders, he provided middle-of-the-order production from the top of the lineup. His most important trait may have been his consistency; he went hitless in back-to-back games only twice last season, three fewer times than major league hits leader Darin Erstad.

Baserunning & Defense

Williams has tremendous speed, which helped him in all facets of the game except for stolen bases, where he was just 12-for-24. However, it was not uncommon to see him racing all over the outfield to make leaping catches and dashing around the bases once the ball was in play. He has a strong, accurate arm and excellent leaping ability, making him the complete outfielder.

2001 Outlook

While the Devil Rays got more than they expected from Williams last year, they're going to be greedy this season, expecting even more. He'll turn 35 during the campaign, but the Rays don't expect him to slow down. He was a part-time player for years and came to Tampa Bay for the opportunity to play every day. Unless something unforeseen happens, he should once again be the Rays' starting center fielder and leadoff man.

Position: CF
Bats: R **Throws:** R
Ht: 6' 2" **Wt:** 187

Opening Day Age: 34
Born: 8/10/66 in New Orleans, LA
ML Seasons: 9

Overall Statistics

	G	AB	R	H	D	T	HR	RBI	SB	BB	SO	Avg	OBP	Slg
2000	146	632	87	173	30	2	21	89	12	34	103	.274	.312	.427
Career	912	2573	395	683	154	16	76	329	84	149	433	.265	.310	.426

Where He Hits the Ball

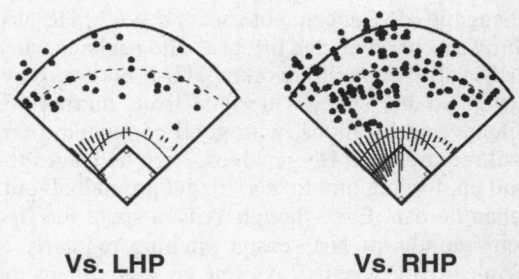

Vs. LHP   **Vs. RHP**

2000 Situational Stats

	AB	H	HR	RBI	Avg		AB	H	HR	RBI	Avg
Home	297	80	6	31	.269	LHP	123	32	5	19	.260
Road	335	93	15	58	.278	RHP	509	141	16	70	.277
First Half	322	91	9	48	.283	Sc Pos	159	45	5	65	.283
Scnd Half	310	82	12	41	.265	Clutch	104	25	2	21	.240

2000 Rankings (American League)

- 1st in lowest stolen-base percentage (50.0)
- 2nd in highest percentage of swings on the first pitch (44.4)
- 3rd in caught stealing (12), errors in center field (6), lowest batting average on a 3-1 count (.000), lowest on-base percentage for a leadoff hitter (.303) and lowest fielding percentage in center field (.983)
- 4th in at-bats
- 5th in lowest percentage of pitches taken (46.2)
- Led the Devil Rays in at-bats, runs scored, hits, singles, doubles, total bases (270), caught stealing (12), plate appearances (682), fewest GDPs per GDP situation (4.6%) and batting average with runners in scoring position

Tampa Bay

Paul Wilson

2000 Season

The Mets seemed to have given up on Paul Wilson, but the Devil Rays were extremely excited to acquire him and Jason Tyner in a late-July deal for Rick White and Bubba Trammell. Wilson had not pitched in the majors since 1996 and had undergone shoulder and elbow surgery. Still, Tampa Bay brought him right to the big leagues after the trade. He responded in impressive fashion even while being handled cautiously. He went 1-2 with a 3.29 ERA in seven starts, closing the season with 14 scoreless innings.

Pitching

Wilson works off his above-average fastball. Depending on the outing, he can use his slider or his changeup as a dependable second pitch. He also throws a curveball and offers a solid package when he has all four pitches working. He is not overpowering, so his success derives from mixing his pitches and locations, with good command a virtual requirement. He gets hurt when he leaves the ball up, forcing him to learn to get groundball outs when he can. Even though Wilson spent the first four months of last season pitching regularly at Triple-A, the Devil Rays felt he was still in the recovery process from surgery and that he should be stronger and sharper for the 2001 season.

Defense

Wilson is a good athlete and has lost a hefty amount of weight since he last pitched in the majors for the Mets, making him quicker and more athletic coming off the mound. He does a decent job of fielding his position but needs to do a better job of keeping the running game in check, as baserunners were six of seven in steals against him last year.

2001 Outlook

Team officials think they may have found a solid starter in Wilson, who has plenty of good years ahead of him. Wilson thinks he has the opportunity to finally show that all the hard work he endured in order to return from two major surgeries wasn't wasted. He'll have the opportunity to open the season in the rotation, though a stint as a long reliever also is possible.

Position: SP
Bats: R **Throws:** R
Ht: 6' 5" **Wt:** 235

Opening Day Age: 28
Born: 3/28/73 in Orlando, FL
ML Seasons: 2

Overall Statistics

	W	L	Pct.	ERA	G	GS	Sv	IP	H	BB	SO	HR	Ratio
2000	1	4	.200	3.35	11	7	0	51.0	38	16	40	1	1.06
Career	6	16	.273	4.86	37	33	0	200.0	195	87	149	16	1.41

How Often He Throws Strikes

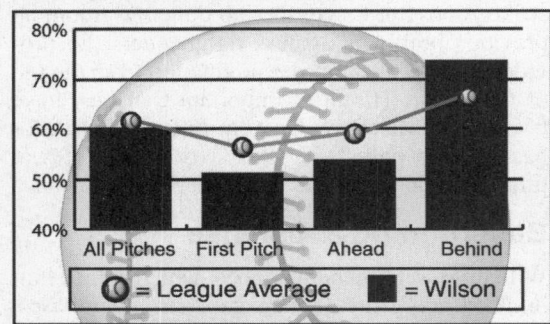

2000 Situational Stats

	W	L	ERA	Sv	IP		AB	H	HR	RBI	Avg
Home	0	2	2.49	0	25.1	LHB	92	21	0	11	.228
Road	1	2	4.21	0	25.2	RHB	90	17	1	3	.189
First Half	0	0	-	0	0.0	Sc Pos	40	9	0	11	.225
Scnd Half	1	4	3.35	0	51.0	Clutch	19	3	0	1	.158

2000 Rankings (American League)

- 6th in fewest GDPs induced per GDP situation (2.7%)

Wilson Alvarez

Position: SP
Bats: L **Throws:** L
Ht: 6' 1" **Wt:** 245

Opening Day Age: 31
Born: 3/24/70 in
Maracaibo, Venezuela
ML Seasons: 10

Overall Statistics

	W	L	Pct.	ERA	G	GS	Sv	IP	H	BB	SO	HR	Ratio
2000							Did Not Play						
Career	86	77	.528	3.96	250	224	1	1433.0	1324	708	1074	153	1.42

2000 Situational Stats

	W	L	ERA	Sv	IP		AB	H	HR	RBI	Avg
Home	—	—	—	—	—	LHB	—	—	—	—	—
Road	—	—	—	—	—	RHB	—	—	—	—	—
First Half	—	—	—	—	—	Sc Pos	—	—	—	—	—
Scnd Half	—	—	—	—	—	Clutch	—	—	—	—	—

2000 Season

Just when the critics of Wilson Alvarez' five-year, $35-million contract thought things couldn't get any worse, they did. After struggling through the first two seasons of the pact with minor injuries and inconsistent performances, Alvarez missed the entire 2000 campaign due to shoulder discomfort that led to rotator cuff surgery.

Pitching & Defense

Alvarez seems to be at his best when he works off his low-90s fastball, moving it around the plate and using it to set up his offspeed stuff. He gets into trouble when he throws too many breaking balls early in the count and falls behind hitters. The key is to have enough confidence in his fastball to just rear back and throw it. Of course, having a healthy arm certainly wouldn't hurt his confidence. Though not very athletic, Alvarez usually gets a glove on balls hit back at him. His pickoff move is decent.

2001 Outlook

It would be hard to understate how much the Devil Rays want and need a healthy Alvarez back in the rotation. Some say he is the key to their entire season. Quite simply, if Alvarez comes back strong, the Rays have a shot to compete and maybe even contend.

Mike DiFelice

Position: C
Bats: R **Throws:** R
Ht: 6' 2" **Wt:** 205

Opening Day Age: 31
Born: 5/28/69 in
Philadelphia, PA
ML Seasons: 5
Pronunciation:
dee-fah-LEECE

Overall Statistics

	G	AB	R	H	D	T	HR	RBI	SB	BB	SO	Avg	OBP	Slg
2000	60	204	23	49	13	1	6	19	0	12	40	.240	.280	.402
Career	292	898	77	225	47	5	19	101	1	54	181	.251	.296	.378

2000 Situational Stats

	AB	H	HR	RBI	Avg		AB	H	HR	RBI	Avg
Home	104	25	4	12	.240	LHP	40	9	0	1	.225
Road	100	24	2	7	.240	RHP	164	40	6	18	.244
First Half	109	32	4	11	.294	Sc Pos	39	6	1	11	.154
Scnd Half	95	17	2	8	.179	Clutch	40	12	2	7	.300

2000 Season

Mike DiFelice played more in 2000 than he did the year before, but that didn't translate into better production. DiFelice dropped 67 points off his average and knocked in two-thirds as many runs as he did in 1999. His defensive performance slipped as well, as he caught just 16 of 51 basestealers.

Hitting, Baserunning & Defense

DiFelice has matured as a hitter and doesn't get fooled nearly as often as he did earlier in his career, but he is not consistent enough to play on an everyday basis. He does seem to have gained some power over the last two seasons, which is good because he is slow on the bases. Behind the plate, DiFelice's strength is catching the ball. He will give up his body to block a pitch or the plate, but he also tends to miss a key pitch every now and then, as evidenced by his 10 passed balls.

2001 Outlook

Unless the Devil Rays trade John Flaherty in a salary-dump deal, DiFelice is headed to a fourth straight season of backup duty. Most likely he will be the official catcher for one or two of the starters, guaranteeing him at least one start every five days. The two backstops do make a good tandem, but DiFelice is likely to remain No. 2 as long as Flaherty is No. 1.

Juan Guzman

Position: SP
Bats: R **Throws:** R
Ht: 5'11" **Wt:** 195

Opening Day Age: 34
Born: 10/28/66 in Santo Domingo, Dominican Republic
ML Seasons: 10
Pronunciation: GOOZ-mahn

Overall Statistics

	W	L	Pct.	ERA	G	GS	Sv	IP	H	BB	SO	HR	Ratio
2000	0	1	.000	43.20	1	1	0	1.2	7	2	3	2	5.40
Career	91	79	.535	4.08	240	240	0	1483.1	1360	667	1243	149	1.37

2000 Situational Stats

	W	L	ERA	Sv	IP		AB	H	HR	RBI	Avg
Home	0	1	43.20	0	1.2	LHB	7	4	2	5	.571
Road	—	—	—	—	—	RHB	4	3	0	3	.750
First Half	0	1	43.20	0	1.2	Sc Pos	5	4	1	7	.800
Scnd Half	—	—	—	—	—	Clutch	—	—	—	—	—

2000 Season

The Devil Rays signed Juan Guzman to a two-year, $12.5 million contract before the 2000 season. They hoped he would be a top-of-the-rotation veteran who could throw 200-plus innings and provide leadership and stability for a young staff. But shoulder discomfort limited him to one start and resulted in midseason surgery.

Pitching & Defense

When healthy, Guzman is a successful, if not dominating starter. He has a low-90s fastball along with a splitter and a slider that can be as tough as anybody's. He has a tendency to surrender home runs when he leaves his fastball up. What had impressed the Rays was his durability and ability to perform under pressure. Guzman doesn't do that much to help himself defensively, since he's not particularly quick or agile. His slow delivery makes him an easy target for would-be thieves.

2001 Outlook

The Devil Rays hope Guzman's arthroscopic shoulder surgery allows him to return to his old form. He began throwing in early December, and has shown the ability to bounce back well from previous arm problems. But he'll be 34 this season, and there's no way to tell how the surgery and a year off will affect him.

Russ Johnson

Position: 3B/2B/SS
Bats: R **Throws:** R
Ht: 5'10" **Wt:** 180

Opening Day Age: 28
Born: 2/22/73 in Baton Rouge, LA
ML Seasons: 4

Overall Statistics

	G	AB	R	H	D	T	HR	RBI	SB	BB	SO	Avg	OBP	Slg
2000	100	230	32	55	8	0	2	20	5	27	40	.239	.320	.300
Career	212	459	65	120	20	0	9	52	9	54	90	.261	.339	.364

2000 Situational Stats

	AB	H	HR	RBI	Avg		AB	H	HR	RBI	Avg
Home	116	29	2	12	.250	LHP	87	23	1	5	.264
Road	114	26	0	8	.228	RHP	143	32	1	15	.224
First Half	97	21	1	12	.216	Sc Pos	64	15	0	18	.234
Scnd Half	133	34	1	8	.256	Clutch	45	12	0	8	.267

2000 Season

Tampa Bay acquired Russ Johnson from Houston in late May to provide depth around the infield and to possibly challenge for the starting job at second base. He provided plenty of depth, but he didn't make enough of an impression to crack the lineup on a regular basis.

Hitting, Baserunning & Defense

Johnson has a keen eye, some power, decent speed and a good glove. He is a line-drive hitter with a knack for producing a good at-bat in clutch situations. But what stands out the most about him is toughness and determination at the plate. Johnson can start at third, second or short, as well as play some outfield. In fact, his versatility makes him so valuable as a utility player that it may actually work against him winning a starting job. He is quick with decent range around the infield and has an average to above-average arm. Johnson has just decent speed but is a smart baserunner.

2001 Outlook

Johnson would like to be the starting second baseman, and he planned to spend the offseason working on his power to help his cause. But the Devil Rays may be just as happy to have him as a utility player, knowing he conceivably could play seven positions.

Quinton McCracken

Position: LF
Bats: B **Throws:** R
Ht: 5' 7" **Wt:** 173

Opening Day Age: 30
Born: 8/16/70 in
Wilmington, NC
ML Seasons: 6
Nickname: Q, Coo Coo

Overall Statistics

	G	AB	R	H	D	T	HR	RBI	SB	BB	SO	Avg	OBP	Slg
2000	15	31	5	4	0	0	0	2	0	6	4	.129	.270	.129
Career	484	1402	221	397	68	15	14	155	70	135	259	.283	.346	.383

2000 Situational Stats

	AB	H	HR	RBI	Avg		AB	H	HR	RBI	Avg
Home	10	1	0	1	.100	LHP	12	3	0	0	.250
Road	21	3	0	1	.143	RHP	19	1	0	2	.053
First Half	26	3	0	2	.115	Sc Pos	7	1	0	2	.143
Scnd Half	5	1	0	0	.200	Clutch	7	1	0	0	.143

2000 Season

Quinton McCracken worked hard to come back from a torn knee ligament he suffered in 1999. But his chances for playing time last year seemed doomed once the Devil Rays signed Greg Vaughn and Gerald Williams. McCracken finished with just 31 at-bats over four stints with Tampa Bay.

Hitting, Baserunning & Defense

McCracken didn't seem to fully regain the quickness and leg strength he displayed before his injury. His days of 20-plus steals probably are over. He makes up for his lack of size with hustle and determination. He is best when he hits the ball on the ground or into the gaps and uses his speed. But he'll occasionally get away from that facet of his game and strike out too much while swinging for the fences. McCracken can play center or left field. While he doesn't have a great arm, he compensates with smart positioning and a quick delivery.

2001 Outlook

Though the extra time off should make his knee even stronger, McCracken dropped out of Tampa Bay's plans, as the Devil Rays released him in late November. Given the surplus of outfielders on the Devil Rays' roster and in their system, McCracken's future will be better served elsewhere.

Bryan Rekar

Position: SP
Bats: R **Throws:** R
Ht: 6' 3" **Wt:** 220

Opening Day Age: 28
Born: 6/3/72 in
Oaklawn, IL
ML Seasons: 6

Overall Statistics

	W	L	Pct.	ERA	G	GS	Sv	IP	H	BB	SO	HR	Ratio
2000	7	10	.412	4.41	30	27	0	173.1	200	39	95	22	1.38
Career	22	34	.393	5.41	104	81	0	507.1	609	157	294	77	1.51

2000 Situational Stats

	W	L	ERA	Sv	IP		AB	H	HR	RBI	Avg
Home	5	4	3.75	0	108.0	LHB	351	103	11	49	.293
Road	2	6	5.51	0	65.1	RHB	335	97	11	39	.290
First Half	3	4	4.12	0	67.2	Sc Pos	159	41	4	66	.258
Scnd Half	4	6	4.60	0	105.2	Clutch	42	18	2	8	.429

2000 Season

Despite off-field problems last year, Bryan Rekar enjoyed his best season in the majors to date. He made 27 starts, a career high, and threw 173.1 innings. Although briefly moved to the bullpen, he proved to be one of the Devil Rays' most consistent starters.

Pitching & Defense

Some Devil Rays say Rekar has the best stuff of all their pitchers, with a moving fastball clocked in the low to mid-90s and a nasty slider. A slight hitch in his windup can be disruptive to a batter's timing. Rekar's breakthrough in the 2000 season was due as much to mental adjustments as anything else. He remained aggressive in the strike zone and eliminated careless mistakes. He has had trouble with a sore back at times and is not a particularly adept fielder. He holds runners well.

2001 Outlook

Rekar finally showed last season that he could be a successful major league starter. His challenge in 2001 will be to prove that he can do it again and with perhaps greater consistency. He also needs to go deeper into games. If he can do all that, there definitely will be a place for him in Tampa Bay's rotation. If not, he might end up in the bullpen, where he hasn't had as much success.

Bobby Smith

Position: 2B
Bats: R **Throws:** R
Ht: 6' 3" **Wt:** 190

Opening Day Age: 26
Born: 5/10/74 in
Oakland, CA
ML Seasons: 3

Overall Statistics

	G	AB	R	H	D	T	HR	RBI	SB	BB	SO	Avg	OBP	Slg
2000	49	175	21	41	8	0	6	26	2	14	59	.234	.293	.383
Career	234	744	83	179	27	4	20	100	11	64	233	.241	.305	.368

2000 Situational Stats

	AB	H	HR	RBI	Avg		AB	H	HR	RBI	Avg
Home	89	22	2	14	.247	LHP	48	12	1	7	.250
Road	86	19	4	12	.221	RHP	127	29	5	19	.228
First Half	74	23	3	14	.311	Sc Pos	47	14	0	17	.298
Scnd Half	101	18	3	12	.178	Clutch	26	5	2	5	.192

2000 Season

The final cut of spring training, Smith started the year with a flourish at Triple-A Durham and had a strong three weeks with the parent club before spraining his right knee July 5. He came back August 19 and struggled the rest of the way, including a 7-for-69 stretch that featured 31 strikeouts.

Hitting, Baserunning & Defense

Smith is a streak hitter, and the bad streaks can be very bad. When he is on a roll, he crushes mistakes and can drive them into gaps and over fences. He smacked 23 homers between Durham and Tampa Bay last year. The Rays converted Smith from third base to second thinking they would take advantage of his corner infield power at a middle infield position, but he has yet to deliver consistently at the big league level. He has a decent arm but isn't particularly smooth in the field. He also doesn't run fast, further limiting his value as a utility player.

2001 Outlook

Smith's best chance to stick with the Rays will be to win the starting second-base job, but he'll have to beat out Russ Johnson and Brent Abernathy. They seem set at third with Vinny Castilla and Aubrey Huff, and they have plenty of utility infielders. Smith has had several chances to win a job before. This may be his last one with Tampa Bay.

Tanyon Sturtze

Position: RP
Bats: R **Throws:** R
Ht: 6' 5" **Wt:** 205

Opening Day Age: 30
Born: 10/12/70 in
Worcester, MA
ML Seasons: 5

Overall Statistics

	W	L	Pct.	ERA	G	GS	Sv	IP	H	BB	SO	HR	Ratio
2000	5	2	.714	4.74	29	6	0	68.1	72	29	44	8	1.48
Career	7	3	.700	5.93	47	12	0	120.0	139	55	71	18	1.62

2000 Situational Stats

	W	L	ERA	Sv	IP		AB	H	HR	RBI	Avg
Home	2	0	3.08	0	38.0	LHB	134	36	4	23	.269
Road	3	2	6.82	0	30.1	RHB	131	36	4	17	.275
First Half	1	2	7.39	0	31.2	Sc Pos	77	24	5	34	.312
Scnd Half	4	0	2.45	0	36.2	Clutch	13	4	0	2	.308

2000 Season

Acquired from the White Sox in May, Tanyon Sturtze took a while to gain command and confidence. He then ran off nearly a half-dozen starts for the Devil Rays, each more impressive than the previous one. He went 3-0 with a 2.28 ERA in the five starts with Tampa before a strained left oblique muscle ended his season a month early.

Pitching & Defense

Sturtze's best pitch is a hard fastball that he keeps down in the strike zone. He can be equally effective when his splitter is working the same way. He also throws a slider and straight changeup. Like other young pitchers, he occasionally has to be reminded to stay aggressive in the strike zone and to keep the ball down. Once he got into the regular routine of the rotation, his strikeout-walk ratio dropped considerably. He's a tremendous athlete, which makes him an extremely good fielder. He needs work on holding runners, however.

2001 Outlook

If he can pick up where he left off, Sturtze was good enough to have a chance to regain a spot in what might be a crowded Tampa Bay rotation. Even if that doesn't work out, the hard-throwing righthander is versatile enough that he could fill an important role in the bullpen.

Jason Tyner

Position: LF
Bats: L **Throws:** L
Ht: 6' 1" **Wt:** 170

Opening Day Age: 23
Born: 4/23/77 in Beaumont, TX
ML Seasons: 1

Overall Statistics

	G	AB	R	H	D	T	HR	RBI	SB	BB	SO	Avg	OBP	Slg
2000	50	124	9	28	4	0	0	13	7	5	16	.226	.261	.258
Career	50	124	9	28	4	0	0	13	7	5	16	.226	.261	.258

2000 Situational Stats

	AB	H	HR	RBI	Avg		AB	H	HR	RBI	Avg
Home	41	7	0	7	.171	LHP	20	3	0	2	.150
Road	83	21	0	6	.253	RHP	104	25	0	11	.240
First Half	41	8	0	5	.195	Sc Pos	28	9	0	13	.321
Scnd Half	83	20	0	8	.241	Clutch	26	6	0	3	.231

2000 Season

Jason Tyner made his way to the major leagues with the Mets, but he appeared to find a home with the Devil Rays after being acquired in late July. Tyner didn't play a lot with Tampa Bay, but the club liked what they saw in his limited at-bats.

Hitting, Baserunning & Defense

The key to Tyner's game is speed. That's what makes him so effective in the outfield, that's what makes him such a dangerous weapon as a baserunner and that's what makes him a potentially disruptive offensive force. The key for Tyner is to hit the ball on the ground or drop line drives into the outfield and then run like crazy. Essentially, he is a Brett Butler-type player. Tyner doesn't have an overly strong arm, but does make up for it with good positioning, although he could use some work on tracking balls. On the bases he is not only fast but also is a technically solid runner. He will continue to develop as a leadoff hitter.

2001 Outlook

Tyner's role for this season seems to be unclear. Assuming the Rays have Greg Vaughn back in left field and Gerald Williams in center, and then acquire a right fielder, Tyner at best would be the fourth or fifth outfielder. His primary role may be to provide defense and speed off the bench.

Esteban Yan

Position: RP/SP
Bats: R **Throws:** R
Ht: 6' 4" **Wt:** 230

Opening Day Age: 26
Born: 6/22/74 in Campina del Seibo, Dominican Republic
ML Seasons: 5
Pronunciation: YAWN

Overall Statistics

	W	L	Pct.	ERA	G	GS	Sv	IP	H	BB	SO	HR	Ratio
2000	7	8	.467	6.21	43	20	0	137.2	158	42	111	26	1.45
Career	15	17	.469	5.76	164	23	1	306.1	346	125	245	51	1.54

2000 Situational Stats

	W	L	ERA	Sv	IP		AB	H	HR	RBI	Avg
Home	2	6	6.20	0	74.0	LHB	253	80	8	33	.316
Road	5	2	6.22	0	63.2	RHB	302	78	18	57	.258
First Half	4	6	6.80	0	92.2	Sc Pos	144	35	5	59	.243
Scnd Half	3	2	5.00	0	45.0	Clutch	91	22	1	11	.242

2000 Season

The Devil Rays decided to move Esteban Yan into the rotation last season after two years in the bullpen. But Yan never really made the adjustment. He again was bothered by soreness in his shoulder, which seems to be an annual event. Worst of all, he allowed a team record 26 homers in 137.2 innings.

Pitching & Defense

When Yan is on, he can be downright nasty. He has a fastball that pushes the mid- to upper-90s with decent movement. He'll also mix in a slider and changeup. Yan tends to get excited on the mound. That adrenaline rush can be a plus when things are going well but a negative when he gets into trouble. He needs to do a better job of throwing strikes and getting ahead of hitters. Yan is not very graceful on the mound and is vulnerable to bunts. Like many Tampa pitchers, he also could pay more attention to the running game.

2001 Outlook

Though Yan was a starter throughout most of his minor league career, the Rays apparently have decided once and for all to keep him in the bullpen. Trades have left him as the likely setup man to closer Roberto Hernandez, a key role given manager Larry Rothschild's reluctance to use Hernandez for more than one inning.

Tampa Bay

Doug Creek (Pos: LHP, Age: 32)

	W	L	Pct.	ERA	G	GS	Sv	IP	H	BB	SO	HR	Ratio
2000	1	3	.250	4.60	45	0	1	60.2	49	39	73	10	1.45
Career	2	7	.222	5.53	120	3	1	135.0	114	96	141	23	1.56

After spending 1998 in Japan and most of 1999 in Triple-A, Creek had a fairly successful season in the Devil Ray bullpen. He limited lefthanded hitters to a .170 average and .250 slugging percentage. 2001 Outlook: B

Mike Duvall (Pos: LHP, Age: 26)

	W	L	Pct.	ERA	G	GS	Sv	IP	H	BB	SO	HR	Ratio
2000	0	0	-	7.71	2	0	0	2.1	5	1	0	0	2.57
Career	1	1	.500	4.47	45	0	0	46.1	55	30	19	5	1.83

Duvall's career strikeout-walk ratio is the worst among hurlers who pitched last year and have at least 25 career innings. He appeared in 40 games for the Devil Rays in 1999. 2001 Outlook: C

Dave Eiland (Pos: RHP, Age: 34)

	W	L	Pct.	ERA	G	GS	Sv	IP	H	BB	SO	HR	Ratio
2000	2	3	.400	7.24	17	10	0	54.2	77	18	17	8	1.74
Career	12	27	.308	5.74	92	70	0	373.0	465	118	153	46	1.56

Few pitchers are successful surrendering four times as many hits as strikeouts. Eiland wasn't last year. He hasn't posted a big league ERA under 5.00 since 1990. Oakland gave him a minor league deal. 2001 Outlook: C

Trevor Enders (Pos: LHP, Age: 26)

	W	L	Pct.	ERA	G	GS	Sv	IP	H	BB	SO	HR	Ratio
2000	0	1	.000	10.61	9	0	0	9.1	14	5	5	2	2.04
Career	0	1	.000	10.61	9	0	0	9.1	14	5	5	2	2.04

Enders went undrafted coming out of college, but after going 24-7 in the minors the last three years, he earned a September callup with Tampa Bay. He thrives with great control. 2001 Outlook: C

Tony Fiore (Pos: RHP, Age: 29)

	W	L	Pct.	ERA	G	GS	Sv	IP	H	BB	SO	HR	Ratio
2000	1	1	.500	8.40	11	0	0	15.0	21	9	8	3	2.00
Career	1	1	.500	8.40	11	0	0	15.0	21	9	8	3	2.00

Since leaving the Phillies' organization in 1999, Fiore has saved a few games in Triple-A. He may be best remembered for throwing at Brian Daubach and getting suspended for three games last year. He re-signed with Tampa in December. 2001 Outlook: C

Ozzie Guillen (Pos: SS/3B, Age: 37, Bats: L)

	G	AB	R	H	D	T	HR	RBI	SB	BB	SO	Avg	OBP	Slg
2000	63	107	22	26	4	0	2	12	1	6	7	.243	.283	.336
Career	1993	6686	773	1764	275	69	28	619	169	239	511	.264	.287	.338

Don Kessinger and Bill Russell are the only other non-pitchers in history to have played at least 16 seasons and collected as many hits as Guillen has without ever slugging at least .375. The Rays signed him to a minor league deal in December. 2001 Outlook: C

Toby Hall (Pos: C, Age: 25, Bats: R)

	G	AB	R	H	D	T	HR	RBI	SB	BB	SO	Avg	OBP	Slg
2000	4	12	1	2	0	0	1	1	0	1	0	.167	.231	.417
Career	4	12	1	2	0	0	1	1	0	1	0	.167	.231	.417

Hall is solid defensively and has hit for average and power in the minors. His strike-zone judgment is troublesome, but he may be Tampa Bay's top catching prospect. 2001 Outlook: C

Cory Lidle (Pos: RHP, Age: 29)

	W	L	Pct.	ERA	G	GS	Sv	IP	H	BB	SO	HR	Ratio
2000	4	6	.400	5.03	31	11	0	96.2	114	29	62	13	1.48
Career	12	8	.600	4.42	90	14	2	183.1	208	51	120	20	1.41

Lidle had an eventful season, returning from elbow surgery, getting called up from Triple-A on four occasions, serving a suspension for throwing at hitters, and becoming a father. 2001 Outlook: B

Felix Martinez (Pos: SS, Age: 26, Bats: B)

	G	AB	R	H	D	T	HR	RBI	SB	BB	SO	Avg	OBP	Slg
2000	106	299	42	64	11	4	2	17	9	32	68	.214	.305	.298
Career	162	422	53	83	13	6	2	25	12	43	97	.197	.284	.270

Martinez started 103 games at shortstop for Tampa Bay last year and led the majors in range factor. But he won't keep the job unless he contributes more with the bat. 2001 Outlook: B

Jim Morris (Pos: LHP, Age: 37)

	W	L	Pct.	ERA	G	GS	Sv	IP	H	BB	SO	HR	Ratio
2000	0	0	-	4.35	16	0	0	10.1	10	7	10	1	1.65
Career	0	0	-	4.80	21	0	0	15.0	13	9	13	2	1.47

Morris was a great story in 1999 when he made his major league debut at age 35. The story turned sour last year when he was demoted to Triple-A, underwent elbow surgery and was later released. The Dodgers have signed him. 2001 Outlook: C

Damian Rolls (Pos: 3B, Age: 23, Bats: R)

	G	AB	R	H	D	T	HR	RBI	SB	BB	SO	Avg	OBP	Slg
2000	4	3	0	1	0	0	0	0	0	0	1	.333	.333	.333
Career	4	3	0	1	0	0	0	0	0	0	1	.333	.333	.333

The Devil Rays acquired Rolls after Kansas City selected him in the Rule 5 draft last winter. He subsequently missed most of the season with a shoulder injury. He's still a work in progress. 2001 Outlook: C

Jeff Sparks (Pos: RHP, Age: 28)

	W	L	Pct.	ERA	G	GS	Sv	IP	H	BB	SO	HR	Ratio
2000	0	1	.000	3.54	15	0	0	20.1	13	18	24	2	1.52
Career	0	1	.000	4.15	23	0	1	30.1	19	30	41	3	1.62

After issuing nine walks in his last three appearances covering 2.2 innings, Sparks was demoted last May and never returned. The Devil Rays released him in November. 2001 Outlook: C

Billy Taylor (Pos: RHP, **Age**: 39)

	W	L	Pct.	ERA	G	GS	Sv	IP	H	BB	SO	HR	Ratio
2000	1	3	.250	8.56	17	0	0	13.2	13	9	13	2	1.61
Career	16	28	.364	4.21	316	0	100	322.2	312	133	304	26	1.38

Taylor saved 26 games for the second straight season, only last year it was in Triple-A. His days as a major league closer almost certainly are behind him unless someone gets desperate. 2001 Outlook: C

Ozzie Timmons (Pos: RF, **Age**: 30, **Bats**: R)

	G	AB	R	H	D	T	HR	RBI	SB	BB	SO	Avg	OBP	Slg
2000	12	41	9	14	3	0	4	13	0	1	7	.341	.357	.707
Career	186	405	62	95	20	1	20	60	4	33	82	.235	.293	.437

Born in Tampa and a product of the University of Tampa, Timmons' homecoming was hardly scintillating last year, though you can't fault his performance. He'll have to keep proving himself somewhere else, as the Rays released him. 2001 Outlook: C

Randy Winn (Pos: LF/CF, **Age**: 26, **Bats**: B)

	G	AB	R	H	D	T	HR	RBI	SB	BB	SO	Avg	OBP	Slg
2000	51	159	28	40	5	0	1	16	6	26	25	.252	.362	.302
Career	239	800	123	215	30	13	4	57	41	72	157	.269	.331	.354

Winn split his third straight season between Triple-A and Tampa Bay. Problem is, his major league time with the Devil Rays has decreased each year. He's 15-for-31 stealing bases the past two years. 2001 Outlook: C

Tampa Bay Devil Rays Minor League Prospects

Organization Overview:

The Devil Rays took the pressure off the farm system by signing free agents Gerald Williams, Greg Vaughn, Jose Canseco and Steve Trachsel. Tampa Bay had made a habit of drafting tools-rich but raw talent that required loads of development time, so few minor leaguers were having an impact. There hasn't been a payoff on the high-priced veterans, with the exception that Trachsel brought Brent Abernathy in a July trade. Hard-throwing Jesus Colome arrived in another deal involving veteran Jim Mecir, and Rick White and Bubba Trammell netted Jason Tyner and Paul Wilson. Now the farm system is flourishing, and Tyner, Wilson, Abernathy and Aubrey Huff may be playing in Tampa Bay in 2001. A highlight of the season may be a Triple-A Durham rotation featuring top prospects Colome, Bobby Seay, Jason Standridge, Matt White and possibly Travis Harper.

Brent Abernathy

Position: 2B
Bats: R **Throws:** R
Ht: 6' 1" **Wt:** 185

Opening Day Age: 23
Born: 9/23/77 in Atlanta, GA

Recent Statistics

	G	AB	R	H	D	T	HR	RBI	SB	BB	SO	Avg
1999 AA Knoxville	136	577	108	168	42	1	13	62	34	55	47	.291
2000 AAA Syracuse	92	358	47	106	21	2	4	35	14	26	32	.296
2000 AAA Durham	27	91	14	24	6	0	1	15	9	11	11	.264
2000 MLE	119	439	53	120	26	1	3	43	17	32	44	.273

The Devil Rays acquired Abernathy in a trade deadline deal that shipped Steve Trachsel and Mark Guthrie to Toronto. His tools have denied him prospect status for most of his career, but Abernathy has excelled with good baseball instincts and a strong work ethic. He does what No. 2 hitters are supposed to do: make contact, get on base and steal some bases. Squeezing more free passes out of his at-bats would enhance his game. Abernathy isn't exceptional defensively, but he can handle second base in the big leagues. With Miguel Cairo getting his walking papers in the fall, the path is clear for Abernathy to grab the second-base job with a good spring.

Jesus Colome

Position: P
Bats: R **Throws:** R
Ht: 6' 2" **Wt:** 170

Opening Day Age: 20
Born: 6/2/80 in San Pedro De Macoris, DR

Recent Statistics

	W	L	ERA	G	GS	Sv	IP	H	R	BB	SO	HR
1999 A Modesto	8	4	3.36	31	22	1	128.2	125	63	60	127	6
2000 AA Midland	9	4	3.59	20	20	0	110.1	99	62	50	95	10
2000 AA Orlando	1	2	6.75	3	3	0	14.2	18	12	7	9	2

The Devil Rays were willing to part with both Jim Mecir and prospect Todd Belitz to acquire Colome in July. Signed out of the Dominican Republic in 1996, Colome throws a fastball that approaches 100 MPH, but has little

movement. He also works with a slider that gives righthanded hitters trouble, but his changeup needs refinement. Before the trade, Colome succeeded in one of the minors' most notorious hitters' parks at Double-A Midland. He went 5-1 (3.36) at Midland's Christensen Stadium. While Colome will stay a starter at Triple-A Durham this spring, he could be a dominating reliever.

Josh Hamilton

Position: OF
Bats: L **Throws:** L
Ht: 6' 4" **Wt:** 209

Opening Day Age: 19
Born: 5/21/81 in Raleigh, NC

Recent Statistics

	G	AB	R	H	D	T	HR	RBI	SB	BB	SO	Avg
1999 R Princeton	56	236	49	82	20	4	10	48	18	13	43	.347
1999 A Hudson Val	16	72	7	14	3	0	7	1	1	14	14	.194
2000 A Chston-SC	96	392	62	118	23	3	13	61	14	26	72	.301

Selected first overall in the 1999 draft, Hamilton is a five-tool prospect with a knowledge of the game that seldom is seen at his age. Hamilton excelled at the plate and in the field. He showed impressive speed and a terrific arm as a center fielder—and an exciting over-the-shoulder catch in the Class-A South Atlantic League All-Star game epitomized his fine defensive work. Polled by *Baseball America*, Sally League managers rated Hamilton the best batting and power prospect in the circuit. He might have hit more homers if he hadn't played in Joseph P. Riley Jr. Park, known for steady winds that blow in off the Ashley River in Charleston, S.C. While torn cartilage that required minor arthroscopic knee surgery in August slowed Hamilton's progress, he may jump to Double-A Orlando to open 2001.

Travis Harper

Position: P
Bats: R **Throws:** R
Ht: 6' 4" **Wt:** 193

Opening Day Age: 24
Born: 5/21/76 in Harrisonburg, VA

Recent Statistics

	W	L	ERA	G	GS	Sv	IP	H	R	BB	SO	HR
2000 AA Orlando	3	1	2.63	9	9	0	51.1	49	19	11	33	1
2000 AAA Durham	7	4	4.24	17	17	0	104.0	98	53	26	48	15
2000 AL Tampa Bay	1	2	4.78	6	5	0	32.0	30	17	15	14	5

Harper's career started slowly as a 1997 third-round pick of the Red Sox who had his contract voided because he had elbow tendinitis. After signing with Tampa Bay in '98, he quickly made up for lost time by reaching Double-A Orlando in '99. He went 10-5 (3.71) between Orlando and Triple-A Durham in 2000. He closed with four decent starts for the Devil Rays, including a two-hit shutout of Toronto on September 24. Harper effectively works the strike zone with a low-90s fastball. His curve and changeup need fine-tuning, but Harper still has won in the high minors because of his smarts and intense makeup. With some improvements to his arsenal, Harper should be pitching in the Tampa Bay rotation in 2001.

Aubrey Huff

Position: 3B   **Opening Day Age:** 24
Bats: L **Throws:** R   **Born:** 12/20/76 in
Ht: 6' 4" **Wt:** 221   Marion, OH

Recent Statistics

	G	AB	R	H	D	THR	RBI	SB	BB	SO	Avg
2000 AAA Durham	108	408	73	129	36	3	20	76	2	51	72	.316
2000 AL Tampa Bay	39	122	12	35	7	0	4	14	0	5	18	.287
2000 MLE	108	389	53	110	31	2	15	56	1	37	75	.283

Drafted in 1998, Huff has hit better than .300 in each of his three minor league seasons. His rapid rise through the system didn't slow in the high minors, where Huff has averaged 21 homers and 77 RBI with a .389 on-base percentage over the last two years. He's a disciplined hitter with a plan at the plate. His quick swing allows him to drive the ball to all fields, and he showed some pop in his Devil Rays debut. His defense is adequate and he isn't a fast runner, but he's an accomplished lefthanded hitter who can handle southpaws. His biggest obstacle is Vinny Castilla, and reportedly the Devil Rays are trying to move him to make room for Huff.

Bobby Seay

Position: P   **Opening Day Age:** 22
Bats: L **Throws:** L   **Born:** 6/20/78 in
Ht: 6' 2" **Wt:** 221   Sarasota, FL

Recent Statistics

	W	L	ERA	G	GS	Sv	IP	H	R	BB	SO	HR
1999 A St. Pete	2	6	3.00	12	11	0	57.0	56	25	23	45	0
1999 AA Orlando	1	2	7.94	6	6	0	17.0	22	15	15	16	2
2000 AA Orlando	8	7	3.88	24	24	0	132.1	132	64	53	106	13

One of two loophole free agents signed by Tampa Bay in 1996, Seay never had surpassed 100 innings in a season because of a series of relatively minor ailments. That changed in 2000, when Seay stayed healthy and turned in his best season. Even in his best seasons prior to 2000, Seay was prone to the home-run ball, but that wasn't the case last summer, when he battled tough with his moving low-90s fastball and above-average curve. Seay pitches inside and doesn't back down from hitters. He needs to improve on setting up hitters, but that will come. Fine-tuning his changeup also will be necessary as Seay faces better hitters at Triple-A Durham in 2001.

Jason Standridge

Position: P   **Opening Day Age:** 22
Bats: R **Throws:** R   **Born:** 11/9/78 in
Ht: 6' 4" **Wt:** 217   Birmingham, AL

Recent Statistics

	W	L	ERA	G	GS	Sv	IP	H	R	BB	SO	HR
1999 A Chston-SC	9	1	2.02	18	18	0	116.0	80	35	31	84	5
1999 A St. Pete	4	4	3.91	8	8	0	48.1	49	21	20	26	0
2000 A St. Pete	2	4	3.38	10	10	0	56.0	45	28	31	41	4
2000 AA Orlando	6	8	3.62	17	17	0	97.0	85	46	43	55	4

His first two pro seasons were difficult, but Standridge blossomed over the next two years. The Devil Rays' first-round pick in 1997 benefited from a switch to a lower arm slot in the spring of '99, and he responded with a 13-5 season for two Class-A clubs. The change gave his low-90s fastball better sink, and he improved its location during a 2000 season in which he made remarkable progress. A sharp-breaking curveball is his out pitch. A changeup is still a work in progress. Standridge finished strong in 2000, going 5-0 in August after a slow start at Double-A Orlando. Standridge is pegged for Triple-A Durham in 2001.

Matt White

Position: P   **Opening Day Age:** 22
Bats: R **Throws:** R   **Born:** 8/13/78 in
Ht: 6' 5" **Wt:** 230   Waynesboro, PA

Recent Statistics

	W	L	ERA	G	GS	Sv	IP	H	R	BB	SO	HR
1999 A St. Pete	9	7	5.18	21	20	0	113.0	125	75	33	92	6
2000 AA Orlando	7	6	3.75	20	20	0	120.0	94	56	58	98	10
2000 AAA Durham	3	2	2.83	6	6	0	35.0	36	14	16	28	1

A loophole free agent from 1996, White looked like a bust after suffering a cracked vertebra in his back in '97. But since his second season at high Class-A St. Petersburg in 1999, it seems the higher the level, the better the young righthander pitches and the more his ERA drops. White enjoyed his best season in 2000, faring better at mixing his mid-90s fastball and power curve. While he is prone to mechanical troubles, White was a more consistent pitcher overall in 2000. His fastball is a bit straight, so he tends to turn to his curve when trouble strikes. White will have time to work on the command of his fastball at Triple-A Durham this summer.

Others to Watch

The athletic **Carl Crawford** (19), who could have played college football or basketball, opted for baseball when the Devil Rays gave a hefty bonus to this 1999 second-round pick. Speed is his game, and he led the Class-A Sally League in hits and steals in 2000. . . Splitting time between baseball and quarterbacking duties at the University of Miami, **Kenny Kelly** (22) has been slow to develop his baseball skills. He brings a lot to the table—bat speed, impressive range and running ability, plus a strong arm—and he finally played a full season in 2000 after abandoning football. Playing at Double-A Orlando was a tough full-season test. . . The nephew of former Cub Ryne Sandberg, **Jared Sandberg** (23) had a breakthrough season in 1999, finishing second in the high Class-A Florida State League with 22 home runs. A back injury hindered him early in 2000 at Double-A Orlando, but he played better as the season progressed. The power was down, but it's there. His back and a tendency to try to pull outside pitches compromised his power last season. . . Righthander **Dan Wheeler** (23) climbed from low Class-A Charleston in 1998 to the majors in '99, calling on excellent command of a less-than-stellar arsenal. While he throws an impressive slider, Wheeler must work the edges of the plate effectively to win at higher levels.

Tampa Bay

The Ballpark in Arlington

Offense

With its large outfield gaps, The Ballpark in Arlington is made for doubles and triples. The ball also carries well from right-center to the right-field line, and line drives and seemingly harmless fly-balls will find the seats. Balls tend to die in the deep power alley to left-center, though Ranger hitters often have used this gap to their advantage. Much like the gaps work in hitters' favor, the small amount of foul territory does as well.

Defense

The mammoth dimensions of the park put a premium on speed in the outfield, particularly in left and center. The relentless summer heat turns the park into a hitters' paradise but makes life difficult for all Rangers players, especially infielders. The grass stays short, and the infield dirt bakes hard in the sun. No one bears the brunt of high game-time temperatures more than catcher Ivan Rodriguez.

Who It Helps the Most

Lefthanded power hitters who lift the ball love the place. Rafael Palmeiro has averaged a homer every 10.1 at-bats at The Ballpark. Fifty-four of his 86 homers over the last two seasons have come at home. Even the Rangers' righthanded hitters demonstrated more home-run power at home in 2000.

Who It Hurts the Most

The Ballpark is larger than many recently opened facilities, but it works against pitchers as much as any hitter-friendly park. Blame the temperature and the vast outfield space for that. No Ranger pitcher was hurt dramatically by The Ballpark, and youngsters Ryan Glynn and Doug Davis, as well as closer John Wetteland, were markedly better at home in 2000. We'll see if Glynn and Davis fare as well there in 2001.

Rookies & Newcomers

The Rangers expect to open this season without a significant rookie, but several are on the way. First baseman Carlos Pena, second baseman Jason Romano, shortstop Mike Young and righthander Spike Lundberg could appear at some point during the season. Lundberg will have to worry the most about the park's dimensions.

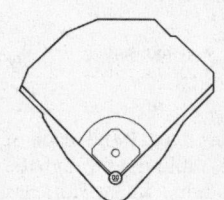

Dimensions: LF-332, LCF-390, CF-400, RCF-381, RF-325

Capacity: 49,166

Elevation: 551 feet

Surface: Grass

Foul Territory: Small

Park Factors

2000 Season

	Home Games			Away Games			
	Rangers	Opp	Total	Rangers	Opp	Total	Index
G	72	72	144	72	72	144	—
Avg	.299	.289	.294	.271	.297	.284	103
AB	2489	2631	5120	2531	2461	4992	103
R	430	441	871	334	432	766	114
H	743	761	1504	687	731	1418	106
2B	150	172	322	142	144	286	110
3B	14	12	26	14	15	29	87
HR	94	100	194	61	84	145	130
BB	287	293	580	232	296	528	107
SO	359	406	765	428	390	818	91
E	70	56	126	52	54	106	119
E-Infield	54	47	101	45	50	95	106
LHB-Avg	.291	.302	.296	.275	.296	.283	104
LHB-HR	49	42	91	33	31	64	135
RHB-Avg	.307	.281	.292	.268	.298	.285	103
RHB-HR	45	58	103	28	53	81	127

1998-2000

	Home Games			Away Games			
	Rangers	Opp	Total	Rangers	Opp	Total	Index
G	217	217	434	217	217	434	—
Avg	.303	.291	.297	.278	.289	.283	105
AB	7459	7893	15352	7698	7378	15076	102
R	1317	1266	2583	1156	1156	2312	112
H	2257	2300	4557	2138	2130	4268	107
2B	428	488	916	425	442	867	104
3B	51	57	108	33	47	80	133
HR	283	277	560	264	227	491	112
BB	836	719	1555	761	779	1540	99
SO	1183	1297	2480	1351	1264	2615	93
E	185	148	333	141	159	300	111
E-Infield	155	125	280	124	140	264	106
LHB-Avg	.295	.292	.294	.276	.283	.280	105
LHB-HR	134	127	261	110	105	215	122
RHB-Avg	.310	.291	.300	.279	.293	.286	105
RHB-HR	149	150	299	154	122	276	104

2000 Rankings (American League)
- Highest home-run factor
- Highest LHB home-run factor
- Second-highest run factor
- Second-highest error factor
- Third-highest double factor
- Third-highest walk factor
- Third-highest RHB batting-average factor
- Third-highest RHB home-run factor
- Second-lowest strikeout factor

Johnny Oates

2000 Season

Johnny Oates agonized through what he considered the worst of his 34 seasons as a player, coach and manager. Oates' club finished with a losing record for only the second time in his nine full seasons as a major league manager. As the club crumbled around him, he pulled back into a shell. He insisted the majors are not a place for player development or experimentation, and the Rangers may have lost some valuable time to look at youngsters in the second half because of that attitude.

Offense

In the classic American League style, Oates plays for the big inning. Only two American League teams attempted fewer stolen bases than the Rangers in 2000, which wasn't a surprise considering that Texas was without Tom Goodwin and Mark McLemore last summer. Little-ball strategies aren't key to Oates' managerial technique, so when his club lacks big-inning prowess as it did in 2000, he struggles for answers. Only three clubs in the Junior Circuit attempted fewer hit-and-runs.

Pitching & Defense

Oates protects pitchers, rarely pushing his starters beyond 120 pitches. The one notable exception is workhorse Rick Helling, who has led the league in pitches thrown the last two years. Oates tries to use a bullpen rotation. It worked better in 1999, when the core four of Jeff Zimmerman, Mike Venafro, Tim Crabtree and John Wetteland turned in very good seasons. All four weren't nearly as effective in 2000, and the Rangers now may lose an ailing Wetteland to retirement. Oates has emphasized defense in Texas, but little went right last summer. The Rangers ranked first among AL teams in errors committed and dead last in fielding percentage.

2001 Outlook

Like most managers, Oates is more comfortable with veterans. That must change, because the Rangers are on the verge of adding more young players. How he handles youngsters—ranging from hurlers Doug Davis and Ryan Glynn to outfielders Ricky Ledee and Ruben Mateo—will be important to the short- and long-term future of this franchise.

Born: 1/21/46 in Sylva, NC

Playing Experience: 1970-1981, Bal, Atl, Phi, LA, NYY

Managerial Experience: 10 seasons

Texas

Manager Statistics

Year	Team, Lg	W	L	Pct	GB	Finish
2000	Texas, AL	71	91	.438	20.5	4th West
10 Seasons		786	729	.518	—	—

2000 Starting Pitchers by Days Rest

	<=3	4	5	6+
Rangers Starts	1	100	24	28
Rangers ERA	6.35	5.73	5.00	5.99
AL Avg Starts	2	88	40	22
AL ERA	4.87	5.03	5.03	5.28

2000 Situational Stats

	Johnny Oates	AL Average
Hit & Run Success %	47.4	35.1
Stolen Base Success %	59.5	68.8
Platoon Pct.	63.6	57.8
Defensive Subs	18	23
High-Pitch Outings	20	13
Quick/Slow Hooks	9/27	18/19
Sacrifice Attempts	66	55

2000 Rankings (American League)

- 1st in steals of home plate (2), hit-and-run success percentage (47.4%), starts with over 140 pitches (1) and mid-inning pitching changes (233)
- 2nd in slow hooks (27) and one-batter pitcher appearances (43)
- 3rd in starts with over 120 pitches (20) and first-batter platoon percentage (66.5%)

Royce Clayton

Traded To
WHITE SOX

Position: SS
Bats: R **Throws:** R
Ht: 6' 0" **Wt:** 183

Opening Day Age: 31
Born: 1/2/70 in Burbank, CA
ML Seasons: 10

2000 Season

A confrontation with teammate Chad Curtis over clubhouse music turned Royce Clayton's season into a nightmare. Feeling management had not backed him, Clayton turned introverted and lifeless. The same thing, for different reasons, happened in St. Louis. He is talented and intelligent, but he is building a history of not handling negative situations well. On the field, his defense was average, and his offense was dreadful. He bombed in a six-week audition as the leadoff hitter and finished with a .301 on-base percentage, fourth-worst in the American League. He had 14 homers on July 14 and none for the duration.

Hitting

Like teammate Ivan Rodriguez, Clayton is not a selective hitter. He never has had more than 55 walks, and his big swing is more befitting a home-run hitter. He has had consecutive 14-homer seasons, but the tradeoff was a combined 81 walks and 192 strikeouts in those two years. Unlike Rodriguez, Clayton does not hit for a high average. He becomes impatient in RBI situations and hit only .222 with runners in scoring position last season. Unfortunately for the Rangers, at age 31 he may be too entrenched in his ways at the plate to change.

Baserunning & Defense

Clayton had four seasons of more than 20 steals in the National League, but moving to Texas' no-fun offense blunted that element of his game. Since joining the Rangers partway through the 1998 campaign, Clayton has only 24 steals in 42 tries. He is a studious defensive player, constantly shifting his placement in response to counts and situations. He has good range, and his throwing shoulder is sound again after problems in '99. His biggest defensive flaw is a poor pivot on double-play attempts.

2001 Outlook

Clayton's clubhouse demeanor became a moot point when the Rangers signed shortstop Alex Rodriguez to a 10-year deal and traded Clayton to the White Sox a few days later for pitchers Aaron Myette and Brian Schmack. Clayton provides security to the Sox, as he is signed through 2002.

Overall Statistics

	G	AB	R	H	D	T	HR	RBI	SB	BB	SO	Avg	OBP	Slg
2000	148	513	70	124	21	5	14	54	11	42	92	.242	.301	.384
Career	1212	4376	546	1128	204	39	70	439	172	333	816	.258	.312	.370

Where He Hits the Ball

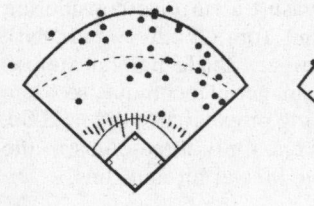
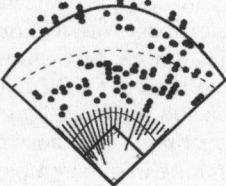

Vs. LHP   **Vs. RHP**

2000 Situational Stats

	AB	H	HR	RBI	Avg		AB	H	HR	RBI	Avg
Home	240	62	9	34	.258	LHP	107	21	4	14	.196
Road	273	62	5	20	.227	RHP	406	103	10	40	.254
First Half	280	67	13	38	.239	Sc Pos	126	28	4	41	.222
Scnd Half	233	57	1	16	.245	Clutch	81	24	2	13	.296

2000 Rankings (American League)

- 4th in sacrifice bunts (12), lowest batting average and lowest on-base percentage
- 6th in GDPs (21) and fielding percentage at shortstop (.977)
- 7th in lowest batting average with runners in scoring position, lowest on-base percentage vs. righthanded pitchers (.312) and lowest batting average on the road
- 8th in errors at shortstop (16)
- Led the Rangers in sacrifice bunts (12), stolen bases, caught stealing (7), strikeouts, GDPs (21), highest groundball/flyball ratio (1.5) and bunts in play (16)

Ryan Glynn

2000 Season

Ryan Glynn moved into the rotation late in the first half and showed just enough to be considered a viable candidate to stay there in 2001. A season-ending four-game losing streak put his record at 5-7 with a 5.58 ERA, but before the September stumble, he was 5-3 with a 4.58 ERA. Two worrisome physical problems arose, however. Glynn had persistent problems with a blister on his right index finger. He also fainted in the dugout after being removed from a start against Boston on a hot August night. Tests showed that he has a low-salt condition that requires constant monitoring.

Pitching

Glynn improved last summer by keeping his emotions under control while on the mound. In '99, he was the classic excitable boy who worked too fast and overthrew when faced with tight situations. When he did that, his control vanished and his slider went flat. While he showed more composure in 2000, he needs additional refinement. Glynn must cut his walk rate from last season's 4.16 per nine innings. He also needs an offspeed pitch to counter lefthanded hitters. They batted .333 against him last year, the third-highest figure allowed by an American League starter.

Defense

Glynn is a good athlete who also played the outfield in college. As he adjusts to the majors, he occasionally shows signs of panic in fielding situations. The Rangers hope experience helps smooth out his defensive game, though they are pleased with his penchant for keeping runners honest. Big league basestealers are 1-for-4 against him, and he logged his first pickoff last year.

2001 Outlook

While Glynn will get every chance at a spot in the rotation, his late-season slide sparks concern. He pitched more than 160 innings for the first time in his career in 2000, and he seemed tired at the finish, even though the Rangers were careful with his pitch count. Glynn did not throw more than 109 pitches in a start in 2000, and the club will continue to gauge increases in pitch counts and innings this summer.

Position: SP
Bats: R **Throws:** R
Ht: 6' 3" **Wt:** 195

Opening Day Age: 26
Born: 11/1/74 in Portsmouth, VA
ML Seasons: 2

Overall Statistics

	W	L	Pct.	ERA	G	GS	Sv	IP	H	BB	SO	HR	Ratio
2000	5	7	.417	5.58	16	16	0	88.2	107	41	33	15	1.67
Career	7	11	.389	6.22	29	26	0	143.1	178	76	72	25	1.77

How Often He Throws Strikes

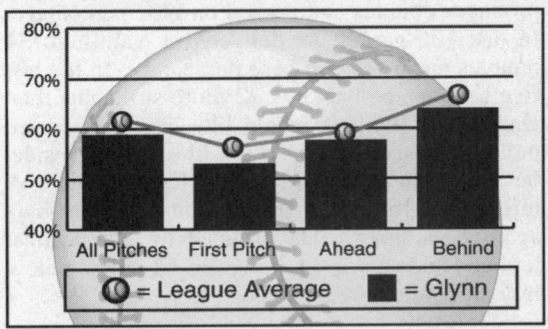

= League Average   = Glynn

2000 Situational Stats

	W	L	ERA	Sv	IP		AB	H	HR	RBI	Avg
Home	2	3	4.43	0	44.2	LHB	174	58	9	32	.333
Road	3	4	6.75	0	44.0	RHB	191	49	6	27	.257
First Half	1	0	1.56	0	17.1	Sc Pos	84	29	6	46	.345
Scnd Half	4	7	6.56	0	71.1	Clutch	18	4	1	2	.222

2000 Rankings (American League)

- 3rd in highest batting average allowed vs. lefthanded batters

Rusty Greer

2000 Season

Injuries marked the beginning and end of Rusty Greer's disappointing season. He went on the disabled list in mid-April with bone spurs in his right ankle that required surgery. He returned in late May and battled through various other ailments before finally missing most of the final 16 games because of plantar fasciitis—inflammation of the band of muscle on the bottom of the foot—in both feet. Between the injuries, Greer played at less-than-full speed. He had a career-low eight homers and 65 RBI in 394 at-bats.

Hitting

Greer has a disciplined opposite-field swing that produces doubles and a good on-base percentage. In just 106 games, he delivered a team-high 34 doubles and a .377 on-base percentage. In the last five seasons, he has only 22 more strikeouts than walks. The Rangers would like him to be more pull-conscious as teams work him up and inside, but he is uncomfortable with that approach. A lefthanded hitter, he usually has good at-bats against southpaws. He dropped to .245 against lefthanders last season, however, 58 points below his career mark.

Baserunning & Defense

Years of diving in left field may have taken a toll on Greer. He was late on many balls last season, and his cautious play sometimes kept him from getting to flys that he may have gobbled up in the past. His arm is limited, but he makes up for that by always throwing to the right base. Greer is a smart baserunner, but his speed has dropped to below average.

2001 Outlook

This is a crucial year for Greer, whose $4.5 million option for 2001 was exercised by the Rangers. He will be 32 on Opening Day, and the club wonders if his body has paid a high price for his aggressive playing style. Texas continues to flirt with the idea of putting Greer into the leadoff spot to take advantage of his good on-base percentage and extra-base ability. If that happens, it would be the third straight season that a majority of his at-bats have come in a different lineup spot.

Position: LF
Bats: L **Throws:** L
Ht: 6' 0" **Wt:** 195

Opening Day Age: 32
Born: 1/21/69 in Fort Rucker, AL
ML Seasons: 7

Overall Statistics

	G	AB	R	H	D	T	HR	RBI	SB	BB	SO	Avg	OBP	Slg
2000	105	394	65	117	34	3	8	65	4	51	61	.297	.377	.459
Career	914	3385	581	1040	226	23	111	568	29	473	506	.307	.392	.486

Where He Hits the Ball

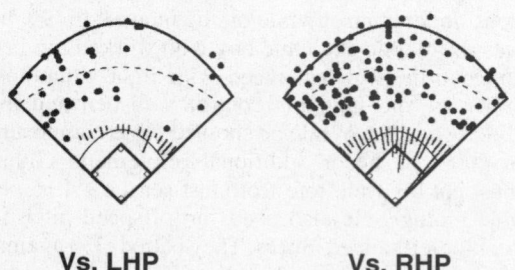

Vs. LHP   **Vs. RHP**

2000 Situational Stats

	AB	H	HR	RBI	Avg		AB	H	HR	RBI	Avg
Home	199	64	3	31	.322	LHP	98	24	1	12	.245
Road	195	53	5	34	.272	RHP	296	93	7	53	.314
First Half	179	52	3	26	.291	Sc Pos	110	36	3	56	.327
Scnd Half	215	65	5	39	.302	Clutch	54	16	0	10	.296

2000 Rankings (American League)

- 4th in errors in left field (3)
- Led the Rangers in doubles, batting average with runners in scoring position, batting average with the bases loaded (.375), batting average on a 3-1 count (.421), highest percentage of pitches taken (61.3) and highest percentage of extra bases taken as a runner (53.1)

Rick Helling

Position: SP
Bats: R **Throws:** R
Ht: 6' 3" **Wt:** 220

Opening Day Age: 30
Born: 12/15/70 in
Devils Lake, ND
ML Seasons: 7

2000 Season

Rick Helling once again served as the staff workhorse. He tied for the American League lead in starts, led in pitches thrown and tied for seventh in innings. He recorded 16 wins while the rest of the Texas rotation won just 34 times in 127 starts. He also led the league in pitches thrown for a second consecutive season. Helling never has missed a start because of injury and has not been on the disabled list in his nine-year professional career. He did slip at the end, however, going 2-4 with a 9.45 ERA for his final six starts.

Pitching

Helling has 49 wins in the last three seasons and continues to mature as a pitcher. Known for his high fastball, he made its average velocity work better for him by throwing it down in the strike zone. He also hides the ball well in his delivery. He added a changeup to help him against lefthanded hitters, who batted only .238 against him in 2000. Helling's competitive urges sometime get the better of him. He challenges hitters at all times, and that has contributed to the 70 homers he's allowed in the last two seasons.

Defense

Helling's athletic abilities show in his fielding; he puts himself in good position and has good hands. He is slow to the plate, but the Rangers prefer that as opposed to getting quicker with a slide-step delivery. They believe catcher Ivan Rodriguez alone deters the running game.

2001 Outlook

Helling has had three consecutive winning seasons despite limited run support. Manager Johnny Oates admitted he will have to be more careful in his handling of his workhorse early in the 2001 season. Helling was 14-8 after a win on August 12 last summer, but had his second consecutive poor finish. He is strong and durable, but it might be better for all involved if he doesn't lead the league in total pitches thrown for a *third* consecutive campaign.

Overall Statistics

	W	L	Pct.	ERA	G	GS	Sv	IP	H	BB	SO	HR	Ratio
2000	16	13	.552	4.48	35	35	0	217.0	212	99	146	29	1.43
Career	60	47	.561	4.65	167	137	0	896.0	873	373	612	139	1.39

How Often He Throws Strikes

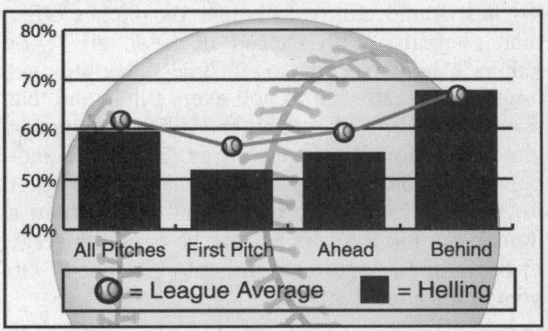

2000 Situational Stats

	W	L	ERA	Sv	IP		AB	H	HR	RBI	Avg
Home	9	6	4.91	0	102.2	LHB	453	108	16	56	.238
Road	7	7	4.09	0	114.1	RHB	389	104	13	54	.267
First Half	10	7	3.85	0	121.2	Sc Pos	208	49	2	75	.236
Scnd Half	6	6	5.29	0	95.1	Clutch	53	17	3	12	.321

2000 Rankings (American League)

- 1st in games started, pitches thrown (3,791) and lowest groundball/flyball ratio allowed (0.6)
- 2nd in most pitches thrown per batter (3.94) and fewest GDPs induced per nine innings (0.4)
- 3rd in walks allowed
- 5th in batters faced (963)
- Led the Rangers in ERA, wins, losses, games started, home runs allowed, walks allowed, strikeouts, pitches thrown (3,791), stolen bases allowed (16), lowest batting average allowed (.252), lowest on-base percentage allowed (.334), most run support per nine innings (5.9), most strikeouts per nine innings (6.1), lowest ERA on the road and lowest batting average allowed vs. lefthanded batters

Gabe Kapler

Position: CF/RF
Bats: R **Throws:** R
Ht: 6' 2" **Wt:** 208

Opening Day Age: 25
Born: 8/31/75 in Hollywood, CA
ML Seasons: 3
Pronunciation: KAP-lur

2000 Season

Few players have made the in-season strides that Gabe Kapler did in 2000. Burdened with a stiff swing, he hit only .245-4-18 in 188 at-bats in the first half. Batting coach Rudy Jaramillo reworked the swing to allow Kapler to stay back, and he hit .344-10-48 in 256 second-half at-bats. His performance included a club-record 28-game hitting streak. He missed the final seven regular-season games because of a torn left biceps muscle for which the club decided on a rehab program rather than surgery.

Hitting

The best measure of Kapler's progress as a hitter is his new-found ability to homer on pitches other than fastballs. With Detroit in 1999, all 18 of Kapler's homers came on fastballs. He stopped lunging in an attempt to pull every pitch, and that switch made him a better hitter. He has struggled in clutch situations, however, hitting .235 in late-and-close situations over his career. Last year, Kapler three times went more than 70 at-bats without a homer, but the Rangers believe he is on the verge of becoming a legitimate threat to produce 25-30 home runs annually.

Baserunning & Defense

Kapler moved from right field to center after Ruben Mateo's leg injury, and he made 82 starts at a position that is difficult to play at The Ballpark in Arlington. He gets a good break on flyballs, but he made too many throwing mistakes in 2000. Of his 10 errors, which tied for most by an American League outfielder, seven came on throws. Kapler runs well enough to record double-digit steals.

2001 Outlook

Was Kapler's second-half surge a fluke? Despite his strong finish, teams repeatedly pitched around Rafael Palmeiro to face Kapler instead. If Mateo isn't fully recovered from his broken leg, he could move to right and Kapler would stay in center. Otherwise look for Kapler to slide over to right while he continues to develop his power stroke.

Overall Statistics

	G	AB	R	H	D	T	HR	RBI	SB	BB	SO	Avg	OBP	Slg
2000	116	444	59	134	32	1	14	66	8	42	57	.302	.360	.473
Career	253	885	122	241	54	6	32	115	21	85	135	.272	.335	.455

Where He Hits the Ball

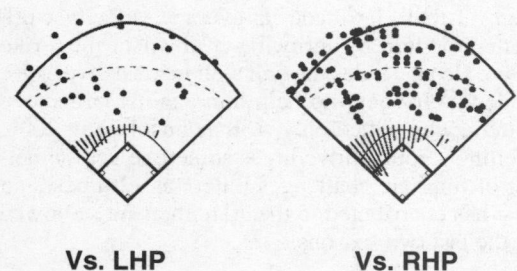

Vs. LHP   Vs. RHP

2000 Situational Stats

	AB	H	HR	RBI	Avg		AB	H	HR	RBI	Avg
Home	225	66	11	46	.293	LHP	98	28	5	13	.286
Road	219	68	3	20	.311	RHP	346	106	9	53	.306
First Half	188	46	4	18	.245	Sc Pos	136	36	2	49	.265
Scnd Half	256	88	10	48	.344	Clutch	63	18	1	9	.286

2000 Rankings (American League)

- 2nd in errors in center field (8)
- 7th in lowest batting average on an 0-2 count (.063)
- Led the Rangers in batting average vs. righthanded pitchers

Mike Lamb

2000 Season

The Rangers never wanted to use Mike Lamb in the majors last season. They tried to re-sign free agent Todd Zeile, but he bolted for the Mets. They gave the job to star-crossed Tom Evans coming out of spring training, but he was lost after the first month because of another shoulder injury. That finally forced Texas to go with Lamb, and he was not ready. He hit for average but exhibited almost no power, collecting just six homers and 33 extra-base hits and failing to deliver an extra-base knock in any of his final 100 at-bats. A converted catcher, Lamb had even more problems in the field. He tied Anaheim's Troy Glaus for the most errors by an American League third baseman with 33.

Hitting

Teammates call Lamb's swing "The Thing." It is an odd two-piece contraption. His lower body moves as if he wants to pull the ball, but he goes after pitches with an all-arms opposite-field swing. The result is little power in either direction. Lamb showed some signs late in the season that he was learning to pull pitches. To be a legitimate major league third baseman at the plate, he must develop more power to either field.

Baserunning & Defense

Lamb's defensive shortcomings stem from bad footwork. He tends to get his feet tangled and clank the ball. Of his 33 errors, 20 came on misplayed balls. He sometimes hesitates as if he's thinking what to do on a particular play, rather than simply reacting. Lamb does not run well, and he has done little in the way of stealing bases since exiting the low minors.

2001 Outlook

The Rangers faced a difficult decision on Lamb. Do they bring in a veteran and risk ruining the psyche of a top prospect who was rushed to the majors? The front office decided to sign veterans and avoid a rebuilding phase. Free agent Ken Caminiti will play third, which clouds Lamb's future. For 2001, he may play part-time with Texas. Or he may be destined for more seasoning at Triple-A Oklahoma.

Position: 3B
Bats: L **Throws:** R
Ht: 6' 1" **Wt:** 195

Opening Day Age: 25
Born: 8/9/75 in West Covina, CA
ML Seasons: 1

Overall Statistics

	G	AB	R	H	D	T	HR	RBI	SB	BB	SO	Avg	OBP	Slg
2000	138	493	65	137	25	2	6	47	0	34	60	.278	.328	.373
Career	138	493	65	137	25	2	6	47	0	34	60	.278	.328	.373

Where He Hits the Ball

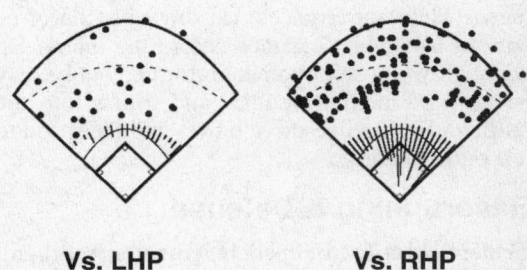

Vs. LHP   **Vs. RHP**

2000 Situational Stats

	AB	H	HR	RBI	Avg		AB	H	HR	RBI	Avg
Home	229	66	4	26	.288	LHP	84	24	1	10	.286
Road	264	71	2	21	.269	RHP	409	113	5	37	.276
First Half	232	68	4	28	.293	Sc Pos	120	27	0	36	.225
Scnd Half	261	69	2	19	.264	Clutch	83	20	0	5	.241

2000 Rankings (American League)

- 1st in errors at third base (33) and lowest fielding percentage at third base (.913)
- 5th in lowest slugging percentage and lowest HR frequency (82.2 ABs per HR)
- 7th in batting average on a 3-2 count (.355) and lowest slugging percentage vs. righthanded pitchers (.374)
- 8th in lowest batting average with runners in scoring position
- Led the Rangers in lowest percentage of swings that missed (12.9) and batting average on a 3-2 count (.355)
- Led AL third basemen in batting average on a 3-2 count (.355) and batting average with two strikes (.258)

Ruben Mateo

2000 Season

Texas' season went south on June 2 when Ruben Mateo broke the femur bone in his right leg running out a grounder. The Rangers went 44-66 after the injury and fell out of the American League West race. The heralded Mateo had begun meeting his advance billing as a legitimate five-tool player, hitting .306 in the 170 at-bats leading up to the injury. He was improving with each game.

Hitting

Mateo tends to take a big uppercut swing, and pitchers took advantage of its holes early in 2000. He was making the necessary adjustments before his season-ending injury. Patience is a problem. Mateo has walked only 14 times in 349 major league plate appearances. He drew just one free pass in his final 17 games before the injury. He could grow into a 25-homer performer, but he may be best at smoking doubles and triples into the outfield. He has line-drive power and the speed to test outfield arms.

Baserunning & Defense

Center field at The Ballpark in Arlington is difficult to play. Mateo made it more difficult with his odd angles on flyballs. He tends to get bad breaks and compounds them by choosing roundabout paths to the ball. His leg injury and the rough edges on his defensive game could force him to right field, as he has the arm for the position. Mateo easily could be a 20-20 performer. He still is learning the art of stealing bases but is perfect on nine stolen-base attempts in the majors.

2001 Outlook

The leg injury hangs huge question marks over Mateo. Will he be ready for spring training? Will there be a psychological barrier that he must hurdle? Will he ever be an everyday player? Mateo has appeared in more than 110 games just once in five professional seasons in the United States.

Position: CF
Bats: R **Throws:** R
Ht: 6' 0" **Wt:** 185

Opening Day Age: 23
Born: 2/10/78 in San Cristobal, Dominican Republic
ML Seasons: 2
Pronunciation: MUH-tay-oh

Overall Statistics

	G	AB	R	H	D	T	HR	RBI	SB	BB	SO	Avg	OBP	Slg
2000	52	206	32	60	11	0	7	19	6	10	34	.291	.339	.447
Career	84	328	48	89	20	1	12	37	9	14	62	.271	.313	.448

Where He Hits the Ball

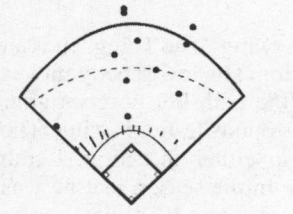 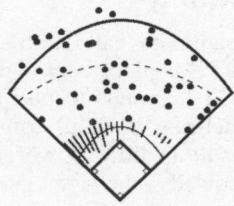

Vs. LHP   **Vs. RHP**

2000 Situational Stats

	AB	H	HR	RBI	Avg		AB	H	HR	RBI	Avg
Home	113	34	3	7	.301	LHP	44	14	3	5	.318
Road	93	26	4	12	.280	RHP	162	46	4	14	.284
First Half	206	60	7	19	.291	Sc Pos	54	11	2	14	.204
Scnd Half	0	0	0	0	-	Clutch	36	8	1	1	.222

2000 Rankings (American League)

- 9th in errors in center field (3)

Darren Oliver

2000 Season

How forgettable was Darren Oliver's 2000 campaign? For starters, he had as many stays on the disabled list as wins. In fact, his two victories were the fewest among American Leaguers with at least 20 starts. Opponents hit a staggering .339 against him, and he lasted at least six innings in only seven starts. He spent nearly all of July and August on the DL with a weak left shoulder, then returned to the rotation in September to determine if he had regained his strength. The results were not encouraging. Oliver went 0-3 with a 7.71 ERA in five September starts. He did not finish the first inning in his final appearance, a fitting conclusion to a lost season.

Pitching

Oliver, who had rotator cuff surgery in 1995, gives every appearance that he lacks confidence in his stuff. No one ever will call him aggressive. He nibbles, preferring to throw a curveball or changeup rather than challenging hitters with his fastball, which has lost velocity. Oliver has only 1.4 strikeouts per walk over the last four years. His curve has become sloppy, causing problems for him versus lefthanded hitters. Lefties have batted .347 against him over the last two seasons.

Defense

Oliver holds runners well, aided by a deceptive pickoff move. He isn't the fastest guy coming off the mound to field his position, but he gets to most groundballs hit in his direction. Because he is quite hittable, he also needs to be surrounded by a sure-handed infield.

2001 Outlook

Owner Tom Hicks pushed general manager Doug Melvin to sign Oliver as a free agent before last season. That created a huge headache for the club. The Rangers have Oliver under contract for two more seasons—a deal that no club would take now—and have no confidence in him. The first step is for him to prove that his left shoulder has rebounded, and even then a return to the bullpen could be in his immediate future.

Position: SP
Bats: R **Throws:** L
Ht: 6' 2" **Wt:** 210

Opening Day Age: 30
Born: 10/6/70 in Kansas City, MO
ML Seasons: 8

Texas

Overall Statistics

	W	L	Pct.	ERA	G	GS	Sv	IP	H	BB	SO	HR	Ratio
2000	2	9	.182	7.42	21	21	0	108.0	151	42	49	16	1.79
Career	56	49	.533	4.88	204	149	2	942.0	1044	408	564	107	1.54

How Often He Throws Strikes

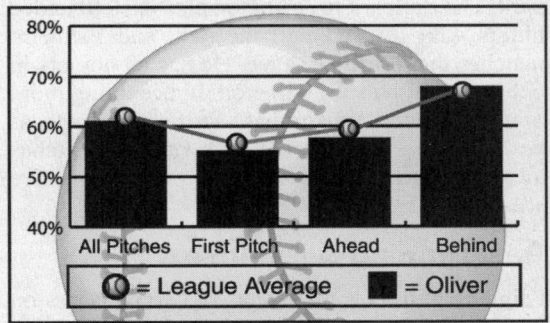

(O) = League Average   ■ = Oliver

2000 Situational Stats

	W	L	ERA	Sv	IP		AB	H	HR	RBI	Avg
Home	1	3	6.39	0	62.0	LHB	110	41	1	15	.373
Road	1	6	8.80	0	46.0	RHB	336	110	15	69	.327
First Half	2	4	6.66	0	73.0	Sc Pos	131	46	2	62	.351
Scnd Half	0	5	9.00	0	35.0	Clutch	19	6	2	5	.316

2000 Rankings (American League)

- 1st in highest batting average allowed with runners in scoring position
- 2nd in highest batting average allowed vs. righthanded batters
- Led the Rangers in most GDPs induced per GDP situation (15.9%)

Rafael Palmeiro

2000 Season

No one suffered more from the departures of Juan Gonzalez and Todd Zeile than Rafael Palmeiro. He went from hitting in an ideal spot between two proven performers to all but standing alone in the middle of the lineup. Palmeiro enjoyed his sixth consecutive season of more than 35 home runs, and he finished among the American League leaders in both homers and RBI. But he had to expand his hitting zone and sacrifice average to do so. Still, he swatted 39 longballs and became the 32nd player in major league history to reach 400 homers.

Hitting

Returning to Texas put Palmeiro in an ideal home park. The Ballpark in Arlington plays to lefthanded hitters who lift and pull the ball, and Palmeiro matches that profile to a tee. He has 63 homers in 638 career at-bats in Arlington. In becoming more of a pull hitter, Palmeiro has sacrificed average, as he sometimes has trouble with offspeed pitches away. He has hit .300 only once in the last five seasons.

Baserunning & Defense

Palmeiro still feels the effects of two surgeries on his right knee before the 1999 season. His speed, once good enough to produce 22 steals, has dropped to well below average, and the Rangers need a pinch-runner for him in late-game situations. Palmeiro's range at first also has decreased. Palmeiro still has good hands and throws better than most first basemen.

2001 Outlook

Palmeiro has improved with age as a power hitter. After hitting only 33 homers in his first 1,423 career at-bats, he has 245 homers in six seasons since passing his 30th birthday. He now has a legitimate chance to retire with 500 homers and 2,800 hits. The Rangers may have aided his bid by signing free agents Alex Rodriguez, Andres Galarraga and Ken Caminiti to provide more help in the lineup. With Galarraga aboard, Palmeiro will receive more time at designated hitter to protect his ailing right knee.

Position: 1B/DH
Bats: L **Throws:** L
Ht: 6' 0" **Wt:** 190

Opening Day Age: 36
Born: 9/24/64 in Havana, Cuba
ML Seasons: 15
Pronunciation: pall-MARE-oh
Nickname: Raffy

Overall Statistics

	G	AB	R	H	D	T	HR	RBI	SB	BB	SO	Avg	OBP	Slg
2000	158	565	102	163	29	3	39	120	2	103	77	.288	.397	.558
Career	2098	7846	1259	2321	455	36	400	1347	88	935	983	.296	.372	.516

Where He Hits the Ball

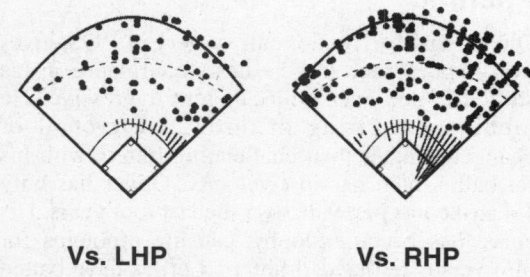

Vs. LHP   **Vs. RHP**

2000 Situational Stats

	AB	H	HR	RBI	Avg		AB	H	HR	RBI	Avg
Home	288	84	26	72	.292	LHP	144	47	10	40	.326
Road	277	79	13	48	.285	RHP	421	116	29	80	.276
First Half	301	90	23	70	.299	Sc Pos	148	45	8	73	.304
Scnd Half	264	73	16	50	.277	Clutch	67	20	3	14	.299

2000 Rankings (American League)

- 1st in lowest groundball/flyball ratio (0.7)
- 3rd in fielding percentage at first base (.995)
- 4th in intentional walks (17) and lowest batting average on a 3-2 count (.098)
- Led the Rangers in home runs, at-bats, runs scored, hits, total bases (315), RBI, sacrifice flies (7), walks, intentional walks (17), times on base (269), pitches seen (2,527), plate appearances (678), slugging percentage, on-base percentage, HR frequency (14.5 ABs per HR), cleanup slugging percentage (.548), slugging percentage vs. lefthanded pitchers (.569), slugging percentage vs. righthanded pitchers (.553), on-base percentage vs. lefthanded pitchers (.415) and on-base percentage vs. righthanded pitchers (.391)

Ivan Rodriguez

2000 Season

His season ended in late July with a fractured thumb, leaving open one big question: Just what is Ivan Rodriguez' ceiling as a player? He hit .347 with 27 homers and 83 RBI in 91 games, putting him on track to exceed his MVP performance of 1999. Rodriguez was on pace to raise his average for the fourth consecutive season while increasing his homers and RBI for the third straight year.

Hitting

The best plan against Rodriguez may be to throw him fastballs right down the middle of the plate. He swings at everything else, generating exceptional extra-base power to the opposite field. He usually offers at the first pitch, and then at each and every pitch to follow. Needless to say, patience is not a virtue in his book. He was on pace for his ninth consecutive sub-40 walk season last year. Sometimes the approach works, as Rodriguez hit .404 when putting the first pitch in play in 2000. However, Rodriguez hits too many "pitcher's pitches" with men on base; he has grounded into 48 double plays in his last 235 games.

Baserunning & Defense

Rodriguez is an adventure on the bases. He likes to run, sometimes until he is tagged. But he makes life even more of an adventure for opposing runners. Rodriguez, who has thrown out 50 percent of baserunners over the last five seasons, does more than shut down running games. His arm forces runners to cut down their leads, making it more difficult to take an extra base. The rest of his defensive game is average. He favors style over substance in blocking pitches in the dirt and has shown little interest in drawing up game plans with his batterymates.

2001 Outlook

The Rangers do not expect lingering problems from the thumb injury. While Rodriguez is only 29 years old, Texas eventually may try to extend the prime years of his career by switching him to a less stressful position. That move, however, is far off on the horizon. For now, the Rangers simply will settle for having the best all-around catcher in the majors.

Position: C
Bats: R **Throws:** R
Ht: 5' 9" **Wt:** 205

Opening Day Age: 29
Born: 11/30/71 in Vega Baja, Puerto Rico
ML Seasons: 10
Nickname: Pudge

Overall Statistics

	G	AB	R	H	D	T	HR	RBI	SB	BB	SO	Avg	OBP	Slg
2000	91	363	66	126	27	4	27	83	5	19	48	.347	.375	.667
Career	1260	4806	715	1459	288	24	171	704	65	256	619	.304	.340	.480

Where He Hits the Ball

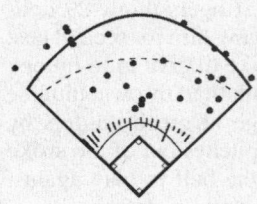
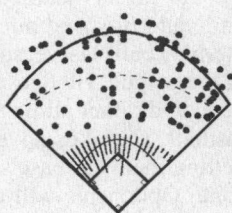

Vs. LHP   **Vs. RHP**

2000 Situational Stats

	AB	H	HR	RBI	Avg		AB	H	HR	RBI	Avg
Home	177	59	16	48	.333	LHP	79	27	8	18	.342
Road	186	67	11	35	.360	RHP	284	99	19	65	.349
First Half	325	119	26	80	.366	Sc Pos	96	30	6	54	.313
Scnd Half	38	7	1	3	.184	Clutch	41	14	4	16	.341

2000 Rankings (American League)

- 4th in most GDPs per GDP situation (18.7%)
- Led AL catchers in triples, caught stealing (5) and batting average with runners in scoring position

Kenny Rogers

2000 Season

Kenny Rogers ranked among the American League's top four hurlers in innings and pitches, which may have been too much of a workload at this stage of his career. After going 4-0 in six June starts, Rogers went 5-8 with a 5.00 ERA in his last 18 outings. He also was hurt by ragged defensive support during the second half. At the close of the season, he underwent surgery to shave down a bone spur in his left elbow.

Pitching

Rogers used to be one of the few hard-throwing lefthanders in baseball. A shoulder injury while with the Yankees in 1996 robbed him of his velocity, but he has learned to get by on soft-tossing guile and offspeed pitches. Rogers threw 29 double-play balls last season, tying him for second best in the league. He doesn't like to give in to hitters; he would rather allow a walk than throw a hittable fastball. He takes advantage of greedy hitters by getting them to chase soft pitches out of the strike zone. Opponents will put the ball in play against Rogers, which puts a burden on the defense.

Defense

A lefthanded shortstop in high school, Rogers ranks among the best and most aggressive fielding pitchers in the majors. He won his first career Gold Glove in 2000. He can take away the sacrifice bunt; the Rangers sometimes hold their breath when he takes a headlong dive for a ball. Rogers also excels at shutting down running games and forcing runners to cut down their primary and secondary leads.

2001 Outlook

Rogers wins. He has double-digit victory totals in seven of his last eight seasons and is 36 games over .500 for his career. He is 36, however, and the Rangers must be careful with his innings. Don't expect him to continue at the pace of the last three seasons, when he had 14 complete games in 99 starts. He needs bullpen help to be strong from start to finish. Rogers could be limited in spring training because of his offseason surgery, but the club expects him to be ready for the start of the season.

Position: SP
Bats: L **Throws:** L
Ht: 6' 1" **Wt:** 217

Opening Day Age: 36
Born: 11/10/64 in Savannah, GA
ML Seasons: 12

Overall Statistics

	W	L	Pct.	ERA	G	GS	Sv	IP	H	BB	SO	HR	Ratio
2000	13	13	.500	4.55	34	34	0	227.1	257	78	127	20	1.47
Career	127	91	.583	4.11	536	251	28	1928.2	1943	729	1241	186	1.39

How Often He Throws Strikes

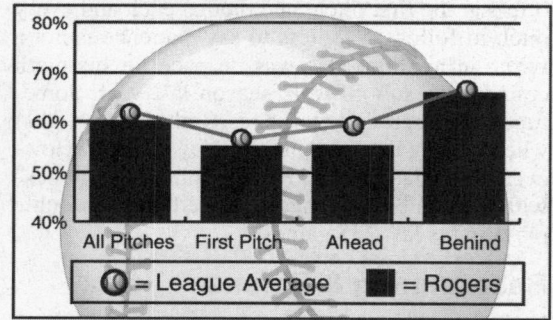

= League Average = Rogers

2000 Situational Stats

	W	L	ERA	Sv	IP		AB	H	HR	RBI	Avg
Home	9	6	4.46	0	121.0	LHB	220	69	6	31	.314
Road	4	7	4.66	0	106.1	RHB	682	188	14	82	.276
First Half	9	6	4.23	0	127.2	Sc Pos	230	62	3	87	.270
Scnd Half	4	7	4.97	0	99.2	Clutch	41	15	2	6	.366

2000 Rankings (American League)

- 1st in batters faced (998) and pickoff throws (176)
- 2nd in GDPs induced (29)
- 3rd in games started, innings pitched and hits allowed
- 4th in hit batsmen (11), pitches thrown (3,613), fewest home runs allowed per nine innings (.79) and most GDPs induced per nine innings (1.1)
- Led the Rangers in losses, complete games (2), innings pitched, hits allowed, batters faced (998), hit batsmen (11), pickoff throws (176), runners caught stealing (6), GDPs induced (29), highest strikeout/walk ratio (1.6), lowest slugging percentage allowed (.431) and highest ground-ball/flyball ratio allowed (1.7)

John Wetteland

2000 Season

Back problems turned 2000 into one of the most trying seasons of John Wetteland's 12-year career. He tied for third in the American League with nine blown saves, allowed a career-high 10 homers and had the worst hits-innings ratio of his big league tenure. It was the second consecutive season that Wetteland has allowed more hits than innings pitched. He did have more than 30 saves for the eighth time, however, and he moved into second place behind John Franco on the list of active career saves leaders.

Pitching

In the best of times, Wetteland threw so hard that opponents could not catch up to his high and straight fastball. But these no longer are the best of times. He has lost velocity, forcing him to rely less on the four-seam fastball and leaving him without the one dominant pitch that marks most closers. He turned into a rare four-pitch closer last season, but he struggled with his consistency. Wetteland's search for a way to neutralize lefthanded hitters led him to the changeup. It did not help—lefthanded batters hit .309 against him.

Defense

Wetteland, who also has had leg problems in recent seasons, does not field his position well. He is slow off the mound and often puts himself in bad fielding position with his follow-through. Like most closers, he tends to ignore runners, as it makes little sense for him to give up more velocity with the slide-step move.

2001 Outlook

Bothered by his back and his recent performance, Wetteland went into the winter questioning his desire to continue playing. He no longer is a dominant closer, but still can be an asset to a club. He is the epitome of a team player, and an excellent role model for young relievers.

Position: RP
Bats: R **Throws:** R
Ht: 6' 2" **Wt:** 215

Opening Day Age: 34
Born: 8/21/66 in San Mateo, CA
ML Seasons: 12
Pronunciation: WET-land

Texas

Overall Statistics

	W	L	Pct.	ERA	G	GS	Sv	IP	H	BB	SO	HR	Ratio
2000	6	5	.545	4.20	62	0	34	60.0	67	24	53	10	1.52
Career	48	45	.516	2.93	618	17	330	765.0	616	252	804	73	1.13

How Often He Throws Strikes

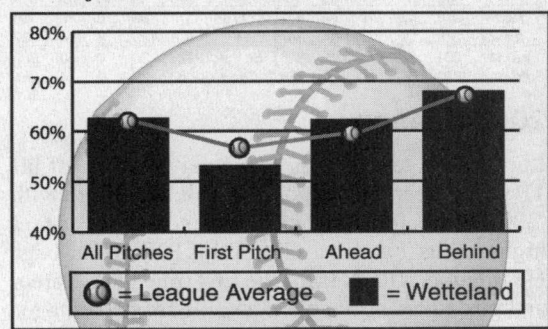

2000 Situational Stats

	W	L	ERA	Sv	IP		AB	H	HR	RBI	Avg
Home	5	1	3.71	15	34.0	LHB	123	38	7	25	.309
Road	1	4	4.85	19	26.0	RHB	112	29	3	14	.259
First Half	3	2	3.57	21	35.1	Sc Pos	66	15	3	28	.227
Scnd Half	3	3	5.11	13	24.2	Clutch	182	53	7	32	.291

2000 Rankings (American League)

- 3rd in save opportunities (43) and blown saves (9)
- 5th in saves and lowest save percentage (79.1)
- 8th in games finished (57)
- Led the Rangers in saves, games finished (57), save opportunities (43), save percentage (79.1), blown saves (9), lowest batting average allowed in relief with runners on base (.241) and relief wins (6)

Luis Alicea

Position: 2B
Bats: B **Throws:** R
Ht: 5' 9" **Wt:** 176

Opening Day Age: 35
Born: 7/29/65 in
Santurce, Puerto Rico
ML Seasons: 11
Pronunciation:
ah-la-SAY-ya

Overall Statistics

	G	AB	R	H	D	T	HR	RBI	SB	BB	SO	Avg	OBP	Slg
2000	139	540	85	159	25	8	6	63	1	59	75	.294	.365	.404
Career	1134	3347	479	871	165	47	42	367	71	445	534	.260	.350	.375

2000 Situational Stats

	AB	H	HR	RBI	Avg		AB	H	HR	RBI	Avg
Home	272	82	4	34	.301	LHP	114	36	0	9	.316
Road	268	77	2	29	.287	RHP	426	123	6	54	.289
First Half	294	93	3	38	.316	Sc Pos	126	36	0	50	.286
Scnd Half	246	66	3	25	.268	Clutch	83	22	0	14	.265

2000 Season

Luis Alicea received the most playing time of his 11-year career and responded well. He flirted with .300 before finishing at .294, and he set career highs in hits, extra-base hits, runs, RBI and at-bats. He filled in at leadoff for the first time in his career and posted a respectable .365 on-base percentage.

Hitting, Baserunning & Defense

A switch-hitter, Alicea produces more power and a better average from the right side. He takes defensive swings as a lefthanded hitter. His speed has decreased. He had only seven steals in 14 tries over the last three seasons with Texas, where manager Johnny Oates dislikes risking outs. Alicea's defense tended to be erratic. That loss of speed has reduced his range to merely average, and he sometimes struggles with the double play. He ranked in the middle of the pack for fielding percentage among American League second baseman.

2001 Outlook

Alicea is 35 and a free agent. He wants to remain a starter, but that's likely only on a second-division club. On a winning team, he could be an effective bench player. He is a good clubhouse presence, especially when it comes to helping young Latin players make the difficult adjustment to big league life.

Frank Catalanotto

Position: 2B/DH/1B
Bats: L **Throws:** R
Ht: 6' 0" **Wt:** 195

Opening Day Age: 26
Born: 4/27/74 in
Smithtown, NY
ML Seasons: 4
Pronunciation:
cat-uh-lah-NOT-toh

Overall Statistics

	G	AB	R	H	D	T	HR	RBI	SB	BB	SO	Avg	OBP	Slg
2000	103	282	55	82	13	2	10	42	6	33	36	.291	.375	.457
Career	305	807	121	229	47	4	27	105	12	63	131	.284	.345	.452

2000 Situational Stats

	AB	H	HR	RBI	Avg		AB	H	HR	RBI	Avg
Home	154	48	6	20	.312	LHP	19	5	0	5	.263
Road	128	34	4	22	.266	RHP	263	77	10	37	.293
First Half	82	32	3	15	.390	Sc Pos	68	22	3	34	.324
Scnd Half	200	50	7	27	.250	Clutch	46	10	0	4	.217

2000 Season

Frank Catalanotto performed well until his playing time increased after the second-half trade of David Segui. He hit .370 with 12 extra-base hits in 108 at-bats during the first four months, but closed by hitting only .241 with 13 extra-base hits in 174 at-bats during the final two months of the season. Catalanotto can hit off the bench. He was 10-for-28 as a pinch-hitter in 2000, and 25-for-84 in a pinch-hitting role over the last three seasons.

Hitting, Baserunning & Defense

Catalanotto knows how to use the opposite field and can drive balls into the gaps. He has improved at pulling pitches. He also showed more patience in 2000, more than doubling his 1999 walk total with 33 last summer. He ran better than the Rangers expected until leg-muscle woes limited him. His defense was below average, as he struggled with footwork problems at second base and difficulties making the throws from third. First base is his best position, but the Rangers are stocked there.

2001 Outlook

His performance during the final two months showed he is best used as a bench player. Catalanotto scheduled November surgery to remove bone chips from his right wrist, but he was expected to be ready for spring training.

Tim Crabtree

Position: RP
Bats: R **Throws:** R
Ht: 6' 4" **Wt:** 220

Opening Day Age: 31
Born: 10/13/69 in Jackson, MI
ML Seasons: 6

Overall Statistics

	W	L	Pct.	ERA	G	GS	Sv	IP	H	BB	SO	HR	Ratio
2000	2	7	.222	5.15	68	0	2	80.1	86	31	54	7	1.46
Career	21	17	.553	4.05	321	0	5	370.2	397	136	272	26	1.44

2000 Situational Stats

	W	L	ERA	Sv	IP		AB	H	HR	RBI	Avg
Home	1	4	6.97	2	41.1	LHB	127	41	1	26	.323
Road	1	3	3.23	0	39.0	RHB	187	45	6	29	.241
First Half	1	5	5.95	0	42.1	Sc Pos	118	31	0	46	.263
Scnd Half	1	2	4.26	2	38.0	Clutch	139	43	3	28	.309

2000 Season

As usual, Tim Crabtree started slowly and never really caught up. He finished with his highest ERA for a season in which he worked at least 45 innings, and he matched his career high by allowing seven homers. A setup man, Crabtree recorded 11 holds but blew seven save opportunities. He pitched his best in September, allowing only 10 hits in 16.1 innings.

Pitching & Defense

The radar gun is Crabtree's biggest enemy. High velocity readings, often touching 98 MPH, may look good, but harder is not always better. His fastball straightens out when thrown at peak velocity. He realized that during the second half and made a significant adjustment in his delivery. He sacrificed a few ticks on the gun for more movement on his heater, and the results were striking. Crabtree is a maximum-effort hurler, which makes pitching on consecutive days difficult.

2001 Outlook

Crabtree has the stuff to be a closer, but he never has experienced the cauldron of regular work in the ninth inning. He could get that chance this season if John Wetteland retires or decides to sign elsewhere. If Wetteland does not return, Crabtree still would have to battle Jeff Zimmerman for the job.

Chad Curtis

Position: LF/RF/DH
Bats: R **Throws:** R
Ht: 5'10" **Wt:** 185

Opening Day Age: 32
Born: 11/6/68 in Marion, IN
ML Seasons: 9

Overall Statistics

	G	AB	R	H	D	T	HR	RBI	SB	BB	SO	Avg	OBP	Slg
2000	108	335	48	91	25	1	8	48	3	37	71	.272	.343	.424
Career	1166	3902	624	1032	192	16	98	451	205	496	655	.264	.349	.397

2000 Situational Stats

	AB	H	HR	RBI	Avg		AB	H	HR	RBI	Avg
Home	157	49	5	29	.312	LHP	116	38	2	17	.328
Road	178	42	3	19	.236	RHP	219	53	6	31	.242
First Half	213	53	7	31	.249	Sc Pos	100	29	2	39	.290
Scnd Half	122	38	1	17	.311	Clutch	55	15	0	6	.273

2000 Season

For a third consecutive team, strident Chad Curtis had a personality clash with a teammate. This time, it was Royce Clayton. Before that, it was Kevin Mitchell in Cleveland and Derek Jeter with the Yankees. Curtis' strong convictions leave little room for compromise, and that can cause problems in the small world of the clubhouse. He served Texas as a capable fourth outfielder with extra-base power, but injuries forced the Rangers to give him more starts and at-bats than planned.

Hitting, Baserunning & Defense

Curtis thinks of himself as a home-run hitter. He hits the occasional longball, but the homers lead to too many big, wild swings. He struck out nearly twice as many times as he walked last season, though that ratio was uncharacteristically high. Curtis, who has bulked up in his quest for power, is no longer a center fielder, and his arm is below average. He had 21 steals in 1998 with the New York Yankees, but he dropped to a career-low three thefts in six tries in 2000.

2001 Outlook

Curtis is signed for the upcoming season, but he has a history of not lasting two full years with the same club. If the Rangers falter, they will look to move him to a contender before the trade deadline.

Doug Davis

Position: RP/SP
Bats: R **Throws:** L
Ht: 6' 3" **Wt:** 190

Opening Day Age: 25
Born: 9/21/75 in
Sacramento, CA
ML Seasons: 2

Overall Statistics

	W	L	Pct.	ERA	G	GS	Sv	IP	H	BB	SO	HR	Ratio
2000	7	6	.538	5.38	30	13	0	98.2	109	58	66	14	1.69
Career	7	6	.538	6.13	32	13	0	101.1	121	58	69	17	1.77

2000 Situational Stats

	W	L	ERA	Sv	IP		AB	H	HR	RBI	Avg
Home	4	3	4.76	0	45.1	LHB	86	27	4	23	.314
Road	3	3	5.91	0	53.1	RHB	293	82	10	38	.280
First Half	3	1	7.48	0	21.2	Sc Pos	117	32	7	51	.274
Scnd Half	4	5	4.79	0	77.0	Clutch	33	8	1	5	.242

2000 Season

After going 15-3 in parts of two seasons in Triple-A, Doug Davis earned a shot at Texas' rotation. He went 4-5 with a 5.54 ERA in 13 starts but performed well against tough competition. In four consecutive starts from August 20 to September 4 against playoff contenders, Davis went 2-1 with a 1.52 ERA. He worked at least six innings in each of those four outings. That included a 142-pitch complete-game win at Boston.

Pitching & Defense

Davis makes the most of marginal stuff. He hides the ball well in his delivery and can throw strikes with his curveball. His ability to effectively mix the curve with his fastball and changeup carried him in the minors, and it's his ticket in the majors, too. Davis has been far more aggressive coming out of the bullpen than as a starter. In 2000, he had 45 walks and 42 strikeouts in 74.2 innings as a starter, compared to just 13 free passes and 24 punchouts in 24 innings in relief. He helps himself on the mound by handling the little nuances, such as holding runners.

2001 Outlook

Davis can determine his fate. Pitch aggressively, and he can be a fourth or fifth starter. Pitch with caution, and he will be in the bullpen.

Bill Haselman

Position: C
Bats: R **Throws:** R
Ht: 6' 3" **Wt:** 223

Opening Day Age: 34
Born: 5/25/66 in Long
Branch, NJ
ML Seasons: 10
Pronunciation:
HASS-ul-mun

Overall Statistics

	G	AB	R	H	D	T	HR	RBI	SB	BB	SO	Avg	OBP	Slg
2000	62	193	23	53	18	0	6	26	0	15	36	.275	.329	.461
Career	469	1294	157	335	81	3	41	167	9	95	247	.259	.311	.421

2000 Situational Stats

	AB	H	HR	RBI	Avg		AB	H	HR	RBI	Avg
Home	106	36	3	17	.340	LHP	35	10	0	5	.286
Road	87	17	3	9	.195	RHP	158	43	6	21	.272
First Half	35	8	0	3	.229	Sc Pos	55	16	0	17	.291
Scnd Half	158	45	6	23	.285	Clutch	31	6	0	3	.194

2000 Season

The season-ending injury to All-Star catcher Ivan Rodriguez in July opened the door for Bill Haselman. A manager-in-training, Haselman figured prominently in the second-half development of righthander Ryan Glynn and lefty Doug Davis. Texas had a 4.95 team ERA with Haselman behind the plate and a 5.80 mark with all other catchers. His season ended with rotator cuff surgery in mid-September.

Hitting, Baserunning & Defense

Haselman, who still can turn on a fastball, hit .282 with six homers and 21 RBI in 149 at-bats after Rodriguez' injury. He is dramatically more effective against lefthanded pitching. He runs like a backup catcher and never has thrown well since a rotator cuff injury early in his career. His key strengths are his game-calling skills and his ability to nurture young pitchers.

2001 Outlook

The Rangers gave Haselman a two-year contract last summer. While his surgery may limit him in spring training, he should be ready on Opening Day. If Rodriguez is healthy, Haselman will receive no more than 30 starts. His influence will be felt by setting up game plans with the pitchers, a task Rodriguez routinely prefers to leave to others.

Ricky Ledee

Position: LF/RF/DH
Bats: L **Throws:** L
Ht: 6' 1" **Wt:** 200

Opening Day Age: 27
Born: 11/22/73 in Ponce, Puerto Rico
ML Seasons: 3
Pronunciation: luh-DAY

Overall Statistics

	G	AB	R	H	D	T	HR	RBI	SB	BB	SO	Avg	OBP	Slg
2000	137	467	59	110	19	5	13	77	13	59	98	.236	.322	.381
Career	267	796	117	198	37	12	23	129	20	94	200	.249	.327	.412

2000 Situational Stats

	AB	H	HR	RBI	Avg		AB	H	HR	RBI	Avg
Home	217	49	6	35	.226	LHP	83	20	3	15	.241
Road	250	61	7	42	.244	RHP	384	90	10	62	.234
First Half	226	55	8	36	.243	Sc Pos	152	47	7	66	.309
Scnd Half	241	55	5	41	.228	Clutch	60	15	3	12	.250

2000 Season

Ricky Ledee was traded twice in 30 days. He went from the Yankees, the only organization he had ever known, to Cleveland and finally to Texas. Ledee hit only .236, third-lowest among American League qualifiers, but showed signs of becoming a run producer. With the Rangers, he hit .309 with runners in scoring position and drove in 38 runs in his final 205 at-bats.

Hitting, Baserunning & Defense

The Rangers want Ledee to adjust his swing to be better able to pull pitches, and be more aggressive overall. Ledee has an opposite-field swing. When Ledee tries to pull pitches with that swing, he rolls over on the ball and grounds out to the right side. Ledee is an intelligent player who shows good judgment on the bases and in the field. He stole 13 bases last season, and could approach 20, though that total is unlikely with Johnny Oates at the helm. Ledee cut down on his miscues in the field last year, but his range and arm are average at best.

2001 Outlook

Ledee's passive personality did not fit within the Yankees' atmosphere of creative tension. The Rangers hope Ledee will bloom under an environment of positive reinforcement, but another trade is not out of the question.

Matt Perisho

Traded To TIGERS

Position: RP/SP
Bats: L **Throws:** L
Ht: 6' 0" **Wt:** 205

Opening Day Age: 25
Born: 6/8/75 in Burlington, IA
ML Seasons: 4

Overall Statistics

	W	L	Pct.	ERA	G	GS	Sv	IP	H	BB	SO	HR	Ratio
2000	2	7	.222	7.37	34	13	0	105.0	136	67	74	20	1.93
Career	2	11	.154	7.29	51	24	0	165.1	218	105	128	28	1.95

2000 Situational Stats

	W	L	ERA	Sv	IP		AB	H	HR	RBI	Avg
Home	1	2	5.80	0	59.0	LHB	142	47	4	25	.331
Road	1	5	9.39	0	46.0	RHB	289	89	16	59	.308
First Half	2	2	5.06	0	53.1	Sc Pos	131	42	3	59	.321
Scnd Half	0	5	9.75	0	51.2	Clutch	6	4	0	0	.667

2000 Season

Matt Perisho teased the Rangers by winning his first start with six shutout innings against Tampa Bay on June 17. It was downhill from there, as opponents began to lay off of his offerings out of the strike zone. He went 0-7 with an 8.74 ERA and 39 walks in his next 12 starts and finished the season out of the rotation. He closed the year with the second-highest ERA in franchise history among pitchers with at least 100 innings.

Pitching & Defense

Perisho figured in the departure of pitching coach Dick Bosman. Perisho, once considered a rising talent, has not developed with the Rangers. He lost confidence in the changeup—his top pitch—last season and collapsed. He allowed a staggering 17.9 baserunners per nine innings. His concentration can wander during games, to which his three errors and .813 fielding percentage in 2000 would attest. He did connect with a pair of pickoffs, however.

2001 Outlook

Out of minor league options and seemingly out of the Rangers' plans, Perisho was dealt to Detroit for two minor league pitchers. The Tigers are looking for a contribution in 2001.

Texas

Justin Thompson

Position: SP
Bats: L **Throws:** L
Ht: 6' 4" **Wt:** 215

Opening Day Age: 28
Born: 3/8/73 in San Antonio, TX
ML Seasons: 4

Overall Statistics

	W	L	Pct.	ERA	G	GS	Sv	IP	H	BB	SO	HR	Ratio
2000							Did Not Play						
Career	36	43	.456	3.98	101	101	0	647.0	629	235	427	71	1.34

2000 Situational Stats

	W	L	ERA	Sv	IP			AB	H	HR	RBI	Avg
Home	—	—	—	—	—	LHB	—	—	—	—	—	—
Road	—	—	—	—	—	RHB	—	—	—	—	—	—
First Half	—	—	—	—	—	Sc Pos	—	—	—	—	—	—
Scnd Half	—	—	—	—	—	Clutch	—	—	—	—	—	—

2000 Season

Texas based the deal that sent Juan Gonzalez to Detroit on getting a true ace in Justin Thompson. The trade proved to be a short-term disaster for the Rangers, because Thompson never made it to the mound for a regular-season game. He had his second major rotator cuff surgery in eight months during May, and he needed another arthroscopic procedure in October to clear out debris in the shoulder. He has not pitched in a major league game since August 15, 1999.

Pitching & Defense

When healthy, Thompson can be an ace. With Detroit in 1997, he was 15-11 with a 3.02 ERA at age 24. He had a devastating curveball, a good high fastball and an effective changeup. Shoulder problems struck in 1999, preventing him from getting the full extension needed to throw an effective curve. In 1997 and '98, his strikeout-walk ratio was a shade better than 2-1. He can be clumsy fielding his position, and his move to the plate is slow.

2001 Outlook

The additional surgery in October ruled out Thompson's availability for spring training, and it will be remarkable if he makes it back before the All-Star break. There are no guarantees he can ever again be the same pitcher he once was.

Jeff Zimmerman

Position: RP
Bats: R **Throws:** R
Ht: 6' 1" **Wt:** 200

Opening Day Age: 28
Born: 8/9/72 in Kelowna, BC, Canada
ML Seasons: 2

Overall Statistics

	W	L	Pct.	ERA	G	GS	Sv	IP	H	BB	SO	HR	Ratio
2000	4	5	.444	5.30	65	0	1	69.2	80	34	74	10	1.64
Career	13	8	.619	3.66	130	0	4	157.1	130	57	141	19	1.19

2000 Situational Stats

	W	L	ERA	Sv	IP			AB	H	HR	RBI	Avg
Home	1	2	5.15	1	36.2	LHB		111	33	6	21	.297
Road	3	3	5.45	0	33.0	RHB		169	47	4	21	.278
First Half	1	4	6.25	0	36.0	Sc Pos		109	23	2	28	.211
Scnd Half	3	1	4.28	1	33.2	Clutch		138	36	5	16	.261

2000 Season

Jeff Zimmerman showed signs that he was pushed too hard in the first half of the 1999 season. Zimmerman was 8-0 with a 0.86 ERA and 18 hits in 52.1 innings during the first half of his rookie campaign. Since then, he is 5-8 with a 5.06 ERA and 112 hits allowed in 105 innings. He never was comfortable with his out pitch, the slider, last season. Opponents hit .286 against Zimmerman, 120 points higher than their average in '99.

Pitching & Defense

Zimmerman was effective throwing the slider to hitters on both sides of the plate early in '99, but he has struggled with the pitch ever since. He began overthrowing it, which takes away its bite. He allowed 10 homers in 2000, the second-highest total among Rangers relievers. His fastball has good screwball movement away from lefthanded hitters. Zimmerman rushed his delivery more than he did during his rookie campaign, but opposing baserunners still were a perfect 8-for-8 against him last year. He is an adequate fielder.

2001 Outlook

The Rangers believe Zimmerman has the makeup to be a closer, but he must solve the slider problem. If John Wetteland doesn't return, Zimmerman could battle Tim Crabtree for the closer's job.

Mark Clark (Pos: RHP, Age: 32)

	W	L	Pct.	ERA	G	GS	Sv	IP	H	BB	SO	HR	Ratio
2000	3	5	.375	7.98	12	8	0	44.0	66	24	16	10	2.05
Career	74	71	.510	4.61	219	197	0	1246.1	1364	367	728	154	1.39

The Rangers kept giving Clark a chance to stake a rotation spot through the first part of June, but he kept failing. Texas ultimately released him in July. 2001 Outlook: C

Kelly Dransfeldt (Pos: SS, Age: 25, Bats: R)

	G	AB	R	H	D	T	HR	RBI	SB	BB	SO	Avg	OBP	Slg
2000	16	26	2	3	2	0	0	2	0	1	14	.115	.148	.192
Career	32	79	5	13	3	0	1	7	0	4	26	.165	.205	.241

Dransfeldt is a strong-armed shortstop who clubbed 27 homers in the minors in 1998. Since then, his power has dwindled. 2001 Outlook: C

Tom Evans (Pos: 3B, Age: 26, Bats: R)

	G	AB	R	H	D	T	HR	RBI	SB	BB	SO	Avg	OBP	Slg
2000	23	54	10	15	4	0	0	5	0	10	13	.278	.394	.352
Career	42	102	17	26	6	0	1	7	0	13	25	.255	.347	.343

Evans underwent rotator cuff surgery last May and was lost for the season. If healthy, he probably would have some value for his doubles power and walks. 2001 Outlook: C

Scarborough Green (Pos: CF/RF, Age: 26, Bats: B)

	G	AB	R	H	D	T	HR	RBI	SB	BB	SO	Avg	OBP	Slg
2000	79	124	21	29	1	1	0	9	10	10	26	.234	.291	.258
Career	117	168	30	36	1	1	0	10	10	13	33	.214	.271	.232

No matter how fast Green runs, an on-base plus slugging percentage below .600 simply won't cut it, especially for an outfielder. The Rangers released him in November, but the Cubs gave him a minor league deal. 2001 Outlook: C

Jonathan Johnson (Pos: RHP, Age: 26)

	W	L	Pct.	ERA	G	GS	Sv	IP	H	BB	SO	HR	Ratio
2000	1	1	.500	6.21	15	0	0	29.0	34	19	23	3	1.83
Career	1	1	.500	7.18	17	1	0	36.1	48	26	29	3	2.04

Johnson signed for a $1.1 million bonus in 1995 as the seventh pick in the draft. So far, the investment has hardly been worth it. He's now a reliever, and not a very good one at that. 2001 Outlook: C

Randy Knorr (Pos: C, Age: 32, Bats: R)

	G	AB	R	H	D	T	HR	RBI	SB	BB	SO	Avg	OBP	Slg
2000	15	34	5	10	2	0	2	2	0	0	3	.294	.294	.529
Career	219	585	69	133	25	3	21	78	0	39	139	.227	.277	.388

Despite his journeyman credentials, Knorr seems to pop up somewhere in the majors each season. Last year it was Texas. This year, who knows? 2001 Outlook: C

Jason McDonald (Pos: RF/LF, Age: 29, Bats: B)

	G	AB	R	H	D	T	HR	RBI	SB	BB	SO	Avg	OBP	Slg
2000	38	94	15	22	5	0	3	13	4	17	25	.234	.357	.383
Career	286	692	113	167	27	5	11	51	33	105	155	.241	.347	.342

McDonald had played 100 games for Oakland in 1999 before signing a minor league deal with Texas last year. While he draws walks and has acceptable speed, he's never hit consistently. 2001 Outlook: C

Mike Munoz (Pos: LHP, Age: 35)

	W	L	Pct.	ERA	G	GS	Sv	IP	H	BB	SO	HR	Ratio
2000	0	1	.000	13.50	7	0	0	4.0	11	3	1	1	3.50
Career	18	20	.474	5.19	453	0	11	364.1	408	174	240	34	1.60

Munoz pitched only in April last year, surrendering 11 hits in 21 at-bats before getting shelved with elbow tendinitis. He re-signed with Texas in mid-December. 2001 Outlook: C

Scott Sheldon (Pos: SS/2B/3B, Age: 32, Bats: R)

	G	AB	R	H	D	T	HR	RBI	SB	BB	SO	Avg	OBP	Slg
2000	58	124	21	35	11	0	4	19	0	10	37	.282	.336	.468
Career	80	165	23	43	11	0	5	22	0	12	49	.261	.315	.418

On September 6, Sheldon played all nine positions in one game. He has a bit of power for someone who can play shortstop or second base. 2001 Outlook: C

Ruben Sierra (Pos: DH, Age: 35, Bats: B)

	G	AB	R	H	D	T	HR	RBI	SB	BB	SO	Avg	OBP	Slg
2000	20	60	5	14	0	0	1	7	1	4	9	.233	.281	.283
Career	1682	6469	892	1737	341	56	240	1054	133	495	971	.269	.317	.450

At age 35, Sierra isn't ancient, though he seemed to get old before he turned 30. While he played well at Triple-A last year, he struggled with Texas, but he re-signed with the team in mid-December. 2001 Outlook: C

Brian Sikorski (Pos: RHP, Age: 26)

	W	L	Pct.	ERA	G	GS	Sv	IP	H	BB	SO	HR	Ratio
2000	1	3	.250	5.73	10	5	0	37.2	46	25	32	9	1.88
Career	1	3	.250	5.73	10	5	0	37.2	46	25	32	9	1.88

The Rangers picked up Sikorski when Houston waived him following the '99 campaign. He allowed as many home runs in 37.2 innings in the majors last year as he did in 100 more frames at Triple-A. 2001 Outlook: C

Pedro Valdes (Pos: RF, Age: 27, Bats: L)

	G	AB	R	H	D	T	HR	RBI	SB	BB	SO	Avg	OBP	Slg
2000	30	54	4	15	5	0	1	5	0	6	7	.278	.350	.426
Career	53	85	7	21	7	1	1	8	0	8	15	.247	.312	.388

Valdes proved he could mash Triple-A pitching long ago. He just never got an extended look in the majors. He left for Japan after last season. 2001 Outlook: D

Mike Venafro (Pos: LHP, Age: 27)

	W	L	Pct.	ERA	G	GS	Sv	IP	H	BB	SO	HR	Ratio
2000	3	1	.750	3.83	77	0	1	56.1	64	21	32	2	1.51
Career	6	3	.667	3.54	142	0	1	124.2	127	43	69	6	1.36

Venafro has appeared in 142 games and posted 36 holds over the past two years. Lefthanded batters hit 99 points lower than did righthanded swingers against him last season. 2001 Outlook: A

B.J. Waszgis (Pos: C, Age: 30, Bats: R)

	G	AB	R	H	D	T	HR	RBI	SB	BB	SO	Avg	OBP	Slg
2000	24	45	6	10	1	0	0	4	0	4	10	.222	.294	.244
Career	24	45	6	10	1	0	0	4	0	4	10	.222	.294	.244

Waszgis finally got called to the majors last July when Ivan Rodriguez was injured. Waszgis signed with Florida after the campaign. 2001 Outlook: C

Texas Rangers Minor League Prospects

Organization Overview:

While it was a disappointing fall from AL West champs in 1999 to the West cellar in 2000, the Rangers have some exciting young talent. The Juan Gonzalez trade netted right fielder Gabe Kapler and some young pitching. The David Segui deal brought left fielder Ricky Ledee, and Ledee, Kapler and homegrown prospect Ruben Mateo form a young, promising outfield. Even more encouraging has to be the emergence of top hitting prospects Carlos Pena and Kevin Mench. The beleaguered Texas bullpen hopes to retool with help from righthanders Darwin Cubillan, Danny Kolb and Francisco Cordero, while the rotation gets younger with Doug Davis and Ryan Glynn trying to solidify roles in 2001. Plus, young hurlers Joaquin Benoit, Jovanny Cedeno, Colby Lewis, Spike Lundberg and Andy Pratt took big steps toward Texas last season.

Francisco Cordero

Position: P
Bats: R **Throws:** R
Ht: 6' 2" **Wt:** 200

Opening Day Age: 23
Born: 8/11/77 in Santo Domingo, DR

Recent Statistics

	W	L	ERA	G	GS	Sv	IP	H	R	BB	SO	HR
2000 AAA Oklahoma	0	0	4.15	3	0	1	4.1	7	3	3	5	0
2000 AL Texas	1	2	5.35	56	0	0	77.1	87	51	48	49	11

Signed by Detroit as a 16-year-old in 1994, Cordero was a key acquisition in the Juan Gonzalez trade. Along with closer John Wetteland and setup man Jeff Zimmerman, the Dominican native gave the Rangers three power pitchers in the pen in 2000, but all three struggled. A propensity to walk hitters caught up with Cordero near midseason. He was sent to Triple-A Oklahoma in early August to regain his control, but injuries in Texas forced a quick return a week later. Cordero throws a 95-97 MPH fastball and a late-breaking slider, and he flashes a changeup for show. Regarded as a closer in training, he must work effectively in the strike zone this spring to secure a role in Texas' wide-open bullpen.

Darwin Cubillan

Position: P
Bats: R **Throws:** R
Ht: 6' 2" **Wt:** 170

Opening Day Age: 26
Born: 11/15/74 in Bobure, Zulia

Recent Statistics

	W	L	ERA	G	GS	Sv	IP	H	R	BB	SO	HR
2000 AAA Syracuse	3	1	0.55	24	0	6	32.2	14	2	13	41	0
2000 AAA Oklahoma	0	0	1.08	8	0	2	16.2	9	2	4	12	0
2000 AL Toronto	1	0	8.04	7	0	0	15.2	20	14	11	14	5
2000 AL Texas	0	0	10.70	13	0	0	17.2	32	22	14	13	4

Signed as a free agent by the Yankees in 1993, Cubillan missed all of 1996 and most of '97 because of reconstructive elbow surgery. After re-emerging at high Class-

A Tampa in 1998, Cubillan repeated there in '99 and pitched remarkably well. He signed with Toronto a year ago as a six-year minor league free agent, and successfully jumped to Triple-A in 2000 before a July trade shipped him and Mike Young to Texas for Esteban Loaiza. Cubillan dominated and earned eight saves at the Triple-A level, primarily throwing a fastball-changeup combination. His arm action on the changeup makes it his best pitch, and better location with it could lead to middle relief work with Texas in 2001.

Danny Kolb

Position: P
Bats: R **Throws:** R
Ht: 6' 4" **Wt:** 215

Opening Day Age: 26
Born: 3/29/75 in Sterling, IL

Recent Statistics

	W	L	ERA	G	GS	Sv	IP	H	R	BB	SO	HR
2000 AAA Oklahoma	4	1	0.98	13	0	4	18.1	11	6	8	18	0
2000 AL Texas	0	0	67.50	1	0	0	0.2	5	5	2	0	0

A sixth-round pick in 1995, Kolb emerged as a prospect with a strong 1996 season in the Class-A Sally League. He struggled with his command for much of the next two seasons, but Kolb got back on track in 1999 at Double-A Tulsa. He can throw in the mid-90s, but at 92-94 MPH his fastball runs in nicely on righthanders. He also throws a good slider, a cut fastball, and a curve he doesn't use much. Elbow problems that flared up late in 1999 led to elbow surgery last June to remove bone chips and repair a ligament. He is expected back for 2001, and if he can keep his power stuff down in the strike zone and harness his command, Kolb can help the big league staff.

Kevin Mench

Position: OF
Bats: R **Throws:** R
Ht: 6' 0" **Wt:** 215

Opening Day Age: 23
Born: 1/7/78 in Wilmington, DE

Recent Statistics

	G	AB	R	H	D	T	HR	RBI	SB	BB	SO	Avg
1999 R Pulaski	65	260	63	94	22	1	16	60	12	28	48	.362
1999 A Savannah	6	23	4	7	1	1	2	8	0	2	4	.304
2000 A Charlotte	132	491	118	164	39	9	27	121	19	78	72	.334

Doubts about Mench's prospect status prior to the 2000 season have been put to rest. This 1999 pick jumped to high Class-A in his second pro season, and adjusting to the wood bat didn't slow him down. With impressive bat speed, Mench powered the ball to all fields en route to his .334-27-121 season and he added 78 walks for a .427 on-base percentage. Exhibiting smarts and polish at the plate, Mench excelled as a situational hitter and run producer. He was just as dominant in the Arizona Fall League, but his defensive game isn't as far along. Still, he tracks balls well and should be adequate in left field.

Aaron Myette

Position: P   **Opening Day Age:** 23
Bats: R **Throws:** R   **Born:** 9/26/77 in New
Ht: 6' 4" **Wt:** 195   Westminster, BC, Canada

Recent Statistics

	W	L	ERA	G	GS	Sv	IP	H	R	BB	SO	HR
2000 AA Birmingham	2	0	3.52	3	3	0	15.1	11	7	8	21	1
2000 AAA Charlotte	5	5	4.35	19	18	0	111.2	103	58	56	85	18
2000 AL Chicago	0	0	0.00	2	0	0	2.2	0	0	4	1	0

The White Sox used one of six first-round picks in 1997 on Myette, who throws a terrific slider and a 91-94 MPH fastball. He allowed hitters a league-low .225 average in going 12-7 at Double-A Birmingham in 1999, but the 2000 season was a nightmare by comparison. Myette broke his hand punching a wall after a rare spring training outing that didn't go well. He was sidelined into May and didn't regain his spring form until July. When he is pitching well, Myette has good command of his fastball inside. Then he gets hitters to swing at and miss the slider, which is his No. 1 pitch. He should be in the 2001 mix for a rotation spot in Texas after his acquisition from Chicago over the winter.

Carlos Pena

Position: 1B   **Opening Day Age:** 22
Bats: L **Throws:** L   **Born:** 5/17/78 in Santo
Ht: 6' 2" **Wt:** 210   Domingo, DR

Recent Statistics

	G	AB	R	H	D	T	HR	RBI	SB	BB	SO	Avg
1999 A Charlotte	136	501	85	128	31	8	18	103	2	74	135	.255
2000 AA Tulsa	138	529	117	158	36	2	28	105	12	101	108	.299
2000 MLE	138	517	99	146	33	1	25	89	8	72	114	.282

Pena has a fluid swing that produces power. After a slight power surge in his second pro season at high Class-A Charlotte in 1999, Pena, a first-round pick in '98, had a breakthrough year last summer. The lefthanded hitter shortened his stroke, using more of a contact swing that didn't compromise his power. He was an effective run producer at Tulsa, leading all of Double-A in runs scored and finishing third in RBI. His patience at the plate resulted in 101 walks and a .414 on-base percentage in 2000, each a career high. Pena is fundamentally sound, and that applies to his defense as well. Pena is known for his soft hands and quick feet around the first-base bag.

Jason Romano

Position: 2B   **Opening Day Age:** 21
Bats: R **Throws:** R   **Born:** 6/24/79 in Tampa,
Ht: 6' 0" **Wt:** 185   FL

Recent Statistics

	G	AB	R	H	D	T	HR	RBI	SB	BB	SO	Avg
1999 A Charlotte	120	459	84	143	27	14	13	71	34	39	72	.312
2000 AA Tulsa	131	535	87	145	35	2	8	70	25	56	84	.271
2000 MLE	131	523	73	133	32	1	6	59	17	40	89	.254

A 1997 draft pick, Romano immediately moved from third base to second. He worked hard on the move and he emerged as a prospect in 1999 by batting .312-13-71 as one of the youngest regulars in the high Class-A

Florida State League. He recorded 54 extra-base hits and 34 steals that season, but the power dropped off at Double-A Tulsa in 2000. At times Romano was overly aggressive, offering at pitches he couldn't handle, but the Rangers expect him to mature into an effective leadoff man. He should combine some home-run pop with above-average speed in the majors. The acquisition of Randy Velarde gives Romano more time to develop.

Mike Young

Position: 2B   **Opening Day Age:** 24
Bats: R **Throws:** R   **Born:** 10/19/76 in
Ht: 6' 0" **Wt:** 185   Covina, CA

Recent Statistics

	G	AB	R	H	D	T	HR	RBI	SB	BB	SO	Avg
2000 AA Tennessee	91	345	51	95	24	5	6	47	16	36	72	.275
2000 AA Tulsa	43	188	30	60	13	5	1	32	9	17	28	.319
2000 AL Texas	2	2	0	0	0	0	0	0	0	0	1	.000
2000 MLE	134	524	73	146	35	8	5	71	18	41	106	.279

Primarily an outfielder in college, Young shifted to short when he joined the Jays as a fifth-round pick in 1997. The Jays later moved him to second base, where he is better suited to play, but then he was dealt to Texas with Darwin Cubillan for Esteban Loaiza last July. His best tools are his arm strength and speed, but he also exhibits a short, quick swing that he uses to drive the ball to all fields. Young also makes good contact and draws walks, which maximizes the use of his speed. While Jason Romano is the second baseman of the future, Young will play both second and short for Triple-A Oklahoma.

Others to Watch

Signed in 1996, Dominican righthander **Joaquin Benoit** (22) has incredible stuff, but refining his four-pitch arsenal and delivery have taken time. He went 4-4 (3.83) at Double-A Tulsa in 2000 before emerging as one of the best pitchers in the Arizona Fall League. . . Fellow Dominican **Jovanny Cedeno** (21) dominated in his second pro season in the Class-A Sally League (11-4, 2.42 and 153 strikeouts). He throws three promising pitches that have good life, including a mid-90s fastball. . . A 31st-round pick in 1996, **Travis Hafner** (23) arrived with power potential and loads of strikeouts. But the whiffs dropped off dramatically and the average and walk rate rose in 2000 at high Class-A Charlotte, where Hafner hit .346-22-109. . . Righthander **Colby Lewis** (21) had Tommy John surgery as a college player in 1998. Still, he led the Rookie-level Appalachian League in ERA in '99 and jumped to the high Class-A Florida State League in 2000. He has three solid pitches including a mid-90s fastball with late break. . . For a second straight season, **Dave "Spike" Lundberg** (23) went 14-7. Despite relying on a finesse game, the righthander allowed fewer hits per nine innings at Double-A in 2000 than he did at Class-A in '99. He also generated more strikeouts per nine in 2000, which can be attributed to his good command of a half-dozen pitches and a slight rise in his velocity.

SkyDome

Offense

The dimensions at SkyDome have stayed the same for several years, but undoubtedly there was a trend towards more longballs in 2000. Slugger Carlos Delgado inverted his previous road-heavy home-run splits to a 30-11 home advantage, which helped skew the park's home-run performance of the past few years. On the other hand, the opposition nearly duplicated its productivity from previous seasons. The long alleys also help create a high percentage of doubles, and speed can play a big offensive role in this park for those who have it.

Defense

SkyDome has kept its Astroturf and its super-cushy underpadding in place, which gives balls a true bounce enabling the infielders to get a good read on the hops. Naturally, balls will scoot into the holes faster at the Dome than in natural grass parks making it a challenge even for defenders who have better than average range. Outfield hops can be a tricky enterprise if the outfielder charges in too far. However, the walls are well-padded for those wishing to climb the 10-foot barrier.

Who It Helps the Most

Even though Carlos Delgado and Tony Batista amassed 40-plus home-run seasons in 2000 and did most of their damage at home, SkyDome is average as a home-run park. It continues to benefit line-drive gap hitters as well as contact hitters with good speed, such as Shannon Stewart.

Who It Hurts the Most

Slower teams struggle defensively at SkyDome, exposing themselves to lots of manufactured runs. Players with limited range will be tested severely, both in the infield and outfield. Pitchers who do not exhibit good command, such as Roy Halladay and Kelvim Escobar, will be stung by the turf.

Rookies & Newcomers

Rookie outfielder Vernon Wells, who is speedy and agile, should find SkyDome helpful to him in the early stages of his career. The ballpark is very doubles-friendly, and that should work in Wells' favor. Both he and Jose Cruz cover a lot of ground in the outfield, a big plus at SkyDome.

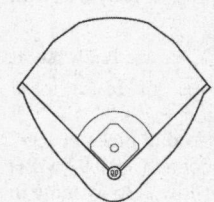

Dimensions: LF-328, LCF-375, CF-400, RCF-375, RF-328

Capacity: 51,000

Elevation: 300 feet

Surface: Turf

Foul Territory: Average

Park Factors

2000 Season

| | Home Games | | | Away Games | | | |
	Blue Jays	Opp	Total	Blue Jays	Opp	Total	Index
G	72	72	144	72	72	144	—
Avg	.279	.280	.280	.270	.287	.278	101
AB	2455	2582	5037	2579	2453	5032	100
R	382	409	791	357	395	752	105
H	686	723	1409	696	704	1400	101
2B	155	159	314	125	137	262	120
3B	8	9	17	12	12	24	71
HR	117	80	197	96	94	190	104
BB	215	241	456	230	246	476	96
SO	417	460	877	498	396	894	98
E	47	47	94	45	47	92	102
E-Infield	43	40	83	35	44	79	105
LHB-Avg	.310	.277	.293	.282	.290	.286	102
LHB-HR	62	35	97	46	48	94	102
RHB-Avg	.258	.282	.270	.262	.284	.272	99
RHB-HR	55	45	100	50	46	96	105

1998-2000

| | Home Games | | | Away Games | | | |
	Blue Jays	Opp	Total	Blue Jays	Opp	Total	Index
G	217	217	434	218	218	436	—
Avg	.274	.268	.271	.273	.278	.275	98
AB	7319	7721	15040	7755	7370	15125	100
R	1143	1142	2285	1129	1126	2255	102
H	2005	2067	4072	2120	2046	4166	98
2B	464	481	945	409	404	813	117
3B	23	28	51	28	51	79	65
HR	300	234	534	298	267	565	95
BB	748	770	1518	730	797	1527	100
SO	1383	1453	2836	1491	1355	2846	100
E	154	119	273	141	148	289	95
E-Infield	134	101	235	116	129	245	96
LHB-Avg	.283	.270	.276	.278	.279	.279	99
LHB-HR	163	108	271	155	127	282	94
RHB-Avg	.267	.266	.266	.270	.276	.273	98
RHB-HR	137	126	263	143	140	283	95

2000 Rankings (American League)

- Highest double factor

Buck Martinez

2000 Season

Tired of the blustery managerial style of Jim Fregosi, the Blue Jays fired Fregosi in October and hired former big league catcher and national broadcaster Buck Martinez to be the organization's eighth full-time manager in their 24-year history. Martinez had been analyzing games for both TSN since 1987 and ESPN since 1992, and he has neither coached nor managed at any level prior to this.

Offense

It's difficult to project what strategy and tactics Martinez will employ this season and beyond. The club has retained the services of batting coach and former manager Cito Gaston, who has had an enormous effect on key players such as Carlos Delgado, Shannon Stewart and Darrin Fletcher. The Blue Jays will be a power-packed team regardless of who's calling the shots from the dugout, but because Martinez has been analyzing games for so long, he's bound to try some creative innovations like restoring the running game or utilizing the hit-and-run more often than his predecessor.

Pitching & Defense

The toughest test Martinez faces will be the handling of his pitching staff. As a former catcher, he has experience to draw upon to tutor his backstops. However, handling the psyche of his staff with the help of new pitching coach Mark Connor will be a new experience. Martinez' tenure in the broadcasting ranks has afforded him a strong knowledge of hitters around the league and how they are to be pitched. Martinez does inherit a talented defense, a unit that should be in the right spots more often than not, given Martinez' strong belief in advance scouting for positioning purposes.

2001 Outlook

Martinez' keen analytical skills, his mastery of the media and strong interpersonal skills bode well for a successful transition from the booth to the bench. Toronto has become a tough market in terms of fan and media expectations, but GM Gord Ash hired Martinez knowing how crucial those relationships are. The great unknown is how Martinez will deal with the adversity of an up-and-down season, which has become the recent standard for Toronto.

Born: 11/07/48 in Redding, California

Playing Experience: 1969-1986, KC, Mil, Tor

Managerial Experience: No major league managing experience

Manager Statistics (Jim Fregosi)

Year	Team, Lg	W	L	Pct	GB	Finish
2000	Toronto, AL	83	79	.512	4.5	3rd East
15 Seasons		1028	1095	.484	—	—

2000 Starting Pitchers by Days Rest

	<=3	4	5	6+
Blue Jays Starts	1	88	43	20
Blue Jays ERA	3.68	4.83	6.26	5.27
AL Avg Starts	2	88	40	22
AL ERA	4.87	5.03	5.03	5.28

2000 Situational Stats

	Jim Fregosi	AL Average
Hit & Run Success %	28.6	35.1
Stolen Base Success %	72.4	68.8
Platoon Pct.	56.0	57.8
Defensive Subs	10	23
High-Pitch Outings	16	13
Quick/Slow Hooks	13/24	18/19
Sacrifice Attempts	45	55

2000 Rankings—Jim Fregosi (American Lg)

- 1st in fewest caught stealings of third base (2) and first-batter platoon percentage (56.0)
- 2nd in saves with over 1 inning pitched (16)
- 3rd in slow hooks (24)

Tony Batista

2000 Season

Tony Batista continued the all-out power assault that stunned both opponents and fans alike after he was traded to Toronto midway into the 1999 season. Batista kept his torrid pace going into the All-Star break, batting .289 with 24 homers and 72 RBI in the first half of 2000. Batista faltered in the second half, however, when the Jays needed him most. Clearly, advance scouts and pitchers began to find holes in his swing.

Hitting

There's not a hitter around today who uses a more unorthodox stance and batting style than Batista. Standing perpendicular to the path between the mound and the plate, Batista looks as though he's waiting for a pitch to be delivered from third base. It's his way of gaining better sight of the ball during the pitcher's delivery, and he times his closure to catch up with the pitch. Batista fully extends his arms on each and every one of his long swings, pulling high or low fastballs from the middle to the inside part of the plate. Pitch him outside and he's a completely different hitter—one who strikes out often with virtually no discipline.

Baserunning & Defense

After replacing injured shortstop Alex Gonzalez during the 1999 season, Batista was moved to third base last spring. He did a good job utilizing his range as a middle infielder at the hot corner. He has an unorthodox throwing style, which is an over-the-top toss that can appear to be a looping lob more than a straight throw. Although he's quick, Batista doesn't have a lot of speed and attempts few thefts.

2001 Outlook

The Batista trade has proven thus far to be one of the most lopsided in recent memory, and the Jays wasted no time signing him to a four-year, $16 million extension after his eye-popping performance in 1999. There should be some concern about his post All-Star numbers, since it's conceivable pitchers now are better prepared to get him out. One has to wonder: with Batista's peculiar batting style, why it took as long as it did.

Position: 3B
Bats: R **Throws:** R
Ht: 6' 0" **Wt:** 185

Opening Day Age: 27
Born: 12/9/73 in Puerto Plata, Dominican Republic
ML Seasons: 5
Pronunciation: bah-TEESE-tah

Overall Statistics

	G	AB	R	H	D	T	HR	RBI	SB	BB	SO	Avg	OBP	Slg
2000	154	620	96	163	32	2	41	114	5	35	121	.263	.307	.519
Career	544	1858	279	496	98	7	100	298	19	124	349	.267	.316	.489

Where He Hits the Ball

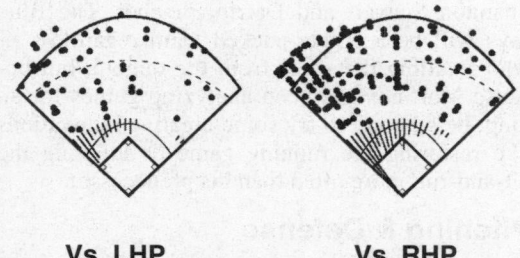

Vs. LHP   **Vs. RHP**

2000 Situational Stats

	AB	H	HR	RBI	Avg		AB	H	HR	RBI	Avg
Home	307	83	25	60	.270	LHP	162	38	6	23	.235
Road	313	80	16	54	.256	RHP	458	125	35	91	.273
First Half	329	95	24	72	.289	Sc Pos	181	52	13	77	.287
Scnd Half	291	68	17	42	.234	Clutch	83	29	7	19	.349

2000 Rankings (American League)

- 3rd in lowest on-base percentage vs. lefthanded pitchers (.287)
- 4th in home runs
- 5th in fielding percentage at third base (.963)
- 6th in at-bats, errors at third base (17), lowest on-base percentage, lowest groundball/flyball ratio (0.8) and lowest batting average on an 0-2 count (.053)
- Led the Blue Jays in home runs, at-bats, GDPs (15) and batting average in the clutch
- Led AL third basemen in at-bats, RBI, batting average with the bases loaded (.400) and slugging percentage vs. righthanded pitchers (.557)

Chris Carpenter

2000 Season

The road to imminent stardom took a serious detour for Chris Carpenter last year, as he posted a league-worst 6.26 ERA and temporarily lost his spot in the rotation. Carpenter's free fall began in the spring as he attempted to come back from elbow surgery after the 1999 campaign. Spring training began with elbow tenderness and ended with a liner off his pitching elbow in late March. Carpenter took another liner off his face during a September contest against the White Sox, but he never went on the disabled list all year.

Pitching

Carpenter works primarily off his two-seam and four-seam fastballs, which clocked in as high as 95 MPH in past seasons. These pitches would set up a knee-buckling curveball to righthanded hitters. His elbow problems have dropped his velocity to a more consistent 91 MPH, and consequently his arching curveball is used less often. Carpenter also had been perfecting an effective circle change, but that pitch deserted him last year. With his repertoire flattening out, Carpenter's walks and home runs shot up while his strikeout rate decreased appreciably. He had very little to come back with once he fell behind in the count, which happened much too often during the 2000 campaign.

Defense

Carpenter has a very good spin move to first base to hold runners close, forcing would-be basestealers to think twice. He has no wasted motion and generally gets the ball to the plate extremely fast, which accounts for the paucity of attempts against him over the past few seasons. He's athletic and quick off the mound, making him a good fielder who can dispose of the slow tappers in front of him.

2001 Outlook

Some of the postseason finger-pointing focused on Carpenter when it came to explaining how the Jays missed out on the playoffs yet again. Carpenter had a lot of pressure placed on him to be the No. 2 starter last spring, and it will be interesting to see how he recovers from such a disappointing year. His first assignment must be to regain his control. His velocity should return after a winter's rest.

Position: SP
Bats: R **Throws:** R
Ht: 6' 6" **Wt:** 225

Opening Day Age: 25
Born: 4/27/75 in Exeter, NH
ML Seasons: 4

Overall Statistics

	W	L	Pct.	ERA	G	GS	Sv	IP	H	BB	SO	HR	Ratio
2000	10	12	.455	6.26	34	27	0	175.1	204	83	113	30	1.64
Career	34	34	.500	5.04	105	88	0	581.2	666	229	410	71	1.54

How Often He Throws Strikes

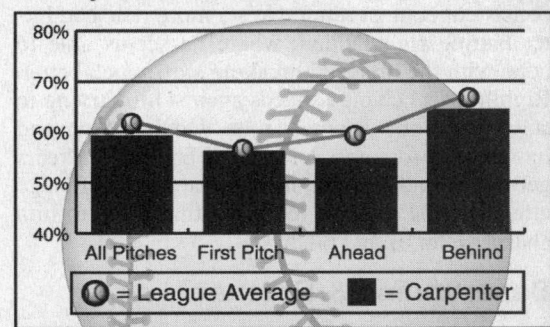

= League Average   = Carpenter

2000 Situational Stats

	W	L	ERA	Sv	IP		AB	H	HR	RBI	Avg
Home	3	6	7.53	0	77.2	LHB	327	96	12	46	.294
Road	7	6	5.25	0	97.2	RHB	376	108	18	70	.287
First Half	7	7	6.13	0	108.2	Sc Pos	181	57	9	87	.315
Scnd Half	3	5	6.48	0	66.2	Clutch	38	9	0	3	.237

2000 Rankings (American League)

- 1st in highest ERA, highest slugging percentage allowed (.496) and highest on-base percentage allowed (.369)
- 3rd in lowest stolen-base percentage allowed (36.4)
- 4th in most home runs allowed per nine innings (1.54)
- 5th in lowest strikeout/walk ratio (1.4) and highest batting average allowed (.290)
- Led the Blue Jays in home runs allowed, runners caught stealing (7), GDPs induced (19), highest groundball/flyball ratio allowed (1.3), lowest stolen-base percentage allowed (36.4) and most GDPs induced per nine innings (1.0)

Jose Cruz

Position: CF
Bats: B **Throws:** R
Ht: 6' 0" **Wt:** 200

Opening Day Age: 26
Born: 4/19/74 in Arroyo, Puerto Rico
ML Seasons: 4

2000 Season

Still looking to prove himself as Toronto's everyday center fielder, Jose Cruz established new single-season marks with 31 home runs, 32 doubles and 76 RBI. Cruz quickly thwarted any challenge for his job from prospect Vernon Wells during spring training. However, Cruz continued to struggle with his batting average, looking particularly inept during the months of June and July.

Hitting

Although Cruz is a switch-hitter, he's one-dimensional from the left side. He has excellent power for a player of average size, but his strike-zone judgment against righthanders is lacking and he's not a consistent contact hitter. He's a more polished hitter batting righthanded, where he seems able to cope with the offspeed breaking stuff much better. Righthanders change speeds against him, trying to stay away from his power zone, which is down and in—as it is for most lefthanded batters. He fears getting behind in the count early, and he'll often go after the first pitch, a tendency that leads to him chasing a lot of bad pitches.

Baserunning & Defense

Cruz is a fast baserunner who picks his spots well when it comes to stealing. He's successful about 75 percent of the time, but he averages less than 20 attempts per season. He covers a lot of ground in the outfield and has a very good glove, though not a great arm. Cruz is just coming into his own defensively, and projects to be one of the better center fielders in the league someday soon.

2001 Outlook

Cruz has heard his name on the trade block more than a few times, as he has come up short of expectations ever since the Jays acquired him in 1997. Despite his power surge, he needs to be a more consistent hitter who keeps his average above the .250 hump if he expects to remain a front-line player. His next arbitration hearing will have the Jays thinking seriously about alternatives such as Vernon Wells again.

Overall Statistics

	G	AB	R	H	D	T	HR	RBI	SB	BB	SO	Avg	OBP	Slg
2000	162	603	91	146	32	5	31	76	15	71	129	.242	.323	.466
Career	477	1699	268	417	84	12	82	231	47	233	436	.245	.335	.454

Where He Hits the Ball

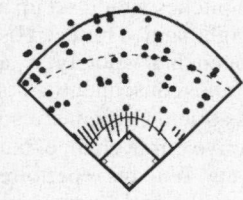
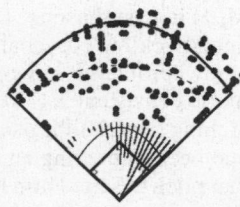

Vs. LHP **Vs. RHP**

2000 Situational Stats

	AB	H	HR	RBI	Avg		AB	H	HR	RBI	Avg
Home	288	72	15	40	.250	LHP	162	47	5	19	.290
Road	315	74	16	36	.235	RHP	441	99	26	57	.224
First Half	346	83	20	47	.240	Sc Pos	133	36	7	47	.271
Scnd Half	257	63	11	29	.245	Clutch	76	19	2	7	.250

2000 Rankings (American League)

- 1st in games played
- 2nd in fielding percentage in center field (.993) and lowest batting average vs. righthanded pitchers
- 5th in lowest batting average
- 8th in lowest batting average on a 3-2 count (.118)
- 9th in errors in center field (3)
- 10th in lowest batting average with two strikes (.143)
- Led the Blue Jays in triples, strikeouts, batting average with the bases loaded (.444), highest percentage of extra bases taken as a runner (48.9) and games played
- Led AL center fielders in games played (162)

Carlos Delgado

2000 Season

After making a valiant run at the Triple Crown in just his fifth full season in the big leagues, Carlos Delgado has joined the ranks of the super elite. In addition to his run at the homer, RBI and batting titles, Delgado led the league in total bases, doubles, extra-base hits and times on base. He placed in the top percentile of so many offensive categories that anyone can summarize his 2000 season in one word—dominant.

Hitting

Even before Delgado's first days on the major league scene, everyone knew about his prodigious power. But his rapid progression as an all-around hitter makes him even more dangerous. Delgado stayed with his open stance and slight crouch of 1999, an approach that allows him to close up fast while waiting longer and hitting to all fields. He perfected the art in 2000, hitting .319 against southpaws while simply ravaging righthanders. He reduced his strikeout totals dramatically with better pitch selection, and now there's hardly a weakness left for pitchers to exploit.

Baserunning & Defense

Although he continues to work hard at the defensive nuances of his position, Delgado is not exactly a surehanded first baseman. He's not quick off the mark and can get tied up on hard-hit grounders to his area. Although he committed the fourth-most errors of any first baseman in the majors in 2000, it's worth noting that he played all 162 games and led the majors in chances. Delgado rarely steals and is not fleet of foot around the bases, either.

2001 Outlook

Delgado is Toronto's marquee player and undisputed team leader. He loves playing in Toronto, and as long as the Jays continually adjust his pay scale upward, he'll remain in town. The Jays did just that in October, restructuring his contract into a four-year, $68 million deal that included a $4.8 million signing bonus and keeps him north of the border through 2004. With the paperwork out of the way, there's no reason to think he can't repeat his prodigious numbers of 2000.

Position: 1B
Bats: L **Throws:** R
Ht: 6' 3" **Wt:** 225

Opening Day Age: 28
Born: 6/25/72 in Aguadilla, Puerto Rico
ML Seasons: 8
Pronunciation: del-GAH-doh

Toronto

Overall Statistics

	G	AB	R	H	D	T	HR	RBI	SB	BB	SO	Avg	OBP	Slg
2000	162	569	115	196	57	1	41	137	0	123	104	.344	.470	.664
Career	829	2901	493	818	214	7	190	604	5	436	728	.282	.383	.557

Where He Hits the Ball

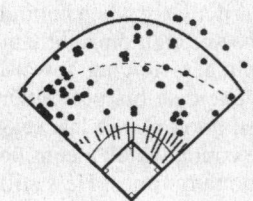

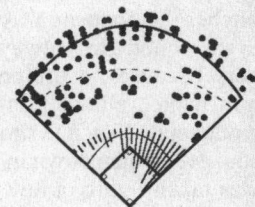

Vs. LHP **Vs. RHP**

2000 Situational Stats

	AB	H	HR	RBI	Avg		AB	H	HR	RBI	Avg
Home	283	102	30	75	.360	LHP	188	60	6	36	.319
Road	286	94	11	62	.329	RHP	381	136	35	101	.357
First Half	320	116	28	80	.363	Sc Pos	172	66	13	102	.384
Scnd Half	249	80	13	57	.321	Clutch	70	18	5	14	.257

2000 Rankings (American League)

- 1st in doubles, total bases (378), hit by pitch (15), times on base (334), pitches seen (2,938), slugging percentage vs. righthanded pitchers (.727) and games played
- 2nd in walks, intentional walks (18), slugging percentage, on-base percentage, batting average with runners in scoring position, cleanup slugging percentage (.664), on-base percentage vs. righthanded pitchers (.492) and errors at first base (13)
- 3rd in batting average vs. righthanded pitchers and lowest fielding percentage at first base (.991)
- Led the Blue Jays in batting average, home runs, runs scored, hits, doubles, total bases (378), RBI, walks and intentional walks (18)

Darrin Fletcher

2000 Season

Darrin Fletcher's third season in Toronto was even better than his first two. Once again he established new career highs in batting average, home runs, on-base percentage and slugging percentage. Fletcher's .320 average was second best among catchers in the league. As the Jays' No. 1 receiver, Fletcher stayed relatively healthy except for one stint on the disabled list with a strained right shoulder, which limited his playing time to only six games during the month of June.

Hitting

Fletcher's dramatic improvement against southpaws in 2000 led to his first plus-.300 season. An open-stance hitter, Fletcher figured out how to take pitches the opposite way, particularly when behind in the count. He's always been tough on righthanders because he prefers pitches moving toward him, which allows him to exercise his pull-hitter tendencies. Fletcher showed good power last season, even when down in the count, which means he was taken lightly a few too many times. He's still somewhat of an overanxious hitter who takes very few walks.

Baserunning & Defense

Fletcher led the league in fielding percentage, which is testimony to his ability to make the right decisions with an accurate, but less than powerful throwing arm. He always was tabbed as a poor defender when it came to throwing out basestealers, but his percentages declined marginally last season. Fletcher is not much of a threat on the basepaths, which is typical of most catchers.

2001 Outlook

The Blue Jays made sure they did not let Fletcher get away after his outstanding 2000 effort, signing him a month after the end of the regular season to a two-year, $7.75 million deal with an option for 2003. He should be Toronto's regular backstop for at least the next couple of campaigns, especially if his performance level continues to exceed expectations. He provides a productive lefthanded bat that generates good numbers, and he continues to improve defensively—commodities that would have been hard to replace at any salary level.

Position: C
Bats: L **Throws:** R
Ht: 6' 2" **Wt:** 205

Opening Day Age: 34
Born: 10/3/66 in Elmhurst, IL
ML Seasons: 12

Overall Statistics

	G	AB	R	H	D	T	HR	RBI	SB	BB	SO	Avg	OBP	Slg
2000	122	416	43	133	19	1	20	58	1	20	45	.320	.355	.514
Career	1066	3359	333	926	188	8	110	505	2	227	343	.276	.326	.435

Where He Hits the Ball

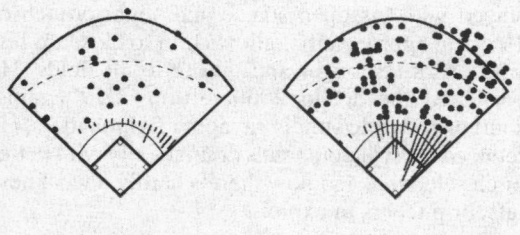

Vs. LHP   Vs. RHP

2000 Situational Stats

	AB	H	HR	RBI	Avg		AB	H	HR	RBI	Avg
Home	220	73	10	34	.332	LHP	79	27	1	12	.342
Road	196	60	10	24	.306	RHP	337	106	19	46	.315
First Half	189	66	10	33	.349	Sc Pos	93	26	3	37	.280
Scnd Half	227	67	10	25	.295	Clutch	68	19	2	14	.279

2000 Rankings (American League)

- 1st in fielding percentage at catcher (.994)
- 9th in batting average with two strikes (.268)
- Led the Blue Jays in batting average on an 0-2 count (.267), lowest percentage of swings that missed (13.4) and highest percentage of swings put into play (47.3)

Brad Fullmer

2000 Season

Brad Fullmer changed Canadian locales last March in a three-way trade of first basemen between Toronto, Montreal and Texas that also involved Lee Stevens and David Segui. Fullmer responded with the best season of his career, which arguably gave his new club the best deal in the trade. Used exclusively as a designated hitter, Fullmer vaulted past 30 homers and 100 RBI in just 482 at-bats, and narrowly missed batting .300.

Hitting

Fullmer is a hard-swinging, no-nonsense type of hitter who relishes just being in the batter's box. He brings a unique determination to every at-bat, making contact often and seldom going down on strikes. Fullmer used to be known as a line-drive hitter in Montreal, where he accumulated lots of doubles. But last season he gained elevation on his shots to the outfield, accounting for the big improvement in home-run production. He's an inside-fastball hitter with amazing bat speed but is much weaker against southpaws who stay outside on him. He'll sit out against the tough lefthanders, which helps keep his average higher.

Baserunning & Defense

Plagued by rotator cuff surgery a few years ago, Fullmer never gained a lot of experience at first base. In Toronto, he's been given the perfect role as a DH, and he's content not to have to play in the field. Fullmer is not fleet-footed and rarely steals a base unless it's given to him. He runs the bases hard, relying on grit and determination.

2001 Outlook

The Jays had to be thrilled with Fullmer's production in his first AL season. Plus, they've found a rare type of designated hitter—they've got one who's happy with the role. Fullmer collected just $310,000 for his efforts in 2000, making him an incredible bargain to boot, but his price tag will move up substantially next season should he reach arbitration. Toronto may try to sign him to a multi-year pact beforehand.

Position: DH
Bats: L **Throws:** R
Ht: 6' 0" **Wt:** 215

Opening Day Age: 26
Born: 1/17/75 in Chatsworth, CA
ML Seasons: 4

Toronto

Overall Statistics

	G	AB	R	H	D	T	HR	RBI	SB	BB	SO	Avg	OBP	Slg
2000	133	482	76	142	29	1	32	104	3	30	68	.295	.340	.558
Career	392	1374	176	388	109	5	57	232	11	93	180	.282	.331	.493

Where He Hits the Ball

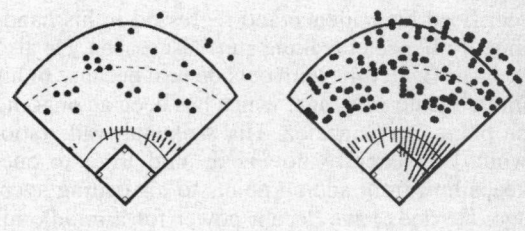

Vs. LHP   **Vs. RHP**

2000 Situational Stats

	AB	H	HR	RBI	Avg		AB	H	HR	RBI	Avg
Home	254	74	16	50	.291	LHP	93	21	5	19	.226
Road	228	68	16	54	.298	RHP	389	121	27	85	.311
First Half	266	81	14	53	.305	Sc Pos	143	46	15	80	.322
Scnd Half	216	61	18	51	.282	Clutch	64	16	2	9	.250

2000 Rankings (American League)

- 2nd in lowest batting average on a 3-1 count (.000)
- 4th in lowest percentage of pitches taken (44.9)
- 8th in slugging percentage vs. righthanded pitchers (.589) and fewest pitches seen per plate appearance (3.43)
- Led the Blue Jays in sacrifice flies (6)
- Led designated hitters in hit by pitch (6), batting average with the bases loaded (.400) and slugging percentage vs. righthanded pitchers (.589)

Alex Gonzalez

2000 Season

In a year following season-ending shoulder surgery, which limited him to only 38 games in 1999, Alex Gonzalez regained his footing and turned in a typical year of moderate offensive production and solid defense. Gonzalez landed on the disabled list in July with a strained groin, which caused him to miss 21 games, but he rebounded with a solid August in which he batted .310. He also established new career highs in homers and RBI.

Hitting

Prior to his injury in 1999, Gonzalez was showing signs of improvement as a hitter, demonstrating greater patience and selectiveness. Perhaps over-eager to show he was fully recovered, Gonzalez sacrificed his patience and regressed in his handling of offspeed breaking stuff last season. He also had a difficult time with outside heat because of his limited plate coverage, which has been an ongoing problem for Gonzalez. His strikeout-walk ratio, which persistently hovers around three-to-one, keeps him from adding points to his batting average. He does have decent power for a middle infielder when he can reach a fastball.

Baserunning & Defense

Gonzalez' calling card is his defense. He flashes good range and a rocket-powered arm, and he dispelled any concerns about his shoulder with continued consistent play in the field in 2000. He can fill the hole to his right and make the unbalanced throw to first as well as nearly any shortstop in the league. Partly due to his manager's reluctance to employ a running game, Gonzalez attempted only eight steals all year, even though he does run well on the bases.

2001 Outlook

Gonzalez was a free agent this winter, and at age 27, he is just now entering his prime. He will begin his second decade in the Toronto organization after signing a four-year contract with the club over the winter worth close to $20 million. He will be Toronto's starting shortstop in 2001, though both Cesar Izturis and Felipe Lopez soon will be challenging for big league jobs.

Position: SS
Bats: R **Throws:** R
Ht: 6' 0" **Wt:** 200

Opening Day Age: 27
Born: 4/8/73 in Miami, FL
ML Seasons: 7

Overall Statistics

	G	AB	R	H	D	T	HR	RBI	SB	BB	SO	Avg	OBP	Slg
2000	141	527	68	133	31	2	15	69	4	43	113	.252	.313	.404
Career	736	2622	328	637	147	15	66	274	67	214	609	.243	.305	.386

Where He Hits the Ball

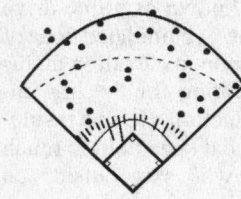
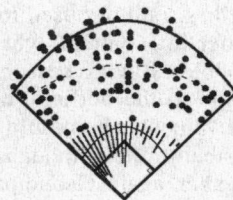

Vs. LHP   **Vs. RHP**

2000 Situational Stats

	AB	H	HR	RBI	Avg		AB	H	HR	RBI	Avg
Home	253	62	5	25	.245	LHP	114	26	2	8	.228
Road	274	71	10	44	.259	RHP	413	107	13	61	.259
First Half	267	64	7	32	.240	Sc Pos	134	36	1	47	.269
Scnd Half	260	69	8	37	.265	Clutch	65	17	2	9	.262

2000 Rankings (American League)

- 1st in sacrifice bunts (16) and bunts in play (26)
- 5th in lowest slugging percentage vs. lefthanded pitchers (.333)
- 7th in lowest fielding percentage at shortstop (.975)
- 8th in errors at shortstop (16)
- Led the Blue Jays in sacrifice bunts (16), highest groundball/flyball ratio (1.4), bunts in play (26) and highest percentage of extra bases taken as a runner (48.9)
- Led AL shortstops in sacrifice bunts (16) and bunts in play (26)

Billy Koch

2000 Season

In his second season in the majors, Billy Koch posted impressive numbers as the Blue Jays' closer, including a 2.63 ERA that was fifth best among the league's relievers. It also was his second 30-plus save season. Koch's high-water mark was a string of 21 consecutive save conversions, which began in early June and continued through late August. The streak threatened to dethrone Tom Henke, who holds the club record with 25 straight.

Pitching

Koch comes right at the hitter, daring each opponent to catch up with his blistering 100-MPH fastball. He does know how to throw a slider and a changeup, but it's that four-seamer that's used almost exclusively. No matter how hard he throws it, hitters will adjust if they know it's always coming. For example, first-pitch hitters batted .447 against him, and he often lived on the edge despite his success converting save opportunities. Koch is less prone to the bouts of wildness that marred his rookie season, but his inability to mix his pitches better is why his strikeout ratio is not as high as it should be for someone who throws as hard as he does.

Defense

Koch reduced the number of steal attempts against him during his second season by using a more economical delivery. He eliminated his high leg kick from the stretch with runners on, and he seems comfortable with something similar to a slide step. Koch is a very good fielding pitcher who makes it tough for bunters because of his agility and quickness off the mound. He's also extremely fast covering first base.

2001 Outlook

Koch signed a three-year, $3.5 million deal prior to the 2000 season, which takes him out of the arbitration process after the 2001 campaign. Most impressive to the Jays was how he harnessed his control and matured rapidly in the closer role. The task ahead is to further develop pitches other than his fastball. If he can do that, Koch then would have all the tools to become the premier closer in the game.

Position: RP
Bats: R **Throws:** R
Ht: 6' 3" **Wt:** 205

Opening Day Age: 26
Born: 12/14/74 in Rockville Center, NY
ML Seasons: 2
Pronunciation: KOTCH

Toronto

Overall Statistics

	W	L	Pct.	ERA	G	GS	Sv	IP	H	BB	SO	HR	Ratio
2000	9	3	.750	2.63	68	0	33	78.2	78	18	60	6	1.22
Career	9	8	.529	2.97	124	0	64	142.1	133	48	117	11	1.27

How Often He Throws Strikes

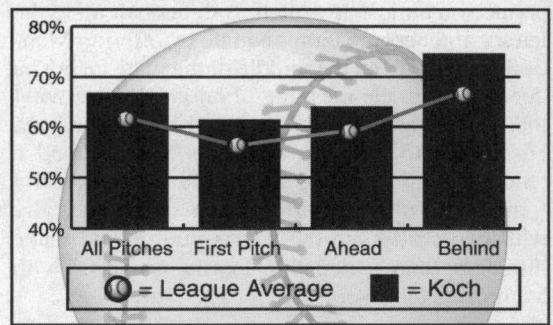

◐ = League Average   ■ = Koch

2000 Situational Stats

	W	L	ERA	Sv	IP		AB	H	HR	RBI	Avg
Home	8	0	2.70	17	40.0	LHB	145	37	2	14	.255
Road	1	3	2.56	16	38.2	RHB	157	41	4	16	.261
First Half	4	1	2.74	20	46.0	Sc Pos	78	19	0	22	.244
Scnd Half	5	2	2.48	13	32.2	Clutch	208	50	4	18	.240

2000 Rankings (American League)

- 2nd in games finished (62)
- 3rd in relief wins (9)
- 5th in relief ERA (2.63)
- Led the Blue Jays in games pitched, saves, games finished (62), save opportunities (38), save percentage (86.8), blown saves (5), first batter efficiency (.212), lowest batting average allowed in relief with runners on base (.235), lowest batting average allowed in relief with runners in scoring position (.244), relief wins (9), relief ERA (2.63), lowest batting average allowed in relief (.258), most strikeouts per nine innings in relief (6.9) and fewest baserunners allowed per nine innings in relief (11.2)

Raul Mondesi

Position: RF
Bats: R **Throws:** R
Ht: 5'11" **Wt:** 215

Opening Day Age: 30
Born: 3/12/71 in San Cristobal, Dominican Republic
ML Seasons: 8
Pronunciation: MAHN-de-see

2000 Season

Feeling queasy over the pending free agency of star outfielder Shawn Green, the Blue Jays dispatched their budding superstar to the Dodgers for Raul Mondesi and reliever Pedro Borbon last winter. Mondesi delivered the much-needed righthanded power missing in the middle of the lineup. He was on his way to establishing new career highs in homers and RBI when bone chips in his right elbow required surgery in late July. He returned near the end of September, but a minor ankle injury quickly ended his season.

Hitting

A dead pull hitter with terrific power, Mondesi will pounce on almost any pitch from the belt up to the letters. Pitchers are tempting fate by offering Mondesi fastballs from the middle of the plate in, but he doesn't know the meaning of an inside-out swing that would take outside pitches the opposite way. His desire to pull the ball goes well beyond a tendency—it's an obsession. He can be easily fooled with offspeed or breaking stuff, especially with two strikes, so the whiffs pile up and make him less than a dependable run producer with teammates on base.

Baserunning & Defense

Mondesi's all-around ability does shine through as a baserunner. He gets up a head of steam rounding the basepaths like few other players in the league, and he's also a good bet to steal successfully. He's a consistent 30-30 threat. Mondesi also garners a lot of credit as a defender because of his cannon-like arm and his ability to cover ground. His judgment is another story, as he tallied seven errors in just 96 games, often due to poor decision-making with his throws.

2001 Outlook

Considering the Jays felt they had to trade either Green or Carlos Delgado before the season rather than sign both, they came out OK acquiring Mondesi. They received production similar to what they expected from Green, yet gained an additional three years of contract stability with Mondesi. The hope now is for a healthy season in 2001.

Overall Statistics

	G	AB	R	H	D	T	HR	RBI	SB	BB	SO	Avg	OBP	Slg
2000	96	388	78	105	22	2	24	67	22	32	73	.271	.329	.523
Career	1012	3875	621	1109	212	39	187	585	162	262	736	.286	.333	.506

Where He Hits the Ball

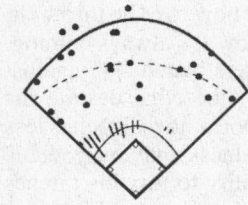
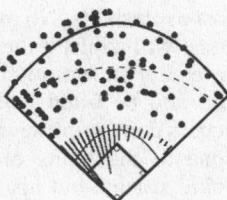

Vs. LHP **Vs. RHP**

2000 Situational Stats

	AB	H	HR	RBI	Avg		AB	H	HR	RBI	Avg
Home	202	51	10	28	.252	LHP	74	23	4	11	.311
Road	186	54	14	39	.290	RHP	314	82	20	56	.261
First Half	345	96	23	63	.278	Sc Pos	96	22	8	43	.229
Scnd Half	43	9	1	4	.209	Clutch	43	12	1	7	.279

2000 Rankings (American League)

- 1st in errors in right field (7), lowest batting average on a 3-2 count (.054) and lowest batting average with two strikes (.121)
- 3rd in lowest batting average with the bases loaded (.000)
- 6th in steals of third (4)
- 9th in highest percentage of swings that missed (27.7)
- Led the Blue Jays in stolen bases, caught stealing (6), fewest GDPs per GDP situation (8.1%) and steals of third (4)
- Led AL right fielders in steals of third (4)

Shannon Stewart

2000 Season

Shannon Stewart continued his ascent among the game's premier leadoff hitters with career highs in runs scored, batting average, slugging percentage, home runs, doubles and RBI. He became a 20-20 man for the first time despite missing 26 games with a recurring hamstring problem. He went on the disabled list in early May, but the soreness remained long after his return. Stewart also scored more than 100 runs for the second straight season.

Hitting

Stewart loves the inside portion of the plate and has quick enough hands to turn on any fastball in his zone. He's always been able to punish lefthanders who try and shave him inside, but his biggest improvement has been against righthanders who want to take him outside. He's a free swinger who isn't always inclined to take a walk, but his quick bat and terrific foot speed make a great combination for accumulating hits. He added body strength over the winter prior to the 2000 season, which quickly translated into more power and made him an even more dangerous threat. If he's not clearing the fences, he's cashing in doubles with his line drives.

Baserunning & Defense

Stewart's speed gives him better-than-average range in left field. His glove has become more reliable each passing season, and he made only two errors in 2000. However, his weak arm can be exploited. Stewart is exceptionally fast on the basepaths. With Toronto's home-run offense, however, a manager is not inclined to use the running game. That was especially true last season, when Stewart was nursing a weakened hamstring. He stole just 20 bases after swiping 51 in 1998.

2001 Outlook

General manager Gord Ash had the foresight to sign Stewart to a three-year deal prior to the 1999 season. Otherwise, his arbitration proceeds would exceed his current salary, which is scheduled to escalate to $2.9 million in 2001. Expect Stewart's running game to return to previous levels, since his hamstring should be fully healed and Buck Martinez was named the new manager. Stewart has the talent to become the game's best leadoff hitter.

Position: LF
Bats: R **Throws:** R
Ht: 6' 1" **Wt:** 205

Opening Day Age: 27
Born: 2/25/74 in Cincinnati, OH
ML Seasons: 6

Toronto

Overall Statistics

	G	AB	R	H	D	T	HR	RBI	SB	BB	SO	Avg	OBP	Slg
2000	136	583	107	186	43	5	21	69	20	37	79	.319	.363	.518
Career	488	1930	328	574	114	17	44	216	121	188	272	.297	.368	.442

Where He Hits the Ball

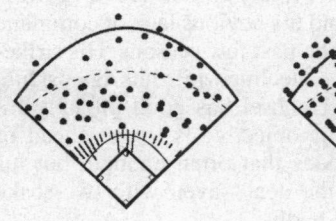
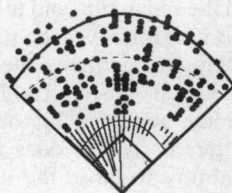

Vs. LHP   **Vs. RHP**

2000 Situational Stats

	AB	H	HR	RBI	Avg		AB	H	HR	RBI	Avg
Home	276	79	12	32	.286	LHP	139	43	3	9	.309
Road	307	107	9	37	.349	RHP	444	143	18	60	.322
First Half	274	93	11	36	.339	Sc Pos	129	35	5	50	.271
Scnd Half	309	93	10	33	.301	Clutch	69	23	0	12	.333

2000 Rankings (American League)

- 1st in fielding percentage in left field (.993)
- 4th in batting average on the road
- Led the Blue Jays in singles, triples, stolen-base percentage (80.0), on-base percentage for a leadoff hitter (.363) and batting average on the road
- Led AL left fielders in hit by pitch (6) and batting average on the road

Steve Trachsel

2000 Season

Acquired from Tampa Bay along with relief pitcher Mark Guthrie as part of a four-player July deadline deal, Steve Trachsel fared poorly in his attempt to solidify the Jays' rotation down the stretch. Trachsel did exceed 200 frames for the fifth straight year, proving that he can eat innings. Yet, the month of June was the only time he was effective, when he posted a 3-2 record with an impressive 2.52 ERA.

Pitching

Without overpowering stuff, Trachsel relies on varying types of fastballs. He uses a two-seamer and a cutter, but depends on a splitter as his out pitch. He also employs a decent curveball and likes to change speeds. He rarely climbs above 91 MPH on the radar gun, and his obvious lack of command has hurt him over the past few seasons. His strike-out ratios continue to decline while hits against him rise each season. Trachsel has good pitching instincts, realizing his objective is to get ahead of hitters early. He does that often enough, but his inability to close the deal—even with two-strike counts—hurts him badly.

Defense

Trachsel is an exceptionally good fielding pitcher who hasn't made an error in two years. He also is quick to cover first base and charges the bunt well. Even though Trachsel is a deliberate pitcher without a deceptive move to first, he tries to keep runners close by wearing them down with an abundance of pickoff tosses. It worked for him last season, as only 17 attempts were made against him and seven of them were cut down.

2001 Outlook

Tampa Bay traded Trachsel because he was a pending free agent who produced mediocre results, and the Blue Jays may have come to the same conclusion. In December, Trachsel signed a two-year, $7 million contract with the Mets. He will figure in somewhere at the bottom of the New York rotation.

Position: SP
Bats: R **Throws:** R
Ht: 6' 4" **Wt:** 205

Opening Day Age: 30
Born: 10/31/70 in Oxnard, CA
ML Seasons: 8
Pronunciation: TRACK-sil

Overall Statistics

	W	L	Pct.	ERA	G	GS	Sv	IP	H	BB	SO	HR	Ratio
2000	8	15	.348	4.80	34	34	0	200.2	232	74	110	26	1.52
Career	68	84	.447	4.42	221	220	0	1347.0	1391	486	939	195	1.39

How Often He Throws Strikes

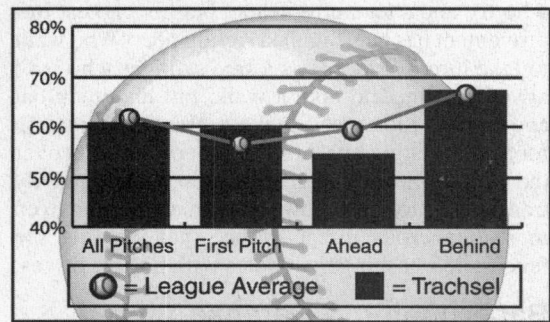

2000 Situational Stats

	W	L	ERA	Sv	IP		AB	H	HR	RBI	Avg
Home	4	8	5.03	0	96.2	LHB	386	115	9	39	.298
Road	4	7	4.59	0	104.0	RHB	404	117	17	67	.290
First Half	6	8	4.76	0	111.2	Sc Pos	187	54	6	80	.289
Scnd Half	2	7	4.85	0	89.0	Clutch	42	9	0	3	.214

2000 Rankings (American League)

- 2nd in losses (15)
- 3rd in games started (34), pickoff throws (161), highest batting average allowed (.294), highest slugging percentage allowed (.473) and lowest winning percentage (.348)
- 4th in highest on-base percentage allowed (.356)
- 6th in hits allowed (232) and fewest strikeouts per nine innings (4.9)
- 7th in complete games (3), least run support per nine innings (4.5) and highest ERA at home (5.03)
- 9th in highest ERA (4.80), lowest strikeout/walk ratio (1.5) and lowest groundball/flyball ratio allowed (1.1)
- 10th in runners caught stealing (7)

David Wells

2000 Season

David Wells reached the 20-win plateau for the first time in his 14-year career, helped by a generous 6.2 run-support factor and his impeccable control. Wells could do no wrong in the first half of the season, and he was rewarded with the starting nod in the All-Star game after compiling a 15-2 record. While he was unable to keep up the pace during the latter months—encountering several difficult outings, particularly at home—at season's end, Wells led the majors in fewest walks per nine innings.

Pitching

His degree of success is directly related to his ability to pinpoint his sweeping curveball. He's a large man, but he doesn't overpower too many hitters with his low-90s fastball, nor does he enjoy the typical success most southpaws do against lefthanded hitters. Instead, he induces a high percentage of grounders by offering mostly downward-moving pitches at various speeds. His approach can work against him on turf, as lots of batted balls find their way through the infield, which is why his ERA and hits-innings pitched ratio seemed high for a 20-game winner. Wells has great stamina, and he has surpassed 200 innings in each of the last six seasons.

Defense

Wells is a better athlete than he appears to be, which he proves with his quick feet in getting to balls hit anywhere near him. He also has better than average reflexes with his glove on those quick comebackers. Last season, Wells improved dramatically in keeping runners close and in check. His methodical delivery still gives basestealers an advantage, however, as 14 of 21 attempts were successful against him.

2001 Outlook

The Jays have Wells tied up through next season and have a club option for 2002. Even though he turned 37 last May, Wells still is among the best lefthanded starters in the league and is the ace of the Toronto staff. After delivering the winningest season of his career, he stands a good chance of seeing that $9 million option exercised next fall.

Position: SP
Bats: L **Throws:** L
Ht: 6' 4" **Wt:** 235

Opening Day Age: 37
Born: 5/20/63 in Torrance, CA
ML Seasons: 14
Nickname: Boomer

Toronto

Overall Statistics

	W	L	Pct.	ERA	G	GS	Sv	IP	H	BB	SO	HR	Ratio
2000	20	8	.714	4.11	35	35	0	229.2	266	31	166	23	1.29
Career	161	107	.601	4.06	479	309	13	2306.2	2342	538	1576	273	1.25

How Often He Throws Strikes

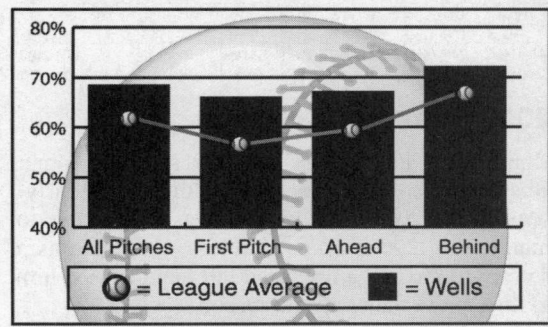

All Pitches · First Pitch · Ahead · Behind
○ = League Average ■ = Wells

2000 Situational Stats

	W	L	ERA	Sv	IP		AB	H	HR	RBI	Avg
Home	9	5	4.98	0	115.2	LHB	197	57	5	26	.289
Road	11	3	3.24	0	114.0	RHB	723	209	18	76	.289
First Half	15	2	3.44	0	128.1	Sc Pos	204	60	5	73	.294
Scnd Half	5	6	4.97	0	101.1	Clutch	96	25	4	9	.260

2000 Rankings (American League)

- 1st in wins, games started, complete games (9), hits allowed, fewest pitches thrown per batter (3.37) and fewest walks per nine innings (1.2)
- 2nd in innings pitched, highest strikeout/walk ratio (5.4) and lowest ERA on the road
- Led the Blue Jays in ERA, wins, games started, complete games (9), innings pitched, hits allowed, batters faced (972), strikeouts, wild pitches (9), pitches thrown (3,272), runners caught stealing (7), GDPs induced (19), highest strikeout/walk ratio (5.4), lowest slugging percentage allowed (.429), lowest on-base percentage allowed (.316), fewest pitches thrown per batter (3.37) and most run support per nine innings (6.2)

Homer Bush

Position: 2B
Bats: R **Throws:** R
Ht: 5'10" **Wt:** 180

Opening Day Age: 28
Born: 11/12/72 in East St Louis, IL
ML Seasons: 4

Overall Statistics

	G	AB	R	H	D	T	HR	RBI	SB	BB	SO	Avg	OBP	Slg
2000	76	297	38	64	8	0	1	18	9	18	60	.215	.271	.253
Career	259	864	126	250	37	4	7	81	47	44	161	.289	.330	.366

2000 Situational Stats

	AB	H	HR	RBI	Avg		AB	H	HR	RBI	Avg
Home	159	34	1	16	.214	LHP	41	13	0	5	.317
Road	138	30	0	2	.217	RHP	256	51	1	13	.199
First Half	243	52	0	14	.214	Sc Pos	71	13	0	17	.183
Scnd Half	54	12	1	4	.222	Clutch	30	7	1	3	.233

2000 Season

Coming off an impressive 1999 season, Homer Bush completely lost his stride with an ugly, early-season slump during which he was barely able to maintain a .200 average. Matters worsened, as a sore right hip and a fractured left hand caused him to miss more than half the season.

Hitting, Baserunning & Defense

Bush regressed markedly last season. A huge percentage of groundballs weren't finding holes early in the year, and Bush's confidence sagged. Soon, most of his at-bats were defensive in nature. With very little power at his disposal, Bush's approach is to use a flat-level swing to make contact and then hope his speed will compensate. He seldom walks, which further diminishes his on-base percentage. With so few opportunities to be on base, Bush's stolen-base totals also took a dive. He has very good range at second base, solid hands and an average arm.

2001 Outlook

Bush seemed to be climbing out of his slump in July, only to be stopped short by the injury to his hand. He was signed to a new three-year, $7.75 million contract before the 2000 season began, and the Jays have to hope that he will return to his 1999 form.

Frank Castillo

Position: SP
Bats: R **Throws:** R
Ht: 6'1" **Wt:** 200

Opening Day Age: 32
Born: 4/1/69 in El Paso, TX
ML Seasons: 9
Pronunciation: cas-TEE-oh

Overall Statistics

	W	L	Pct.	ERA	G	GS	Sv	IP	H	BB	SO	HR	Ratio
2000	10	5	.667	3.59	25	24	0	138.0	112	56	104	18	1.22
Career	66	79	.455	4.52	232	218	1	1290.0	1343	407	896	157	1.36

2000 Situational Stats

	W	L	ERA	Sv	IP		AB	H	HR	RBI	Avg
Home	3	4	4.09	0	55.0	LHB	253	57	10	27	.225
Road	7	1	3.25	0	83.0	RHB	255	55	8	23	.216
First Half	6	5	4.17	0	99.1	Sc Pos	113	22	4	32	.195
Scnd Half	4	0	2.09	0	38.2	Clutch	15	3	1	3	.200

2000 Season

After spending all of 1999 in the minors, journeyman Frank Castillo joined the Blue Jays as a minor league signing and cashed in with a surprisingly effective big league season. Injuries to his right forearm and elbow sidelined him for a month in the second half, yet he won his last nine decisions dating back to June 12.

Pitching & Defense

Castillo has endured elbow and shoulder difficulties recently, causing a loss of velocity since his earlier days with the Cubs. However, he was able to get his cutter and two-seam fastball up to 89 MPH this season, which helped the rest of his arsenal. Castillo has a decent hook and a good changeup. He also throws a slider, which taxed his elbow again. Batters have difficulty timing him. They tend to overswing, leading to lots of flyballs and a stingy .220 opponent batting average in 2000. Castillo is a good fielder, but his deliberate motion makes him easy to steal against.

2001 Outlook

Many fans may think of Castillo as a tired veteran, but he's only 32 years old on April 1. He's proven that if he can stay healthy, he can be effective. Boston signed Castillo to a two-year deal worth $4.5 million.

Marty Cordova

Position: LF/RF/DH
Bats: R **Throws:** R
Ht: 6' 0" **Wt:** 206

Opening Day Age: 31
Born: 7/10/69 in Las Vegas, NV
ML Seasons: 6
Pronunciation: core-DOE-vuh

Overall Statistics

	G	AB	R	H	D	T	HR	RBI	SB	BB	SO	Avg	OBP	Slg
2000	62	200	23	49	7	0	4	18	3	18	35	.245	.317	.340
Career	690	2522	359	692	146	14	83	403	55	251	533	.274	.346	.442

2000 Situational Stats

	AB	H	HR	RBI	Avg		AB	H	HR	RBI	Avg
Home	115	29	3	15	.252	LHP	66	14	2	8	.212
Road	85	20	1	3	.235	RHP	134	35	2	10	.261
First Half	144	39	2	12	.271	Sc Pos	48	12	1	15	.250
Scnd Half	56	10	2	6	.179	Clutch	24	8	0	0	.333

2000 Season

After being released by Boston before the season began, Marty Cordova immediately was signed to a minor league contract and called up to Toronto a week into the season. He served as a backup outfielder and part-time designated hitter. Despite hitting .302 in 63 May at-bats, Cordova never really was given the chance to catch on full-time.

Hitting, Baserunning & Defense

Cordova has limited power for a corner outfielder, which always has been the chief complaint against him. His bothersome injuries in recent years also have worked against him. At best, he's a line-drive hitter who strokes the ball to all fields, but usually he tries to pull the ball in search of that elusive power. This tendency makes him an inconsistent hitter who either grounds out often or strikes out. Cordova's range in the outfield has become limited because of foot injuries, and those injuries have had a negative effect on his baserunning as well.

2001 Outlook

Cordova was designated for assignment by the Blue Jays immediately after the season, which means he'll be looking for employment elsewhere for 2001. His downward spiral since receiving AL Rookie of the Year honors in 1995 makes him a hard sell.

Kelvim Escobar

Position: SP/RP
Bats: R **Throws:** R
Ht: 6' 1" **Wt:** 210

Opening Day Age: 24
Born: 4/11/76 in La Guaira, Venezuela
ML Seasons: 4

Overall Statistics

	W	L	Pct.	ERA	G	GS	Sv	IP	H	BB	SO	HR	Ratio
2000	10	15	.400	5.35	43	24	2	180.0	186	85	142	26	1.51
Career	34	31	.523	5.04	125	64	16	464.2	489	220	379	51	1.53

2000 Situational Stats

	W	L	ERA	Sv	IP		AB	H	HR	RBI	Avg
Home	7	7	4.32	1	98.0	LHB	341	96	15	55	.282
Road	3	8	6.59	1	82.0	RHB	356	90	11	50	.253
First Half	6	9	5.26	0	114.2	Sc Pos	181	47	7	74	.260
Scnd Half	4	6	5.51	2	65.1	Clutch	76	17	2	9	.224

2000 Season

Hard-throwing Kelvim Escobar endured another bumpy ride in 2000, working both in the rotation and out of the bullpen. He finished second on the club in strikeouts and innings pitched, but sustained bouts of wildness contributed to the first losing season of his short career.

Pitching & Defense

Escobar has not been able to break through as a starter, primarily because of his inability to control his breaking pitches. He continues to throw an explosive 95-MPH fastball and relies on a two-strike splitter as his out pitch. Such a two-pitch arsenal is enough for most relief pitchers, but his 5.42 ERA as a starter is the result of his limited resources over so many more innings. He still has problems establishing the curveball and he uses his changeup sparingly. Escobar is extremely poor at holding runners and is an average fielder at best.

2001 Outlook

Escobar's place on the Toronto staff is anything but certain. His last starting assignment was on August 11, and he could wind up as a setup man for the long haul if the rest of Toronto's starting staff comes into camp healthy in the spring.

Craig Grebeck

Position: 2B
Bats: R **Throws:** R
Ht: 5' 7" **Wt:** 155

Opening Day Age: 36
Born: 12/29/64 in Johnstown, PA
ML Seasons: 11
Pronunciation: GRAY-beck
Nickname: Little Hurt

Overall Statistics

	G	AB	R	H	D	T	HR	RBI	SB	BB	SO	Avg	OBP	Slg
2000	66	241	38	71	19	0	3	23	0	25	33	.295	.364	.411
Career	729	1947	238	516	115	8	19	185	4	226	265	.265	.345	.362

2000 Situational Stats

	AB	H	HR	RBI	Avg		AB	H	HR	RBI	Avg
Home	108	32	2	12	.296	LHP	92	25	2	10	.272
Road	133	39	1	11	.293	RHP	149	46	1	13	.309
First Half	127	35	3	10	.276	Sc Pos	64	21	0	18	.328
Scnd Half	114	36	0	13	.316	Clutch	29	9	0	4	.310

2000 Season

Usually relegated to backup duty at second base, Craig Grebeck often was pressed into starting service when Homer Bush suffered through slumps and injuries in 2000. Grebeck returned to his bench role after the Jays acquired Mickey Morandini in early August. Still, Grebeck batted .310 with runners on base and hit at a .316 clip in the second half.

Hitting, Baserunning & Defense

Grebeck's entire career is based on scrappy play in all phases of the game. He has a tendency to get on base frequently and seldom strikes out. He draws a large percentage of his walks because of his small stature. Grebeck also has surprising line-drive power, which he has exhibited more regularly over the last two seasons, and he is a good contact hitter. He does not steal, but he runs around the bags with decent speed. He's been an average fielder throughout his career, but had a subpar defensive season last summer.

2001 Outlook

Over the past few seasons, Grebeck has been signed on a year-to-year basis. He always finds employment as a role player, but he's usually a late signee, and it's not yet clear where he will end up in 2001.

Todd Greene

Position: DH
Bats: R **Throws:** R
Ht: 5'10" **Wt:** 208

Opening Day Age: 29
Born: 5/8/71 in Augusta, GA
ML Seasons: 5

Overall Statistics

	G	AB	R	H	D	T	HR	RBI	SB	BB	SO	Avg	OBP	Slg
2000	34	85	11	20	2	0	5	10	0	5	18	.235	.278	.435
Career	223	680	83	167	33	0	31	92	5	30	137	.246	.281	.431

2000 Situational Stats

	AB	H	HR	RBI	Avg		AB	H	HR	RBI	Avg
Home	31	5	2	2	.161	LHP	50	13	2	6	.260
Road	54	15	3	8	.278	RHP	35	7	3	4	.200
First Half	17	6	1	2	.353	Sc Pos	22	4	0	5	.182
Scnd Half	68	14	4	8	.206	Clutch	12	4	1	4	.333

2000 Season

After being cast off by Anaheim during spring training, Toronto signed Todd Greene to a minor league contract and brought him up in late May. Used as a righthanded-hitting designated hitter, Greene produced little in a role that never gave him more than 30 at-bats in any given month.

Hitting, Baserunning & Defense

Greene is a one-dimensional fastball hitter who can unleash a lot of power on any pitcher who plays his game. Unfortunately for Greene, there aren't too many big league hurlers willing to play along. He's never been able to cope with the offspeed or breaking stuff, and consequently he strikes out frequently when he faces a steady diet of offspeed pitches. Greene has been plagued with serious elbow and shoulder problems since his catching days in the minors, all but prohibiting him from playing a defensive role. He runs hard, but he's slow.

2001 Outlook

Greene tantalized scouts with his prodigious power when he was a prospect seven years ago, but injuries and a lack of strike-zone judgment have derailed his career. He's viewed strictly as a part-timer now, though the Blue Jays liked what they saw last season just enough to sign Greene to a one-year, $475,000 deal on November 1.

Joey Hamilton

Position: SP
Bats: R **Throws:** R
Ht: 6' 4" **Wt:** 230

Opening Day Age: 30
Born: 9/9/70 in
Statesboro, GA
ML Seasons: 7
Nickname: Big Daddy

Overall Statistics

	W	L	Pct.	ERA	G	GS	Sv	IP	H	BB	SO	HR	Ratio
2000	2	1	.667	3.55	6	6	0	33.0	28	12	15	3	1.21
Career	64	53	.547	4.07	174	166	0	1065.2	1058	394	710	96	1.36

2000 Situational Stats

	W	L	ERA	Sv	IP		AB	H	HR	RBI	Avg
Home	1	0	2.25	0	20.0	LHB	73	18	1	3	.247
Road	1	1	5.54	0	13.0	RHB	47	10	2	9	.213
First Half	0	0	-	0	0.0	Sc Pos	24	5	0	6	.208
Scnd Half	2	1	3.55	0	33.0	Clutch	3	0	0	0	.000

2000 Season

The disappointment surrounding Joey Hamilton's aborted 1999 season increased to exasperation in 2000, as he had difficulty recovering from shoulder surgery and then ripped his hamstring in the pre-season. He eventually made it back to the rotation in August and pitched decently over six starts.

Pitching & Defense

Hamilton has all the tools when it comes to pitching assortment. He features a low-90s two-seam fastball, a good curve, a late-breaking slider and a two-strike splitter. He consistently works the lower half of the strike zone and produces good ground-ball ratios. He walks too many batters, and he has yet to learn how to stay out of trouble against lefthanded hitters. Not exactly in great shape, Hamilton is an average fielder. Still, he does keep runners close with a quick move from the stretch, presenting few opportunities for basestealers.

2001 Outlook

Hamilton is under contract through the 2001 season. Primarily because of shoulder problems, he has started just 24 games since becoming a Blue Jay two years ago. In his limited appearances, he has shown flashes of being a dependable starter. The trick is to stay healthy, and thus far his track record is not good.

Esteban Loaiza

Position: SP
Bats: R **Throws:** R
Ht: 6' 3" **Wt:** 210

Opening Day Age: 29
Born: 12/31/71 in
Tijuana, Mexico
ML Seasons: 6
Pronunciation:
low-EYE-zuh

Overall Statistics

	W	L	Pct.	ERA	G	GS	Sv	IP	H	BB	SO	HR	Ratio
2000	10	13	.435	4.56	34	31	1	199.1	228	57	137	29	1.43
Career	49	52	.485	4.72	174	147	1	912.1	1039	279	561	116	1.44

2000 Situational Stats

	W	L	ERA	Sv	IP		AB	H	HR	RBI	Avg
Home	6	5	4.42	1	93.2	LHB	415	119	16	50	.287
Road	4	8	4.68	0	105.2	RHB	377	109	13	42	.289
First Half	5	5	5.19	1	102.1	Sc Pos	175	46	9	63	.263
Scnd Half	5	8	3.90	0	97.0	Clutch	49	12	2	4	.245

2000 Season

The Blue Jays traded two minor leaguers—Darwin Cubillan and Mike Young—to Texas for Esteban Loaiza in July. Loaiza hit the skids with Texas, but regrouped upon his arrival in Toronto, posting a respectable 3.62 ERA in 14 starts.

Pitching & Defense

Loaiza throws a good fastball, which appears to sneak up on hitters because of his fluid delivery. He can register 94 MPH on the gun at times, but more often he airs it out in the 91-92 MPH range. He complements his four-seam heater with an 87-MPH slider, and Loaiza can catch hitters off guard with an effective changeup. He has good control, but early in the season he was getting pounded with too many first-pitch fastballs and fastballs thrown when down in the count. He mixed up his offerings better during the second half. Usually a pretty good fielding pitcher, he erred three times last year. He's tough to read from the stretch and has a decent move to first.

2001 Outlook

Loaiza doesn't gain free agency until after the 2001 season, but he'll cost in excess of $3 million in his final year of arbitration. Toronto likely will keep him as insurance in case its younger starters falter as they did in 2000.

Dave Martinez

Position: RF/1B
Bats: L **Throws:** L
Ht: 5'10" **Wt:** 190

Opening Day Age: 36
Born: 9/26/64 in New York, NY
ML Seasons: 15

Overall Statistics

	G	AB	R	H	D	T	HR	RBI	SB	BB	SO	Avg	OBP	Slg
2000	132	457	60	125	19	5	5	47	8	50	73	.274	.346	.370
Career	1799	5558	762	1531	227	69	89	560	180	546	849	.275	.341	.389

2000 Situational Stats

	AB	H	HR	RBI	Avg		AB	H	HR	RBI	Avg
Home	212	59	3	22	.278	LHP	72	21	1	9	.292
Road	245	66	2	25	.269	RHP	385	104	4	38	.270
First Half	230	55	3	23	.239	Sc Pos	132	34	1	41	.258
Scnd Half	227	70	2	24	.308	Clutch	70	22	1	4	.314

2000 Season

Acquired via a waiver trade from the Rangers during the first week of August, Dave Martinez actually wore four different uniforms over the course of the season. He replaced the injured Raul Mondesi in right field and helped keep Toronto's playoff hopes alive down the stretch by batting .398 in 20 August games as a Blue Jay.

Hitting, Baserunning & Defense

While Martinez is a patient lefthanded batter with little power, he found himself in the uncustomary role of batting third in Toronto's power-packed lineup. Martinez will hit line drives to all fields and can hold his own against lefthanded pitching. Although he's not much of a basestealing threat at age 36, Martinez can take advantage of poor-throwing outfielders. His defense is well above average, and he managed to pile up 15 outfield assists in just 120 games with his strong throwing arm.

2001 Outlook

Even at age 36, Martinez remains productive in a part-time role. The Braves' front office has coveted him for a few years, and this offseason Martinez was signed to a two-year, $3 million deal by Atlanta. Martinez can fill in at all three outfield spots or first base.

Lance Painter

Position: RP
Bats: L **Throws:** L
Ht: 6'1" **Wt:** 200

Opening Day Age: 33
Born: 7/21/67 in Bedford, England
ML Seasons: 8

Overall Statistics

	W	L	Pct.	ERA	G	GS	Sv	IP	H	BB	SO	HR	Ratio
2000	2	0	1.000	4.73	42	2	0	66.2	69	22	53	9	1.37
Career	24	16	.600	5.14	269	28	3	403.0	441	153	300	56	1.47

2000 Situational Stats

	W	L	ERA	Sv	IP		AB	H	HR	RBI	Avg
Home	1	0	3.75	0	36.0	LHB	103	30	4	28	.291
Road	1	0	5.87	0	30.2	RHB	152	39	5	13	.257
First Half	1	0	4.42	0	38.2	Sc Pos	83	24	2	31	.289
Scnd Half	1	0	5.14	0	28.0	Clutch	25	8	1	2	.320

2000 Season

Traded from St. Louis to Toronto in a five-player swap during the offseason, Lance Painter was used both as a lefthanded setup man and middle reliever. He was a more effective pitcher at SkyDome than away from home, though his season was marked by inconsistency and a two-week stay on the disabled list with a sore elbow after making two emergency starts in May.

Pitching & Defense

Painter's mastery over lefthanded hitters was not in evidence as he crossed over to the American League for the first time in his career. His 92-MPH fastball is predictable at times, and using that pitch when behind in the count can lead to all sorts of trouble. When his location is up to par and he stays ahead, Painter can appear overpowering, registering high strikeout percentages with a nasty slider. He's got a good move to first and fields his position well.

2001 Outlook

Painter has just completed his six-year minimum service time to gain free agency, and it's doubtful he will be re-signed by Toronto. He's probably just as eager to hit the market as the Jays are to replace him.

Other Toronto Blue Jays

Clayton Andrews (Pos: LHP, **Age**: 22)

	W	L	Pct.	ERA	G	GS	Sv	IP	H	BB	SO	HR	Ratio
2000	1	2	.333	10.02	8	2	0	20.2	34	9	12	6	2.08
Career	1	2	.333	10.02	8	2	0	20.2	34	9	12	6	2.08

Andrews was selected in the 1996 draft and reached the majors at age 21 last year. He and his good breaking ball joined the Reds via an offseason trade. 2001 Outlook: C

Pedro Borbon (Pos: LHP, **Age**: 33)

	W	L	Pct.	ERA	G	GS	Sv	IP	H	BB	SO	HR	Ratio
2000	1	1	.500	6.48	59	0	1	41.2	45	38	29	5	1.99
Career	10	7	.588	4.41	218	0	5	163.1	144	95	129	13	1.46

It was a long, arduous journey back from major elbow surgery in 1996 for Borbon. He seemed to be recovering, but after pitching in 59 games last year, he was expected to undergo more surgery. 2001 Outlook: C

Alberto Castillo (Pos: C, **Age**: 31, **Bats**: R)

	G	AB	R	H	D	T	HR	RBI	SB	BB	SO	Avg	OBP	Slg
2000	66	185	14	39	7	0	1	16	0	21	36	.211	.287	.265
Career	251	622	54	142	20	0	7	61	1	66	130	.228	.303	.294

After playing a bit over his head with St. Louis in 1999, Castillo returned to his previous level of performance after getting traded to Toronto before last season. 2001 Outlook: B

Matt DeWitt (Pos: RHP, **Age**: 23)

	W	L	Pct.	ERA	G	GS	Sv	IP	H	BB	SO	HR	Ratio
2000	1	0	1.000	8.56	8	0	0	13.2	20	9	6	4	2.12
Career	1	0	1.000	8.56	8	0	0	13.2	20	9	6	4	2.12

The Blue Jays made DeWitt primarily a reliever after they acquired him from St. Louis last offseason. He saved some games in Triple-A, but suffered a broken leg in August. 2001 Outlook: C

Leo Estrella (Pos: RHP, **Age**: 26)

	W	L	Pct.	ERA	G	GS	Sv	IP	H	BB	SO	HR	Ratio
2000	0	0	-	5.79	2	0	0	4.2	9	0	3	1	1.93
Career	0	0	-	5.79	2	0	0	4.2	9	0	3	1	1.93

The Blue Jays acquired Estrella from the Mets in exchange for Tony Phillips a couple years ago. Estrella has won 10 or more games each of the past three seasons, plus he tossed a pair of no-hitters in the minors last summer. He was traded to Cincinnati in November. 2001 Outlook: C

John Frascatore (Pos: RHP, **Age**: 31)

	W	L	Pct.	ERA	G	GS	Sv	IP	H	BB	SO	HR	Ratio
2000	2	4	.333	5.42	60	0	0	73.0	87	33	30	14	1.64
Career	19	17	.528	4.09	262	5	1	354.2	375	141	197	46	1.45

Frascatore seems destined to be remembered as the "other" player Toronto acquired in the Tony Batista trade. Frascatore can soak up some innings in middle relief, however. 2001 Outlook: B

Charlie Greene (Pos: C, **Age**: 30, **Bats**: R)

	G	AB	R	H	D	T	HR	RBI	SB	BB	SO	Avg	OBP	Slg
2000	3	9	0	1	0	0	0	0	0	0	5	.111	.111	.111
Career	55	75	5	13	2	0	0	2	0	5	25	.173	.222	.200

Greene is a journeyman receiver who doesn't hit for average but has a fine defensive reputation. He'll sometimes be recalled when injury strikes, but never shows he should stay. The Padres signed him in November to a minor league deal. 2001 Outlook: C

Eric Gunderson (Pos: LHP, **Age**: 35)

	W	L	Pct.	ERA	G	GS	Sv	IP	H	BB	SO	HR	Ratio
2000	0	1	.000	7.11	6	0	0	6.1	15	2	2	0	2.68
Career	8	11	.421	4.95	254	5	2	229.0	274	84	137	29	1.56

After getting released the year before by Texas, Gunderson signed with Toronto before getting traded to the Giants last July. He worked mostly in the minors, hoping for a spot as a situational lefty. 2001 Outlook: C

Mark Guthrie (Pos: LHP, **Age**: 35)

	W	L	Pct.	ERA	G	GS	Sv	IP	H	BB	SO	HR	Ratio
2000	3	6	.333	4.67	76	0	0	71.1	70	37	63	8	1.50
Career	38	46	.452	4.18	578	43	12	835.2	865	320	658	85	1.42

Guthrie was swapped twice last year, landing in Toronto at the trade deadline. The interest teams display is probably due to the side from which he throws rather than his effectiveness. 2001 Outlook: A

Roy Halladay (Pos: RHP, **Age**: 23)

	W	L	Pct.	ERA	G	GS	Sv	IP	H	BB	SO	HR	Ratio
2000	4	7	.364	10.64	19	13	0	67.2	107	42	44	14	2.20
Career	13	14	.481	5.77	57	33	1	231.0	272	123	139	35	1.71

Halladay is a mystery, beginning with the fact that he's been so highly-regarded despite mediocre hits allowed and strikeout ratios. His stuff is supposedly great, but last year was ugly. 2001 Outlook: B

Mickey Morandini (Pos: 2B, **Age**: 34, **Bats**: L)

	G	AB	R	H	D	T	HR	RBI	SB	BB	SO	Avg	OBP	Slg
2000	126	409	41	105	15	4	0	29	6	36	77	.257	.322	.313
Career	1298	4558	597	1222	209	54	32	351	123	437	714	.268	.338	.359

Morandini returned to Philadelphia last spring after a trade from Montreal, but got sent back to Canada in August. He started 31 times for the Blue Jays down the stretch and re-signed with them in December. 2001 Outlook: B

Chad Mottola (Pos: RF, **Age**: 29, **Bats**: R)

	G	AB	R	H	D	T	HR	RBI	SB	BB	SO	Avg	OBP	Slg
2000	3	9	1	2	0	0	0	2	0	0	4	.222	.300	.222
Career	38	88	11	19	3	0	3	8	2	6	20	.216	.274	.352

Once the fifth overall pick of a draft, Mottola burst through as a 30-30 man and International League MVP last season. At his age he's no longer a top prospect, though he can help as a spare outfielder. 2001 Outlook: B

Peter Munro (Pos: RHP, Age: 25)

	W	L	Pct.	ERA	G	GS	Sv	IP	H	BB	SO	HR	Ratio
2000	1	1	.500	5.96	9	3	0	25.2	38	16	16	1	2.10
Career	1	3	.250	6.00	40	5	0	81.0	108	39	54	7	1.81

Munro was traded to Texas last August to complete one of those Dave Martinez deals. Munro experienced elbow problems last year, but possesses a decent fastball when healthy. 2001 Outlook: C

Paul Quantrill (Pos: RHP, Age: 32)

	W	L	Pct.	ERA	G	GS	Sv	IP	H	BB	SO	HR	Ratio
2000	2	5	.286	4.52	68	0	1	83.2	100	25	47	7	1.49
Career	41	62	.398	3.97	450	64	16	854.1	998	250	497	90	1.46

Quantrill hasn't been as effective since breaking his leg in an offseason snowmobiling accident two years ago. His ERA has risen the past three seasons, though he can pitch seemingly every day. 2001 Outlook: A

Dewayne Wise (Pos: LF, Age: 23, Bats: L)

	G	AB	R	H	D	T	HR	RBI	SB	BB	SO	Avg	OBP	Slg
2000	28	22	3	3	0	0	0	0	1	1	5	.136	.208	.136
Career	28	22	3	3	0	0	0	0	1	1	5	.136	.208	.136

Wise was a Rule 5 draftee last year. His best, and maybe only, attribute right now is his speed. With just 78 at-bats above Class-A, he'll likely spend this season in the minors. 2001 Outlook: C

Chris Woodward (Pos: SS, Age: 24, Bats: R)

	G	AB	R	H	D	T	HR	RBI	SB	BB	SO	Avg	OBP	Slg
2000	37	104	16	19	7	0	3	14	1	10	28	.183	.254	.337
Career	51	130	17	25	8	0	3	16	1	12	34	.192	.259	.323

Woodward's major league average dropped nearly in half from his mark in Triple-A last year. He played all four infield positions for the Blue Jays, and his versatility may help him land a job. 2001 Outlook: B

Toronto Blue Jays Minor League Prospects

Organization Overview:

The Blue Jays had an impressive draft record during the 1990s, and their first-round picks during the decade included Shawn Green, Shannon Stewart, Billy Koch, Steve Karsay, Vernon Wells and Chris Carpenter. Toronto also ranks high among big league teams when it comes to signing and developing players now on major league rosters. Even after trading away a portion of their middle-infield depth during the 2000 pennant chase, they still have two premium shortstop prospects in Felipe Lopez and Cesar Izturis. Depth in the minors has been extremely important to the Blue Jays, who have dropped out of the ranks of big-market players and don't spend money to fill holes like they did several years ago. Free-agent spending and investments in player development could rise with the team's purchase by Rogers Communications, a corporate giant in Canada.

Pasqual Coco

Position: P   **Opening Day Age:** 23
Bats: R **Throws:** R   **Born:** 9/24/77 in Santo
Ht: 6' 1" **Wt:** 185   Domingo, DR

Recent Statistics

	W	L	ERA	G	GS	Sv	IP	H	R	BB	SO	HR
2000 AA Tennessee	12	7	3.76	27	26	0	167.2	154	83	68	142	16
2000 AL Toronto	0	0	9.00	1	1	0	4.0	5	4	5	2	1

Signed as a 16-year-old in 1994, Coco pitched in the Dominican Summer League before beginning his North American career in 1997 at Class-A St. Catharines in the New York-Penn League. The tall, slender righthander showed dramatic improvement in his second year at St. Catharines—and that was a springboard for his 11-1 (2.21) start at Class-A Hagerstown in '99. Coco finished '99 in the high Class-A Florida State League, where he went 4-6 for an organization-best 15 wins. With good arm action on an improved fastball-changeup combination, he moved up to Double-A Tennessee in 2000 and proved he was ready for the jump. Coco's fastball reaches the low-90s, and when he fine-tunes his slider, he could become a No. 2 or 3 starter in the majors.

Bob File

Position: P   **Opening Day Age:** 24
Bats: R **Throws:** R   **Born:** 1/28/77 in
Ht: 6' 4" **Wt:** 215   Philadelphia, PA

Recent Statistics

	W	L	ERA	G	GS	Sv	IP	H	R	BB	SO	HR
1999 A Dunedin	4	1	1.70	47	0	26	53.0	30	13	14	48	2
2000 AA Tennessee	4	3	3.12	36	0	20	34.2	29	20	13	40	1
2000 AAA Syracuse	2	0	0.93	20	0	8	19.1	14	2	2	10	1

File has been used as a closer in each of his three minor league seasons. In 1999 as a 22-year-old, he saved 26 games, allowed less than one baserunner per inning to reach and posted a 1.70 ERA for a talented Class-A Dunedin team that dominated the Florida State League. File wasn't as dominant in 2000, but he was just as effective. In 54 innings, he saved 28 games and recorded a 2.33 ERA between Double-A Tennessee and Triple-A Syracuse. File, in 139 career innings, has surrendered just five homers. His fastball has good movement, and both his heater and slider are above-average pitches. He needs to work on getting lefties out, but he should get a chance to help Toronto's bullpen—though he won't supplant Billy Koch as the Jays' closer.

Cesar Izturis

Position: SS   **Opening Day Age:** 21
Bats: B **Throws:** R   **Born:** 2/10/80 in
Ht: 5' 9" **Wt:** 175   Barquisimeto, VZ

Recent Statistics

	G	AB	R	H	D	T	HR	RBI	SB	BB	SO	Avg
1999 A Dunedin	131	536	77	165	28	12	3	77	32	22	58	.308
2000 AAA Syracuse	132	435	54	95	16	5	0	27	21	20	44	.218
2000 MLE	132	429	50	89	16	4	0	25	17	18	46	.207

Despite being one of the youngest players in the high Class-A Florida State League in 1999, where he held his own with the bat and the glove, Izturis jumped to Triple-A Syracuse in 2000. While he struggled at the plate, Izturis impressed with solid defensive play and a strong arm as a shortstop. The Venezuelan native, who joined the Toronto organization as a non-drafted free agent in 1996, is ready defensively for the major leagues. To get his bat big league-ready, Izturis must make better contact and keep the ball out of the air. Drawing more walks would better utilize his speed and enhance his value as a hitter. Just 21 years old, Izturis is likely to return to Syracuse for the start of the 2001 season.

Joe Lawrence

Position: C   **Opening Day Age:** 24
Bats: R **Throws:** R   **Born:** 2/13/77 in Lake
Ht: 6' 2" **Wt:** 200   Charles, LA

Recent Statistics

	G	AB	R	H	D	T	HR	RBI	SB	BB	SO	Avg
1999 AA Knoxville	70	250	52	66	16	2	7	24	7	56	48	.264
2000 A Dunedin	101	375	69	113	32	1	13	67	21	69	74	.301
2000 AA Tennessee	39	133	22	35	9	0	9	37	7	30	27	.263

Primarily a third baseman since he was a first-round pick in 1996, Lawrence moved behind the plate in 2000. The Jays believed he had the tools, arm and makeup to make the switch, and it filled an organizational void at the position. The positional change forced Lawrence back to Class-A Dunedin, where he played in 1998, and he demonstrated solid improvement in his all-around game behind the plate. His bat always has been consistent; he makes good contact and sprays line drives. Those liners eventually may take flight, as the Jays believe Lawrence will develop more power as he matures.

Felipe Lopez

Position: SS
Bats: B **Throws:** R
Ht: 6' 1" **Wt:** 175

Opening Day Age: 20
Born: 5/12/80 in
Bayamon, PR

Recent Statistics

	G	AB	R	H	D	T	HR	RBI	SB	BB	SO	Avg
1999 A Hagerstown	134	537	87	149	27	4	14	80	21	61	157	.277
2000 AA Tennessee	127	463	52	119	18	4	9	41	12	31	110	.257
2000 MLE	127	457	49	113	18	3	8	39	9	25	117	.247

The Jays dealt from strength during the 2000 pennant race, parting with promising middle infielders in trades with Tampa Bay and Texas. But they wouldn't deal Lopez, their first-round pick in 1998, who was one of the best prospects in the Double-A Southern League at age 20. His arm is strong and his defensive skills are well developed. Offensively, he made good progress and showed he had the tools to handle Double-A ball, but his slow start, slight drop-off in performance from 1999, and some of his league-high 44 errors were more a matter of concentration. The Jays want him to maintain a higher level of concentration, which he'll need in the majors. Otherwise, Lopez needs to improve his plate discipline and fine-tune his little-ball skills.

Andy Thompson

Position: OF
Bats: R **Throws:** R
Ht: 6' 3" **Wt:** 215

Opening Day Age: 25
Born: 10/8/75 in
Oconomowoc, WI

Recent Statistics

	G	AB	R	H	D	T	HR	RBI	SB	BB	SO	Avg
2000 AAA Syracuse	121	426	59	105	27	2	22	65	9	50	95	.246
2000 AL Toronto	2	6	2	1	0	0	0	1	0	3	2	.167
2000 MLE	121	420	54	99	27	1	20	60	7	46	99	.236

A power-hitting threat drafted in 1994, Thompson didn't come around until his breakout year in 1999. That season he delivered 33 doubles and 31 homers in 483 at-bats between Double-A Knoxville and Triple-A Syracuse. Last summer, he wasn't as productive in a full season at Syracuse. Thompson's intense makeup tends to work against him in his battle to adjust to better pitching, and he was too pull-conscious for much of 2000. The Jays want him to think more about driving the ball and less about home runs. Adequate defensively with an accurate arm, he is capable of manning left field in the majors.

Vernon Wells

Position: OF
Bats: R **Throws:** R
Ht: 6' 1" **Wt:** 210

Opening Day Age: 22
Born: 12/8/78 in
Shreveport, LA

Recent Statistics

	G	AB	R	H	D	T	HR	RBI	SB	BB	SO	Avg
2000 AAA Syracuse	127	493	76	120	31	7	16	66	23	48	88	.243
2000 AL Toronto	3	2	0	0	0	0	0	0	0	0	0	.000
2000 MLE	127	486	70	113	31	5	14	61	18	44	92	.233

A legitimate five-tool prospect, Wells turned in a phenomenal season in 1999 as he passed through three levels en route to Triple-A Syracuse. It was quite a year for a 20-year-old, but his follow-up campaign wasn't as impressive. Wells has moved quickly through the Toronto system, which hasn't allowed him or opposing pitchers much time to make adjustments to one another. Pitchers at the Triple-A level and above *do* adjust quickly to hitters, and Wells learned that lesson last summer. Despite his low average, he improved at driving the ball, but his ability to make constant adjustments to pitchers and his baserunning need work. Wells has a strong arm, and his speed and good reads on balls hit his way allow him to play a shallow center field.

Jayson Werth

Position: C
Bats: R **Throws:** R
Ht: 6' 5" **Wt:** 191

Opening Day Age: 21
Born: 5/20/79 in
Springfield, IL

Recent Statistics

	G	AB	R	H	D	T	HR	RBI	SB	BB	SO	Avg
1999 A Frederick	66	236	41	72	10	1	3	30	16	37	37	.305
1999 AA Bowie	35	121	18	33	5	1	1	11	7	17	26	.273
2000 A Frederick	24	83	16	23	3	0	2	18	5	10	15	.277
2000 AA Bowie	85	276	47	63	16	2	5	26	9	54	50	.228
2000 MLE	85	269	41	56	14	1	4	23	6	40	54	.208

Baltimore's first-round choice in 1997, Werth has proven to be a quick and mobile catcher. His arm isn't that strong, but his quickness and athleticism behind the plate make up for it. Despite his size, Werth largely has been a successful contact hitter with solid plate discipline. In fact, he's nearly leadoff material at this point in his career, as the fleet-footed catcher has a career .373 on-base percentage and 66 stolen bases in 81 attempts as a minor leaguer. Werth is young, so the power still may come. The Blue Jays will benefit if it does, as Toronto acquired Werth from the Orioles for a minor league pitcher during the winter meetings in December.

Others to Watch

One of the more advanced high school products around is lefthander **Matt Ford** (19), who works with a high-80s fastball and an outstanding changeup. He has excellent command. His curveball needs work, but Ford has fanned well more than a hitter an inning over two seasons and is 9-3 (3.20) for his career. . . A native of the Netherlands Antilles who signed at age 16, **Diegomar Markwell** (20) took big strides in his fourth go-round in the short-season New York-Penn League. The 6-foot-3 southpaw displayed an average fastball and an above-average curveball. He'll start the 2001 season in a full-season league. . . The Jays' first-round pick in 2000, outfielder **Miguel Negron** (18), is a decent fielder who can run. Bothered by nagging injuries in his debut season, he needs to get stronger and develop patience as a hitter. Negron is a contact hitter with a chance be a perennial .300 hitter. . . He's big at 6-foot-3, 195 pounds, but catching prospect **Josh Phelps** (22) is both strong *and* quick behind the plate. He also has a quick bat, making him a solid power prospect who has hit for average at a pitching-friendly park at Class-A Dunedin the last two seasons.

National League Players

Bank One Ballpark

Offense

BOB seems to play as a fairly neutral park for offense. Left field, especially the left-center gap, is the easiest part for hitters to reach for home runs. The ball does not seem to carry as well to right field, and very few homers clear the high fence in center. Bank One Ballpark is a good park for doubles and especially triples, with deep alleys and some tricky angles in the corners. Because of the desert summer temperatures, the roof usually is closed from around mid-May until the final weekend of the season. The ball seems to carry better when the roof is open, probably because the air is warmer.

Defense

The left field wall was intentionally built so outfielders can rob hitters of home runs. The picnic overhangs, to the left and right of dead center field, can deflect what seems like a catchable flyball back toward the infield, but they rarely come into play. The corners, in front of the bullpens, have a variety of angles and fielders need to let the ball come out before playing it. The Diamondbacks seem to finally have found a strain of grass that can grow despite the roof being closed much of the summer, so there should be fewer bad hops in the outfield.

Who It Helps the Most

Brian Anderson, a flyball pitcher, has made good use of the larger parts of the park to keep hitters from reaching the fence. The close left-field gap helps Jay Bell and Matt Williams. Steve Finley seemed to see the ball better at home last year.

Who It Hurts the Most

Todd Stottlemyre has compiled a 3.72 ERA on the road compared to a 5.38 ERA at home the past two seasons. Greg Colbrunn has also fared better away from home over the same span, hitting 49 points higher on the road.

Rookies & Newcomers

Danny Klassen has been much better at BOB than on the road in his limited chances. Curt Schilling was a bit better at home in his two months as a Diamondback.

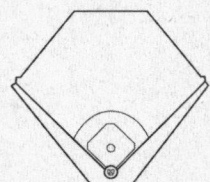

Dimensions: LF-330, LCF-374, CF-407, RCF-374, RF-334

Capacity: 48,500

Elevation: 1090 feet

Surface: Grass

Foul Territory: Average

Park Factors

2000 Season

	Home Games			Away Games			
	D'backs	Opp	Total	D'backs	Opp	Total	Index
G	72	72	144	75	75	150	—
Avg	.281	.265	.273	.248	.261	.254	107
AB	2425	2490	4915	2576	2494	5070	101
R	370	341	711	356	346	702	106
H	681	659	1340	638	652	1290	108
2B	130	118	248	122	118	240	107
3B	20	16	36	17	11	28	133
HR	75	81	156	90	88	178	90
BB	244	218	462	245	234	479	99
SO	411	525	936	471	585	1056	91
E	46	34	80	51	49	100	83
E-Infield	42	29	71	43	35	78	95
LHB-Avg	.291	.242	.272	.245	.267	.253	108
LHB-HR	41	26	67	49	27	76	93
RHB-Avg	.269	.275	.273	.250	.259	.255	107
RHB-HR	34	55	89	41	61	102	89

1998-2000

	Home Games			Away Games			
	D'backs	Opp	Total	D'backs	Opp	Total	Index
G	220	220	440	223	223	446	—
Avg	.272	.259	.266	.252	.258	.255	104
AB	7402	7675	15077	7743	7399	15142	101
R	1078	996	2074	1057	1032	2089	101
H	2014	1990	4004	1950	1912	3862	105
2B	358	367	725	369	345	714	102
3B	74	57	131	50	32	82	160
HR	234	236	470	263	262	525	90
BB	728	635	1363	749	754	1503	91
SO	1369	1451	2820	1616	1571	3187	89
E	127	141	268	151	152	303	90
E-Infield	109	117	226	124	114	238	96
LHB-Avg	.276	.253	.267	.257	.265	.260	103
LHB-HR	111	71	182	124	77	201	92
RHB-Avg	.268	.262	.265	.246	.255	.251	105
RHB-HR	123	165	288	139	185	324	88

2000 Rankings (National League)

- Second-highest RHB batting-average factor
- Third-highest batting-average factor
- Third-highest hit factor

Bob Brenly

2000 Season

Bob Brenly was Arizona's TV analyst and also worked games for the Fox network. He had been working in television after spending four seasons—1992 to 1995—as a coach with the Giants. Despite not having been in uniform for a while, Brenly stayed up on the game, showing his ability to evaluate talent and strategy in his broadcasts.

Offense

Asked for his biggest influence, Brenly has cited former Giants manager Roger Craig. One thing Brenly says he learned from Craig is the need to be unpredictable, which keeps opponents guessing and the players loose and attentive. That means hit-and-runs, double steals and squeeze plays. But being unpredictable, Brenly warns, means doing those things sparingly. He says he prefers to have regulars as opposed to platooning but wants to make sure players get occasional rest through the season. Brenly says individual matchups are more important that straight right-left decisions.

Pitching & Defense

A former catcher, Brenly is expected to be attuned to his pitchers. He wants to limit innings for the starters early in the season. He expects to establish roles for relievers from the seventh inning on. The Craig influence may also be seen in teaching some pitchers the split-finger fastball. Brenly is not a big believer in a wide variety of defenses. He'd rather keep things simple and stress execution.

2001 Outlook

Brenly's mandate is to lighten the mood and create a better atmosphere for the players. His four-year, $2 million contract with an option for 2005 gives him a chance to do that. His baseball acumen and ability to communicate are unquestioned, but he hasn't managed on any level. There is little evidence that a first-time manager can improve an already good team. Eleven times since 1990 a manager began his career at the start of a season with a team that had a winning record the year before. Only in three cases did the team improve: the 1997 Astros (Larry Dierker), the 1994 Astros (Terry Collins) and the 1992 Brewers (Phil Garner). Like Brenly, Dierker was a former broadcaster.

Born: 2/25/54 in Coshocton, OH

Playing Experience: 1981-1989, SF, Tor

Managerial Experience: No major league managing experience

Manager Statistics (Buck Showalter)

Year	Team, Lg	W	L	Pct	GB	Finish
2000	Arizona, NL	85	77	.525	12.0	3rd West
7 Seasons		563	504	.528	—	—

2000 Starting Pitchers by Days Rest

	<=3	4	5	6+
Diamondbacks Starts	0	93	31	29
Diamondbacks ERA	—	4.08	4.28	5.62
NL Avg Starts	2	80	50	21
NL ERA	5.00	4.61	4.60	5.18

2000 Situational Stats

	Buck Showalter	NL Average
Hit & Run Success %	40.7	33.8
Stolen Base Success %	68.8	68.8
Platoon Pct.	60.4	53.2
Defensive Subs	11	19
High-Pitch Outings	18	14
Quick/Slow Hooks	13/14	14/16
Sacrifice Attempts	89	87

2000 Rankings—Buck Showalter (National Lg)

- 1st in starts with over 140 pitches (1) and first-batter platoon percentage (60.4)
- 3rd in fewest caught stealing of second base (34), double steals (5) and hit-and-run success percentage (40.7)

Arizona

Brian Anderson

2000 Season

Signed to a three-year contract before last season, Brian Anderson established himself as a solid starter. His record was deceiving, since he had 10 starts in which he allowed two or fewer earned runs but did not get the win. Counting a blown save in his first start of the season, Anderson could have had 20 wins with decent luck. Over his final eight starts, he posted a 2.86 ERA but just a 2-2 record.

Pitching

Once a fastball-changeup pitcher who tried to throw a curveball and a slider, Anderson finally has found a third pitch that suits him: a cut fastball. Its good lateral movement—toward a righthanded hitter—can keep batters from cheating toward the outside part of the plate, where Anderson likes to work with his changeup and fastball. He has an average fastball but good arm action on his changeup. He still uses the slider on occasion. Sometimes his excellent control works against him, as he challenges hitters instead of pitching around them when called for. Consistently throwing strikes also leads to a high number of home runs allowed.

Defense & Hitting

Anderson makes up for less-than-overwhelming stuff by helping himself with the glove and bat. He has excellent reactions and can field balls well off the mound. His good pickoff moves and quick delivery to the plate keep opponents from running on him. A switch-hitter, he can bunt, hit-and-run or fake-bunt-and-slash. He is fast enough and smart enough to be used as a pinch-runner.

2001 Outlook

Anderson enters this season with more confidence than ever. He has proven he belongs as a starter, and not just a fifth starter. Because of his great control he doesn't run up high pitch counts. He stays in good condition, so his arm should be in good shape despite a career-high innings total in 2000. With a little more consistency and a lot more luck, Anderson could be a big winner.

Position: SP
Bats: B **Throws:** L
Ht: 6' 1" **Wt:** 183

Opening Day Age: 28
Born: 4/26/72 in Geneva, OH
ML Seasons: 8

Overall Statistics

	W	L	Pct.	ERA	G	GS	Sv	IP	H	BB	SO	HR	Ratio
2000	11	7	.611	4.05	33	32	0	213.1	226	39	104	38	1.24
Career	51	38	.573	4.63	154	136	1	863.1	945	175	413	149	1.30

How Often He Throws Strikes

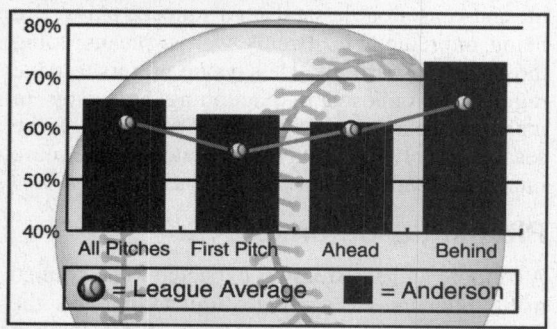

○ = League Average ■ = Anderson

2000 Situational Stats

	W	L	ERA	Sv	IP		AB	H	HR	RBI	Avg
Home	6	3	3.51	0	110.1	LHB	188	50	7	19	.266
Road	5	4	4.63	0	103.0	RHB	634	176	31	77	.278
First Half	8	3	4.31	0	117.0	Sc Pos	144	36	7	51	.250
Scnd Half	3	4	3.74	0	96.1	Clutch	64	18	4	6	.281

2000 Rankings (National League)

- 2nd in home runs allowed, balks (4) and fewest walks per nine innings (1.6)
- 3rd in fewest pitches thrown per batter (3.42)
- 4th in fewest strikeouts per nine innings (4.4)
- 5th in GDPs induced (25), most GDPs induced per GDP situation (19.7%) and most home runs allowed per nine innings (1.60)
- Led the Diamondbacks in sacrifice bunts (9), hits allowed, home runs allowed, balks (4), GDPs induced (25), fewest pitches thrown per batter (3.42), most run support per nine innings (5.2), most GDPs induced per nine innings (1.1), fewest walks per nine innings (1.6) and most GDPs induced per GDP situation (19.7%)

Jay Bell

2000 Season

Jay Bell set career highs in home runs and RBI in 1999, producing one of the top homer seasons ever by a second baseman. But last year he fell to totals much like those of 1998, his first year with Arizona. He probably was affected by the low on-base percentage of Tony Womack batting in front of him. But Bell's 20-homer drop-off also seemed to be caused by simply not hitting the ball as hard. In addition, by the end of the season Bell seemed to have lost a step defensively.

Hitting

Bell was once a classic No. 2 hitter who bunted often and tried to move runners along. He evolved into a 20-plus homer player from 1997-99. But last year his strength seemed to decline, and pitches he used to hit out of the park often died in left field. He needs to return to his physical condition of 1999 to regain his power. Bell has reduced his strikeouts but still will chase pitches out of the zone with two strikes. He'll take a walk, however, and thus remain a capable No. 2 hitter.

Baserunning & Defense

Although last year was only Bell's second full season at second base, he might be ready for another position change. He has a decent arm and sure hands, so he won't make many errors, and he turns the double play passably. But his range is woeful, especially on turf. He simply doesn't get to many balls, particularly to his left. While he isn't fast, he does steal bases at a respectable percentage.

2001 Outlook

Bell seems to be on the career path of former teammate Jeff King, at least in terms of progressing defensively around the diamond toward first base. But Bell, who has a no-trade clause and two years at $8 million per season left on his contract, doesn't possess the power needed from a first baseman. The combination leaves Arizona in a bad position. The Diamondbacks probably will stick with Bell at second base and try to live with his lack of range.

Position: 2B
Bats: R **Throws:** R
Ht: 6' 0" **Wt:** 184

Opening Day Age: 35
Born: 12/11/65 in Eglin AFB, FL
ML Seasons: 15

Overall Statistics

	G	AB	R	H	D	T	HR	RBI	SB	BB	SO	Avg	OBP	Slg
2000	149	565	87	151	30	6	18	68	7	70	88	.267	.348	.437
Career	1830	6805	1050	1828	368	66	180	800	91	761	1317	.269	.344	.421

Where He Hits the Ball

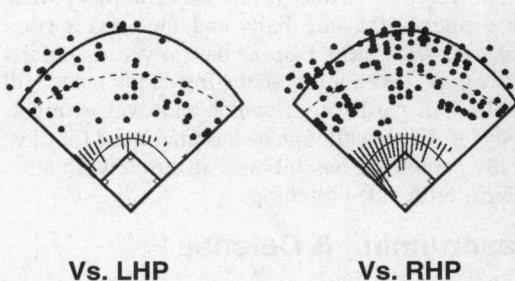

Vs. LHP	Vs. RHP

2000 Situational Stats

	AB	H	HR	RBI	Avg		AB	H	HR	RBI	Avg
Home	286	79	9	38	.276	LHP	147	51	6	21	.347
Road	279	72	9	30	.258	RHP	418	100	12	47	.239
First Half	330	86	9	31	.261	Sc Pos	125	35	2	42	.280
Scnd Half	235	65	9	37	.277	Clutch	75	23	3	12	.307

2000 Rankings (National League)

- 2nd in fielding percentage at second base (.988)
- 5th in most pitches seen per plate appearance (4.16)
- 7th in pitches seen (2,701)
- 8th in batting average vs. lefthanded pitchers and lowest batting average vs. righthanded pitchers
- 9th in on-base percentage vs. lefthanded pitchers (.430)
- 10th in slugging percentage vs. lefthanded pitchers (.571)
- Led the Diamondbacks in strikeouts, pitches seen (2,701), most pitches seen per plate appearance (4.16), batting average vs. lefthanded pitchers and slugging percentage vs. lefthanded pitchers (.571)

Erubiel Durazo

2000 Season

Counted on as the lefthanded half of a platoon at first base, Erubiel Durazo's 2000 season was almost entirely wasted because of right wrist problems. The trouble first cropped up in spring training and eventually led to surgery in late May to repair torn cartilage. He lasted just three days in his return, went back on the disabled list, then continued to struggle and was sent to the minors for 10 days. Eventually, a bone chip was discovered in the wrist, and late-August surgery ended his season.

Hitting

Durazo's great strengths are strike-zone judgement and power to all fields. He has a keen ability to take close pitches that are balls and thus has a good strikeout-walk ratio. Durazo has power to all parts of the park. He can turn on the inside pitch and still hit the ball hard to left-center and even straightaway left field. Although he has platooned for most of his career, he has hit well in his few chances against lefthanded pitching.

Baserunning & Defense

Durazo's ability at first base is limited. He picks the low throw out of the dirt well but only has moderate range. His biggest shortcoming is his throwing arm; he short-arms the ball and has trouble on the feed to second base when starting double plays. His throwing problems also have led to hesitation instead of quick reaction, which can cost him an out or a chance at the lead runner. Durazo does not run well.

2001 Outlook

The wrist problems of last year were most evident when Durazo would take called strikes instead of pulling the trigger on a swing. If the wrist clears up and Durazo can swing pain-free, he should rediscover his quick bat and the ability to pull the ball and hit the other way. His power also should return. A position change is in order, however. The free-agent acquisition of Mark Grace means that Durazo likely will move to right field. Durazo got a taste of his new position in winter ball, but the jury still is out as to whether he has the arm to keep the opposition honest.

Position: 1B
Bats: L **Throws:** L
Ht: 6' 3" **Wt:** 225

Opening Day Age: 27
Born: 1/23/74 in Hermosillo, Mexico
ML Seasons: 2
Pronunciation: ur-ROO-bee-ell dew-RAH-zoh

Overall Statistics

	G	AB	R	H	D	T	HR	RBI	SB	BB	SO	Avg	OBP	Slg
2000	67	196	35	52	11	0	8	33	1	34	43	.265	.373	.444
Career	119	351	66	103	15	2	19	63	2	60	86	.293	.395	.510

Where He Hits the Ball

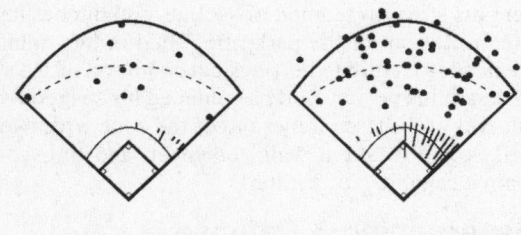

Vs. LHP   Vs. RHP

2000 Situational Stats

	AB	H	HR	RBI	Avg		AB	H	HR	RBI	Avg
Home	100	25	3	16	.250	LHP	22	7	0	2	.318
Road	96	27	5	17	.281	RHP	174	45	8	31	.259
First Half	145	40	7	27	.276	Sc Pos	58	13	3	26	.224
Scnd Half	51	12	1	6	.235	Clutch	31	8	0	2	.258

2000 Rankings (National League)

- 10th in lowest cleanup slugging percentage (.481)
- Led the Diamondbacks in fewest GDPs per GDP situation (5.8%) and batting average on a 3-1 count (.600)

Steve Finley

2000 Season

Steve Finley made a bid for MVP honors over the first half of last season. He almost single-handedly carried the Diamondbacks' offense before cooling off. He made the All-Star team for the second time and set a career high in home runs. He might have approached his best batting average but was hit by a pitch on September 12. He tried to play the rest of the season despite suffering severe bone bruises in his left wrist.

Hitting

Finley has become less pull-oriented than he was between 1996 and 1999, when his home runs increased while his batting average dropped. He still turns on inside pitches, especially from the belt down, for homers. But he also will go with pitches to left field for hits, which helps his batting average. His power is almost all from center field to the right field line. He has improved against lefthanded pitching.

Baserunning & Defense

Now a four-time Gold Glove winner, Finley still makes the occasional spectacular catch, crashing into or leaping over the wall. But his range in center field often is disguised by his good jump on balls off the bat, allowing him to get to the spot of the catch early. Although he doesn't possess significant arm strength, Finley gets rid of the ball quickly, throws to the right spot and is accurate. He usually prevents runners from taking the extra base, normally by cutting off balls in the gap rather than throwing them out. Finley has good speed and can steal 10 or more bases but is no longer the guy who once stole 44 in a season.

2001 Outlook

A herniated disk in his lower back has bothered Finley the past two seasons, so he opted for surgery in mid-November and hopes to be in the best physical condition of his career by spring training. Still, his style of play always will result in a fair number of minor injuries, though he can be counted on to play through the pain and stay in the lineup. As long as he's on the field, he should continue to produce offensively and be an upper-echelon center fielder.

Position: CF
Bats: L **Throws:** L
Ht: 6' 2" **Wt:** 180

Opening Day Age: 36
Born: 3/12/65 in Union City, TN
ML Seasons: 12

Overall Statistics

	G	AB	R	H	D	T	HR	RBI	SB	BB	SO	Avg	OBP	Slg
2000	152	539	100	151	27	5	35	96	12	65	87	.280	.361	.544
Career	1690	6327	1005	1737	302	90	188	745	254	534	853	.275	.332	.440

Where He Hits the Ball

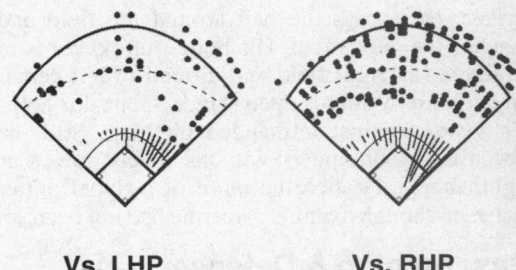

Vs. LHP   **Vs. RHP**

2000 Situational Stats

	AB	H	HR	RBI	Avg		AB	H	HR	RBI	Avg
Home	260	87	17	54	.335	LHP	157	43	11	34	.274
Road	279	64	18	42	.229	RHP	382	108	24	62	.283
First Half	313	94	25	70	.300	Sc Pos	129	32	9	58	.248
Scnd Half	226	57	10	26	.252	Clutch	84	22	7	23	.262

2000 Rankings (National League)

- 1st in highest percentage of extra bases taken as a runner (73.9)
- 3rd in lowest batting average on the road
- 4th in fielding percentage in center field (.992)
- 9th in sacrifice flies (9)
- Led the Diamondbacks in home runs, intentional walks (7), HR frequency (15.4 ABs per HR), batting average with the bases loaded (.300) and highest percentage of extra bases taken as a runner (73.9)
- Led NL center fielders in sacrifice flies (9), slugging percentage vs. lefthanded pitchers (.535), batting average at home and highest percentage of extra bases taken as a runner (73.9)

Luis Gonzalez

2000 Season

Although his batting average wasn't as impressive as in 1999, when he finished second in the batting race with a .336 average, Luis Gonzalez' 2000 season was the best of his career. He set personal highs in home runs, RBI, walks and doubles. Gonzalez was batting .229 on May 7, but thereafter hit .330 with 95 RBI, 38 doubles and 23 homers in his final 132 games. He was the only National League player to start all 162 games.

Hitting

Gonzalez is a good No. 3 hitter, with a smooth, flat swing. His walk and strikeout totals will be roughly the same, as he is willing to draw a free pass, but he sometimes will chase breaking pitches with two strikes. He sprays the ball around the field and reaches the gaps often. His home-run power is to straightaway right field and around to left-center on occasion. With his open stance, Gonzalez helps his vision against lefthanded pitching. Still, he doesn't hit southpaws with as much power as righthanders. He became more of a flyball hitter last year, though over his career he had not been so.

Baserunning & Defense

Gonzalez is a fair runner but not a basestealer. His defense in left field has improved; he tracks flyballs well and has learned to play the short left field fence at Bank One Ballpark, at times leaping to take away home runs. But Gonzalez has an average arm and often only reaches the cutoff man. He can prevent runners from taking an extra base by hustling to the ball and getting it to the infield quickly.

2001 Outlook

Unlike most players, Gonzalez continues to improve after age 30, maturing as a hitter over the past couple years. His quick stroke and intelligent approach should enable him to continue to produce as a .300 hitter with good gap power. His defense is acceptable, especially considering his offense. With two years remaining on his contract, he should continue to be an Arizona mainstay.

Position: LF
Bats: L **Throws:** R
Ht: 6' 2" **Wt:** 190

Opening Day Age: 33
Born: 9/2/67 in Tampa, FL
ML Seasons: 11

Overall Statistics

	G	AB	R	H	D	T	HR	RBI	SB	BB	SO	Avg	OBP	Slg
2000	162	618	106	192	47	2	31	114	2	78	85	.311	.392	.544
Career	1437	5096	750	1434	329	44	164	775	100	552	687	.281	.355	.460

Where He Hits the Ball

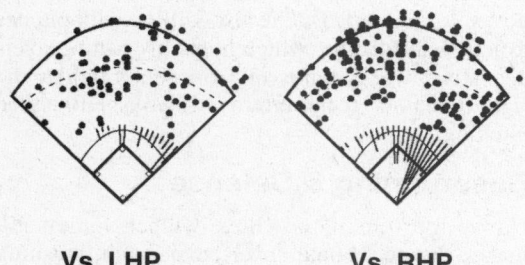

Vs. LHP   **Vs. RHP**

2000 Situational Stats

	AB	H	HR	RBI	Avg		AB	H	HR	RBI	Avg
Home	305	104	14	56	.341	LHP	177	45	8	31	.254
Road	313	88	17	58	.281	RHP	441	147	23	83	.333
First Half	336	104	18	53	.310	Sc Pos	144	49	8	78	.340
Scnd Half	282	88	13	61	.312	Clutch	85	30	5	23	.353

2000 Rankings (National League)

- 1st in fielding percentage in left field (.990) and games played
- 2nd in sacrifice flies (12) and plate appearances (722)
- 4th in at-bats and doubles
- Led the Diamondbacks in batting average, at-bats, runs scored, hits, doubles, total bases (336), RBI, sacrifice flies (12), walks, hit by pitch (12), times on base (282), plate appearances (722), slugging percentage, on-base percentage, batting average with runners in scoring position, batting average vs. righthanded pitchers, slugging percentage vs. righthanded pitchers (.583), on-base percentage vs. righthanded pitchers (.415) and batting average at home

Randy Johnson

2000 Season

In some ways Randy Johnson was better in 2000 than during his 1999 Cy Young Award season. He enjoyed his best April ever, compiling a 6-0 record and sparkling 0.91 ERA. Although he endured some poor starts in the second half and lost the ERA title with a disastrous final outing, he finished 19-7 with 347 strikeouts, the seventh most ever. Most importantly, he did it in 4,026 pitches, 180 fewer than the previous year. It all added up to a second straight Cy Young Award—his third such honor.

Pitching

Johnson has incorporated a two-seam, sinking fastball into his repertoire. Instead of piling up pitch counts along with strikeouts, Johnson can use the two-seamer to get quick outs or a double-play ball when in trouble. Of course, it doesn't hurt that he still can throw 98-100 MPH. His slider, which can break almost to the hitter's shoetops, is as hard as most pitchers' fastballs. Because of his height, Johnson is very dependent on consistent mechanics, and at times he can open up his delivery a bit early and lose command. He rarely faces lefthanded batters, so to be effective he must be able to come inside to righthanders.

Defense & Hitting

Johnson has improved his hitting. He occasionally can drive a ball for extra bases, though he is a slow baserunner. He picks off a fair number of runners, usually when they're guessing. Johnson is slow to the plate and can be run on. He isn't a good fielder, sometimes hurrying throws that lead to errors and not always covering first or backing up other bases.

2001 Outlook

Realizing he can't throw 150 pitches in a game as he did in the 1990s, Johnson makes use of his ability to limit his pitch counts with the two-seam fastball. His reduced pitch total in 2000—the equivalent of almost two starts—should help him this season, along with his usual emphasis on conditioning. Despite his drop-off in the second half last season, he showed no signs of losing his velocity. Johnson remains an unqualified ace and a candidate for a fourth Cy Young Award.

Position: SP
Bats: R **Throws:** L
Ht: 6'10" **Wt:** 230

Opening Day Age: 37
Born: 9/10/63 in Walnut Creek, CA
ML Seasons: 13
Nickname: Big Unit

Overall Statistics

	W	L	Pct.	ERA	G	GS	Sv	IP	H	BB	SO	HR	Ratio
2000	19	7	.731	2.64	35	35	0	248.2	202	76	347	23	1.12
Career	179	95	.653	3.19	366	357	2	2498.2	1932	1089	3040	222	1.21

How Often He Throws Strikes

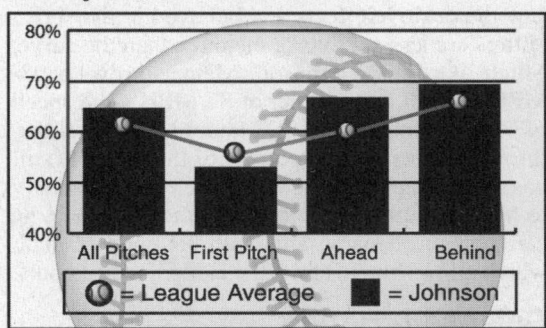

● = League Average   ■ = Johnson

2000 Situational Stats

	W	L	ERA	Sv	IP		AB	H	HR	RBI	Avg
Home	11	3	2.51	0	132.2	LHB	83	19	0	4	.229
Road	8	4	2.79	0	116.0	RHB	817	183	23	74	.224
First Half	14	2	1.80	0	144.2	Sc Pos	202	42	5	56	.208
Scnd Half	5	5	3.81	0	104.0	Clutch	108	24	4	8	.222

2000 Rankings (National League)

- 1st in games started, complete games (8), shutouts (3), strikeouts, pitches thrown (4,026), runners caught stealing (16), most strikeouts per nine innings (12.6) and winning percentage
- 2nd in ERA, stolen bases allowed (26), highest strikeout/walk ratio (4.6) and lowest ERA on the road
- 3rd in wins, innings pitched, lowest on-base percentage allowed (.288), most pitches thrown per batter (4.02) and lowest fielding percentage at pitcher (.900)
- Led the Diamondbacks in ERA, wins, games started, complete games (8), shutouts (3), innings pitched, batters faced (1,001), walks allowed, strikeouts and wild pitches (5)

Arizona

Matt Mantei

Position: RP
Bats: R **Throws:** R
Ht: 6' 1" **Wt:** 190

Opening Day Age: 27
Born: 7/7/73 in Tampa, FL
ML Seasons: 5
Pronunciation: MAN-tie

2000 Season

Matt Mantei's first half of last season was a mess. He opened the year on the disabled list because of biceps tendinitis before returning to the DL in early May with a sore right shoulder. Then he simply struggled, and Byung-Hyun Kim took over Arizona's closer's duties. Mantei did return to form in July and was brilliant over the final three months, converting 15 of 16 save chances while striking out 21 and allowing four hits over 15.1 innings.

Pitching

Mantei now throws a slider instead of a curveball, an exchange that began in spring training last year. It didn't take hold until midseason, when Mantei saw the positive effects and believed in the slider. Hitters are less apt to take the pitch than the curve. Much like Randy Johnson, Mantei throws a 98-MPH fastball and a slider at 89 MPH—the speed of some pitchers' fastball. Mantei spots the slider, throwing it perhaps 10 percent of the time. He still has some bouts with control problems, especially to his first hitter or two of the game. However, he can get out of many jams with his good fastball, which allows him to climb the ladder for strikeouts.

Defense & Hitting

Mantei is not a sure-handed fielder but usually gets the job done. As with many closers, he is more worried about retiring the hitter than holding baserunners. He thus has a slow delivery to the plate, making it fairly easy for runners to steal bases. Mantei rarely bats.

2001 Outlook

Mantei showed he could be an elite closer over last season's second half. He has the proper mental makeup for the role and the hard fastball, as well as confidence in his slider. Although he hates to be labeled injury-prone, he has a long history of health problems, albeit a wide variety of ailments as opposed to one recurring injury. His contract status could be a factor this year; if the Diamondbacks do not sign Mantei to a long-term deal, he'll be eligible for free agency after the season.

Overall Statistics

	W	L	Pct.	ERA	G	GS	Sv	IP	H	BB	SO	HR	Ratio
2000	1	1	.500	4.57	47	0	17	45.1	31	35	53	4	1.46
Career	6	9	.400	3.70	180	0	58	197.0	138	136	255	13	1.39

How Often He Throws Strikes

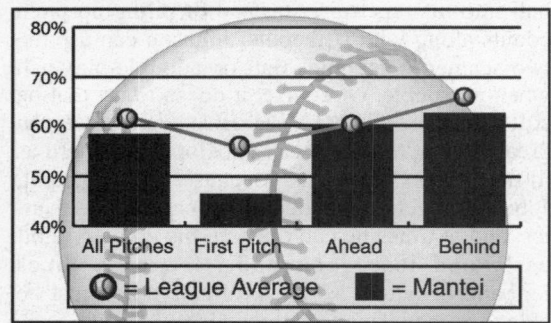

2000 Situational Stats

	W	L	ERA	Sv	IP		AB	H	HR	RBI	Avg
Home	0	0	2.74	5	23.0	LHB	71	13	2	12	.183
Road	1	1	6.45	12	22.1	RHB	90	18	2	10	.200
First Half	1	1	7.36	4	22.0	Sc Pos	53	11	1	16	.208
Scnd Half	0	0	1.93	13	23.1	Clutch	82	15	1	11	.183

2000 Rankings (National League)

- 7th in save percentage (85.0)
- Led the Diamondbacks in saves, games finished (38), wild pitches (5), save opportunities (20) and save percentage (85.0)

Armando Reynoso

2000 Season

Armando Reynoso served as Arizona's fifth starter last year and matched his career high with 30 starts. Despite compiling a losing record and a career-high 12 defeats, he tied Brian Anderson for the second-most wins on the team. Eight of Reynoso's final 11 outings were quality starts, but the Diamondbacks mustered just one run in three of those contests. That stretch also included a five-decision losing streak, and he never lowered his ERA below 5.00 after May 9.

Pitching

With below-average velocity, Reynoso relies on a wide repertoire and his ability to change speeds. He throws a sinking fastball, an occasional curve and changeup at a variety of speeds. He has to hit the corners and sometimes suffers with umpires who call tight strike zones. Reynoso historically encounters much of his troubles in the first inning. With his tendency to go deep into counts, Reynoso can be counted on for only six to seven innings per start.

Defense & Hitting

Reynoso is a surehanded fielder who gets off the mound well and has one of the best righthanded pickoff moves in the game. He also uses his quick feet for a good pickoff move to second base. He gets to plenty of balls around the mound, registering a highly respectable 34 assists and three double plays last year. Reynoso is an OK bunter but a poor hitter who strikes out often.

2001 Outlook

The Diamondbacks declined to pick up Reynoso's $5 million option for 2001, but they quickly locked him back up with a two-year, $6.5 million offer in early December. He seems fully recovered from 1997 elbow and shoulder surgery and should be able to make 30 starts again. His ERA will be high, especially because of his frequent first-inning struggles. But he is a strong competitor who can find a way to reach double-digits in victories from his fifth spot in the Arizona rotation.

Position: SP
Bats: R **Throws:** R
Ht: 6' 0" **Wt:** 204

Opening Day Age: 34
Born: 5/1/66 in San Luis Potosi, Mexico
ML Seasons: 10
Pronunciation: ray-NOH-so

Overall Statistics

	W	L	Pct.	ERA	G	GS	Sv	IP	H	BB	SO	HR	Ratio
2000	11	12	.478	5.27	31	30	0	170.2	179	52	89	22	1.35
Career	67	56	.545	4.68	187	177	1	1031.1	1124	362	537	125	1.44

How Often He Throws Strikes

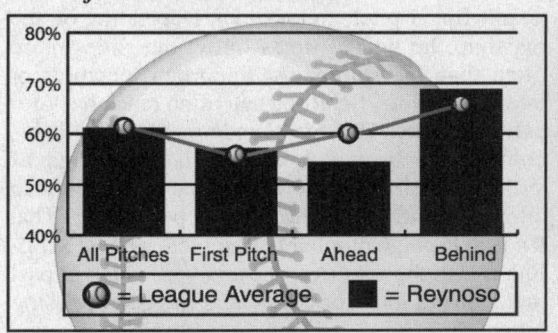

= League Average   ■ = Reynoso

2000 Situational Stats

	W	L	ERA	Sv	IP		AB	H	HR	RBI	Avg
Home	7	4	5.27	0	85.1	LHB	315	85	11	46	.270
Road	4	8	5.27	0	85.1	RHB	341	94	11	39	.276
First Half	5	6	5.81	0	83.2	Sc Pos	129	40	5	60	.310
Scnd Half	6	6	4.76	0	87.0	Clutch	32	11	2	5	.344

2000 Rankings (National League)

- 1st in pickoff throws (190)
- 5th in fewest strikeouts per nine innings (4.7)
- 6th in highest ERA at home
- 7th in highest ERA
- 9th in fewest GDPs induced per nine innings (0.6)
- 10th in highest ERA on the road
- Led the Diamondbacks in losses, pickoff throws (190) and lowest stolen-base percentage allowed (50.0)

Curt Schilling

2000 Season

Curt Schilling helped force his trade last summer by threatening to walk away from the Phillies once his contract expired in 2001. So after more than eight seasons in Philadelphia, Schilling was dealt to Arizona, where he had been raised. The July 26 trade—for Omar Daal, Travis Lee, Vicente Padilla and Nelson Figueroa—was supposed to give Arizona the top 1-2 pitching punch in baseball. But after Schilling won four of his first five decisions with the Diamondbacks, he lost five straight as the team fell from contention.

Pitching

Schilling throws a fastball in the 92-94 MPH range, a split-finger pitch and a slider. Depending on the matchup, he will at times throw the slider more often than the splitter. At important junctures or late in the game, Schilling can often reach back for extra velocity. His most underrated facet is his control. He throws a very high percentage of strikes, which not only reduces his walks but also allows him to use fewer pitches per inning. That leads to his high number of complete games. Schilling is a studious hurler who analyzes video of past matchups to look for edges against each opposing hitter.

Defense & Hitting

While Schilling doesn't make many pickoff throws, he has a fairly quick delivery to the plate that helps keep the running game in control. He is a fundamentally sound fielder. If 2000 is any indication, his hitting is improving; he actually batted .258 after the trade. But his career statistics indicate that his success may have been an aberration.

2001 Outlook

After his shoulder surgery in December of 1999, Schilling was told it would require a year for him to get back to full strength. At times last year he couldn't dial up his fastball a notch, as he was used to doing. That should be corrected this season, and he will be determined to make up for last year's losing record. The Diamondbacks hope that is the case, as they anteed up for a three-year, $32 million contract extension in mid-December that will keep Schilling in Arizona through 2004.

Position: SP
Bats: R **Throws:** R
Ht: 6' 4" **Wt:** 231

Opening Day Age: 34
Born: 11/14/66 in Anchorage, AK
ML Seasons: 13
Pronunciation: SHILL-ing

Overall Statistics

	W	L	Pct.	ERA	G	GS	Sv	IP	H	BB	SO	HR	Ratio
2000	11	12	.478	3.81	29	29	0	210.1	204	45	168	27	1.18
Career	110	95	.537	3.43	355	244	13	1902.0	1687	499	1739	180	1.15

How Often He Throws Strikes

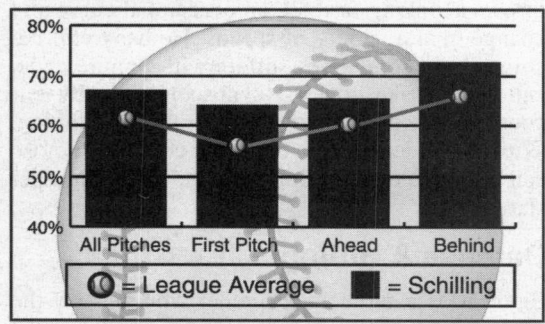

= League Average   = Schilling

2000 Situational Stats

	W	L	ERA	Sv	IP		AB	H	HR	RBI	Avg
Home	6	6	3.43	0	110.1	LHB	428	104	10	43	.243
Road	5	6	4.23	0	100.0	RHB	373	100	17	45	.268
First Half	4	5	4.26	0	88.2	Sc Pos	166	47	6	59	.283
Scnd Half	7	7	3.48	0	121.2	Clutch	76	22	2	12	.289

2000 Rankings (National League)

- 1st in complete games (8)
- 3rd in shutouts (2) and lowest stolen-base percentage allowed (25.0)
- 4th in highest strikeout/walk ratio (3.7) and lowest on-base percentage allowed (.294)
- 5th in fewest walks per nine innings (1.9)
- 8th in fewest pitches thrown per batter (3.56)
- Led the Diamondbacks in lowest batting average allowed vs. lefthanded batters (.233)

Todd Stottlemyre

2000 Season

For the second straight year, a significant arm injury cut into Todd Stottlemyre's season. In 1999, he suffered a 70 percent tear in his rotator cuff but managed to come back without surgery. In 2000, it was elbow tendinitis, which struck after he had started 8-2 with a 4.63 ERA. He first returned after 15 days on the disabled list, displaying good stuff in two of his three June starts. But the tendinitis came back and he was out for 10 weeks. In the season's final week, Stottlemyre had surgery to reposition his ulnar nerve, moving it from the elbow joint to under a muscle, which should prevent the tendinitis from recurring.

Pitching

Stottlemyre's fastball is in the low-90 MPH range, and he also will throw a curve and occasional changeup. But his best pitch is his slider, which is better now than ever. It's hard with a big break. Because of his torn rotator cuff, Stottlemyre's pitch count is monitored carefully. He never exceeded 101 pitches last year. He is known for his competitive nature as much as his stuff, but at times his intensity level has led him to make some mistakes, such as trying to pitch through pain.

Defense & Hitting

A lefthanded swinger, Stottlemyre is a competent hitter who can put the ball in play. He has a lifetime batting average over .200 and connected for his first major league home run last year. He is also capable of sacrificing when called upon. He fields his position well and has a decent pickoff move, though baserunners will take some chances when he's on the hill.

2001 Outlook

Stottlemyre is a wild-card in Arizona's fortunes. His $8 million salary and injury history make him practically untradeable. He has been good when healthy the past two years, and a full season of Stottlemyre makes the Arizona rotation formidable. But his recent history makes it unrealistic to count on getting 30-35 starts out of him. He was cleared to begin throwing in December, and the Diamondbacks hope he can be ready for the start of the season.

Position: SP
Bats: L   **Throws:** R
Ht: 6' 3"   **Wt:** 215

Opening Day Age: 35
Born: 5/20/65 in Yakima, WA
ML Seasons: 13
Pronunciation: STAH-till-my-er

Arizona

Overall Statistics

	W	L	Pct.	ERA	G	GS	Sv	IP	H	BB	SO	HR	Ratio
2000	9	6	.600	4.91	18	18	0	95.1	98	36	76	18	1.41
Career	138	119	.537	4.25	367	335	1	2171.1	2174	809	1575	242	1.37

How Often He Throws Strikes

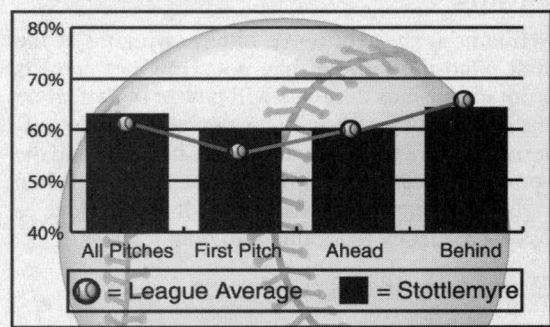

2000 Situational Stats

	W	L	ERA	Sv	IP		AB	H	HR	RBI	Avg
Home	3	4	6.07	0	43.0	LHB	143	39	10	21	.273
Road	6	2	3.96	0	52.1	RHB	222	59	8	31	.266
First Half	8	5	4.24	0	76.1	Sc Pos	78	25	6	36	.321
Scnd Half	1	1	7.58	0	19.0	Clutch	11	3	1	1	.273

2000 Rankings (National League)
- Did not rank near the top or bottom in any category

Matt Williams

2000 Season

With a week left in spring training, Matt Williams fouled a ball off his foot and broke a bone. He then strained a quadriceps during his comeback. When he finally began playing regularly after the All-Star break, he battled plantar fasciaitis in his left arch and an arthritis-like disease (Ankylosing Spondylitis) that affected his ability to grip the bat. Awful with men in scoring position, he was dropped from the cleanup spot for much of the stretch run. He wound up driving in 95 fewer runs than in 1999. Only one player with more than 300 at-bats has ever had an RBI decline that large: Hack Wilson in 1931 (from 191 RBI to 61).

Hitting

Williams is an aggressive hitter, swinging at the first pitch more often than not. How he recovers from his various ailments will have a big effect on his production, especially his power. When he suffers from sore legs or feet, he loses his base, and the spondylitis can limit how hard he swings. When right, Williams drives the ball to all fields. He does have a tendency to ground into double plays.

Baserunning & Defense

Williams' defense has been more consistent than his bat in recent years. He reacts well at third base, especially to his left, and has soft hands that help him snag tough hops. When his feet are OK, his footwork is very good, and he gets in position to get off a good throw. His arm strength is fine and he makes nice feeds to second base to begin double plays. He has snuck in stolen bases at times but is slowing down and won't run much.

2001 Outlook

Health will be Williams' main concern. He will try to avoid surgery to treat the plantar fasciaitis, which first cropped up in late 1999. And he needs to find a successful treatment for the Ankylosing Spondylitis. He prefers not to take medication, which can have harmful side effects. Should Williams, who is signed through 2003, be able to deal with these issues, he again could be productive.

Position: 3B
Bats: R **Throws:** R
Ht: 6' 2" **Wt:** 214

Opening Day Age: 35
Born: 11/28/65 in Bishop, CA
ML Seasons: 14

Overall Statistics

	G	AB	R	H	D	T	HR	RBI	SB	BB	SO	Avg	OBP	Slg
2000	96	371	43	102	18	2	12	47	1	20	51	.275	.315	.431
Career	1656	6243	893	1677	292	33	346	1097	49	410	1226	.269	.316	.492

Where He Hits the Ball

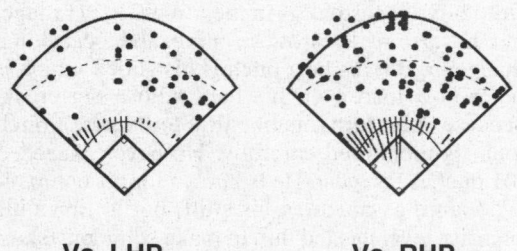

Vs. LHP **Vs. RHP**

2000 Situational Stats

	AB	H	HR	RBI	Avg		AB	H	HR	RBI	Avg
Home	180	45	5	14	.250	LHP	106	33	5	14	.311
Road	191	57	7	33	.298	RHP	265	69	7	33	.260
First Half	93	25	2	4	.269	Sc Pos	94	18	4	33	.191
Scnd Half	278	77	10	43	.277	Clutch	61	19	1	6	.311

2000 Rankings (National League)

- 2nd in lowest batting average with runners in scoring position
- 5th in lowest cleanup slugging percentage (.442)
- Led the Diamondbacks in batting average on an 0-2 count (.192)

Tony Womack

2000 Season

Moved to shortstop last spring, Tony Womack again was Arizona's leadoff man. But he had one of the lowest on-base percentages in the National League. He also didn't lead the league in stolen bases for the first time since 1996. Part of that may have been due to playing with a cyst behind his left knee over the second half of the season. He had surgery to repair the cyst before the season ended and is expected to be fine for spring training.

Hitting

Womack's hitting style does not take advantage of his speed. He could benefit from hitting more groundballs and goes for long stretches without attempting to bunt for a hit. He is most vulnerable to simple fastballs high and away, which he usually will hit for harmless flyballs to left field. If he does hit a ball into the right-center gap or either corner, Womack can turn it into a triple. He can be expected to hit around .280, but since he rarely walks, his on-base percentage is very low.

Baserunning & Defense

The active leader in career stolen-base percentage, Womack is one of the fastest players in the game. He is selective, waiting for the right count and time before taking off. However, he will get picked off on occasion because he takes an aggressive lead. At shortstop, Womack has proven to be capable. He possesses athleticism, OK range (especially to his left), and enough arm for the position. His biggest weakness is turning the double play.

2001 Outlook

Womack's speed always makes him a tempting leadoff man, but he needs to get on base more, which would lead to more productive seasons for the hitters behind him in the lineup. Womack prefers to play shortstop, but he probably would be better at second base or in right field. Still, the Diamondbacks have said they have no plan to shift his position again.

Position: SS
Bats: L **Throws:** R
Ht: 5' 9" **Wt:** 159

Opening Day Age: 31
Born: 9/25/69 in Danville, VA
ML Seasons: 7

Arizona

Overall Statistics

	G	AB	R	H	D	T	HR	RBI	SB	BB	SO	Avg	OBP	Slg
2000	146	617	95	167	21	14	7	57	45	30	74	.271	.307	.384
Career	641	2593	396	716	101	41	20	201	239	174	352	.276	.322	.370

Where He Hits the Ball

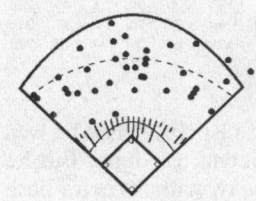 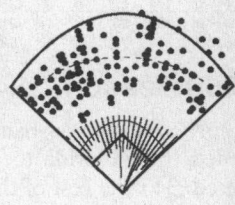

Vs. LHP   **Vs. RHP**

2000 Situational Stats

	AB	H	HR	RBI	Avg		AB	H	HR	RBI	Avg
Home	316	85	4	36	.269	LHP	123	34	1	17	.276
Road	301	82	3	21	.272	RHP	494	133	6	40	.269
First Half	359	102	5	33	.284	Sc Pos	139	40	2	50	.288
Scnd Half	258	65	2	24	.252	Clutch	76	23	1	13	.303

2000 Rankings (National League)

- 1st in triples
- 2nd in lowest on-base percentage for a leadoff hitter (.306)
- 4th in stolen bases and lowest on-base percentage
- 5th in at-bats and lowest on-base percentage vs. righthanded pitchers (.301)
- 6th in fielding percentage at shortstop (.970) and steals of third (5)
- Led the Diamondbacks in singles, triples, stolen bases, caught stealing (11), highest ground-ball/flyball ratio (1.5), stolen-base percentage (80.4), on-base percentage for a leadoff hitter (.306), bunts in play (18), lowest percentage of swings that missed (14.4) and steals of third (5)

Danny Bautista

Position: RF/LF/CF
Bats: R **Throws:** R
Ht: 5'11" **Wt:** 170

Opening Day Age: 28
Born: 5/24/72 in Santo Domingo, Dominican Republic
ML Seasons: 8
Pronunciation: bah-TEESE-tah

Overall Statistics

	G	AB	R	H	D	T	HR	RBI	SB	BB	SO	Avg	OBP	Slg
2000	131	351	54	100	20	7	11	59	6	25	50	.285	.333	.476
Career	526	1318	176	336	62	11	36	169	21	68	241	.255	.292	.401

2000 Situational Stats

	AB	H	HR	RBI	Avg		AB	H	HR	RBI	Avg
Home	157	50	5	23	.318	LHP	131	35	4	13	.267
Road	194	50	6	36	.258	RHP	220	65	7	46	.295
First Half	132	28	6	17	.212	Sc Pos	76	24	3	47	.316
Scnd Half	219	72	5	42	.329	Clutch	64	21	4	12	.328

2000 Season

Danny Bautista was batting just .191 when he was traded from Florida to Arizona last June. But he batted .317 the rest of the way, with 30 extra-base hits in 262 at-bats. Expected to be a spare outfielder or platoon player at the time of the deal, Bautista wound up getting most of the playing time in right field and backing up Steve Finley in center.

Hitting, Baserunning & Defense

Bautista hits the ball hard but doesn't have great home-run power. He is a free swinger who will not walk much. He showed last year that he can hit righthanders as well as southpaws. He runs well and can steal bases but is prone to baserunning mistakes. He is a very good outfielder with a powerful arm and the range to play center field.

2001 Outlook

The Diamondbacks picked up the $675,000 option on Bautista immediately after last season ended. With Arizona expected to move Erubial Durazo to right field, Bautista again will back up the team's regular outfielders. Whether he could start for a full year is unknown, but he makes an ideal fourth outfielder, since he can play all three positions and is used to coming off the bench.

Greg Colbrunn

Position: 1B
Bats: R **Throws:** R
Ht: 6'0" **Wt:** 205

Opening Day Age: 31
Born: 7/26/69 in Fontana, CA
ML Seasons: 9

Overall Statistics

	G	AB	R	H	D	T	HR	RBI	SB	BB	SO	Avg	OBP	Slg
2000	116	329	48	103	22	1	15	57	0	43	45	.313	.405	.523
Career	819	2416	287	697	130	9	81	369	29	143	390	.288	.337	.450

2000 Situational Stats

	AB	H	HR	RBI	Avg		AB	H	HR	RBI	Avg
Home	156	44	6	26	.282	LHP	137	39	6	25	.285
Road	173	59	9	31	.341	RHP	192	64	9	32	.333
First Half	119	37	6	19	.311	Sc Pos	85	27	2	38	.318
Scnd Half	210	66	9	38	.314	Clutch	59	15	1	8	.254

2000 Season

Greg Colbrunn was supposed to be Arizona's starting first baseman against lefthanded pitching last year. But as Erubiel Durazo's health wavered, Alex Cabrera emerged and Travis Lee also played some first, so Colbrunn saw his job description change. Still, from early August through the end of the season, Colbrunn played full-time and mostly batted cleanup. He responded by hitting .328 with nine homers and 35 RBI over that period.

Hitting, Baserunning & Defense

Colbrunn showed last year he can hit righthanded pitching if exposed to it consistently. He is an aggressive hitter who almost always gets the barrel of the bat on the ball. He also has learned to take a walk when pitched around. Colbrunn is an average first baseman without much range. He isn't fast and has attempted three stolen bases the past two years. A minor league backstop, he has been Arizona's emergency catcher but has not been needed there.

2001 Outlook

The signing of Mark Grace means Colbrunn likely will return to a reserve role. His experience as a pinch-hitter makes him valuable as a bench player, though he may have to share opportunities with free-agent signee Midre Cummings. Last year Arizona signed Colbrunn to a two-year extension.

Craig Counsell

Position: 2B/3B
Bats: L **Throws:** R
Ht: 6' 0" **Wt:** 175

Opening Day Age: 30
Born: 8/21/70 in South Bend, IN
ML Seasons: 5

Overall Statistics

	G	AB	R	H	D	T	HR	RBI	SB	BB	SO	Avg	OBP	Slg
2000	67	152	23	48	8	1	2	11	3	20	18	.316	.400	.421
Career	316	826	110	219	43	8	7	78	8	104	106	.265	.352	.362

2000 Situational Stats

	AB	H	HR	RBI	Avg		AB	H	HR	RBI	Avg
Home	60	17	0	1	.283	LHP	15	4	0	0	.267
Road	92	31	2	10	.337	RHP	137	44	2	11	.321
First Half	59	18	2	6	.305	Sc Pos	28	7	0	9	.250
Scnd Half	93	30	0	5	.323	Clutch	31	15	0	1	.484

2000 Season

Released by the Dodgers midway through spring training, Craig Counsell hooked on with Arizona. He batted .348 in 50 games at Triple-A Tucson before being called up May 31. After Lenny Harris and Andy Fox were traded, Counsell remained as Arizona's lefthanded-hitting utility infielder.

Hitting, Baserunning & Defense

Counsell is a patient hitter who will try to coax a walk or get hit by a pitch. He hits the ball mostly on the ground and has little power. He runs well and could bat leadoff since his on-base percentage is decent, though he doesn't have enough speed to produce a high stolen-base total. Once considered exclusively a second baseman, Counsell showed last year he has the arm to play shortstop and third base and thus can handle the utility role. He doesn't have the range to play shortstop regularly, however.

2001 Outlook

Versatility and his lefthanded bat make Counsell a good bet to stick as a reserve infielder. The Diamondbacks need someone able to play third base because of concerns about Matt Williams' health. Counsell can serve that role, and his smarts, work ethic and adaptability can keep him in the big leagues.

Geraldo Guzman

Position: SP
Bats: R **Throws:** R
Ht: 6' 1" **Wt:** 160

Opening Day Age: 28
Born: 11/28/72 in Arroyo Seco Tenares, Dominican Republic
ML Seasons: 1

Overall Statistics

	W	L	Pct.	ERA	G	GS	Sv	IP	H	BB	SO	HR	Ratio
2000	5	4	.556	5.37	13	10	0	60.1	66	22	52	8	1.46
Career	5	4	.556	5.37	13	10	0	60.1	66	22	52	8	1.46

2000 Situational Stats

	W	L	ERA	Sv	IP		AB	H	HR	RBI	Avg
Home	2	3	4.13	0	28.1	LHB	103	34	5	18	.330
Road	3	1	6.47	0	32.0	RHB	128	32	3	13	.250
First Half	1	0	1.13	0	8.0	Sc Pos	48	15	2	22	.313
Scnd Half	4	4	6.02	0	52.1	Clutch	14	3	2	2	.214

2000 Season

In early 1999, Geraldo Guzman was working as a carpenter, having been released by the Expos in 1991. The Diamondbacks discovered him in a sandlot league and sent him to Double-A. He worked his way into the rotation, was promoted to Triple-A and then got the call as an emergency starter for the Diamondbacks on July 6. He won his first two starts before struggling the rest of the way.

Pitching, Defense & Hitting

Guzman has a fastball with late life and a big-breaking slider that he can throw to either side of the plate. But he needs to build his endurance so his velocity can stay in the 92-94 MPH range all year. He has yet to develop a consistent third pitch. His offense is very poor; he even has trouble making contact on bunt attempts. His inexperience in the field is evident, and he won't get to many grounders hit back up the box.

2001 Outlook

After seven years off, Guzman should have plenty of mileage left in his arm. He might remain a starter this season, though his two-pitch repertoire and tendency to wear down make him more suited for the bullpen. That role also will require adjustments. He may be better off with a return to the minor leagues to hone his craft.

Arizona

Byung-Hyun Kim

Position: RP
Bats: R **Throws:** R
Ht: 5'11" **Wt:** 176

Opening Day Age: 22
Born: 1/19/79 in
Kwangju, South Korea
ML Seasons: 2

Overall Statistics

	W	L	Pct.	ERA	G	GS	Sv	IP	H	BB	SO	HR	Ratio
2000	6	6	.500	4.46	61	1	14	70.2	52	46	111	9	1.39
Career	7	8	.467	4.50	86	1	15	98.0	72	66	142	11	1.41

2000 Situational Stats

	W	L	ERA	Sv	IP		AB	H	HR	RBI	Avg
Home	3	1	4.19	10	34.1	LHB	113	27	3	17	.239
Road	3	5	4.71	4	36.1	RHB	147	25	6	19	.170
First Half	2	3	2.11	14	42.2	Sc Pos	76	15	2	26	.197
Scnd Half	4	3	8.04	0	28.0	Clutch	160	30	5	22	.188

2000 Season

The sidearming Byung-Hyun Kim filled in ably as Arizona's closer the first half of last season and could have merited a spot in the All-Star Game. But he faltered in the second half and at one point was sent back to Triple-A Tucson. He continued to have problems, especially with his control, the remainder of the season.

Pitching, Defense & Hitting

Kim's sidearm, almost underhand, stuff is difficult to hit. He throws 92 MPH, unusually hard for someone with a low arm angle. He also has a rising, wide-breaking slider. But Kim loses command at times and tends to nibble instead of challenging hitters. He is a good fielder but can lose concentration. Though he reduced his delivery time during his demotion, he still is relatively easy to run on. He has yet to show a decent swing as a hitter.

2001 Outlook

Kim's only obstacle might be the mental facet of the game. He makes no secret of his preference to start. The Diamondbacks have promised to consider it, but their decision to pick up the 2001 option for Armando Reynoso was not a promising sign. Kim's ability to pitch often could make him a very valuable reliever.

Damian Miller

Position: C
Bats: R **Throws:** R
Ht: 6'2" **Wt:** 212

Opening Day Age: 31
Born: 10/13/69 in
LaCrosse, WI
ML Seasons: 4

Overall Statistics

	G	AB	R	H	D	T	HR	RBI	SB	BB	SO	Avg	OBP	Slg
2000	100	324	43	89	24	0	10	44	2	36	74	.275	.347	.441
Career	268	854	100	235	58	2	26	118	3	68	207	.275	.329	.439

2000 Situational Stats

	AB	H	HR	RBI	Avg		AB	H	HR	RBI	Avg
Home	164	47	6	22	.287	LHP	104	28	3	10	.269
Road	160	42	4	22	.263	RHP	220	61	7	34	.277
First Half	165	47	8	28	.285	Sc Pos	90	23	4	35	.256
Scnd Half	159	42	2	16	.264	Clutch	51	14	1	10	.275

2000 Season

After batting .280 through early July, Damian Miller earned the No. 1 catching job. He raised his average as high as .299 at one point and set career highs in average, hits and walks. But playing more than he ever had in the majors, he slumped in September and missed the final two weeks with a sore foot.

Hitting, Baserunning & Defense

Miller is a line-drive hitter with occasional power who will still strike out fairly frequently. He has a history of hitting for a high average against lefthanded pitching. He is a good receiver who has at times been the personal catcher for Randy Johnson. Miller gets rid of the ball quickly on throws to second base and is agile behind the plate while blocking balls. He isn't much of a runner, though he did swipe a pair of bases last season.

2001 Outlook

Because of salary concerns, Miller will have the chance to be Arizona's No. 1 catcher. But how he holds up playing every day remains a question. He seems to be slow recovering from injuries and runs hot and cold as a hitter. Although he has just a little over three years of big league experience, Miller is 31 and needs to capitalize on this short window of opportunity.

Dan Plesac

Position: RP
Bats: L **Throws:** L
Ht: 6' 5" **Wt:** 217

Opening Day Age: 39
Born: 2/4/62 in Gary, IN
ML Seasons: 15
Pronunciation:
PLEE-sack
Nickname: Sac,
Sac-Man

Overall Statistics

	W	L	Pct.	ERA	G	GS	Sv	IP	H	BB	SO	HR	Ratio
2000	5	1	.833	3.15	62	0	0	40.0	34	26	45	4	1.50
Career	56	62	.475	3.65	884	14	154	957.0	887	349	895	92	1.29

2000 Situational Stats

	W	L	ERA	Sv	IP		AB	H	HR	RBI	Avg
Home	2	0	2.50	0	18.0	LHB	77	20	3	14	.260
Road	3	1	3.68	0	22.0	RHB	72	14	1	10	.194
First Half	1	0	3.80	0	21.1	Sc Pos	59	13	3	23	.220
Scnd Half	4	1	2.41	0	18.2	Clutch	41	12	3	12	.293

2000 Season

After working hard last spring training to improve his performance against righthanded hitters, Dan Plesac posted his best ERA since 1992. While he still was used to get tough lefthanded hitters out, he often was left in to face righthanders, holding them to a .194 batting average.

Pitching, Defense & Hitting

Plesac, whose fastball can touch 92 MPH, uses a slider as an out pitch against lefties. He'll sometimes throw that pitch exclusively in a given at-bat. But against righthanders, he uses more changeups and two-seam fastballs. He's also adjusted his position on the rubber to allow him to come inside. His delivery makes it difficult for him to field a chopper to the right side and on occasion to even cover first base. He holds his own against the running game but does very little with a bat.

2001 Outlook

When Plesac reported for spring training last year, he intended for it to be his final season. But his success in 2000 convinced him not to retire, and he signed a one-year, $2.4 million contract with Toronto in early December. He should continue to be an effective lefthanded specialist. It's a narrow role, but one a contending team like Toronto needs to fill.

Russ Springer

Position: RP
Bats: R **Throws:** R
Ht: 6' 4" **Wt:** 205

Opening Day Age: 32
Born: 11/7/68 in
Alexandria, LA
ML Seasons: 9

Overall Statistics

	W	L	Pct.	ERA	G	GS	Sv	IP	H	BB	SO	HR	Ratio
2000	2	4	.333	5.08	52	0	0	62.0	63	34	59	11	1.56
Career	19	32	.373	5.01	333	27	7	514.0	525	242	473	72	1.49

2000 Situational Stats

	W	L	ERA	Sv	IP		AB	H	HR	RBI	Avg
Home	2	1	6.03	0	37.1	LHB	70	17	3	15	.243
Road	0	3	3.65	0	24.2	RHB	171	46	8	33	.269
First Half	2	2	5.73	0	33.0	Sc Pos	82	20	3	37	.244
Scnd Half	0	2	4.34	0	29.0	Clutch	40	15	4	14	.375

2000 Season

Arizona gave Springer a two-year, $4 million contract to lure him back—he had been an expansion-draft pick before being traded to Atlanta—for a setup role. But early struggles relegated him to mopup and long-relief duties. He allowed 15 of 39 inherited runners to score and gave up 11 home runs in just 62 innings.

Pitching, Defense & Hitting

Springer has a hard fastball, but its straight and he sometimes has trouble throwing to the right spot. He can mix in a sharp curve but also needs to throw that pitch for a strike more consistently. His project this year may be to try a split-finger fastball, which would help him against hitters who sit on his fastball. Springer fields his position capably but does not have much of a pickoff move. He picked up a single last year, his first hit since 1996.

2001 Outlook

New manager Bob Brenly, who once played for split-finger guru Roger Craig, thinks Springer may benefit from the pitch. Still, Springer will not initially be counted on for a late-inning role, since pitchers who performed well as setup men last year will take those spots. Springer was excellent over the second half of the 1999 season, which was the last time he was an impending free agent.

Arizona

Kelly Stinnett

Position: C
Bats: R **Throws:** R
Ht: 5'11" **Wt:** 225

Opening Day Age: 31
Born: 2/4/70 in Lawton, OK
ML Seasons: 7
Pronunciation: STIH-net

Overall Statistics

	G	AB	R	H	D	T	HR	RBI	SB	BB	SO	Avg	OBP	Slg
2000	76	240	22	52	7	0	8	33	0	19	56	.217	.291	.346
Career	424	1206	139	281	52	4	39	140	6	123	326	.233	.318	.380

2000 Situational Stats

	AB	H	HR	RBI	Avg		AB	H	HR	RBI	Avg
Home	114	26	2	18	.228	LHP	48	12	1	4	.250
Road	126	26	6	15	.206	RHP	192	40	7	29	.208
First Half	153	35	8	28	.229	Sc Pos	61	16	2	23	.262
Scnd Half	87	17	0	5	.195	Clutch	34	5	1	4	.147

2000 Season

Kelly Stinnett split time with Damian Miller the last two months of 1998 and all of 1999. But Stinnett was hitting .227 early last July and was relegated to backup duties until September. He then started 18 games while Miller battled injuries. Stinnett's final average was a career low.

Hitting, Baserunning & Defense

In terms of pure power, Stinnett boasts as much as almost any player. But he rarely makes solid contact. He is most susceptible to good breaking pitches and has yet to find a way to stay back on offspeed stuff. He is a very good receiver. He has good reactions behind the plate and blocks balls very well. He relies on arm strength more than a quick release when throwing out runners. Despite his squat build, Stinnett runs well and can beat out an occasional chopper, although he won't steal many bases.

2001 Outlook

Arizona may look to trade Stinnett, rather than pay him a six-figure salary to back up Damian Miller. Unless his offense improves, he is best suited for a reserve role. He should keep a major league job for a while because of his defensive capabilities.

Greg Swindell

Position: RP
Bats: R **Throws:** L
Ht: 6'3" **Wt:** 230

Opening Day Age: 36
Born: 1/2/65 in Fort Worth, TX
ML Seasons: 15
Pronunciation: swin-DELL

Overall Statistics

	W	L	Pct.	ERA	G	GS	Sv	IP	H	BB	SO	HR	Ratio
2000	2	6	.250	3.20	64	0	1	76.0	71	20	64	7	1.20
Career	121	114	.515	3.80	566	269	5	2146.2	2224	488	1477	241	1.26

2000 Situational Stats

	W	L	ERA	Sv	IP		AB	H	HR	RBI	Avg
Home	1	4	3.15	0	40.0	LHB	107	17	2	8	.159
Road	1	2	3.25	1	36.0	RHB	181	54	5	23	.298
First Half	1	2	2.29	1	39.1	Sc Pos	71	17	3	23	.239
Scnd Half	1	4	4.17	0	36.2	Clutch	77	20	2	8	.260

2000 Season

Greg Swindell was a reliable middle man and setup reliever last season for the Diamondbacks. His 64 appearances tied the team record, and 24 of those outings lasted more than an inning. His won-loss record was misleading, since he allowed a run in only 18 of his appearances. He had one stretch, from early June until early July, in which he faced 55 batters without issuing a walk.

Pitching, Defense & Hitting

Though lefthanded, Swindell can be trusted against righthanded batters. He gets them out by using a forkball-type pitch, especially once he's ahead in the count. He'll also use a changeup that turns over, almost like a screwball. His control is very good (15 unintentional walks and one hit batter in 2000). Swindell is tough to run on, primarily because of his quick delivery. He's a capable hitter but rarely sets foot in the batter's box these days.

2001 Outlook

Despite his age, Swindell will be entering just his sixth season as a full-time reliever. He has adapted well to the role. He's been protected from too-frequent use the past two years, so he should be able to continue in the same vein in 2001. He is a valuable middle reliever who can eat innings.

Other Arizona Diamondbacks

Rod Barajas (**Pos**: C, **Age**: 25, **Bats**: R)

	G	AB	R	H	D	T	HR	RBI	SB	BB	SO	Avg	OBP	Slg
2000	5	13	1	3	0	0	1	3	0	0	4	.231	.231	.462
Career	10	29	4	7	1	0	2	6	0	1	5	.241	.267	.483

Barajas' catching skills rate among the best in Arizona's system. His batting average plunged at Triple-A last year, but he has a history of previous success along with some power. 2001 Outlook: C

Alex Cabrera (**Pos**: 1B/RF, **Age**: 29, **Bats**: R)

	G	AB	R	H	D	T	HR	RBI	SB	BB	SO	Avg	OBP	Slg
2000	31	80	10	21	2	1	5	14	0	4	21	.263	.299	.500
Career	31	80	10	21	2	1	5	14	0	4	21	.263	.299	.500

Cabrera looked like the second coming of Erubiel Durazo, with more power, last season. But after slugging 44 homers between the minors and Arizona, he signed with Japan in the offseason. 2001 Outlook: D

Jason Conti (**Pos**: RF, **Age**: 26, **Bats**: L)

	G	AB	R	H	D	T	HR	RBI	SB	BB	SO	Avg	OBP	Slg
2000	47	91	11	21	4	3	1	15	3	7	30	.231	.293	.374
Career	47	91	11	21	4	3	1	15	3	7	30	.231	.293	.374

Conti makes contact, has extra-base power and will steal some bases. With two season at Triple-A under his belt, he'll hope to stick with the Diamondbacks as a spare outfielder. 2001 Outlook: C

David Dellucci (**Pos**: RF, **Age**: 27, **Bats**: L)

	G	AB	R	H	D	T	HR	RBI	SB	BB	SO	Avg	OBP	Slg
2000	34	50	2	15	3	0	0	2	0	4	9	.300	.352	.360
Career	238	602	75	172	30	13	7	71	5	52	143	.286	.349	.414

Dellucci returned from a career-threatening wrist injury last year but didn't seem to drive the ball the way he had before the surgery. He still hit .300. 2001 Outlook: B

Nelson Figueroa (**Pos**: RHP, **Age**: 26)

	W	L	Pct.	ERA	G	GS	Sv	IP	H	BB	SO	HR	Ratio
2000	0	1	.000	7.47	3	3	0	15.2	17	5	7	4	1.40
Career	0	1	.000	7.47	3	3	0	15.2	17	5	7	4	1.40

The Diamondbacks included Figueroa in the package which netted Curt Schilling from Philadelphia. While he isn't imposing physcially, Figueroa has had success at every level. 2001 Outlook: C

Hanley Frias (**Pos**: SS/2B, **Age**: 27, **Bats**: B)

	G	AB	R	H	D	T	HR	RBI	SB	BB	SO	Avg	OBP	Slg
2000	75	112	18	23	5	0	2	6	2	17	18	.205	.310	.304
Career	173	311	53	72	9	3	4	25	6	47	45	.232	.332	.318

Frias' offense is lacking, but he's a jack-of-all-trades on the infield. His defense allowed him to spend his first full season in the majors last year. 2001 Outlook: B

Darren Holmes (**Pos**: RHP, **Age**: 34)

	W	L	Pct.	ERA	G	GS	Sv	IP	H	BB	SO	HR	Ratio
2000	0	1	.000	13.03	18	0	1	19.1	37	9	16	6	2.38
Career	32	29	.525	4.47	454	6	58	583.1	621	233	488	55	1.46

Holmes passed through St. Louis, Baltimore and Arizona (twice) last year. He did all that while surrendering a .416

batting average. Quite a feat. And he became a free agent in October. 2001 Outlook: C

Danny Klassen (**Pos**: 3B, **Age**: 25, **Bats**: R)

	G	AB	R	H	D	T	HR	RBI	SB	BB	SO	Avg	OBP	Slg
2000	29	76	13	18	3	0	2	8	1	8	24	.237	.318	.355
Career	59	185	25	40	5	1	5	16	2	17	57	.216	.289	.335

Klassen split time between Arizona and Triple-A last year. Primarily a shortstop in the minors, he saw most of his action at third base with the Diamondbacks, filling in for an injured Matt Williams. 2001 Outlook: C

Matt Mieske (**Pos**: LF, **Age**: 33, **Bats**: R)

	G	AB	R	H	D	T	HR	RBI	SB	BB	SO	Avg	OBP	Slg
2000	73	89	10	16	1	2	2	7	0	8	18	.180	.253	.303
Career	663	1547	225	406	78	10	56	226	7	124	313	.262	.318	.434

The Diamondbacks signed Mieske after Houston released him last August. He batted just .130 against lefthanders last season and Arizona did not offer him arbitration. 2001 Outlook: C

Mike Morgan (**Pos**: RHP, **Age**: 41)

	W	L	Pct.	ERA	G	GS	Sv	IP	H	BB	SO	HR	Ratio
2000	5	5	.500	4.87	60	4	5	101.2	123	40	56	10	1.60
Career	139	185	.429	4.22	537	410	8	2700.1	2857	912	1366	261	1.40

Morgan signed a deal with Arizona in early November that will bring him back for a 21st big league season. He helped as a starter and middle reliever last year, and even saved his first games since 1991. 2001 Outlook: B

Johnny Ruffin (**Pos**: RHP, **Age**: 29)

	W	L	Pct.	ERA	G	GS	Sv	IP	H	BB	SO	HR	Ratio
2000	0	0	-	9.00	5	0	0	9.0	14	3	5	4	1.89
Career	10	6	.625	4.12	136	0	3	192.1	182	89	159	25	1.41

It seems as though it was the Reagan administration when Ruffin was one of the top prospects in the White Sox system, but he's still only 29. He saved 20 games at Triple-A last year, but Arizona released him in November. 2001 Outlook: C

Rob Ryan (**Pos**: RF, **Age**: 27, **Bats**: L)

	G	AB	R	H	D	T	HR	RBI	SB	BB	SO	Avg	OBP	Slg
2000	27	27	4	8	1	1	0	2	0	4	7	.296	.406	.407
Career	47	56	8	15	2	1	2	7	0	5	15	.268	.339	.446

Ryan has been a consistent .300 hitter at every level of the minor leagues. Combined with a nifty batting eye, he's constantly on base. But he's too old to be considered an exciting prospect. 2001 Outlook: C

Turner Ward (**Pos**: RF, **Age**: 35, **Bats**: B)

	G	AB	R	H	D	T	HR	RBI	SB	BB	SO	Avg	OBP	Slg
2000	15	52	5	9	4	0	0	4	1	5	7	.173	.241	.250
Career	609	1533	209	385	72	11	39	217	33	185	241	.251	.332	.389

Ward's batting average in 82 Triple-A at-bats was over 200 points higher than his mark with Arizona last year. At his age, the retirement home may be looming with his next slump or injury. Arizona released him shortly after the season ended. 2001 Outlook: C

Arizona Diamondbacks Minor League Prospects

Organization Overview:

The suddenly aging Diamondbacks aren't going to be able to turn to the farm system to fill in their holes. Injuries and trades have done their part to deplete the depth in the system. Arizona's aggressiveness in the free-agent market also has cost the team a plethora of high draft picks since the franchise's inception. Arizona has managed to become a prominent factor in the international market, with deep financial resources aiding a talented scouting department. Byung-Hyun Kim, Erubiel Durazo, Geraldo Guzman, Vicente Padilla have been productive coups outside of the draft. Despite lacking a first-rounder last year, the early returns on their fourth and fifth-rounders, Josh Kroeger and Brad Cresse, are promising. Several of the organization's top pitching prospects suffered injury setbacks last year, including Nick Bierbrodt, Jeremy Ward, Ben Norris, Andrew Good and the biggest blow of them all, John Patterson.

Nick Bierbrodt

Position: P
Bats: L **Throws:** L
Ht: 6' 5" **Wt:** 190
Opening Day Age: 22
Born: 5/16/78 in Tarzana, CA

Recent Statistics

	W	L	ERA	G	GS	Sv	IP	H	R	BB	SO	HR
1999 AA El Paso	5	6	4.62	14	14	0	76.0	78	45	37	55	3
1999 AAA Tucson	1	4	7.27	11	11	0	43.1	57	42	30	43	9
2000 AAA Tucson	2	1	4.82	4	3	0	18.2	13	10	14	11	3
2000 R Diamondbcks	0	0	4.50	4	3	0	8.0	4	4	5	10	0
2000 AA El Paso	1	3	7.13	7	7	0	35.1	37	30	24	36	1

Since being drafted with the first pick in franchise history in 1996, Bierbrodt's ascent has been slow and arduous at times. After splitting his 1999 campaign between Double-A and Triple-A, injuries prevented the southpaw from making any progress last year. Nagging elbow and ribcage injuries limited Bierbrodt to only 13 starts at three different levels. Bierbrodt's best pitch is his changeup, but a sinking fastball and good curveball can be potent weapons, too. The Diamondbacks were encouraged by his health at year's end but the elbow again flared up in Dominican League play, and he was shut down.

Alex Cintron

Position: SS
Bats: B **Throws:** R
Ht: 6' 2" **Wt:** 180
Opening Day Age: 22
Born: 12/17/78 in Humacao, PR

Recent Statistics

	G	AB	R	H	D	T	HR	RBI	SB	BB	SO	Avg
1999 A High Desert	128	499	78	153	25	4	3	64	15	19	65	.307
2000 AA El Paso	125	522	83	157	30	6	4	59	9	29	56	.301
2000 MLE	125	501	65	136	26	4	3	46	6	19	59	.271

A little known 36th-rounder in 1997, Cintron rapidly has established himself as one of Arizona's best prospects. Even at 6-foot-3, 180 pounds, the wiry shortstop doesn't forfeit any range or quickness for the position. His size and athletic ability are on par with the new generation of shortstops taking over the game. A switch-hitter with excellent bat control, Cintron offers good power to the alleys that could develop into more home runs as he matures as a hitter. The rangy Puerto Rican needs to refine his basestealing techniques, but he already is an accomplished bunter.

Brad Cresse

Position: C
Bats: R **Throws:** R
Ht: 6' 2" **Wt:** 210
Opening Day Age: 22
Born: 7/31/78 in Long Beach, CA

Recent Statistics

	G	AB	R	H	D	T	HR	RBI	SB	BB	SO	Avg
2000 A High Desert	48	173	35	56	7	0	17	56	0	17	50	.324
2000 AA El Paso	15	42	9	11	1	0	1	10	0	6	12	.262

When Cresse singled in the game-winning run of the College World Series last summer, he capped off a stellar career at LSU. His success carried over into the minor league ranks after the Diamondbacks selected him in the fifth round of the amateur draft. Cresse had gone undrafted after his junior season, as scouts didn't project his defense, let alone his bat, to make an impact in the pros. In a testament to his work ethic, Cresse showed dramatic improvement as a senior, recapturing the status he had established as a sophomore. The son of long-time Dodgers coach, Mark Cresse, he made strides behind the plate to improve his defense and showcased his power potential by launching 17 home runs in his Class A California League debut. He earned a promotion to Double-A and finished 2000 in the Arizona Fall League.

Jack Cust

Position: OF
Bats: L **Throws:** R
Ht: 6' 1" **Wt:** 205
Opening Day Age: 22
Born: 1/16/79 in Flemington, NJ

Recent Statistics

	G	AB	R	H	D	T	HR	RBI	SB	BB	SO	Avg
1999 A High Desert	125	455	107	152	42	3	32	112	1	96	145	.334
2000 AA El Paso	129	447	100	131	32	6	20	75	12	117	150	.293
2000 MLE	129	430	79	114	28	4	15	59	7	78	160	.265

Cust has done nothing but mash since being drafted in the first round in 1997. He obliterated the high Class-A California League in '99 with 77 extra-base hits as a 20-year-old. Last year, he ripped 32 doubles and 20 home runs. He is a patient, disciplined hitter who generates longball power with a quick, uppercut swing. He's drawn over 200 walks in the last two seasons, but his approach has also resulted in back-to-back 145-plus strikeout campaigns. An average arm and limited range make the converted first baseman a liability in left field. Cust will be knocking on the door in Triple-A with his formidable big stick.

Lyle Overbay

Position: 1B **Opening Day Age:** 24
Bats: L **Throws:** L **Born:** 1/28/77 in
Ht: 6' 2" **Wt:** 215 Centralia, WA

Recent Statistics

	G	AB	R	H	D	T	HR	RBI	SB	BB	SO	Avg
1999 R Missoula	75	306	66	105	25	7	12	101	10	40	53	.343
2000 A South Bend	71	259	47	86	19	3	6	47	9	27	36	.332
2000 AA El Paso	62	244	43	86	16	2	8	49	3	28	39	.352
2000 MLE	62	232	33	74	14	1	6	38	2	18	41	.319

Overbay was plucked out of the University of Nevada in the 18th round of the '99 draft. He wasted little time showing he was overlooked on draft day by racking up a remarkable 100 RBI in his short-season debut. He effectively forced his way onto the fast track, splitting last year between the Midwest League and Double-A. The Diamondbacks are encouraged by his lefthanded line-drive stroke and the gap power he showed in his first two years, and they feel his professional hitting style and advanced strike-zone judgment could lead to more over-the-fence power. A converted collegiate outfielder, he is making a smooth transition to first base. He put the final touching on his 2000 season in the Arizona Fall League and will put pressure on Greg Colbrunn, Erubiel Durazo and Alex Cabrera in the next year and a half.

John Patterson

Position: P **Opening Day Age:** 23
Bats: R **Throws:** R **Born:** 1/30/78 in Orange,
Ht: 6' 6" **Wt:** 197 TX

Recent Statistics

	W	L	ERA	G	GS	Sv	IP	H	R	BB	SO	HR
1999 AA El Paso	8	6	4.77	18	18	0	100.0	98	61	42	117	16
1999 AAA Tucson	1	5	7.04	7	6	0	30.2	43	26	18	29	3
2000 AAA Tucson	0	2	7.80	3	2	0	15.0	21	14	9	10	1

Arizona's premier pitching prospect, Patterson had his train derailed last spring with the news of Tommy John surgery. Signed for $6.075 million after the Expos drafted him with the fifth overall pick in 1996, they lost his rights through a never-before-used loophole. As the lanky righty made his way up the ladder, he looked like he was worth every penny of his bonus. Patterson has the mid-90s fastball of the most dominant power pitchers, yet also can summon the hammer curve and change to knock hitters out. The surgery is expected to get him back by mid-May 2001 and shouldn't affect his velocity.

Bret Prinz

Position: P **Opening Day Age:** 23
Bats: R **Throws:** R **Born:** 6/15/77 in
Ht: 6' 3" **Wt:** 200 Chicago Heights, IL

Recent Statistics

	W	L	ERA	G	GS	Sv	IP	H	R	BB	SO	HR
1999 A South Bend	6	10	4.48	30	23	0	138.2	129	82	52	98	16
2000 A South Bend	1	0	0.00	6	0	1	7.1	2	2	1	10	0
2000 AA El Paso	9	1	3.56	53	0	26	60.2	71	24	16	69	6

Until the Diamondbacks converted Prinz to the bullpen, he was a borderline pitching prospect. The shift to closer jumpstarted his career, however, as he rapidly adapted into the role. An 18th-rounder in 1998, the righty dropped his arm angle to a sidearm release, subsequently increasing his velocity into the mid-90s. The Organization Player of the Year overmatched the Midwest League early on before moving up to the Double-A Texas League. While he nailed down 26 saves at El Paso, Prinz surrendered 71 hits in 60.2 innings—numbers that conflict with his 16 walks, 69 Ks and powerful fastball. He finished his breakout campaign working on his breaking and offspeed offerings in the Arizona Fall League.

Carlos Urquiola

Position: OF **Opening Day Age:** 20
Bats: L **Throws:** R **Born:** 4/22/80 in
Ht: 5' 8" **Wt:** 150 Caracas, VZ

Recent Statistics

	G	AB	R	H	D	T	HR	RBI	SB	BB	SO	Avg
1999 A South Bend	93	384	66	139	13	3	0	35	20	22	32	.362
2000 A High Desert	40	165	34	60	6	2	0	12	24	15	16	.364
2000 AA El Paso	68	225	33	68	8	1	0	18	13	20	17	.302
2000 MLE	68	216	26	59	7	0	0	14	9	13	18	.273

One of the few basestealing threats coming in the system, Urquiola has swiped 57 bases in the past two years. The diminutive 20-year-old possesses almost no power. A slap-hitter, Urquiola knows his limitations and sprays the ball to all fields. He also keeps the ball on the ground to utilize his speed. After winning the Class-A Midwest League batting title in '99 with a .362 average, he proved his bat was no fluke, earning a promotion to Double-A. Arizona still is trying to find the best position for the former second baseman. Center field or left field are options that can take advantage of his blazing speed, but he still needs work.

Others to Watch

Drafted in the eighth round of the '99 draft, lefthander **Chris Capuano's** (22) debut was delayed so he could complete his degree at Duke University. He still managed to go 10-4, 2.21 ERA in the Midwest League, allowing just 68 hits in 101.2 innings despite joining the organization in June. . . Arizona's 1999 first-rounder, righthander **Casey Daigle** (19), made his long-awaited debut last year after a broken finger sidelined him for more than a year. He has one of the best arms in the system. . . Signed out of the Dominican for a lucrative signing bonus, shortstop **Jerry Gil** (18) hit .225 in the Rookie-level Pioneer League. At 6-foot-3 and 185-pounds, he's a raw athlete and projects to add power. . . Outfielder **Brian Gordon** (22) emerged last year with a broad base of skills, reaching double digits in doubles, triples, homers and steals. . . The fourth overall pick in the '99 draft, **Corey Myers** (20), has been disappointing. Shifted from shortstop to third base, his .125 average in the Midwest League earned him a demotion to Rookie-ball. . . Outfielder **Luis Terrero** (20) lacks command of the strike zone, but he offers plus-defensive tools, as well as good bat speed and power potential.

Ted Turner Field

Offense

Turner Field's large dimensions have forced the Braves to alter their offensive attack over the past two years. Always among the NL leaders in home runs, the Braves were in the middle of the pack last year. The deep alley in right hurts lefthanded power hitters unless they jerk the ball down the line. The outfield is spacious, which creates numerous bloop hits. The ball carries best to left field, but has a tendency to die in center early in the season.

Defense

The spacious gaps led the Braves last year to opt for such speedy outfielders as Andruw Jones, Brian Jordan and Reggie Sanders. This is interesting to note, considering that the team is tossing out the possibility of Chipper Jones and B.J. Surhoff manning the outfield next season. The outfield wall produces pure bounces except in right field, where a chain link fence protects the out-of-town scoreboard, creating soft, inconsistent returns. The near-perfect grass surface is one of the game's best, as well as one of its fastest.

Who It Helps the Most

Turner Field surrenders few cheap homers, especially to lefthanded hitters. That fact instills confidence in righthanded pitchers and allows them to challenge hitters from both sides of the plate. Over the last three years, Greg Maddux has a 2.58 ERA at home, compared to a 3.30 figure on the road.

Who It Hurts the Most

Lefthanded sluggers who hit most of their homers to right-center find themselves owning little more than warning track power here. Surhoff hit just one home run in 60 at-bats at Turner in 2000. Lefthanded pitchers also have to be careful when facing righthanded hitters who have a tendency to pull the ball down the line for home runs.

Rookies & Newcomers

The Braves' young pitchers have little difficulty adjusting to Turner Field. That should bode well if such prospects as Matt McClendon, Derrick Lewis or Damian Moss receive a shot. Top position prospect Marcus Giles is a line-drive hitting second baseman who should love the park's spacious gaps.

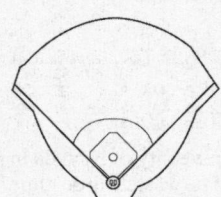

Dimensions: LF-335, LCF-380, CF-401, RCF-390, RF-330

Capacity: 49,714

Elevation: 1050 feet

Surface: Grass

Foul Territory: Small

Park Factors

2000 Season

	Home Games			Away Games			
	Braves	Opp	Total	Braves	Opp	Total	Index
G	72	72	144	72	72	144	—
Avg	.278	.255	.266	.264	.257	.261	102
AB	2362	2512	4874	2511	2413	4924	99
R	353	301	654	356	326	682	96
H	657	641	1298	662	621	1283	101
2B	111	109	220	132	116	248	90
3B	12	8	20	13	11	24	84
HR	75	72	147	83	76	159	93
BB	267	206	473	264	210	474	101
SO	401	494	895	491	478	969	93
E	60	87	147	60	66	126	117
E-Infield	54	72	126	52	61	113	112
LHB-Avg	.296	.280	.288	.244	.267	.254	113
LHB-HR	21	26	47	18	22	40	113
RHB-Avg	.266	.242	.253	.276	.253	.264	96
RHB-HR	54	46	100	65	54	119	87

1998-2000

	Home Games			Away Games			
	Braves	Opp	Total	Braves	Opp	Total	Index
G	217	217	434	217	217	434	—
Avg	.274	.244	.259	.266	.250	.258	100
AB	7105	7446	14551	7634	7236	14870	98
R	1084	798	1882	1116	894	2010	94
H	1946	1819	3765	2027	1807	3834	98
2B	385	299	684	400	317	717	97
3B	34	30	64	37	27	64	102
HR	246	180	426	282	185	467	93
BB	773	614	1387	801	669	1470	96
SO	1267	1608	2875	1430	1556	2986	98
E	153	203	356	146	180	326	109
E-Infield	135	164	299	128	154	282	106
LHB-Avg	.276	.247	.262	.259	.259	.259	101
LHB-HR	82	64	146	76	67	143	102
RHB-Avg	.272	.243	.257	.270	.245	.257	100
RHB-HR	164	116	280	206	118	324	90

2000 Rankings (National League)

- Third-highest LHB batting-average factor
- Second-lowest RHB home-run factor

Bobby Cox

2000 Season

For the second time in as many seasons, Bobby Cox got the most out of a team that wound up missing numerous key components. Despite losing a top starting pitcher for the entire season, two key relievers for most of the campaign, his second baseman for the second half and shuffling an outfield that looked like an urgent care center, Cox guided the Braves to 95 wins and their ninth straight division title.

Offense

Cox' offense succeeds because he allows hitters to work their way out of slumps instead of forcing them to sit. With the addition of Quilvio Veras and Rafael Furcal at the top of lineup, Cox showed a willingness to run more often than in the past. But after Veras was lost in July, the manager relied more on his conservative, station-to-station approach that succeeds with home runs. With his deep bullpen, Cox uses veteran pinch-hitters frequently and as well as anyone.

Pitching & Defense

Due to the presence of veteran starters, Cox does not receive the deserved recognition for his ability to handle pitchers. He trusts his veterans and is willing to go with them for an extra batter or two. Cox tied Baltimore's Mike Hargrove with the fewest quick hooks in the majors last year with just seven. His deep bullpen allows Cox to use as many as four relievers a night, leading to frequent double switches. He is a strong believer in having a steady defense up the middle and rarely employs exaggerated defensive shifts.

2001 Outlook

Late-season rumors claimed Cox was ready to step down as Atlanta's skipper after more than 10 years on the job. Those who know Cox well, however, believe he will remain at the helm for another three or four years. He likes his team and wants badly to add another world championship to a legacy that includes ranking 13th in major league history with 1,616 managerial wins.

Born: 5/21/41 in Tulsa, OK

Playing Experience: 1968-1969, NYY

Managerial Experience: 19 seasons

Manager Statistics

Year	Team, Lg	W	L	Pct	GB	Finish
2000	Atlanta, NL	95	67	.586	—	1st East
19 Seasons		1616	1271	.559	—	—

2000 Starting Pitchers by Days Rest

	<=3	4	5	6+
Braves Starts	7	101	28	21
Braves ERA	3.89	3.78	3.75	6.10
NL Avg Starts	2	80	50	21
NL ERA	5.00	4.61	4.60	5.18

2000 Situational Stats

	Bobby Cox	NL Average
Hit & Run Success %	34.4	33.8
Stolen Base Success %	72.5	68.8
Platoon Pct.	58.6	53.2
Defensive Subs	11	19
High-Pitch Outings	6	14
Quick/Slow Hooks	7/16	14/16
Sacrifice Attempts	109	87

2000 Rankings (National League)

- 1st in steals of third base (24), double steals (10), squeeze plays (11), pitchouts (59), pitchouts with a runner moving (17) and starts on three days rest (7)
- 2nd in stolen base attempts (204), steals of second base (123) and sacrifice bunt attempts (109)
- 3rd in stolen-base percentage (72.5) and 2+ pitching changes in low-scoring games (27)

Atlanta

Andy Ashby

Position: SP
Bats: R **Throws:** R
Ht: 6' 5" **Wt:** 202

Opening Day Age: 33
Born: 7/11/67 in
Kansas City, MO
ML Seasons: 10

2000 Season

Andy Ashby was the epitome of fire and ice after the Braves acquired him from Philadelphia during last year's All-Star break. He hadn't pitched well for the Phillies in the first half, but impressed his new Atlanta teammates by going 3-0 with two complete games in his first three outings. He then faltered to an 0-4 record over five starts from August 13 to September 3 before finishing strongly by winning four of his last five starts in September. However, manager Bobby Cox was not impressed enough to keep Ashby in the rotation for the playoffs.

Pitching

When his confidence is peaking, Ashby can dominate righthanded hitters with his hard, two-seam fastball that has a tendency to dart inside. He can mix that offering with his four-seam fastball, slider and split-finger fastball, all of which have good movement. Unfortunately, Ashby had difficulty keeping his pitches low in the strike zone last year. He also didn't fare well on the road, posting a 5.98 ERA, the fourth-worst mark in the league. He has shown a tendency to lose velocity and wear down over the course of a season, though last year was an exception.

Defense & Hitting

Ashby does not hurt himself with his glove. He is light on his feet while on the mound and is one of the more aggressive pitchers in the game when it comes to trying to nail the lead baserunner on a bunt. He also does a laudable job of holding runners close, thereby reducing the number of successful stolen-base attempts. Although he is not a good hitter, Ashby is a capable bunter in sacrifice situations.

2001 Outlook

Ashby signed a three-year, $22.5 million contract with the pitching-rich Dodgers in early December. He remains a capable pitcher, particularly as a No. 3 or 4 starter, yet he has had difficulty living up to expectations in high-profile situations at Philadelphia and Atlanta. Consistency continues to be the primary ingredient preventing Ashby from being one of the top two starters in a rotation.

Overall Statistics

	W	L	Pct.	ERA	G	GS	Sv	IP	H	BB	SO	HR	Ratio
2000	12	13	.480	4.92	31	31	0	199.1	216	61	106	29	1.39
Career	84	87	.491	4.10	254	241	1	1542.1	1573	457	1016	175	1.32

How Often He Throws Strikes

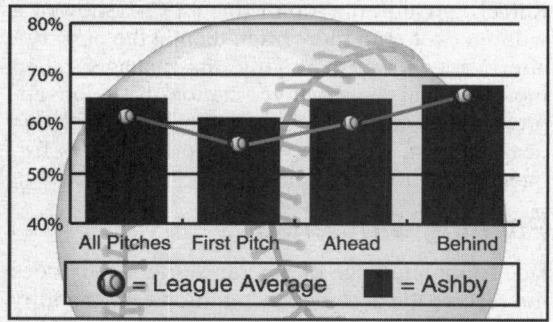

○ = League Average   ■ = Ashby

2000 Situational Stats

	W	L	ERA	Sv	IP		AB	H	HR	RBI	Avg
Home	6	6	4.05	0	109.0	LHB	371	116	16	54	.313
Road	6	7	5.98	0	90.1	RHB	401	100	13	57	.249
First Half	4	7	5.68	0	101.1	Sc Pos	180	53	5	75	.294
Scnd Half	8	6	4.13	0	98.0	Clutch	57	11	1	3	.193

2000 Rankings (National League)

- 2nd in fewest pitches thrown per batter (3.38)
- 3rd in fewest GDPs induced per nine innings (0.5)
- 4th in highest ERA on the road (5.98)
- 7th in fewest strikeouts per nine innings (4.8)
- 8th in losses (13) and errors at pitcher (3)
- 9th in highest stolen-base percentage allowed (71.4)

Rafael Furcal

2000 Season

An impressive showing in spring training earned 19-year-old Rafael Furcal a spot on the Atlanta roster. Since the young middle infielder was making the jump from Class-A to the major leagues, manager Bobby Cox wanted to start the rookie two or three times a week. Instead, injuries to Walt Weiss and Quilvio Veras landed Furcal in a starting role that he parlayed into National League Rookie of the Year accolades.

Hitting

The switch-hitting Furcal is a patient batter who keeps the ball on the ground, allowing his outstanding speed to help him get on base. He saw 4.10 pitches per plate appearance while waiting for an offering he could handle. A premier bunter, Furcal led the league by putting 33 bunts in play last season. While most players of his ilk are considered slap hitters, Furcal has the ability to drive the ball. He hit all four of his home runs after September 1, and Cox believes Furcal will reach double digits in roundtrippers in the near future.

Baserunning & Defense

Furcal impressed his coaching staff and scouts alike with his ability to move between shortstop and second base with ease. He has good range at both positions and owns the strongest arm among National League infielders. No one is better at getting the ball in the hole at short and retiring the runner at first base. Furcal is one of the game's fastest players. His 40 stolen bases set a major league record for swipes by a 19-year-old, breaking Ty Cobb's mark of 23 set in 1906.

2001 Outlook

With Weiss expected to retire and Veras returning from injury, Furcal will be Atlanta's starting shortstop, provided the Braves do not make a run at a premier free agent. Should the team sign a free agent, there has been talk of possibly moving Furcal to third base and Chipper Jones into the outfield. Regardless of where he lands, Furcal will reside near the top of the Atlanta lineup.

Position: SS/2B
Bats: B **Throws:** R
Ht: 5'10" **Wt:** 165

Opening Day Age: 20
Born: 8/24/80 in Loma de Cabrera, Dominican Republic
ML Seasons: 1

Overall Statistics

	G	AB	R	H	D	T	HR	RBI	SB	BB	SO	Avg	OBP	Slg
2000	131	455	87	134	20	4	4	37	40	73	80	.295	.394	.382
Career	131	455	87	134	20	4	4	37	40	73	80	.295	.394	.382

Where He Hits the Ball

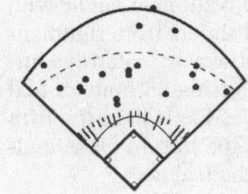
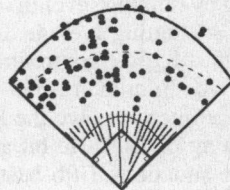

Vs. LHP   **Vs. RHP**

2000 Situational Stats

	AB	H	HR	RBI	Avg		AB	H	HR	RBI	Avg
Home	234	79	1	19	.338	LHP	96	24	0	5	.250
Road	221	55	3	18	.249	RHP	359	110	4	32	.306
First Half	168	51	0	12	.304	Sc Pos	116	29	1	33	.250
Scnd Half	287	83	4	25	.289	Clutch	58	18	1	8	.310

2000 Rankings (National League)

- 1st in bunts in play (33)
- 2nd in caught stealing (14), fewest GDPs per GDP situation (3.0%), highest percentage of extra bases taken as a runner (72.5) and lowest fielding percentage at shortstop (.950)
- 3rd in highest groundball/flyball ratio (2.2) and errors at shortstop (23)
- Led the Braves in stolen bases, caught stealing (14), highest groundball/flyball ratio (2.2), most pitches seen per plate appearance (4.10), fewest GDPs per GDP situation (3.0%), batting average vs. righthanded pitchers, on-base percentage vs. righthanded pitchers (.404), batting average at home, bunts in play (33) and highest percentage of pitches taken (59.9)

Atlanta

Andres Galarraga

Signed By
RANGERS

2000 Season

After missing all of the 1999 campaign while undergoing treatment for non-Hodgkin's lymphoma, Andres Galarraga overcame long odds to re-emerge as one of the team's offensive catalysts. The Big Cat put together a torrid start in April and May to earn his fifth trip to the All-Star Game before cooling off after the break. He placed third on the team in home runs and reached the century mark in RBI for the fifth time since 1995.

Hitting

Galarraga remains one of the game's premier hitters with his quick, powerful stroke that produces hits to all fields. Aggressive in his unique, open stance, he continued to dominate lefthanded pitching by ranking seventh in the National League with a .347 batting average. Hard sliders from righthanders still give him trouble, however. Galarraga improves in crunch time—10 of his 28 homers tied the contest or gave the Braves the lead in the fifth inning or later. He hit at a .365 clip in close-and-late situations, fifth-best in the league.

Baserunning & Defense

A Gold Glove winner in 1989 and 1990, Galarraga was not as fluid last year around first base. Although he remains agile for his size, he committed 14 errors and had a .988 fielding percentage, both of which ranked next-to-last among NL first basemen. Galarraga still is one of the more proficient fielders at digging throws out of the dirt, but his handiwork on hit balls has become suspect. He's also slowed down on the basepaths. He was successful on three of eight stolen-base attempts, resulting in the second-lowest theft total of his career.

2001 Outlook

He had said he would consider retirement if he didn't remain with the Braves, but the Rangers convinced Galarraga to sign for one year at $6.25 million. While he remains one of the league's more productive and dangerous power hitters, he'll turn 40 on June 18. The Rangers are hoping The Ballpark in Arlington can revive the pop in his bat that disappeared in the second half of 2000. He will be the regular DH and play some first base, as well as help mentor Texas first-base prospect Carlos Pena.

Position: 1B
Bats: R **Throws:** R
Ht: 6' 3" **Wt:** 235

Opening Day Age: 39
Born: 6/18/61 in Caracas, Venezuela
ML Seasons: 15
Pronunciation: ON-dress gahl-lah-RAH-guh
Nickname: Big Cat

Overall Statistics

	G	AB	R	H	D	T	HR	RBI	SB	BB	SO	Avg	OBP	Slg
2000	141	494	67	149	25	1	28	100	3	36	126	.302	.369	.526
Career	1915	7123	1078	2070	389	31	360	1272	124	503	1741	.291	.348	.506

Where He Hits the Ball

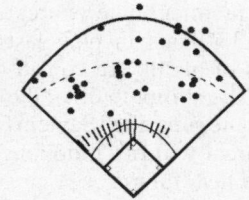 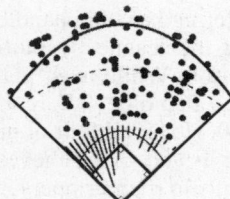

Vs. LHP　　　　**Vs. RHP**

2000 Situational Stats

	AB	H	HR	RBI	Avg		AB	H	HR	RBI	Avg
Home	224	71	14	52	.317	LHP	118	41	3	18	.347
Road	270	78	14	48	.289	RHP	376	108	25	82	.287
First Half	296	87	20	62	.294	Sc Pos	166	49	10	77	.295
Scnd Half	198	62	8	38	.313	Clutch	63	23	7	17	.365

2000 Rankings (National League)

- 2nd in errors at first base (14) and lowest fielding percentage at first base (.988)
- 3rd in hit by pitch (17) and lowest percentage of extra bases taken as a runner (27.7)
- 5th in batting average in the clutch, lowest percentage of pitches taken (46.8) and highest percentage of swings that missed (30.4)
- Led the Braves in hit by pitch (17), strikeouts, batting average in the clutch and cleanup slugging percentage (.470)
- Led NL first basemen in hit by pitch (17)

Tom Glavine

Position: SP
Bats: L **Throws:** L
Ht: 6' 0" **Wt:** 185

Opening Day Age: 35
Born: 3/25/66 in
Concord, MA
ML Seasons: 14
Pronunciation: GLA-vin

2000 Season

Tom Glavine made a serious bid last year to capture his third Cy Young Award by leading the National League in victories and posting his fifth 20-win campaign. The lefthander won his first five decisions while compiling a 1.80 ERA. He then went 6-0 with a 2.95 ERA in July, becoming the 96th pitcher to reach the 200-win mark with his final triumph that month. Most importantly, Glavine was 10-2 with a 3.01 ERA in 14 starts following an Atlanta loss.

Pitching

No one is more intense on the mound than Glavine. After watching umpires fail to give him the outside corner in 1999, he made the adjustment by developing a cut fastball similar to Greg Maddux'. The pitch enabled him to work inside more effectively. It's just as accurate as his heavy, sinking fastball and devastating changeup, helping Glavine rank 10th in the league by allowing just 2.43 walks per nine innings. Glavine also remains durable, as evidenced by his 3,706 pitches last year, a total surpassed by only Randy Johnson and Livan Hernandez. Despite the high pitch counts, Glavine allowed only 10.9 baserunners per nine innings, sixth-best in the NL.

Defense & Hitting

Glavine is much more than a good pitcher. He helps himself by fielding his position as well as any hurler in the game, handling 52 chances without an error in 2000. The lefthander also does a good job of holding runners on base. Glavine takes pride in his hitting and can help himself at the plate. He had 14 sacrifices last year, but his two RBI represented his lowest output since 1987.

2001 Outlook

Glavine has shown no signs of slowing down after 13 full seasons in the major leagues. He can make the necessary adjustments to hitters and umpires, and his stuff is as good as it's ever been. Determined to leave a lasting impression on the game, Glavine should remain one of the premier pitchers for the next several seasons and solidify his eventual place in Cooperstown.

Overall Statistics

	W	L	Pct.	ERA	G	GS	Sv	IP	H	BB	SO	HR	Ratio
2000	21	9	.700	3.40	35	35	0	241.0	222	65	152	24	1.19
Career	208	125	.625	3.39	434	434	0	2900.2	2751	965	1811	202	1.28

How Often He Throws Strikes

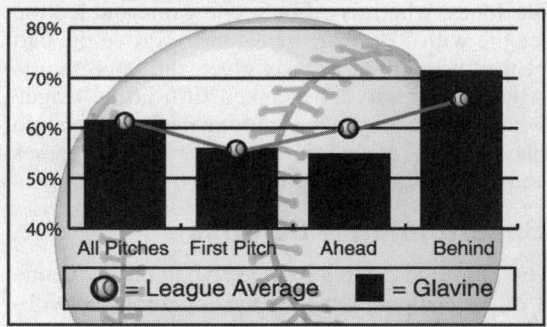

2000 Situational Stats

	W	L	ERA	Sv	IP		AB	H	HR	RBI	Avg
Home	12	3	3.05	0	130.0	LHB	190	46	4	18	.242
Road	9	6	3.81	0	111.0	RHB	719	176	20	66	.245
First Half	9	5	3.61	0	132.0	Sc Pos	182	46	4	55	.253
Scnd Half	12	4	3.14	0	109.0	Clutch	55	7	1	2	.127

2000 Rankings (National League)

- 1st in wins and games started
- 2nd in sacrifice bunts (14)
- 3rd in shutouts (2) and pitches thrown (3,706)
- 4th in innings pitched and winning percentage
- 5th in batters faced (992), runners caught stealing (10) and lowest on-base percentage allowed (.296)
- Led the Braves in sacrifice bunts (14), wins, games started, walks allowed, pitches thrown (3,706), runners caught stealing (10), lowest stolen-base percentage allowed (61.5), most run support per nine innings (5.6), most GDPs induced per nine innings (0.7), lowest batting average allowed vs. lefthanded batters and winning percentage

Atlanta

Andruw Jones

Position: CF
Bats: R **Throws:** R
Ht: 6' 1" **Wt:** 210

Opening Day Age: 23
Born: 4/23/77 in Willemstad, Curacao
ML Seasons: 5

2000 Season

The Braves finally received the breakthrough season they had been expecting from Andruw Jones. The 23-year-old parlayed his .322 batting average in June into his finest year yet, featuring career marks in runs, home runs and RBI. He also played in his first All-Star Game and remains the National League's best defender in center field.

Hitting

After battling concentration lapses during his first three full seasons in the majors, everything seemed to click for Jones. No longer a free swinger, he rarely chases bad pitches and is not a guaranteed out when thrown a breaking ball. Instead, the durable Jones, who missed only one game and led the league with 729 plate appearances, drove the ball nearly every time he was given the opportunity. Always aggressive, he ranked fifth in the league with a .387 average when putting the first pitch into play. He also placed third with 59 multihit games and 199 hits, and fifth with 355 total bases.

Baserunning & Defense

His failure to catch a routine flyball during Game 1 of the National League Division Series notwithstanding, Jones is the best outfielder of this generation. His instincts are unmatched, enabling him to get to balls that most other center fielders watch fall in the gaps. He has learned how to take the shortest route to flyballs, and owns one of the strongest and most accurate arms of any outfielder in the game. The lone criticism centers on his nonchalant basket catches, a la Willie Mays. Jones is an excellent baserunner who stole 21 bases in 26 attempts.

2001 Outlook

Many observers believe that Jones is on the verge of moving into the elite group of superstar players. He possesses as much natural ability as anyone in the major leagues, and he now is combining experience and maturity to take his game to a higher level. He has learned from his mistakes, and his varied tools make him the total package. He won't turn 24 until late April, which means he could be very special very soon.

Overall Statistics

	G	AB	R	H	D	T	HR	RBI	SB	BB	SO	Avg	OBP	Slg
2000	161	656	122	199	36	6	36	104	21	59	100	.303	.366	.541
Career	666	2335	379	635	129	21	116	361	95	238	468	.272	.344	.494

Where He Hits the Ball

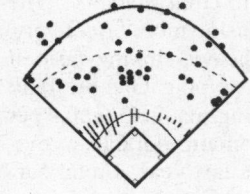

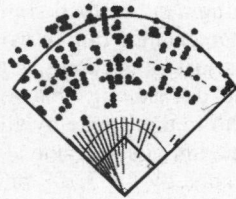

Vs. LHP   **Vs. RHP**

2000 Situational Stats

	AB	H	HR	RBI	Avg		AB	H	HR	RBI	Avg
Home	318	94	15	42	.296	LHP	134	42	4	13	.313
Road	338	105	21	62	.311	RHP	522	157	32	91	.301
First Half	346	108	23	54	.312	Sc Pos	173	48	8	69	.277
Scnd Half	310	91	13	50	.294	Clutch	86	28	6	23	.326

2000 Rankings (National League)

- 1st in at-bats and plate appearances (729)
- 2nd in fielding percentage in center field (.996)
- 3rd in hits
- 4th in games played
- 5th in runs scored, total bases (355) and highest percentage of extra bases taken as a runner (71.2)
- 10th in pitches seen (2,682)
- Led the Braves in home runs, at-bats, runs scored, hits, singles, triples, total bases (355), pitches seen (2,682), plate appearances (729), batting average with the bases loaded (.417), slugging percentage vs. righthanded pitchers (.565) and games played
- Led NL center fielders in batting average, at-bats, hits, doubles and total bases (355)

Chipper Jones

2000 Season

After earning National League MVP honors in 1999, Chipper Jones put together an impressive encore that left no doubt he is one of baseball's best all-around players. Despite fighting through painful bone chips in his right elbow throughout the season, Jones equalled his career high in RBI while hitting better than .300 and clubbing more than 30 homers for the fourth time in five seasons. That production earned the third baseman a six-year, $90 million contract extension in August.

Hitting

The switch-hitting Jones has become more aggressive against lefthanded pitchers recently, resulting in a .415 average versus southpaws in 2000. He has been consistent thanks in part to a rigorous offseason conditioning program. He had two diverse career-long streaks in 2000—a 19-game hitting streak in early June and a 3-for-41 stretch with runners in scoring position in August. Nevertheless, Jones became only the third third baseman in history to produce five consecutive 100-RBI seasons, joining Pie Traynor and Al Rosen. Jones also is one of the game's toughest batters to strike out, rare for a player with his type of power.

Baserunning & Defense

If there is a flaw in Jones' game, it's his defense. Critics were everywhere when he committed a key error in the final game of the regular season that wound up costing the Braves home-field advantage in the playoffs. He also had a crucial miscue in the postseason, prompting Jones to say he would move to first base or the outfield if it would help the team. He has good range, a strong arm and good instincts. Jones is a heady baserunner who stole 14 bases in 2000 after swiping 25 the year before.

2001 Outlook

Jones will continue to hit third in Atlanta's lineup, but his place at third base could be in jeopardy. He said he would be willing to move to the outfield, manning left field if Brian Jordan remains with the team or playing right if Jordan is dealt. Regardless of the glove he wears, Jones joins Andruw Jones as the two most important pieces to the Braves' lineup. Another run at MVP honors is probable.

Position: 3B
Bats: B **Throws:** R
Ht: 6' 4" **Wt:** 210

Opening Day Age: 28
Born: 4/24/72 in DeLand, FL
ML Seasons: 7

Overall Statistics

	G	AB	R	H	D	T	HR	RBI	SB	BB	SO	Avg	OBP	Slg
2000	156	579	118	180	38	1	36	111	14	95	64	.311	.404	.566
Career	935	3469	660	1051	204	18	189	635	97	554	527	.303	.396	.536

Where He Hits the Ball

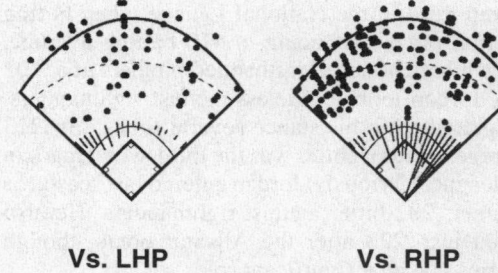

Vs. LHP   **Vs. RHP**

2000 Situational Stats

	AB	H	HR	RBI	Avg		AB	H	HR	RBI	Avg
Home	288	93	18	69	.323	LHP	130	54	12	33	.415
Road	291	87	18	42	.299	RHP	449	126	24	78	.281
First Half	303	97	22	68	.320	Sc Pos	177	46	9	73	.260
Scnd Half	276	83	14	43	.301	Clutch	67	20	4	17	.299

2000 Rankings (National League)

- 1st in batting average vs. lefthanded pitchers and slugging percentage vs. lefthanded pitchers (.777)
- 2nd in on-base percentage vs. lefthanded pitchers (.480), errors at third base (23) and lowest fielding percentage at third base (.944)
- Led the Braves in batting average, home runs, doubles, RBI, sacrifice flies (10), walks, intentional walks (10), times on base (277), slugging percentage, on-base percentage, HR frequency (16.1 ABs per HR), batting average vs. lefthanded pitchers, slugging percentage vs. lefthanded pitchers (.777), on-base percentage vs. lefthanded pitchers (.480) and highest percentage of swings put into play (49.9)

Brian Jordan

2000 Season

After suiting up for the season opener against the Rockies, Brian Jordan missed the next two weeks with a strained right ribcage muscle. He returned from the disabled list on April 19 and played well in May and June before faltering in July. A sprained ankle and twisted knee suffered on July 25 took him out of the lineup again, however, while a torn right rotator cuff, sore wrist and sore knees hampered him during the last three months. His highlight occurred May 21 when he drove in a career-high seven runs versus San Diego.

Hitting

Jordan is an aggressive hitter who feasts on fastballs and can handle being pitched inside. He ranked third in the National League when hitting the first pitch, producing a .410 batting average. But while he touched lefthanded pitchers at a .402 clip, Jordan looked clueless against righthanders. Despite altering his stance several times, his .223 average versus righties was the third-worst mark in the league. Curiously, Jordan entered last season as a career .282 hitter against righthanders. He also batted just .223 after the All-Star break, though injuries played a significant role.

Baserunning & Defense

To his credit, Jordan did not allow last year's troubles at the plate to affect his performance in the field. He led NL right fielders with a .990 fielding percentage and continued to display a strong and accurate arm that makes runners think twice about taking the extra base. His excellent speed and uncanny instincts allow him to cover a lot of ground and take away many potential extra-base hits in Turner Field's spacious right-field alley. He also applies his speed and aggressiveness on the basepaths, making him an outstanding baserunner.

2001 Outlook

Jordan experienced the same frustrations with injuries last year that he encountered earlier in his career. Because he has three years remaining on a contract that is scheduled to pay him $7 million in 2001, the Braves were listening to offers for the outfielder. Jordan remains one of the game's most productive right fielders when healthy.

Position: RF
Bats: R **Throws:** R
Ht: 6' 1" **Wt:** 205

Opening Day Age: 34
Born: 3/29/67 in Baltimore, MD
ML Seasons: 9

Overall Statistics

	G	AB	R	H	D	T	HR	RBI	SB	BB	SO	Avg	OBP	Slg
2000	133	489	71	129	26	0	17	77	10	38	80	.264	.320	.421
Career	929	3371	517	963	176	28	124	559	109	228	534	.286	.337	.465

Where He Hits the Ball

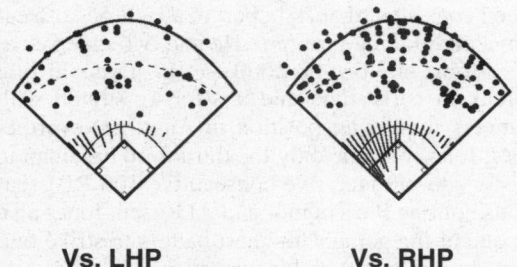

Vs. LHP   **Vs. RHP**

2000 Situational Stats

	AB	H	HR	RBI	Avg		AB	H	HR	RBI	Avg
Home	232	65	7	39	.280	LHP	112	45	5	27	.402
Road	257	64	10	38	.249	RHP	377	84	12	50	.223
First Half	274	81	13	50	.296	Sc Pos	144	39	7	63	.271
Scnd Half	215	48	4	27	.223	Clutch	63	16	3	8	.254

2000 Rankings (National League)

- 1st in fielding percentage in right field (.990)
- 2nd in lowest on-base percentage vs. righthanded pitchers (.283)
- 3rd in lowest batting average vs. righthanded pitchers
- 4th in highest percentage of extra bases taken as a runner (71.4) and lowest batting average with two strikes (.136)
- 5th in lowest slugging percentage vs. righthanded pitchers (.355) and lowest batting average on a 3-2 count (.087)
- Led the Braves in batting average on a 3-1 count (.625) and batting average on an 0-2 count (.292)
- Led NL right fielders in batting average on an 0-2 count (.292)

Javy Lopez

2000 Season

After hitting .400 with nine home runs and 21 RBI last July, Javy Lopez was on pace to establish career highs in several categories. But fatigue plagued the Braves' lone dependable catcher during the final two months. He started to press at the plate and lost his patience, causing his production to tumble. Even so, his 24 homers and 89 RBI both represented the second-best totals of his seven-year career.

Hitting

Lopez is well aware that his contributions at the plate are a significant part of his responsibilities with Atlanta. He studies his statistics like an accountant, and works constantly to improve his swing and ability to make contact. While he showed some effects from missing the last two months of 1999 with a partially torn knee ligament, Lopez still is one of the strongest players in the game. He's a threat to hit the longball every time he stands in the batter's box, especially when he can connect with a low fastball. He also remains a high-average hitter since learning to lay off breaking pitches in the dirt a few years ago.

Baserunning & Defense

Fatigue took its toll in other areas of Lopez' game last season. While he showed he has learned how to call a game as well as any catcher in the National League, his glovework diminished. He nailed only 21 percent of potential basestealers, the third-lowest rate in the circuit, and he became sloppy when blocking balls in the dirt late in the campaign. Lopez' speed has decreased to the point where it is considered below average. The lost step contributed to Lopez grounding into 20 double plays, which tied for the second most in the NL.

2001 Outlook

An offseason of rest and training should help Lopez regain anything he may have lost late last season. With his ability to hit for power and average, as well as his improved knowledge in calling a game, he is one of the most important parts to the Braves' championship puzzle. A career year would not be a surprise.

Position: C
Bats: R **Throws:** R
Ht: 6' 3" **Wt:** 200

Opening Day Age: 30
Born: 11/5/70 in Ponce, Puerto Rico
ML Seasons: 9
Pronunciation: HAH-vee LOE-pezz

Overall Statistics

	G	AB	R	H	D	T	HR	RBI	SB	BB	SO	Avg	OBP	Slg
2000	134	481	60	138	21	1	24	89	0	35	80	.287	.337	.484
Career	790	2761	343	800	130	10	143	467	7	184	493	.290	.338	.499

Where He Hits the Ball

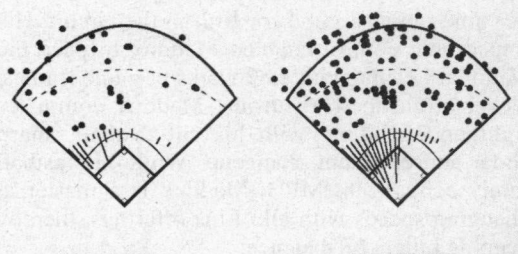

Vs. LHP   **Vs. RHP**

2000 Situational Stats

	AB	H	HR	RBI	Avg		AB	H	HR	RBI	Avg
Home	242	61	12	41	.252	LHP	101	28	5	22	.277
Road	239	77	12	48	.322	RHP	380	110	19	67	.289
First Half	273	79	12	44	.289	Sc Pos	137	41	6	64	.299
Scnd Half	208	59	12	45	.284	Clutch	68	17	1	10	.250

2000 Rankings (National League)

- 2nd in GDPs (20)
- 3rd in lowest percentage of runners caught stealing as a catcher (20.7)
- Led the Braves in GDPs (20), batting average with runners in scoring position and batting average on the road
- Led NL catchers in GDPs (20) and highest groundball/flyball ratio (1.5)

Atlanta

Greg Maddux

Position: SP
Bats: R **Throws:** R
Ht: 6' 0" **Wt:** 185

Opening Day Age: 34
Born: 4/14/66 in San Angelo, TX
ML Seasons: 15

2000 Season

After a subpar 1999, Greg Maddux returned to his dominating ways last season, tossing 36 consecutive shutout innings late in the campaign. He won at least 19 games for the seventh time in his career, joined Cy Young and Gaylord Perry as the only pitchers to win 15 or more games in 13 straight seasons and went 5-1 in September.

Pitching

Maddux continues to succeed with pinpoint control and incredible movement on his deep repertoire of pitches. He keeps the ball low in the strike zone, forcing batters to hit the ball on the ground, as evidenced by his 2.66 groundball-flyball ratio, best in the league, and his 0.69 home runs allowed per nine innings, good for fifth in the circuit. His impeccable control enabled Maddux to pace the National League with 1.52 walks per nine frames. Never afraid to work inside, Maddux dominates righthanded hitters with his cut fastball, sharp slider and excellent changeup. While his fastball rarely eclipses 90 MPH, Maddux is a master at changing speeds with all of his offerings, thereby keeping hitters off-balance.

Defense & Hitting

Maddux is the all-time leader for putouts among pitchers. He captured Gold Gloves every year in the 90s and committed just one error last season. Like most Atlanta pitchers, Maddux is capable of helping himself at the plate. His greatest weakness involves holding runners. Baserunners stole 32 bases and succeeded on 82 percent of their attempts against him, both of which represented the worst numbers in the league.

2001 Outlook

With his knowledge of the game and his uncanny ability to place pitches exactly where he wants them, Maddux should remain one of the major league's premier hurlers and could earn another Cy Young Award for his mantle. Since he is not overpowering, advancing age does not figure to rob him of any significant velocity. Along with lefthander Tom Glavine, Maddux continues to form one half of the most successful left-right combination in the big leagues.

Overall Statistics

	W	L	Pct.	ERA	G	GS	Sv	IP	H	BB	SO	HR	Ratio
2000	19	9	.679	3.00	35	35	0	249.1	225	42	190	19	1.07
Career	240	135	.640	2.83	471	467	0	3318.0	2986	733	2350	176	1.12

How Often He Throws Strikes

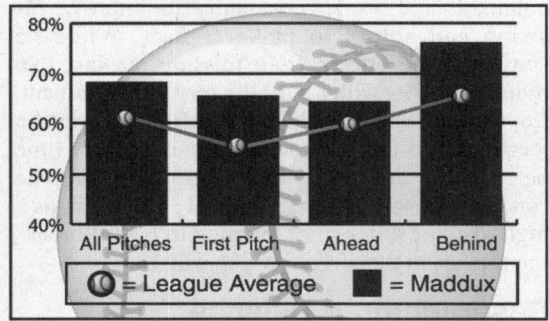

○ = League Average ■ = Maddux

2000 Situational Stats

	W	L	ERA	Sv	IP		AB	H	HR	RBI	Avg
Home	10	4	2.96	0	118.2	LHB	401	108	10	35	.269
Road	9	5	3.03	0	130.2	RHB	546	117	9	50	.214
First Half	10	3	3.32	0	132.2	Sc Pos	210	50	1	60	.238
Scnd Half	9	6	2.62	0	116.2	Clutch	86	20	1	6	.233

2000 Rankings (National League)

- 1st in games started, shutouts (3), stolen bases allowed (32), highest groundball/flyball ratio allowed (2.7), fewest pitches thrown per batter (3.18), fewest walks per nine innings (1.5) and highest stolen-base percentage allowed (82.1) 235
- 2nd in innings pitched and lowest on-base percentage allowed (.276)
- 3rd in wins, complete games (6), batters faced (1,012), highest strikeout/walk ratio (4.5), lowest slugging percentage allowed (.338) and lowest ERA on the road
- Led the Braves in ERA, games started, complete games (6), shutouts (3), innings pitched, hits allowed, batters faced (1,012) and hit batsmen (10)

Kevin Millwood

2000 Season

After establishing himself in 1999 as one of the premier young starting pitchers, Kevin Millwood took a step backward last year. The righthander won eight fewer games and saw his ERA increase by almost two full runs. His troubles jeopardized his spot in the postseason rotation. After beginning 2-0 with a 3.38 ERA in his first five starts, Millwood produced ERAs of over five in May, June and July. He rebounded with a solid second half and went 3-0 with a 1.64 ERA in three starts against Arizona.

Pitching

As he continues to grow and mature, Millwood is developing a physique similar to Roger Clemens. His stuff is similar as well, featuring a mid-90s fastball and a hard slider. His breaking ball and changeup, however, deserted him at times last year after showing vast improvement in 1999. Millwood has proven to be durable, tying for the league lead last season with 35 starts. He also ranked third in the circuit by surrendering a .261 on-base percentage to batters leading off an inning. However, his failure to keep pitches low in the strike zone led to a meager groundball-flyball ratio of 0.71, second lowest in the league.

Defense & Hitting

Two years ago, Millwood learned how to help himself by improving his fielding. He did not commit an error last season, and did a better job of holding runners at first base. Millwood is a better hitter than his paltry .119 mark from 2000 would indicate. He did show he is more than capable of advancing runners by tying for second in the league with 14 sacrifice bunts.

2001 Outlook

With his natural abilities, eagerness to improve and solid support system, Millwood is likely to bounce back to his 1999 form. His flaws regarding his two secondary pitches are correctable, while his velocity and all-around power cannot be taught. A minimum of 15 wins is attainable for this righthander if he regains the feel of his offspeed pitches and continues to learn from his mistakes.

Position: SP
Bats: R **Throws:** R
Ht: 6' 4" **Wt:** 220

Opening Day Age: 26
Born: 12/24/74 in Gastonia, NC
ML Seasons: 4

Overall Statistics

	W	L	Pct.	ERA	G	GS	Sv	IP	H	BB	SO	HR	Ratio
2000	10	13	.435	4.66	36	35	0	212.2	213	62	168	26	1.29
Career	50	31	.617	3.78	112	105	0	666.1	611	198	578	69	1.21

How Often He Throws Strikes

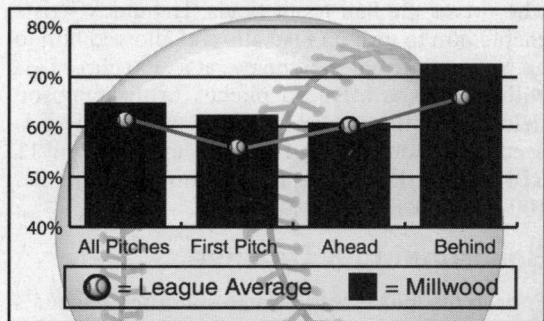

= League Average   ■ = Millwood

2000 Situational Stats

	W	L	ERA	Sv	IP		AB	H	HR	RBI	Avg
Home	6	7	4.81	0	110.1	LHB	357	103	11	50	.289
Road	4	6	4.49	0	102.1	RHB	468	110	15	56	.235
First Half	5	8	5.34	0	114.2	Sc Pos	165	49	7	74	.297
Scnd Half	5	5	3.86	0	98.0	Clutch	66	20	2	12	.303

2000 Rankings (National League)

- 1st in games started
- 2nd in sacrifice bunts (14) and lowest groundball/flyball ratio allowed (0.7)
- 7th in pickoff throws (140)
- 8th in losses
- Led the Braves in sacrifice bunts (14), losses, games started, home runs allowed and most strikeouts per nine innings (7.1)

Atlanta

B.J. Surhoff

2000 Season

B.J. Surhoff did not hide his tears when the Braves acquired him from Baltimore at the trading deadline. After hitting safely in 42 of his last 49 games with the Orioles, Surhoff batted .290 as the Braves' left fielder in August before suffering a pulled right quadriceps on September 7. The injury kept him sidelined for all but a few pinch-hit appearances the rest of the campaign.

Hitting

Surhoff was slotted anywhere from second to sixth in the batting order with the Braves. His best place may be third, but Chipper Jones owns that spot in the Atlanta lineup. Surhoff is a productive hitter who drives the ball to all fields. His quick wrists enable him to turn on fastballs and allowed him to hit National League southpaws at a .300 clip. He is willing to take offspeed pitches to the opposite field, but will wait for a fastball when power is needed. Although he had just one home run and 11 RBI with Atlanta, Surhoff remains a 20-homer, 100-RBI threat.

Baserunning & Defense

Prior to his injury, Surhoff had solidified Atlanta's defense in left field. His range may be limited, but that isn't a problem with Andruw Jones manning center. Surhoff excels at reading the ball off the bat and holds many potential doubles to singles. His arm also rates better than average among left fielders. While he's no longer a threat to steal 20 bases, Surhoff doesn't clog the basepaths, either. He's slowed down and isn't able to take the extra base as often as in previous years.

2001 Outlook

Surhoff didn't want to leave the Orioles due to his son's lingering health concerns and the quality of care he was receiving in Baltimore. However, the Braves believe Surhoff is a perfect fit in left field. He also could see time at first base if free-agent acquisition Rico Brogna falters as the everyday replacement for Andres Galarraga. With Reggie Sanders expected to depart, Surhoff should be an integral part to the Atlanta lineup no matter where he plays in the field, unless of course he requests a trade under the rules of the Basic Agreement.

Position: LF
Bats: L **Throws:** R
Ht: 6' 1" **Wt:** 200

Opening Day Age: 36
Born: 8/4/64 in Bronx, NY
ML Seasons: 14

Overall Statistics

	G	AB	R	H	D	T	HR	RBI	SB	BB	SO	Avg	OBP	Slg
2000	147	539	69	157	36	2	14	68	10	41	58	.291	.344	.443
Career	1863	6734	878	1895	359	38	160	961	127	523	679	.281	.332	.417

Where He Hits the Ball

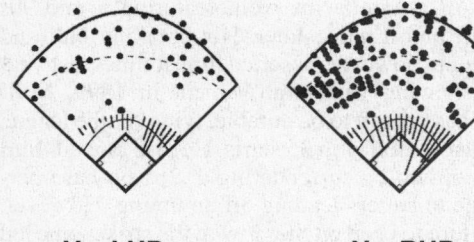

Vs. LHP   **Vs. RHP**

2000 Situational Stats

	AB	H	HR	RBI	Avg		AB	H	HR	RBI	Avg
Home	249	71	7	31	.285	LHP	149	44	6	18	.295
Road	290	86	7	37	.297	RHP	390	113	8	50	.290
First Half	342	97	11	50	.284	Sc Pos	151	44	1	52	.291
Scnd Half	197	60	3	18	.305	Clutch	77	15	3	9	.195

2000 Rankings (National League)

- Did not rank near the top or bottom in any category

Quilvio Veras

2000 Season

A torn anterior cruciate ligament in his right knee suffered in mid-July brought Quilvio Veras' productive first season with Atlanta to an abrupt halt. Prior to the injury, the second baseman was on pace to set career highs in runs, doubles, home runs and RBI. Veras ranked second among National League leadoff hitters with a .413 on-base percentage at the time of his mishap.

Hitting

Veras, who battled leg injuries during his last four seasons with San Diego, gives the Braves their best leadoff hitter since Otis Nixon owned the job in the early 1990s. Veras vastly improved Atlanta's team speed and combined with rookie Rafael Furcal at the top of the lineup to create a merry-go-round on the basepaths. Veras is one of the game's most patient hitters and does not fret when behind in the count. In fact, the second baseman led the league with a .471 average on full counts and ranked second with a .298 mark with two strikes. He also is one of the game's premier bunters.

Baserunning & Defense

Despite boasting above-average speed, Veras gets thrown out too often when attempting to steal. He was caught 12 times in 84 games last year, a total that tied for seventh most in the league overall. Even so, he makes opposing pitchers nervous with his quick first step and ability to score from first base on a routine double. Veras also improved Atlanta's infield defense. He has good range, turns the double play efficiently and possesses a solid arm for second base. He and Furcal form one of the game's more exciting middle infield tandems.

2001 Outlook

Veras appeared to experience few problems with his knee two months after undergoing surgery and should be ready to contribute in spring training. He gives the Braves a different type of production than the team had received from its recent second basemen. Although durability continues to plague Veras, his speed-oriented offense and solid range provide a good fit at Turner Field.

Position: 2B
Bats: B **Throws:** R
Ht: 5'10" **Wt:** 183

Opening Day Age: 29
Born: 4/3/71 in Santo Domingo, Dominican Republic
ML Seasons: 6
Pronunciation: KILL-vee-oh VARE-ess

Overall Statistics

	G	AB	R	H	D	T	HR	RBI	SB	BB	SO	Avg	OBP	Slg
2000	84	298	56	92	15	0	5	37	25	51	50	.309	.413	.409
Career	696	2522	430	685	115	13	29	214	176	403	410	.272	.376	.362

Where He Hits the Ball

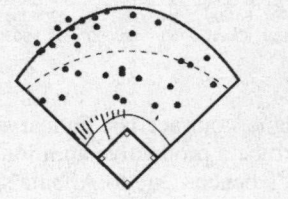

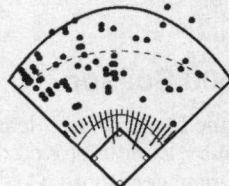

Vs. LHP   **Vs. RHP**

2000 Situational Stats

	AB	H	HR	RBI	Avg		AB	H	HR	RBI	Avg
Home	133	44	2	19	.331	LHP	76	27	3	16	.355
Road	165	48	3	18	.291	RHP	222	65	2	21	.293
First Half	297	92	5	37	.310	Sc Pos	73	23	0	30	.315
Scnd Half	1	0	0	0	.000	Clutch	39	11	1	5	.282

2000 Rankings (National League)

- 1st in batting average on a 3-2 count (.471)
- 2nd in batting average with two strikes (.298)
- 3rd in on-base percentage for a leadoff hitter (.404)
- 7th in caught stealing (12)
- 10th in lowest stolen-base percentage (67.6)
- Led the Braves in on-base percentage for a leadoff hitter (.404), batting average on a 3-2 count (.471) and batting average with two strikes (.298)
- Led NL second basemen in batting average on a 3-2 count (.471) and batting average with two strikes (.298)

Bobby Bonilla

Position: LF
Bats: B **Throws:** R
Ht: 6' 3" **Wt:** 240

Opening Day Age: 38
Born: 2/23/63 in New York, NY
ML Seasons: 15
Pronunciation: buh-NEE-yuh
Nickname: Bobby Bo

Overall Statistics

	G	AB	R	H	D	T	HR	RBI	SB	BB	SO	Avg	OBP	Slg
2000	114	239	23	61	13	3	5	28	0	37	51	.255	.356	.397
Career	2020	7039	1067	1973	401	61	282	1152	44	889	1151	.280	.359	.475

2000 Situational Stats

	AB	H	HR	RBI	Avg		AB	H	HR	RBI	Avg
Home	120	31	4	13	.258	LHP	43	16	1	8	.372
Road	119	30	1	15	.252	RHP	196	45	4	20	.230
First Half	159	43	4	18	.270	Sc Pos	64	17	1	22	.266
Scnd Half	80	18	1	10	.225	Clutch	36	12	0	6	.333

2000 Season

Signed to a minor league contract last January, Bobby Bonilla proved to be a productive addition to manager Bobby Cox's bench. Due to Atlanta's plethora of injuries in the outfield, the switch-hitting Bonilla started 62 games in left field. He also served as the Braves' primary pinch-hitter and led the team with 10 RBI in that role.

Hitting, Baserunning & Defense

The 38-year-old Bonilla still has some power, as well as the ability to post decent numbers for short periods. He dominated lefthanded pitchers last season, batting 142 points higher against southpaws than righthanders. His speed has declined, though he possesses fine baserunning awareness. Defensively, Bonilla is below average in left field, as evidenced by his four errors. His days as a fill-in at third base likely are over.

2001 Outlook

Bonilla showed last season that he has made the adjustment to playing a reserve role. He even displayed some leadership qualities by discussing his observations regularly with Cox. Bonilla could play for a couple more seasons if he continues to produce as a pinch-hitter and avoids being a disruption in the clubhouse, though Atlanta also signed outfielder Dave Martinez in mid-December.

Kerry Ligtenberg

Position: RP
Bats: R **Throws:** R
Ht: 6' 2" **Wt:** 215

Opening Day Age: 29
Born: 5/11/71 in Rapid City, SD
ML Seasons: 3
Pronunciation: LITE-enn-berg

Overall Statistics

	W	L	Pct.	ERA	G	GS	Sv	IP	H	BB	SO	HR	Ratio
2000	2	3	.400	3.61	59	0	12	52.1	43	24	51	7	1.28
Career	6	5	.545	3.08	149	0	43	140.1	106	52	149	17	1.13

2000 Situational Stats

	W	L	ERA	Sv	IP		AB	H	HR	RBI	Avg
Home	0	1	3.71	5	26.2	LHB	63	13	2	4	.206
Road	2	2	3.51	7	25.2	RHB	127	30	5	19	.236
First Half	2	1	3.86	7	28.0	Sc Pos	58	8	2	16	.138
Scnd Half	0	2	3.33	5	24.1	Clutch	81	18	4	16	.222

2000 Season

Having missed the entire 1999 slate following Tommy John surgery, Kerry Ligtenberg returned last year to serve as a capable closer and setup man. A combination of ineffectiveness and inactivity led to a demotion to Triple-A Richmond in May. But he came back 11 days later in a better frame of mind and proceeded to go 1-1 with nine saves and a 1.98 ERA from June 5 to August 25.

Pitching, Defense & Hitting

The owner of a split-finger fastball, slider and four-seam fastball that reaches the low 90s, Ligtenberg does an excellent job of keeping the ball on the ground. The sidewinder thrives in difficult situations, holding hitters to a .138 average with runners in scoring position last year. He also does a decent job defending his position, and his quick delivery makes it difficult for runners to get a good jump, however the six who tried to steal succeeded. Not unlike most relievers, Ligtenberg rarely bats.

2001 Outlook

Ligtenberg's re-emergence took the pressure off John Rocker and made the Atlanta bullpen one of the team's strengths. The situation should remain unchanged this season, with Ligtenberg picking up a handful of saves while serving as one of the majors' best late-inning situational pitchers.

Kevin McGlinchy

Position: RP
Bats: R   **Throws:** R
Ht: 6' 5"   **Wt:** 220

Opening Day Age: 23
Born: 6/28/77 in
Malden, MA
ML Seasons: 2

Overall Statistics

	W	L	Pct.	ERA	G	GS	Sv	IP	H	BB	SO	HR	Ratio
2000	0	0	-	2.16	10	0	0	8.1	11	6	9	1	2.04
Career	7	3	.700	2.75	74	0	0	78.2	77	36	76	7	1.44

2000 Situational Stats

	W	L	ERA	Sv	IP		AB	H	HR	RBI	Avg
Home	0	0	3.86	0	2.1	LHB	13	3	0	0	.231
Road	0	0	1.50	0	6.0	RHB	22	8	1	6	.364
First Half	0	0	3.38	0	5.1	Sc Pos	19	3	1	6	.158
Scnd Half	0	0	0.00	0	3.0	Clutch	1	1	1	5	1.000

2000 Season

Looking to build on a steady rookie showing, Kevin McGlinchy instead faced frustration in 2000. Tendinitis in his throwing shoulder landed him on the disabled list from mid-April to mid-May before shelving him on May 24. He wound up working a total of 19 innings in three minor league rehabilitation assignments, and returned to the bigs for three effective outings at the end of September.

Pitching, Defense & Hitting

McGlinchy's limited arsenal fits perfectly into the Braves' situational late-game matchups. Manager Bobby Cox calls upon McGlinchy to overpower righthanded hitters with his mid-90s fastball. He keeps batters honest with an effective slider that looks similar to his heater before dropping into the dirt. His biggest weakness involves an occasional lack of concentration that will cause him to leave the ball up in the strike zone. A decent fielder, McGlinchy swung the bat well in the minors.

2001 Outlook

The Braves are confident that McGlinchy's shoulder tendinitis isn't a chronic problem. He showed in 1999 that his arm can bounce back nightly, especially when he doesn't pitch more than an inning at a time. His return would bolster a bullpen that ranked as one of the best last season.

Terry Mulholland

Position: RP/SP
Bats: R   **Throws:** L
Ht: 6' 3"   **Wt:** 220

Opening Day Age: 38
Born: 3/9/63 in
Uniontown, PA
ML Seasons: 14

Overall Statistics

	W	L	Pct.	ERA	G	GS	Sv	IP	H	BB	SO	HR	Ratio
2000	9	9	.500	5.11	54	20	1	156.2	198	41	78	24	1.53
Career	112	124	.475	4.28	469	307	5	2146.2	2306	555	1124	225	1.33

2000 Situational Stats

	W	L	ERA	Sv	IP		AB	H	HR	RBI	Avg
Home	4	5	5.55	1	73.0	LHB	119	35	2	18	.294
Road	5	4	4.73	0	83.2	RHB	523	163	22	79	.312
First Half	9	8	5.71	1	115.0	Sc Pos	172	46	5	69	.267
Scnd Half	0	1	3.46	0	41.2	Clutch	49	13	2	9	.265

2000 Season

Terry Mulholland filled virtually every role on the Braves' pitching staff last season. He started for most of the first half after John Smoltz was injured during spring training, then moved to the bullpen shortly after Andy Ashby was acquired in July. Mulholland's best efforts came as a starter, although he did come through on occasion in relief.

Pitching, Defense & Hitting

The crafty Mulholland always has allowed hitters to make contact. Last season, however, more hits started to fall. While lefthanded hitters touched the southpaw at a .294 clip, righties hit .312 against him, the fourth-worst norm in the league. He also allowed 24 home runs, one shy of his career high. He still has four effective pitches, and his effort is beyond repute. Mulholland arguably is the toughest pitcher in baseball to run against. On the other hand, his fielding and hitting are mediocre at best.

2001 Outlook

With Smoltz, Odalis Perez and Rudy Seanez expected to return from lengthy injuries, the Atlanta front office felt little need to re-sign Mulholland. The Pirates took a chance on the versatile lefty, signing him to a two-year, $6 million deal in hopes that he can stabilize their bullpen.

Atlanta

Odalis Perez

Position: SP
Bats: L **Throws:** L
Ht: 6' 0" **Wt:** 150

Opening Day Age: 22
Born: 6/7/78 in La Matas de Farfan, Dominican Republic
ML Seasons: 2
Pronunciation: oh-DALL-iss

Overall Statistics

	W	L	Pct.	ERA	G	GS	Sv	IP	H	BB	SO	HR	Ratio
2000					Did Not Play								
Career	4	7	.364	5.82	28	17	0	103.2	110	57	87	13	1.61

2000 Situational Stats

	W	L	ERA	Sv	IP		AB	H	HR	RBI	Avg
Home	—	—	—	—	—	LHB	—	—	—	—	—
Road	—	—	—	—	—	RHB	—	—	—	—	—
First Half	—	—	—	—	—	Sc Pos	—	—	—	—	—
Scnd Half	—	—	—	—	—	Clutch	—	—	—	—	—

2000 Season

Odalis Perez missed all of last season after undergoing Tommy John surgery the previous summer. The lefthander, who started 17 games for the Braves in 1999 before tearing an elbow ligament, looked strong while throwing all of his pitches during fall instructional league.

Pitching, Defense & Hitting

Perez has two plus-pitches—a fastball clocked as high as 94 MPH during instructional league and a tight, sharp-breaking curveball that most scouts consider to be his best offering. His aggressiveness and willingness to throw inside have produced comparisons to fellow Dominican Pedro Martinez. The Braves feared the skinny Perez would hurt his arm in the minors, but feel he has remedied the problem by adding muscle in his legs and hips, thereby reducing the strain on his arm. Perez is quick off the mound and consistent with his glove. He is a mediocre hitter.

2001 Outlook

The majors' second-youngest player in 1999, Perez gives every indication that he will play a significant role in the Braves' future. He is expected to be at full strength by Opening Day. Atlanta would love for him to earn the fifth slot in the rotation, although he has proven just as capable in relief.

Mike Remlinger

Position: RP
Bats: L **Throws:** L
Ht: 6' 1" **Wt:** 210

Opening Day Age: 35
Born: 3/23/66 in Middletown, NY
ML Seasons: 8
Pronunciation: REM-lin-jurr

Overall Statistics

	W	L	Pct.	ERA	G	GS	Sv	IP	H	BB	SO	HR	Ratio
2000	5	3	.625	3.47	71	0	12	72.2	55	37	72	6	1.27
Career	34	35	.493	4.15	292	59	15	568.1	509	298	520	68	1.42

2000 Situational Stats

	W	L	ERA	Sv	IP		AB	H	HR	RBI	Avg
Home	4	1	3.19	4	36.2	LHB	79	16	1	15	.203
Road	1	2	3.75	8	36.0	RHB	187	39	5	21	.209
First Half	2	2	3.54	7	40.2	Sc Pos	75	20	0	26	.267
Scnd Half	3	1	3.38	5	32.0	Clutch	176	30	2	19	.170

2000 Season

Mike Remlinger continued to establish himself as one of the game's better setup men. He solidified an unstable bullpen and recorded a career-high 12 saves. He also ranked second in the league with 23 holds while limiting opposing hitters to a .207 batting average.

Pitching, Defense & Hitting

A starter early in his career, Remlinger is at his best when he can display his entire repertoire. The lefthander can reach the low 90s with his fastball and mix in a hard, late-breaking slider. His above-average changeup became his best pitch last August. Remlinger goes right after hitters and does an excellent job of getting ahead in the count. An average fielder, his ability to hold runners has improved to the point where last year opponents attempted just one steal on his watch. A career .077 hitter, he hasn't recorded a base hit since 1998.

2001 Outlook

Remlinger will remain an integral part of the Braves' bullpen in 2001. The vast majority of his appearances will come in the seventh or eighth innings when Atlanta has the lead. His efforts again should enable Tom Glavine and Greg Maddux to flirt with 20 wins and closer John Rocker to register 30-plus saves.

John Rocker

Position: RP
Bats: R **Throws:** L
Ht: 6' 4" **Wt:** 225

Opening Day Age: 26
Born: 10/17/74 in Statesboro, GA
ML Seasons: 3

Overall Statistics

	W	L	Pct.	ERA	G	GS	Sv	IP	H	BB	SO	HR	Ratio
2000	1	2	.333	2.89	59	0	24	53.0	42	48	77	5	1.70
Career	6	10	.375	2.53	180	0	64	163.1	111	107	223	14	1.33

2000 Situational Stats

	W	L	ERA	Sv	IP		AB	H	HR	RBI	Avg
Home	1	1	3.19	15	31.0	LHB	37	9	2	6	.243
Road	0	1	2.45	9	22.0	RHB	163	33	3	12	.202
First Half	1	0	4.62	12	25.1	Sc Pos	60	8	1	14	.133
Scnd Half	0	2	1.30	12	27.2	Clutch	129	23	1	11	.178

2000 Season

John Rocker weathered the storm last year that he had created prior to the 2000 season. After returning from a suspension early in the campaign, the hard-throwing lefthander endured control problems and a brief demotion to Triple-A Richmond in early June. By the end of the year he was back to his dominating ways, including a final stretch in which he allowed an earned run in just four of his last 35 outings.

Pitching, Defense & Hitting

Rocker throws as hard as anyone, with a sinking fastball that reaches the high 90s. He battles control problems but can be unhittable when in a groove. Even though his slider and changeup are inconsistent, Rocker rarely gives in when his fastball is on target. Due to his high leg kick that causes him to fall off the mound, Rocker is no better than an average fielder. He has not batted in his first three big league seasons.

2001 Outlook

Provided he keeps his mouth shut, Rocker should take another step toward being one of the league's most effective closers. He has the necessary tools and the mental makeup to dominate late in games, traits that should make 40 saves a possibility in 2001.

Reggie Sanders

Pivotal Season

Position: LF/RF
Bats: R **Throws:** R
Ht: 6' 1" **Wt:** 185

Opening Day Age: 33
Born: 12/1/67 in Florence, SC
ML Seasons: 10

Overall Statistics

	G	AB	R	H	D	T	HR	RBI	SB	BB	SO	Avg	OBP	Slg
2000	103	340	43	79	23	1	11	37	21	32	78	.232	.302	.403
Career	1041	3703	634	996	199	41	162	540	215	443	963	.269	.351	.476

2000 Situational Stats

	AB	H	HR	RBI	Avg		AB	H	HR	RBI	Avg
Home	157	41	4	12	.261	LHP	72	19	2	13	.264
Road	183	38	7	25	.208	RHP	268	60	9	24	.224
First Half	201	36	4	13	.179	Sc Pos	84	19	2	26	.226
Scnd Half	139	43	7	24	.309	Clutch	47	13	1	5	.277

2000 Season

Reggie Sanders appeared to be the perfect fit in left field for the Braves after arriving from San Diego last offseason. It didn't work out that way, however. The injury bug bit him again, forcing two stints on the disabled list. Aside from a productive September that saw Sanders hit .337 with five homers and 18 RBI in 22 games, his batting average resided below the Mendoza line.

Hitting, Baserunning & Defense

Sanders possesses an excellent combination of speed and power. He was terrific in 1999, hitting 26 homers with 36 stolen bases, but didn't hit his first home run last year until June 4. Despite 21 steals, he made several poor baserunning mistakes over the course of last season. While streaky at the plate, Sanders is a consistent outfielder who can play all three positions.

2001 Outlook

Sanders appears certain to open the 2001 season playing for his third team in as many years. When he isn't fighting injuries, Sanders can post some solid numbers, but he is not a player a team can build around. Nevertheless, as one of the game's good guys and because of his ever-present potential, Sanders should find a starting job somewhere.

Atlanta

John Smoltz

Position: SP
Bats: R **Throws:** R
Ht: 6' 3" **Wt:** 220

Opening Day Age: 33
Born: 5/15/67 in
Warren, MI
ML Seasons: 12

Overall Statistics

	W	L	Pct.	ERA	G	GS	Sv	IP	H	BB	SO	HR	Ratio
2000					Did Not Play								
Career	157	113	.581	3.35	356	356	0	2414.1	2092	774	2098	195	1.19

2000 Situational Stats

	W	L	ERA	Sv	IP		AB	H	HR	RBI	Avg
Home	—	—	—	—	—	LHB	—	—	—	—	—
Road	—	—	—	—	—	RHB	—	—	—	—	—
First Half	—	—	—	—	—	Sc Pos	—	—	—	—	—
Scnd Half	—	—	—	—	—	Clutch	—	—	—	—	—

2000 Season

The Braves' worst fears regarding John Smoltz became reality in spring training. The righthander altered his arm angle in 1999 due to recurring arm discomfort. The change helped him reach double digits in wins for the 10th time, it also may have led to a torn elbow ligament, necessitating Tommy John surgery and the loss of Smoltz' 2000 season.

Pitching, Defense & Hitting

Smoltz is a power pitcher, plain and simple. While he dropped his slider during the 1999 slate, he added a knuckleball and improved his changeup to go with his mid-90s fastball. Though it remains to be seen if he can still throw with the same velocity after surgery, his two new pitches should reduce the strain on his arm. He also shouldn't lose any of his tenacity. An excellent all-around athlete, Smoltz fields his position and hits as well as any pitcher in the league.

2001 Outlook

Smoltz was pitching off the mound late last year and is expected to be at full strength in spring training. Twice before in his career he showed the ability to recover quickly following surgery. The Braves picked up his $8 million option for 2001, so expect him to be no less than Atlanta's fourth starter this year.

Walt Weiss

Position: SS
Bats: B **Throws:** R
Ht: 6' 0" **Wt:** 188

Opening Day Age: 37
Born: 11/28/63 in
Tuxedo, NY
ML Seasons: 14
Pronunciation: WICE

Overall Statistics

	G	AB	R	H	D	T	HR	RBI	SB	BB	SO	Avg	OBP	Slg
2000	80	192	29	50	6	2	0	18	1	26	32	.260	.353	.313
Career	1495	4686	623	1207	182	31	25	386	96	658	658	.258	.351	.326

2000 Situational Stats

	AB	H	HR	RBI	Avg		AB	H	HR	RBI	Avg
Home	96	31	0	10	.323	LHP	67	20	0	10	.299
Road	96	19	0	8	.198	RHP	125	30	0	8	.240
First Half	119	34	0	10	.286	Sc Pos	49	10	0	18	.204
Scnd Half	73	16	0	8	.219	Clutch	16	5	0	2	.313

2000 Season

Injuries limited Walt Weiss to 192 at-bats last year, his lowest total since 1991. Weiss' strained hamstring in May, sprained thumb in June and strained knee ligament in July and August meant rookie Rafael Furcal saw most of the activity at shortstop for the Braves.

Hitting, Baserunning & Defense

Weiss had difficulty getting into a groove at the plate last year. Despite his minimal power, he remains a capable offensive producer while hitting in the difficult eighth slot in the lineup. His calling card remains his glove, which is one of the steadiest in the majors. He has an uncanny ability to anticipate plays and make strong, accurate throws. Weiss is a smart baserunner who compensates for average speed with his knowledge on the basepaths.

2001 Outlook

An inability to stay healthy and the loss of a step on defense left Weiss contemplating retirement at the end of last season. He's a free agent, and Atlanta appears set with Furcal at shortstop, provided a high-profile acquisition isn't made. That acquisition will not be Weiss, who should expect nothing more than a part-time role with another team.

Other Atlanta Braves

Paul Bako (**Pos**: C, **Age**: 28, **Bats**: L)

	G	AB	R	H	D	T	HR	RBI	SB	BB	SO	Avg	OBP	Slg
2000	81	221	18	50	10	1	2	20	0	27	64	.226	.312	.308
Career	250	741	57	188	36	3	7	67	2	76	203	.254	.321	.339

Bako was a favorite receiver for Greg Maddux last season, but Eddie Perez has traditionally held that job. Bako's batting average has been heading in the wrong direction. 2001 Outlook: C

Stan Belinda (**Pos**: RHP, **Age**: 34)

	W	L	Pct.	ERA	G	GS	Sv	IP	H	BB	SO	HR	Ratio
2000	1	3	.250	7.71	56	0	1	46.2	55	22	51	14	1.65
Career	41	37	.526	4.15	585	0	79	685.1	590	285	622	85	1.28

Belinda has now surrendered 25 homers in his last 89.1 innings. It's hard to inspire much confidence like that, and he was released by two organizations last year. 2001 Outlook: C

John Burkett (**Pos**: RHP, **Age**: 36)

	W	L	Pct.	ERA	G	GS	Sv	IP	H	BB	SO	HR	Ratio
2000	10	6	.625	4.89	31	22	0	134.1	162	51	110	13	1.59
Career	129	107	.547	4.35	350	330	1	2074.1	2278	533	1348	195	1.36

Burkett managed to post a decent record despite allowing a .303 batting average. Why? He received great run support. He is a free agent, and on a poor team his limitations could be exposed. 2001 Outlook: B

Mark DeRosa (**Pos**: SS, **Age**: 26, **Bats**: R)

	G	AB	R	H	D	T	HR	RBI	SB	BB	SO	Avg	OBP	Slg
2000	22	13	9	4	1	0	0	3	0	2	1	.308	.400	.385
Career	34	24	11	5	1	0	0	3	0	2	4	.208	.269	.250

Since he plays the same position and is more than four years older than brilliant rookie Rafael Furcal, it would appear the best DeRosa can hope for is a reserve role if Walt Weiss departs. 2001 Outlook: B

Mike Hubbard (**Pos**: C, **Age**: 30, **Bats**: R)

	G	AB	R	H	D	T	HR	RBI	SB	BB	SO	Avg	OBP	Slg
2000	2	1	0	0	0	0	0	0	0	0	1	.000	.000	.000
Career	99	181	10	29	1	0	3	10	0	4	56	.160	.182	.215

Eddie Perez is coming back from rotator cuff surgery and Fernando Lunar and Paul Bako are other options, so Hubbard faced high obstacles in hoping to land a backup job with the Braves. He signed a minor league contract with the Rangers in early November. 2001 Outlook: D

Wally Joyner (**Pos**: 1B, **Age**: 38, **Bats**: L)

	G	AB	R	H	D	T	HR	RBI	SB	BB	SO	Avg	OBP	Slg
2000	119	224	24	63	12	0	5	32	0	31	31	.281	.365	.402
Career	1980	6979	959	2024	404	25	201	1092	59	820	807	.290	.364	.441

The Braves declined Joyner's option and he became a free agent. At his age he'll probably never again be a regular, but he can help a team as a pinch-hitter or late-inning defensive replacement. 2001 Outlook: B

Scott Kamieniecki (**Pos**: RHP, **Age**: 36)

	W	L	Pct.	ERA	G	GS	Sv	IP	H	BB	SO	HR	Ratio
2000	3	4	.429	5.59	52	0	2	58.0	64	42	46	9	1.83
Career	53	59	.473	4.52	250	138	5	975.2	1006	446	542	105	1.49

After getting released by Cleveland, Kamieniecki pitched decently for the Braves last August, compiling a 1.80 ERA that month. He blew up thereafter (12.86), however, and the Braves have better options. 2001 Outlook: C

Keith Lockhart (**Pos**: 2B/3B, **Age**: 36, **Bats**: L)

	G	AB	R	H	D	T	HR	RBI	SB	BB	SO	Avg	OBP	Slg
2000	113	275	32	73	12	3	2	32	4	29	31	.265	.331	.353
Career	685	1699	221	465	93	13	33	216	29	139	177	.274	.327	.402

With the emergence of Rafael Furcal and the return of Quilvio Veras from injury, Lockhart won't be the Braves' first option. He can be a decent utility infielder and lefthanded bat off the bench. 2001 Outlook: A

Greg McMichael (**Pos**: RHP, **Age**: 34)

	W	L	Pct.	ERA	G	GS	Sv	IP	H	BB	SO	HR	Ratio
2000	0	0	-	4.41	15	0	0	16.1	12	4	14	3	0.98
Career	31	29	.517	3.25	453	0	53	523.1	483	193	459	42	1.29

In his second tour of duty with the Braves, McMichael managed only 15 appearances before undergoing rotator cuff surgery. He's passed through five organizations the past three years and will be looking for yet another team over the winter. 2001 Outlook: C

Gabe Molina (**Pos**: RHP, **Age**: 25)

	W	L	Pct.	ERA	G	GS	Sv	IP	H	BB	SO	HR	Ratio
2000	0	0	-	9.00	11	0	0	15.0	28	10	9	3	2.53
Career	1	2	.333	7.58	31	0	0	38.0	56	26	23	7	2.00

Molina was obtained from Baltimore in the B.J. Surhoff deal at last year's trading deadline. While Molina has saved games in the minors, he'll be seeking a middle relief role with the Braves. 2001 Outlook: C

Eddie Perez (**Pos**: C, **Age**: 32, **Bats**: R)

	G	AB	R	H	D	T	HR	RBI	SB	BB	SO	Avg	OBP	Slg
2000	7	22	0	4	1	0	0	3	0	0	2	.182	.182	.227
Career	320	840	88	216	45	1	24	104	1	50	126	.257	.305	.399

Perez underwent season-ending rotator cuff surgery last May. Assuming he recovers, he's the logical choice to serve as Javy Lopez' backup catcher, especially if Greg Maddux has any input. 2001 Outlook: A

Rudy Seanez (**Pos**: RHP, **Age**: 32)

	W	L	Pct.	ERA	G	GS	Sv	IP	H	BB	SO	HR	Ratio
2000	2	4	.333	4.29	23	0	2	21.0	15	9	20	3	1.14
Career	16	11	.593	4.59	204	0	10	209.2	191	111	197	20	1.44

The saga of Rudy Seanez continues. He always had great potential and he seemed to turn a corner with Atlanta. But the injuries keep piling up, and now he's a free agent coming off surgery. 2001 Outlook: C

Chris Seelbach (Pos: RHP, **Age**: 28)

	W	L	Pct.	ERA	G	GS	Sv	IP	H	BB	SO	HR	Ratio
2000	0	1	.000	10.80	2	0	0	1.2	3	0	1	0	1.80
Career	0	1	.000	10.80	2	0	0	1.2	3	0	1	0	1.80

Seelbach was the Braves' fourth-round pick way back in 1991. He reached Triple-A in 1994, where he's been parked in neutral ever since. He's still trying to harness his control. 2001 Outlook: C

Steve Sisco (Pos: 2B, **Age**: 31, **Bats**: R)

	G	AB	R	H	D	T	HR	RBI	SB	BB	SO	Avg	OBP	Slg
2000	25	27	4	5	0	0	1	2	0	3	4	.185	.267	.296
Career	25	27	4	5	0	0	1	2	0	3	4	.185	.267	.296

A career minor leaguer for nine seasons, Sisco finally reached the majors last year when the Braves sustained some injuries. He can play either middle infield position and hits with a little pop. He was traded to Baltimore in mid-December. 2001 Outlook: C

Dave Stevens (Pos: RHP, **Age**: 31)

	W	L	Pct.	ERA	G	GS	Sv	IP	H	BB	SO	HR	Ratio
2000	0	0	-	12.00	2	0	0	3.0	5	1	4	2	2.00
Career	15	16	.484	6.02	183	6	21	251.0	298	132	170	49	1.71

A long time ago, it seems, Stevens was a fairly decent closer prospect. But he's worked most of the past couple years in the minors and didn't do anything that exciting last season. 2001 Outlook: C

Pedro Swann (Pos: RF, **Age**: 30, **Bats**: L)

	G	AB	R	H	D	T	HR	RBI	SB	BB	SO	Avg	OBP	Slg
2000	4	2	0	0	0	0	0	0	0	0	2	.000	.000	.000
Career	4	2	0	0	0	0	0	0	0	0	2	.000	.000	.000

Swann returned for his second tour of duty in the Braves organization last year. He's a lefthanded-hitting outfielder without eye-catching power, though he can hit for a fairly decent average. 2001 Outlook: D

Tim Unroe (Pos: 1B, **Age**: 30, **Bats**: R)

	G	AB	R	H	D	T	HR	RBI	SB	BB	SO	Avg	OBP	Slg
2000	4	5	0	0	0	0	0	0	0	1	2	.000	.167	.000
Career	79	95	13	21	3	0	3	11	2	11	32	.221	.308	.347

Unroe has mashed the ball in Triple-A and can play first base, third base and the outfield. He can even fill in at second base in a pinch, but his plate discipline is lacking. He refused a minor league assignment and became a free agent. 2001 Outlook: C

Ismael Villegas (Pos: RHP, **Age**: 24)

	W	L	Pct.	ERA	G	GS	Sv	IP	H	BB	SO	HR	Ratio
2000	0	0	-	13.50	1	0	0	2.2	4	2	2	2	2.25
Career	0	0	-	13.50	1	0	0	2.2	4	2	2	2	2.25

Villegas was the payoff for Tyler Houston in 1996. Villegas was used strictly in relief last season. He hasn't complied a yearly ERA below 4.00 since 1995. 2001 Outlook: C

Don Wengert (Pos: RHP, **Age**: 31)

	W	L	Pct.	ERA	G	GS	Sv	IP	H	BB	SO	HR	Ratio
2000	0	1	.000	7.20	10	0	0	10.0	12	5	7	2	1.70
Career	14	30	.318	5.77	156	44	3	422.2	536	151	222	71	1.63

For the fourth straight year, Wengert will begin a new season with a different organization. The question is where. He declared free agency after winning four games in Triple-A last year. 2001 Outlook: D

Atlanta Braves Minor League Prospects

Organization Overview:

The Braves' scouting and player development departments could run a clinic on cultivating young arms. The latest crop appears to be stronger than ever, so much so that losing Bruce Chen, Jimmy Osting, Luis Rivera, Robbie Bell and Ruben Quevedo in the last two years barely has left a dent in the system's depth. It was determined that Atlanta signed up-and-coming shortstop Wilson Betemit at the age of 14, and the organization incurred a six-month ban on scouting or signing in the Dominican Republic, as well as a substantial fine. However, as long as the Braves continue to outsmart the rest of baseball by stealing guys like Kevin Millwood, Matt McClendon, Tim Spooneybarger, Scott Sobkowiak, Adam Wainwright and Matt Belisle in the draft, it just won't matter what their restrictions are. The Braves continue to produce homegrown talent to fill needs at the big league level. Last year Rafael Furcal provided a spark at the top of the lineup, and Jason Marquis showcased overpowering stuff out of the pen.

Matt Belisle

Position: P | **Opening Day Age:** 20
Bats: B **Throws:** R | **Born:** 6/6/80 in
Ht: 6' 3" **Wt:** 195 | Mccallum, TX

Recent Statistics

	W	L	ERA	G	GS	Sv	IP	H	R	BB	SO	HR
1999 R Danville	2	5	4.79	14	14	0	71.1	86	50	23	60	3
2000 A Macon	9	5	2.37	15	15	0	102.1	79	37	18	97	7
2000 A Myrtle Bch	3	4	3.43	12	12	0	78.2	72	32	11	71	5

Belisle started to garner attention from scouts prior to his senior season in high school, but a torn ACL caused some teams to lose interest before the draft. Once thought of as a sure-fire, top-of-the-draft selection, he slipped to the Braves' second-round pick in 1998. After a brief tune-up in the Appalachian League in '99, Belisle showed no ill-effects from the knee injury. He pitched the first half of the season in the SAL and was there long enough to earn recognition around the loop as the best control pitcher. His sinking 94-95 MPH heater, outstanding curve and changeup earned him a promotion to advanced Class-A just two years removed from high school.

Marcus Giles

Position: 2B | **Opening Day Age:** 22
Bats: R **Throws:** R | **Born:** 5/18/78 in San
Ht: 5' 8" **Wt:** 180 | Diego, CA

Recent Statistics

	G	AB	R	H	D	T	HR	RBI	SB	BB	SO	Avg
1999 A Myrtle Bch	126	497	80	162	40	7	13	73	9	54	89	.326
2000 AA Greenville	132	458	73	133	28	2	17	62	25	72	71	.290
2000 MLE	132	442	59	117	25	1	13	50	17	50	76	.265

Much like his older brother Brian was in Cleveland, Marcus has grown accustomed to being overlooked. A 53rd-rounder in '96, Marcus resembles Brian, who was a 17th-rounder, in more ways than one. Both are short and muscular, generating above-average power with quick strokes, and they practice the same intense work ethic. Although his average dipped below .300 for the first time, Marcus continues to flourish at the plate. In Double-A, the 5-foot-8 second baseman drew more walks than Ks, stole a career-high 25 bases and steadily improved his glove work. He has excelled at each level and could very well join Rafael Furcal up the middle in Atlanta within a year.

Wes Helms

Position: 3B | **Opening Day Age:** 24
Bats: R **Throws:** R | **Born:** 5/12/76 in
Ht: 6' 4" **Wt:** 230 | Gastonia, NC

Recent Statistics

	G	AB	R	H	D	T	HR	RBI	SB	BB	SO	Avg
2000 AAA Richmond	136	539	74	155	27	7	20	88	0	27	92	.288
2000 NL Atlanta	6	5	0	1	0	0	0	0	0	0	2	.200
2000 MLE	136	518	58	134	23	5	15	69	0	21	96	.259

Helms reached Triple-A three years ago, so the fact that he still is there could be considered a disappointment. That is, until you take into account the circumstances. The powerful 6-foot-4 slugger suffered a pair of shoulder injuries in '99 that bumped him off schedule, and then of course there is a perennial MVP candidate presenting a formidable obstacle in Atlanta. On the heels of re-establishing his prospect profile with a strong year in Richmond, Helms is coming up to a pivotal season. He is out of options and was to work on learning first base and outfield during winter ball in Venezuela to fortify his status on the 25-man roster before spring. There also exists the possibility in Atlanta that Chipper Jones may be moved to the outfield, leaving a vacancy at third that Helms may be looked upon to fill.

George Lombard

Position: OF | **Opening Day Age:** 25
Bats: L **Throws:** R | **Born:** 9/14/75 in Atlanta,
Ht: 6' 0" **Wt:** 212 | GA

Recent Statistics

	G	AB	R	H	D	T	HR	RBI	SB	BB	SO	Avg
2000 AAA Richmond	112	424	72	117	25	7	10	48	32	55	130	.276
2000 NL Atlanta	27	39	8	4	0	0	0	2	4	1	14	.103
2000 MLE	112	408	56	101	21	5	7	37	23	43	136	.248

Coming off of an impressive performance in the Arizona Fall League in '99, expectations were high for Lombard in 2000. Instead, the athletic outfielder underachieved again, and did nothing to further his status during his second Triple-A stint. A second rounder in '94, his combination of speed and power still is intriguing, and the Braves hope their patience will pay dividends because Lombard is out of options.

Atlanta

Jason Marquis

Position: P
Bats: L **Throws:** R
Ht: 6' 1" **Wt:** 185

Opening Day Age: 22
Born: 8/21/78 in
Manhasset, NY

Recent Statistics

	W	L	ERA	G	GS	Sv	IP	H	R	BB	SO	HR
2000 AA Greenville	4	2	3.57	11	11	0	68.0	68	35	23	49	10
2000 AAA Richmond	0	3	9.00	6	6	0	20.0	26	21	13	18	2
2000 NL Atlanta	1	0	5.01	15	0	0	23.1	23	16	12	17	4

The flame-throwing Marquis arrived in Atlanta well ahead of schedule, making his debut in the Braves' pen on June 6 last season. Atlanta turned to the 22-year-old righty because of his overpowering arsenal of legitimate 97-98 MPH gas and a hard slider. While his role in the pen may have filled a temporary hole, his future is as a starter, especially considering his ability to command three big league pitches. Pitching in relief for the first time and relying primarily on the heat, Marquis lost the feel for his offspeed stuff when he returned to the rotation in Triple-A Richmond. Often lost in the shuffle of the Braves high-profile young guns, he has arrived and heads into spring training as a potential starter.

Matt McClendon

Position: P
Bats: R **Throws:** R
Ht: 6' 6" **Wt:** 220

Opening Day Age: 23
Born: 10/13/77 in
Corpus Christi, TX

Recent Statistics

	W	L	ERA	G	GS	Sv	IP	H	R	BB	SO	HR
1999 A Jamestown	1	1	3.91	7	7	0	23.0	18	11	11	24	2
2000 A Myrtle Bch	3	1	1.59	6	6	0	39.2	24	7	8	43	1
2000 AA Greenville	7	6	3.78	22	21	0	131.0	124	59	54	90	6

The Reds drafted McClendon in the first round out of high school in '96, but he spurned their offer to pitch for the Florida Gators. He never lived up to the expectations, posting ERAs over 6.00, and his prospect star faded. But the Braves kept a close eye on him and nabbed him in the fifth round in '99, feeling that his struggles could be attributed to a heavy workload. In his pro debut, Atlanta limited his innings before letting him air out his 93-94 MPH fastball, curve and changeup last year. He climbed his way to Double-A, but is working on staying consistent with his breaking pitches and the mechanical adjustments applied after college. He's likely to be headed back to Double-A, with an ETA in Atlanta of 2002.

Christian Parra

Position: P
Bats: R **Throws:** R
Ht: 6' 1" **Wt:** 255

Opening Day Age: 23
Born: 2/28/78 in
Sullivan, MO

Recent Statistics

	W	L	ERA	G	GS	Sv	IP	H	R	BB	SO	HR
1999 A Jamestown	1	2	3.10	9	9	0	49.1	46	21	19	62	2
1999 A Macon	1	1	3.31	6	6	0	32.2	33	15	12	37	3
2000 A Myrtle Bch	17	4	2.28	26	25	0	157.2	98	46	56	163	6

To say that Parra emerged from obscurity would be a vast understatement. He doesn't own a prototypical pitcher's frame, which helps explain why he wasn't drafted after junior college. But, he can flat-out pitch. Consistently timed in the 90-91 MPH range, Parra mixes his curve, slider and change effectively and can locate all four pitches with near pinpoint precision. In his first full season, Parra allowed an eye-catching 60 fewer hits than innings pitched while earning the Pitcher of the Year award in the advanced Class-A Carolina League.

Horacio Ramirez

Position: P
Bats: L **Throws:** L
Ht: 6' 1" **Wt:** 170

Opening Day Age: 21
Born: 11/24/79 in
Carson, CA

Recent Statistics

	W	L	ERA	G	GS	Sv	IP	H	R	BB	SO	HR
1999 A Macon	6	3	2.67	17	14	0	77.2	70	30	25	43	6
2000 A Myrtle Bch	15	8	3.22	27	26	0	148.1	136	57	42	125	14

Ramirez didn't garner any attention until last season, and still is relatively unknown. That should change soon. Myrtle Beach pitching coach Bruce Dal Canton deserves a lot of the credit for developing an unbelievable staff of young arms in the Carolina League, and Ramirez was one of his prized projects last year. Despite never making more than 20 starts in a season prior to '99, the 1997 fifth-rounder now is held in high regard as one of the top southpaws in the organization. Ramirez commands three Major League-quality offerings, fooling hitters with a deceptive 89-90 MPH fastball, an excellent slider and changeup delivered from a free and easy motion.

Others to Watch

After a three-month layoff during a court case over **Wilson Betemit's** (20) free-agency status, the 18-year-old switch-hitting shortstop didn't miss a beat, reporting to the New York-Penn League in great shape. The Braves liken his tools to Edgar Renteria. . . **Jung Bong** (20) was one of the most improved pitchers in the system during the second half, displaying more consistency with his curve and change to complement a low-90s heater. . . **Matt Butler** (21) made his successful full-season debut using a 92-93 MPH fastball, good breaking ball and a recently developed changeup to go 13-7, 2.94 ERA. . . **Nathan Kent** (22) was a virtual unknown after getting drafted in the 49th round in 1999, until he emerged in Macon with three quality pitches, including a 93-MPH heater. . . **Scott Sobkowiak** (23) was on the fast track, but surgery to remove bone chips in his elbow forced him out of action after four Double-A starts. The righthander features a sinking 95-MPH fastball and a power curve. . . 1998 29th-rounder **Tim Spooneybarger** (21) used some electric stuff to dominate in the Carolina League. He possesses the best curve in the organization and overpowers opponents with a lively mid-90s fastball. . . Atlanta was stunned to find **Adam Wainwright** (19) at the end of the first round last June. Rated one of the top prospects in both the GCL and Appalachian League, he exhibited a feel for pitching beyond his youth to accompany his 94-MPH fastball, curve and change.

Wrigley Field

Offense

Last season was far from ordinary at Wrigley Field. There were few extended hot spells, and the wind didn't blow out as often as in years past. The result was that Wrigley depressed scoring. It often plays as a pitchers' park during the cooler months of April and May, but a hitters' wind usually prevails over the midsummer months. The power alleys are among the most inviting in the majors.

Defense

The Cubs have to give their pitchers some opportunity to succeed, and keeping the grass long is one way they do it. Pitchers who keep the ball on the ground can induce an above-average number of double plays, and the grass gives immobile infielders an extra step. The corner outfielders must be able to deal with the outfield wall's odd contours near the foul lines, where a flyball may be either a home run or an easily catchable ball, depending on how close it is to the foul pole. The bullpen mounds in foul territory can trip up a novice.

Who It Helps the Most

Sammy Sosa is helped the most, especially since he has the power to take advantage of either power alley (he fared better on the road last year, but almost all the Cubs did). Ricky Gutierrez found he had just enough power to reach the left-field bleachers. Kevin Tapani pitched better here last year, as he often does. Kerry Wood avoids being hurt by the park by keeping the ball out of play.

Who It Hurts the Most

Rick Aguilera, a rather extreme flyball pitcher, was badly hurt by the park, even last year. Todd Van Poppel had trouble adjusting as well. Contact hitters such as Joe Girardi and Eric Young derived little benefit.

Rookies & Newcomers

Matt Stairs, if healthy, could take good advantage of Wrigley. Of course, that's assuming the park returns to its normal ways in 2001. Rondell White should hit more homers, due in part to his escape from Olympic Stadium. Corey Patterson would have a good shot to reach the 20-homer plateau in a full season.

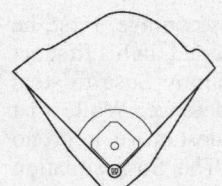

Dimensions: LF-355, LCF-368, CF-400, RCF-368, RF-353

Capacity: 38,884

Elevation: 595 feet

Surface: Grass

Foul Territory: Small

Park Factors

2000 Season

| | Home Games | | | Away Games | | | |
	Cubs	Opp	Total	Cubs	Opp	Total	Index
G	74	74	148	71	71	142	—
Avg	.261	.252	.256	.253	.288	.270	95
AB	2484	2572	5056	2489	2418	4907	99
R	329	364	693	356	466	822	81
H	649	647	1296	629	696	1325	94
2B	115	109	224	135	143	278	78
3B	9	7	16	11	20	31	50
HR	75	95	170	87	111	198	83
BB	291	299	590	270	302	572	100
SO	495	532	1027	510	489	999	100
E	41	49	90	49	44	93	93
E-Infield	29	37	66	40	39	79	80
LHB-Avg	.231	.234	.232	.223	.269	.246	94
LHB-HR	17	34	51	33	41	74	67
RHB-Avg	.278	.263	.271	.270	.299	.284	95
RHB-HR	58	61	119	54	70	124	93

1998-2000

| | Home Games | | | Away Games | | | |
	Cubs	Opp	Total	Cubs	Opp	Total	Index
G	223	223	446	219	219	438	—
Avg	.268	.266	.267	.251	.278	.265	101
AB	7483	7920	15403	7664	7461	15125	100
R	1071	1165	2236	1055	1225	2280	96
H	2004	2108	4112	1925	2076	4001	101
2B	355	386	741	354	395	749	97
3B	46	34	80	38	61	99	79
HR	265	290	555	263	284	547	100
BB	845	808	1653	785	796	1581	103
SO	1533	1610	3143	1664	1427	3091	100
E	156	145	301	151	146	297	100
E-Infield	118	113	231	123	125	248	91
LHB-Avg	.270	.269	.269	.251	.276	.263	103
LHB-HR	81	104	185	97	104	201	92
RHB-Avg	.266	.264	.265	.251	.280	.266	100
RHB-HR	184	186	370	166	180	346	104

2000 Rankings (National League)

- Lowest run factor
- Second-lowest double factor
- Second-lowest triple factor
- Second-lowest home-run factor
- Second-lowest LHB home-run factor
- Third-lowest infield-error factor

Chicago (NL)

Don Baylor

2000 Season

Give Don Baylor credit for his courage. First, he agreed to manage the Cubs; second, in his first act as manager, he challenged Sammy Sosa to steal more bases and play better defense. While that might not have been the shrewdest move, it left no doubt that Baylor was boss. The Sosa situation threatened to force the team to trade him, but ultimately it was resolved. Oddly, this development coincided with the Cubs' complete disintegration, as they finished with the major leagues' worst record, 65-97, a two game drop from the year before.

Offense

Perhaps it's to be expected that Don Baylor, after having managed in Colorado, would view any other park as a pitchers' park. But his fondness for the bunt came as something of a surprise. The Cubs led the majors in sacrifices, and Baylor often called for it early in games. The club had a decent record in one-run games, so the results were defensible. He adopted his predecessor's most questionable strategy, often batting Sammy Sosa ahead of Mark Grace—putting his best RBI man in front of his best on-base man, instead of the other way around.

Pitching & Defense

Baylor gave shots to several young pitchers, with poor results. He was willing to let his starters work deep into games, even a youngster such as Ruben Quevedo or a recovering ligament transplantee such as Kerry Wood. In both cases, he may have had little choice and cannot be entirely blamed for their failures. Baylor called fewer pitchouts with the Cubs than he did in Colorado, and his success rate was a less-than-impressive 33.3 percent last season. One thing he did differently in 2000 was call for more intentional walks.

2001 Outlook

The Cubs can only go up, but the same could have been said a year ago. They can look forward to beginning the year with Rondell White and possibly Corey Patterson in the outfield. Baylor's most pressing tasks will be to sort out the pitching staff and find a replacement for Mark Grace, who signed with Arizona in December.

Born: 6/28/49 in Austin, TX

Playing Experience: 1970-1988, Bal, Oak, Ana, NYY, Bos, Min

Managerial Experience: 7 seasons

Manager Statistics

Year	Team, Lg	W	L	Pct	GB	Finish
2000	Chicago, NL	65	97	.401	30.0	6th Central
7 Seasons		505	566	.472	—	—

2000 Starting Pitchers by Days Rest

	<=3	4	5	6+
Cubs Starts	4	83	28	33
Cubs ERA	3.75	5.28	4.59	6.46
NL Avg Starts	2	80	50	21
NL ERA	5.00	4.61	4.60	5.18

2000 Situational Stats

	Don Baylor	NL Average
Hit & Run Success %	25.3	33.8
Stolen Base Success %	71.5	68.8
Platoon Pct.	50.9	53.2
Defensive Subs	20	19
High-Pitch Outings	15	14
Quick/Slow Hooks	13/24	14/16
Sacrifice Attempts	115	87

2000 Rankings (National League)

- 1st in sacrifice bunt attempts (115)
- 2nd in fewest caught stealings of second base (33), slow hooks (24) and starts on three days rest (4)
- 3rd in double steals (5), sacrifice-bunt percentage (84.4), starting lineups used (130) and one-batter pitcher appearances (41)

Rick Aguilera

2000 Season

Seen as one of the few constants on the team going into the season, veteran closer Rick Aguilera nearly lost the faith of new manager Don Baylor during a very rough stretch in May. He pitched decently for the rest of the year before a broken thumb ended his season in early September. Overall, it was his worst year yet as a closer, and his ERA didn't even reflect that he allowed nearly half of the runners he inherited to score.

Pitching

In his late 30s, Aguilera has come to rely more and more on his forkball. The fact that he gave up 11 home runs in fewer than 50 innings last year illustrates that the forkball doesn't have the sinking action it once had. He also has an average fastball and slider, but he has to have precise command to make it all work. He's tougher on lefthanded hitters than most righthanded pitchers.

Defense & Hitting

Aguilera has a good record at the plate, although he hasn't had much of a chance to add to it since becoming a closer in 1990. Baserunners don't have to worry about Aguilera picking them off; he's nailed only one runner in his career. He's fairly easy to run on but is a good fielder who rarely errs.

2001 Outlook

Aguilera's contract was up at the end of last year and the Cubs declined to offer him arbitration. Chicago also signed Tom Gordon and slated him as the team's closer for 2001. In light of Aguilera's age and unimpressive 2000 season, he may find it hard to find a club willing to pay him closer money. He was effective in the second half, so it's possible his early slump had more to do with a physical problem than age. Aguilera may be reaching the point in his career where he must choose between a less glamorous role and retirement.

Position: RP
Bats: R **Throws:** R
Ht: 6' 5" **Wt:** 210

Opening Day Age: 39
Born: 12/31/61 in San Gabriel, CA
ML Seasons: 16
Pronunciation: ag-yuh-LAIR-uh
Nickname: Aggie

Overall Statistics

	W	L	Pct.	ERA	G	GS	Sv	IP	H	BB	SO	HR	Ratio
2000	1	2	.333	4.91	54	0	29	47.2	47	18	38	11	1.36
Career	86	81	.515	3.57	732	89	318	1291.1	1233	351	1030	138	1.23

How Often He Throws Strikes

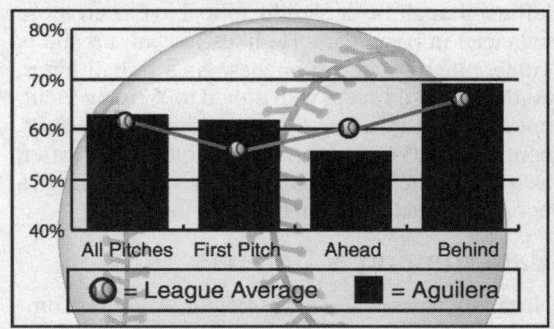

2000 Situational Stats

	W	L	ERA	Sv	IP		AB	H	HR	RBI	Avg
Home	1	1	6.23	13	21.2	LHB	74	19	3	11	.257
Road	0	1	3.81	16	26.0	RHB	113	28	8	22	.248
First Half	1	2	6.52	17	29.0	Sc Pos	46	12	1	19	.261
Scnd Half	0	0	2.41	12	18.2	Clutch	120	28	8	24	.233

2000 Rankings (National League)

- 2nd in blown saves (8)
- 3rd in lowest save percentage (78.4)
- 5th in save opportunities (37)
- 6th in saves
- Led the Cubs in saves, games finished (44), save opportunities (37), save percentage (78.4) and blown saves (8)

Shane Andrews

2000 Season

Andrews hit well after signing with the Cubs in September of 1999 and won the third-base job coming out of spring training last spring. He got off to a hot start before going on the disabled list in late May with lower back pain, a chronic problem for him. He underwent surgery in June to repair a herniated disk. He returned in August, reclaimed his third base job (mostly by default), and hit well for the last five weeks of the season.

Hitting

Andrews is strikeout-prone and doesn't hit for much of an average, but he has good power to all fields. Last year he did most of his damage against lefties, though his left-right splits have been more balanced in past years. He likes the ball up and is vulnerable to offspeed pitches. As a flyball hitter, Andrews would seem well-suited to Wrigley Field, but he didn't take much advantage of the friendly confines in 2000. The wind didn't blow out as often as it had in the past, though, and he could receive a boost this year if he remains with the Cubs.

Baserunning & Defense

Normally an above-average fielder, Andrews committed a lot of errors early last season—perhaps due in part to his back. An underappreciated glove man in past years, his range now has eroded to the point where he's just average. Andrews has decent hands and a strong throwing arm. He has no speed and advances only by virtue of his bat, not his legs.

2001 Outlook

A free agent at the conclusion of the 2000 season, Andrews probably won't be back with the Cubs. Chicago all but assured his departure when they traded Tim Worrell for San Francisco's Bill Mueller in mid-November, and then did not offer Andrews arbitration. Andrews' encouraging return late last summer may induce another club to pick him up to fill a smaller role, but his days as a regular probably are over.

Position: 3B
Bats: R **Throws:** R
Ht: 6' 1" **Wt:** 220

Opening Day Age: 29
Born: 8/28/71 in Dallas, TX
ML Seasons: 6
Nickname: Mongo, Caveman

Overall Statistics

	G	AB	R	H	D	T	HR	RBI	SB	BB	SO	Avg	OBP	Slg
2000	66	192	25	44	5	0	14	39	1	27	59	.229	.329	.474
Career	562	1691	194	374	75	4	86	263	7	190	512	.221	.299	.423

Where He Hits the Ball

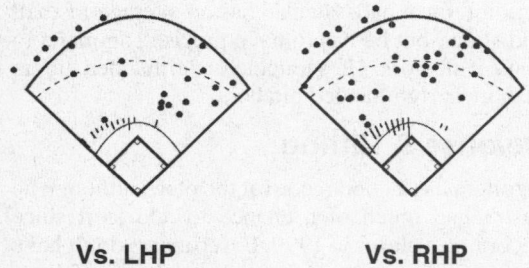

Vs. LHP   **Vs. RHP**

2000 Situational Stats

	AB	H	HR	RBI	Avg		AB	H	HR	RBI	Avg
Home	91	20	7	20	.220	LHP	61	18	7	21	.295
Road	101	24	7	19	.238	RHP	131	26	7	18	.198
First Half	118	25	10	27	.212	Sc Pos	54	13	6	28	.241
Scnd Half	74	19	4	12	.257	Clutch	32	8	4	11	.250

2000 Rankings (National League)

- 5th in most GDPs per GDP situation (18.0%)
- 10th in errors at third base (12)

Damon Buford

2000 Season

Last year, for the first time in his big league career, Damon Buford played every day. He performed about as well as he always had, flashing good defense while hitting for an unimpressive average with a little pop. His first-half power numbers were a pleasant surprise, but a prolonged second-half slump brought them down to his customary levels. As one of the few Cubs who could cover center field, he was allowed to keep his job almost all season.

Hitting

Buford takes a power hitter's approach, pulling the ball with regularity while making inconsistent contact. The problem is that he doesn't have quite enough power to make up for his frequent strikeouts and middling average. He hits lefthanders well but never has hit righthanders enough to deserve to face them regularly. Last season was no exception. He doesn't reach base enough or generate adequate power to bat anywhere but the bottom third of the order.

Baserunning & Defense

Few others cover as much ground as Buford, who gets excellent jumps and puts his speed to good use. His throwing has improved but is no better than average. He's never mastered the nuances of reading pitchers and isn't much of a threat to steal, though he is a good baserunner.

2001 Outlook

It must be tough for Buford to accept that no matter how well he plays, his days as the Cubs' center fielder are numbered. Super-prospect Corey Patterson is on the way, and manager Don Baylor seemingly can't wait for him to arrive. Buford may not like it, but he is better suited to the backup role to which he ultimately will be relegated. As a platoon player and fourth outfielder, he could be quite useful.

Position: CF
Bats: R **Throws:** R
Ht: 5'10" **Wt:** 180

Opening Day Age: 30
Born: 6/12/70 in Baltimore, MD
ML Seasons: 8
Pronunciation: BYEW-ford

Overall Statistics

	G	AB	R	H	D	T	HR	RBI	SB	BB	SO	Avg	OBP	Slg
2000	150	495	64	124	18	3	15	48	4	47	118	.251	.324	.390
Career	664	1768	269	433	84	9	51	210	56	169	407	.245	.316	.389

Where He Hits the Ball

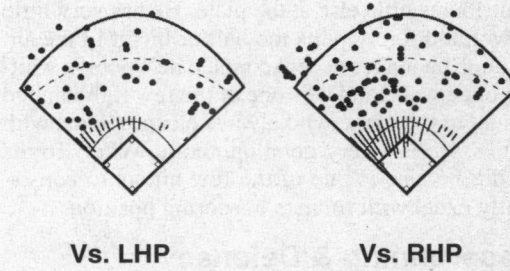

Vs. LHP   **Vs. RHP**

2000 Situational Stats

	AB	H	HR	RBI	Avg		AB	H	HR	RBI	Avg
Home	242	65	9	26	.269	LHP	135	44	4	20	.326
Road	253	59	6	22	.233	RHP	360	80	11	28	.222
First Half	286	78	12	30	.273	Sc Pos	106	29	3	35	.274
Scnd Half	209	46	3	18	.220	Clutch	98	17	3	6	.173

2000 Rankings (National League)

- 2nd in lowest batting average vs. righthanded pitchers
- 3rd in lowest on-base percentage vs. righthanded pitchers (.297)
- 4th in lowest slugging percentage vs. righthanded pitchers (.347)
- 7th in errors in center field (4), lowest batting average on the road and lowest fielding percentage in center field (.987)
- 8th in lowest batting average
- Led the Cubs in triples, hit by pitch (8) and lowest percentage of swings on the first pitch (19.4)
- Led NL center fielders in batting average vs. lefthanded pitchers and lowest percentage of swings on the first pitch (19.4)

Joe Girardi

2000 Season

Joe Girardi returned to his roots last year, signing a free-agent contract with the Cubs, his original major league team. The veteran receiver was brought back primarily to nurse along the Cubs' young pitchers. If Girardi's presence was beneficial, the youngsters' ERAs failed to reflect it, but Girardi got mostly favorable reviews anyhow. He kept his average up for most of the year and was hitting .297 on August 6 when his nose was broken by a pitch. He returned to the lineup less than a week later, but hit only .223 the rest of the way.

Hitting

Girardi generally lines enough fastballs into short right-center to post a decent batting average, but he contributes little else at the plate. He has very little power and rarely pulls the ball or hits it in the air. Though he makes decent contact, he's poor at waiting out a walk, and he's one of the few righthanded hitters in the game who always has problems with lefties. He is a very good bunter, however. To his credit, he also is one of the few hitters to consistently excel with runners in scoring position.

Baserunning & Defense

Girardi is fairly agile behind the plate and blocks balls in the dirt capably enough. His accurate arm and quick release help keep the running game in check. Whatever speed he once had is gone, and at this point in his career, he's a non-threat on the bases.

2001 Outlook

Girardi's future with the Cubs is very much up in the air. The team signed free agent catcher Todd Hundley to a four-year, $22.5 million deal, and at that price, Hundley will make most of the starts behind the plate. Chicago did not offer arbitration to Jeff Reed, so for now Girardi will be Hundley's primary backup. By now, everyone knows exactly what to expect from Girardi, and he's always able to fulfill those expectations, more or less.

Position: C
Bats: R **Throws:** R
Ht: 5'11" **Wt:** 200

Opening Day Age: 36
Born: 10/14/64 in Peoria, IL
ML Seasons: 12
Pronunciation: jeh-RAR-dee

Overall Statistics

	G	AB	R	H	D	T	HR	RBI	SB	BB	SO	Avg	OBP	Slg
2000	106	363	47	101	15	1	6	40	1	32	61	.278	.339	.375
Career	1093	3641	412	986	166	24	32	383	43	239	518	.271	.318	.356

Where He Hits the Ball

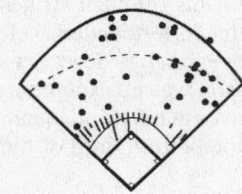 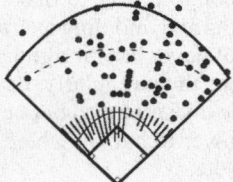

Vs. LHP Vs. RHP

2000 Situational Stats

	AB	H	HR	RBI	Avg		AB	H	HR	RBI	Avg
Home	194	50	4	21	.258	LHP	114	23	2	7	.202
Road	169	51	2	19	.302	RHP	249	78	4	33	.313
First Half	212	64	4	21	.302	Sc Pos	77	24	0	29	.312
Scnd Half	151	37	2	19	.245	Clutch	68	17	0	3	.250

2000 Rankings (National League)

- 1st in lowest slugging percentage vs. lefthanded pitchers (.272)
- 2nd in lowest batting average vs. lefthanded pitchers
- 4th in fielding percentage at catcher (.993) and lowest on-base percentage vs. lefthanded pitchers (.300)
- Led the Cubs in GDPs (12)

Mark Grace

Position: 1B
Bats: L **Throws:** L
Ht: 6' 2" **Wt:** 200

Opening Day Age: 36
Born: 6/28/64 in
Winston-Salem, NC
ML Seasons: 13

2000 Season

Mark Grace didn't have a lot of fun last season. In the final year of his contract, the longtime Cub broke a finger in spring training, tore a hamstring in May and saw signs late in the summer that the club didn't intend to retain him. The distraction seemed to bother him, as he batted .232 without a homer over his last 138 at-bats to finish under .300 for the first time in six years.

Hitting

At the plate, Grace has everything but middle-of-the-order home-run power. He has an excellent eye and is quite content to take a walk if he doesn't get a good pitch to hit. He hits line drives to all fields and finds the gaps often enough to be among the leaders in doubles year after year. He still makes excellent contact and struck out a career-low 28 times in 2000. He waits on changeups and breaking balls extremely well, even from southpaws, who give him little trouble.

Baserunning & Defense

Despite distinctly below-average speed, Grace is a heady baserunner who knows his limits. He takes advantage of opportunities to advance less than in years past. He has a reputation as one of the finest defensive first basemen in the game, and while he may no longer deserve that label, he's still very good. He led major league first basemen in fielding percentage last year, and his soft hands still put his fellow infielders at ease. His range afield isn't what it once was but still is well above average, and his arm is adequate for the position.

2001 Outlook

Starting anew in Arizona, Grace is a good bet to rebound and get his average back into his customary .300 range. His two-year, $6 million deal with a mutual option for 2003 most likely will keep him comfortable until he retires. He still stings the ball consistently enough to be a productive hitter. The move to Bank One Ballpark does not figure to give him much of a boost, however, as it has played almost identical to Wrigley Field for lefthanded hitters over the past three years.

Overall Statistics

	G	AB	R	H	D	T	HR	RBI	SB	BB	SO	Avg	OBP	Slg
2000	143	510	75	143	41	1	11	82	1	95	28	.280	.394	.429
Career	1910	7156	1057	2201	456	43	148	1004	67	946	561	.308	.386	.445

Where He Hits the Ball

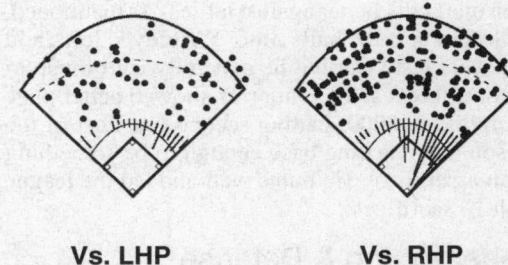

Vs. LHP   **Vs. RHP**

2000 Situational Stats

	AB	H	HR	RBI	Avg		AB	H	HR	RBI	Avg
Home	260	77	3	36	.296	LHP	131	40	6	23	.305
Road	250	66	8	46	.264	RHP	379	103	5	59	.272
First Half	246	70	7	34	.285	Sc Pos	134	41	1	63	.306
Scnd Half	264	73	4	48	.277	Clutch	89	19	2	11	.213

2000 Rankings (National League)

- 1st in fielding percentage at first base (.997) and highest percentage of swings put into play (59.1)
- 3rd in lowest cleanup slugging percentage (.401)
- 4th in highest percentage of pitches taken (62.4)
- 5th in lowest percentage of swings that missed (8.3)
- 8th in doubles and batting average with the bases loaded (.556)
- 9th in walks
- 10th in intentional walks (11)
- Led the Cubs in doubles, sacrifice flies (8), walks, fewest GDPs per GDP situation (4.6%), batting average with the bases loaded (.556), highest percentage of pitches taken (62.4) and highest percentage of swings put into play (59.1)

Chicago (NL)

Ricky Gutierrez

2000 Season

Signed as a free agent to plug the Cubs' hole at shortstop, Ricky Gutierrez came through with his best major league season. He got off to a hot start, as he often does, but broke from his usual pattern by remaining productive over most of the second half. Gutierrez more than doubled his previous career high in homers, and he slugged better than .400 for the first time in his eight big league campaigns.

Hitting

If teams defensed Gutierrez with a five-man infield, he might never hit .200 again. Most of his hits are liners or grounders through the infield. He hits to all fields against both lefties and righties, but has been markedly better against lefties. As mentioned, he lofted a few balls into Wrigley's left-field bleachers last year, but he generally isn't much of a power threat at all. Gutierrez showed better plate discipline in 2000, batting second for most of the season and reaching base enough to be something of an asset there. He bunts well and led the league with 16 sacrifices.

Baserunning & Defense

Gutierrez adjusted well from artificial turf to Wrigley's thick grass, which helped to camouflage his average range. Getting that extra split-second to get into position to receive the ball also helped him cut his errors. Gutierrez posted the highest fielding percentage among everyday National League shortstops in 2000. His hands and arm are more than adequate for the position. He doesn't have a basestealer's speed, but did well in his limited attempts.

2001 Outlook

The Cubs picked up Gutierrez' $3.4 million option for 2001 in early November, and he will try to prove last year wasn't a fluke. It might have been a bit over his head, however, and there's no guarantee that he'll continue to get the job done in the No. 2 slot, or that he'll reach double-digits in homers again. Even if the Cubs have to drop him down in the order, he'll remain their starting shortstop for 2001.

Position: SS
Bats: R **Throws:** R
Ht: 6' 1" **Wt:** 195

Opening Day Age: 30
Born: 5/23/70 in Miami, FL
ML Seasons: 8
Pronunciation: goo-tee-AIR-ez

Overall Statistics

	G	AB	R	H	D	T	HR	RBI	SB	BB	SO	Avg	OBP	Slg
2000	125	449	73	124	19	2	11	56	8	66	58	.276	.375	.401
Career	817	2598	347	682	99	22	24	242	45	293	463	.263	.342	.345

Where He Hits the Ball

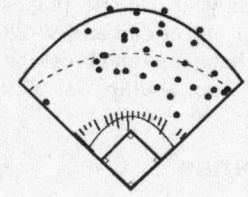
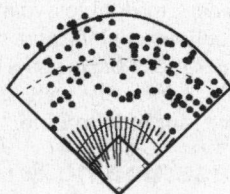

Vs. LHP   Vs. RHP

2000 Situational Stats

	AB	H	HR	RBI	Avg		AB	H	HR	RBI	Avg
Home	216	62	7	21	.287	LHP	90	32	1	13	.356
Road	233	62	4	35	.266	RHP	359	92	10	43	.256
First Half	216	61	7	30	.282	Sc Pos	116	37	2	45	.319
Scnd Half	233	63	4	26	.270	Clutch	79	11	2	10	.139

2000 Rankings (National League)

- 1st in sacrifice bunts (16) and fielding percentage at shortstop (.986)
- 3rd in lowest batting average in the clutch
- 5th in highest groundball/flyball ratio (2.2)
- 10th in highest percentage of swings put into play (50.4)
- Led the Cubs in sacrifice bunts (16), highest groundball/flyball ratio (2.2), batting average with runners in scoring position and batting average on a 3-2 count (.340)
- Led NL shortstops in sacrifice bunts (16) and lowest percentage of swings on the first pitch (20.8)

Jon Lieber

2000 Season

Over the first four months of the 2000 season, Jon Lieber was one of the best pitchers in baseball. He entered August with a 10-5 record and a 3.49 ERA, as well as 172.2 innings pitched—second in the majors only to Randy Johnson. Then he completely collapsed in August and September, dropping six of eight decisions and posting a 6.43 ERA in 12 starts. Though he ended up leading the majors in innings while posting a winning record with a last-place team, his season could have been a lot better.

Pitching

Year after year, Lieber is two-thirds great and one-third lousy; he consistently has one of the widest platoon splits of any major league starter. With a righthanded hitter at the plate, he's one of the best pitchers in baseball, but with a lefty at the dish, he's distinctly below average. His terrific command of a fastball and slider makes him tough on righties, but he lacks a decent second pitch against lefties. Lieber showed improved stamina within games last season, which perhaps encouraged manager Don Baylor to work him so hard.

Defense & Hitting

Lieber finishes his delivery in good position to field comebackers and covers the middle of the infield very well. He cuts off the running game through good use of the slide step. A decent bunter, he showed big improvement at the plate, contributing 18 hits, including four doubles.

2001 Outlook

Lieber was worked much harder last year than ever before, and it remains to be seen how his arm will hold up. He's never been a fitness fanatic, and his late-season dive is a legitimate cause for concern. If he's sound, he could have his best year yet if the team behind him improves at all.

Position: SP
Bats: L **Throws:** R
Ht: 6' 3" **Wt:** 225

Opening Day Age: 30
Born: 4/2/70 in Council Bluffs, IA
ML Seasons: 7
Pronunciation: LEE-burr

Overall Statistics

	W	L	Pct.	ERA	G	GS	Sv	IP	H	BB	SO	HR	Ratio
2000	12	11	.522	4.41	35	35	0	251.0	248	54	192	36	1.20
Career	60	69	.465	4.32	217	170	2	1137.0	1224	258	886	148	1.30

How Often He Throws Strikes

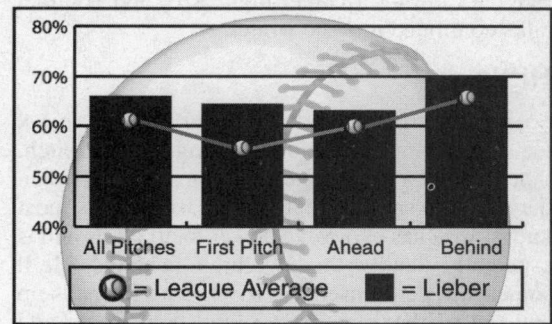

2000 Situational Stats

	W	L	ERA	Sv	IP		AB	H	HR	RBI	Avg
Home	6	5	3.71	0	128.2	LHB	436	124	18	64	.284
Road	6	6	5.15	0	122.1	RHB	530	124	18	61	.234
First Half	8	5	3.63	0	143.2	Sc Pos	191	51	5	78	.267
Scnd Half	4	6	5.45	0	107.1	Clutch	107	20	6	8	.187

2000 Rankings (National League)

- 1st in games started, innings pitched and batters faced (1,047)
- 3rd in complete games (6), hits allowed and home runs allowed
- Led the Cubs in ERA, wins, games started, complete games (6), innings pitched, hits allowed, batters faced (1,047), home runs allowed, hit batsmen (10), strikeouts, balks (2), pitches thrown (3,669), pickoff throws (138), GDPs induced (17), highest strikeout/walk ratio (3.6), lowest batting average allowed (.257), lowest slugging percentage allowed (.424), lowest on-base percentage allowed (.301), highest ground-ball/flyball ratio allowed (1.7) and lowest stolen-base percentage allowed (64.3)

Sammy Sosa

2000 Season

After all the accolades Sammy Sosa earned and received the previous two seasons, no one expected that his 2000 season would be as tumultuous as it ultimately turned out to be. It began in January when new manager Don Baylor challenged Sosa to run more and upgrade his defensive play. When negotiations for a contract extension stalled in June, Sosa—in the next-to-last year of his contract—told the club to either sign him to an extension or trade him. The Cubs shopped him, but the public outcry against trading the Cubs' biggest hero was overwhelming, and the player and club soon smoothed things over. Sosa completed another fine season, leading the majors with 50 home runs and hitting a career-high .320, and contract talks continued into the winter.

Hitting

Sosa is far from the wild swinger he used to be. He's gotten into the habit of taking the first pitch, though quite a few pitchers got hurt last year when they tried to sneak a first strike past him. As most know, Sosa has explosive power to all fields and is especially deadly on knee-high fastballs. He'll sometimes get himself out by chasing fastballs up and out of the zone or breaking balls down and away, but he doesn't do it nearly as often as he used to. The drop in his home-run total was due more to the oddly unfriendly winds at Wrigley last summer than any decline in his skills.

Baserunning & Defense

Bulkier than he was in his 30-steal days, Sosa no longer is much of a stolen-base threat. Despite Baylor's urging, Sosa virtually stopped running in the second half last year. He has the range to be a good right fielder, but misses more than his share of catchable balls. His throwing accuracy has improved but he's lost some arm strength.

2001 Outlook

If the reconciliation between Sosa and the Cubs' front office results in the contract extension he's been seeking, Sosa ought to remain happy and productive for years to come. He loves being the center of attention, and with the Cubs, he'll have little competition in that department.

Position: RF
Bats: R **Throws:** R
Ht: 6' 0" **Wt:** 220

Opening Day Age: 32
Born: 11/12/68 in San Pedro de Macoris, Dominican Republic
ML Seasons: 12

Overall Statistics

	G	AB	R	H	D	T	HR	RBI	SB	BB	SO	Avg	OBP	Slg
2000	156	604	106	193	38	1	50	138	7	91	168	.320	.406	.634
Career	1565	5893	947	1606	244	36	386	1079	231	519	1537	.273	.333	.523

Where He Hits the Ball

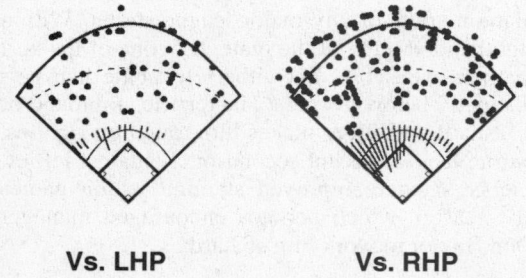

Vs. LHP   **Vs. RHP**

2000 Situational Stats

	AB	H	HR	RBI	Avg		AB	H	HR	RBI	Avg
Home	291	89	22	59	.306	LHP	124	43	8	23	.347
Road	313	104	28	79	.332	RHP	480	150	42	115	.313
First Half	338	103	23	74	.305	Sc Pos	160	50	15	91	.313
Scnd Half	266	90	27	64	.338	Clutch	102	28	8	23	.275

2000 Rankings (National League)

- 1st in home runs, pitches seen (2,877) and errors in right field (10)
- 2nd in total bases (383), RBI and strikeouts
- 3rd in HR frequency (12.1 ABs per HR), on-base percentage vs. lefthanded pitchers (.461) and lowest fielding percentage in right field (.970)
- Led the Cubs in batting average, home runs, runs scored, hits, total bases (383), RBI, sacrifice flies (8), intentional walks (19), times on base (286), strikeouts, GDPs (12), pitches seen (2,877), plate appearances (705), slugging percentage, on-base percentage, HR frequency (12.1 ABs per HR), most pitches seen per plate appearance (4.08), batting average in the clutch and batting average vs. lefthanded pitchers

Kevin Tapani

Position: SP
Bats: R **Throws:** R
Ht: 6' 1" **Wt:** 190

Opening Day Age: 37
Born: 2/18/64 in Des Moines, IA
ML Seasons: 12
Pronunciation: TAP-uh-nee
Nickname: Tap

2000 Season

Give Kevin Tapani a little credit—for a 36-year-old with a bad back who pitched in a home-run park with a dismal team behind him, he did OK last year. His sore back didn't prevent him from taking the mound every fifth day, at least until September, when a knee injury did him in. Despite missing almost a month, he pitched nearly 200 innings and usually kept his club in the game.

Pitching

Health problems have cut into his innings during each of the last two seasons, but when he's on the mound, Tapani is as effective as he ever was. He's the consummate savvy veteran, getting by with average stuff by hitting his spots and mixing his pitches. He has an average fastball, a decent splitter and changeup, and good command. He's vulnerable to the longball when a hitter guesses along with him, but he rarely hurts himself with bases on balls. Lefthanded hitters generally fare no better against Tapani than righthanded hitters do, and lefties hit just .231 against him in 2000.

Defense & Hitting

Tapani fielded his position well last year before his knee problem cropped up. He's always surehanded and hasn't committed an error in four years. He helps himself with the bat on occasion but isn't a consistent threat, though he can lay down a bunt when needed. He doesn't have much of a pickoff move, but does a reasonable job of keeping the running game in check by getting the ball to the plate quickly.

2001 Outlook

Tapani will be counted upon to lend stability to the Cubs' rotation this year. If he stays healthy, he is the type of pitcher who could help a contending team for the stretch run, so the Cubs might shop him around as the trade deadline approaches.

Overall Statistics

	W	L	Pct.	ERA	G	GS	Sv	IP	H	BB	SO	HR	Ratio
2000	8	12	.400	5.01	30	30	0	195.2	208	47	150	35	1.30
Career	134	111	.547	4.34	332	325	0	2096.2	2221	514	1333	236	1.30

How Often He Throws Strikes

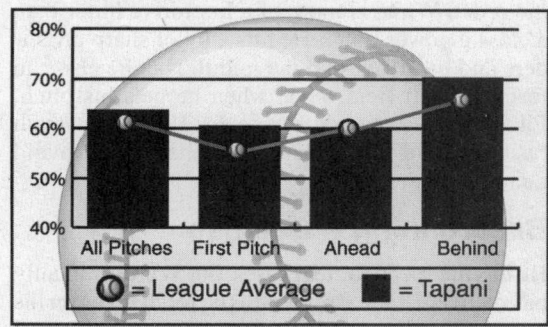

◎ = League Average   ■ = Tapani

2000 Situational Stats

	W	L	ERA	Sv	IP		AB	H	HR	RBI	Avg
Home	6	6	4.32	0	125.0	LHB	312	72	9	32	.231
Road	2	6	6.24	0	70.2	RHB	455	136	26	74	.299
First Half	5	7	4.74	0	125.1	Sc Pos	144	50	10	70	.347
Scnd Half	3	5	5.50	0	70.1	Clutch	62	14	4	7	.226

2000 Rankings (National League)

- 2nd in highest batting average allowed with runners in scoring position
- 4th in home runs allowed and most home runs allowed per nine innings (1.61)
- 6th in lowest winning percentage
- 8th in fewest walks per nine innings (2.2) and least run support per nine innings (4.5)
- 9th in highest batting average allowed vs. righthanded batters
- 10th in highest strikeout/walk ratio (3.2) and highest ERA
- Led the Cubs in losses, stolen bases allowed (17), runners caught stealing (8), most GDPs induced per nine innings (0.7) and most strikeouts per nine innings (6.9)

Chicago (NL)

379

Rondell White

2000 Season

It was a cruel irony that Rondell White suffered a season-ending shoulder injury only weeks after finally escaping Olympic Stadium. The sore-kneed outfielder, who'd been plagued by the Big O's unforgiving artificial turf for his entire career, was dealt to the Cubs at the trading deadline. He hit well for his new club until an ill-fated stolen-base attempt in late August resulted in a dislocated left shoulder. Overall, it was a fairly typical year for White, who also missed time with hamstring problems but hit well when in the lineup.

Hitting

Although he's well-suited to his usual third spot in the order, White is more of a line-drive hitter than a classic power hitter. He hits a lot of sharp grounders and line drives up the middle, but he also can reach the left-field fence when he gets his pitch. Pitchers have learned not to feed him first-pitch fastballs, and lefthanders wish they could avoid facing him altogether.

Baserunning & Defense

He has the speed to steal bases, but White gradually has realized that it isn't worth the toll it takes on his knees. He still runs the bases better than almost all middle-of-the-order hitters. He has the range, if not the durability, to cover center field, and is one of the most wide-ranging left fielders the Cubs have had in recent years. He has a very poor throwing arm, however—one of the weakest in the game.

2001 Outlook

The Cubs hold the option on White's contract for the 2001 season and are expecting him to form a potent one-two punch with Sammy Sosa this year. If Wrigley Field's grass helps keep White in the lineup, he easily could enjoy the best season of his career. Olympic Stadium routinely turned his homers into doubles, so his power numbers could get a boost.

Position: LF
Bats: R **Throws:** R
Ht: 6' 0" **Wt:** 210

Opening Day Age: 29
Born: 2/23/72 in Milledgeville, GA
ML Seasons: 8

Overall Statistics

	G	AB	R	H	D	T	HR	RBI	SB	BB	SO	Avg	OBP	Slg
2000	94	357	59	111	26	0	13	61	5	33	79	.311	.374	.493
Career	761	2823	427	830	167	23	103	391	88	205	506	.294	.349	.479

Where He Hits the Ball

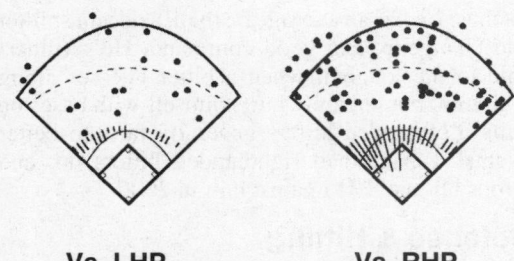

Vs. LHP　　　　**Vs. RHP**

2000 Situational Stats

	AB	H	HR	RBI	Avg		AB	H	HR	RBI	Avg
Home	194	57	3	35	.294	LHP	74	25	3	11	.338
Road	163	54	10	26	.331	RHP	283	86	10	50	.304
First Half	290	89	11	54	.307	Sc Pos	100	35	2	46	.350
Scnd Half	67	22	2	7	.328	Clutch	47	15	4	10	.319

2000 Rankings (National League)

- 9th in batting average with runners in scoring position (.350)

Kerry Wood

2000 Season

All things considered, Kerry Wood's 2000 season was rather encouraging. Coming off Tommy John surgery, he returned a month ahead of schedule, suffered no arm problems and showed that he still could be dominant at times. His command was inconsistent, but he gradually improved as the year progressed and had a fairly good second half despite a strained oblique muscle that shelved him for three weeks in August.

Pitching

Reconstructive surgery has cost Wood little velocity—he still hits the mid-90s consistently. The hard curveball and slider that made him so unhittable as a rookie were not in evidence last year. Probably at the Cubs' insistence, he relied far less on breaking balls. Instead, he used changeups and two-seamers, but lacked command of them and often got into trouble using them. His overall command sometimes wavers, and there are games where he simply can't find the strike zone. Wood regularly reaches the 100-pitch mark by the sixth or seventh inning—his 1998 20-strikeout game and last season's September 12 win over the Reds are Wood's only two complete games at any level of pro ball.

Defense & Hitting

Wood has a decent pickoff move, but runners do test him despite the many high fastballs he throws. In the field, he rarely hurts himself. He's a very good hitting pitcher—perhaps the only serious power threat among major league hurlers. He doesn't strike out often and can bunt when needed.

2001 Outlook

If Wood's arm remains healthy, he can only improve. The Cubs may be less reluctant to let him throw breaking balls or work deep into games this year, so he'll almost certainly be more effective and have more chances to pick up victories. The only concern is that the Cubs may have allowed him to push himself too hard last year, but his fine late-season work seemed to show that he hadn't exceeded his limits.

Position: SP
Bats: R **Throws:** R
Ht: 6' 5" **Wt:** 230

Opening Day Age: 23
Born: 6/16/77 in Irving, TX
ML Seasons: 2

Overall Statistics

	W	L	Pct.	ERA	G	GS	Sv	IP	H	BB	SO	HR	Ratio
2000	8	7	.533	4.80	23	23	0	137.0	112	87	132	17	1.45
Career	21	13	.618	4.03	49	49	0	303.2	229	172	365	31	1.32

How Often He Throws Strikes

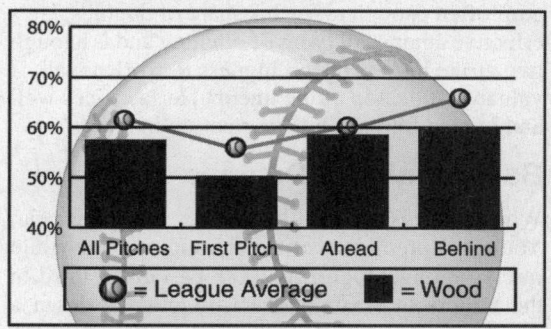

◖ = League Average   ■ = Wood

2000 Situational Stats

	W	L	ERA	Sv	IP		AB	H	HR	RBI	Avg
Home	4	2	4.05	0	60.0	LHB	224	50	6	27	.223
Road	4	5	5.38	0	77.0	RHB	271	62	11	42	.229
First Half	3	6	5.25	0	73.2	Sc Pos	128	32	6	53	.250
Scnd Half	5	1	4.26	0	63.1	Clutch	45	12	1	3	.267

2000 Rankings (National League)

- Led the Cubs in walks allowed, wild pitches (5), lowest batting average allowed vs. lefthanded batters, lowest batting average allowed vs. righthanded batters, lowest batting average allowed with runners in scoring position and winning percentage

Chicago (NL)

381

Eric Young

Position: 2B
Bats: R **Throws:** R
Ht: 5' 8" **Wt:** 175

Opening Day Age: 33
Born: 5/18/67 in New Brunswick, NJ
ML Seasons: 9
Nickname: E.Y.

2000 Season

It's funny how things work out sometimes. The Cubs acquired Eric Young from the Dodgers before the 1999 season when they were forced to take on Young's contract in order to get starter Ismael Valdes. Valdes was a complete flop and was traded back to Los Angeles during the season, but Young had a fine year as the Cubs' second baseman and leadoff man. Perhaps most importantly, he was able to play every day and overcome the leg problems that plagued him the previous two seasons.

Hitting

Young's a prototypical slap hitter, using a short, quick stroke to send liners to all fields. He splits the gaps often enough to log his share of doubles. He's effective against all types of pitching and is a tough two-strike hitter. His willingness to work a walk is valuable at the top of the lineup. He sacrifices well and bunted for base hits more often in 2000.

Baserunning & Defense

When his legs are healthy, as they were last year, Young is a premier basestealer, running often while rarely getting caught. In 2000, he ranked third in the majors in steals and wasn't gunned down a single time in his last 28 attempts, dating from the day before the All-Star break through the end of the season. Decent range is his only asset in the field. His hands are stiff, his arm is weak and his double-play pivot is slow.

2001 Outlook

As Young enters his mid-30s, he's showing no signs of decline. He may begin to slow down in a few years, but he appears to be solid for the time being. Few players are more consistent from year to year, and as long as he keeps his legs in shape, the Cubs shouldn't need to worry about the top of their lineup.

Overall Statistics

	G	AB	R	H	D	T	HR	RBI	SB	BB	SO	Avg	OBP	Slg
2000	153	607	98	180	40	2	6	47	54	63	39	.297	.367	.399
Career	1088	3921	664	1139	195	35	49	385	346	447	278	.290	.369	.396

Where He Hits the Ball

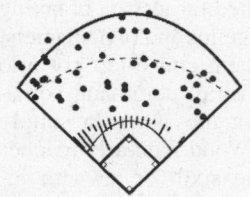
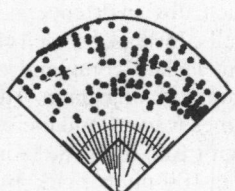

Vs. LHP   **Vs. RHP**

2000 Situational Stats

	AB	H	HR	RBI	Avg		AB	H	HR	RBI	Avg
Home	316	93	5	31	.294	LHP	138	47	2	8	.341
Road	291	87	1	16	.299	RHP	469	133	4	39	.284
First Half	345	106	6	30	.307	Sc Pos	120	32	0	40	.267
Scnd Half	262	74	0	17	.282	Clutch	100	21	0	9	.210

2000 Rankings (National League)

- 2nd in lowest percentage of swings that missed (7.6), highest percentage of swings put into play (58.9) and steals of third (7)
- 3rd in stolen bases, stolen-base percentage (88.5), errors at second base (15) and bunts in play (30)
- Led the Cubs in at-bats, singles, stolen bases, caught stealing (7), hit by pitch (8), GDPs (12), stolen-base percentage (88.5), batting average on an 0-2 count (.306), on-base percentage for a leadoff hitter (.370), batting average with two strikes (.247), bunts in play (30), lowest percentage of swings that missed (7.6), steals of third (7) and highest percentage of extra bases taken as a runner (66.0)

Roosevelt Brown

Position: LF
Bats: L **Throws:** R
Ht: 5'11" **Wt:** 195

Opening Day Age: 25
Born: 8/3/75 in Vicksburg, MS
ML Seasons: 2

Overall Statistics

	G	AB	R	H	D	T	HR	RBI	SB	BB	SO	Avg	OBP	Slg
2000	45	91	11	32	8	0	3	14	0	4	22	.352	.378	.538
Career	78	155	17	46	14	1	4	24	1	6	36	.297	.321	.477

2000 Situational Stats

	AB	H	HR	RBI	Avg		AB	H	HR	RBI	Avg
Home	38	14	1	8	.368	LHP	4	1	0	0	.250
Road	53	18	2	6	.340	RHP	87	31	3	14	.356
First Half	19	5	0	0	.263	Sc Pos	23	5	1	12	.217
Scnd Half	72	27	3	14	.375	Clutch	17	3	1	1	.176

2000 Season

As one of the more advanced hitters in the upper levels of the Cubs' farm system, Roosevelt Brown has earned extended looks during each of the past two Septembers. He made the club out of spring training last year as a fifth outfielder. After seeing little playing time, Brown was sent down on May 2. He was recalled in late August, played regularly against righthanders and hit very well, positioning himself for a larger role in 2001.

Hitting, Baserunning & Defense

Brown is an aggressive, flyball hitter with decent straightaway power. He hasn't been allowed to face many lefties in the majors after hitting them well in the minors. He has decent speed, but not enough of it to be much of a basestealer or center fielder. He can get by in left or right field and has a strong enough arm to play right. After going 1-for-13 as a pinch-hitter in 1999, he did much better coming off the bench last year, batting .286 with a homer and five RBI in 14 at-bats.

2001 Outlook

Brown is the leading candidate to back up the outfield corners and serve as the team's top pinch-hitting threat. He'd be well-suited for the role. He'd also be first in line to take over for Rondell White if the oft-injured left fielder is sidelined.

Kyle Farnsworth

Position: RP
Bats: R **Throws:** R
Ht: 6' 4" **Wt:** 215

Opening Day Age: 24
Born: 4/14/76 in Wichita, KS
ML Seasons: 2

Overall Statistics

	W	L	Pct.	ERA	G	GS	Sv	IP	H	BB	SO	HR	Ratio
2000	2	9	.182	6.43	46	5	1	77.0	90	50	74	14	1.82
Career	7	18	.280	5.57	73	26	1	207.0	230	102	144	42	1.60

2000 Situational Stats

	W	L	ERA	Sv	IP		AB	H	HR	RBI	Avg
Home	1	3	4.81	0	43.0	LHB	124	32	9	24	.258
Road	1	6	8.47	1	34.0	RHB	185	58	5	36	.314
First Half	1	5	9.07	0	42.2	Sc Pos	102	30	4	45	.294
Scnd Half	1	4	3.15	1	34.1	Clutch	57	21	2	16	.368

2000 Season

After coming on strongly in the final two months of 1999, Kyle Farnsworth regressed last year, to the point where the Cubs completely changed his role. He made the starting rotation out of spring training but was hit hard in April. He was sent to the bull-pen, where he was hit even harder, and then to Triple-A Iowa, where he was groomed as a closer. Recalled in late July, he pitched short relief in the second half with generally encouraging results.

Pitching, Defense & Hitting

Short relief seems like a good fit for Farnsworth, since he has a closer's mid-90s heat and little to go with it. He'll work in a two-seamer and a breaking ball, but his command is inconsistent. Still, it may be enough for him to make it as a reliever—he struck out more than a batter an inning and held hitters to a .220 average in relief after his recall. He has plenty of rough edges to smooth over—he's a nervous, erratic fielder, his long delivery gives basestealers a good jump and he's a terrible hitter.

2001 Outlook

Farnsworth will begin the season again hoping to build on the previous year's late-season success. The signing of Tom Gordon means it's unlikely he'll grab the closer's role, so he'll face the ups and downs of short relief as he matures.

Chicago (NL)

Willie Greene

Position: 3B
Bats: L **Throws:** R
Ht: 5'11" **Wt:** 190

Opening Day Age: 29
Born: 9/23/71 in Milledgeville, GA
ML Seasons: 9

Overall Statistics

	G	AB	R	H	D	T	HR	RBI	SB	BB	SO	Avg	OBP	Slg
2000	105	299	34	60	15	2	10	37	4	36	69	.201	.289	.365
Career	655	1902	254	446	76	12	86	307	17	260	477	.234	.326	.423

2000 Situational Stats

	AB	H	HR	RBI	Avg		AB	H	HR	RBI	Avg
Home	162	38	7	23	.235	LHP	45	11	0	3	.244
Road	137	22	3	14	.161	RHP	254	49	10	34	.193
First Half	161	38	7	21	.236	Sc Pos	80	21	3	28	.263
Scnd Half	138	22	3	16	.159	Clutch	62	9	0	4	.145

2000 Season

The Cubs brought in Willie Greene to compete for their third-base job last spring. A hand injury delayed the start of his season, enabling Shane Andrews to fill the opening. Greene returned on April 26 and hit well for a few weeks, becoming the regular third baseman against righthanded pitchers after Andrews went down with an injury. In Andrews' absence, Greene's bat completely wilted, and the Cubs played him until Andrews returned.

Hitting, Baserunning & Defense

Greene's lefthanded power has intrigued many teams, but he's always been undone by his two fatal weaknesses: an inability to hit either offspeed pitches or southpaws. He hit .244 in limited time against lefthanders last year, but owns a career slugging percentage of just .300 against them. He's an average third baseman, with good hands and a strong arm but below-average range. His speed on the bases is unimpressive.

2001 Outlook

The acquisition of Bill Mueller means Greene probably won't be back with the Cubs this year. A lefthanded power hitting third baseman should interest someone, however. Greene may not thrive unless he finds a role that won't overexpose his narrow offensive talents.

Felix Heredia

Position: RP
Bats: L **Throws:** L
Ht: 6'0" **Wt:** 180

Opening Day Age: 24
Born: 6/18/76 in Barahona, Dominican Republic
ML Seasons: 5
Pronunciation: her-RAY-dee-uh

Overall Statistics

	W	L	Pct.	ERA	G	GS	Sv	IP	H	BB	SO	HR	Ratio
2000	7	3	.700	4.76	74	0	2	58.2	46	33	52	6	1.35
Career	19	11	.633	4.71	291	2	5	242.2	233	136	220	19	1.52

2000 Situational Stats

	W	L	ERA	Sv	IP		AB	H	HR	RBI	Avg
Home	6	1	3.51	2	33.1	LHB	82	16	2	15	.195
Road	1	2	6.39	0	25.1	RHB	127	30	4	20	.236
First Half	3	3	5.63	1	32.0	Sc Pos	60	16	3	30	.267
Scnd Half	4	0	3.71	1	26.2	Clutch	94	26	2	19	.277

2000 Season

Late last year the Cubs realized they might be able to make better use of Felix Heredia. The lefthander with the live arm served as a one-batter specialist since joining the club in mid-1998. He faced just one batter in one-third of his first 54 appearances last year, but that happened in only two of his last 20 games. He performed capably however he was used, and he pitched better than his ERA showed.

Pitching, Defense & Hitting

Heredia showed better command of his big-breaking slider last year. When he's able to mix it with his 90-MPH fastball, he can be very effective, but his command sometimes wavers. He's very tough on lefties but has improved against righthanded hitters enough to handle a larger role. He didn't allow a single steal all year, and only one runner even tried to go on him. He comes off the mound in poor position to field and handled only six chances in 2000. At the plate, he's had mixed results in limited at-bats.

2001 Outlook

The Cubs will enter the spring with Tom Gordon, not Heredia, as the top candidate for the closer's job. Heredia is young, throws hard and is tough to hit. At worst, he'll remain a key lefthanded specialist or setup man along with Jeff Fassero.

Jose Nieves

Position: 3B/SS
Bats: R **Throws:** R
Ht: 6' 1" **Wt:** 180

Opening Day Age: 25
Born: 6/16/75 in Guacara, Venezuela
ML Seasons: 3
Pronunciation: nee-AY-vuss

Overall Statistics

	G	AB	R	H	D	T	HR	RBI	SB	BB	SO	Avg	OBP	Slg
2000	82	198	17	42	6	3	5	24	1	11	43	.212	.251	.348
Career	138	380	33	87	15	4	7	42	1	19	68	.229	.270	.345

2000 Situational Stats

	AB	H	HR	RBI	Avg		AB	H	HR	RBI	Avg
Home	86	19	1	8	.221	LHP	80	17	1	12	.213
Road	112	23	4	16	.205	RHP	118	25	4	12	.212
First Half	114	27	4	17	.237	Sc Pos	45	10	0	13	.222
Scnd Half	84	15	1	7	.179	Clutch	42	9	0	6	.214

2000 Season

During a two-month trial in 1999, Jose Nieves seemed like Manny Alexander's even more evil twin, booting balls in the field and flailing at pitches out of the strike zone. He did a little better last year in a smaller role but still didn't impress. He played mainly third base—primarily against lefthanders while Shane Andrews was out early in the year—backed up at shortstop and pinch-hit.

Hitting, Baserunning & Defense

Nieves' fatal weakness at the plate is an inability to make consistent contact. Part of the problem is his willingness to chase bad pitches, but he swings and misses at more than his share of good pitches, too. He wasn't as error-prone last year as he was during his rookie campaign. His inexperience showed at third, but he did a decent job at shortstop. He has the arm and athleticism for either position. Despite decent speed, he's a poor basestealer.

2001 Outlook

Unfortunately for Nieves, the Cubs' third-base spot is no longer open, as the team traded for Bill Mueller in mid-November. On a better club, Nieves might have trouble holding on to his job as a utility infielder, but in Chicago, that is likely to be his role once again. He'll need to step up his game substantially in order to hold any significant role.

Ruben Quevedo

Position: SP
Bats: R **Throws:** R
Ht: 6' 1" **Wt:** 230

Opening Day Age: 22
Born: 1/5/79 in Valencia Carabobo, Venezuela
ML Seasons: 1

Overall Statistics

	W	L	Pct.	ERA	G	GS	Sv	IP	H	BB	SO	HR	Ratio
2000	3	10	.231	7.47	21	15	0	88.0	96	54	65	21	1.70
Career	3	10	.231	7.47	21	15	0	88.0	96	54	65	21	1.70

2000 Situational Stats

	W	L	ERA	Sv	IP		AB	H	HR	RBI	Avg
Home	1	5	5.16	0	45.1	LHB	145	36	9	24	.248
Road	2	5	9.91	0	42.2	RHB	209	60	12	51	.287
First Half	0	3	12.67	0	16.1	Sc Pos	78	25	6	49	.321
Scnd Half	3	7	6.28	0	71.2	Clutch	30	14	4	11	.467

2000 Season

Ruben Quevedo was one of the youngest pitchers in the majors last year, and it showed. The main prospect acquired from the Braves in the Terry Mulholland trade in 1999, Quevedo was called up from Triple-A Iowa to the Cubs' bullpen on April 12 and sent back down on April 25. He continued to bounce up and down between Chicago and Iowa before landing a rotation spot in late July. He reeled off four good starts, but got lit up from early August until the end of the season.

Pitching, Defense & Hitting

Quevedo throws a fastball in the low 90s, a curve, a slider and a changeup. He works up in the strike zone, yields mostly flyballs and gets by when he changes speeds effectively. With the Cubs, he had frequent control problems, something that wasn't an issue in the minors. Oddly, he's been tougher on lefthanded hitters, both in the minors and the big leagues. He seems to hold runners well, but is a poor hitter and bunter and a below-average fielder.

2001 Outlook

One of the more advanced pitchers in the upper levels of the Cubs' system, Quevedo stands to benefit from the club's rebuilding process. He's no lock to land a rotation spot out of spring training, but he's expected to soon make an impact.

Chicago (NL)

Steve Rain

Position: RP
Bats: R **Throws:** R
Ht: 6' 6" **Wt:** 260

Opening Day Age: 25
Born: 6/2/75 in Los Angeles, CA
ML Seasons: 2

Overall Statistics

	W	L	Pct.	ERA	G	GS	Sv	IP	H	BB	SO	HR	Ratio
2000	3	4	.429	4.35	37	0	0	49.2	46	27	54	10	1.47
Career	3	5	.375	5.46	53	0	0	64.1	74	34	66	11	1.68

2000 Situational Stats

	W	L	ERA	Sv	IP		AB	H	HR	RBI	Avg
Home	2	1	3.42	0	23.2	LHB	74	16	3	8	.216
Road	1	3	5.19	0	26.0	RHB	110	30	7	21	.273
First Half	1	0	2.40	0	15.0	Sc Pos	46	6	1	16	.130
Scnd Half	2	4	5.19	0	34.2	Clutch	63	14	4	14	.222

2000 Season

Righthander Steve Rain, who was hit frighteningly hard in a brief trial in 1999, fared better last summer. He was called up in mid-June and pitched well in middle relief for six weeks. He tailed off in August and September, but finished with decent numbers.

Pitching, Defense & Hitting

To be effective, Rain must get hitters to chase his slider. When his command is off, he has only an average fastball and changeup to fall back on. He's quite hittable, so painting the corners is how he must get by. He had better success against lefties last year, something he rarely accomplished in the minors. A big man at 6-foot-6, he's not very mobile in the field, although he keeps his mistakes to a minimum and cuts off the running game well. He has virtually no experience at the plate.

2001 Outlook

In the minors, Rain has been very effective at times, but he has been wildly inconsistent overall. He could come into camp, pitch well and land a setup job or just as easily he could bomb out and earn a return trip to Triple-A.

Jeff Reed

Position: C
Bats: L **Throws:** R
Ht: 6' 2" **Wt:** 200

Opening Day Age: 38
Born: 11/12/62 in Joliet, IL
ML Seasons: 17

Overall Statistics

	G	AB	R	H	D	T	HR	RBI	SB	BB	SO	Avg	OBP	Slg
2000	90	229	26	49	10	0	4	25	0	44	68	.214	.342	.310
Career	1234	3101	311	774	144	10	61	323	7	391	566	.250	.334	.361

2000 Situational Stats

	AB	H	HR	RBI	Avg		AB	H	HR	RBI	Avg
Home	103	17	0	8	.165	LHP	25	3	0	1	.120
Road	126	32	4	17	.254	RHP	204	46	4	24	.225
First Half	109	23	3	15	.211	Sc Pos	52	12	0	19	.231
Scnd Half	120	26	1	10	.217	Clutch	50	10	1	9	.200

2000 Season

Jeff Reed had an uneventful year as the Cubs' part-time catcher. Playing slightly less often than semi-regular catcher Joe Girardi, Reed slumped, contributing less at the plate than he had in the past.

Hitting, Baserunning & Defense

What sets Reed apart from most backup catchers is the fact that he bats lefthanded. Although he isn't a particularly strong hitter—his main strength at this point is the ability to work a walk—he can be used as a pinch-hitter, a role he's filled well. He hasn't faced lefties in years, though. Most of his hits come on line drives over the infield. Reed is about as mobile behind the plate and on the bases as your average 38-year-old catcher. He throws with average strength and accuracy.

2001 Outlook

Reed became a free agent over the winter. Chicago signed Todd Hundley and won't bring Reed back, but he could catch on with a team looking for an experienced backup. At his age, and with his eroding numbers over the last few years, he could be facing the end of the line soon.

Todd Van Poppel

Position: RP
Bats: R **Throws:** R
Ht: 6' 5" **Wt:** 230

Opening Day Age: 29
Born: 12/9/71 in Hinsdale, IL
ML Seasons: 7

Overall Statistics

	W	L	Pct.	ERA	G	GS	Sv	IP	H	BB	SO	HR	Ratio
2000	4	5	.444	3.75	51	2	2	86.1	80	48	77	10	1.48
Career	26	42	.382	5.88	186	82	3	595.2	614	347	430	90	1.61

2000 Situational Stats

	W	L	ERA	Sv	IP		AB	H	HR	RBI	Avg
Home	2	3	5.25	2	36.0	LHB	145	34	3	15	.234
Road	2	2	2.68	0	50.1	RHB	176	46	7	27	.261
First Half	2	3	2.23	2	36.1	Sc Pos	87	20	5	32	.230
Scnd Half	2	2	4.86	0	50.0	Clutch	105	28	4	16	.267

2000 Season

Last year, something went right for Todd Van Poppel. The star-crossed No. 1 pick, who'd spent all of 1999 in the minors, signed a Triple-A contract with the Cubs and pitched so well at Iowa that he earned a callup in May. He quickly nailed down a spot as a middle reliever by reeling off 10 scoreless appearances and pitched decently all year.

Pitching, Defense & Hitting

Van Poppel's stuff—a high-80s fastball, a curve and a changeup—gives him enough ammunition to succeed, but only if he has his command. Last year, he had it more often than not, but it still comes and goes. Even when he's effective, he works long counts and throws a lot of pitches. He tends to work up in the strike zone and gets a lot of flyballs. He's a poor hitter and a decent fielder, although his high leg kick and lack of an effective pickoff move make him easy to run on.

2001 Outlook

Van Poppel's move to the National League in 1998 seems to have done him good. The Cubs hope his good streak continues, as they signed him to a one-year deal worth $850,000. Since the Cubs signed Tom Gordon to fill the closer's role, Van Poppel should remain in long relief. But if Gordon gets injured, Van Poppel could get the call to close.

Tim Worrell

Traded To
GIANTS

Position: RP
Bats: R **Throws:** R
Ht: 6' 4" **Wt:** 231

Opening Day Age: 33
Born: 7/5/67 in Pasadena, CA
ML Seasons: 8
Pronunciation: wor-RELL

Overall Statistics

	W	L	Pct.	ERA	G	GS	Sv	IP	H	BB	SO	HR	Ratio
2000	5	6	.455	2.99	59	0	3	69.1	72	29	57	10	1.46
Career	25	38	.397	4.29	298	49	7	597.2	601	235	460	68	1.40

2000 Situational Stats

	W	L	ERA	Sv	IP		AB	H	HR	RBI	Avg
Home	2	1	2.50	3	36.0	LHB	120	27	2	8	.225
Road	3	5	3.51	0	33.1	RHB	152	45	8	22	.296
First Half	2	3	2.70	1	30.0	Sc Pos	82	15	0	17	.183
Scnd Half	3	3	3.20	2	39.1	Clutch	157	39	4	16	.248

2000 Season

Tim Worrell began his year with the Orioles, but he was released on May 1 after five shaky outings. The Cubs signed him to a minor league contract and called him up in late May. He soon settled into a setup role and was one of the team's few reliable relievers for the rest of the year. Though he didn't pitch as well as his ERA indicated and often got into jams, he usually pitched his way out of them.

Pitching, Defense & Hitting

Worrell has a good fastball and hard slider, and he works in an occasional changeup. He focuses on the outer corner of the plate but can be taken deep when he gets a fastball up or comes too far inside to a power hitter. Worrell was more effective against lefty hitters last year, but that probably was a one-year aberration. The improvement in his command was real, as he issued only 18 unintentional walks. He's a decent fielder who holds runners well, but he rarely contributes with the bat.

2001 Outlook

The Cubs signed Worrell to a two-year extension late last season, but they traded him to the Giants for third baseman Bill Mueller in mid-November. Batters hit Worrell just as well last season as they ever had, and he'll be hard-pressed to keep his ERA from rising in 2001.

Jamie Arnold (**Pos**: RHP, **Age**: 27)

	W	L	Pct.	ERA	G	GS	Sv	IP	H	BB	SO	HR	Ratio
2000	0	3	.000	6.18	14	4	1	39.1	38	24	16	1	1.58
Career	2	7	.222	5.73	50	7	2	108.1	119	58	42	7	1.63

Arnold was part of the package the Cubs received for Ismael Valdes in August. Arnold is still young enough to emerge, but his strikeout and walk rates have headed in the wrong directions. 2001 Outlook: C

Tarrik Brock (**Pos**: LF, **Age**: 27, **Bats**: L)

	G	AB	R	H	D	T	HR	RBI	SB	BB	SO	Avg	OBP	Slg
2000	13	12	1	2	0	0	0	0	1	4	4	.167	.375	.167
Career	13	12	1	2	0	0	0	0	1	4	4	.167	.375	.167

The Cubs had another Brock in the outfield once. Who was he? Oh yeah, the guy with 3,000 hits and all those stolen bases. It's unlikely they'll ever regret losing Tarrik, whenever he moves on. 2001 Outlook: D

Brant Brown (**Pos**: LF/1B, **Age**: 29, **Bats**: L)

	G	AB	R	H	D	T	HR	RBI	SB	BB	SO	Avg	OBP	Slg
2000	95	162	11	28	7	0	5	16	3	13	62	.173	.237	.309
Career	424	1056	142	261	52	11	45	146	15	74	316	.247	.301	.445

The Cubs put Brown out of his misery when they outrighted him to Triple-A at the end of August. Before then, he had mustered a .164 average versus righties and slugged only .114 after the All-Star break. He signed a minor league deal with Milwaukee in early December. 2001 Outlook: C

Daniel Garibay (**Pos**: LHP, **Age**: 28)

	W	L	Pct.	ERA	G	GS	Sv	IP	H	BB	SO	HR	Ratio
2000	2	8	.200	6.03	30	8	0	74.2	88	39	46	9	1.70
Career	2	8	.200	6.03	30	8	0	74.2	88	39	46	9	1.70

The Cubs signed Garibay following the 1999 season, after seven reasonably successful years in Mexico. But he certainly didn't look like the second-coming of Fernando Valenzuela last year. 2001 Outlook: C

Raul Gonzalez (**Pos**: LF, **Age**: 27, **Bats**: R)

	G	AB	R	H	D	T	HR	RBI	SB	BB	SO	Avg	OBP	Slg
2000	3	2	0	0	0	0	0	0	0	0	2	.000	.000	.000
Career	3	2	0	0	0	0	0	0	0	0	2	.000	.000	.000

Gonzalez has played for three organizations the past few years, and he flashed developing power and a nice stroke in Double-A in 1998-99. But he was ordinary at Triple-A last season. 2001 Outlook: D

Jeff Huson (**Pos**: 3B/2B/SS, **Age**: 36, **Bats**: L)

	G	AB	R	H	D	T	HR	RBI	SB	BB	SO	Avg	OBP	Slg
2000	70	130	19	28	7	1	0	11	2	13	9	.215	.287	.285
Career	827	1879	242	439	65	13	8	150	64	191	228	.234	.304	.295

He went 4-for-8 over the final two days of last season to finish over the Mendoza line. His next hit against a lefthander will be his first since 1999. The Cubs did not offer him arbitration, so he's a free agent. 2001 Outlook: C

Matt Karchner (**Pos**: RHP, **Age**: 33)

	W	L	Pct.	ERA	G	GS	Sv	IP	H	BB	SO	HR	Ratio
2000	1	1	.500	6.14	13	0	0	14.2	19	11	5	3	2.05
Career	21	13	.618	4.21	223	0	27	241.1	242	132	166	30	1.55

The Jon Garland-for-Karchner trade is looking worse all the time, at least from the Cubs' perspective. Karchner gave them a total of 60.2 innings and five wins over two-plus years before getting released. 2001 Outlook: C

Cole Liniak (**Pos**: 3B, **Age**: 24, **Bats**: R)

	G	AB	R	H	D	T	HR	RBI	SB	BB	SO	Avg	OBP	Slg
2000	3	3	0	0	0	0	0	0	0	0	2	.000	.000	.000
Career	15	32	3	7	2	0	0	2	0	1	6	.219	.242	.281

Liniak's minor-league record suggests a low-average power-hitter who can play third base. Similar to Shane Andrews, though without as many walks or the bad back. He was traded to Toronto in mid-December. 2001 Outlook: C

Mike Mahoney (**Pos**: C, **Age**: 28, **Bats**: R)

	G	AB	R	H	D	T	HR	RBI	SB	BB	SO	Avg	OBP	Slg
2000	4	7	1	2	1	0	0	1	0	1	0	.286	.444	.429
Career	4	7	1	2	1	0	0	1	0	1	0	.286	.444	.429

The Braves released Mahoney after the 1999 season, and he suddenly became a .300 hitter at age 27 last year. He's a good receiver, so if he can come close to repeating that performance, he has a chance. 2001 Outlook: C

Oswaldo Mairena (**Pos**: LHP, **Age**: 25)

	W	L	Pct.	ERA	G	GS	Sv	IP	H	BB	SO	HR	Ratio
2000	0	0	-	18.00	2	0	0	2.0	7	2	0	1	4.50
Career	0	0	-	18.00	2	0	0	2.0	7	2	0	1	4.50

Mairena is a small lefthander from Nicaragua whom the Cubs received from the Yankees in the Glenallen Hill trade. Mairena has fewer than 26 innings above Double-A, so he probably needs more seasoning. 2001 Outlook: C

Gary Matthews Jr. (**Pos**: LF/CF, **Age**: 26, **Bats**: B)

	G	AB	R	H	D	T	HR	RBI	SB	BB	SO	Avg	OBP	Slg
2000	80	158	24	30	1	2	4	14	3	15	28	.190	.264	.297
Career	103	194	28	38	1	2	4	21	5	24	37	.196	.288	.284

Acquired from the Padres last March, Matthews hasn't hit well for two years. He's now 230 homers behind his father. Unless Rondell White gets injured, he may not get many chances to inch closer. 2001 Outlook: C

Chad Meyers (**Pos**: 2B, **Age**: 25, **Bats**: R)

	G	AB	R	H	D	T	HR	RBI	SB	BB	SO	Avg	OBP	Slg
2000	36	52	8	9	2	0	0	5	1	3	11	.173	.228	.212
Career	79	194	25	42	11	0	0	9	5	12	38	.216	.275	.273

The Cubs recalled Meyers on three occasions last season. His speed and versatility give him some value, which is negated if he doesn't get on base or hit for any power. A hairline fracture in his left foot derailed his winter ball season. 2001 Outlook: B

Phil Norton (Pos: LHP, Age: 25)

	W	L	Pct.	ERA	G	GS	Sv	IP	H	BB	SO	HR	Ratio
2000	0	1	.000	9.35	2	2	0	8.2	14	7	6	5	2.42
Career	0	1	.000	9.35	2	2	0	8.2	14	7	6	5	2.42

Though he hadn't particularly distinguished himself at Triple-A, Norton received a couple of sacrificial starts last August, with predictable results. 2001 Outlook: C

Augie Ojeda (Pos: SS, Age: 26, Bats: B)

	G	AB	R	H	D	T	HR	RBI	SB	BB	SO	Avg	OBP	Slg
2000	28	77	10	17	3	1	2	8	0	10	9	.221	.307	.364
Career	28	77	10	17	3	1	2	8	0	10	9	.221	.307	.364

The Cubs acquired Ojeda from the Orioles in a minor league swap after the 1999 season. He has a little bit of pop for a shortstop, and his defense may land him a backup role in the majors. 2001 Outlook: B

Jerry Spradlin (Pos: RHP, Age: 33)

	W	L	Pct.	ERA	G	GS	Sv	IP	H	BB	SO	HR	Ratio
2000	4	5	.444	6.00	58	1	7	90.0	101	32	67	11	1.48
Career	17	19	.472	4.75	310	1	11	371.2	371	122	292	40	1.33

The Cubs signed him in September, making them his fourth team over the past two seasons. The Royals gave him a few save chances in May, but he certainly didn't sieze the opportunity and the Cubs released him in late November. 2001 Outlook: B

Danny Young (Pos: LHP, Age: 29)

	W	L	Pct.	ERA	G	GS	Sv	IP	H	BB	SO	HR	Ratio
2000	0	1	.000	21.00	4	0	0	3.0	5	6	0	1	3.67
Career	0	1	.000	21.00	4	0	0	3.0	5	6	0	1	3.67

Young had endured nine minor league seasons for the right to get rocked for one week in the majors last spring. At least he was able to visit Japan with the rest of the Cubs in March. 2001 Outlook: D

Chicago Cubs Minor League Prospects

Organization Overview:

In September, Chicago's faithful got a glimpse of the future when multi-tooled center fielder Corey Patterson made his big league debut. Farm director-turned-assistant GM Jim Hendry also has assembled a solid crop of upper-level prospects on the brink of injecting a stale lineup with some much-needed youth and excitement. The farm is deep in several problem areas for the parent club, including corner infielders, shortstops and young hurlers. Hee Seop Choi has emerged as Mark Grace's long-term replacement, and the Cubs hope at least one of a rising trio of third-base prospects will separate themselves and erase the memories of the Gary Scott/Kevin Orie tribulations at the hot corner. A wave of pitching could bolster the staff within a year.

Hee Seop Choi

Position: 1B
Bats: L **Throws:** L
Ht: 6' 5" **Wt:** 235
Opening Day Age: 22
Born: 3/16/79 in Chon Nam, Korea

Recent Statistics

	G	AB	R	H	D	T	HR	RBI	SB	BB	SO	Avg
1999 A Lansing	79	290	71	93	18	6	18	70	2	50	68	.321
2000 A Daytona	96	345	60	102	25	6	15	70	4	37	78	.296
2000 AA West Tenn	36	122	25	37	9	0	10	25	3	25	38	.303

Choi has advanced at a brisk pace through the system. The lefty can drive the ball out of any part of the park, but he is far from a feast-or-famine masher. A former pitcher in Korea, Choi has become adept at first base and was named the best defensive first baseman in the Florida State League. He is a professional hitter with a disciplined approach who already draws a fair amount of walks and doesn't fan excessively. After a standout showing in the Arizona Fall League, Choi is poised to take over as the Cubs' everyday first baseman by 2002.

Ben Christensen

Position: P
Bats: R **Throws:** R
Ht: 6' 4" **Wt:** 205
Opening Day Age: 23
Born: 2/7/78 in Waterloo, IA

Recent Statistics

	W	L	ERA	G	GS	Sv	IP	H	R	BB	SO	HR
1999 R Cubs	0	1	3.00	3	3	0	9.0	8	3	5	10	0
1999 A Eugene	0	2	5.91	5	5	0	21.1	21	14	14	21	2
1999 A Daytona	1	3	6.35	4	4	0	22.2	25	16	11	18	4
2000 A Daytona	4	2	2.10	10	10	0	64.1	43	18	15	63	6
2000 AA West Tenn	3	1	2.76	7	7	0	42.1	36	18	15	42	2

The dominating pitcher from Wichita State had a dark cloud cast over his career following a controversial and well-publicized beanball incident. Chicago took a risk by selecting him in the first round in 1999, but the Cubs have been thrilled with his maturity. Considered a student of the game, Christensen is a fierce competitor on the mound, where he commands his polished repertoire. He overmatched the Florida State League in his debut with a sinking 90-93 MPH fastball, a changeup and a pair of nasty sliders that he varies speeds on. After a promotion to Double-A, he was shut down after seven starts due to shoulder tendinitis. The layoff was expected to get his arm ready for a charge toward Wrigley in 2001.

Bobby Hill

Position: SS
Bats: B **Throws:** R
Ht: 5' 10" **Wt:** 170
Opening Day Age: 22
Born: 4/3/78 in San Jose, CA

Recent Statistics

	G	AB	R	H	D	T	HR	RBI	SB	BB	SO	Avg
2000 IND Newark	132	481	109	157	22	9	13	82	81	101	57	.326

The White Sox' second-round pick in 1999, Hill was unable to come to terms and signed with Newark of the independent Atlantic League. The move allowed him to re-enter the draft in 2000, and again he was selected in the second round by Chicago—although it was the Cubs who were bidding for his services this time around. After another holdout, the Cubs inked the shortstop to a $1.425 million deal in November. Often compared to a young Chuck Knoblauch, the switch-hitter owns Miami's school record for steals, and he hit better than .400 as a sophomore. A .390 mark helped lead the 'Canes to the national championship in '99. The Cubs plan to shift Hill to second, where he's expected to blitz through their system. He could be primed for a starting position in the middle of the Cubs' infield by the start of 2002.

Mike Meyers

Position: P
Bats: R **Throws:** R
Ht: 6' 2" **Wt:** 210
Opening Day Age: 23
Born: 10/18/77 in London, ON, Canada

Recent Statistics

	W	L	ERA	G	GS	Sv	IP	H	R	BB	SO	HR
1999 A Daytona	10	3	1.93	19	17	0	107.1	68	30	40	122	9
1999 AA West Tenn	4	0	1.09	5	5	0	33.0	21	5	10	51	1
2000 AA West Tenn	5	2	2.44	9	9	0	59.0	41	18	26	51	4
2000 AAA Iowa	2	6	7.28	13	12	0	59.1	74	51	30	44	9

Meyers entered last season with an attention-grabbing 2.18 career ERA, and was off to a strong start in Double-A with a 2.44 ERA through nine starts. That performance convinced Chicago to promote the righty to Triple-A Iowa. Despite averaging better than a strikeout per inning over his four professional years, Meyers isn't an overpowering pitcher. He relies on location and changing speeds. In Triple-A, he found out the importance of being precise with his command, but he wasn't able to make the adjustments and was touched for a .316 opponent average. He eventually was shut down with a sore elbow. The move was considered precautionary, and the Cubs expect the former 26th-rounder to resume mixing up his 88-91 MPH moving fastball, plus-curveball and changeup against Triple-A hitters this year.

Joey Nation

Position: P
Bats: L **Throws:** L
Ht: 6' 2" **Wt:** 205
Opening Day Age: 22
Born: 9/28/78 in Oklahoma City, OK

Recent Statistics

	W	L	ERA	G	GS	Sv	IP	H	R	BB	SO	HR
2000 AA West Tenn	11	10	3.31	27	27	0	166.0	137	72	65	165	17
2000 NL Chicago	0	2	6.94	2	2	0	11.2	12	9	8	8	2

Acquired from Atlanta with Ruben Quevedo and Micah Bowie for Terry Mulholland and Jose Hernandez in '99, Nation led the organization in Ks last year. His fastball registers a tick above average, but he needs to improve his command over the offering. He hits his spots with his best pitch, a changeup, and a good curveball. The Cubs like Nation's competitiveness on the hill and see him as an effective middle to end of the rotation starter.

Corey Patterson

Position: OF
Bats: L **Throws:** R
Ht: 5' 10" **Wt:** 180
Opening Day Age: 21
Born: 8/13/79 in Atlanta, GA

Recent Statistics

	G	AB	R	H	D	T	HR	RBI	SB	BB	SO	Avg
2000 AA West Tenn	118	444	73	116	26	5	22	82	27	45	115	.261
2000 NL Chicago	11	42	9	7	1	0	2	2	1	3	14	.167
2000 MLE	118	441	72	113	25	4	21	81	21	38	123	.256

Widely regarded as the best position prospect in baseball, Patterson leapfrogged the advanced Class-A Florida State League. Just two years removed from high school, the multi-tooled center fielder earned high praise from Chicago's brass during spring training, and he got a chance to showcase those tools in September. The third overall pick in '98, Patterson is expected to evolve into the total package. However, he does have some areas to iron out before realizing his full potential. After a sluggish adjustment period to Double-A, he rebounded in the second half, but hit just .197 against lefties. The organization would like to see him make the most of his wheels by dropping more bunts and using left field. An aggressive hitter, Patterson needs to be more selective and narrow the strike zone. The franchise is eagerly anticipating Patterson's arrival, possibly as early as this season.

Carlos Zambrano

Position: P
Bats: L **Throws:** R
Ht: 6' 4" **Wt:** 220
Opening Day Age: 19
Born: 6/1/81 in Puerto Cabello, Carabobo, Vz

Recent Statistics

	W	L	ERA	G	GS	Sv	IP	H	R	BB	SO	HR
1999 A Lansing	13	7	4.17	27	24	0	153.1	150	87	62	98	9
2000 AA West Tenn	3	1	1.34	9	9	0	60.1	39	14	21	43	2
2000 AAA Iowa	2	5	3.97	34	0	6	56.2	54	30	40	46	3

Armed with one of the liveliest fastballs in the minors, Zambrano blitzed through the system from the Midwest League to Triple-A in a year. A big horse on the mound, he manhandled Double-A hitters with his overpowering mid-90s gas. He continued to mow down opponents while making adjustments to the higher levels as a teenager. His role is undetermined as his complementary pitches—a slider and advanced changeup—give him three offerings, plus he can maintain the life and velocity on his fastball into the late innings as a starter. His rapid ascent is a good indication of the Cubs' belief in him.

Julio Zuleta

Position: 1B
Bats: R **Throws:** R
Ht: 6' 6" **Wt:** 230
Opening Day Age: 26
Born: 3/28/75 in Panama City, Panama

Recent Statistics

	G	AB	R	H	D	T	HR	RBI	SB	BB	SO	Avg
2000 AAA Iowa	107	392	76	122	25	1	26	94	5	31	77	.311
2000 NL Chicago	30	68	13	20	8	0	3	12	0	2	19	.294
2000 MLE	107	378	61	108	22	0	22	76	3	25	80	.286

After six years in the organization, the late-blooming Zuleta started to mash the ball in 1999. An imposing 6-foot-6, 230 pounds, he originally was signed as a wiry catcher. Now at first base, he's no longer stuck behind Mark Grace, who was signed by Arizona in the offseason. The strapping Zuleta cranked 50 home runs in the past two seasons, including three during a promising taste of the big leagues. He's a bit of a free swinger, though, who crushes lefties and could serve as a valuable power source to the Cubs in a platoon role this year at first base with Matt Stairs.

Others to Watch

Until 2000, **Juan Cruz'** results didn't match his scouting report. The 20-year-old righthanded Dominican native emerged with an overpowering arsenal consisting of a lively 93-97 MPH fastball. The slender 6-foot-2 Cruz may evoke some comparisons to Pedro Martinez with his loose, quick arm action and physical resemblance. . . **Ross Gload** (24) surprised everyone when he came over from the Marlins in the Henry Rodriguez trade and tore up Triple-A to the tune of a .404 batting average and an unheard of .942 slugging percentage. The lefthanded hitting Gload mashed 30 homers between the two systems. . . Developing third basemen **Ryan Gripp** (22), **Eric Hinske** (23) and **Dave Kelton** (21) are bright spots at a position that Chicago has struggled to find an answer for, though they did trade with the Giants for Bill Mueller in the offseason. Gripp had 56 extra-base hits in the Midwest League and batted .333. Hinske's bat should carry him to the big leagues, after hitting 40 jacks in the past two seasons, and Kelton projects to have the highest upside of the three. He was bothered by a sore shoulder early on and started slowly in the Florida State League, before turning it on in the second half. Kelton displays good range, and the Cubs expect him to hit for power and average as he matures. . . Lefty **Will Ohman** (23) capped his rapid ascent through the minors with a September stint in Chicago. After limiting Double-A hitters to a .200 average, he could be ready to pair with Felix Heredia as southpaws out of the Cubs' bullpen.

Cinergy Field

Offense

Construction has begun on a new ballpark directly behind Cinergy Field. One of the immediate results is that at Cinergy home plate will be moved back 10 feet and the outfield fence will be moved in accordingly to accommodate the ongoing construction. As of presstime, the height of the fence and the exact dimensions still are being determined, so how the park will play on offense is a bit of a question mark. Otherwise, the same spongy artificial turf and the friendly power alleys remain the same.

Defense

Cincinnati has built much of its defense on its middle infielders being able to play on the quick, phony turf. Ken Griffey's outstanding range is perfect to play centerfield in Cinergy's rather deep gaps. The Reds' corner outfielders always have trouble negotiating the down-the-line bullpens, and extra bases frequently happen by accident when balls bounce over outfielders' heads.

Who It Helps the Most

Though no Kingdome, Griffey found the friendly right-field fence to his liking. The ballpark's dimensions also help hitters like Larkin and Sean Casey, who can drive the ball to the opposite field and into gaps that are both reachable and spacious.

Who It Hurts the Most

Groundball pitchers like Danny Graves can be hurt because of the quick artificial turf. Infielders with average range like third baseman Aaron Boone can also be at a disadvantage because the ball can take off on the carpet.

Rookies & Newcomers

Cincinnati has a bevy of young outfield prospects who all would fit in well in Cinergy Field's landscape. However, the Reds will play there for only two more seasons before moving into their new grass stadium, where the dimensions will be more varied.

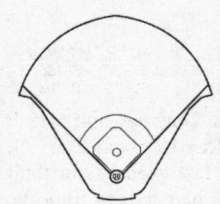

Dimensions: LF-330, LCF-375, CF-404, RCF-375, RF-330

Capacity: 52,953

Elevation: 550 feet

Surface: Turf

Foul Territory: Small

Park Factors

2000 Season

	Home Games			Away Games			
	Reds	Opp	Total	Reds	Opp	Total	Index
G	73	73	146	75	75	150	—
Avg	.284	.271	.278	.264	.247	.256	109
AB	2444	2564	5008	2657	2447	5104	101
R	385	370	755	362	318	680	114
H	695	696	1391	702	604	1306	109
2B	144	156	300	135	140	275	111
3B	14	18	32	20	15	35	93
HR	82	98	180	96	72	168	109
BB	268	293	561	239	311	550	104
SO	402	458	860	503	466	969	90
E	46	39	85	55	44	99	88
E-Infield	37	31	68	41	36	77	91
LHB-Avg	.301	.279	.290	.263	.246	.255	114
LHB-HR	35	36	71	51	31	82	93
RHB-Avg	.274	.266	.270	.265	.247	.257	105
RHB-HR	47	62	109	45	41	86	125

1998-2000

	Home Games			Away Games			
	Reds	Opp	Total	Reds	Opp	Total	Index
G	222	222	444	223	223	446	—
Avg	.269	.251	.259	.268	.251	.260	100
AB	7361	7620	14981	7898	7284	15182	99
R	1114	1055	2169	1107	968	2075	105
H	1978	1909	3887	2120	1829	3949	99
2B	420	445	865	419	399	818	107
3B	40	41	81	54	44	98	84
HR	237	273	510	262	220	482	107
BB	845	875	1720	736	833	1569	111
SO	1386	1488	2874	1575	1422	2997	97
E	154	126	280	155	173	328	86
E-Infield	124	105	229	117	140	257	90
LHB-Avg	.278	.260	.269	.287	.254	.270	99
LHB-HR	91	87	178	113	80	193	99
RHB-Avg	.264	.244	.254	.258	.249	.254	100
RHB-HR	146	186	332	149	140	289	113

2000 Rankings (National League)

- Second-highest batting-average factor
- Second-highest hit factor
- Second-highest LHB batting-average factor
- Second-highest RHB home-run factor
- Third-highest run factor
- Third-highest RHB batting-average factor
- Third-lowest strikeout factor

Bob Boone

2000 Season

No one was a closer observer of the Reds' disappointing year than Bob Boone, who was GM Jim Bowden's top personnel advisor. There were rumblings throughout the season that Boone in fact was lobbying for Jack McKeon's job, speculation that was confirmed weeks after the season when Boone was named manager. Boone's first managerial stint was a disappointing period with a Kansas City club that had little talent. He now inherits a team that has become a revolving door of players under Bowden's frenetic leadership.

Offense

Boone knows the value of being aggressive on the bases, and he has a variety of speed weapons to put in motion frequently. While in Kansas City, Boone was fond of constantly changing lineups, though that could have been a reflection of how few givens he had to consider each night. As there are few obviously settled spots in the Reds' lineup, it's likely that he again will be juggling batting orders and platooning at many positions.

Pitching & Defense

By necessity, Boone will lean heavily on his bullpen, as the Reds' likely starting rotation lacks any real innings-eaters. Boone would seem to have a good feel for when to remove pitchers, coming from a background where he caught more games than any catcher in history. He also appreciates defense. With a roster that will have several interchangeable parts, he will not hesitate to substitute for defense when he has the lead in the late innings.

2001 Outlook

Boone inherits an uneasy team, what with factions of players having supported either of two coaches—Ron Oester and Ken Griffey Sr.—for the managing job. He also walks into a situation where the Reds' management continues to cut corners because the team has so much money tied up in Ken Griffey Jr. and Barry Larkin. Boone is very confident in his own judgment, and the stage could be set for frequent disputes with the equally omniscient Bowden.

Born: 11/19/47 in San Diego, CA

Playing Experience: 1972-1990, Phi, Ana, KC

Managerial Experience: 3 seasons

Manager Statistics (Jack McKeon)

Year	Team, Lg	W	L	Pct	GB	Finish
2000	Cincinnati, NL	85	77	.525	10.0	2nd Central
12 Seasons		771	735	.512	—	—

2000 Starting Pitchers by Days Rest

	<=3	4	5	6+
Reds Starts	1	71	62	20
Reds ERA	13.50	4.84	4.18	4.28
NL Avg Starts	2	80	50	21
NL ERA	5.00	4.61	4.60	5.18

2000 Situational Stats

	Jack McKeon	NL Average
Hit & Run Success %	31.3	33.8
Stolen Base Success %	72.3	68.8
Platoon Pct.	51.4	53.2
Defensive Subs	41	19
High-Pitch Outings	10	14
Quick/Slow Hooks	16/9	14/16
Sacrifice Attempts	82	87

2000 Rankings—Jack McKeon (National Lg)

- 1st in defensive substitutions (41), starts with over 140 pitches (1) and saves with over 1 inning pitched (24)
- 2nd in first-batter platoon percentage (51.4)
- 3rd in fewest caught stealings of second base (34) and double steals (5)

Rob Bell

2000 Season

Cincinnati did not want Rob Bell to begin last year in the majors, but injuries and a solid spring training earned him a spot in the rotation. However, a series of inconsistent efforts sent him back to the minors in late June. When Bell returned, he was much more effective, ending up with 140.1 innings and seven wins.

Pitching

The Reds have liked Bell's array of stuff since making him a key part of the deal with Atlanta in 1998 that also brought Denny Neagle and Michael Tucker to Cincinnati. Bell throws his fastball in the mid-90s and employs both a heavy two-seamer and an improved cutter. He also throws a power curve that eventually could develop into a major weapon. Bell continues to struggle with a consistent offspeed pitch, something which he will concentrate on this spring. He also will struggle with his release point and needs to cut down on his walks and high pitch counts. He has the stuff to be a high-strikeout pitcher who is tough to hit.

Defense & Hitting

Bell's high leg kick and lack of a pickoff move makes him very vulnerable to basestealers, who last year were successful in 19 of 20 attempts. He also does not get into good fielding position, though he is athletic enough to improve his defensive skills. Bell shows little aptitude for hitting, managing only three baseknocks last year in 45 at-bats.

2001 Outlook

By necessity, the Reds had to rush Bell into their rotation last year and he suffered through the expected growing pains. However, he has a very high ceiling and last season's frustrating times should pay dividends during the course of this season. The offseason departures of both Ron Villone and Steve Parris put more pressure on Bell, who will be just 24 on Opening Day. But it would not surprise anyone to see him break through and win 13-15 games and be on his way to being one of the league's better young starting pitchers.

Position: SP
Bats: R **Throws:** R
Ht: 6' 5" **Wt:** 225

Opening Day Age: 24
Born: 1/17/77 in Newburgh, NY
ML Seasons: 1

Overall Statistics

	W	L	Pct.	ERA	G	GS	Sv	IP	H	BB	SO	HR	Ratio
2000	7	8	.467	5.00	26	26	0	140.1	130	73	112	32	1.45
Career	7	8	.467	5.00	26	26	0	140.1	130	73	112	32	1.45

How Often He Throws Strikes

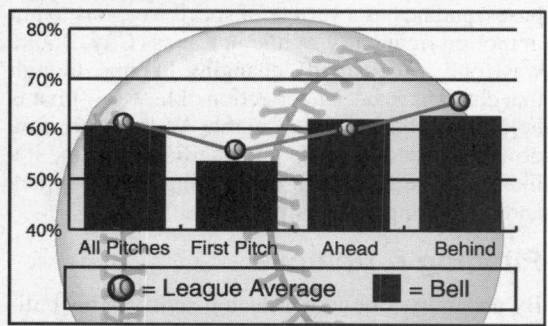

= League Average   = Bell

2000 Situational Stats

	W	L	ERA	Sv	IP		AB	H	HR	RBI	Avg
Home	5	2	4.82	0	80.1	LHB	234	53	12	28	.226
Road	2	6	5.25	0	60.0	RHB	300	77	20	45	.257
First Half	4	6	5.28	0	75.0	Sc Pos	127	26	8	41	.205
Scnd Half	3	2	4.68	0	65.1	Clutch	16	4	3	4	.250

2000 Rankings (National League)

- 6th in home runs allowed and wild pitches (11)
- 7th in lowest batting average allowed with runners in scoring position
- 8th in stolen bases allowed (19)
- Led the Reds in home runs allowed, stolen bases allowed (19) and lowest batting average allowed vs. lefthanded batters

Aaron Boone

2000 Season

On his way to a bust-out year in which he seemed headed for 25 homers and 90 RBI, Aaron Boone's season suddenly was cut short on July 6 when he blew out his left knee and was forced to miss the rest of the season. At the time of the injury, he was on pace to set career highs in all major offensive categories and had a chance to hit .300.

Hitting

Once a prospect whose biggest flaw was lack of power, Boone has bulked up considerably over the last three years. At the same time, he has become much quicker in turning on inside pitches, making him a legitimate home-run threat. He now is more adept at laying off breaking pitches which he can't handle and trying to work counts into fastball situations. Boone always has had trouble against lefthanders, but he made strides last year with a much better sense of trying to go where pitches were located.

Baserunning & Defense

By no means a burner, Boone has surprisingly good speed and until he was injured, he was a very good percentage basestealer. He also shows sound judgment on the bases, rarely trying for an extra base and not being successful. His range is ordinary at third, and he can struggle on plays where he has to charge the ball. Boone has good reactions, however, and possesses a consistently accurate throwing arm.

2001 Outlook

Cincinnati expects Boone to be fully recovered from his knee injury when spring training opens, and he will get the rare opportunity to play for his father Bob, the new Reds' manager. Boone has established himself to the point where Cincinnati no longer openly talks about shopping for a third baseman. It is now his job to lose.

Position: 3B
Bats: R   **Throws:** R
Ht: 6' 2"   **Wt:** 200

Opening Day Age: 28
Born: 3/9/73 in La Mesa, CA
ML Seasons: 4

Overall Statistics

	G	AB	R	H	D	T	HR	RBI	SB	BB	SO	Avg	OBP	Slg
2000	84	291	44	83	18	0	12	43	6	24	52	.285	.356	.471
Career	297	993	129	278	58	7	28	148	30	71	172	.280	.339	.437

Where He Hits the Ball

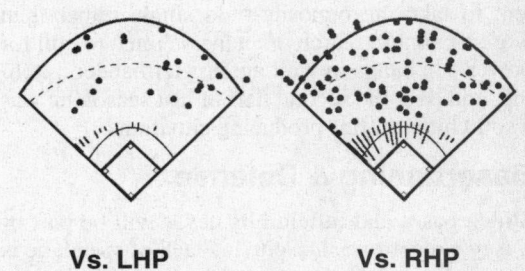

Vs. LHP   **Vs. RHP**

2000 Situational Stats

	AB	H	HR	RBI	Avg		AB	H	HR	RBI	Avg
Home	155	42	5	19	.271	LHP	53	16	1	9	.302
Road	136	41	7	24	.301	RHP	238	67	11	34	.282
First Half	291	83	12	43	.285	Sc Pos	70	20	1	26	.286
Scnd Half	0	0	0	0	-	Clutch	55	17	3	12	.309

2000 Rankings (National League)

- Led the Reds in hit by pitch (10)
- Led NL third basemen in hit by pitch (10)

Sean Casey

2000 Season

A day before the season opened, Sean Casey suffered a hairline fracture of his thumb. The injury would sideline him for two and a half weeks and largely trigger a sluggish start in which he did not reach 20 RBI until June 28. However, Casey got things going over the second half and ended up hitting over .300 for the second straight year.

Hitting

Casey's ability to come back from the thumb injury eased concerns that he might become gunshy about being jammed by inside pitches. He has shown the ability to fight off hard stuff and can open his swing to drive the ball to the opposite field. Still a work in progress in terms of power, Casey often is content to take the opposite-field single rather than work a count in search of an inside pitch to pull for power. He hangs in well against lefthanded pitching, and over the second half of last season he was a solid hitter in run-producing situations.

Baserunning & Defense

Stolen bases and infield hits never will be part of Casey's repertoire. Despite his lack of speed, he is aggressive on the bases and has good judgment when trying to gain an extra base. He has worked to improve his skills at first base, where his range is just average but where he has become more adept at picking balls out of the dirt and reliably making the routine play.

2001 Outlook

Along with Ken Griffey Jr. and Pokey Reese, the popular Casey is one of the Reds' foundation players around whom their next several seasons likely will be built. As long as he can make it out of spring training unscathed, this could be the year he breaks through to the next level and reaches the 30-homer and 100-RBI levels.

Position: 1B
Bats: L **Throws:** R
Ht: 6' 4" **Wt:** 225

Opening Day Age: 26
Born: 7/2/74 in Willingboro, NJ
ML Seasons: 4

Overall Statistics

	G	AB	R	H	D	T	HR	RBI	SB	BB	SO	Avg	OBP	Slg
2000	133	480	69	151	33	2	20	85	1	52	80	.315	.385	.517
Career	386	1386	217	432	96	6	52	237	2	157	215	.312	.386	.502

Where He Hits the Ball

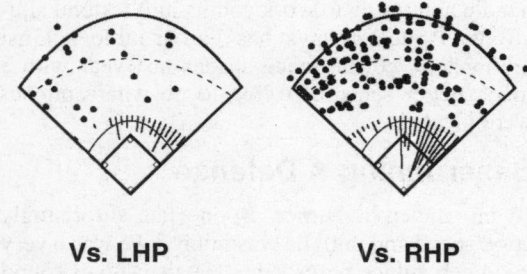

Vs. LHP   Vs. RHP

2000 Situational Stats

	AB	H	HR	RBI	Avg		AB	H	HR	RBI	Avg
Home	244	77	9	50	.316	LHP	104	26	1	18	.250
Road	236	74	11	35	.314	RHP	376	125	19	67	.332
First Half	238	61	5	23	.256	Sc Pos	120	44	3	59	.367
Scnd Half	242	90	15	62	.372	Clutch	81	24	2	11	.296

2000 Rankings (National League)

- 4th in batting average with runners in scoring position
- 5th in fielding percentage at first base (.995)
- Led the Reds in batting average, batting average with runners in scoring position, batting average vs. righthanded pitchers, batting average on a 3-1 count (.538) and batting average on the road
- Led NL first basemen in highest groundball/fly-ball ratio (1.6)

Danny Graves

2000 Season

There were few pitchers in baseball who were more valuable than Danny Graves last season. An All-Star for the first time, Graves achieved the rare reliever's double-double of 10 wins and 30 saves while placing among the league leaders in relief innings. Graves showed signs of wearing down over the last two months, but that didn't keep him from finishing with a career-best 2.56 ERA.

Pitching

Graves' best pitch is a hard, sinking fastball that he throws in the low to mid-90s. The pitch is effective against both lefthanded and righthanded hitters. Graves has improved his changeup to the point where it has become as much of an out pitch as the fastball. He at times will show a slider or a curve, which he occasionally will use as another offspeed pitch. However, most of the time Graves is aggressive about coming at hitters with the sinker—it is both his best weapon and also a pitch that can get him in trouble when it flattens out or when he loses control of the strike zone.

Defense & Hitting

Like most closers, Graves is easy to run on because he focuses his attention on the batter and not a baserunner. He is a decent athlete who knows how to make the routine plays. Never known as a hitter, he shocked the Reds last year by making his only hit of the season—and first career hit—a home run.

2001 Outlook

With 57 saves in the last two seasons, Graves unquestionably is the Reds' closer. However, Cincinnati can't keep running him out for close to 100 innings a year. He is capable of pitching two-inning saves on occasion, but his effectiveness clearly will be enhanced if the Reds can limit him primarily to one-inning appearances.

Position: RP
Bats: R **Throws:** R
Ht: 5'11" **Wt:** 185

Opening Day Age: 27
Born: 8/7/73 in Saigon, Vietnam
ML Seasons: 5

Overall Statistics

	W	L	Pct.	ERA	G	GS	Sv	IP	H	BB	SO	HR	Ratio
2000	10	5	.667	2.56	66	0	30	91.1	81	42	53	8	1.35
Career	22	13	.629	3.32	233	0	65	339.1	317	149	199	28	1.37

How Often He Throws Strikes

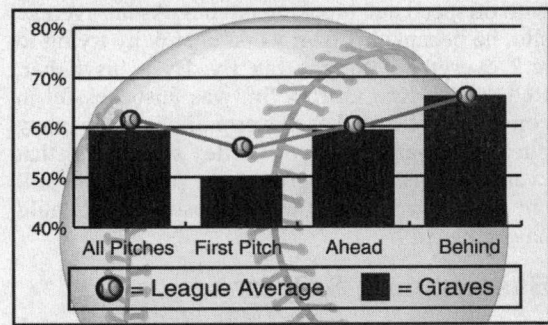

2000 Situational Stats

	W	L	ERA	Sv	IP		AB	H	HR	RBI	Avg
Home	7	3	2.68	12	50.1	LHB	166	44	4	22	.265
Road	3	2	2.41	18	41.0	RHB	167	37	4	22	.222
First Half	9	1	1.99	14	54.1	Sc Pos	121	32	2	37	.264
Scnd Half	1	4	3.41	16	37.0	Clutch	260	62	4	31	.238

2000 Rankings (National League)

- 2nd in relief innings (91.1)
- 3rd in relief wins (10)
- 5th in saves, relief ERA (2.56) and fewest strikeouts per nine innings in relief (5.2)
- 6th in save percentage (85.7)
- 7th in save opportunities (35) and games finished (57)
- Led the Reds in saves, games finished (57), save opportunities (35), save percentage (85.7), blown saves (5), relief wins (10) and relief ERA (2.56)

Cincinnati

Ken Griffey Jr.

2000 Season

After forcing a trade that brought him to Cincinnati, Ken Griffey did not have the smoothest of rides in his first National League season. Griffey's batting average languished below .240 for nearly 100 games before a late spurt got him up to his final .271 mark. He also had troubles with the media, made his final start on September 11, and sat out the rest of the season—except for three pinch-hit appearances—with rather nebulous injury problems.

Hitting

NL pitchers went right after Griffey, crowding him inside with hard stuff and then working him away with offspeed and breaking pitches. As his average slid, he became his own worst enemy by trying to jerk everything for the big fly. Even his father, Reds coach Ken Griffey Sr., was unsuccessful in convincing his son that he was pulling off too many pitches. It's a measure of Griffey's greatness that even with his long unproductive periods, he still put up power numbers which most players would have coveted.

Baserunning & Defense

Griffey always has been an outstanding baserunner, however he seems to be becoming more conservative on the basepaths. He is an indifferent basestealer and attempted only 10 steals last season. He is one of the all-time great center fielders with superb range and the ability to get good jumps on balls. His average arm is made effective by his quick release. Still, he was introduced to the NL by not being voted a Gold Glove for the first time in 11 seasons.

2001 Outlook

Even for a premier player like Griffey, the adjustment to a new team and new league was a difficult one. He did enjoy stretches in mid-summer when he was as good as ever, and now that the novelty of his move has worn off, he should settle in and be more consistent. If he gets out of the box fast this year, look for him to hit .300 and close in on 50 home runs.

Position: CF
Bats: L **Throws:** L
Ht: 6' 3" **Wt:** 205

Opening Day Age: 31
Born: 11/21/69 in Donora, PA
ML Seasons: 12
Nickname: Junior, The Kid

Overall Statistics

	G	AB	R	H	D	T	HR	RBI	SB	BB	SO	Avg	OBP	Slg
2000	145	520	100	141	22	3	40	118	6	94	117	.271	.387	.556
Career	1680	6352	1163	1883	342	33	438	1270	173	841	1101	.296	.380	.568

Where He Hits the Ball

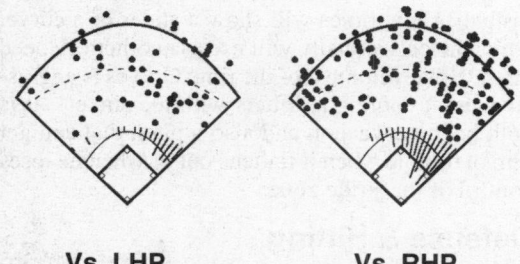

Vs. LHP   Vs. RHP

2000 Situational Stats

	AB	H	HR	RBI	Avg		AB	H	HR	RBI	Avg
Home	256	74	22	62	.289	LHP	152	40	11	32	.263
Road	264	67	18	56	.254	RHP	368	101	29	86	.274
First Half	302	72	28	72	.238	Sc Pos	131	33	10	71	.252
Scnd Half	218	69	12	46	.317	Clutch	92	24	6	22	.261

2000 Rankings (National League)

- 2nd in errors in center field (5)
- 5th in intentional walks (17) and lowest ground-ball/flyball ratio (0.7)
- Led the Reds in home runs, runs scored, total bases (289), RBI, sacrifice flies (8), walks, intentional walks (17), times on base (244), strikeouts, pitches seen (2,449), plate appearances (631), slugging percentage, on-base percentage, HR frequency (13.0 ABs per HR), most pitches seen per plate appearance (3.88), fewest GDPs per GDP situation (4.4%), batting average on an 0-2 count (.250), slugging percentage vs. righthanded pitchers (.573) and on-base percentage vs. righthanded pitchers (.404)

Pete Harnisch

2000 Season

Pete Harnisch was forced to battle through shoulder troubles, which recurred twice during the season and ended up limiting him to only 22 starts. The injury also limited his ability to pitch deep into games, and he reached the 100-pitch mark just six times. However, Harnisch usually was able to hold on when he was on the mound, as Cincinnati won 11 of his starts.

Pitching

Harnisch never has had overpowering velocity, and he rarely gets out of the high 80s anymore. However his shoulder discomfort affects both his command and his feel for his great changeup—two things without which he becomes very hittable. Harnisch cannot win if he's not hitting his spots, and he does not have the confidence to change speeds on any count. He will show a big-breaking curve, which he largely uses as a second offspeed weapon, and will occasionally mix in a slider. Because he usually is around the plate with not overpowering stuff, Harnisch can often be a longball victim.

Defense & Hitting

Always a great competitor, Harnisch does many of the little things a pitcher needs to do. He fields his position very well and is surprisingly agile in coming off the mound to field bunts. He also has become very good at holding runners, with basestealers only attempting nine thefts against him last year. Harnisch can help himself with the bat, last year hitting the second homer of his career and adding eight RBI.

2001 Outlook

Harnisch's value extends beyond his solid pitching. He has become a team leader for the Reds, and with a winter of conditioning to strengthen his shoulder, Cincinnati thinks he will be able to take a regular starting turn this year. His ability to chew up innings and put double-digit wins on the board are paramount on a team that traded both Ron Villone and Steve Parris in the offseason.

Position: SP
Bats: R **Throws:** R
Ht: 6' 0" **Wt:** 228

Opening Day Age: 34
Born: 9/23/66 in Commack, NY
ML Seasons: 13
Pronunciation: HARN-ish

Overall Statistics

	W	L	Pct.	ERA	G	GS	Sv	IP	H	BB	SO	HR	Ratio
2000	8	6	.571	4.74	22	22	0	131.0	133	46	71	23	1.37
Career	110	100	.524	3.84	314	311	0	1923.2	1774	699	1351	214	1.29

How Often He Throws Strikes

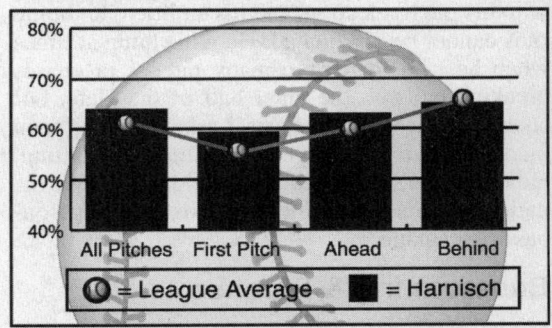

2000 Situational Stats

	W	L	ERA	Sv	IP		AB	H	HR	RBI	Avg
Home	4	3	6.30	0	65.2	LHB	226	60	6	23	.265
Road	4	3	3.17	0	65.1	RHB	284	73	17	45	.257
First Half	1	5	7.51	0	38.1	Sc Pos	110	25	2	41	.227
Scnd Half	7	1	3.59	0	92.2	Clutch	19	4	1	1	.211

2000 Rankings (National League)
- 8th in wild pitches (10)
- Led the Reds in complete games (3)

Barry Larkin

2000 Season

An odd year in which Barry Larkin was nearly traded and then was subsequently signed to a new contract extension finally ended with him again missing significant time with injury. He was sidelined for 60 games with knee and finger injuries, missing most of the season's final five weeks. Larkin still ended up batting over .300 for the ninth time in his career and tied for third on the club in runs scored.

Hitting

One of the game's most reliable hitters, Larkin's skills have shown few signs of erosion. He has extra-base power to all fields, is usually disciplined with his pitch selection, and his ability to hit home runs cannot be discounted. He will slump at times when he tries to lift too many pitches or chases breaking balls on the outer half of the plate. For such a savvy, veteran player, Larkin also has been inconsistent in recent years in situational hitting. However, he remains a very tough out, and his patience is evidenced by his consistently high on-base percentages.

Baserunning & Defense

Despite troubles with his knee, Larkin has not slowed at all in the field, where his range and arm are both among the best in the game among shortstops. He did have a stretch of erratic throwing last season, though that could have been related to a finger problem on his throwing hand. Larkin remains an excellent basestealer with an outstanding success rate, last year swiping 14 bases in 20 attempts. He is aggressive about taking an extra base.

2001 Outlook

For years, Larkin annually has been involved in trade rumors, but with last summer's contract episode, he seems set to finish his career in Cincinnati. He must avoid what have become frequent injuries, but his skills still are sharp, and he will remain one of the key components in the Reds' nucleus.

Position: SS
Bats: R **Throws:** R
Ht: 6' 0" **Wt:** 185

Opening Day Age: 36
Born: 4/28/64 in Cincinnati, OH
ML Seasons: 15

Overall Statistics

	G	AB	R	H	D	T	HR	RBI	SB	BB	SO	Avg	OBP	Slg
2000	102	396	71	124	26	5	11	41	14	48	31	.313	.389	.487
Career	1809	6687	1134	2008	361	70	179	834	359	812	664	.300	.377	.456

Where He Hits the Ball

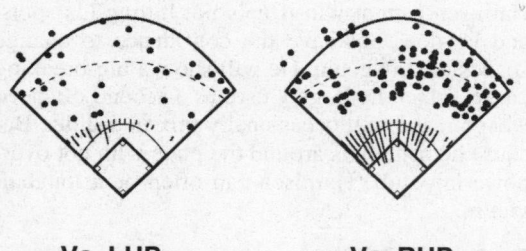

Vs. LHP   **Vs. RHP**

2000 Situational Stats

	AB	H	HR	RBI	Avg		AB	H	HR	RBI	Avg
Home	187	57	6	26	.305	LHP	75	23	3	9	.307
Road	209	67	5	15	.321	RHP	321	101	8	32	.315
First Half	256	81	8	28	.316	Scd Pos	96	23	1	20	.240
Scnd Half	140	43	3	13	.307	Clutch	64	16	0	4	.250

2000 Rankings (National League)

- 4th in fielding percentage at shortstop (.973) and highest percentage of swings put into play (54.2)
- 6th in lowest percentage of swings that missed (9.5) and steals of third (5)
- Led the Reds in caught stealing (6), lowest percentage of swings that missed (9.5), highest percentage of swings put into play (54.2), steals of third (5) and highest percentage of extra bases taken as a runner (51.2)
- Led NL shortstops in highest percentage of swings put into play (54.2)

Pokey Reese

2000 Season

National League pitchers adjusted to Pokey Reese, who eventually was dropped out of the leadoff spot following a 3-for-22 stretch in late May. Reese struggled over the last couple of months, usually batting in the seventh or eighth spot, and he missed the season's final week and a half after getting hit on the left wrist by a Russ Ortiz' pitch. He again was outstanding in the field, earning his second straight Gold Glove at second base.

Hitting

In order to become the leadoff hitter the Reds hope he can be, Reese needs to improve his patience and pitch selection. He has strengthened himself physically to the point where he has surprising power and the ability to handle above-average hard stuff. However, he is overly anxious and swings too often early in the count. He also fell in love with trying to lift the ball, something he cannot do on a regular basis and still hope to be successful. His new ability to hit home runs often caused him to lengthen his swing, which makes him vulnerable to not only fastballs, but also breaking balls and off-speed stuff off the plate.

Baserunning & Defense

Reese continues to grow as a basestealer. He was successful on 29 of 32 attempts last year, an excellent percentage illustrative of his ability to pick his spots and use his outstanding quickness to get consistently good jumps. Reese has few peers at second base, where his range is the best in the National League and where he has become slick in turning the double play. Many of the errors he does make come on plays which few other second basemen would even attempt.

2001 Outlook

In some ways, Reese's 2000 season was more impressive than his breakout '99 campaign. He improved his leadoff on-base percentage from the .316 figure he posted in 1999 to .345 last season. If he can grow as a hitter, he can be of the best at his position for the next several years.

Position: 2B
Bats: R **Throws:** R
Ht: 5'11" **Wt:** 180

Opening Day Age: 27
Born: 6/10/73 in Columbia, SC
ML Seasons: 4

Overall Statistics

	G	AB	R	H	D	T	HR	RBI	SB	BB	SO	Avg	OBP	Slg
2000	135	518	76	132	20	6	12	46	29	45	86	.255	.319	.386
Career	471	1633	229	420	74	13	27	140	95	125	277	.257	.314	.368

Where He Hits the Ball

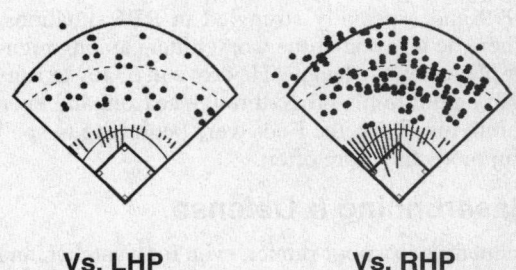

Vs. LHP   **Vs. RHP**

2000 Situational Stats

	AB	H	HR	RBI	Avg		AB	H	HR	RBI	Avg
Home	258	67	3	24	.260	LHP	109	28	1	9	.257
Road	260	65	9	22	.250	RHP	409	104	11	37	.254
First Half	322	86	6	31	.267	Sc Pos	115	23	2	35	.200
Scnd Half	196	46	6	15	.235	Clutch	93	24	3	13	.258

2000 Rankings (National League)

- 1st in stolen-base percentage (90.6)
- 2nd in lowest percentage of swings on the first pitch (10.8)
- 5th in lowest batting average with runners in scoring position
- 6th in errors at second base (14) and lowest fielding percentage at second base (.980)
- 7th in lowest on-base percentage
- 8th in stolen bases
- Led the Reds in triples, stolen bases, stolen-base percentage (90.6), highest percentage of pitches taken (58.7), lowest percentage of swings on the first pitch (10.8) and batting average on a 3-2 count (.306)

Eddie Taubensee

Position: C
Bats: L **Throws:** R
Ht: 6' 3" **Wt:** 230

Opening Day Age: 32
Born: 10/31/68 in Beeville, TX
ML Seasons: 10
Pronunciation: TAW-ben-see

2000 Season

A year after seemingly establishing himself as a front-line player, Eddie Taubensee's production plummeted in all categories. His tough season was compounded by a back problem that troubled him for much of the year and ultimately sidelined him for the season in early August. His .380 slugging percentage was his lowest mark since 1992.

Hitting

Teams stopped throwing Taubensee first-pitch fastballs, choosing instead to come at him with more breaking stuff and offspeed pitches. His bat speed also was affected by his back trouble, and he was consistently handled with hard stuff. He had difficulty pulling the ball with the power he showed in 1999 and especially struggled in RBI situations, where he was one of the worst hitters among regular players in the league. He drove in 63 fewer runs than he did in his break-through season, and even before his injury, the Reds were beginning to spell him more and more often.

Baserunning & Defense

Taubensee is a poor runner, even for a catcher, and his back troubles further diminished whatever speed he still has. He has worked hard to become a better receiver, and Reds pitchers have learned to trust his game-calling skills much more than they did a few years ago. His arm is poor. After finishing with the worst caught stealing percentage (15 percent) in baseball in 1999, he was among the worst at 19 percent in 2000.

2001 Outlook

If Taubensee isn't putting up solid offensive numbers, he's no better than a part-time player because his defensive skills are not his strong suit. But even if he can put his back problems behind him, there's no guarantee that he can repeat his big 1999 campaign, which is partly why the Reds picked up his $1.8 million option for 2001 and then dealt him to Cleveland for two minor league pitchers in November. With Sandy Alomar Jr. heading off to Chicago, Taubensee could be the Tribe's main backstop if he's healthy.

Overall Statistics

	G	AB	R	H	D	T	HR	RBI	SB	BB	SO	Avg	OBP	Slg
2000	81	266	29	71	12	0	6	24	0	21	44	.267	.324	.380
Career	923	2758	335	755	149	8	91	408	11	245	555	.274	.331	.433

Where He Hits the Ball

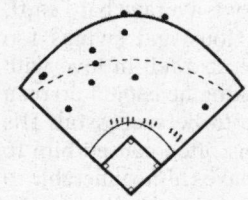

Vs. LHP

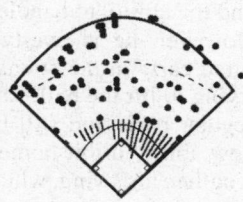

Vs. RHP

2000 Situational Stats

	AB	H	HR	RBI	Avg		AB	H	HR	RBI	Avg
Home	107	26	0	4	.243	LHP	38	13	1	4	.342
Road	159	45	6	20	.283	RHP	228	58	5	20	.254
First Half	213	56	4	19	.263	Sc Pos	63	13	1	16	.206
Scnd Half	53	15	2	5	.283	Clutch	46	14	2	7	.304

2000 Rankings (National League)

- Did not rank near the top or bottom in any category

Ron Villone

Position: SP/RP
Bats: L **Throws:** L
Ht: 6' 3" **Wt:** 237

Opening Day Age: 31
Born: 1/16/70 in Englewood, NJ
ML Seasons: 6
Pronunciation: VA-lone

2000 Season

In his second season as a starting pitcher, Ron Villone experienced mixed results. His ineffectiveness early in the season resulted in him getting temporarily bumped back to the bullpen. He ended up rejoining the rotation and managed a career-high 10 victories, though he offset those wins with 10 losses.

Pitching

Villone struggles to maintain consistent mechanics. The result is that his control can end up killing him. He averaged nearly five walks per nine innings last year, and he pitches behind in the count far too often to be consistently effective. When he finds his release point, he can be overpowering with a riding fastball in the mid-90s and a hard curve. He also has greatly improved his changeup. However, Villone has trouble making in-game adjustments, and if he starts struggling, he rarely is able to right the ship. He posts high pitch counts, which means that the bullpen is on call throughout a given start.

Defense & Hitting

Villone often gets himself in awkward fielding position and is slow coming off the mound to field bunts. He has an above-average pickoff move but is slow delivering the ball home, which makes him vulnerable to good basestealers. Villone has worked hard to improve his hitting and last year enjoyed his best season as a batter, managing seven hits and four RBI.

2001 Outlook

Though he has the stuff to be a solid 12-15 game winner, Villone also has enough flaws to make him something of a fringe pitcher. With the likelihood of him becoming a costly arbitration case, the Reds cut their losses by dealing him to Colorado in exchange for a pair of minor leaguers in early November. Some scouts still believe Villone's future could be in the bullpen, and Coors Field certainly will test his mettle as a starter. If he does remain a starter, he won't have to be more than a bottom-of-the-rotation guy for the Rockies, who also signed fellow lefties Mike Hampton and Denny Neagle in the offseason.

Overall Statistics

	W	L	Pct.	ERA	G	GS	Sv	IP	H	BB	SO	HR	Ratio
2000	10	10	.500	5.43	35	23	0	141.0	154	78	77	22	1.65
Career	23	21	.523	4.67	221	45	5	451.1	427	268	330	54	1.54

How Often He Throws Strikes

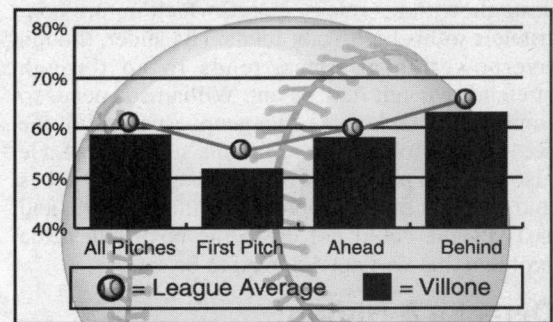

○ = League Average   ■ = Villone

2000 Situational Stats

	W	L	ERA	Sv	IP			AB	H	HR	RBI	Avg
Home	5	7	7.16	0	71.2	LHB	117	30	6	18	.256
Road	5	3	3.63	0	69.1	RHB	421	124	16	68	.295
First Half	7	6	5.98	0	87.1	Sc Pos	129	41	5	62	.318
Scnd Half	3	4	4.53	0	53.2	Clutch	24	10	3	6	.417

2000 Rankings (National League)

- 1st in lowest fielding percentage at pitcher (.871)
- 2nd in errors at pitcher (4)
- 9th in highest batting average allowed with runners in scoring position
- Led the Reds in walks allowed, hit batsmen (9) and runners caught stealing (5)

Cincinnati

Scott Williamson

2000 Season

With their starting rotation in tatters, the Reds tried Scott Williamson as a starting pitcher and in eight of his 10 starts, the Reds were given a good chance to win. The experiment came a year after Williamson was National League Rookie of the Year as a reliever and during a season where his inconsistency in the bullpen was a source of much frustration.

Pitching

When he's at his best, Williamson brings his fastball in the mid- to upper 90s and is capable of blowing people away with pure heat. His command of the strike zone remains very uneven. He can struggle with his release point, which in turn contributes to his high walk totals. His slider, though overpowering at times, tends to go through stretches when it flattens out. Williamson needs to improve the feel on his changeup, especially if the Reds intend to use him again in a starting role. He also needs to pitch more often through minor aches and pains. A finger problem hurt him in 1999, and last year he could not go to the post with a toe problem that was not believed to be serious.

Defense & Hitting

Williamson's deliberate delivery and his lack of any creditable pickoff move gives his catchers a challenge stopping opposing basestealers, though he did pick off four runners in 2000. Williamson does an adequate job of fielding his position. He is virtually helpless at the plate, with only one hit to show for 23 lifetime at-bats.

2001 Outlook

With the Cincinnati roster constantly in a state of upheaval under GM Jim Bowden, Williamson's role likely will remain unclear until spring training. The team did trade away a pair of starters in Ron Villone and Steve Parris in the offseason, but Williamson's best value likely remains in the bullpen, where his stuff can be nasty and where his great arm has made him the target of trade efforts by a number of clubs.

Position: RP/SP
Bats: R **Throws:** R
Ht: 6' 0" **Wt:** 185

Opening Day Age: 25
Born: 2/17/76 in Fort Polk, LA
ML Seasons: 2

Overall Statistics

	W	L	Pct.	ERA	G	GS	Sv	IP	H	BB	SO	HR	Ratio
2000	5	8	.385	3.29	48	10	6	112.0	92	75	136	7	1.49
Career	17	15	.531	2.89	110	10	25	205.1	146	118	243	15	1.29

How Often He Throws Strikes

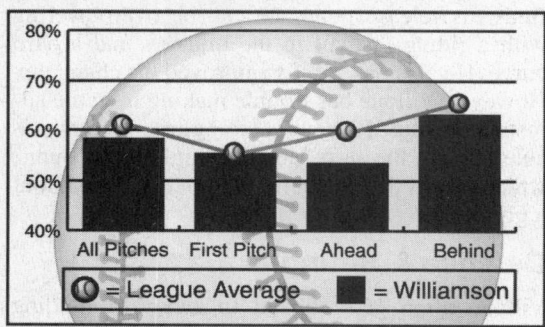

O = League Average   ■ = Williamson

2000 Situational Stats

	W	L	ERA	Sv	IP		AB	H	HR	RBI	Avg
Home	0	6	4.37	4	59.2	LHB	171	43	5	25	.251
Road	5	2	2.06	2	52.1	RHB	240	49	2	21	.204
First Half	2	6	3.61	6	62.1	Sc Pos	135	22	2	37	.163
Scnd Half	3	2	2.90	0	49.2	Clutch	146	31	2	20	.212

2000 Rankings (National League)

- 2nd in wild pitches (21), lowest batting average allowed with runners in scoring position and most strikeouts per nine innings in relief (13.2)
- 3rd in lowest batting average allowed vs. righthanded batters
- 7th in lowest batting average allowed in relief with runners in scoring position (.173)
- 10th in most baserunners allowed per nine innings in relief (14.6)
- Led the Reds in strikeouts, wild pitches (21), pickoff throws (120), lowest batting average allowed with runners in scoring position, lowest batting average allowed in relief (.218) and most strikeouts per nine innings in relief (13.2)

Dmitri Young

2000 Season

One of the more overlooked hitters in the National League, Dmitri Young started poorly for a second straight year and then had a big second half that allowed him to hit over .300. It was the third straight campaign that he topped the .300 plateau. Young also had his best RBI year, and his 88 ribbies were the second-best total on the Cincinnati club.

Hitting

When he's in his groove, Young can be a line-drive machine from either side of the plate. A better overall hitter batting lefthanded, Young has developed some righthanded power. For someone who has become a consistent .300 threat, Young is an impatient hitter who looks for a fastball early in the count and drives it where it's pitched. His gap power to all fields explains why he hits so many doubles. Indifferent conditioning may be one reason why he always seems to get off to poor starts. If he could put together a whole year and work more deep counts, he could challenge the .330 neighborhood and drive in 100 runs.

Baserunning & Defense

Young did not steal a base last year, and he has become something of a liability on the basepaths. His outfield range also is sub-par, whether he plays left or right field. Young does not get good jumps on balls and is prone to mishandling some plays, especially when he arrives late. His throwing arm is below average.

2001 Outlook

Young has the ability be a significant player, and age still is on his side. However, he also could frustrate, primarily because he has not worked himself into the best physical shape and he's prone to very uneven stretches. The Reds would love to see him firmly entrench himself as one of their everyday outfielders. But until Young proves he's worthy of such a label, he likely will remain just a very good three-quarters-of-the-time player.

Position: LF/1B
Bats: B **Throws:** R
Ht: 6' 2" **Wt:** 235

Opening Day Age: 27
Born: 10/11/73 in Vicksburg, MS
ML Seasons: 5

Overall Statistics

	G	AB	R	H	D	T	HR	RBI	SB	BB	SO	Avg	OBP	Slg
2000	152	548	68	166	37	6	18	88	0	36	80	.303	.346	.491
Career	549	1819	253	537	129	12	51	263	11	155	313	.295	.351	.463

Where He Hits the Ball

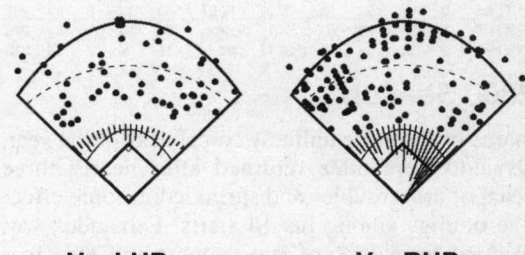

Vs. LHP   **Vs. RHP**

2000 Situational Stats

	AB	H	HR	RBI	Avg		AB	H	HR	RBI	Avg
Home	267	87	6	47	.326	LHP	141	47	5	26	.333
Road	281	79	12	41	.281	RHP	407	119	13	62	.292
First Half	302	84	9	42	.278	Sc Pos	146	49	2	66	.336
Scnd Half	246	82	9	46	.333	Clutch	96	30	5	14	.313

2000 Rankings (National League)

- 1st in highest percentage of swings on the first pitch (48.4)
- 2nd in lowest percentage of pitches taken (43.1)
- 3rd in fewest pitches seen per plate appearance (3.28)
- 4th in fielding percentage in left field (.978)
- Led the Reds in at-bats, hits, singles, doubles, triples, highest groundball/flyball ratio (1.8), batting average in the clutch, batting average vs. lefthanded pitchers, slugging percentage vs. lefthanded pitchers (.546), on-base percentage vs. lefthanded pitchers (.364), batting average at home and games played
- Led NL left fielders in GDPs (16) and highest groundball/flyball ratio (1.8)

Osvaldo Fernandez

Position: SP
Bats: R **Throws:** R
Ht: 6' 2" **Wt:** 193

Opening Day Age: 32
Born: 11/4/68 in
Holguin, Cuba
ML Seasons: 3

Overall Statistics

	W	L	Pct.	ERA	G	GS	Sv	IP	H	BB	SO	HR	Ratio
2000	4	3	.571	3.62	15	14	0	79.2	69	31	36	6	1.26
Career	14	20	.412	4.42	56	53	0	307.2	336	103	173	35	1.43

2000 Situational Stats

	W	L	ERA	Sv	IP		AB	H	HR	RBI	Avg
Home	1	2	3.32	0	40.2	LHB	141	30	4	14	.213
Road	3	1	3.92	0	39.0	RHB	149	39	2	16	.262
First Half	2	2	4.73	0	51.1	Sc Pos	58	16	1	23	.276
Scnd Half	2	1	1.59	0	28.1	Clutch	16	5	2	3	.313

2000 Season

In one of the more unlikely comebacks of the year, Osvaldo Fernandez returned after nearly three years of arm troubles and sprinkled in some effective outings among his 14 starts. Fernandez was plagued by a lack of run support and also was sidelined for a period by groin troubles.

Pitching, Defense & Hitting

With good control and a seasoned feel for hitting spots and changing speeds, Fernandez can be effective. Though he cannot hold his stuff for much more than 85 pitches, he is economical with his sinking fastball, forkball and change. He also can spot his average fastball inside when needed. He is fairly slow to the plate and easy to run on, and he will sting a team with an occasional error in the field. Fernandez is no factor with the bat.

2001 Outlook

With his checkered medical history and advancing age, Fernandez isn't someone around whom to build a staff. However, he had stretches last year where he showed he can still be a serviceable starting pitcher, capable of winning 10 games if given good run support and bullpen help. Given the trades of both Ron Villone and Steve Parris, Fernandez could be called upon to make 20 or more starts for the Reds in 2001.

Brian Hunter (Overrated)

Position: CF/LF/RF
Bats: R **Throws:** R
Ht: 6' 3" **Wt:** 180

Opening Day Age: 30
Born: 3/5/71 in
Portland, OR
ML Seasons: 7

Overall Statistics

	G	AB	R	H	D	T	HR	RBI	SB	BB	SO	Avg	OBP	Slg
2000	104	240	47	64	5	1	1	14	20	27	40	.267	.342	.308
Career	763	2903	433	765	118	24	20	192	241	205	496	.264	.312	.341

2000 Situational Stats

	AB	H	HR	RBI	Avg		AB	H	HR	RBI	Avg
Home	130	40	1	10	.308	LHP	94	21	0	4	.223
Road	110	24	0	4	.218	RHP	146	43	1	10	.295
First Half	126	37	0	9	.294	Sc Pos	49	12	0	13	.245
Scnd Half	114	27	1	5	.237	Clutch	29	7	0	1	.241

2000 Season

A late-season acquisition for Cincinnati, Brian Hunter added another basestealer to the Reds' roster and also served as a part-time outfielder. He ended up with 20 steals in 23 attempts for the Rockies and Reds in 2000 and managed a decent .342 on-base percentage.

Hitting, Baserunning & Defense

Hunter showed signs of improving his pitch selection last year, but he remains too anxious a hitter for someone with so little power and he can be easily overpowered. He never has fully utilized his speed to boost his batting average, partly because he hits far too many pitches in the air. Hunter remains one of the game's better basestealers, thanks to that excellent speed and his ability to get jumps. He lacks the instincts to be a center fielder and is better suited for left, where his arm is above average.

2001 Outlook

Hunter has been a tease for whichever team he's played for. However, his reputation has sunk to the point where he is viewed as a spare player whose biggest asset is providing a pair of fast feet off the bench. His release by the Reds in late November means he will be playing for his fifth team in three years in 2001.

Jason LaRue

Position: C
Bats: R **Throws:** R
Ht: 5'11" **Wt:** 200

Opening Day Age: 27
Born: 3/19/74 in
Houston, TX
ML Seasons: 2

Overall Statistics

	G	AB	R	H	D	T	HR	RBI	SB	BB	SO	Avg	OBP	Slg
2000	31	98	12	23	3	0	5	12	0	5	19	.235	.299	.418
Career	67	188	24	42	10	0	8	22	4	16	51	.223	.305	.404

2000 Situational Stats

	AB	H	HR	RBI	Avg		AB	H	HR	RBI	Avg
Home	37	4	1	6	.108	LHP	20	6	2	7	.300
Road	61	19	4	6	.311	RHP	78	17	3	5	.218
First Half	0	0	0	0	-	Sc Pos	22	7	1	7	.318
Scnd Half	98	23	5	12	.235	Clutch	7	1	0	0	.143

2000 Season

Reds pitchers quickly learned to love throwing to Jason LaRue, and for one brief shining moment when he homered twice in one game against the Cubs, it seemed maybe he could emerge as a hitter. However, LaRue's lack of punch largely kept him in a reserve role.

Hitting, Baserunning & Defense

LaRue has some power when he's able to get his arms extended, and he can catch up to a fastball. His big swing is easy for pitchers to exploit. He can't catch up to many pitches on the inner half of the plate and will chase offspeed or breaking pitches off the plate or in the dirt. He has slightly better than average speed for a catcher. LaRue's strength is his defense. He is an outstanding handler of pitchers and frames pitches well. He has good technique in blocking balls and has a strong and usually accurate arm, though he needs work on his throwing mechanics.

2001 Outlook

Having a former catcher in Bob Boone managing him should do wonders for LaRue's solid receiving skills. He still has to prove he can shorten his swing and make more consistent contact, but with Eddie Taubensee traded to Cleveland, LaRue could get a chance to win everyday status behind the plate.

Alex Ochoa

Position: LF/RF
Bats: R **Throws:** R
Ht: 6' 0" **Wt:** 195

Opening Day Age: 28
Born: 3/29/72 in Miami Lakes, FL
ML Seasons: 6
Pronunciation:
oh-CHO-uh

Overall Statistics

	G	AB	R	H	D	T	HR	RBI	SB	BB	SO	Avg	OBP	Slg
2000	118	244	50	77	21	3	13	58	9	24	27	.316	.378	.586
Career	537	1327	207	376	85	12	30	178	29	116	177	.283	.344	.433

2000 Situational Stats

	AB	H	HR	RBI	Avg		AB	H	HR	RBI	Avg
Home	130	37	9	34	.285	LHP	90	27	5	26	.300
Road	114	40	4	24	.351	RHP	154	50	8	32	.325
First Half	90	28	4	21	.311	Sc Pos	65	25	5	47	.385
Scnd Half	154	49	9	37	.318	Clutch	54	15	3	9	.278

2000 Season

Though he may never achieve the stardom once predicted for him, Alex Ochoa may have turned his career around in 2000. He had his best season as a major leaguer, setting career highs in most categories. By late last season, he had become a regular part of the Reds' outfield.

Hitting, Baserunning & Defense

Over the last two years, Ochoa has added several pounds of muscle, and the result is that he has become a much more serious extra-base threat. He now is capable of pulling inside fastballs for home runs and has added power to the opposite field. His .586 slugging percentage last year was a career mark by 120 points. Ochoa's pitch selection also has improved, as he's learned to lay off breaking pitches. He has above-average speed and has learned to become a basestealing threat. An outstanding outfielder in either right or left, he owns one of the game's best arms.

2001 Outlook

At the very least, Ochoa proved last year that he is a good extra outfielder who can hit all types of pitches. He could challenge for everyday status this year, especially with his power now at a point where hitting 20 or more homers no longer is a reach.

Cincinnati

Steve Parris

Traded To BLUE JAYS

Position: SP
Bats: R **Throws:** R
Ht: 6' 0" **Wt:** 195

Opening Day Age: 33
Born: 12/17/67 in Joliet, IL
ML Seasons: 5

Overall Statistics

	W	L	Pct.	ERA	G	GS	Sv	IP	H	BB	SO	HR	Ratio
2000	12	17	.414	4.81	33	33	0	192.2	227	71	117	30	1.55
Career	35	35	.500	4.49	96	89	0	528.2	564	199	368	71	1.44

2000 Situational Stats

	W	L	ERA	Sv	IP		AB	H	HR	RBI	Avg
Home	7	6	4.07	0	90.2	LHB	383	119	17	46	.311
Road	5	11	5.47	0	102.0	RHB	389	108	13	52	.278
First Half	5	11	5.26	0	99.1	Sc Pos	214	47	5	68	.220
Scnd Half	7	6	4.34	0	93.1	Clutch	19	8	0	3	.421

2000 Season

It was a tale of two seasons for Steve Parris. He got off to a nightmare of a start by losing 11 of his first 14 decisions and was on pace for a possible 20-loss debacle. However, he reversed himself and closed the year by winning nine of his last 15 decisions over the last three months.

Pitching, Defense & Hitting

Much of Parris' early-season trouble was control. When he is pitching from behind in the count or missing in the wrong part of the strike zone, he gets beat up because his stuff does not overpower hitters. He was able to regain a more consistent release point with both his sinker and his change and again became an efficient pitcher. Parris handles himself well in the field but is fairly easy to run on. He is not an automatic out at bat.

2001 Outlook

Parris was eligible for arbitration at the end of the year, so Cincinnati traded him to Toronto in late November for minor league hurlers Clayton Andrews and Leo Estrella. Parris is a fine-line pitcher who does not have top-of-the-rotation stuff, but is a very useful third or fourth starter who should be able to win a dozen or more games for the Blue Jays.

Dennys Reyes

Position: RP
Bats: R **Throws:** L
Ht: 6' 3" **Wt:** 246

Opening Day Age: 23
Born: 4/19/77 in Higuera de Zaragoza, Mexico
ML Seasons: 4
Pronunciation: RAY-ess

Overall Statistics

	W	L	Pct.	ERA	G	GS	Sv	IP	H	BB	SO	HR	Ratio
2000	2	1	.667	4.53	62	0	0	43.2	43	29	36	5	1.65
Career	9	11	.450	4.18	160	16	2	219.2	209	133	221	17	1.56

2000 Situational Stats

	W	L	ERA	Sv	IP		AB	H	HR	RBI	Avg
Home	1	0	4.09	0	22.0	LHB	73	13	2	13	.178
Road	1	1	4.98	0	21.2	RHB	91	30	3	18	.330
First Half	2	1	6.11	0	28.0	Sc Pos	53	17	2	28	.321
Scnd Half	0	0	1.72	0	15.2	Clutch	40	10	0	5	.250

2000 Season

Once pegged to have a future as a starter, Dennys Reyes instead has become more established as a lefthanded situational middle reliever. He rarely is called upon to pitch more than an inning, last year tossing only 43.2 frames in his 62 appearances.

Pitching, Defense & Hitting

Reyes is not strictly a lefthanded specialist, as his cut fastball can be equally effective—or ineffective, as the case may be—against all hitters. He will change speeds with the cutter and also mix in a slow overhand curve. However, he lacks the velocity to come inside very often and becomes hittable because batters can crowd the plate and take his pitches to the opposite field. He is not a good fielder and does not have any pickoff move for a runner to worry about. Reyes is no factor as a hitter.

2001 Outlook

Nothing ever is certain on the ever-changing Reds roster, as evidenced by their trading frenzy in November. At the very least, Reyes knows he will be in Cincinnati next year, as he signed a one-year, $625,000 deal in mid-December. Whether he becomes a starter or remains a situational reliever depends upon a number of factors, including his offseason conditioning.

Benito Santiago

Position: C
Bats: R **Throws:** R
Ht: 6' 1" **Wt:** 195

Opening Day Age: 36
Born: 3/9/65 in Ponce, Puerto Rico
ML Seasons: 15
Pronunciation: sahn-tee-AH-go

Overall Statistics

	G	AB	R	H	D	T	HR	RBI	SB	BB	SO	Avg	OBP	Slg
2000	89	252	22	66	11	1	8	45	2	19	45	.262	.310	.409
Career	1556	5397	591	1406	242	29	178	722	81	343	1015	.261	.305	.415

2000 Situational Stats

	AB	H	HR	RBI	Avg		AB	H	HR	RBI	Avg
Home	154	44	7	36	.286	LHP	82	22	2	10	.268
Road	98	22	1	9	.224	RHP	170	44	6	35	.259
First Half	129	30	3	17	.233	Sc Pos	64	17	2	35	.266
Scnd Half	123	36	5	28	.293	Clutch	47	10	1	10	.213

2000 Season

Acquired as a reserve player, Benito Santiago ended up catching much more regularly than anticipated due to an injury to Eddie Taubensee. He ended up reviving his veteran career with solid production both offensively and defensively.

Hitting, Baserunning & Defense

Santiago remains a dangerous fastball hitter who can catch up with quality hard stuff and pull those pitches for power. He always has been overly aggressive and will struggle against breaking stuff and offspeed offerings. After all these years, he remains one of the game's best throwing catchers, last year gunning down nearly 40 percent of those runners who tried to steal against him. He has better-than-average speed for a catcher, despite his advanced age.

2001 Outlook

At this stage of his career, Santiago largely is viewed as a part-time player. The free agent has the power-hitting and catching skills to still be a useful bench player for most teams. Though the Reds did ship off Taubensee to Cleveland in the offseason, they still have Jason LaRue waiting in the wings, so Santiago most likely will be looking for work elsewhere.

Chris Stynes

Traded To RED SOX

Position: 3B/2B
Bats: R **Throws:** R
Ht: 5'10" **Wt:** 185

Opening Day Age: 28
Born: 1/19/73 in Queens, NY
ML Seasons: 6

Overall Statistics

	G	AB	R	H	D	T	HR	RBI	SB	BB	SO	Avg	OBP	Slg
2000	119	380	71	127	24	1	12	40	5	32	54	.334	.386	.497
Career	422	1165	187	344	49	3	26	117	41	93	124	.295	.351	.409

2000 Situational Stats

	AB	H	HR	RBI	Avg		AB	H	HR	RBI	Avg
Home	170	60	8	25	.353	LHP	88	35	3	12	.398
Road	210	67	4	15	.319	RHP	292	92	9	28	.315
First Half	98	44	6	16	.449	Sc Pos	83	24	2	27	.289
Scnd Half	282	83	6	24	.294	Clutch	57	15	2	7	.263

2000 Season

Chris Stynes gave the Reds a big boost off the bench. He stepped in at third when Aaron Boone was lost with an injury and for several weeks was among the hottest hitters in the league, while often filling the leadoff spot. Stynes set career highs in all key categories.

Hitting, Baserunning & Defense

For the second season in his career, Stynes showed the ability to hit for a high average by hitting balls where they're pitched, hanging in against breaking balls and being aggressive early in the count on fastball strikes. He has become stronger physically and is more of a threat to pull with power. Stynes has average speed but is willing to take chances on the basepaths. He can play second, third and the outfield corners, with third being his best position. His arm can be erratic, however, which can make him a bit of a liability at the hot corner.

2001 Outlook

Stynes was deemed expendable and was dealt to Boston for outfielder Michael Coleman and utility player Donnie Sadler. Stynes should remain a valuable pinch-hitter and spot starter at a number of positions for the Red Sox, but there remains doubt that he could sustain production on an everyday basis for a full season.

Cincinnati

Scott Sullivan (Rubber Arm)

Position: RP
Bats: R **Throws:** R
Ht: 6' 3" **Wt:** 210

Opening Day Age: 30
Born: 3/13/71 in
Carrollton, AL
ML Seasons: 6

Overall Statistics

	W	L	Pct.	ERA	G	GS	Sv	IP	H	BB	SO	HR	Ratio
2000	3	6	.333	3.47	79	0	3	106.1	87	38	96	14	1.18
Career	18	18	.500	3.70	294	0	8	431.0	363	158	361	50	1.21

2000 Situational Stats

	W	L	ERA	Sv	IP		AB	H	HR	RBI	Avg
Home	2	5	3.34	0	59.1	LHB	159	34	5	15	.214
Road	1	1	3.64	3	47.0	RHB	226	53	9	28	.235
First Half	1	3	4.39	2	55.1	Sc Pos	99	19	4	31	.192
Scnd Half	2	3	2.47	1	51.0	Clutch	172	44	7	20	.256

2000 Season

Amazingly durable, Scott Sullivan was one of baseball's busiest relievers for a third straight year. He has worked more than 100 innings in each of those three campaigns, something no other active reliever in baseball has done. He had one of the best strikeout-walk ratios of his career and added three saves.

Pitching, Defense & Hitting

Sullivan's stock in trade is his sidearm fastball, which he throws in the low 90s. The pitch is especially difficult on righthanded hitters, who have hit just .217 against Sullivan over the past five years. He has worked on improving his arsenal against lefties, developing a more consistent cut fastball and also mixing in a slider. He gets in trouble when his fastball sits over the plate, a reason why he allowed 14 homers last year. His delivery often leaves him out of position to field but basestealers rarely ran off him in 2000. He is not often called upon to hit.

2001 Outlook

Few relievers in baseball are better staff savers than Sullivan. He can pitch virtually every day and in a variety of roles with consistent effectiveness. He is especially vital to a Reds pitching staff that lacks innings-eaters in the starting rotation.

Michael Tucker

Position: RF/LF/CF
Bats: L **Throws:** R
Ht: 6' 2" **Wt:** 185

Opening Day Age: 29
Born: 6/25/71 in South
Boston, VA
ML Seasons: 6

Overall Statistics

	G	AB	R	H	D	T	HR	RBI	SB	BB	SO	Avg	OBP	Slg
2000	148	270	55	72	13	4	15	36	13	44	64	.267	.381	.511
Career	719	1995	322	523	101	23	69	252	56	232	493	.262	.345	.440

2000 Situational Stats

	AB	H	HR	RBI	Avg		AB	H	HR	RBI	Avg
Home	125	40	7	17	.320	LHP	24	4	2	2	.167
Road	145	32	8	19	.221	RHP	246	68	13	34	.276
First Half	139	39	10	23	.281	Sc Pos	70	12	0	16	.171
Scnd Half	131	33	5	13	.252	Clutch	54	12	2	5	.222

2000 Season

Used as a spot starter, pinch-hitter and defensive replacement, Michael Tucker supplied some surprising power. He hit a career-high 15 home runs in 270 at-bats, while adding a very good on-base percentage. He set a career mark playing in 148 games, offering the Reds a solid fourth outfielder.

Hitting, Baserunning & Defense

Tucker never has been able to claim an everyday job, partly because of his difficulty against lefthanded pitching. He also strikes out far too much for a player with his limited power. He continues to be vulnerable against high fastballs and frequently tries to pull pitches he cannot handle. Tucker has a quick first step and has become a solid, high-percentage basestealer who last year was successful on 13 of 19 attempts. He at times rushes plays into miscues in the field but is otherwise a solid outfielder with an above-average arm.

2001 Outlook

Until another front-line outfielder comes along, Tucker should remain busy. The release of Brian Hunter could translate into more opportunities for Tucker. He seems destined to remain a utility player, however, because he never has produced for a significant period of time and because he owns a career .239 batting average against lefties.

Other Cincinnati Reds

Kimera Bartee (**Pos**: LF, **Age**: 28, **Bats**: R)

	G	AB	R	H	D	T	HR	RBI	SB	BB	SO	Avg	OBP	Slg
2000	11	4	2	0	0	0	0	0	1	0	2	.000	.200	.000
Career	231	401	69	90	12	5	4	32	36	34	136	.224	.288	.309

Bartee spent most of 2000 in Triple-A and offers the same speed and defense as always. The Angels claimed him off wiavers in mid-December. 2001 Outlook: C

Mike Bell (**Pos**: 3B, **Age**: 26, **Bats**: R)

	G	AB	R	H	D	T	HR	RBI	SB	BB	SO	Avg	OBP	Slg
2000	19	27	5	6	0	0	2	4	0	4	7	.222	.323	.444
Career	19	27	5	6	0	0	2	4	0	4	7	.222	.323	.444

Bell hit a few more home runs last season than he had before. He opted for free agency and was signed by the Rockies. 2001 Outlook: B

Juan Castro (**Pos**: SS/2B, **Age**: 28, **Bats**: R)

	G	AB	R	H	D	T	HR	RBI	SB	BB	SO	Avg	OBP	Slg
2000	82	224	20	54	12	2	4	23	0	14	33	.241	.283	.366
Career	294	656	64	135	27	6	6	46	1	47	119	.206	.257	.293

The Reds acquired Castro from the Dodgers in a deal last April. He can play second, third and short and signed a two-year extension last June. 2001 Outlook: B

Norm Charlton (**Pos**: LHP, **Age**: 38)

	W	L	Pct.	ERA	G	GS	Sv	IP	H	BB	SO	HR	Ratio
2000	0	0	-	27.00	2	0	0	3.0	6	6	1	1	4.00
Career	47	52	.475	3.75	561	37	96	851.2	762	398	760	66	1.36

Not satisfied when Tampa Bay released him last March, Charlton hooked on with the Reds, who released him by the end of April. 2001 Outlook: D

Brady Clark (**Pos**: RF, **Age**: 27, **Bats**: R)

	G	AB	R	H	D	T	HR	RBI	SB	BB	SO	Avg	OBP	Slg
2000	11	11	1	3	1	0	0	2	0	0	2	.273	.273	.364
Career	11	11	1	3	1	0	0	2	0	0	2	.273	.273	.364

Clark played his first pro season as he was just turning 24 in 1997. But he's been drawing walks, banging doubles and batting .300 almost ever since. 2001 Outlook: C

D.T. Cromer (**Pos**: 1B, **Age**: 30, **Bats**: L)

	G	AB	R	H	D	T	HR	RBI	SB	BB	SO	Avg	OBP	Slg
2000	35	47	7	16	4	0	2	8	0	1	14	.340	.360	.553
Career	35	47	7	16	4	0	2	8	0	1	14	.340	.360	.553

Cromer wasn't quite the prospect that his brother Brandon was, but D.T. reached the majors first, joining their other brother, Tripp. 2001 Outlook: C

Elmer Dessens (**Pos**: RHP, **Age**: 29)

	W	L	Pct.	ERA	G	GS	Sv	IP	H	BB	SO	HR	Ratio
2000	11	5	.688	4.28	40	16	1	147.1	170	43	85	10	1.45
Career	13	13	.500	5.03	101	24	1	250.1	302	72	143	22	1.49

Dessens spent '99 in Japan, signed with the Reds and posted the club's second-most wins. 2001 Outlook: B

Keith Glauber (**Pos**: RHP, **Age**: 29)

	W	L	Pct.	ERA	G	GS	Sv	IP	H	BB	SO	HR	Ratio
2000	0	0	-	3.68	4	0	0	7.1	5	2	4	0	0.95
Career	0	0	-	3.00	7	0	0	15.0	11	3	8	0	0.93

Glauber hasn't been able to gain any traction, bouncing between Double-A and Triple-A the past four seasons. At best he's a middle relief candidate. 2001 Outlook: C

Brooks Kieschnick (**Pos**: 1B, **Age**: 28, **Bats**: L)

	G	AB	R	H	D	T	HR	RBI	SB	BB	SO	Avg	OBP	Slg
2000	14	12	0	0	0	0	0	0	0	1	5	.000	.077	.000
Career	78	131	15	28	4	0	5	18	1	16	34	.214	.299	.359

Kieschnick went hitless in his few at-bats with the Reds. The former first-round pick of the Cubs has power but is far past prospect status. He was signed by the Rockies to a minor league contract in early December. 2001 Outlook: C

Larry Luebbers (**Pos**: RHP, **Age**: 31)

	W	L	Pct.	ERA	G	GS	Sv	IP	H	BB	SO	HR	Ratio
2000	0	2	.000	6.20	14	1	1	20.1	27	12	9	1	1.92
Career	5	10	.333	4.96	36	23	1	143.1	147	66	63	16	1.49

Luebbers doesn't strike out many batters and can be hit. He is a poor choice to work out of the bullpen, but the Reds used him there last year. 2001 Outlook: C

Hector Mercado (**Pos**: LHP, **Age**: 26)

	W	L	Pct.	ERA	G	GS	Sv	IP	H	BB	SO	HR	Ratio
2000	0	0	-	4.50	12	0	0	14.0	12	8	13	2	1.43
Career	0	0	-	4.50	12	0	0	14.0	12	8	13	2	1.43

Mercado missed all of 1998 and most of 1999 with elbow problems. In 2000 he worked in 59 games between Cincinnati and Triple-A. 2001 Outlook: C

John Riedling (**Pos**: RHP, **Age**: 25)

	W	L	Pct.	ERA	G	GS	Sv	IP	H	BB	SO	HR	Ratio
2000	3	1	.750	2.35	13	0	1	15.1	11	8	18	1	1.24
Career	3	1	.750	2.35	13	0	1	15.1	11	8	18	1	1.24

Riedling became more successful after moving to the bullpen in 1999. His strikeout rate jumped last year and he had one poor outing with the Reds. 2001 Outlook: B

Chris Sexton (**Pos**: SS/2B, **Age**: 29, **Bats**: R)

	G	AB	R	H	D	T	HR	RBI	SB	BB	SO	Avg	OBP	Slg
2000	35	100	9	21	4	0	0	10	4	13	12	.210	.310	.250
Career	70	159	18	35	4	1	1	17	8	24	22	.220	.328	.277

Originally drafted by the Reds in 1993, Sexton returned to Cincinnati last season. He draws walks and offers infield versatility, but little power. The Reds re-signed him to a minor league deal in mid-November. 2001 Outlook: C

Scott Winchester (**Pos**: RHP, **Age**: 27)

	W	L	Pct.	ERA	G	GS	Sv	IP	H	BB	SO	HR	Ratio
2000	1	0	1.000	3.68	5	0	0	7.1	10	2	3	1	1.64
Career	3	6	.333	5.65	26	16	0	92.1	120	31	46	14	1.64

Winchester returned from shoulder surgery the year before to pitch most of last season at Triple-A. It appears his days as a starter are now history. 2001 Outlook: C

Mark Wohlers (**Pos**: RHP, **Age**: 31)

	W	L	Pct.	ERA	G	GS	Sv	IP	H	BB	SO	HR	Ratio
2000	1	2	.333	4.50	20	0	0	28.0	19	17	20	3	1.29
Career	32	24	.571	3.78	408	0	112	414.1	350	221	457	23	1.38

Wohlers' control wasn't great last year, but much better than the previous two seasons. He agreed to a one-year, $1.5 million deal with the Reds in mid-December, with a mutual option for 2002. 2001 Outlook: B

Cincinnati

Cincinnati Reds Minor League Prospects

Organization Overview:

The Reds turned their focus toward the future when they unloaded their ace, Denny Neagle, to the Yankees for a super package of prospects: Drew Henson, Jackson Melian, Ed Yarnall and Brian Reith. Rob Bell stepped in and injected a fresh power arm into a staggering staff, but there isn't another upper-level pitching prospect on the verge of breaking through to make an impact. Cincinnati's 2000 draft could be responsible for rejuvenating the system before long, although their top three picks signed too late to debut in 2000, and one, highly touted Dustin Moseley, remains unsigned. Third-rounder David Gil reached Double-A by season's end.

Ben Broussard

Position: OF   **Opening Day Age:** 24
Bats: L **Throws:** L   **Born:** 9/24/76 in
Ht: 6' 2" **Wt:** 220   Beaumont, TX

Recent Statistics

	G	AB	R	H	D	THR	RBI	SB	BB	SO	Avg
1999 R Billings	38	145	39	59	11	2	14	48	1	34	30	.407
1999 A Clinton	5	20	8	11	4	1	2	6	0	3	4	.550
1999 AA Chattanooga	35	127	26	27	5	0	8	21	1	11	41	.213
2000 AA Chattanooga	87	286	64	73	8	4	14	51	15	72	78	.255
2000 MLE	87	277	51	64	7	2	11	41	10	51	83	.231

Between college, the minors and the California Fall League, Broussard amassed an amazing 60 home runs in 1999. His performance convinced the Reds he was ready to handle Double-A in his first full pro season. Broussard picked up right where he left off, before a wrist injury hampered his progress. He displays sound plate discipline, but struggled against southpaws, hitting just .171. A collegiate first baseman, he is adapting to the outfield, but he has good mobility for a man of his size. In just over a full season in the minors, Broussard's numbers stack up well. His wrist injury is a concern, and he needs to prove himself in the higher levels.

Travis Dawkins

Position: SS-2B   **Opening Day Age:** 21
Bats: R **Throws:** R   **Born:** 5/12/79 in
Ht: 6' 1" **Wt:** 180   Newberry, SC

Recent Statistics

	G	AB	R	H	D	THR	RBI	SB	BB	SO	Avg
2000 AA Chattanooga	95	368	54	85	20	6	6	31	22	40	71	.231
2000 NL Cincinnati	14	41	5	9	2	0	0	3	0	2	7	.220
2000 MLE	95	358	43	75	18	4	4	25	15	28	76	.209

In 1999, Dawkins shot up the organizational ladder from Class-A to the majors, raising expectations along the way. After hitting .300 in Double-A the year before, he never seemed to get on track in 2000 and his production suffered mightily in his first full campaign in Double-A. But he didn't turn 21 until after the season began, so there's no need to push the panic button. He's nearly major league-ready in the field, with outstanding range, soft hands and a strong arm. Dawkins won't hit for much power, but he is a great baserunner who is capable of swiping more than 30 bases a year.

Adam Dunn

Position: OF   **Opening Day Age:** 21
Bats: L **Throws:** R   **Born:** 11/9/79 in
Ht: 6' 6" **Wt:** 235   Houston, TX

Recent Statistics

	G	AB	R	H	D	THR	RBI	SB	BB	SO	Avg
1999 A Rockford	93	313	62	96	16	2	11	44	21	46	64	.307
2000 A Dayton	122	420	101	118	29	1	16	79	24	100	101	.281

Dunn, a former University of Texas backup quarterback, hung up the helmet and pads and set his sights on the diamond full time in 2000. With football out of the picture, the Reds believe Dunn has the highest ceiling of their prospects and are enthralled with his approach. Already an advanced hitter, Dunn drew an amazing 100 walks in his first full season. Even at 6-foot-6 and 235 pounds he can run the bases, and he made encouraging progress in the outfield. Not blessed with a strong throwing arm, he is working on improving his footwork and taking better angles to make him a serviceable left fielder. Although he's only hit 31 bombs in 858 at-bats, he has the swing, strength and plate discipline to suggest his power will increase as he develops.

Drew Henson

Position: 3B   **Opening Day Age:** 21
Bats: R **Throws:** R   **Born:** 2/13/80 in San
Ht: 6' 5" **Wt:** 222   Diego, CA

Recent Statistics

	G	AB	R	H	D	THR	RBI	SB	BB	SO	Avg
1999 A Tampa	69	254	37	71	12	0	13	37	3	26	71	.280
2000 A Tampa	5	21	4	7	2	0	1	1	0	1	7	.333
2000 AA Norwich	59	223	39	64	9	2	7	39	0	20	75	.287
2000 AA Chattanooga	16	64	7	11	8	0	1	9	2	4	25	.172
2000 MLE	75	278	38	66	15	1	5	40	1	16	106	.237

Although he plays baseball for only three months out of the year, Henson was aggressively promoted through the Yankees' system until he was dealt to the Reds. A full-time student at the University of Michigan, Henson also assumed the starting QB role for the Wolverines in 2000. The ball seems to explode off of his bat upon contact and his power potential is enormous. The big, strong third baseman fell into a slump after leaving the Yankees' organization, and Henson even hinted that he had a strong desire to play for New York. He stays in good baseball shape by taking BP at a homemade batting cage and one of the few things that he needs to improve on is pitch recognition. A broken foot sidelined Henson for the first three weeks of the football season, but he was under center by Week 4. A legitimate NFL prospect, Henson has kept his career aspirations to himself thus far, but he will be facing a crucial decision by 2002.

Austin Kearns

Position: OF
Bats: R **Throws:** R
Ht: 6' 3" **Wt:** 220

Opening Day Age: 20
Born: 5/20/80 in Lexington, KY

Recent Statistics

	G	AB	R	H	D	T	HR	RBI	SB	BB	SO	Avg
1999 A Rockford	124	426	72	110	36	5	13	48	21	50	120	.258
2000 A Dayton	136	484	110	148	37	2	27	104	18	90	93	.306

Voted the best outfield arm in the Midwest League, Kearns is developing into a prototypical right fielder. In his second consecutive year in the Midwest League, the 20-year-old made dramatic strides at the plate. The most disciplined hitter in the organization, Kearns demonstrated professional plate awareness, drawing 90 walks while fanning 93 times. While his power was slow to come around, he exploded with a mid-summer surge, blasting 11 bombs in a 10-game span, which also included eight consecutive games with a home run. The next step for Kearns is Double-A, and as long as he continues on last season's path he'll move quickly.

Brandon Larson

Position: 3B
Bats: R **Throws:** R
Ht: 6' 0" **Wt:** 210

Opening Day Age: 24
Born: 5/24/76 in San Angelo, TX

Recent Statistics

	G	AB	R	H	D	T	HR	RBI	SB	BB	SO	Avg
1999 A Rockford	69	250	38	75	18	1	13	52	12	25	67	.300
1999 AA Chattanooga	43	172	28	49	10	0	12	42	4	10	51	.285
2000 AAA Louisville	17	63	11	18	7	1	2	4	0	4	16	.286
2000 AA Chattanooga	111	427	61	116	26	0	20	64	15	31	122	.272
2000 MLE	128	473	57	117	30	0	17	54	11	25	146	.247

Cincinnati made Larson its first-round pick in 1997 after he cranked 40 jacks for Louisiana State. After that, Larson couldn't seem to stay out of the emergency room. Finally last year, Larson kept a clean bill of health and began to show some pop. Larson made great strides and eliminated the peaks and valleys of his first three seasons. His 47 home runs in the past two years are an indication that the injuries didn't rob him of any of his pure power. He's ticketed for Triple-A, where he'll continue to make up for lost time.

Chris Reitsma

Position: P
Bats: R **Throws:** R
Ht: 6' 5" **Wt:** 214

Opening Day Age: 23
Born: 12/31/77 in Minneapolis, MN

Recent Statistics

	W	L	ERA	G	GS	Sv	IP	H	R	BB	SO	HR
1999 A Sarasota	4	10	5.61	19	19	0	96.1	116	71	31	79	11
2000 A Sarasota	3	4	3.66	11	11	0	64.0	57	29	17	47	3
2000 AA Trenton	7	2	2.58	14	14	0	90.2	78	28	21	58	7

The first Canadian ever drafted in the first round, Cincinnati acquired Reitsma from the Red Sox for Dante Bichette. Drafted by the Devil Rays in the '99 Rule 5 draft, he failed to make the 25-man roster and was returned to Boston. Injuries never allowed Reitsma to flash any of his first-round talent over a substantial period of time, but the Reds have been encouraged by his arm strength. With two elbow fractures in his past, Reitsma went to the Arizona Fall League to hone his low to mid-90s heater and plus-changeup and refine his mechanics. The 23-year-old will be knocking on the door in Triple-A, with a possible setup relief job awaiting.

Ed Yarnall

Position: P
Bats: L **Throws:** L
Ht: 6' 3" **Wt:** 234

Opening Day Age: 25
Born: 12/4/75 in Lima, PA

Recent Statistics

	W	L	ERA	G	GS	Sv	IP	H	R	BB	SO	HR
2000 AAA Columbus	2	1	4.56	10	10	0	49.1	43	27	26	34	4
2000 AAA Louisville	3	4	3.86	11	11	0	67.2	72	32	34	59	7
2000 AL New York	0	0	15.00	2	1	0	3.0	5	5	3	1	1

Jim Bowden hopes a change of scenery will revive Yarnall's fledgling career. Last year was a disappointment for Yarnall, who had the Yankees' fifth starter job all but gift wrapped for him prior to spring training. He was on the heels of leading the Triple-A International League in ERA and a promising September showcase in New York in '99, but 2000 was marred with inconsistent outings. When he's right, Yarnall mixes up a deceptive 89-92 MPH fastball with good life in the strike zone, a solid curve and change. After getting shelled during spring training, his confidence suffered and he never recovered. Originally selected in the third round by the Mets in 1996, Cincinnati is Yarnall's fourth organization in four years. He'll get another shot at joining the rotation this spring, and the November trades of Ron Villone and Steve Parris may help to pave Yarnall's way.

Others to Watch

Despite struggling in Double-A, **Alejandro Diaz** (22) is loaded with the upside potential that the Reds envisioned when they signed him to a $1.175 million deal before the 1999 season. Diaz' tools are raw, as the defensively gifted center fielder drew just 14 walks and was caught stealing on 20 of 38 attempts last year. . . 1999 first-rounder **Ty Howington** (20) owns one of the best arms in the system. Although his performance doesn't support it, the hard-throwing lefty impressed with a fastball that reaches the mid-90s, a biting curveball and a developing changeup. . . Also part of the Neagle trade, **Jackson Melian** (21) has been a high-profile prospect since signing with New York as a 16-year-old out of Venezuela. Hamstring injuries prevented him from making any significant progress, but his power potential is intriguing. . . Easily forgotten in the Neagle trade, righthander **Brian Reith** (23) is tough to miss at 6-foot-5, but his performance sets him apart, too. He's a polished pitcher with good command of a 90-92-MPH fastball, slider and changeup. . . **Dane Sardinha** (21) didn't sign in time to play last season, but the second rounder is polished and already has been tagged the Reds' catcher of the future with his balance of offense and defense.

Coors Field

Offense

Another reason besides the altitude behind the offensive-friendly aspects of Coors Field is the large size of the playing field. Pitchers suffered because outfielders are too concerned about the ball being hit over their head. That allows too many catchable popups to fall in. It also allows baserunners to take extra bases because the outfielders are so deep that they don't get to the ball quickly enough. Pitchers can have success, but they have to forget about their ERA and concentrate on throwing strikes.

Defense

The Rockies new administration realized that the key to survival is having athletes. Speed in the outfield is paramount. As one scout suggested, what the Rockies need is an outfield of three center fielders, at least two with power. A new sod was installed in the offseason, and it will be groomed thicker and taller to try and slow groundballs.

Who It Helps the Most

There is not a hitter who doesn't find Coors Field comfortable, but none enjoyed it more than Jeff Cirillo (.403 home, .239 road) and Jeffrey Hammonds (.399, .275). Cirillo's gap power is ideal for the wide spaces in the outfield.

Who It Hurts the Most

Rockies pitchers finished 15th in the National League in ERA, but were third in road ERA (4.39), behind only Cincinnati and Atlanta. There's no way of getting around the struggle Coors creates for pitchers. Starting pitchers, however, seem to have more problems than relievers. Brian Bohanon is a perfect example. He had a rotation-best 4.68 ERA overall, but what went unnoticed was his NL-leading 2.79 figure on the road.

Rookies & Newcomers

The headline-grabbing additions of the offseason were starters Mike Hampton and Denny Neagle and outfielder Ron Gant. Both pitchers will face the Coors Field challenge that many have failed to pass, but Gant should thrive in the rare air. Juan Pierre should become a Coors Field creation. He's a speedster, and as he gets stronger and drives the ball he'll challenge for the doubles and triples lead.

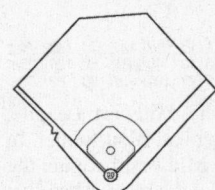

Dimensions: LF-347, LCF-390, CF-415, RCF-375, RF-350

Capacity: 50,381

Elevation: 5280 feet

Surface: Grass

Foul Territory: Small

Park Factors

2000 Season

| | Home Games | | | Away Games | | | |
	Rockies	Opp	Total	Rockies	Opp	Total	Index
G	75	75	150	75	75	150	—
Avg	.332	.303	.317	.251	.253	.252	126
AB	2654	2721	5375	2573	2424	4997	108
R	571	492	1063	316	327	643	165
H	880	824	1704	647	613	1260	135
2B	167	159	326	129	131	260	117
3B	31	19	50	17	16	33	141
HR	102	122	224	46	77	123	169
BB	306	275	581	252	264	516	105
SO	380	470	850	458	446	904	87
E	45	91	136	44	56	100	136
E-Infield	37	73	110	39	51	90	122
LHB-Avg	.326	.287	.309	.266	.253	.261	119
LHB-HR	54	51	105	30	33	63	159
RHB-Avg	.338	.313	.324	.236	.253	.245	132
RHB-HR	48	71	119	16	44	60	181

1998-2000

| | Home Games | | | Away Games | | | |
	Rockies	Opp	Total	Rockies	Opp	Total	Index
G	225	225	450	225	225	450	—
Avg	.328	.311	.320	.252	.262	.257	124
AB	8038	8226	16264	7709	7278	14987	109
R	1588	1538	3126	906	1014	1920	163
H	2639	2562	5201	1944	1908	3852	135
2B	498	471	969	391	392	783	114
3B	75	66	141	42	46	88	148
HR	339	361	700	188	206	394	164
BB	795	880	1675	668	857	1525	101
SO	1129	1375	2504	1384	1365	2749	84
E	151	210	361	145	160	305	118
E-Infield	111	169	280	123	144	267	105
LHB-Avg	.336	.309	.323	.270	.272	.271	119
LHB-HR	150	140	290	87	85	172	156
RHB-Avg	.322	.313	.317	.238	.256	.247	129
RHB-HR	189	221	410	101	121	222	169

2000 Rankings (National League)

- Highest batting-average factor
- Highest run factor
- Highest hit factor
- Highest home-run factor
- Highest LHB batting-average factor
- Highest LHB home-run factor
- Highest RHB batting-average factor
- Highest RHB home-run factor
- Second-highest error factor
- Second-highest infield-error factor
- Third-highest double factor
- Third-highest triple factor
- Third-highest walk factor
- Lowest strikeout factor

Buddy Bell

2000 Season

Buddy Bell went through a learning process in 2000. He had managed three years in Detroit, but this was his first year in the National League, and of course the first time he had dealt with Coors Field. He adjusted well, learning that the grind of 81 games in Colorado requires a manager to make liberal use of his bench because the game can get mentally and physically tiring in the rare air. He guided the Rockies to their first winning season in three years, and most importantly got the team back on track after a July that saw the Rockies win just seven games and lose 22.

Offense

Bell changed the look of the Rockies. They no longer were the Blake Street Bombers, finishing 13th in the NL in home runs. Todd Helton was the only member of the team with more than 20 long-balls. The Rockies, however, still led the NL in runs scored. Bell had a more athletic team than the Rockies had fielded the previous year, and he took advantage of the superior physical ability. The Rockies were aggressive on the bases, forcing the opposition to make mistakes.

Pitching & Defense

Bell believes pitching coach Marcel Lachemann is the best in the business, and lets him run a staff that will include newcomers Mike Hampton, Denny Neagle and Ron Villone. What Bell and Lachemann learned quickly is Coors Field is not a ballpark where you can coax an extra inning out of a pitcher. Bell stresses the fundamentals on defense, and he won't substitute in the field very often.

2001 Outlook

The Rockies returned to respectability in 2000 and are looking to move into contention in 2001. Bell has a better feel for the team, and general manager Dan O'Dowd began fine-tuning the roster after the 2000 All-Star break, which allowed the Rockies to be big players in the offseason free-agent market. The key for improvement rests with the pitching staff, where the Rockies should get a huge shot in the arm from Hampton, Neagle and Villone. They'll also hope for a pleasant surprise from John Wasdin, John Thomson or Kevin Jarvis.

Born: 8/27/51 in Pittsburgh, PA

Playing Experience: 1972-1989, Cle, Tex, Cin, Hou

Managerial Experience: 4 seasons

Manager Statistics

Year	Team, Lg	W	L	Pct	GB	Finish
2000	Colorado, NL	82	80	.506	15.0	4th West
4 Seasons		266	357	.427	—	—

2000 Starting Pitchers by Days Rest

	<=3	4	5	6+
Rockies Starts	4	92	35	23
Rockies ERA	5.28	5.69	4.86	6.52
NL Avg Starts	2	80	50	21
NL ERA	5.00	4.61	4.60	5.18

2000 Situational Stats

	Buddy Bell	NL Average
Hit & Run Success %	36.6	33.8
Stolen Base Success %	68.2	68.8
Platoon Pct.	64.1	53.2
Defensive Subs	8	19
High-Pitch Outings	10	14
Quick/Slow Hooks	12/18	14/16
Sacrifice Attempts	100	87

2000 Rankings (National League)

- 1st in steals of home plate (2), relief appearances (480), mid-inning pitching changes (207) and one-batter pitcher appearances (57)
- 2nd in steals of third base (18), double steals (8), intentional walks (53), pinch-hitters used (285) and starts on three days rest (4)
- 3rd in stolen base attempts (192), hit-and-run attempts (93) and first-batter platoon percentage (64.1)

Pedro Astacio

2000 Season

With the threat of deportation hanging over him because of domestic abuse charges, Pedro Astacio never put together that solid run of games that allowed him to win a career-best 17 decisions in 1999. He did, however, retain his status at the top of the Rockies' rotation. He won six consecutive decisions from mid-April through May, and twirled three complete games on the season. He continued to establish himself as a strikeout pitcher, ranking behind only Randy Johnson and Rick Ankiel among National League starters with an average of 8.85 strikeouts per nine innings.

Pitching

Astacio has command of three quality pitches, but it is his moving 92-93 MPH fastball that makes everything else work. He has to be aggressive with the fastball, and he needs to work quickly. He has the command of a sweeping curveball and a changeup that allows him to use both pitches when he is behind in the count. He will throw an occasional slider, but it is more of a last resort when his change or curveball aren't clicking.

Defense & Hitting

Astacio is athletic and moves deftly off the mound. He does, however, have concentration lapses that can hurt him in the field. He has a quick move to first and a rapid delivery, which allows the catchers a solid chance to throw out potential basestealers. Astacio now has 68 career hits, but the offensive aspect of his game suffered last year, when he had only eight knocks and one sacrifice bunt.

2001 Outlook

Astacio should be a key cog in the rotation, though his future in Colorado was up in the air for a while as the team pursued Darren Dreifort. He no longer has to worry about being the staff ace with the signing of Mike Hampton. Astacio will benefit from being able to slip into the No. 2 role just ahead of Denny Neagle. From that slot, Astacio is certain to rack up strikeouts and eat innings, both critical tasks on a team that envisions itself as a potential contender.

Position: SP
Bats: R **Throws:** R
Ht: 6' 2" **Wt:** 210

Opening Day Age: 31
Born: 11/28/69 in Hato Mayor, Dominican Republic
ML Seasons: 9
Pronunciation: uh-STAH-see-oh

Overall Statistics

	W	L	Pct.	ERA	G	GS	Sv	IP	H	BB	SO	HR	Ratio
2000	12	9	.571	5.27	32	32	0	196.1	217	77	193	32	1.50
Career	95	82	.537	4.44	282	239	0	1573.0	1617	518	1222	196	1.36

How Often He Throws Strikes

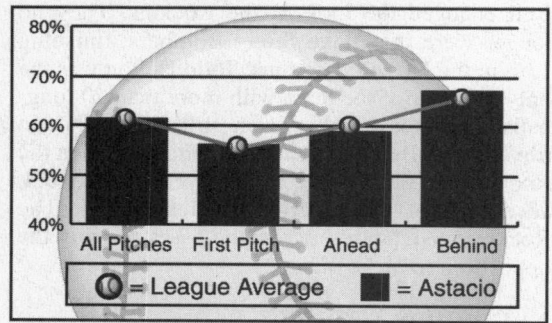

2000 Situational Stats

	W	L	ERA	Sv	IP		AB	H	HR	RBI	Avg
Home	7	4	6.54	0	96.1	LHB	358	104	17	57	.291
Road	5	5	4.05	0	100.0	RHB	414	113	15	52	.273
First Half	7	5	4.87	0	122.0	Sc Pos	187	56	6	72	.299
Scnd Half	5	4	5.93	0	74.1	Clutch	70	22	4	8	.314

2000 Rankings (National League)

- 3rd in hit batsmen (15) and most strikeouts per nine innings (8.8)
- 4th in highest ERA at home
- 6th in home runs allowed
- 7th in most run support per nine innings (6.4) and most home runs allowed per nine innings (1.47)
- 8th in strikeouts, highest ERA and highest slugging percentage allowed (.474)
- 10th in highest on-base percentage allowed (.356)
- Led the Rockies in wins, games started, complete games (3), innings pitched, hits allowed, batters faced (875), home runs allowed, hit batsmen (15), strikeouts, wild pitches (8), pitches thrown (3,184) and stolen bases allowed (15)

Brian Bohanon

2000 Season

Brian Bohanon took a little time to find his groove in 2000. After having several bone chips removed from his left elbow following the 1999 season, Bohanon thought he was ready on Opening Day, but he wasn't. He wound up in the bullpen in mid-May, regained his arm strength, and then was the Rockies' most dependable starter in the final four months. He equaled his career-high with 12 victories for the second season in a row. Bohanon was particularly strong after the All-Star Break (8-4, 3.28), and led National League pitchers with a 2.79 ERA on the road.

Pitching

There's nothing about Bohanon that would seem to make him standout, but what radar guns can't register is his heart. His fastball usually is clocked in the low 80s, occasionally touching 90 if he's real strong. He survives—particularly at Coors Field—because he doesn't give up. He will make up pitches as a game goes along. A changeup that has been his bread-and-butter wasn't sharp last year, but he broke out a split-finger pitch he hadn't used in three seasons and added it as his offspeed offering. He is capable of pitching in relief but prefers to start.

Defense & Hitting

Bohanon has athletic skills, though his bulky body does restrict his mobility. He is slow getting to first base, but he does field his position well and last year logged 35 total chances. His move to first is ordinary at best. Bohanon can handle the bat. He smacked two homers, three doubles and drove in 11 runs, and he even pinch-hit last year.

2001 Outlook

Bohanon is a definite in a Rockies rotation that once again will feature its share of new faces. He has shown no fear of pitching in Coors Field, and he has the uncanny ability to not let a bad game at home affect his approach on the road. He most likely will pitch out of the No. 4 spot in the rotation and should approach 200 innings if his elbow stays healthy.

Position: SP
Bats: L **Throws:** L
Ht: 6' 2" **Wt:** 240

Opening Day Age: 32
Born: 8/1/68 in Denton, TX
ML Seasons: 11
Pronunciation: boe-HAN-un

Overall Statistics

	W	L	Pct.	ERA	G	GS	Sv	IP	H	BB	SO	HR	Ratio
2000	12	10	.545	4.68	34	26	0	177.0	181	79	98	24	1.47
Career	49	52	.485	5.00	284	138	2	1019.0	1102	442	624	122	1.52

How Often He Throws Strikes

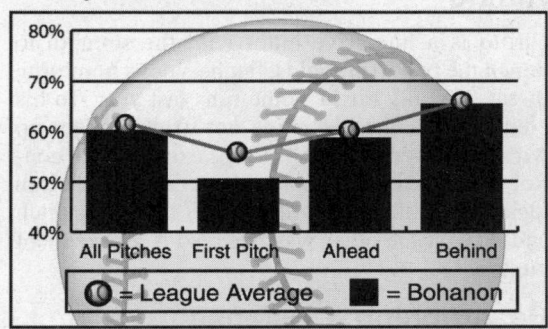

2000 Situational Stats

	W	L	ERA	Sv	IP		AB	H	HR	RBI	Avg
Home	6	5	6.65	0	86.2	LHB	163	32	5	24	.196
Road	6	5	2.79	0	90.1	RHB	517	149	19	64	.288
First Half	4	6	6.33	0	81.0	Sc Pos	167	42	3	58	.251
Scnd Half	8	4	3.28	0	96.0	Clutch	21	5	1	2	.238

2000 Rankings (National League)

- 1st in lowest ERA on the road
- 3rd in highest ERA at home
- 4th in lowest strikeout/walk ratio (1.2)
- 5th in most GDPs induced per nine innings (1.1) and highest stolen-base percentage allowed (78.9)
- Led the Rockies in ERA, wins, walks allowed, stolen bases allowed (15), GDPs induced (22), lowest batting average allowed (.266), lowest slugging percentage allowed (.429), lowest on-base percentage allowed (.346), fewest home runs allowed per nine innings (1.22), most GDPs induced per nine innings (1.1), lowest ERA on the road and lowest batting average allowed with runners in scoring position

Jeff Cirillo

2000 Season

After five-plus seasons in Milwaukee, Jeff Cirillo found Coors Field the perfect place for him. He signed a four-year, $30 million contract extension at the All-Star break, tying him to the Rockies through 2006, including an option. A career .311 hitter, he struggled in making the adjustment to facing pitching outside of Coors, but he finished with his second .326 average and a career-best 115 RBI. His .391 average with runners in scoring position was second in the majors to teammate Todd Helton. Cirillo also had 53 doubles, becoming the first player in history to have seasons with 45-plus doubles in both leagues.

Hitting

Cirillo is a line-drive hitter with the strength to punch the ball to all fields, but he's not a home-run threat. He only hit 11 home runs last year. To his credit he has the discipline not to get caught up with the power numbers. He has excellent bat control, and if he could run a tad better he would be an ideal No. 2 hitter. He will fight off the inside pitch and drive it the other way. He also is an excellent bunter.

Baserunning & Defense

Cirillo has average speed, but his feel for the game allows him to take advantage of lapses by the defense. He runs hard, which often leads to him picking up the unexpected base. He is a quality third baseman with better lateral movement to his left. He has a strong, accurate arm and comes in well on the bunt play.

2001 Outlook

Cirillo will be out there every day at third base for Colorado. He could bat second, but figures to get most of his appearances in the No. 5 hole, where he will benefit from hitting between the lefthanded sticks of Larry Walker and Todd Hollandsworth. His offensive numbers will improve as he learns to make quicker adjustments to the difference between facing pitchers at Coors Field and on the road.

Position: 3B
Bats: R **Throws:** R
Ht: 6' 1" **Wt:** 195

Opening Day Age: 31
Born: 9/23/69 in Pasadena, CA
ML Seasons: 7
Pronunciation: suh-RILL-o

Overall Statistics

	G	AB	R	H	D	T	HR	RBI	SB	BB	SO	Avg	OBP	Slg
2000	157	598	111	195	53	2	11	115	3	67	72	.326	.392	.477
Career	946	3409	555	1059	239	15	77	487	35	397	444	.311	.386	.457

Where He Hits the Ball

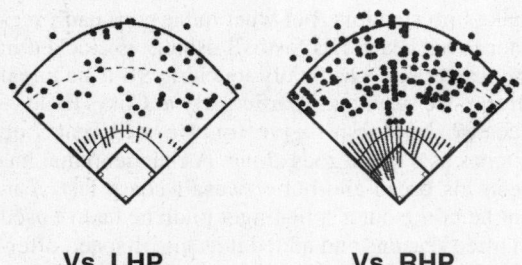

Vs. LHP   Vs. RHP

2000 Situational Stats

	AB	H	HR	RBI	Avg		AB	H	HR	RBI	Avg
Home	318	128	9	75	.403	LHP	132	50	2	32	.379
Road	280	67	2	40	.239	RHP	466	145	9	83	.311
First Half	300	99	9	64	.330	Sc Pos	169	66	4	98	.391
Scnd Half	298	96	2	51	.322	Clutch	87	22	1	13	.253

2000 Rankings (National League)

- 1st in batting average at home
- 2nd in doubles, sacrifice flies (12), batting average with runners in scoring position, batting average with the bases loaded (.667) and batting average vs. lefthanded pitchers
- 4th in GDPs (19) and fielding percentage at third base (.964)
- 5th in errors at third base (15)
- Led the Rockies in singles, sacrifice flies (12), GDPs (19), highest groundball/flyball ratio (1.5), batting average with the bases loaded (.667), batting average vs. lefthanded pitchers, batting average on a 3-1 count (.583), batting average at home and highest percentage of extra bases taken as a runner (63.6)

Jeffrey Hammonds

2000 Season

Jeffrey Hammonds finally showed signs of fulfilling the expectations that made him a first-round draft choice of Baltimore, but once again his season was pockmarked by injuries. A first-time All-Star selection, he enjoyed career highs in many offensive categories. He was, however, sidelined by injuries three times, including missing the final two weeks with right shoulder inflammation. He also missed one game and parts of two others in May with a strained left hip flexor, and was out for 17 games after suffering a hamstring pull on Opening Day. Still, he managed to squeeze in a career-best 454 at-bats and steal 14 bases, one shy of his top mark.

Hitting

Hammonds can hit fastballs, and that worked to his advantage last year when he found himself in the middle of the Rockies lineup, often behind Todd Helton. Helton was intentionally walked ahead of Hammonds 17 times, which put Hammonds in a good hitting situation. He has power potential, but his real strength is the ability to drive the ball into the gaps. He gets himself out by getting overanxious and chasing breaking pitches out of the strike zone.

Baserunning & Defense

Hammonds is a plus-runner, but a history of leg injuries has slowed him down. He is a student of the game and makes very few mistakes on the bases. He will take the extra base and reaffirmed his basestealing potential last year. He can play any of the three outfield positions, but is best-suited to left. He has a decent, but not great, arm.

2001 Outlook

The Rockies did not tender salary arbitration to Hammonds, and the team signed Ron Gant to split time in left field with Todd Hollandsworth. Hammonds would like the chance to build off his solid production of last year, but an opportunity to play every day will have to come on another club. He is an asset because of his multi-dimensional game, but the question will be how he handles the daily demands, something he has not proven he can do thus far in his career.

Position: RF/LF
Bats: R **Throws:** R
Ht: 6' 0" **Wt:** 200

Opening Day Age: 30
Born: 3/5/71 in Scotch Plains, NJ
ML Seasons: 8

Colorado

Overall Statistics

	G	AB	R	H	D	T	HR	RBI	SB	BB	SO	Avg	OBP	Slg
2000	122	454	94	152	24	2	20	106	14	44	83	.335	.395	.529
Career	681	2151	369	607	117	11	88	341	56	193	414	.282	.343	.470

Where He Hits the Ball

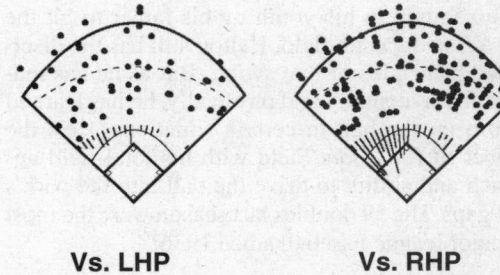

Vs. LHP   **Vs. RHP**

2000 Situational Stats

	AB	H	HR	RBI	Avg		AB	H	HR	RBI	Avg
Home	218	87	14	71	.399	LHP	98	37	6	31	.378
Road	236	65	6	35	.275	RHP	356	115	14	75	.323
First Half	224	80	14	65	.357	Sc Pos	159	56	7	83	.352
Scnd Half	230	72	6	41	.313	Clutch	73	25	5	17	.342

2000 Rankings (National League)

- 2nd in batting average at home
- 3rd in batting average on an 0-2 count (.368)
- 4th in batting average and lowest cleanup slugging percentage (.407)
- 7th in lowest stolen-base percentage (66.7)
- 8th in batting average with runners in scoring position
- 9th in batting average with two strikes (.265)
- Led the Rockies in caught stealing (7), strikeouts and batting average on a 3-2 count (.341)
- Led NL left fielders in batting average, batting average on an 0-2 count (.368), batting average at home and batting average with two strikes (.265)

Todd Helton

2000 Season

Todd Helton enjoyed a season that even Coors critics couldn't debunk. In becoming the first player in National League history—and only the fifth in major league history—to have 200 hits, 40 home runs, 100 RBI, 100 runs, 100 extra-base hits and 100 walks in a season, Helton hit .353 outside Coors Field. An All-Star selection for he first time, he led the majors with a .372 average and 147 RBI. The biggest turn of events for him was that he started strong and hit lefthanders, two areas that troubled him in his previous seasons in the big leagues.

Hitting

Helton is as pure a hitter as there is in the game today. Taught in his youth by his father to hit the ball to the opposite field, Helton still has the disciplined principles of that swing. But as he has matured, both mentally and physically, he has learned to turn on the ball in certain situations. He's the perfect fit for Coors Field with his total-field approach and ability to drive the ball into the park's vast gaps. His 59 doubles last season were the most in major league baseball since 1936.

Baserunning & Defense

Helton is an athlete, although he has below-average running speed, and it's obvious with the way he plays first base. He isn't afraid to range to his right and is as good as they come when it comes to charging bunt plays and looking for the force at second base. His biggest problems early in his career came with popups, but he has worked hard to master that aspect of the game. Helton is not going to steal many bases, but once he gets started he moves pretty well and always is looking to take the extra base.

2001 Outlook

Helton positioned himself in the superstar category in 2000. It's hard to believe he can match last year's numbers, as nobody in history has had back-to-back seasons like that. But he's going to hit in the mid-.300 range, produce a lot of runs and play virtually every day.

Position: 1B
Bats: L **Throws:** L
Ht: 6' 2" **Wt:** 206

Opening Day Age: 27
Born: 8/20/73 in Knoxville, TN
ML Seasons: 4

Overall Statistics

	G	AB	R	H	D	T	HR	RBI	SB	BB	SO	Avg	OBP	Slg
2000	160	580	138	216	59	2	42	147	5	103	61	.372	.463	.698
Career	506	1781	343	594	137	9	107	368	15	232	203	.334	.411	.601

Where He Hits the Ball

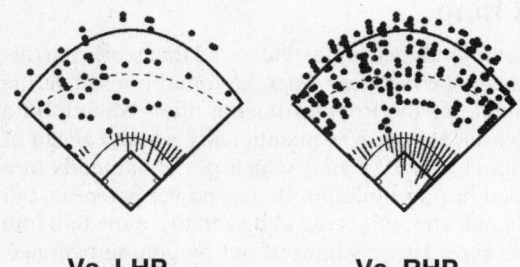

Vs. LHP   **Vs. RHP**

2000 Situational Stats

	AB	H	HR	RBI	Avg		AB	H	HR	RBI	Avg
Home	302	118	27	88	.391	LHP	143	47	7	31	.329
Road	278	98	15	59	.353	RHP	437	169	35	116	.387
First Half	298	114	21	70	.383	Sc Pos	153	60	15	110	.392
Scnd Half	282	102	21	77	.362	Clutch	84	33	9	22	.393

2000 Rankings (National League)

- 1st in batting average, hits, doubles, total bases (405), RBI, times on base (323), slugging percentage, on-base percentage, batting average with runners in scoring position, batting average in the clutch, batting average vs. righthanded pitchers, batting average on an 0-2 count (.484), cleanup slugging percentage (.770) and batting average with two strikes (.336)
- 2nd in runs scored, intentional walks (22), slugging percentage vs. righthanded pitchers (.732) and on-base percentage vs. righthanded pitchers (.467)
- 3rd in batting average at home, batting average on the road and fielding percentage at first base (.995)

Neifi Perez

Position: SS
Bats: B **Throws:** R
Ht: 6' 0" **Wt:** 175

Opening Day Age: 26
Born: 2/2/75 in Villa Mella, Dominican Republic
ML Seasons: 5
Pronunciation: NAY-fee

2000 Season

Nothing underscored Neifi Perez' performance more than the first Gold Glove of his career, an opportunity provided when the Mets' Rey Ordonez was sidelined by a broken forearm. Given a chance to hit second in the final two-plus months of the season, Perez also excelled in that role. He finished the season with a career-high 71 runs. His 11 triples were tied for second in the National League, with 10 of those three-baggers coming from the left side, a bit ironic considering he enjoyed more success righthanded (.357) than lefthanded (.266) last year.

Hitting

Perez is a free-swinger, but he makes contact and has good bat control. He led the team with nine bunt hits last year, employing a swinging-bunt approach that pushes the ball past the mound and catches the second baseman or shortstop off guard. He has more power from the right side, and he hit for a better average righthanded. He can drive any fastball, including Randy Johnson's. He will chase pitches, but pitchers have to be careful because Perez routinely expands his strike zone with success.

Baserunning & Defense

Perez has slightly better than average speed but is not a basestealing threat. He does, however, run the bases aggressively (41 triples the last four years), and when the ball is hit to the outfield, he's looking for a way to get an extra base. He is a pleasure to watch defensively. He has wonderful instincts, excellent range and a strong, accurate arm. He rarely botches a routine play. The errors he draws come on attempts to make the spectacular play, particularly on double-play pivots, where he has no fear.

2001 Outlook

Perez promises to get better as he gains experience and becomes more comfortable with a leadership role. The team can count on him to play every day; he's taken the field in 481 of the Rockies' 486 games since he assumed the full-time shortstop duties at the start of the 1998 season. He ignores nagging injuries, taking pride in being a consistent member of the starting lineup.

Overall Statistics

	G	AB	R	H	D	T	HR	RBI	SB	BB	SO	Avg	OBP	Slg
2000	162	651	92	187	39	11	10	71	3	30	63	.287	.314	.427
Career	581	2346	330	655	106	41	36	234	27	117	238	.279	.311	.405

Where He Hits the Ball

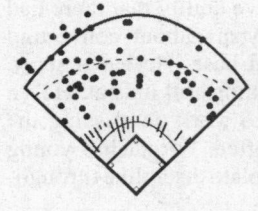
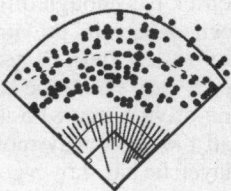

Vs. LHP   **Vs. RHP**

2000 Situational Stats

	AB	H	HR	RBI	Avg		AB	H	HR	RBI	Avg
Home	341	110	7	47	.323	LHP	154	55	7	26	.357
Road	310	77	3	24	.248	RHP	497	132	3	45	.266
First Half	319	90	4	42	.282	Sc Pos	164	44	0	55	.268
Scnd Half	332	97	6	29	.292	Clutch	96	26	2	12	.271

2000 Rankings (National League)

- 1st in games played
- 2nd in at-bats and triples
- 3rd in fielding percentage at shortstop (.978)
- 4th in lowest batting average with the bases loaded (.071), lowest on-base percentage vs. righthanded pitchers (.297) and lowest percentage of pitches taken (46.4)
- 5th in sacrifice flies (11) and bunts in play (29)
- Led the Rockies in at-bats, triples, plate appearances (699), fewest GDPs per GDP situation (7.1%), bunts in play (29) and games played
- Led NL shortstops in at-bats, hits, singles, doubles, total bases (278), sacrifice flies (11), plate appearances (699) and batting average vs. lefthanded pitchers

Ben Petrick

Position: C
Bats: R **Throws:** R
Ht: 6' 0" **Wt:** 205

Opening Day Age: 23
Born: 4/7/77 in Salem, OR
ML Seasons: 2
Pronunciation: PEET-trick

2000 Season

The Rockies' catcher of the future finally arrived in the final two months of the season. After a brief and disappointing callup early in 2000 when Scott Servais injured his ankle, Ben Petrick returned to the minor leagues for some more work. He came back to the parent club for good on July 16. Initially the plan was to let him become acclimated, but an injury to Brent Mayne resulted in Petrick starting 15 of 17 games in one stretch in late August and early September. He not only flashed his offensive prowess, but also impressed the Rockies and scouts from opposing teams with his strides behind the plate.

Hitting

Petrick has enough offensive ability that there had been debate in previous years about converting him to left field or second base. He has a short, quick stroke, and the ball jumps off his bat. He's a line-drive hitter who has to work on pushing the ball the other way more often. For such a young player, he has shown good plate discipline throughout his career.

Baserunning & Defense

Petrick has the speed for 20-plus stolen bases and has solid instincts on the basepaths. Defense has been the big question mark in the past, but he answered that question in the second half last year. The key was bullpen coach and catching instructor Fred Kendall, who saw too much athletic ability and too strong a work ethic to write off Petrick's ability to be a big league catcher. Kendall gave him encouragement to work on his defense, and helped him gain better balance. It showed. During his second half callup last year, he showed agility to block balls, got in sync with pitchers in pitch selection and quickened his release.

2001 Outlook

Petrick figures to open the season in a catching platoon with Brent Mayne, but it won't be a strict platoon because the Rockies want to make sure the righthanded-hitting Petrick gets plenty of playing time. Don't be surprised if Petrick assumes the No. 1 job by the middle of the regular season.

Overall Statistics

	G	AB	R	H	D	T	HR	RBI	SB	BB	SO	Avg	OBP	Slg
2000	52	146	32	47	10	1	3	20	1	20	33	.322	.401	.466
Career	71	208	45	67	13	1	7	32	2	30	46	.322	.406	.495

Where He Hits the Ball

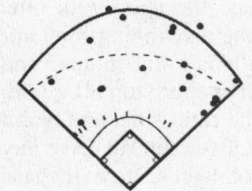
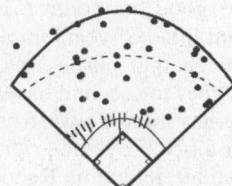

Vs. LHP   **Vs. RHP**

2000 Situational Stats

	AB	H	HR	RBI	Avg		AB	H	HR	RBI	Avg
Home	89	29	2	15	.326	LHP	48	17	1	4	.354
Road	57	18	1	5	.316	RHP	98	30	2	16	.306
First Half	15	4	0	0	.267	Sc Pos	39	9	0	17	.231
Scnd Half	131	43	3	20	.328	Clutch	27	8	2	4	.296

2000 Rankings (National League)

- Did not rank near the top or bottom in any category

Juan Pierre

2000 Season

It wouldn't be fair to say that Juan Pierre came out of nowhere, but that statement in not far from the truth. A 13th-round draft choice in 1998, Pierre opened the season at Double-A Carolina, where he played 107 games. After a four-game audition at Triple-A Colorado Springs, he found himself in the big leagues on August 7. He logged 51 games for Colorado and gave no indication of being intimidated, hitting .310 and going 12-for-24 against lefthanded pitchers, including three knocks off Randy Johnson.

Hitting

Pierre knows his strengths. He's a contact hitter who will make a living with his legs. He slaps at the ball and is headed out of the box towards first base before he makes contact. Pierre has only one home run in 1,505 professional at-bats. He does need to get stronger so he can sting the ball better and force infielders to play him more honestly. This will open up his bunting game and force outfielders to play deeper, which will allow more balls to get through the gaps. Pierre did spend the winter in Denver in a strengthening program, but he was quick to point out the plan is not designed for him to hit more home runs.

Baserunning & Defense

Pierre is a big-time stolen base threat. He was a bit timid in his big league debut, but he has a chance to one day challenge for a stolen-base title. He had 151 stolen bases in 315 minor league games. He is a true center fielder but has to be more aggressive at Coors Field, where the ball tends to float. His arm is slightly below average, but Pierre charges balls and gets rid of his throws quickly, which helps to lessen concerns about arm strength.

2001 Outlook

Pierre will have to prove in spring training that he is ready for an Opening Day shot in the big leagues. There is some feeling he might need a couple of months at Colorado Springs to get tuned up, but given his work ethic and how quickly he has advanced through the farm system, don't bet against him being part of the big league roster from the get-go.

Position: CF
Bats: L **Throws:** L
Ht: 6' 0" **Wt:** 170

Opening Day Age: 23
Born: 8/14/77 in Mobile, AL
ML Seasons: 1

Overall Statistics

	G	AB	R	H	D	T	HR	RBI	SB	BB	SO	Avg	OBP	Slg
2000	51	200	26	62	2	0	0	20	7	13	15	.310	.353	.320
Career	51	200	26	62	2	0	0	20	7	13	15	.310	.353	.320

Where He Hits the Ball

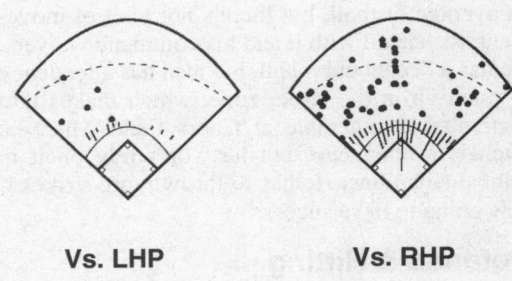

Vs. LHP   **Vs. RHP**

2000 Situational Stats

	AB	H	HR	RBI	Avg		AB	H	HR	RBI	Avg
Home	108	37	0	14	.343	LHP	24	12	0	5	.500
Road	92	25	0	6	.272	RHP	176	50	0	15	.284
First Half	0	0	0	0	-	Sc Pos	49	17	0	20	.347
Scnd Half	200	62	0	20	.310	Clutch	31	6	0	3	.194

2000 Rankings (National League)

- Did not rank near the top or bottom in any category

Brian Rose

2000 Season

Once the pride of the Boston farm system, Brian Rose was traded from the Red Sox to the Rockies on July 27 in a deal that also netted Jeff Frye and John Wasdin for Mike Lansing, Rolando Arrojo and Rick Croushore. Rose opened the season in the Red Sox' rotation, but he was back toiling in Triple-A Pawtucket before being dealt to Colorado. He was inserted into the Rockies' rotation for the final two months, and Colorado went 6-6 in his 12 starts.

Pitching

There was a lot of hype surrounding Rose in Boston, but he hasn't shown much in limited big league opportunities during the last four seasons. He has an average fastball, but there's not a lot of movement associated with it and his command waivers. He has a decent curveball, but also has a tendency to pitch up in the strike zone, which makes him particularly vulnerable at Coors Field. His best pitch is a changeup, but he won't rely on it in critical situations. He has to throw more strikes if he's going to have success.

Defense & Hitting

Rose is a dead-bodied pitcher. He doesn't move around the mound very well and isn't overly successful when it comes to holding runners. Having never gotten much of a chance to swing the bat with the Red Sox, his lack of hitting skills are hard to ignore. He went 1-for-24 at the plate last season and had trouble with even the fundamental chore of putting down a sacrifice bunt.

2001 Outlook

Rose will be a long-shot candidate for the Rockies' rotation, but he will have to battle newly-acquired Ron Villone and Masato Yoshii for a regular spot at the bottom of the rotation. Rose does have one option left, and it's not out of the question he could spend time at Triple-A Colorado Springs. He is going to have to pick up his tempo on the mound and be more aggressive with his fastball if he's going to be more than a fill-in.

Position: SP
Bats: R **Throws:** R
Ht: 6' 3" **Wt:** 215

Opening Day Age: 25
Born: 2/13/76 in New Bedford, MA
ML Seasons: 4

Overall Statistics

	W	L	Pct.	ERA	G	GS	Sv	IP	H	BB	SO	HR	Ratio
2000	7	10	.412	5.79	27	24	0	116.2	130	51	64	21	1.55
Career	15	20	.429	5.67	58	51	0	255.1	290	96	136	49	1.51

How Often He Throws Strikes

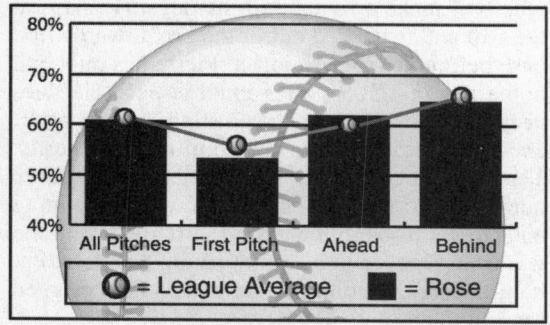

2000 Situational Stats

	W	L	ERA	Sv	IP		AB	H	HR	RBI	Avg
Home	3	6	8.08	0	49.0	LHB	232	74	11	42	.319
Road	4	4	4.12	0	67.2	RHB	235	56	10	32	.238
First Half	3	5	6.11	0	53.0	Sc Pos	116	36	8	53	.310
Scnd Half	4	5	5.51	0	63.2	Clutch	9	2	0	0	.222

2000 Rankings (National League)
- Did not rank near the top or bottom in any category

Larry Walker

Position: RF/LF
Bats: L **Throws:** R
Ht: 6' 3" **Wt:** 237

Opening Day Age: 34
Born: 12/1/66 in Maple Ridge, Canada
ML Seasons: 12

Colorado

2000 Season

Injuries have haunted Larry Walker throughout his career, and last season certainly was no exception. He did hit .309, but after back-to-back National League batting titles, and just three years removed from an NL MVP Award, he drove in only 51 runs and hit only nine homers, his lowest totals since his first full big league season in Montreal a decade earlier. Walker underwent arthroscopic surgery on his right elbow in late September, and then went under the knife again on his right knee in October.

Hitting

Walker is a force at the plate, even if he's not at full strength. He uses all fields, which is a valuable approach at Coors Field considering the generous dimensions of the outfield and the way the ball carries. He will chase the high fastball, and righthanded pitchers have success pounding him inside. But opposing hurlers do have to get the ball in on his hands because if they leave it over the plate, Walker can drive it over the fence. He really struggles when he is chasing breaking balls out of the zone, committing too soon with a swing that gets long.

Baserunning & Defense

A Gold Glove-caliber outfielder with an accurate arm and quick release, he still led the Rockies with 11 outfield assists despite the right elbow soreness that limited him to 87 games last year. He reads the ball well and will play games on hitters, particularly at Coors Field where he can fake a runner into thinking he's going to make a play on a shot that winds up going off the right-field scoreboard. On the bases, he is not a speedster but still has some of the best instincts in the game.

2001 Outlook

This year will be a big test for the competitiveness and pride of Walker. He's no longer the man the team revolves around, and he finds his name being mentioned in trade talks. He has security—five years remain on his six-year, $75 million contract—but he no longer has a special aura.

Overall Statistics

	G	AB	R	H	D	T	HR	RBI	SB	BB	SO	Avg	OBP	Slg
2000	87	314	64	97	21	7	9	51	5	46	40	.309	.409	.506
Career	1385	4906	950	1528	335	43	271	906	195	578	847	.311	.390	.563

Where He Hits the Ball

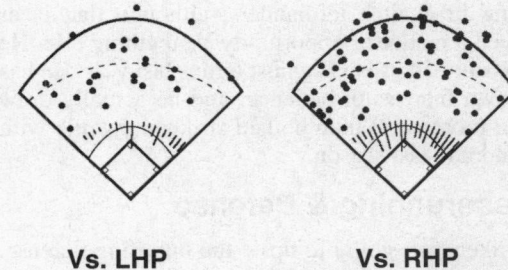

Vs. LHP   **Vs. RHP**

2000 Situational Stats

	AB	H	HR	RBI	Avg		AB	H	HR	RBI	Avg
Home	156	56	7	36	.359	LHP	85	29	2	17	.341
Road	158	41	2	15	.259	RHP	229	68	7	34	.297
First Half	203	66	4	28	.325	Sc Pos	69	27	4	41	.391
Scnd Half	111	31	5	23	.279	Clutch	42	7	1	2	.167

2000 Rankings (National League)

- 7th in triples
- Led the Rockies in hit by pitch (9)

Todd Walker

2000 Season

Todd Walker escaped Minnesota, where his personality clash with manager Tom Kelly was so strong that he welcomed a demotion to the minors and said he would rather stay in Salt Lake City than get called up. Instead, he was shipped to the Rockies shortly after the All-Star break and began to resurrect his career. In 57 games with the Rockies he hit .316 with seven home runs and 36 RBI. He wasted no time taking advantage of Coors Field, hitting .350 there.

Hitting

Walker is a professional hitter. He has a short, quick swing and understands the value of using all fields for his line drives. He has yet to prove he can hang in against lefthanders, although that is as much a matter of opportunity as anything else. He had only 14 at-bats against lefties last year. He has shown increasing patience, and he actually drew one more walk than he had strikeouts while with Colorado last season.

Baserunning & Defense

Walker isn't going to upset the opposing defense. He's an average runner at best. He does, however, run hard all the time and does have a feel for navigating the basepaths, which allows him to get an extra sack or two. His defense has been criticized ever since he was in college. In his time with the Rockies, however, he worked with infield coach Toby Harrah and got away from a straight-ahead approach to groundballs. He now puts himself in better position to make the throw once he fielded the ball. He seemed at least adequate by season's end.

2001 Outlook

Walker will open the season in a platoon with Terry Shumpert at second base. Given the preponderance of righthanded pitching, he will get the bulk of the playing time. It's not out of the question that he could assume a full-time role as the season progresses, freeing Shumpert for a valuable utility role with the Rockies.

Position: 2B
Bats: L **Throws:** R
Ht: 6' 0" **Wt:** 181

Opening Day Age: 27
Born: 5/25/73 in Bakersfield, CA
ML Seasons: 5

Overall Statistics

	G	AB	R	H	D	T	HR	RBI	SB	BB	SO	Avg	OBP	Slg
2000	80	248	42	72	11	4	9	44	7	27	29	.290	.355	.476
Career	443	1545	212	445	102	12	30	174	53	141	220	.288	.346	.428

Where He Hits the Ball

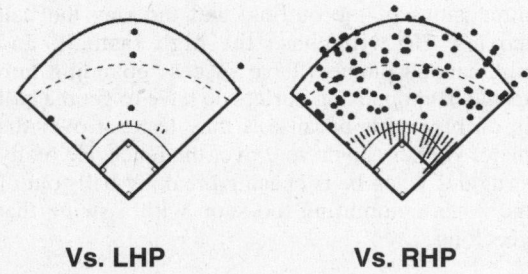

Vs. LHP   **Vs. RHP**

2000 Situational Stats

	AB	H	HR	RBI	Avg		AB	H	HR	RBI	Avg
Home	143	44	5	28	.308	LHP	14	5	1	5	.357
Road	105	28	4	16	.267	RHP	234	67	8	39	.286
First Half	77	18	2	8	.234	Sc Pos	67	16	2	33	.239
Scnd Half	171	54	7	36	.316	Clutch	42	10	0	5	.238

2000 Rankings (National League)

- Did not rank near the top or bottom in any category

Masato Yoshii

2000 Season

After two decent years with the Mets following 13 years in Japan, Masato Yoshii struggled in his debut with the Rockies. He ranked 10th in the National League in run support per nine innings (6.13), but the stat was misleading. In his 23 starts without a win, including 15 losses and eight no-decisions, the Rockies averaged only 3.83 runs a game. The one team he was able to control was Arizona. He won all three of his starts and had 1.37 ERA against the Diamondbacks, but was 3-15 against the rest of the major leagues.

Pitching

Yoshii is a high-fastball pitcher. At the start of last season, the Rockies tried to get him to sink the ball more out of concerns about Coors Field. He struggled, even on the road. By mid-season, though, pitching coach Marcel Lachemann told Yoshii to go back to what he was comfortable with. He changes speeds off an average fastball, and has a decent slider. When he has his command and keeps hitters off balance, he can survive pitching up, even at Coors Field.

Defense & Hitting

Yoshii is fundamentally solid in the field, but not spectacular. He finishes his delivery in position to field shots back up the middle, comes off the mound well to field bunts and has a decent move to first. He's not going to win the Silver Slugger Award, but he can handle the bat well enough to at least be respectable.

2001 Outlook

The Rockies paid the buyout on Yoshii's $4 million option for 2001, but then re-signed him to an one-year deal at a lesser amount with an option for 2002. He will get a chance to retain a spot in the rotation, but he's going to have to earn a starting role in spring training. He did undergo postseason surgery to remove bone spurs from his right elbow that bothered him in September, but he was expected to be ready by the time camp opens.

Position: SP
Bats: R **Throws:** R
Ht: 6' 2" **Wt:** 210

Opening Day Age: 35
Born: 4/20/65 in Osaka, Japan
ML Seasons: 3
Pronunciation: muh-SAH-toh YOH-shee

Colorado

Overall Statistics

	W	L	Pct.	ERA	G	GS	Sv	IP	H	BB	SO	HR	Ratio
2000	6	15	.286	5.86	29	29	0	167.1	201	53	88	32	1.52
Career	24	31	.436	4.72	89	87	0	513.0	535	164	310	79	1.36

How Often He Throws Strikes

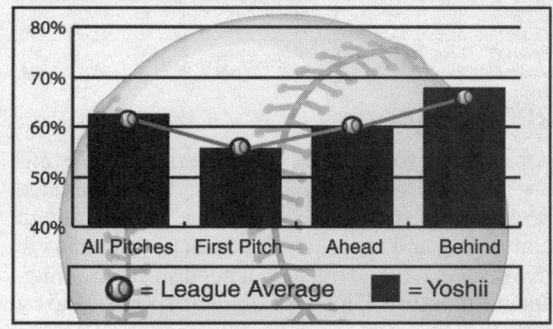

= League Average   = Yoshii

2000 Situational Stats

	W	L	ERA	Sv	IP		AB	H	HR	RBI	Avg
Home	2	3	5.85	0	67.2	LHB	305	86	14	42	.282
Road	4	12	5.87	0	99.2	RHB	351	115	18	59	.328
First Half	4	9	5.55	0	99.0	Sc Pos	152	44	6	65	.289
Scnd Half	2	6	6.32	0	68.1	Clutch	29	10	3	7	.345

2000 Rankings (National League)

- 2nd in highest batting average allowed (.306), highest slugging percentage allowed (.537), most home runs allowed per nine innings (1.72), highest batting average allowed vs. righthanded batters and lowest winning percentage
- 3rd in highest ERA
- Led the Rockies in sacrifice bunts (12), losses, home runs allowed, fewest pitches thrown per batter (3.60) and fewest walks per nine innings (2.9)

Bobby Chouinard

Position: RP
Bats: R **Throws:** R
Ht: 6' 1" **Wt:** 190

Opening Day Age: 28
Born: 5/1/72 in Manila, Philippines
ML Seasons: 4

Overall Statistics

	W	L	Pct.	ERA	G	GS	Sv	IP	H	BB	SO	HR	Ratio
2000	2	2	.500	3.86	31	0	0	32.2	35	9	23	4	1.35
Career	11	8	.579	4.41	103	13	1	173.1	187	64	105	22	1.45

2000 Situational Stats

	W	L	ERA	Sv	IP		AB	H	HR	RBI	Avg
Home	1	1	4.42	0	18.1	LHB	49	11	1	4	.224
Road	1	1	3.14	0	14.1	RHB	79	24	3	12	.304
First Half	0	0	-	0	0.0	Sc Pos	28	9	0	11	.321
Scnd Half	2	2	3.86	0	32.2	Clutch	49	11	3	6	.224

2000 Season

After asking for his release from Arizona in February of 2000 following his arrest for aggravated assault against his wife, Chouinard went through counseling and approached the Rockies about a job in May. He worked out at extended spring training, spent a month at Triple-A Colorado Springs, and by mid-July he was back in the big leagues.

Pitching, Defense & Hitting

Chouinard has a fastball in the low 90s with good sinking action, critical for Coors Field. He also features a hard slider. The key for him is his ability to throw strikes. He issued only seven unintentional walks in 32.2 innings last year. He holds runners well and finishes his delivery in good fielding position. He has a good stroke, but like most relievers there are few opportunities for him to display his bat skills in a game.

2001 Outlook

Chouinard will serve a one-year jail term for the assault conviction in four, three-month increments during the next four offseasons. He will train under Rockies supervision each day during the offseason so he can stay in pitching shape, and he will be allowed to pitch during the season. He has the inside track on the righthanded setup role in the Colorado bullpen.

Jeff Frye

Position: 2B/RF
Bats: R **Throws:** R
Ht: 5' 9" **Wt:** 170

Opening Day Age: 34
Born: 8/31/66 in Oakland, CA
ML Seasons: 7

Overall Statistics

	G	AB	R	H	D	T	HR	RBI	SB	BB	SO	Avg	OBP	Slg
2000	106	326	49	100	19	0	1	16	5	36	54	.307	.377	.374
Career	593	1980	292	583	129	10	14	179	54	200	261	.294	.361	.391

2000 Situational Stats

	AB	H	HR	RBI	Avg		AB	H	HR	RBI	Avg
Home	164	54	0	7	.329	LHP	117	42	1	5	.359
Road	162	46	1	9	.284	RHP	209	58	0	11	.278
First Half	209	60	1	13	.287	Sc Pos	65	18	0	14	.277
Scnd Half	117	40	0	3	.342	Clutch	50	16	0	3	.320

2000 Season

In the final year of his cotract, Jeff Frye found himself with limited playing time in the final two months of the season. The Rockies took him back in a trade with Boston, but Frye had only 87 at-bats and played in only 37 games with Colorado. Even with all the upheaval and periods of inactivity, he did finish the season above .300 for the third time in his seven-year career in the majors.

Hitting, Baserunning & Defense

Frye is a contact hitter who uses all fields, but he doesn't have threatening power. He can hit second in the order because he does have good bat control. He is a slightly below-average runner and presents little threat on the bases. His weak arm pretty much limits him to playing second base, though he did grab some time in right field last year. He is steady but not spectacular at the keystone but hangs in well on the double-play pivot.

2001 Outlook

Frye signed a one-year, $1 million contract with Toronto in mid-December. He has the attitude a team would like from a utility player. But he hasn't shown the ability to play anywhere except second base for any period of time, making him a luxury on a team's bench.

Todd Hollandsworth

Position: CF/LF/RF
Bats: L **Throws:** L
Ht: 6' 2" **Wt:** 215

Opening Day Age: 27
Born: 4/20/73 in
Dayton, OH
ML Seasons: 6

Butch Huskey

Position: DH/RF/1B/LF
Bats: R **Throws:** R
Ht: 6' 3" **Wt:** 244

Opening Day Age: 29
Born: 11/10/71 in
Anadarko, OK
ML Seasons: 7

Todd Hollandsworth

Overall Statistics

	G	AB	R	H	D	T	HR	RBI	SB	BB	SO	Avg	OBP	Slg
2000	137	428	81	115	20	0	19	47	18	41	99	.269	.333	.449
Career	580	1741	262	472	86	12	52	202	55	142	384	.271	.327	.424

2000 Situational Stats

	AB	H	HR	RBI	Avg		AB	H	HR	RBI	Avg
Home	218	57	13	28	.261	LHP	56	14	0	6	.250
Road	210	58	6	19	.276	RHP	372	101	19	41	.272
First Half	211	52	7	16	.246	Sc Pos	109	20	2	26	.183
Scnd Half	217	63	12	31	.290	Clutch	78	17	1	7	.218

2000 Season

Todd Hollandsworth was so comfortable in Colorado following his July 31 trade from Los Angeles
that he decided to ignore free agency and told agent
Jeff Moorad to work out the best two-year deal
with the Rockies. After a brief adjustment period,
Hollandsworth finished with a flourish, hitting
.357 with 10 home runs in 98 September at-bats. It
wasn't all Coors Field, either; he hit .300 at Coors
Field in two months and .351 on the road.

Hitting, Baserunning & Defense

Hitting coach Clint Hurdle lowered Hollandsworth's hands and cut down on his body
movement. It allowed Hollandsworth to quicken
his swing, and made him better able to lay off bad
breaking pitches. Now he needs to begin taking
advantage of left field. He is a plus-runner with an
aggressive approach on the bases. He has the potential to steal 30 bases. Hollandsworth can play all
three outfield positions, as well as first base, but an
average arm makes him best-suited for left.

2001 Outlook

After signing a two-year, $5.5 million contract
with Colorado in late October, Hollandsworth figures to share the duties in left field with Ron Gant
or take over center if Juan Pierre needs more time
in Triple-A.

Butch Huskey

Overall Statistics

	G	AB	R	H	D	T	HR	RBI	SB	BB	SO	Avg	OBP	Slg
2000	109	307	40	80	21	0	9	45	1	41	63	.261	.346	.417
Career	642	2078	259	555	98	4	86	336	21	164	384	.267	.318	.442

2000 Situational Stats

	AB	H	HR	RBI	Avg		AB	H	HR	RBI	Avg
Home	149	41	6	29	.275	LHP	120	37	3	13	.308
Road	158	39	3	16	.247	RHP	187	43	6	32	.230
First Half	215	48	5	27	.223	Sc Pos	94	23	2	36	.245
Scnd Half	92	32	4	18	.348	Clutch	34	7	0	6	.206

2000 Season

Butch Huskey took advantage of a chance to resurrect his career when a mid-July trade sent him from
Minnesota to Colorado. The Twins had sent him to
the minor leagues. After initially struggling when
he joined the Rockies, Huskey finished strong,
hitting .441 in September and finishing with a .348
average in 45 games following the swap.

Hitting, Baserunning & Defense

Huskey has a big swing and can drive the ball. He
gets himself in trouble when he tries to pull everything. Pitchers will work him away, resulting in too
many groundballs to short. He does, however, have
enough strength to drive the ball the other way
when he is patient. A former football player who
turned down a football scholarship to Oklahoma,
Huskey is a below-average runner. He can play left
and right field, as well as third and first base, but
his real value is with a bat in his hands, not a glove.

2001 Outlook

Huskey can provide a team with a righthanded
threat off the bench. He plays enough positions to
have value as a fifth outfielder or backup infielder
on the corners, but doesn't show the defensive
consistency to earn an everyday opportunity.

Jose Jimenez

Position: RP
Bats: R **Throws:** R
Ht: 6' 3" **Wt:** 190

Opening Day Age: 27
Born: 7/7/73 in San Pedro de Macoris, Dominican Republic
ML Seasons: 3
Pronunciation: HIM-enn-ezz

Overall Statistics

	W	L	Pct.	ERA	G	GS	Sv	IP	H	BB	SO	HR	Ratio
2000	5	2	.714	3.18	72	0	24	70.2	63	28	44	4	1.29
Career	13	16	.448	4.87	105	31	24	255.0	258	107	169	20	1.43

2000 Situational Stats

	W	L	ERA	Sv	IP		AB	H	HR	RBI	Avg
Home	4	1	4.20	9	40.2	LHB	105	25	2	10	.238
Road	1	1	1.80	15	30.0	RHB	159	38	2	18	.239
First Half	4	0	3.09	15	35.0	Sc Pos	71	14	1	23	.197
Scnd Half	1	2	3.28	9	35.2	Clutch	151	39	3	17	.258

2000 Season

Jose Jimenez found himself working in relief last spring for Colorado. With David Lee struggling early and Jerry Dipoto sidelined by a bulging disk that required surgery, Jimenez stepped into the closer's role. He did a quality job, tying for ninth in the league with 24 saves. His save total was the third-best single-season mark in club history, seven shy of the club record set by Dave Veres in 1999.

Pitching, Defense & Hitting

Jimenez has a heavy sinker that is consistently in the low 90s. He also throws a sharp slider, but doesn't have an offspeed pitch, which is why he is better suited for the bullpen than the rotation. He does throw strikes when he keeps his tempo upbeat. He gets in trouble when he starts walking around the mound between pitches. He doesn't have a particularly good move, but he does have a quick delivery that gives the catcher a chance to throw out runners. At the plate? He has struck out in 28 of 63 big league at-bats. Enough said.

2001 Outlook

Jimenez now has a feel for the bullpen and will get a chance to close again. He has a resilient arm to go along with the overpowering, groundball-inducing sinker that allows him to survive at Coors Field and dominate at sea level.

Brent Mayne

Position: C
Bats: L **Throws:** R
Ht: 6' 1" **Wt:** 192

Opening Day Age: 32
Born: 4/19/68 in Loma Linda, CA
ML Seasons: 11
Nickname: Mayner

Overall Statistics

	G	AB	R	H	D	T	HR	RBI	SB	BB	SO	Avg	OBP	Slg
2000	117	335	36	101	21	0	6	64	1	47	48	.301	.381	.418
Career	882	2400	243	648	136	3	26	282	12	251	385	.270	.340	.362

2000 Situational Stats

	AB	H	HR	RBI	Avg		AB	H	HR	RBI	Avg
Home	156	49	3	37	.314	LHP	46	9	1	12	.196
Road	179	52	3	27	.291	RHP	289	92	5	52	.318
First Half	185	59	4	38	.319	Sc Pos	95	34	1	55	.358
Scnd Half	150	42	2	26	.280	Clutch	59	18	0	7	.305

2000 Season

Brent Mayne is coming off back-to-back seasons of hitting .301 in the most active years of his career. He drove in a career-best 64 runs in 2000, most ever for a Rockies catcher. He was in the national spotlight on August 22 when the Rockies ran out of pitchers, and Mayne took the mound in the 12th inning against Atlanta. He became the first position player to win a big league game since August 25, 1968 when Yankee Rocky Colavito did it.

Hitting, Baserunning & Defense

Mayne has learned his offensive limitations, which allows him to be a contributor at the plate. His bat speed is average at best, but he no longer tries to pull everything. He has decent speed for a catcher and with his gap-drive offensive approach, he will leg out a few doubles. Mayne has developed into a quality big league catcher. He works hard to call a good game behind the plate. He does have a bit of a loop in his hand action on throws to second, but if the pitcher gives him a chance he can keep the average baserunners from taking liberties.

2001 Outlook

With the emergence of Ben Petrick in the final two months last year, Mayne's role figures to be reduced this season. Look for him to start roughly half the games.

Mike Myers

Position: RP
Bats: L **Throws:** L
Ht: 6' 4" **Wt:** 214

Opening Day Age: 31
Born: 6/26/69 in Arlington Heights, IL
ML Seasons: 6

Overall Statistics

	W	L	Pct.	ERA	G	GS	Sv	IP	H	BB	SO	HR	Ratio
2000	0	1	.000	1.99	78	0	1	45.1	24	24	41	2	1.06
Career	6	13	.316	4.31	403	0	10	263.1	253	125	239	33	1.44

2000 Situational Stats

	W	L	ERA	Sv	IP		AB	H	HR	RBI	Avg
Home	0	0	2.05	0	26.1	LHB	91	11	1	7	.121
Road	0	1	1.89	1	19.0	RHB	59	13	1	7	.220
First Half	0	1	0.83	1	21.2	Sc Pos	46	6	0	11	.130
Scnd Half	0	0	3.04	0	23.2	Clutch	44	6	0	4	.136

2000 Season

In Mike Myers' first year with the Rockies, he had the best year of his career. He equaled the franchise record with 78 appearances, the fifth year in a row he has had at least 70, and had the lowest relief ERA in Rockies history. He even had a 2.05 ERA in 43 appearances at Coors Field. He was second in the National League in lowest percentage of inherited runners scored, allowing only nine of 64 (14.1 percent) to cross the plate.

Pitching, Defense & Hitting

Myers is a situational lefty. At the urging of Hall of Famer Al Kaline, he adopted a sidearming approach that makes it difficult for lefties to hang in against him. More importantly, though, Myers began coming inside on the hands to righthanded hitters and held them to a .220 average last year. He has that sidearm fastball and sweeping slider. He moves around well on the mound and fields his position, but the sidearm delivery makes him vulnerable to basestealers if he doesn't hold them close. Limited to primarily one-batter appearances, he has only one at-bat in his big league career.

2001 Outlook

Myers has found a niche for himself, and he will continue to be the reliever who gets the call to face the tough lefthanded hitter in a pressure situation.

Terry Shumpert

Position: LF/2B/3B
Bats: R **Throws:** R
Ht: 6' 0" **Wt:** 200

Opening Day Age: 34
Born: 8/16/66 in Paducah, KY
ML Seasons: 11

Overall Statistics

	G	AB	R	H	D	T	HR	RBI	SB	BB	SO	Avg	OBP	Slg
2000	115	263	52	68	11	7	9	40	8	28	40	.259	.340	.456
Career	575	1409	214	356	78	18	37	171	66	120	267	.253	.315	.412

2000 Situational Stats

	AB	H	HR	RBI	Avg		AB	H	HR	RBI	Avg
Home	130	40	7	25	.308	LHP	94	26	3	15	.277
Road	133	28	2	15	.211	RHP	169	42	6	25	.249
First Half	131	37	4	26	.282	Sc Pos	74	17	1	29	.230
Scnd Half	132	31	5	14	.235	Clutch	47	13	1	7	.277

2000 Season

Terry Shumpert finally found a home, as he has become the Rockies' Mr. Fix-It. In his first full season in the big leagues since 1994, he played all four infield positions, making his major league debut at first base, plus left field. He also hit in all nine spots in the batting order and handled the pinch-hit role well, four times delivering go-ahead RBI in that situation.

Hitting, Baserunning & Defense

Shumpert has become comfortable with his abilities. Instead of trying to pull everything, which was a problem in his youth, he takes what the pitcher offers. He will turn on a fastball, and at Coors Field he can sting a pitcher who makes a mistake. He is not a burner, but has a feel on the bases (22-for-26 in stolen bases the last two years). His range is average at shortstop and his arm is not quite what a team wants from third base, but he works at getting in position to makes plays. Second base his is best position.

2001 Outlook

The Rockies exercised their $725,000 option on Shumpert for 2001. He will platoon at second with Todd Walker, but his real value remains his versatility. He will get playing time at all four infield positions, as well as in the outfield.

Julian Tavarez

Position: RP/SP
Bats: L **Throws:** R
Ht: 6' 2" **Wt:** 190
Opening Day Age: 27
Born: 5/22/73 in Santiago, Dominican Republic
ML Seasons: 8
Pronunciation: tuh-VAR-ez

Overall Statistics

	W	L	Pct.	ERA	G	GS	Sv	IP	H	BB	SO	HR	Ratio
2000	11	5	.688	4.43	51	12	1	120.0	124	53	62	11	1.48
Career	40	24	.625	4.41	364	24	2	552.2	612	205	318	53	1.48

2000 Situational Stats

	W	L	ERA	Sv	IP		AB	H	HR	RBI	Avg
Home	4	1	3.96	1	72.2	LHB	180	47	3	28	.261
Road	7	4	5.13	0	47.1	RHB	283	77	8	31	.272
First Half	5	2	6.45	1	37.2	Sc Pos	127	32	4	47	.252
Scnd Half	6	3	3.50	0	82.1	Clutch	66	16	3	10	.242

2000 Season

After a poor start to his season in relief, Julian Tavarez showed promise during the final two months when the Rockies needed a starter. The Rockies won nine of his 12 starts, and he posted a 5-3 record with a 3.80 ERA in that role. The demands of a career-high 120 innings, however, showed in September, when he lost three of his last four starts. He allowed 16 earned runs in 16.2 innings over those final four starts.

Pitching, Defense & Hitting

Tavarez has a hard sinker and tight slider, but if he wants to continue his career as a starting pitcher he is going to have to refine an offspeed pitch. When he is aggressive and working fast, he throws strikes and keeps hitters off balance, but he has a tendency to lose concentration. Tavarez fields his position well and has a quick move to first. He is not a factor with a bat in his hands. He went 3-for-35 last season, and all three hits were swinging bunts capped by head-first slides into first.

2001 Outlook

Tavarez signed a two-year deal with the Cubs in mid-November worth a guaranteed $5 million. With incentives, the money could escalate to $7 million. Chicago is expected to put him in the rotation and see what he can do.

Gabe White

Position: RP
Bats: L **Throws:** L
Ht: 6' 2" **Wt:** 200
Opening Day Age: 29
Born: 11/20/71 in Sebring, FL
ML Seasons: 6

Overall Statistics

	W	L	Pct.	ERA	G	GS	Sv	IP	H	BB	SO	HR	Ratio
2000	11	2	.846	2.36	68	0	5	84.0	64	15	84	6	0.94
Career	21	14	.600	4.10	225	15	16	334.0	307	84	295	53	1.17

2000 Situational Stats

	W	L	ERA	Sv	IP		AB	H	HR	RBI	Avg
Home	10	2	3.13	2	46.0	LHB	105	21	4	20	.200
Road	1	0	1.42	3	38.0	RHB	198	43	2	19	.217
First Half	6	0	1.76	1	46.0	Sc Pos	72	18	5	35	.250
Scnd Half	5	2	3.08	4	38.0	Clutch	145	29	3	21	.200

2000 Season

Gabe White was traded from Cincinnati to the Rockies during the opening week of the season, and next thing he knew he was on his way to a career year. Armed with a career 4.68 ERA prior to last year, he compiled a 2.17 ERA with Colorado, going 10-2 with a 2.80 ERA at Coors Field. The 10 wins were a franchise record at Coors. White also set a franchise record by running off 29.1 scoreless innings between May 6 and July 9.

Pitching, Defense & Hitting

White has a solid-but-average fastball with sinking action and a changeup. The key for him is hitting his locations. He walked only 14 batters in 83 innings last season as a Rockie. Having struggled against lefthanders in his previous big league opportunities, he was more aggressive against them last season, going inside and hard and limiting them to a .200 average. He fields his position well and has yet to commit an error in the majors. His chances to swing the bat are limited, but he did hit a home run and a single in nine at-bats last season.

2001 Outlook

White will be a workhorse because of his ability to get out both righthanded and lefthanded hitters. He should be able to pick up the occasional save, but his primary responsibility will be as a setup man.

Other Colorado Rockies

Rigo Beltran (Pos: LHP, **Age**: 31)

	W	L	Pct.	ERA	G	GS	Sv	IP	H	BB	SO	HR	Ratio
2000	0	0	-	40.50	1	1	0	1.1	6	3	1	2	6.75
Career	2	3	.400	4.34	76	5	1	105.2	109	43	106	13	1.44

Beltran started at Triple-A last year, with poor results. A return to relief duty is likely. 2001 Outlook: C

Darren Bragg (Pos: LF, **Age**: 31, **Bats**: L)

	G	AB	R	H	D	T	HR	RBI	SB	BB	SO	Avg	OBP	Slg
2000	71	149	16	33	7	1	3	21	4	17	41	.221	.296	.342
Career	633	1925	268	496	115	10	39	222	45	253	425	.258	.347	.389

Bragg signed with Colorado last year but was released in July. He didn't play center field at all. 2001 Outlook: C

Bubba Carpenter (Pos: LF, **Age**: 32, **Bats**: L)

	G	AB	R	H	D	T	HR	RBI	SB	BB	SO	Avg	OBP	Slg
2000	15	27	4	6	0	0	3	5	0	4	13	.222	.323	.556
Career	15	27	4	6	0	0	3	5	0	4	13	.222	.323	.556

Carpenter had toiled in Triple-A since 1993 before reaching the majors last year. After the Rockies designated him for assignment in July, he signed in Korea. The Mets then signed him in December. 2001 Outlook: D

Giovanni Carrara (Pos: RHP, **Age**: 33)

	W	L	Pct.	ERA	G	GS	Sv	IP	H	BB	SO	HR	Ratio
2000	0	1	.000	12.83	8	0	0	13.1	21	11	15	5	2.40
Career	3	7	.300	8.24	41	14	0	110.1	153	67	70	30	1.99

Carrara plied his trade in Japan in 1998 before going 19-9 at Triple-A the past two years. He's now a free agent. 2001 Outlook: C

Mike DeJean (Pos: RHP, **Age**: 30)

	W	L	Pct.	ERA	G	GS	Sv	IP	H	BB	SO	HR	Ratio
2000	4	4	.500	4.89	54	0	0	53.1	54	30	34	9	1.58
Career	14	9	.609	4.95	224	1	4	256.1	289	110	130	30	1.56

Elbow and stomach ailments didn't prevent DeJean from appearing in 50 games for a fourth straight year. He sported a 2.66 road ERA last year. 2001 Outlook: A

Jerry Dipoto (Pos: RHP, **Age**: 32)

	W	L	Pct.	ERA	G	GS	Sv	IP	H	BB	SO	HR	Ratio
2000	0	0	-	3.95	17	0	0	13.2	16	5	9	1	1.54
Career	27	24	.529	4.05	390	0	49	495.1	527	221	352	33	1.51

Dipoto missed most of last year with a bulging disk in his neck. If healthy, he should return to an important role in the bullpen, most likely as a setup man. 2001 Outlook: B

Kevin Jarvis (Pos: RHP, **Age**: 31)

	W	L	Pct.	ERA	G	GS	Sv	IP	H	BB	SO	HR	Ratio
2000	3	4	.429	5.95	24	19	0	115.0	138	33	60	26	1.49
Career	15	23	.395	6.43	109	59	1	414.0	530	148	225	83	1.64

Jarvis signed with the Rockies last year as a six-year minor league free agent. He managed to lower his career ERA in his first year in Colorado. 2001 Outlook: C

Aaron Ledesma (Pos: 3B, **Age**: 29, **Bats**: R)

	G	AB	R	H	D	T	HR	RBI	SB	BB	SO	Avg	OBP	Slg
2000	32	40	4	9	2	0	0	3	0	2	9	.225	.279	.275
Career	284	754	94	223	38	4	2	76	11	44	111	.296	.338	.365

Ledesma played at Triple-A most of last year. His anemic power makes it kind of silly to play him anywhere but the middle infield. 2001 Outlook: C

David Lee (Pos: RHP, **Age**: 28)

	W	L	Pct.	ERA	G	GS	Sv	IP	H	BB	SO	HR	Ratio
2000	0	0	-	11.12	7	0	1	5.2	10	6	6	3	2.82
Career	3	2	.600	4.45	43	0	1	54.2	53	35	44	7	1.61

It's conceivable that Lee could see action as Colorado's closer. The sidearmer blew his chance last April but has succeeded in the minors. 2001 Outlook: C

Jeff Manto (Pos: 1B, **Age**: 36, **Bats**: R)

	G	AB	R	H	D	T	HR	RBI	SB	BB	SO	Avg	OBP	Slg
2000	7	5	2	4	2	0	1	4	0	2	0	.800	.857	1.800
Career	289	713	97	164	35	2	31	97	3	97	182	.230	.329	.415

Manto's slugging percentage in 2000 was the highest recorded by someone with at least five at-bats in a year. He signed with Cleveland last April. 2001 Outlook: C

Adam Melhuse (Pos: 1B, **Age**: 29, **Bats**: B)

	G	AB	R	H	D	T	HR	RBI	SB	BB	SO	Avg	OBP	Slg
2000	24	24	3	4	0	1	0	4	0	3	6	.167	.259	.250
Career	24	24	3	4	0	1	0	4	0	3	6	.167	.259	.250

Melhuse was acquired from the Dodgers last June. The switch-hitter has produced great walk rates with some power and he has defensive versatility. 2001 Outlook: C

Carlos Mendoza (Pos: LF, **Age**: 26, **Bats**: L)

	G	AB	R	H	D	T	HR	RBI	SB	BB	SO	Avg	OBP	Slg
2000	13	10	0	1	0	0	0	0	0	1	4	.100	.182	.100
Career	28	22	6	4	0	0	0	1	0	5	6	.182	.379	.182

Mendoza batted .354 at Triple-A last year but failed to hit a home run. He draws walks and can leg out triples, though he is not a polished basestealer. 2001 Outlook: C

David Moraga (Pos: LHP, **Age**: 25)

	W	L	Pct.	ERA	G	GS	Sv	IP	H	BB	SO	HR	Ratio
2000	0	0	-	40.50	4	0	0	2.2	10	2	2	1	4.50
Career	0	0	-	40.50	4	0	0	2.2	10	2	2	1	4.50

The Rockies acquired Moraga off waivers from Montreal last June. He has yet to record an ERA below 6.19 at any stop above Double-A. 2001 Outlook: C

Elvis Pena (Pos: SS, **Age**: 24, **Bats**: B)

	G	AB	R	H	D	T	HR	RBI	SB	BB	SO	Avg	OBP	Slg
2000	10	9	1	3	1	0	0	1	1	1	1	.333	.400	.444
Career	10	9	1	3	1	0	0	1	1	1	1	.333	.400	.444

Pena has very little experience above Double-A. But he can get on base and steal bases. 2001 Outlook: C

Pete Walker (Pos: RHP, **Age**: 31)

	W	L	Pct.	ERA	G	GS	Sv	IP	H	BB	SO	HR	Ratio
2000	0	0	-	17.36	3	0	0	4.2	10	4	2	1	3.00
Career	1	0	1.000	7.04	17	0	0	23.0	34	12	8	4	2.00

Walker did well in Colorado Springs the past two years, but failed in his brief callup with the Rockies. Until then, his last trip to the majors was 1996. 2001 Outlook: C

John Wasdin (Pos: RHP, **Age**: 28)

	W	L	Pct.	ERA	G	GS	Sv	IP	H	BB	SO	HR	Ratio
2000	1	6	.143	5.38	39	4	1	80.1	90	24	71	14	1.42
Career	28	27	.509	5.07	214	42	3	524.0	547	160	352	88	1.35

Wasdin came to Colorado in a trade last July. Wasdin had pitched well for Boston the past few years. He throws strikes and can be used as a swingman. 2001 Outlook: A

Colorado Rockies Minor League Prospects

Organization Overview:

A youth movement began to take form in Coors Field last year. Todd Helton came into full blossom as one of the game's premier hitters and Juan Pierre provided the top of the order with some electricity. Ben Petrick also started to evolve under the tutelage of veteran Brent Mayne. With Jason Jennings, Chi-Hui Tsao, Shawn Chacon, Jason Young and the as of yet unsigned first-rounder Matt Harrington leading the way, the Rockies are working on developing their first batch of major league-caliber arms. Their efforts to develop their young hurlers largely could be for trade bait, however, as the parent club opened the vaults in the offseason to ink high-profile hurlers Mike Hampton and Denny Neagle and also traded for Ron Villone.

Robert Averette

Position: P   **Opening Day Age:** 24
Bats: R **Throws:** R   **Born:** 9/30/76 in
Ht: 6' 2" **Wt:** 195   Sylacauga, AL

Recent Statistics

	W	L	ERA	G	GS	Sv	IP	H	R	BB	SO	HR
1999 A Rockford	9	5	2.58	19	19	0	125.2	117	54	40	98	2
1999 AA Chattanooga	2	1	5.20	6	6	0	36.1	42	22	19	15	1
2000 AAA Louisville	0	1	8.38	2	2	0	9.2	9	10	10	4	1
2000 AA Chattanooga	12	6	2.44	19	19	0	136.1	126	51	28	87	6
2000 AA Carolina	1	3	3.19	5	5	0	31.0	25	12	10	29	3

Virtually unnoticed in Cincinnati after he was selected in the 21st round three years ago, Averette was acquired by the Rockies last year. He spent his first full year in Double-A, after splitting each of the previous two years between the Midwest League and Southern League. Averette uses a maximum effort delivery, but is not overpowering. His over-the-top curveball was named the best breaking pitch in the Southern League, a pitch that he complements with an 88-91 MPH sinking fastball and a change that induce loads of ground balls. A full season at Triple-A probably is on tap for the 6-foot-2 righty.

Brent Butler

Position: 2B   **Opening Day Age:** 23
Bats: R **Throws:** R   **Born:** 2/11/78 in
Ht: 6' 0" **Wt:** 180   Laurinburg, NC

Recent Statistics

	G	AB	R	H	D	T	HR	RBI	SB	BB	SO	Avg
1999 AA Arkansas	139	528	68	142	21	1	13	54	0	26	47	.269
2000 AAA Colo Sprngs	122	438	73	128	35	1	8	54	1	44	46	.292
2000 MLE	122	439	60	129	34	0	8	44	0	36	44	.294

Butler had his most productive season in three years. Brought over from St. Louis in a seven-player trade that sent Darryl Kile to the Cardinals, Butler must continue to emerge to help even out what looks to be a lopsided deal. The former third-rounder whetted everyone's taste buds with his breakthrough season in the Midwest League as a 19-year-old in 1997. However, last year he

bucked the trend of his declining numbers in the thin air, hitting-catered environment of Triple-A Colorado Springs. Encouraging was the fact that Butler evened out his strikeout-walk ratio that had steadily spiraled downward for three years. Only blessed with average speed, the 23-year-old has one steal in two years. Once thought of as an above-average offensive shortstop, his switch to second base adds versatility, and Todd Walker's presence buys him a year of seasoning in Triple-A.

Shawn Chacon

Position: P   **Opening Day Age:** 23
Bats: R **Throws:** R   **Born:** 12/23/77 in
Ht: 6' 3" **Wt:** 212   Anchorage, AK

Recent Statistics

	W	L	ERA	G	GS	Sv	IP	H	R	BB	SO	HR
1999 A Salem	5	5	4.13	12	12	0	72.0	69	44	34	66	3
2000 AA Carolina	10	10	3.16	27	27	0	173.2	151	71	85	172	10

The Rockies' version of "Generation K" was supposed to be their trio of 1997 draft picks. Only Chacon remains in the system and he re-established himself last year and could turn out to be the best of them after all. Chacon made just 24 starts in the Carolina League between 1998 and '99, thanks to a loss of focus and some minor elbow problems. In 2000, he emerged with his best season since being drafted, setting personal bests with 27 starts and 173.2 innings. The 6-foot-3 righthander is back on track, impressing the brass with a low to mid-90s fastball, slider and change that help limit opponents to a stingy .236 average. His off-field troubles seemed to disappear, and his ability to return better than ever is a testament to his great stuff. He may make the parent club by 2002.

Randey Dorame

Position: P   **Opening Day Age:** 22
Bats: L **Throws:** L   **Born:** 1/23/79 in
Ht: 6' 2" **Wt:** 205   Huatabampo, Mexico

Recent Statistics

	W	L	ERA	G	GS	Sv	IP	H	R	BB	SO	HR
1999 A Vero Beach	0	2	5.73	3	2	0	11.0	15	9	1	5	2
1999 A San Berndno	14	3	2.51	24	24	0	154.1	130	52	37	159	9
2000 A Vero Beach	7	1	2.21	9	9	0	57.0	50	15	13	49	3
2000 AA San Antonio	3	4	3.86	9	9	0	58.1	53	29	18	28	5
2000 AA Carolina	0	2	5.06	2	2	0	10.2	7	6	4	9	3

Signed by the Dodgers out of Mexico in 1997, Dorame was acquired by the Rockies in the Tom Goodwin deal. Not overpowering, the southpaw relies on control and changing speeds. Dorame locates an average fastball and mixes in a great curveball and changeup to keep hitters from sitting on his fastball. In going from an organization that traditionally is groomed for pitching to the Rockies, remaining sharp with his command will be key to his survival. He probably will begin this year in Double-A before being thrown to the wolves in Triple-A Colorado Springs. At this pace, his ETA looks like 2002.

Craig House

Position: P
Bats: R **Throws:** R
Ht: 6' 2" **Wt:** 210

Opening Day Age: 23
Born: 7/8/77 in Naha AFB, Okinawa, Japan

Recent Statistics

	W	L	ERA	G	GS	Sv	IP	H	R	BB	SO	HR
2000 A Salem	2	0	2.25	13	0	8	16.0	7	4	10	24	0
2000 AA Carolina	0	2	3.80	18	0	9	21.1	14	11	15	28	0
2000 AAA Colo Spmgs	0	0	3.24	8	0	4	8.1	6	4	2	8	0
2000 NL Colorado	1	1	7.24	16	0	0	13.2	13	11	17	8	3

Usually pitchers who light up the radar guns with near-100-MPH heat are well known and highly drafted. But House wasn't picked until the 12th round in 1999. The Rockies shifted him to the bullpen and he began flirting with triple-digits. In just over a year, House rode his fastball to the majors. His unorthodox herky-jerky delivery may have been another reason teams weren't quick to draft him, and his mechanics also could be the source of his control problems that came to the forefront in the majors. A closer in the making, House has mowed down minor leaguers to the tune of 13.2 strikeouts per nine innings. The Rockies had hoped a trip to the Arizona Fall League would help him get his arsenal under control, but shoulder tendinitis ended his AFL campaign early.

Jason Jennings

Position: P
Bats: L **Throws:** R
Ht: 6' 2" **Wt:** 230

Opening Day Age: 22
Born: 7/17/78 in Dallas, TX

Recent Statistics

	W	L	ERA	G	GS	Sv	IP	H	R	BB	SO	HR
1999 A Portland	1	0	1.00	2	2	0	9.0	5	1	2	11	0
1999 A Asheville	2	2	3.70	12	12	0	58.1	55	27	8	69	3
2000 A Salem	7	10	3.47	22	22	0	150.1	136	66	42	133	6
2000 AA Carolina	1	3	3.44	6	6	0	36.2	32	19	11	33	4

The Rockies spent their first pick two years ago on *Baseball America's* College Player of the Year. An accomplished slugger at Baylor University, Jennings now does all of his damage on the mound. In his first full season, the 6-foot-2, 230-pound righty exhibited a polished workhorse-like repertoire, logging 150.1 innings and three complete games in Class-A before making his final six starts in Double-A. An outstanding command of a heavy sinking fastball in the 89-92 MPH range, a good slider and change cater to his rapid ascent toward the majors. The former DH won't be an easy out, and will be a longball threat in Denver's thin air.

Chin-Hui Tsao

Position: P
Bats: R **Throws:** R
Ht: 6' 2" **Wt:** 178

Opening Day Age: 19
Born: 6/2/81 in Hualien, Taiwan

Recent Statistics

	W	L	ERA	G	GS	Sv	IP	H	R	BB	SO	HR
2000 A Asheville	11	8	2.73	24	24	0	145.0	119	54	40	187	8

Colorado's first venture into the Far East has been an overwhelming success, and its inroads may pay even more dividends in the future. Signed after the '99 season for $2.2 million, Tsao was considered one of the top prospects available on the Pacific Rim. Referred to as a national hero in his native Taiwan for his dominant pitching performances in international competition, Tsao grabbed everyone's attention during his spring training debut when he fired a hitless inning of relief. Despite his electrifying introduction to the American game, Tsao spent his first year in the Class-A South Atlantic League. Animated on the mound, the Rockies were encouraged by the progress their 19-year-old prized prospect displayed in adapting to a new culture. He still is working on the fundamentals, but his dynamic arsenal is convincing, as are the results: Tsao has command of a moving 93-94 MPH fastball, an untouchable slider and a good changeup. He struck out an organization-best 187 hitters at a rate of better than 11 Ks per nine innings and earned the Most Valuable Pitcher award in the SAL.

Others to Watch

Josh Bard (23) made a lot of progress in his professional debut, hitting .282 and displaying a line-drive stroke from both sides of the plate last year. The 1999 third-rounder is considered a heady catcher with solid receiving skills. . . **Aaron Cook** (22) took a big step forward last year with his power repertoire, and command of a mid-90s fastball, slider and changeup. A 1997 second rounder, Cook issued just 1.69 walks per nine in 185.2 innings between his two Class-A stops. . . **Chuck Crowder** (24) was impressive in his first year after being drafted in the fourth round out of Georgia Tech. The southpaw features a moving fastball in the low-90s, curve and change, but is working on smoothing out his mechanics. . . The Rockies remain enthralled with **Choo Freeman** (21) and his athletic ability, but his raw tools have been slow to come around as he progresses through the system. The '98 first-round pick showed very little improvement in moving up to the advanced Class-A Carolina League over his 1999 numbers in the South Atlantic League. . . The pure-hitting **Jody Gerut** (23) used a line-drive stroke and advanced strike-zone judgment to stroke 32 doubles in Double-A. He drew 76 walks to only 54 whiffs, and is a polished defensive outfielder. . . **Juan Uribe** (20) is so smooth with the leather that he has earned incumbent shortstop Neifi Perez' praise as his successor one day. The slick-fielding Dominican demonstrated the best infield arm in the Carolina League, and he shows offensive potential with a quick bat and gap power. . . A second-round pick out of Stanford, **Jason Young** (21), signed after the season for a club-record $2.75 million. Young mixes three quality pitches for strikes. His fastball approaches the mid-90s, regularly hitting the 90-93 MPH range with tailing action. His changeup may be his best pitch and his knuckle-curve still is coming around.

Colorado

Pro Player Stadium

Offense

The home/road gap narrowed significantly in 2000 as several Marlins hitters broke through psychological barriers at their primary workplace. A big difference was the club's performance at home, considering their road performance was similar to that of 1999. The Marlins averaged 4.36 runs per contest and hit 62 homers at Pro Player last season compared to 4.04 and 43 in 1999. The Marlins even hit six points higher at Pro Player Stadium, their best homefield advantage since 1997. John Boles did manage somewhat differently at home, significantly increasing stolen base attempts.

Defense

The biggest challenge remains the Teal Tower, a 28-foot scoreboard in left-center field that causes odd caroms almost nightly. Floyd has learned to handle the silliness in left field, and Wilson's speed comes in handy while racing down drives into the Bermuda Triangle in deep left-center.

Who It Helps the Most

In general, pitchers are helped. A.J. Burnett's ERA was two times higher on the road. Dan Miceli's difference was nearly as drastic. But Chuck Smith and Ricky Bones, both pronounced groundball pitchers, preferred the home mound as well. Perhaps it's the thick grass. The same stuff probably helped Luis Castillo hit 73 points higher at home.

Who It Hurts the Most

First baseman Derrek Lee went nearly two full years between home runs at the Pro, yet hit 20 points higher at home last season. Preston Wilson hit 19 of his 31 homers on the road. Among pitchers, Antonio Alfonseca totally reversed his struggles from the previous year and posted an ERA that was a full run lower on the road. Also preferring the road were Vic Darensbourg and Brad Penny.

Rookies & Newcomers

The Marlins have a number of young pitchers in their system, including Josh Beckett, who may make their way to the majors this season. They probably will welcome working in Pro Player. Returning free agent Charles Johnson is a career .231 hitter at Pro Player Stadium.

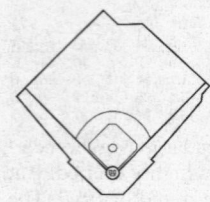

Dimensions: LF-330, LCF-385, CF-404, RCF-385, RF-345

Capacity: 35,521

Elevation: 10 feet

Surface: Grass

Foul Territory: Large

Park Factors

2000 Season

	Home Games			Away Games			Index
	Marlins	Opp	Total	Marlins	Opp	Total	
G	72	72	144	72	72	144	—
Avg	.262	.253	.257	.256	.280	.268	96
AB	2397	2486	4883	2527	2412	4939	99
R	314	327	641	329	378	707	91
H	628	629	1257	646	676	1322	95
2B	114	122	236	120	130	250	95
3B	14	22	36	12	17	29	126
HR	62	70	132	81	78	159	84
BB	257	284	541	228	302	530	103
SO	536	511	1047	548	438	986	107
E	48	57	105	61	59	120	88
E-Infield	44	45	89	50	52	102	87
LHB-Avg	.302	.248	.274	.272	.280	.276	99
LHB-HR	18	18	36	20	29	49	74
RHB-Avg	.240	.256	.248	.247	.280	.263	94
RHB-HR	44	52	96	61	49	110	88

1998-2000

	Home Games			Away Games			Index
	Marlins	Opp	Total	Marlins	Opp	Total	
G	216	216	432	218	218	436	—
Avg	.256	.263	.259	.256	.295	.275	94
AB	7302	7562	14864	7567	7309	14876	101
R	898	1058	1956	932	1266	2198	90
H	1867	1989	3856	1934	2156	4090	95
2B	352	385	737	364	411	775	95
3B	55	64	119	44	50	94	127
HR	151	220	371	211	246	457	81
BB	744	886	1630	637	952	1589	103
SO	1501	1464	2965	1636	1217	2853	104
E	165	173	338	180	141	321	106
E-Infield	142	145	287	145	117	262	111
LHB-Avg	.264	.268	.266	.264	.303	.283	94
LHB-HR	50	77	127	59	102	161	77
RHB-Avg	.250	.260	.255	.250	.290	.270	95
RHB-HR	101	143	244	152	144	296	84

2000 Rankings (National League)
- Second-lowest RHB batting-average factor
- Third-lowest home-run factor
- Third-lowest LHB home-run factor

John Boles

2000 Season

While other managers were fired for being too soft on their players, John Boles surprised many with his ability to swing the hammer when necessary. He delivered a memorable spring diatribe in which he challenged his young team to increase its intensity and goals. He followed with a few more clubhouse meetings during the season. Not coincidentally, the Marlins became the first team since the 1967-69 Mets to improve by at least 10 wins in consecutive seasons. Not bad for a club that scored the second-fewest runs in the majors and was out-plated by 66 runs overall for the season.

Offense

No team ran as often as the Marlins did in 2000. Four players stole at least 19 bases, led by major league leader Luis Castillo. Boles did not experiment much with his lineup after settling early on with Mark Kotsay in the No. 2 slot and Preston Wilson hitting cleanup. The Marlins finished 15th in the league in sacrifice bunts. This, despite the fact that Florida finished 29th in the majors in runs scored. He liked to use pitcher Jesus Sanchez as a pinch-runner but otherwise eschewed the practice.

Pitching & Defense

Boles defined the bullpen roles early and pretty much stuck with them the whole way. He may have been guilty of overusing Dan Miceli in the opening month; Miceli never was the same after a bout with forearm tendinitis. Ricky Bones faded after a big first half as well. Closer Antonio Alfonseca was handled with extreme care, handed just five inherited runners all year and generally used with a two- or three-run lead. Among starters, only Ryan Dempster earned the right to approach 120 pitches with regularity. Boles can sully a lineup card with double switches as well as anybody.

2001 Outlook

Boles was rewarded with a one-year contract extension last September that will take him through 2002. Going into the final season of a deal with no future assurances tends to be a distraction, but Boles won't have to worry about that now. Instead, he can work on guiding the Marlins to their second winning record in their brief history.

Born: 8/19/48 in Chicago, Illinois

Playing Experience: No major league experience

Managerial Experience: 3 seasons

Manager Statistics

Year	Team, Lg	W	L	Pct	GB	Finish
2000	Florida, NL	79	82	.491	15.5	3rd East
3 Seasons		183	215	.460	—	—

2000 Starting Pitchers by Days Rest

	<=3	4	5	6+
Marlins Starts	0	62	77	13
Marlins ERA	—	4.50	4.62	4.83
NL Avg Starts	2	80	50	21
NL ERA	5.00	4.61	4.60	5.18

2000 Situational Stats

	John Boles	NL Average
Hit & Run Success %	25.3	33.8
Stolen Base Success %	75.3	68.8
Platoon Pct.	52.9	53.2
Defensive Subs	26	19
High-Pitch Outings	8	14
Quick/Slow Hooks	17/11	14/16
Sacrifice Attempts	61	87

2000 Rankings (National League)

- 1st in stolen base attempts (223), steals of second base (154) and steals of home plate (2)
- 2nd in stolen-base percentage (75.3)
- 3rd in quick hooks (17)

Antonio Alfonseca

2000 Season

Having secured the closer's role with a solid second half in 1999, Antonio Alfonseca turned in a strangely satisfying season. The "Dragonslayer" blew just four saves in 49 chances, leading the majors in total saves and tying Bryan Harvey's single-season franchise mark. But virtually all of Alfonseca's secondary numbers were less than scintillating. His nightly tightrope act often left observers gasping.

Pitching

Credit Marlins manager John Boles for his careful use of an exceedingly flawed closer. Alfonseca was asked to deal with just five inherited runners all year, and he often was handed a lead of three runs or more. Good thing, because the excitable Dominican allowed a .305 batting average with runners in scoring position and a .325 mark with runners in scoring position and two outs. He did fare much better than in the past against lefthanders and on artificial turf. His success on turf might seem strange considering his nearly 2-1 ground-ball-flyball ratio. His fastball topped out at 98 MPH and stayed at 95-96 with tremendous sink. His slider is just average, while his changeup rates below average. He doesn't get a lot of strikeouts and struggles to make hitters expand their zone. He is pretty much a one-pitch guy, but then, so is Mariano Rivera.

Defense & Hitting

Though awkward, Alfonseca is an average fielder with reliable hands. Unlike most closers, he doesn't allow many stolen bases, thanks to a move to home plate that can be as quick as 1.15 seconds. Hitless in nine career at-bats, he did not add to that futility in 2000.

2001 Outlook

With no obvious challengers in the fold, Alfonseca will open the year as Florida's closer. Arbitration will make him a first-time millionaire, so the Marlins will be watching closely for signs of a letdown in focus or conditioning. Still, since taking over for Matt Mantei in July of 1999, Alfonseca has converted 66 of 72 save opportunities (.917), so he must be doing something right.

Position: RP
Bats: R **Throws:** R
Ht: 6' 5" **Wt:** 235

Opening Day Age: 28
Born: 4/16/72 in La Romana, Dom. Rep.
ML Seasons: 4
Pronunciation: AL-fonn-say-kuh
Nickname: Pulpo, Dragonslayer

Overall Statistics

	W	L	Pct.	ERA	G	GS	Sv	IP	H	BB	SO	HR	Ratio
2000	5	6	.455	4.24	68	0	45	70.0	82	24	47	7	1.51
Career	14	20	.412	3.95	216	0	74	244.0	272	96	158	24	1.51

How Often He Throws Strikes

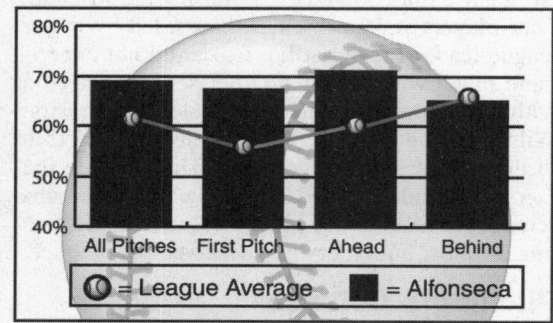

2000 Situational Stats

	W	L	ERA	Sv	IP		AB	H	HR	RBI	Avg
Home	2	4	4.70	23	38.1	LHB	130	36	2	16	.277
Road	3	2	3.69	22	31.2	RHB	152	46	5	19	.303
First Half	3	4	4.60	28	43.0	Sc Pos	82	25	2	28	.305
Scnd Half	2	2	3.67	17	27.0	Clutch	224	63	3	26	.281

2000 Rankings (National League)

- 1st in saves and save percentage (91.8)
- 2nd in save opportunities (49)
- 4th in balks (2) and games finished (62)
- 7th in highest batting average allowed in relief (.291)
- 8th in relief losses (6)
- Led the Marlins in saves, games finished (62), save opportunities (49), save percentage (91.8), blown saves (4), most GDPs induced per GDP situation (15.9%) and relief losses (6)

A.J. Burnett

Position: SP
Bats: R **Throws:** R
Ht: 6' 5" **Wt:** 205

Opening Day Age: 24
Born: 1/3/77 in North Little Rock, AR
ML Seasons: 2

2000 Season

Expected to build on his late-season audition in 1999, A.J. Burnett endured a miserable spring, then missed the first half of last season following a freak injury suffered during fielding drills. He tore a ligament in his pitching thumb and didn't make his 2000 big league debut until July 20, using the down time to add strength to his lower trunk. His performance thereafter was inconsistent. He dueled Rick Ankiel pitch for pitch in late August, piling up a career-high 10 strikeouts. He then fell into a miserable four-start rut, but never used his thumb injury as an excuse.

Pitching

When he's on, Burnett's stuff sizzles. His fastball tops out at 96 MPH and stays within the 92-93 range. His signature pitch, the spike curveball, came and went, which was a little surprising. Umpires often missed the big bender and Burnett grew somewhat passive with the pitch as he tried to throw it for more strikes. He pretty much ate up righthanded hitters. Lefties hit 83 points higher, however, thanks to a changeup that still needs work as well as their ability to neutralize his curve. Burnett struggled mightily on the road with an ERA of 7.46. Walks remain a problem, though he did a nice job of clamping down with runners in scoring position.

Defense & Hitting

Noted more for his basketball than baseball talents in high school, Burnett has good reactions, is quick footed and is a plus-fielder. He still needs to improve his times to the plate and his pickoff move. He's also the best hitter among Marlins pitchers. He batted .280 last year, including a homer off Ankiel. Burnett's bunting could be better.

2001 Outlook

If he stays healthy, there's no reason to believe Burnett can't occupy the No. 2 slot behind Ryan Dempster in the Marlins' rotation. Burnett is four months older than Dempster, and the Marlins are hoping he'll enjoy a similar breakthrough in his third time around the National League. The strut still is there, even after getting knocked around a bit.

Overall Statistics

	W	L	Pct.	ERA	G	GS	Sv	IP	H	BB	SO	HR	Ratio
2000	3	7	.300	4.79	13	13	0	82.2	80	44	57	8	1.50
Career	7	9	.438	4.35	20	20	0	124.0	117	69	90	11	1.50

How Often He Throws Strikes

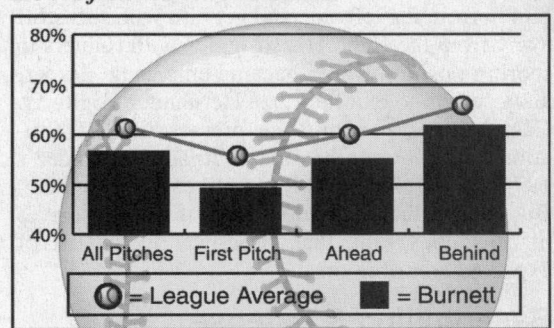

= League Average   = Burnett

2000 Situational Stats

	W	L	ERA	Sv	IP		AB	H	HR	RBI	Avg
Home	2	3	2.83	0	47.2	LHB	149	45	2	13	.302
Road	1	4	7.46	0	35.0	RHB	160	35	6	22	.219
First Half	0	0	-	0	0.0	Sc Pos	80	17	1	24	.213
Scnd Half	3	7	4.79	0	82.2	Clutch	21	8	1	3	.381

2000 Rankings (National League)

- Did not rank near the top or bottom in any category

Luis Castillo

Position: 2B
Bats: B **Throws:** R
Ht: 5'11" **Wt:** 175

Opening Day Age: 25
Born: 9/12/75 in San Pedro de Macoris, Dominican Republic
ML Seasons: 5
Pronunciation: cas-TEE-oh

2000 Season

Though Luis Castillo was left off the All-Star team, he played at that level for most of last season. The speedy switch-hitter kept his average near .360 until wearing down in September. He led the majors in stolen bases, breaking Chuck Carr's franchise mark in the process. Castillo did everything a leadoff-hitter second baseman is supposed to do.

Hitting

Power is not part of Castillo's arsenal. He's more than content to slap groundballs, bunt and use his blazing speed to beat out infield hits. He has more gap power from the right side and has improved his lefthanded swing tremendously. Pitchers still bust him in from the left side and get him with soft stuff away from the right. His struggles with runners in scoring position (.211) became epic as he desperately sought to exit the Enzo Hernandez Highway. Castillo readily admits he presses in RBI situations, a big reason he didn't surpass Hernandez's 1971 season total of 12 RBI until early September. But the Marlins really don't care if Castillo drives in runs; they rank that far down on his list of expected contributions.

Baserunning & Defense

A nagging hamstring injury slowed Castillo early and late last season, hurting his stolen-base percentage. His instincts on the bases have improved greatly and his raw speed is a significant weapon. If not for all the standout second basemen in the National League, Castillo might have a Gold Glove by now. His strong, accurate arm allows him to make highlight plays up the middle by throwing against his body. He still needs to improve on plays to his left, where he's reluctant to dive for balls after a history of shoulder problems.

2001 Outlook

After making an initial pass through salary arbitration, Castillo will have a fat wallet for the first time in his career. His progress has been spurred by a relentless work ethic, and the Marlins don't expect that to change. Prospect Pablo Ozuna has stalled a bit in the minors, which means Castillo should have several more years to become further entrenched in South Florida.

Overall Statistics

	G	AB	R	H	D	T	HR	RBI	SB	BB	SO	Avg	OBP	Slg
2000	136	539	101	180	17	3	2	17	62	78	86	.334	.418	.388
Career	424	1606	251	464	53	10	4	71	148	208	303	.289	.370	.342

Where He Hits the Ball

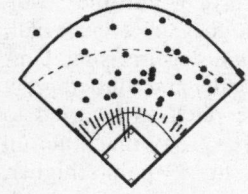 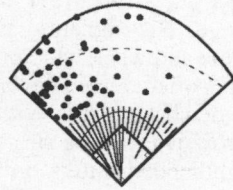

Vs. LHP   **Vs. RHP**

2000 Situational Stats

	AB	H	HR	RBI	Avg		AB	H	HR	RBI	Avg
Home	258	96	1	7	.372	LHP	148	43	2	3	.291
Road	281	84	1	10	.299	RHP	391	137	0	14	.350
First Half	260	96	1	4	.369	Sc Pos	90	19	0	15	.211
Scnd Half	279	84	1	13	.301	Clutch	72	22	0	4	.306

2000 Rankings (National League)

- 1st in singles, stolen bases, caught stealing (22), highest groundball/flyball ratio (4.7), most pitches seen per plate appearance (4.30), on-base percentage for a leadoff hitter (.419) and lowest HR frequency (269.5 ABs per HR)
- 2nd in batting average vs. righthanded pitchers and steals of third (7)
- 3rd in bunts in play (30) and lowest percentage of swings that missed (7.9)
- Led the Marlins in batting average, runs scored, hits, singles, sacrifice bunts (9), stolen bases, caught stealing (22), walks, times on base (258), pitches seen (2,690), on-base percentage, highest groundball/flyball ratio (4.7) and most pitches seen per plate appearance (4.30)

Ryan Dempster

Position: SP
Bats: R **Throws:** R
Ht: 6' 1" **Wt:** 201

Opening Day Age: 23
Born: 5/3/77 in Sechelt, Canada
ML Seasons: 3

2000 Season

Ryan Dempster took a major step forward in a breakout year. The affable Western Canadian made his first All-Star team, threw a one-hitter against the National League champion Mets and broke Kevin Brown's franchise mark for strikeouts in a single season. In the process, Dempster stepped into the void left by Alex Fernandez' season-ending injury and no one noticed any drop-off.

Pitching

Punishing offseason workouts gave Dempster a frame more akin to some of his heroes from pro wrestling. The velocity on his fastball increased as well; he topped out at 95 MPH and was able to pitch consistently in the low-90s into the late innings. While his changeup has come a long way, it's a nasty slider that ranks as Dempster's out pitch. He gets ahead with his fastball, then retires even All-Stars with a slider that NL managers ranked behind only Randy Johnson's and Robb Nen's. He needs to reduce his walks (97) and home runs allowed (30), but he knows how to pitch to the situation. He allowed a .111 on-base percentage with the bases loaded. Once wild without purpose, he now throws inside to back hitters off the plate. He drew the ire of Reds outfielder Michael Tucker with a well-placed fastball in the ribs, but that only made the Marlins appreciate Dempster even more.

Defense & Hitting

For such a solid athlete, Dempster should be much better with his bat and glove. He's a career .079 hitter in 139 at-bats, though he did manage to drop four sacrifice bunts last year. He is an average fielder who keeps baserunners off balance by varying his holds.

2001 Outlook

At 23, Dempster is considered one of the game's top young pitchers. He speaks openly about making another 10 All-Star teams and probably expects to make another leap forward in his fourth big league season. Even if Fernandez can't come back from his latest round of shoulder woes, the Marlins won't lack an ace. Dempster is it.

Overall Statistics

	W	L	Pct.	ERA	G	GS	Sv	IP	H	BB	SO	HR	Ratio
2000	14	10	.583	3.66	33	33	0	226.1	210	97	209	30	1.36
Career	22	23	.489	4.46	72	69	0	428.0	428	228	370	57	1.53

How Often He Throws Strikes

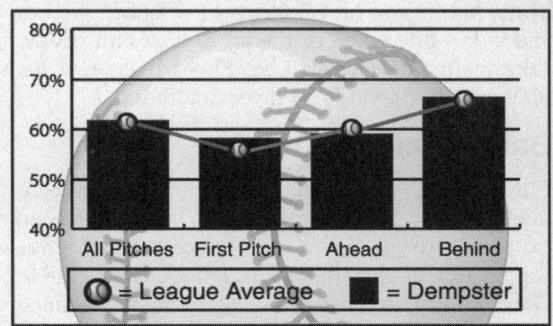

○ = League Average   ■ = Dempster

2000 Situational Stats

	W	L	ERA	Sv	IP		AB	H	HR	RBI	Avg
Home	6	3	3.40	0	111.1	LHB	379	93	16	40	.245
Road	8	7	3.91	0	115.0	RHB	484	117	14	53	.242
First Half	9	5	3.65	0	123.1	Sc Pos	210	44	5	63	.210
Scnd Half	5	5	3.67	0	103.0	Clutch	64	17	1	5	.266

2000 Rankings (National League)

- 2nd in errors at pitcher (4)
- 4th in strikeouts and fewest GDPs induced per nine innings (0.5)
- 5th in lowest fielding percentage at pitcher (.909)
- Led the Marlins in ERA, wins, games started, complete games (2), innings pitched, hits allowed, batters faced (974), walks allowed, hit batsmen (5), strikeouts, pitches thrown (3,599), stolen bases allowed (13), runners caught stealing (9), GDPs induced (13), highest strikeout/walk ratio (2.2), lowest batting average allowed (.243), lowest slugging percentage allowed (.404), lowest on-base percentage allowed (.322) and highest groundball/flyball ratio allowed (1.1)

Cliff Floyd

2000 Season

Another lost April forced Cliff Floyd to play catch up all year. However, his attitude and effort never wavered. His troublesome left knee had to be drained several times and cost him most of August. But Floyd returned in September to hit .351 and whet appetites for a breakthrough follow-up.

Hitting

Few players in the game hit the ball as consistently hard as Floyd does. Those Willie McCovey comparisons really weren't too far off. Floyd hits lefthanders better than righthanders and he has the plate discipline to consistently post good strikeout-walk ratios. He still tends to chase fastballs up and away, but he can hit all forms of offspeed pitches and won't bite when teams try to bust him inside. Like teammate Derrek Lee, Floyd overcame his phobia of hitting at Pro Player Stadium.

Baserunning & Defense

Floyd doesn't get enough credit for his baserunning prowess. He'll take the extra base and has an excellent first step for such a big man. He was caught stealing just three times in 27 tries in 2000. Once almost laughable in the field, he stunned teammates and staffers alike with a steady diet of diving catches, regularly racing in to skim sinking liners off the grass. For that transformation he credited fungo master Rusty Kuntz. He did, however, commit a career-high nine errors and posted his worst fielding percentage as a regular outfielder. Floyd's arm remains below average but has gotten more accurate through long hours of extra work.

2001 Outlook

Floyd is entering the third year of a four-year, $19 million contract. He desperately wants to justify the organization's faith in his tools. He had surgery on his right wrist in late November to repair tendons and remove scar tissue but is expected to recover in time for spring training. He is entrenched in left field with Florida, and if he stays healthy enough to play 150 or more games, there's no reason to doubt he'll post career bests across the board.

Position: LF
Bats: L **Throws:** R
Ht: 6' 4" **Wt:** 235

Opening Day Age: 28
Born: 12/5/72 in Chicago, IL
ML Seasons: 8

Overall Statistics

	G	AB	R	H	D	T	HR	RBI	SB	BB	SO	Avg	OBP	Slg
2000	121	420	75	126	30	0	22	91	24	50	82	.300	.378	.529
Career	660	2057	301	565	138	13	73	326	82	212	420	.275	.346	.461

Where He Hits the Ball

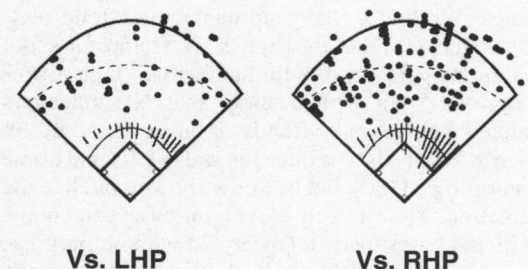

Vs. LHP   **Vs. RHP**

2000 Situational Stats

	AB	H	HR	RBI	Avg		AB	H	HR	RBI	Avg
Home	191	58	13	50	.304	LHP	126	42	5	26	.333
Road	229	68	9	41	.297	RHP	294	84	17	65	.286
First Half	290	80	16	59	.276	Sc Pos	133	41	7	67	.308
Scnd Half	130	46	6	32	.354	Clutch	73	25	6	17	.342

2000 Rankings (National League)

- 1st in lowest fielding percentage in left field (.951)
- 2nd in stolen-base percentage (88.9) and errors in left field (9)
- 8th in fewest GDPs per GDP situation (3.9%)
- Led the Marlins in stolen-base percentage (88.9), fewest GDPs per GDP situation (3.9%), batting average with runners in scoring position, batting average vs. lefthanded pitchers, slugging percentage vs. lefthanded pitchers (.524) and on-base percentage vs. lefthanded pitchers (.383)
- Led NL left fielders in stolen bases and stolen-base percentage (88.9)

Alex Gonzalez

2000 Season

Long gone were the good vibes of Alex Gonzalez' rookie All-Star season. In their place were a series of injuries, sustained pouting and deep confusion at the plate. He spent much of the campaign just trying to avoid the interstate and for a long while it appeared his batting average would be historically low. Just when a solid July got him going, a sprained knee cost him August and any semblance of momentum.

Hitting

Mercifully dropped from the No. 2 slot after a slow start, Gonzalez was even worse lower in the order. He still insists on swinging for the fences and posted another poor strikeout-walk ratio. He was nearly demoted to Triple-A on several occasions before he got serious enough to work with the three-headed hitting monster of batting coach Jack Maloof and special assistants Andre Dawson and Tony Perez. Finally persuaded to abandon the toe-tap timing device that wasn't working, Gonzalez spread out in the box and got better looks at the strike zone. That produced a .317 average in July, but after getting hurt he got frustrated and went back to his old unproductive style.

Baserunning & Defense

Gonzalez is not slow, as evidenced by his 12 career triples, but he lacks basestealing instincts and isn't a particularly daring baserunner. He can make highlight plays in the field, especially to his backhand side, but increasingly took his bat out to shortstop. His throwing became more erratic as the year wore on and he came to favor a sidearm flip style. He needs to improve on charging balls, and his overall concentration could be much better.

2001 Outlook

Gonzalez' moodiness and prolonged slumps have created division within the organization. Some wanted the club to sign a more stable presence for the position, while others see Gonzalez' potential as too great to abandon so quickly. He'll be 24 on Opening Day, and a return to form—soon—is essential to his long-term future with the Marlins.

Position: SS
Bats: R **Throws:** R
Ht: 6' 0" **Wt:** 170

Opening Day Age: 24
Born: 2/15/77 in Cagua, Venezuela
ML Seasons: 3

Florida

Overall Statistics

	G	AB	R	H	D	T	HR	RBI	SB	BB	SO	Avg	OBP	Slg
2000	109	385	35	77	17	4	7	42	7	13	77	.200	.229	.319
Career	270	1031	127	245	47	12	24	108	10	37	220	.238	.273	.376

Where He Hits the Ball

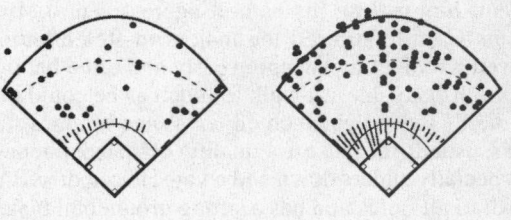

Vs. LHP   **Vs. RHP**

2000 Situational Stats

	AB	H	HR	RBI	Avg		AB	H	HR	RBI	Avg
Home	187	34	5	21	.182	LHP	98	24	2	10	.245
Road	198	43	2	21	.217	RHP	287	53	5	32	.185
First Half	261	47	4	27	.180	Sc Pos	90	22	3	36	.244
Scnd Half	124	30	3	15	.242	Clutch	54	5	0	2	.093

2000 Rankings (National League)

- 1st in lowest batting average in the clutch
- 2nd in lowest batting average with two strikes (.120)
- 4th in lowest fielding percentage at shortstop (.958)
- 6th in errors at shortstop (19)
- 8th in batting average on a 3-1 count (.667)
- Led the Marlins in batting average on a 3-1 count (.667)

Mark Kotsay

2000 Season

Mark Kotsay somehow lost his starting job in right field in spring training to mumps-ravaged Brant Brown, mainly because the Marlins were looking for a little more pop at the position. But Brown wasn't the answer and Kotsay's strong overall game helped him reclaim the job by late April. Kotsay put together his best season yet and answered most of the organization's questions about his ability to play regularly.

Hitting

Freed from the inherent power requests of hitting fifth, Kotsay took to the No. 2 hole with ease and enthusiasm. He wasn't asked to perform the typical tasks of a No. 2 hitter because the Marlins didn't want him to lose his natural aggressiveness. But Luis Castillo still led the majors in stolen bases, even with Kotsay swinging early and often behind him. Kotsay doesn't walk as much as he could but doesn't strike out much either. When he does fan it's usually because of quality offspeed pitches, especially sliders down and away. He can drive the ball to all fields and has a strong groundball bias.

Baserunning & Defense

As word has spread about Kotsay's defense, opponents have challenged him less frequently on the bases. His assists dropped from 20 in 1998 and 19 in 1999 to 14, but that had nothing to do with any drop-off in accuracy or arm strength. His routes are impeccable and he's not afraid to crash into walls to steal hits. A Gold Glove would seem to be in his future. Kotsay has good speed and a good idea on the bases. Previous bouts with shin splints were cured with orthotic shoe inserts. All but a handful of his at-bats came at the top of the order, and he responded with career highs in stolen bases and runs scored.

2001 Outlook

Unlike last year, Kotsay should run unopposed for the starting right-field job. Like so many of his teammates, he will be enjoying his first arbitration-induced salary bump. Prospect Julio Ramirez was traded to the White Sox, so there's little pressure from below.

Position: RF
Bats: L **Throws:** L
Ht: 6' 0" **Wt:** 190

Opening Day Age: 25
Born: 12/2/75 in Whittier, CA
ML Seasons: 4

Overall Statistics

	G	AB	R	H	D	T	HR	RBI	SB	BB	SO	Avg	OBP	Slg
2000	152	530	87	158	31	5	12	57	19	42	46	.298	.347	.443
Career	468	1655	221	463	80	22	31	179	39	109	164	.280	.322	.411

Where He Hits the Ball

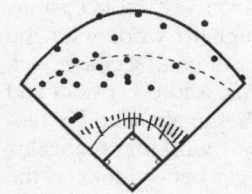 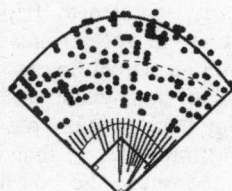

Vs. LHP   **Vs. RHP**

2000 Situational Stats

	AB	H	HR	RBI	Avg		AB	H	HR	RBI	Avg
Home	261	76	5	30	.291	LHP	104	32	1	13	.308
Road	269	82	7	27	.305	RHP	426	126	11	44	.296
First Half	292	90	7	35	.308	Sc Pos	123	28	2	36	.228
Scnd Half	238	68	5	22	.286	Clutch	86	24	2	12	.279

2000 Rankings (National League)

- 2nd in fielding percentage in right field (.989)
- 4th in fewest pitches seen per plate appearance (3.31) and lowest batting average on a 3-1 count (.048)
- 6th in highest percentage of swings put into play (53.5)
- 8th in highest percentage of swings on the first pitch (38.6)
- 9th in GDPs (17)
- Led the Marlins in triples, GDPs (17), batting average on the road and highest percentage of swings put into play (53.5)
- Led NL right fielders in highest percentage of swings put into play (53.5)

Derrek Lee

2000 Season

After losing an all-out spring training battle at first base with Kevin Millar, Derrek Lee gradually gained playing time until he reclaimed the full-time job in mid-May. He hit a career-high 28 homers, reduced his strikeout rate and improved his batting average. In the process, he reminded Marlins officials why they had acquired him as the key component in the Kevin Brown salary-dump deal.

Hitting

A lanky ex-basketball star who turned down a scholarship to play for Dean Smith, Lee likes to extend his arms. While he crushes balls out over the plate, he's quick enough to turn on fastballs on the inner half. Pitchers can make him chase high fastballs, especially inside, as well as sliders low and away. Lee overcame a strange mental block about hitting at home. He went nearly two years between home runs at Pro Player Stadium before a two-homer breakout game against the Cubs in late June. He hit seven more homers there the rest of the year. Lee likes to work the count in his favor, preferring to take the first pitch. He tends to get discouraged with borderline strike calls, which cause him to expand his zone. His work as a run producer needs improvement, as he hit just .238 with runners in scoring position.

Baserunning & Defense

Even when he wasn't hitting, Lee was worth having in the lineup for his defense alone. He draws mention as a future Gold Glove candidate for his immense wing span, soft hands and quick reactions, all of which reduce the throwing errors by his fellow infielders. His speed is average at best, which for the most part keeps him a station-to-station baserunner.

2001 Outlook

Still just 25, Lee hopes to build on the gains of his break-out year. The starting job at first is his from Opening Day, which should help him relax. He fell just short of first-time arbitration status, so another big season will be necessary before he can land that first big contract.

Position: 1B
Bats: R **Throws:** R
Ht: 6' 5" **Wt:** 225

Opening Day Age: 25
Born: 9/6/75 in Sacramento, CA
ML Seasons: 4

Overall Statistics

	G	AB	R	H	D	T	HR	RBI	SB	BB	SO	Avg	OBP	Slg
2000	158	477	70	134	18	3	28	70	0	63	123	.281	.368	.507
Career	391	1203	162	299	59	5	51	168	7	136	337	.249	.331	.433

Where He Hits the Ball

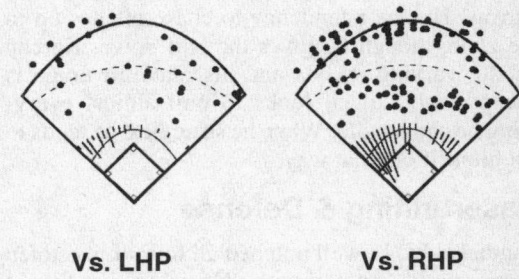

Vs. LHP   **Vs. RHP**

2000 Situational Stats

	AB	H	HR	RBI	Avg		AB	H	HR	RBI	Avg
Home	209	61	9	28	.292	LHP	101	23	6	8	.228
Road	268	73	19	42	.272	RHP	376	111	22	62	.295
First Half	220	59	18	37	.268	Sc Pos	130	31	7	45	.238
Scnd Half	257	75	10	33	.292	Clutch	82	30	8	16	.366

2000 Rankings (National League)

- 4th in batting average in the clutch
- 6th in lowest fielding percentage at first base (.993)
- 7th in errors at first base (8)
- Led the Marlins in slugging percentage, HR frequency (17.0 ABs per HR), batting average in the clutch and slugging percentage vs. righthanded pitchers (.527)
- Led NL first basemen in triples

Mike Lowell

2000 Season

The Marlins finally got the chance to see the player they thought they were getting from the Yankees when they surrendered three pitching prospects in February of 1999. Fully recovered from a brush with testicular cancer, Mike Lowell regained his gap power and the bounce in his step. He showed leadership skills and a nose for the RBI.

Hitting

Streaky to a fault, Lowell has acquired a reputation as an RBI guy even though his statistics don't entirely support that. He hit just .226 in close & late situations and .273 with runners in scoring position. For a time his numbers in day games were far superior to those at night, but that gap has begun to narrow. He has a tendency to chase pitches up in the zone, though he loves the ball down. He can handle varying speeds and his plate coverage is exceptional. Lowell looks to pull almost everything he can handle. When he struggles, he tends to get himself out that way.

Baserunning & Defense

Sundial slow, Lowell notched all four of his stolen bases in the final month. He is an intelligent baserunner and knows how to stretch a long single into a double. He showed improved quickness at third base, where he is better on balls in the hole than down the line. He is serviceable at charging slow rollers but is no Scott Rolen in that department.

2001 Outlook

Lowell may never be an All-Star quality third baseman, but with little help developing behind him in the organization, the position is his for the foreseeable future. He is fundamentally sound in all areas and has acquired an obvious level of respect within the young clubhouse. He is one of the Marlins' building blocks and should be a middle-of-the-order staple for years to come.

Position: 3B
Bats: R **Throws:** R
Ht: 6' 4" **Wt:** 205

Opening Day Age: 27
Born: 2/24/74 in San Juan, Puerto Rico
ML Seasons: 3

Overall Statistics

	G	AB	R	H	D	T	HR	RBI	SB	BB	SO	Avg	OBP	Slg
2000	140	508	73	137	38	0	22	91	4	54	75	.270	.344	.474
Career	245	831	106	219	53	0	34	138	4	80	145	.264	.333	.450

Where He Hits the Ball

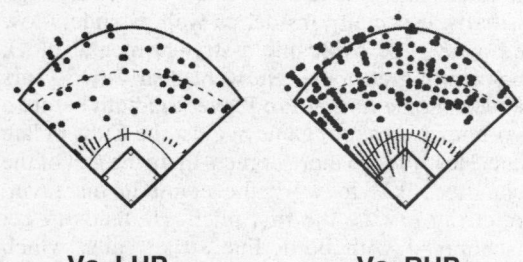

Vs. LHP   **Vs. RHP**

2000 Situational Stats

	AB	H	HR	RBI	Avg		AB	H	HR	RBI	Avg
Home	244	62	11	38	.254	LHP	105	27	5	16	.257
Road	264	75	11	53	.284	RHP	403	110	17	75	.273
First Half	264	67	12	43	.254	Sc Pos	150	41	7	69	.273
Scnd Half	244	70	10	48	.287	Clutch	84	19	5	16	.226

2000 Rankings (National League)

- 3rd in fielding percentage at third base (.968)
- 4th in lowest groundball/flyball ratio (0.7)
- 5th in sacrifice flies (11)
- Led the Marlins in doubles, sacrifice flies (11), hit by pitch (9) and batting average with the bases loaded (.444)

Brad Penny

2000 Season

Coming off a standout showing in the Arizona Fall League, Brad Penny won a wide-open battle for the fifth starter's spot in spring training last year. He then experienced an uneven rookie season while making the jump from Double-A. He got off to a solid start before going through a frustrating run as "Rain Man," when delays shortened all but one of his outings in a four-start span. A bout of shoulder weakness landed him on the disabled list in July. He spent all of August on a rehab assignment before returning to make four September starts.

Pitching

As per his reputation in the minors, Penny showed a tendency to throw almost exclusively fastballs and shun a solid curve and developing changeup. He became enamored with a cut fastball at midseason, despite the middling results it yielded. While his four-seamer could hit 96 MPH, he was much more effective when throwing sinkers in the low 90s and complementing the offerings with soft stuff. He did a much better job of mixing his pitches in September after returning from his first Triple-A experience. He showed better mound presence and did not let his emotions get the best of him.

Defense & Hitting

Penny is a lumbering fielder and needs to improve his pickoff move. Like many young pitchers, he sometimes ignores baserunners in order to concentrate on his command. Penny doesn't get cheated at the plate, and he was used as a pinch-hitter in an extra-inning game. His bunting needs work.

2001 Outlook

Still just 22 years old, Penny will enter this season as one of the favorites to claim a spot at the back of the rotation. The Marlins still believe he has the makeup and ability to become an upper-rotation workhorse, though he must improve the mental part of his game for that to happen. The club was encouraged by his late-season progress last year.

Position: SP
Bats: R **Throws:** R
Ht: 6' 4" **Wt:** 200

Opening Day Age: 22
Born: 5/24/78 in Broken Arrow, OK
ML Seasons: 1

Florida

Overall Statistics

	W	L	Pct.	ERA	G	GS	Sv	IP	H	BB	SO	HR	Ratio
2000	8	7	.533	4.81	23	22	0	119.2	120	60	80	13	1.50
Career	8	7	.533	4.81	23	22	0	119.2	120	60	80	13	1.50

How Often He Throws Strikes

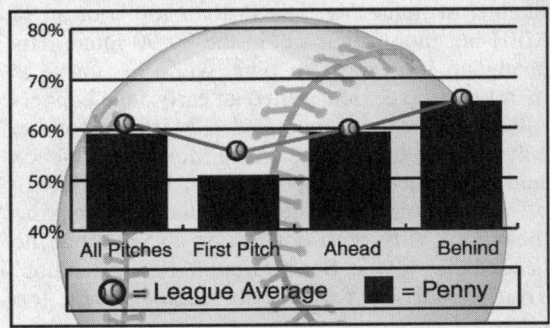

Ⓚ = League Average ■ = Penny

2000 Situational Stats

	W	L	ERA	Sv	IP		AB	H	HR	RBI	Avg
Home	5	2	5.66	0	55.2	LHB	193	48	2	16	.249
Road	3	5	4.08	0	64.0	RHB	263	72	11	46	.274
First Half	4	7	5.32	0	88.0	Sc Pos	116	27	5	48	.233
Scnd Half	4	0	3.41	0	31.2	Clutch	17	6	2	5	.353

2000 Rankings (National League)

- 10th in lowest fielding percentage at pitcher (.933)
- Led the Marlins in hit batsmen (5)

Jesus Sanchez

2000 Season

Another strong winter-ball season in his native Dominican Republic earned Jesus Sanchez one more shot at the Marlins' rotation last year. Having failed miserably in a relief role in 1999, he tantalized as the only lefthanded starter on the club. He seemed to be getting it when he tossed shutouts against the Orioles and Cardinals within a five-start span after the All-Star break. Predictably, however, he gave back those gains with a horrific September.

Pitching

A marked flyball pitcher, Sanchez can serve up his share of longballs (32) or, when he's on, set entire lineups to muttering. His fastball tops out at 94 MPH but more often sits in the 89-90 range. His changeup is average to plus, while his curve is merely average. He credited an early June conversation with countryman Pedro Martinez for his July and August success. From Martinez, Sanchez said he learned the importance of backing hitters off the plate with inside fastballs, then making them look silly with changeups away. When he heeded that advice, Sanchez could be outstanding. Trouble was, he reverted to mediocrity far too often.

Defense & Hitting

Though armed with one of the best pickoff moves in the league, Sanchez gave up a surprising number of stolen bases. Opponents just decided to go on his first move, figuring they couldn't solve him anyway, and it worked. He is a below-average fielder. Helpless at the plate his first two seasons, Sanchez was a much-improved hitter. He hit .232 and had three sacrifice bunts. He also served as a pinch-runner on several occasions despite his share of misadventures on the basepaths.

2001 Outlook

Sanchez will come to spring training as Florida's third or fourth starter but could easily move lower or even drop back to the bullpen. His inconsistency has proved maddening. But after an initial run through the salary arbitration process, waiting around for that cosmic click will be more expensive.

Position: SP
Bats: L **Throws:** L
Ht: 5'10" **Wt:** 155

Opening Day Age: 26
Born: 10/11/74 in Bani, Dominican Republic
ML Seasons: 3

Overall Statistics

	W	L	Pct.	ERA	G	GS	Sv	IP	H	BB	SO	HR	Ratio
2000	9	12	.429	5.34	32	32	0	182.0	197	76	123	32	1.50
Career	21	28	.429	5.11	126	71	0	431.1	459	227	322	66	1.59

How Often He Throws Strikes

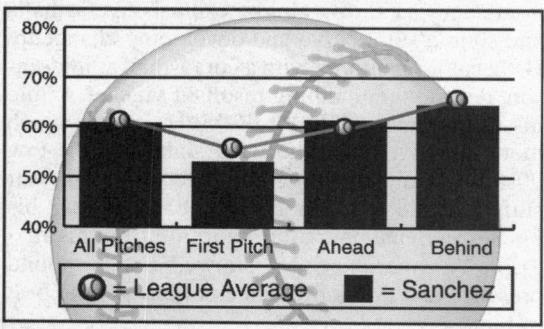

2000 Situational Stats

	W	L	ERA	Sv	IP		AB	H	HR	RBI	Avg
Home	4	6	4.42	0	91.2	LHB	112	28	3	15	.250
Road	5	6	6.28	0	90.1	RHB	592	169	29	96	.285
First Half	5	7	5.47	0	105.1	Sc Pos	158	39	4	65	.247
Scnd Half	4	5	5.17	0	76.2	Clutch	28	7	1	4	.250

2000 Rankings (National League)

- 3rd in shutouts (2) and highest ERA on the road
- 5th in highest ERA and highest slugging percentage allowed (.497)
- 6th in home runs allowed, lowest groundball/flyball ratio allowed (0.9), most home runs allowed per nine innings (1.58) and lowest fielding percentage at pitcher (.923)
- 8th in errors at pitcher (3)
- 9th in lowest winning percentage
- Led the Marlins in losses, complete games (2), shutouts (2), home runs allowed, pickoff throws (126), GDPs induced (13), fewest pitches thrown per batter (3.64), most run support per nine innings (5.4), most GDPs induced per nine innings (0.6) and fewest walks per nine innings (3.8)

Preston Wilson

2000 Season

Last season was the year those five tools came together in stunning fashion. How good was Preston Wilson? So good that nobody in the organization really cared that he tied Bobby Bonds for the second-highest strikeout total ever. Just to be safe, Marlins manager John Boles reduced Wilson's playing time in the final week to keep him from setting the record. Wilson broke Gary Sheffield's franchise mark for single-season RBI and was the majors' only 30-homer, 30-stolen base man.

Hitting

Despite all the strikeouts, Wilson has a fairly solid approach at the plate. That's why Boles resisted the temptation to drop Wilson out of the cleanup spot. He tends to chase high fastballs and good breaking balls away, but he no longer tries to pull everything. He has more than enough power to take balls out to right-center and finally learned to do just that. His RBI numbers, impressive as they were, could have been even higher if he'd hit better than .244 with runners in scoring position. He hit .411 when putting the first pitch in play. Once on pace to strike out 220-plus times, Wilson made much better contact down the stretch.

Baserunning & Defense

The former high school running back has an awkward running style, but then so does Michael Johnson. In Wilson's case, he is more than fast enough to score from first on balls in the gap, and his 72-percent success rate on steal attempts was more than satisfactory. Defensively, Wilson has come a long way. His routes can make things exciting at times, but his speed enables him to outrun mistakes and close with the best of them. His arm is lively if erratic.

2001 Outlook

Though Wilson may not stay in the cleanup spot permanently, he's a fixture in center field. He's a not-so-distant future All-Star, and with a strong follow-up season he could be looking at a mega-salary increase on his first pass through arbitration-land next winter. At 26, he still has time to get his high strikeout totals under control.

Position: CF
Bats: R **Throws:** R
Ht: 6' 2" **Wt:** 193

Opening Day Age: 26
Born: 7/19/74 in Bamberg, SC
ML Seasons: 3

Overall Statistics

	G	AB	R	H	D	T	HR	RBI	SB	BB	SO	Avg	OBP	Slg
2000	161	605	94	160	35	3	31	121	36	55	187	.264	.331	.486
Career	332	1138	168	303	58	7	58	195	48	107	364	.266	.336	.482

Where He Hits the Ball

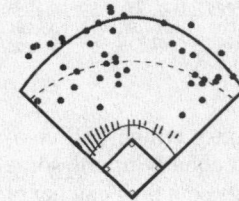 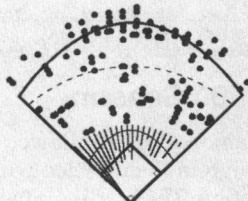

Vs. LHP **Vs. RHP**

2000 Situational Stats

	AB	H	HR	RBI	Avg		AB	H	HR	RBI	Avg
Home	297	79	12	62	.266	LHP	144	36	9	31	.250
Road	308	81	19	59	.263	RHP	461	124	22	90	.269
First Half	334	87	19	67	.260	Sc Pos	193	47	10	86	.244
Scnd Half	271	73	12	54	.269	Clutch	103	23	4	20	.223

2000 Rankings (National League)

- 1st in strikeouts
- 2nd in caught stealing (14) and errors in center field (5)
- 3rd in highest percentage of swings that missed (32.2)
- 4th in games played
- 5th in lowest percentage of swings put into play (33.1)
- Led the Marlins in home runs, at-bats, total bases (294), RBI, strikeouts, plate appearances (674), cleanup slugging percentage (.490) and games played
- Led NL center fielders in RBI, caught stealing (14), strikeouts, cleanup slugging percentage (.490) and games played (161)

Ramon Castro

Position: C
Bats: R **Throws:** R
Ht: 6' 3" **Wt:** 225

Opening Day Age: 25
Born: 3/1/76 in Vega Baja, Puerto Rico
ML Seasons: 2

Overall Statistics

	G	AB	R	H	D	T	HR	RBI	SB	BB	SO	Avg	OBP	Slg
2000	50	138	10	33	4	0	2	14	0	16	36	.239	.318	.312
Career	74	205	14	45	8	0	4	18	0	26	50	.220	.306	.317

2000 Situational Stats

	AB	H	HR	RBI	Avg		AB	H	HR	RBI	Avg
Home	66	13	0	4	.197	LHP	25	5	0	2	.200
Road	72	20	2	10	.278	RHP	113	28	2	12	.248
First Half	0	0	0	0	-	Sc Pos	32	9	1	13	.281
Scnd Half	138	33	2	14	.239	Clutch	18	4	0	3	.222

2000 Season

Ramon Castro followed a lousy winter-ball campaign in Puerto Rico with an equally troublesome spring. The Marlins reluctantly sent their catcher of the future to Triple-A Calgary for more seasoning. He responded with a first half worthy of a Futures Game selection. Recalled in July, he showed less power than expected and even struggled defensively at times.

Hitting, Baserunning & Defense

Blessed with decent natural power, Castro frequently lapses into his pull-happy ways. He steps in the bucket, pulls off balls and litters the field with weak flies. Coaches constantly plead with him to trust his hands and take pitches up the middle and to right-center. His .145 average with two strikes and .197 mark at home were particularly worrisome. His game calling improved as the year went along, but it's his strong throwing arm that will keep him around. He needs to do a better job blocking balls. He is extremely slow.

2001 Outlook

The Marlins were able to convince free agent Charles Johnson to take a hometown discount and sign up for a second tour of duty. Castro will back Johnson up, and also could be used as trade bait.

Reid Cornelius

Position: SP
Bats: R **Throws:** R
Ht: 6' 0" **Wt:** 200

Opening Day Age: 30
Born: 6/2/70 in Thomasville, AL
ML Seasons: 3

Overall Statistics

	W	L	Pct.	ERA	G	GS	Sv	IP	H	BB	SO	HR	Ratio
2000	4	10	.286	4.82	22	21	0	125.0	135	50	50	19	1.48
Career	8	17	.320	4.91	45	33	0	211.0	226	85	101	30	1.47

2000 Situational Stats

	W	L	ERA	Sv	IP		AB	H	HR	RBI	Avg
Home	1	3	4.33	0	54.0	LHB	212	60	11	30	.283
Road	3	7	5.20	0	71.0	RHB	266	75	8	33	.282
First Half	3	2	3.76	0	55.0	Sc Pos	101	27	2	40	.267
Scnd Half	1	8	5.66	0	70.0	Clutch	24	9	3	4	.375

2000 Season

Reid Cornelius was recalled from Triple-A in late May after Alex Fernandez went on the disabled list. Cornelius proved baffling at times, at one point taking a no-hitter into the seventh inning against Tampa Bay. But his fortunes turned as hitters adjusted to his soft-tossing ways, and he was saddled with the worst run support of any Marlins starter. He was winless in 13 starts after July 2.

Pitching, Defense & Hitting

Once a power-pitching prodigy, Cornelius has adjusted well after elbow problems robbed him of his mid-90s fastball. He now is the rare crafty righthander. The changeup allows Cornelius to handle lefthanded hitters as well as righties. He also mixes in a good curve. He is a solid bunter but not much of a threat at the plate. He does a good job holding runners and played errorless defense last year while taking part in three double plays.

2001 Outlook

A lot would have to go wrong for Cornelius to return to Florida's rotation. He might pitch out of the bullpen but has made just nine relief appearances in the last five seasons, including the minor leagues. Fernandez' health again could factor into Cornelius' fate.

Alex Fernandez

Position: SP
Bats: R **Throws:** R
Ht: 6' 1" **Wt:** 225

Opening Day Age: 31
Born: 8/13/69 in Miami Beach, FL
ML Seasons: 10

Overall Statistics

	W	L	Pct.	ERA	G	GS	Sv	IP	H	BB	SO	HR	Ratio
2000	4	4	.500	4.13	8	8	0	52.1	59	16	27	7	1.43
Career	107	87	.552	3.74	263	261	0	1760.1	1693	552	1252	190	1.28

2000 Situational Stats

	W	L	ERA	Sv	IP		AB	H	HR	RBI	Avg
Home	3	3	3.43	0	39.1	LHB	84	21	3	11	.250
Road	1	1	6.23	0	13.0	RHB	118	38	4	12	.322
First Half	4	4	4.13	0	52.1	Sc Pos	39	8	0	15	.205
Scnd Half	0	0	-	0	0.0	Clutch	20	8	0	1	.400

2000 Season

Alex Fernandez made just eight starts before going on the disabled list last May with a strained elbow ligament. The injury likely resulted from compensations he had made in his delivery as he recovered from major shoulder surgery in 1997. A course of rest and treatment wasn't enough and he was shut down for good at midseason.

Pitching, Defense & Hitting

Until this latest setback, Fernandez thought he had made it all the way back from his career-threatening surgery on his rotator cuff. His velocity returned to the low 90s and his control was pinpoint. He even threw 121 pitches in his fourth start of the season. When healthy, he shuts down lefthanded batters with offspeed stuff and goes for the kill with two strikes or with runners in scoring position. He fields his position well, holds runners well enough and always has been able to swing the bat.

2001 Outlook

Fernandez hopes to rejoin the Marlins rotation by May 1, but there are no guarantees that he can. This will be the final season of the five-year, $35 million deal he signed to come home. He would love to stay, but he will have to prove he can stay healthy and remain an upper-echelon pitcher before Florida would take another big-money chance on him.

Braden Looper

Position: RP
Bats: R **Throws:** R
Ht: 6' 5" **Wt:** 225

Opening Day Age: 26
Born: 10/28/74 in Weatherford, OK
ML Seasons: 3

Overall Statistics

	W	L	Pct.	ERA	G	GS	Sv	IP	H	BB	SO	HR	Ratio
2000	5	1	.833	4.41	73	0	2	67.1	71	36	29	3	1.59
Career	8	5	.615	4.10	149	0	2	153.2	172	68	83	11	1.56

2000 Situational Stats

	W	L	ERA	Sv	IP		AB	H	HR	RBI	Avg
Home	5	1	4.42	0	38.2	LHB	78	28	2	17	.359
Road	0	0	4.40	2	28.2	RHB	187	43	1	30	.230
First Half	3	1	2.66	1	40.2	Sc Pos	105	27	2	46	.257
Scnd Half	2	0	7.09	1	26.2	Clutch	118	30	1	24	.254

2000 Season

Handed the seventh- or eighth-inning role in a well-defined bullpen, Braden Looper thrived in the first half before wearing down drastically after the break. He credited the arrival of veteran setup man Dan Miceli with aiding his mental approach and seemed to suffer in Miceli's injury-related absence. Looper again proved durable, falling just two appearances short of Robb Nen's club record and reporting no signs of arm trouble.

Pitching, Defense & Hitting

Once touted as a prototypical closer, Looper no longer seems to fit that bill. He gives up too many hits and registers too few strikeouts for the role. He also struggles with lefthanded hitters, who see the ball extremely well against him. The velocity on his fastball fluctuates from 93-98 MPH and his slider tends to flatten out. He does throw a heavy ball, producing a nearly 3-1 groundball-flyball ratio. He is an average fielder at best and rarely bats.

2001 Outlook

While Looper remains another year away from becoming eligible for salary arbitration, few in the organization still would view him as a low-cost alternative to Antonio Alfonseca. The best-case scenario might be a promotion from seventh- to eighth-inning duty.

Dan Miceli

Position: RP
Bats: R **Throws:** R
Ht: 6' 0" **Wt:** 216

Opening Day Age: 30
Born: 9/9/70 in Newark, NJ
ML Seasons: 8
Pronunciation: muh-SELL-ee
Nickname: The Godfather

Overall Statistics

	W	L	Pct.	ERA	G	GS	Sv	IP	H	BB	SO	HR	Ratio
2000	6	4	.600	4.25	45	0	0	48.2	45	18	40	4	1.29
Career	31	31	.500	4.71	388	9	31	449.0	447	206	401	57	1.45

2000 Situational Stats

	W	L	ERA	Sv	IP		AB	H	HR	RBI	Avg
Home	5	2	2.76	0	29.1	LHB	89	24	2	11	.270
Road	1	2	6.52	0	19.1	RHB	97	21	2	12	.216
First Half	3	2	3.74	0	21.2	Sc Pos	47	12	1	19	.255
Scnd Half	3	2	4.67	0	27.0	Clutch	129	31	2	13	.240

2000 Season

Acquired from the Padres in an offseason deal for Brian Meadows, Dan Miceli approached cult-hero status with a sizzling first five weeks. But after making 18 appearances in the Marlins' first 35 games, he was slowed by arm troubles for the second straight year. This time it was an inflamed forearm that caused him to miss all but three outings over a two-month period. His effectiveness tailed off noticeably in the second half.

Pitching, Defense & Hitting

Miceli had a big impact on the young Marlins relievers, showing them the value of swagger, location and the moxie to throw any pitch on any count. His 3-2 changeup to Mark Grace for an early season strikeout only increased the respect factor. Miceli's fastball was in the range of 91-93 MPH when he was healthy, and he displayed a decent curve. The martial arts expert is agile around the mound and holds runners well enough for a reliever. He has only one hit in 19 career at-bats.

2001 Outlook

With one season at $2 million left on his contract, Miceli probably isn't going anywhere. He again will be asked to set up for Antonio Alfonseca, but his second-half struggles likely preclude his role from growing any larger.

Kevin Millar

Position: 1B/LF/3B
Bats: R **Throws:** R
Ht: 6' 0" **Wt:** 210

Opening Day Age: 29
Born: 9/24/71 in Los Angeles, CA
ML Seasons: 3

Overall Statistics

	G	AB	R	H	D	T	HR	RBI	SB	BB	SO	Avg	OBP	Slg
2000	123	259	36	67	14	3	14	42	0	36	47	.259	.364	.498
Career	230	612	85	168	31	7	23	109	1	77	111	.275	.364	.461

2000 Situational Stats

	AB	H	HR	RBI	Avg		AB	H	HR	RBI	Avg
Home	133	32	6	18	.241	LHP	71	18	6	14	.254
Road	126	35	8	24	.278	RHP	188	49	8	28	.261
First Half	159	45	8	23	.283	Sc Pos	76	21	2	27	.276
Scnd Half	100	22	6	19	.220	Clutch	54	16	2	9	.296

2000 Season

Determined to increase his power and build on the solid gains of his rookie season, Kevin Millar reported to spring training with 15 extra pounds of muscle. He outhit Derrek Lee and opened the year starting at first base, but he could not hold off his more talented rival. As Millar's playing time diminished, he struggled in a bench role, hitting just .209 in 43 pinch-hit at-bats.

Hitting, Baserunning & Defense

Millar knows what to do with a middle-in fastball and can make pitchers pay for mistakes. But he is susceptible to high fastballs and sliders away. He has extremely limited range but does a decent job with the balls he gets to. Millar filled in on occasion at third base and left field. He moves a little better at third, which he played a bit in the minors. He is a below-average baserunner.

2001 Outlook

Millar was on the borderline of qualifying for Super Two salary arbitration status. His strong rookie season could push his salary beyond what the Marlins would like to pay a glorified pinch-hitter, and there are other teams that could use him on a more regular basis. For now he'll serve as insurance in case Lee drops into another prolonged funk.

Vladimir Nunez

Position: SP
Bats: R **Throws:** R
Ht: 6' 4" **Wt:** 224

Opening Day Age: 26
Born: 3/15/75 in Havana, Cuba
ML Seasons: 3
Pronunciation: NOON-yez

Overall Statistics

	W	L	Pct.	ERA	G	GS	Sv	IP	H	BB	SO	HR	Ratio
2000	0	6	.000	7.90	17	12	0	68.1	88	34	45	12	1.79
Career	7	16	.304	5.68	65	24	1	182.1	190	90	133	23	1.54

2000 Situational Stats

	W	L	ERA	Sv	IP		AB	H	HR	RBI	Avg
Home	0	2	7.16	0	32.2	LHB	112	38	6	22	.339
Road	0	4	8.58	0	35.2	RHB	164	50	6	36	.305
First Half	0	6	8.35	0	60.1	Sc Pos	79	27	5	47	.342
Scnd Half	0	0	4.50	0	8.0	Clutch	9	3	0	1	.333

2000 Season

Vladimir Nunez opened last year as Florida's No. 3 starter but lasted barely two months before getting shipped to the minors. The once-ballyhooed Cuban defector drove club officials crazy with his insistence on experimenting with a variety of arm angles and release points. Recalled in September, he pitched out of the bullpen with middling results.

Pitching, Defense & Hitting

Three months in Triple-A finally convinced Nunez he's not El Duque Lite. Nunez learned to pitch consistently from the same arm angle, which gave him better movement on his two-seam fastball. While he throws hard enough and has a good slider, he largely shelved his changeup and split-finger working in relief. He threw a few four-seamers but now realizes he has to be careful about catching too much of the strike zone. He is an above-average fielder, especially for a man his size. He could do a much better job holding baserunners. He tends to get sloppy with his pickoff move and can be slow to home plate.

2001 Outlook

Nunez planned to play winter ball in the Dominican and was hopeful of regaining his spot in the rotation. But that won't be easy. The best-case scenario is likely a spot in middle relief.

Mike Redmond

Position: C
Bats: R **Throws:** R
Ht: 6' 1" **Wt:** 185

Opening Day Age: 29
Born: 5/5/71 in Seattle, WA
ML Seasons: 3

Overall Statistics

	G	AB	R	H	D	T	HR	RBI	SB	BB	SO	Avg	OBP	Slg
2000	87	210	17	53	8	1	0	15	0	13	19	.252	.316	.300
Career	208	570	49	165	26	1	3	54	0	44	69	.289	.354	.354

2000 Situational Stats

	AB	H	HR	RBI	Avg		AB	H	HR	RBI	Avg
Home	105	30	0	9	.286	LHP	81	26	0	4	.321
Road	105	23	0	6	.219	RHP	129	27	0	11	.209
First Half	128	33	0	6	.258	Sc Pos	53	14	0	15	.264
Scnd Half	82	20	0	9	.244	Clutch	28	6	0	1	.214

2000 Season

After prospect Ramon Castro fell on his face in spring training, Mike Redmond shared Florida's catching duties through the season's first half. Once Castro was recalled, Redmond served as his caddie, seeing only spot time against southpaws and serving as Ryan Dempster's personal catcher.

Hitting, Baserunning & Defense

Marlin catchers comprised the last position in the majors to homer in 2000, in part due to Redmond's popgun bat. After hitting better than .300 each of his first two seasons, his average, on-base percentage and slugging percentage slid significantly as pitchers learned to pound him inside with hard stuff. But soft-tossing lefties still don't know how to get him out. Marlins pitchers love throwing to him, and he deserves as much credit as anyone for the emergence of Dempster into an All-Star and flighty Antonio Alfonseca into an elite closer. Redmond is slow, but he hustles on the bases.

2001 Outlook

Redmond was one of several Marlins on the cusp of Super Two arbitration status. Any significant raise could jeopardize his standing as a backup on a low-budget ballclub. The organization worships his makeup but the signing of Charles Johnson makes Redmond little more than a luxury.

Henry Rodriguez

Position: LF
Bats: L **Throws:** L
Ht: 6' 2" **Wt:** 225

Opening Day Age: 33
Born: 11/8/67 in Santo Domingo, Dominican Republic
ML Seasons: 9

Overall Statistics

	G	AB	R	H	D	T	HR	RBI	SB	BB	SO	Avg	OBP	Slg
2000	112	367	47	94	21	1	20	61	1	36	99	.256	.327	.482
Career	925	3003	388	783	176	9	160	520	10	272	789	.261	.322	.485

2000 Situational Stats

	AB	H	HR	RBI	Avg		AB	H	HR	RBI	Avg
Home	166	41	7	24	.247	LHP	53	13	2	4	.245
Road	201	53	13	37	.264	RHP	314	81	18	57	.258
First Half	217	55	17	43	.253	Sc Pos	87	22	7	42	.253
Scnd Half	150	39	3	18	.260	Clutch	64	15	6	13	.234

2000 Season

It was a tale of two halves for Henry Rodriguez in 2000. He opened with the Cubs and was on pace to challenge his career-high of 36 homers after two months. Nagging injuries then began to slow him, and a deadline trade to the Marlins came as a shock. He showed little with Florida even before a mysterious bout with migraines reduced him to occasional pinch-hitting duties down the stretch.

Hitting, Baserunning & Defense

Known as a streaky hitter, H-Rod likes to jump on first-pitch fastballs. When pitchers can set him up, they tend to put him away with sweeping curves and high heat. He likes the ball out over the plate and down in the zone, but his power grew increasingly rare after the All-Star break. His lack of speed leaves him a below-average baserunner and an even worse defender. At times it looks like he isn't even trying. His arm is poor as well.

2001 Outlook

The Marlins wasted no time buying out Rodriguez' expensive option for $600,000. At 33, he probably will have to scrounge for employment, with an incentive-laden contract the most likely scenario. Though he never has played in the American League, he admits he is open to the possibility of working as a DH.

Chuck Smith

Position: SP
Bats: R **Throws:** R
Ht: 6' 1" **Wt:** 185

Opening Day Age: 31
Born: 10/21/69 in Memphis, TN
ML Seasons: 1

Overall Statistics

	W	L	Pct.	ERA	G	GS	Sv	IP	H	BB	SO	HR	Ratio
2000	6	6	.500	3.23	19	19	0	122.2	111	54	118	6	1.35
Career	6	6	.500	3.23	19	19	0	122.2	111	54	118	6	1.35

2000 Situational Stats

	W	L	ERA	Sv	IP		AB	H	HR	RBI	Avg
Home	2	4	2.19	0	61.2	LHB	179	43	2	21	.240
Road	4	2	4.28	0	61.0	RHB	268	68	4	26	.254
First Half	0	2	2.76	0	32.2	Sc Pos	95	23	2	38	.242
Scnd Half	6	4	3.40	0	90.0	Clutch	28	7	0	3	.250

2000 Season

After spending nearly 10 years knocking around the minors, including stints in Taiwan and the Northern League, Chuck Smith finally got his major league chance. Rescued from the Rangers' Triple-A club in mid-June, Smith stayed in Florida's rotation the rest of the year. His record was deceiving due to poor run support.

Pitching, Defense & Hitting

Smith gets tremendous natural movement on all the pitches in his vast repertoire. He throws a four-seamer that can reach 94 MPH, a two-seamer in the low 90s, a sweeping spike curve and a Vulcan changeup with split-finger action. He's not afraid to challenge hitters and knows how to put them away. His command escaped him at times, but he always seemed to get it back. Smith is active on the mound and has a good pickoff move. He largely is helpless with the bat, managing just one sacrifice bunt in nearly four months of work.

2001 Outlook

Late last season, Marlins manager John Boles said Smith had shown enough to be penciled in as the No. 3 starter. Smith finally may have come into his own at age 31. It won't be easy to hold off the Marlins' endless wave of young starters, but he just might have the makeup and stuff to do it.

Other Florida Marlins

Armando Almanza (Pos: LHP, Age: 28)

	W	L	Pct.	ERA	G	GS	Sv	IP	H	BB	SO	HR	Ratio
2000	4	2	.667	4.86	67	0	0	46.1	38	43	46	3	1.75
Career	4	3	.571	4.06	81	0	0	62.0	46	52	66	4	1.58

Almanza appeared in a ton of games last year, but you can only be so effective when you walk a batter an inning. Though he's a flyball pitcher, he wasn't hurt by the home run. 2001 Outlook: B

Manny Aybar (Pos: RHP, Age: 26)

	W	L	Pct.	ERA	G	GS	Sv	IP	H	BB	SO	HR	Ratio
2000	2	2	.500	4.31	54	0	0	79.1	74	35	45	11	1.37
Career	14	17	.452	5.06	151	27	3	325.2	334	142	217	38	1.46

After switching between four teams in the space of eight months, Aybar will hope for greater stability this year. The rubber-armed hurler can seemingly throw every day. 2001 Outlook: A

Dave Berg (Pos: SS/2B/3B, Age: 30, Bats: R)

	G	AB	R	H	D	T	HR	RBI	SB	BB	SO	Avg	OBP	Slg
2000	82	210	23	53	14	1	1	21	3	25	46	.252	.340	.343
Career	272	696	83	197	43	2	6	67	8	78	151	.283	.358	.376

Berg can play any infield position and not hurt you, though his range may be a bit limited. He does nothing exceptional on offense. 2001 Outlook: B

Ricky Bones (Pos: RHP, Age: 31)

	W	L	Pct.	ERA	G	GS	Sv	IP	H	BB	SO	HR	Ratio
2000	2	3	.400	4.54	56	0	0	77.1	94	27	59	6	1.56
Career	59	78	.431	4.84	314	164	1	1214.1	1351	431	523	160	1.47

After getting released by Baltimore in 1999, Bones hooked on with the Marlins. He remains very hittable but signed a new contract with Florida in November. 2001 Outlook: B

Chris Clapinski (Pos: 2B, Age: 29, Bats: B)

	G	AB	R	H	D	T	HR	RBI	SB	BB	SO	Avg	OBP	Slg
2000	34	49	12	15	4	1	1	7	0	5	7	.306	.370	.490
Career	70	105	18	28	5	3	1	9	1	14	19	.267	.358	.400

Clapinski is limited as a player, but he's beaten the odds by making it to the majors after originally signing as a nondrafted free agent. 2001 Outlook: C

Vic Darensbourg (Pos: LHP, Age: 30)

	W	L	Pct.	ERA	G	GS	Sv	IP	H	BB	SO	HR	Ratio
2000	5	3	.625	4.06	56	0	0	62.0	61	28	59	7	1.44
Career	5	11	.313	4.88	171	0	1	167.2	163	79	149	15	1.44

Darensbourg rebounded from a poor 1999 to pitch better last season. He's worked between 56 and 59 games each of the past three years. He signed a three-year extension with the Marlins in December. 2001 Outlook: A

Andy Fox (Pos: SS/3B, Age: 30, Bats: L)

	G	AB	R	H	D	T	HR	RBI	SB	BB	SO	Avg	OBP	Slg
2000	100	250	29	58	8	2	4	20	10	22	53	.232	.302	.328
Career	473	1246	169	311	46	10	22	111	41	125	248	.250	.332	.356

A fine athlete, Fox looked like he was coming into his own in 1998 with Arizona. He was traded to the Marlins last June and played seven positions overall. Florida re-signed him to a one-year deal in mid-November and likely will keep him in a utility role. 2001 Outlook: A

Jason Grilli (Pos: RHP, Age: 24)

	W	L	Pct.	ERA	G	GS	Sv	IP	H	BB	SO	HR	Ratio
2000	1	0	1.000	5.40	1	1	0	6.2	11	2	3	0	1.95
Career	1	0	1.000	5.40	1	1	0	6.2	11	2	3	0	1.95

A former first-round pick of the Giants, Grilli came to the Marlins in the Livan Hernandez deal in 1999. Despite a fastball that touches the mid-90s, Grilli surrenders a lot of hits. 2001 Outlook: C

Mendy Lopez (Pos: SS, Age: 26, Bats: R)

	G	AB	R	H	D	T	HR	RBI	SB	BB	SO	Avg	OBP	Slg
2000	4	3	0	0	0	0	0	0	0	1	1	.000	.250	.000
Career	85	229	20	58	10	3	1	18	5	13	46	.253	.298	.336

Lopez hit for a hefty average along with decent power for a shortstop at Triple-A last year. He also has experience at second and third. He signed with Houston in November. 2001 Outlook: C

Ron Mahay (Pos: LHP, Age: 29)

	W	L	Pct.	ERA	G	GS	Sv	IP	H	BB	SO	HR	Ratio
2000	1	1	.500	7.19	23	2	0	41.1	57	25	32	10	1.98
Career	7	2	.778	4.35	86	3	2	111.2	110	54	83	17	1.47

The Marlins acquired Mahay from Oakland for cash considerations last May. Once a minor league outfielder, he was troubled by walks and homers last season, a combustible combination. He signed with San Diego in November. 2001 Outlook: C

Sandy Martinez (Pos: C, Age: 28, Bats: L)

	G	AB	R	H	D	T	HR	RBI	SB	BB	SO	Avg	OBP	Slg
2000	10	18	1	4	2	0	0	0	0	0	8	.222	.222	.333
Career	213	557	39	130	32	4	6	51	1	37	144	.233	.287	.338

Martinez' defensive skills always have been solid, and at age 27 he surprised by hitting .300 with power at Triple-A last year. He has signed a minor league deal with Montreal for this season. 2001 Outlook: C

Mark Smith (Pos: LF/RF, Age: 30, Bats: R)

	G	AB	R	H	D	T	HR	RBI	SB	BB	SO	Avg	OBP	Slg
2000	104	192	22	47	8	1	5	27	2	17	54	.245	.310	.375
Career	301	702	89	171	34	2	23	102	15	70	160	.244	.317	.396

After knocking 20 homers in Japan in 1999, Smith returned to the majors in the same peripheral role he always had. He has signed a minor league deal with Montreal for this season. 2001 Outlook: C

Joe Strong (Pos: RHP, Age: 38)

	W	L	Pct.	ERA	G	GS	Sv	IP	H	BB	SO	HR	Ratio
2000	1	1	.500	7.32	18	0	1	19.2	26	12	18	3	1.93
Career	1	1	.500	7.32	18	0	1	19.2	26	12	18	3	1.93

Strong was an exceptional story last year, making his major league debut at the age of 37 after having worked previously in Taiwan, Korea and Mexico. He re-signed with Florida in early November. 2001 Outlook: D

Florida

Florida Marlins Minor League Prospects

Organization Overview:

Last year contained no drastic salary dumping moves for the Marlins; in fact they actually *traded for* Henry Rodriguez and Chuck Smith. But that wasn't the biggest news out of South Florida. Only a full season removed from a 108-loss season, the young Marlins hovered around .500 all season, finishing with 79 wins, just 15.5 games behind the division-leading Braves. With all of the talent that already has advanced to the majors, the system is having a hard time keeping up with producing prospects. The farm is far from barren, however, as power-arms still lead the way. Even after signing Josh Beckett to a $7 million deal in 1999, the financially-strapped Marlins remained aggressive in the 2000 draft, anteing up for their first three picks, Adrian Gonzalez, Jason Stokes and Rob Henkel.

Wes Anderson

Position: P **Opening Day Age:** 21
Bats: R **Throws:** R **Born:** 9/10/79 in Pine
Ht: 6' 4" **Wt:** 175 Bluff, AR

Recent Statistics

	W	L	ERA	G	GS	Sv	IP	H	R	BB	SO	HR
1999 A Kane County	9	5	3.21	23	23	0	137.1	111	55	51	134	8
2000 A Brevard Cty	6	9	3.42	22	21	0	115.2	108	55	66	91	5

Flourishing in the shadows of the system's high-profile power arms, Anderson quietly has established himself as a bright young prospect with a lively fastball. A 14th-round pick in 1997, the 21-year-old righty mows hitters down with a mid-90s fastball, a filthy slider and a changeup from a free and easy delivery. Tall and lean, Anderson was sidetracked for the second straight year with shoulder tendinitis. Although he's expected to recover, the injury may have hindered his control last year as his strikeout-walk ratio suffered a noticeable decline from the previous season. At 21, he's still ahead of schedule and should pitch a full season at Double-A this year, provided he's healthy.

Josh Beckett

Position: P **Opening Day Age:** 20
Bats: R **Throws:** R **Born:** 5/15/80 in Spring,
Ht: 6' 4" **Wt:** 190 TX

Recent Statistics

	W	L	ERA	G	GS	Sv	IP	H	R	BB	SO	HR
2000 A Kane County	2	3	2.12	13	12	0	59.1	45	18	15	61	4

A Texas phenom in the high school ranks, Beckett attracted attention with his mid- to high-90s heat, and drew the inevitable comparisons to some of the state's legends: Roger Clemens, Nolan Ryan and Kerry Wood. Florida used the second overall pick in '99 on him and locked him up with a four-year contract after that season. He made his much-anticipated debut in big league camp

last spring and didn't disappoint. His poise, 95-MPH smoke, knee-buckling 12-to-6 curve and polished changeup fueled the hype about his regular season debut in the Midwest League. He overmatched the Class-A circuit with his devastating three-pitch arsenal, but he was hampered with lingering tendinitis. He was making progress and strengthening his shoulder in instructional league, putting him back on the fast track this year.

Cesar Crespo

Position: OF **Opening Day Age:** 21
Bats: B **Throws:** R **Born:** 5/23/79 in Rio
Ht: 5' 11" **Wt:** 170 Piedras, PR

Recent Statistics

	G	AB	R	H	D	T	HR	RBI	SB	BB	SO	Avg
1999 A Brevard Cty	115	427	63	122	17	2	6	40	22	62	86	.286
2000 AA Portland	134	482	96	124	21	6	9	60	41	77	118	.257
2000 MLE	134	463	74	105	17	5	6	46	28	51	126	.227

A highly coveted third-round pick by the Mets out of Puerto Rico in '97, Crespo is developing into a versatile prospect. Drafted as a shortstop, the switch-hitter can play all three outfield slots and has the hands and range to handle the middle of the infield. He has excellent bat speed and is effective at reaching base and using his foot speed. His 41 steals were second in the Double-A Eastern League last year. He demonstrates occasional power from both sides of the plate, and could develop more pop with added strength. Crespo could break into the majors as a utility player within a year.

Geoff Goetz

Position: P **Opening Day Age:** 21
Bats: L **Throws:** L **Born:** 4/3/79 in Pompton
Ht: 5' 11" **Wt:** 163 Plains, NJ

Recent Statistics

	W	L	ERA	G	GS	Sv	IP	H	R	BB	SO	HR
1999 A Kane County	5	3	4.26	16	12	0	50.2	52	28	24	43	4
2000 A Brevard Cty	6	2	1.75	27	0	5	67.0	43	19	36	61	1
2000 AA Portland	1	2	5.96	17	0	1	22.2	27	15	11	21	3

Shoulder injuries never allowed the former Mets first-rounder to showcase his best stuff before last year. In an effort to aid Goetz' progress, the Marlins, who acquired the southpaw in the Mike Piazza deal, shifted him to a relief role. He pitched every third day with a 55-pitch limit. The results were an overwhelming success, as Goetz emerged as a dominating force out of the pen in the Class-A Florida State League. Armed with a sharp curve that rated as the best breaking pitch in the FSL, a 90-MPH fastball and a deceptive change, he permitted just 43 hits in 67 innings before earning a promotion to Double-A. Goetz pitched more regularly in Portland and showed he needs to sharpen the command of his fastball. Once he hones his control, he won't be far from jumping into the Marlins' pen.

Abraham Nunez

Position: DH
Bats: B **Throws:** R
Ht: 6' 2" **Wt:** 186

Opening Day Age: 21
Born: 2/5/80 in Haina, DR

Recent Statistics

	G	AB	R	H	D	T	HR	RBI	SB	BB	SO	Avg
1999 A High Desert	130	488	106	133	29	6	22	93	40	86	122	.273
2000 A Brevard Cty	31	103	17	20	4	0	1	9	11	28	34	.194
2000 AA Portland	74	221	39	61	17	3	6	42	8	44	64	.276
2000 MLE	74	211	30	51	14	2	4	32	5	29	68	.242

Arizona tried to block Nunez from being the player to be named in the Matt Mantei deal. A shoulder injury prevented him from showing off his electrifying five-tool potential for most of the year. As a designated hitter, he still managed to provide a glimpse of the talent that caught everyone's eye in '99 when he ripped 22 homers, stole 40 bases and drew 86 walks. But, it wasn't until instructional league that he was able to resume firing missiles in from the outfield with one of the strongest outfield arms in the minors. He could still be on track to challenge for a big league job by 2002.

Pablo Ozuna

Position: 2B
Bats: R **Throws:** R
Ht: 6' 0" **Wt:** 160

Opening Day Age: 22
Born: 8/25/78 in Santo Domingo, DR

Recent Statistics

	G	AB	R	H	D	T	HR	RBI	SB	BB	SO	Avg
2000 AA Portland	118	464	74	143	25	6	7	59	35	40	55	.308
2000 NL Florida	14	24	2	8	1	0	0	0	1	0	2	.333
2000 MLE	118	442	57	121	21	4	5	45	24	26	58	.274

Ozuna spent his second full year in Double-A at the age of 21. One of the keys to the Edgar Renteria trade with the Cardinals in 1998, he established himself as a prospect in '98 by tearing up the Midwest League to the tune of .357, with 62 steals. He skipped a level to the Eastern League after the trade, but it hasn't affected his hitting. He improved his strike-zone judgment last year and boosted his on-base percentage over 50 points. A converted shortstop, he committed 25 errors in his first season at second base, and with speedster Luis Castillo blocking his path in Florida, another defensive change isn't out of the question. Ozuna is headed to Triple-A.

Nate Rolison

Position: 1B
Bats: L **Throws:** R
Ht: 6' 6" **Wt:** 240

Opening Day Age: 24
Born: 3/27/77 in Hattiesburg, MS

Recent Statistics

	G	AB	R	H	D	T	HR	RBI	SB	BB	SO	Avg
2000 AAA Calgary	123	443	88	146	37	3	23	88	3	70	117	.330
2000 NL Florida	8	13	0	1	0	0	0	2	0	1	4	.077
2000 MLE	123	410	58	113	29	2	13	58	1	47	122	.276

Rolison isn't the first power-hitting first baseman to get overlooked coming up through the organization, but he's making it hard to ignore his production. Last year after posting a .582 slugging percentage with 37 doubles and 23 jacks, the Marlins rewarded him with a September

cup-of-coffee. A 1995 second-rounder, he did little to distinguish himself in consecutive trips to the Double-A Eastern League before breaking out last year. Rolison became a more well-rounded hitter after adjusting his strike zone. He suffered a broken hamate bone in his right wrist in winter ball, but he's expected to be ready by the start of spring training. A massive 6-foot-6 and 240 pounds, he is improving his agility around the bag, but Derrek Lee's emergence makes Rolison expendable.

Claudio Vargas

Position: P
Bats: R **Throws:** R
Ht: 6' 3" **Wt:** 210

Opening Day Age: 21
Born: 5/19/79 in Valverde Mao, DR

Recent Statistics

	W	L	ERA	G	GS	Sv	IP	H	R	BB	SO	HR
1999 A Kane County	5	5	3.88	19	19	0	99.2	97	47	41	88	8
2000 A Brevard Cty	10	5	3.28	24	23	0	145.1	126	64	44	143	10
2000 AA Portland	1	1	3.60	3	2	0	15.0	16	9	6	13	1

Signed as a 16-year-old out of the Dominican Republic in 1995, Vargas spent two seasons tuning up in the Dominican Summer League before coming stateside to showcase his lively arm. He began to turn some heads in 1999 as he filled out his frame. But last year he did more than fill out. Vargas went 10-5 with a 3.28 ERA while limiting opponents to a .235 average in the Florida State League. He earned a late-season promotion to Double-A en route to claiming the organization's minor league Pitcher of the Year award. He effectively keeps the ball down and in the park by throwing a heavy fastball in the low-90s range, along with an advanced changeup and curveball combination. Vargas will continue his rapid ascent in Double-A this year with an eye on a 2002 opportunity in South Florida.

Others to Watch

The Marlins used the first overall pick last June on San Diego high school first baseman **Adrian Gonzalez** (18), and had him signed to a $3 million deal before his name was announced. The smooth-swinging lefty is an advanced hitter for his age. . . Using a polished four-pitch attack out of the bullpen, **Bryan Moore** (24) recorded 27 saves in Class-A while exhibiting outstanding command and resilience with his 88-92 MPH darting fastball and diving splitter. . . Righthander **Blaine Neal** (23) spent the 1998 season as a first baseman struggling at the plate with a .190 average. Back on the mound, the 6-foot-5 power pitcher projects as a potential closer with mid-90s heat. He's also armed with a deadly slider. . . Some think Florida's second-round pick last year, first baseman **Jason Stokes** (19), was one of the best power-hitting prospects in the draft. But signability may have caused him to slide. He signed after the season and showcased his tremendous power in Instructional League. . . **Josh Wilson** (20) is a smooth shortstop with quick feet and sound instincts. He demonstrates surprising power for his size, hit .344 in the New York-Penn League and runs well, too.

Florida

Enron Field

Offense

Enron Field's effect on offense is highly exaggerated. The Astros had a home-road run differential of +72. The Rockies, a truly mediocre offensive club, had a home-road run difference of +298. Most of the positive difference that Enron has on offenses is the ease at which home runs fly out. The Astros hit 21 more home runs at home than on the road—roughly one every four games—but this was one of the most powerful teams in baseball.

Defense

Enron's short fences down the lines account for much of the difference in both home runs and doubles from other parks. Enron also has a minimum of foul territory, which costs pitchers outs on foul balls. Both factors tend to favor hurlers who can sink the ball down in the strike zone and pitch to the outside half of the plate. The quirky angles of Enron's outfield walls quickly expose defensive weaknesses.

Who It Helps the Most

Jeff Bagwell, a pull hitter who hits the ball high in the air, was unstoppable at home in 2000—a big change from his Astrodome-hampered past. Most of the Astros' young power hitters—Lance Berkman, Darryl Ward and Chris Truby—benefited significantly from playing at home. Chris Holt, with his hard sinker, was easily the team's most effective pitcher at Enron.

Who It Hurts the Most

Just as Enron's reputation is somewhat exaggerated, so is its effect on the Astros' shell-shocked pitching duo of Jose Lima and Octavio Dotel. Both struggled at home, but both were miserably ineffective on the road also. No Astro regular starter had an ERA of more than one run greater at home than on the road. Richard Hidalgo's home-run numbers suffered significantly at Enron, but he made it up with a reversed ratio of doubles.

Rookies & Newcomers

The Astros won't see many changes in their starting lineup in 2001. But it's easy to see that newcomers such as Brad Ausmus will be attracted by Enron. The opposite is true for pitchers.

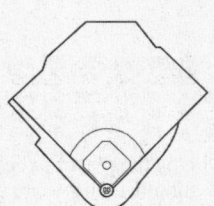

Dimensions: LF-315, LCF-362, CF-435, RCF-373, RF-326

Capacity: 40,950

Elevation: 22 feet

Surface: Grass

Foul Territory: Small

Park Factors

2000 Season

	Home Games			Away Games			
	Astros	Opp	Total	Astros	Opp	Total	Index
G	72	72	144	75	75	150	—
Avg	.282	.290	.286	.273	.272	.273	105
AB	2422	2617	5039	2644	2548	5192	101
R	463	462	925	403	404	807	119
H	682	760	1442	722	693	1415	106
2B	138	154	292	121	134	255	118
3B	24	27	51	10	16	26	202
HR	123	119	242	104	98	202	123
BB	313	273	586	308	280	588	103
SO	478	492	970	547	463	1010	99
E	54	41	95	67	56	123	80
E-Infield	46	33	79	52	48	100	82
LHB-Avg	.283	.320	.307	.293	.287	.290	106
LHB-HR	39	58	97	26	46	72	142
RHB-Avg	.281	.267	.275	.265	.260	.263	105
RHB-HR	84	61	145	78	52	130	113

1998-1999 (Astrodome)

	Home Games			Away Games			
	Astros	Opp	Total	Astros	Opp	Total	Index
G	149	149	298	146	146	292	—
Avg	.275	.253	.264	.268	.271	.269	98
AB	4980	5208	10188	5134	4983	10117	99
R	768	571	1339	749	620	1369	96
H	1369	1319	2688	1377	1348	2725	97
2B	307	271	578	260	230	490	117
3B	26	28	54	20	29	49	109
HR	131	117	248	165	138	303	81
BB	645	419	1064	587	453	1040	102
SO	1035	1218	2253	1038	967	2005	112
E	96	123	219	100	118	218	98
E-Infield	73	110	183	86	100	186	96
LHB-Avg	.274	.258	.264	.280	.270	.273	97
LHB-HR	29	45	74	41	49	90	77
RHB-Avg	.275	.250	.264	.265	.271	.268	99
RHB-HR	102	72	174	124	89	213	83

2000 Rankings (National League)

- Highest triple factor
- Second-highest run factor
- Second-highest double factor
- Second-highest home-run factor
- Second-highest LHB home-run factor
- Third-lowest error factor

Larry Dierker

2000 Season

Larry Dierker led the Astros to the playoffs in each of his first three years. He quickly learned the realities of his job when the Astros got off to the worst start in the major leagues. Perhaps the most disturbing faction of discontent came from within the clubhouse, as players questioned his ability to make game decisions. A better second half, with a number of young and hungry players on the field, quieted some of the criticism. At the end of the year, many were surprised when the Astros announced that Dierker would return in 2001.

Offense

The Astros' switch from the Astrodome to run-friendly Enron Field may have been at the heart of many of the questions concerning Dierker's game management strategy. He always has been an advocate of drawing walks, running and stealing bases, and moving runners to score runs. Those strategies were necessary in the Astrodome, but they don't fit into Enron's pinball environment. In general, Dierker likes to use a set lineup, but injuries to key players forced him to juggle his lineup daily.

Pitching & Defense

It's impossible to judge Dierker's use of pitchers based on the 2000 season. His hallmark previously was letting his starters pitch deep into games, preferably to work out of their own problems. Between injuries and ineffectiveness in both the starting rotation and the bullpen, Dierker's decision-making process was more a matter of survival and damage control in 2000. That also could be the case in 2001, especially as the team awaits the recovery of Shane Reynolds from December knee surgery.

2001 Outlook

The Astros' meltdown in 2000 lies on the shoulders of Dierker's veteran players and upper management. The veterans who have been his most vocal critics in the clubhouse and the worst players on the field still are in place. The perception in Houston is that McLane's decision to bring Dierker back rests more on his desire not to waste the $1.5 million that will be paid for the last two years of Dierker's contract than on any real confidence in him. It's a volatile mix that will not survive another slow start.

Born: 9/22/46 in Hollywood, CA

Playing Experience: 1964-1977, Hou, StL

Managerial Experience: 4 seasons

Manager Statistics

Year	Team, Lg	W	L	Pct	GB	Finish
2000	Houston, NL	72	90	.444	23.0	4th Central
4 Seasons		342	279	.551	—	—

2000 Starting Pitchers by Days Rest

	<=3	4	5	6+
Astros Starts	1	85	55	11
Astros ERA	18.90	5.80	5.27	4.50
NL Avg Starts	2	80	50	21
NL ERA	5.00	4.61	4.60	5.18

2000 Situational Stats

	Larry Dierker	NL Average
Hit & Run Success %	34.5	33.8
Stolen Base Success %	68.7	68.8
Platoon Pct.	48.4	53.2
Defensive Subs	23	19
High-Pitch Outings	19	14
Quick/Slow Hooks	8/29	14/16
Sacrifice Attempts	77	87

2000 Rankings (National League)
- 1st in slow hooks (29)
- 3rd in steals of third base (16) and starts with over 120 pitches (19)

Moises Alou

2000 Season

How often do 34-year-old outfielders put up their career year after missing an entire season with major knee problems? That's exactly what Moises Alou did in 2000, finishing second in the National League batting race at .355. With his 30 home runs, he joined teammates Jeff Bagwell and Richard Hidalgo in leading the Astros to a National League-record 249 longballs.

Hitting

Alou has learned to hit virtually every type of pitch in every type of situation. He is the unique power hitter who both rarely strikes out and rarely walks. In fact, his strikeouts dropped from 87 to 45 from 1998 to 2000—after missing all of 1999—and his walks fell from 84 to 52. That's an incredible metamorphosis for a player of Alou's experience. Alou was perhaps the most effective first-pitch hitter in baseball in 2000, hitting .495 with a .763 slugging percentage when he made contact with the first offering.

Baserunning & Defense

The less said about Alou's defense the better. He started out the 2000 season in left field and proved more stationary than the Enron Field scoreboard. Alou even admitted publicly that he was scared to dive for balls with his surgically repaired knee, especially for a team that then had the worst record in the majors. As the season progressed, Alou moved to right field and became more comfortable and more aggressive, although he still was a liability. He is pretty much a station-to-station baserunner.

2001 Outlook

In light of last summer's production, the $6 million Alou has coming in the last year of his contract in 2001 is a bargain-basement price. The Astros probably are no longer looking to deal him following the trade that sent outfielder Roger Cedeno to the Tigers. Alou also has a no-trade clause that he has used to block deals in the past, and there is no guarantee he will change that approach now. If he stays at Enron, another .330-25-100 season is well within reach.

Position: RF/LF
Bats: R **Throws:** R
Ht: 6' 3" **Wt:** 195

Opening Day Age: 34
Born: 7/3/66 in Atlanta, GA
ML Seasons: 9
Pronunciation: MOY-sezz ah-LOO

Overall Statistics

	G	AB	R	H	D	T	HR	RBI	SB	BB	SO	Avg	OBP	Slg
2000	126	454	82	161	28	2	30	114	3	52	45	.355	.416	.623
Career	1045	3725	617	1127	229	28	175	726	76	389	521	.303	.369	.520

Where He Hits the Ball

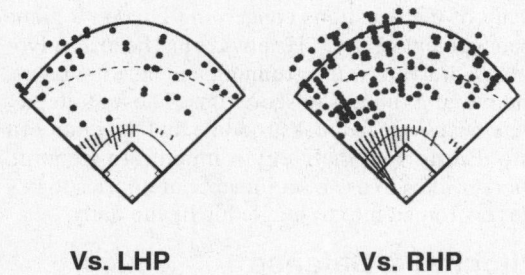

Vs. LHP   **Vs. RHP**

2000 Situational Stats

	AB	H	HR	RBI	Avg		AB	H	HR	RBI	Avg
Home	222	77	17	64	.347	LHP	100	37	8	27	.370
Road	232	84	13	50	.362	RHP	354	124	22	87	.350
First Half	198	71	15	48	.359	Sc Pos	144	49	7	83	.340
Scnd Half	256	90	15	66	.352	Clutch	60	14	2	9	.233

2000 Rankings (National League)

- 1st in GDPs (21)
- 2nd in batting average and batting average on the road
- 3rd in batting average vs. righthanded pitchers and highest percentage of swings on the first pitch (43.2)
- Led the Astros in batting average, singles, sacrifice flies (9), GDPs (21), batting average vs. righthanded pitchers, on-base percentage vs. righthanded pitchers (.417), batting average on the road, highest percentage of swings put into play (46.2) and batting average with two strikes (.230)
- Led NL right fielders in batting average, sacrifice flies (9) and GDPs (21)

Jeff Bagwell

2000 Season

Baseball fans and pundits had been wondering what Jeff Bagwell would do outside the vast spaces of the Astrodome for years, and they found out in 2000. He quietly went about establishing career highs in home runs and runs scored, leading the major leagues in the latter category with an incredible 152 runs. Not surprisingly, he was the biggest beneficiary of Enron's offensive boost, smacking 28 longballs at home against a more human 19 on the road.

Hitting

Bagwell's unique hitting style has changed little over the years, except perhaps for reducing his stride and lower-body action. He has incredible strength in his hands and arms, and combines an aggressive, all-out swing with one of the best batting eyes in the game. Patience was less of a virtue for Bagwell in 2000, but he still managed to top the century mark in free passes for the sixth time in the last seven years.

Baserunning & Defense

Twice Bagwell has claimed membership in the 30-30 club, and he may be the slowest player ever to steal 30 bases in a season on two different occasions. A smart baserunner in the past, he struggled in 2000. It isn't likely that Bagwell will steal 30 bases again. . . not with older legs and a power-laden lineup around him. Bagwell's defense is above average. Many of his errors are from over-aggressiveness, and he has a flair for the spectacular play.

2001 Outlook

Bagwell's contract status had been a constant source of both conversation and distraction in Houston since early in the 2000 season. But that no longer will be the case, as the normally penny-pinching Astros decided to pony up for a five-year, $85 million contract extension through 2006 rather than risk losing their future Hall of Famer to another organization at the peak of his career. Short of injury, the only thing that realistically could have kept Bagwell from another huge season was if the contract situation had remained unresolved.

Position: 1B
Bats: R **Throws:** R
Ht: 6' 0" **Wt:** 195

Opening Day Age: 32
Born: 5/27/68 in Boston, MA
ML Seasons: 10

Overall Statistics

	G	AB	R	H	D	T	HR	RBI	SB	BB	SO	Avg	OBP	Slg
2000	159	590	152	183	37	1	47	132	9	107	116	.310	.424	.615
Career	1476	5349	1073	1630	351	22	310	1093	167	992	1022	.305	.417	.552

Where He Hits the Ball

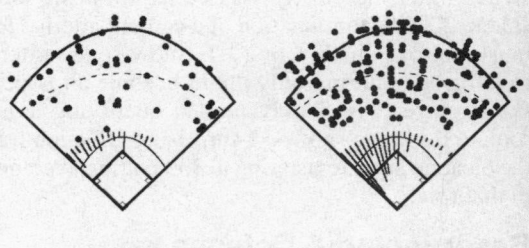

Vs. LHP　　　　**Vs. RHP**

2000 Situational Stats

	AB	H	HR	RBI	Avg		AB	H	HR	RBI	Avg
Home	286	101	28	72	.353	LHP	112	41	9	39	.366
Road	304	82	19	60	.270	RHP	478	142	38	93	.297
First Half	327	96	23	64	.294	Sc Pos	152	46	10	81	.303
Scnd Half	263	87	24	68	.331	Clutch	90	24	5	13	.267

2000 Rankings (National League)

- 1st in runs scored and on-base percentage vs. lefthanded pitchers (.496)
- 2nd in times on base (305)
- 3rd in home runs, RBI, walks, pitches seen (2,812), plate appearances (719) and slugging percentage vs. lefthanded pitchers (.688)
- Led the Astros in home runs, at-bats, runs scored, hits, total bases (363), RBI, walks, intentional walks (11), times on base (305), strikeouts, pitches seen (2,812), plate appearances (719), on-base percentage, HR frequency (12.6 ABs per HR), highest groundball/flyball ratio (0.8), most pitches seen per plate appearance (3.91), batting average vs. lefthanded pitchers and batting average on an 0-2 count (.268)

Lance Berkman

Position: RF/LF
Bats: B **Throws:** L
Ht: 6' 1" **Wt:** 205

Opening Day Age: 25
Born: 2/10/76 in Waco, TX
ML Seasons: 2

2000 Season

There was no obvious place for Lance Berkman to play at the start of the season, and there even was speculation that he might have to mark most of his time at Triple-A New Orleans. An injury to Roger Cedeno along with Darryl Ward's weight and defensive woes gave Berkman an opening, and he quickly established himself as a bona-fide big league power hitter.

Hitting

Berkman has a chance to become a true multi-skilled offensive threat, combining the power to hit home runs with the plate discipline and ability to hit for a high average. Although Berkman is a switch-hitter, he clearly was better from the left side in 2000, a continuation of a career pattern. He must improve quickly, or a J.T. Snow-style switch to lefthanded hitting only might become an issue. For a player who barely missed qualifying as a rookie, Berkman showed a surprising affection for the cleanup spot, registering a .339 batting average in that role.

Baserunning & Defense

Berkman started the year off in right field, the first time he had played that position regularly, but was switched back to left when the defensive work of Moises Alou and Daryle Ward proved inadequate for Enron Field's tricky angles. Berkman is a hard-working defender with a strong arm who is prone to misjudging flyballs on occasion. He has below-average speed on the bases, but he is far from a base clogger and will take an extra sack if the opportunity presents itself.

2001 Outlook

Berkman clearly is ahead of Ward in the running for the third outfield spot in Houston and Cedeno was traded to the Tigers in mid-December. Alou and Richard Hidalgo already are secure at the other two outfield positions. With a hot spring, Berkman could even step back into the cleanup role he was so comfortable with in 2000.

Overall Statistics

	G	AB	R	H	D	T	HR	RBI	SB	BB	SO	Avg	OBP	Slg
2000	114	353	76	105	28	1	21	67	6	56	73	.297	.388	.561
Career	148	446	86	127	30	1	25	82	11	68	94	.285	.375	.525

Where He Hits the Ball

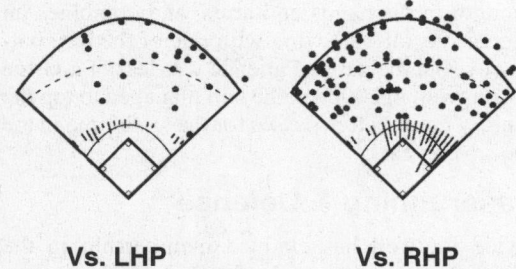

Vs. LHP   **Vs. RHP**

2000 Situational Stats

	AB	H	HR	RBI	Avg		AB	H	HR	RBI	Avg
Home	166	53	10	33	.319	LHP	78	17	2	11	.218
Road	187	52	11	34	.278	RHP	275	88	19	56	.320
First Half	167	50	12	33	.299	Sc Pos	100	20	4	44	.200
Scnd Half	186	55	9	34	.296	Clutch	54	19	4	14	.352

2000 Rankings (National League)

- 3rd in cleanup slugging percentage (.696)
- 5th in errors in right field (6)
- 6th in lowest batting average with runners in scoring position
- Led the Astros in batting average in the clutch and cleanup slugging percentage (.696)
- Led NL left fielders in cleanup slugging percentage (.696) and steals of third (3)

Craig Biggio

2000 Season

Prior to 2000, Craig Biggio had a well-deserved reputation as perhaps the most durable post-Ripken player in baseball, never having been on the disabled list during his 12-plus year Astros career. That ended after 101 games when Biggio tore two ligaments in his left knee turning a double play. But even before that, there were significant concerns that Biggio had lost both a step in the field and some of his trademark bat quickness.

Hitting

The power that made Biggio such a multi-tiered offensive threat throughout his career was noticeably missing before the injury, a concern made worse by the switch to the friendly confines of Enron Field. A slashing hitter who peppered the left-field wall while leading baseball with 56 doubles in 1999, Biggio was no longer able to consistently turn on pitches last year. Biggio's plate discipline continues to make him a valuable top-of-the-order hitter, though.

Baserunning & Defense

Before the injury, there actually was more concern over Biggio's defense than his offense. Usually scouts talk about a player losing a step in the field, but for Biggio they were talking about losing *two* steps. A balky knee won't help Biggio return to his former Gold Glove level, either. Biggio's stolen-base totals had been declining for a couple of years prior to 2000, and this is another area that likely will be affected by age and injury.

2001 Outlook

Biggio will have to address pre-injury concerns about his declining performance, along with proving his surgically repaired knee is healthy, right from the start of the 2001 season. The biggest concern will be his defense, but also under scrutiny will be his power. Biggio has three years left on the lucrative contract he signed prior to 2000, so he's not going anywhere. The Astros signed Jose Vizcaino in the offseason partly to cover second if Biggio needs more recovery time at the start of the season.

Position: 2B
Bats: R **Throws:** R
Ht: 5'11" **Wt:** 180

Opening Day Age: 35
Born: 12/14/65 in Smithtown, NY
ML Seasons: 13
Pronunciation: BIDG-jee-oh

Houston

Overall Statistics

	G	AB	R	H	D	T	HR	RBI	SB	BB	SO	Avg	OBP	Slg
2000	101	377	67	101	13	5	8	35	12	61	73	.268	.388	.393
Career	1800	6766	1187	1969	402	43	160	741	358	847	1046	.291	.381	.434

Where He Hits the Ball

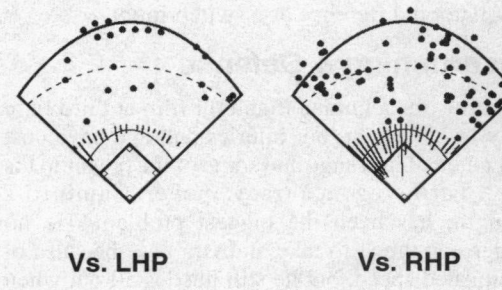

Vs. LHP   **Vs. RHP**

2000 Situational Stats

	AB	H	HR	RBI	Avg		AB	H	HR	RBI	Avg
Home	170	44	2	15	.259	LHP	68	16	0	3	.235
Road	207	57	6	20	.275	RHP	309	85	8	32	.275
First Half	305	77	5	29	.252	Sc Pos	65	18	1	26	.277
Scnd Half	72	24	3	6	.333	Clutch	50	8	0	2	.160

2000 Rankings (National League)

- 2nd in on-base percentage for a leadoff hitter (.413)
- 3rd in fielding percentage at second base (.987)
- 4th in hit by pitch (16)
- 5th in lowest percentage of extra bases taken as a runner (31.8)
- 6th in batting average on a 3-1 count (.667) and lowest batting average in the clutch
- 7th in batting average on a 3-2 count (.361)
- Led the Astros in triples, on-base percentage for a leadoff hitter (.413), bunts in play (11) and batting average on a 3-2 count (.361)
- Led NL second basemen in batting average on a 3-1 count (.667)

Ken Caminiti

Position: 3B
Bats: B **Throws:** R
Ht: 6' 0" **Wt:** 200

Opening Day Age: 37
Born: 4/21/63 in Hanford, CA
ML Seasons: 14
Pronunciation: kam-un-NET-ee
Nickname: The Gun

2000 Season

Ken Caminiti was on course for one of his best offensive seasons before rupturing a tendon in his right wrist on a swing and undergoing surgery. He was slated to possibly return in September but abruptly left the club for personal reasons. It has been reported that Caminiti entered a substance abuse facility during the offseason.

Hitting

Like many veteran hitters, Caminiti has learned how to recognize what pitches he can drive and what pitches he needs to lay off. The result is more power and more walks. The most surprising thing about Caminiti's offensive evolution since his first stint with the Astros is that he no longer has any real platoon difference as a switch-hitter.

Baserunning & Defense

Caminiti was a human highlight film at third base early in his career, but injuries and age have cost him much of his range and some of the power in his arm. Throwing accuracy, never Caminiti's strength, has been the biggest problem. He no longer is a threat to take an extra base because of diminished speed, but he still hustles all out when he's on the basepaths.

2001 Outlook

The Astros did not pick up Caminiti's $5.5 million option for 2001, and he agreed to terms with the Rangers on a two-year, $9.5 million deal. If healthy, he will be Texas' regular third baseman. He's no longer a vacuum cleaner at the hot corner, but if he can come back strong both physically and mentally, he'll be a key part of a formidable lineup that also includes Alex Rodriguez, Rafael Palmeiro, Andres Galarraga and Ivan Rodriguez.

Overall Statistics

	G	AB	R	H	D	T	HR	RBI	SB	BB	SO	Avg	OBP	Slg
2000	59	208	42	63	13	0	15	45	3	42	37	.303	.419	.582
Career	1642	5932	858	1629	331	16	224	942	88	684	1078	.275	.349	.449

Where He Hits the Ball

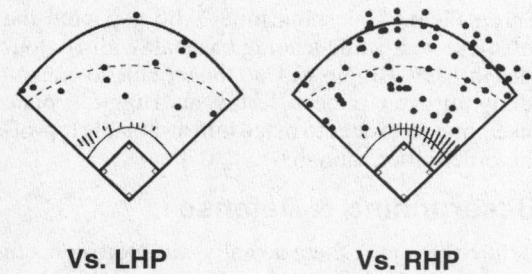

Vs. LHP   **Vs. RHP**

2000 Situational Stats

	AB	H	HR	RBI	Avg		AB	H	HR	RBI	Avg
Home	91	22	9	27	.242	LHP	40	12	1	11	.300
Road	117	41	6	18	.350	RHP	168	51	14	34	.304
First Half	208	63	15	45	.303	Sc Pos	60	18	4	28	.300
Scnd Half	0	0	0	0	--	Clutch	31	9	2	7	.290

2000 Rankings (National League)

- 9th in cleanup slugging percentage (.585)
- Led NL third basemen in cleanup slugging percentage (.585)

Scott Elarton

2000 Season

Scott Elarton underwent shoulder surgery after the 1999 season, which made him a minor question mark entering spring training. He started the season slowly, but became more aggressive as he gained confidence in his arm. Elarton's 17-7 record is somewhat deceiving in that he received an average of more than seven runs of offensive support over his 30 starts, one of the highest totals in baseball. But that record did move Elarton's career mark to 28-13, and paints him has a future top-of-the-rotation starter.

Pitching

Elarton is an extremely intelligent and polished pitcher, especially for a someone only in his mid-20s. He throws three average to above-average pitches with solid command. Elarton's fastball picked up velocity throughout the season; it usually sits in the low 90s and can peak in the 94-95 MPH range. Elarton has experimented with a slider, but he depends on a sharp curveball as his top breaking pitch. He also throws a deceptive changeup.

Defense & Hitting

Despite his 6-foot-7, 240-pound frame, Elarton is an agile athlete and an above-average fielder. He hasn't made an error in the majors. At the plate, Elarton concentrates on making contact and hit a respectable .159 in 2000 while tying for the staff lead with six runs scored.

2001 Outlook

On one hand, it would be unrealistic to expect Elarton to get the same type of run support in 2001 and duplicate his 17-7 record. On the other hand, the fact that he will start the 2001 season strong and healthy—likely with the No. 1 starter's mantel on his broad shoulders—could boost Elarton to even more impressive achievements. The Astros will count on both his performance on the mound and his leadership abilities to guide their pitching staff back to respectability in 2001. His importance to the staff will be magnified over the first month of the season, as Shane Reynolds is expected to be out until May while recovering from December knee surgery.

Position: SP
Bats: R **Throws:** R
Ht: 6' 7" **Wt:** 240

Opening Day Age: 25
Born: 2/23/76 in Lamar, CO
ML Seasons: 3

Houston

Overall Statistics

	W	L	Pct.	ERA	G	GS	Sv	IP	H	BB	SO	HR	Ratio
2000	17	7	.708	4.81	30	30	0	192.2	198	84	131	29	1.46
Career	28	13	.683	4.14	100	47	3	373.2	349	147	308	42	1.33

How Often He Throws Strikes

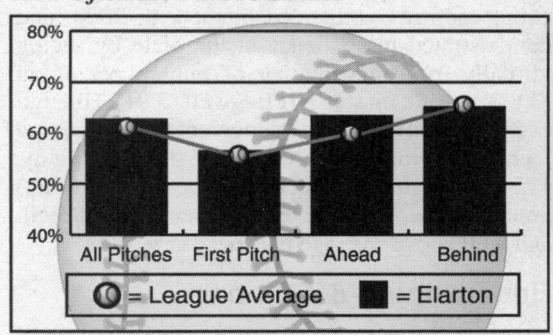

2000 Situational Stats

	W	L	ERA	Sv	IP		AB	H	HR	RBI	Avg
Home	10	4	5.02	0	107.2	LHB	356	93	16	47	.261
Road	7	3	4.55	0	85.0	RHB	397	105	13	57	.264
First Half	8	3	5.74	0	84.2	Sc Pos	176	48	5	73	.273
Scnd Half	9	4	4.08	0	108.0	Clutch	45	9	1	3	.200

2000 Rankings (National League)

- 3rd in most run support per nine innings (7.1), winning percentage and lowest groundball/flyball ratio allowed (0.8)
- 6th in wins and highest stolen-base percentage allowed (75.0)
- 8th in highest ERA at home
- Led the Astros in ERA, wins, walks allowed, lowest batting average allowed (.263), lowest slugging percentage allowed (.454), lowest on-base percentage allowed (.339), most run support per nine innings (7.1), most strikeouts per nine innings (6.1), lowest ERA on the road, lowest batting average allowed vs. lefthanded batters and winning percentage

Richard Hidalgo

2000 Season

The Astros' young Venezuelan established himself as one of the best young players in baseball in 2000, with an incredible .314-44-122 season while playing center field much of the year. While Hidalgo is a severe flyball hitter, critics can't credit Enron Field for his success either, as he hit 28 of his 44 home runs on the road. Hidalgo was at his best in September, slamming 27 extra-base hits during the month en route to a mind-boggling .971 September slugging percentage.

Hitting

There appears to be no real holes in Hidalgo's approach at the plate. He showed no platoon differential against righthanded pitchers in 2000, and demonstrated his patience at the plate by seeing virtually the same number of pitches per at-bat (3.88) as walk master Jeff Bagwell (3.91). Hidalgo even boosted his on-base percentage by getting plunked 21 times. He has grown from a skinny, 175-pound 16-year-old to a rock-solid 190-200 pound athlete, which gives him incredible strength and well above-average bat speed.

Baserunning & Defense

Hidalgo doesn't physically resemble a center fielder, but he does a solid job on defense. He gets outstanding jumps on flyballs, which makes up for his average running speed. Hidalgo's arm always has been considered one of the best in baseball, and his combination of strength and accuracy keeps runners from taking any liberties. He isn't as instinctive on the bases as he is on defense, but he hustles and doesn't run into many outs.

2001 Outlook

A high-ranking Astros official said before the 2000 season that Hidalgo had the potential to be a Sammy Sosa-type talent. That evaluation doesn't seem too far off base at the moment. A key in 2001 will be Hidalgo's ability to continue to play center field while keeping his sometimes-balky knees healthy. At only 26 years old, last year's .314-44-122 performance could be just a stepping stone for Hidalgo.

Position: CF/RF/LF
Bats: R **Throws:** R
Ht: 6' 3" **Wt:** 190

Opening Day Age: 25
Born: 7/2/75 in Caracas, Venezuela
ML Seasons: 4

Overall Statistics

	G	AB	R	H	D	T	HR	RBI	SB	BB	SO	Avg	OBP	Slg
2000	153	558	118	175	42	3	44	122	13	56	110	.314	.391	.636
Career	354	1214	206	345	87	5	68	219	25	133	238	.284	.363	.532

Where He Hits the Ball

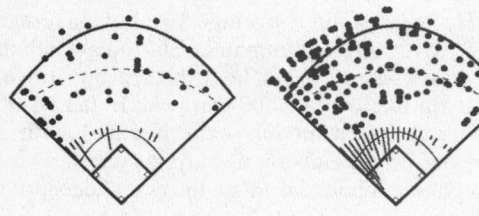

Vs. LHP   **Vs. RHP**

2000 Situational Stats

	AB	H	HR	RBI	Avg		AB	H	HR	RBI	Avg
Home	269	85	16	59	.316	LHP	117	39	5	14	.333
Road	289	90	28	63	.311	RHP	441	136	39	108	.308
First Half	280	80	23	61	.286	Sc Pos	158	47	5	77	.297
Scnd Half	278	95	21	61	.342	Clutch	72	15	2	8	.208

2000 Rankings (National League)

- 2nd in hit by pitch (21), errors in center field (5) and lowest groundball/flyball ratio (0.6)
- 4th in home runs
- 5th in total bases (355), slugging percentage, slugging percentage vs. righthanded pitchers (.646) and lowest fielding percentage in center field (.985)
- Led the Astros in doubles, sacrifice flies (9), hit by pitch (21), slugging percentage, slugging percentage vs. righthanded pitchers (.646), lowest percentage of swings that missed (17.2), highest percentage of extra bases taken as a runner (62.0) and lowest percentage of swings on the first pitch (24.7)

Jose Lima

2000 Season

The *Scouting Notebook 2000* states, "Jose Lima has allowed 64 home runs the past two seasons despite pitching in the Astrodome, and he will be more prone to surrendering longballs in Enron Field." Lima's 48 home runs allowed—27 at Enron—were an all-time National League record. But the truth is, Lima was horrible by all breakdowns in 2000: by month, home-road, lefty-righty, by inning, you name it. In fact, lefthanded hitters had a .426 on-base percentage and .689 slugging percentage against Lima, the rough equivalent of having Todd Helton at bat every time.

Pitching

Lima is a fastball-changeup pitcher who has a well above-average ratio of flyballs to groundballs. His fastball is in the 88-92 MPH range and fairly straight. Lima depends on his changeup extensively, and this is where many observers felt he had problems in 2000. His pitching patterns became too predictable and hitters sat on his change. Another problem is that Lima is very shy about coming inside, enabling hitters to attack the plate. His curveball is fair and is not a successful weapon against the lefthanded hitters who dominate him.

Defense & Hitting

While Lima is agile on the mound, his defense is only average. He has some success holding runners, but that may be more a sign of the opposition's desire to stay at first base and wait for the longball when he's on the hill. Lima is a good hitter who also is an accomplished bunter.

2001 Outlook

Not only did Lima's performance on the mound deteriorate substantially in 2000, his demeanor on the bench and in the clubhouse was affected accordingly. Always an emotional pitcher in the best of times, Lima's tirades and childish behavior while getting pummeled were a distraction for the club. He has two more years on a three-year, $18 million contract he signed prior to the 2000 season, and Shane Reynolds is expected to miss at least the first month of the season recovering from knee surgery. The Astros have no choice but to put him on the mound in 2001—and hope for better results.

Position: SP
Bats: R **Throws:** R
Ht: 6' 2" **Wt:** 205

Opening Day Age: 28
Born: 9/30/72 in Santiago, Dominican Republic
ML Seasons: 7
Pronunciation: LEE-muh

Overall Statistics

	W	L	Pct.	ERA	G	GS	Sv	IP	H	BB	SO	HR	Ratio
2000	7	16	.304	6.65	33	33	0	196.1	251	68	124	48	1.62
Career	53	56	.486	4.87	210	122	5	904.0	998	203	646	146	1.33

How Often He Throws Strikes

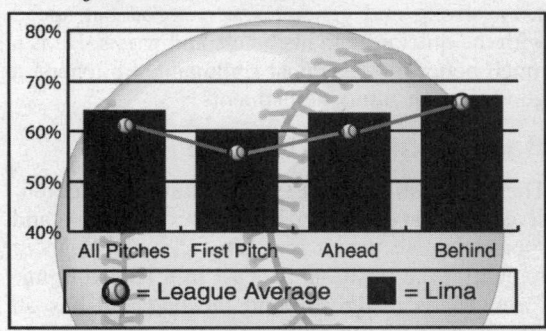

○ = League Average   ■ = Lima

2000 Situational Stats

	W	L	ERA	Sv	IP		AB	H	HR	RBI	Avg
Home	5	8	6.92	0	108.0	LHB	360	131	25	69	.364
Road	2	8	6.32	0	88.1	RHB	441	120	23	69	.272
First Half	2	13	7.36	0	106.1	Sc Pos	177	49	8	80	.277
Scnd Half	5	3	5.80	0	90.0	Clutch	31	9	1	4	.290

2000 Rankings (National League)

- 1st in home runs allowed, highest ERA, highest batting average allowed (.313), highest slugging percentage allowed (.578), most home runs allowed per nine innings (2.20), highest ERA at home and highest batting average allowed vs. lefthanded batters .250
- 2nd in hits allowed and highest ERA on the road
- 3rd in lowest winning percentage
- Led the Astros in sacrifice bunts (8), losses, games started, hits allowed, home runs allowed, highest strikeout/walk ratio (1.8), fewest pitches thrown per batter (3.56) and fewest walks per nine innings (3.1)

Houston

Julio Lugo

2000 Season

Injuries and poor performance by other Astros forced Julio Lugo into a primary role in Houston's middle infield, and the former draft-and-follow answered the call, especially on offense. Lugo's .283 batting average ranked him among the upper half of National League shortstops, as did his 22 stolen bases. The best may be yet to come, as Lugo hit half of his 10 home runs after September 1.

Hitting

Lugo has a slashing, downward swing that results in a high contact rate and an above-average number of groundballs. What surprises people is Lugo's power when he gets a pitch he can turn on. Lugo is wiry, strong and generates very good bat speed with the quickness in his hands and wrists. He is a much better hitter against righthanded pitchers, a good sign for future adjustments.

Baserunning & Defense

The big question about Lugo's future is his defensive ability at shortstop. Most Astros officials and scouts believe that it is a long shot for Lugo to remain at the position, at least in a Houston uniform. He is unsure around the bag and has an erratic arm. It's worth noting that Lugo is much smoother and dependable at second base, giving rise to speculation that much of his trouble at short is mental. Lugo also has played outfield in the past and has both the speed and arm strength to be a solid center fielder. He showed good aggressiveness and judgment on the bases as a rookie, and he easily could improve on his 22 stolen bases.

2001 Outlook

Lugo's offensive potential is too great to immediately move him off shortstop, even if second base appears to be his best position defensively. Tim Bogar's offense is worse than Lugo's defense, and prospect Adam Everett might not even be at Bogar's level with the bat. Free agent Jose Vizcaino also was signed, meaning that Bogar may not be back in Houston in 2001. The Astros' shortstop position will be a wide-open battle when players arrive for spring training.

Position: SS/2B
Bats: R **Throws:** R
Ht: 5'10" **Wt:** 165

Opening Day Age: 25
Born: 11/16/75 in Barahona, Dominican Republic
ML Seasons: 1

Overall Statistics

	G	AB	R	H	D	T	HR	RBI	SB	BB	SO	Avg	OBP	Slg
2000	116	420	78	119	22	5	10	40	22	37	93	.283	.346	.431
Career	116	420	78	119	22	5	10	40	22	37	93	.283	.346	.431

Where He Hits the Ball

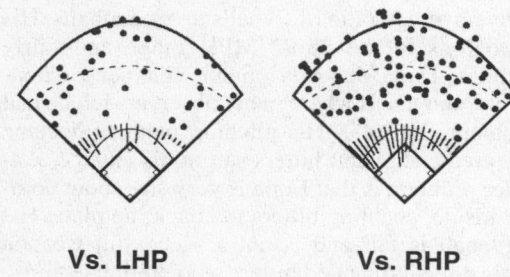

Vs. LHP   **Vs. RHP**

2000 Situational Stats

	AB	H	HR	RBI	Avg		AB	H	HR	RBI	Avg
Home	219	60	6	24	.274	LHP	113	27	1	8	.239
Road	201	59	4	16	.294	RHP	307	92	9	32	.300
First Half	113	31	1	9	.274	Sc Pos	94	20	2	28	.213
Scnd Half	307	88	9	31	.287	Clutch	50	15	0	4	.300

2000 Rankings (National League)

- 5th in batting average on a 3-1 count (.667), lowest slugging percentage vs. lefthanded pitchers (.327) and lowest on-base percentage vs. lefthanded pitchers (.301)
- 8th in on-base percentage for a leadoff hitter (.376)
- Led the Astros in triples, stolen-base percentage (71.0), batting average on a 3-1 count (.667) and steals of third (4)
- Led NL shortstops in batting average on a 3-1 count (.667)

Mitch Meluskey

Position: C
Bats: B **Throws:** R
Ht: 6' 0" **Wt:** 185

Opening Day Age: 27
Born: 9/18/73 in Yakima, WA
ML Seasons: 3
Pronunciation: muh-LUSK-ee

2000 Season

On paper, Meluskey's 2000 season looks like an unqualified success. He was one of the top rookies in the National League and finished with 35 extra-base hits in just 337 at-bats. But Meluskey's season was marred by his defensive struggles and an ugly incident in which he slugged teammate Matt Mieske during batting practice in June.

Hitting

Meluskey is a virtual clone of another young Astros slugger, outfielder Lance Berkman. Like Berkman, Meluskey is an outstanding lefthanded hitter who combines above-average power with excellent plate discipline. From the right side of the plate, Meluskey definitely is platoon material, perhaps affected by on-and-off shoulder problems he has had throughout his career.

Baserunning & Defense

Despite being a professional for nine years, Meluskey still has not mastered many of the basic defensive fundamentals behind the plate. Many of his 12 errors in 2000 were the result of poor footwork when throwing, and he also struggled with framing the ball. Meluskey's combative personality doesn't always sit well with pitchers, and he has been accused of letting his successes and failures at the plate affect his defensive efforts. On the basepaths, Meluskey is a below-average runner who generally is content to take the conservative route around the daimond.

2001 Outlook

Meluskey was part of a six-player deal with Detroit in mid-December that also included sending Roger Cedeno and Chris Holt to the Tigers for Brad Ausmus, Doug Brocail and Nelson Cruz. If Meluskey wasn't such a tremendous offensive catcher, his defensive shortcomings and his problems with his teammates—which weren't limited to his run-in with Mieske—might prevent him from becoming a big league regular. But catchers with his potential at the plate are few and far between, which should insure that Meluskey will be productive as Detroit's starting backstop.

Overall Statistics

	G	AB	R	H	D	T	HR	RBI	SB	BB	SO	Avg	OBP	Slg
2000	117	337	47	101	21	0	14	69	1	55	74	.300	.401	.487
Career	135	378	52	110	23	0	15	72	2	61	84	.291	.392	.471

Where He Hits the Ball

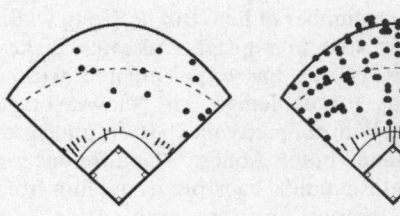

Vs. LHP   **Vs. RHP**

2000 Situational Stats

	AB	H	HR	RBI	Avg		AB	H	HR	RBI	Avg
Home	166	47	11	34	.283	LHP	57	11	0	10	.193
Road	171	54	3	35	.316	RHP	280	90	14	59	.321
First Half	201	60	9	43	.299	Sc Pos	107	40	4	52	.374
Scnd Half	136	41	5	26	.301	Clutch	50	15	1	10	.300

2000 Rankings (National League)

- 1st in lowest fielding percentage at catcher (.982)
- 2nd in errors at catcher (12)
- 3rd in batting average with runners in scoring position and batting average with the bases loaded (.625)
- Led the Astros in batting average with runners in scoring position, batting average with the bases loaded (.625) and highest percentage of pitches taken (60.0)
- Led NL catchers in batting average with runners in scoring position, batting average with the bases loaded (.625) and highest percentage of pitches taken (60.0)

Houston

Shane Reynolds

2000 Season

Normally the Astros' lead starter and innings eater, Shane Reynolds suffered through his worst big league season along with most of the rest of the Houston staff. Enron Field wasn't Reynolds' crutch, though. His back started bothering him in spring training, and he was shut down at the end of July with a degenerative disk problem.

Pitching

Reynolds is a combination control and strikeout pitcher. He uses his 88-90 MPH fastball to get ahead of hitters early in the count, then puts them away with one of the best split-finger pitches in the game. Because Reynolds works aggressively early in the count with his fastball, he tends to give up an above-average number of hits. But he rarely walks hitters and is able to register strikeouts in key situations. Reynolds has experimented with a slider recently to supplement his below-average curveball, but both are pretty much show pitches to keep righthanded hitters honest. The difference in 2000 was that Reynolds' back prevented him from getting his fastball-splitter combination low enough in the strike zone.

Defense & Hitting

Reynolds is an above-average hitter and is capable of driving a mistake pitch up an alley or over the fence. Even with a bad back, he hit .225 and knocked a double and a home run in 2000. Reynolds fields balls well coming off the mound but is only fair at covering first base.

2001 Outlook

Reynolds is one of the best-conditioned pitchers in baseball and was expected to make a complete recovery from his back woes. Then a freak injury while jogging forced him to have surgery on his left knee in late December. The recovery is expected to keep him out of the rotation until May, so for the first time since 1995 he will not be Houston's Opening Day starter. The Astros desperately need the stability that he brings to the starting rotation. He is signed through the 2002 season with a club option for 2003, so he should be a part of the Houston rotation for at least three more years.

Position: SP
Bats: R **Throws:** R
Ht: 6' 3" **Wt:** 210

Opening Day Age: 33
Born: 3/26/68 in Bastrop, LA
ML Seasons: 9

Overall Statistics

	W	L	Pct.	ERA	G	GS	Sv	IP	H	BB	SO	HR	Ratio
2000	7	8	.467	5.22	22	22	0	131.0	150	45	93	20	1.49
Career	86	69	.555	3.85	233	207	0	1365.2	1450	296	1160	134	1.28

How Often He Throws Strikes

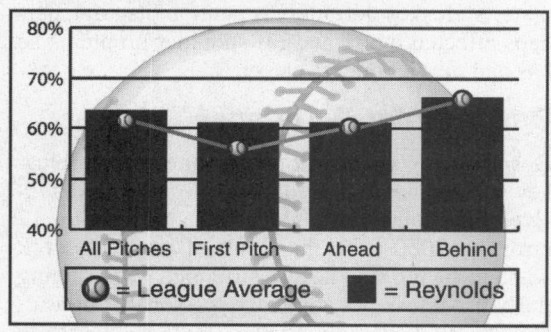

= League Average   = Reynolds

2000 Situational Stats

	W	L	ERA	Sv	IP		AB	H	HR	RBI	Avg
Home	3	4	5.17	0	55.2	LHB	234	65	6	29	.278
Road	4	4	5.26	0	75.1	RHB	289	85	14	47	.294
First Half	6	5	4.17	0	114.1	Sc Pos	129	31	9	56	.240
Scnd Half	1	3	12.42	0	16.2	Clutch	23	7	2	4	.304

2000 Rankings (National League)

- Led the Astros in lowest batting average allowed with runners in scoring position

Billy Wagner

2000 Season

Billy Wagner's 2000 season was essentially over from the start. In retrospect, it was really over at the end of the 1999 season, when Wagner suffered from elbow tenderness down the stretch. After Wagner blew more than half his save opportunities and saw his ERA grow to 6.18 in mid-June, he admitted to elbow pain. He was shut down and underwent elbow ligament surgery, which officially ended his season.

Pitching

When healthy, Wagner is one of the most unique pitchers in baseball history. Barely 5-foot-11, he combines a deceptive delivery with a riding 95-98 MPH fastball that is devastating. His 1998 and '99 strikeouts-innings pitched ratios are the two highest in major league history, and he arguably was baseball's best reliever in 1999. Wagner throws a higher percentage of fastballs—around 85 percent—than any pitcher in baseball, but began experimenting with a slider to replace his inconsistent curveball in 1999. It will be interesting to see which breaking ball he uses after his surgery.

Defense & Hitting

Since strikeouts account for more than half his outs in a normal year, and the majority of the other outs are on flyballs, his defense is fairly irrelevant. As a closer, Wagner almost never comes to the plate. Actually, Wagner is a live-bodied athlete who probably would be above average in both areas if his role and style allowed it.

2001 Outlook

Wagner was soft-tossing when the season ended and is considered on schedule to being at full strength by the start of spring training. The Astros are sure to start him off conservatively at the beginning of the year, much as the Giants did with Robb Nen at the start of the 2000 season after Nen's elbow surgery. Don't be surprised if the hypercompetitive Wagner makes a 2001 comeback that is similar to Nen's in 2000.

Position: RP
Bats: L **Throws:** L
Ht: 5'11" **Wt:** 180

Opening Day Age: 29
Born: 7/25/71 in Tannersville, VA
ML Seasons: 6

Overall Statistics

	W	L	Pct.	ERA	G	GS	Sv	IP	H	BB	SO	HR	Ratio
2000	2	4	.333	6.18	28	0	6	27.2	28	18	28	6	1.66
Career	19	18	.514	2.73	252	0	107	280.2	186	126	422	28	1.11

How Often He Throws Strikes

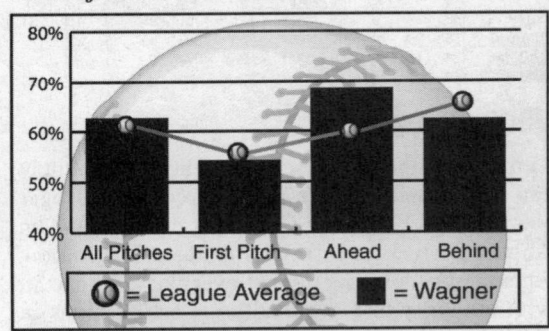

○ = League Average   ■ = Wagner

2000 Situational Stats

	W	L	ERA	Sv	IP		AB	H	HR	RBI	Avg
Home	0	3	6.28	3	14.1	LHB	28	9	3	13	.321
Road	2	1	6.08	3	13.1	RHB	82	19	3	10	.232
First Half	2	4	6.18	6	27.2	Sc Pos	44	9	1	15	.205
Scnd Half	0	0	-	0	0.0	Clutch	72	22	4	18	.306

2000 Rankings (National League)

- 1st in blown saves (9)
- Led the Astros in blown saves (9)

Tim Bogar

Position: SS
Bats: R **Throws:** R
Ht: 6' 2" **Wt:** 198

Opening Day Age: 34
Born: 10/28/66 in
Indianapolis, IN
ML Seasons: 8

Overall Statistics

	G	AB	R	H	D	T	HR	RBI	SB	BB	SO	Avg	OBP	Slg
2000	110	304	32	63	9	2	7	33	1	35	56	.207	.292	.319
Career	689	1501	176	340	67	9	22	159	13	141	271	.227	.297	.327

2000 Situational Stats

	AB	H	HR	RBI	Avg		AB	H	HR	RBI	Avg
Home	146	37	3	17	.253	LHP	81	23	2	10	.284
Road	158	26	4	16	.165	RHP	223	40	5	23	.179
First Half	136	18	2	11	.132	Sc Pos	77	22	1	25	.286
Scnd Half	168	45	5	22	.268	Clutch	39	5	0	1	.128

2000 Season

Tim Bogar once again proved that he absolutely can't hit when he isn't playing regularly. Bogar was batting .128 when Craig Biggio was hurt on August 1. Over the last two months of the season, when he was playing almost every day, Bogar hit with authority and eventually set career highs in home runs and RBI.

Hitting, Baserunning & Defense

Bogar's swing is long and slow, and he has to get into a groove to be productive as a hitter—a groove that he can't get into against righthanded pitchers or by playing once or twice a week. Bogar is one of the most surehanded, dependable defensive shortstops in the game. He hasn't lost a step and retains his quickness and above-average arm strength. Bogar has below-average speed on the bases.

2001 Outlook

The Astros' shortstop situation is no more clear entering 2001 than it was at the beginning of the 2000 season. Bogar essentially has the opposite tools and skills as Julio Lugo, the Astros' good-hit, poor-field rookie who came up in 2000. Bogar is considered an outstanding presence in the clubhouse, but he is a free agent and the club signed Jose Vizcaino, who could fill a role similar to Bogar's.

Roger Cedeno

Traded To
TIGERS

Position: CF/LF/RF
Bats: B **Throws:** R
Ht: 6' 1" **Wt:** 205

Opening Day Age: 26
Born: 8/16/74 in
Valencia Edo.
Carabobo, Venezuela
ML Seasons: 6
Pronunciation:
suh-DAYN-yoh

Overall Statistics

	G	AB	R	H	D	T	HR	RBI	SB	BB	SO	Avg	OBP	Slg
2000	74	259	54	73	2	5	6	26	25	43	47	.282	.383	.398
Career	540	1399	238	388	59	13	17	117	114	182	305	.277	.362	.375

2000 Situational Stats

	AB	H	HR	RBI	Avg		AB	H	HR	RBI	Avg
Home	134	33	3	16	.246	LHP	48	15	3	10	.313
Road	125	40	3	10	.320	RHP	211	58	3	16	.275
First Half	163	42	4	19	.258	Sc Pos	47	11	2	20	.234
Scnd Half	96	31	2	7	.323	Clutch	41	8	1	3	.195

2000 Season

When he was healthy, Roger Cedeno performed as advertised offensively, reaching base at nearly a .400 clip and leading the team in steals. But he missed nearly two and a half months with a ruptured tendon in a finger on his left hand, and lost his starting position to Lance Berkman. Cedeno's defense was the biggest disappointment.

Hitting, Baserunning & Defense

Cedeno is a patient hitter with a slashing swing and some raw power. Cedeno is ineffectual against lefthanded pitchers and is essentially a platoon player, though he did manage a .313 average against southpaws in limited at-bats last year. Cedeno has problems on defense with his jumps and routes on flyballs. He proved just as poor in right field as he did in center. Cedeno has first-class speed on the bases and is a threat to lead the league in steals if given a full season of at-bats.

2001 Outlook

Cedeno was part of a six-player trade with the Tigers in mid-December. He is pegged as a possible replacement in right field if Juan Gonzalez does not return to Detroit. Cedeno's speed should come in handy both in covering the spacious outfield at Comerica Park and in fulfilling his anticipated leadoff duties for the Tigers.

Octavio Dotel

Position: RP/SP
Bats: R **Throws:** R
Ht: 6' 0" **Wt:** 175

Opening Day Age: 25
Born: 11/25/75 in Santo Domingo, Dominican Republic
ML Seasons: 2

Overall Statistics

	W	L	Pct.	ERA	G	GS	Sv	IP	H	BB	SO	HR	Ratio
2000	3	7	.300	5.40	50	16	16	125.0	127	61	142	26	1.50
Career	11	10	.524	5.39	69	30	16	210.1	196	110	227	38	1.45

2000 Situational Stats

	W	L	ERA	Sv	IP		AB	H	HR	RBI	Avg
Home	0	2	5.25	9	61.2	LHB	216	61	12	38	.282
Road	3	5	5.54	7	63.1	RHB	264	66	14	40	.250
First Half	1	5	5.61	1	94.2	Sc Pos	133	34	6	51	.256
Scnd Half	2	2	4.75	15	30.1	Clutch	116	32	8	27	.276

2000 Season

At times in 2000, Octavio Dotel showed the ability to blow away big league hitters with his raw stuff, especially as the team's closer after Billy Wagner's injury ended his season. At other times, Dotel was wild either outside the strike zone or in the middle of it. Dotel can't blame Enron Field for his trouble, as his ERA was worse on the road.

Pitching, Defense & Hitting

Dotel has two power pitches, a live 95-MPH fastball and a hard slider. As a starter he showed the ability to cruise through the first three or four innings, but often was terrorized his second and third time through the order. Dotel is an extreme flyball pitcher who works high in the strike zone. He won't get to too many balls in the field, and he does little to curb the running game. Dotel is one of the worst hitting pitchers in baseball, but has been able to get the sacrifice bunt down.

2001 Outlook

Dotel has made no secret of his dislike for relief duty, and the Astros may be forced to use him in the rotation while Shane Reynolds recovers from knee surgery. Dotel's two-pitch repertoire and his tendency to implode after a couple of innings make him much better suited to the bullpen, but his role for 2001 may not be determined until the spring.

Tony Eusebio

Position: C
Bats: R **Throws:** R
Ht: 6' 2" **Wt:** 210

Opening Day Age: 33
Born: 4/27/67 in San Jose de los Llanos, Dominican Republic
ML Seasons: 8
Pronunciation: you-SAY-bee-oh

Overall Statistics

	G	AB	R	H	D	T	HR	RBI	SB	BB	SO	Avg	OBP	Slg
2000	74	218	24	61	18	0	7	33	0	25	45	.280	.361	.459
Career	539	1585	163	440	79	5	25	227	1	165	290	.278	.347	.381

2000 Situational Stats

	AB	H	HR	RBI	Avg		AB	H	HR	RBI	Avg
Home	103	25	2	13	.243	LHP	63	14	2	9	.222
Road	115	36	5	20	.313	RHP	155	47	5	24	.303
First Half	127	26	2	12	.205	Sc Pos	63	16	0	22	.254
Scnd Half	91	35	5	21	.385	Clutch	30	6	1	7	.200

2000 Season

Tony Eusebio was enjoying the best offensive season of his career in 2000—which included piling up a 24-game hitting streak in July and August—when his year abruptly ended on September 1. He separated his right shoulder tumbling into the cavernous Enron Field dugout while chasing a pop fly, which resulted in surgery.

Hitting, Baserunning & Defense

Eusebio has a distinctive inside-out swing that produces a steady stream of line drives to the right side of the field. He's very strong in the upper body and began lifting the ball more frequently in 2000, resulting in 18 doubles and seven home runs. Eusebio has evolved into a competent defensive catcher. He isn't especially mobile or quick, but works well with pitchers and has a strong throwing arm. Eusebio ranks among the slowest runners in baseball and is no threat on the bases.

2001 Outlook

The Astros have Eusebio under contract for another year and will welcome him back for his 17th season in the Houston organization. He will back up Brad Ausmus, who was acquired in a six-player deal with the Tigers that sent Mitch Meluskey to Detroit. The Astros are counting on Eusebio's usual pop from his reserve role.

Chris Holt

Position: SP
Bats: R **Throws:** R
Ht: 6' 4" **Wt:** 205

Opening Day Age: 29
Born: 9/18/71 in Dallas, TX
ML Seasons: 4

Overall Statistics

	W	L	Pct.	ERA	G	GS	Sv	IP	H	BB	SO	HR	Ratio
2000	8	16	.333	5.35	34	32	0	207.0	247	75	136	22	1.56
Career	21	42	.333	4.51	103	90	1	585.1	656	196	346	51	1.46

2000 Situational Stats

	W	L	ERA	Sv	IP		AB	H	HR	RBI	Avg
Home	4	6	4.91	0	113.2	LHB	378	126	13	68	.333
Road	4	10	5.88	0	93.1	RHB	434	121	9	52	.279
First Half	3	10	4.99	0	115.1	Sc Pos	209	66	8	100	.316
Scnd Half	5	6	5.79	0	91.2	Clutch	39	10	2	7	.256

2000 Season

Chris Holt actually was one of the team's more effective pitchers at Enron Field, recording a home ERA that was nearly a run better than his road mark. Holt's won-lost record has reached the point of being a psychological stumbling block for him. While his 8-16 record in 2000 is reflective of his 21-42 career mark, Holt's ERA combined with Houston's offense should produce a .500 pitcher.

Pitching, Defense & Hitting

Holt's best pitch is a low-90s sinking fastball that generates a high percentage of groundball outs, which makes him effective at Enron Field. His curveball and changeup are not as good as his fastball, so he is less effective against lefthanders. While he isn't very mobile, Holt has good quickness on groundballs up the middle. Holt is a poor hitter and bunter who fails to make much contact.

2001 Outlook

Holt was part of the six-player deal that also sent Roger Cedeno and Mitch Meluskey to Detroit for Brad Ausmus, Doug Brocail and Nelson Cruz. Holt's anticipated salary slot is way too high for a 21-42 career pitcher, but his pitching style and ability to eat innings have the Tigers pencilling him in as their No. 4 starter.

Wade Miller

Position: SP
Bats: R **Throws:** R
Ht: 6' 2" **Wt:** 185

Opening Day Age: 24
Born: 9/13/76 in Reading, PA
ML Seasons: 2

Overall Statistics

	W	L	Pct.	ERA	G	GS	Sv	IP	H	BB	SO	HR	Ratio
2000	6	6	.500	5.14	16	16	0	105.0	104	42	89	14	1.39
Career	6	7	.462	5.54	21	17	0	115.1	121	47	97	18	1.46

2000 Situational Stats

	W	L	ERA	Sv	IP		AB	H	HR	RBI	Avg
Home	4	3	5.00	0	54.0	LHB	165	51	10	30	.309
Road	2	3	5.29	0	51.0	RHB	239	53	4	24	.222
First Half	0	1	5.14	0	7.0	Sc Pos	100	28	1	38	.280
Scnd Half	6	5	5.14	0	98.0	Clutch	31	13	2	6	.419

2000 Season

After Octavio Dotel was moved to the bullpen to replace injured closer Billy Wagner, Wade Miller was called up from New Orleans in July and put into the rotation. His 6-6 record and 5.14 ERA are somewhat deceptive in that he bunched a string of quality starts around a few very poor outings. Miller easily has the best baserunners-per-nine innings ratio among Astros starters at 12.8.

Pitching, Defense & Hitting

Miller has a hard sinking fastball in the 92-94 MPH range that enables him to keep the ball consistently on the ground, a big plus in Enron Field. He uses both a power curveball and a power slider to dominate righthanded batters. While he is an agile and competent fielder, Miller has yet to figure out how to handle big league pitching at the plate, going 4-for-40 in his rookie season.

2001 Outlook

With Chris Holt's departure, Dotel's role up in the air and Shane Reynolds on the shelf until May recovering from knee surgery, Miller appears to be a lock to join the Astros' rotation full-time in 2001. He was one of the team's most effective starters over the last two months of the 2000 season, and his ability to throw three power pitches for strikes promises more impressive stretches in the future.

Joe Slusarski

Position: RP
Bats: R **Throws:** R
Ht: 6' 4" **Wt:** 195

Opening Day Age: 34
Born: 12/19/66 in
Indianapolis, IN
ML Seasons: 6

Overall Statistics

	W	L	Pct.	ERA	G	GS	Sv	IP	H	BB	SO	HR	Ratio
2000	2	7	.222	4.21	54	0	3	77.0	80	22	54	8	1.32
Career	13	20	.394	4.97	106	34	3	289.2	317	121	162	41	1.51

2000 Situational Stats

	W	L	ERA	Sv	IP		AB	H	HR	RBI	Avg
Home	1	1	4.38	3	39.0	LHB	135	43	1	22	.319
Road	1	6	4.03	0	38.0	RHB	163	37	7	29	.227
First Half	1	5	4.10	1	37.1	Sc Pos	96	27	3	41	.281
Scnd Half	1	2	4.31	2	39.2	Clutch	96	25	4	14	.260

2000 Season

Joe Slusarski emerged from the long list of retread minor league pitchers to become a dependable big league reliever at age 34. His 77 innings were the most he had accumulated in any big league season since 1991 with Oakland. Slusarski's 4.21 ERA easily was the lowest figure on the shell-shocked Astros staff among pitchers who spent a majority of the season in Houston.

Pitching, Defense & Hitting

Slusarski's stuff is ideal for his role and his home ballpark. He has a smooth, easy delivery that enables him to spot his pitches low around the strike zone and keep the ball out of the air. Slusarski throws an 88-MPH sinker as his lead pitch, and complements it with a very effective changeup and a good slider. He went 1-for-9 with five strikeouts as a hitter in 2000, the first year he ever had batted in the majors.

2001 Outlook

With the Astros' bullpen no longer in such disarray, Slusarski will have to fight for a setup role in spring training. He fits easily into the mold of other recent successful setup men, such as Mark Petkovsek and Anthony Telford, who didn't combine opportunity, knowledge and command of their stuff until their late-20s and early-30s.

Bill Spiers

Position: 3B/SS/2B
Bats: L **Throws:** R
Ht: 6' 2" **Wt:** 190

Opening Day Age: 34
Born: 6/5/66 in
Orangeburg, SC
ML Seasons: 12
Pronunciation: SPY-ers

Overall Statistics

	G	AB	R	H	D	T	HR	RBI	SB	BB	SO	Avg	OBP	Slg
2000	124	355	41	107	17	3	3	43	7	49	38	.301	.386	.392
Career	1248	3405	477	921	158	35	37	388	97	354	496	.270	.340	.370

2000 Situational Stats

	AB	H	HR	RBI	Avg		AB	H	HR	RBI	Avg
Home	169	57	2	23	.337	LHP	32	8	0	3	.250
Road	186	50	1	20	.269	RHP	323	99	3	40	.307
First Half	183	56	1	21	.306	Sc Pos	76	27	2	40	.355
Scnd Half	172	51	2	22	.297	Clutch	68	22	0	8	.324

2000 Season

Chris Spiers' 2000 season was virtually identical to his 1998 and '99 campaigns. He has played in 123-127 games each year, accumulating 355-393 at-bats. With Ken Caminiti and Craig Biggio out with injuries, and two rookies—Julio Lugo and Chris Truby—getting extensive playing time, Spiers was called upon for more of a leadership role in the infield.

Hitting, Baserunning & Defense

The vast majority of Spiers' at-bats come against righthanded pitchers. He is a patient contact hitter who keeps the ball on the ground and is adept at the hit-and-run and advancing runners. Spiers continues to be one of the top utility men in baseball. He is equally adept at third, short or second and hasn't lost a step of range in the field.

2001 Outlook

Spiers is one of the leaders in the Houston clubhouse, and the Astros picked up the option on his contract for 2001. His weakness against lefthanders, along with his tendency to break down physically if he plays too much, will keep the Astros from extending him a regular job. Look for Spiers to at least platoon with the righthanded-hitting Chris Truby in 2001, along with filling in around the diamond as needed.

Houston

Chris Truby

Position: 3B
Bats: R **Throws:** R
Ht: 6' 2" **Wt:** 190

Opening Day Age: 27
Born: 12/9/73 in Palm Springs, CA
ML Seasons: 1

Overall Statistics

	G	AB	R	H	D	T	HR	RBI	SB	BB	SO	Avg	OBP	Slg
2000	78	258	28	67	15	4	11	59	2	10	56	.260	.295	.477
Career	78	258	28	67	15	4	11	59	2	10	56	.260	.295	.477

2000 Situational Stats

	AB	H	HR	RBI	Avg		AB	H	HR	RBI	Avg
Home	144	36	9	44	.250	LHP	76	27	4	22	.355
Road	114	31	2	15	.272	RHP	182	40	7	37	.220
First Half	64	17	1	6	.266	Sc Pos	81	24	6	47	.296
Scnd Half	194	50	10	53	.258	Clutch	30	7	2	7	.233

2000 Season

Chris Truby wasn't guaranteed a shot at making his major league debut in 2000, but Ken Caminiti's injury gave him the opportunity and Truby made the most of it. He hit well with men on base, slugging .585 in those situations, and he drove in runs at a better rate than Caminiti.

Hitting, Baserunning & Defense

Although Truby has impressive power, he is an overaggressive, early-count hitter who only walked 10 times in a half season's worth of at-bats. He also was unable to hit righthanded pitchers well—they limited him to a .220 batting average. Truby is an above-average defensive third baseman, with quick feet, good fundamentals and a strong, accurate throwing arm. Although he has below-average speed, Truby is considered a good baserunner with solid instincts.

2001 Outlook

Caminiti signed with the Rangers in the offseason, so the ideal situation for the Astros would appear to be a straight platoon at third base between Truby and the lefthanded-hitting Bill Spiers. This won't offer Truby any more at-bats than he received in 2000. Nor will it answer questions about whether Truby is the long-term solution at third.

Daryle Ward

Position: LF/1B
Bats: L **Throws:** L
Ht: 6' 2" **Wt:** 230

Opening Day Age: 25
Born: 6/27/75 in Lynwood, CA
ML Seasons: 3

Overall Statistics

	G	AB	R	H	D	T	HR	RBI	SB	BB	SO	Avg	OBP	Slg
2000	119	264	36	68	10	2	20	47	0	15	61	.258	.295	.538
Career	187	417	48	110	16	2	28	77	0	25	94	.264	.303	.513

2000 Situational Stats

	AB	H	HR	RBI	Avg		AB	H	HR	RBI	Avg
Home	105	29	13	25	.276	LHP	23	7	2	8	.304
Road	159	39	7	22	.245	RHP	241	61	18	39	.253
First Half	159	34	12	28	.214	Sc Pos	68	11	3	21	.162
Scnd Half	105	34	8	19	.324	Clutch	55	10	3	5	.182

2000 Season

After his clutch performance late in 1999, Daryle Ward faced growing expectations in 2000. Although he hit 20 home runs and slugged .538, the season had to count as a disappointment. Ward was passed by fellow prospect Lance Berkman and saw his playing time significantly diminish in the second half of the season.

Hitting, Baserunning & Defense

Ward still has tremendous power at the plate. His irregular playing time transformed him into an impatient hitter, but he has the potential to hit in the .300 range with 35-plus home runs as a regular. The ongoing project to get Ward into the lineup as a left fielder hasn't earned him more at-bats. He simply is a brutal defender, with no range, instincts or arm strength. Ward's inability or unwillingness to lose weight is a major part of his defensive problems. At his weight, Ward is not a threat on the bases.

2001 Outlook

Ward is perceived as a disappointment in Houston, but there is virtually no chance that he will be moved to another club unless the Astros are overwhelmed by a team seeking a young offensive-minded first baseman. He again will serve as the club's primary backup to Jeff Bagwell and fill in in the outfield as needed.

Other Houston Astros

Glen Barker (**Pos**: CF, **Age**: 29, **Bats**: B)

	G	AB	R	H	D	T	HR	RBI	SB	BB	SO	Avg	OBP	Slg
2000	84	67	18	15	2	1	2	6	9	7	23	.224	.307	.373
Career	165	140	41	36	4	1	3	17	26	18	42	.257	.348	.364

Barker's best asset is his speed. While it helps him play center field and steal bases, his speed doesn't help him reach base or hit for power. 2001 Outlook: C

Jose Cabrera (**Pos**: RHP, **Age**: 29)

	W	L	Pct.	ERA	G	GS	Sv	IP	H	BB	SO	HR	Ratio
2000	2	3	.400	5.92	52	0	2	59.1	74	17	41	10	1.53
Career	6	3	.667	4.32	93	0	2	108.1	108	33	88	14	1.30

Cabrera's fastball reaches the low 90s. He spent most of last season in the Houston bullpen, doubling his previous career high in appearances. 2001 Outlook: B

Frank Charles (**Pos**: C, **Age**: 32, **Bats**: R)

	G	AB	R	H	D	T	HR	RBI	SB	BB	SO	Avg	OBP	Slg
2000	4	7	1	3	1	0	0	2	0	0	2	.429	.429	.571
Career	4	7	1	3	1	0	0	2	0	0	2	.429	.429	.571

Charles was a minor league lifer before the Astros gave him a handful of at-bats during last season's final month. Unfortunately, it may wind up being his only action in the big leagues. 2001 Outlook: D

Raul Chavez (**Pos**: C, **Age**: 28, **Bats**: R)

	G	AB	R	H	D	T	HR	RBI	SB	BB	SO	Avg	OBP	Slg
2000	14	43	3	11	2	0	1	5	0	3	6	.256	.298	.372
Career	32	75	4	19	2	0	1	7	2	4	12	.253	.284	.320

Chavez signed a minor league contract with the Astros last January. He got some time in the majors when Mitch Meluskey was disabled. He offers little as a hitter. 2001 Outlook: C

Tripp Cromer (**Pos**: 3B, **Age**: 33, **Bats**: R)

	G	AB	R	H	D	T	HR	RBI	SB	BB	SO	Avg	OBP	Slg
2000	9	8	2	1	0	0	0	0	0	1	1	.125	.222	.125
Career	193	520	54	117	22	0	12	47	0	27	101	.225	.266	.337

The Astros promoted Cromer last August 2 when Craig Biggio was injured. But by the end of the month Cromer was placed on the disabled list for personal reasons and he eventually became a free agent. 2001 Outlook: C

Wayne Franklin (**Pos**: LHP, **Age**: 27)

	W	L	Pct.	ERA	G	GS	Sv	IP	H	BB	SO	HR	Ratio
2000	0	0	-	5.48	25	0	0	21.1	24	12	21	2	1.69
Career	0	0	-	5.48	25	0	0	21.1	24	12	21	2	1.69

Franklin's innings-per-game rate provides some indication of his role. He did record eight holds while limiting batters to a .120 average in close and late situations. 2001 Outlook: C

Jason Green (**Pos**: RHP, **Age**: 25)

	W	L	Pct.	ERA	G	GS	Sv	IP	H	BB	SO	HR	Ratio
2000	1	1	.500	6.62	14	0	0	17.2	15	20	19	3	1.98
Career	1	1	.500	6.62	14	0	0	17.2	15	20	19	3	1.98

Green's strikeout-walk ratio, so strong in the minors last year, deteriorated with Houston. The Astros waived him after the season and Colorado picked him up. 2001 Outlook: C

Kip Gross (**Pos**: RHP, **Age**: 36)

	W	L	Pct.	ERA	G	GS	Sv	IP	H	BB	SO	HR	Ratio
2000	0	1	.000	10.38	2	1	0	4.1	9	2	3	2	2.54
Career	7	8	.467	3.90	73	12	0	147.2	168	66	81	14	1.58

Gross spent five seasons in Japan before returning to the states a couple years ago. While he pitched well at Triple-A in 2000, at his age he may not be in great demand as a free agent this offseason. 2001 Outlook: C

Scott Linebrink (**Pos**: RHP, **Age**: 24)

	W	L	Pct.	ERA	G	GS	Sv	IP	H	BB	SO	HR	Ratio
2000	0	0	-	6.00	11	0	0	12.0	18	8	6	4	2.17
Career	0	0	-	6.00	11	0	0	12.0	18	8	6	4	2.17

Linebrink was a second-round pick of the Giants in 1997 who was traded to the Astros for Doug Henry last July. After Linebrink missed much of 1999 due to injury, he worked mostly in relief last year. 2001 Outlook: C

Mike Maddux (**Pos**: RHP, **Age**: 39)

	W	L	Pct.	ERA	G	GS	Sv	IP	H	BB	SO	HR	Ratio
2000	2	2	.500	6.26	21	0	0	27.1	31	12	17	6	1.57
Career	39	37	.513	4.05	472	48	20	861.2	873	284	564	67	1.34

The Astros released Maddux last July and he retired soon thereafter. Though he won 201 fewer career games than brother Greg has, Mike still leads in games pitched, 472-471. 2001 Outlook: D

Rusty Meacham (**Pos**: RHP, **Age**: 33)

	W	L	Pct.	ERA	G	GS	Sv	IP	H	BB	SO	HR	Ratio
2000	0	0	-	11.57	5	0	0	4.2	8	2	3	3	2.14
Career	22	14	.611	4.30	194	9	9	307.2	342	83	185	36	1.38

After pitching for the Mariners in 1996, it took four years and five organizations before Meacham could make it back to the majors. Only he knows if it was worth it. 2001 Outlook: C

Yorkis Perez (Pos: LHP, **Age**: 33)

	W	L	Pct.	ERA	G	GS	Sv	IP	H	BB	SO	HR	Ratio
2000	2	1	.667	5.16	33	0	0	22.2	25	14	21	4	1.72
Career	14	15	.483	4.56	314	0	1	254.2	230	133	234	25	1.43

The Astros traded Traver Miller to the Phillies in exchange for Perez last March, but eventually released Perez in July. Since he's lefthanded and not yet ancient, he could resurface. 2001 Outlook: C

Brian Powell (Pos: RHP, **Age**: 27)

	W	L	Pct.	ERA	G	GS	Sv	IP	H	BB	SO	HR	Ratio
2000	2	1	.667	5.74	9	5	0	31.1	34	13	14	8	1.50
Career	5	9	.357	6.18	27	21	0	115.0	135	49	60	25	1.60

Powell was part of the package acquired from Detroit in the Brad Ausmus deal in 1999. Powell has managed to win in the minors despite a poor strikeout rate and not having overpowering stuff. 2001 Outlook: C

Jay Powell (Pos: RHP, **Age**: 29)

	W	L	Pct.	ERA	G	GS	Sv	IP	H	BB	SO	HR	Ratio
2000	1	1	.500	5.67	29	0	0	27.0	29	19	16	1	1.78
Career	24	17	.585	3.93	308	0	15	331.2	318	168	276	18	1.47

Powell landed on the disabled list last May with shoulder tendinitis, a condition that eventually required surgery. If he's healthy, he could provide a big boost to Houston's middle relief. 2001 Outlook: B

Marc Valdes (Pos: RHP, **Age**: 29)

	W	L	Pct.	ERA	G	GS	Sv	IP	H	BB	SO	HR	Ratio
2000	5	5	.500	5.08	53	0	2	56.2	69	25	35	3	1.66
Career	11	15	.423	4.88	135	22	4	243.2	274	117	132	17	1.60

Even though Valdes wasn't traded from Tampa Bay to the Astros until May 27, he came within one game of leading Houston in pitching appearances. He was designated for assignment in mid-December. 2001 Outlook: B

Eddie Zosky (Pos: 3B, **Age**: 33, **Bats**: R)

	G	AB	R	H	D	T	HR	RBI	SB	BB	SO	Avg	OBP	Slg
2000	4	4	0	0	0	0	0	0	0	0	1	.000	.000	.000
Career	44	50	4	8	1	2	0	3	0	1	13	.160	.173	.260

Zosky was a first-round pick of the Blue Jays in 1989. He's never hit a lot and his range at shortstop is limited, but he also can play second and third. He cleared waivers and became a free agent. 2001 Outlook: C

Houston Astros Minor League Prospects

Organization Overview:

Enron Field didn't welcome the Astros with open arms in its inaugural season, as Houston sunk from a World Series contender to a disappointing 72 wins. Paring payroll had as much to do with their demise as the hitter-friendly confines of the new park. A rebuilding mode began to take shape as homegrown youngsters Richard Hidalgo, Lance Berkman, Julio Lugo, Chris Truby, Mitch Meluskey, who was traded to the Tigers, and Daryle Ward all showed offensive promise, while the system watched a stable of pitching prospects emerge. Two farmhands, Roy Oswalt and Adam Everett, played vital roles in helping Team USA to the gold medal in the Summer Olympics. Houston's scouting department has shown a penchant for finding smallish power pitchers and Oswalt qualifies under the Billy Wagner/Mike Nannini/Tim Redding mold.

Morgan Ensberg

Position: 3B **Opening Day Age:** 26
Bats: R **Throws:** R **Born:** 8/26/75 in
Ht: 6' 2" **Wt:** 210 Redondo Beach, CA

Recent Statistics

	G	AB	R	H	D	THR	RBI	SB	BB	SO	Avg
2000 AA Round Rock	137	483	95	145	34	0	28	90	9	92	107	.300
2000 NL Houston	4	7	0	2	0	0	0	0	0	0	1	.286
2000 MLE	137	471	79	133	32	0	24	75	6	65	114	.282

The home-run leader on Southern Cal's College World Series championship team of 1998, Ensberg went to the Astros as an eighth-round pick that year. He's been a patient hitter in the pros, but it wasn't until last summer that his power emerged. He also walked 92 times and posted a .416 on-base percentage. Ensberg gets too pull-conscious, and breaking pitches on the outer half of the plate give him trouble. Despite soft hands and a strong arm, Ensberg is an average third baseman. He's not as good defensively as Chris Truby, who will also battle for Caminiti's job, but after recording 62 extra-base hits at Round Rock, Ensberg's a better hitting prospect.

Adam Everett

Position: SS **Opening Day Age:** 24
Bats: R **Throws:** R **Born:** 2/2/77 in Austell,
Ht: 6' 0" **Wt:** 156 GA

Recent Statistics

	G	AB	R	H	D	THR	RBI	SB	BB	SO	Avg
1999 AA Trenton	98	338	56	89	11	0	10	44	21	41	64	.263
2000 AAA New Orleans	126	453	82	111	25	2	5	37	13	75	100	.245
2000 MLE	126	446	72	104	24	1	4	32	9	65	104	.233

Drafted with the 12th overall pick by the Red Sox in '98, Everett was acquired by the Astros following the 1999 season as part of the trade for Carl Everett. He has drawn raves about his fielding skills, and he earned the starting shortstop job on the Olympic team based on his range, hands and arm. After a lackluster offensive performance in Triple-A, Everett struggled with the bat in Australia. Some have questioned whether he's strong enough to hit in the majors, but he exhibits good bat control and has some gap power potential. Julio Lugo handled the shortstop duties well as a rookie, so there's no need to rush Everett and his major league-caliber glove.

Keith Ginter

Position: 2B **Opening Day Age:** 24
Bats: R **Throws:** R **Born:** 5/5/76 in Norwalk,
Ht: 5' 10" **Wt:** 190 CA

Recent Statistics

	G	AB	R	H	D	THR	RBI	SB	BB	SO	Avg
2000 AA Round Rock	125	462	108	154	30	3	26	92	24	82	127	.333
2000 NL Houston	5	8	3	2	0	0	1	3	0	1	3	.250
2000 MLE	125	449	90	141	28	2	22	76	16	58	136	.314

Ginter was not considered much of a prospect after hitting 22 home runs in his first 651 career at-bats prior to 2000. Drafted in the 10th round in 1998, the second baseman busted out with a monster season last year in the Double-A Texas League. The Texas Tech product flirted with .400 into June before finishing atop the circuit with a .333 mark. He's always understood the value of working the count and taking a walk, as evidenced by his league-best .457 on-base percentage. Glovework at the keystone isn't his strongest asset, but he cut his errors from 21 in 1999 to 17 last season. He's in the unenviable position of being behind one of the game's best second basemen, but he certainly has turned some heads.

Tony McKnight

Position: P **Opening Day Age:** 23
Bats: L **Throws:** R **Born:** 6/29/77 in
Ht: 6' 5" **Wt:** 205 Texarkana, AR

Recent Statistics

	W	L	ERA	G	GS	Sv	IP	H	R	BB	SO	HR
2000 AA Round Rock	0	2	4.78	6	6	0	32.0	39	19	10	24	4
2000 AAA New Orleans	4	8	4.56	19	19	0	118.1	129	66	36	63	10
2000 NL Houston	4	1	3.86	6	6	0	35.0	35	19	9	23	4

McKnight hasn't traveled the normal high-profile path of a first-rounder, but he finally is establishing himself as the type of pitcher they drafted in 1995. A heavy workload as an amateur took its toll, and elbow and shoulder injuries hampered him throughout his first three pro seasons. Two years ago, McKnight developed in the tough pitching environment of the Texas League and made his major league debut last year. He held his own in six big league starts, and while his fastball is above-average, he depends on location instead of blowing away hitters. A plus-curve is his best offering and a changeup rounds out his assortment of pitches. His track record makes injuries a concern, but his arm has been able to withstand an average of 166.2 innings pitched over the last three years.

Mike Nannini

Position: P
Bats: R **Throws:** R
Ht: 5' 11" **Wt:** 170

Opening Day Age: 20
Born: 8/9/80 in Detroit, MI

Recent Statistics

		W	L	ERA	G	GS	Sv	IP	H	R	BB	SO	HR
1999 A	Auburn	5	3	1.90	11	11	0	75.2	55	19	17	86	2
1999 A	Michigan	4	10	4.43	15	15	0	87.1	107	56	31	68	8
2000 A	Michigan	7	4	3.55	15	15	0	101.1	85	45	33	86	4
2000 A	Kissimmee	7	3	3.33	12	12	0	78.1	83	34	14	56	3

After taking a step backward in 1999, Nannini took two forward last year. A supplemental first-round pick in 1998, he powered his way into the high Class-A Florida State League before his 20th birthday. The Astros love Nannini's poise on the mound and were impressed with adjustments he made in 2000. Not only can he mow down opponents with a 93-96 MPH fastball, but Nannini also demonstrates a feel for locating a potentially filthy slider and changeup down in the zone. He didn't guarantee himself a promotion to Double-A this year, but another split season could be on the horizon.

Roy Oswalt

Position: P
Bats: R **Throws:** R
Ht: 6' 0" **Wt:** 170

Opening Day Age: 23
Born: 8/29/77 in Kosciusko, MS

Recent Statistics

		W	L	ERA	G	GS	Sv	IP	H	R	BB	SO	HR
1999 A	Michigan	13	4	4.46	22	22	0	151.1	144	78	54	143	8
2000 A	Kissimmee	4	3	2.98	8	8	0	45.1	52	15	11	47	1
2000 AA	Round Rock	11	4	1.94	19	18	0	129.2	106	37	22	141	5

Oswalt was a 23rd round draft-and-follow in 1996 with a reputation as a flame-thrower. Signed in 1997, injuries beset his progress until 1999. At just 6-foot, 170-pounds, he pumps his heater into the mid-90s, and he showed the polish to help lead Team USA to the Gold in the Sydney Games. Oswalt's ability to spot his three-pitch arsenal with pinpoint accuracy was noted by league managers, who named him the best control pitcher in the Texas League. He spun two shutouts after his promotion to Double-A, including a dominant 15-K effort in his debut. Although he started the year in the FSL, he managed to lead the league in ERA while finishing second in wins and punchouts.

Tim Redding

Position: P
Bats: R **Throws:** R
Ht: 6' 0" **Wt:** 180

Opening Day Age: 23
Born: 2/12/78 in Rochester, NY

Recent Statistics

		W	L	ERA	G	GS	Sv	IP	H	R	BB	SO	HR
1999 A	Michigan	8	6	4.97	43	11	14	105.0	84	69	76	141	4
2000 A	Kissimmee	12	5	2.68	24	24	0	154.2	125	62	57	170	5
2000 AA	Round Rock	2	0	3.46	5	5	0	26.0	14	12	22	22	4

Equipped with one of the best arms in the system, Florida State league managers recognized Redding's fastball as the circuit's best. His blazing mid-90s fastball could be considered an imposing figure in itself, but the develop-ment of his slider and changeup will decide whether he's destined for a relief role or not. After splitting '99 between the rotation and pen, Redding spent last year as a starter in the Class-A Florida State League. While posting the league's third best ERA, he paced the loop with 170 strikeouts. A 1997 20th rounder, Redding could ride the fast track to Houston.

Wilfredo Rodriguez

Position: P
Bats: L **Throws:** L
Ht: 6' 3" **Wt:** 180

Opening Day Age: 22
Born: 3/20/79 in Bolivar, VZ

Recent Statistics

		W	L	ERA	G	GS	Sv	IP	H	R	BB	SO	HR
1999 A	Kissimmee	15	7	2.88	25	24	0	153.1	108	55	62	148	8
2000 A	Kissimmee	3	5	4.75	9	9	0	53.0	43	29	30	52	5
2000 AA	Round Rock	2	4	5.77	11	11	0	57.2	54	42	52	55	10

Rodriguez came into the 2000 season as one of the top lefthanded pitching prospects in baseball. He was coming off back-to-back dominating seasons and was garnering praise for his lively mid- to high-90s gas. He features a curve and changeup. Rodriguez never got untracked last year after being bothered by shoulder tendinitis and a hamstring injury. His season began in extended spring training and ended with Rodriguez struggling to find his mechanics and command. His uncharacteristic spell of wildness can be attributed to his injuries. Coming off a wasted season, there is no reason to think he won't be able to regain his dominant form in Double-A this year.

Others to Watch

Righthander **Jimmy Barrett** (19) showed a live fastball in the Appalachian League by striking out 72 in 66.2 innings a year after he was drafted in the third round. . . Catcher **John Buck** (20) could be on the verge of a breakthrough season after ripping 33 doubles and 10 homers in the Midwest League last year. The 1998 seventh-rounder was impressive on defense and at the plate in 2000. . . Lefthander **Carlos Hernandez** (20) used a sneaky 89-90 MPH fastball and a great curveball to ring up 115 hitters in 110.2 innings, while allowing just 93 hits. The diminutive 5-foot-10, 145-pounder tossed a no-hitter and effectively changes speeds, but needs to refine his control. . . In two years since being drafted as a sixth-round outfielder **Jason Lane** (24) has garnered two league MVP awards. Last season in the Midwest League, he was among the leaders in all offensive categories, including .299-23-104. . . A broken right arm has been a major concern for righthander **Brad Lidge** (24), who possesses an overpowering arsenal featuring a lively mid-90s heater. He has shown the stuff to emerge as a dominating reliever if he can recover. . . Live-armed righthander **Robert Stiehl** (20) was the Astros' first pick last June, and he made the most of his first 10.2 innings after signing for $1.4 million. A converted catcher, he blew away 20 hitters while surrendering just five hits in his debut season.

Dodger Stadium

Offense

When one thinks of a pitchers' park, one should think of Dodger Stadium. While the park's dimensions seem fairly straightforward at first glance, the power alleys are deep. The foul areas are large, even after adding a section of luxury seats behind home plate last year. A new warning track surface may have been the most dramatic addition last season, as there were significantly more ground-rule doubles bouncing off the rubber and into the crowd.

Defense

That synthetic surface on the warning track caused problems for defensive players. Many stumbled when stepping from the grass to the rock-hard track, and anyone who dared to slide on it never did so again. The stuff was put in to protect the pricey irrigation system that helps keep the field green and soft during the dry summer months. The field is indeed not as hard as it used to be, reducing bad hops on the infield.

Who It Helps the Most

All pitchers are helped, especially at night when the heavy ocean air swoops in and drags balls down at the warning track. Flyball hurlers like Ismael Valdes are assisted the most. Pull hitters might get a bit of an edge, as balls hit down the line have only a three-foot wall to clear.

Who It Hurts the Most

Flyball hitters who tend to smack the ball between the alleys probably are hurt the most. Eric Karros hit almost 30 points higher on the road last season. Adrian Beltre has hit fewer home runs and almost 40 points lower at home in his brief career.

Rookies & Newcomers

Young pitchers like Eric Gagne and Luke Prokopec will tend to have better numbers than they might in a less forgiving park. Should Angel Pena ever make it to the big leagues, his power numbers will be reduced. Though Shawn Green had a disappointing season, he hit just fine at home last year. It was all those unfamiliar parks that did him in.

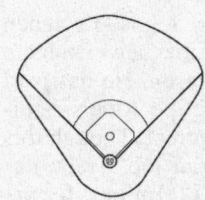

Dimensions: LF-330, LCF-385, CF-395, RCF-385, RF-330

Capacity: 56,000

Elevation: 340 feet

Surface: Grass

Foul Territory: Large

Park Factors

2000 Season

	Home Games			Away Games			
	Dodgers	Opp	Total	Dodgers	Opp	Total	Index
G	75	75	150	72	72	144	—
Avg	.253	.233	.243	.264	.269	.266	91
AB	2452	2550	5002	2530	2411	4941	97
R	340	315	655	400	342	742	85
H	620	595	1215	667	648	1315	89
2B	103	110	213	137	134	271	78
3B	9	8	17	16	10	26	65
HR	101	79	180	95	85	180	99
BB	282	291	573	320	238	558	101
SO	505	561	1066	469	485	954	110
E	70	55	125	56	61	117	103
E-Infield	58	42	100	48	53	101	95
LHB-Avg	.250	.225	.237	.256	.280	.268	88
LHB-HR	41	36	77	34	38	72	102
RHB-Avg	.255	.240	.248	.269	.260	.265	94
RHB-HR	60	43	103	61	47	108	96

1998-2000

	Home Games			Away Games			
	Dodgers	Opp	Total	Dodgers	Opp	Total	Index
G	223	223	446	220	220	440	—
Avg	.258	.240	.249	.257	.265	.261	95
AB	7307	7618	14925	7716	7373	15089	98
R	973	934	1907	1084	1072	2156	87
H	1886	1825	3711	1984	1957	3941	93
2B	290	335	625	366	389	755	84
3B	27	18	45	44	49	93	49
HR	257	235	492	255	234	489	102
BB	735	807	1542	820	813	1633	95
SO	1391	1589	2980	1486	1516	3002	100
E	194	165	359	178	186	364	97
E-Infield	165	131	296	152	152	304	96
LHB-Avg	.248	.242	.245	.242	.282	.265	92
LHB-HR	75	98	173	67	102	169	104
RHB-Avg	.263	.238	.251	.264	.252	.259	97
RHB-HR	182	137	319	188	132	320	101

2000 Rankings (National League)

- Third-highest strikeout factor
- Lowest batting-average factor
- Lowest hit factor
- Lowest double factor
- Lowest RHB batting-average factor
- Second-lowest LHB batting-average factor

Los Angeles

Jim Tracy

2000 Season

After a second season as Davey Johnson's bench coach, Jim Tracy was named the new Dodgers manager a month into the offseason. He has paid his dues, including a stint as Felipe Alou's right-hand man for four years in Montreal. Though this is his first big league managerial job, Tracy has been at the helm for almost 1,000 minor league games. He posted a .508 lifetime winning percentage and led Double-A Harrisburg to a title in 1993.

Offense

Many of the complaints about Johnson centered on his Earl Weaver-esque propensity to wait for the three-run homer. Tracy will be expected to play more little ball, and his initial comments indicated that he will emphasize the importance of bunting, moving runners, hitting the other way, etc. Yet he is inheriting a club composed largely of free-swinging sluggers like Eric Karros and free-swinging popguns like Tom Goodwin. Whether he will have any influence on this high-priced veteran ballclub is going to be the big question.

Pitching & Defense

Tracy also talked about the importance of fielding well, but he is inheriting a team with only two or three players who are above-average glove men. It is one thing to stress the fundamentals to kids on their way up the food chain; it's quite another to do so with multi-millionaires under long-term contracts. As for pitching, the club signed Andy Ashby and re-signed Darren Dreifort, so the rotation is solid from top to bottom. Then the Dodgers hired Jim Colborn as their pitching coach, and they hope he can keep the volatile Chan Ho Park focused.

2001 Outlook

After having just two skippers in their first 38 years in Los Angeles, the Dodgers have made Tracy their fourth new manager since the middle of 1996. Tracy was hired because he's quiet and gets along with general manager Kevin Malone. We'll see how long that plays if the club regresses. There is talk that Tommy Lasorda will be brought back to the dugout as the new bench coach, though one must wonder if the loquacious Hall-of-Famer will be happy as the second banana.

Born: 12/31/55 in Hamilton, OH

Playing Experience: 1980-1981, ChC

Managerial Experience: No major league managing experience

Manager Statistics (Davey Johnson)

Year	Team, Lg	W	L	Pct	GB	Finish
2000	Los Angeles, NL	86	76	.531	11.0	2nd West
14 Seasons		1148	888	.563	—	—

2000 Starting Pitchers by Days Rest

	<=3	4	5	6+
Dodgers Starts	3	86	35	29
Dodgers ERA	7.82	3.71	5.04	4.52
NL Avg Starts	2	80	50	21
NL ERA	5.00	4.61	4.60	5.18

2000 Situational Stats

	Davey Johnson	NL Average
Hit & Run Success %	22.2	33.8
Stolen Base Success %	69.3	68.8
Platoon Pct.	56.1	53.2
Defensive Subs	11	19
High-Pitch Outings	10	14
Quick/Slow Hooks	20/15	14/16
Sacrifice Attempts	80	87

2000 Rankings—Davey Johnson (National Lg)

- 2nd in quick hooks (20)

Adrian Beltre

2000 Season

Despite turning back the hands of time when it was uncovered that someone with the Dodgers had lied about his age when they signed him, Adrian Beltre continued making progress in his second full year in the majors. Though the young Dominican jumped off to a bad start, he got it going after the All-Star break and led the team in both average and RBI during August.

Hitting

Beltre uncoils in a hurry and uses the whole field. As his body matures, many of his gappers should fly up and over the wall, to both left- and right-center field. Right now, most of his homers come on balls he can yank. He sits on fastballs and can be fooled rather easily with breaking stuff away. Though he is a bit of a wild swinger, he showed a good command of the strike zone during his meteoric rise through the minor league system. One assumes that his patience will only improve with more big league experience.

Baserunning & Defense

Beltre really can motor, though that speed has not yet translated into basestealing success. A more aggressive managerial strategy could allow him to double his stolen-base output rather easily. He seldom makes baserunning blunders. Don't be fooled by the error total; the kid can play some defense. Many of his errors come on throws that should never be made, and his stone-handed first sacker doesn't help. Beltre struggles with balls hit directly at him, as he has not yet learned to just attack and trust his natural ability. He already does that on bunts and balls hit to his left, when he occasionally will field grounders on the far side of the shortstop hole.

2001 Outlook

Though the numbers do not necessarily reflect it, Beltre is moving forward and is about ready to have a breakout year. Were someone within the coaching staff to connect with him, it would only accelerate the process. If he continues to make patience a priority, there's a .320-30-100 season-with 25-plus steals lurking just around the corner.

Position: 3B
Bats: R **Throws:** R
Ht: 5'11" **Wt:** 170

Opening Day Age: 21
Born: 4/7/79 in Santo Domingo, Dominican Republic
ML Seasons: 3
Pronunciation: BELL-tray

Overall Statistics

	G	AB	R	H	D	T	HR	RBI	SB	BB	SO	Avg	OBP	Slg
2000	138	510	71	148	30	2	20	85	12	56	80	.290	.360	.475
Career	367	1243	173	338	66	7	42	174	33	131	222	.272	.344	.438

Where He Hits the Ball

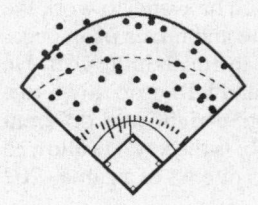

Vs. LHP

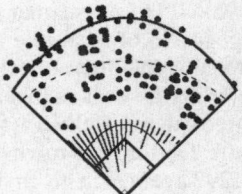

Vs. RHP

2000 Situational Stats

	AB	H	HR	RBI	Avg		AB	H	HR	RBI	Avg
Home	228	64	7	26	.281	LHP	119	33	4	21	.277
Road	282	84	13	59	.298	RHP	391	115	16	64	.294
First Half	259	65	8	38	.251	Sc Pos	137	44	8	69	.321
Scnd Half	251	83	12	47	.331	Clutch	89	16	3	16	.180

2000 Rankings (National League)

- 2nd in errors at third base (23)
- 3rd in lowest fielding percentage at third base (.944)
- Led the Dodgers in most pitches seen per plate appearance (3.95), batting average on an 0-2 count (.273), steals of third (4), lowest percentage of swings on the first pitch (19.5) and batting average with two strikes (.265)
- Led NL third basemen in most pitches seen per plate appearance (3.95), batting average with two strikes (.265) and steals of third (4)

Kevin Brown

Position: SP
Bats: R **Throws:** R
Ht: 6' 4" **Wt:** 200

Opening Day Age: 36
Born: 3/14/65 in McIntyre, GA
ML Seasons: 14

2000 Season

Kevin Brown's season opened unfavorably when he fractured his right pinky while trying to bunt in his second start. He returned just two weeks later with a splint on his pitching hand. He later took the mound despite suffering from bruised ribs. Though he was all over the National League leader boards, Brown managed just 13 wins. The reason was lack of run support; he allowed a 2.40 ERA in his 14 no-decisions.

Pitching

The epitome of nasty in both stuff and demeanor, Brown's main pitches are a heavy sinking fastball that bores down and in on righthanders and a hard slider that breaks in the other direction. He will use a 95-MPH four-seamer when he wants to work the upper part of the strike zone and mixes in an occasional split-finger offering to finish hitters off. He is crafty as well as mean, and will drop down to a three-quarter delivery to give righties a different look. Getting to Brown early is the key. He allowed a .292 average in his first 15 pitches of a game, .202 thereafter.

Defense & Hitting

Brown will go after any ball he can reach and chases down foul pops like no other pitcher. He sometimes tries to do too much and gets himself in trouble, as he is not the most graceful athlete. For a guy with good control, he has trouble with throws to bases and his pickoff move is not very good. Brown strikes out a lot at the plate, though he's not an automatic out.

2001 Outlook

The only reason that the Dodgers are not getting their money's worth out of Brown is that his surrounding cast has not gelled. Brown's home record since joining the club is 16-4 with a 1.87 ERA. The surly righthander clearly is one of the best five pitchers in the game and should remain so for the foreseeable future. After all, he never has shown any signs of arm trouble.

Overall Statistics

	W	L	Pct.	ERA	G	GS	Sv	IP	H	BB	SO	HR	Ratio
2000	13	6	.684	2.58	33	33	0	230.0	181	47	216	21	0.99
Career	170	114	.599	3.21	382	380	0	2660.2	2494	730	1917	161	1.21

How Often He Throws Strikes

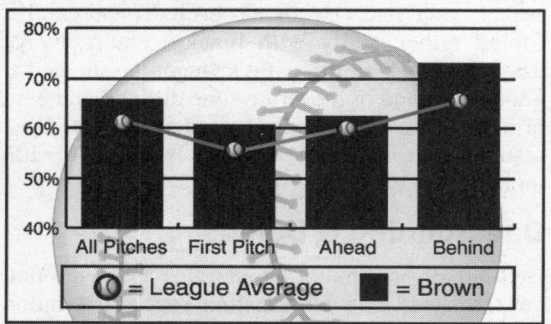

◯ = League Average ■ = Brown

2000 Situational Stats

	W	L	ERA	Sv	IP		AB	H	HR	RBI	Avg
Home	7	1	1.79	0	115.2	LHB	411	93	5	33	.226
Road	6	5	3.38	0	114.1	RHB	437	88	16	39	.201
First Half	8	2	2.38	0	125.0	Sc Pos	178	34	3	46	.191
Scnd Half	5	4	2.83	0	105.0	Clutch	70	15	3	7	.214

2000 Rankings (National League)

- 1st in ERA, highest strikeout/walk ratio (4.6), lowest batting average allowed (.213), lowest on-base percentage allowed (.261), lowest ERA at home and fewest GDPs induced per nine innings (0.4)
- 2nd in sacrifice bunts (14), lowest slugging percentage allowed (.337), errors at pitcher (4) and lowest batting average allowed vs. righthanded batters
- 3rd in strikeouts and highest stolen-base percentage allowed (80.0)
- Led the Dodgers in sacrifice bunts (14), ERA, complete games (5), innings pitched, pickoff throws (142), stolen bases allowed (20) and highest strikeout/walk ratio (4.6)

Alex Cora

2000 Season

Though he was expected to win the starting short-stop job, Alex Cora was outplayed by Kevin Elster last spring and started his third straight campaign in Triple-A. Cora hit .373 at Albuquerque and was recalled after just a month. He continued his hot hitting and had a .282 average at the end of June. Alas, the league quickly caught up to him and he hit just .218 over the final three months. His fine glovework was the only thing that kept him in the lineup.

Hitting

Cora is the classic good-glove, no-stick shortstop. While he packs a little punch, he normally is quite content to slap the ball the other way. He is completely overmatched versus lefthanders and usually was benched against them. Lefties beat him with hard stuff and breaking balls, which he will chase out of the strike zone. Cora could help himself a great deal by developing a better idea of the strike zone.

Baserunning & Defense

Though no basestealer, Cora is a heady runner with enough speed to take the extra sack. Of course, his main problem is getting to first. Defense is his game and he is able to play anywhere in the infield. But it was a revelation to see him play shortstop on a regular basis. He has great range, especially to his left, his hands are very good and he has a strong, accurate arm. While Cora's errors came from youthful exuberance, he is the guy to whom one wants the ball hit at crucial times.

2001 Outlook

While his defense provided much comfort to the pitching staff, Cora is going to have to hit better than he did over the second half of last year. He has flashed offensive improvement at Triple-A the last two years, so there is hope he will do the same in the big leagues, as his older brother Joey did as he matured. It's hard not to root for a guy with Alex' grit and determination.

Position: SS
Bats: L **Throws:** R
Ht: 6' 0" **Wt:** 180

Opening Day Age: 25
Born: 10/18/75 in Caguas, Puerto Rico
ML Seasons: 3

Overall Statistics

	G	AB	R	H	D	T	HR	RBI	SB	BB	SO	Avg	OBP	Slg
2000	109	353	39	84	18	6	4	32	4	26	53	.238	.302	.357
Career	149	416	42	93	19	7	4	35	4	28	65	.224	.286	.332

Where He Hits the Ball

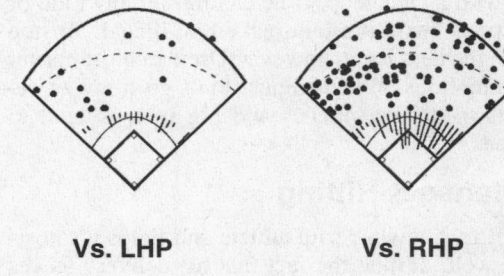

Vs. LHP   **Vs. RHP**

2000 Situational Stats

	AB	H	HR	RBI	Avg		AB	H	HR	RBI	Avg
Home	168	37	2	10	.220	LHP	62	14	0	5	.226
Road	185	47	2	22	.254	RHP	291	70	4	27	.241
First Half	130	33	1	6	.254	Sc Pos	87	17	1	26	.195
Scnd Half	223	51	3	26	.229	Clutch	46	16	0	4	.348

2000 Rankings (National League)

- 5th in fielding percentage at shortstop (.972)
- Led the Dodgers in triples and batting average in the clutch

Darren Dreifort

2000 Season

As usual, Darren Dreifort came out of spring training smoking. He has a 2.83 lifetime ERA in the season's first month before he historically hits the wall, and last year was no different. What *was* different was that he was able to finish the campaign, taking his turn in the rotation until the season's last days.

Pitching

Dreifort's stuff ranks right up there with teammate Kevin Brown's. Dreifort throws a mid-90s fastball that moves so much, he simply needs to aim for the middle of the plate. His high-80s slider is one of the hardest in the game, and it vanishes down and away against righthanders. He's also begun to dabble with a changeup. If he can master any kind of offspeed pitch, it might make him illegal. To step up to the next level, however, Dreifort must master his emotions. When things don't go his way, he starts to groove pitches and big innings tend to ensue.

Defense & Hitting

Dreifort is a wonderful athlete and fields his position well, despite the fact that his delivery leaves him a bit off balance. His pickoff move is OK, though his big leg kick makes him somewhat vulnerable to the stolen base. The former college designated hitter broke out against the Cubs on August 8. Not only did he become the first pitcher since 1990 to hit two home runs in one game, the two blasts combined for an estimated 903 feet! He would be an even better hitter if he would shorten his stroke a little.

2001 Outlook

As he entered free agency, Dreifort figured to be one of the hottest commodities on the market. But the Dodgers were able to keep him in the fold with a five-year, $55 million package in mid-December. The team feels he is on his way to becoming a No. 1 caliber starter. The fact that he has a losing career record and never has pitched 200 innings in a season can be overlooked. His stuff is just too good to ignore.

Position: SP
Bats: R **Throws:** R
Ht: 6' 2" **Wt:** 211

Opening Day Age: 28
Born: 5/3/72 in Wichita, KS
ML Seasons: 6
Pronunciation: DRY-fort

Overall Statistics

	W	L	Pct.	ERA	G	GS	Sv	IP	H	BB	SO	HR	Ratio
2000	12	9	.571	4.16	32	32	0	192.2	175	87	164	31	1.36
Career	39	45	.464	4.28	188	87	10	667.0	636	281	581	68	1.37

How Often He Throws Strikes

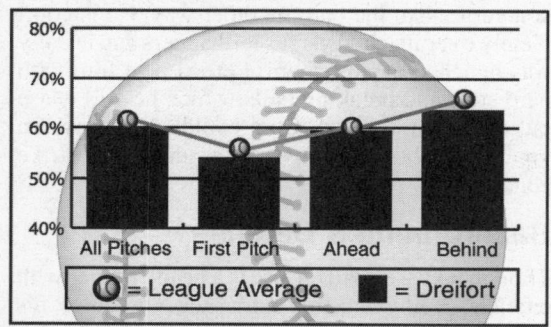

= League Average = Dreifort

2000 Situational Stats

	W	L	ERA	Sv	IP		AB	H	HR	RBI	Avg
Home	6	5	4.44	0	97.1	LHB	356	94	19	57	.264
Road	6	4	3.87	0	95.1	RHB	378	81	12	35	.214
First Half	4	7	5.14	0	98.0	Sc Pos	201	39	8	64	.194
Scnd Half	8	2	3.14	0	94.2	Clutch	29	7	1	2	.241

2000 Rankings (National League)

- 3rd in wild pitches (17) and balks (3)
- 5th in hit batsmen (12), runners caught stealing (10), most run support per nine innings (6.5), lowest batting average allowed vs. righthanded batters and lowest batting average allowed with runners in scoring position
- 8th in stolen bases allowed (19), highest ground-ball/flyball ratio allowed (1.8) and most home runs allowed per nine innings (1.45)
- 9th in lowest batting average allowed (.238) and lowest ERA on the road
- 10th in home runs allowed
- Led the Dodgers in home runs allowed, hit batsmen (12), wild pitches (17), balks (3) and runners caught stealing (10)

Tom Goodwin

2000 Season

One Colorado official called Tom Goodwin the Rockies' MVP through the first couple months of last season. Goodwin was hitting over .340 in mid-June when he suddenly couldn't buy a hit. The Dodgers came calling at the trade deadline, and he returned to where his career began. Back near sea level, his production suffered, as he hit .251 with a paltry .310 on-base percentage for Los Angeles.

Hitting

Goodwin is a slap hitter with very little power. However, he can use the whole field, and balls that get past the outfielders often are triples. He has a fair view of the strike zone, though he could do a better job of drawing walks. His biggest deficiency is an inability to make contact. He struck out 117 times last year and his speed doesn't do much good when he's strolling back to the dugout. He's simply overmatched against the toughest righthanders.

Baserunning & Defense

As one scout put it, Goodwin "can run .300." In fact, some say he's the fastest runner in the game today. He runs effortlessly and has become a better basestealer as he's matured. In center field, his foot speed allows him to run down his mistakes. He can fly from side to side, gets back to the wall in good shape and is athletic enough to hit the turf and still come up with balls hit in front of him. The same scout says that Goodwin "can't throw a lick."

2001 Outlook

As is typical of the current Dodger administration, it bought high with Goodwin. The team now has a speedy outfielder who has hit .269 lifetime anywhere outside Colorado. At Dodger Stadium, his career average is .239. Los Angeles must find spots for both he and Devon White, two overpriced center fielders who might be platooned. Goodwin will steal his share of bases, but his true value will be determined by how often he can reach first base.

Position: CF/LF
Bats: L **Throws:** R
Ht: 6' 1" **Wt:** 175

Opening Day Age: 32
Born: 7/27/68 in Fresno, CA
ML Seasons: 10

Overall Statistics

	G	AB	R	H	D	T	HR	RBI	SB	BB	SO	Avg	OBP	Slg
2000	147	528	94	139	11	9	6	58	55	68	117	.263	.346	.352
Career	941	3130	525	853	94	32	18	230	307	309	522	.273	.339	.340

Where He Hits the Ball

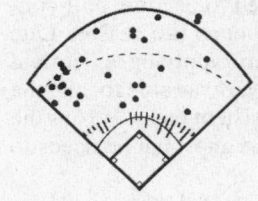 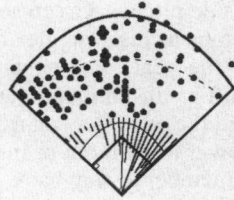

Vs. LHP   **Vs. RHP**

2000 Situational Stats

	AB	H	HR	RBI	Avg		AB	H	HR	RBI	Avg
Home	268	81	4	37	.302	LHP	106	36	2	15	.340
Road	260	58	2	21	.223	RHP	422	103	4	43	.244
First Half	275	79	4	42	.287	Sc Pos	113	34	3	53	.301
Scnd Half	253	60	2	16	.237	Clutch	68	22	1	11	.324

2000 Rankings (National League)

- 2nd in stolen bases (55), steals of third (7), lowest slugging percentage vs. righthanded pitchers (.325) and lowest batting average on the road (.223)
- 3rd in highest percentage of extra bases taken as a runner (72.3) and highest percentage of pitches taken (62.5)
- 5th in triples (9), stolen-base percentage (84.6), fielding percentage in center field (.991) and lowest slugging percentage (.352)
- Led NL center fielders in triples (9), stolen bases (55), highest percentage of pitches taken (62.5) and steals of third (7)

Shawn Green

2000 Season

Last season began with such optimism and promise for Shawn Green. He was coming home again—he went to high school in southern California—with a huge long-term deal, and the fans loved him. Through the end of May, Green was hitting .337 and was on pace to bash 32 homers with 126 RBI. Then it all just stopped. He started slumping and never really shook out of it, hitting just .239 over the last four months of the season.

Hitting

Green's swing is naturally a bit long, and pitchers took advantage of it by busting him inside. Though he strikes out quite a bit, he also has a good eye. When things are going well, he will lay off those inside pitches. Green seemed to become pull-conscious as his struggles continued last season. Late in the year, opponents were applying an infield shift against him, but he never was able to take the ball the other way on a consistent basis. He has the power to hit it out or into the gaps, but he needs to remember to stay back.

Baserunning & Defense

Green glides so gracefully that it's a bit surprising to see how quickly he chews up ground. That speed and his great instincts make him a fine basestealer who also will take the extra base when the opportunity presents itself. In right field, he is the antithesis of the man he replaced, Raul Mondesi. Both are very good, but Green is DiMaggio to Mondy's Clemente. Green gets a great jump and can move well in any direction. His throws are accurate and always to the right base.

2001 Outlook

Green really struggled in his first season in the National League. He wasn't able to adjust when the scouting reports got around after his first few months through the circuit. Don't be surprised if he gains some revenge, however. Though he will not put up the same ridiculous numbers that he had with Toronto, Green has the power, plate discipline and speed to be a perennial MVP candidate.

Position: RF
Bats: L **Throws:** L
Ht: 6' 4" **Wt:** 200

Opening Day Age: 28
Born: 11/10/72 in Des Plaines, IL
ML Seasons: 8

Overall Statistics

	G	AB	R	H	D	T	HR	RBI	SB	BB	SO	Avg	OBP	Slg
2000	162	610	98	164	44	4	24	99	24	90	121	.269	.367	.472
Career	878	3123	500	882	208	19	143	475	100	296	631	.282	.349	.499

Where He Hits the Ball

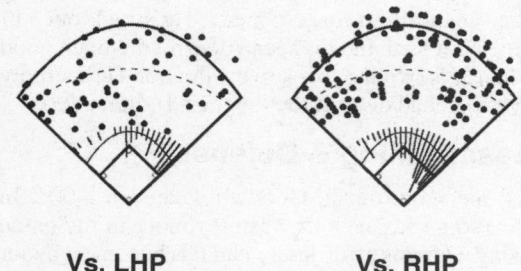

Vs. LHP   Vs. RHP

2000 Situational Stats

	AB	H	HR	RBI	Avg		AB	H	HR	RBI	Avg
Home	297	89	15	53	.300	LHP	185	48	4	24	.259
Road	313	75	9	46	.240	RHP	425	116	20	75	.273
First Half	320	94	13	59	.294	Sc Pos	167	43	6	70	.257
Scnd Half	290	70	11	40	.241	Clutch	97	29	2	10	.299

2000 Rankings (National League)

- 1st in games played
- 4th in pitches seen (2,784) and plate appearances (714)
- 5th in doubles, errors in right field (6) and lowest fielding percentage in right field (.980)
- Led the Dodgers in doubles, stolen bases, intentional walks (9), pitches seen (2,784), plate appearances (714), stolen-base percentage (82.8), batting average with the bases loaded (.467), cleanup slugging percentage (.519) and games played
- Led NL right fielders in at-bats, doubles, plate appearances (714), batting average with the bases loaded (.467) and games played (162)

Mark Grudzielanek

2000 Season

Mark Grudzielanek was hitting .303 on July 6 when he was struck by a nasty viral bug that was circulating throughout the Dodger clubhouse. He was out for 10 days and lost a lot of weight. The already lean infielder never fully recovered, and he hit just .246 over the second half.

Hitting

Grudzielanek is a slasher at the plate. He goes up there hacking and can spray balls to any and all parts of the park, enabling him to average 33 doubles the last five seasons. Miscast as a leadoff hitter, he has settled into the No. 2 spot in the order, where his natural opposite-field stroke can be quite useful. Though he doesn't have a good eye, he recently has made strides at recognizing breaking pitches before they slide away and out of the strike zone. Because of that, he has set new career highs in walks in each of the past two seasons.

Baserunning & Defense

Grudzielanek is quick more than he is fast. He isn't the smartest guy on the basepaths and must be monitored carefully lest he run the club out of an inning. He made the transition to second base relatively well. While his arm was a bit short for the shortstop position, it's more than adequate for second base. He also has plenty of range for the position, especially going to his left, but he did commit 17 errors at the keystone in 2000. Grudzielanek was surprisingly good on double plays, starting them as well as making the pivot.

2001 Outlook

The Dodgers locked Grudzielanek up for several years before last season began, so he will be their second baseman for the foreseeable future. He is not a bad guy to plug into the No. 2 hole, though the organization hopes that he can cut down on his miscues in the field in 2001. Grudzielanek also provides Los Angeles with a backup shortstop should the need arise. He plays hard and his dirty uniform is a welcome sight on a club that does not always appear to give maximum effort.

Position: 2B
Bats: R **Throws:** R
Ht: 6' 1" **Wt:** 185

Opening Day Age: 30
Born: 6/30/70 in Milwaukee, WI
ML Seasons: 6
Pronunciation: gruzz-ell-AH-neck

Overall Statistics

	G	AB	R	H	D	T	HR	RBI	SB	BB	SO	Avg	OBP	Slg
2000	148	617	101	172	35	6	7	49	12	45	81	.279	.335	.389
Career	814	3269	437	935	179	21	35	277	102	165	425	.286	.329	.386

Where He Hits the Ball

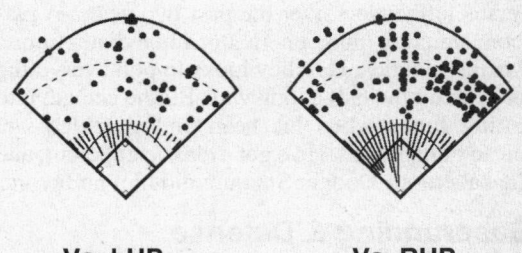

Vs. LHP   **Vs. RHP**

2000 Situational Stats

	AB	H	HR	RBI	Avg		AB	H	HR	RBI	Avg
Home	287	81	4	21	.282	LHP	168	42	2	12	.250
Road	330	91	3	28	.276	RHP	449	130	5	37	.290
First Half	353	107	5	31	.303	Sc Pos	119	28	0	36	.235
Scnd Half	264	65	2	18	.246	Clutch	93	21	1	9	.226

2000 Rankings (National League)

- 2nd in errors at second base (17) and lowest fielding percentage at second base (.976)
- 5th in at-bats
- 8th in highest groundball/flyball ratio (1.8) and lowest HR frequency (88.1 ABs per HR)
- 9th in singles
- 10th in lowest slugging percentage vs. lefthanded pitchers (.357) and lowest on-base percentage vs. lefthanded pitchers (.317)
- Led the Dodgers in at-bats, hits, singles, triples, hit by pitch (9), highest groundball/flyball ratio (1.8), lowest percentage of swings that missed (12.1), highest percentage of swings put into play (49.3) and highest percentage of extra bases taken as a runner (50.8)

Todd Hundley

2000 Season

Todd Hundley came out the box looking to make amends for his disastrous 1999 campaign. Despite sitting out almost all of June with a strained ribcage muscle, he had 17 homers at the break. But he also missed almost all of July when a foul tip broke his right thumb. He was never able to regain his stroke after his second return. He reverted to his low-average, low-contact ways, hitting .239 in the season's final two months.

Hitting

For the second straight year, Hundley abandoned switch-hitting during the season to stick with the left side. After the change, he still looked helpless against southpaws. He's hit .180 with four homers versus lefthanders over the past two years. A platoon situation may be in his immediate future. Against righties, Hundley looks to pull everything and can hit the ball a long way. But he can get into hitting funks when his head and shoulders get ahead of his hands. He's got a classic uppercut, and the cavernous Dodger Stadium did him no favors.

Baserunning & Defense

The burly catcher is as station-to-station as they come. Hundley is not very good defensively. He doesn't slide well to block balls in the dirt and gets lazy with his glovework. His throwing, while still atrocious, actually improved as the season progressed. Still, he remains just as likely to bounce balls to second base and into center field as he is to hit the middle infielder's mitt.

2001 Outlook

The Dodgers divulged they were going in a different direction behind the plate, and Hundley agreed to a four-year, $23.5 million deal with the Cubs in early December. Chicago hopes he can assume a majority of the catching duties and add some punch to its everyday lineup. He certainly stands to benefit offensively from the move to a much more accommodating venue. Hundley has battled through a number of injuries over the past few seasons, but he should add a lot to Chicago in terms of character, toughness and power. His father, Randy, was a backstop for the Cubs for 10 years.

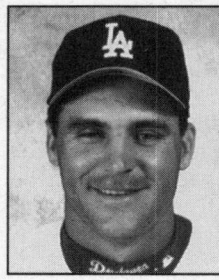

Position: C
Bats: B **Throws:** R
Ht: 5'11" **Wt:** 199

Opening Day Age: 31
Born: 5/27/69 in Martinsville, VA
ML Seasons: 11

Overall Statistics

	G	AB	R	H	D	T	HR	RBI	SB	BB	SO	Avg	OBP	Slg
2000	90	299	49	85	16	0	24	70	0	45	69	.284	.375	.579
Career	1033	3224	438	775	148	7	172	522	14	388	806	.240	.325	.451

Where He Hits the Ball

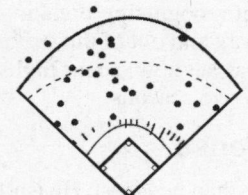
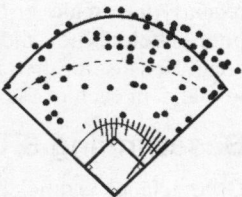

Vs. LHP   **Vs. RHP**

2000 Situational Stats

	AB	H	HR	RBI	Avg		AB	H	HR	RBI	Avg
Home	142	33	10	30	.232	LHP	76	18	4	17	.237
Road	157	52	14	40	.331	RHP	223	67	20	53	.300
First Half	158	50	17	43	.316	Sc Pos	77	28	10	53	.364
Scnd Half	141	35	7	27	.248	Clutch	48	10	2	7	.208

2000 Rankings (National League)

- 1st in errors at catcher (13)
- 2nd in lowest percentage of runners caught stealing as a catcher (20.0)
- 5th in batting average with runners in scoring position
- Led the Dodgers in batting average with runners in scoring position and highest percentage of pitches taken (58.9)

Eric Karros

2000 Season

After threatening to break up near the end of every July, Eric Karros and the Dodgers finally agreed to tie the knot before last season. The parties agreed upon a three-year, $24 million extension in February of 2000 that contains a no-trade clause through 2001. Karros then went out and produced the 30 homers and 100 RBI that have become expected. In fact, it was the fifth time in the last six years that he has reached those benchmarks. His average, however, was his lowest since 1993.

Hitting

Karros is very streaky, as is evidenced by his monthly batting averages: .222, .320, .220, .301, .250, and .182. He also had homerless streaks of 19 and 27 games in the second half of last season. When he regains his power stroke, the longballs come in bunches. He is somewhat odd for a righthanded hitter in that he likes the ball down and in. He will jump all over a high inside fastball as well. Breaking balls down and away can send him fishing, but a pitcher is advised to alter his pattern. Karros is a sharp guy who makes constant adjustments at the plate.

Baserunning & Defense

While Karros carries the proverbial piano on his back, he seldom runs his club out of an inning. He likes to steal the occasional base when opponents forget about him. However, a chronically creaky left knee has reduced those attempts. Though fundamentally sound, Karros is a mediocre first sacker at best. What he lacks in range, he compounds by having extremely poor hands. His inability to dig throws out of the dirt puts a lot of pressure on the Dodger infielders.

2001 Outlook

Like the sun, the seasons and the swallows that always return to nearby Capistrano, the Dodgers have come to depend on the power numbers Karros annually provides. He should be able to keep posting those figures for at least a couple more seasons, though it would not be shocking if the knee caused him to miss some playing time in the not-too-distant future.

Position: 1B
Bats: R **Throws:** R
Ht: 6' 4" **Wt:** 226

Opening Day Age: 33
Born: 11/4/67 in Hackensack, NJ
ML Seasons: 10
Pronunciation: CARE-ose

Overall Statistics

	G	AB	R	H	D	T	HR	RBI	SB	BB	SO	Avg	OBP	Slg
2000	155	584	84	146	29	0	31	106	4	63	122	.250	.321	.459
Career	1338	5040	658	1363	254	9	242	840	50	439	930	.270	.328	.468

Where He Hits the Ball

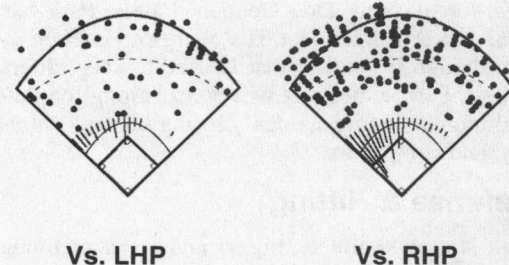

Vs. LHP   **Vs. RHP**

2000 Situational Stats

	AB	H	HR	RBI	Avg		AB	H	HR	RBI	Avg
Home	289	68	16	52	.235	LHP	140	40	5	22	.286
Road	295	78	15	54	.264	RHP	444	106	26	84	.239
First Half	313	83	25	70	.265	Sc Pos	174	42	9	78	.241
Scnd Half	271	63	6	36	.232	Clutch	91	20	7	24	.220

2000 Rankings (National League)

- 2nd in sacrifice flies (12) and lowest percentage of extra bases taken as a runner (27.5)
- 3rd in lowest groundball/flyball ratio (0.7)
- 4th in fielding percentage at first base (.995)
- 5th in lowest batting average at home
- 6th in lowest on-base percentage vs. righthanded pitchers (.301)
- 7th in GDPs (18), lowest batting average and lowest batting average vs. righthanded pitchers
- 9th in errors at first base (7)
- Led the Dodgers in sacrifice flies (12), strikeouts, GDPs (18) and batting average vs. lefthanded pitchers

Chan Ho Park

2000 Season

An historically slow starter, Chan Ho Park pitched dramatically better in last year's second half. He allowed just six home runs after the All-Star break (compared to 15 before) and improved his strike-out-walk ratio from 1.5 to 2.1. In the season's final two months, he went 7-2 with a microscopic 1.79 ERA. He ended the campaign with a 25-inning scoreless streak.

Pitching

Park has great stuff and still is learning to use it. His fastball, though relatively straight, can reach 95 MPH. He has a knee-buckling curveball that he has gotten away from in recent years. When he gets that pitch over, his style is reminiscent of Nolan Ryan or a young Doc Gooden. Lately, Park has gone more with a slider. His changeup is improving, though it's still primarily used to keep hitters honest. Park sometimes will breeze along for several innings before suddenly losing his concentration and composure.

Defense & Hitting

Park is a good athlete, bigger and faster than one might think. He gets off the mound very quickly, though he doesn't always make sound decisions once he has the ball. He's one of the best pitchers in the game at controlling the running game. He has a decent move and delivers the pitch very quickly. Opposing basestealers were just 3-for-11 against him last year and are under .500 over his career. Park likes to hit and never gets cheated. When he connects, he can hit the ball a long way, and he clubbed his first two homers last season. He also managed to hit .214, exactly the same average he allowed.

2001 Outlook

Much of Park's improvement last season must be attributed to being teamed up with Chad Kreuter, who quickly gained the 27-year-old's trust. The veteran catcher was able to keep Park from falling into a funk. Park is due to make big bucks in arbitration, but the Dodgers hope to tie him up for several more years down the road.

Position: SP
Bats: R **Throws:** R
Ht: 6' 2" **Wt:** 204

Opening Day Age: 27
Born: 6/30/73 in Kong Ju City, Korea
ML Seasons: 7

Overall Statistics

	W	L	Pct.	ERA	G	GS	Sv	IP	H	BB	SO	HR	Ratio
2000	18	10	.643	3.27	34	34	0	226.0	173	124	217	21	1.31
Career	65	43	.602	3.88	185	141	0	949.2	818	469	880	101	1.36

How Often He Throws Strikes

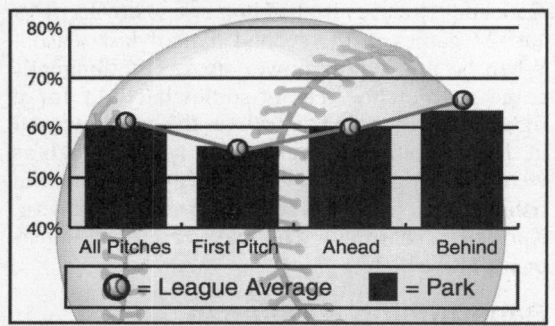

2000 Situational Stats

	W	L	ERA	Sv	IP		AB	H	HR	RBI	Avg
Home	10	4	2.34	0	119.0	LHB	399	91	12	41	.228
Road	8	6	4.29	0	107.0	RHB	410	82	9	39	.200
First Half	9	6	4.17	0	121.0	Sc Pos	201	32	1	50	.159
Scnd Half	9	4	2.23	0	105.0	Clutch	55	9	2	3	.164

2000 Rankings (National League)

- 1st in lowest batting average allowed vs. righthanded batters and lowest batting average allowed with runners in scoring position
- 2nd in walks allowed, strikeouts and lowest batting average allowed (.214)
- 3rd in lowest ERA at home
- 4th in wild pitches (13), pitches thrown (3,696), lowest slugging percentage allowed (.344), lowest stolen-base percentage allowed (27.3) and highest walks per nine innings (4.9)
- 5th in wins, hit batsmen (12) and most strikeouts per nine innings (8.6)
- Led the Dodgers in wins, losses, games started, batters faced (963), walks allowed, hit batsmen (12), strikeouts and pitches thrown (3,696)

Jeff Shaw

2000 Season

Jeff Shaw never had been on the disabled list in his 11-year career, and it required an 8.00 ERA to force him to go on the DL last season. Following a short stint to allow some elbow tendinitis to subside, he returned better than ever. After blowing more saves in the first half than he had during all of 1999, Shaw was virtually flawless after the All-Star break. He went 15-for-15 in save opportunities and allowed just three runs over the final three months of the 2000 campaign.

Pitching

Shaw throws in the low 90s and possesses great control of his fastball. He likes to bust the first one up and in on the hands for a strike. He also has a solid slider and likes to get hitters out with a split-finger pitch. The elbow troubles, which often accompany the splitter, were causing Shaw to leave his out pitch up over the plate, where it's quite hittable. He allowed a .328 average before the break, but only a .194 mark once he was healthy. Shaw truly has a closer's mentality; he just wants the ball with the game on the line.

Defense & Hitting

Shaw fields his position well. He gets off the mound quickly, makes sound decisions and is quite athletic. He has little in the way of a pickoff move, however, and takes some time to deliver the ball to the plate. Opposing basestealers are 27-for-30 (90 percent) against him over the last five years. Shaw's last base hit came in 1994, and he hardly ever is asked to pick up a bat.

2001 Outlook

Shaw's spectacular second half was hidden by his horrible first three months of the Dodgers' disappointing season. If Los Angeles is to make a run this year, he will be an integral part of the bullpen mix. Should the club fail to contend, however, it would not be out of the question to see him moved for some much-needed young talent.

Position: RP
Bats: R **Throws:** R
Ht: 6' 2" **Wt:** 200

Opening Day Age: 34
Born: 7/7/66 in Washington Courthouse, OH
ML Seasons: 11

Overall Statistics

	W	L	Pct.	ERA	G	GS	Sv	IP	H	BB	SO	HR	Ratio
2000	3	4	.429	4.24	60	0	27	57.1	61	16	39	7	1.34
Career	31	49	.388	3.54	556	19	160	773.1	758	216	487	81	1.26

How Often He Throws Strikes

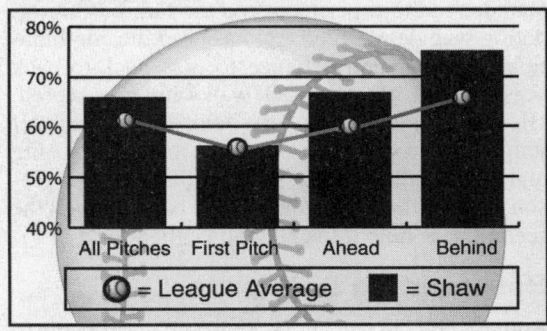

○ = League Average   ■ = Shaw

2000 Situational Stats

	W	L	ERA	Sv	IP		AB	H	HR	RBI	Avg
Home	3	2	3.93	12	34.1	LHB	112	34	3	10	.304
Road	0	2	4.70	15	23.0	RHB	118	27	4	13	.229
First Half	2	4	8.00	12	27.0	Sc Pos	58	11	2	17	.190
Scnd Half	1	0	0.89	15	30.1	Clutch	159	45	6	19	.283

2000 Rankings (National League)

- 3rd in blown saves (7)
- 4th in lowest save percentage (79.4)
- 8th in save opportunities (34) and saves
- 9th in games finished (51)
- Led the Dodgers in saves, games finished (51), save opportunities (34), save percentage (79.4), blown saves (7) and lowest batting average allowed in relief with runners in scoring position (.190)

Gary Sheffield

2000 Season

Despite being hobbled by a sprained right ankle suffered in early April, Gary Sheffield carried the Dodgers over the first half of last season. The suspensions that were handed down after the battle with fans in the stands at Wrigley Field on May 16 seemed to weigh most heavily on Sheffield, who argued to the end that he was serving as a peacemaker in the incident. The suspension, a case of the flu and a bad back limited Sheffield to just 199 at-bats after the All-Star break.

Hitting

Sheffield has one of the quickest bats in baseball. He tried to steady his bat early last spring, but soon abandoned the experiment and the familiar intimidating waggle returned. He has used the combination of power and patience to post back-to-back seasons with 100-plus RBI, walks and runs scored. His main power is to left field, but he can hit longballs out to any part of the park. Opposing clubs quite often used a shift against him last season, but Sheffield was able to drill balls through the second base hole if the situation called for it.

Baserunning & Defense

Bothered by the bad ankle, Sheffield wasn't able to steal bases as often as he had in the past. He doesn't always run hard and is criticized for his apparent lack of effort at times. But he seems to know when to turn it on and is a savvy baserunner. His instincts in the outfield are just fair; he began as a shortstop and never has completely adjusted to the outfield. He has a strong, accurate arm and will seldom throw to the wrong bag.

2001 Outlook

Having now put up 500 at-bats back-to-back for the first time in his career, Sheffield has matured as he's moved into his 30s. He has played through nagging injuries and become a vocal presence in the disjointed Dodger clubhouse. He wants to win, but if the chaos in Los Angeles continues and he doesn't connect with new skipper Jim Tracy, Sheffield could re-emerge as an irritant.

Position: LF
Bats: R **Throws:** R
Ht: 5'11" **Wt:** 205

Opening Day Age: 32
Born: 11/18/68 in Tampa, FL
ML Seasons: 13

Overall Statistics

	G	AB	R	H	D	T	HR	RBI	SB	BB	SO	Avg	OBP	Slg
2000	141	501	105	163	24	3	43	109	4	101	71	.325	.438	.643
Career	1449	5146	884	1508	265	19	279	916	160	858	621	.293	.397	.515

Where He Hits the Ball

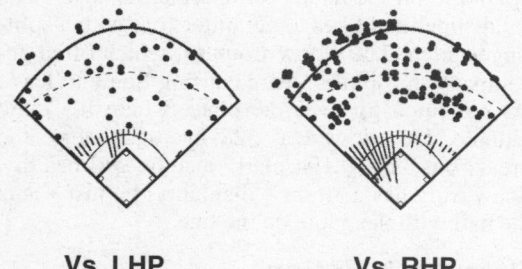

Vs. LHP   **Vs. RHP**

2000 Situational Stats

	AB	H	HR	RBI	Avg		AB	H	HR	RBI	Avg
Home	237	73	23	52	.308	LHP	123	35	7	17	.285
Road	264	90	20	57	.341	RHP	378	128	36	92	.339
First Half	302	101	27	71	.334	Sc Pos	126	45	10	66	.357
Scnd Half	199	62	16	38	.312	Clutch	70	16	4	9	.229

2000 Rankings (National League)

- 1st in errors in left field (10)
- 2nd in HR frequency (11.7 ABs per HR) and lowest fielding percentage in left field (.954)
- 3rd in on-base percentage and slugging percentage vs. righthanded pitchers (.685)
- 4th in slugging percentage
- 5th in on-base percentage vs. righthanded pitchers (.442)
- Led the Dodgers in batting average, home runs, runs scored, total bases (322), RBI, caught stealing (6), walks, times on base (268), slugging percentage, on-base percentage, HR frequency (11.7 ABs per HR), batting average vs. righthanded pitchers and slugging percentage vs. lefthanded pitchers (.512)

Terry Adams

Position: RP
Bats: R **Throws:** R
Ht: 6' 3" **Wt:** 215

Opening Day Age: 28
Born: 3/6/73 in Mobile, AL
ML Seasons: 6

Overall Statistics

	W	L	Pct.	ERA	G	GS	Sv	IP	H	BB	SO	HR	Ratio
2000	6	9	.400	3.52	66	0	2	84.1	80	39	56	6	1.41
Career	25	35	.417	3.93	342	0	39	415.0	409	207	343	31	1.48

2000 Situational Stats

	W	L	ERA	Sv	IP		AB	H	HR	RBI	Avg
Home	4	4	2.88	0	40.2	LHB	159	36	1	12	.226
Road	2	5	4.12	2	43.2	RHB	168	44	5	25	.262
First Half	3	3	2.89	2	46.2	Sc Pos	93	19	2	29	.204
Scnd Half	3	6	4.30	0	37.2	Clutch	180	46	4	23	.256

2000 Season

Acquired in the trade that sent Eric Young and Ismael Valdes to the Cubs, Terry Adams had something to prove to the many that criticized the deal. Though suffering from a troublesome pitching shoulder on occasion, Adams proved to be an effective setup man.

Pitching, Defense & Hitting

Adams goes right after hitters with a fastball that can reach 97 MPH. Because it's rather straight, he needs to mix in a hard slider. When he is off his game, it is often because he cannot get the breaking pitch over for strikes. Hitters then sit on the fastball, which Adams sometimes will obligingly groove. He looks rather awkward getting off the mound and has made six errors the last three years. However, he has a compact delivery and is able to control the running game pretty well. Adams is seldom asked to bat, for good reason.

2001 Outlook

Adams has made a habit of fading down the stretch. His lifetime ERA is a full two runs higher after the break than it is before. He does not seem to have the makeup to close games regularly, but new skipper Jim Tracy might disagree. When healthy, Adams certainly has the stuff to handle the job.

Mike Fetters

Position: RP
Bats: R **Throws:** R
Ht: 6' 4" **Wt:** 226

Opening Day Age: 36
Born: 12/19/64 in Van Nuys, CA
ML Seasons: 12

Overall Statistics

	W	L	Pct.	ERA	G	GS	Sv	IP	H	BB	SO	HR	Ratio
2000	6	2	.750	3.24	51	0	5	50.0	35	25	40	7	1.20
Career	25	35	.417	3.59	473	6	90	589.2	572	273	413	49	1.43

2000 Situational Stats

	W	L	ERA	Sv	IP		AB	H	HR	RBI	Avg
Home	4	1	3.67	2	27.0	LHB	95	18	6	11	.189
Road	2	1	2.74	3	23.0	RHB	76	17	1	7	.224
First Half	3	1	2.42	3	22.1	Sc Pos	46	10	1	11	.217
Scnd Half	3	1	3.90	2	27.2	Clutch	90	18	4	9	.200

2000 Season

Mike Fetters was one of the Dodgers' most pleasant surprises last season. Signed to help shore up a 1999 trouble spot in the bullpen, he allowed just 12 hits in the first half. He was so effective that when stopper Jeff Shaw blew up and eventually went on the disabled list, Fetters received a few chances to close games. He converted five of seven save opportunities.

Pitching, Defense & Hitting

Fetters still throws in the low 90s and often will groove the first one in order to get ahead in the count. His bread-and-butter pitch is a splitter that is usually out of the strike zone, so he walks his fair share of hitters. The pitch breaks down and away from lefties, who hit .189 against him last season. He gets off the mound rather well for an overweight guy, but his herky-jerky delivery leaves him vulnerable to the stolen base. He has yet to step to the plate in the big leagues.

2001 Outlook

The Dodgers rewarded Fetters with a two-year, $4.25 million deal with a club option for 2003 in mid-October. Now the team must hold its breath. Fetters has been on the disabled list several times in his career with elbow troubles and was seldom able to pitch in back-to-back games last season.

Eric Gagne

Position: SP
Bats: R **Throws:** R
Ht: 6' 2" **Wt:** 195

Opening Day Age: 25
Born: 1/7/76 in
Montreal, Canada
ML Seasons: 2

Overall Statistics

	W	L	Pct.	ERA	G	GS	Sv	IP	H	BB	SO	HR	Ratio
2000	4	6	.400	5.15	20	19	0	101.1	106	60	79	20	1.64
Career	5	7	.417	4.45	25	24	0	131.1	124	75	109	23	1.52

2000 Situational Stats

	W	L	ERA	Sv	IP		AB	H	HR	RBI	Avg
Home	1	4	5.37	0	57.0	LHB	190	50	11	33	.263
Road	3	2	4.87	0	44.1	RHB	203	56	9	26	.276
First Half	1	5	5.43	0	64.2	Sc Pos	96	19	3	37	.198
Scnd Half	3	1	4.66	0	36.2	Clutch	3	0	0	0	.000

2000 Season

Fully expected to win a rotation spot last spring, Eric Gagne instead was sent to Triple-A. When he returned to fill in for an injured Kevin Brown, Gagne showed his inexperience by pitching tentatively and running up such high pitch counts that he seldom lasted more than five innings. He shuttled between LA and Albuquerque before finally settling in with the big club at the end of the season.

Pitching, Defense & Hitting

The native Canadian has all the stuff to make it in the major leagues. He can reach 94 MPH with his four-seam fastball, and his two-seamer bores in a good eight inches on righthanded hitters. Gagne also has a fine curveball and his changeup, while erratic, shows great promise. What he lacks is command. He needs to quicken his delivery, as opposing basestealers ran almost at will. He can field his position just fine and is no easy out at the plate.

2001 Outlook

Gagne has little left to prove in the minors, and he's tasted major league success the last month of the past two seasons. Now the Dodgers need to show some patience and let the kid mature into the No. 2 or 3 starter he will eventually become.

Matt Herges

Position: RP
Bats: L **Throws:** R
Ht: 6' 0" **Wt:** 200

Opening Day Age: 30
Born: 4/1/70 in
Champaign, IL
ML Seasons: 2

Overall Statistics

	W	L	Pct.	ERA	G	GS	Sv	IP	H	BB	SO	HR	Ratio
2000	11	3	.786	3.17	59	4	1	110.2	100	40	75	7	1.27
Career	11	5	.688	3.33	76	4	1	135.0	124	48	93	12	1.27

2000 Situational Stats

	W	L	ERA	Sv	IP		AB	H	HR	RBI	Avg
Home	5	2	2.32	0	54.1	LHB	170	45	4	24	.265
Road	6	1	3.99	1	56.1	RHB	232	55	3	33	.237
First Half	6	0	3.27	0	52.1	Sc Pos	127	34	2	51	.268
Scnd Half	5	3	3.09	1	58.1	Clutch	91	22	2	10	.242

2000 Season

Not even expected to make the Dodgers out of spring training, Matt Herges probably was the club's most valuable player the first month of last season. He did not allow an earned run in his first 12 relief appearances, a span of 19.1 innings. While he didn't fare as well in four spot starts, he proved to be both durable and dependable.

Pitching, Defense & Hitting

Herges is not very tall and has a compact delivery, so his 92-MPH fastball sneaks up on hitters. He gets some movement on it and can locate it anywhere in the strike zone. Herges also has a tight little curveball that he can get over the plate. His best attribute may be his fearlessness. Because he gets the ball to the plate so quickly, opposing basestealers were just 7-for-13 against him. Herges is a good athlete and fields his position adequately. He failed to make contact in eight of 14 plate appearances last year.

2001 Outlook

After a long and arduous eight-year journey through the Dodgers' minor league system, Herges looks like he's going to stay awhile. While he conceivably could be converted into a starter, his durability and the acquisition of Andy Ashby may keep him in middle relief.

Chad Kreuter

Position: C
Bats: B **Throws:** R
Ht: 6' 2" **Wt:** 200

Opening Day Age: 36
Born: 8/26/64 in Greenbrae, CA
ML Seasons: 13
Pronunciation: CREW-ter

Overall Statistics

	G	AB	R	H	D	T	HR	RBI	SB	BB	SO	Avg	OBP	Slg
2000	80	212	32	56	13	0	6	28	1	54	48	.264	.416	.410
Career	823	2201	260	525	106	7	46	245	4	307	508	.239	.334	.356

2000 Situational Stats

	AB	H	HR	RBI	Avg		AB	H	HR	RBI	Avg
Home	101	22	4	10	.218	LHP	59	17	4	8	.288
Road	111	34	2	18	.306	RHP	153	39	2	20	.255
First Half	114	31	5	14	.272	Sc Pos	54	13	1	22	.241
Scnd Half	98	25	1	14	.255	Clutch	31	8	0	1	.258

2000 Season

Chad Kreuter provided what the Dodgers needed, a veteran backup catcher who could control the running game and settle down the Dodgers' hypersensitive rotation. The fact that he reached base safely in 53 of 64 starts was a pleasant surprise.

Hitting, Baserunning & Defense

The switch-hitting Kreuter exhibited much more patience last season than he ever had before, walking more than he struck out. He makes contact from both sides and has gap power, though he can take the occasional hanging breaking pitch deep, especially from the right side. While he moves well for a catcher, he basically is a station-to-station guy. The 13-year veteran did a wonderful job with the pitching staff, especially Chan Ho Park, with whom he developed a special rapport as his designated catcher. The staff ERA with Kreuter catching was 3.52 (4.10 overall). He is fundamentally sound and threw out 40 percent of opposing basestealers.

2001 Outlook

The Dodgers signed the 36-year-old to a two-year, $2.3 million deal with an option for 2003 immediately following his career season. The departure of free agent Todd Hundley means Kreuter will assume a majority of the backstop duties in 2001, possibly sharing some time with Paul LoDuca.

Antonio Osuna

Position: RP
Bats: R **Throws:** R
Ht: 5'11" **Wt:** 206

Opening Day Age: 27
Born: 4/12/73 in Sinaloa, Mexico
ML Seasons: 6
Pronunciation: oh-SOO-nuh

Overall Statistics

	W	L	Pct.	ERA	G	GS	Sv	IP	H	BB	SO	HR	Ratio
2000	3	6	.333	3.74	46	0	0	67.1	57	35	70	7	1.37
Career	24	21	.533	3.28	265	0	10	327.0	261	141	346	32	1.23

2000 Situational Stats

	W	L	ERA	Sv	IP		AB	H	HR	RBI	Avg
Home	1	4	3.57	0	35.1	LHB	110	25	1	13	.227
Road	2	2	3.94	0	32.0	RHB	139	32	6	20	.230
First Half	1	4	3.15	0	34.1	Sc Pos	66	16	0	24	.242
Scnd Half	2	2	4.36	0	33.0	Clutch	86	20	4	18	.233

2000 Season

After missing almost all of 1999 with right elbow problems, Antonio Osuna finally made it back to the big leagues last May. He was used primarily in middle relief and was up to the task. He contributed more than the club had any right to expect.

Pitching, Defense & Hitting

Pitching out of the stretch and with an extremely compact delivery, Osuna gets a surprising amount of heat on his fastball. He may have lost a couple of ticks on the gun since undergoing elbow surgery in September of 1999, but he still can reach the low to mid-90s. His fastball is quite straight, however, and he likes to use the upper part of the strike zone. He developed a splitter during his rehab and it could become a valuable part of his arsenal as he develops a feel for the pitch. His breaking ball is weak, and he has trouble getting it over the plate. Osuna's move is not very good, and he is just an average fielder. He is seldom asked to pick up a bat.

2001 Outlook

Another year removed from the operating table, Osuna should only improve. His middle-relief role with the Dodgers is pretty secure. Should the splitter become a strikeout pitch, one can envision a scenario where he again receives opportunities to close some games.

Los Angeles

Carlos Perez

Position: SP
Bats: L **Throws:** L
Ht: 6' 3" **Wt:** 210

Opening Day Age: 30
Born: 1/14/71 in Nigua,
Dominican Republic
ML Seasons: 5

Overall Statistics

	W	L	Pct.	ERA	G	GS	Sv	IP	H	BB	SO	HR	Ratio
2000	5	8	.385	5.56	30	22	0	144.0	192	33	64	25	1.56
Career	40	53	.430	4.44	142	127	0	822.2	900	211	448	108	1.35

2000 Situational Stats

	W	L	ERA	Sv	IP		AB	H	HR	RBI	Avg
Home	1	2	3.84	0	65.2	LHB	142	42	6	21	.296
Road	4	6	7.01	0	78.1	RHB	450	150	19	68	.333
First Half	4	4	5.05	0	98.0	Sc Pos	150	50	6	59	.333
Scnd Half	1	4	6.65	0	46.0	Clutch	21	6	2	3	.286

2000 Season

Carlos Perez won more than twice as many games and lowered his ERA by almost two full runs over 1999. Of course, he remained one of the worst pitchers in baseball. After accepting a demotion in April, the southpaw balked at further trips to Triple-A. So rather than eat his contract, the Dodgers shuttled Perez between the rotation and bullpen before September shoulder surgery shut him down.

Pitching, Defense & Hitting

Never a hard thrower, Perez has been topping out in the mid-80s the last two years. Because the reduced velocity makes his fastball look too much like his changeup, hitters can sit on one and have time to adjust to the other. While he has good control, he has to nibble so much that he often finds himself behind in the count. His move is mediocre at best. He gets off the mound in good shape, though he can be a bit gangly. He is not a bad hitter, and he rapped out a double and triple last year.

2001 Outlook

Perhaps Perez had been suffering shoulder pain the last couple years and just hadn't said anything until it became unbearable. That would explain the horrible performance and severely reduced velocity. The Dodgers owe him $7.5 million, so they will try to get whatever they can out of him.

F.P. Santangelo

Position: CF/LF
Bats: B **Throws:** R
Ht: 5'10" **Wt:** 165

Opening Day Age: 33
Born: 10/24/67 in
Livonia, MI
ML Seasons: 6
Pronunciation:
san-TAN-jel-oh

Overall Statistics

	G	AB	R	H	D	T	HR	RBI	SB	BB	SO	Avg	OBP	Slg
2000	81	142	19	28	4	0	1	9	3	21	33	.197	.322	.246
Career	633	1620	242	401	83	14	21	154	36	229	302	.248	.365	.355

2000 Situational Stats

	AB	H	HR	RBI	Avg		AB	H	HR	RBI	Avg
Home	70	9	0	0	.129	LHP	57	8	0	4	.140
Road	72	19	1	9	.264	RHP	85	20	1	5	.235
First Half	120	22	0	7	.183	Sc Pos	28	7	0	8	.250
Scnd Half	22	6	1	2	.273	Clutch	21	1	0	0	.048

2000 Season

Expected to be a crucial component off the Dodger bench, F.P. Santangelo got off to a horrible start. His average stood at a paltry .119 at the end of May. Just when he was finding his stroke, a series of thumb injuries essentially finished his season.

Hitting, Baserunning & Defense

Santangelo is a slap-hitting switch-hitter who occasionally can leg out a double. He will use the whole field from both sides of the plate and has a pretty good eye. Used mostly as a pinch-hitter in 2000, he usually hacked at the first fastball he saw. He is quick on the bases and can swipe the occasional bag. Santangelo's principal asset is his versatility with the glove. He can handle any outfield position and plays a decent second base. While his arm is nothing special, he gets good breaks on grounders and flies, and he doesn't hurt a club in the middle of the diamond.

2001 Outlook

Signed to a two-year, $1.6 million contract in January of 2000, Santangelo will look to make amends for his lost season. He has been a solid little utility man in the past, and there is no reason to believe that last year was anything but an aberration.

Ismael Valdes

Position: SP
Bats: R **Throws:** R
Ht: 6' 4" **Wt:** 225

Opening Day Age: 27
Born: 8/21/73 in Ciudad Victoria, Mexico
ML Seasons: 7
Pronunciation: ISH-mail val-DEZZ
Nickname: Rocket

Overall Statistics

	W	L	Pct.	ERA	G	GS	Sv	IP	H	BB	SO	HR	Ratio
2000	2	7	.222	5.64	21	20	0	107.0	124	40	74	22	1.53
Career	63	61	.508	3.59	197	170	1	1132.0	1087	326	830	126	1.25

2000 Situational Stats

	W	L	ERA	Sv	IP		AB	H	HR	RBI	Avg
Home	2	3	4.55	0	55.1	LHB	202	66	14	35	.327
Road	0	4	6.79	0	51.2	RHB	220	58	8	26	.264
First Half	1	2	4.83	0	50.1	Sc Pos	88	27	4	39	.307
Scnd Half	1	5	6.35	0	56.2	Clutch	16	4	0	0	.250

2000 Season

Though he argued that it was not necessary, the Cubs placed Ismael Valdes on the disabled list with shoulder tendinitis before last season even began. When he returned in early May, he was completely ineffective and Chicago eventually sent him back to Los Angeles, where he pitched just as poorly.

Pitching, Defense & Hitting

Valdes relies on command more than pure stuff, so when he had trouble with his location last season, he was hit hard. His four-seam fastball was topping out in the mid-80s, and he was leaving the two-seamer and changeup out over the plate, allowing lefties to hit .327 against him. Valdes tends to fall in love with his curveball and has a propensity to leave it hanging. He is only an average fielder but did a good job against basestealers in 2000. He's a weak hitter.

2001 Outlook

The drop in velocity and trouble with command are warning signs that Valdes' shoulder is bothering him more than he's reporting. The Dodgers did not offer him arbitration, so he now is a free agent with an 11-21 record over the last two seasons. Potential buyers should note that he is 29-36 with a 4.47 ERA outside of Dodger Stadium in his career.

Devon White

Position: CF
Bats: B **Throws:** R
Ht: 6' 2" **Wt:** 190

Opening Day Age: 38
Born: 12/29/62 in Kingston, Jamaica
ML Seasons: 16
Nickname: Devo

Overall Statistics

	G	AB	R	H	D	T	HR	RBI	SB	BB	SO	Avg	OBP	Slg
2000	47	158	26	42	5	1	4	13	3	9	30	.266	.310	.386
Career	1815	6954	1073	1826	353	69	194	799	328	513	1431	.263	.318	.417

2000 Situational Stats

	AB	H	HR	RBI	Avg		AB	H	HR	RBI	Avg
Home	61	21	2	4	.344	LHP	65	20	2	7	.308
Road	97	21	2	9	.216	RHP	93	22	2	6	.237
First Half	83	24	3	9	.289	Sc Pos	37	8	1	10	.216
Scnd Half	75	18	1	4	.240	Clutch	25	7	2	5	.280

2000 Season

Last season was a lost one for Devon White, who tore the rotator cuff in his left shoulder in early May. After going on the disabled list for the first time since 1997, he came back in July but never regained full strength. He collected his fewest at-bats since 1986.

Hitting, Baserunning & Defense

The switch-hitter is now quite a bit better from the right side, where White has a level swing that produces more line drives. As a lefty, he has trouble with any breaking pitch, as well as plus-fastballs. He does not make enough consistent contact from either side, however. He has lost a step or two, which has made him more conservative both on the bases and in center field. A better than 75 percent basestealer during his career, he went just 3-for-9 last year. In the outfield, he has trouble with balls hit over his head.

2001 Outlook

The Dodgers would love to dump White's casual attitude and high salary, but they would seem to be stuck with him. Now that they have Tom Goodwin to patrol center field, where does White fit in? How to deal with a disgruntled White sitting on the bench will provide new manager Jim Tracy with an interesting challenge.

Other Los Angeles Dodgers

Bruce Aven (Pos: LF/RF, Age: 29, Bats: R)

	G	AB	R	H	D	T	HR	RBI	SB	BB	SO	Avg	OBP	Slg
2000	81	168	20	42	11	0	7	29	2	8	39	.250	.284	.440
Career	231	568	81	156	31	2	19	101	5	53	126	.275	.343	.437

Aven had hit fairly well for Florida in 1999, but was traded to the Pirates and Dodgers last season. He can play any outfield position and doesn't seem to have a huge platoon split. 2001 Outlook: B

Geronimo Berroa (Pos: LF, Age: 36, Bats: R)

	G	AB	R	H	D	T	HR	RBI	SB	BB	SO	Avg	OBP	Slg
2000	24	31	2	8	0	1	0	5	0	4	8	.258	.343	.323
Career	779	2506	379	692	113	9	101	382	19	276	510	.276	.349	.449

For a guy whose whole major league existence basically depends on his ability to hit, Berroa hasn't done much at the plate the past three years. He's also been susceptible to injuries as he's gotten older. 2001 Outlook: C

Jeff Branson (Pos: SS, Age: 34, Bats: L)

	G	AB	R	H	D	T	HR	RBI	SB	BB	SO	Avg	OBP	Slg
2000	18	17	3	4	1	0	0	0	0	1	6	.235	.278	.294
Career	681	1534	170	377	72	11	34	156	9	122	308	.246	.300	.374

Branson has been toiling at Triple-A the past couple years, hoping for another shot in the majors. He may have gotten that last big league paycheck last season, though LA did re-sign him to a minor league contract in early November. 2001 Outlook: C

Chris Donnels (Pos: LF, Age: 34, Bats: L)

	G	AB	R	H	D	T	HR	RBI	SB	BB	SO	Avg	OBP	Slg
2000	27	34	8	10	3	0	4	9	0	6	7	.294	.390	.735
Career	310	630	70	152	30	4	11	62	5	81	126	.241	.326	.354

Donnels returned to the majors last year for the first time since 1995. His role with the Dodgers would seem to be covered by Dave Hansen, though he can offer a good lefthanded bat to somebody. 2001 Outlook: C

Kevin Elster (Pos: SS, Age: 36, Bats: R)

	G	AB	R	H	D	T	HR	RBI	SB	BB	SO	Avg	OBP	Slg
2000	80	220	29	50	8	0	14	32	0	38	52	.227	.341	.455
Career	940	2844	332	648	136	12	88	376	14	295	562	.228	.300	.377

It only *seems* as though Elster has nine lives. After making one impressive comeback in 1996, he didn't play at all in 1999 but returned to start for the Dodgers on Opening Day last year. He's now a free agent. 2001 Outlook: C

Shawn Gilbert (Pos: LF, Age: 33, Bats: R)

	G	AB	R	H	D	T	HR	RBI	SB	BB	SO	Avg	OBP	Slg
2000	15	20	5	3	1	0	1	3	0	2	7	.150	.227	.350
Career	51	47	9	7	1	0	2	4	2	3	17	.149	.200	.298

Gilbert has hit well in the Pacific Coast League, and even spent a month with the Dodgers last season. But at this stage of his career, it's hard to see the free agent in any team's future. 2001 Outlook: C

Dave Hansen (Pos: 1B/3B, Age: 32, Bats: L)

	G	AB	R	H	D	T	HR	RBI	SB	BB	SO	Avg	OBP	Slg
2000	102	121	18	35	6	2	8	26	0	26	32	.289	.415	.570
Career	786	1217	126	326	54	5	25	147	2	184	216	.268	.364	.382

Hansen was terrific in his role last year, getting on base and delivering seven pinch-hit homers. Not surprisingly, the Dodgers then signed him for this season with a club option for 2002. 2001 Outlook: A

Orel Hershiser (Pos: RHP, Age: 42)

	W	L	Pct.	ERA	G	GS	Sv	IP	H	BB	SO	HR	Ratio
2000	1	5	.167	13.14	10	6	0	24.2	42	14	13	5	2.27
Career	204	150	.576	3.48	510	466	5	3130.1	2939	1007	2014	235	1.26

Hershiser's final season hardly was a glowing success, as he returned to Los Angeles a shell of his old Dodger self. He retired soon after the Dodgers released him last June. 2001 Outlook: D

Mike Judd (Pos: RHP, Age: 25)

	W	L	Pct.	ERA	G	GS	Sv	IP	H	BB	SO	HR	Ratio
2000	0	1	.000	15.75	1	1	0	4.0	4	3	5	2	1.75
Career	3	2	.600	8.41	16	5	0	46.0	57	24	45	10	1.76

Traded from the Yankees to the Dodgers for Billy Brewer in 1996, Judd reached the majors in 1997 following a fine minor league campaign. Since then, his career has stalled in Triple-A. 2001 Outlook: C

Jim Leyritz (Pos: DH, Age: 37, Bats: R)

	G	AB	R	H	D	T	HR	RBI	SB	BB	SO	Avg	OBP	Slg
2000	65	115	5	24	1	0	2	12	0	14	26	.209	.305	.270
Career	903	2527	325	667	107	2	90	387	7	337	581	.264	.362	.415

So what's stranger, the fact that so many teams swap Leyritz or that so many clubs trade for him? If he keeps hitting .209 with no power, he'll find fewer suitors. The Dodgers did not offer him arbitration. 2001 Outlook: C

Paul LoDuca (Pos: C, Age: 28, Bats: R)

	G	AB	R	H	D	T	HR	RBI	SB	BB	SO	Avg	OBP	Slg
2000	34	65	6	16	2	0	2	8	0	6	8	.246	.301	.369
Career	76	174	19	42	4	0	5	20	1	16	18	.241	.306	.351

LoDuca has been a .300-hitting machine in the minors with some great walk-strikeout ratios. He can catch, play the outfield and even fill in at third base. He would seem to have value but hasn't stuck yet, though he could see a fair amount of time at catcher with Todd Hundley going to the Cubs. 2001 Outlook: B

Onan Masaoka (Pos: LHP, Age: 23)

	W	L	Pct.	ERA	G	GS	Sv	IP	H	BB	SO	HR	Ratio
2000	1	1	.500	4.00	29	0	0	27.0	23	15	27	2	1.41
Career	3	5	.375	4.23	83	0	1	93.2	78	62	88	10	1.49

After staying with the Dodgers for all of 1999, Masaoka split last season between Los Angeles and the minors. His control, always tenuous, deserted him on occasion. 2001 Outlook: C

Mike Metcalfe (**Pos**: LF, **Age**: 28, **Bats**: B)

	G	AB	R	H	D	T	HR	RBI	SB	BB	SO	Avg	OBP	Slg
2000	4	12	0	1	0	0	0	0	0	1	2	.083	.154	.083
Career	8	13	0	1	0	0	0	0	2	1	3	.077	.143	.077

A former third-round draft pick, Metcalfe has stolen a lot of bases in the minors but also has been caught a lot. He has switched between second base and the outfield and has little power, but the Devil Rays signed him to a minor league deal anyway. 2001 Outlook: C

Trever Miller (**Pos**: LHP, **Age**: 27)

	W	L	Pct.	ERA	G	GS	Sv	IP	H	BB	SO	HR	Ratio
2000	0	0	-	10.47	16	0	0	16.1	27	12	11	3	2.39
Career	5	6	.455	5.43	105	5	2	136.0	170	70	86	16	1.76

After getting traded from Houston to Philadelphia last March, Miller was acquired off waivers by Los Angeles in May, before soon departing for the minors. He's always had troubles with righthanded hitters. 2001 Outlook: C

Gregg Olson (**Pos**: RHP, **Age**: 34)

	W	L	Pct.	ERA	G	GS	Sv	IP	H	BB	SO	HR	Ratio
2000	0	1	.000	5.09	13	0	0	17.2	21	7	15	4	1.58
Career	40	38	.513	3.28	594	0	217	647.1	572	310	564	42	1.36

The Dodgers knew Olson's injury history but still signed him to a two-year deal last season. He then missed over half the campaign with a strained forearm. He remains a likely setup man this season. 2001 Outlook: B

Al Reyes (**Pos**: RHP, **Age**: 29)

	W	L	Pct.	ERA	G	GS	Sv	IP	H	BB	SO	HR	Ratio
2000	1	0	1.000	4.58	19	0	0	19.2	15	12	18	2	1.37
Career	13	7	.650	4.27	173	0	2	211.0	179	113	202	28	1.38

The Dodgers acquired Reyes from the Orioles last June, in part to unload Alan Mills' contract. Reyes is a candidate for middle relief. He appeared in at least 50 games in both 1998 and 1999. 2001 Outlook: C

Jeff Williams (**Pos**: LHP, **Age**: 28)

	W	L	Pct.	ERA	G	GS	Sv	IP	H	BB	SO	HR	Ratio
2000	0	0	-	15.88	7	0	0	5.2	12	8	3	1	3.53
Career	2	0	1.000	6.94	12	3	0	23.1	24	17	10	3	1.76

Williams, a native of Australia, experienced weakness in his left wrist last year and spent two months on the disabled list. He had surgery after the season and is expected to compete for a spot this spring. 2001 Outlook: C

Los Angeles

Los Angeles Dodgers Minor League Prospects

Organization Overview:

Kevin Malone's tenure as general manager has been marred with anemic teams, ill-fated signings and trades and just overall turmoil. The Davey Johnson-era came and went, and Jim Tracy has been hired as his replacement. There are hopes that the former bench coach can bring some of this managerial intuition, learned from his days under Felipe Alou in Montreal, to stabilize the chaotic team chemistry that has plagued the franchise since Mike Piazza's day. The Adrian Beltre debacle nearly led to the rising star fleeing Chavez Ravine via free agency, and ended up costing the organization in fines and signing embargoes for six months. On the farm, the Dodgers are in the process of restocking a system that has lacked depth, but a strong draft and a group of power arms, like Joel Hanrahan, Heath Totten, Ricardo Rodriguez, Maximo Regalado and Ben Diggins, have them heading in the right direction.

Luke Allen

Position: 3B
Bats: L **Throws:** R
Ht: 6' 2" **Wt:** 208

Opening Day Age: 22
Born: 8/4/78 in Covington, GA

Recent Statistics

	G	AB	R	H	D	T	HR	RBI	SB	BB	SO	Avg
1999 AA San Antonio	137	533	90	150	16	12	14	82	14	44	102	.281
2000 AA San Antonio	90	339	55	90	15	5	7	60	14	40	71	.265
2000 MLE	90	323	43	74	12	2	5	47	9	26	76	.229

Allen spent his second consecutive season in Double-A. A nondrafted free agent in 1996, he is learning to play third base and to hone his power potential at the same time. He played against older, more experienced competition both years. The Dodgers are intrigued with his pop from the left side, although he has never topped 14 home runs in a season. At third, he committed 53 errors in 1999, before cutting back to 27 last year. He owns plenty of arm strength but needs to improve his glovework and mobility to become an adequate defender. After only playing in 90 games due to a minor injury, Allen could afford to spend more time in the Texas League before moving to Triple-A.

Hiram Bocachica

Position: 2B
Bats: R **Throws:** R
Ht: 5' 11" **Wt:** 165

Opening Day Age: 25
Born: 3/4/76 in Ponce, PR

Recent Statistics

	G	AB	R	H	D	T	HR	RBI	SB	BB	SO	Avg
2000 AAA Albuquerque	124	482	99	155	38	4	23	84	10	40	100	.322
2000 NL Los Angeles	8	10	2	3	0	0	0	0	0	0	2	.300
2000 MLE	124	447	67	120	28	2	15	57	6	26	104	.268

A former Expos first-rounder out of Puerto Rico, Bocachica finally began to put all of his tools together in his seventh professional season. One of the knocks on him has been his approach, but his newfound focus helped him to achieve his best results to date. Bocachica was drafted as a shortstop and has since visited center field and now second base, where he shows good range and decent hands. Scouts always envisioned him as an offensive middle infielder with speed and the ability to drive the ball with great bat speed. Last year's 65 extra-base hits and .560 slugging percentage reflect that sentiment. Now, out of options, Bocachica has a solid chance of scoring a job in Los Angeles in a utility role.

Chin-Feng Chen

Position: OF
Bats: R **Throws:** R
Ht: 6' 1" **Wt:** 189

Opening Day Age: 23
Born: 10/28/77 in Tainan City, Taiwan

Recent Statistics

	G	AB	R	H	D	T	HR	RBI	SB	BB	SO	Avg
1999 A San Berndno	131	510	98	161	22	10	31	123	31	75	129	.316
2000 AA San Antonio	133	516	66	143	27	3	6	67	23	61	131	.277
2000 MLE	133	492	51	119	22	1	4	52	15	40	140	.242

After signing out of Taiwan in '99 and tearing apart the high Class-A California League in his U.S. debut, Chen came back to earth last year in Double-A. Not only was he not able to replicate his 30-30 effort from '99, he didn't even reach double-digits in home runs, and his stolen base rate dropped from 82 percent to 61 percent. Following a hot start, he ended up with a disappointing .376 slugging percentage and he hit just six homers after belting 31 longballs in 1999 at high Class-A San Bernardino. Chen was trying to make in-season adjustments by covering the outer half of the plate, but he was unable to handle inside stuff and he whiffed 131 times. He generates electric bat speed from a lean, athletic frame, and the ball explodes off of his bat, which is why the Dodgers aren't too concerned with his disappointing 2000 season. He may have to prove himself in Double-A before taking the next step.

Ben Diggins

Position: P
Bats: R **Throws:** R
Ht: 6' 7" **Wt:** 230

Opening Day Age: 21
Born: 6/13/79 in Leota, KS

Recent Statistics

	W	L	ERA	G	GS	Sv	IP	H	R	BB	SO	HR
2000				Did Not Play								

Drafted by the Cardinals with the 32nd pick out of high school as a power-hitting slugger, Diggins opted for pitching at the University of Arizona. A draft-eligible sophomore, the Dodgers made him a two-time first-rounder last year, signing him after an extended holdout for $2.2 million as a smoke-throwing righthanded hurler. He is only beginning to tap into his unlimited potential, although some still believe his ceiling is higher on offense. Armed with a lively 94-96 MPH fastball that has

touched 98 MPH, Diggins showed the makings of a plus-slider in instructional league. At his size, he's been compared to another former two-way standout, Dave Winfield. He'll begin his career in the South Atlantic League as a starter, with most scouts feeling Diggins will eventually be converted into a dominating two-pitch closer.

Carlos Garcia

Position: P   **Opening Day Age:** 22
Bats: R **Throws:** R   **Born:** 9/23/78 in
Ht: 6' 1" **Wt:** 172   Guaymas Sonora, Mexico

Recent Statistics

	W	L	ERA	G	GS	Sv	IP	H	R	BB	SO	HR
2000 A San Berndno	14	7	2.57	27	27	0	182.0	162	61	49	106	5

Signed as a free agent out of Mexico in 1996, Garcia spent two years tuning up for his minor league debut in the Triple-A equivalent Mexican League. A control pitcher, he made an immediate impact by claiming the California League's Pitcher of the Year honors by finishing with a 14-7, 2.57 record. After compiling 153.1 innings in '99 for Mexico City, Garcia continued to establish himself as a workhorse by amassing 182 innings last season. He survives with a sinking high-80s fastball that touches 92, along with a polished curve and change. Garcia demonstrates an advanced feel for pitching by mixing speeds and location, and he induces a lot of groundballs. He only surrendered five homers. Garcia's know-how should help him succeed in Double-A.

Luke Prokopec

Position: P   **Opening Day Age:** 23
Bats: L **Throws:** R   **Born:** 2/23/78 in
Ht: 5' 11" **Wt:** 166   Blackwood, Australia

Recent Statistics

	W	L	ERA	G	GS	Sv	IP	H	R	BB	SO	HR
2000 AA San Antonio	7	3	2.45	22	22	0	128.2	118	40	23	124	8
2000 NL Los Angeles	1	1	3.00	5	3	0	21.0	19	10	9	12	2

Going nowhere as a minor league outfielder with a .227 average, Prokopec converted to pitching in his third minor league season. The Australian native took immediately to the mound, showing a surprising aptitude for pitching. Prokopec wasn't ready for Double-A two years ago and it showed, as he allowed 172 hits and a 5.42 ERA. Not only was he ready for the challenge last year, he was much improved, posting the second-best ERA in the circuit along with an eye-catching strikeout-walk ratio. His best pitch, a sharp curveball, was named the best breaking ball in the Texas League, and he mixes it strategically with an average fastball and solid changeup. He earned a taste of the big leagues last year, and showed tremendous poise in three starts. Prokopec will attack Triple-A with an opportunity to pitch for the Dodgers before the end of the season.

Joe Thurston

Position: SS   **Opening Day Age:** 21
Bats: L **Throws:** R   **Born:** 9/29/79 in
Ht: 5' 11" **Wt:** 175   Fairfield, CA

Recent Statistics

	G	AB	R	H	D	THR	RBI	SB	BB	SO	Avg
1999 A Yakima	71	277	48	79	10	3	0	32	27	27	34	.285
1999 A San Berndno	2	3	0	0	0	0	0	0	0	0	1	.000
2000 A San Berndno	138	551	97	167	31	8	4	70	43	56	61	.303

A fourth-round pick in 1999, Thurston was regarded as an excellent defensive prospect. Last year, however, he exceeded expectations by excelling with the bat, too. Named the most exciting player in the California League and nicknamed "Joey Ballgame," he played in all but two games for San Bernardino. A lefthanded-hitting shortstop, Thurston displays a knack for putting the ball in play and getting on base, and he led the league with 167 hits. He's also a plus-runner, as evidenced by his 43 steals, but he needs to refine his technique after getting caught 25 times. Thurston draws praise for his work ethic and has all of the assets of an outstanding defensive shortstop with a solid arm, great range and good hands and footwork. He'll advance one level at a time, with a chance to compete for a big league job by 2003.

Others to Watch

Third baseman **Willy Aybar** (18) showed impressive strength and power potential as a teenager. He also displayed promising control of the strike zone in his pro debut, walking 36 times. . . Third baseman **Brennan King** (20) is a smooth-swinging prospect who has drawn comparisons to a young Travis Fryman. His defense is ahead of his bat at this time, but he is expected to develop power as he fills out his 6-foot-3 frame. . . Lefthander **Hong-Chih Kuo** (19) was signed out of Taiwan for $1.25 million, but he only logged three innings of work before an injury to his left elbow cut his debut season short last year. There was enough time to turn heads with his lively 95-98 MPH fastball, and he should return in late spring. . . Acquired from the Blue Jays as a throw-in with Shawn Green, **Jorge Nunez** (23) has an exciting package of tools that he is trying to cultivate. His speed and arm strength are his strongest tools, but he committed the second most errors in baseball last year with 58. . . Righthander **Maximo Regalado** (24) started bringing it in the mid-90s neighborhood after a shift to the bullpen. He toiled in the lower levels as a starter for three years, but recorded 30 saves and 72 Ks in 54 innings between two stops last year. . . Shortstop **Jason Repko** (20) was limited to 17 at-bats last year due to injuries, but his health has returned and the Dodgers are excited about his five-tool potential and the energy that he brings to the top of the order. . . The Dodgers think so highly of righthander **Ricardo Rodriguez** (21), they added him to the 40-man roster after his debut season. He overpowered the Rookie-level Pioneer League, registering 129 Ks in 95.2 innings with a blazing fastball/slider combo.

Miller Park

Offense

It's impossible to say whether Miller Park will be a better hitters' park than old Milwaukee County Stadium. The old park was neutral overall and tended to be a pitchers' park early in the year before it warmed up, and a hitters' park in the warmer weather. Miller's dimensions from alley to alley are very similar to those of the old park, but the new park is deeper from the alleys to the foul poles. The ability to close the roof and shut out the cold could be a major boost to the hitters, which may cancel out the impact of the larger measurements.

Defense

Miller Park has very little foul territory down the lines, especially on the first-base line. The corner outfielders will have more territory to cover and will need to have more mobility and stronger throwing arms.

Who It Helps the Most

The park may help hitters who haven't done well in cold weather, such as Mark Loretta and Jose Hernandez. Loretta hasn't hit well in April and Hernandez has struggled in both April and September. Geoff Jenkins and Richie Sexson have good power to the alleys and hit the ball out to all fields, so they may be able to benefit from the park's offense-boosting attributes without losing too many home runs to the deep corners.

Who It Hurts the Most

Jeromy Burnitz, a rather extreme pull hitter, may lose some home runs to the deeper right-field corner. John Snyder, who was much more effective at County Stadium last year, may miss the old park.

Rookies & Newcomers

Richie Sexson will be hoping the park won't cost him too many home runs; Ben Sheets and the Brewers' other young pitchers such as Allen Levrault, Kyle Peterson and Horacio Estrada will be happy to see the park turn out to be a pitchers' park.

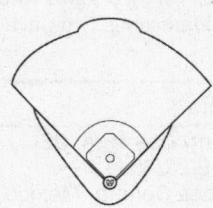

Dimensions: LF-315, LCF-376, CF-402, RCF-376, RF-315

Capacity: 53,192

Elevation: 635 feet

Surface: Grass

Foul Territory: Small

Park Factors

2000 Season (County Stadium)

	Home Games			Away Games			
	Brewers	Opp	Total	Brewers	Opp	Total	Index
G	75	75	150	73	73	146	—
Avg	.230	.264	.247	.255	.273	.263	94
AB	2492	2666	5158	2526	2396	4922	102
R	330	359	689	342	383	725	93
H	572	703	1275	643	653	1296	96
2B	119	120	239	139	110	249	92
3B	17	10	27	8	20	28	92
HR	73	64	137	88	93	181	72
BB	295	330	625	276	322	598	100
SO	534	427	961	578	459	1037	88
E	63	71	134	43	49	92	142
E-Infield	58	56	114	31	38	69	161
LHB-Avg	.234	.266	.252	.271	.272	.272	93
LHB-HR	33	28	61	53	31	84	64
RHB-Avg	.227	.262	.245	.246	.273	.259	95
RHB-HR	40	36	76	35	62	97	78

1998-2000 (County Stadium)

	Home Games			Away Games			
	Brewers	Opp	Total	Brewers	Opp	Total	Index
G	222	222	444	221	221	442	—
Avg	.252	.277	.265	.261	.273	.267	99
AB	7405	7904	15309	7716	7406	15122	101
R	980	1172	2152	1054	1122	2176	98
H	1868	2188	4056	2015	2024	4039	100
2B	373	373	746	402	392	794	93
3B	33	36	69	33	57	90	76
HR	202	247	449	243	277	520	85
BB	838	841	1679	810	876	1686	98
SO	1367	1345	2712	1665	1404	3069	87
E	161	167	328	155	149	304	107
E-Infield	132	129	261	122	118	240	108
LHB-Avg	.249	.276	.262	.266	.268	.267	98
LHB-HR	109	84	193	144	83	227	83
RHB-Avg	.255	.277	.266	.258	.276	.267	100
RHB-HR	93	163	256	99	194	293	87

2000 Rankings (National Lg./County Stadium)

- Highest error factor
- Highest infield-error factor
- Lowest home-run factor
- Lowest LHB home-run factor
- Lowest RHB home-run factor
- Second-lowest strikeout factor
- Third-lowest batting-average factor
- Third-lowest RHB batting-average factor

Davey Lopes

2000 Season

Davey Lopes' first season at the helm of the Brewers was anything but easy. His job was to patch together a club that had been completely overhauled over the winter. At first, everything went wrong. Injuries hit the pitching staff, rookie first baseman Kevin Barker flopped and shortstop Mark Loretta got hurt in June. But there were many positive developments in the second half: slugger Richie Sexson was acquired, Curtis Leskanic established himself as the closer, the rest of the bullpen got sorted out and performed admirably and Jeff D'Amico emerged as a potential ace. By the end of the year, there was hope.

Offense

As Phil Garner did in 1992, Lopes came in vowing to jump-start a moribund offense by reviving the running game. A strange approach, considering the lack of team speed. With a dearth of baserunners and few true RBI men, Lopes used the hit-and-run a lot and held off on sending runners until there were two outs.

Pitching & Defense

Lopes' biggest accomplishment was finding the proper roles for his pitchers. He transformed Valerio de los Santos, Ray King, Juan Acevedo and Dave Weathers into reliable middle men. He named Curtis Leskanic the closer when Bob Wickman was traded. On the other hand, he pitched Jamey Wright heavily despite Wright's iffy shoulder and showed more patience with John Snyder than perhaps was warranted. Lopes seems to be good at stealing signs; he calls a lot of pitchouts and catches a lot of runners that way. He uses the intentional walk when the situation warrants.

2001 Outlook

The Brewers' primary task last year was to sort out their talent and give it some shape, and Lopes did that very well. Now he'll need to take the next step and work with the new design from the start of the season. He'll need to identify the remaining holes, decide how to deal with the center-field situation and hope that Richie Sexson can reach the fences in the new park. Plus, he'll need to keep healthy the club's young pitchers.

Born: 5/03/45 in East Providence, RI

Playing Experience: 1972-1987, LA, Oak, ChC, Hou

Managerial Experience: 1 season

Manager Statistics

Year	Team, Lg	W	L	Pct	GB	Finish
2000	Milwaukee, NL	73	89	.451	22.0	3rd Central
1 Season		73	89	.448	—	—

2000 Starting Pitchers by Days Rest

	<=3	4	5	6+
Brewers Starts	0	81	57	14
Brewers ERA	—	5.12	4.76	6.66
NL Avg Starts	2	80	50	21
NL ERA	5.00	4.61	4.60	5.18

2000 Situational Stats

	Davey Lopes	NL Average
Hit & Run Success %	30.3	33.8
Stolen Base Success %	62.1	68.8
Platoon Pct.	47.5	53.2
Defensive Subs	8	19
High-Pitch Outings	10	14
Quick/Slow Hooks	10/16	14/16
Sacrifice Attempts	78	87

2000 Rankings (National League)

- 1st in fewest caught stealings of third base (3) and intentional walks (56)
- 2nd in pitchouts (50), pitchouts with a runner moving (15) and pinch-hitters used (285)

Ron Belliard

2000 Season

It was a disappointing sophomore season for second baseman Ron Belliard. He came to camp carrying some extra weight and wasn't able to play a part in the running attack that new manager Davey Lopes envisioned. Batting leadoff, Belliard kept his average around .300 for the first three months, but he slumped in July and never really recovered. Lopes dropped him to the bottom third of the order in August. Late in the year, Belliard revealed that he'd been suffering from back problems, which only lent ammunition to those who questioned his conditioning and work habits.

Hitting

Belliard is well suited to hit at the top of the order. He has a good batting eye, hits for a good average and when healthy has flashed enough extra-base pop to be able to put himself in scoring position. A line-drive hitter, he uses the entire field and has shown in that past that he can shorten up well with two strikes. He's also a decent bunter.

Baserunning & Defense

Belliard has fairly good speed and was a good basestealer in the minors, so his lack of major league success on the bases has been somewhat frustrating. Some feel that his weight is holding him back, so to speak. He has good range in the field and turns the double play well, but he led the National League with 19 errors in 2000. His only other defensive weakness is a puzzling inability to take throws at first base on bunt plays.

2001 Outlook

Belliard opted to rehab his back over the winter rather than undergo surgery, and the Brewers expect him to be fully recovered by this spring. His immediate future is tough to predict—he could work himself into better shape and hit the way he did early last year, or the back problems could recur and ruin his season. The Brewers will have their fingers crossed.

Position: 2B
Bats: R **Throws:** R
Ht: 5' 8" **Wt:** 180

Opening Day Age: 25
Born: 4/7/75 in Bronx, NY
ML Seasons: 3

Overall Statistics

	G	AB	R	H	D	T	HR	RBI	SB	BB	SO	Avg	OBP	Slg
2000	152	571	83	150	30	9	8	54	7	82	84	.263	.354	.389
Career	284	1033	144	286	59	13	16	112	11	146	143	.277	.365	.406

Where He Hits the Ball

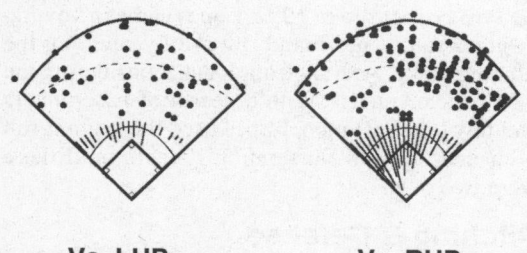

Vs. LHP   **Vs. RHP**

2000 Situational Stats

	AB	H	HR	RBI	Avg		AB	H	HR	RBI	Avg
Home	279	70	4	28	.251	LHP	124	35	1	9	.282
Road	292	80	4	26	.274	RHP	447	115	7	45	.257
First Half	342	98	6	36	.287	Sc Pos	114	35	1	47	.307
Scnd Half	229	52	2	18	.227	Clutch	97	24	0	7	.247

2000 Rankings (National League)

- 1st in errors at second base (19) and lowest fielding percentage at second base (.976)
- 5th in triples
- 9th in lowest batting average at home
- 10th in lowest on-base percentage for a leadoff hitter (.343)
- Led the Brewers in triples, highest ground-ball/flyball ratio (1.6), batting average with runners in scoring position, batting average on an 0-2 count (.186), on-base percentage for a leadoff hitter (.343), on-base percentage vs. lefthanded pitchers (.400), highest percentage of pitches taken (59.9) and lowest percentage of swings on the first pitch (23.0)
- Led NL second basemen in triples

Henry Blanco

2000 Season

The Brewers watched opposing basestealers run wild in 1999, so when the season was over they sent for Henry Blanco, a relative unknown who was one of the major league's premier defensive catchers. In his first year with the Brewers, he missed time due to injuries and the death of his father at midseason, but he did everything expected of him with the glove. His bat wasn't as bad as advertised, either.

Hitting

Blanco never was much of an offensive threat in the minors and was downright pathetic outside of Coors Field in 1999. So it was quite a surprise that he didn't damage the Brewers' offense last year. A flyball hitter, he pulled the ball more often in 2000 and showed decent doubles power. He hit well against lefties in limited at-bats, something he rarely did in the past.

Baserunning & Defense

It's no exaggeration to say that Blanco is the National League's version of Pudge Rodriguez behind the plate. With excellent footwork, a quick release and a powerful, deadly-accurate arm, he's easily the best-throwing catcher in the National League. A converted third baseman, he's also good at keeping balls in the dirt in front of him. Like most catchers, he's no roadrunner.

2001 Outlook

As pleased as the Brewers were with Blanco, he could end up as a major disappointment this season. He suffered a rotator-cuff injury late in the 2000 campaign, and although surgery wasn't required, a re-aggravation could rob him of his only good tool. Furthermore, he may have been hitting over his head last summer. He could get the chance to play more, but it's entirely possible that he'll hit so poorly that he won't be able to stay in the lineup. The Brewers signed backup Raul Casanova to a one-year deal in early December just in case.

Position: C
Bats: R **Throws:** R
Ht: 5'11" **Wt:** 170

Opening Day Age: 29
Born: 8/29/71 in Caracas, Venezuela
ML Seasons: 3

Overall Statistics

	G	AB	R	H	D	T	HR	RBI	SB	BB	SO	Avg	OBP	Slg
2000	93	284	29	67	24	0	7	31	0	36	60	.236	.318	.394
Career	184	552	60	130	36	3	14	60	1	70	99	.236	.320	.388

Where He Hits the Ball

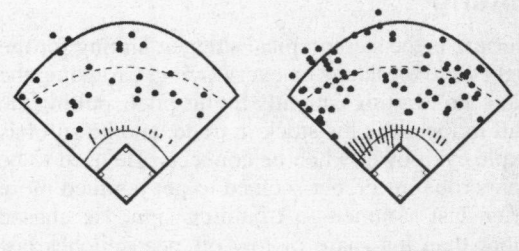

Vs. LHP   **Vs. RHP**

2000 Situational Stats

	AB	H	HR	RBI	Avg		AB	H	HR	RBI	Avg
Home	135	29	3	8	.215	LHP	62	19	2	8	.306
Road	149	38	4	23	.255	RHP	222	48	5	23	.216
First Half	166	39	5	21	.235	Sc Pos	71	13	1	21	.183
Scnd Half	118	28	2	10	.237	Clutch	50	12	1	6	.240

2000 Rankings (National League)

- 6th in lowest batting average on a 3-1 count (.091)
- 7th in lowest batting average with the bases loaded (.091)
- 8th in batting average on a 3-2 count (.357)
- Led the Brewers in batting average on a 3-2 count (.357)

Jeromy Burnitz

2000 Season

Jeromy Burnitz seemed to personify the Brewers' struggles in 2000. Counted upon to anchor a rag-tag batting order, Burnitz wasn't up to the task for most of the year. The club opened talks for a long-term deal in June, but Burnitz, frustrated with the club's lack of progress on the field, cut off negotiations in July. He remained in a deep slump for much of the year and was able to post decent power numbers only by hitting a bunch of home runs over the last three weeks of September. His—and the Brewers'—season ended on a more positive note, as Burnitz said that the club's late resurgence had made him more open to the idea of remaining a Brewer. ●

Hitting

Burnitz is the stereotypical slugger, aiming for the right-field bleachers on every swing. Crowding the plate and waiting patiently for his pitch, pulling the ball in the air is his stock in trade, and he still has explosive power when he connects. He used to be dangerous inside but seemed to get jammed more often last summer—a troubling sign. He chased more than his share of low offspeed pitches last year.

Baserunning & Defense

Burnitz is a quality right fielder with good mobility and a powerful throwing arm. He will be perfectly suited to defend the deeper right-field corner at new Miller Park. He has fairly good speed for a big man, but apart from surprising people with some steals early in 1997, hasn't been much of a stolen-base threat.

2001 Outlook

Burnitz now goes into the final year of his contract, and it remains an open question whether the club will be able to sign him to an extension. If an impasse is reached by midsummer, the club may consider trading him to a contender in order to avoid losing him outright. Hopefully for Brewers' fans, Burnitz will rebound, the club will continue to improve and the contract situation will be settled.

Position: RF
Bats: L **Throws:** R
Ht: 6' 0" **Wt:** 205

Opening Day Age: 31
Born: 4/15/69 in Westminster, CA
ML Seasons: 8
Pronunciation: burr-NITZ

Overall Statistics

	G	AB	R	H	D	T	HR	RBI	SB	BB	SO	Avg	OBP	Slg
2000	161	564	91	131	29	2	31	98	6	99	121	.232	.356	.456
Career	839	2747	472	711	156	19	154	504	48	429	672	.259	.365	.498

Where He Hits the Ball

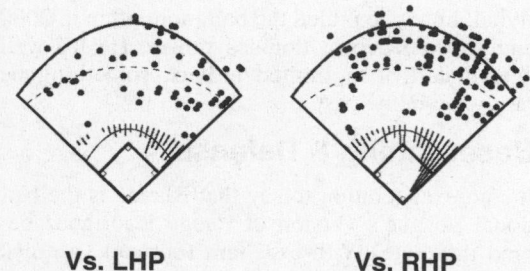

Vs. LHP   **Vs. RHP**

2000 Situational Stats

	AB	H	HR	RBI	Avg		AB	H	HR	RBI	Avg
Home	285	66	12	55	.232	LHP	160	38	7	31	.238
Road	279	65	19	43	.233	RHP	404	93	24	67	.230
First Half	321	70	17	53	.218	Sc Pos	146	37	4	65	.253
Scnd Half	243	61	14	45	.251	Clutch	87	14	5	18	.161

2000 Rankings (National League)

- 2nd in lowest batting average
- 3rd in lowest batting average at home
- 4th in pitches seen (2,784), errors in right field (7), games played and lowest fielding percentage in right field (.979)
- 5th in lowest batting average vs. righthanded pitchers
- 6th in lowest batting average on the road
- Led the Brewers in RBI, sacrifice flies (9), walks, intentional walks (10), times on base (244), pitches seen (2,784), plate appearances (686), most pitches seen per plate appearance (4.06) and games played
- Led NL right fielders in sacrifice flies (9)

Jeff D'Amico

2000 Season

It was one of the best and most remarkable seasons a Brewers pitcher ever had. Jeff D'Amico, who'd missed almost all of 1998 and '99 while recovering from a pair of shoulder surgeries, returned with everything but a cape. He started the year in the minors but was called up in May and immediately had several good starts. After two poor ones, he was diagnosed with shoulder tendinitis, and the Brewers cautiously shut him down for almost a month. But D'Amico returned in July, went 5-0 with 0.76 ERA and was one of baseball's best pitchers over the second half, nearly capturing the National League ERA title.

Pitching

D'Amico came back from his shoulder troubles without his old 90-MPH heat, but he made up for it with improved command, a better changeup and a big, slow curve. His location is so precise that he not only throws strikes, but also throws quality strikes, working ahead of the hitters while conserving his pitches. He routinely pitched late into games without running up high pitch counts in 2000, and lefthanded hitters found him just as difficult to solve as righthanded hitters did.

Defense & Hitting

Though he has no pickoff move, D'Amico controls the running game well by delivering his pitches quickly. A big man, he's not very mobile, but he's reliable, and his next major league error will be his first. He's a lousy hitter, but did luck into a home run.

2001 Outlook

The Brewers re-signed D'Amico to a one-year, $2.3 million contract in mid-December. As always, the question is whether he can hold up for a full season. He still hasn't done so at any level since being drafted in 1993. He didn't throw a destructive number of pitches last year, however, and he did stay strong through most of September. So there's reason for optimism. The Brewers will be holding their breath hoping he can deliver a full season of last year's caliber of performance.

Position: SP
Bats: R **Throws:** R
Ht: 6' 7" **Wt:** 250

Opening Day Age: 25
Born: 12/27/75 in St. Petersburg, FL
ML Seasons: 4
Pronunciation: duh-MEEK-oh

Overall Statistics

	W	L	Pct.	ERA	G	GS	Sv	IP	H	BB	SO	HR	Ratio
2000	12	7	.632	2.66	23	23	0	162.1	143	46	101	14	1.16
Career	27	20	.574	4.00	64	63	0	385.0	371	120	249	60	1.28

How Often He Throws Strikes

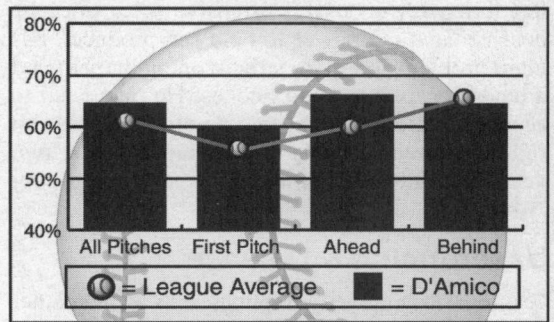

◎ = League Average ■ = D'Amico

2000 Situational Stats

	W	L	ERA	Sv	IP		AB	H	HR	RBI	Avg
Home	8	5	3.19	0	96.0	LHB	248	60	5	27	.242
Road	4	2	1.90	0	66.1	RHB	354	83	9	23	.234
First Half	4	4	2.45	0	51.1	Sc Pos	125	28	2	36	.224
Scnd Half	8	3	2.76	0	111.0	Clutch	70	15	2	4	.214

2000 Rankings (National League)

- 2nd in least run support per nine innings (3.8)
- 3rd in ERA
- 5th in lowest stolen-base percentage allowed (27.3) and fewest pitches thrown per batter (3.50)
- Led the Brewers in ERA, wins, strikeouts, highest strikeout/walk ratio (2.2), lowest batting average allowed (.238), lowest on-base percentage allowed (.297), lowest stolen-base percentage allowed (27.3), fewest pitches thrown per batter (3.50), most strikeouts per nine innings (5.6), fewest walks per nine innings (2.6), lowest ERA at home, lowest batting average allowed vs. lefthanded batters, lowest batting average allowed vs. righthanded batters and winning percentage

Milwaukee

Marquis Grissom

2000 Season

Few Brewers were more frustrating to watch in 2000 than aging center fielder Marquis Grissom. Expected to be the sparkplug of an aggressive, running offense, Grissom completely flopped as the leadoff man, leaving a gaping hole in the lineup that never was filled. Bothered by a hip flexor and a hamstring injury, he didn't find his hitting stroke until the season was lost.

Hitting

Grissom never has been a strong leadoff man, and last year, when the dive in his batting average plunged his on-base percentage into the statistical nether-regions, he became a major liability. This left him with no useful offensive role, since he doesn't have the power to be a run producer. His main problems are poor strike-zone judgment and a tendency to chase bad pitches. He may need to accept a platoon role at this point—he hasn't hit righthanders acceptably in either of the last two years, but did well against lefties last year hitting .304.

Baserunning & Defense

Grissom has enjoyed a reputation as a fine center fielder, but more and more often his legs prevent him from playing to the best of his abilities. His range, which usually is his strength, was only fair last year and his weak throwing arm always is a liability. His 20 stolen bases last year were offset by being caught 10 times. He is especially tentative with a lefthander on the mound.

2001 Outlook

What to do with Grissom is becoming a major dilemma for the Brewers. He's clearly on the downslide. He turns 34 in April and has had just one decent season in the last four, but his contract runs through 2002, and the cash-strapped team can't very well bench one of its highest-paid players. His defenders might contend that his leg woes—rather than the erosion of his skills—were the reason for his offensive collapse, but his critics would contend that Grissom, even when healthy, hasn't been worth the money he's being paid.

Position: CF
Bats: R **Throws:** R
Ht: 5'11" **Wt:** 188

Opening Day Age: 33
Born: 4/17/67 in Atlanta, GA
ML Seasons: 12
Pronunciation: mar-KEESE
Nickname: Grip

Overall Statistics

	G	AB	R	H	D	T	HR	RBI	SB	BB	SO	Avg	OBP	Slg
2000	146	595	67	145	18	2	14	62	20	39	99	.244	.288	.351
Career	1581	6198	906	1695	285	46	145	663	402	451	882	.273	.323	.404

Where He Hits the Ball

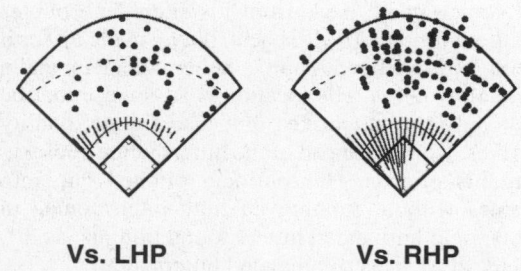

Vs. LHP   **Vs. RHP**

2000 Situational Stats

	AB	H	HR	RBI	Avg		AB	H	HR	RBI	Avg
Home	307	77	4	23	.251	LHP	125	38	2	18	.304
Road	288	68	10	39	.236	RHP	470	107	12	44	.228
First Half	355	90	9	44	.254	Sc Pos	138	35	3	48	.254
Scnd Half	240	55	5	18	.229	Clutch	98	22	2	10	.224

2000 Rankings (National League)

- 1st in lowest on-base percentage, lowest on-base percentage for a leadoff hitter (.288) and lowest on-base percentage vs. righthanded pitchers (.273)
- 3rd in fielding percentage in center field (.992) and lowest slugging percentage vs. righthanded pitchers (.336)
- 4th in lowest slugging percentage and lowest batting average vs. righthanded pitchers
- 5th in lowest batting average
- Led the Brewers in at-bats, singles, stolen bases, caught stealing (10), stolen-base percentage (66.7), batting average vs. lefthanded pitchers and highest percentage of extra bases taken as a runner (67.5)

Jimmy Haynes

2000 Season

The Brewers collected power arms last year with the aim of helping them to learn to harness their natural stuff. With some, they succeeded; with Jimmy Haynes, they failed, just as two other clubs had failed before. He got off to a good start, winning five of his first seven decisions, but he was inconsistent and mostly poor from then on. Though he won a career-high 12 games and didn't miss a start, it was a frustrating year overall, one in which he showed no progress.

Pitching

Haynes' raw stuff always has generated high expectations. With a good fastball, a nice overhand curve and a slider, he can be tough when he's locked in. But all too often, his command wavers. He pitches from behind, is too wild to put hitters away with two strikes and uses himself up too quickly. In 2000, he was nothing more than a five-inning pitcher, with a 4.20 ERA through the first five innings and a 10.40 ERA from the sixth on. As the season wore on, his middle-inning troubles became increasingly severe.

Defense & Hitting

Haynes is quick both to first base and home and is tough to run on. He has a habit of throwing over to first a lot. He's an aggressive fielder and isn't afraid to try for the lead runner. Haynes hit regularly for the first time last summer. He collected four doubles but fared poorly overall.

2001 Outlook

It was deeply disappointing to see Haynes not only fail to progress, but actually regress last year. The Brewers hardly have a surplus of high-ceiling arms, so they'll likely stick with Haynes and hope that he'll figure it out. They may show less patience in 2001 if he continues to struggle.

Position: SP
Bats: R **Throws:** R
Ht: 6' 4"   **Wt:** 203

Opening Day Age: 28
Born: 9/5/72 in LaGrange, GA
ML Seasons: 6

Overall Statistics

	W	L	Pct.	ERA	G	GS	Sv	IP	H	BB	SO	HR	Ratio
2000	12	13	.480	5.33	33	33	0	199.1	228	100	88	21	1.65
Career	38	47	.447	5.63	139	118	1	722.0	822	378	467	90	1.66

How Often He Throws Strikes

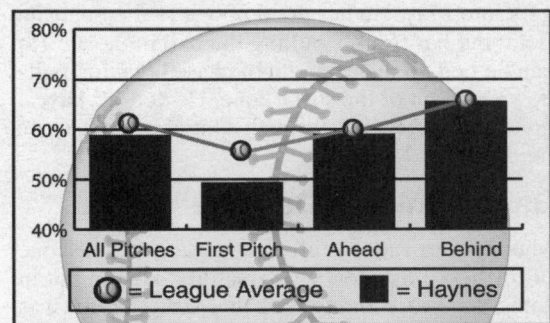

2000 Situational Stats

	W	L	ERA	Sv	IP		AB	H	HR	RBI	Avg
Home	4	6	5.45	0	100.2	LHB	329	105	11	48	.319
Road	8	7	5.20	0	98.2	RHB	445	123	10	61	.276
First Half	9	7	4.42	0	116.0	Sc Pos	206	58	1	79	.282
Scnd Half	3	6	6.59	0	83.1	Clutch	30	9	3	4	.300

2000 Rankings (National League)

- 1st in lowest strikeout/walk ratio (0.9) and highest on-base percentage allowed (.378)
- 2nd in fewest strikeouts per nine innings (4.0)
- 3rd in GDPs induced (29)
- 4th in most GDPs induced per nine innings (1.3)
- 5th in walks allowed, pickoff throws (148), highest batting average allowed (.295) and highest ERA at home
- Led the Brewers in wins, losses, games started, innings pitched, hits allowed, batters faced (897), home runs allowed, walks allowed, pitches thrown (3,322), pickoff throws (148), runners caught stealing (9), GDPs induced (29), most run support per nine innings (4.9) and lowest ERA on the road

Jose Hernandez

2000 Season

The latest in a long line of Milwaukee free-agent busts, Jose Hernandez was signed to a three-year, $10 million deal before the 2000 season. The club inked him to replace Jeff Cirillo at third base, as well as to provide righthanded power to a left-leaning lineup. But Hernandez got off to a dismal start at the plate and in the field and never fully recovered. He was felled in August by a strained back and didn't play very often or effectively thereafter.

Hitting

Hernandez always has been a pronounced warm-weather hitter, so it was curious to see him sign with Milwaukee, where the spring chill often lingers into May. He has good power to the opposite field, but has trouble pulling the ball in the air. He can be tied up inside and will chase breaking balls down and out of the strike zone. He doesn't have a good eye and swings through a lot of pitches, so he rarely walks.

Baserunning & Defense

Making Hernandez a full-timer largely negated one of his best attributes, his versatility. He did put in some time at shortstop when Mark Loretta was hurt, and played the position adequately. He recovered from an early fielding slump to play fairly well at third base, showing good range and a strong arm. He has average speed and steals an occasional base, but just as often runs himself into trouble.

2001 Outlook

Hernandez probably will remain in the lineup no matter how poorly he hits. Like Marquis Grissom, he earns a lot of money and has no obvious replacement on the roster. The move to climate-controlled Miller Park may help him get off to a better start in 2001.

Position: 3B/SS
Bats: R **Throws:** R
Ht: 6' 1" **Wt:** 180

Opening Day Age: 31
Born: 7/14/69 in Vega Alta, Puerto Rico
ML Seasons: 9
Pronunciation: her-NAN-dezz

Overall Statistics

	G	AB	R	H	D	T	HR	RBI	SB	BB	SO	Avg	OBP	Slg
2000	124	446	51	109	22	1	11	59	3	41	125	.244	.315	.372
Career	869	2435	354	608	102	24	84	316	27	195	680	.250	.308	.415

Where He Hits the Ball

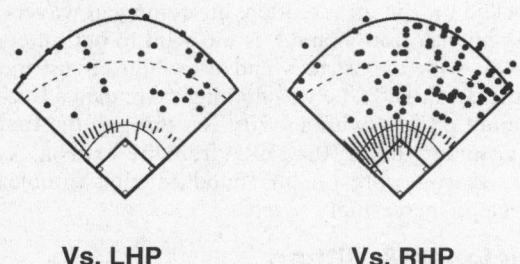

Vs. LHP   **Vs. RHP**

2000 Situational Stats

	AB	H	HR	RBI	Avg		AB	H	HR	RBI	Avg
Home	210	50	8	33	.238	LHP	113	24	2	10	.212
Road	236	59	3	26	.250	RHP	333	85	9	49	.255
First Half	303	74	10	40	.244	Sc Pos	125	34	2	46	.272
Scnd Half	143	35	1	19	.245	Clutch	82	23	1	8	.280

2000 Rankings (National League)

- 3rd in lowest batting average vs. lefthanded pitchers
- 4th in lowest slugging percentage vs. lefthanded pitchers (.327)
- 7th in lowest on-base percentage vs. lefthanded pitchers (.310)
- 8th in errors at third base (13) and highest percentage of swings that missed (28.1)
- 9th in lowest batting average on a 3-2 count (.127) and lowest batting average with two strikes (.146)
- 10th in strikeouts
- Led the Brewers in batting average with the bases loaded (.533)
- Led NL third basemen in caught stealing (7)

Geoff Jenkins

2000 Season

Geoff Jenkins continued his rise to stardom last year. Following his breakout 1999 season, in which his exposure to southpaws was limited, Jenkins was given the full-time job in left field and moved up to the third spot in the order. He had a terrific April, but he broke his right middle finger in early May. He returned only three weeks later and picked up where he'd left off, pounding the ball for the rest of the season.

Hitting

Jenkins has a lightning-quick bat and can get good wood on just about anything on the inner half of the plate. He isn't strictly a pull hitter, however, and reaches the left-field wall with regularity, though he did pull the ball more often in 2000. He hung in well against lefties, especially for someone who hadn't seen them much. First-pitch fastballs make his eyes light up.

Baserunning & Defense

Even more surprising than Jenkins' development at the plate has been his evolution as an outfielder. He came up as an iffy fielder with a surgically-repaired shoulder, but he's become one of the best defensive left fielders in the majors. An aggressive, hard-charging flycatcher, his only errors are those of aggression, and he throws very well. Jenkins has pretty good speed and makes the most of it on the bases, going 16-for-18 as a basestealer the last two years.

2001 Outlook

Jenkins' broken finger cost him a shot at 40 homers, which he could attain in 2001 if he stays healthy and is able to adjust to the club's new ballpark. If the Brewers can solve their problems at the top of the order, his RBI count should benefit as well. In other words, he's poised to put up the kind of season that could earn him the recognition he deserves as one of the game's top young hitters.

Position: LF
Bats: L **Throws:** R
Ht: 6' 1" **Wt:** 204

Opening Day Age: 26
Born: 7/21/74 in Olympia, WA
ML Seasons: 3

Overall Statistics

	G	AB	R	H	D	T	HR	RBI	SB	BB	SO	Avg	OBP	Slg
2000	135	512	100	155	36	4	34	94	11	33	135	.303	.360	.588
Career	354	1221	203	355	91	8	64	204	17	88	283	.291	.349	.536

Where He Hits the Ball

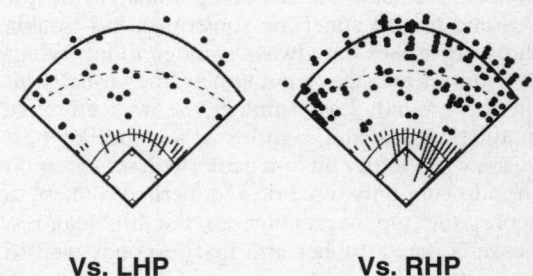

Vs. LHP   **Vs. RHP**

2000 Situational Stats

	AB	H	HR	RBI	Avg		AB	H	HR	RBI	Avg
Home	248	69	15	42	.278	LHP	120	34	5	21	.283
Road	264	86	19	52	.326	RHP	392	121	29	73	.309
First Half	236	70	14	46	.297	Sc Pos	131	33	8	56	.252
Scnd Half	276	85	20	48	.308	Clutch	86	21	2	13	.244

2000 Rankings (National League)

- 2nd in batting average on a 3-1 count (.714)
- 3rd in errors in left field (7) and lowest percentage of pitches taken (43.3)
- 4th in lowest fielding percentage in left field (.975)
- 5th in hit by pitch (15)
- Led the Brewers in batting average, home runs, runs scored, hits, doubles, total bases (301), hit by pitch (15), strikeouts, slugging percentage, on-base percentage, HR frequency (15.1 ABs per HR), fewest GDPs per GDP situation (8.4%), batting average vs. righthanded pitchers, batting average on a 3-1 count (.714), slugging percentage vs. lefthanded pitchers (.500) and slugging percentage vs. righthanded pitchers (.615)

Milwaukee

Curtis Leskanic

Position: RP
Bats: R **Throws:** R
Ht: 6' 0" **Wt:** 186

Opening Day Age: 32
Born: 4/2/68 in Homestead, PA
ML Seasons: 8
Pronunciation: les-CAN-ik

2000 Season

When Brewers closer Bob Wickman was traded away late last July, manager Davey Lopes didn't hesitate to name his successor. The clear winner was Curtis Leskanic, who'd been the club's most dominant reliever over the previous two months. Leskanic had come over in a winter trade and got off to a rocky start before going on the disabled list in May with a groin infection. But he clearly earned Lopes' unqualified support and vindicated the decision by going 7-1 and converting 11 of 12 save opportunities after becoming the closer.

Pitching

Leskanic's pitches have good velocity and exceptional movement. With a moving fastball in the low 90s and a hard slider, he sometimes has trouble throwing strikes but always is tough to hit. Whatever hitters manage to put in play, they usually hit on the ground. Last summer, he was effective against lefties and righties alike—unlike past years, when lefties hit him hard. He deserves credit for allowing only three of 31 inherited runners to score, the top percentage in the big leagues. Leskanic has a rubber arm that responds well to frequent work.

Defense & Hitting

A good athlete, Leskanic fields his position well and is quick to cover first. He's moderately tough to run on and is a decent hitter with a bit of power, though he rarely gets to display it.

2001 Outlook

The Brewers locked up Leskanic for three more years in late November, inking him to an incentive-laden deal that starts at $7.2 million and escalates to $12.9 million if he reaches certain plateaus over the next three seasons. He seems to have solved his problem with lefthanded hitters, and certainly has won the confidence of Lopes. He'll open the year as the closer and is a good bet to save a decent number of games this season.

Overall Statistics

	W	L	Pct.	ERA	G	GS	Sv	IP	H	BB	SO	HR	Ratio
2000	9	3	.750	2.56	73	0	12	77.1	58	51	75	7	1.41
Career	40	23	.635	4.59	429	11	32	547.1	530	272	490	59	1.47

How Often He Throws Strikes

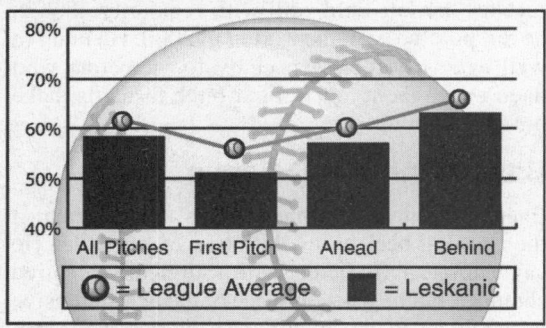

◉ = League Average ■ = Leskanic

2000 Situational Stats

	W	L	ERA	Sv	IP		AB	H	HR	RBI	Avg
Home	6	1	1.96	5	41.1	LHB	103	22	2	13	.214
Road	3	2	3.25	7	36.0	RHB	171	36	5	12	.211
First Half	0	2	3.02	1	41.2	Sc Pos	87	10	2	16	.115
Scnd Half	9	1	2.02	11	35.2	Clutch	126	22	1	7	.175

2000 Rankings (National League)

- 1st in lowest percentage of inherited runners scored (9.7)
- 2nd in lowest batting average allowed in relief with runners in scoring position (.115)
- 4th in relief wins (9), lowest batting average allowed in relief with runners on base (.182) and relief ERA (2.56)
- Led the Brewers in games pitched, games finished (39), lowest batting average allowed in relief with runners on base (.182), lowest batting average allowed in relief with runners in scoring position (.115), lowest percentage of inherited runners scored (9.7), relief wins (9), relief ERA (2.56) and lowest batting average allowed in relief (.212)

Mark Loretta

2000 Season

After battling Jose Valentin for the shortstop position for the better part of four years, Mark Loretta landed the job uncontested last year, only to lose nearly half the season to injury. An offseason trade sent Valentin packing and ended Loretta's days of shuttling around the infield. Loretta vindicated the club's decision, playing his usual steady defense while hitting over .300 in the No. 2 hole—until early June, that is, when a broken toe shelved him for more than two months. He returned in late August, but didn't hit as well the rest of the way.

Hitting

Loretta is the consummate bat-control artist, using a short, quick stroke to send liners to all fields. He can catch up with anyone's fastball, and can hold his own with two strikes. He flashed a bit more power in 2000, making an effort to pull the inside pitch more often. He can lay down a sacrifice when necessary. He's patient and takes pitches but doesn't draw a high number of walks because he puts the ball in play so often.

Baserunning & Defense

Though his range is no better than average, Loretta is the most surehanded shortstop in baseball. He committed only two errors in 90 games at short last year, and just seven in 130 games there in 1998-99. He has a quick release and an accurate arm, as well as very soft hands. He has average speed and is not a basestealer. Loretta has performed well at first, second and third base, but his versatility presumably won't be needed from now on.

2001 Outlook

Loretta's goal is the same as it was a year ago: to play a full season as the Brewers' starting shortstop. If he's able to stay healthy—something he always was able to do until last year—he should be a reliable contributor at the plate and in the field. He's a good bet to enjoy his best season yet.

Position: SS
Bats: R **Throws:** R
Ht: 6' 0" **Wt:** 180

Opening Day Age: 29
Born: 8/14/71 in Santa Monica, CA
ML Seasons: 6

Overall Statistics

	G	AB	R	H	D	T	HR	RBI	SB	BB	SO	Avg	OBP	Slg
2000	91	352	49	99	21	1	7	40	0	37	38	.281	.350	.406
Career	608	1995	286	582	107	11	25	224	21	196	226	.292	.358	.394

Where He Hits the Ball

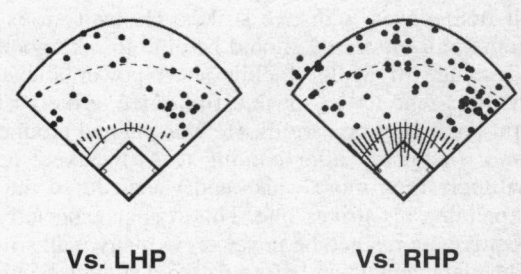

Vs. LHP   **Vs. RHP**

2000 Situational Stats

	AB	H	HR	RBI	Avg		AB	H	HR	RBI	Avg
Home	152	38	3	16	.250	LHP	78	26	1	11	.333
Road	200	61	4	24	.305	RHP	274	73	6	29	.266
First Half	200	61	5	23	.305	Sc Pos	73	24	2	29	.329
Scnd Half	152	38	2	17	.250	Clutch	47	14	0	6	.298

2000 Rankings (National League)

- 1st in lowest percentage of swings that missed (6.9)
- Led the Brewers in sacrifice bunts (8), batting average with two strikes (.220), bunts in play (14), lowest percentage of swings that missed (6.9) and highest percentage of swings put into play (48.5)
- Led NL shortstops in lowest percentage of swings that missed (6.9)

Milwaukee

Richie Sexson

2000 Season

Is Richie Sexson to be *The Man Who Saved Mil-waukee*? He was received that way in August after coming over in a deadline deal and absolutely mashing the ball for the final two months of the season. He survived an up-and-down first half with the Indians, during which the club considered sending him to the minors. But the Brewers won the bidding war for him, touting him as a potential cornerstone of their rebuilding effort. Returned to his natural position, first base, and installed in the cleanup spot, he drove in 47 runs in 57 games for Milwaukee.

Hitting

The long-armed Sexson has prodigious power to all fields, even with two strikes. He isn't an extreme pull hitter and should be able to take good advantage of Miller Field's short power alleys. Pitchers who try to sneak a first-pitch strike past him had better be careful. He was pitched around more frequently after coming to Milwaukee; he willingly took more walks and wasn't lured into expanding his strike zone. This was an especially positive sign, since he never drew many walks in Cleveland and never before had to deal with being pitched around.

Baserunning & Defense

Lost amid all the homers was Sexson's defense at first base, which was surprisingly good. He has good hands and a very good throwing arm for a first baseman, and he often handled relays from the outfield. On the bases, he is not a complete plodder, but he takes a while to get going and is no basestealer.

2001 Outlook

It's no wonder that Sexson, who played out of position and batted at the bottom of the order in Cleveland, flourished after Milwaukee restored him to his natural spots in the field and the lineup. Because Sexson is just 26, all signs point to 2001 being his best season yet.

Position: 1B/LF/DH
Bats: R **Throws:** R
Ht: 6' 7" **Wt:** 225

Opening Day Age: 26
Born: 12/29/74 in Portland, OR
ML Seasons: 4

Overall Statistics

	G	AB	R	H	D	T	HR	RBI	SB	BB	SO	Avg	OBP	Slg
2000	148	537	89	146	30	1	30	91	2	59	159	.272	.349	.499
Career	336	1201	190	325	61	9	72	242	6	99	320	.271	.330	.516

Where He Hits the Ball

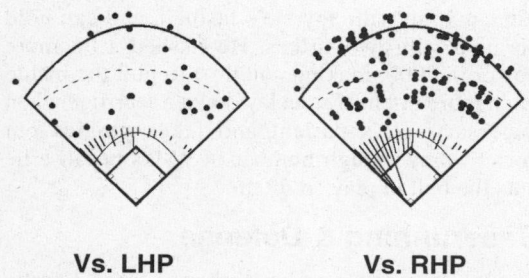

Vs. LHP   Vs. RHP

2000 Situational Stats

	AB	H	HR	RBI	Avg		AB	H	HR	RBI	Avg
Home	255	72	15	41	.282	LHP	118	26	5	19	.220
Road	282	74	15	50	.262	RHP	419	120	25	72	.286
First Half	295	73	15	37	.247	Sc Pos	133	39	6	55	.293
Scnd Half	242	73	15	54	.302	Clutch	97	30	8	18	.309

2000 Rankings (National League)

- 7th in batting average on a 3-1 count (.667)
- Led the Brewers in cleanup slugging percentage (.559)

Jamey Wright

2000 Season

Young Jamey Wright finally escaped from Coors Field, liberated in the Jeff Cirillo deal before the 2000 season. He nearly didn't have a 2000 season, though, as he came down with a sore shoulder in spring training and was diagnosed with a slightly torn rotator cuff. Luckily, surgery was not required, and he was able to rehab and return by late May. He remained in the rotation for the rest of the year and was inconsistent but impressive at times, and he finished as one of the club's best starters overall.

Pitching

Wright's low-90s power sinker is difficult both to control and hit, as evidenced by his .261 opponent batting average, nine wild pitches, 88 walks and a major league-high 18 hit batsmen. He gets plenty of hitters to chase his hard slider and keeps them off-balance with a slow curve. He's one of the most extreme groundball pitchers in the majors, inducing 25 twin-killings in 2000. Wright threw a lot of pitches for someone with an iffy shoulder, but he was able to maintain his strength through the end of the season.

Defense & Hitting

Wright's delivery takes him off to the first-base side of the mound, but he has good reactions and fields his position well. He has quick feet and a very good pickoff move for a righthander. He's also quick to the plate and is very difficult to run on overall. Wright is a very weak hitter.

2001 Outlook

Many think Wright has a bright future, and cite Kevin Brown as an example of a pitcher whose stuff was so electric it took years to harness. As Wright refines his control, he can only get better. He'll begin the year as one of the Brewers' top starters. The only concern is that his shoulder may flare up again after last summer's heavy work.

Position: SP
Bats: R **Throws:** R
Ht: 6' 5" **Wt:** 221

Opening Day Age: 26
Born: 12/24/74 in Oklahoma City, OK
ML Seasons: 5

Overall Statistics

	W	L	Pct.	ERA	G	GS	Sv	IP	H	BB	SO	HR	Ratio
2000	7	9	.438	4.10	26	25	0	164.2	157	88	96	12	1.49
Career	32	42	.432	5.22	118	116	0	706.1	805	349	335	73	1.63

How Often He Throws Strikes

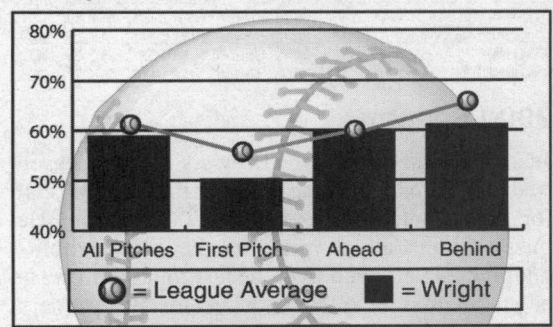

Legend: ◒ = League Average ■ = Wright

Chart categories: All Pitches, First Pitch, Ahead, Behind (Y-axis: 40% to 80%)

2000 Situational Stats

	W	L	ERA	Sv	IP		AB	H	HR	RBI	Avg
Home	4	3	3.68	0	88.0	LHB	247	66	6	31	.267
Road	3	6	4.58	0	76.2	RHB	355	91	6	39	.256
First Half	4	2	3.45	0	60.0	Sc Pos	148	43	3	58	.291
Scnd Half	3	7	4.47	0	104.2	Clutch	45	9	1	1	.200

2000 Rankings (National League)

- 1st in hit batsmen (18)
- 2nd in most GDPs induced per nine innings (1.4) and lowest strikeout/walk ratio (1.1)
- 3rd in highest groundball/flyball ratio allowed (2.1) and fewest home runs allowed per nine innings (.66)
- 4th in balks (2), highest on-base percentage allowed (.368) and least run support per nine innings (4.1)
- 5th in GDPs induced (25) and lowest slugging percentage allowed (.354)
- Led the Brewers in hit batsmen (18), wild pitches (9), balks (2), lowest slugging percentage allowed (.354) and highest groundball/flyball ratio allowed (2.1)

Juan Acevedo

Position: RP
Bats: R **Throws:** R
Ht: 6' 2" **Wt:** 228

Opening Day Age: 30
Born: 5/5/70 in Juarez, Mexico
ML Seasons: 5
Pronunciation:
ah-suh-VAY-doh

Overall Statistics

	W	L	Pct.	ERA	G	GS	Sv	IP	H	BB	SO	HR	Ratio
2000	3	7	.300	3.81	62	0	0	82.2	77	31	51	11	1.31
Career	24	25	.490	4.45	204	34	19	396.2	409	150	232	56	1.41

2000 Situational Stats

	W	L	ERA	Sv	IP		AB	H	HR	RBI	Avg
Home	1	1	2.33	0	46.1	LHB	122	35	4	15	.287
Road	2	6	5.70	0	36.1	RHB	191	42	7	30	.220
First Half	0	3	3.83	0	44.2	Sc Pos	88	24	3	34	.273
Scnd Half	3	4	3.79	0	38.0	Clutch	117	30	6	17	.256

2000 Season

Juan Acevedo came to the Brewers in an offseason trade for Fernando Vina, as part of their casting call for power pitchers before the 2000 season. He missed almost all of April with shoulder tendinitis but pitched very well over the last four months. He began in middle relief and became the primary righthanded setup man in August when Curtis Leskanic moved into the closer's role.

Pitching, Defense & Hitting

Acevedo has a high, riding fastball in the low 90s and a cutter. He's a flyball pitcher who's vulnerable to the longball. He seems to be at his best working only one inning each time he takes the mound. Lefthanded hitters gave him problems last year, but he's been effective against them in the past. Acevedo has a good move to first and is tough to run on. He's a decent fielder, but a completely hopeless hitter with a .081 career average.

2001 Outlook

Did Acevedo find his proper role last year, or will his inconsistency return? There have been several other occasions when Acevedo has excelled in a new role, only to prove unable to sustain his success the following year. Until he proves otherwise, however, the Brewers will consider him no more than a very capable setup man.

Raul Casanova

Position: C
Bats: B **Throws:** R
Ht: 6' 0" **Wt:** 195

Opening Day Age: 28
Born: 8/23/72 in Humacao, Puerto Rico
ML Seasons: 4

Overall Statistics

	G	AB	R	H	D	T	HR	RBI	SB	BB	SO	Avg	OBP	Slg
2000	86	231	20	57	13	3	6	36	1	26	48	.247	.331	.407
Career	228	662	57	153	26	4	16	72	2	63	124	.231	.304	.355

2000 Situational Stats

	AB	H	HR	RBI	Avg		AB	H	HR	RBI	Avg
Home	118	29	4	23	.246	LHP	57	14	1	12	.246
Road	113	28	2	13	.248	RHP	174	43	5	24	.247
First Half	88	23	4	16	.261	Sc Pos	65	15	2	31	.231
Scnd Half	143	34	2	20	.238	Clutch	51	13	1	7	.255

2000 Season

When the Brewers needed a backup catcher in June, Raul Casanova got the call. He'd been up earlier in the season but hadn't hit at all and was waived. No one claimed him, so he returned to Triple-A Indianapolis. But after his June recall, he got hot with the bat, earning decent playing time against righthanded pitchers. He cooled in the second half.

Hitting, Baserunning & Defense

Casanova, a switch-hitter, is a similar hitter from both sides. He is a good fastball hitter, but will chase breaking balls. A line-drive hitter, he shows infrequent power. He fared well as a pinch-hitter in a dozen tries. Rough footwork and an inconsistent release hampered his throwing last summer, although he has a fairly strong arm. All he does on the bases is clog them.

2001 Outlook

The Brewers' acquisition of former Toronto catcher Kevin Brown in late July was not a good sign for Casanova. Still, Milwaukee re-signed Casanova to a one-year deal in early December and he again will have the inside track at being Henry Blanco's primary backup.

Valerio de los Santos

Position: RP
Bats: L **Throws:** L
Ht: 6' 2" **Wt:** 180

Opening Day Age: 25
Born: 10/6/75 in Las Matas, Dominican Republic
ML Seasons: 3

Overall Statistics

	W	L	Pct.	ERA	G	GS	Sv	IP	H	BB	SO	HR	Ratio
2000	2	3	.400	5.13	66	2	0	73.2	72	33	70	15	1.43
Career	2	4	.333	4.77	86	2	0	103.2	95	42	93	20	1.32

2000 Situational Stats

	W	L	ERA	Sv	IP		AB	H	HR	RBI	Avg
Home	2	1	4.50	0	40.0	LHB	110	30	5	19	.273
Road	0	2	5.88	0	33.2	RHB	173	42	10	31	.243
First Half	1	3	6.18	0	43.2	Sc Pos	74	22	3	36	.297
Scnd Half	1	0	3.60	0	30.0	Clutch	50	12	2	11	.240

2000 Season

Valerio de los Santos' first full major league season was an ongoing experiment to find his proper role. After missing most of 1999 due to back surgery, he began the year in the Brewers' rotation but was sent to the bullpen after only two starts. He didn't fit as a specialist, but he settled in as a middle reliever and pitched very well in the second half.

Pitching, Defense & Hitting

De los Santos is a two-pitch pitcher, working up and down with a low-90s fastball and a splitter. He isn't strong against lefties since he lacks an effective breaking pitch. He gets a lot of flyballs and can be vulnerable to the home run. He doesn't throw to first often, but has a quick delivery and is very tough to run on. A decent fielder, he's a weak hitter who's only 2-for-15 at the plate in his pro career.

2001 Outlook

De los Santos seemed to find a niche in middle relief last year, and has the talent to take on a longer role if and when he's ready. He was primarily a starter in the minors and could return to the rotation in the future. Whether it's in his present role or a larger one, he could be an important member of the staff this year.

Charlie Hayes

Position: 3B/1B
Bats: R **Throws:** R
Ht: 6' 0" **Wt:** 215

Opening Day Age: 35
Born: 5/29/65 in Hattiesburg, MS
ML Seasons: 13

Overall Statistics

	G	AB	R	H	D	T	HR	RBI	SB	BB	SO	Avg	OBP	Slg
2000	121	370	46	93	17	0	9	46	1	57	84	.251	.348	.370
Career	1516	5212	576	1369	249	16	144	736	47	413	902	.263	.317	.399

2000 Situational Stats

	AB	H	HR	RBI	Avg		AB	H	HR	RBI	Avg
Home	171	37	2	15	.216	LHP	117	30	4	14	.256
Road	199	56	7	31	.281	RHP	253	63	5	32	.249
First Half	224	59	6	32	.263	Sc Pos	96	21	3	37	.219
Scnd Half	146	34	3	14	.233	Clutch	74	19	0	15	.257

2000 Season

Coming off a terrible year in 1999, Charlie Hayes was signed to back up the infield corners and provide bench depth. The poor play of first baseman Kevin Barker and third baseman Jose Hernandez forced him into a larger role, however. He played semi-regularly at first and third through July, often hitting cleanup against lefthanders. He slumped in August and virtually disappeared in September. Overall, he didn't hit for much power but did well as pinch-hitter.

Hitting, Baserunning & Defense

Hayes' power clearly is on the wane, and it's been several years since he hit righthanders well enough to deserve to face them. He's still reasonably productive against lefties. He showed better plate discipline than ever last year, drawing a career-high 57 walks in part-time play. He no longer has much range at either first or third base, but has a strong arm and good hands at either position. His baserunning isn't a factor.

2001 Outlook

Hayes was not offered arbitration and became a free agent over the winter. He likely won't be back with Milwaukee. His minor resurgence in 2000 may be enough to land him a bench role somewhere.

Milwaukee

Tyler Houston

Position: 1B/3B/C
Bats: L **Throws:** R
Ht: 6' 1" **Wt:** 210

Opening Day Age: 30
Born: 1/17/71 in Long Beach, CA
ML Seasons: 5

Overall Statistics

	G	AB	R	H	D	T	HR	RBI	SB	BB	SO	Avg	OBP	Slg
2000	101	284	30	71	15	0	18	43	2	17	72	.250	.292	.493
Career	460	1153	120	294	51	3	42	161	9	79	265	.255	.302	.414

2000 Situational Stats

	AB	H	HR	RBI	Avg		AB	H	HR	RBI	Avg
Home	129	31	6	17	.240	LHP	22	4	2	8	.182
Road	155	40	12	26	.258	RHP	262	67	16	35	.256
First Half	130	33	9	20	.254	Sc Pos	66	13	4	24	.197
Scnd Half	154	38	9	23	.247	Clutch	54	6	2	3	.111

2000 Season

The Brewers got their money's worth out of Tyler Houston last season. Signed to a minor league contract over the winter, he opened the season as their backup catcher. He suffered calf and ankle injuries in May and June, and he didn't catch much in the second half. Playing mostly first and third base and pinch-hitting, he had a couple of three-week hot streaks in which he hit homers in bunches.

Hitting, Baserunning & Defense

Houston rarely faces southpaws. At the plate, he's impatient, strikeout-prone and never draws walks or hits for much of an average. His middling power is his only real offensive asset. He likes to hit the first pitch, pulls the ball and often hits it through the hole with a runner on first. His track record as a pinch-hitter is unimpressive. He has good hands and decent range at first or third, but he's not a strong defensive catcher. Basestealers take liberties on him when he's behind the plate. Speed is not part of his game.

2001 Outlook

Houston's lefthanded bat and ability to play several positions make him a useful bench player, so he may be asked back. If not, he ought to be able to catch on somewhere else.

Ray King

Position: RP
Bats: L **Throws:** L
Ht: 6' 1" **Wt:** 230

Opening Day Age: 27
Born: 1/15/74 in Chicago, IL
ML Seasons: 2

Overall Statistics

	W	L	Pct.	ERA	G	GS	Sv	IP	H	BB	SO	HR	Ratio
2000	3	2	.600	1.26	36	0	0	28.2	18	10	19	1	0.98
Career	3	2	.600	2.52	46	0	0	39.1	29	20	24	3	1.25

2000 Situational Stats

	W	L	ERA	Sv	IP		AB	H	HR	RBI	Avg
Home	3	1	1.50	0	18.0	LHB	49	10	1	2	.204
Road	0	1	0.84	0	10.2	RHB	51	8	0	4	.157
First Half	0	0	4.50	0	2.0	Sc Pos	26	4	0	5	.154
Scnd Half	3	2	1.01	0	26.2	Clutch	55	9	0	4	.164

2000 Season

Lefthander Ray King was one of the biggest surprises on the Brewers' staff during the second half of 2000. He was wild in a short trial with the Cubs late in 1999, and failed to make the club last spring. In mid-April, the Cubs dealt him to the Brewers. After brief callups in April and May, he came up for good in July and quickly settled in as a situational lefty and middle reliever.

Pitching, Defense & Hitting

King's sharp slider is his out pitch. With a 90-MPH fastball, he's basically a two-pitch pitcher. The key for him last year was that he was able to keep his slider close enough to make batters chase it, but he kept it off the plate enough to keep them from hitting it. When he's on, he keeps the ball down and gets groundballs. Only one runner has tried to steal on King in the majors, and he was thrown out. King fields his position well but has struck out eight times without a hit in 11 pro at-bats.

2001 Outlook

The second half of last season was one of the few times in King's career that he's shown good command for a decent stretch. He'll begin 2001 in the same role he served in last summer, but there's no guarantee the plate won't start jumping around on him again.

Luis Lopez

Position: SS/2B
Bats: B **Throws:** R
Ht: 5'11" **Wt:** 166

Opening Day Age: 30
Born: 9/4/70 in Cidra,
Puerto Rico
ML Seasons: 7
Pronunciation:
LOE-pezz

Overall Statistics

	G	AB	R	H	D	T	HR	RBI	SB	BB	SO	Avg	OBP	Slg
2000	78	201	24	53	14	0	6	27	1	9	35	.264	.309	.423
Career	498	1166	131	285	63	4	15	113	9	77	252	.244	.300	.344

2000 Situational Stats

	AB	H	HR	RBI	Avg		AB	H	HR	RBI	Avg
Home	135	31	3	18	.230	LHP	47	12	2	5	.255
Road	66	22	3	9	.333	RHP	154	41	4	22	.266
First Half	92	24	2	10	.261	Sc Pos	57	13	1	21	.228
Scnd Half	109	29	4	17	.266	Clutch	42	16	3	9	.381

2000 Season

Luis Lopez came to the Brewers in a minor offseason deal before the 2000 campaign. The normally light-hitting reserve infielder had a surprising season with the bat, and he played his usual solid defense.

Hitting, Baserunning & Defense

Lopez, a smallish switch-hitter, came into the season with nine career homers, but added six more in 2000. Mostly a slap hitter from either side, he showed occasional power to right field from the left side of the plate. He remains an impatient hitter, but he's a good bunter. Lopez has good range and hands at both second base and shortstop. His arm is a little short for the left side of the infield, but he compensates with a quick release. His speed is unimpressive, but he gets the green light, perhaps because he looks like the type of player who ought to be able to steal bases.

2001 Outlook

Lopez inked a two-year, $1.4 million deal with the Brewers in late October. He probably never will get the chance to play full-time, but should continue to be useful in a bench role.

James Mouton

Position: CF/LF
Bats: R **Throws:** R
Ht: 5' 9" **Wt:** 175

Opening Day Age: 32
Born: 12/29/68 in
Denver, CO
ML Seasons: 7
Pronunciation:
moo-TAHN

Overall Statistics

	G	AB	R	H	D	T	HR	RBI	SB	BB	SO	Avg	OBP	Slg
2000	87	159	28	37	7	1	2	17	13	30	43	.233	.363	.327
Career	648	1432	203	352	67	7	16	137	102	163	298	.246	.328	.336

2000 Situational Stats

	AB	H	HR	RBI	Avg		AB	H	HR	RBI	Avg
Home	68	19	1	8	.279	LHP	68	18	1	7	.265
Road	91	18	1	9	.198	RHP	91	19	1	10	.209
First Half	93	21	1	8	.226	Sc Pos	38	9	1	13	.237
Scnd Half	66	16	1	9	.242	Clutch	31	6	0	4	.194

2000 Season

When new manager Davey Lopes announced his plan for a speed-based offense, critics cringed at the thought of a Milwaukee roster stocked with one-dimensional speed demons. As it turned out, the signing of James Mouton was as far as it went. Mouton backed up all three outfield positions and pinch-hit, and proved capable of getting on base. A sore left wrist grounded him in September, leading to surgery after the season.

Hitting, Baserunning & Defense

Mouton's chances to be anything more than a backup were done in by his complete inability to hit righthanded pitching. He's a spray hitter who slaps the ball around, bunts very well and has become more adept at working walks over the last few years. He has excellent speed and is a good basestealer against righthanded pitchers, but he doesn't read lefties well. In the outfield, Mouton has passable range and is very surehanded, but his arm is barely adequate in center or right.

2001 Outlook

Mouton became a free agent over the winter, but the Brewers re-signed him to a minor league deal in early December. They have poor team speed and few outfielders who can cover center field so he still could be useful in plugging those holes.

John Snyder

Position: SP
Bats: R **Throws:** R
Ht: 6' 3" **Wt:** 200

Opening Day Age: 26
Born: 8/16/74 in Southfield, MI
ML Seasons: 3

Overall Statistics

	W	L	Pct.	ERA	G	GS	Sv	IP	H	BB	SO	HR	Ratio
2000	3	10	.231	6.17	23	23	0	127.0	147	77	69	8	1.76
Career	19	24	.442	6.01	63	62	0	342.2	410	149	188	49	1.63

2000 Situational Stats

	W	L	ERA	Sv	IP		AB	H	HR	RBI	Avg
Home	1	2	3.49	0	59.1	LHB	217	62	5	29	.286
Road	2	8	8.51	0	67.2	RHB	280	85	3	52	.304
First Half	3	3	4.76	0	58.2	Sc Pos	142	55	2	70	.387
Scnd Half	0	7	7.38	0	68.1	Clutch	27	8	1	1	.296

2000 Season

The Brewers acquired John Snyder from the White Sox in January, hoping he could regain the form he displayed in early 1999 before arm problems—and elbow surgery—ruined his season. He began the 2000 campaign on the disabled list with a strained oblique muscle and was hit hard when activated in May. He turned it around and pitched well until the All-Star break, but he was continually lit up the rest of the year. He was winless in his final 16 starts.

Pitching, Defense & Hitting

Snyder doesn't have great stuff or command. He has a below-average fastball, a sinking two-seamer, an overhand curve, a slider and a changeup. He often pitches from behind in the count, and walks frequently hurt him. He also struggled badly with men on base. Holding runners is not a strength of his. In his first year as a hitter, he went 3-for-38 with only one successful sacrifice.

2001 Outlook

The Brewers must like something about Snyder, because they stuck with him last year long after most teams would have pulled the plug. Snyder has shown no signs of coming around, but the Brewers have shown no signs of giving up on him. It's hard to say how long the stalemate will continue.

Dave Weathers

Position: RP
Bats: R **Throws:** R
Ht: 6' 3" **Wt:** 230

Opening Day Age: 31
Born: 9/25/69 in Lawrenceburg, TN
ML Seasons: 10

Overall Statistics

	W	L	Pct.	ERA	G	GS	Sv	IP	H	BB	SO	HR	Ratio
2000	3	5	.375	3.07	69	0	1	76.1	73	32	50	7	1.38
Career	34	41	.453	5.12	320	67	3	682.2	798	311	471	64	1.62

2000 Situational Stats

	W	L	ERA	Sv	IP		AB	H	HR	RBI	Avg
Home	3	3	3.14	0	43.0	LHB	94	21	1	10	.223
Road	0	2	2.97	1	33.1	RHB	187	52	6	24	.278
First Half	3	3	3.42	1	50.0	Sc Pos	79	20	0	25	.253
Scnd Half	0	2	2.39	0	26.1	Clutch	123	37	3	16	.301

2000 Season

Righthander David Weathers signed a two-year deal with Milwaukee over the winter and responded with his best overall season. He not only improved his effectiveness, but also proved he could handle a more important role. Formerly a long man, he moved into a middle-relief and setup role. He was one of the most frequently-used pitchers in the league for most of the season, except for August, when he was sidelined with a strained oblique muscle.

Pitching, Defense & Hitting

Weathers throws a 90-MPH fastball and a sinker, but his slider is his out pitch. He gained more confidence in his sinker in 2000 and finally was able to conquer lefthanded hitters, who'd previously made his life miserable. He always had trouble pitching on consecutive days until last year. The opposition used to run wild on him, but new catcher Henry Blanco helped put that to a stop. In the field, Weathers was errorless for a fifth straight year, although he'll never be called graceful. He's no threat at the plate.

2001 Outlook

Weathers is signed through this season and should remain a respectable middle man for the Brewers.

Other Milwaukee Brewers

Kevin Barker (**Pos**: 1B, **Age**: 25, **Bats**: L)

	G	AB	R	H	D	T	HR	RBI	SB	BB	SO	Avg	OBP	Slg
2000	40	100	14	22	5	0	2	9	1	20	21	.220	.352	.330
Career	78	217	27	55	8	0	5	32	2	29	40	.253	.341	.359

Barker's average nosedived at Triple-A and with Milwaukee last season. He may have been more passive at the plate, as his walk rate improved significantly. He's young enough to bounce back a bit. 2001 Outlook: C

Kevin L. Brown (**Pos**: C, **Age**: 27, **Bats**: R)

	G	AB	R	H	D	T	HR	RBI	SB	BB	SO	Avg	OBP	Slg
2000	5	17	3	4	3	0	0	1	0	1	5	.235	.278	.412
Career	66	145	23	39	12	1	3	19	0	12	41	.269	.327	.428

Brown was once a decent prospect in the Texas system. The Brewers acquired him from Toronto for Alvin Morrow last July. If he can catch a break, Brown might be able to surprise. 2001 Outlook: C

Jim Bruske (**Pos**: RHP, **Age**: 36)

	W	L	Pct.	ERA	G	GS	Sv	IP	H	BB	SO	HR	Ratio
2000	1	0	1.000	6.48	15	0	0	16.2	22	12	8	5	2.04
Career	9	1	.900	4.13	105	1	2	144.0	154	68	95	16	1.54

What a great name for someone playing in Milwaukee. Unfortunately, Bruske strained his elbow and was ineffective for the Brewers and at Triple-A last year. He became a free agent after the season. 2001 Outlook: C

Mike Buddie (**Pos**: RHP, **Age**: 30)

	W	L	Pct.	ERA	G	GS	Sv	IP	H	BB	SO	HR	Ratio
2000	0	0	-	4.50	5	0	0	6.0	8	1	5	0	1.50
Career	4	1	.800	5.44	31	2	0	49.2	57	14	26	6	1.43

Buddie became a Brewer last year after eight-plus seasons in the Yankee organization. He pitched better after leaving the Yankees and he'll fight for a middle relief role. 2001 Outlook: C

Lou Collier (**Pos**: CF, **Age**: 27, **Bats**: R)

	G	AB	R	H	D	T	HR	RBI	SB	BB	SO	Avg	OBP	Slg
2000	14	32	9	7	1	0	1	2	0	6	4	.219	.333	.344
Career	216	538	60	129	23	6	5	60	6	52	117	.240	.310	.333

After beginning his professional career as a shortstop, Collier primarily played third base and the outfield last year. While the versatility can't hurt, he doesn't hit enough for his new positions. 2001 Outlook: C

Kane Davis (**Pos**: RHP, **Age**: 25)

	W	L	Pct.	ERA	G	GS	Sv	IP	H	BB	SO	HR	Ratio
2000	0	3	.000	12.60	8	2	0	15.0	27	13	4	4	2.67
Career	0	3	.000	12.60	8	2	0	15.0	27	13	4	4	2.67

The Brewers acquired Davis in the six-player deal with Cleveland last July that also brought Richie Sexson. Davis allowed a whopping .494 on-base percentage in his brief major league experience last year. 2001 Outlook: C

Angel Echevarria (**Pos**: 1B, **Age**: 29, **Bats**: R)

	G	AB	R	H	D	T	HR	RBI	SB	BB	SO	Avg	OBP	Slg
2000	41	51	3	10	2	0	1	6	0	7	11	.196	.293	.294
Career	203	312	44	88	14	0	13	56	1	30	58	.282	.354	.452

Echevarria was acquired off waivers from Colorado last July. The Rockies were evidently smart enough to recognize his averages at Colorado Springs were a bit inflated by the altitude. 2001 Outlook: C

Chris Jones (**Pos**: RF, **Age**: 35, **Bats**: R)

	G	AB	R	H	D	T	HR	RBI	SB	BB	SO	Avg	OBP	Slg
2000	12	16	3	3	2	0	0	1	0	1	4	.188	.235	.313
Career	548	1021	155	257	43	11	30	131	26	74	287	.252	.303	.404

Jones saw some action with the Brewers last July, thereby making Milwaukee his eighth major league team in 10 years. Jones now is a free agent who offers little that someone 10 years younger couldn't. 2001 Outlook: D

Lyle Mouton (**Pos**: LF, **Age**: 31, **Bats**: R)

	G	AB	R	H	D	T	HR	RBI	SB	BB	SO	Avg	OBP	Slg
2000	42	97	14	27	7	1	2	16	1	10	29	.278	.349	.433
Career	307	788	95	224	43	2	22	115	9	71	202	.284	.345	.428

While he's no more than a spare outfielder, Mouton did bat .429 last year in 28 at-bats with runners in scoring position. Despite that, the Brewers released him in late November. 2001 Outlook: C

Hector Ramirez (**Pos**: RHP, **Age**: 29)

	W	L	Pct.	ERA	G	GS	Sv	IP	H	BB	SO	HR	Ratio
2000	0	1	.000	10.00	6	0	0	9.0	11	5	4	1	1.78
Career	1	3	.250	5.40	21	0	0	30.0	30	16	13	2	1.53

After flunking a trial with the Brewers last May, Ramirez refused a minor league assignment, then later pitched in Triple-A for Baltimore and Houston. Pretty soon he'll run out of teams. 2001 Outlook: C

Paul Rigdon (**Pos**: RHP, **Age**: 25)

	W	L	Pct.	ERA	G	GS	Sv	IP	H	BB	SO	HR	Ratio
2000	5	5	.500	5.15	17	16	0	87.1	89	35	63	18	1.42
Career	5	5	.500	5.15	17	16	0	87.1	89	35	63	18	1.42

The Brewers acquired Rigdon last July in the same deal that netted Richie Sexson. Rigdon is a tall righthander who has consistently been successful in the minors and may stick in the Brewer rotation. 2001 Outlook: B

Rafael Roque (**Pos**: LHP, **Age**: 27)

	W	L	Pct.	ERA	G	GS	Sv	IP	H	BB	SO	HR	Ratio
2000	0	0	-	10.13	4	0	0	5.1	7	7	4	1	2.63
Career	5	8	.385	5.36	56	18	1	137.2	145	73	104	26	1.58

After serving as Milwaukee's Opening Day starter in 1999, Roque spent most of last season in the minors. He reportedly wasn't throwing as hard for the Brewers as he had before. 2001 Outlook: C

Milwaukee

Bob Scanlan (**Pos**: RHP, **Age**: 34)

	W	L	Pct.	ERA	G	GS	Sv	IP	H	BB	SO	HR	Ratio
2000	0	0	-	27.00	2	0	0	1.2	6	0	1	0	3.60
Career	20	34	.370	4.46	272	39	17	510.1	546	195	240	41	1.45

Scanlan was reborn in Triple-A last year, saving 35 games with a terrific ERA. His strikeout rate remains weak, however, and it's unlikely any team would use him in anything other than middle relief. 2001 Outlook: C

Everett Stull (**Pos**: RHP, **Age**: 29)

	W	L	Pct.	ERA	G	GS	Sv	IP	H	BB	SO	HR	Ratio
2000	2	3	.400	5.82	20	4	0	43.1	41	30	33	7	1.64
Career	2	4	.333	6.65	24	4	0	47.1	50	36	35	8	1.82

Stull signed a minor league deal with Milwaukee after working with the Braves last spring training. He still has a great arm, but still has problems with command, too. 2001 Outlook: C

Mark Sweeney (**Pos**: DH, **Age**: 31, **Bats**: L)

	G	AB	R	H	D	T	HR	RBI	SB	BB	SO	Avg	OBP	Slg
2000	71	73	9	16	6	0	1	6	0	12	18	.219	.337	.342
Career	480	707	85	184	35	3	12	86	7	105	140	.260	.356	.369

Sweeney will keep a major league job as long as he can deliver as a pinch-hitter. After batting .355 in that role in 1999, he slumped to .185 off the bench last year. He refused a minor league assignment and became a free agent shortly after the season ended. 2001 Outlook: C

Matt Williams (**Pos**: LHP, **Age**: 29)

	W	L	Pct.	ERA	G	GS	Sv	IP	H	BB	SO	HR	Ratio
2000	0	0	-	7.00	11	0	0	9.0	7	13	7	2	2.22
Career	0	0	-	7.00	11	0	0	9.0	7	13	7	2	2.22

The Brewers selected Williams in the Rule 5 Draft in 1999. He pitched for Milwaukee in April, allowed a ton of walks, and the Brewers soon returned him to the Yankee organization. 2001 Outlook: C

Milwaukee Brewers Minor League Prospects

Organization Overview:

When Dean Taylor took over as general manager, his new regime was committed to overhauling the farm system. He inherited an unorganized system in disarray, with very little talent brewing in the upper levels. In all fairness, injuries have cursed the Brewers for years, as several top draft picks with high hopes were attacked with arm injuries, including Jeff D'Amico, Kyle Peterson, Jose Garcia and J.M. Gold. D'Amico's return to form was a pleasant surprise, and a much needed boost for the franchise, which now is able to boast a developing young core of homegrown players. The rapid emergence of Ben Sheets, along with the intriguing development of pure power pitcher Nick Neugebauer, provide a ray of hope as Taylor and his staff mold the organization back to respectability.

Horacio Estrada

Position: P **Opening Day Age:** 25
Bats: L **Throws:** L **Born:** 10/19/75 in San
Ht: 6' 0" **Wt:** 160 Joaquin, VZ

Recent Statistics

	W	L	ERA	G	GS	Sv	IP	H	R	BB	SO	HR
2000 AAA Indianapols	14	4	3.33	25	25	0	159.1	149	63	45	103	14
2000 NL Milwaukee	3	0	6.29	7	4	0	24.1	30	18	20	13	5

Estrada will enter this spring in the same boat he was in a year ago—with a chance to make the Brewers' rotation. Last year, the Venezuelan southpaw, signed at the age of 16 way back in 1992, pitched his way off of the Opening Day staff before going on to a solid season in Triple-A. He was much improved in his second tour of the International League, meriting a pair of callups to Milwaukee as a spot starter. Animated on the mound, Estrada has proven to be durable since undergoing shoulder surgery in '98. He isn't overpowering, and he needs to be sharp with his curve and change to be effective. After pacing the IL in wins (14) and shutouts (2), he won the clinching game of the Triple-A World Series. He is out of options and would be the only lefty in the rotation.

Allen Levrault

Position: P **Opening Day Age:** 23
Bats: R **Throws:** R **Born:** 8/15/77 in Fall
Ht: 6' 3" **Wt:** 230 River, MA

Recent Statistics

	W	L	ERA	G	GS	Sv	IP	H	R	BB	SO	HR
2000 AAA Indianapols	6	8	4.24	21	18	0	108.1	98	55	46	78	9
2000 NL Milwaukee	0	1	4.50	5	1	0	12.0	10	7	7	9	0

Levrault's track record shows that he hasn't adjusted well to midseason promotions. In '98, his ERA soared over three points after a bump up to Double-A, and in '99 his ERA ballooned to 8.65 in Triple-A. Those setbacks aside, he remains a solid prospect coming off a decent

year in Triple-A Indianapolis. The big righthander turned some heads with his intense demeanor during a pair of stints with Milwaukee. He has the build and makeup of a power pitcher. His fastball reaches the low 90s, but it's his changeup that sets up hitters. Levrault is fine-tuning his curveball to polish off his repertoire. His best chance to join the Brewers staff in 2001 may come as a reliever, a role that could fit his style to a tee.

Jose Mieses

Position: P **Opening Day Age:** 21
Bats: R **Throws:** R **Born:** 10/14/79 in Santo
Ht: 6' 1" **Wt:** 165 Domingo, DR

Recent Statistics

	W	L	ERA	G	GS	Sv	IP	H	R	BB	SO	HR
2000 A Beloit	13	6	2.53	21	21	0	135.0	107	43	37	132	8
2000 A Mudville	4	1	2.65	6	6	0	34.0	25	11	18	40	1

In his first full season out of the Dominican Summer League, Mieses continued to establish himself as one of the Brewers' most intriguing young pitching prospects. The slightly-built righthander won an organization-best 17 games between Beloit and Mudville, a year after grabbing attention by going 10-2 in the Pioneer League. Mieses' control was regarded as the best in the Midwest League this year, where he teased hitters with an 88-91 MPH fastball, curveball and a deceptive, diving palmball. He did not turn 21 until after the season, but he didn't seem to be phased at all by an in-season promotion to the high Class-A California League. The Dominican native issued less than three walks per nine innings, while registering more Ks than innings pitched. He'll be challenged in the upper levels, but his 2000 performance certainly didn't do anything to hinder his progress towards Miller Park by 2002.

Nick Neugebauer

Position: P **Opening Day Age:** 20
Bats: R **Throws:** R **Born:** 7/15/80 in
Ht: 6' 3" **Wt:** 225 Riverside, CA

Recent Statistics

	W	L	ERA	G	GS	Sv	IP	H	R	BB	SO	HR
1999 A Beloit	7	5	3.90	18	18	0	80.2	50	41	80	125	4
2000 A Mudville	4	4	4.19	18	18	0	77.1	43	40	87	117	0
2000 AA Huntsville	1	3	3.73	10	10	0	50.2	35	28	47	57	2

One of the toughest pitchers to hit in all of baseball, Neugebauer allowed just 78 knocks in 128 innings last year. There may be a fear factor involved, as not only does his massive frame present an intimidating figure on the mound, but his wildness also makes it difficult to dig in. Everything about Neugebauer is power. The burly righthander brings it in the mid- to upper 90s, hitting 100 MPH on occasion, with a deadly slider, and a less-advanced curve and change. After ringing up 12.2 strikeout victims per nine last year, his two-year total stands at 299

Milwaukee

in 208.2 innings. While he may be untouchable, he's also been issuing free passes at an alarming rate. He took a trip to the Arizona Fall League, where he showed signs of taming his wild, raw stuff—the only thing preventing him from being considered the most dominant prospect in baseball. Youth is on his side, but he should need the next two years to harness his command in the upper levels before taking on the even more selective big league hitters.

Kyle Peterson

Position: P   **Opening Day Age:** 24
Bats: L **Throws:** R   **Born:** 4/9/76 in Elkhorn,
Ht: 6' 3" **Wt:** 215   NE

Recent Statistics

	W	L	ERA	G	GS	Sv	IP	H	R	BB	SO	HR
1999 AAA Louisville	7	6	3.55	18	18	0	109.0	90	52	42	95	13
1999 NL Milwaukee	4	7	4.56	17	12	0	77.0	87	46	25	34	3
2000 A Beloit	1	1	1.80	3	3	0	15.0	10	4	4	17	2
2000 AA Huntsville	0	1	7.71	1	1	0	4.2	6	7	4	1	1

The Brewers hoped that Peterson had set the tone for what was to come from their 1997 first-round pick after his encouraging rookie season in '99. Those expectations quickly changed when he underwent arthroscopic surgery on his right shoulder to shave cartilage from his rotator cuff, effectively ending his season before it started. A Stanford product, he enjoyed a rapid ascent from the college ranks to The Show, needing just 264.1 minor league innings before cracking the Brewers' rotation for 12 starts in '99. Peterson is equipped with the typical Stanford hurler resume, meaning he's an intelligent pitcher, and in his case not overpowering, both of which could help him return to form. He made some rehab starts late in the season and was scheduled to attend the AFL, but he was shut down with stiffness in order to get him prepared for spring.

Jeff Pickler

Position: 2B   **Opening Day Age:** 25
Bats: L **Throws:** R   **Born:** 1/6/76 in Garden
Ht: 5' 10" **Wt:** 180   Grove, CA

Recent Statistics

	G	AB	R	H	D	T	HR	RBI	SB	BB	SO	Avg
1999 A Stockton	80	311	40	105	14	3	1	42	7	23	29	.338
1999 AA Huntsville	51	183	20	51	8	1	1	23	9	15	25	.279
2000 AA Huntsville	71	254	34	77	11	0	0	26	15	30	28	.303
2000 AAA Indianapolis	56	189	34	58	6	1	1	20	14	24	27	.307
2000 MLE	127	429	56	121	15	0	0	38	21	41	56	.282

Often overlooked as a prospect, there is one thing to know about Pickler: he can flat-out hit. Since winning the SEC batting championship at Tennessee with a gaudy .445 mark in '98, he has proven that. Drafted in the 11th round in '98, he hasn't let wood bats and pro pitching deter his progress at the plate, as he now boasts a .323 average as a pro. A lefthanded hitter, he demonstrates excellent bat control and advanced strike-zone judgment. He doesn't produce a lot of power with his line-drive swing, but he puts the ball in play with regularity. Pickler's tools won't jump off the board, but he runs

well, has a good glove and his instincts are sound. He doesn't offer a lot of versatility, and Ronnie Belliard is blocking his path in Milwaukee.

Ben Sheets

Position: P   **Opening Day Age:** 22
Bats: R **Throws:** R   **Born:** 7/18/78 in Baton
Ht: 6' 1" **Wt:** 195   Rouge, LA

Recent Statistics

	W	L	ERA	G	GS	Sv	IP	H	R	BB	SO	HR
1999 R Ogden	0	1	5.63	2	2	0	8.0	8	5	2	12	2
1999 A Stockton	1	0	3.58	5	5	0	27.2	23	11	14	28	1
2000 AA Huntsville	5	3	1.88	13	13	0	72.0	55	17	25	60	4
2000 AAA Indianapolis	3	5	2.87	14	13	0	81.2	77	31	31	59	4

The 10th overall pick in '99, Sheets dominated the minors in his first full season out of Northeast Louisiana. The organization is counting on the righthander, who was signed for a $2.45 million bonus, to reverse a trend of poor draft choices, bad luck and injuries. He thrust himself into the forefront of the club's pitching plans for this season after capping off a tremendous 2000 campaign as the ace of the Olympic team. Dealing a polished three-pitch arsenal made up of a low- to mid-90s heater, big 12-to-6 breaking curve and changeup, Sheets allowed just a .234 batting average between Double- and Triple-A. In addition to representing Milwaukee in the Futures Game, he sealed the gold medal for Team USA with a dramatic shutout over archrival Cuba, posting a stingy 0.41 ERA in 22 innings in Sydney. Provided he doesn't fall flat on his face in spring, Sheets is all but guaranteed a spot in the Brewers' rotation.

Others to Watch

Righthander **Jose Garcia** (22) regained his low-90s fastball, potential plus-curveball and changeup after missing all of '99 with an elbow injury. . . Former first-rounder **J.M. Gold** (20) underwent Tommy John surgery last summer, but he was making encouraging progress and was expected to again be airing out his mid-90s gas by spring training. . . Outfielder **Cristian Guerrero** (19) is most well-known for his bloodlines, but he'll etch a name for himself if he continues to swing like he did last year. The wiry 6-foot-4, 200-pounder shows five-tool potential and boasted a .569 slugging percentage at low Class-A Ogden. . . Athletic shortstop **Billy Hall** (21) is an exciting player still honing his plate discipline, while flashing a strong arm and a quick bat. . . Righthander **Jack Krawczyk** (25) doesn't posses the overpowering stuff of a closer, but the all-time NCAA saves leader is a master a changing speeds and baffling hitters. His fastball sits in the mid-80s, and he relied almost exclusively on his "dead fish" changeup to record 15 saves and a 1.47 ERA in Mudville. . . A natural leadoff hitter and outfielder, **David Krynzel** (19) was the most promising prospect in the Rookie-level Pioneer League after being selected as the 11th overall pick in June. One of the fastest players available in the draft, he hit .359.

Olympic Stadium

Offense

With high outfield walls and generous foul territory, Olympic Stadium is a pitchers' park. It's become more neutral in the last two years, however, since the roof has been re-covered. Its dimensions make it a below-average home-run park, though it did not play that way last season. Baserunners get better traction and like to run here.

Defense

The park requires speed in the outfield, where hard-hit liners often split the gaps and go to the wall. The center fielder must be diligent about backing up the corner men on anything hit in front of them, since there's always the danger that a flyball will bounce over them or a grounder will get through the wickets. In the latter case, there's no grass to slow the ball, which will roll to the wall unless cut off. The infield turf doesn't slow the ball either and can create bad hops for infielders.

Who It Helps the Most

Line-drive hitters such as Jose Vidro and Michael Barrett take advantage of the outfield gaps. Vladimir Guerrero's frozen ropes rattle around like pinballs, and the high walls do little to impede his moon shots. Tony Armas Jr. and Felipe Lira were both helped by the park last year.

Who It Hurts the Most

Wilton Guerrero, a switch-hitting groundball hitter, and Peter Bergeron, a lefthanded groundball hitter, have each been hurt by the park. It was expected that the Big O would reduce Lee Stevens' power numbers, but that hasn't been the case thus far.

Rookies & Newcomers

Newcomer Fernando Tatis is capable of generating a lot of doubles at Olympic Stadium. Outfielder Milton Bradley may have the type of line-drive stroke well suited for the park. Andy Tracy doesn't seem like a player who'd be able to take advantage of the park, but it didn't make much difference last year. Fernando Seguignol hit well here in 1999 but reversed that trend last season. Young pitchers like Scott Downs and Guillermo Mota are more likely than not to be helped.

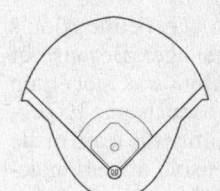

Dimensions: LF-325, LCF-375, CF-404, RCF-375, RF-325

Capacity: 46,500

Elevation: 90 feet

Surface: Turf

Foul Territory: Large

Park Factors

2000 Season

	Home Games			Away Games			
	Expos	Opp	Total	Expos	Opp	Total	Index
G	72	72	144	72	72	144	—
Avg	.270	.275	.273	.265	.287	.276	99
AB	2412	2534	4946	2525	2426	4951	100
R	333	395	728	331	404	735	99
H	652	697	1349	670	696	1366	99
2B	143	130	273	130	138	268	102
3B	14	19	33	18	18	36	92
HR	76	89	165	82	69	151	109
BB	200	236	436	225	261	486	90
SO	430	488	918	493	425	918	100
E	58	48	106	64	48	112	95
E-Infield	49	40	89	48	38	86	103
LHB-Avg	.273	.305	.289	.251	.312	.279	104
LHB-HR	31	49	80	30	33	63	132
RHB-Avg	.268	.255	.261	.277	.270	.274	95
RHB-HR	45	40	85	52	36	88	94

1998-2000

	Home Games			Away Games			
	Expos	Opp	Total	Expos	Opp	Total	Index
G	217	217	434	217	217	434	—
Avg	.259	.267	.263	.262	.276	.269	98
AB	7217	7635	14852	7567	7231	14798	100
R	936	1098	2034	956	1167	2123	96
H	1871	2036	3907	1986	1994	3980	98
2B	412	401	813	395	391	786	103
3B	48	45	93	56	42	98	95
HR	211	206	417	231	226	457	91
BB	610	721	1331	608	780	1388	96
SO	1291	1427	2718	1422	1339	2761	98
E	206	167	373	197	159	356	105
E-Infield	158	138	296	151	132	283	105
LHB-Avg	.262	.284	.274	.250	.281	.266	103
LHB-HR	51	93	144	71	98	169	86
RHB-Avg	.258	.254	.256	.270	.272	.271	95
RHB-HR	160	113	273	160	128	288	94

2000 Rankings (National League)
- Third-highest LHB home-run factor
- Second-lowest walk factor

Felipe Alou

2000 Season

In many ways, the 2000 season was Felipe Alou's most difficult as the Expos' manager. Because of the club's new ownership, Alou was uncertain whether 2000 would be his last as manager. Expectations for the club were higher after the team made some uncharacteristically expensive offseason acquisitions. After the team got off to a good start, a wave of injuries decimated the pitching staff and sent the team into a tailspin that never ended. Alou's demeanor never changed, but on occasion—and for the first time in memory—he managed like a man afraid of losing his job.

Offense

Getting the green light from Alou is a privilege not easily earned. Only a handful of Expos were allowed to run last year. Although the club had decent speed, it finished last in the league in steals. Alou usually is patient with youngsters. His handling of Michael Barrett was an exception; Alou stuck with Peter Bergeron through thick and thin, which is more typical. His lack of emphasis on the value of the base on balls, both at the top of the lineup and overall, is notable.

Pitching & Defense

In the past, Alou handled his pitchers as carefully as any manager in baseball. That seemed to change last year, as he worked a number of hurlers hard. Defense, especially up the middle, is very important to Alou. He'll put up with a no-hit, good-field type player in the middle of the diamond, but will consider moving even a strong hitter if Alou deems his glove inadequate. He usually devotes at least two bench spots to purely defensive players.

2001 Outlook

The Expos have committed to bring back Alou this year, but in many ways the franchise is in greater disarray than ever. Most of last year's high-priced acquisitions turned out disastrously, and it's unlikely further money will be spent. Uncertainty over the club's future in Montreal also hangs over the franchise. While the club can expect to be healthier, and thus stronger, there is less optimism for the immediate future than there was a year ago.

Born: 5/12/35 in Haina, Dominican Republic

Playing Experience: 1958-1974, SF, Atl, Oak, NYY, Mon, Mil

Managerial Experience: 9 seasons

Manager Statistics

Year	Team, Lg	W	L	Pct	GB	Finish
2000	Montreal, NL	67	95	.414	28.0	4th East
9 Seasons		670	685	.494	—	—

2000 Starting Pitchers by Days Rest

	<=3	4	5	6+
Expos Starts	1	70	55	24
Expos ERA	4.50	5.23	4.81	6.16
NL Avg Starts	2	80	50	21
NL ERA	5.00	4.61	4.60	5.18

2000 Situational Stats

	Felipe Alou	NL Average
Hit & Run Success %	37.0	33.8
Stolen Base Success %	54.7	68.8
Platoon Pct.	60.9	53.2
Defensive Subs	32	19
High-Pitch Outings	5	14
Quick/Slow Hooks	22/16	14/16
Sacrifice Attempts	103	87

2000 Rankings (National League)

- 1st in quick hooks (22)
- 2nd in defensive substitutions (32) and mid-inning pitching changes (190)
- 3rd in relief appearances (452) and saves with over 1 inning pitched (15)

Michael Barrett

2000 Season

The Expos weren't sure what to do with Michael Barrett last year, and at times it seemed that their indecision infected his play. Last winter, the club announced he'd be its starting third baseman and wouldn't be shuttled between third base and catcher any longer. Montreals commitment lasted six weeks. He got off to a poor start, was demoted in May, was recalled in June, was moved back to catcher, was demoted and recalled in August, and used at both the hot corner and behind the plate in September. No matter where he played, he never got the bat going.

Hitting

Barrett bulked up over the winter in an effort to develop more power, but it didn't work. He isn't much of a pull hitter—getting most of his doubles on line drives to the gaps—and doesn't lift the ball enough to be much of a home-run threat. This approach probably won't yield many homers no matter how much muscle he adds. He makes good contact, rarely walking or striking out, but didn't hit the ball hard consistently enough last year.

Baserunning & Defense

Barrett's early-season fielding slump seemed to haunt him for the rest of the year. He has the range and arm to be a good third baseman, but seemed more tentative last year. His throwing was disappointing behind the plate, where he is relatively inexperienced and a bit rough. It's unclear how much the sore elbow he reported in September had to do with his fielding problems. He's an average runner on the bases.

2001 Outlook

The one thing the Expos vowed not to do last winter—hinder Barrett's development by vacillating about his role—they did. That should not be an issue this year, as the acqusition of Fernando Tatis means Barrett won't be spending any time at third. Barrett played catcher for Mayaguez in the Puerto Rican Winter League during the offseason, and at this point, the chances are very good that he'll go back behind the plate for the Expos on a regular basis.

Position: 3B/C
Bats: R **Throws:** R
Ht: 6' 2" **Wt:** 200

Opening Day Age: 24
Born: 10/22/76 in Atlanta, GA
ML Seasons: 3

Overall Statistics

	G	AB	R	H	D	T	HR	RBI	SB	BB	SO	Avg	OBP	Slg
2000	89	271	28	58	15	1	1	22	0	23	35	.214	.277	.288
Career	223	727	84	192	49	4	10	76	0	58	80	.264	.322	.384

Where He Hits the Ball

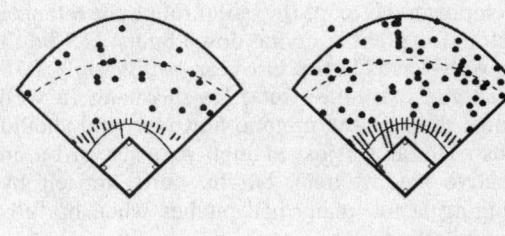

Vs. LHP   Vs. RHP

2000 Situational Stats

	AB	H	HR	RBI	Avg		AB	H	HR	RBI	Avg
Home	131	33	0	15	.252	LHP	81	13	0	5	.160
Road	140	25	1	7	.179	RHP	190	45	1	17	.237
First Half	160	35	1	14	.219	Sc Pos	70	16	0	20	.229
Scnd Half	111	23	0	8	.207	Clutch	47	12	1	8	.255

2000 Rankings (National League)

- 8th in errors at third base (13)

Peter Bergeron

2000 Season

Last year's spring training featured a battle between two rookies, Peter Bergeron and Milton Bradley, for the Expos' center field position and leadoff duties. Bergeron won, and despite having only 58 games of Triple-A experience, Montreal immediately made him a regular. He struggled at the plate for most of the season but managed to hold the job, partly because Bradley squandered his opportunities to dislodge him. Overall, Bergeron impressed with his defense but looked a bit rough at the plate and on the bases. Still, at age 22, his potential was obvious.

Hitting

Bergeron is a lefthanded groundball hitter without much power. He slaps the ball through the left side a lot and is great at laying down bunts. He didn't fare well versus lefties last year, batting only .218 with three extra-base hits. He did hang in well against them in the minors, however, and should adjust. He shows just enough patience to be an effective leadoff man, but he hurts himself by swinging at too many bad pitches when he falls behind in the count.

Baserunning & Defense

Despite having good speed, Bergeron didn't steal bases effectively, swiping only 11 bags in 24 attempts. He had trouble reading lefthanders' moves and didn't attempt a single steal off them. He puts his speed to good use in center field, cutting off the gaps well. His throwing arm had been questioned following offseason shoulder surgery, but he proved to be a strong thrower and led the National League in outfield assists.

2001 Outlook

Bergeron and Bradley may stage a rematch this year. If Bradley makes the club, Bergeron could be shifted to left field. In any case, he'll remain a regular and almost certainly will improve upon last year's numbers. He's capable of hitting for a better average right away and could become a good leadoff man down the road.

Position: CF/LF
Bats: L **Throws:** R
Ht: 6' 0" **Wt:** 185

Opening Day Age: 23
Born: 11/9/77 in Greenfield, MA
ML Seasons: 2

Overall Statistics

	G	AB	R	H	D	T	HR	RBI	SB	BB	SO	Avg	OBP	Slg
2000	148	518	80	127	25	7	5	31	11	58	100	.245	.320	.349
Career	164	563	92	138	27	7	5	32	11	67	105	.245	.324	.345

Where He Hits the Ball

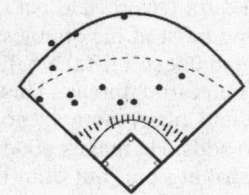 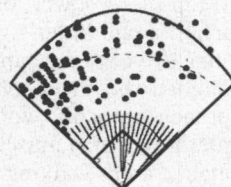

Vs. LHP   **Vs. RHP**

2000 Situational Stats

	AB	H	HR	RBI	Avg		AB	H	HR	RBI	Avg
Home	245	55	3	14	.224	LHP	87	19	0	2	.218
Road	273	72	2	17	.264	RHP	431	108	5	29	.251
First Half	285	66	3	14	.232	Sc Pos	85	17	2	23	.200
Scnd Half	233	61	2	17	.262	Clutch	62	13	0	5	.210

2000 Rankings (National League)

- 1st in lowest stolen-base percentage (45.8)
- 2nd in sacrifice bunts (14), errors in center field (5), bunts in play (32) and lowest batting average at home
- 3rd in lowest slugging percentage and lowest fielding percentage in center field (.982)
- Led the Expos in sacrifice bunts (14), stolen bases, caught stealing (13), walks, highest groundball/flyball ratio (2.2), stolen-base percentage (45.8), most pitches seen per plate appearance (3.73), batting average on a 3-1 count (.615), on-base percentage for a leadoff hitter (.321), bunts in play (32) and highest percentage of pitches taken (56.4)

Milton Bradley

2000 Season

Milton Bradley arrived at spring training last season with only 87 games of experience above A-ball under his belt, hoping to land the Expos' center field job. He didn't manage to beat out the more advanced Peter Bergeron, but he did make decent progress over the course of the season. Bradley hit well enough at Triple-A to earn a callup at the All-Star break, but then irked manager Felipe Alou for not hustling on the basepaths and was sent back down two weeks later. He was recalled in mid-August and played regularly in center field for three weeks before missing most of September with a strained oblique muscle. He didn't hit, which was understandable in light of his age and inexperience.

Hitting

Bradley was auditioned as a top-of-the-order hitter last year, batting mostly first or second. At this point, he lacks the plate discipline to be effective in that role. He could grow into it, since he's a spray hitter who hit equally well from either side of the plate in the high minors. But he also has power potential and could develop into a run-producer as he matures.

Baserunning & Defense

Bradley is more polished in center field, where he combines good range and athleticism with a strong, accurate arm. He's as rough on the bases as he is at the plate, however. He's been a poor percentage basestealer in the minors and didn't try to run much with Montreal last year, attempting just three swipes in 42 games.

2001 Outlook

Bradley looked like he needed a year of seasoning in Triple-A, but the Expos never have been averse to letting a youngster learn on the job. Another concern is his ability to control his temper, which in the past has been an issue on more than one occasion. These concerns aside, Bradley may see significant time with the big club this year and could turn the corner at any time.

Position: CF
Bats: B   **Throws:** R
Ht: 6' 0"   **Wt:** 180

Opening Day Age: 22
Born: 4/15/78 in Harbor City, FL
ML Seasons: 1

Overall Statistics

	G	AB	R	H	D	T	HR	RBI	SB	BB	SO	Avg	OBP	Slg
2000	42	154	20	34	8	1	2	15	2	14	32	.221	.288	.325
Career	42	154	20	34	8	1	2	15	2	14	32	.221	.288	.325

Where He Hits the Ball

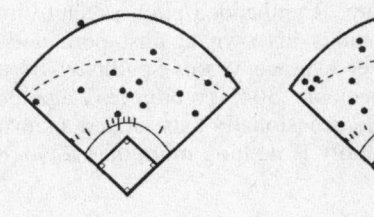

Vs. LHP   Vs. RHP

2000 Situational Stats

	AB	H	HR	RBI	Avg		AB	H	HR	RBI	Avg
Home	74	18	1	6	.243	LHP	46	12	1	9	.261
Road	80	16	1	9	.200	RHP	108	22	1	6	.204
First Half	0	0	0	0	-	Sc Pos	33	12	2	15	.364
Scnd Half	154	34	2	15	.221	Clutch	16	4	0	1	.250

2000 Rankings (National League)

- Did not rank near the top or bottom in any category

Orlando Cabrera

2000 Season

Expos shortstop Orlando Cabrera's season was interrupted by his father's death in May and a serious shoulder separation in July. Each had an understandable impact on his overall numbers, which were not any better than the previous year's. His absence during the latter half of July coincided with the team's overall collapse, when his steady glove in the middle infield was missed.

Hitting

Cabrera goes up there hacking. He rarely walks or strikes out, since he usually puts the ball in play before the count reaches two strikes or three balls. He uses the entire field and can show power to left field on occasion, but gets into trouble when he tries to power up. Righthanded pitchers shut him down, but he holds his own against portsiders. While his career average versus southpaws is a more than respectable .304, it's only .237 against righthanders. He occasionally bats second against lefties but generally is nothing more than a No. 8 hitter.

Baserunning & Defense

It's a mystery why Cabrera hasn't yet earned the green light; he has the speed to steal bases and did so quite effectively in the minors, stealing as many as 51 one season. He may add thievery to his game as soon as he's allowed to, though he'll need to improve his success rate. At short, he's a powerful thrower with decent range. His fielding percentage was third best among National League shortstops.

2001 Outlook

Hopefully this will be the year that Cabrera makes it through the season without a serious injury. He's still young—just 26 this year—so there's time for him to develop into a decent hitter. It looks like he'll get the chance to do that, as there are no serious challengers to his job within the organization. While his bat isn't much of an asset, he's by far the best defensive shortstop the Expos have.

Position: SS
Bats: R **Throws:** R
Ht: 5'10" **Wt:** 175

Opening Day Age: 26
Born: 11/2/74 in Cartagena, Colombia
ML Seasons: 4

Overall Statistics

	G	AB	R	H	D	T	HR	RBI	SB	BB	SO	Avg	OBP	Slg
2000	125	422	47	100	25	1	13	55	4	25	28	.237	.279	.393
Career	324	1083	143	274	64	11	24	118	13	62	96	.253	.295	.399

Where He Hits the Ball

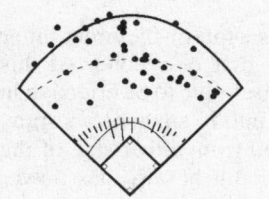
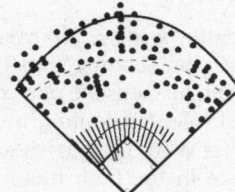

Vs. LHP   **Vs. RHP**

2000 Situational Stats

	AB	H	HR	RBI	Avg		AB	H	HR	RBI	Avg
Home	225	52	7	33	.231	LHP	105	30	2	9	.286
Road	197	48	6	22	.244	RHP	317	70	11	46	.221
First Half	263	64	8	34	.243	Sc Pos	102	27	7	44	.265
Scnd Half	159	36	5	21	.226	Clutch	58	10	1	7	.172

2000 Rankings (National League)

- 2nd in fielding percentage at shortstop (.981)
- 5th in highest percentage of swings put into play (53.8)
- 8th in lowest batting average in the clutch
- 10th in lowest percentage of swings that missed (10.5) and most GDPs per GDP situation (16.9%)
- Led the Expos in lowest percentage of swings that missed (10.5) and highest percentage of swings put into play (53.8)

Vladimir Guerrero

Future MVP

2000 Season

It seemed almost too good to be true. If Vladimir Guerrero could be *that* good at ages 22 and 23, how good could he be at age 24? Guerrero answered that question last year and didn't disappoint anyone, with the possible exception of opposing pitchers. He went two weeks into the season before striking out, set new personal highs in both batting average and home runs, and finished near the top of the National League in every Triple Crown category.

Hitting

Guerrero is perhaps the most aggressive hitter in the game, offering at almost anything he can reach. It works for him because he can drive pitches most hitters can't even touch, whether it's a pitch inches off the ground or another up and out of the strike zone. He hits the ball hard as consistently as any batsman around and possesses frightful power to all fields. Guerrero feasts on first-pitch fastballs, and it's a wonder he ever sees one anymore.

Baserunning & Defense

Guerrero has the tools to be a good baserunner and outfielder, but hasn't mastered the subtleties of either aspect of the game. For example, he has a fearsome throwing arm, but still throws flat-footed even when he has time to gather momentum. His mistakes are often due to overaggressiveness rather than lack of effort. He needs to learn when to charge and when to lay back on turf bounces, and he must work on keeping his glove down on hard-hit grounders. Hip, knee and leg problems probably contributed to his lackluster 9-for-19 showing on the bases last year, but he runs well and his baserunning overall is an asset.

2001 Outlook

If Guerrero can be that good at age 24, what can he do *this* year? It's clear Guerrero hasn't reached his ceiling yet. Since he's under contract to the Expos for three more years, Montreal will see how high the ceiling rises through at least age 27.

Position: RF
Bats: R **Throws:** R
Ht: 6' 3"   **Wt:** 205

Opening Day Age: 25
Born: 2/9/76 in Nizao Bani, Dominican Republic
ML Seasons: 5
Nickname: Miqueas

Overall Statistics

	G	AB	R	H	D	T	HR	RBI	SB	BB	SO	Avg	OBP	Slg
2000	154	571	101	197	28	11	44	123	9	58	74	.345	.410	.664
Career	572	2156	357	695	124	25	136	404	37	174	273	.322	.378	.592

Where He Hits the Ball

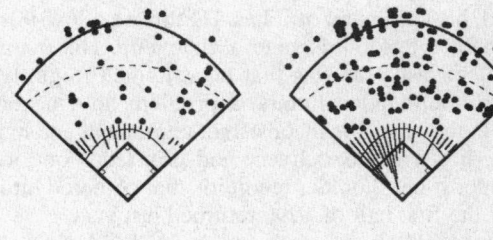

Vs. LHP   **Vs. RHP**

2000 Situational Stats

	AB	H	HR	RBI	Avg		AB	H	HR	RBI	Avg
Home	293	99	25	62	.338	LHP	133	50	12	32	.376
Road	278	98	19	61	.353	RHP	438	147	32	91	.336
First Half	314	116	23	76	.369	Sc Pos	143	46	9	70	.322
Scnd Half	257	81	21	47	.315	Clutch	80	27	5	13	.338

2000 Rankings (National League)

- 1st in intentional walks (23), errors in right field (10), fewest pitches seen per plate appearance (3.13) and lowest percentage of pitches taken (40.7)
- 2nd in triples, slugging percentage vs. lefthanded pitchers (.744), lowest fielding percentage in right field (.969) and highest percentage of swings on the first pitch (47.9)
- 3rd in batting average, total bases (379), slugging percentage and batting average vs. lefthanded pitchers
- Led the Expos in batting average, home runs, runs scored, triples, total bases (379), RBI, walks, intentional walks (23), hit by pitch (8), times on base (263) and slugging percentage

Montreal

Dustin Hermanson

Position: SP
Bats: R **Throws:** R
Ht: 6' 2" **Wt:** 200

Opening Day Age: 28
Born: 12/21/72 in
Springfield, OH
ML Seasons: 6

2000 Season

Dustin Hermanson's puzzling slide continued last year. In his defense, his sudden conversion to the closer's role in May, the equally sudden return to the starting rotation in June, and the club's miserable second half didn't help. But it's clear that Hermanson isn't the same pitcher he was a few years ago. His strikeout rate declined for the third straight season, and he was far more hittable than he's ever been. He changed the grip on his changeup late in the year and posted a 3.10 ERA in his last nine starts, but even then, his strikeout rate continued to plummet.

Pitching

While Hermanson's stuff hasn't visibly deteriorated, his command of it has. He throws a low-90s fastball, a hard slider and a changeup. His main problem last year was that he struggled mightily against lefthanded hitters, a problem he'd never had in the past. His inconsistent command, and his tinkering with his delivery and grip leads one to wonder if the shoulder tendinitis that bothered him over the first half of 1999 returned last year.

Defense & Hitting

Few righthanders have a better pickoff move than Hermanson, who nabbed four runners last year. While he isn't especially quick to the plate, his good move makes him tough to run on. He's a good athlete with a decent glove, but he had a poor year in the field. At the plate, he's an easy out, although he did contribute a few hits last season.

2001 Outlook

What ails Hermanson? Will it continue to plague him in 2000? Only time will tell. Three years ago, he seemed like a potential ace, but that was a long time ago. The Expos traded him in mid-December along with Steve Kline to St. Louis for Fernando Tatis and Britt Reames. Hermanson figures to be a regular part of a deep St. Louis rotation. He has enjoyed success pitching at Busch Stadium, and the Cards hope that a change of venue will be the best medicine.

Overall Statistics

	W	L	Pct.	ERA	G	GS	Sv	IP	H	BB	SO	HR	Ratio
2000	12	14	.462	4.77	38	30	4	198.0	226	75	94	26	1.52
Career	47	48	.495	4.17	170	122	4	805.0	801	292	559	93	1.36

How Often He Throws Strikes

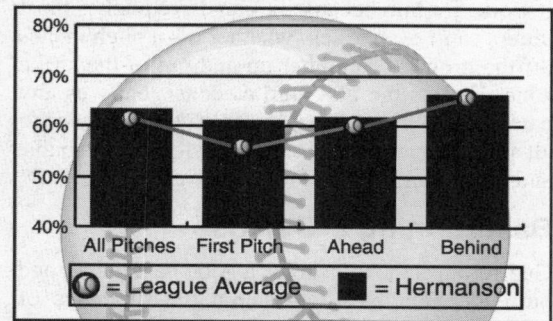

= League Average   ■ = Hermanson

2000 Situational Stats

	W	L	ERA	Sv	IP		AB	H	HR	RBI	Avg
Home	8	7	4.91	3	102.2	LHB	318	102	17	60	.321
Road	4	7	4.63	1	95.1	RHB	460	124	9	51	.270
First Half	6	7	5.60	4	91.2	Sc Pos	202	67	7	87	.332
Scnd Half	6	7	4.06	0	106.1	Clutch	68	17	3	10	.250

2000 Rankings (National League)

- 3rd in fewest strikeouts per nine innings (4.3)
- 5th in lowest strikeout/walk ratio (1.3)
- Led the Expos in wins, losses, complete games (2), home runs allowed, walks allowed, pickoff throws (130), runners caught stealing (7), lowest stolen-base percentage allowed (53.3), fewest pitches thrown per batter (3.57), most run support per nine innings (5.0), most GDPs induced per nine innings (0.7) and lowest batting average allowed vs. righthanded batters

Steve Kline

2000 Season

The 2000 season was a roller-coaster ride for southpaw Steve Kline. He excelled over the first two months of the season in his customary role as the Expos' lefthanded setup man, posting a 1.33 ERA through May. After closer Ugueth Urbina was injured and Dustin Hermanson struggled as his fill-in, Kline took over the closer's duties in June. He saved five straight games—on consecutive days—early that month, but soon succumbed to overwork. In the second half, his effectiveness dropped off, his save chances dwindled and he was bumped back to his setup role in August.

Pitching

Kline's hard sinker-slider repertoire seemingly produces nothing but strikeouts and groundballs. He induced 16 double plays last year, the highest total among National League relievers. He's tougher on lefties but effective enough against righthanded hitters to be more than a specialist. He has the arm to work on consecutive days, but several spells of heavy use clearly took a lot out of him last year. He has the stuff to be a closer, but does he have the stamina? He might if he were handled more judiciously.

Defense & Hitting

Kline used the slide step more last year and became nearly impossible to run on, allowing only one steal all season. He's a good athlete and reliable fielder, committing one error in each of the past four years. He rarely gets a chance to bat, and he's hitless with four strikeouts in eight career at-bats.

2001 Outlook

Kline was traded to the Cardinals in mid-December along with Dustin Hermanson for Fernando Tatis and Britt Reames. Kline figures to fill St. Louis' need for a lefty setup man. Assuming that last year's second-half fade was nothing more than simple overwork, he should bounce back nicely in his new environment. When he's at full strength, he's one of the most effective lefthanded relievers around.

Position: RP
Bats: B **Throws:** L
Ht: 6' 1" **Wt:** 215

Opening Day Age: 28
Born: 8/22/72 in Sunbury, PA
ML Seasons: 4

Overall Statistics

	W	L	Pct.	ERA	G	GS	Sv	IP	H	BB	SO	HR	Ratio
2000	1	5	.167	3.50	83	0	14	82.1	88	27	64	8	1.40
Career	15	19	.441	3.84	289	1	15	276.1	279	124	246	30	1.46

How Often He Throws Strikes

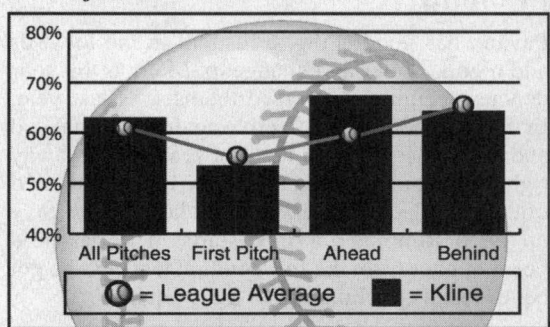

2000 Situational Stats

	W	L	ERA	Sv	IP		AB	H	HR	RBI	Avg
Home	1	2	3.89	8	41.2	LHB	107	26	1	12	.243
Road	0	3	3.10	6	40.2	RHB	209	62	7	33	.297
First Half	1	2	2.10	11	51.1	Sc Pos	79	26	3	39	.329
Scnd Half	0	3	5.81	3	31.0	Clutch	177	51	3	27	.288

2000 Rankings (National League)

- 1st in games pitched
- 3rd in worst first batter efficiency (.378)
- 6th in highest percentage of inherited runners scored (42.5)
- 7th in most GDPs induced per GDP situation (19.3%)
- 8th in relief innings (82.1)
- Led the Expos in games pitched, saves, games finished (42), save opportunities (18), holds (12), blown saves (4), most GDPs induced per GDP situation (19.3%), relief innings (82.1) and relief ERA (3.50)

Montreal

Carl Pavano

2000 Season

Last year nearly became the long-awaited break-through season for Carl Pavano, the man acquired along with Tony Armas Jr. for Pedro Martinez after the 1997 campaign. Pavano was the Expos' top starter for the first three months of the season before going down with elbow trouble, an injury that had cut short his 1999 season as well. He tried to return after the All-Star Break, but the elbow pain that's come and gone for four years would not subside. He underwent arthroscopic surgery to remove a bone spur from his elbow in August, which the Expos hope will fix the problem once and for all.

Pitching

Pavano has good stuff—a fastball in the low-90s and a good slider and changeup. Many of his tendencies seemingly reversed themselves last year. In the past, he'd been effective against righthanded and lefthanded hitters alike; last year he blew away righties but got pounded by lefties. In the past, he'd often struggled in the first inning; last year he gave up five first-inning runs in 15 starts. In the past he'd been tougher from the full windup; last year he got better results pitching out of the stretch.

Defense & Hitting

Generally reliable afield, Pavano has a high leg kick and gives up more than his share of stolen bases. Over the past three years, only 16 of 56 (28.6 percent) of would-be basestealers have been nabbed on his watch. Pavano contributes little with the bat but an occasional sacrifice.

2001 Outlook

If last year's surgery truly has cured Pavano's elbow problems, this could be the season that he finally stays healthy and makes good on his potential. A healthy Pavano easily could be one of Montreal's top starters and perhaps one of the better ones in the National League. He didn't throw more than 104 innings in either of the past two years and hasn't made it through a full season since 1996, so it's quite possible that his arm problems may continue.

Position: SP
Bats: R **Throws:** R
Ht: 6' 5" **Wt:** 230

Opening Day Age: 25
Born: 1/8/76 in New Britain, CT
ML Seasons: 3

Overall Statistics

	W	L	Pct.	ERA	G	GS	Sv	IP	H	BB	SO	HR	Ratio
2000	8	4	.667	3.06	15	15	0	97.0	89	34	64	8	1.27
Career	20	21	.488	4.32	58	56	0	335.2	336	112	217	34	1.33

How Often He Throws Strikes

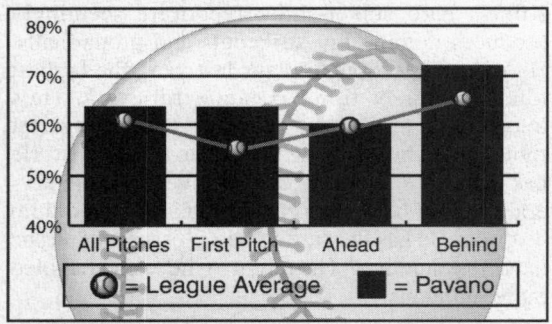

2000 Situational Stats

	W	L	ERA	Sv	IP		AB	H	HR	RBI	Avg
Home	6	3	3.19	0	62.0	LHB	173	54	7	22	.312
Road	2	1	2.83	0	35.0	RHB	186	35	1	10	.188
First Half	8	4	3.06	0	97.0	Sc Pos	87	17	0	21	.195
Scnd Half	0	0	-	0	0.0	Clutch	24	8	2	3	.333

2000 Rankings (National League)

- 9th in most GDPs induced per GDP situation (18.0%)

Lee Stevens

2000 Season

Like the Expos, Lee Stevens' 2000 season had a good start and a lousy finish. He was acquired in March in a three-way deal for Brad Fullmer to improve the club's infield defense. He provided good run production in the first half, but a hand injury in July sapped his power, and a torn ligament in his left big toe ended his season in September.

Hitting

Stevens had been a platoon player before 1999, so it was an open question whether he would continue to hit lefthanders last year. He answered to everyone's satisfaction, damaging lefties and righties alike. Stevens likes the ball down, and pitchers try to get him to chase balls in the dirt. The risk is that if the pitch is more than a few inches off the ground, Stevens can golf it into the gaps. Back in Texas, the short right-field porch made pitchers keep the ball away from him, so he often went the opposite way. In Montreal, he saw more inside pitches and began to pull the ball more.

Baserunning & Defense

Stevens was brought in primarily for his glove, and while he committed a career-high 11 errors, the Expos got what they expected—one of the better-fielding first basemen in the majors. While he had a few problems adjusting to artificial turf, his soft hands and ability to scoop throws were appreciated by the other infielders. He moves well laterally and has a good throwing arm. His speed, however, is below average.

2001 Outlook

Stevens was signed to a two-year, $8 million extension through 2002 in August, ensuring that he'll anchor the Expos' infield and provide lefthanded power for the next two seasons, at least. He should be able to match last year's numbers with ease and ought to exceed them if he's able to avoid the injuries that slowed him last year.

Position: 1B
Bats: L **Throws:** L
Ht: 6' 4" **Wt:** 235

Opening Day Age: 33
Born: 7/10/67 in Kansas City, MO
ML Seasons: 8

Overall Statistics

	G	AB	R	H	D	T	HR	RBI	SB	BB	SO	Avg	OBP	Slg
2000	123	449	60	119	27	2	22	75	0	48	105	.265	.337	.481
Career	744	2432	313	641	137	12	104	379	6	217	586	.264	.323	.458

Where He Hits the Ball

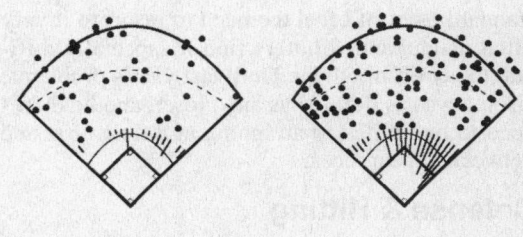

Vs. LHP   **Vs. RHP**

2000 Situational Stats

	AB	H	HR	RBI	Avg		AB	H	HR	RBI	Avg
Home	236	61	14	43	.258	LHP	114	32	7	28	.281
Road	213	58	8	32	.272	RHP	335	87	15	47	.260
First Half	290	76	17	56	.262	Sc Pos	130	31	4	49	.238
Scnd Half	159	43	5	19	.270	Clutch	60	13	0	5	.217

2000 Rankings (National League)

- 3rd in errors at first base (11) and lowest fielding percentage at first base (.991)
- 4th in batting average with the bases loaded (.625)
- 6th in highest percentage of swings that missed (29.1)
- 10th in lowest batting average with two strikes (.149)
- Led the Expos in strikeouts and batting average with the bases loaded (.625)

Ugueth Urbina

Position: RP
Bats: R **Throws:** R
Ht: 6' 2" **Wt:** 205

Opening Day Age: 27
Born: 2/15/74 in
Caracas, Venezuela
ML Seasons: 6
Pronunciation:
ooo-GET ur-BEE-nuh
Nickname: Oogy

2000 Season

Montreal closer Ugueth Urbina's 2000 season was ruined by two separate arm surgeries—for the same problem. He developed a sore elbow in May and underwent surgery later in the month for the removal of a bone chip. He rehabbed over the summer in hopes of returning by season's end. In late June, his arm locked up, and X-rays revealed more bone chips. He went under the knife again in July, ending his season.

Pitching

When he's right, Urbina comes at the hitter with nothing but hard stuff—a high-octane fastball and a hard, biting slider. He has the arm to blow high heat past anyone. He has a changeup but, understandably, doesn't feel the need to resort to it very often. Righthanded hitters find it especially difficult to lay off his slider. Until last year's problems, Urbina was as durable as any closer, and he didn't need to be limited to an inning at a time or rested between appearances.

Defense & Hitting

Even by closers' standards, the non-pitching aspects of Urbina's game are subpar. As a fielder, he hardly ever touches the ball, or needs to. He doesn't pay attention to runners and is possibly the easiest pitcher to run on in the majors. At the plate, he's 0-for-17 with 10 strikeouts over the last four years.

2001 Outlook

Despite the surgery, the Expos picked up Urbina's option for 2001. He is expected to be back at full strength in time for the start of the season. He had similar surgery over the winter of 1996-97 and came back strong the following year. If he's able to bounce back, there's no reason he can't return to his past status as one of the game's top finishers.

Overall Statistics

	W	L	Pct.	ERA	G	GS	Sv	IP	H	BB	SO	HR	Ratio
2000	0	1	.000	4.05	13	0	8	13.1	11	5	22	1	1.20
Career	29	25	.537	3.43	251	21	110	360.0	287	161	423	42	1.24

How Often He Throws Strikes

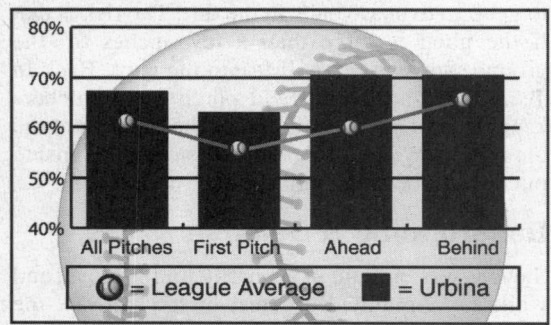

= League Average = Urbina

2000 Situational Stats

	W	L	ERA	Sv	IP		AB	H	HR	RBI	Avg
Home	0	0	2.70	6	10.0	LHB	26	7	1	4	.269
Road	0	1	8.10	2	3.1	RHB	23	4	0	3	.174
First Half	0	1	4.05	8	13.1	Sc Pos	16	6	1	7	.375
Scnd Half	0	0	-	0	0.0	Clutch	36	8	1	7	.222

2000 Rankings (National League)

- Did not rank near the top or bottom in any category

Javier Vazquez

Position: SP
Bats: R **Throws:** R
Ht: 6' 2" **Wt:** 195

Opening Day Age: 24
Born: 7/25/76 in Ponce, Puerto Rico
ML Seasons: 3

2000 Season

Coming into 2000, the Expos hoped that young Javier Vazquez could build on his strong second half from the year before. Did he ever! He jumped out to a 6-1 start, survived a long stretch of poor run support in midseason, and closed with a rush. Both his won-lost record and ERA were deceptive, as he notched 24 quality starts, the fifth-best total in the National League, and saw his ERA inflated by a handful of poor starts. Outlasting Carl Pavano and leapfrogging Dustin Hermanson, he staked his claim as the Expos' ace.

Pitching

Vazquez changes speeds exceptionally well for a pitcher who will be only 25 this summer. He works primarily with a low-90s fastball and a changeup that he'll throw to both righties and lefties. He added a cut fastball last year and also throws a curve. His command used to be inconsistent, but he issued only slightly more than two unintentional walks per nine innings last year. He hadn't been pushed to finish games until last season, when he rose to the challenge and maintained his effectiveness in the late innings. He stepped up his game in critical situations last year, something he'd failed to do the year before.

Defense & Hitting

Vazquez helps himself in just about all areas of the game. He's one of the game's best-hitting pitchers, rarely striking out and able to bunt when necessary. He's also an able glove man who has a good move to first and checks the running game well.

2001 Outlook

The only real concern heading into 2001 is that Vazquez might be affected by last year's heavier workload. His season-ending run of high-pitch outings is a cause for concern, since he averaged nearly 123 pitches per start in September. If a winter of rest is all his arm needs, he could be among the National League's top winners this year.

Overall Statistics

	W	L	Pct.	ERA	G	GS	Sv	IP	H	BB	SO	HR	Ratio
2000	11	9	.550	4.05	33	33	0	217.2	247	61	196	24	1.42
Career	25	32	.439	4.96	92	91	0	544.2	597	181	448	75	1.43

How Often He Throws Strikes

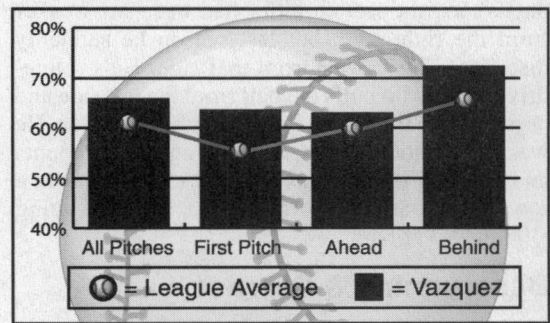

⊙ = League Average   ■ = Vazquez

2000 Situational Stats

	W	L	ERA	Sv	IP		AB	H	HR	RBI	Avg
Home	5	4	3.82	0	103.2	LHB	394	110	7	38	.279
Road	6	5	4.26	0	114.0	RHB	471	137	17	57	.291
First Half	7	4	4.07	0	108.1	Sc Pos	221	52	3	63	.235
Scnd Half	4	5	4.03	0	109.1	Clutch	64	18	1	8	.281

2000 Rankings (National League)

- 4th in hits allowed
- Led the Expos in ERA, games started, complete games (2), innings pitched, hits allowed, batters faced (945), strikeouts, pitches thrown (3,496), GDPs induced (17), highest strikeout/walk ratio (3.2), lowest batting average allowed (.286), lowest slugging percentage allowed (.434), lowest on-base percentage allowed (.335), highest groundball/flyball ratio allowed (1.5), fewest home runs allowed per nine innings (.99), most strikeouts per nine innings (8.1), fewest walks per nine innings (2.5), lowest ERA at home, lowest ERA on the road, lowest batting average allowed vs. lefthanded batters and lowest batting average allowed with runners in scoring position

Montreal

Jose Vidro

2000 Season

Last spring, coming off a fine 1999 season, Jose Vidro expected to have little competition for the Expos' second-base job. The club, citing Vidro's glovework, had other ideas, and brought in veteran Mickey Morandini to challenge for the spot. Vidro beat him out easily, and Morandini was sold to Philadelphia before the season started. Vidro went on to have an even better season, substantially improving both in the field and at the plate, though he faded a bit in the second half.

Hitting

The main difference in Vidro's hitting last year was his production from the right side of the plate. In past years, the switch-hitter had been far weaker from the right side, but last season he suddenly discovered his power from that side. He's a line-drive hitter who pulls the ball from the left side and uses more of the whole field from the right side. He was more patient last year, working deeper counts and drawing more walks. For the second year in a row, he was at his best in the No. 2 hole, batting .396 in 283 at-bats.

Baserunning & Defense

Vidro looked more comfortable in the field last year, showing more range and a quicker double-play pivot. He's not a natural second baseman, but his anticipation and reliability make up for his slow feet. His strong arm allows him to play relatively deep. Vidro's got average speed and rarely is a threat to run.

2001 Outlook

It's safe to say Vidro can come to spring training in 2001 without having to worry about beating out a Craig Counsell. He's only 26, and ought to remain one of the most productive second basemen in the National League. Perhaps he'll even begin to receive some long-overdue recognition for his skills.

Position: 2B
Bats: B **Throws:** R
Ht: 5'11" **Wt:** 190

Opening Day Age: 26
Born: 8/27/74 in Mayaguez, Puerto Rico
ML Seasons: 4
Pronunciation: VEE-droh

Overall Statistics

	G	AB	R	H	D	T	HR	RBI	SB	BB	SO	Avg	OBP	Slg
2000	153	606	101	200	51	2	24	97	5	49	69	.330	.379	.540
Career	443	1474	211	437	120	5	38	191	8	116	173	.296	.350	.462

Where He Hits the Ball

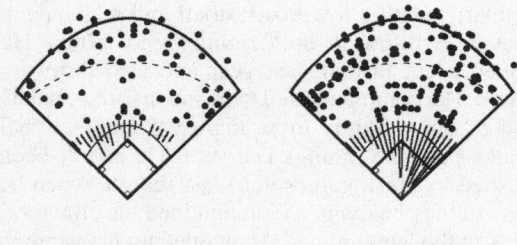

Vs. LHP   **Vs. RHP**

2000 Situational Stats

	AB	H	HR	RBI	Avg		AB	H	HR	RBI	Avg
Home	307	113	11	50	.368	LHP	161	60	7	25	.373
Road	299	87	13	47	.291	RHP	445	140	17	72	.315
First Half	325	122	15	62	.375	Sc Pos	143	44	8	71	.308
Scnd Half	281	78	9	35	.278	Clutch	76	27	5	14	.355

2000 Rankings (National League)

- 2nd in hits
- 3rd in doubles
- 4th in batting average vs. lefthanded pitchers and fielding percentage at second base (.986)
- 5th in slugging percentage vs. lefthanded pitchers (.602) and batting average at home
- Led the Expos in at-bats, runs scored, hits, singles, doubles, sacrifice flies (6), GDPs (17), pitches seen (2,424), plate appearances (663), batting average in the clutch, batting average on a 3-2 count (.327), batting average on an 0-2 count (.275), batting average at home and lowest percentage of swings on the first pitch (28.2)
- Led NL second basemen in hits, doubles, GDPs (17) and batting average vs. lefthanded pitchers

Tony Armas Jr.

Position: SP
Bats: R **Throws:** R
Ht: 6' 4" **Wt:** 205

Opening Day Age: 22
Born: 4/29/78 in Puerto Piritu, Venezuela
ML Seasons: 2

Overall Statistics

	W	L	Pct.	ERA	G	GS	Sv	IP	H	BB	SO	HR	Ratio
2000	7	9	.438	4.36	17	17	0	95.0	74	50	59	10	1.31
Career	7	10	.412	4.19	18	18	0	101.0	82	52	61	10	1.33

2000 Situational Stats

	W	L	ERA	Sv	IP		AB	H	HR	RBI	Avg
Home	4	3	3.65	0	44.1	LHB	143	38	6	22	.266
Road	3	6	4.97	0	50.2	RHB	197	36	4	15	.183
First Half	4	6	4.20	0	60.0	Sc Pos	75	16	5	29	.213
Scnd Half	3	3	4.63	0	35.0	Clutch	15	4	1	4	.267

2000 Season

The 2000 season gave Expos fans their first good look at young righthander Tony Armas Jr., the son of the former major league outfielder. Armas fought a sore elbow, shoulder tendinitis and inconsistency, but was impressive overall.

Pitching, Defense & Hitting

Armas has all the elements one looks for in a young pitcher: good stuff, a deep arsenal and solid command. He mainly relies on a live fastball in the low-90s and an excellent curve, but also throws a splitter, slider and change. His walk rate was a bit high last year, and while he was very tough his first time through the order, he tended to get hit hard the second time around. Armas is a decent fielder who holds runners well and possesses a workable pickoff move. Unlike his father, he's a terrible hitter and hasn't yet mastered bunting.

2001 Outlook

After a season in which he missed time with both elbow and shoulder woes, the main concern with Armas this year will be his health. The Expos are counting on him to fill a spot in the middle of their rotation and continue to progress.

Geoff Blum

Position: 3B/SS/2B/1B
Bats: B **Throws:** R
Ht: 6' 3" **Wt:** 195

Opening Day Age: 27
Born: 4/26/73 in Redwood City, CA
ML Seasons: 2

Overall Statistics

	G	AB	R	H	D	T	HR	RBI	SB	BB	SO	Avg	OBP	Slg
2000	124	343	40	97	20	2	11	45	1	26	60	.283	.335	.449
Career	169	476	61	129	27	4	19	63	2	43	85	.271	.333	.464

2000 Situational Stats

	AB	H	HR	RBI	Avg		AB	H	HR	RBI	Avg
Home	156	48	5	19	.308	LHP	72	21	5	12	.292
Road	187	49	6	26	.262	RHP	271	76	6	33	.280
First Half	94	23	2	11	.245	Sc Pos	85	23	4	36	.271
Scnd Half	249	74	9	34	.297	Clutch	63	15	1	5	.238

2000 Season

Against all odds, Geoff Blum completed his rise from minor league journeyman to starting third baseman last year. After riding the pine most of the first half, he filled in at short when Orlando Cabrera was injured in July. Given the chance to replace the floundering Michael Barrett at third base in August, Blum seized the opportunity and held the job the rest of the year, hitting surprisingly well.

Hitting, Baserunning & Defense

Apparently Blum is a late bloomer. Never much of a hitter in the minors, his major-league totals are rather respectable. He's a flyball hitter who pulls the ball and hits equally well from either side of the plate. His range isn't ideal for short or second, but his arm is strong enough for third base. He saw action at all four infield spots last year and didn't embarrass himself. He has average speed and isn't much of a basestealing threat.

2001 Outlook

Blum seemed to have the inside track on the third-base job before the Expos acquired Fernando Tatis in a mid-December trade. Blum's versatility actually might hurt his chances to remain a regular.

Scott Downs

Position: SP
Bats: L **Throws:** L
Ht: 6' 2" **Wt:** 190

Opening Day Age: 25
Born: 3/17/76 in
Louisville, KY
ML Seasons: 1

Overall Statistics

	W	L	Pct.	ERA	G	GS	Sv	IP	H	BB	SO	HR	Ratio
2000	4	3	.571	5.29	19	19	0	97.0	122	40	63	13	1.67
Career	4	3	.571	5.29	19	19	0	97.0	122	40	63	13	1.67

2000 Situational Stats

	W	L	ERA	Sv	IP		AB	H	HR	RBI	Avg
Home	3	1	5.33	0	49.0	LHB	70	19	5	12	.271
Road	1	2	5.25	0	48.0	RHB	321	103	8	40	.321
First Half	3	3	5.97	0	75.1	Sc Pos	82	25	1	36	.305
Scnd Half	1	0	2.91	0	21.2	Clutch	18	6	0	0	.333

2000 Season

After going 13-2 with a 2.35 ERA between Class-A and Double-A in 1999, Scott Downs jumped to the majors last spring, landing the final spot in the Cubs' rotation. He was hit hard over the first two months of the season before settling down. He then was swapped to Montreal at the trade deadline for outfielder Rondell White. But after his first appearance in a Montreal uniform, a sprained elbow ligament ended Downs' season.

Pitching, Defense & Hitting

Many lefthanders have been successful with similar repertoires: an average fastball, a good breaking ball and good command. Downs already knows how to keep the ball just off the outside corner. He helps himself by holding runners close and getting the ball to the plate quickly, which helps keep the double play in order. He's also an alert fielder, but a weak hitter and unimpressive bunter.

2001 Outlook

The state of Downs' elbow will determine where he'll begin this season. Before getting hurt last year, it appeared he was learning how to approach major league hitters. He could stick in Montreal's rotation but probably won't get enough support to enjoy immediate success.

Hideki Irabu

Position: SP
Bats: R **Throws:** R
Ht: 6' 4" **Wt:** 240

Opening Day Age: 31
Born: 5/5/69 in Hyogo, Japan
ML Seasons: 4
Pronunciation:
hih-DECK-ee
ee-ROB-oo

Overall Statistics

	W	L	Pct.	ERA	G	GS	Sv	IP	H	BB	SO	HR	Ratio
2000	2	5	.286	7.24	11	11	0	54.2	77	14	42	9	1.66
Career	31	25	.554	5.10	85	75	0	450.1	474	156	357	77	1.40

2000 Situational Stats

	W	L	ERA	Sv	IP		AB	H	HR	RBI	Avg
Home	2	2	6.98	0	29.2	LHB	90	32	5	19	.356
Road	0	3	7.56	0	25.0	RHB	137	45	4	19	.328
First Half	2	4	7.58	0	48.2	Sc Pos	65	20	0	26	.308
Scnd Half	0	1	4.50	0	6.0	Clutch	5	2	0	0	.400

2000 Season

Hideki Irabu's 2000 season was a washout, almost from start to finish. Irabu pitched poorly in April and May before going down with torn knee cartilage. He underwent surgery and returned in July, but developed a sore elbow after just one start. August surgery to remove bone chips ended his lost campaign.

Pitching, Defense & Hitting

When he's right, Irabu mixes high low-90s fastballs, splitters and sliders. He gives up a lot of flyballs and home runs and rarely induces double plays. He doesn't have the stamina to be much more than a six-inning pitcher. His poor conditioning hurts him most in the field, where he's sure-handed but immobile. He has no pickoff move or slide step and is one of the easiest of all pitchers to run on. He can't swing a bat but can lay down a bunt.

2001 Outlook

Irabu has a year left on his contract, and there's no market for him, so it looks like the Expos will have to keep him for another year. He has a good career record on artificial turf, so the Expos will hope that a healthy Irabu can fare better at Olympic Stadium.

Mike Mordecai

Position: 3B/SS
Bats: R **Throws:** R
Ht: 5'10" **Wt:** 185

Opening Day Age: 33
Born: 12/13/67 in Birmingham, AL
ML Seasons: 7

Overall Statistics

	G	AB	R	H	D	T	HR	RBI	SB	BB	SO	Avg	OBP	Slg
2000	86	169	20	48	16	0	4	16	2	12	34	.284	.335	.450
Career	468	782	92	187	43	5	18	76	6	66	141	.239	.298	.376

2000 Situational Stats

	AB	H	HR	RBI	Avg		AB	H	HR	RBI	Avg
Home	75	22	2	8	.293	LHP	68	21	0	5	.309
Road	94	26	2	8	.277	RHP	101	27	4	11	.267
First Half	95	29	4	13	.305	Sc Pos	35	6	1	11	.171
Scnd Half	74	19	0	3	.257	Clutch	30	10	0	4	.333

2000 Season

Utilityman Mike Mordecai enjoyed his best season last year, batting a career-high .284. He played his customary role, making occasional spot starts in the infield (mostly at third base) and often coming in late in the game as a defensive replacement or part of a double-switch.

Hitting, Baserunning & Defense

Mordecai slugged .450 last year, something that likely won't happen again. He's a weak hitter with a quick stroke who likes to pull inside pitches through the left side of the infield. His versatility keeps him in the big leagues. He has the hands and arm to play any infield position, though his range is just average. He's very good on the pivot; second base is probably his best position. Speed is not among his assets.

2001 Outlook

The Expos picked up Mordecai's option for 2001, which means that he'll spend another year coming off the bench to snare grounders for them in the late innings. His playing time could diminish, as the club's third-base situation no longer is unsettled with the acquisition of Fernando Tatis.

Guillermo Mota

Position: RP
Bats: R **Throws:** R
Ht: 6'4" **Wt:** 205

Opening Day Age: 27
Born: 7/25/73 in San Pedro de Macoris, Dominican Republic
ML Seasons: 2

Overall Statistics

	W	L	Pct.	ERA	G	GS	Sv	IP	H	BB	SO	HR	Ratio
2000	1	1	.500	6.00	29	0	0	30.0	27	12	24	3	1.30
Career	3	5	.375	4.01	80	0	0	85.1	81	37	51	8	1.38

2000 Situational Stats

	W	L	ERA	Sv	IP		AB	H	HR	RBI	Avg
Home	0	0	4.85	0	13.0	LHB	41	10	3	5	.244
Road	1	1	6.88	0	17.0	RHB	69	17	0	13	.246
First Half	0	1	11.12	0	11.1	Sc Pos	29	9	0	14	.310
Scnd Half	1	0	2.89	0	18.2	Clutch	38	7	1	3	.184

2000 Season

Last year a healthy Guillermo Mota finally displayed the blazing heater that had been notably absent the year before. After a poor spring, he was recalled in May and bounced between Montreal and Triple-A for most of the first half. His big breakthrough came after he was recalled in September and pitched very well the rest of the month.

Pitching, Defense & Hitting

Mota's calling card is a live fastball in the mid- to upper-90s. He can go up the ladder with it, and few hitters can get on top of it or pull it. He's inconsistent with his slider and changeup, but doesn't always need them. Mota, a former minor league shortstop, hit a home run in his first major league at-bat. Understandably, he's an excellent fielder. He's developed a good move to first, and no one even tried to steal on him last year.

2001 Outlook

Mota was much more effective than his ERA indicated last year and can be an effective short reliever if he pitches as well this year. The Expos are counting on him to make their Opening Day roster and play an important role for them.

Montreal

Fernando Seguignol

Position: 1B/LF/RF
Bats: B **Throws:** R
Ht: 6'5" **Wt:** 230

Opening Day Age: 26
Born: 1/19/75 in Bocas del Toro, Panama
ML Seasons: 3

Overall Statistics

	G	AB	R	H	D	T	HR	RBI	SB	BB	SO	Avg	OBP	Slg
2000	76	162	22	45	8	0	10	22	0	9	46	.278	.326	.512
Career	127	309	42	83	21	0	17	35	0	17	94	.269	.324	.502

2000 Situational Stats

	AB	H	HR	RBI	Avg		AB	H	HR	RBI	Avg
Home	63	13	1	5	.206	LHP	81	29	6	12	.358
Road	99	32	9	17	.323	RHP	81	16	4	10	.198
First Half	19	8	1	3	.421	Sc Pos	39	7	1	11	.179
Scnd Half	143	37	9	19	.259	Clutch	24	5	3	6	.208

2000 Season

Amid Montreal's second-half collapse, Fernando Seguignol got a chance to play and took advantage of it. He was called up from Triple-A in late June, and played some left field while Rondell White was out. He served as one of the club's top pinch-hitters and excelled in that role. When first baseman Lee Stevens went down late in the year, Seguignol stepped in and hit fairly well.

Hitting, Baserunning & Defense

Seguignol's ability to hit for power from both sides of the plate is the reason he's in the big leagues. He has poor strike-zone judgment and will chase low breaking balls. He hits to all fields from the right side and pulls the ball more often from the left side. A converted outfielder, he's able to play left or right but doesn't move well enough to play there regularly. Seguignol is an average first baseman at best, and he doesn't run well enough to steal bases.

2001 Outlook

Seguignol probably earned himself a reserve spot with his pinch-hitting last year. He could continue to help in that role, and also as a backup outfielder and first baseman, but his defensive limitations probably will prevent him from playing regularly unless someone gets hurt.

Scott Strickland

Position: RP
Bats: R **Throws:** R
Ht: 5'11" **Wt:** 180

Opening Day Age: 24
Born: 4/26/76 in Houston, TX
ML Seasons: 2

Overall Statistics

	W	L	Pct.	ERA	G	GS	Sv	IP	H	BB	SO	HR	Ratio
2000	4	3	.571	3.00	49	0	9	48.0	38	16	48	3	1.13
Career	4	4	.500	3.41	66	0	9	66.0	53	27	71	6	1.21

2000 Situational Stats

	W	L	ERA	Sv	IP		AB	H	HR	RBI	Avg
Home	1	2	4.09	4	22.0	LHB	62	18	2	10	.290
Road	3	1	2.08	5	26.0	RHB	115	20	1	14	.174
First Half	2	0	4.24	0	17.0	Sc Pos	50	10	1	19	.200
Scnd Half	2	3	2.32	9	31.0	Clutch	101	20	1	12	.198

2000 Season

It was not your average season for Scott Strickland. He suffered an apparent season-ending shoulder injury in May, only to return in July and become the club's closer and most effective reliever. There was an even odder postscript: at the end of the year, an examination revealed that the torn labrum he'd been diagnosed with in May had either healed or never existed, eliminating the need for offseason surgery.

Pitching, Defense & Hitting

Strickland has good command of a moving fastball in the low-90s and a good slider. While he has serious problems with lefties, righthanded hitters have equally serious difficulties with him. His ability to work on consecutive days is unproven, since he was asked to do so only eight times last year. He seems to be a decent fielder with an acceptable move to first. He hasn't shown anything at the plate yet.

2001 Outlook

If it's true that Strickland's shoulder is fine, he could be in line for a good season in 2001. With closer Ugueth Urbina questionable, Strickland again could be counted on to pick up some saves.

Anthony Telford

Position: RP
Bats: R **Throws:** R
Ht: 6' 0" **Wt:** 195

Opening Day Age: 35
Born: 3/6/66 in San Jose, CA
ML Seasons: 7

Overall Statistics

	W	L	Pct.	ERA	G	GS	Sv	IP	H	BB	SO	HR	Ratio
2000	5	4	.556	3.79	64	0	3	78.1	76	23	68	10	1.26
Career	20	23	.465	3.94	305	9	7	424.2	431	156	307	43	1.38

2000 Situational Stats

	W	L	ERA	Sv	IP		AB	H	HR	RBI	Avg
Home	2	1	4.50	2	40.0	LHB	121	34	7	20	.281
Road	3	3	3.05	1	38.1	RHB	175	42	3	13	.240
First Half	5	3	4.15	1	47.2	Sc Pos	79	14	1	21	.177
Scnd Half	0	1	3.23	2	30.2	Clutch	126	35	4	15	.278

2000 Season

Anthony Telford had another solid season as the Expos' main setup man last year, though it ended on something of a down note. He faltered out of the gate and went on the DL in May—for the first time in his career—with a sore shoulder. He returned in June and pitched well for the next three months, but missed most of September when the shoulder flared up again. He underwent arthroscopic surgery at season's end but should be ready for spring training.

Pitching, Defense & Hitting

Telford mixes an average fastball, a curve, a slider and an occasional changeup. What makes him useful is his ability to pitch effectively on consecutive days and for more than an inning at a time. Lefthanded hitters can give him problems. Telford has improved his control of the running game but still lacks an effective pickoff move. He recovered from a poor fielding year in '99 to enjoy an errorless season last year.

2001 Outlook

Provided that he's fully recovered from last year's surgery by the start of the season, Telford should remain an unsung but important member of the Expos' bullpen.

Andy Tracy

Position: 3B/1B
Bats: L **Throws:** R
Ht: 6' 3" **Wt:** 220

Opening Day Age: 27
Born: 12/11/73 in Bowling Green, OH
ML Seasons: 1

Overall Statistics

	G	AB	R	H	D	T	HR	RBI	SB	BB	SO	Avg	OBP	Slg
2000	83	192	29	50	8	1	11	32	1	22	61	.260	.339	.484
Career	83	192	29	50	8	1	11	32	1	22	61	.260	.339	.484

2000 Situational Stats

	AB	H	HR	RBI	Avg		AB	H	HR	RBI	Avg
Home	87	22	6	14	.253	LHP	30	6	1	5	.200
Road	105	28	5	18	.267	RHP	162	44	10	27	.272
First Half	48	7	2	6	.146	Sc Pos	53	15	4	23	.283
Scnd Half	144	43	9	26	.299	Clutch	39	6	1	1	.154

2000 Season

Andy Tracy wasn't considered much of a prospect before bashing 37 home runs at Double-A in 1999. Though he was no spring chicken at age 26 last year, the Expos decided to take a closer look at his lefthanded power. They called him up to stay after the All-Star break and gave him semi-regular playing time. He split time between first and third base and performed well as a pinch-hitter, showing potential as a role player.

Hitting, Baserunning & Defense

Tracy, a patient hitter who piles up strikeouts, has power to all fields. He hasn't seen many southpaws in the majors, but he's handled them well in the past. Tracy was mostly a first baseman in the minors and was error-prone in limited time at third last year. His future clearly is at first, where he performed capably. Tracy has average speed and basestealing is not part of his game.

2001 Outlook

With a decent debut season, Tracy put himself in good position to make the club as a pinch-hitter and backup corner infielder this year. He probably won't play regularly unless first baseman Lee Stevens gets hurt.

Montreal

Other Montreal Expos

Matt Blank (Pos: LHP, Age: 24)

	W	L	Pct.	ERA	G	GS	Sv	IP	H	BB	SO	HR	Ratio
2000	0	1	.000	5.14	13	0	0	14.0	12	5	4	1	1.21
Career	0	1	.000	5.14	13	0	0	14.0	12	5	4	1	1.21

Blank opened last season in the Montreal bullpen but was disabled in May with a strained forearm. He was later diagnosed with a stress fracture. If healthy, he could stick once again with the Expos. 2001 Outlook: C

Trace Coquillette (Pos: 3B, Age: 26, Bats: R)

	G	AB	R	H	D	T	HR	RBI	SB	BB	SO	Avg	OBP	Slg
2000	34	59	6	12	4	0	1	8	0	7	19	.203	.284	.322
Career	51	108	8	25	7	0	1	12	1	11	26	.231	.306	.324

Coquillette's power suddenly disappeared last year, but if it returns he might be useful as a utility guy. He can help out at a variety of positions and has batted .300 on occasion in the past. He signed a minor league deal with the Cubs in mid-December. 2001 Outlook: C

Tomas de la Rosa (Pos: SS, Age: 23, Bats: R)

	G	AB	R	H	D	T	HR	RBI	SB	BB	SO	Avg	OBP	Slg
2000	32	66	7	19	3	1	2	9	2	7	11	.288	.365	.455
Career	32	66	7	19	3	1	2	9	2	7	11	.288	.365	.455

Yes, de la Rosa was only 22 and playing shortstop at Triple-A last year, but he struggled offensively there. Though he hit better with Montreal, the doubts will linger. 2001 Outlook: C

Scott Forster (Pos: LHP, Age: 29)

	W	L	Pct.	ERA	G	GS	Sv	IP	H	BB	SO	HR	Ratio
2000	0	1	.000	7.88	42	0	0	32.0	28	25	23	5	1.66
Career	0	1	.000	7.88	42	0	0	32.0	28	25	23	5	1.66

Forster is a 29-year-old lefthander who has worked primarily out of the bullpen the past two seasons. He's also posted some ugly walk ratios during that time. He signed a minor league deal with the Mets in December. 2001 Outlook: C

Wilton Guerrero (Pos: LF/CF/RF, Age: 26, Bats: B)

	G	AB	R	H	D	T	HR	RBI	SB	BB	SO	Avg	OBP	Slg
2000	127	288	30	77	7	2	2	23	8	19	41	.267	.312	.326
Career	491	1364	162	387	46	27	10	113	29	54	196	.284	.311	.379

It's clear Wilton didn't inherit his brother Vladimir's power gene. Since Wilton also doesn't hit for an exceptional average or draw a lot of walks, he's an offensive liability as an outfielder. 2001 Outlook: B

Mike Johnson (Pos: RHP, Age: 25)

	W	L	Pct.	ERA	G	GS	Sv	IP	H	BB	SO	HR	Ratio
2000	5	6	.455	6.39	41	13	0	101.1	107	53	70	18	1.58
Career	7	14	.333	6.97	71	32	2	206.2	241	99	137	44	1.65

After five strong starts at Triple-A, Johnson spent the rest of last year with Montreal. He received a chance to start in the middle of the year, but posted a 7.17 ERA in that role. 2001 Outlook: C

Terry Jones (Pos: LF/CF, Age: 30, Bats: B)

	G	AB	R	H	D	T	HR	RBI	SB	BB	SO	Avg	OBP	Slg
2000	108	168	30	42	8	2	0	13	7	10	32	.250	.292	.321
Career	197	453	70	108	16	5	1	32	24	34	95	.238	.291	.302

The Expos acquired Jones after the Yankees waived him last spring. He's a switch-hitter with some speed but little power and an ugly career on-base percentage. 2001 Outlook: C

Yovanny Lara (Pos: RHP, Age: 25)

	W	L	Pct.	ERA	G	GS	Sv	IP	H	BB	SO	HR	Ratio
2000	0	0	-	6.35	6	0	0	5.2	5	8	3	0	2.29
Career	0	0	-	6.35	6	0	0	5.2	5	8	3	0	2.29

Lara underwent rotator cuff surgery last September. If he's healthy, he'll probably return to the minors, since he has only 5.2 innings of experience above Double-A. 2001 Outlook: C

Felipe Lira (Pos: RHP, Age: 28)

	W	L	Pct.	ERA	G	GS	Sv	IP	H	BB	SO	HR	Ratio
2000	5	8	.385	5.40	53	7	0	101.2	129	36	51	11	1.62
Career	26	46	.361	5.25	159	79	1	572.1	645	220	345	83	1.51

Lira refused a minor league assignment after last season and became a free agent. He's always been hittable, and allowed a .310 batting average last year. He was winless in six decisions as a starter, but the Expos re-signed him to a minor league deal. 2001 Outlook: C

Graeme Lloyd (Pos: LHP, Age: 33)

	W	L	Pct.	ERA	G	GS	Sv	IP	H	BB	SO	HR	Ratio
2000					Did Not Play								
Career	16	22	.421	3.62	366	0	11	358.0	351	107	198	37	1.28

Lloyd signed a three-year, $9 million contract last offseason and then missed the entire year due to shoulder problems. Even before the injury, the Expos' signing of the middle reliever was questioned. Lefty Steve Kline was dealt to St. Louis, however, so Lloyd could be the lefthanded setup man. 2001 Outlook: A

Trey Moore (Pos: LHP, Age: 28)

	W	L	Pct.	ERA	G	GS	Sv	IP	H	BB	SO	HR	Ratio
2000	1	5	.167	6.62	8	8	0	35.1	55	21	24	7	2.15
Career	3	10	.231	5.61	21	19	0	96.1	133	38	59	12	1.78

Moore missed all of the 1999 campaign recovering from rotator cuff surgery, and he pitched well enough last year to earn a promotion in August. His shoulder might still be troublesome. 2001 Outlook: C

Talmadge Nunnari (Pos: 1B, Age: 25, Bats: L)

	G	AB	R	H	D	T	HR	RBI	SB	BB	SO	Avg	OBP	Slg
2000	18	5	2	1	0	0	0	1	0	6	2	.200	.583	.200
Career	18	5	2	1	0	0	0	1	0	6	2	.200	.583	.200

Nunnari has been a high-average hitter with single-digit home run power in the minor leagues. That's not the kind of combination most teams look for in their first basemen. 2001 Outlook: C

Charlie O'Brien (**Pos**: C, **Age**: 39, **Bats**: R)

	G	AB	R	H	D	T	HR	RBI	SB	BB	SO	Avg	OBP	Slg
2000	9	19	1	4	1	0	1	2	0	2	7	.211	.286	.421
Career	800	2232	216	493	119	4	56	261	1	209	354	.221	.303	.353

O'Brien's career likely ended when the Expos released him last June. If so, it wasn't a bad one for a guy who only once played more than 75 games in a season. 2001 Outlook: D

Jim Poole (**Pos**: LHP, **Age**: 34)

	W	L	Pct.	ERA	G	GS	Sv	IP	H	BB	SO	HR	Ratio
2000	1	0	1.000	10.97	23	0	0	10.2	21	4	8	5	2.34
Career	22	12	.647	4.31	431	0	4	363.0	376	156	256	41	1.47

Poole signed with the Cleveland organization after the Expos released him last June. He'll have to do better against lefthanded hitters (.448 average) if he's to become the new Tony Fossas. 2001 Outlook: C

Jeremy Powell (**Pos**: RHP, **Age**: 24)

	W	L	Pct.	ERA	G	GS	Sv	IP	H	BB	SO	HR	Ratio
2000	0	3	.000	7.96	11	4	0	26.0	35	9	19	6	1.69
Career	5	16	.238	5.84	35	27	0	148.0	175	64	77	25	1.61

Powell is a big righthander who is still fairly young. But he's often been pounded whenever he's been promoted to the major leagues the past three years. That can't be good for his confidence. The Padres signed him in early December. 2001 Outlook: C

Brad Rigby (**Pos**: RHP, **Age**: 27)

	W	L	Pct.	ERA	G	GS	Sv	IP	H	BB	SO	HR	Ratio
2000	0	0	-	11.85	10	0	2	13.2	27	8	5	6	2.56
Career	5	13	.278	5.50	73	14	2	175.0	221	61	75	31	1.61

The Expos acquired Rigby in a deal for Miguel Batista last April. Rigby has endured back problems in the past and he struggled in Triple-A last season. 2001 Outlook: C

Julio Santana (**Pos**: RHP, **Age**: 27)

	W	L	Pct.	ERA	G	GS	Sv	IP	H	BB	SO	HR	Ratio
2000	1	5	.167	5.67	36	4	0	66.2	69	33	58	11	1.53
Career	11	21	.344	5.71	123	42	0	371.2	427	176	217	55	1.62

Santana was once one of the Texas Rangers' top prospects. Since then injuries and ineffectiveness have plagued him. He's still only 27 years of age and joined the Mets via the Rule 5 draft. 2001 Outlook: C

Sean Spencer (**Pos**: LHP, **Age**: 25)

	W	L	Pct.	ERA	G	GS	Sv	IP	H	BB	SO	HR	Ratio
2000	0	0	-	5.40	8	0	0	6.2	7	3	6	2	1.50
Career	0	0	-	8.64	10	0	0	8.1	12	6	8	2	2.16

Spencer was acquired from the Mariners last August in the Chris Widger deal. He's a short lefthander who has never started a game as a professional. He'll try to stick as a middle reliever. 2001 Outlook: C

Mike Thurman (**Pos**: RHP, **Age**: 27)

	W	L	Pct.	ERA	G	GS	Sv	IP	H	BB	SO	HR	Ratio
2000	4	9	.308	6.42	17	17	0	88.1	112	46	52	9	1.79
Career	16	25	.390	4.91	65	59	0	313.2	320	128	177	36	1.43

Thurman twice was placed on the disabled list with elbow tendinitis last season. The injury may help explain why he allowed a far greater average (.315) and suffered a dip in control compared to 1999. 2001 Outlook: B

Yohanny Valera (**Pos**: C, **Age**: 24, **Bats**: R)

	G	AB	R	H	D	T	HR	RBI	SB	BB	SO	Avg	OBP	Slg
2000	7	10	1	0	0	0	0	1	0	1	5	.000	.167	.000
Career	7	10	1	0	0	0	0	1	0	1	5	.000	.167	.000

Valera was signed by the Expos as a free agent last offseason following seven years in the Mets' organization. He hasn't hit for a high average nor drawn many walks during his professional career. He inked a minor league deal with Tampa Bay in mid-November. 2001 Outlook: C

Lenny Webster (**Pos**: C, **Age**: 36, **Bats**: R)

	G	AB	R	H	D	T	HR	RBI	SB	BB	SO	Avg	OBP	Slg
2000	39	81	6	17	3	0	0	5	0	6	14	.210	.264	.247
Career	587	1450	157	368	73	2	33	176	1	140	209	.254	.324	.375

Webster spent two stints on the disabled list last season with shoulder and elbow woes, before undergoing shoulder surgery in October. The Expos did not offer him arbitration, making him a free agent. 2001 Outlook: C

Montreal Expos Minor League Prospects

Organization Overview:

Another year, another wave of homegrown rookies debut in Montreal. Two years ago when Jeffrey Loria purchased the financially-strapped franchise, he promised to put an end to the salary-dumping moves that led to the departure of several promising young stars. However, Brad Fullmer was moved prior to the season for Lee Stevens, who is nearly seven years older. Then the multi-talented, oft-injured Rondell White was shipped off to the Cubs at the deadline for 25-year-old Scott Downs, a solid pitcher but not a frontline starter. Drafting Stanford's Justin Wayne with the fifth pick, and a tough sign in Grady Sizemore in the third round, and inking them to $2.95 and $2 million bonuses, respectively, showed an uncommon willingness to pay the going rate.

Donnie Bridges

Position: P
Bats: R **Throws:** R
Ht: 6' 4" **Wt:** 220
Opening Day Age: 22
Born: 12/10/78 in
Hattiesburg, MS

Recent Statistics

	W	L	ERA	G	GS	Sv	IP	H	R	BB	SO	HR
1999 A Cape Fear	6	1	2.28	8	8	0	47.1	37	12	17	44	2
1999 A Jupiter	4	6	4.09	18	18	0	99.0	116	53	36	63	5
2000 A Jupiter	5	5	3.19	11	11	0	73.1	58	29	20	66	0
2000 AA Harrisburg	11	7	2.39	19	19	0	128.0	104	39	49	84	5

The first of seven Expos first-rounders in 1997, it took Bridges three years to step to the forefront of that class. His ascent began in the Florida State League, the same level his '99 season ended at, but after just 11 starts Montreal realized a difference. He earned a promotion to the Double-A Eastern League, where he finished with the second best ERA in the loop. An aggressive fastball/slider pitcher, Bridges' heater displays great movement and regularly sits in the 91-95 MPH range. But his tight-breaking slider is his out pitch, while his change showed marked improvement. Oddly enough, the Expos sent Bridges to the Arizona Fall League to add even more to his heavy workload. By succeeding in Double-A at age 21, Bridges elevated his status and is now riding the fast track to Montreal. It will be worth watching to see if he can sustain another year of workhorse duties.

Scott Hodges

Position: 3B
Bats: L **Throws:** R
Ht: 6' 0" **Wt:** 190
Opening Day Age: 22
Born: 12/26/78 in
Louisville, KY

Recent Statistics

	G	AB	R	H	D	THR	RBI	SB	BB	SO	Avg
1999 A Cape Fear	127	449	62	116	31	2	8	59	8	45	105	.258
2000 A Jupiter	111	422	75	129	32	1	14	83	8	49	66	.306
2000 AA Harrisburg	6	17	2	3	0	0	1	5	1	2	4	.176

An unheralded member of the Expos deep 1997 draft class, Hodges started to show signs of breaking out in 2000. He bettered his career average by nearly 50 points, finishing in the top 10 in a pitching-dominated league. After whiffing in excess of 100 times in '99, the lefthanded hitting third baseman made a dramatic improvement with his strike-zone judgment. He possesses outstanding defensive skills and a strong arm. He's roped more than 30 doubles in each of the last two seasons, suggesting that his power will continue to increase.

Brandon Phillips

Position: SS
Bats: R **Throws:** R
Ht: 5' 10" **Wt:** 170
Opening Day Age: 19
Born: 6/28/81 in
Raleigh, NC

Recent Statistics

	G	AB	R	H	D	THR	RBI	SB	BB	SO	Avg
1999 R Expos	47	169	23	49	11	3	1	21	12	15	35	.290
2000 A Cape Fear	126	484	74	117	17	8	11	72	23	38	97	.242

With Milton Bradley on the brink of establishing himself in Montreal, Phillips' all-around tools stand out as the best in the system. Drafted in the second round out of a Georgia high school, his performance hasn't caught up with his talent just yet. Then you consider that he was an 18-year-old holding his own in the full-season South Atlantic League last year. With only 47 games of Rookie-level experience on his resume, Phillips showcased a broad base of skills, earning the title as best defensive shortstop in the loop along the way. Still raw, and oozing with athletic ability, he has the potential to be a special player as he becomes more consistent and stops trying to be too flashy. Phillips is ahead of most prospects at his age already, but should enjoy a slow, but steady, climb up the ladder beginning in the Florida State League.

Brian Schneider

Position: C
Bats: L **Throws:** R
Ht: 6' 1" **Wt:** 200
Opening Day Age: 24
Born: 11/26/76 in
Jacksonville, FL

Recent Statistics

	G	AB	R	H	D	THR	RBI	SB	BB	SO	Avg
2000 AAA Ottawa	67	238	22	59	22	3	4	31	1	16	42	.248
2000 NL Montreal	45	115	6	27	6	0	0	11	0	7	24	.235
2000 MLE	67	232	18	53	20	2	3	25	0	13	44	.228

Schneider's bat showed signs of life in 1999 after the '95 fifth-rounder did little offensively to distinguish himself in four years. A valuable commodity as a lefthanded hitting catcher, he took over catching duties in Montreal in the final two months of 2000. Schneider has yet to prove that the 17 home runs he launched in '99 weren't a fluke. He makes consistent contact, not walking or whiffing frequently. He is a slightly above average catch-and-throw receiver with a strong arm and good fundamentals behind the plate. He needs to find the power stroke that caught the Expos' attention two years ago to avoid getting overlooked as a starting option.

Britt Reames

Position: P **Opening Day Age:** 27
Bats: R **Throws:** R **Born:** 8/19/73 in
Ht: 5' 11" **Wt:** 175 Seneca, SC

Recent Statistics

	W	L	ERA	G	GS	Sv	IP	H	R	BB	SO	HR
2000 AA Arkansas	2	3	6.13	8	8	0	39.2	46	28	18	39	4
2000 AAA Memphis	6	2	2.28	13	13	0	75.0	55	20	20	77	2
2000 NL St. Louis	2	1	2.88	8	7	0	40.2	30	17	23	31	4

It was a long and tumultuous road from the 17th round of the 1995 draft to the majors, but Reames' perseverance paid off last year in the heat of a playoff race. The smallish righthander established himself as a noteworthy prospect in '96 when he went 15-7 with a 1.90 ERA in the Class-A Midwest League. Before the excitement and hype of his breakout season could set in, however, he underwent Tommy John surgery and missed nearly three seasons. He put it all back together again in Triple-A last year by developing a tough changeup to complement his sneaky fastball and good curveball. After logging 155.1 innings in 2000, he was traded to Montreal along with Fernando Tatis for Dustin Hermanson and Steve Kline. He could be part of the Montreal rotation in 2001.

T.J. Tucker

Position: P **Opening Day Age:** 22
Bats: R **Throws:** R **Born:** 8/20/78 in
Ht: 6' 3" **Wt:** 245 Clearwater, FL

Recent Statistics

	W	L	ERA	G	GS	Sv	IP	H	R	BB	SO	HR
2000 AA Harrisburg	2	1	3.60	8	8	0	45.0	33	19	17	24	7
2000 NL Montreal	0	1	11.57	2	2	0	7.0	11	9	3	2	5

Tucker has garnered the most attention of the seven '97 first-rounders. Also a highly recruited place kicker, he takes his game-on-the-line football competitiveness to the mound with him, but doesn't just try to blow hitters away. He works with a straight fastball, ranging between 88-94 MPH, and owns above average command of an overhand curve and changeup. His velocity is deceptively disguised with an easy and effortless motion, although he did require surgery to remove bone chips after just 10 starts last year.

Justin Wayne

Position: P **Opening Day Age:** 21
Bats: R **Throws:** R **Born:** 4/16/79 in
Ht: 6' 3" **Wt:** 200 Honolulu, HI

Recent Statistics

	W	L	ERA	G	GS	Sv	IP	H	R	BB	SO	HR
2000 A Jupiter	0	3	5.81	5	5	0	26.1	26	22	11	24	2

One of the most polished, near-major league ready pitchers in the 2000 draft, Wayne brings a well-developed four-pitch repertoire to the system. An All-American at Stanford, he already has begun to face the inevitable comparisons to another Stanford righthander, Mike Mussina. Wayne finished his three-year college career with an eye-popping 31-5 record and brings the same cerebral approach to the mound that Mussina exhibits. Wayne's fastball can get into the low 90s, but his changeup and slider also are advanced pitches that help him put hitters away. He started his career in the Florida State League and should see aggressive advancement through the system, with a 2001 debut a possibility.

Brad Wilkerson

Position: OF **Opening Day Age:** 23
Bats: L **Throws:** L **Born:** 6/1/77 in Daviess,
Ht: 6' 0" **Wt:** 200 KY

Recent Statistics

	G	AB	R	H	D	T	HR	RBI	SB	BB	SO	Avg
1999 AA Harrisburg	138	422	66	99	21	3	8	49	3	88	100	.235
2000 AA Harrisburg	66	229	53	77	36	2	6	44	8	42	38	.336
2000 AAA Ottawa	63	212	40	53	11	1	12	35	5	45	60	.250
2000 MLE	129	429	78	118	44	1	13	66	8	67	102	.275

A sandwich first-round pick in '98, Wilkerson didn't sign in time to debut that summer. Coming off of a stellar two-way career at the University of Florida, his pro debut left a lot to be desired. He returned to Double-A last year with something to prove. In just half of a season, he earned respect as the circuit's best batting prospect, followed by a promotion to Ottawa. A smooth hitter, he demonstrates outstanding plate discipline. A natural right fielder with a strong arm, he is learning to play left due to Vladimir Guerrero's presence, but his athletic ability allowed him to start in center for Team USA during the Olympics. It won't be long before the hard-working Wilkerson forces his way into Felipe Alou's lineup.

Others to Watch

Drafted in the fourth round of the '99 draft, **Matt Cepicky's** (23) calling card is power. Cepicky is showing that he is not a one-dimensional player, however, something that should help him as he progresses to Montreal over the next couple of years. . . Lefty **Josh Girdley** (20) has been held back in short-season ball for two years, but the former first-rounder is poised for a breakthrough season with his projectable 89-93 MPH fastball, plus-curveball and improving change. . . Another southpaw, **Luke Lockwood** (19) came on last year at three levels, using a fastball clocked in the upper 80s with good life, a curve and change. His makeup is off the scale and he projects to add some inches to his fastball. . . The 11th overall pick in '98, **Josh McKinley** (21) started to show some signs of blossoming last year. Struggling with his throws from the left side of the infield, he may have found a home at second base, and Montreal is encouraged by his progress. . . At 6-foot-6, 225-pounds, **Valentino Pascucci** (22) offers intriguing power potential that helped him earn a promotion in his first full season. The '99 15th-rounder is a patient hitter who stroked 34 doubles. . . After opening up the bank vault for Justin Wayne, Montreal gave third-rounder **Grady Sizemore** (18) $2 million to sway him away from a two-sport scholarship to the University of Washington. A pure athlete, he hit .293 in his Rookie-level debut.

Montreal

549

Shea Stadium

Offense

Now the National League's third-oldest venue, Shea Stadium continues to be one of the game's best pitchers' parks. That said, the Mets had a slightly higher batting average (.267) at home than away (.263) last year. Despite its symmetrical dimensions and power alleys that are modest in depth, the stadium does not relinquish a lot of home runs because the ball doesn't carry well. Batting averages suffer, especially among righthanded pull hitters. The ball seems to carry best toward right field. Shea's foul territory is spacious, especially when compared to most of the newer parks.

Defense

The grass surface and symmetrical dimensions do not require fielders to possess blazing speed. The infield surface tends to slow groundballs for fielders. Without a large area in the outfield, fly chasers do not have to overcompensate in any particular phase. Poor lighting that makes flyballs difficult to pick up is the toughest challenge for fielders.

Who It Helps the Most

Pitchers, especially lefties, love Shea Stadium. The southpaws in the Mets' starting rotation last year are a classic example. Al Leiter's ERA was more than a run lower at Shea. Righthanders also benefit, as evidenced by Bobby J. Jones' 3.60 home ERA versus 6.44 on the road.

Who It Hurts the Most

Righthanded hitters tend to curse Shea's existence. Mike Piazza hit more than 100 points higher on the road—.377 to .269. Edgardo Alfonzo's averages were .343 away from Shea and .302 at home. Fortunately for the Mets, visitors have more trouble, which enabled New York to tie the Giants for best home record in the majors last season at 55-26.

Rookies & Newcomers

Shea's reputation as a pitchers' park has righty Grant Roberts itching to make the Mets' rotation. Free-agent acquisition Kevin Appier also should find his new home to his liking. Considering the way Alex Escobar covered ground in the Eastern League last year, the five-tool outfielder should easily adjust defensively in Shea.

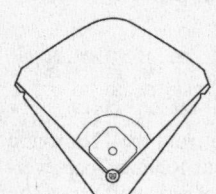

Dimensions: LF-338, LCF-378, CF-410, RCF-378, RF-338

Capacity: 55,777

Elevation: 20 feet

Surface: Grass

Foul Territory: Large

Park Factors

2000 Season

	Home Games			Away Games			
	Mets	Opp	Total	Mets	Opp	Total	Index
G	71	71	142	71	71	142	—
Avg	.267	.236	.251	.263	.266	.264	95
AB	2329	2465	4794	2474	2387	4861	99
R	352	284	636	357	358	715	89
H	622	582	1204	650	634	1284	94
2B	126	116	242	125	134	259	95
3B	3	9	12	11	19	30	41
HR	82	61	143	89	80	169	86
BB	294	225	519	309	262	571	92
SO	449	548	997	474	471	945	107
E	59	52	111	49	61	110	101
E-Infield	47	43	90	40	53	93	97
LHB-Avg	.235	.229	.231	.232	.262	.250	93
LHB-HR	15	17	32	17	26	43	80
RHB-Avg	.275	.239	.258	.271	.267	.270	96
RHB-HR	67	44	111	72	54	126	87

1998-2000

	Home Games			Away Games			
	Mets	Opp	Total	Mets	Opp	Total	Index
G	216	216	432	217	217	434	—
Avg	.263	.245	.254	.274	.258	.266	95
AB	7111	7419	14530	7617	7192	14809	99
R	1017	876	1893	1088	982	2070	92
H	1868	1819	3687	2085	1857	3942	94
2B	361	384	745	430	400	830	91
3B	15	48	63	29	55	84	76
HR	212	188	400	238	231	469	87
BB	851	739	1590	908	769	1677	97
SO	1318	1631	2949	1428	1465	2893	104
E	134	152	286	126	147	273	105
E-Infield	106	125	231	103	122	225	103
LHB-Avg	.278	.247	.262	.265	.261	.263	100
LHB-HR	76	55	131	76	84	160	85
RHB-Avg	.254	.244	.249	.279	.257	.268	93
RHB-HR	136	133	269	162	147	309	88

2000 Rankings (National League)
- Lowest triple factor
- Third-lowest RHB home-run factor

Bobby Valentine

2000 Season

Bobby Valentine proved his critics wrong last year. After hearing the constant criticism about being eccentric and egotistical, Valentine guided the Mets to the World Series. He kept the pressure on the Braves throughout the regular season before rallying the troops after a dismal first half of September. He then got maximum production from his team in the playoffs before the Mets lost three one-run games in the Subway Series.

Offense

Love him or hate him, Valentine knows what he's doing. He is a master at connecting the pieces of the puzzle and emerging with an eye-popping mosaic. Valentine depended on the longball and the hit-and-run more often last year due to his team's lack of speed. He also showed during the playoffs that he is not afraid to make radical alterations to the lineup. He trusts his hunches, such as keeping the productive but raw Timo Perez on the playoff roster. Though not the most popular manager in the game, Valentine gets his players to perform because they know he is doing everything possible to emerge as the victor.

Pitching & Defense

While he demands an airtight defense, Valentine is not afraid to hide a defensive player such as Benny Agbayani in the outfield in hopes of getting more offensive production. He's a firm believer in having a deep rotation and bullpen. He prefers ground-ball pitchers such as Al Leiter and is careful not to overload them early in the season. He uses his bullpen frequently, which makes rubber-armed hurlers like Turk Wendell and Armando Benitez so valuable.

2001 Outlook

Valentine and general manager Steve Phillips each signed three year deals with an option for a fourth year in late October, even though their personalities seem to mesh like oil and water. Many observers wondered if the controversial skipper would reject the Mets' offseason overtures and pursue another job. The new deal means Valentine will be committed to leading New York to the playoffs for a franchise record third straight season.

Born: 5/13/50 in Stamford, CT

Playing Experience: 1969-1979, LA, Ana, SD, NYM, Sea

Managerial Experience: 13 seasons

Manager Statistics

Year	Team, Lg	W	L	Pct	GB	Finish
2000	New York, NL	94	68	.580	1.0	2nd East
13 Seasons		960	906	.514	—	—

2000 Starting Pitchers by Days Rest

	<=3	4	5	6+
Mets Starts	3	72	53	24
Mets ERA	5.40	4.22	3.84	3.67
NL Avg Starts	2	80	50	21
NL ERA	5.00	4.61	4.60	5.18

2000 Situational Stats

	Bobby Valentine	NL Average
Hit & Run Success %	32.7	33.8
Stolen Base Success %	58.9	68.8
Platoon Pct.	34.6	53.2
Defensive Subs	32	19
High-Pitch Outings	18	14
Quick/Slow Hooks	15/14	14/16
Sacrifice Attempts	84	87

2000 Rankings (National League)

- 1st in hit-and-run attempts (107) and pinch-hitters used (299)
- 2nd in sacrifice-bunt percentage (85.7), defensive substitutions (32) and 2+ pitching changes in low-scoring games (28)
- 3rd in pitchouts (49)

Edgardo Alfonzo

2000 Season

Other players in the Big Apple may receive more attention, but no one is more productive on a daily basis than Edgardo Alfonzo. The Mets' best infielder and most consistent hitter, Alfonzo played through a bruised right hip and several other ailments to earn a trip to the All-Star Game and put together his best season. The unflappable second baseman struggled briefly in July, when he hit an uncharacteristic .242, yet finished the year increasing his on-base and slugging percentages each by 40 points over 1999.

Hitting

Alfonzo is a machine who succeeds despite hitting a lot of flyballs. He connects with power on low, inside pitches, and goes to the opposite field with pitches in the middle of the strike zone and higher. His strong knowledge of the strike zone and great plate coverage result in few weaknesses in his swing. Alfonzo is one of the league's more patient hitters. He remains productive on the road as well as with two strikes, including a .293 mark on 0-2 counts. He also comes through in the clutch, as evidenced by his .377 average after the sixth inning last year, which led the National League.

Baserunning & Defense

Alfonzo's glove is the glue of the strong Mets' infield. After not misplaying a groundball in 1999, the former third baseman was nearly as consistent last year by committing just 10 miscues in 1,240.2 innings. He has soft hands, one of the league's strongest arms at second base and turns the double play well. His natural baseball instincts are most obvious in the field and on the basepaths, where he succeeds despite mediocre speed.

2001 Outlook

It will not be long before Alfonzo's name becomes automatic when All-Star rosters and Gold Glove recipients are announced. While he is one of the best No. 2 hitters in the league, his numbers were equally impressive last year when he spent the season in the third hole. In either spot in the batting order, Alfonzo is a complete player who is just beginning to show how good he really is.

Position: 2B
Bats: R **Throws:** R
Ht: 5'11" **Wt:** 187

Opening Day Age: 27
Born: 11/8/73 in St. Teresa, Venezuela
ML Seasons: 6

Overall Statistics

	G	AB	R	H	D	T	HR	RBI	SB	BB	SO	Avg	OBP	Slg
2000	150	544	109	176	40	2	25	94	3	95	70	.324	.425	.542
Career	827	2950	472	874	164	14	87	433	34	345	381	.296	.370	.450

Where He Hits the Ball

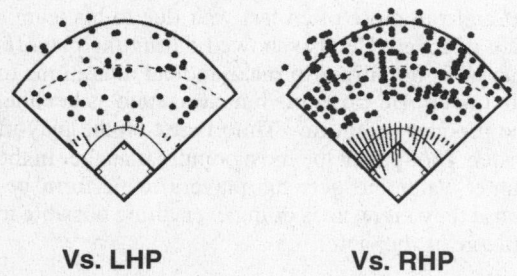

Vs. LHP   **Vs. RHP**

2000 Situational Stats

	AB	H	HR	RBI	Avg		AB	H	HR	RBI	Avg
Home	255	77	13	45	.302	LHP	104	31	5	17	.298
Road	289	99	12	49	.343	RHP	440	145	20	77	.330
First Half	305	97	13	58	.318	Sc Pos	135	46	5	63	.341
Scnd Half	239	79	12	36	.331	Clutch	70	25	3	10	.357

2000 Rankings (National League)

- 3rd in batting average with two strikes (.297)
- 5th in on-base percentage and lowest percentage of swings on the first pitch (14.6)
- 6th in batting average on the road, fielding percentage at second base (.985), batting average on a 3-2 count (.371) and lowest groundball/flyball ratio (0.7)
- 7th in batting average in the clutch and on-base percentage vs. righthanded pitchers (.433)
- 8th in errors at second base (10)
- Led the Mets in runs scored, hits, singles, doubles, walks, times on base (276), pitches seen (2,632), plate appearances (650), on-base percentage and batting average with runners in scoring position

Derek Bell

New York (NL)

Position: RF
Bats: R **Throws:** R
Ht: 6' 2" **Wt:** 215

Opening Day Age: 32
Born: 12/11/68 in
Tampa, FL
ML Seasons: 10

2000 Season

Acquired from Houston prior to last season, Derek Bell was one of the Mets' hottest hitters during the first half. He set a club record by scoring at least one run in 11 straight games while batting .465 during a 12-game hitting streak. He later slumped and batted under .200 after the All-Star break. A bruised left knee affected him in August and he was lost for the playoffs when he sprained his right ankle in Game 1 of the Division Series.

Hitting

Bell's success comes from consistently hitting the ball on the ground. He has great bat speed that produces above-average power, yet his home-run and RBI production always seem to be a disappointment. Despite having played eight full seasons in the majors, he remains impatient at the plate. One of the streakiest players in the game, Bell's decline in the second half can be attributed to his inability to hit lefthanded pitchers. After batting .299 versus southpaws the previous three years, he produced a paltry .156 mark in 2000. While he handles fastballs well, he has trouble with outside breaking pitches, particularly sliders.

Baserunning & Defense

After averaging 27 stolen bases between 1993 and 1996, Bell is no longer a major threat on the basepaths. He appeared to lose another half-step last season, yet remains effective when running the sacks and covering right field. He has an above-average arm with a reputation that keeps runners from taking the extra base. Bell also remains effective in making sliding catches, particularly ones near the foul line.

2001 Outlook

Thanks in part to the emergence of Timo Perez in September, the high-strung Bell seemed to disappear from the New York clubhouse after the All-Star break and is headed to his fifth team. He signed a two-year, $9.75 million deal with the Pirates in mid-December to be their starting right fielder. He remains a productive player in the field and at the plate, but the inconsistency that has plagued him throughout his career makes him a risky pickup.

Overall Statistics

	G	AB	R	H	D	T	HR	RBI	SB	BB	SO	Avg	OBP	Slg
2000	144	546	87	145	31	1	18	69	8	65	125	.266	.348	.425
Career	1164	4422	628	1235	229	15	129	655	170	352	917	.279	.338	.425

Where He Hits the Ball

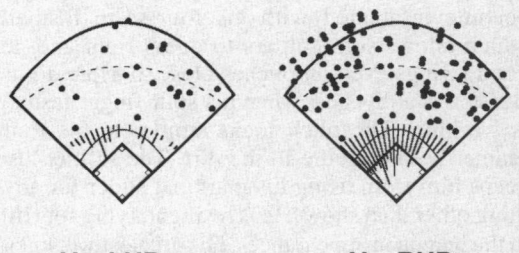

Vs. LHP   **Vs. RHP**

2000 Situational Stats

	AB	H	HR	RBI	Avg		AB	H	HR	RBI	Avg
Home	257	78	8	34	.304	LHP	109	17	0	5	.156
Road	289	67	10	35	.232	RHP	437	128	18	64	.293
First Half	327	104	12	53	.318	Sc Pos	120	32	5	53	.267
Scnd Half	219	41	6	16	.187	Clutch	76	17	4	11	.224

2000 Rankings (National League)

- 2nd in lowest batting average with the bases loaded (.000)
- 4th in fielding percentage in right field (.988) and lowest batting average on the road
- 6th in highest groundball/flyball ratio (2.1)
- Led the Mets in at-bats, stolen bases, strikeouts, highest groundball/flyball ratio (2.1), batting average at home and steals of third (2)
- Led NL right fielders in highest groundball/flyball ratio (2.1), games pitched, innings pitched, hits allowed, batters faced (10), walks allowed and pitches thrown (36)

Armando Benitez

Position: RP
Bats: R **Throws:** R
Ht: 6' 4" **Wt:** 229

Opening Day Age: 28
Born: 11/3/72 in Ramon Santana, Dominican Republic
ML Seasons: 7
Pronunciation: buh-NEE-tezz

2000 Season

In his second year as the Mets' closer, Armando Benitez improved his consistency and set the team record with 41 saves. He survived a brief period when he surrendered several key home runs to provide the necessary hammer for New York in the game's last inning. Despite battling a case of gout in his right big toe late in the season, Benitez was dominant in August by saving 11 games. He also led the National League in games finished and paced all relievers by limiting opponents to a .148 average.

Pitching

Benitez can be overpowering and is one of the hardest throwers in the game. He has a tendency to become infatuated with his four-seam fastball, which allows some hitters to guess right and get good swings even on pitches close to triple digits. Benitez is at his best when his split-finger fastball is working. The pitch looks similar to his four-seamer before diving in the dirt. The splitter also keeps him from using his marginal slider for anything other than show. He is resilient, tying for fifth in the league in appearances. His greatest weakness is his inclination to get rattled when his best offerings are hit, even if they're fouled off.

Defense & Hitting

Benitez gets few opportunities to field his position since his pitches seem to result in either strikeouts or flyballs. When a ball does come in his direction, he has proven to be consistent with the glove as well as capable when covering first base. He started to pay a little more attention to baserunners last year after ignoring them in the past. Predictably, Benitez' hitting prowess is lacking.

2001 Outlook

While late-game home runs reared their head after vanishing in 1999, Benitez is one of the game's best closers. He was successful on 41 of 46 save attempts last year and was nothing short of dominant during the late summer. Now that he's established himself as the Mets' closer, he should retain the job for the foreseeable future.

Overall Statistics

	W	L	Pct.	ERA	G	GS	Sv	IP	H	BB	SO	HR	Ratio
2000	4	4	.500	2.61	76	0	41	76.0	39	38	106	10	1.01
Career	19	23	.452	3.04	360	0	100	367.2	228	208	517	41	1.19

How Often He Throws Strikes

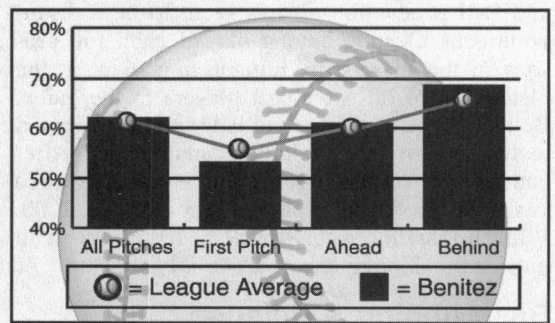

2000 Situational Stats

	W	L	ERA	Sv	IP		AB	H	HR	RBI	Avg
Home	3	3	2.38	25	41.2	LHB	120	16	1	10	.133
Road	1	1	2.88	16	34.1	RHB	143	23	9	27	.161
First Half	2	3	3.38	19	42.2	Sc Pos	69	14	5	30	.203
Scnd Half	2	1	1.62	22	33.1	Clutch	172	27	6	28	.157

2000 Rankings (National League)

- 1st in games finished (68) and lowest batting average allowed in relief (.148)
- 2nd in lowest batting average allowed vs. lefthanded batters, save percentage (89.1) and lowest batting average allowed in relief with runners on base (.171)
- 3rd in save opportunities (46) and saves
- 4th in most strikeouts per nine innings in relief (12.6) and fewest baserunners allowed per nine innings in relief (9.1)
- 5th in games pitched and first batter efficiency (.143)
- Led the Mets in saves, games finished (68), save opportunities (46), save percentage (89.1) and relief ERA (2.61)

Mike Bordick

Position: SS
Bats: R **Throws:** R
Ht: 5'11" **Wt:** 175

Opening Day Age: 35
Born: 7/21/65 in Marquette, MI
ML Seasons: 11

2000 Season

After the Mets lost Rey Ordonez in late May with a broken forearm and used Kurt Abbott and Melvin Mora for nearly two months at shortstop, Mike Bordick was a godsend when he arrived from Baltimore on July 28. Prior to the trade, Bordick was considered the Orioles' MVP. He drove in 29 runs in April and made his first All-Star Game appearance. His bat was not as productive in New York, however, especially during a dismal showing at the plate throughout the postseason.

Hitting

His postseason woes aside, last year was Bordick's best offensive campaign. He established his career high in home runs before he was traded and also set new personal standards for slugging percentage and RBI. He always has been a contact hitter with the ability to execute the hit-and-run as well as anyone in the game. He also is an excellent bunter, a skill that manager Bobby Valentine employed frequently. As he showed in the postseason, Bordick has a tendency to strike out a lot when he falls into the habit of chasing high pitches.

Baserunning & Defense

Some observers were concerned when Bordick committed five errors in his first 20 games with the Mets, but he improved down the stretch and did a solid job of forming an effective double-play combination with Edgardo Alfonzo. Bordick makes most routine plays as well as the occasional impressive one. He is as adept at charging the ball and making the throw on the run as he is going into the hole and making a long, strong strike to first. On the basepaths, he has average speed and does a good job of taking the extra base.

2001 Outlook

While the Mets were said to be considering signing a free agent to play shortstop, Bordick was not the first name on the list. He appears to be in high demand with a handful of teams looking for a dependable if unspectacular gloveman who can provide some production at the bottom of the lineup. Given his improved output in recent seasons, Bordick should maintain a starting job for another couple years.

Overall Statistics

	G	AB	R	H	D	T	HR	RBI	SB	BB	SO	Avg	OBP	Slg
2000	156	583	88	166	30	1	20	80	9	49	99	.285	.341	.443
Career	1443	4831	568	1264	207	25	71	506	77	415	641	.262	.324	.359

Where He Hits the Ball

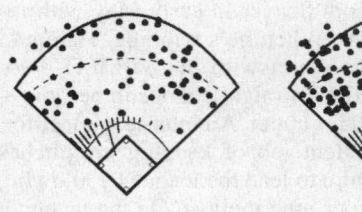 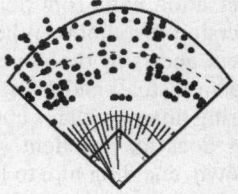

Vs. LHP   **Vs. RHP**

2000 Situational Stats

	AB	H	HR	RBI	Avg		AB	H	HR	RBI	Avg
Home	270	76	9	34	.281	LHP	153	47	5	21	.307
Road	313	90	11	46	.288	RHP	430	119	15	59	.277
First Half	333	101	14	54	.303	Sc Pos	137	34	3	54	.248
Scnd Half	250	65	6	26	.260	Clutch	84	28	2	12	.333

2000 Rankings (National League)

- Did not rank near the top or bottom in any category

Mike Hampton

Position: SP
Bats: R **Throws:** L
Ht: 5'10" **Wt:** 180

Opening Day Age: 28
Born: 9/9/72 in
Brooksville, FL
ML Seasons: 8

2000 Season

Traded to the Mets prior to last season, Mike Hampton overcame a slow start and the pressures of pitching in New York to emerge as one of the team's key contributors. He allowed 36 walks and owned a 6.52 ERA in his first seven starts, yet rebounded to rank fifth in the National League in ERA. He capped the campaign by winning two games and earning the MVP Award in the League Championship Series.

Pitching

Hampton is a three-pitch hurler whose best offering is his cut fastball. The cutter abandoned him early last season, leading to one of the more dismal stretches in his career. He credits a 15-minute conversation with Tom Seaver in early May with reversing his slump. When he's winning, Hampton gets ahead in the count with his 87-MPH, two-seam fastball and his straight changeup before retiring hitters with his cutter. An intense competitor, he does an excellent job of keeping his pitches down, enabling him to lead the league by allowing 0.41 home runs per nine innings. On the negative side, the southpaw has trouble finding a way to win when he doesn't have his best stuff.

Defense & Hitting

Hampton has quick reflexes that allow him to catch most hard-hit balls back through the box. The lefthander also is quick off the mound to field bunts and cover first base. Although Greg Maddux has a lock on the NL Gold Glove, Hampton may be the better fielder. A former Silver Slugger winner, Hampton also helps himself at the plate and runs the bases as well as many everyday players.

2001 Outlook

Despite going 11-4 with a 2.05 ERA at Shea Stadium, Hampton never embraced the idea of pitching in New York. After being wooed by numerous suiters, the free agent settled on an eight-year, $121 million pact with Colorado in early December. Considered two of the premier lefthanders on the market, Hampton and Denny Neagle give the Rockies playoff aspirations, though Hampton's ERA at Coors Field is 6.48 in five career starts. He is 4-1 in those outings, however.

Overall Statistics

	W	L	Pct.	ERA	G	GS	Sv	IP	H	BB	SO	HR	Ratio
2000	15	10	.600	3.14	33	33	0	217.2	194	99	151	10	1.35
Career	85	53	.616	3.44	241	187	1	1260.2	1234	489	852	88	1.37

How Often He Throws Strikes

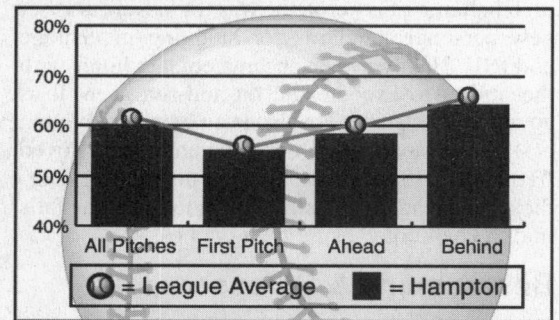

= League Average   = Hampton

2000 Situational Stats

	W	L	ERA	Sv	IP		AB	H	HR	RBI	Avg
Home	11	4	2.05	0	132.0	LHB	148	39	3	16	.264
Road	4	6	4.83	0	85.2	RHB	658	155	7	63	.236
First Half	9	5	3.36	0	120.2	Sc Pos	201	44	1	63	.219
Scnd Half	6	5	2.88	0	97.0	Clutch	87	23	2	9	.264

2000 Rankings (National League)

- 1st in lowest slugging percentage allowed (.325) and fewest home runs allowed per nine innings (.41)
- 2nd in highest groundball/flyball ratio allowed (2.5) and lowest ERA at home
- 4th in GDPs induced (26)
- 5th in ERA and runners caught stealing (10)
- Led the Mets in ERA, games started, complete games (3), innings pitched, batters faced (929), walks allowed, wild pitches (10), GDPs induced (26), lowest slugging percentage allowed (.325), highest groundball/flyball ratio allowed (2.5), lowest stolen-base percentage allowed (47.4), fewest home runs allowed per nine innings (.41) and most GDPs induced per nine innings (1.1)

Al Leiter

Position: SP
Bats: L **Throws:** L
Ht: 6' 3" **Wt:** 220

Opening Day Age: 35
Born: 10/23/65 in Toms River, NJ
ML Seasons: 14
Pronunciation: LITE-er

New York (NL)

2000 Season

Al Leiter stepped forward as the ace of the Mets' rotation last year. The lefthander kept the team close during the first two months while turmoil threatened to tear the club apart. He went 10-1 in his first 16 starts and maintained that level into the postseason. His masterful performance in Game 2 of the Division Series got the team on track in the playoffs. He also started two games in the World Series.

Pitching

Leiter is a big-game pitcher who has the concentration and ability to ignore the pressure and scrutiny that come with playing in New York. He's one of the few remaining workhorses who stays strong after eclipsing the 100-pitch mark. He owns one of baseball's best cutters, a pitch that runs in on the fists of righthanded hitters. Leiter actually throws two different cutters, with one featuring a short, sharp break and another with a bigger bend. His fastball also runs up and in, which helped him limit lefthanded batters to a .119 average last year. When he opts to go outside, Leiter usually will throw his above-average changeup.

Defense & Hitting

Not blessed with a good pickoff move, Leiter throws over to first base more than most pitchers. His 186 pickoff throws last year ranked second in the National League. Only two pitchers surrendered more than Leiter's 22 stolen bases, however. He is a decent fielder who can be a step slow covering first base due to the long stride in his delivery. While few pitchers are less adept with the bat than Leiter, he is a decent bunter.

2001 Outlook

He may be a 35-year-old who has thrown a lot of pitches over the past six seasons, but Leiter has gotten stronger in recent years. He has returned to the outstanding form he showed prior to suffering a knee injury midway through the 1998 campaign and is one of the game's most dominating pitchers when in a groove. Leiter should continue to be the Mets' heart and soul every fifth day in 2001, and his continued steady production will help lessen the sting of Mike Hampton's departure.

Overall Statistics

	W	L	Pct.	ERA	G	GS	Sv	IP	H	BB	SO	HR	Ratio
2000	16	8	.667	3.20	31	31	0	208.0	176	76	200	19	1.21
Career	106	79	.573	3.73	264	234	2	1502.2	1312	759	1307	113	1.38

How Often He Throws Strikes

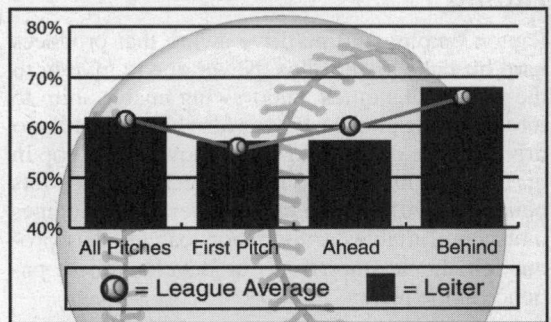

2000 Situational Stats

	W	L	ERA	Sv	IP		AB	H	HR	RBI	Avg
Home	9	3	2.67	0	101.0	LHB	118	14	3	12	.119
Road	7	5	3.70	0	107.0	RHB	653	162	16	67	.248
First Half	10	2	2.99	0	120.1	Sc Pos	173	39	3	59	.225
Scnd Half	6	6	3.49	0	87.2	Clutch	72	14	2	3	.194

2000 Rankings (National League)

- 1st in lowest batting average allowed vs. lefthanded batters
- 2nd in pickoff throws (186) and fewest GDPs induced per nine innings (0.4)
- 3rd in stolen bases allowed (22) and runners caught stealing (13)
- 4th in most strikeouts per nine innings (8.7)
- 5th in strikeouts, lowest batting average allowed (.228), lowest ERA at home and most pitches thrown per batter (3.98)
- Led the Mets in wins, hit batsmen (11), strikeouts, pitches thrown (3,479), pickoff throws (186), stolen bases allowed (22), runners caught stealing (13), lowest batting average allowed (.228) and most strikeouts per nine innings (8.7)

Jay Payton

2000 Season

Perseverance finally paid off for Jay Payton. After undergoing three right elbow operations and surgery on his left shoulder that cost him nearly three years of development, the outfielder made the most of his opportunity last season. Replacing the injured Darryl Hamilton, Payton emerged as the answer in center field and was a late candidate for National League Rookie of the Year where he finished a distant third. He ranked first among NL rookies in hits. He also placed second in homers and extra-base hits and finished near the top in batting average, slugging percentage and on-base percentage.

Hitting

Payton employs a line-drive swing that produces hard hit balls to all fields. Never one to give in to the pitcher, his quick, short swing enables him to turn on inside pitches. Payton also has the ability to drive outside offerings. He has shown some pop in his bat since his days at Georgia Tech, and the Mets believe he will hit with more power as he becomes more comfortable in the major leagues. His production should improve as he develops more patience at the plate.

Baserunning & Defense

Payton's earliest contributions last year came in the field. Unable to hit or throw while recovering from the elbow surgeries, he spent all his time on the diamond chasing flyballs. The results left him an above-average defender who is at his best when going back on balls. The surgeries stole some of his arm strength, but Payton's tosses usually are accurate. He has the speed to be a good basestealer but has not enjoyed much success in that area. He was caught on 11 of 16 stolen-base attempts last year.

2001 Outlook

Payton rewarded the Mets for not giving up on him while injuries hampered his progress after he was drafted in the first round in 1994. He still has adjustments to make at the plate, particularly against sliders and high fastballs, but his tremendous talent and heart are obvious. He will return to center field this season and should have a big future in New York if he remains healthy.

Position: CF
Bats: R **Throws:** R
Ht: 5'10" **Wt:** 185

Opening Day Age: 28
Born: 11/22/72 in Zanesville, OH
ML Seasons: 3

Overall Statistics

	G	AB	R	H	D	T	HR	RBI	SB	BB	SO	Avg	OBP	Slg
2000	149	488	63	142	23	1	17	62	5	30	60	.291	.331	.447
Career	177	518	66	151	25	1	17	63	6	31	66	.292	.332	.442

Where He Hits the Ball

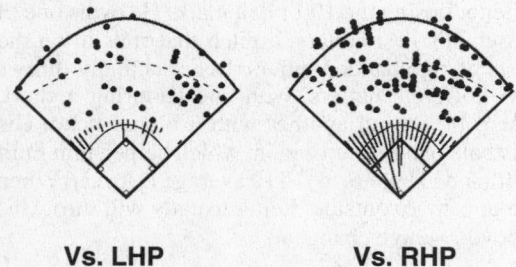

Vs. LHP   Vs. RHP

2000 Situational Stats

	AB	H	HR	RBI	Avg		AB	H	HR	RBI	Avg
Home	240	67	9	34	.279	LHP	104	38	5	14	.365
Road	248	75	8	28	.302	RHP	384	104	12	48	.271
First Half	221	63	8	27	.285	Sc Pos	126	31	4	45	.246
Scnd Half	267	79	9	35	.296	Clutch	82	17	3	7	.207

2000 Rankings (National League)

- 1st in errors in center field (6)
- 2nd in lowest fielding percentage in center field (.981)
- 5th in fewest pitches seen per plate appearance (3.35)
- 8th in batting average on a 3-2 count (.357) and lowest on-base percentage vs. righthanded pitchers (.306)
- 9th in caught stealing (11) and highest percentage of swings on the first pitch (38.2)
- 10th in lowest percentage of pitches taken (48.4)
- Led the Mets in sacrifice flies (8) and caught stealing (11)
- Led NL center fielders in batting average with two strikes (.243)

Mike Piazza

2000 Season

Mike Piazza was the National League's leading MVP candidate through the first five months of last season. But numerous minor injuries took their toll and led to a difficult September. Nevertheless, despite playing with a bruised hip and shin in August, getting beaned by Roger Clemens in July and struck in the head with a bat earlier in the season, Piazza put together one of his best all-around campaigns.

Hitting

Piazza has a classic swing that fans memorize. He loves to pull low pitches on the inner half of the plate, producing long, majestic home runs. If he can extend his arms on outside pitches, he simply drives the ball the other way with similar results. Though one of the game's more consistent hitters, Piazza gets on rolls in which he is almost impossible to retire. He makes consistent contact for a power hitter, fanning just 69 times in 482 at-bats last year. He also hits well on the road, producing a league-best .377 average last year.

Baserunning & Defense

No one questions the effort Piazza provides behind the plate. He is a true warrior who weathers the physical punishment as well as anyone. He does a decent job of calling a game and handling the pitching staff, but the overall results are no better than average. No catcher was easier to run against last year. A new catching technique picked up prior to last season took pressure off his left thumb, which improved his abilities as a receiver and enabled him to hit with power throughout the campaign. He needs that power, because he is a slow and conservative baserunner.

2001 Outlook

Eight full seasons into his major league career, Piazza has established himself as the best offensive catcher in baseball annals. While his body continues to feel the effects of playing behind the plate, his bat remains productive, making him one of the game's elite performers. A change of position might be worth considering in the next two or three years. In the meantime, he'll remain the Mets' primary backstop and their most important player.

Position: C
Bats: R **Throws:** R
Ht: 6' 3" **Wt:** 215

Opening Day Age: 32
Born: 9/4/68 in Norristown, PA
ML Seasons: 9
Pronunciation: pee-AH-zuh

Overall Statistics

	G	AB	R	H	D	T	HR	RBI	SB	BB	SO	Avg	OBP	Slg
2000	136	482	90	156	26	0	38	113	4	58	69	.324	.398	.614
Career	1117	4135	701	1356	199	4	278	881	17	439	632	.328	.392	.580

Where He Hits the Ball

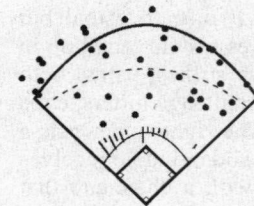 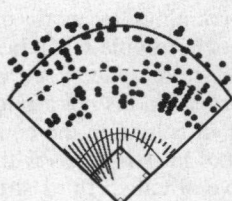

Vs. LHP   **Vs. RHP**

2000 Situational Stats

	AB	H	HR	RBI	Avg		AB	H	HR	RBI	Avg
Home	238	64	17	53	.269	LHP	79	28	11	20	.354
Road	244	92	21	60	.377	RHP	403	128	27	93	.318
First Half	264	92	24	72	.348	Scr Pos	140	40	9	68	.286
Scnd Half	218	64	14	41	.294	Clutch	75	27	6	17	.360

2000 Rankings (National League)

- 1st in batting average on the road and fielding percentage at catcher (.997)
- Led the Mets in batting average, home runs, total bases (296), RBI, GDPs (15), slugging percentage, HR frequency (12.7 ABs per HR), batting average in the clutch, batting average on a 3-1 count (.714), cleanup slugging percentage (.596), slugging percentage vs. righthanded pitchers (.568), batting average on the road and steals of third (2)
- Led NL catchers in batting average, home runs, total bases (296), RBI, slugging percentage, HR frequency (12.7 ABs per HR), batting average in the clutch, batting average vs. righthanded pitchers and batting average on a 3-1 count (.714)

Rick Reed

2000 Season

A midseason injury seemed to get Rick Reed back on track last year. After jumping off to a strong start in April, the righthander battled an ailing left side and posted just one victory in May and June while his ERA resided above 6.20. He missed nearly three weeks in July with a non-displaced fracture of his left wrist. Reed finished the year on a strong note, however, ranking among the league's top 10 in walks per nine innings, winning percentage and strikeout-walk ratio.

Pitching

Reed succeeds with four pitches and impeccable control. He surrendered fewer walks than all but four pitchers in the majors last year with at least 110 innings. He works off his two-seam fastball but gets in trouble when he leaves his curveball up in the strike zone. Reed throws strikes, paints both corners and is not afraid to challenge hitters, even when behind in the count. The righthander gets a lot of his strikeouts with his slider, but he receives several called third strikes with a changeup that ranks as his fourth-best offering. He is one of the league's more focused pitchers, which makes his late-season tendency to surrender two-out hits to the bottom of the order surprising.

Defense & Hitting

An excellent all-around athlete, Reed helps himself in the field and at the plate. He is one of the league's more accomplished pitchers with the glove and does a good job of limiting the running game. He handles the bat as well as any pitcher. He is a consistent bunter in sacrifice situations and can provide some power on occasion.

2001 Outlook

Unlike Mike Hampton, Reed said during the season that he would like to remain with New York despite being a free agent. The two sides agreed to a three-year, $21.75 million deal in early December that also includes a team option for 2004. The Mets would like to see Reed go a little deeper in games, but there is no denying his ability to perform consistently every fifth day. Most teams long to have a No. 3 or 4 starter of Reed's caliber.

Position: SP
Bats: R **Throws:** R
Ht: 6' 1" **Wt:** 195

Opening Day Age: 35
Born: 8/16/65 in Huntington, WV
ML Seasons: 12

Overall Statistics

	W	L	Pct.	ERA	G	GS	Sv	IP	H	BB	SO	HR	Ratio
2000	11	5	.688	4.11	30	30	0	184.0	192	34	121	28	1.23
Career	60	45	.571	3.93	181	160	1	1020.1	1043	199	636	132	1.22

How Often He Throws Strikes

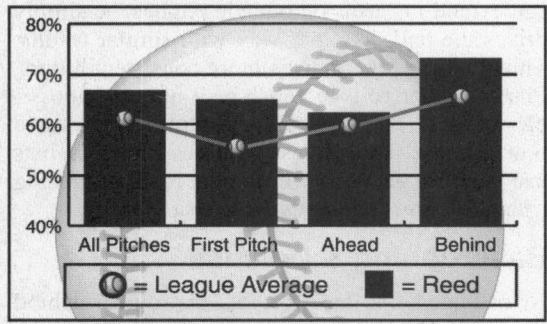

○ = League Average ■ = Reed

2000 Situational Stats

	W	L	ERA	Sv	IP		AB	H	HR	RBI	Avg
Home	5	3	4.08	0	81.2	LHB	344	94	13	40	.273
Road	6	2	4.13	0	102.1	RHB	377	98	15	41	.260
First Half	4	2	4.76	0	90.2	Sc Pos	132	34	5	47	.258
Scnd Half	7	3	3.47	0	93.1	Clutch	41	9	1	3	.220

2000 Rankings (National League)

- 2nd in sacrifice bunts (14)
- 3rd in fewest walks per nine innings (1.7)
- 6th in highest strikeout/walk ratio (3.6) and winning percentage
- 10th in lowest on-base percentage allowed (.302)
- Led the Mets in sacrifice bunts (14), home runs allowed, lowest on-base percentage allowed (.302), fewest pitches thrown per batter (3.58), most run support per nine innings (5.8), fewest walks per nine innings (1.7), most GDPs induced per GDP situation (14.4%), bunts in play (17) and winning percentage

Glendon Rusch

2000 Season

The emergence of Glendon Rusch as a reliable starter served as a key to the Mets' National League pennant. He earned the fifth starter's job in spring training before moving up a notch while Bobby J. Jones was shelved during the first half. Rusch wound up posting career bests in wins, ERA and starts. He continued to contribute as a reliever in the postseason by getting New York out of several late-inning jams.

Pitching

Rusch is a finesse pitcher who has the ability to strike out hitters when necessary. His success depends on how effectively he can control his plus-curveball, changeup and cut fastball as well as his mid- to upper-80s fastball. The lefthander displayed impressive command last year, ranking fifth in the league with a 3.6 strikeout-walk ratio and seventh with 2.1 walks per nine innings. There were times he felt as if he had to throw a perfect game, for no National League hurler received less run support than Rusch's 3.7 runs per nine frames. He needs to keep runners off the basepaths, for he surrendered a .338 average with runners in scoring position, fourth worst in the circuit.

Defense & Hitting

The greatest improvement needed in Rusch's game involves his defense. He did a better job making the routine plays around the mound last year, but still struggles to complete the difficult throw to retire the lead runner. For a lefty, his move to first base is mediocre, enabling opponents to steal 11 bases in 16 tries. At the plate, it is obvious that Rusch was raised in an American League organization.

2001 Outlook

After two difficult seasons in Kansas City's rotation before spending most of 1999 at Triple-A, Rusch looked like a more mature pitcher with the Mets last year. He appeared to be more comfortable by not having to be one of the top two starters in the rotation, and with Kevin Appier and Al Leiter manning the top two spots in 2001, that won't be a problem this year. On the heels of his successful first year in the Big Apple, Rusch should be ready to make greater strides this season.

Position: SP
Bats: L **Throws:** L
Ht: 6' 1" **Wt:** 200

Opening Day Age: 26
Born: 11/7/74 in Seattle, WA
ML Seasons: 4
Pronunciation: RUSH

Overall Statistics

	W	L	Pct.	ERA	G	GS	Sv	IP	H	BB	SO	HR	Ratio
2000	11	11	.500	4.01	31	30	0	190.2	196	44	157	18	1.26
Career	23	36	.390	5.13	94	81	1	520.2	601	149	371	69	1.44

How Often He Throws Strikes

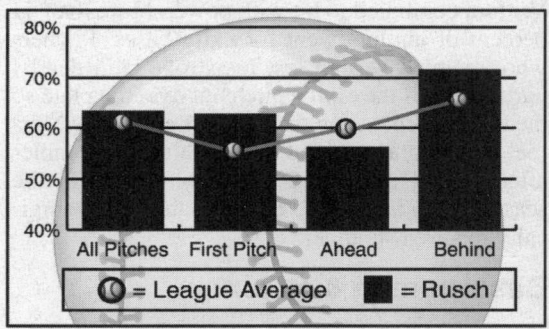

= League Average   = Rusch

2000 Situational Stats

	W	L	ERA	Sv	IP		AB	H	HR	RBI	Avg
Home	7	4	4.34	0	93.1	LHB	158	48	3	19	.304
Road	4	7	3.70	0	97.1	RHB	577	148	15	64	.256
First Half	6	7	4.43	0	101.2	Sc Pos	145	49	5	65	.338
Scnd Half	5	4	3.54	0	89.0	Clutch	43	8	2	4	.186

2000 Rankings (National League)

- 1st in least run support per nine innings (3.7)
- 4th in highest batting average allowed with runners in scoring position
- 5th in highest strikeout/walk ratio (3.6)
- 6th in lowest ERA on the road
- 7th in fewest walks per nine innings (2.1)
- 8th in most pitches thrown per batter (3.92)
- Led the Mets in losses, hits allowed, highest strikeout/walk ratio (3.6) and lowest ERA on the road

Robin Ventura

2000 Season

Robin Ventura's second season with the Mets proved to be his most frustrating campaign to date. After an outstanding debut in New York in 1999, Ventura saw his production in all phases of the game decrease. His batting average was the lowest of his 12-year career. He underwent right shoulder surgery prior to the season, then battled a bruised right rotator cuff that landed him on the disabled list for two weeks in late July. He said the ailments did not affect his performance, though the numbers and his lack of consistency suggest otherwise.

Hitting

While his average may have been low last year, Ventura continued to hit with power. More than 44 percent of his hits went for extra bases. Pitchers who assumed he had lost his stroke paid dearly, particularly if they left a pitch out over the plate so the third baseman could extend his arms. The Mets feel that Ventura started to overthink his troubles after getting into some bad habits early in the season when he tried to compensate for his surgically repaired shoulder.

Baserunning & Defense

Ventura's defense slipped along with his batting average last year. He committed 17 errors, compared to nine in 1999. His .954 fielding percentage was fourth worst among National League third basemen. That's a huge departure from the man who won six Gold Gloves over the previous nine years. Ventura's ailing shoulder had to affect many of his errant throws, although he refused to place the blame on any injury. While his baserunning was acceptable, he succeeded on just three-of-eight stolen-base attempts.

2001 Outlook

The Mets hope a quiet offseason that includes regaining confidence and additional strength in his shoulder will be the panacea necessary to get Ventura back to his All-Star ways. At age 33, he should have several prime years remaining as a cornerstone in the Mets' lineup. A repeat of last season not only would be surprising, but also a discouraging harbinger.

Position: 3B
Bats: L **Throws:** R
Ht: 6' 1" **Wt:** 198

Opening Day Age: 33
Born: 7/14/67 in Santa Maria, CA
ML Seasons: 12

Overall Statistics

	G	AB	R	H	D	T	HR	RBI	SB	BB	SO	Avg	OBP	Slg
2000	141	469	61	109	23	1	24	84	3	75	91	.232	.338	.439
Career	1556	5599	807	1530	280	13	227	945	19	817	859	.273	.364	.450

Where He Hits the Ball

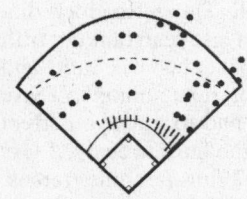
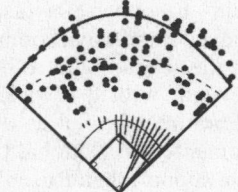

Vs. LHP   **Vs. RHP**

2000 Situational Stats

	AB	H	HR	RBI	Avg		AB	H	HR	RBI	Avg
Home	224	52	12	38	.232	LHP	102	23	5	22	.225
Road	245	57	12	46	.233	RHP	367	86	19	62	.234
First Half	289	69	16	53	.239	Sc Pos	125	32	5	60	.256
Scnd Half	180	40	8	31	.222	Clutch	77	14	2	10	.182

2000 Rankings (National League)

- 3rd in lowest batting average
- 4th in errors at third base (17), lowest batting average at home and lowest fielding percentage at third base (.954)
- Led the Mets in intentional walks (12)
- Led NL third basemen in intentional walks (12) and highest percentage of pitches taken (58.6)

Todd Zeile

2000 Season

Former third baseman Todd Zeile acquired a new first baseman's mitt after signing with the Mets as a free agent prior to last season. He then proceeded to make general manager Steve Phillips look good by becoming a decent replacement for the departed John Olerud. Hitting mostly sixth in the batting order, Zeile ranked fourth on the team in home runs and RBI. His batting average and RBI totals matched his career norms, while his home-run total was a little higher than average.

Hitting

No batter is more patient than Zeile. He swung at the first pitch in only 9.4 percent of his at-bats, ranked first in the National League by taking 65.8 percent of all pitches and placed third by averaging 4.22 pitches per plate appearance. Ironically, his batting average was just .032 when he got behind 0-2, the third-worst mark in the league. Zeile is quick to hack, however, when he gets his favorite offering—a fastball on the inner half of the plate. He has a short swing that produces power to all fields with his strong wrists.

Baserunning & Defense

Zeile was not the disaster at first base that many observers expected. Granted, he had difficulty with popups in foul territory, particularly ones down the right-field line, but he otherwise held his own at the new position. A catcher during the early stages of his professional career before shifting to third base, he has steady hands on groundballs, even though his range is limited. Though not fleet of foot, he possesses enough speed to record three triples last season and score from first on Benny Agbayani's game-winning double in Game 3 of the World Series.

2001 Outlook

Zeile, who is playing for his eighth major league team in 12 campaigns, is slated to return as the Mets' first baseman this year. With a season under his belt, his defense at first base should improve further. His production also might be better if the Mets acquire another slugger, thereby allowing Zeile simply to play his game.

Position: 1B
Bats: R **Throws:** R
Ht: 6' 1" **Wt:** 200

Opening Day Age: 35
Born: 9/9/65 in Van Nuys, CA
ML Seasons: 12
Pronunciation: ZEAL

Overall Statistics

	G	AB	R	H	D	T	HR	RBI	SB	BB	SO	Avg	OBP	Slg
2000	153	544	67	146	36	3	22	79	3	74	85	.268	.356	.467
Career	1626	5889	789	1576	323	20	205	884	50	728	948	.268	.348	.434

Where He Hits the Ball

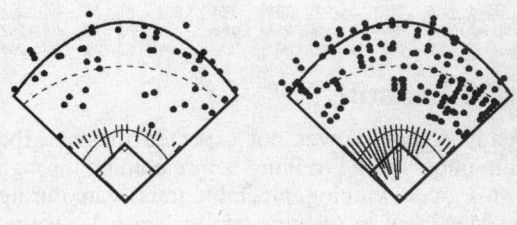

Vs. LHP   **Vs. RHP**

2000 Situational Stats

	AB	H	HR	RBI	Avg		AB	H	HR	RBI	Avg
Home	257	72	8	38	.280	LHP	117	29	10	21	.248
Road	287	74	14	41	.258	RHP	427	117	12	58	.274
First Half	298	91	14	52	.305	Sc Pos	144	36	4	54	.250
Scnd Half	246	55	8	27	.224	Clutch	90	28	5	20	.311

2000 Rankings (National League)

- 1st in lowest percentage of swings on the first pitch (9.4) and highest percentage of pitches taken (65.8)
- 3rd in most pitches seen per plate appearance (4.22) and lowest batting average on an 0-2 count (.032)
- 4th in errors at first base (10)
- 5th in lowest fielding percentage at first base (.992)
- Led the Mets in triples, GDPs (15), most pitches seen per plate appearance (4.22), batting average vs. lefthanded pitchers, slugging percentage vs. lefthanded pitchers (.564), on-base percentage vs. lefthanded pitchers (.364), highest percentage of pitches taken (65.8) and games played

Benny Agbayani

Position: LF/RF
Bats: R **Throws:** R
Ht: 6' 0" **Wt:** 225

Opening Day Age: 29
Born: 12/28/71 in Honolulu, HI
ML Seasons: 3
Pronunciation:
ag-by-YAWN-ee
Nickname: The
Hawaiian Punch

Overall Statistics

	G	AB	R	H	D	T	HR	RBI	SB	BB	SO	Avg	OBP	Slg
2000	119	350	59	101	20	1	15	60	5	54	68	.289	.391	.480
Career	231	641	102	182	38	4	29	102	11	87	133	.284	.375	.491

2000 Situational Stats

	AB	H	HR	RBI	Avg		AB	H	HR	RBI	Avg
Home	167	49	9	33	.293	LHP	91	25	3	11	.275
Road	183	52	6	27	.284	RHP	259	76	12	49	.293
First Half	148	44	7	29	.297	Sc Pos	101	29	2	46	.287
Scnd Half	202	57	8	31	.282	Clutch	61	16	2	6	.262

2000 Season

Benny Agbayani was not expected to make the team out of spring training before coming through with a game-winning, pinch hit grand slam during the Mets' season-opening trip to Japan. Hawaiian Punch was then expected to be traded, yet remained due to Darryl Hamilton's injury. He hit so well that he earned the starting job in left field.

Hitting, Baserunning & Defense

Agbayani is an excellent low-ball, fastball hitter who is capable of catching fire. That's exactly what happened in mid-June. After not starting for more than two weeks, he became the first Met since Gary Carter to slug three homers in consecutive at-bats. Outside breaking pitches give Agbayani trouble. Though not blessed with the greatest range or speed, he is a capable fielder. There are times, however, when he makes circus catches on routine flyballs. He's good for about five steals a season.

2001 Outlook

Agbayani is one of manager Bobby Valentine's favorite players. He's an overachiever with several limitations, but he plays with gusto and will help his team more often than he hurts it. If he continues to hit and improve in left field, he should own the starting job throughout this season.

John Franco

Position: RP
Bats: L **Throws:** L
Ht: 5'10" **Wt:** 185

Opening Day Age: 40
Born: 9/17/60 in
Brooklyn, NY
ML Seasons: 17

Overall Statistics

	W	L	Pct.	ERA	G	GS	Sv	IP	H	BB	SO	HR	Ratio
2000	5	4	.556	3.40	62	0	4	55.2	46	26	56	6	1.29
Career	82	74	.526	2.68	940	0	420	1097.0	1007	430	857	62	1.31

2000 Situational Stats

	W	L	ERA	Sv	IP		AB	H	HR	RBI	Avg
Home	2	1	3.81	3	26.0	LHB	67	14	0	2	.209
Road	3	3	3.03	1	29.2	RHB	141	32	6	17	.227
First Half	3	3	3.60	3	35.0	Sc Pos	54	10	1	13	.185
Scnd Half	2	1	3.05	1	20.2	Clutch	146	33	2	12	.226

2000 Season

After serving as the Mets' closer for the previous 10 seasons, John Franco looked rejuvenated at age 40 last year while establishing himself as the team's eighth-inning setup man. He had considered leaving New York prior to the campaign but stayed and made the most of the opportunity.

Pitching, Defense & Hitting

Franco's bread-and-butter pitch is a changeup with movement reminiscent of a screwball. He uses both sides of the plate with his slider and is not afraid to move the ball up and down in the strike zone. A soft-tosser who also owns a sinking fastball, Franco's greatest attribute is his guile. He never backs down and always wants the ball with the game on the line. He made his first error since 1991 last year, and his attention to the running game has waned over the past couple of years. He has just four at-bats over the past six seasons.

2001 Outlook

Franco has more saves than any lefthanded pitcher in history and he'll have a chance to add to that total as the Mets signed him to a three-year, $10.5 million deal in late November. Chances are he will add another three or four saves this year, and possibly more if Armando Benitez should go down for any length of time.

Lenny Harris

Position: 3B/1B
Bats: L **Throws:** R
Ht: 5'10" **Wt:** 220

Opening Day Age: 36
Born: 10/28/64 in
Miami, FL
ML Seasons: 13

Overall Statistics

	G	AB	R	H	D	T	HR	RBI	SB	BB	SO	Avg	OBP	Slg
2000	112	223	31	58	7	4	4	26	13	20	22	.260	.317	.381
Career	1421	3282	399	895	136	18	31	305	123	231	271	.273	.321	.353

2000 Situational Stats

	AB	H	HR	RBI	Avg		AB	H	HR	RBI	Avg
Home	90	25	2	13	.278	LHP	19	3	0	3	.158
Road	133	33	2	13	.248	RHP	204	55	4	23	.270
First Half	106	18	1	13	.170	Sc Pos	52	12	1	20	.231
Scnd Half	117	40	3	13	.342	Clutch	61	14	0	6	.230

2000 Season

Lenny Harris joined the Mets for the second time in 13 major league seasons when he was dealt to New York from Arizona on June 2. After hitting just .188 with the Diamondbacks, Harris batted over .310 in each of the last three months, with a .466 on-base percentage in July.

Hitting, Baserunning & Defense

Harris is a solid lefthanded pinch-hitter against righties. He is a pesky, low-ball hitter who doesn't settle for a lot of free passes, but he can hang in when he's behind in the count. In 1999, he came within two pinch-hits of John Vander Wal's big league record. He is one of the swiftest Mets, as evidenced by the fact that he tied Derek Bell for the team lead with eight stolen bases. One of the game's most versatile utility men, Harris hit in all nine slots of the batting order and played five different positions last year. In fact, in one four-game stretch late last August, Harris started in left field, second base and first base.

2001 Outlook

Harris received a two-year contract worth $2.2 million in November. He can expect to see action in 100 games by serving as a pinch-hitter and playing second base and the corner positions of the infield and outfield.

Bobby J. Jones

Position: SP
Bats: R **Throws:** R
Ht: 6' 4" **Wt:** 225

Opening Day Age: 31
Born: 2/10/70 in
Fresno, CA
ML Seasons: 8

Overall Statistics

	W	L	Pct.	ERA	G	GS	Sv	IP	H	BB	SO	HR	Ratio
2000	11	6	.647	5.06	27	27	0	154.2	171	49	85	25	1.42
Career	74	56	.569	4.13	193	190	0	1215.2	1255	353	714	137	1.32

2000 Situational Stats

	W	L	ERA	Sv	IP		AB	H	HR	RBI	Avg
Home	7	3	3.60	0	75.0	LHB	303	80	15	46	.264
Road	4	3	6.44	0	79.2	RHB	306	91	10	34	.297
First Half	3	4	6.79	0	59.2	Sc Pos	172	40	3	46	.233
Scnd Half	8	2	3.98	0	95.0	Clutch	16	3	0	2	.188

2000 Season

Bobby Jones struggled in his first eight starts last season, going 1-3 with a 10.19 ERA. He found himself back in the minors on June 13. But after two outings at Triple-A, he returned to go 10-3 the rest of the way. His highlight came in Game 4 of the Division Series, when he tossed a one-hit shutout against San Francisco.

Pitching, Defense & Hitting

Jones has a deep repertoire of pitches that he mixes well to keep hitters off-balance. He relies on control and command of his 85-MPH fastball, cutter, curveball and changeup, and he gets stronger as the game progresses. He wastes little time showing what he's got, for most of his losses occur when he gets knocked out early in the contest. He fields his position well but had a difficult time holding runners with Piazza as his batterymate. He can be productive at the plate.

2001 Outlook

Jones could not have picked a better time to pitch well down the stretch and in the postseason. He entered the free-agent market proving to teams that his past shoulder problems appear to be history, which should land him a job in the middle of a starting rotation.

Rey Ordonez

Position: SS
Bats: R **Throws:** R
Ht: 5' 9" **Wt:** 159

Opening Day Age: 28
Born: 11/11/72 in
Havana, Cuba
ML Seasons: 5
Pronunciation: RAY
or-DOAN-yez

Overall Statistics

	G	AB	R	H	D	T	HR	RBI	SB	BB	SO	Avg	OBP	Slg
2000	45	133	10	25	5	0	0	9	0	17	16	.188	.278	.226
Career	623	2016	191	489	66	11	4	174	23	129	224	.243	.287	.292

2000 Situational Stats

	AB	H	HR	RBI	Avg		AB	H	HR	RBI	Avg
Home	56	12	0	6	.214	LHP	26	5	0	4	.192
Road	77	13	0	3	.169	RHP	107	20	0	5	.187
First Half	133	25	0	9	.188	Sc Pos	36	5	0	7	.139
Scnd Half	0	0	0	0	-	Clutch	24	3	0	1	.125

2000 Season

Rey Ordonez' season ended prematurely last year when he fractured his left forearm on May 29 and subsequently underwent surgery. He had struggled before the injury and had seen his batting average dip to a paltry .188. He also committed six errors after making only four miscues in all of 1999.

Hitting, Baserunning & Defense

Ordonez is a throwback, the classic good-field, no-hit shortstop that was prevalent before the arrival of Rodriguez, Jeter, Garciaparra, et al. Ordonez earned three straight Gold Gloves prior to last season and he would have added another had he stayed healthy. He is the most creative defensive player in the game and makes spectacular plays look routine. His defense is so good that his poor stick is overlooked, although last year during his limited time he was a liability at the plate. He is not an outstanding baserunner, perhaps because he doesn't get on base often enough.

2001 Outlook

The Mets never worried about Ordonez' offensive shortcomings in the past, but their philosophy may be changing. His future in New York depends upon whether the team signs a prominent free agent. Should that happen, Ordonez will be making the highlight reel in another city.

Timoniel Perez

Position: LF/RF
Bats: L **Throws:** L
Ht: 5' 9" **Wt:** 167

Opening Day Age: 23
Born: 4/8/77 in Bani,
Dominican Republic
ML Seasons: 1

Overall Statistics

	G	AB	R	H	D	T	HR	RBI	SB	BB	SO	Avg	OBP	Slg
2000	24	49	11	14	4	1	1	3	1	3	5	.286	.333	.469
Career	24	49	11	14	4	1	1	3	1	3	5	.286	.333	.469

2000 Situational Stats

	AB	H	HR	RBI	Avg		AB	H	HR	RBI	Avg
Home	18	6	0	0	.333	LHP	8	1	1	1	.125
Road	31	8	1	3	.258	RHP	41	13	0	2	.317
First Half	0	0	0	0	-	Sc Pos	7	1	0	2	.143
Scnd Half	49	14	1	3	.286	Clutch	5	1	0	0	.200

2000 Season

Timo Perez emerged as the new Melvin Mora, only better. After hitting a combined .357 in the minors last year, Perez impressed manager Bobby Valentine with his all-around abilities. Perez took over for an injured Derek Bell in Game 1 of the Division Series and responded by batting .300 with 10 runs scored in nine playoff games.

Hitting, Baserunning & Defense

Perez is fearless on the field. Opposing pitchers pay the price when they try to challenge him with a fastball early in the count. While he has a tendency to buckle his knees on curveballs, Perez also will hang in and deliver a hit against the same offering. He is an excellent bunter who is capable of laying them down for hits. Despite his above-average speed, he doesn't yet run the bases as well as he should, though he does use his legs to his advantage in the outfield.

2001 Outlook

Is Perez as good as he appeared to be late last season? Probably not. Still, he turns just 24 on April 8, and he could develop into the disruptive leadoff hitter New York needs. While he might step in to take Derek Bell's place in right field, Perez' role this year could depend upon the Mets' activity in free agency.

Todd Pratt

Position: C
Bats: R **Throws:** R
Ht: 6' 3" **Wt:** 230

Opening Day Age: 34
Born: 2/9/67 in Bellevue, NE
ML Seasons: 8

Overall Statistics

	G	AB	R	H	D	T	HR	RBI	SB	BB	SO	Avg	OBP	Slg
2000	80	160	33	44	6	0	8	25	0	22	31	.275	.378	.463
Career	333	770	99	200	40	2	24	119	2	79	196	.260	.335	.410

2000 Situational Stats

	AB	H	HR	RBI	Avg		AB	H	HR	RBI	Avg
Home	62	15	2	11	.242	LHP	43	11	1	5	.256
Road	98	29	6	14	.296	RHP	117	33	7	20	.282
First Half	86	20	6	16	.233	Sc Pos	46	10	2	19	.217
Scnd Half	74	24	2	9	.324	Clutch	34	5	1	5	.147

2000 Season

Todd Pratt relieved Mike Piazza behind the plate on 71 occasions, helping Piazza stay fresh or recover from one of his numerous bumps and bruises. Pratt also responded with the bat by establishing career highs in home runs and RBI.

Hitting, Baserunning & Defense

Mets manager Bobby Valentine did not hesitate to write Pratt's name in the lineup for Game 1 of the World Series. After all, the skipper knew Pratt is an excellent defensive catcher who has shown he can come through with a big hit. He kills fastballs and is equally effective against righthanders and lefthanders. While his throwing arm is significantly more effective than Piazza's, Pratt struggles to block pitches in the dirt. He can fill in at first base and left field if necessary. He may be the only member of the team who is slower than Piazza.

2001 Outlook

This journeyman receiver appears to have found a home with the Mets after previously moving through six organizations. Pratt serves as a strong complement to Piazza and his bat doesn't hurt the team when Piazza is forced to sit for several days. Signed through 2001, another 40 starts and several relief appearances appear to be on Pratt's agenda once again.

Bubba Trammell

Traded To PADRES

Position: RF/LF
Bats: R **Throws:** R
Ht: 6' 2" **Wt:** 220

Opening Day Age: 29
Born: 11/6/71 in Knoxville, TN
ML Seasons: 4
Pronunciation: TRAM-mull

Overall Statistics

	G	AB	R	H	D	T	HR	RBI	SB	BB	SO	Avg	OBP	Slg
2000	102	245	28	65	13	2	10	45	4	29	49	.265	.345	.457
Career	287	850	119	232	55	3	40	132	7	103	166	.273	.351	.486

2000 Situational Stats

	AB	H	HR	RBI	Avg		AB	H	HR	RBI	Avg
Home	146	42	6	24	.288	LHP	82	25	4	17	.305
Road	99	23	4	21	.232	RHP	163	40	6	28	.245
First Half	165	46	7	27	.279	Sc Pos	75	22	3	35	.293
Scnd Half	80	19	3	18	.238	Clutch	42	11	4	11	.262

2000 Season

Bubba Trammell went from the outhouse to the penthouse when he was traded from Tampa Bay to the Mets last July 28. A solid acquisition for general manager Steve Phillips, Trammell bolstered New York's bench while seeing action at both corner outfield positions. He paid his greatest dividend with his two-run, pinch-hit single in Game 1 of the World Series.

Hitting, Baserunning & Defense

No one questions Trammell's power. He loves to extend his arms and will make a pitcher pay if a fastball is thrown over the plate. His problems arise from a lack of patience, particularly when he enters a mild slump. Although he has decent speed and was successful on all four of his stolen-base attempts last year, he isn't a threat to run wild. He struggles defensively. Despite possessing a strong arm, he has difficulty taking the right angles toward hard-hit balls.

2001 Outlook

Following his first full season in the majors, Trammell was traded to the Padres for Donne Wall. Trammell is expected to see time in left field and pick up a few spot starts at first base, and he should add some pop to a club that hit just 157 homers last year.

Turk Wendell (Rubber Arm)

Position: RP
Bats: L **Throws:** R
Ht: 6' 2" **Wt:** 205

Opening Day Age: 33
Born: 5/19/67 in Pittsfield, MA
ML Seasons: 8
Pronunciation: WENN-dull

Overall Statistics

	W	L	Pct.	ERA	G	GS	Sv	IP	H	BB	SO	HR	Ratio
2000	8	6	.571	3.59	77	0	1	82.2	60	41	73	9	1.22
Career	29	25	.537	3.83	414	6	31	498.0	445	250	421	51	1.40

2000 Situational Stats

	W	L	ERA	Sv	IP		AB	H	HR	RBI	Avg
Home	5	2	1.99	1	45.1	LHB	102	23	3	6	.225
Road	3	4	5.54	0	37.1	RHB	189	37	6	21	.196
First Half	4	4	3.60	0	50.0	Sc Pos	62	11	2	16	.177
Scnd Half	4	2	3.58	1	32.2	Clutch	143	34	4	11	.238

2000 Season

Turk Wendell got off to a poor start last year by surrendering three game-winning homers in May. He regained control of his slider shortly thereafter to re-establish himself as the Mets' righthanded setup man. As a result, he ranked fourth in the National League in appearances and fifth in relief wins.

Pitching, Defense & Hitting

Wendell's out pitch is his sharp-breaking slider. His problems arise when he falls in love with the pitch and abandons his fastball, which appeared to lose a foot or so last year. He succeeds by retiring the first batter. In fact, only the Padres' Kevin Walker did a better job of getting the first hitter out, as Wendell surrendered a .119 average. He's a good fielder with a decent move to first base. Conversely, his bat is among the worst in baseball.

2001 Outlook

One of the Mets' primary objectives heading into the offseason was to re-sign Wendell as a free agent and they got their man with a three-year deal that could be worth a total of $9,999,999.99 (he wears No. 99) with bonuses. He is among the more consistent eighth-inning pitchers in the league and does a solid job along with John Franco of holding the lead for Armando Benitez.

Rick White

Position: RP
Bats: R **Throws:** R
Ht: 6' 4" **Wt:** 230

Opening Day Age: 32
Born: 12/23/68 in Springfield, OH
ML Seasons: 5

Overall Statistics

	W	L	Pct.	ERA	G	GS	Sv	IP	H	BB	SO	HR	Ratio
2000	5	9	.357	3.52	66	0	3	99.2	83	38	67	9	1.21
Career	18	26	.409	3.94	225	18	9	406.2	426	134	254	37	1.38

2000 Situational Stats

	W	L	ERA	Sv	IP		AB	H	HR	RBI	Avg
Home	3	1	2.75	0	52.1	LHB	153	41	5	17	.268
Road	2	8	4.37	3	47.1	RHB	218	42	4	26	.193
First Half	3	5	3.23	2	64.0	Sc Pos	95	19	3	33	.200
Scnd Half	2	4	4.04	1	35.2	Clutch	109	28	4	15	.257

2000 Season

Rick White was one of the Mets' unsung heroes after arriving from Tampa Bay on July 28. The 31-year-old solidified New York's bullpen by posting a 1.26 ERA in his first 14.1 innings. His presence gave the Mets another option in the latter innings without having to use setup men Turk Wendell and John Franco before the eighth.

Pitching, Defense & Hitting

White is a rare short reliever in that he consistently employs more than two pitches. A former bar bouncer, he is not afraid to challenge hitters. His fastball features a hard, sinking action in the low 90s. His curveball is usually effective, and he complements his fastball and breaking ball with a slider and forkball. His effectiveness, particularly his command of the strike zone, seems to wane after an inning, making him strictly a situational pitcher. He fields his position decently and holds runners well for a righthander. He has just three singles and a double to show for his 36 career at-bats.

2001 Outlook

White now has put together two solid seasons in the majors. With the dearth of quality relievers, he should have a job for several more seasons, though the Mets' pen is deep with the acquisition of Donne Wall to complement Franco and Wendell.

Other New York Mets

Kurt Abbott (Pos: SS/2B, Age: 31, Bats: R)

	G	AB	R	H	D	T	HR	RBI	SB	BB	SO	Avg	OBP	Slg
2000	79	157	22	34	7	1	6	12	1	14	51	.217	.283	.389
Career	696	2035	273	521	109	23	62	242	21	133	568	.256	.305	.424

After seeing fewer at-bats in the majors last season than he had since 1993, Abbott signed a minor league contract with the Braves in December. He provides middle-infield insurance for Atlanta. 2001 Outlook: B

Dennis Cook (Pos: LHP, Age: 38)

	W	L	Pct.	ERA	G	GS	Sv	IP	H	BB	SO	HR	Ratio
2000	6	3	.667	5.34	68	0	2	59.0	63	31	53	8	1.59
Career	62	44	.585	3.90	566	71	9	942.0	886	366	688	120	1.33

Cook still has a year remaining on his contract, so he should continue to serve an integral role in the Mets' bullpen as a situational lefty. He's gone 24-12 with 50 holds over the past three seasons. 2001 Outlook: A

Matt Franco (Pos: 1B/3B, Age: 31, Bats: L)

	G	AB	R	H	D	T	HR	RBI	SB	BB	SO	Avg	OBP	Slg
2000	101	134	9	32	4	0	2	14	0	21	22	.239	.340	.313
Career	468	638	74	163	23	2	13	72	1	86	101	.255	.344	.359

Franco has managed to stick around on the Mets' bench for parts of the past five seasons. He wouldn't seem to have the kind of power you'd want from a corner infielder, though he does draw walks. 2001 Outlook: C

Darryl Hamilton (Pos: LF/CF, Age: 36, Bats: L)

	G	AB	R	H	D	T	HR	RBI	SB	BB	SO	Avg	OBP	Slg
2000	43	105	20	29	4	1	1	6	2	14	20	.276	.358	.362
Career	1276	4451	692	1306	197	36	50	449	160	474	474	.293	.361	.388

Hamilton spent four months on the disabled list with foot and toe problems last year. With Jay Payton in center field, Hamilton will likely serve as an extra outfielder for the Mets and as injury insurance. 2001 Outlook: B

Mark Johnson (Pos: 1B, Age: 33, Bats: L)

	G	AB	R	H	D	T	HR	RBI	SB	BB	SO	Avg	OBP	Slg
2000	21	22	2	4	0	0	1	6	0	5	9	.182	.333	.318
Career	315	819	120	192	40	1	31	110	12	129	223	.234	.342	.399

Johnson was already overaged when he played decently in 127 games with the Pirates in 1996. He's almost dropped off the radar screen the past three years, waiting for some team to call in an emergency. 2001 Outlook: C

Bobby M. Jones (Pos: LHP, Age: 28)

	W	L	Pct.	ERA	G	GS	Sv	IP	H	BB	SO	HR	Ratio
2000	0	1	.000	4.15	11	1	0	21.2	18	14	20	2	1.48
Career	14	20	.412	5.77	80	45	0	294.2	333	169	208	40	1.70

The Mets appeared to corner the market on Bobby Joneses when they acquired Bobby M. from the Rockies last January. The lefthander may stick around if one of the other veteran southpaws leave. 2001 Outlook: C

David Lamb (Pos: 3B, Age: 25, Bats: B)

	G	AB	R	H	D	T	HR	RBI	SB	BB	SO	Avg	OBP	Slg
2000	7	5	1	1	0	0	0	0	0	1	1	.200	.333	.200
Career	62	129	19	29	5	1	1	13	0	11	19	.225	.286	.302

The Devil Rays kept Lamb on their roster for most of 1999 after selecting him in the Rule 5 draft, then waived him last February. While his defensive versatility is a plus, his batting skills aren't. He signed a minor league deal with Anaheim in the first week of December. 2001 Outlook: C

Pat Mahomes (Pos: RHP, Age: 30)

	W	L	Pct.	ERA	G	GS	Sv	IP	H	BB	SO	HR	Ratio
2000	5	3	.625	5.46	53	5	0	94.0	96	66	76	15	1.72
Career	34	31	.523	5.55	227	56	5	546.2	568	308	355	94	1.60

After winning all eight of his decisions in 1999, Mahomes wasn't nearly as impressive last season. Shaky control and too many longballs again reared their ugly head for him. 2001 Outlook: B

Jim Mann (Pos: RHP, Age: 26)

	W	L	Pct.	ERA	G	GS	Sv	IP	H	BB	SO	HR	Ratio
2000	0	0	-	10.13	2	0	0	2.2	6	1	0	1	2.63
Career	0	0	-	10.13	2	0	0	2.2	6	1	0	1	2.63

The Mets acquired Mann in the Rule 5 draft after the 1999 season. He had been with the Blue Jays organization. He's worked in middle relief for most of his professional career. He signed a minor league deal with Houston in the first week of December. 2001 Outlook: C

Joe McEwing (Pos: LF/2B/3B/CF, Age: 28, Bats: R)

	G	AB	R	H	D	T	HR	RBI	SB	BB	SO	Avg	OBP	Slg
2000	87	153	20	34	14	1	2	19	3	9	29	.222	.248	.366
Career	249	686	90	179	43	5	11	64	10	47	119	.261	.313	.386

After playing extensively with St. Louis in 1999, McEwing was traded to the Mets last March. He can fill in almost anywhere on the field, but needs to get on base more often than he did last year. 2001 Outlook: B

Ryan McGuire (Pos: RF, Age: 29, Bats: L)

	G	AB	R	H	D	T	HR	RBI	SB	BB	SO	Avg	OBP	Slg
2000	1	2	0	0	0	0	0	0	0	1	0	.000	.333	.000
Career	303	551	56	121	31	4	6	45	2	79	122	.220	.316	.323

McGuire's window of opportunity may have passed as a big league regular. He played primarily in the outfield in the minors last year, and signed a minor league deal with Florida after the season. 2001 Outlook: C

Jon Nunnally (Pos: LF, Age: 29, Bats: L)

	G	AB	R	H	D	T	HR	RBI	SB	BB	SO	Avg	OBP	Slg
2000	48	74	16	14	5	1	2	6	3	17	26	.189	.337	.365
Career	364	885	162	218	47	12	42	125	19	146	239	.246	.354	.469

With the exception of a second-half spree with the Reds in 1997, Nunnally never seemed to hit as well as his minor league numbers might indicate. He signed to play in Japan last June. 2001 Outlook: D

Bill Pulsipher (**Pos**: LHP, **Age**: 27)

	W	L	Pct.	ERA	G	GS	Sv	IP	H	BB	SO	HR	Ratio
2000	0	2	.000	12.15	2	2	0	6.2	12	6	7	1	2.70
Career	13	19	.406	5.04	64	46	0	293.0	320	118	181	39	1.49

Still trying to return to his form prior to 1996 elbow surgery, Pulsipher's second tour with the Mets wasn't a success. He was traded to Arizona last June and signed with Tampa Bay in November. 2001 Outlook: C

Jerrod Riggan (**Pos**: RHP, **Age**: 26)

	W	L	Pct.	ERA	G	GS	Sv	IP	H	BB	SO	HR	Ratio
2000	0	0	-	0.00	1	0	0	2.0	3	0	1	0	1.50
Career	0	0	-	0.00	1	0	0	2.0	3	0	1	0	1.50

Riggan finally reached Double-A at an advanced age last season and was nothing short of sensational. He'll have to prove at the next level that last year's excellence wasn't a fluke. 2001 Outlook: C

Rich Rodriguez (**Pos**: LHP, **Age**: 38)

	W	L	Pct.	ERA	G	GS	Sv	IP	H	BB	SO	HR	Ratio
2000	0	1	.000	7.78	32	0	0	37.0	59	15	18	7	2.00
Career	26	18	.591	3.75	517	2	7	581.1	583	232	350	59	1.40

After signing a two-year deal with the Mets prior to last season, Rodriguez was really rather dreadful. The Mets would already seem to have their share of venerable lefthanded relievers. 2001 Outlook: C

Dennis Springer (**Pos**: RHP, **Age**: 36)

	W	L	Pct.	ERA	G	GS	Sv	IP	H	BB	SO	HR	Ratio
2000	0	1	.000	8.74	2	2	0	11.1	20	5	5	2	2.21
Career	23	46	.333	5.23	125	95	1	635.0	682	254	288	105	1.47

After leading Florida with nearly 200 innings in 1999, Springer spent most of last season at Triple-A. He's not particularly old for a guy who throws mostly knuckleballs, so his career may linger. 2001 Outlook: C

Jorge Toca (**Pos**: 1B, **Age**: 26, **Bats**: R)

	G	AB	R	H	D	T	HR	RBI	SB	BB	SO	Avg	OBP	Slg
2000	8	7	1	3	1	0	0	4	0	0	1	.429	.429	.571
Career	12	10	1	4	1	0	0	4	0	0	3	.400	.400	.500

Toca, born in Cuba, was signed by the Mets in 1998. He can play first base or the outfield, but didn't show as much power last year as he had in 1999. He also doesn't walk as much as you'd like. 2001 Outlook: C

Jorge Velandia (**Pos**: 2B/SS, **Age**: 26, **Bats**: R)

	G	AB	R	H	D	T	HR	RBI	SB	BB	SO	Avg	OBP	Slg
2000	33	31	2	3	1	0	0	2	0	2	8	.097	.176	.129
Career	118	112	6	16	4	0	0	4	2	5	29	.143	.193	.179

The Mets obtained Velandia from Oakland in a swap for Nelson Cruz last August. Velandia offers little as a hitter, but can play either middle infield position. 2001 Outlook: C

Vance Wilson (**Pos**: C, **Age**: 28, **Bats**: R)

	G	AB	R	H	D	T	HR	RBI	SB	BB	SO	Avg	OBP	Slg
2000	4	4	0	0	0	0	0	0	0	0	2	.000	.000	.000
Career	5	4	0	0	0	0	0	0	0	0	2	.000	.000	.000

Wilson returned last season from a broken arm suffered in 1999 to play 100 games for the first time in his seven-year professional career. He displayed some decent power for a catcher. 2001 Outlook: C

New York Mets Minor League Prospects

Organization Overview:

After running away with the wild-card, the Mets went on to lose the Subway Series to the Yankees. The same success wasn't shared throughout the system in terms of developing prospects, as the depth has been somewhat depleted by trades and free-agent signings. Still, home-grown players like Benny Agbayani, rookie standout Jay Payton, team MVP Edgardo Alfonzo and postseason sparkplug Timo Perez all made an impact in the Mets' first trip to the World Series since 1986. On the farm, Alex Escobar made a triumphant return from injuries and Brian Cole continued to bloom into an intriguing player. The Mets signed a duo of first-rounders, lefthander Billy Traber and righty Bob Keppel, as compensation for losing John Olerud via free agency.

Eric Cammack

Position: P
Bats: R **Throws:** R
Ht: 6' 1" **Wt:** 185

Opening Day Age: 25
Born: 8/14/75 in Nederland, TX

Recent Statistics

	W	L	ERA	G	GS	Sv	IP	H	R	BB	SO	HR
2000 AAA Norfolk	6	2	1.70	47	0	9	63.2	38	14	31	67	2
2000 NL New York	0	0	6.30	8	0	0	10.0	7	7	10	9	1

Cammack's rise through the system has been relatively obscure since coming out of Lamar as a 13th-rounder in 1997. Pitching out of the bullpen may be the cause for his lack of mainstream notoriety, but the Mets are well aware of his accomplishments. The key to his success is mixing up a diverse four-pitch repertoire that keeps hitters guessing. Cammack deals an 89-92 MPH fastball, curveball, slider and change from a deceptive motion. Because he doesn't blow hitters away, he'll have to be fine with his command and tricky with his offspeed stuff against big league hitters. Cammack's brief stint in New York wasn't convincing, but he has a good chance to work his way into the Mets' pen this year.

Ken Chenard

Position: P
Bats: R **Throws:** R
Ht: 6' 3" **Wt:** 185

Opening Day Age: 22
Born: 8/30/78 in Apple Valley, CA

Recent Statistics

	W	L	ERA	G	GS	Sv	IP	H	R	BB	SO	HR
1999 R Kingsport	6	3	3.07	14	13	0	76.1	64	32	25	80	6
2000 A Capital City	4	5	2.86	21	21	0	94.1	75	39	48	112	2

Chenard is developing as a potential frontline pitching prospect, although the shoulder injuries that sidelined him twice during the season have raised concerns about his durability. The hard-throwing righty punched out 112 in 94.1 innings in the South Atlantic League last year using his 90-95 MPH gas, a potential plus-curveball and changeup. Injuries limited his innings, but his ability was evident as he surrendered just 75 hits. Undrafted out of high school, the Mets took a chance on him with a 46th-round draft-and-follow choice in 1998. He blossomed into a top pick at a California junior college, and the Mets signed him shortly before the '99 draft. Arm troubles continue to haunt the system's prized pitching gems, but hopefully Chenard will be spared from the knife, allowing him to progress at a rapid pace. A healthy season should catapult him atop the Mets' prospect lists.

Brian Cole

Position: OF
Bats: R **Throws:** R
Ht: 5' 9" **Wt:** 168

Opening Day Age: 22
Born: 9/28/78 in Meridian, MS

Recent Statistics

	G	AB	R	H	D	T	HR	RBI	SB	BB	SO	Avg
1999 A Capital City	125	500	97	158	41	4	18	71	50	37	77	.316
2000 A St. Lucie	91	375	73	117	26	5	15	61	54	29	51	.312
2000 AA Binghamton	46	176	31	49	9	2	4	25	15	13	28	.278

After earning *Baseball America's* Junior College Player of the Year Award in 1998, Cole went virtually unnoticed, going as an 18th-rounder in the '98 draft. He swiped 69 bags last year between the high Class-A Florida State League and the Double-A Eastern League after stealing 50 bases in '99. Cole also continues to surprise those who doubted his power potential. Despite an outstanding stolen-base success rate, Cole needs to improve his strike-zone judgment to become a better tablesetter. Rated the most exciting player in the FSL before his promotion last season, he could be ready for the majors by next year.

Alex Escobar

Position: OF
Bats: R **Throws:** R
Ht: 6' 1" **Wt:** 180

Opening Day Age: 22
Born: 9/6/78 in Valencia, VZ

Recent Statistics

	G	AB	R	H	D	T	HR	RBI	SB	BB	SO	Avg
1999 R Mets	2	8	1	3	2	0	0	1	0	1	2	.375
1999 A St. Lucie	1	3	1	2	0	0	1	3	1	1	1	.667
2000 AA Binghamton	122	437	79	126	25	7	16	67	24	57	114	.288
2000 MLE	122	419	64	108	21	5	12	55	16	39	122	.258

Prior to the 2000 season, Escobar had just one full season under his belt after signing out of Venezuela in 1995, yet he was still regarded as the Mets' best position prospect. It was that one full season ('98), however, that established him as a multi-faceted prospect worth watching. Shoulder and back injuries restricted Escobar to three games in '99, but he jumped back on track at full speed last season in Double-A, showing little effects of his layoff by ripping the Eastern League for a .487 slugging percentage. Despite his injury-riddled past and inexperience, Escobar and his five-tool potential will play in Triple-A this year, buying the Mets time to figure out a way to fit him into the crowded outfield picture by 2002.

Dicky Gonzalez

Position: P **Opening Day Age:** 22
Bats: R **Throws:** R **Born:** 12/21/78 in
Ht: 5' 11" **Wt:** 170 Bayamon, PR

Recent Statistics

	W	L	ERA	G	GS	Sv	IP	H	R	BB	SO	HR
1999 AAA Norfolk	0	1	2.70	1	1	0	6.2	5	2	1	3	0
1999 A St. Lucie	14	9	2.83	25	25	0	168.2	156	66	30	143	11
2000 AA Binghamton	13	5	3.84	26	25	0	147.2	130	75	36	138	14

Gonzalez silences skeptics with each promotion. His early success was written off because he didn't possess the size or blazing fastball to survive at higher levels. Not only did he survive the test at Double-A, he thrived. A control pitcher, he has added inches to his fastball, which can touch the 90-92 MPH range now. Changing speeds and locating his curve, slider and change is his bread-and-butter, though. His strikeout-walk ratio was nearly 4-1 last year, and he has issued just 1.7 walks per nine in 646.2 career innings. Gonzalez has answered each challenge—the next one will be Triple-A this season.

Grant Roberts

Position: P **Opening Day Age:** 23
Bats: R **Throws:** R **Born:** 9/13/77 in El
Ht: 6' 3" **Wt:** 205 Cajon, CA

Recent Statistics

	W	L	ERA	G	GS	Sv	IP	H	R	BB	SO	HR
2000 AAA Norfolk	7	8	3.38	25	25	0	157.1	154	67	63	115	6
2000 NL New York	0	0	11.57	4	1	0	7.0	11	10	4	6	0

Roberts has responded well from elbow surgery in '98, after his most dominating season. His stuff can be overpowering, with a 93-94 MPH sinking fastball, a deceptive backdoor slider and a change. But it wasn't until last year that he began to put the entire package together, posting an impressive 3.38 ERA. Roberts pitched tentatively in his major league debut, but he will be given every opportunity to join the rotation for good this spring.

Pat Strange

Position: P **Opening Day Age:** 20
Bats: R **Throws:** R **Born:** 8/23/80 in
Ht: 6' 5" **Wt:** 243 Springfield, MA

Recent Statistics

	W	L	ERA	G	GS	Sv	IP	H	R	BB	SO	HR
1999 A Capital Cty	12	5	2.63	28	21	1	154.0	138	57	29	113	4
2000 A St. Lucie	10	1	3.58	19	13	0	88.0	78	48	32	77	4
2000 AA Binghamton	4	3	4.55	10	10	0	55.1	62	30	30	36	2

Since the Mets drafted Strange in the second round in 1998, he has emerged as one of the most consistent prospects on the farm. The big righthander went 10-1 with a 3.58 ERA in the Florida State League, prompting managers around the circuit to select him as the best pitching prospect and the Mets to promote him to Double-A. Strange combines the build and stuff to overpower his opponents with the ability to locate his pitches on both sides of the plate. An intelligent, tough worker

on the mound, he fires a heavy fastball in the low 90s and changes speeds with a good breaking ball and two types of changeups. Strange stumbled a bit upon his promotion and doesn't turn 21 until near the end of the season, so the Mets won't rush him.

Tyler Walker

Position: P **Opening Day Age:** 24
Bats: R **Throws:** R **Born:** 5/15/76 in San
Ht: 6' 3" **Wt:** 225 Francisco, CA

Recent Statistics

	W	L	ERA	G	GS	Sv	IP	H	R	BB	SO	HR
1999 A St. Lucie	6	5	2.94	13	13	0	79.2	64	31	29	64	6
1999 AA Binghamton	6	4	6.22	13	13	0	68.0	78	49	32	59	11
2000 AA Binghamton	7	6	2.75	22	22	0	121.0	82	43	55	111	3
2000 AAA Norfolk	1	3	2.39	5	5	0	26.1	29	7	9	17	0

Like Dicky Gonzalez, Walker's frame doesn't scream out pitching prospect, but the big righthander's performance does. On the heels of a breakthrough season that he split between Double-A and Triple-A, Walker suffered a torn labrum and was shut down during his Arizona Fall League stint. A converted college reliever, the Mets' 1997 second-round pick overmatched the Eastern League with the combination of a low-90s sinking fastball, curveball and changeup. In truly dominant fashion, Walker allowed an amazing .191 batting average, including .159 versus lefties in Double-A. Surgery should keep him out until May, and he'll resume his climb to the bigs via Triple-A, provided there are no setbacks.

Others to Watch

Third baseman **Enrique Cruz** (19) was voted the best position prospect in the Appalachian League last year after hitting .251 with nine bombs. He excites the Mets with his live bat and above-average power potential. . . Righthander **Jeremy Griffiths** (23) presents an imposing figure on the hill at 6-foot-7, and he overpowers hitters with an easy 93-MPH fastball and an assortment of breaking pitches. He walked just 39 while fanning 138 in 128.2 innings at Class-A Capital City. . . Righthander **Rafael Lopez** (20) combined to strike out 66 in 78.1 innings last year between Rookie and Class-A stops, while walking just 13. At 6-foot-4, his live arm has the potential to add velocity onto his low-90s fastball. . . Righthander **Nick Maness** (22) showed flashes of harnessing his lively repertoire and filling into his projectable label. After allowing just 116 hits in 145.1 innings at high Class-A St. Lucie, he stood out in the Arizona Fall League with a 90-MPH fastball, curve and promising changeup. . . Another Mets young gun with arm concerns, lefthander **Neal Musser** (20) is polished with a moving high-80s fastball, good breaking ball and changeup. He demonstrated sound command and has posted a 2.06 ERA in two seasons. . . Outfielder **Marvin Seale** (21) took a major leap forward last year in the South Atlantic League by stealing 52 bases and establishing himself as a potential leadoff hitter. Still learning to switch-hit, he struck out 125 times.

Veterans Stadium

Offense

The Vet pads offensive totals a bit, as hitters tend to pick up the ball well, particularly during night games. The ball scoots to the wall quickly on the rock-hard artificial turf, guaranteeing high doubles and triples totals. One factor to consider for 2001, however—the Phils were considering natural grass field surface options during the offseason that could be implemented by opening day.

Defense

Error totals tend to be low at the Vet, as the artificial turf affords infielders true hops. It's important for the home club to utilize speedy, quick middle infielders who can cover the necessary ground to be competent turf defenders. The artificial turf has physically worn down some of the Phils' everyday players in recent seasons. Chief among them is star third baseman Scott Rolen, who is often rested in home day games following night games. Other key players have indicated their desire to get off of the artificial turf when their contracts expire.

Who It Helps the Most

Speedy, slashing line drive gap hitters like Bobby Abreu, Doug Glanville and Scott Rolen are helped most by Veterans Stadium. Balls that would be singles on grass fields skip to the wall and become doubles or triples. Fly ball pitchers who locate the ball well can thrive in the Vet. Bruce Chen and Randy Wolf fit this profile.

Who It Hurts the Most

Slow-footed infielders have difficulty getting to balls on the hard turf. Flyball pitchers who don't locate the ball well pay the price, as Paul Byrd did in 2000. Groundball pitchers like Vicente Padilla can get singled to death because of the fast surface.

Rookies & Newcomers

Jimmy Rollins is expected to win the Phils' starting shortstop job, and his style of play is tailored to an artificial turf field. His doubles and triples totals should be inflated, his error total will be minimized by the lack of bad hops, and his throwing arm is strong enough to retire hitters from deep in the hole. Reggie Taylor is another turf-style player that could make the 2001 club in a supporting role.

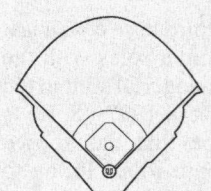

Dimensions: LF-330, LCF-371, CF-408, RCF-371, RF-330

Capacity: 62,363

Elevation: 20 feet

Surface: Turf

Foul Territory: Large

Philadelphia

Park Factors

2000 Season

	Home Games			Away Games			
	Phillies	Opp	Total	Phillies	Opp	Total	Index
G	72	72	144	72	72	144	—
Avg	.257	.264	.261	.246	.270	.258	101
AB	2392	2511	4903	2472	2348	4820	102
R	319	390	709	292	352	644	110
H	615	664	1279	609	633	1242	103
2B	147	190	337	114	115	229	145
3B	21	21	42	16	9	25	165
HR	58	88	146	63	90	153	94
BB	278	305	583	261	258	519	110
SO	518	565	1083	474	442	916	116
E	40	38	78	47	58	105	74
E-Infield	32	32	64	35	48	83	77
LHB-Avg	.266	.240	.253	.248	.282	.265	96
LHB-HR	20	26	46	12	29	41	103
RHB-Avg	.252	.278	.266	.246	.263	.254	105
RHB-HR	38	62	100	51	61	112	91

1998-2000

	Home Games			Away Games			
	Phillies	Opp	Total	Phillies	Opp	Total	Index
G	217	217	434	217	217	434	—
Avg	.270	.263	.266	.253	.269	.261	102
AB	7304	7605	14909	7552	7230	14782	101
R	1060	1131	2191	904	1080	1984	110
H	1973	1998	3971	1910	1942	3852	103
2B	415	475	890	349	390	739	119
3B	61	48	109	45	33	78	139
HR	194	272	466	179	264	443	104
BB	822	850	1672	733	752	1485	112
SO	1485	1668	3153	1452	1327	2779	112
E	120	139	259	156	163	319	81
E-Infield	105	107	212	128	129	257	82
LHB-Avg	.289	.264	.276	.253	.279	.267	104
LHB-HR	79	100	179	51	89	140	123
RHB-Avg	.259	.262	.260	.253	.262	.257	101
RHB-HR	115	172	287	128	175	303	96

2000 Rankings (National League)

- Highest double factor
- Highest strikeout factor
- Second-highest triple factor
- Second-highest walk factor
- Second-lowest error factor
- Second-lowest infield-error factor

Larry Bowa

2000 Season

Larry Bowa was the Mariners' third base coach last season, and previously held similar roles with the Phillies and Angels. His first managerial stint in the majors was with the Padres back in 1987-88. He is a gung-ho, high-intensity type that has shown trademark aggressiveness in both roles. Prone to temper tantrums as a player and in his first stint as a big league manager, he swears that he's matured. Truth be told, the Phils' brass hopes he's plenty fiery, as long as it's within reason.

Offense

Bowa likes to play the game right—hit behind the runner, throw to the right base, etc. He likes to stick with a set lineup. Expect the Phils' regulars to get a lot fewer planned days off in 2001 compared to last season. He believes in dealing with team issues behind closed doors, and will look to his everyday position players like Scott Rolen, Mike Lieberthal and Bobby Abreu to assume the mantle of leader once worn by the likes of Bowa, Bob Boone and Darren Daulton. It will be interesting to see how much patience he will have with developing players like shortstop Jimmy Rollins, who evokes a more talented version of Phillies' 1970 rookie shortstop Larry Bowa.

Pitching & Defense

Bowa is a stickler for the fundamentals. He's not likely to have a lot of patience for indifferent defense, especially from his infielders, or for bases on balls from his pitchers. Bowa is likely to respect traditional bullpen roles. One of his first decisions will be who gets the closer role, with free agents Ricky Bottalico and Jose Mesa the early favorites. Bowa not surprisingly holds defensive performance in particularly high regard. His mentoring of Jimmy Rollins will be interesting to watch.

2001 Outlook

Bowa begins a two-year deal with a team option in place for 2003. His presence will sell a few more season tickets, not an insignificant factor surrounding his hire. His baseball acumen is unquestioned. He knows how to play the game, and has never had trouble communicating. The true test will come with the inevitable adversity.

Born: 12/06/45 in Sacramento, CA

Playing Experience: 1970-1985, Phi, ChC, NYM

Managerial Experience: 2 seasons

Manager Statistics (Terry Francona)

Year	Team, Lg	W	L	Pct	GB	Finish
2000	Philadelphia, NL	65	97	.401	30.0	5th East
42 Seasons		285	363	.440	—	—

2000 Starting Pitchers by Days Rest

	<=3	4	5	6+
Phillies Starts	0	72	64	16
Phillies ERA	—	4.32	4.47	3.70
NL Avg Starts	2	80	50	21
NL ERA	5.00	4.61	4.60	5.18

2000 Situational Stats

	Terry Francona	NL Average
Hit & Run Success %	36.7	33.8
Stolen Base Success %	77.3	68.8
Platoon Pct.	52.7	53.2
Defensive Subs	14	19
High-Pitch Outings	25	14
Quick/Slow Hooks	11/19	14/16
Sacrifice Attempts	89	87

2000 Rankings—Terry Francona (National Lg)

- 1st in stolen-base percentage (77.3), fewest caught stealings of second base (25), fewest caught stealings of third base (3) and starts with over 120 pitches (25)
- 2nd in squeeze plays (7)

Bobby Abreu

Position: RF
Bats: L **Throws:** R
Ht: 6' 0" **Wt:** 197

Opening Day Age: 27
Born: 3/11/74 in Aragua, Venezuela
ML Seasons: 5
Pronunciation: uh-BRAY-oo

Philadelphia

2000 Season

Bobby Abreu continued to establish himself as one of the most versatile, productive offensive performers in the National League. He showcased an impressive combination of on-base and power skills as a No. 3 hitter for most of the season, but he also excelled as a leadoff man over a 19-game stretch late in the year. Though he struggled against lefthanded pitching average-wise, he did manage to finally club his first three career homers off of southpaws, likely signaling better things to come.

Hitting

Abreu's swing is as pure as they come. Against righthanders, he is a lethal force, working the count into his favor regularly and launching the resulting fastballs to all fields with authority. He has a much different approach against lefthanded pitching. He is content to slap the ball the other way and back through the middle for singles, only rarely attempting to pull the ball for distance. He's taking baby steps in this area, and will make greater strides in the near future. Once he does, he'll be a batting title contender and 30-plus homer player.

Baserunning & Defense

Abreu is deceptively fast. He has a long, loping stride, but he can get up to full speed extremely quickly. He's also an instinctive baserunner and a high-percentage basestealer with an innate feel for situational play. Defensively, he has solid range for a right fielder. He ranked among National League leaders in assists with 13, just three behind leader Peter Bergeron.

2001 Outlook

Abreu is a budding superstar whose game will reach a truly rarified level when he learns to drive the ball for distance against lefthanders. He'll benefit from the departure of manager Terry Francona, who chose to publicly berate him late in the 2000 season. Abreu has resisted the Phils' attempts to lock him into a long-term contract, and it is proving to be a wise strategy. Look for a career year from Abreu—a .350-30-120 monster—within the next couple of years.

Overall Statistics

	G	AB	R	H	D	T	HR	RBI	SB	BB	SO	Avg	OBP	Slg
2000	154	576	103	182	42	10	25	79	28	100	116	.316	.416	.554
Career	531	1829	312	572	117	29	65	273	81	316	413	.313	.413	.515

Where He Hits the Ball

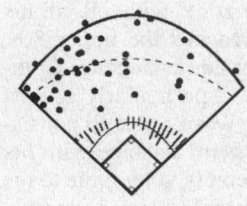 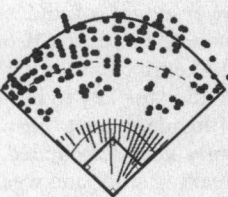

Vs. LHP   **Vs. RHP**

2000 Situational Stats

	AB	H	HR	RBI	Avg		AB	H	HR	RBI	Avg
Home	284	96	14	41	.338	LHP	136	33	3	10	.243
Road	292	86	11	38	.295	RHP	440	149	22	69	.339
First Half	306	100	10	42	.327	Sc Pos	125	30	6	50	.240
Scnd Half	270	82	15	37	.304	Clutch	89	27	4	13	.303

2000 Rankings (National League)

- 2nd in pitches seen (2,833) and highest percentage of pitches taken (63.7)
- 3rd in fielding percentage in right field (.989) and lowest percentage of swings on the first pitch (11.1)
- 4th in triples, most pitches seen per plate appearance (4.17) and on-base percentage vs. righthanded pitchers (.445)
- 5th in batting average vs. righthanded pitchers
- Led the Phillies in batting average, runs scored, hits, doubles, triples, total bases (319), caught stealing (8), walks, intentional walks (9), times on base (283), GDPs (12), pitches seen (2,833), slugging percentage, on-base percentage and most pitches seen per plate appearance (4.17)

Kent Bottenfield

2000 Season

Following a career year that saw him post an 18-7 record for the Cardinals, Kent Bottenfield was dealt to the Angels prior to last season along with Adam Kennedy for Jim Edmonds. He got off to a 7-8, 5.71 start before the Angels sent him to the Phillies for Ron Gant. He was only marginally more effective for Philadelphia. He then sprained an ankle in late September, costing him his last two starts.

Pitching

Bottenfield is a journeyman-type pitcher who cut his major league teeth as a setup man. He still carries the tools that served him well in that role—a lively, sinking fastball and an ability to navigate the lower edges of the strike zone with all of his pitches. His fastball only reaches the upper 80s, and he mixes it with a slider and changeup. Command is the key to his success, particularly against lefthanders. Last season, he wasn't able to consistently keep lefthanded hitters off balance with his breaking stuff, and was extremely vulnerable to the longball against them. Bottenfield is a durable hurler that can go well beyond 100 pitches when locating the ball well.

Defense & Hitting

Bottenfield's size makes him a frequent target for bunts. In fact, in his first start for the Phillies last season, a barrage of bunts turned an otherwise solid effort into a loss. He controls the running game quite well, courtesy of a compact motion that he often supplements with a slide-step delivery with men on base. He is an average hitter for a pitcher, and is reliable at laying down sacrifice bunts.

2001 Outlook

Bottenfield became a free agent at the end of the 2000 season, but the Phillies had expressed interest in retaining his services for the right price. At best, he is a bottom-of-the-rotation starter capable of keeping his club in contention deep into ballgames. Bottenfield needs to get in better physical condition, however, and avoid the nagging injuries that dogged him during the second half of 2000.

Position: SP
Bats: R **Throws:** R
Ht: 6' 3" **Wt:** 240

Opening Day Age: 32
Born: 11/14/68 in Portland, OR
ML Seasons: 8

Overall Statistics

	W	L	Pct.	ERA	G	GS	Sv	IP	H	BB	SO	HR	Ratio
2000	8	10	.444	5.40	29	29	0	171.2	185	77	106	30	1.53
Career	44	44	.500	4.43	279	107	9	859.2	889	369	527	107	1.46

How Often He Throws Strikes

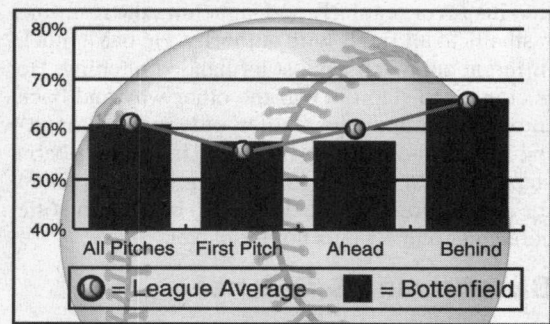

= League Average = Bottenfield

2000 Situational Stats

	W	L	ERA	Sv	IP		AB	H	HR	RBI	Avg
Home	4	7	5.71	0	110.1	LHB	352	107	13	53	.304
Road	4	3	4.84	0	61.1	RHB	324	78	17	50	.241
First Half	5	7	5.72	0	102.1	Sc Pos	139	44	2	62	.317
Scnd Half	3	3	4.93	0	69.1	Clutch	31	8	1	3	.258

2000 Rankings (National League)

- 10th in fewest GDPs induced per GDP situation (3.3%)

Jeff Brantley

2000 Season

After Jeff Brantley missed most of the 1999 season with a torn labrum in his throwing shoulder, Philadelphia signed him to an incentive-laden $250,000 contract almost as an afterthought. The team never dreamed that Mike Jackson would require shoulder surgery that would end his season before it began. Brantley ended up serving as the Phils' closer for the vast majority of 2000, replacing Wayne Gomes in May. But don't be fooled by Brantley's saves total—batters hit .288 and slugged .491 against him, with 12 homers in only 55.1 innings.

Pitching

Even in his prime, Brantley relied more on a resilient arm and a bulldog demeanor than on raw stuff. Today, the arm resiliency and most of the stuff are gone, leaving only the nasty makeup. He often struggled to reach 85 MPH with his fastball last season. He also features a splitter that functions as his chief strikeout pitch, a slider that he will use when ahead in the count against righties and a changeup that is mostly for show. With his stuff missing on many occasions in 2000, command became a problem for the first time since the early stages of his career. He fell behind in the count regularly, and the resulting 2-0 and 3-1 fastballs often wound up on the other side of the wall.

Defense & Hitting

Brantley is not particularly athletic at this stage in his career, but he remains an adequate fielder at his position. He doesn't hold runners on base particularly well, despite the fact that teams often opted to play for the big inning against him. He is not asked to hit very often, and won't be asked to anytime soon.

2001 Outlook

It will continue to be a year-to-year proposition for Brantley. He fully believes he can remain healthy and be a full-time major league closer, though he is unlikely to draw any more than a spring training invitation and a make-good minor league contract from any club. The Phillies did not offer him arbitration, and it remains unlikely that they will extend an offer, given that they signed both Ricky Bottalico and Jose Mesa in the offseason.

Position: RP
Bats: R **Throws:** R
Ht: 5'10" **Wt:** 197

Opening Day Age: 37
Born: 9/5/63 in Florence, AL
ML Seasons: 13

Overall Statistics

	W	L	Pct.	ERA	G	GS	Sv	IP	H	BB	SO	HR	Ratio
2000	2	7	.222	5.86	55	0	23	55.1	64	29	57	12	1.68
Career	43	45	.489	3.35	597	18	172	838.1	728	357	717	100	1.29

How Often He Throws Strikes

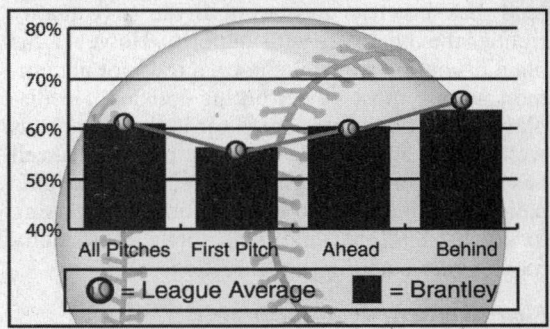

2000 Situational Stats

	W	L	ERA	Sv	IP		AB	H	HR	RBI	Avg
Home	2	3	3.82	14	35.1	LHB	103	30	2	19	.291
Road	0	4	9.45	9	20.0	RHB	119	34	10	17	.286
First Half	1	2	5.13	13	26.1	Sc Pos	48	16	0	23	.333
Scnd Half	1	5	6.52	10	29.0	Clutch	145	39	6	26	.269

2000 Rankings (National League)

- 3rd in relief losses (7) and highest relief ERA (5.86)
- 4th in fewest GDPs induced per GDP situation (1.9%)
- 5th in most baserunners allowed per nine innings in relief (15.5)
- 8th in lowest save percentage (82.1) and highest batting average allowed in relief (.288)
- Led the Phillies in saves, games finished (47), save opportunities (28), save percentage (82.1), blown saves (5), relief losses (7) and most strikeouts per nine innings in relief (9.3)

Pat Burrell

2000 Season

On May 23, Pat Burrell finally had his long-awaited major league coming-out party, and he certainly did not disappoint. His second major league hit was his only triple of the season, a laser shot at Enron Field that almost hit the flagpole in center. He was batting a meager .189 on June 16, but then went on a 23-for-60 tear that raised his average to .276 by July 2. Pat the Bat had arrived. Just ask Armando Benitez, who yielded a pair of homers to him during that streak.

Hitting

The ball simply explodes off of Burrell's bat to all fields. He focuses on pulling lefthanders and already has shown an uncanny ability to drive quality righties the other way with authority. However, his plate discipline was quite poor, a trait not uncommon among most power-hitting rookies. He displayed a particular weakness for high fastballs, as well as low and outside breaking pitches. Burrell has a proven minor league track record of extreme patience at the plate, so it would not be surprising to see his strikeout and walk totals consistently move in more appropriate directions.

Baserunning & Defense

Burrell remains quite slow, but he has worked hard over the past few offseasons to build his flexibility and first-step quickness. He'll never be a basestealer, but now is nimble enough to function well in the outfield. He appeared quite uncomfortable defensively in his two months as a first baseman, but he played quite well after his move to the outfield. He showed only adequate range, but he has a very strong throwing arm.

2001 Outlook

The sky is the limit for Burrell, and he should begin to take steps towards his peak in 2001. He was a bit old for a marquee rookie last season, so it's not a stretch to expect him to jump into the 35-40 homer club right away. He'll likely bat No. 5, and if a true leadoff man is introduced in Philadelphia, Burrell could be part of a heart-of-the-order combo that generates scads of runs in 2001 and beyond.

Position: 1B/LF
Bats: R **Throws:** R
Ht: 6' 4" **Wt:** 225

Opening Day Age: 24
Born: 10/10/76 in Eureka Springs, AR
ML Seasons: 1

Overall Statistics

	G	AB	R	H	D	T	HR	RBI	SB	BB	SO	Avg	OBP	Slg
2000	111	408	57	106	27	1	18	79	0	63	139	.260	.359	.463
Career	111	408	57	106	27	1	18	79	0	63	139	.260	.359	.463

Where He Hits the Ball

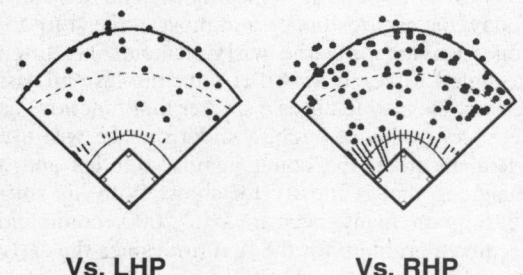

Vs. LHP   Vs. RHP

2000 Situational Stats

	AB	H	HR	RBI	Avg		AB	H	HR	RBI	Avg
Home	202	54	7	38	.267	LHP	85	24	5	21	.282
Road	206	52	11	41	.252	RHP	323	82	13	58	.254
First Half	156	41	6	33	.263	Sc Pos	134	41	4	60	.306
Scnd Half	252	65	12	46	.258	Clutch	66	16	4	15	.242

2000 Rankings (National League)

- 1st in batting average with the bases loaded (.727)
- 5th in strikeouts
- 8th in lowest percentage of swings put into play (34.3)
- 9th in highest percentage of swings that missed (27.8)
- Led the Phillies in strikeouts, batting average with runners in scoring position and batting average with the bases loaded (.727)
- Led NL first basemen in strikeouts and batting average with the bases loaded (.727)

Bruce Chen

2000 Season

Longtime top Atlanta pitching prospect Bruce Chen finally got his chance to take a regular turn in a major league rotation after being sent to the Phillies on July 12 in the Andy Ashby deal. Chen's numbers were better with the Braves, but his performance with the Phils was more impressive. He consistently pitched deep into ballgames, and would have posted much better numbers if not for poor run support and a couple of particularly poor September outings. By season's end, he had passed Randy Wolf as the Phils' most reliable starting pitcher.

Pitching

Chen is a strikeout pitcher, but not a power pitcher. His fastball checks in at only 86-88 MPH, but he mixes it well with an above-average curveball and a solid changeup, consistently painting the corners with all three. He is an extreme flyball pitcher, who can get into deep trouble when he leaves his fastball up in the strike zone. Though he held righties to an impressive .235 average last season, they did crush 15 homers off of him in only 388 at-bats. Chen's ability to maintain low pitch counts makes him a complete-game candidate.

Defense & Hitting

Chen doesn't hold runners on base particularly well for a lefthander, though he has made some strides in that area. After allowing six steals in only 51 innings in 1999, he allowed the same number in 134 innings last season. He's fairly athletic on the mound and fields his position well. At bat, he's one of the worst to ever come to the plate. He's an .042 career hitter with 30 strikeouts in 48 career at-bats.

2001 Outlook

The acquisition of Chen was a major coup for the Phillies. He possesses all of the attributes of a winning big league starter, and won't turn 24 until the middle of the 2001 season. If he can moderate his vulnerability to the longball, especially later in starts as he begins to tire, he could be a big winner and potential staff ace. A run at 15 wins in 2001 is a very reachable goal.

Position: RP/SP
Bats: B **Throws:** L
Ht: 6' 2" **Wt:** 210

Opening Day Age: 23
Born: 6/19/77 in Panama City, Panama
ML Seasons: 3

Philadelphia

Overall Statistics

	W	L	Pct.	ERA	G	GS	Sv	IP	H	BB	SO	HR	Ratio
2000	7	4	.636	3.29	37	15	0	134.0	116	46	112	18	1.21
Career	11	6	.647	3.90	57	26	0	205.1	177	82	174	32	1.26

How Often He Throws Strikes

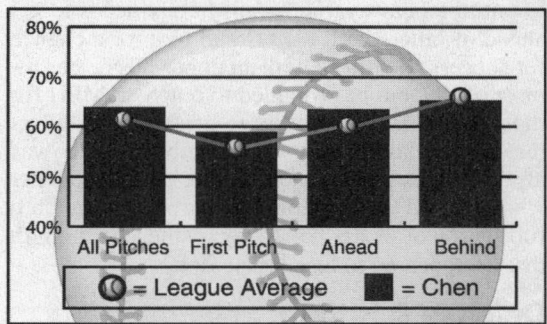

2000 Situational Stats

	W	L	ERA	Sv	IP		AB	H	HR	RBI	Avg
Home	3	2	4.11	0	65.2	LHB	112	25	3	9	.223
Road	4	2	2.50	0	68.1	RHB	388	91	15	42	.235
First Half	4	0	2.50	0	39.2	Sc Pos	100	17	4	29	.170
Scnd Half	3	4	3.63	0	94.1	Clutch	47	10	0	2	.213

2000 Rankings (National League)

- Led the Phillies in lowest batting average allowed vs. righthanded batters (.232) and lowest batting average allowed in relief with runners in scoring position (.175)

Omar Daal

Position: SP
Bats: L **Throws:** L
Ht: 6' 3" **Wt:** 195

Opening Day Age: 29
Born: 3/1/72 in
Maracaibo, Venezuela
ML Seasons: 8
Pronunciation: DOLL

2000 Season

Nightmare City. Omar Daal went from a 16-win 1999 season that included a playoff start to a September 2000 sideshow that featured Brian Kingman—the majors' last 20-loss guy—comically following Daal from town to town, praying that he wouldn't lose his 20th game and interrupt Kingman's 15 minutes of fame. Daal obliged, earning a quality no-decision and a win in his last two starts to finish at 4-19. He pitched horribly for the Diamondbacks and only slightly better for the Phillies after the July 26 Curt Schilling trade.

Pitching

Daal relies heavily on his curveball and changeup to put hitters away, but he absolutely needs to get ahead of hitters with his fastball to have a chance for success. He did so with an upper-80s heater for most of '99, but he struggled to reach 85 MPH for most of 2000. His inability to get ahead of hitters turned him alternately into a nibbler who was afraid to walk hitters, and a batting-practice pitcher who allowed 26 homers. Daal expects to pitch a full season of winter ball to regain the arm strength that he appeared to lose last season.

Defense & Hitting

Daal has quick reflexes and is an above-average defender on the mound. He controls the running game extremely well. He has a deceptive move to first base that causes runners to rarely even try to steal on him. Only two basestealers were successful in six attempts last season. Daal is an exceptional hitter that can hit a mistake fastball for distance. He's a solid bunter that handles the bat well.

2001 Outlook

The Phils made a mutually beneficial decision when they tore up Daal's existing contract, instead guaranteeing a much lower amount ($2.75 million) for 2001 and adding a club option for $4.5 million in 2002. The Phils need starting pitching, and if Daal can return to anything even resembling his 1999 form, he'll be worth the investment. The addition of just a few MPH on his fastball should again make him a respectable mid-rotation starter.

Overall Statistics

	W	L	Pct.	ERA	G	GS	Sv	IP	H	BB	SO	HR	Ratio
2000	4	19	.174	6.14	32	28	0	167.0	208	72	96	26	1.68
Career	40	51	.440	4.49	302	92	1	758.0	775	301	541	83	1.42

How Often He Throws Strikes

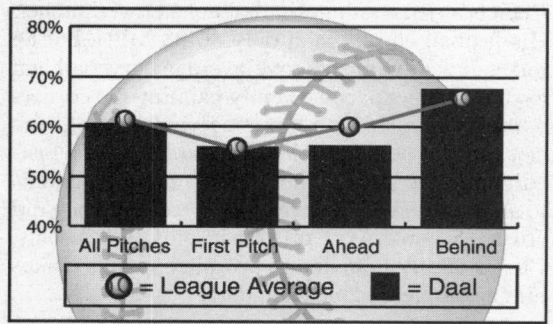

= League Average = Daal

2000 Situational Stats

	W	L	ERA	Sv	IP		AB	H	HR	RBI	Avg
Home	3	10	6.91	0	86.0	LHB	121	36	6	28	.298
Road	1	9	5.33	0	81.0	RHB	561	172	20	90	.307
First Half	2	10	7.36	0	91.2	Sc Pos	175	60	7	91	.343
Scnd Half	2	9	4.66	0	75.1	Clutch	36	13	2	3	.361

2000 Rankings (National League)

- 1st in losses (19) and lowest winning percentage (.174)
- 2nd in errors at pitcher (4), highest ERA (6.14), highest on-base percentage allowed (.376) and highest ERA at home (6.91)
- 3rd in highest batting average allowed (.305), least run support per nine innings (3.9) and highest batting average allowed with runners in scoring position (.343)
- Led the Phillies in losses (9)

Doug Glanville

2000 Season

Along with Ruben Rivera and Marquis Grissom, Doug Glanville was one of the weakest offensive outfielders in the National League, largely due to his utter lack of on-base skills. In April and May of 1999, Glanville walked 27 times, but he has walked just 52 times since. On August 1, 2000, he woke up with a .260 average, a .294 on-base percentage and .345 slugging percentage, before stepping it up in garbage time. His leadoff role finally was taken from him in August, likely for good.

Hitting

Glanville swings early and often. He has put the first pitch in play a total of 147 times in the past two years, a very high total for a leadoff man. Early in his excellent 1999 season, he appeared to be grasping the nature of a leadoff hitter's role, working the count more often. He has seemingly given up on that facet of the game, and on many occasions admitted to not being one of those "high on-base percentage guys" while being interviewed last season. He occasionally drives the ball for distance from gap-to-gap, usually on fastballs, underscoring the incremental benefit that working the count would have upon his offensive game.

Baserunning & Defense

Glanville has above-average raw speed and solid baserunning instincts. He is one of the more prolific basestealers in the major leagues today, usually with one of the higher success rates. Defensively, he has shown impressive range in the past but appeared to be a bit off of his game in 2000. His jumps on balls hit into the gap seemed a step slow, and he appeared to skimp on hustle on occasion. His range and arm are slightly above average for a center fielder.

2001 Outlook

Glanville was the most attractive piece of trade bait possessed by the Phils entering the offseason. He conclusively has proven that he is not a leadoff man, and Philadelphia might look to deal him for one, or for pitching help. He'd be best suited as a number six or seven hitter on a deeper offensive club that values his complementary skills.

Position: CF
Bats: R **Throws:** R
Ht: 6' 2" **Wt:** 172

Opening Day Age: 30
Born: 8/25/70 in Hackensack, NJ
ML Seasons: 5

Philadelphia

Overall Statistics

	G	AB	R	H	D	T	HR	RBI	SB	BB	SO	Avg	OBP	Slg
2000	154	637	89	175	27	6	8	52	31	31	76	.275	.307	.374
Career	657	2500	385	730	120	25	32	219	109	148	304	.292	.333	.398

Where He Hits the Ball

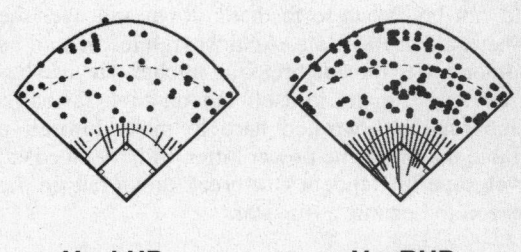

Vs. LHP   **Vs. RHP**

2000 Situational Stats

	AB	H	HR	RBI	Avg		AB	H	HR	RBI	Avg
Home	315	87	3	20	.276	LHP	139	33	1	13	.237
Road	322	88	5	32	.273	RHP	498	142	7	39	.285
First Half	349	92	5	29	.264	Sc Pos	129	33	1	41	.256
Scnd Half	288	83	3	23	.288	Clutch	105	24	1	9	.229

2000 Rankings (National League)

- 2nd in lowest on-base percentage vs. lefthanded pitchers (.285)
- 3rd in at-bats, singles, lowest on-base percentage, lowest on-base percentage for a leadoff hitter (.312) and lowest slugging percentage vs. lefthanded pitchers (.302)
- 6th in fielding percentage in center field (.990) and lowest slugging percentage
- 7th in stolen bases and errors in center field (4)
- 9th in sacrifice bunts (12), bunts in play (19) and lowest batting average vs. lefthanded pitchers
- 10th in plate appearances (689) and stolen-base percentage (79.5)
- Led the Phillies in at-bats, singles, sacrifice bunts (12), sacrifice flies (7) and stolen bases

Mike Lieberthal

2000 Season

Mike Lieberthal earned an All-Star Game berth, while pacing the Phillies in homers and RBI for most of the season's first half. He was bedeviled by injuries for most of the second half, however, first spraining an ankle and then undergoing surgery on September 13 to remove bone spurs from his right elbow. After the break, Lieberthal batted a puny .210 with only two homers in 100 at-bats.

Hitting

Lieberthal is an aggressive hitter who combines exceptional extra-base power for a catcher with the ability to make consistent contact. He is lethal against lefthanded pitching and is content to spank lefties' breaking pitches the other way for singles. He can lay waste to fastballs down and over the inner half of the plate. Against righties he can be vulnerable to outside breaking pitches. He also has a tendency to get himself out on high fastballs. Lieberthal has worked hard to make himself a viable major league power hitter. Still, he needs to overcome his tendency to break down late in the season to become a true star.

Baserunning & Defense

Lieberthal is not a basestealing threat, but he does run fairly well for a catcher and isn't afraid to take the extra base when the situation dictates. He is one of the most underrated defensive catchers in the game. Only 44 baserunners stole successfully against him last season. He handles pitchers well, according to no less an authority than the ornery Curt Schilling, who questioned those skills early in his career.

2001 Outlook

Lieberthal is one of the central pieces of the Phils' nucleus. He's signed through 2002, with the club holding a $7.25 million option for 2003. It is no coincidence that Philadelphia has fallen apart at about the same time he physically broke down in both 1999 and 2000. For him to truly be the top-flight catcher he can be, Lieberthal needs to reach a level of physical conditioning that will enable him to carry a 130-game workload without incident.

Position: C
Bats: R **Throws:** R
Ht: 6' 0" **Wt:** 190

Opening Day Age: 29
Born: 1/18/72 in Glendale, CA
ML Seasons: 7
Pronunciation: LEE-ber-thal

Overall Statistics

	G	AB	R	H	D	T	HR	RBI	SB	BB	SO	Avg	OBP	Slg
2000	108	389	55	108	30	0	15	71	2	40	53	.278	.352	.470
Career	563	1959	265	528	118	6	82	321	7	163	299	.270	.331	.461

Where He Hits the Ball

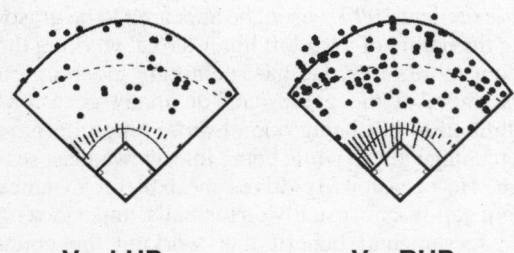

Vs. LHP   **Vs. RHP**

2000 Situational Stats

	AB	H	HR	RBI	Avg		AB	H	HR	RBI	Avg
Home	199	52	8	42	.261	LHP	80	28	4	19	.350
Road	190	56	7	29	.295	RHP	309	80	11	52	.259
First Half	289	87	13	56	.301	Sc Pos	122	33	5	56	.270
Scnd Half	100	21	2	15	.210	Clutch	70	17	4	14	.243

2000 Rankings (National League)

- 2nd in batting average on a 3-2 count (.459) and lowest cleanup slugging percentage (.399)
- 3rd in fielding percentage at catcher (.994)
- 4th in lowest percentage of extra bases taken as a runner (27.9)
- Led the Phillies in GDPs (12) and batting average on a 3-2 count (.459)
- Led NL catchers in batting average on a 3-2 count (.459) and lowest percentage of swings that missed (15.9)

Robert Person

Position: SP
Bats: R **Throws:** R
Ht: 6' 0" **Wt:** 194

Opening Day Age: 31
Born: 10/6/69 in St. Louis, MO
ML Seasons: 6

2000 Season

At age 30, Robert Person pitched enough innings to qualify for an ERA title for the first time in his career last season. He battled shoulder soreness throughout most of the season's first half, and was on the disabled list with an injured right shoulder from June 19 through the All-Star break. His stuff remained intact throughout—he was one of the tougher pitchers to hit in the National League, limiting hitters to a .229 average.

Pitching

Person is a straight-ahead power pitcher. He relies heavily on a low to mid-90s fastball and a knee-buckling slider that he often uses as his out pitch. When he is getting ahead of hitters, he can be downright scary. However, hitters wisely tend to be defensive against Person, who usually obliges them by running a higher than average number of deep counts. He often approaches 100 pitches by the fifth inning, and his humble average of just over six innings per start last season was easily the best of his career. His ability to overmatch lefties suggests that his upside is quite high. It's a testament to the quality of his repertoire that as the most prolific flyball pitcher in the National League last year, he only gave up 13 home runs in 173.1 innings.

Defense & Hitting

Person has a deliberate delivery that enables basestealers to take advantage of him. He allowed 12 steals last season, and nine in 10 attempts in 148 innings in 1999. He is athletic, but he's often out of position to make plays on balls hit back through the middle. He's basically an automatic out at the plate.

2001 Outlook

The Phillies are counting on Person to take a regular turn in their rotation in 2001. In fact, they will lean on him heavily in 2001, as the other top three holdover starters—Bruce Chen, Randy Wolf and Omar Daal—all are lefthanded. Considering his age, it's difficult to envision Person stepping up his game above its current level. Still, he should give the Phillies 10-12 wins and 160-180 representative innings per season in the near term.

Overall Statistics

	W	L	Pct.	ERA	G	GS	Sv	IP	H	BB	SO	HR	Ratio
2000	9	7	.563	3.63	28	28	0	173.1	144	95	164	13	1.38
Career	32	30	.516	4.62	150	86	8	589.2	544	299	519	82	1.43

How Often He Throws Strikes

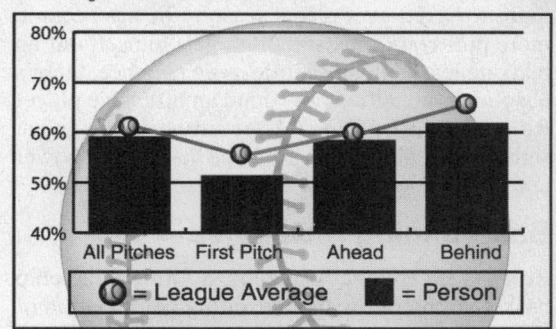

= League Average   = Person

2000 Situational Stats

	W	L	ERA	Sv	IP		AB	H	HR	RBI	Avg
Home	6	2	3.28	0	96.0	LHB	287	51	6	24	.178
Road	3	5	4.07	0	77.1	RHB	342	93	7	40	.272
First Half	5	2	3.17	0	88.0	Sc Pos	153	29	1	47	.190
Scnd Half	4	5	4.11	0	85.1	Clutch	27	8	0	5	.296

2000 Rankings (National League)

- 1st in lowest groundball/flyball ratio allowed (0.7)
- 2nd in most pitches thrown per batter (4.14)
- 3rd in lowest batting average allowed with runners in scoring position
- 4th in fewest home runs allowed per nine innings (.68) and lowest batting average allowed vs. lefthanded batters
- 5th in highest walks per nine innings (4.9)
- Led the Phillies in ERA, walks allowed, strikeouts, wild pitches (10), pickoff throws (87), stolen bases allowed (12), runners caught stealing (8), lowest batting average allowed (.229), lowest slugging percentage allowed (.372) and lowest on-base percentage allowed (.332)

Scott Rolen

2000 Season

As he was in 1999, Scott Rolen was productive on a per at-bat basis last season but saw his campaign shortened significantly by nagging back and ankle injuries. He spent two weeks on the disabled list for the latter injury beginning in late May, and had to frequently rest for the former, generally not playing day games after night games on artificial turf. His walk total dropped to a career low last season, and has been cut almost in half since 1998.

Hitting

When he's locked in, Rolen will work the count and crush the resulting fastballs with authority to all fields. However, as his patience has increasingly wavered over recent seasons, he has become more pull-conscious and often gets himself out on bad pitches. With just a little more patience, there's absolutely no telling how good an offensive player Rolen could become. After struggling against righthanded pitching in 1999, he hit for both power and average against them last season.

Baserunning & Defense

Rolen is exceptionally athletic, a former blue-chip basketball recruit with an exciting combination of size and speed. He is a borderline reckless baserunner who has a knack for knowing when to take the extra base, though his lingering back soreness has made him less of a factor as a basestealer. He still had a solid 88.9 percent success rate, picking his spots well. He is hands down the best defensive third baseman in the game. He has exceptional first-step quickness, a cannon arm, and the range of a shortstop.

2001 Outlook

Rolen's back is the key. If he continues to require rest 1-2 days per week, he'll remain a very good 110-120 game player. If he can put his injury behind him, so to speak, and work the count the way he did in 1997 and '98, Rolen could emerge as one of the brightest stars in the game. The 2001 season likely is a crossroads year. Look for Rolen to break loose and possibly price himself out of the Phils' future plans with a massive all-around campaign.

Position: 3B
Bats: R **Throws:** R
Ht: 6' 4" **Wt:** 226

Opening Day Age: 25
Born: 4/4/75 in Jasper, IN
ML Seasons: 5
Pronunciation: ROH-len

Overall Statistics

	G	AB	R	H	D	T	HR	RBI	SB	BB	SO	Avg	OBP	Slg
2000	128	483	88	144	32	6	26	89	8	51	99	.298	.370	.551
Career	593	2196	385	623	147	14	108	386	50	300	519	.284	.375	.511

Where He Hits the Ball

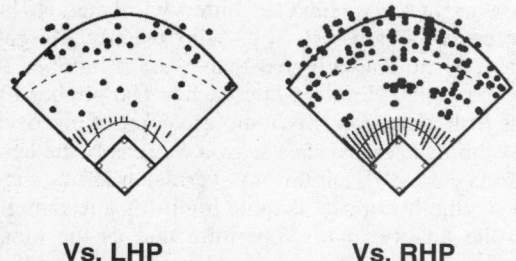

Vs. LHP   **Vs. RHP**

2000 Situational Stats

	AB	H	HR	RBI	Avg		AB	H	HR	RBI	Avg
Home	220	72	12	48	.327	LHP	106	30	8	20	.283
Road	263	72	14	41	.274	RHP	377	114	18	69	.302
First Half	255	76	16	52	.298	Sc Pos	161	46	7	63	.286
Scnd Half	228	68	10	37	.298	Clutch	73	28	7	17	.384

2000 Rankings (National League)

- 2nd in batting average in the clutch and fielding percentage at third base (.971)
- 6th in fewest GDPs per GDP situation (3.7%)
- Led the Phillies in home runs, RBI, intentional walks (9), HR frequency (18.6 ABs per HR), fewest GDPs per GDP situation (3.7%), batting average in the clutch, batting average on an 0-2 count (.276), cleanup slugging percentage (.566) and batting average with two strikes (.246)
- Led NL third basemen in triples, fewest GDPs per GDP situation (3.7%), batting average in the clutch, batting average on an 0-2 count (.276) and slugging percentage vs. righthanded pitchers (.544)

Jimmy Rollins

2000 Season

Jimmy Rollins spent a full season as the Phils' Triple-A shortstop before starting 11 games at shortstop in the majors in the second half of September. The 1996 second-round pick's batting average lingered below the Mendoza Line in the minors for most of the season's first two months, but he rebounded to bat .274 overall with 24 steals and substantial extra-base pop. He was one of the last cuts from the US Olympic team, and then acquitted himself quite well in his brief trial with the parent club.

Hitting

Despite his diminutive stature, this switch-hitter is far from a mere spray hitter. Rollins drives the ball to all fields, routinely reaching the gaps. He is equally adept from both sides of the plate, which should smooth his offensive transition to everyday major league play. Still, he has never batted .300 or walked more than 51 times in a professional season, indicating that he is not the prototypical lead-off man at this stage in his development. It's highly likely that he will exceed those walk and batting average standards once he matures. He could benefit from hitting the ball on the ground more often.

Baserunning & Defense

Rollins' raw speed is enhanced by both his innate feel for the game and his ability to consistently get a quality jump. He projects as an eventual 30-40 stolen base threat. He has above-average range and his arm strength is adequate, but he's not a likely future Gold Glover at shortstop. A couple of minor league levels behind him resides Anderson Machado, a higher-ceiling defensive prospect who could eventually move Rollins over to second base.

2001 Outlook

The Phils would love to see Rollins take both the starting shortstop job and leadoff spot in the batting order and run with them in spring training. That's a pretty tough daily double for a 22-year-old, but he appears to be up to the task. Look for Rollins to rank among the top National League Rookie of the Year candidates in 2001, and serve as a catalyst for a rejuvenated Phillies offense.

Position: SS
Bats: B **Throws:** R
Ht: 5' 8" **Wt:** 160

Opening Day Age: 22
Born: 11/27/78 in Oakland, CA
ML Seasons: 1

Overall Statistics

	G	AB	R	H	D	T	HR	RBI	SB	BB	SO	Avg	OBP	Slg
2000	14	53	5	17	1	1	0	5	3	2	7	.321	.345	.377
Career	14	53	5	17	1	1	0	5	3	2	7	.321	.345	.377

Where He Hits the Ball

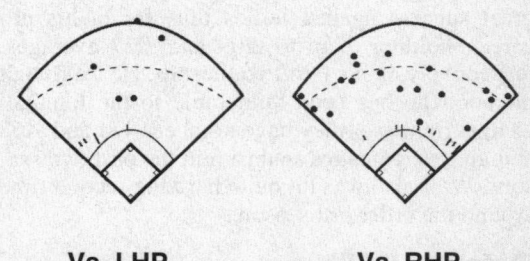

Vs. LHP **Vs. RHP**

2000 Situational Stats

	AB	H	HR	RBI	Avg		AB	H	HR	RBI	Avg
Home	26	10	0	3	.385	LHP	12	4	0	0	.333
Road	27	7	0	2	.259	RHP	41	13	0	5	.317
First Half	0	0	0	0	-	Sc Pos	13	5	0	5	.385
Scnd Half	53	17	0	5	.321	Clutch	9	2	0	1	.222

2000 Rankings (National League)

- Did not rank near the top or bottom in any category

Randy Wolf

2000 Season

Randy Wolf took the ball every fifth day in his first full major league season, and was one of the more effective starting pitchers in the National League before he hit a rough patch in August. He allowed 46 hits and 16 walks in 26.1 innings in that fateful month, but to his credit, he righted the ship and finished strong in September. He paced the team in wins, innings and finished second in strikeouts.

Pitching

Wolf combines a high-80s fastball with an excellent changeup and a solid curveball, though he needs to consistently change speeds and work the edges of the plate. When he struggles, it's generally a result of poor location of his fastball. He has had great success against lefties thus far in his pro career, holding them to .209 and .227 averages, respectively, in his first two seasons. He's a flyball pitcher who has been vulnerable to the longball against righties—they have notched .474 and .463 slugging percentages against him the past two seasons. Wolf also was hit quite hard the second time around the order last season.

Defense & Hitting

Wolf is quite athletic on the mound, and fields his position well. He has a compact delivery and an above-average move to first base, enabling him to effectively eliminate the running game. A .207 career hitter with some extra-base pop, he is not an automatic out at the plate.

2001 Outlook

Wolf is still a kid at 24, but has made strides towards becoming one of the premier lefthanded starters in the NL. He's already established himself as a seven-inning horse who consistently keeps his club in ballgames. Look for him to advance along the learning curve a bit more in 2001, with a 15-win season a reasonable possibility. Barring a major offseason acquisition, Wolf could be the Phils' Opening Day starter.

Position: SP
Bats: L **Throws:** L
Ht: 6' 0" **Wt:** 194

Opening Day Age: 24
Born: 8/22/76 in Canoga Park, CA
ML Seasons: 2

Overall Statistics

	W	L	Pct.	ERA	G	GS	Sv	IP	H	BB	SO	HR	Ratio
2000	11	9	.550	4.36	32	32	0	206.1	210	83	160	25	1.42
Career	17	18	.486	4.80	54	53	0	328.0	336	150	276	45	1.48

How Often He Throws Strikes

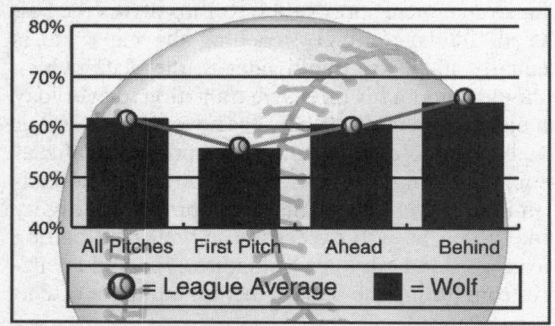

⊙ = League Average ■ = Wolf

2000 Situational Stats

	W	L	ERA	Sv	IP		AB	H	HR	RBI	Avg
Home	5	4	5.16	0	97.2	LHB	110	25	1	12	.227
Road	6	5	3.64	0	108.2	RHB	670	185	24	89	.276
First Half	8	5	3.68	0	115.0	Sc Pos	193	51	6	76	.264
Scnd Half	3	4	5.22	0	91.1	Clutch	65	19	3	15	.292

2000 Rankings (National League)

- 4th in lowest groundball/flyball ratio allowed (0.8)
- 5th in lowest ERA on the road
- 6th in lowest stolen-base percentage allowed (30.0) and most pitches thrown per batter (3.97)
- 7th in highest ERA at home
- 8th in pitches thrown (3,529)
- Led the Phillies in wins, losses, games started, innings pitched, hits allowed, batters faced (889), home runs allowed, hit batsmen (8), pitches thrown (3,529), GDPs induced (20), highest strikeout/walk ratio (1.9), highest groundball/flyball ratio allowed (0.8), lowest stolen-base percentage allowed (30.0) and fewest pitches thrown per batter (3.97)

Marlon Anderson

Position: 2B
Bats: L **Throws:** R
Ht: 5'11" **Wt:** 198

Opening Day Age: 27
Born: 1/6/74 in Montgomery, AL
ML Seasons: 3

Overall Statistics

	G	AB	R	H	D	T	HR	RBI	SB	BB	SO	Avg	OBP	Slg
2000	41	162	10	37	8	1	1	15	2	12	22	.228	.282	.309
Career	187	657	62	165	37	5	7	73	17	37	89	.251	.292	.355

2000 Situational Stats

	AB	H	HR	RBI	Avg		AB	H	HR	RBI	Avg
Home	115	27	1	13	.235	LHP	21	4	0	0	.190
Road	47	10	0	2	.213	RHP	141	33	1	15	.234
First Half	0	0	0	0	-	Sc Pos	46	6	1	14	.130
Scnd Half	162	37	1	15	.228	Clutch	28	7	0	1	.250

2000 Season

Marlon Anderson lost his everyday second-base job in spring training and didn't return to Philadelphia until August 6. Though Anderson performed well, particularly with the bat, at Triple-A Scranton-Wilkes Barre, it was more of the same for him at the major league level. He swung at everything, showed no on-base skills at all, failed to incorporate his speed into his offensive game, and exhibited subpar defensive range and mechanics.

Hitting, Baserunning & Defense

Anderson is an aggressive hitter who does not work the count. While he does possess decent pop to the gaps, he often puts the pitcher's pitch into play, negating his power to a large extent. He pulls the ball too often, resulting in weak grounders to second and lazy flyballs to the outfield. Anderson runs quite well, but has never used speed to his full advantage, particularly at the big league level. Defensively, he has bad footwork and doesn't get to as many balls as he should, considering his speed.

2001 Outlook

Anderson has now logged more than the equivalent of a full season in Philadelphia, and has shown few signs of succeeding at second. Look for the Phils to try to move him, use him in a platoon or make him a lefthanded bat off of the bench in 2001.

Alex Arias

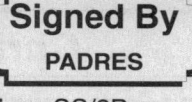

Position: SS/3B
Bats: R **Throws:** R
Ht: 6' 3" **Wt:** 202

Opening Day Age: 33
Born: 11/20/67 in New York, NY
ML Seasons: 9
Pronunciation: AIR-ee-us

Overall Statistics

	G	AB	R	H	D	T	HR	RBI	SB	BB	SO	Avg	OBP	Slg
2000	70	155	17	29	9	0	2	15	1	16	28	.187	.271	.284
Career	699	1629	184	439	75	6	16	184	9	163	187	.269	.341	.352

2000 Situational Stats

	AB	H	HR	RBI	Avg		AB	H	HR	RBI	Avg
Home	68	13	1	8	.191	LHP	50	12	1	5	.240
Road	87	16	1	7	.184	RHP	105	17	1	10	.162
First Half	86	16	1	9	.186	Sc Pos	35	10	0	13	.286
Scnd Half	69	13	1	6	.188	Clutch	29	5	0	4	.172

2000 Season

Coming off of a career season in 1999 in which he batted .303, Alex Arias logged the poorest of his nine seasons as a major league utilityman in 2000. He never got untracked offensively, batting .122 over the season's first two months. The Phillies ultimately used others at short, leaving Arias as a little-used deep reserve.

Hitting, Baserunning & Defense

Arias is a contact hitter who sprays singles to all fields but has little extra-base power or speed. As long as he works counts and gets his singles, he fits quite well in a bench role. He appeared to lose confidence at the plate during the 2000 season, however, and rarely hit the ball with authority. Though Arias is not a steals guy, he is a solid baserunner with decent straight-ahead speed. Defensively, he is surehanded and can hold his own at second or third base, though the Phils envision him primarily as a shortstop. He doesn't have the range or arm to play on a full-time basis, however.

2001 Outlook

Arias signed with the Padres during the offseason. He will have a chance to be San Diego's regular shortstop while the Padres groom Santiago Perez. The Padres also will rely on Arias for his veteran leadership in the clubhouse.

Chris Brock

Position: RP
Bats: R **Throws:** R
Ht: 6' 0" **Wt:** 185

Opening Day Age: 31
Born: 2/5/70 in
Orlando, FL
ML Seasons: 4

Overall Statistics

	W	L	Pct.	ERA	G	GS	Sv	IP	H	BB	SO	HR	Ratio
2000	7	8	.467	4.34	63	5	1	93.1	85	41	69	21	1.35
Career	13	16	.448	4.91	102	30	1	258.1	274	108	180	44	1.48

2000 Situational Stats

	W	L	ERA	Sv	IP		AB	H	HR	RBI	Avg
Home	4	5	3.59	0	52.2	LHB	126	28	4	11	.222
Road	3	3	5.31	1	40.2	RHB	230	57	17	35	.248
First Half	5	4	3.69	0	61.0	Sc Pos	80	16	3	23	.200
Scnd Half	2	4	5.57	1	32.1	Clutch	122	31	6	17	.254

2000 Season

Chris Brock was acquired by the Phillies from the Giants prior to the 2000 season. An injury to staff ace Curt Schilling forced Brock into the rotation, where he was winless in five starts, allowing seven homers in 31 innings. He performed better as a setup man the rest of the way.

Pitching, Defense & Hitting

Brock is a typical fifth-starter and swingman type. He possesses a slightly above-average high-80s fastball that he needs to keep low in the zone to be successful, and he mixes it with a slider and changeup that he uses liberally against lefthanded hitters. Brock is a flyball pitcher who gets into trouble when he falls behind in the count, and when he elevates his fastball in the strike zone. He has performed much better out of the bullpen in his career. Brock is an average fielder who doesn't hold baserunners especially well, though he allowed just six steals in 93.1 innings last season. He's an excellent fastball hitter with a dash of power, and he bunts well.

2001 Outlook

The Phils' bullpen is a major area of concern entering the 2001 season, though the club signed Ricky Bottalico, Rheal Cormier and Jose Mesa. Brock is possibly the most reliable returning member.

Paul Byrd

Position: SP
Bats: R **Throws:** R
Ht: 6' 1" **Wt:** 184

Opening Day Age: 30
Born: 12/3/70 in
Louisville, KY
ML Seasons: 6

Overall Statistics

	W	L	Pct.	ERA	G	GS	Sv	IP	H	BB	SO	HR	Ratio
2000	2	9	.182	6.51	17	15	0	83.0	89	35	53	17	1.49
Career	29	28	.509	4.62	144	59	0	461.1	452	179	292	71	1.37

2000 Situational Stats

	W	L	ERA	Sv	IP		AB	H	HR	RBI	Avg
Home	2	2	6.69	0	36.1	LHB	144	48	11	32	.333
Road	0	7	6.36	0	46.2	RHB	185	41	6	31	.222
First Half	2	7	6.30	0	70.0	Sc Pos	72	29	5	46	.403
Scnd Half	0	2	7.62	0	13.0	Clutch	13	5	1	10	.385

2000 Season

Paul Byrd suffered through a nightmarish 2000 season after making the All-Star Game and winning 15 times a year earlier. An especially brutal first two months earned him a June 2 demotion to the minors. He returned to the majors quickly, but after a second consecutive relief outing on July 26, he blew out his shoulder. He underwent arthroscopic surgery on August 2, ending his season.

Pitching, Defense & Hitting

Byrd's fastball only reaches the mid-80s. He needs to effectively mix his slider, curve, and particularly his changeup on the edges of the strike zone to have any kind of success. He is a flyball pitcher who is in big trouble when he falls behind hitters or has trouble locating his fastball. That was the case in 2000, when lefties lit him up to the tune of a .333 average and a .681 slugging percentage. He does not hold runners well but is a scrappy defender who fields his position adequately. He is a non-factor at the plate, though he bunts fairly well.

2001 Outlook

After the season, Byrd was outrighted off of the Phillies' 40-man roster. If he proves his health by the spring, he could be offered a minor league deal. Truth be told, Byrd possesses the grit and the command to be an effective situational bullpen righty.

Wayne Gomes

Position: RP
Bats: R **Throws:** R
Ht: 6' 2" **Wt:** 227

Opening Day Age: 28
Born: 1/15/73 in
Hampton, VA
ML Seasons: 4
Pronunciation: GOAMZ

Overall Statistics

	W	L	Pct.	ERA	G	GS	Sv	IP	H	BB	SO	HR	Ratio
2000	4	6	.400	4.40	65	0	7	73.2	72	35	49	6	1.45
Career	23	18	.561	4.44	246	0	27	283.2	281	150	217	24	1.52

2000 Situational Stats

	W	L	ERA	Sv	IP		AB	H	HR	RBI	Avg
Home	2	4	4.89	2	38.2	LHB	108	33	2	20	.306
Road	2	2	3.86	5	35.0	RHB	167	39	4	23	.234
First Half	4	4	3.31	7	49.0	Sc Pos	97	24	1	36	.247
Scnd Half	0	2	6.57	0	24.2	Clutch	121	28	4	19	.231

2000 Season

Wayne Gomes began the season as the Phillies' closer, and did a fair job early on, saving four games and posting an impressive 1.13 ERA in April. As has been his custom, he struggled with his control and ran out of gas in the second half. Gomes was on the disabled list for three weeks just after the break with right elbow tendinitis.

Pitching, Defense & Hitting

Gomes' stuff is good enough for him to flourish in a late-inning role. He features a lively low-90s fastball and a knee-buckling curve that functions as his primary out pitch. Strike one, however, has proved elusive for him throughout his career. He needs to get ahead with his fastball to make his curve effective. His curve wasn't as sharp as usual for most of the year, dropping his overall strikeout rate to an unacceptable level for a pitcher with poor control. Runners took liberties against Gomes, stealing six bases in seven attempts last season. He's a fair fielder, and a poor hitter who rarely bats.

2001 Outlook

Gomes needs to come to spring training in shape to position himself as a durable 80-90 inning setup man/middle reliever. The Phillies signed Ricky Bottalico, Rheal Cormier and Jose Mesa, so Gomes' job is by no means guaranteed.

Mike Jackson

Position: RP
Bats: R **Throws:** R
Ht: 6' 2"   **Wt:** 225

Opening Day Age: 36
Born: 12/22/64 in
Houston, TX
ML Seasons: 14

Overall Statistics

	W	L	Pct.	ERA	G	GS	Sv	IP	H	BB	SO	HR	Ratio
2000					Did Not Play								
Career	53	61	.465	3.26	835	7	138	1017.2	801	414	905	101	1.19

2000 Situational Stats

	W	L	ERA	Sv	IP		AB	H	HR	RBI	Avg
Home	—	—	—	—	—	LHB	—	—	—	—	—
Road	—	—	—	—	—	RHB	—	—	—	—	—
First Half	—	—	—	—	—	Sc Pos	—	—	—	—	—
Scnd Half	—	—	—	—	—	Clutch	—	—	—	—	—

2000 Season

Mike Jackson was thought to be one of the final pieces in a contending puzzle when signed to an incentive-laden free-agent contract prior to the season, but he literally got hurt before his very first regular-season appearance. After a pair of aborted rehabilitation attempts, Jackson underwent arthroscopic right shoulder surgery on May 26, ending his season before it began.

Pitching, Defense & Hitting

Before his injury, Jackson's out pitch was a nasty slider, which was particularly tough on righthanded hitters. He always possessed just enough fastball—usually reaching the low 90s—to keep both left and righthanded hitters honest, effectively setting up his premier offspeed pitch. Precise command within the strike zone has been his hallmark. From 1993 to '99, Jackson never walked as many as 30 batters in a season. His growing list of injuries has turned him into a below-average defender on the mound. As a short reliever, Jackson's offense never has been an issue.

2001 Outlook

Jackson was outrighted from the Phillies' 40-man roster in October, and the Astros signed him to a one-year deal in mid-December. He will join a number of new faces in the Houston bullpen.

Kevin Jordan

Position: 2B/3B
Bats: R **Throws:** R
Ht: 6' 1" **Wt:** 201

Opening Day Age: 31
Born: 10/9/69 in San Francisco, CA
ML Seasons: 6

Travis Lee

Position: 1B/RF/LF
Bats: L **Throws:** L
Ht: 6' 3" **Wt:** 214

Opening Day Age: 25
Born: 5/26/75 in San Diego, CA
ML Seasons: 3

Overall Statistics

	G	AB	R	H	D	T	HR	RBI	SB	BB	SO	Avg	OBP	Slg
2000	109	337	30	74	16	2	5	36	0	17	41	.220	.257	.323
Career	492	1296	129	336	65	5	22	162	2	59	160	.259	.295	.368

2000 Situational Stats

	AB	H	HR	RBI	Avg		AB	H	HR	RBI	Avg
Home	171	38	2	13	.222	LHP	113	24	1	14	.212
Road	166	36	3	23	.217	RHP	224	50	4	22	.223
First Half	197	49	2	18	.249	Sc Pos	104	22	1	30	.212
Scnd Half	140	25	3	18	.179	Clutch	78	11	0	8	.141

Overall Statistics

	G	AB	R	H	D	T	HR	RBI	SB	BB	SO	Avg	OBP	Slg
2000	128	404	53	95	24	1	9	54	8	65	79	.235	.342	.366
Career	394	1341	181	335	60	5	40	176	33	190	252	.250	.342	.391

2000 Situational Stats

	AB	H	HR	RBI	Avg		AB	H	HR	RBI	Avg
Home	205	45	2	22	.220	LHP	73	15	0	8	.205
Road	199	50	7	32	.251	RHP	331	80	9	46	.242
First Half	218	51	8	40	.234	Sc Pos	122	24	0	38	.197
Scnd Half	186	44	1	14	.237	Clutch	61	12	0	4	.197

2000 Season

Kevin Jordan opened the season as the Phillies' insurance policy at first, second and third base. He was pressed into service much more than expected because of Scott Rolen's ongoing back woes and the inability of Phillies' second basemen to hit lefthanders. An effective bench resource in prior seasons, Jordan rarely hit the ball with authority.

Hitting, Baserunning & Defense

Jordan loves to swing the bat. He now has all of 59 walks in 1,381 career plate appearances. He served as a very useful pinch-hitter for most of the last few seasons because of his ability to hit righthanders. He doesn't possess much extra-base power, though he can occasionally launch a mistake fastball for distance. He appeared to suffer from a major loss of bat speed last season. Though he is fairly sure-handed, his range is subpar and his throwing arm is only adequate. Once a fairly speedy runner in the minors, he's been quite slow since breaking his leg in Triple-A several years ago.

2001 Outlook

Jordan's versatility is all he has going for him these days, but that might be enough to make Philadelphia's roster. It would be a surprise if he matches his 2000 total of 337 at-bats over the remainder of his major league career.

2000 Season

Travis Lee started well enough, homering six times by the end of May for the Diamondbacks, but already had begun his free-fall when traded to the Phillies in July. He didn't homer for Philadelphia until September 21 despite playing on a full-time basis, first as a left fielder and then as a first baseman.

Hitting, Baserunning & Defense

Lee's insistence on pulling the ball has made him a relatively easy mark for all types of pitching, particularly lefthanders. He had a grand total of one base hit to the left side of the field against lefties in 2000. Against righties, he is much more patient, but with little positive effect. He becomes increasingly tentative as the count builds. Lee is a fast runner for a big man, and he is quite instinctive on the bases. He's a versatile defender who moves well around the bag at first base and can play competent defense at all three outfield positions.

2001 Outlook

The tools that made Lee a $10 million bonus baby are there, and Lee won't turn 26 until early in the 2001 season. It's unlikely that the Phils will entrust first base to him on a full-time basis at the outset, but with a hot start he could earn the job.

Vicente Padilla (Future Closer)

Position: RP
Bats: R **Throws:** R
Ht: 6' 2" **Wt:** 200

Opening Day Age: 23
Born: 9/27/77 in Chinandega, Nicaragua
ML Seasons: 2

Overall Statistics

	W	L	Pct.	ERA	G	GS	Sv	IP	H	BB	SO	HR	Ratio
2000	4	7	.364	3.72	55	0	2	65.1	72	28	51	3	1.53
Career	4	8	.333	4.24	60	0	2	68.0	79	31	51	4	1.62

2000 Situational Stats

	W	L	ERA	Sv	IP		AB	H	HR	RBI	Avg
Home	2	5	4.05	0	33.1	LHB	95	32	2	19	.337
Road	2	2	3.38	2	32.0	RHB	159	40	1	15	.252
First Half	2	0	2.15	0	29.1	Sc Pos	70	18	1	29	.257
Scnd Half	2	7	5.00	2	36.0	Clutch	151	44	2	29	.291

2000 Season

Vicente Padilla was a key piece of the the July 26 Curt Schilling deal. He was extremely effective with Arizona prior to the deal, notching a 2.31 ERA in 35 innings. His performance slipped with the Phils, however, as they used him in more crucial game situations when he wasn't ready.

Pitching, Defense & Hitting

Padilla primarily is a two-pitch power hurler, combining a low to mid-90s fastball with a hard curve. He can be very tough when his mechanics are in sync. Late in the 2000 season his mechanics wavered, and all of his offerings flattened out, making him quite hittable. His current repertoire seems sufficient against righties, but he does not have an out pitch against lefties. For a young man, Padilla is not exceptionally fit. He has a relatively slow delivery, and runners can get good jumps on him. He is an ordinary fielder. He has a 1.000 career batting average; he was 1-for-1 with Arizona.

2001 Outlook

The Phillies have big plans for Padilla, and he does possess the raw talent to be successful in a short-relief role. However, the gradual late-season deterioration of his mechanics was distressing. If he finds an answer for lefthanders, he could be on his way toward a successful career as a closer.

Tomas Perez

Position: SS
Bats: R **Throws:** R
Ht: 5'11" **Wt:** 177

Opening Day Age: 27
Born: 12/29/73 in Barquisimeto, Venezuela
ML Seasons: 5

Overall Statistics

	G	AB	R	H	D	T	HR	RBI	SB	BB	SO	Avg	OBP	Slg
2000	45	140	17	31	7	1	1	13	1	11	30	.221	.278	.307
Career	223	665	63	154	26	8	3	49	3	55	108	.232	.291	.308

2000 Situational Stats

	AB	H	HR	RBI	Avg		AB	H	HR	RBI	Avg
Home	76	15	0	4	.197	LHP	23	7	0	1	.304
Road	64	16	1	9	.250	RHP	117	24	1	12	.205
First Half	4	2	0	2	.500	Sc Pos	42	7	0	11	.167
Scnd Half	136	29	1	11	.213	Clutch	25	3	1	2	.120

2000 Season

Tomas Perez pushed Desi Relaford at shortstop last spring but was the last player cut before the club broke camp. After a brief cup-of-coffee in April, Perez was summoned to the majors on August 4 to play shortstop after the Phils gave up on Relaford. Perez received a month-long audition, and while he proved surehanded defensively, his range was sub-par and his bat even more anemic than Relaford's.

Hitting, Baserunning & Defense

Perez is a wild-swinger who sprays the ball with minimal extra-base pop. He also showed an ability to drive mistake fastballs for distance at Triple-A last season. That ability was much less in evidence once he graduated to the majors, however, where his willingness to expand his strike zone caused Perez to get himself out often. He has above-average straight-ahead speed but has been successful in just over 50 percent of his stolen-base attempts as a pro. He boasts sure hands and a decent arm, but he has below-average range at shortstop.

2001 Outlook

Jimmy Rollins represents the future at shortstop for the Phillies, but Perez showed enough in his brief major league stay and his fine Triple-A campaign to potentially usurp the infield utility role vacated by Alex Arias, who signed with the Padres.

Other Philadelphia Phillies

Scott Aldred (Pos: LHP, Age: 32)

	W	L	Pct.	ERA	G	GS	Sv	IP	H	BB	SO	HR	Ratio
2000	1	3	.250	5.75	23	0	0	20.1	23	10	21	3	1.62
Career	20	39	.339	6.02	229	67	1	499.2	581	230	312	78	1.62

Aldred didn't pitch after May due to a sore shoulder that resulted in arthroscopic surgery. He has settled down as a reliever in recent years, so some team may take a chance on him. 2001 Outlook: C

Clemente Alvarez (Pos: C, Age: 32, Bats: R)

	G	AB	R	H	D	T	HR	RBI	SB	BB	SO	Avg	OBP	Slg
2000	2	5	1	1	0	0	0	0	0	0	1	.200	.200	.200
Career	2	5	1	1	0	0	0	0	0	0	1	.200	.200	.200

Alvarez is the epitome of a journeyman minor league receiver. His glove has helped him last through 14 minor league seasons despite woeful batting averages and slugging percentages. 2001 Outlook: D

Gary Bennett (Pos: C, Age: 28, Bats: R)

	G	AB	R	H	D	T	HR	RBI	SB	BB	SO	Avg	OBP	Slg
2000	31	74	8	18	5	0	2	5	0	13	15	.243	.371	.392
Career	83	210	19	55	9	0	3	30	0	24	38	.262	.339	.348

Bennett suddenly became a .300 hitter at Triple-A last year, though nothing in his past would indicate the outburst was anything but a fluke. 2001 Outlook: C

Jason Boyd (Pos: RHP, Age: 28)

	W	L	Pct.	ERA	G	GS	Sv	IP	H	BB	SO	HR	Ratio
2000	0	1	.000	6.55	30	0	0	34.1	39	24	32	2	1.83
Career	0	1	.000	6.13	34	0	0	39.2	44	26	36	2	1.76

Boyd passed from Pittsburgh to Milwaukee to Philadelphia through waivers last March. He then had shoulder problems and a broken hand and worked at three levels. Otherwise, it was an uneventful season. 2001 Outlook: C

Mark Brownson (Pos: RHP, Age: 25)

	W	L	Pct.	ERA	G	GS	Sv	IP	H	BB	SO	HR	Ratio
2000	1	0	1.000	7.20	5	0	0	5.0	7	3	3	1	2.00
Career	2	2	.500	6.94	11	9	0	48.0	65	13	32	11	1.63

After six seasons in the Colorado organization, Brownson was plucked off the waiver wire by Philadelphia following the 1999 season. He saw more action in relief last year than he had since 1996. 2001 Outlook: C

Kirk Bullinger (Pos: RHP, Age: 31)

	W	L	Pct.	ERA	G	GS	Sv	IP	H	BB	SO	HR	Ratio
2000	0	0	-	5.40	3	0	0	3.1	4	0	4	0	1.20
Career	1	0	1.000	7.30	15	0	0	12.1	20	2	6	1	1.78

Bullinger has reached the majors with three different organizations the past three years. He'll probably be in yet another system in 2001, but he's no more than a middle relief candidate. 2001 Outlook: C

Rob Ducey (Pos: LF, Age: 35, Bats: L)

	G	AB	R	H	D	T	HR	RBI	SB	BB	SO	Avg	OBP	Slg
2000	117	165	26	32	5	1	6	26	1	31	49	.194	.318	.345
Career	646	1206	180	292	75	13	28	134	22	150	321	.242	.328	.396

The Phillies and Blue Jays completed deals involving Ducey on two occasions last season. He didn't hit righthanders well and batted just .170 from the seventh inning on. 2001 Outlook: C

Mark Holzemer (Pos: LHP, Age: 31)

	W	L	Pct.	ERA	G	GS	Sv	IP	H	BB	SO	HR	Ratio
2000	0	1	.000	7.71	25	0	0	25.2	36	8	19	4	1.71
Career	2	5	.286	7.69	94	4	1	100.2	138	47	64	15	1.84

Holzemer's track record dooms him to almost nothing better than a role as a situational lefthander. Righthanded hitters have hammered him for a .363 average in his major league career. 2001 Outlook: C

Brian Hunter (Pos: 1B, Age: 33, Bats: R)

	G	AB	R	H	D	T	HR	RBI	SB	BB	SO	Avg	OBP	Slg
2000	87	140	14	30	5	0	8	23	0	20	39	.214	.313	.421
Career	699	1555	187	364	90	7	67	259	4	141	335	.234	.298	.430

The Phillies acquired Hunter after Atlanta waived him last April. For a guy whose bat will decide whether he stays in the big leagues, Hunter didn't help himself last season though the Phils re-signed him to a one-year deal. 2001 Outlook: C

Tom Jacquez (Pos: LHP, Age: 25)

	W	L	Pct.	ERA	G	GS	Sv	IP	H	BB	SO	HR	Ratio
2000	0	0	-	11.05	9	0	1	7.1	10	3	6	2	1.77
Career	0	0	-	11.05	9	0	1	7.1	10	3	6	2	1.77

Jacquez pitched at UCLA at the same time as Jim Parque. Jacquez moved to the bullpen full time last year and became a little less hittable, though he'll probably never blow anyone away. 2001 Outlook: C

David Newhan (Pos: 2B, Age: 27, Bats: L)

	G	AB	R	H	D	T	HR	RBI	SB	BB	SO	Avg	OBP	Slg
2000	24	37	8	6	1	0	1	2	0	8	13	.162	.311	.270
Career	56	80	15	12	2	0	3	8	2	9	24	.150	.236	.288

Newhan came to the Phillies as part of the Desi Relaford deal. He can play the infield and the outfield and has hit 20 homers and stolen 20 bases in the minors, so he's a utility candidate. 2001 Outlook: C

Cliff Politte (Pos: RHP, Age: 27)

	W	L	Pct.	ERA	G	GS	Sv	IP	H	BB	SO	HR	Ratio
2000	4	3	.571	3.66	12	8	0	59.0	55	27	50	8	1.39
Career	7	6	.538	5.07	33	16	0	113.2	119	60	87	16	1.57

After scuffling the previous two seasons, Politte got his career back on track by pitching well at Triple-A and with the Phillies last year. He could be a candidate for Philadelphia's rotation. 2001 Outlook: B

Tom Prince (Pos: C, Age: 36, Bats: R)

	G	AB	R	H	D	T	HR	RBI	SB	BB	SO	Avg	OBP	Slg
2000	46	122	14	29	9	0	2	16	1	13	31	.238	.321	.361
Career	372	821	75	167	53	2	11	95	4	74	180	.203	.280	.313

Prince returned from torn ligaments in his wrist the previous year to have more at-bats than in any season since 1993. There's little reason to feel his 14-year career as a backup won't reach 15, though Philadelphia did not offer him arbitration. 2001 Outlook: B

Chris Pritchett (Pos: 1B, Age: 31, Bats: L)

	G	AB	R	H	D	T	HR	RBI	SB	BB	SO	Avg	OBP	Slg
2000	5	11	0	1	0	0	0	0	0	1	3	.091	.167	.091
Career	61	149	16	33	3	1	3	11	3	7	31	.221	.255	.315

Pritchett's lefthanded bat doesn't pack the power most teams would like to get from their first basemen. He's not a high-average hitter, either. He'll be looking for another team this season. 2001 Outlook: D

Steve Schrenk (Pos: RHP, Age: 32)

	W	L	Pct.	ERA	G	GS	Sv	IP	H	BB	SO	HR	Ratio
2000	2	3	.400	7.33	20	0	0	23.1	25	13	19	3	1.63
Career	3	6	.333	5.25	52	2	1	73.2	66	27	55	9	1.26

Schrenk has been plugging along at Triple-A for most of the past eight seasons. His talent will never blow anyone away, but he's gained a lot of pitching savvy over the years. He signed a minor league deal with Oakland in early December. 2001 Outlook: C

Kevin Sefcik (Pos: LF/CF, Age: 30, Bats: R)

	G	AB	R	H	D	T	HR	RBI	SB	BB	SO	Avg	OBP	Slg
2000	99	153	15	36	6	2	0	10	4	13	19	.235	.300	.301
Career	424	770	92	212	36	10	6	56	21	80	102	.275	.351	.371

Sefcik can play any outfield position and even fill in at second base if necessary. He has some speed but little power. His value is limited if he has trouble reaching base, as he did last year. He refused assignment and became a free agent. 2001 Outlook: B

Amaury Telemaco (Pos: RHP, Age: 27)

	W	L	Pct.	ERA	G	GS	Sv	IP	H	BB	SO	HR	Ratio
2000	1	3	.250	6.66	13	2	0	24.1	25	14	22	6	1.60
Career	17	23	.425	5.03	138	42	0	361.1	382	128	236	58	1.41

After reaching the majors in 1996 with the Cubs at age 22, Telemaco has failed to progress. He compiled a 10.80 ERA in 11 relief appearances with the Phillies last year. He re-signed with the Phillies for 2001 in mid-December for $375,000. 2001 Outlook: C

Ed Vosberg (Pos: LHP, Age: 39)

	W	L	Pct.	ERA	G	GS	Sv	IP	H	BB	SO	HR	Ratio
2000	1	1	.500	4.13	31	0	0	24.0	21	18	23	4	1.63
Career	10	15	.400	4.34	244	3	13	219.2	239	105	168	21	1.57

For the second year in a row, Vosberg switched teams in midseason. Last year he was traded from Colorado to the Phillies. He's no more than a situational lefty and became a free agent in October. 2001 Outlook: C

Philadelphia Phillies Minor League Prospects

Organization Overview:

Two years ago the Phillies were on the verge of contending, but a nosedive sent them to the basement of the National League last season, where they tied with the Cubs for the worst record with only 65 wins. While the Philadelphia parent club floundered, the minor league affiliates flourished across the board, posting the second-best composite winning percentage in baseball at .568. The Phillies were able to acquire a slew of prospects for veteran righties Curt Schilling and Andy Ashby. But many believe they settled for less than market value on Schilling, unless Travis Lee blossoms. And they gave up promising rookie Adam Eaton to San Diego just eight months earlier to obtain Ashby. Pat Burrell, Scott Rolen, Bobby Abreu, Lee and rising prospect Jimmy Rollins provide a solid foundation for new manager Larry Bowa to work with, although the pitching staff lacks a true ace and dominating closer.

Brad Baisley

Position: P
Bats: R **Throws:** R
Ht: 6' 9" **Wt:** 205

Opening Day Age: 21
Born: 8/24/79 in Dade City, FL

Recent Statistics

	W	L	ERA	G	GS	Sv	IP	H	R	BB	SO	HR
1999 A Piedmont	10	7	2.26	23	23	0	147.2	116	56	55	110	5
2000 A Clearwater	3	9	3.74	16	15	1	89.0	95	47	34	60	9

The top pitching prospect in the system entering the 2000 season, Baisley was on the brink of breaking out as a frontline presence before tendinitis sidelined him for most of the summer. The wiry righthander is expected to gain velocity on his 89-93 MPH fastball. He also drops in a good curveball and developing changeup, further complicating matters for opposing hitters. At his height, the downward plane of the ball adds an extra dimension to his attack. Brett Myers and Ryan Madson may have passed him in terms of prospect status, but Baisley's strong showing in instructional league put him back on track for a date with Double-A this year.

Brandon Duckworth

Position: P
Bats: B **Throws:** R
Ht: 6' 2" **Wt:** 185

Opening Day Age: 25
Born: 1/23/76 in Salt Lake City, UT

Recent Statistics

	W	L	ERA	G	GS	Sv	IP	H	R	BB	SO	HR
1999 A Clearwater	11	5	4.84	27	17	1	132.0	164	84	40	101	13
2000 AA Reading	13	7	3.16	27	27	0	165.0	145	70	52	178	17

Duckworth has continued to silence his doubters since going undrafted out of Cal State Fullerton in 1997. The righthander never has been overpowering, but he demonstrates excellent command and a polished feel for changing speeds. After spending parts of his first two years in the Class-A Florida State League without distinguishing himself, he turned some heads with his performance in the Double-A Eastern League last year. He was voted the fifth best prospect in the circuit and his sharp, downward breaking curveball was regarded as the best in the loop. While he will rely on his curve, he'll throw any of his offerings at any point in the count, including a 90-92 MPH fastball or his change. Duckworth will get a look with Philadelphia in 2001.

Ryan Madson

Position: P
Bats: L **Throws:** R
Ht: 6' 6" **Wt:** 180

Opening Day Age: 20
Born: 8/28/80 in Long Beach, CA

Recent Statistics

	W	L	ERA	G	GS	Sv	IP	H	R	BB	SO	HR
1999 A Batavia	5	5	4.72	15	15	0	87.2	80	51	43	75	5
2000 A Piedmont	14	5	2.59	21	21	0	135.2	113	50	45	123	5

Similar to Brad Baisley in stature and upside, Madson began to come into his own last year in the Class-A South Atlantic League. A ninth-round draft pick in '98, teams were scared away by his commitment to USC, but the Phillies' gamble is starting to pay dividends. He flashed enticing potential in his first two years in short season leagues but established himself on a more consistent basis last year. He began to grow into his tall projectable frame. The added strength, coupled with sound mechanics, helped him to post an eye-catching 14-5, 2.59 ERA. Madson's fastball explodes in the 88-93 MPH range, complemented by a solid curveball and changeup. The Phillies are excited about his future and believe he's only scratched the surface of his ability.

Brett Myers

Position: P
Bats: R **Throws:** R
Ht: 6' 4" **Wt:** 215

Opening Day Age: 20
Born: 8/17/80 in Jacksonville, FL

Recent Statistics

	W	L	ERA	G	GS	Sv	IP	H	R	BB	SO	HR
1999 R Phillies	2	1	2.33	7	5	0	27.0	17	8	7	30	0
2000 A Piedmont	13	7	3.18	27	27	0	175.1	165	78	69	140	7

Drafted with the 12th overall pick in the 1999 draft, Myers signed for $2.05 million and blew away the Gulf Coast League in his professional debut. The Phillies were attracted to the 6-foot-4, 215-pounder out of a Florida high school based on his power-pitching frame, makeup and repertoire. Armed with a lively fastball that registers in the low to mid-90s, a hard-breaking curveball and rudimentary changeup, Myers showcased dominant potential last year. He also displayed surprising polish for a teenager in his first year against full-season competition. His health and command should determine just how fast he joins the rotation in Philadelphia.

Doug Nickle

Position: P
Bats: R **Throws:** R
Ht: 6' 4" **Wt:** 210

Opening Day Age: 26
Born: 10/2/74 in Sonoma, CA

Recent Statistics

	W	L	ERA	G	GS	Sv	IP	H	R	BB	SO	HR
2000 AA Reading	8	3	2.44	49	0	16	77.1	55	25	22	58	4
2000 NL Philadelphia	0	0	13.50	4	0	0	2.2	5	4	2	0	0

A relatively unknown minor league starter, Nickle's career was jump-started when the Angels dealt him to the Phillies for Gregg Jefferies during the 1998 season. Philadelphia shifted the 1997 13th-rounder to the bullpen, where he has thrived since '99. His overpowering arsenal helped him earn the title as the best reliever in the Double-A Eastern League last year. Opponents managed to hit at just a .196 clip against his 94-MPH fastball and knuckle-curve. Nickle got a taste of the bigs in September, and he could be back for a second helping this year.

Jimmy Osting

Position: P
Bats: R **Throws:** L
Ht: 6' 5" **Wt:** 190

Opening Day Age: 23
Born: 4/7/77 in Louisville, KY

Recent Statistics

	W	L	ERA	G	GS	Sv	IP	H	R	BB	SO	HR
1999 A Macon	14	4	2.88	27	22	2	147.0	130	52	30	131	13
2000 A Myrtle Bch	2	2	3.13	4	4	0	23.0	25	8	5	17	0
2000 AAA Richmond	0	2	11.57	3	3	0	9.1	15	12	11	2	2
2000 AA Greenville	2	6	2.65	11	11	0	71.1	67	30	29	52	6
2000 AA Reading	4	2	2.38	10	9	0	56.2	53	17	26	31	1

The Phillies enjoyed immediate returns from the Andy Ashby trade, acquiring Bruce Chen and Osting from the Braves in July. While Chen's already in the rotation, Osting could solidify the trade. Osting missed all of the '98 season due to Tommy John surgery, but he has regained his form with two promising seasons. The southpaw split last year between two Double-A circuits, but the results didn't vary much. He effectively changes speeds off of an average 86-90 MPH fastball while painting both sides of the plate, but he is working on getting more bite and a better arch on his curve. His progress in Double-A is a good indication that he's not far from breaking into the big league staff.

Reggie Taylor

Position: OF
Bats: L **Throws:** R
Ht: 6' 1" **Wt:** 178

Opening Day Age: 24
Born: 1/12/77 in Newberry, SC

Recent Statistics

	G	AB	R	H	D	T	HR	RBI	SB	BB	SO	Avg
2000 AAA Scranton-WB	98	422	60	116	10	8	15	43	23	21	87	.275
2000 NL Philadelphia	9	11	1	1	0	0	0	0	1	0	8	.091
2000 MLE	98	413	51	107	10	6	13	37	17	18	93	.259

Six years after the Phillies drafted Taylor in the first round, he has yet to establish himself in the majors. Following consecutive seasons in the Double-A Eastern League, Taylor was regarded as one of the 10 best prospects in the Triple-A International League. A separated shoulder suffered in winter ball caused his season to start late. It was the same shoulder that kept him out of action for half of '98, but didn't prevent him from being named the outfielder with the best arm in the IL. Taylor's athletic ability, power and speed thrill scouts, but until he gets a better grasp on the strike zone, it will be hard for him to achieve his full potential in the show.

Eric Valent

Position: OF
Bats: L **Throws:** L
Ht: 6' 0" **Wt:** 191

Opening Day Age: 23
Born: 4/4/77 in La Mirada, CA

Recent Statistics

	G	AB	R	H	D	T	HR	RBI	SB	BB	SO	Avg
1999 A Clearwater	134	520	91	150	31	9	20	106	5	58	110	.288
2000 AA Reading	128	469	81	121	22	5	22	90	2	70	89	.258
2000 MLE	128	458	67	110	21	4	18	75	1	50	97	.240

Perhaps he is most well known for being the organization's compensation for losing J.D. Drew, but Valent is carving his own identity with steady play. His .258 batting average last year doesn't tell the whole story. He has demonstrated a professional understanding of the strike zone, drawing 70 walks last year. His 55 home runs since being drafted out of UCLA in the supplemental first round of the '98 draft are a promising sign of things to come. His work ethic gives him an extra advantage, and despite not being fleet-footed, he is considered a solid outfielder with a strong arm. Valent should spend another year in Triple-A, but he'll be in the on-deck circle if the Phillies need an extra bat.

Others to Watch

Outfielder **Marlon Byrd** (23) emerged as a prospect by hitting .309 with 59 extra-base hits and 41 steals in Class-A Piedmont. Strong and stocky, he hits with power to all fields and his work habits are unparalleled. . . Righthander **Dave Coggin** (24) reappeared on the prospect radar screen last year, making five big league starts. A four-pitch pitcher, his heat sits in the low 90s. . . Switch-hitting shortstop **Anderson Machado** (20) was lauded for his performance in the high Class-A Florida State League as a teenager. He reminds some of a young Dave Concepcion, and stole 32 bases in his first full season. . . Outfielder **Jorge Padilla** (21) started to tap into his potential by impressing the Phillies with his dedication to physical conditioning. It showed on the field, as he raised his average nearly 100 points from '99 in the South Atlantic League. . . A Cuban defector, outfielder **Josue Perez** (23) joined the Phillies as a free agent for $850,000 in '99. They are pleased with his tools in center field and progress at the plate. . . The 15th overall pick last June, second baseman **Chase Utley** (22) exhibited the pure-hitting stroke that made him an All-American at UCLA in his pro debut. He hit .307 in the New York-Penn League while adjusting to wood bats, but was too pull-conscious at times. He's expected to make a quick journey up the ladder.

PNC Park

Offense

Three Rivers Stadium, the Pirates' home from 1970 to 2000, was the ultimate neutral park. PNC Park might be the same way, as owner Kevin McClatchy wants something between Houston's hitter-friendly Enron Field and Detroit's pitcher-friendly Comerica Park. The dimensions will be 325 feet to left, 389 to left-center, 410 to deep left-center, 399 to dead center, 375 to right-center and 320 to right. Lefthanded hitters would appear to have a slight edge with the short porch in right field, though the fence will be 21-feet high there and only six feet in left. Foul territory will be considerably smaller in PNC Park than it was at Three Rivers.

Defense

The Pirates will be moving from the fast track of artificial turf at Three Rivers to a slower grass surface at PNC Park. That should put less of a premium on an infielder's range. The outfield dimensions won't be drastically different, though the deeper alley in left-center will all but require having a center fielder with range.

Who It Helps the Most

The Pirates infield of Kevin Young, Warren Morris, Aramis Ramirez and Pat Meares was awful last season, but on grass their lack of range won't be so badly exposed. The shorter right-field fence should add a few homers for lefthanded hitters like Brian Giles and John Vander Wal.

Who It Hurts the Most

Adrian Brown is a speed player and playing on grass will reduce his ability to chop balls through the infield for hits. Righthander Kris Benson, who was 7-4 with a 2.78 ERA in 17 home starts last season, may be hurt by the short porch in left.

Rookies & Newcomers

The Pirates lack prospects at the upper levels, so they will try to improve through free agency and trades. Free-agent acquisition Derek Bell's home-run totals could dip due to the deep left-center field dimensions. Groundball pitcher Terry Mulholland will try to take advantage of the natural grass surface.

Dimensions: LF-325, LCF-389, CF-399, RCF-375, RF-320

Capacity: 38,127

Elevation: 730 feet

Surface: Grass

Foul Territory: Small

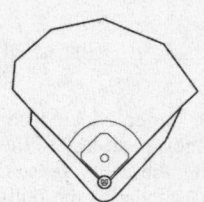

Park Factors

2000 Season (Three Rivers Stadium)

	Home Games			Away Games			Index
	Pirates	Opp	Total	Pirates	Opp	Total	
G	72	72	144	75	75	150	—
Avg	.261	.269	.265	.272	.287	.279	95
AB	2433	2547	4980	2659	2546	5205	100
R	355	389	744	371	424	795	97
H	635	685	1320	722	731	1453	95
2B	150	142	292	145	141	286	107
3B	17	14	31	11	19	30	108
HR	74	77	151	72	73	145	109
BB	239	312	551	271	327	598	96
SO	466	516	982	466	453	919	112
E	58	67	125	65	44	109	119
E-Infield	50	52	102	52	36	88	121
LHB-Avg	.277	.285	.281	.276	.316	.296	95
LHB-HR	32	31	63	28	34	62	114
RHB-Avg	.252	.260	.256	.269	.269	.269	95
RHB-HR	42	46	88	44	39	83	106

1998-2000 (Three Rivers Stadium)

	Home Games			Away Games			Index
	Pirates	Opp	Total	Pirates	Opp	Total	
G	220	220	440	223	223	446	98
Avg	.263	.257	.260	.254	.274	.264	98
AB	7300	7614	14914	7753	7512	15265	99
R	1043	1036	2079	961	1137	2098	100
H	1917	1954	3871	1971	2058	4029	97
2B	429	421	850	364	413	777	112
3B	59	33	92	40	51	91	103
HR	208	216	424	185	214	399	109
BB	698	819	1517	699	894	1593	97
SO	1500	1571	3071	1527	1395	2922	108
E	179	183	362	201	153	354	104
E-Infield	153	154	307	166	127	293	106
LHB-Avg	.274	.261	.267	.257	.302	.279	96
LHB-HR	92	86	178	81	95	176	106
RHB-Avg	.256	.254	.255	.253	.257	.255	100
RHB-HR	116	130	246	104	119	223	112

2000 Rankings (National League/Three Rivers)
- Second-highest strikeout factor
- Third-highest infield-error factor

Lloyd McClendon

2000 Season

Owner Kevin McClatchy talked about his Pirates possibly winning 90 games when last season started. Instead, Pittsburgh fell on its face and finished 69-93. That cost manager Gene Lamont his job when he was fired October 2 and replaced by Pirates hitting coach Lloyd McClendon. McClendon's managerial experience is limited to one-year stints in the Florida Instructional League, California Fall League and Arizona Fall League. However, the Pirates believe he will be a much better motivator and communicator than Lamont was.

Offense

McClendon says he doesn't have a set offensive strategy, preferring to adapt to his talent. With that in mind, it is hard to tell which way McClendon will lean in his rookie season, since the Pirates have neither great power nor speed. They were 12th in the National League last season in both home runs and stolen bases. Look for the Pirates to be a free-swinging outfit under McClendon, since they annually posted one of the lowest on-base percentages while he was the hitting coach.

Pitching & Defense

The knock on McClendon is that he doesn't know pitching. He begs to differ. He came up through the Mets' farm system as a catcher and says he learned a lot about both the mental and mechanical aspects of pitching. A key will be getting righthanders Francisco Cordova and Jason Schmidt healthy and back into the starting rotation after both underwent arthroscopic surgery last August. McClendon also says one of his top priorities is improving the defense after the Pirates finished 12th in the league in fielding last year.

2001 Outlook

The Pirates weren't ready to win 90 games last season. Still, they have more talent than their 93 losses would indicate. It would be unrealistic to think McClendon can turn the Pirates into contenders in his first season. However, it is safe to assume the Pirates could get close to .500 and maybe even surpass that mark for the first time since 1992. The club should at least play with more spark, something lacking during much of the Lamont regime.

Born: 1/11/59 in Gary, IN

Playing Experience: 1987-1994, Cin, ChC, Pit

Managerial Experience: No major league managing experience

Manager Statistics (Gene Lamont)

Year	Team, Lg	W	L	Pct	GB	Finish
2000	Pittsburgh, NL	69	93	.426	26.0	5th Central
8 Seasons		553	562	.496	—	—

2000 Starting Pitchers by Days Rest

	<=3	4	5	6+
Pirates Starts	1	75	57	19
Pirates ERA	3.00	4.86	5.81	3.70
NL Avg Starts	2	80	50	21
NL ERA	5.00	4.61	4.60	5.18

2000 Situational Stats

	Gene Lamont	NL Average
Hit & Run Success %	31.4	33.8
Stolen Base Success %	68.3	68.8
Platoon Pct.	51.2	53.2
Defensive Subs	4	19
High-Pitch Outings	13	14
Quick/Slow Hooks	16/13	14/16
Sacrifice Attempts	78	87

2000 Rankings—Gene Lamont (National Lg)

- 2nd in squeeze plays (7), relief appearances (466) and one-batter pitcher appearances (44)
- 3rd in intentional walks (47) and mid-inning pitching changes (172)

Jimmy Anderson

2000 Season

Jimmy Anderson was the last man to make the Pirates' roster last spring training, beating out veteran Pete Schourek for the No. 5 spot in the starting rotation. In order to keep Anderson, the cost-conscious Pirates released Schourek and ate his $2 million salary. Anderson struggled early in his rookie season and was sent to the minor leagues in mid-June for three starts. He returned to the Pirates just before the All-Star break and remained in their rotation for the rest of the year.

Pitching

Anderson doesn't have overpowering stuff and won't strike many hitters out. In order to be successful, he needs to have pinpoint control of a slider and sinking fastball that rarely tops 90 MPH. His fastball, because of its lack of velocity, is hittable if it catches too much of the plate. Anderson also has trouble throwing his slider for strikes consistently. Still, he does a good job keeping his pitches low in the strike zone, resulting in plenty of groundballs and few home runs.

Defense & Hitting

Though he is a bit on the pudgy side, Anderson fields his position well. He is quick around the mound and adept at snagging comebackers through the box, though he doesn't hold runners well for a lefty. Anderson also takes his hitting seriously and makes consistent contact for a pitcher. He wasn't always reliable in sacrifice bunt situations last year, however.

2001 Outlook

While he was bit of a disappointment last year, Anderson will get another opportunity to establish himself at the back end of the Pirates' rotation this season. The fact that he posted an outstanding 2.96 groundball-flyball ratio in 2000 leads one to believe he should be aided by the Pirates' move from the artificial turf of Three Rivers Stadium to the grass surface of PNC Park. Better defense behind him also would help.

Position: SP
Bats: L **Throws:** L
Ht: 6' 1" **Wt:** 207

Opening Day Age: 25
Born: 1/22/76 in Portsmouth, VA
ML Seasons: 2

Overall Statistics

	W	L	Pct.	ERA	G	GS	Sv	IP	H	BB	SO	HR	Ratio
2000	5	11	.313	5.25	27	26	0	144.0	169	58	73	13	1.58
Career	7	12	.368	5.04	40	30	0	173.1	194	74	86	15	1.55

How Often He Throws Strikes

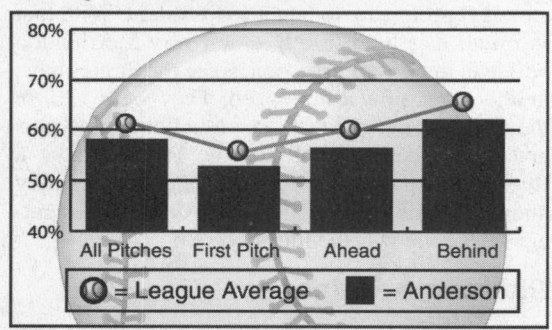

= League Average   = Anderson

2000 Situational Stats

	W	L	ERA	Sv	IP		AB	H	HR	RBI	Avg
Home	3	7	3.99	0	76.2	LHB	119	36	5	19	.303
Road	2	4	6.68	0	67.1	RHB	456	133	8	62	.292
First Half	2	5	5.89	0	62.2	Sc Pos	168	51	6	68	.304
Scnd Half	3	6	4.76	0	81.1	Clutch	18	2	0	1	.111

2000 Rankings (National League)

- 4th in lowest winning percentage
- 7th in GDPs induced (23)
- Led the Pirates in GDPs induced (23)

Kris Benson

2000 Season

Kris Benson produced a solid sophomore season after being thrust into the role of Pittsburgh's No. 1 starter when Jason Schmidt and Francisco Cordova both required arm surgery. Benson won only 10 games because he continually endured mediocre run support, bad defense and a shaky bullpen. The lack of help seemed to wear him down mentally as he was 2-6 with a 5.01 ERA after the All-Star break after going 8-6 with a 3.05 ERA in the first half.

Pitching

Benson has everything needed to become a premier pitcher, including four above-average pitches. He throws a four-seam fastball that routinely hits 95 MPH, along with a two-seam fastball with good sinking action. He also has a curveball with a tight break, a slider with extremely good movement and a changeup that has improved dramatically. Benson has pretty good command of all his pitches, though he still has a tendency to leave his fastball up in the strike zone at times. He put on 15 pounds prior to last season but still his numbers declined in the second half, leaving lingering questions about his stamina over the long haul.

Defense & Hitting

Benson isn't very good defensively since he is somewhat slow off the mound when fielding bunts and covering first base. He pays close attention to runners and has a decent pickoff move. At the plate, Benson occasionally will put a charge into the ball. He is very reliable laying down bunts and takes pride in that part of his game.

2001 Outlook

Benson possesses the kind of talent you'd expect from someone selected first overall in the 1996 draft, and he's the man the Pirates will build their starting rotation around. He has the look of a big winner and a future Cy Young candidate. It's only a matter of time before the talented Benson breaks through with the first in a long line of big seasons. This certainly could be the year.

Position: SP
Bats: R **Throws:** R
Ht: 6' 4" **Wt:** 200

Opening Day Age: 26
Born: 11/7/74 in Superior, WI
ML Seasons: 2

Overall Statistics

	W	L	Pct.	ERA	G	GS	Sv	IP	H	BB	SO	HR	Ratio
2000	10	12	.455	3.85	32	32	0	217.2	206	86	184	24	1.34
Career	21	26	.447	3.95	63	63	0	414.1	390	169	323	40	1.35

How Often He Throws Strikes

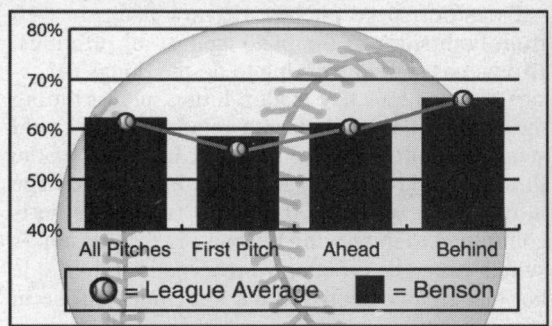

2000 Situational Stats

	W	L	ERA	Sv	IP		AB	H	HR	RBI	Avg
Home	7	4	2.78	0	123.0	LHB	395	109	16	53	.276
Road	3	8	5.23	0	94.2	RHB	432	97	8	39	.225
First Half	8	6	3.05	0	129.2	Sc Pos	194	44	6	64	.227
Scnd Half	2	6	5.01	0	88.0	Clutch	80	23	3	8	.288

2000 Rankings (National League)

- 6th in lowest ERA at home
- 9th in highest groundball/flyball ratio allowed (1.8)
- 10th in innings pitched, hit batsmen (10), pickoff throws (135) and lowest batting average allowed vs. righthanded batters
- Led the Pirates in sacrifice bunts (9), ERA, losses, games started, complete games (2), innings pitched, batters faced (936), walks allowed, hit batsmen (10), strikeouts, pitches thrown (3,422), pickoff throws (135), runners caught stealing (6), lowest batting average allowed (.249), lowest slugging percentage allowed (.391) and lowest on-base percentage allowed (.325)

Adrian Brown

Position: CF/RF
Bats: B **Throws:** R
Ht: 6' 0" **Wt:** 185

Opening Day Age: 27
Born: 2/7/74 in
McComb, MS
ML Seasons: 4

2000 Season

After spending parts of three seasons with the Pirates as a reserve outfielder, Adrian Brown finally stuck for a full year. His season turned out to be surprisingly good. After being sidelined for most of July with a strained hamstring, Brown was activated in early August and became the regular center fielder and leadoff hitter. He finished strongly and emerged as one of the few bright spots during the Pirates' dismal season.

Hitting

Brown has come a long way as an offensive performer since first getting to the major leagues in 1997 and being completely fooled by breaking balls and offspeed pitches. He now hangs in well from both sides of the plate against all offerings. Brown has started learning to do the things necessary to be an effective leadoff hitter, such as hitting the ball on the ground with regularity. He could stand to improve his walk totals, however, as the Pirates would like to see his on-base percentage move closer to the .400 range. Brown says he is committed to improving his bunting this season. A switch-hitter, he is better from his natural right side but has greatly improved his lefthanded stroke in recent years.

Baserunning & Defense

Brown has above-average speed and utilizes it well. He knows when to pick his spots to run and is rarely caught stealing. He was nabbed only once in 14 attempts last season. Brown also routinely takes the extra base while advancing on singles and doubles. With his hamstring bothering him, he had his trouble in center field late last season, failing to reach balls he normally would track down. When healthy, he possesses outstanding range and a good arm.

2001 Outlook

Brown made a strong case late last season to be the starting center fielder and leadoff man in Pittsburgh. Still, the Pirates don't seem totally convinced of his ability to play regularly. At worst, Brown will be a very good reserve outfielder.

Overall Statistics

	G	AB	R	H	D	T	HR	RBI	SB	BB	SO	Avg	OBP	Slg
2000	104	308	64	97	18	3	4	28	13	29	34	.315	.373	.432
Career	309	833	135	229	33	6	9	60	30	84	109	.275	.344	.361

Where He Hits the Ball

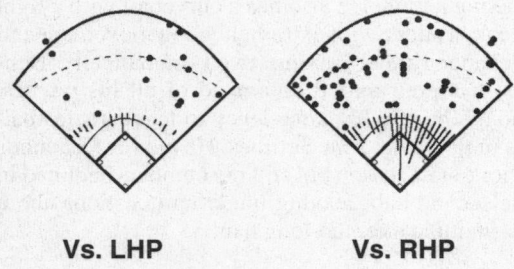

Vs. LHP   **Vs. RHP**

2000 Situational Stats

	AB	H	HR	RBI	Avg		AB	H	HR	RBI	Avg
Home	135	39	2	12	.289	LHP	52	19	1	4	.365
Road	173	58	2	16	.335	RHP	256	78	3	24	.305
First Half	99	32	1	7	.323	Sc Pos	65	22	0	24	.338
Scnd Half	209	65	3	21	.311	Clutch	64	18	0	6	.281

2000 Rankings (National League)

- 4th in batting average on an 0-2 count (.348)
- 8th in lowest batting average on a 3-2 count (.121)
- 10th in on-base percentage for a leadoff hitter (.368)
- Led the Pirates in batting average on a 3-1 count (.500), batting average on an 0-2 count (.348) and on-base percentage for a leadoff hitter (.368)

Francisco Cordova

2000 Season

Francisco Cordova endured an erratic year that ended on an operating table. He twice went on the disabled list with a sore elbow and was demoted from the starting rotation to the bullpen in early August because of ineffectiveness. Cordova hadn't pitched in relief since his rookie season of 1996. Finally, he was found to have a small bone spur on his elbow and underwent season-ending arthroscopic surgery in mid-August.

Pitching

When healthy, Cordova has good control of three pitches and his sinking fastball reaches 93 MPH with great movement. However, his velocity and command were inconsistent last year as he battled through elbow problems. At his best, Cordova effectively changes speeds with his fastball, continually adding and subtracting from its velocity from pitch to pitch. He also has a sharp slider and a functional changeup, throwing all three of his pitches from a variety of arm angles and inducing many groundballs.

Defense & Hitting

Cordova has gotten heavier in recent years and his weight has affected his agility around the mound. He is slow to react to balls hit back through the box and is no longer quick while covering first base. Cordova does have a quick move to first and can be difficult to steal on. He is an awful hitter who often bails out of the batter's box before the pitch is even thrown. Incredibly, he did not have a sacrifice bunt in 37 plate appearances last season.

2001 Outlook

The Pirates believe Cordova will be ready to go at the start of spring training, since his surgery was considered minor. However, he has had two bad seasons in a row and must be considered a risk. The Pirates declined a $3.85 million option on him for 2001, but they turned around and signed him at a lower price in late November. His rehab is on schedule, and the team would love to see 25-30 starts out of him next year.

Position: SP
Bats: R **Throws:** R
Ht: 6' 1" **Wt:** 197

Opening Day Age: 28
Born: 4/26/72 in Veracruz, Mexico
ML Seasons: 5
Pronunciation: core-DOE-vuh

Overall Statistics

	W	L	Pct.	ERA	G	GS	Sv	IP	H	BB	SO	HR	Ratio
2000	6	8	.429	5.21	18	17	0	95.0	107	38	66	12	1.53
Career	42	47	.472	3.96	166	112	12	753.2	755	235	537	75	1.31

How Often He Throws Strikes

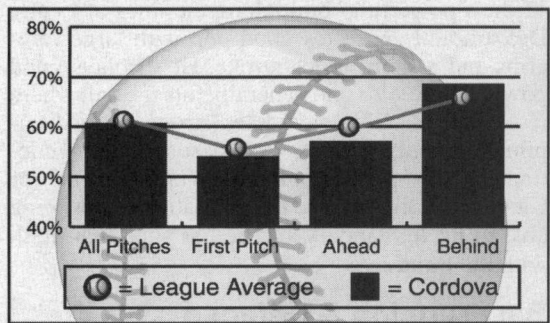

= League Average   = Cordova

2000 Situational Stats

	W	L	ERA	Sv	IP		AB	H	HR	RBI	Avg
Home	4	3	4.59	0	49.0	LHB	172	60	4	18	.349
Road	2	5	5.87	0	46.0	RHB	203	47	8	32	.232
First Half	5	7	4.68	0	84.2	Sc Pos	95	26	4	36	.274
Scnd Half	1	1	9.58	0	10.1	Clutch	14	5	0	1	.357

2000 Rankings (National League)

- 8th in errors at pitcher (3)

Brian Giles

2000 Season

Brian Giles enjoyed another fine season, proving his breakthrough year with the Pirates in 1999 was no fluke. Giles became the first player in Pirates history to hit .300 with 30 homers and 100 RBI in consecutive seasons. He opened the campaign as Pittsburgh's right fielder, moved to center field in late May after rookie Chad Hermansen flopped and then spent the final two months in left field to make room for the emerging Adrian Brown.

Hitting

Giles is the total package as a hitter. He hits for power and average while also showing great patience and a keen batting eye. Though only 5-foot-11, he's powerfully built along the lines of Lenny Dykstra and generates good pop with large forearms and a short, quick stroke. He displays good power to all fields and generally hits the ball where it is pitched. Giles possesses strong plate discipline, certainly a virtue last season since he continually was pitched around. While playing for Cleveland, Giles gained the reputation of not being able to hit lefthanders, but he has shed that myth with the Pirates.

Baserunning & Defense

Giles has average speed and runs with a choppy gait. However, he will steal a base when the opposition isn't paying attention and is aggressive on the bases. Giles plays a capable center field, though he doesn't have the fluidity or instincts usually associated with the position. He rates above average in left, where his mediocre arm isn't a big factor.

2001 Outlook

Giles is the man the Pirates plan to build around. They extended his contract through the 2005 season last May. He has become an outstanding offensive player over the past two seasons and should be a fixture in the middle of Pittsburgh's lineup. He also is becoming a team leader with his outspokenness and odd sense of humor.

Position: CF/LF/RF
Bats: L **Throws:** L
Ht: 5'10" **Wt:** 200

Opening Day Age: 30
Born: 1/20/71 in El Cajon, CA
ML Seasons: 6
Pronunciation: JYLES

Overall Statistics

	G	AB	R	H	D	T	HR	RBI	SB	BB	SO	Avg	OBP	Slg
2000	156	559	111	176	37	7	35	123	6	114	69	.315	.432	.594
Career	596	1937	370	583	118	14	113	395	38	364	288	.301	.410	.551

Where He Hits the Ball

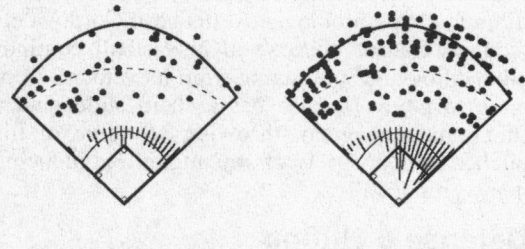

Vs. LHP   **Vs. RHP**

2000 Situational Stats

	AB	H	HR	RBI	Avg		AB	H	HR	RBI	Avg
Home	269	87	16	55	.323	LHP	150	44	5	28	.293
Road	290	89	19	68	.307	RHP	409	132	30	95	.323
First Half	319	101	21	72	.317	Sc Pos	164	49	8	79	.299
Scnd Half	240	75	14	51	.313	Clutch	86	24	3	21	.279

2000 Rankings (National League)

- 2nd in walks
- 3rd in times on base (297) and on-base percentage vs. righthanded pitchers (.446)
- Led the Pirates in home runs, doubles, triples, total bases (332), RBI, sacrifice flies (8), walks, intentional walks (13), times on base (297), GDPs (15), plate appearances (688), slugging percentage, on-base percentage, HR frequency (16.0 ABs per HR), batting average vs. righthanded pitchers, cleanup slugging percentage (.580), slugging percentage vs. righthanded pitchers (.648), on-base percentage vs. righthanded pitchers (.446), batting average at home, lowest percentage of swings that missed (11.6) and games played

Jason Kendall

2000 Season

Jason Kendall made a remarkable comeback after suffering a gruesome dislocated right ankle in 1999 that had threatened his career. He returned so strongly that he earned the starting catcher's assignment for the National League in the 2000 All-Star Game, subbing for the injured Mike Piazza. Furthermore, Kendall became the first catcher ever to steal 20 bases in three different seasons.

Hitting

Kendall immediately adjusts to pitching patterns and no one seems able to retire him the same way twice. He sprays line drives to all fields and is a perennial .300 hitter. Kendall is developing power as he gets older, learning to turn on inside pitches and looking like he will eventually hit 20 homers one season. He also has a good eye and will take a walk, though one disturbing trend is that his strikeout total keeps rising each year. The strikeout increase stems in part from the pressure to carry a weak offense, which causes him to swing at more bad pitches.

Baserunning & Defense

Kendall always has been noted for being the rare catcher with good speed. He showed no drop-off in that department last season and even shaved a tenth of a second off his time from home plate to first base. Kendall is agile behind the plate and is one of the best in the game at blocking balls. However, his throwing suffered greatly in the second half of last season, leading to speculation he was hiding an arm injury. He also has the troubling tendency to drop throws from the outfield.

2001 Outlook

Pittsburgh signed Kendall to a six-year, $60 million contract extension in mid-November, making him the highest-paid player in franchise history. With the upcoming opening of PNC Park, the Pirates didn't want to risk letting their main draw walk away as a free agent at the end of the 2001 season and get only amateur draft picks as compensation. With money no longer an issue, Kendall can resume his role as the second-best hitting catcher in the National League.

Position: C
Bats: R **Throws:** R
Ht: 6' 0" **Wt:** 195

Opening Day Age: 26
Born: 6/26/74 in San Diego, CA
ML Seasons: 5

Pittsburgh

Overall Statistics

	G	AB	R	H	D	T	HR	RBI	SB	BB	SO	Avg	OBP	Slg
2000	152	579	112	185	33	6	14	58	22	79	79	.320	.412	.470
Career	653	2294	393	720	148	21	45	265	93	252	245	.314	.402	.456

Where He Hits the Ball

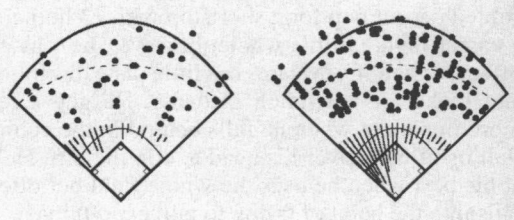

Vs. LHP   **Vs. RHP**

2000 Situational Stats

	AB	H	HR	RBI	Avg		AB	H	HR	RBI	Avg
Home	289	88	7	32	.304	LHP	127	42	2	14	.331
Road	290	97	7	26	.334	RHP	452	143	12	44	.316
First Half	304	97	7	28	.319	Sc Pos	114	35	1	36	.307
Scnd Half	275	88	7	30	.320	Clutch	88	31	3	14	.352

2000 Rankings (National League)

- 3rd in errors at catcher (10) and lowest fielding percentage at catcher (.991)
- 4th in singles, lowest percentage of swings on the first pitch (13.3) and lowest stolen-base percentage (64.7)
- 5th in hit by pitch (15)
- Led the Pirates in batting average, at-bats, runs scored, hits, singles, stolen bases, caught stealing (12), hit by pitch (15), pitches seen (2,680), highest groundball/flyball ratio (1.3), stolen-base percentage (64.7), most pitches seen per plate appearance (3.95), batting average in the clutch, batting average vs. lefthanded pitchers, slugging percentage vs. lefthanded pitchers (.496), on-base percentage vs. lefthanded pitchers (.411)

Pat Meares

2000 Season

Pat Meares spent last season as the Pirates' starting shortstop. That was the role he was supposed to fill after toiling for six years with Minnesota and signing a free-agent contract with Pittsburgh prior to the 1999 campaign. But surgery to repair torn tendons in his left hand limited him to 21 games that year. In his first full season in the National League, Meares never got into any kind of groove until he hit .297 last September.

Hitting

Meares essentially was a one-handed swinger last year. He was unable to fully grip the bat with his left hand as he was recovering from the previous season's surgery. Despite the pain, he demonstrated decent pop for a shortstop with 13 homers, a career high. On the whole, however, he was an offensive liability. Meares has little plate discipline and looks for first-pitch fastballs. He gets even more impatient when he falls behind in the count, flailing at balls over his head and in the dirt. He's at his best when he uses the whole field but often falls into the habit of trying to pull everything.

Baserunning & Defense

Meares possesses average speed at best and rarely tries to steal. He is a poor baserunner, continually watching the ball rather than his third-base coach. He experienced a tough year in the field last season, though he settled down in the second half. His range is only adequate, but he compensates with a strong arm. Still, Meares often seems to lack the instincts typically associated with a shortstop.

2001 Outlook

The Pirates inexplicably signed Meares to a four-year, $15 million contract extension in 1999 that keeps him with the club through 2003. He is all but untradeable at that price. Though the Pirates would like to upgrade at shortstop, economics dictate that they will stick with Meares for at least this season.

Position: SS
Bats: R **Throws:** R
Ht: 6' 0" **Wt:** 187

Opening Day Age: 32
Born: 9/6/68 in Salina, KS
ML Seasons: 8
Pronunciation: MEERS

Overall Statistics

	G	AB	R	H	D	T	HR	RBI	SB	BB	SO	Avg	OBP	Slg
2000	132	462	55	111	22	2	13	47	1	36	91	.240	.305	.381
Career	895	3017	374	792	146	23	54	357	43	140	543	.263	.304	.380

Where He Hits the Ball

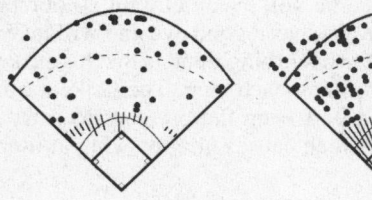

Vs. LHP   Vs. RHP

2000 Situational Stats

	AB	H	HR	RBI	Avg		AB	H	HR	RBI	Avg
Home	222	55	7	28	.248	LHP	121	28	3	9	.231
Road	240	56	6	19	.233	RHP	341	83	10	38	.243
First Half	281	69	7	33	.246	Sc Pos	94	23	3	33	.245
Scnd Half	181	42	6	14	.232	Clutch	72	23	3	8	.319

2000 Rankings (National League)

- 2nd in lowest on-base percentage
- 4th in lowest batting average
- 5th in errors at shortstop (20)
- 6th in lowest on-base percentage vs. lefthanded pitchers (.306) and lowest fielding percentage at shortstop (.967)
- 7th in lowest batting average vs. lefthanded pitchers and lowest on-base percentage vs. righthanded pitchers (.304)

Warren Morris

Position: 2B
Bats: L **Throws:** R
Ht: 5'11" **Wt:** 179

Opening Day Age: 27
Born: 1/11/74 in
Alexandria, LA
ML Seasons: 2

2000 Season

Few players experienced a bigger decline from 1999 to 2000 than Warren Morris. In his second season as the Pirates' second baseman, Morris had a poor all-around year after finishing third in the National League Rookie of the Year voting in '99. He hit .217 in May of last season, .225 in July and his home runs plunged from 15 the previous campaign to three last year.

Hitting

Pitchers around the league adjusted to Morris in his second season, but he didn't adjust back until late in the year. He had demonstrated the ability to turn on inside fastballs as a rookie. However, last year Morris was fed a steady diet of fastballs and breaking pitches on the outside corner, and he spent most of the season lifting weak flyballs to the opposite field. When Morris is on his game, he is aggressive at the plate and sprays line drives all over the field while hitting an occasional home run. The Pirates inexplicably handed him 237 at-bats as the leadoff hitter last season. He proved ill-suited for that role, since he doesn't take many pitches; he managed only a .327 on-base percentage while batting in the No. 1 slot.

Baserunning & Defense

Morris is an average runner who doesn't steal many bases because he has problems getting a good jump. He also can be tentative on the basepaths. Morris had a shaky first half in the field last year but settled down after the All-Star break. He was tagged as a bad defensive player coming up through the minor leagues. Still, he has adequate hands and range while displaying a knack for turning the double play.

2001 Outlook

After Morris looked like the Pirates' starting second baseman for the next 10 years in 1999, his shaky sophomore season has made his future in Pittsburgh tenuous. The Pirates admit they would consider upgrading at second base, which could make him expendable, but Morris showed enough as a rookie that it's hard to give up on him so quickly.

Overall Statistics

	G	AB	R	H	D	T	HR	RBI	SB	BB	SO	Avg	OBP	Slg
2000	144	528	68	137	31	2	3	43	7	65	78	.259	.341	.343
Career	291	1039	133	284	51	5	18	116	10	124	166	.273	.351	.384

Where He Hits the Ball

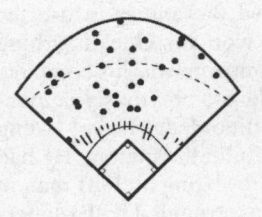
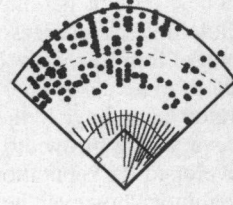

Vs. LHP   **Vs. RHP**

2000 Situational Stats

	AB	H	HR	RBI	Avg		AB	H	HR	RBI	Avg
Home	265	66	3	21	.249	LHP	87	20	0	8	.230
Road	263	71	0	22	.270	RHP	441	117	3	35	.265
First Half	284	72	2	21	.254	Sc Pos	114	28	0	38	.246
Scnd Half	244	65	1	22	.266	Clutch	95	27	1	11	.284

2000 Rankings (National League)

- 2nd in lowest slugging percentage and lowest HR frequency (176.0 ABs per HR)
- 3rd in errors at second base (15)
- 4th in lowest fielding percentage at second base (.979)
- 5th in lowest on-base percentage for a leadoff hitter (.327)
- 6th in lowest slugging percentage vs. righthanded pitchers (.356)
- 7th in lowest batting average at home

Aramis Ramirez

2000 Season

For the third straight season, Aramis Ramirez had difficulty nailing down the Pirates' third-base job. He began the year as the starter, but by late April he was mired with a .167 batting average and was shipped back to Triple-A Nashville. Ramirez returned to the Pirates in mid-June much improved. However, he missed the season's final month after partially dislocating his left shoulder in late August.

Hitting

Ramirez has the potential to be an offensive force. He has excellent bat speed and eventually should turn his gap shots into more home runs. Like many young hitters, he has a tendency to pull too many pitches, though he showed the ability to use the whole field as last season wore on. One disturbing point of Ramirez' 2000 campaign was his complete lack of plate discipline. He had previously demonstrated a good eye in the minor leagues, yet swung at everything thrown to him in the majors. He had developed the reputation for being an RBI man in the minors, however, he has struggled with runners in scoring position at the major league level. His numbers with men on base should improve with experience.

Baserunning & Defense

Ramirez is a below-average runner who goes station-to-station on the basepaths. He's an enigma with the glove. Some observers insist he is a potential Gold Glove winner because of his strong arm, soft hands and good reactions. However, he doesn't take that part of the game seriously and makes far too many careless errors due to a lack of concentration.

2001 Outlook

Ramirez has been rapped as immature and arrogant, but he is very young and showed signs of maturity and humility last year after returning from the minor leagues. While he has room to grow, he made enough strides last season to head into spring training as the Pirates' starting third baseman.

Position: 3B
Bats: R **Throws:** R
Ht: 6' 1" **Wt:** 219

Opening Day Age: 22
Born: 6/25/78 in Santo Domingo, Dominican Republic
ML Seasons: 3
Pronunciation: AIR-emm-iss

Overall Statistics

	G	AB	R	H	D	T	HR	RBI	SB	BB	SO	Avg	OBP	Slg
2000	73	254	19	65	15	2	6	35	0	10	36	.256	.293	.402
Career	163	561	44	134	26	4	12	66	0	34	117	.239	.290	.364

Where He Hits the Ball

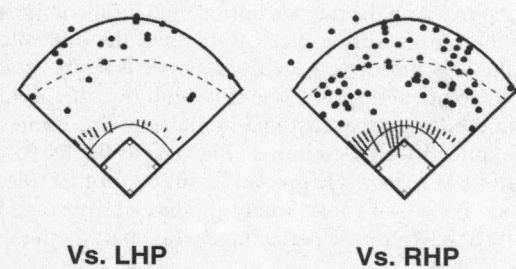

Vs. LHP   **Vs. RHP**

2000 Situational Stats

	AB	H	HR	RBI	Avg		AB	H	HR	RBI	Avg
Home	121	33	4	22	.273	LHP	63	15	1	4	.238
Road	133	32	2	13	.241	RHP	191	50	5	31	.262
First Half	123	27	2	15	.220	Sc Pos	63	14	3	31	.222
Scnd Half	131	38	4	20	.290	Clutch	34	11	1	9	.324

2000 Rankings (National League)

- 6th in errors at third base (14)

Todd Ritchie

2000 Season

After being signed as a minor league free agent and winning 15 games in 1999, Todd Ritchie couldn't match that surprising performance in his second season with the Pirates. He went on the disabled list for three weeks at the beginning of August with a strained muscle under his right armpit. It was suspected the injury had caused his inconsistency over the first four months.

Pitching

Ritchie is a power pitcher who relies on a heavy sinking fastball that reaches 95 MPH and breaks plenty of bats when it's moving. He also features a hard slider that can be an effective pitch when he keeps it down in the strike zone. He occasionally mixes in an overhand curveball and possesses an improved changeup. Ritchie's problem always has been control. He has taken steps to fix that the past two years by eliminating a violent head jerk in his delivery. His biggest troubles last year occurred when he left too many pitches up in the strike zone, resulting in an increased home-run rate.

Defense & Hitting

Ritchie is a good athlete and an outstanding defender. He has good reactions to balls hit up the middle and is quick to pounce on bunts and to cover first base. He has a good pickoff move. Ritchie makes more consistent contact with the bat than most pitchers and he delivered 13 hits last season. However, his bunting declined as he routinely failed to come through in sacrifice situations.

2001 Outlook

Though Ritchie probably isn't as good as he was in 1999, he is better than he showed in 2000. He is a serviceable No. 3 or No. 4 starter, and the Pirates can use all the arms they can find. They figure to use Ritchie as a part of their rotation for a while, since they signed him last May to a two-year, $5 million contact extension through 2002.

Position: SP
Bats: R **Throws:** R
Ht: 6' 3" **Wt:** 222

Opening Day Age: 29
Born: 11/7/71 in Portsmouth, VA
ML Seasons: 4

Overall Statistics

	W	L	Pct.	ERA	G	GS	Sv	IP	H	BB	SO	HR	Ratio
2000	9	8	.529	4.81	31	31	0	187.0	208	51	124	26	1.39
Career	26	20	.565	4.32	116	57	0	458.0	494	142	296	55	1.39

How Often He Throws Strikes

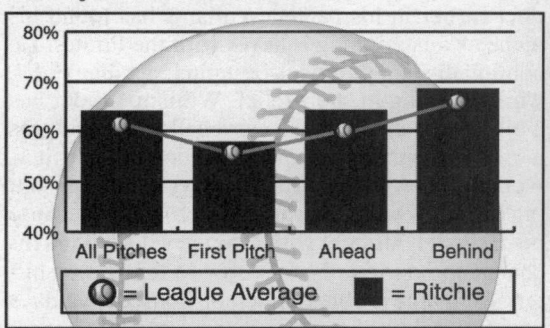

= League Average   = Ritchie

2000 Situational Stats

	W	L	ERA	Sv	IP		AB	H	HR	RBI	Avg
Home	5	4	4.33	0	108.0	LHB	334	104	13	51	.311
Road	4	4	5.47	0	79.0	RHB	403	104	13	54	.258
First Half	5	5	4.42	0	110.0	Sc Pos	186	49	9	79	.263
Scnd Half	4	3	5.38	0	77.0	Clutch	44	8	1	3	.182

2000 Rankings (National League)

- 7th in fewest pitches thrown per batter (3.53)
- 9th in highest slugging percentage allowed (.468)
- 10th in highest batting average allowed (.282)
- Led the Pirates in hits allowed, home runs allowed, highest strikeout/walk ratio (2.4), lowest stolen-base percentage allowed (63.6), fewest pitches thrown per batter (3.53) and fewest walks per nine innings (2.5)

Mike Williams

2000 Season

Mike Williams regained his job as the Pirates closer in spring training after a shaky finish the previous season. He had been removed from the role in 1999 in the midst of compiling an 11.00 ERA after August 1. But in 2000 he wound up converting a career-high 24 saves in 29 chances for a club that rarely provided save opportunities. Though Williams had 12 saves in each half of the season, his ERA was 2.15 before the All-Star break and 4.98 after. None of his final six saves were of the 1-2-3 variety.

Pitching

After flopping as a starting pitcher with Philadelphia earlier in his career, Williams has found his niche as a late-inning reliever with the Pirates. He continually can throw his best pitch, a killer slider, while working in short relief. Williams' slider has a big break, almost like a curveball, and it induces a string of strikeouts and groundouts when it is working. However, he can't always control his out pitch. That's when he runs into problems because his fastball is straight with average velocity and his changeup is primarily for show to lefthanded hitters. Williams is able to pitch on consecutive days without any problem and has the mental toughness to overcome poor outings.

Defense & Hitting

Williams is a good defender. He's quick off the mound and has good reflexes. Though he pays closer attention to baserunners than most closers, he still can be run on because his delivery to home is slow. He hardly ever bats as the closer and isn't much of a hitter.

2001 Outlook

Though Williams is not a dominant closer, he has gotten the job done for the Pirates the past two seasons. Look for him to return to the same role in 2001. He is eligible for free agency at the end of the season, at which point the Pirates may try to upgrade the position.

Position: RP
Bats: R **Throws:** R
Ht: 6' 2" **Wt:** 204

Opening Day Age: 32
Born: 7/29/68 in Radford, VA
ML Seasons: 9

Overall Statistics

	W	L	Pct.	ERA	G	GS	Sv	IP	H	BB	SO	HR	Ratio
2000	3	4	.429	3.50	72	0	24	72.0	56	40	71	8	1.33
Career	23	37	.383	4.50	276	55	48	580.0	584	246	443	69	1.43

How Often He Throws Strikes

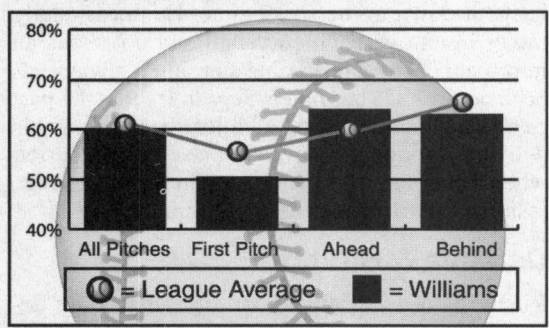

◐ = League Average   ■ = Williams

2000 Situational Stats

	W	L	ERA	Sv	IP		AB	H	HR	RBI	Avg
Home	2	0	2.80	12	35.1	LHB	104	24	6	20	.231
Road	1	4	4.17	12	36.2	RHB	153	32	2	14	.209
First Half	2	1	2.15	12	37.2	Sc Pos	73	21	1	25	.288
Scnd Half	1	3	4.98	12	34.1	Clutch	146	33	3	24	.226

2000 Rankings (National League)

- 2nd in games finished (63)
- 8th in save percentage (82.8)
- 9th in saves
- Led the Pirates in saves, games finished (63), stolen bases allowed (13), save opportunities (29), save percentage (82.8), lowest batting average allowed in relief (.218) and fewest baserunners allowed per nine innings in relief (12.5)

Kevin Young

2000 Season

Kevin Young's offensive numbers declined across the board last year after he underwent knee surgery the previous offseason. The drop-off caused him to lose his hold on the cleanup hitter's job in the Pirate lineup. He also was rested more often at first base to lessen the strain on his knee. Young then missed a large portion of September due to a strained groin muscle. Strangely, the injury occurred when he checked his swing while drawing a walk.

Hitting

Young never has been the classic cleanup-hitting first baseman in the Mark McGwire mold. Still, Young has shown the ability to hit home runs in the past. He's also generated his share of extra-base hits by using the whole field. However, his slugging percentage decreased by nearly 100 points last season. He continually experienced trouble getting around on the inside pitch as an already long swing got even longer. Never a disciplined hitter, Young at times lost command of the strike zone and often swung at just about everything.

Baserunning & Defense

Young is a good baserunner when healthy. He's deceptively fast with the moxie to swipe 15 to 20 bases a year. His stolen-base total was down last year because of the knee problem. He also became more of a station-to-station runner. Young's defense has nosedived the past two years as he made 23 errors in 1999 and 17 last year. A third baseman in the minor leagues, he once boasted as much range as any first baseman in the game. But his range disappeared last season.

2001 Outlook

Young is signed for three more years, so he isn't going anywhere. However, the Pirates have to be concerned with the way he looked last season following knee surgery, when he appeared to age five years. Young insists moving from Three Rivers Stadium's artificial turf to PNC Park's grass surface will help his knee and rejuvenate his career. The Pirates can only hope that's the case.

Position: 1B
Bats: R **Throws:** R
Ht: 6' 3" **Wt:** 222

Opening Day Age: 31
Born: 6/16/69 in Alpena, MI
ML Seasons: 9

Overall Statistics

	G	AB	R	H	D	T	HR	RBI	SB	BB	SO	Avg	OBP	Slg
2000	132	496	77	128	27	0	20	88	8	32	96	.258	.311	.433
Career	865	2896	415	771	172	16	112	483	63	232	637	.266	.327	.453

Where He Hits the Ball

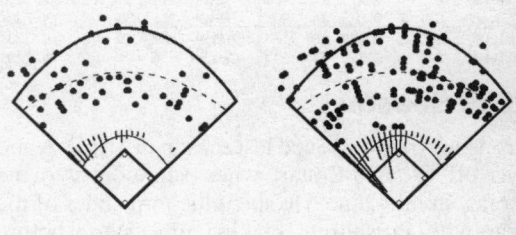

Vs. LHP   **Vs. RHP**

2000 Situational Stats

	AB	H	HR	RBI	Avg		AB	H	HR	RBI	Avg
Home	228	59	11	45	.259	LHP	129	34	7	14	.264
Road	268	69	9	43	.257	RHP	367	94	13	74	.256
First Half	317	83	13	56	.262	Sc Pos	156	41	5	71	.263
Scnd Half	179	45	7	32	.251	Clutch	86	16	4	15	.186

2000 Rankings (National League)

- 1st in errors at first base (17), lowest cleanup slugging percentage (.345) and lowest fielding percentage at first base (.986)
- 5th in lowest on-base percentage
- 8th in lowest groundball/flyball ratio (0.7)
- 9th in lowest on-base percentage vs. righthanded pitchers (.307)
- 10th in lowest batting average on a 3-1 count (.111)
- Led the Pirates in strikeouts and GDPs (15)

Bronson Arroyo

Position: SP
Bats: R **Throws:** R
Ht: 6' 5" **Wt:** 180

Opening Day Age: 24
Born: 2/24/77 in Key West, FL
ML Seasons: 1

Overall Statistics

	W	L	Pct.	ERA	G	GS	Sv	IP	H	BB	SO	HR	Ratio
2000	2	6	.250	6.40	20	12	0	71.2	88	36	50	10	1.73
Career	2	6	.250	6.40	20	12	0	71.2	88	36	50	10	1.73

2000 Situational Stats

	W	L	ERA	Sv	IP		AB	H	HR	RBI	Avg
Home	2	1	4.07	0	42.0	LHB	110	33	2	20	.300
Road	0	5	9.71	0	29.2	RHB	181	55	8	33	.304
First Half	0	2	9.33	0	18.1	Sc Pos	81	27	2	37	.333
Scnd Half	2	4	5.40	0	53.1	Clutch	4	1	0	0	.250

2000 Season

Bronson Arroyo opened last season in Triple-A and was off to an 8-2 start when summoned to the Pirates in mid-June. He spent the remainder of the year with Pittsburgh, making nine starts before being sent to the bullpen as a long reliever in early August. He also pocketed three starts in September.

Pitching, Defense & Hitting

Arroyo doesn't have one dominant pitch. What he does have, though, is variety—a 91-MPH fastball, curveball, slider and changeup. Because he isn't overpowering, Arroyo needs command of all his pitches to succeed. While he won't blow anyone away and was overmatched as a rookie, he has a decent feel for pitching and knows how to win, as evidenced by his 57-30 career record in the minor leagues. He is an exceptional athlete who fields his position and handles the bat well. He also does an adequate job of stopping the running game.

2001 Outlook

Arroyo could have used a full season at Nashville last year but was promoted to the big leagues because of injuries. Look for the Pirates to send him back to Triple-A this season before letting him push for a spot at the end of their rotation in 2002.

Mike Benjamin

Position: 3B/SS/2B
Bats: R **Throws:** R
Ht: 6' 0" **Wt:** 172

Opening Day Age: 35
Born: 11/22/65 in Euclid, OH
ML Seasons: 12

Overall Statistics

	G	AB	R	H	D	T	HR	RBI	SB	BB	SO	Avg	OBP	Slg
2000	93	233	28	63	18	2	2	19	5	12	45	.270	.313	.391
Career	710	1806	220	424	107	14	24	166	44	99	398	.235	.282	.349

2000 Situational Stats

	AB	H	HR	RBI	Avg		AB	H	HR	RBI	Avg
Home	132	33	0	10	.250	LHP	80	26	0	10	.325
Road	101	30	2	9	.297	RHP	153	37	2	9	.242
First Half	149	42	1	9	.282	Sc Pos	57	16	1	17	.281
Scnd Half	84	21	1	10	.250	Clutch	43	18	0	4	.419

2000 Season

Mike Benjamin enjoyed a fine season as the Pirates' top utility infielder. He filled in at third base in May, sharing time with Luis Sojo, when Aramis Ramirez was sent back to Triple-A. However, Benjamin's primary role last year was to back up at second base and shortstop.

Hitting, Baserunning & Defense

Benjamin has become an adequate hitter and has batted .262 over the past three seasons, a significant increase over his prior career mark of .204 through 1997. Benjamin attributes his improved hitting to more playing time. He has good speed and is an exceptional baserunner who rarely makes a mistake on the basepaths. He is outstanding defensively at any infield spot with good range, sure hands and a solid arm. He ended last season with a 102-game errorless streak at second base.

2001 Outlook

The Pirates gave Benjamin a two-year, $1.85 million contract extension last August, ensuring he wouldn't leave as a free agent in the offseason. Benjamin's recent offensive surge has made him one of the top utility infielders in the game. He also will continue to be a clubhouse leader for this perennially young team.

Emil Brown

Position: RF/LF/CF
Bats: R **Throws:** R
Ht: 6' 2" **Wt:** 193

Opening Day Age: 26
Born: 12/29/74 in Chicago, IL
ML Seasons: 4

Overall Statistics

	G	AB	R	H	D	T	HR	RBI	SB	BB	SO	Avg	OBP	Slg
2000	50	119	13	26	5	0	3	16	3	11	34	.218	.299	.336
Career	135	267	31	55	9	1	5	25	8	22	80	.206	.292	.303

2000 Situational Stats

	AB	H	HR	RBI	Avg		AB	H	HR	RBI	Avg
Home	62	13	2	11	.210	LHP	32	7	0	2	.219
Road	57	13	1	5	.228	RHP	87	19	3	14	.218
First Half	3	0	0	0	.000	Sc Pos	35	8	1	14	.229
Scnd Half	116	26	3	16	.224	Clutch	19	2	1	2	.105

2000 Season

Emil Brown split a third straight season between the Pirates and the minor leagues after spending all of 1997 in the major leagues as a Rule 5 draft pick from Oakland. He was called up three different times from Triple-A Nashville in 2000 and had a career-high 119 at-bats in the majors.

Hitting, Baserunning & Defense

Brown has showed the ability to hit for a high average with moderate power in the minor leagues but has been overmatched by major league pitching. His plate discipline improved last season at Nashville, but it did so at the sake of power, as Brown's home-run total dropped at Triple-A from 18 to five. He has above-average speed and is a basestealing threat. He has good range and an outstanding arm, enabling him to play any of the three outfield positions. Right field seems to be his best spot.

2001 Outlook

Brown is out of minor league options, so he figures to either be traded or stick with the Pirates as a fifth outfielder. He is a five-tool player with as much raw talent as anyone in the organization. He is 26, though, so time is running short for him to turn that potential into production.

Josias Manzanillo

Position: RP
Bats: R **Throws:** R
Ht: 6' 0" **Wt:** 205

Opening Day Age: 33
Born: 10/16/67 in San Pedro de Macoris, Dominican Republic
ML Seasons: 7
Pronunciation:
hose-EYE-us man-za-NEE-oh

Overall Statistics

	W	L	Pct.	ERA	G	GS	Sv	IP	H	BB	SO	HR	Ratio
2000	2	2	.500	3.38	43	0	0	58.2	50	32	39	6	1.40
Career	7	8	.467	4.41	148	1	3	206.1	191	103	177	24	1.42

2000 Situational Stats

	W	L	ERA	Sv	IP		AB	H	HR	RBI	Avg
Home	0	2	2.97	0	30.1	LHB	68	17	1	4	.250
Road	2	0	3.81	0	28.1	RHB	140	33	5	23	.236
First Half	0	0	4.43	0	20.1	Sc Pos	61	10	2	22	.164
Scnd Half	2	2	2.82	0	38.1	Clutch	52	15	4	11	.288

2000 Season

Josias Manzanillo signed with the Pirates as a minor league free agent just before spring training last year. He was a physical question mark after missing the second half of 1999 due to elbow surgery. He opened last season at Triple-A Nashville before being summoned to the majors in mid-May. He eventually became the Pirates' top righthanded setup man.

Pitching, Defense & Hitting

While Manzanillo has a live fastball, his best pitch is an outstanding slider with late break. He is particularly tough with runners in scoring position but also prone to bouts of wildness. Manzanillo is an emotional pitcher who unnerves hitters by jumping for joy after key strikeouts and sprinting to the dugout at the end of every inning. He is quick off the mound and good defensively. He also possesses a quick move home that helps stop the running game. He rarely bats as a short reliever.

2001 Outlook

A veteran of nine organizations, Manzanillo seems to have found a home with the Pirates. He pitched well enough last season to warrant a return in 2001. He may move from his setup role to middle relief if Pittsburgh upgrades its bullpen.

Keith Osik

Position: C/3B
Bats: R **Throws:** R
Ht: 6' 0" **Wt:** 192

Opening Day Age: 32
Born: 10/22/68 in Port Jefferson, NY
ML Seasons: 5
Pronunciation: OH-sick

Overall Statistics

	G	AB	R	H	D	T	HR	RBI	SB	BB	SO	Avg	OBP	Slg
2000	46	123	11	36	6	1	4	22	3	14	11	.293	.387	.455
Career	248	633	59	156	36	4	7	63	5	61	100	.246	.322	.349

2000 Situational Stats

	AB	H	HR	RBI	Avg			AB	H	HR	RBI	Avg
Home	51	14	1	8	.275	LHP		35	13	3	9	.371
Road	72	22	3	14	.306	RHP		88	23	1	13	.261
First Half	28	8	2	5	.286	Sc Pos		27	9	0	14	.333
Scnd Half	95	28	2	17	.295	Clutch		21	5	0	1	.238

2000 Season

Keith Osik returned to his role as backup catcher after inheriting the No. 1 job in the second half of 1999 when Jason Kendall dislocated his right ankle. Osik enjoyed his finest season last year, filling in capably at third base in September when Aramis Ramirez was injured.

Hitting, Baserunning & Defense

Osik spent many hours reconstructing his swing following a disappointing '99 season in which he hit .186. He watched hours of videotape and concluded that he had been muscling up on the bat too much. He went back to his old style of concentrating on hitting line drives to all fields, an approach that worked well. He also showed a knack for delivering hits with runners in scoring position. Like most catchers, Osik doesn't run well. He is a solid defender with an adequate arm. He has played every position except shortstop and center field in his major league career and was sometimes spectacular in his limited action at third last season.

2001 Outlook

Osik likely will return as Pittsburgh's backup catcher again. The Pirates don't see Osik as a true No. 1 receiver but then again, they don't need to with Jason Kendall behind the plate for the foreseeable future.

Scott Sauerbeck

Position: RP
Bats: R **Throws:** L
Ht: 6' 3" **Wt:** 197

Opening Day Age: 29
Born: 11/9/71 in Cincinnati, OH
ML Seasons: 2

Overall Statistics

	W	L	Pct.	ERA	G	GS	Sv	IP	H	BB	SO	HR	Ratio
2000	5	4	.556	4.04	75	0	1	75.2	76	61	83	4	1.81
Career	9	5	.643	3.08	140	0	3	143.1	129	99	138	10	1.59

2000 Situational Stats

	W	L	ERA	Sv	IP			AB	H	HR	RBI	Avg
Home	3	2	4.72	0	34.1	LHB		117	26	2	12	.222
Road	2	2	3.48	1	41.1	RHB		164	50	2	25	.305
First Half	3	0	3.57	0	40.1	Sc Pos		94	22	0	30	.234
Scnd Half	2	4	4.58	1	35.1	Clutch		111	27	3	18	.243

2000 Season

Scott Sauerbeck became the Pirates' top lefthanded setup man after Jason Christiansen was traded to St. Louis on July 30. Sauerbeck again was a workhorse, leading the club in appearances for a second straight season. He pitched in 75 games despite missing 15 days in June with a sprained pitching elbow.

Pitching, Defense & Hitting

Sauerbeck is tough on lefthanded hitters with his excellent curveball. He is more than a situational southpaw, however, since his tailing fastball and fine changeup permit him to combat righthanded batters. Sauerbeck offers good deception by changing arm angles. He also induces many groundballs and allows few homers because of his ability to keep the ball down. He does the little things well, such as fielding his position and holding runners on. He has batted just three times over two seasons, so it's hard to get a line on his hitting ability.

2001 Outlook

Sauerbeck will join free agent Terry Mulholland as the Pirates' top lefthanded relievers this season. Plucked from the Mets in the Rule 5 draft in 1998, Sauerbeck has proven to be a real find and should continue to be a key member of Pittsburgh's bullpen for years to come.

Jason Schmidt

Position: SP
Bats: R **Throws:** R
Ht: 6' 5" **Wt:** 213

Opening Day Age: 28
Born: 1/29/73 in
Lewiston, ID
ML Seasons: 6

Overall Statistics

	W	L	Pct.	ERA	G	GS	Sv	IP	H	BB	SO	HR	Ratio
2000	2	5	.286	5.40	11	11	0	63.1	71	41	51	6	1.77
Career	43	47	.478	4.58	137	128	0	799.1	846	344	586	82	1.49

2000 Situational Stats

	W	L	ERA	Sv	IP		AB	H	HR	RBI	Avg
Home	1	3	7.50	0	30.0	LHB	100	25	1	10	.250
Road	1	2	3.51	0	33.1	RHB	150	46	5	25	.307
First Half	2	5	5.40	0	63.1	Sc Pos	63	18	2	27	.286
Scnd Half	0	0	-	0	0.0	Clutch	10	6	2	4	.600

2000 Season

Jason Schmidt was tabbed as Pittsburgh's Opening Day starter for the first time in his career. The Pirates felt he would break through as a big winner. Instead, Schmidt struggled early and did not pitch after June 9. He underwent surgery to repair a frayed rotator cuff in his pitching shoulder in mid-August.

Pitching, Defense & Hitting

No one ever has questioned Schmidt's stuff. His fastball reaches 95 MPH and he can spot it effectively. He also has a good hard slider and a changeup that has improved each season. He goes through stretches where he leaves pitches up in the strike zone, however. Schmidt is a poor defender with bad reactions, though he can be hard to steal against by varying his delivery times. He isn't much of a hitter and is never a sure bet to lay down a sacrifice bunt.

2001 Outlook

Schmidt hasn't quite lived up to expectations and now is coming off shoulder surgery. He's a big question mark, and the Pirates face the tough decision of whether to offer him salary arbitration or possibly let him walk away as a free agent if he doesn't agree to terms.

Jose Silva

Position: RP/SP
Bats: R **Throws:** R
Ht: 6' 5" **Wt:** 235

Opening Day Age: 27
Born: 12/19/73 in
Tijuana, Mexico
ML Seasons: 5

Overall Statistics

	W	L	Pct.	ERA	G	GS	Sv	IP	H	BB	SO	HR	Ratio
2000	11	9	.550	5.56	51	19	0	136.0	178	50	98	16	1.68
Career	21	25	.457	5.37	116	53	4	372.0	447	135	269	38	1.56

2000 Situational Stats

	W	L	ERA	Sv	IP		AB	H	HR	RBI	Avg
Home	6	5	5.07	0	65.2	LHB	231	82	10	43	.355
Road	5	4	6.01	0	70.1	RHB	331	96	6	43	.290
First Half	5	3	3.28	0	68.2	Sc Pos	160	51	9	75	.319
Scnd Half	6	6	7.89	0	67.1	Clutch	88	32	2	10	.364

2000 Season

Jose Silva opened last season as a setup reliever following shoulder surgery the previous November. He then moved into the starting rotation in mid-June. He compiled a 3.40 ERA in 32 relief appearances and a 6.45 ERA in 19 starts.

Pitching, Defense & Hitting

Silva has the stuff to be a big winner as a starter or a top-notch closer. His fastball hits 94 MPH but seems faster because of his smooth delivery. He also has an over-the-top curveball that is unhittable when he gets it over the plate. However, he continues to have problems with consistency and control. Silva isn't very mobile in the field and doesn't have good reactions. However, he does have a rather quick move home, which helps negate the running game. He improved as a hitter last season and became more consistent at laying down sacrifice bunts.

2001 Outlook

Silva is in line for one more chance to prove he belongs in the Pirates' rotation because they are thin in that area. Some believe he could be a great closer. However, Silva has to start turning potential into production sometime soon because he now is arbitration-eligible and a more expensive proposition.

John Vander Wal

Position: RF/1B/LF
Bats: L **Throws:** L
Ht: 6' 2" **Wt:** 197

Opening Day Age: 34
Born: 4/29/66 in Grand Rapids, MI
ML Seasons: 10

Overall Statistics

	G	AB	R	H	D	T	HR	RBI	SB	BB	SO	Avg	OBP	Slg
2000	134	384	74	115	29	0	24	94	11	72	92	.299	.410	.563
Career	983	1702	234	448	98	12	61	291	28	244	394	.263	.355	.442

2000 Situational Stats

	AB	H	HR	RBI	Avg		AB	H	HR	RBI	Avg
Home	175	54	13	51	.309	LHP	50	10	2	7	.200
Road	209	61	11	43	.292	RHP	334	105	22	87	.314
First Half	182	51	10	45	.280	Sc Pos	109	38	9	70	.349
Scnd Half	202	64	14	49	.317	Clutch	79	18	2	13	.228

2000 Season

The Pirates acquired John Vander Wal and two minor league pitchers from San Diego in a trade for Al Martin in spring training. One of the top pinch-hitters in baseball history, Vander Wal wound up with the most playing time of his 10-year career. He responded by driving in nearly 100 runs in just 384 at-bats.

Hitting, Baserunning & Defense

Vander Wal demonstrated last season he is capable of generating impressive numbers with semi-regular playing time. He hits the ball extremely hard and has good power to the opposite field. He always has displayed fine plate discipline and produced a lofty .410 on-base percentage last year. He isn't fast but will steal a base when the opposition isn't paying attention. Vander Wal is a below-average defensive outfielder with limited range and a weak arm but is competent at first base.

2001 Outlook

The Pirates signed Vander Wal to a two-year contract worth up to $4 million with incentives on July 31 to keep him from free agency. While his 116 career pinch-hits tie him for fifth place on the all-time list, he proved last year that he deserves a bigger role. The signing of Derek Bell means Vander Wal probably won't get that larger role.

Enrique Wilson

Position: 3B/2B/SS
Bats: B **Throws:** R
Ht: 5'11" **Wt:** 180

Opening Day Age: 25
Born: 7/27/75 in Santo Domingo, Dominican Republic
ML Seasons: 4

Overall Statistics

	G	AB	R	H	D	T	HR	RBI	SB	BB	SO	Avg	OBP	Slg
2000	80	239	27	70	15	1	5	27	2	18	24	.293	.340	.427
Career	230	676	83	191	43	2	9	64	9	47	75	.283	.327	.392

2000 Situational Stats

	AB	H	HR	RBI	Avg		AB	H	HR	RBI	Avg
Home	120	37	3	16	.308	LHP	63	22	2	9	.349
Road	119	33	2	11	.277	RHP	176	48	3	18	.273
First Half	117	38	2	12	.325	Sc Pos	68	18	1	22	.265
Scnd Half	122	32	3	15	.262	Clutch	41	10	2	3	.244

2000 Season

Enrique Wilson began the season with Cleveland in a familiar position, stuck yet again in a utility infielder's role behind All-Stars Roberto Alomar at second base, Travis Fryman at third and Omar Vizquel at shortstop. Wilson then was traded on July 28 to the Pirates along with Alex Ramirez for Wil Cordero and played frequently at all three positions before spraining his right ankle and finishing with just 35 at-bats in September.

Hitting, Baserunning & Defense

Wilson is a line-drive hitter who makes consistent contact while flashing gap power. He had the reputation of being a better lefthanded hitter but reversed that trend last season. Though Wilson was a stolen-base threat in the minor leagues, he hasn't run much in the majors, partly because he's gotten heavier. He has the arm to play shortstop, but his weight has decreased his range. He is good at second base and adequate at third.

2001 Outlook

Pittsburgh wants to improve its middle infield, and Wilson will get a chance to show he deserves to play. The Pirates wanted to use the final two months last season to determine if he was a regular, but his ankle injury ruined that plan. The Pirates still aren't sure exactly what they have in him.

Brad Clontz (Pos: RHP, Age: 29)

	W	L	Pct.	ERA	G	GS	Sv	IP	H	BB	SO	HR	Ratio
2000	0	0	-	5.14	5	0	0	7.0	7	11	8	1	2.57
Career	22	8	.733	4.34	272	0	8	277.2	276	120	210	30	1.43

Clontz struggled with his control, underwent elbow surgery and was released by the Pirates after the season. He remains ineffective against lefthanded batters, limiting his usefulness. 2001 Outlook: C

Ivan Cruz (Pos: 1B, Age: 32, Bats: L)

	G	AB	R	H	D	T	HR	RBI	SB	BB	SO	Avg	OBP	Slg
2000	8	11	0	1	0	0	0	0	0	0	8	.091	.091	.091
Career	24	41	3	10	1	0	1	5	0	2	14	.244	.279	.341

Though he's proven he can mash minor league pitching, Cruz has never received a lengthy audition in the majors. At age 32, the best he can hope for is a job as a lefthanded bat off the bench. 2001 Outlook: C

Mike Garcia (Pos: RHP, Age: 32)

	W	L	Pct.	ERA	G	GS	Sv	IP	H	BB	SO	HR	Ratio
2000	0	2	.000	11.12	13	0	0	11.1	21	7	9	1	2.47
Career	1	2	.333	7.36	20	0	0	18.1	23	10	18	2	1.80

After a hot spring, Garcia cooled off considerably, as the National League rocked him for a .429 average. He was eventually demoted and released before being sold to a Korean team. 2001 Outlook: D

Alex Hernandez (Pos: 1B, Age: 23, Bats: L)

	G	AB	R	H	D	T	HR	RBI	SB	BB	SO	Avg	OBP	Slg
2000	20	60	4	12	3	0	1	5	1	0	13	.200	.200	.300
Career	20	60	4	12	3	0	1	5	1	0	13	.200	.200	.300

Hernandez possesses good tools and hit well at Double-A last year, but wasn't at all impressive in a September callup. The Pirates have plenty of other outfield candidates. 2001 Outlook: C

Adam Hyzdu (Pos: RF, Age: 29, Bats: R)

	G	AB	R	H	D	T	HR	RBI	SB	BB	SO	Avg	OBP	Slg
2000	12	18	2	7	2	0	1	4	0	0	4	.389	.389	.667
Career	12	18	2	7	2	0	1	4	0	0	4	.389	.389	.667

The dream still lives for Hyzdu, a first-round pick of the Giants way back in 1990. After over 4,000 minor league at-bats, he finally reached the majors last September. He could help as a pinch-hitter. 2001 Outlook: D

Rich Loiselle (Pos: RHP, Age: 29)

	W	L	Pct.	ERA	G	GS	Sv	IP	H	BB	SO	HR	Ratio
2000	2	3	.400	5.10	40	0	0	42.1	43	30	32	5	1.72
Career	9	17	.346	3.76	184	3	48	206.0	213	107	169	19	1.55

Considering he was coming back from reconstructive elbow surgery and also battled shoulder problems, Loiselle didn't pitch that poorly in 2000. If healthy, he could surprise, though likely not as a closer. 2001 Outlook: B

Abraham Nunez (Pos: SS, Age: 25, Bats: B)

	G	AB	R	H	D	T	HR	RBI	SB	BB	SO	Avg	OBP	Slg
2000	40	91	10	20	1	0	1	8	0	8	14	.220	.283	.264
Career	173	442	44	96	13	2	2	33	14	51	92	.217	.300	.269

When he arrived in a trade from Toronto after the '96 season, Nunez looked to be the Bucs' shortstop of the future. He still might be, considering he'll be 25 this year, but his average needs to top .220. 2001 Outlook: B

Brian O'Connor (Pos: LHP, Age: 24)

	W	L	Pct.	ERA	G	GS	Sv	IP	H	BB	SO	HR	Ratio
2000	0	0	-	5.11	6	1	0	12.1	12	11	7	2	1.86
Career	0	0	-	5.11	6	1	0	12.1	12	11	7	2	1.86

O'Connor finally conquered Double-A last year, and actually made a spot start for Pittsburgh in May before a September callup. His strikeout-to-walk ratio remains worrysome. 2001 Outlook: C

Jose Parra (Pos: RHP, Age: 28)

	W	L	Pct.	ERA	G	GS	Sv	IP	H	BB	SO	HR	Ratio
2000	0	1	.000	6.94	6	2	0	11.2	17	7	9	3	2.06
Career	6	11	.353	6.62	53	19	0	153.2	198	62	95	31	1.69

After spending the previous two years in Korea and Japan, Parra returned to the big leagues for the first time since 1996. The results certainly didn't indicate Parra should discard his passport. 2001 Outlook: C

Chris Peters (Pos: LHP, Age: 29)

	W	L	Pct.	ERA	G	GS	Sv	IP	H	BB	SO	HR	Ratio
2000	1	0	1.000	2.86	18	0	1	28.1	23	14	16	2	1.31
Career	17	21	.447	4.57	123	43	2	348.2	373	142	210	47	1.48

Peters never was a hard thrower, and now he'll be trying to put last year's shoulder and elbow woes behind him. But he throws strikes, can start or relieve, and isn't helpless versus righties. 2001 Outlook: B

Alex Ramirez (Pos: RF/LF, Age: 26, Bats: R)

	G	AB	R	H	D	T	HR	RBI	SB	BB	SO	Avg	OBP	Slg
2000	84	227	26	56	11	2	9	30	2	12	49	.247	.285	.432
Career	135	332	38	86	17	3	12	48	3	15	78	.259	.293	.437

Once pegged by *Baseball America* as the Indians' left fielder of the future, Cleveland traded Ramirez to Pittsburgh last July. He will take his power potential to Japan next season. 2001 Outlook: D

Dan Serafini (Pos: LHP, Age: 27)

	W	L	Pct.	ERA	G	GS	Sv	IP	H	BB	SO	HR	Ratio
2000	2	5	.286	5.51	14	11	0	65.1	79	28	35	11	1.64
Career	14	13	.519	6.06	91	29	1	233.1	294	102	114	32	1.70

The former first-round pick has now bounced around four organizations the past three years. Although he pitched better after his mid-season trade to Pittsburgh, the lefty is still trying to establish himself. 2001 Outlook: C

Pittsburgh

Matt Skrmetta (**Pos**: RHP, **Age**: 28)

	W	L	Pct.	ERA	G	GS	Sv	IP	H	BB	SO	HR	Ratio
2000	2	2	.500	11.66	14	0	0	14.2	19	9	11	3	1.91
Career	2	2	.500	11.66	14	0	0	14.2	19	9	11	3	1.91

The Pirates acquired Skrmetta in a deal for Jarrod Patterson last August. Though Skrmetta earned some saves in Triple-A, his first exposure to the big leagues showed he was overmatched. The Reds signed him to a minor league deal in late November. 2001 Outlook: C

Brian Smith (**Pos**: RHP, **Age**: 28)

	W	L	Pct.	ERA	G	GS	Sv	IP	H	BB	SO	HR	Ratio
2000	0	0	-	10.38	3	0	0	4.1	6	2	3	1	1.85
Career	0	0	-	10.38	3	0	0	4.1	6	2	3	1	1.85

Smith is a short righthander whom the Pirates selected in the Rule 5 draft last year. He was dominant at Double-A, but is now 28 years old and must hope a bullpen role opens for him. 2001 Outlook: C

Steve Sparks (**Pos**: RHP, **Age**: 26)

	W	L	Pct.	ERA	G	GS	Sv	IP	H	BB	SO	HR	Ratio
2000	0	0	-	6.75	3	0	0	4.0	4	5	2	0	2.25
Career	0	0	-	6.75	3	0	0	4.0	4	5	2	0	2.25

This isn't the same Steve Sparks who throws a knuckleball for Detroit. He's a 6-foot-4 thrower who spent most of 2000 at Double-A before getting a cup of coffee with the Pirates. Expect more Triple-A time. 2001 Outlook: C

Jeff Wallace (**Pos**: LHP, **Age**: 24)

	W	L	Pct.	ERA	G	GS	Sv	IP	H	BB	SO	HR	Ratio
2000	2	0	1.000	7.07	38	0	0	35.2	42	34	27	5	2.13
Career	3	0	1.000	4.67	90	0	0	86.2	76	80	82	7	1.80

He's big and he's lefthanded, but until he can walk fewer than one batter per inning, Wallace will hardly inspire confidence striding in from the bullpen. He was claimed off waivers by the Reds on December 1. 2001 Outlook: B

John Wehner (**Pos**: 3B, **Age**: 33, **Bats**: R)

	G	AB	R	H	D	T	HR	RBI	SB	BB	SO	Avg	OBP	Slg
2000	21	50	10	15	3	0	1	9	0	4	6	.300	.352	.420
Career	418	753	96	190	32	4	4	52	13	63	124	.252	.310	.321

Wehner has now strung together a 10-year big league career, despite only 753 at-bats. If he manages to extend the streak to 11 campaigns, don't expect anything close to last year's average. 2001 Outlook: C

Marc Wilkins (**Pos**: RHP, **Age**: 30)

	W	L	Pct.	ERA	G	GS	Sv	IP	H	BB	SO	HR	Ratio
2000	4	2	.667	5.07	52	0	0	60.1	54	43	37	4	1.61
Career	19	13	.594	4.12	231	2	3	277.1	256	147	207	21	1.45

Wilkins is the definition of middle-relief filler. Although he posted an ugly strikeout-to-walk ratio last year, Oakland saw enough to claim him off waivers but then released him in mid-December. 2001 Outlook: C

Pittsburgh Pirates Minor League Prospects

Organization Overview:

Last year was a discouraging one at the major league level for the Pirates. The Pirates thought Chad Hermansen and Aramis Ramirez were on the verge of contributing, but both spent most of the season in Triple-A for a third straight year. Pittsburgh *did* parlay its questionable offseason signing of Wil Cordero into two solid youngsters, Enrique Wilson and Alex Ramirez. On the whole, things were much more positive throughout the organization's minor league system, however. Class-A Hickory boasted a plethora of prospects, including two potential impact players in J.R. House and Bobby Bradley. The Pirates are well-stocked behind the plate with Craig Wilson, Humberto Cota, House and Ryan Doumit, and have accumulated a hopeful corps of young shortstops including Jack Wilson, Jose Castillo and Edwin Yan.

Bobby Bradley

Position: P **Opening Day Age:** 20
Bats: R **Throws:** R **Born:** 12/15/80 in West
Ht: 6' 1" **Wt:** 164 Palm Beach, FL

Recent Statistics

	W	L	ERA	G	GS	Sv	IP	H	R	BB	SO	HR
1999 R Pirates	1	1	2.90	6	6	0	31.0	31	13	4	31	2
2000 A Hickory	8	2	2.29	14	14	0	82.2	62	31	21	118	3

Expectations were sky-high for the Pirates' 1999 first-round pick, yet Bradley managed to exceed those expectations in his full-season debut. He displayed dominance and poise beyond his years. In his first 12 starts, he overmatched the South Atlantic League with his impressive arsenal consisting of a low-90s fastball, a plus-*plus* curveball and changeup. Bradley's curveball was named the best breaking ball in the SAL, but that might be shortchanging the tight-breaking unhittable pitch. A sprained elbow ligament kept him on the shelf from June on—a precautionary measure—but he was throwing pain-free during Instructional League. He is expected to be back on the fast track this year and could enjoy a Rick Ankiel-like ascent to the NL if he stays healthy.

Humberto Cota

Position: C **Opening Day Age:** 22
Bats: R **Throws:** R **Born:** 2/7/79 in San Luis
Ht: 6' 0" **Wt:** 175 Rio Colorado, Mex

Recent Statistics

	G	AB	R	H	D	T	HR	RBI	SB	BB	SO	Avg
1999 A Chston-SC	85	336	42	94	21	9	9	61	1	20	51	.280
1999 A Hickory	37	133	28	36	11	2	2	20	3	21	20	.271
2000 AA Altoona	112	429	49	112	20	1	8	44	6	21	80	.261
2000 MLE	112	418	40	101	19	0	6	36	4	14	86	.242

Of the organization's catching prospects, Cota is the most advanced defensively. Released by Atlanta in 1997 due to a serious shoulder injury, the Pirates acquired the Mexico-native from Tampa Bay two years later. Cota

shows no ill-effects from the injury and is a fundamentally sound receiver. While he's exhibited some offensive potential, his marginal plate discipline may preclude him from becoming an offensive weapon. He spent last year in Double-A as a 21-year-old, so his poor strikeout-walk ratio and declining power numbers aren't as much of a concern. His presence, along with Craig Wilson and phenom J.R. House, can allow the Pirates' brass to rest easier if they do lose Jason Kendall.

J.J. Davis

Position: OF **Opening Day Age:** 22
Bats: R **Throws:** R **Born:** 10/25/78 in
Ht: 6' 4" **Wt:** 250 Glendora, CA

Recent Statistics

	G	AB	R	H	D	T	HR	RBI	SB	BB	SO	Avg
1999 A Hickory	86	317	58	84	26	1	19	65	2	44	99	.265
2000 A Lynchburg	130	485	77	118	36	1	20	80	9	52	171	.243

Davis owns the best raw power in the system, but injuries have prevented him from making consistent progress. After playing in just 86 games in Class-A, Davis underwent elbow surgery, putting an end to his 1999 season. Nevertheless, he was promoted to the advanced Class-A Carolina League last year, where he showcased his tape-measure power, as well as his inexperience. He mashed a career-best 20 home runs and an encouraging 36 doubles, but he fanned 171 times. A pitcher/first baseman in high school, he is starting to get better jumps on flyballs in right field, and his arm is strong. Improving his pitch selection is a priority.

Chad Hermansen

Position: OF **Opening Day Age:** 23
Bats: R **Throws:** R **Born:** 9/10/77 in Salt
Ht: 6' 2" **Wt:** 185 Lake City, UT

Recent Statistics

	G	AB	R	H	D	T	HR	RBI	SB	BB	SO	Avg
2000 AAA Nashville	78	294	47	66	12	1	11	38	16	25	89	.224
2000 NL Pittsburgh	33	108	12	20	4	1	2	8	0	6	37	.185
2000 MLE	78	286	36	58	11	0	8	29	11	19	94	.203

Last year was supposed to be the year that Hermansen took Pittsburgh's center field job for good. The spring training deal that sent Al Martin to San Diego opened up a starting job for the 1995 first-rounder, but after a dismal month he found himself back in Triple-A. Hermansen has a quick bat and can mash fastballs, but hasn't been able to adjust to good offspeed and breaking offerings. Hermansen averaged 26 home runs a season in the four years leading up to the 2000 season, before suffering his most disappointing campaign. The Pirates remain high on him, although his confidence was non-existent upon returning to Nashville for a third season last year. Improving his approach at the plate will be the key to deciding his future.

J.R. House

Position: C
Bats: R **Throws:** R
Ht: 6' 1" **Wt:** 202
Opening Day Age: 21
Born: 11/11/79 in Charleston, WV

Recent Statistics

	G	AB	R	H	D	THR	RBI	SB	BB	SO	Avg
1999 R Pirates	33	113	13	37	9	3	5	23	1	11	23	.327
1999 A Williamsprt	26	100	11	30	6	0	1	13	0	9	21	.300
1999 A Hickory	4	11	1	3	0	0	0	0	0	0	3	.273
2000 A Hickory	110	420	78	146	29	1	23	90	1	46	91	.348

House missed a month of the season with mononucleosis. Known as a tough hitters' league, the SAL provided little challenge for him. He took the loop's batting title, home-run crown and MVP award while posting an eye-catching .414 and .586 on-base and slugging percentages. All of this from a 1999 fifth-round pick out of a Florida high school. House also was recruited as a QB, which caused his draft status to slide. The Pirates applaud his leadership and game-calling skills, although his throwing is considered average. He generates outstanding power with excellent bat speed, and his quick transition to the pro ranks was no match for SAL hurlers.

Tike Redman

Position: OF
Bats: L **Throws:** L
Ht: 5' 11" **Wt:** 166
Opening Day Age: 24
Born: 3/10/77 in Tuscaloosa, AL

Recent Statistics

	G	AB	R	H	D	THR	RBI	SB	BB	SO	Avg
2000 AAA Nashville	121	506	62	132	24	11	4	51	24	32	73	.261
2000 NL Pittsburgh	9	18	2	6	1	0	1	1	1	1	7	.333
2000 MLE	121	490	48	116	22	8	3	40	17	25	77	.237

Redman was a fifth-rounder in '96 and he's progressed up the ladder at a steady pace. Redman's game revolves around speed, but that doesn't mean he'll get the bat knocked out of his hands. He generates enough pop to punch the ball into the gaps with a smooth lefthanded stroke, and has averaged 23 doubles and 11 triples over the past three seasons. He made strides in bunting, stealing and working the count in the Arizona Fall League, drawing 15 walks while sporting a .386 on-base percentage and succeeding on 11 of 14 steal attempts. He's considered the best defensive outfielder in the system with his gap-to-gap range and strong, accurate arm. A .322 career OBP isn't good for a leadoff hitter, an area he must improve before competing for time in Pittsburgh.

Craig Wilson

Position: C
Bats: R **Throws:** R
Ht: 6' 2" **Wt:** 217
Opening Day Age: 24
Born: 11/30/76 in Fountain Valley, CA

Recent Statistics

	G	AB	R	H	D	THR	RBI	SB	BB	SO	Avg
1999 AA Altoona	111	362	57	97	21	3	20	69	1	40	104	.268
2000 AAA Nashville	124	396	83	112	24	2	33	86	1	44	121	.283
2000 MLE	124	382	65	98	22	1	26	67	0	34	128	.257

Wilson was a little-known prospect when he came over in a 1996 nine-player trade with the Jays. But four years later, he is one of the few players acquired by the Pirates still with a good chance to contribute as a major leaguer. For Wilson, defense has been a question mark, not his bat. Each year he seems to increase his power output. Elbow surgery in '98 has hindered his progress behind home plate for the past two years, and he's shared time between catching, first base and DH. His power would be a major plus at the position, but he doesn't possess a quick release and tends to get long with his throws. His plate discipline also is an area that needs to be addressed.

Jack Wilson

Position: SS
Bats: R **Throws:** R
Ht: 6' 0" **Wt:** 170
Opening Day Age: 23
Born: 12/29/77 in Westlake Village, CA

Recent Statistics

	G	AB	R	H	D	THR	RBI	SB	BB	SO	Avg
1999 A Peoria	64	251	47	86	22	4	3	28	11	15	23	.343
1999 A Potomac	64	257	44	76	10	1	2	18	7	19	31	.296
2000 A Potomac	13	47	7	13	0	1	2	7	2	5	10	.277
2000 AA Arkansas	88	343	65	101	20	8	6	34	2	36	59	.294
2000 AA Altoona	33	139	17	35	7	2	1	16	1	14	17	.252
2000 MLE	121	469	71	123	24	6	5	42	1	35	80	.262

The Pirates acquired Wilson from the Cardinals in July for hard-throwing lefty Jason Christiansen. A ninth-round pick by St. Louis in 1998 out of a California junior college, Wilson made rapid progress through the system. His glove was expected to carry him up the rungs of the organization, but Wilson's bat has been surprisingly advanced at each level. A consistent contact hitter, he displays good bat control and a hint of gap power. Regarded as the best defensive shortstop in the Texas League in a manager's poll, Wilson committed just 17 errors and is considered major league-ready with the leather.

Others to Watch

Tony Alvarez (21) is an aggressive up-and-comer who has displayed versatility in the field by playing first and third base, as well as all three outfield positions. He projects to add more power to go with the wheels that helped him steal 52 bases. . . Lefthander **Sean Burnett** (18) showed why *Baseball America* regarded him as the high schooler with the best command by walking just three in his GCL debut. . . Shortstop **Jose Castillo** (20) made a successful jump from the GCL to the full-season SAL last year, ripping 56 extra-base hits. Still raw and inexperienced, the Venezuelan-native owns a cannon-like arm, but committed 60 errors and drew only 29 walks. . . Catcher **Ryan Doumit** (19) hit .313 in the New York-Penn League, impressing with his all-around receiving skills and a powerful throwing arm. . . Outfielder **Aron Weston** (20) posted just a .340 slugging percentage last year, but the wiry and athletic 6-foot-5, 173-pound, 1999 third-rounder is attracting attention with his power and speed. . . Lefthander **Dave Williams** (22) succeeded last year by changing speeds and locating an average 88-90 MPH fastball. He doesn't project to be a big strikeout pitcher, but with the help of a plus-changeup and curveball he posted a SAL-best 193 Ks.

Busch Stadium

Offense

For years, Busch Stadium ranked among the worst home-run parks in the major leagues. But the field has undergone revisions over the past decade, and the new Busch Stadium is now one of baseball's better parks for the longball. Still, it is not a launching pad. It is a fair park where the ball carries well down both lines and where it flies everywhere when the weather heats up in midsummer. The infield is kept fairly hard to add to the offensive dimension.

Defense

The Cardinals have built a pitching staff that features some solid strikeout hurlers, which lessens the impact of the increased power shown at Busch. And speed is less of a necessity on the grass surface and in the slightly smaller outfield gaps. The addition of Jim Edmonds gives the Cardinals the outstanding center fielder needed to play what are fairly deep power alleys in both left-center and right-center.

Who It Helps the Most

Edmonds was a perfect fit for St. Louis, since his power to the opposite field was rewarded and where he warmed to what is one of the best home-crowd atmospheres in baseball. Ray Lankford, in an otherwise poor season, hit nearly 100 points better at home. The splitter of closer Dave Veres was also well suited to the grass infield at Busch.

Who It Hurts the Most

Edgar Renteria hit only four of his career-high 16 home runs at home. Matt Morris' earned run average was over four runs worse in St. Louis than on the road, while Garret Stephenson earned only six of his 16 victories at Busch Stadium.

Rookies & Newcomers

St. Louis is not likely to have many new faces, having tied up most of its nucleus to long-term contracts. They did trade for Dustin Hermanson, who has held opponents to a .187 batting average at Busch. A big question will be how Matt Morris pitches at home. He will likely be in the rotation from the start of this season and he must pitch better at Busch Stadium than he has in the past.

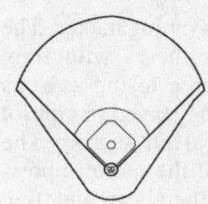

Dimensions: LF-330, LCF-372, CF-402, RCF-372, RF-330

Capacity: 49,676

Elevation: 535 feet

Surface: Grass

Foul Territory: Large

Park Factors

2000 Season

	Home Games			Away Games			
	Cardinals	Opp	Total	Cardinals	Opp	Total	Index
G	75	75	150	72	72	144	—
Avg	.274	.254	.264	.269	.262	.266	99
AB	2463	2544	5007	2509	2375	4884	98
R	416	371	787	398	327	725	104
H	676	647	1323	676	623	1299	98
2B	108	149	257	135	122	257	98
3B	13	12	25	10	13	23	106
HR	121	99	220	96	83	179	120
BB	344	303	647	276	253	529	119
SO	549	546	1095	589	448	1037	103
E	54	56	110	49	54	103	103
E-Infield	43	41	84	34	49	83	97
LHB-Avg	.295	.262	.278	.291	.264	.278	100
LHB-HR	58	37	95	45	34	79	123
RHB-Avg	.261	.249	.255	.254	.261	.257	99
RHB-HR	63	62	125	51	49	100	118

1998-2000

	Home Games			Away Games			
	Cardinals	Opp	Total	Cardinals	Opp	Total	Index
G	223	223	446	220	220	440	—
Avg	.267	.260	.264	.259	.273	.266	99
AB	7505	7860	15365	7634	7275	14909	102
R	1176	1116	2292	1122	1036	2158	105
H	2003	2046	4049	1980	1983	3963	101
2B	360	422	782	407	391	798	95
3B	42	32	74	37	45	82	88
HR	322	248	570	279	211	490	113
BB	979	873	1852	841	811	1652	109
SO	1593	1485	3078	1752	1334	3086	97
E	199	150	349	158	163	321	107
E-Infield	165	116	281	119	132	251	110
LHB-Avg	.283	.255	.268	.265	.271	.268	100
LHB-HR	110	90	200	89	72	161	124
RHB-Avg	.258	.263	.261	.256	.273	.264	99
RHB-HR	212	158	370	190	139	329	107

2000 Rankings (National League)
- Highest walk factor
- Third-highest home-run factor
- Third-highest RHB home-run factor

St. Louis

Tony La Russa

2000 Season

It's amazing what a difference winning makes. The same Cardinals fans who grew uneasy with Tony La Russa over the previous three losing seasons hailed his handling of a club that stayed in control of the National League Central all season. The Cardinals' division title was all the more impressive because they were without their heart and soul, Mark McGwire, for most of the entire second half. St. Louis really came together when La Russa and General Manager Walt Jocketty overhauled the bullpen in late May to solidify what was the club's weakest area.

Offense

Ideally, La Russa would prefer a team with more speed and versatility than the Cardinals' lineup, which includes several high-strikeout batters and few genuine basestealers. The addition of Fernando Vina gave the Cards a much-needed leadoff hitter. La Russa does not shy away from putting runners in motion, and he finished second among NL managers in hit-and-run attempts for the second straight year. No one uses a bench better than La Russa, who was forced to juggle lineups due to St. Louis' series of injuries last season.

Pitching & Defense

One of La Russa's key decisions was to insert Matt Morris into a relief role. The combination of Morris and closer Dave Veres led the Cardinals' bullpen down the stretch, though the lack of a consistent lefthanded reliever prevented La Russa from matching up relievers in the late innings, as he would like to do. He showed his ability to adapt to the situation at hand, often employing his closer in the eighth inning rather than saving him for the ninth. Given a stable rotation for the first time in St. Louis, he was much more patient with his starters than in the recent past.

2001 Outlook

There is no better pennant-race manager than La Russa. If the Cardinals stay reasonably free of injuries this year, they should be the team to beat again in the National League Central. He has lost none of his fire or intensity and now has a roster that is a good blend of youth and experience.

Born: 10/04/44 in Tampa, FL

Playing Experience: 1963-1973, Oak, Atl, ChC

Managerial Experience: 22 seasons

Manager Statistics

Year	Team, Lg	W	L	Pct	GB	Finish
2000	St. Louis, NL	95	67	.586	—	1st Central
22 Seasons		1734	1578	.523	—	—

2000 Starting Pitchers by Days Rest

	<=3	4	5	6+
Cardinals Starts	2	81	59	14
Cardinals ERA	2.19	4.18	4.32	4.50
NL Avg Starts	2	80	50	21
NL ERA	5.00	4.61	4.60	5.18

2000 Situational Stats

	Tony La Russa	NL Average
Hit & Run Success %	43.9	33.8
Stolen Base Success %	63.0	68.8
Platoon Pct.	53.3	53.2
Defensive Subs	25	19
High-Pitch Outings	11	14
Quick/Slow Hooks	17/8	14/16
Sacrifice Attempts	107	87

2000 Rankings (National League)

- 1st in starting lineups used (137) and starts with over 140 pitches (1)
- 2nd in hit-and-run attempts (98), hit-and-run success percentage (43.9) and saves with over 1 inning pitched (18)
- 3rd in sacrifice bunt attempts (107), pitchouts with a runner moving (11) and quick hooks (17)

Rick Ankiel

Position: SP
Bats: L **Throws:** L
Ht: 6' 1" **Wt:** 210

Opening Day Age: 21
Born: 7/19/79 in Fort Pierce, FL
ML Seasons: 2
Pronunciation: ANN-keel

2000 Season

A nightmarish postseason overshadowed what was a solid rookie year for Rick Ankiel. He was part of the Cards' rotation all year, making 30 starts, winning 11 games and ranking among the league leaders in strikeouts and opponents' batting average. The Cardinals won nine of his last 10 starts. Unfortunately, all that progress was forgotten when Ankiel set records for wildness in his two playoff appearances.

Pitching

As far as stuff is concerned, Ankiel is among the best young lefthanders in the game. He throws in the mid- to high 90s with a riding fastball he can work inside and which he is learning to sink. He also throws a curve with a big 12-to-6 break, which he can offer at varying speeds. He shows a slider and also has improved his feel for a changeup. He is tough against lefthanded hitters, who hit only one homer off him in 95 at-bats last year. Control is what stands between Ankiel and the ability to be an ace. His trouble is not command, but rather throwing strikes consistently. When he starts missing, his mechanics deteriorate and he starts missing the strike zone by a lot, which is why he was among league leaders in walks and wild pitches.

Defense & Hitting

Though Ankiel is a good athlete, he is prone to hurrying plays in the field and throwing erratically at times. His pickoff move is a work in progress, though he delivers to the plate quickly. He is on his way to being one of the best hitting pitchers in the game. He had 17 hits last year, batting .250 with two homers and nine RBI. He swings the bat so well that Tony La Russa has used him occasionally as a pinch-hitter.

2001 Outlook

St. Louis does not think that Ankiel's awful postseason performance will have any carryover effect on his psyche. He is a tough-minded player with maturity beyond his 21 years. If he is able to maintain more consistent pitching mechanics, he is fully capable of breaking through this season with 15-17 wins.

Overall Statistics

	W	L	Pct.	ERA	G	GS	Sv	IP	H	BB	SO	HR	Ratio
2000	11	7	.611	3.50	31	30	0	175.0	137	90	194	21	1.30
Career	11	8	.579	3.46	40	35	1	208.0	163	104	233	23	1.28

How Often He Throws Strikes

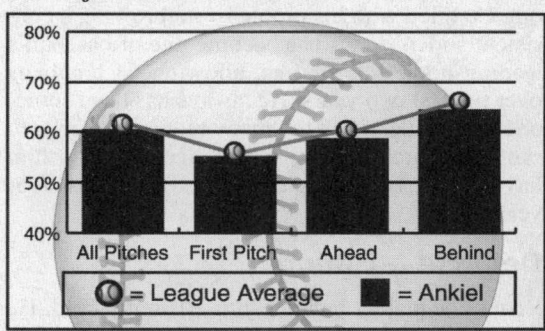

All Pitches · First Pitch · Ahead · Behind

○ = League Average ■ = Ankiel

2000 Situational Stats

	W	L	ERA	Sv	IP		AB	H	HR	RBI	Avg
Home	7	2	3.36	0	101.2	LHB	95	24	1	5	.253
Road	4	5	3.68	0	73.1	RHB	530	113	20	65	.213
First Half	6	4	3.74	0	91.1	Sc Pos	140	32	4	48	.229
Scnd Half	5	3	3.23	0	83.2	Clutch	17	4	1	1	.235

2000 Rankings (National League)

- 1st in errors at pitcher (7) and most pitches thrown per batter (4.20)
- 2nd in most strikeouts per nine innings (10.0)
- 3rd in lowest batting average allowed (.219)
- 4th in balks (2) and lowest batting average allowed vs. righthanded batters
- 5th in wild pitches (12)
- Led the Cardinals in ERA, walks allowed, strikeouts, wild pitches (12), balks (2), lowest batting average allowed (.219), lowest slugging percentage allowed (.365), fewest home runs allowed per nine innings (1.08), most strikeouts per nine innings (10.0), lowest ERA at home and lowest batting average allowed vs. righthanded batters

St. Louis

Andy Benes

2000 Season

In his second stint with St. Louis, Andy Benes lost nearly a month due to knee troubles. He still managed to reach double-figures in wins for the sixth straight year and the 10th time in his career. Nevertheless, his earned run average was a career high and his effectiveness deteriorated late in the season. He went winless from July 14 until September 26.

Pitching

Benes' velocity rarely passes the low 90s these days, which means he must rely more on location and changing speeds, something he had resisted until recently. His fastball also tends to straighten out. Coupled with his problems in throwing a consistent slider, Benes has become one of baseball's leading home-run victims, allowing 64 longballs over the last two years. He always has been someone who walks a few too many hitters and tends to run high pitch counts, which accounts for him having only two complete games in the last four years.

Defense & Hitting

Benes adequately handles himself in the field. He doesn't have any special pickoff move but has worked hard on his slide step to better hold runners. Last year basestealers were caught 32 percent of the time on his watch. Benes has seven career home runs, but he struggles to make contact overall, managing just four hits last year.

2001 Outlook

Because he is so hittable, Benes no longer is a No. 1 or 2 starter. However, with St. Louis, he doesn't have to be anything more than a fourth or fifth starter. If he's provided good run support, he should continue to win 12-14 games a year. With their potential depth in starting pitching, the Cardinals may consider shopping him for outfield help because durable veteran pitchers always have value.

Position: SP
Bats: R **Throws:** R
Ht: 6' 6" **Wt:** 245

Opening Day Age: 33
Born: 8/20/67 in Evansville, IN
ML Seasons: 12
Pronunciation: BENN-ess
Nickname: Big Train, Rain Man

Overall Statistics

	W	L	Pct.	ERA	G	GS	Sv	IP	H	BB	SO	HR	Ratio
2000	12	9	.571	4.88	30	27	0	166.0	174	68	137	30	1.46
Career	143	128	.528	3.86	358	351	1	2301.0	2175	797	1858	249	1.29

How Often He Throws Strikes

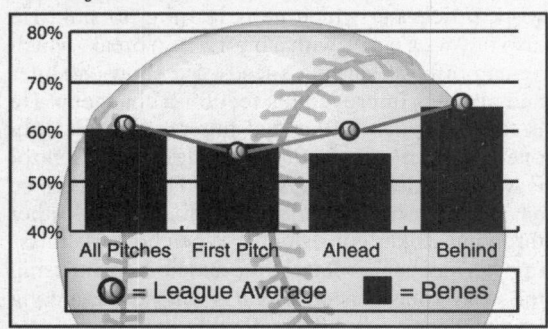

Legend: ⊙ = League Average ■ = Benes

2000 Situational Stats

	W	L	ERA	Sv	IP		AB	H	HR	RBI	Avg
Home	5	3	5.03	0	68.0	LHB	265	71	15	39	.268
Road	7	6	4.78	0	98.0	RHB	368	103	15	51	.280
First Half	9	3	4.47	0	108.2	Sc Pos	146	40	5	58	.274
Scnd Half	3	6	5.65	0	57.1	Clutch	27	8	1	5	.296

2000 Rankings (National League)

- 2nd in most run support per nine innings (7.2)
- 3rd in most home runs allowed per nine innings (1.63)
- 4th in highest slugging percentage allowed (.499)
- 5th in lowest groundball/flyball ratio allowed (0.9)
- 7th in most pitches thrown per batter (3.96)
- Led the Cardinals in stolen bases allowed (15), most run support per nine innings (7.2) and most GDPs induced per nine innings (0.9)

J.D. Drew

2000 Season

J.D. Drew showed solid improvement in his second full season in the major leagues. Playing most of the time against righthanded pitching, Drew flirted with .300 last season. He got better as the year progressed, hitting .309 in his last 60 starts and showing the ability to deliver in clutch situations.

Hitting

Strikeouts continue to plague Drew, who still can be overpowered inside and who has a tendency to try and pull too many pitches on the outer half of the plate. He began using more of the opposite field in the final few months last season. He is a good breaking-ball hitter and has begun to display increasingly better pitch selection. Drew's power has only begun to emerge. As he matures physically and develops a better idea of the strike zone, he should become a 30-plus home-run hitter. He must work on being able to hang in better versus lefthanded pitching, as he did not produce a single home run against southpaws last season.

Baserunning & Defense

With excellent speed and instincts on the bases, Drew is a fine basestealer who has the tools to possibly become a 30-30 man. He played much of last season in right field, where his range is better suited than in center. He has a strong enough arm to play right though he needs to improve how quickly he gets rid of the ball. Drew also makes too many defensive miscues, often because he tries to rush plays or attempts the spectacular play.

2001 Outlook

This could be the season when Drew emerges into the stardom that has been predicted for him for years. He needs to show he can play every day against lefthanders and he needs to become less erratic in the field. He has matured over the last year into a much more coachable player. The Cardinals still think his all-around baseball skills will make him an upper-echelon performer.

Position: RF/CF/LF
Bats: L **Throws:** R
Ht: 6' 1" **Wt:** 195

Opening Day Age: 25
Born: 11/20/75 in Valdosta, GA
ML Seasons: 3

Overall Statistics

	G	AB	R	H	D	T	HR	RBI	SB	BB	SO	Avg	OBP	Slg
2000	135	407	73	120	17	2	18	57	17	67	99	.295	.401	.479
Career	253	811	154	224	36	9	36	109	36	121	186	.276	.376	.476

Where He Hits the Ball

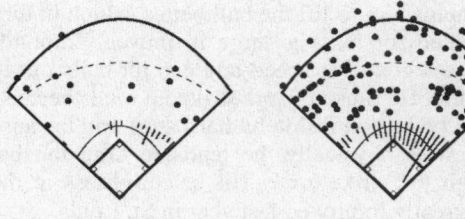

Vs. LHP   Vs. RHP

2000 Situational Stats

	AB	H	HR	RBI	Avg		AB	H	HR	RBI	Avg
Home	208	65	11	33	.313	LHP	74	19	0	4	.257
Road	199	55	7	24	.276	RHP	333	101	18	53	.303
First Half	222	65	14	41	.293	Sc Pos	84	23	6	39	.274
Scnd Half	185	55	4	16	.297	Clutch	48	12	2	9	.250

2000 Rankings (National League)

- 4th in fewest GDPs per GDP situation (3.2%)
- 5th in lowest stolen-base percentage (65.4)
- 7th in errors in right field (5)
- Led the Cardinals in stolen-base percentage (65.4)
- Led NL right fielders in sacrifice bunts (5), fewest GDPs per GDP situation (3.2%) and bunts in play (11)

St. Louis

623

Jim Edmonds

2000 Season

Few players ever have made a bigger impact in their first season with a club than Jim Edmonds. He had a career year and finished fourth in the voting for the National League MVP Award. He became the first Cardinals outfielder ever to hit 40 home runs while also leading the club in runs scored, RBI and walks. Edmonds was a Triple Crown threat until his average tumbled in July and August. However, he finished strong with 19 RBI in September and a big Division Series performance against Atlanta.

Position: CF
Bats: L **Throws:** L
Ht: 6' 1" **Wt:** 212

Opening Day Age: 30
Born: 6/27/70 in Fullerton, CA
ML Seasons: 8

Hitting

Edmonds has moved a bit off the plate, allowing him to get his arms extended more consistently. That helps him to lift the ball better, which in turn accounted for his big surge in power. Edmonds possesses good bat speed and can hit balls out to any field. He runs up large strikeout totals because he can be busted inside by hard stuff and because as he tires physically, he tends to drag the bat through the strike zone. His selectiveness at the plate greatly improved last year in St. Louis.

Baserunning & Defense

Though his speed is only slightly above average, Edmonds is a threat to steal. He has good baserunning instincts and will look to take an extra base. Defensively, there are few center fielders in his class. He gets as good a jump on balls as anybody in the game. He routinely makes spectacular catches, both on balls hit in front of him and over his head. He also has a very accurate throwing arm.

2001 Outlook

It's hard to believe that a year ago Edmonds was viewed in Anaheim as a divisive player and available to any takers. He quickly became one of the Cardinals' franchise players and was rewarded with a six-year, $57 million contact last May that takes him through 2006. He is in his prime and should be a mainstay in the St. Louis lineup for years to come.

Overall Statistics

	G	AB	R	H	D	T	HR	RBI	SB	BB	SO	Avg	OBP	Slg
2000	152	525	129	155	25	0	42	108	10	103	167	.295	.411	.583
Career	861	3169	593	923	186	12	163	516	36	377	725	.291	.368	.512

Where He Hits the Ball

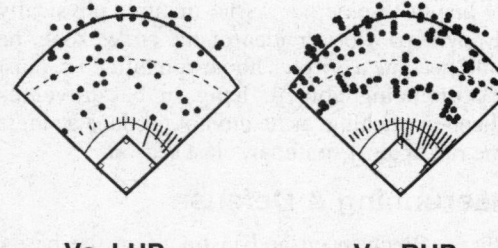

Vs. LHP   **Vs. RHP**

2000 Situational Stats

	AB	H	HR	RBI	Avg		AB	H	HR	RBI	Avg
Home	250	74	22	57	.296	LHP	152	41	11	31	.270
Road	275	81	20	51	.295	RHP	373	114	31	77	.306
First Half	290	99	25	59	.341	Sc Pos	145	40	13	69	.276
Scnd Half	235	56	17	49	.238	Clutch	63	20	3	8	.317

2000 Rankings (National League)

- 2nd in most pitches seen per plate appearance (4.29)
- 3rd in runs scored, strikeouts and fewest GDPs per GDP situation (3.1%)
- 4th in walks and HR frequency (12.5 ABs per HR)
- Led the Cardinals in home runs, runs scored, total bases (306), RBI, walks, times on base (264), strikeouts, pitches seen (2,761), plate appearances (643), slugging percentage, on-base percentage, HR frequency (12.5 ABs per HR), most pitches seen per plate appearance (4.29), fewest GDPs per GDP situation (3.1%), batting average in the clutch and batting average vs. lefthanded pitchers

Darryl Kile

Position: SP
Bats: R **Throws:** R
Ht: 6' 5" **Wt:** 212

Opening Day Age: 32
Born: 12/2/68 in
Garden Grove, CA
ML Seasons: 10

2000 Season

No move the Cardinals made last season was more important than acquiring Darryl Kile. He was the definition of an ace for St. Louis, earning 20 victories and ranking among the league leaders in several categories, including innings, complete games and strikeouts. Kile also was at his best down the stretch, winning seven of his last eight decisions and finishing fifth in the National League Cy Young Award voting.

Pitching

The biggest reason for Kile's turnaround was a renewed confidence in his fastball. For much of last year he had an effective two-seam, sinking fastball that he consistently threw for strikes. When he gets ahead with the fastball, his great curveball then becomes one of baseball's most devastating pitches. Kile also has improved his slider to the point where he can use it effectively against lefthanded hitters. In addition, he's become adept at using his curve as an offspeed pitch. His one flaw is a tendency to get blown out on those occasions when he brings less than his best stuff. His ERA in his nine losses was 9.35; he had a 2.39 ERA in his other 25 starts.

Defense & Hitting

Prior to last season, Kile had been easy to run on because of his curveball and his fairly slow delivery. However, he has worked hard at holding runners in order to limit the number of times they try to steal, and he clearly benefitted from having Mike Matheny behind the plate. He is only an average fielder who can be out of position on defensive plays. Kile handles the bat fairly well, managing nine hits and eight sacrifices last season.

2001 Outlook

The Cardinals got all they could have hoped for from Kile in 2000. They also got a lot from him away from the field, where his preparation and work ethic made him a staff leader. St. Louis tied him up with a three-year, $23 million contract in October that included a $5 million signing bonus and an option for 2004. With a productive offense to back him up, Kile should be good for 17-20 wins annually for the next several seasons.

Overall Statistics

	W	L	Pct.	ERA	G	GS	Sv	IP	H	BB	SO	HR	Ratio
2000	20	9	.690	3.91	34	34	0	232.1	215	58	192	33	1.18
Career	112	104	.519	4.27	311	283	0	1853.1	1825	825	1439	183	1.43

How Often He Throws Strikes

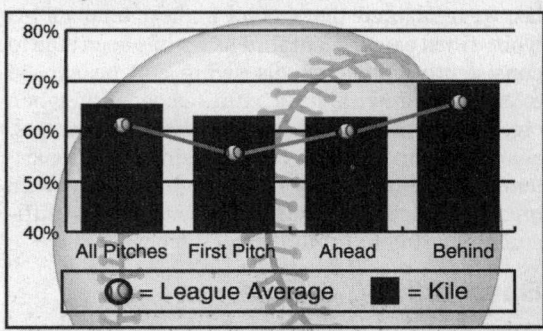

O = League Average   ■ = Kile

2000 Situational Stats

	W	L	ERA	Sv	IP		AB	H	HR	RBI	Avg
Home	11	5	3.67	0	125.0	LHB	406	93	15	44	.229
Road	9	4	4.19	0	107.1	RHB	464	122	18	57	.263
First Half	11	5	4.51	0	121.2	Sc Pos	165	42	8	68	.255
Scnd Half	9	4	3.25	0	110.2	Clutch	75	21	4	11	.280

2000 Rankings (National League)

- 1st in lowest stolen-base percentage allowed (15.4)
- 2nd in wins
- 4th in hit batsmen (13) and runners caught stealing (11)
- 5th in complete games (5), home runs allowed and winning percentage
- Led the Cardinals in wins, games started, complete games (5), innings pitched, hits allowed, batters faced (960), home runs allowed, hit batsmen (13), pitches thrown (3,520), highest strikeout/walk ratio (3.3), lowest on-base percentage allowed (.301), lowest stolen-base percentage allowed (15.4), fewest pitches thrown per batter (3.67) and fewest walks per nine innings (2.2)

St. Louis

Ray Lankford

2000 Season

Ray Lankford's career slid further back last season. After an awful start and struggling all year against lefthanded pitching, Lankford ended up being employed largely as a platoon player. Though his 26 homers represented the third-highest output of his career, Lankford's RBI total did not reach 70 for a second straight year and his batting average was over 40 points below his mark for the previous three seasons.

Hitting

Lankford has strung together 10 straight seasons with 100 or more Ks, and he continues to struggle to make contact. His 148 strikeouts in 393 at-bats last year marked the second-highest total of his whiff-filled career. Lankford never has been able to consistently cut down his swing and he can be overpowered with hard stuff, especially when crowded on the inner half of the plate. Lefthanders, against whom he hit an embarrassing .135, consistently get him out by pitching him away with breaking pitches. He also compounded his difficulty by trying to lift too many pitches.

Baserunning & Defense

Once a 40-steal man, Lankford's basestealing ability has become very limited due to his knee troubles and reluctance to run. He has above-average speed on the bases. His range in left field still is respectable. Lankford does not have a great throwing arm but is usually accurate with his pegs.

2001 Outlook

What once seemed to be a stellar career in the making has reached the crossroads. Nothing illustrated Lankford's sagging fortunes better than the fact that he was sharing playing time much of last year with journeyman Craig Paquette. The Cardinals still owe Lankford two more years on his contract. That fact probably will hinder what are likely to be serious efforts to deal him in the offseason so the Cardinals may be forced to hope that he can approach the numbers he was putting up three years ago.

Position: LF
Bats: L **Throws:** L
Ht: 5'11" **Wt:** 200

Opening Day Age: 33
Born: 6/5/67 in Modesto, CA
ML Seasons: 11

Overall Statistics

	G	AB	R	H	D	T	HR	RBI	SB	BB	SO	Avg	OBP	Slg
2000	128	392	73	99	16	3	26	65	5	70	148	.253	.367	.508
Career	1397	4953	854	1366	307	48	207	768	244	707	1289	.276	.367	.483

Where He Hits the Ball

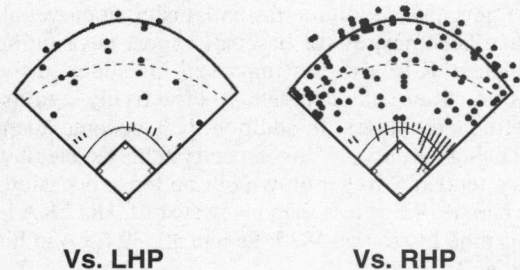

Vs. LHP　　　　　**Vs. RHP**

2000 Situational Stats

	AB	H	HR	RBI	Avg		AB	H	HR	RBI	Avg
Home	190	57	18	44	.300	LHP	74	10	2	10	.135
Road	202	42	8	21	.208	RHP	318	89	24	55	.280
First Half	216	54	14	36	.250	Sc Pos	113	22	1	35	.195
Scnd Half	176	45	12	29	.256	Clutch	58	12	2	6	.207

2000 Rankings (National League)

- 1st in highest percentage of swings that missed (35.9) and lowest percentage of swings put into play (26.7)
- 3rd in lowest batting average with runners in scoring position and lowest fielding percentage in left field (.973)
- 4th in strikeouts
- 6th in errors in left field (5)
- Led NL left fielders in strikeouts and highest percentage of extra bases taken as a runner (62.5)

Mark McGwire

Position: 1B
Bats: R **Throws:** R
Ht: 6' 5" **Wt:** 250

Opening Day Age: 37
Born: 10/1/63 in Pomona, CA
ML Seasons: 15
Nickname: Sack, Big Mac

2000 Season

After two of the highest-profile seasons ever, Mark McGwire's year was crippled by a knee injury that basically sidelined him for half of 2000. His last start came on July 6. At the time, he was on his way to another monster year with 30 homers and 69 RBI. But he had only 15 at-bats the rest of the way. Despite missing three months, McGwire still was able to move past Jimmie Foxx, Mickey Mantle and Mike Schmidt into seventh place on the all-time career home-run list.

Hitting

McGwire's awesome power shows no sign of any decline. He remains a very patient hitter who frequently walks and rarely goes out of the strike zone to fish for pitches. His ability to lift virtually every pitch makes him a threat to go deep whenever he is able to make contact. He is very selective at the plate, which means he can hit over .300 in addition to all the power. A legendary pull hitter, McGwire can take his share of pitches to center and right-center without losing any of his power.

Baserunning & Defense

One of baseball's slowest runners, McGwire rarely hits anything other than singles and home runs. He's managed only 50 doubles in the last three seasons and just six triples in his entire career. McGwire usually uses good judgment on the bases. He has good hands at first, but his range has slipped and he has always had problems with his throwing accuracy.

2001 Outlook

The Cardinals hope that McGwire's knee condition will improve following surgery in October and an entire winter of rest and rehabilitation. However, he is at an age where injuries can linger and his knee could be a career-threatening problem. If he does come back and play every day, McGwire can be counted on for at least 50 home runs, enough to push him past the 600-homer threshold. However, there are some questions beyond 2001, as his contract expires and he has made some noise about possibly retiring.

Overall Statistics

	G	AB	R	H	D	T	HR	RBI	SB	BB	SO	Avg	OBP	Slg
2000	89	236	60	72	8	0	32	73	1	76	78	.305	.483	.746
Career	1777	5888	1119	1570	248	6	554	1350	12	1261	1478	.267	.398	.593

Where He Hits the Ball

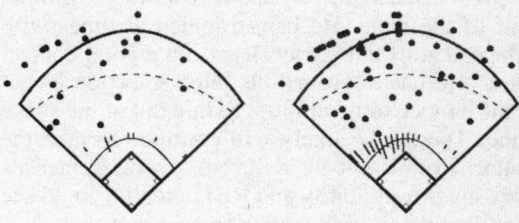

Vs. LHP   **Vs. RHP**

2000 Situational Stats

	AB	H	HR	RBI	Avg		AB	H	HR	RBI	Avg
Home	120	41	18	38	.342	LHP	53	17	8	13	.321
Road	116	31	14	35	.267	RHP	183	55	24	60	.301
First Half	221	67	30	69	.303	Sc Pos	64	20	9	41	.313
Scnd Half	15	5	2	4	.333	Clutch	29	8	4	6	.276

2000 Rankings (National League)

- 2nd in cleanup slugging percentage (.769) and lowest batting average on a 3-2 count (.056)
- 8th in intentional walks (12)
- Led the Cardinals in intentional walks (12) and cleanup slugging percentage (.769)

St. Louis

Edgar Renteria

2000 Season

Though perhaps not in the class of the American League's superstar shortstops, Edgar Renteria had a breakthrough season last year in which he emerged as perhaps the best all-around shortstop in the National League. He had career-best totals in home runs, RBI and runs scored while leading the Cardinals in steals and playing excellent infield defense.

Hitting

With physical maturity, Renteria has emerged as a power-hitting threat. The Cardinals think his 16 homers and 32 doubles last year are signs of things to come. He has greatly improved his bat speed and strength and can turn around hard stuff on the inner half of the plate. He has struggled at times with offspeed stuff but always has been a good contact hitter. He has improved his pitch selection to become a much tougher hitter to lure out of the strike zone. Though he likely will continue to take the majority of his at-bats in the No. 2 spot, Renteria's growing power ability and RBI potential could see him drop down in the order on occasion.

Baserunning & Defense

Because of the firepower behind him in the Cardinals' lineup, Renteria picks his basestealing spots carefully. He likely could steal 40 bases a year given the opportunity. At times he is guilty of forcing the action too much but overall shows consistently good speed and judgment on the bases. The one flaw in his otherwise excellent shortstop play is a tendency to be erratic throwing the ball. Fourteen of his 27 errors last year came on throws. His range is above average, and he has excellent hands.

2001 Outlook

At just 25, Renteria is a five-year veteran and seems on the verge of taking the next step and becoming one of the elite shortstops in baseball. The Cardinals think he has 20-homer, 90-RBI potential. They also love his work ethic and even temperament, which is why they signed him to a four-year, $20 million contract with options for 2004 and 2005 in February of 2000 that will keep him part of the St. Louis nucleus for years to come.

Position: SS
Bats: R **Throws:** R
Ht: 6' 1" **Wt:** 180

Opening Day Age: 25
Born: 8/7/75 in Barranquilla, Colombia
ML Seasons: 5
Pronunciation: ren-ter-REE-uh

Overall Statistics

	G	AB	R	H	D	T	HR	RBI	SB	BB	SO	Avg	OBP	Slg
2000	150	562	94	156	32	1	16	76	21	63	77	.278	.346	.423
Career	697	2712	423	767	125	11	39	253	147	242	413	.283	.341	.380

Where He Hits the Ball

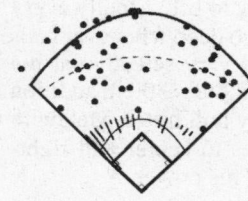
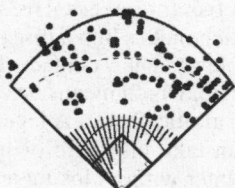

Vs. LHP   **Vs. RHP**

2000 Situational Stats

	AB	H	HR	RBI	Avg		AB	H	HR	RBI	Avg
Home	279	71	4	28	.254	LHP	139	36	5	16	.259
Road	283	85	12	48	.300	RHP	423	120	11	60	.284
First Half	326	89	10	38	.273	Sc Pos	145	35	5	59	.241
Scnd Half	236	67	6	38	.284	Clutch	72	15	1	8	.208

2000 Rankings (National League)

- 2nd in errors at shortstop (27)
- 3rd in lowest stolen-base percentage (61.8) and lowest fielding percentage at shortstop (.958)
- 4th in GDPs (19)
- 5th in caught stealing (13)
- 8th in highest percentage of extra bases taken as a runner (65.4)
- 9th in sacrifice flies (9)
- Led the Cardinals in at-bats, hits, doubles, sacrifice flies (9), stolen bases, caught stealing (13), GDPs (19), plate appearances (643), highest groundball/flyball ratio (1.4), on-base percentage vs. lefthanded pitchers (.381), steals of third (3), and highest percentage of extra bases taken as a runner (65.4)

Garrett Stephenson

2000 Season

Garrett Stephenson made the most of his first full season as a major league starter with a breakout 16-victory, 200-inning campaign. He began the season in fine style, getting off to an 8-0 start. After tailing off in June and July, he rebounded to go 4-0 in August. His big year ended on a down note when he left his first playoff start with an elbow injury and was sidelined the rest of the postseason.

Pitching

Stephenson doesn't break bats with his assortment of sinkers, changeups and sliders. However, he is another example of how a pitcher can blossom in his late 20s when he acquires a feel for changing speeds and learns to throw strikes. Stephenson effectively changes speeds regardless of the count, works both sides of the plate, has good control and keeps his pitch counts down. He is hittable when he loses control of the strike zone and throws pitches that catch too much of the plate. He has matured into a good competitor and has shown the ability to pitch out of trouble and keep his team in most games that he works.

Defense & Hitting

Stephenson is quick off the mound and usually in position to make most defensive plays. He holds runners well and has a compact delivery to the plate, which gives his catcher a chance to throw out basestealers. Stephenson is no threat as a hitter but handles the bat well enough to lead the Cardinals in sacrifices last year.

2001 Outlook

The Cardinals were optimistic that Stephenson's postseason arm troubles will be behind him when spring training opens. If healthy, he should be entering his prime years. He will again need excellent run support to remain a 16-game winner. However, St. Louis was 20-11 in Stephenson's 31 starts last year, a record which underscores that his season was no fluke. The addition of Dustin Hermanson from Montreal gives the Cardinals a very deep rotation, however, and Stephenson also could serve as quality trade bait sometime in the near future.

Position: SP
Bats: R **Throws:** R
Ht: 6' 5" **Wt:** 208

Opening Day Age: 29
Born: 1/2/72 in Takoma Park, MD
ML Seasons: 5

Overall Statistics

	W	L	Pct.	ERA	G	GS	Sv	IP	H	BB	SO	HR	Ratio
2000	16	9	.640	4.49	32	31	0	200.1	209	63	123	31	1.36
Career	30	21	.588	4.44	79	67	0	432.0	447	152	283	57	1.39

How Often He Throws Strikes

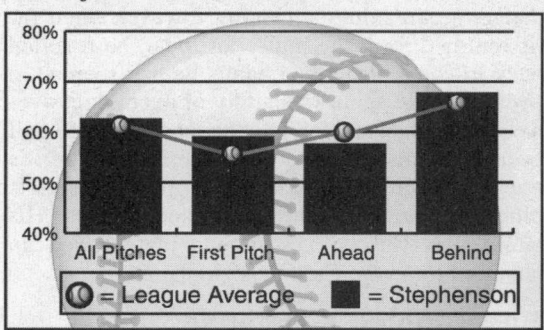

○ = League Average   ■ = Stephenson

2000 Situational Stats

	W	L	ERA	Sv	IP		AB	H	HR	RBI	Avg
Home	6	5	4.75	0	106.0	LHB	377	117	10	40	.310
Road	10	4	4.20	0	94.1	RHB	398	92	21	58	.231
First Half	9	5	4.63	0	107.0	Sc Pos	163	44	8	66	.270
Scnd Half	7	4	4.34	0	93.1	Clutch	45	11	1	5	.244

2000 Rankings (National League)

- 3rd in shutouts (2)
- 4th in balks (2) and most run support per nine innings (6.9)
- 7th in sacrifice bunts (13)
- 8th in wins, lowest stolen-base percentage allowed (33.3) and lowest groundball/flyball ratio allowed (1.0)
- 10th in home runs allowed and fewest GDPs induced per nine innings (0.6)
- Led the Cardinals in sacrifice bunts (13), shutouts (2) and balks (2)

St. Louis

Fernando Tatis

2000 Season

One of the few disappointments for St. Louis last season was the play of Fernando Tatis, who was hampered for much of the year by a groin injury that wound up limiting him to only 96 games. At the time he was injured in late April, Tatis was leading the National League in runs batted in. However, his power numbers ended up being cut in half from his breakthrough 1999 campaign. He concluded the season largely riding the bench.

Hitting

Tatis has big-time power to all fields and the kind of bat speed that can handle hard stuff. He remains vulnerable to offspeed offerings but has become a dangerous breaking-ball hitter. However, when Tatis returned from the injury last year, he reverted back to some of the bad habits he had seemed to overcome. He again was guilty of overaggressiveness at the plate and fell into the rut of trying to pull everything instead of driving the ball where it's pitched. When he tries to pull too often, Tatis starts piling up too many strikeouts and popups. His late-season stubbornness at the plate ended up landing him in the Cardinals' doghouse.

Baserunning & Defense

The groin injury took away Tatis' quickness on the bases last year. But when he is healthy, he has better-than-average speed and the instincts to be a solid basestealer. He has excellent defensive skills, including very good hands and solid range at third base. He possesses an exceptional throwing arm that he has begun to harness more consistently.

2001 Outlook

The Cardinals had signed Tatis to a four-year, $14 million deal in March of 2000, but the need for a quality starter sparked a four-player deal that sent Tatis and Britt Reames to Montreal for Dustin Hermanson and Steve Kline. Tatis will be the Expos' everyday third baseman. Manager Tony La Russa was not pleased with Tatis' approach and attitude late last season. But the Cardinals think much of the problem was Tatis' own frustration over his injury-plagued campaign. The Expos now hope that a change of scenery can help him return to the All-Star caliber player he was in 1999.

Position: 3B
Bats: R **Throws:** R
Ht: 5'10" **Wt:** 170

Opening Day Age: 26
Born: 1/1/75 in San Pedro de Macoris, Dominican Republic
ML Seasons: 4
Pronunciation: tah-TEESE

Overall Statistics

	G	AB	R	H	D	T	HR	RBI	SB	BB	SO	Avg	OBP	Slg
2000	96	324	59	82	21	1	18	64	2	57	94	.253	.379	.491
Career	455	1616	261	446	94	7	71	258	39	189	387	.276	.361	.475

Where He Hits the Ball

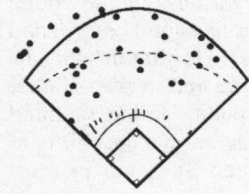 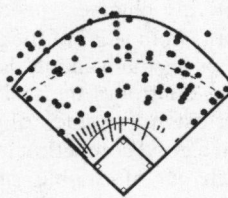

Vs. LHP   **Vs. RHP**

2000 Situational Stats

	AB	H	HR	RBI	Avg		AB	H	HR	RBI	Avg
Home	164	43	11	42	.262	LHP	88	23	8	16	.261
Road	160	39	7	22	.244	RHP	236	59	10	48	.250
First Half	103	37	8	34	.359	Sc Pos	95	21	4	42	.221
Scnd Half	221	45	10	30	.204	Clutch	39	9	1	2	.231

2000 Rankings (National League)

- 3rd in lowest percentage of swings put into play (32.4)
- 9th in lowest batting average on a 3-1 count (.111)
- 10th in highest percentage of swings that missed (27.3)
- Led the Cardinals in batting average with the bases loaded (.300)
- Led NL third basemen in hit by pitch (10)

Dave Veres

2000 Season

In a bullpen that was totally revamped last season, Dave Veres did a solid job as the Cardinals' closer in his first year with St. Louis. He was successful on 29 of his 36 save opportunities, with 13 of his saves requiring more than one inning of work. He also had an excellent strikeout-walk ratio and lowered his ERA by 2.29 runs from his 1999 campaign with Colorado.

Pitching

There is nothing mysterious about Veres' primary pitching weapons—he throws one of baseball's best split-finger fastballs. When he can get ahead in the count with his good fastball, Veres is a tough pitcher to hit. He will throw the splitter on any count and usually for strikes. His feel for the splitter occasionally deserts him, and at times he will overthrow his slider, particularly when he starts falling behind with his fastball. He is an outstanding competitor and durable enough to frequently pitch more than one inning in a given appearance. He also has the ability to be available to pitch three or four days in succession. In fact, his splitter tends to improve the more he works because he avoids overthrowing when he's tired from regular activity.

Defense & Hitting

Veres has solid defensive skills and helps himself with his glove, especially with his ability to field bunts. Unlike many closers, Veres works hard to hold runners and his quick delivery gives his catcher a chance to throw out basestealers. He can handle himself with the bat, though he had only one plate appearance last season.

2001 Outlook

While he is not widely considered among the game's elite closers, Veres is more than just a journeyman. He has saved 60 games over the past two seasons and his value is increased by his durability. St. Louis feels comfortable about him continuing in the closer's role for at least another year or two, as they signed him to a one-year, $5.25 million extension for 2002 with a club option for 2003.

Position: RP
Bats: R **Throws:** R
Ht: 6' 2" **Wt:** 220

Opening Day Age: 34
Born: 10/19/66 in Montgomery, AL
ML Seasons: 7
Pronunciation: VEERZ

Overall Statistics

	W	L	Pct.	ERA	G	GS	Sv	IP	H	BB	SO	HR	Ratio
2000	3	5	.375	2.85	71	0	29	75.2	65	25	67	6	1.19
Career	26	24	.520	3.32	432	0	75	513.0	501	185	462	50	1.34

How Often He Throws Strikes

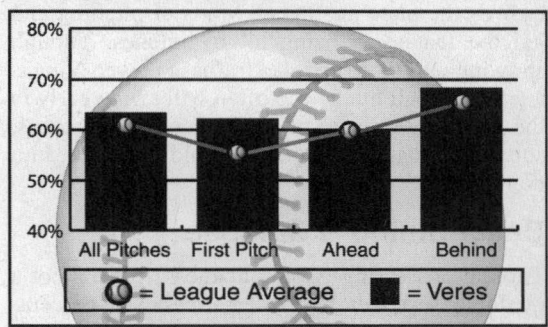

○ = League Average   ■ = Veres

2000 Situational Stats

	W	L	ERA	Sv	IP		AB	H	HR	RBI	Avg
Home	2	2	2.66	15	40.2	LHB	119	25	1	6	.210
Road	1	3	3.09	14	35.0	RHB	153	40	5	30	.261
First Half	1	2	3.05	18	44.1	Sc Pos	86	20	2	31	.233
Scnd Half	2	3	2.59	11	31.1	Clutch	178	42	5	29	.236

2000 Rankings (National League)

- 3rd in blown saves (7)
- 5th in games finished (61)
- 6th in save opportunities (36) and saves
- 7th in lowest save percentage (80.6)
- 8th in errors at pitcher (3)
- 9th in lowest batting average allowed vs. lefthanded batters and relief ERA (2.85)
- Led the Cardinals in games pitched, saves, games finished (61), save opportunities (36), save percentage (80.6), blown saves (7), relief wins (3), relief innings (75.2), relief ERA (2.85), most strikeouts per nine innings in relief (8.0) and fewest baserunners allowed per nine innings in relief (11.4)

Fernando Vina

Position: 2B
Bats: L **Throws:** R
Ht: 5' 9" **Wt:** 174

Opening Day Age: 31
Born: 4/16/69 in Sacramento, CA
ML Seasons: 8
Pronunciation: VEEN-yah

2000 Season

Though nagging rib and hamstring injuries sidelined him for nearly 40 games last year, Fernando Vina otherwise was a solid addition to the Cardinals as their leadoff hitter and second baseman. He hit .300 for the second time in his career, had a respectable on-base percentage and led all National League second basemen in fielding percentage.

Hitting

Vina brings a variety of assets to the leadoff spot. He's one of the toughest players in baseball to strike out and one of the game's better bunters. Last year he reached base on nine bunt singles. He crowds the plate against all kinds of pitching and led the league in being hit by pitches. Though showing only occasional extra-base power, Vina is a good fastball hitter who often will swing early in the count. He does not work many long counts, something that the Cardinals would like to see him do more of.

Baserunning & Defense

Though possessing good quickness, Vina is not a quality basestealer. His career stolen-base percentage is a rather mediocre 63.3 percent. He also tends to press the action too frequently on the bases and is prone to making baserunning errors. There are few second basemen that are better defensively. Vina possesses outstanding range and a strong arm with a quick release. No one in baseball is more adept at turning the double play.

2001 Outlook

Another of Cardinals General Manager Walt Jocketty's productive acquisitions, Vina quickly fit in well with St. Louis and was signed to a three-year, $15 million contract extension in early May of 2000 with a $1 million signing bonus and an option for 2004. The one worry about Vina is his tendency to wear down physically. He will be a solid part of the Cardinals' lineup, but they need him to play 125-plus games a year, something he's done only twice in his big league career.

Overall Statistics

	G	AB	R	H	D	T	HR	RBI	SB	BB	SO	Avg	OBP	Slg
2000	123	487	81	146	24	6	4	31	10	36	36	.300	.380	.398
Career	754	2613	401	746	116	32	26	203	76	192	188	.285	.356	.384

Where He Hits the Ball

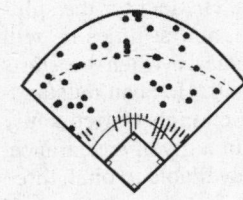 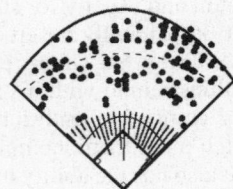

Vs. LHP   **Vs. RHP**

2000 Situational Stats

	AB	H	HR	RBI	Avg		AB	H	HR	RBI	Avg
Home	230	66	1	12	.287	LHP	120	32	0	3	.267
Road	257	80	3	19	.311	RHP	367	114	4	28	.311
First Half	267	79	3	21	.296	Sc Pos	95	26	3	30	.274
Scnd Half	220	67	1	10	.305	Clutch	46	10	0	4	.217

2000 Rankings (National League)

- 1st in hit by pitch (28) and fielding percentage at second base (.988)
- 2nd in fewest pitches seen per plate appearance (3.27)
- 3rd in highest percentage of swings put into play (55.6) and lowest HR frequency (121.8 ABs per HR)
- 4th in batting average on a 3-2 count (.424)
- 5th in batting average on an 0-2 count (.324)
- Led the Cardinals in batting average, singles, triples, hit by pitch (28), batting average vs. righthanded pitchers, batting average on an 0-2 count (.324), on-base percentage for a leadoff hitter (.382), batting average on the road and bunts in play (24)

Eric Davis

Position: RF
Bats: R **Throws:** R
Ht: 6' 3" **Wt:** 185

Opening Day Age: 38
Born: 5/29/62 in Los Angeles, CA
ML Seasons: 16

Overall Statistics

	G	AB	R	H	D	T	HR	RBI	SB	BB	SO	Avg	OBP	Slg
2000	92	254	38	77	14	0	6	40	1	36	60	.303	.389	.429
Career	1552	5165	921	1398	232	23	278	912	348	727	1360	.271	.361	.486

2000 Situational Stats

	AB	H	HR	RBI	Avg		AB	H	HR	RBI	Avg
Home	133	36	2	16	.271	LHP	105	41	3	18	.390
Road	121	41	4	24	.339	RHP	149	36	3	22	.242
First Half	160	49	6	28	.306	Sc Pos	84	27	1	33	.321
Scnd Half	94	28	0	12	.298	Clutch	38	10	0	2	.263

2000 Season

Used almost exclusively as a platoon player against lefthanded pitching, Eric Davis provided the Cardinals with solid production in his part-time role. He was among the league's best hitters against southpaws, batting .390 versus lefties while making 61 starts in right field.

Hitting, Baserunning & Defense

Davis has tended to hit more balls to the opposite field in recent years as his bat speed has started to decline. However, he can pull an occasional inside pitch with power and is a tough out in the clutch, hitting .321 with runners in scoring position. Hampered by knee and back troubles, Davis is no longer a stolen-base threat but can still take the extra base. Shoulder troubles have downgraded his throwing arm, though his range remains acceptable due to the good jump he gets on most balls.

2001 Outlook

Davis is a part-time player at this stage of his career, and he became a free agent. By the end of last season, there was growing reason to believe that he was leaning toward retiring from a solid major league career in which his legacy likely will be the considerable charitable work he's done in the fight against colon cancer.

Pat Hentgen

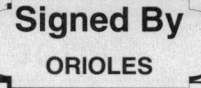

Position: SP
Bats: R **Throws:** R
Ht: 6' 2" **Wt:** 195

Opening Day Age: 32
Born: 11/13/68 in Detroit, MI
ML Seasons: 10
Pronunciation: HENT-gen

Overall Statistics

	W	L	Pct.	ERA	G	GS	Sv	IP	H	BB	SO	HR	Ratio
2000	15	12	.556	4.72	33	33	0	194.1	202	89	118	24	1.50
Career	120	88	.577	4.21	285	255	0	1750.0	1789	646	1113	215	1.39

2000 Situational Stats

	W	L	ERA	Sv	IP		AB	H	HR	RBI	Avg
Home	6	6	4.71	0	93.2	LHB	337	85	7	40	.252
Road	9	6	4.74	0	100.2	RHB	396	117	17	55	.295
First Half	8	6	5.16	0	104.2	Sc Pos	172	42	7	70	.244
Scnd Half	7	6	4.22	0	89.2	Clutch	12	5	1	2	.417

2000 Season

Pat Hentgen was the stable starter St. Louis hoped for when it acquired him last year. He worked nearly 200 innings and won 15 games, becoming one of just six active pitchers with 10 or more wins each of the last eight seasons. Hentgen wore down at the end of the year, however, and largely was unused in St. Louis' playoff competition.

Pitching, Defense & Hitting

Hentgen's velocity now tops out at around 90 MPH, which means he can't solely rely on the four-seam fastball that once was his signature. He worked on throwing more two-seamers last year and also limited how many cut fastballs he delivered to lefthanders. He'll occasionally spot a changeup or big-breaking curve. He does a good job of holding runners on base and remains a very reliable fielder. He also managed eight hits in his first season in the National League.

2001 Outlook

The Cardinals were pleased with Hentgen last year but not pleased enough to pick up his $6 million option for 2001. The pitching-starved Orioles signed him to a two-year, $9.6 million deal in late December. While Hentgen is not likely to be a Cy Young candidate again, he is a stable veteran who can win 12-15 games in the right situation.

St. Louis

Carlos Hernandez

Position: C
Bats: R **Throws:** R
Ht: 5'10" **Wt:** 215

Opening Day Age: 33
Born: 5/24/67 in San Felix, Bolivar, Venezuela
ML Seasons: 10
Pronunciation: her-NAN-dezz

Overall Statistics

	G	AB	R	H	D	T	HR	RBI	SB	BB	SO	Avg	OBP	Slg
2000	75	242	23	62	15	0	3	35	2	21	35	.256	.322	.355
Career	488	1244	102	315	51	1	24	141	5	63	196	.253	.298	.354

2000 Situational Stats

	AB	H	HR	RBI	Avg		AB	H	HR	RBI	Avg
Home	111	33	2	15	.297	LHP	68	15	0	6	.221
Road	131	29	1	20	.221	RHP	174	47	3	29	.270
First Half	185	47	2	24	.254	Sc Pos	63	19	1	31	.302
Scnd Half	57	15	1	11	.263	Clutch	42	10	0	6	.238

2000 Season

Acquired at the trading deadline as insurance, Carlos Hernandez ended up catching throughout the postseason for St. Louis after Mike Matheny was lost. Hernandez struggled throughout the second half of the campaign but still hit .275 after joining the Cardinals.

Hitting, Baserunning & Defense

In his only full major league season as a regular in 1998, Hernandez displayed decent power with nine home runs. He is more of a spray hitter who usually puts the ball in play and can be a tough out in clutch situations. He does not worry the opposition with his running. Hernandez has solid catching mechanics, both with his throwing and in his ability to block pitches in the dirt. He also is adept at framing pitches.

2001 Outlook

Hernandez appeared to have established himself as a solid everyday catcher when he helped San Diego to the pennant in 1998. But he missed all of 1999 due to injury and may never again get a chance to be a regular. If St. Louis retains him, he likely will share playing time and could be expendable if the Cardinals decide to stick with Matheny and Eli Marrero.

Mike James

Position: RP
Bats: R **Throws:** R
Ht: 6'3" **Wt:** 205

Opening Day Age: 33
Born: 8/15/67 in Fort Walton, FL
ML Seasons: 5

Overall Statistics

	W	L	Pct.	ERA	G	GS	Sv	IP	H	BB	SO	HR	Ratio
2000	2	2	.500	3.16	51	0	2	51.1	40	24	41	7	1.25
Career	15	12	.556	3.37	235	0	11	264.2	230	127	211	23	1.35

2000 Situational Stats

	W	L	ERA	Sv	IP		AB	H	HR	RBI	Avg
Home	1	1	1.96	0	23.0	LHB	64	13	3	10	.203
Road	1	1	4.13	2	28.1	RHB	119	27	4	13	.227
First Half	0	1	3.60	1	20.0	Sc Pos	55	11	0	14	.200
Scnd Half	2	1	2.87	1	31.1	Clutch	52	11	3	8	.212

2000 Season

After two years of serious elbow troubles, Mike James pitched his way back to the majors and did a good job in the middle of the St. Louis bullpen. He experienced some minor early-season shoulder trouble, but pitched well from mid-June on, owning an ERA under 3.00 over the last three months.

Pitching, Defense & Hitting

James has had to make some changes in his approach since undergoing major elbow surgery. He has slightly altered his three-quarter motion to lessen the strain on his elbow. With his velocity down, he throws more cut fastballs, sliders and occasional changeups. James must hit precise spots with his new assortment because he is vulnerable to home runs when he misses his spots. He is a good athlete who does an adequate job of fielding his position and holding runners. He is no factor as a hitter.

2001 Outlook

By the end of last season, St. Louis had grown more confident in James' ability to pitch effectively. A job is likely his to lose when spring training begins. Though he never again may be the overpowering setup man he sometimes was in Anaheim, James still is a useful reliever who can be tough to hit at times.

Eli Marrero

Position: C
Bats: R **Throws:** R
Ht: 6' 1" **Wt:** 180
Opening Day Age: 27
Born: 11/17/73 in Havana, Cuba
ML Seasons: 4
Pronunciation: muh-RARE-oh

Overall Statistics

	G	AB	R	H	D	T	HR	RBI	SB	BB	SO	Avg	OBP	Slg
2000	53	102	21	23	3	1	5	17	5	9	16	.225	.302	.422
Career	267	718	85	157	36	3	17	78	26	57	127	.219	.277	.348

2000 Situational Stats

	AB	H	HR	RBI	Avg		AB	H	HR	RBI	Avg
Home	53	13	2	6	.245	LHP	20	4	2	6	.200
Road	49	10	3	11	.204	RHP	82	19	3	11	.232
First Half	86	21	5	17	.244	Sc Pos	28	6	2	14	.214
Scnd Half	16	2	0	0	.125	Clutch	10	0	0	1	.000

2000 Season

After being relegated to reserve duty by the solid play of Mike Matheny, Eli Marrero had his season largely ended when he tore a thumb ligament in early July. Marrero had shown glimpses of reviving his bat by hitting five homers. He also played solid defense, going errorless in 38 games behind the plate.

Hitting, Baserunning & Defense

Marrero had to try and rebuild his whole swing after bottoming out two years ago. He has decent bat speed and occasionally can pull for power. He remains vulnerable to chasing breaking balls and too often gets himself out by swinging early in the count. For a catcher, Marrero has better-than-average speed and has legitimate stolen-base ability. He also has excellent catching skills and is adept at framing pitches. His quick release and strong arm helped him nail nearly 60 percent of opposing base stealers in 2000.

2001 Outlook

Marrero is young enough to ignite a once promising career that has been stalled by injuries and a lack of hitting the past two years. However, he will enter spring training fighting to hold on to a backup role. St. Louis could consider using him in trade efforts if he doesn't reverse his recent slide.

Mike Matheny  Gold Glover

Position: C
Bats: R **Throws:** R
Ht: 6' 3" **Wt:** 205
Opening Day Age: 30
Born: 9/22/70 in Reynoldsburg, OH
ML Seasons: 7
Pronunciation: ma-THEEN-ee

Overall Statistics

	G	AB	R	H	D	T	HR	RBI	SB	BB	SO	Avg	OBP	Slg
2000	128	417	43	109	22	1	6	47	0	32	96	.261	.317	.362
Career	630	1752	159	415	84	5	28	192	6	101	385	.237	.287	.338

2000 Situational Stats

	AB	H	HR	RBI	Avg		AB	H	HR	RBI	Avg
Home	191	52	2	21	.272	LHP	104	26	2	14	.250
Road	226	57	4	26	.252	RHP	313	83	4	33	.265
First Half	224	56	3	23	.250	Sc Pos	109	24	1	37	.220
Scnd Half	193	53	3	24	.275	Clutch	48	9	0	2	.188

2000 Season

A little-noticed offseason acquisition by St. Louis, Mike Matheny proved to be an important member of the Cardinals' division-winning lineup last year. He set career highs in most offensive categories. More importantly, he was an excellent handler of the Cardinals' pitching staff and earned his first Gold Glove.

Hitting, Baserunning & Defense

Matheny got his average over .260 for the first time, largely due to hitting to the opposite field. He also came up big in September, batting over .300 and helping key the Cardinals' drive to the playoffs. He is no threat on the bases with his catcher's speed. Matheny is one of baseball's best handlers of pitchers and has a strong arm and very quick release, which helped him throw out a major league high 51 percent of opposing basestealers.

2001 Outlook

Matheny suffered one of last season's toughest breaks when he severed tendons in a finger in a household accident on the eve of the playoffs. He is expected to make a full recovery, however, and the Cardinals exercised the option on his contract for 2001. They anticipate him doing the bulk of the catching again this season. Whatever offense he can supply will be viewed as a bonus.

St. Louis

635

Matt Morris

Position: RP
Bats: R **Throws:** R
Ht: 6' 5" **Wt:** 210

Opening Day Age: 26
Born: 8/9/74 in Middletown, NY
ML Seasons: 3

Overall Statistics

	W	L	Pct.	ERA	G	GS	Sv	IP	H	BB	SO	HR	Ratio
2000	3	3	.500	3.57	31	0	4	53.0	53	17	34	3	1.32
Career	22	17	.564	3.05	81	50	4	383.2	362	128	262	23	1.28

2000 Situational Stats

	W	L	ERA	Sv	IP		AB	H	HR	RBI	Avg
Home	1	3	6.10	1	20.2	LHB	94	24	2	10	.255
Road	2	0	1.95	3	32.1	RHB	109	29	1	10	.266
First Half	0	2	3.15	2	20.0	Sc Pos	46	13	3	19	.283
Scnd Half	3	1	3.82	2	33.0	Clutch	121	31	3	15	.256

2000 Season

After missing all of 1999 due to Tommy John surgery on his elbow, Matt Morris returned to the Cardinals late last May and became their most reliable setup man. Morris was second among Cards relievers in innings pitched, recorded seven holds and added four saves.

Pitching, Defense & Hitting

A little more than 13 months after undergoing reconstructive elbow surgery, Morris was back in the majors possessing much of the same overpowering stuff he boasted prior to his injury. His four-seam fastball was consistently in the mid-90s. He had regained the sharpness of his sinking two-seamer and was able to throw strikes with his overhand curve and much-improved straight change. Morris is fairly easy to run on with his deliberate move to the plate. He is an adequate fielder and can handle the bat.

2001 Outlook

The Cardinals anticipate that Morris' stint as a reliever will be short-lived. They project him to be a member of the starting rotation. Barring any physical setbacks, Morris quickly should reassume his status as one of the National League's best young pitchers with the clear potential to be a 15-17 game winner.

Craig Paquette

Position: 3B/1B/LF/RF/2B
Bats: R **Throws:** R
Ht: 6' 0" **Wt:** 190

Opening Day Age: 32
Born: 3/28/69 in Long Beach, CA
ML Seasons: 8
Pronunciation: pah-KET

Overall Statistics

	G	AB	R	H	D	T	HR	RBI	SB	BB	SO	Avg	OBP	Slg
2000	134	384	47	94	24	2	15	61	4	27	83	.245	.294	.435
Career	608	1966	235	470	97	9	80	293	23	92	495	.239	.273	.420

2000 Situational Stats

	AB	H	HR	RBI	Avg		AB	H	HR	RBI	Avg
Home	196	51	13	37	.260	LHP	113	25	2	14	.221
Road	188	43	2	24	.229	RHP	271	69	13	47	.255
First Half	242	61	9	40	.252	Sc Pos	115	28	5	44	.243
Scnd Half	142	33	6	21	.232	Clutch	57	13	2	8	.228

2000 Season

There wasn't a more valuable player on the St. Louis bench last year than Craig Paquette. He appeared in 134 games, a career high, getting extensive playing time at third base while filling in at first, second, right field and left field. His home-run and RBI totals were both the second highest of his career.

Hitting, Baserunning & Defense

Paquette is a very good fastball hitter who can pull inside pitches with power. He also has developed power to the opposite field. He is a free swinger who tends to strike out too frequently but is a dangerous mistake hitter. Paquette's best defensive position probably is third base, where he has decent range and hands. His powerful arm can be erratic at times and his outfield range is below average. He can steal the occasional base but is otherwise a subpar runner.

2001 Outlook

As a last-minute replacement on Opening Day for Mark McGwire, Paquette homered. In the final regular season game, his dramatic homer helped St. Louis steal home-field advantage in the playoffs from the Braves. He now may get a chance to be the Cards' primary third baseman with Fernando Tatis headed to Montreal.

Placido Polanco

Position: 2B/3B/SS
Bats: R **Throws:** R
Ht: 5'10" **Wt:** 168

Opening Day Age: 25
Born: 10/10/75 in Santo Domingo, Dominican Republic
ML Seasons: 3
Pronunciation: plah-SEE-doh poh-LAHNK-oh

Overall Statistics

	G	AB	R	H	D	T	HR	RBI	SB	BB	SO	Avg	OBP	Slg
2000	118	323	50	102	12	3	5	39	4	16	26	.316	.347	.418
Career	251	657	84	192	24	8	7	69	7	36	59	.292	.329	.385

2000 Situational Stats

	AB	H	HR	RBI	Avg		AB	H	HR	RBI	Avg
Home	145	42	2	15	.290	LHP	87	29	4	17	.333
Road	178	60	3	24	.337	RHP	236	73	1	22	.309
First Half	168	53	3	16	.315	Sc Pos	79	27	3	36	.342
Scnd Half	155	49	2	23	.316	Clutch	55	12	1	7	.218

2000 Season

One of St. Louis' unsung key players last year was Placido Polanco, who was a solid fill-in at third, short and second and hit .313 as a starter. In his first full season, Polanco set career highs in all categories and led the Cardinals with a .342 average with runners in scoring position. He also made only three errors.

Hitting, Baserunning & Defense

With a compact, quick swing and solid pitch selection, Polanco is a tough out in any situation. He rarely strikes out, is a good breaking-ball hitter and has surprising power. His ability to consistently put the ball in play makes him especially valuable as a pinch-hitter. His best defensive position is second base, where he turns the double play adequately. He also has good hands at the other infield positions. Polanco does not have exceptional speed but is capable of stealing a base.

2001 Outlook

There were few National League utility players better than Polanco last year, and he will have a job this spring. By hitting over .300, he showed the potential of possibly being an everyday infielder, though he will have to fight Craig Paquette for the vacancy at third base created by the departure of Fernando Tatis.

Mike Timlin

Position: RP
Bats: R **Throws:** R
Ht: 6' 4" **Wt:** 210

Opening Day Age: 35
Born: 3/10/66 in Midland, TX
ML Seasons: 10

Overall Statistics

	W	L	Pct.	ERA	G	GS	Sv	IP	H	BB	SO	HR	Ratio
2000	5	4	.556	4.18	62	0	12	64.2	67	35	52	8	1.58
Career	37	40	.481	3.59	525	3	111	626.0	593	246	502	53	1.34

2000 Situational Stats

	W	L	ERA	Sv	IP		AB	H	HR	RBI	Avg
Home	5	0	3.66	5	32.0	LHB	107	33	3	25	.308
Road	0	4	4.68	7	32.2	RHB	140	34	5	13	.243
First Half	2	3	5.08	9	28.1	Sc Pos	72	21	3	29	.292
Scnd Half	3	1	3.47	3	36.1	Clutch	131	39	4	22	.298

2000 Season

One of St. Louis' late-season, stretch-drive acquisitions, Mike Timlin did a solid job in the Cardinals' bullpen in August and September. Though he saved only one game for St. Louis, his earned run average improved by a run and a half after arriving from Baltimore, and he was the Cardinals' best reliever for much of September.

Pitching, Defense & Hitting

Scouts love Timlin's stuff. He can throw in the mid-90s, and when he's right he throws one of the game's best sliders. However, he invariably hits stretches when he is either wild or his stuff becomes hittable. Questions also arise about Timlin's effectiveness in tight situations; he allowed a .321 batting average with runners on base last year. He is solid in the field and for a reliever holds runners fairly well. He has never batted in his 10-year major league career.

2001 Outlook

If he's mainly confined to setup work, Timlin is a solid veteran reliever. In a changing Cardinals bullpen, he could be a key as a stable part of their late-inning equation.

St. Louis

Other St. Louis Cardinals

Alan Benes (**Pos**: RHP, **Age**: 29)

	W	L	Pct.	ERA	G	GS	Sv	IP	H	BB	SO	HR	Ratio
2000	2	2	.500	5.67	30	0	0	46.0	54	23	26	7	1.67
Career	25	23	.521	4.32	92	58	0	416.2	400	182	339	49	1.40

Benes' star potential has dimmed considerably. Like teammate Matt Morris, Benes was returning from injury last year. But Benes didn't enjoy as much success and may stay in the bullpen. 2001 Outlook: B

Justin Brunette (**Pos**: LHP, **Age**: 25)

	W	L	Pct.	ERA	G	GS	Sv	IP	H	BB	SO	HR	Ratio
2000	0	0	-	5.79	4	0	0	4.2	8	5	2	0	2.79
Career	0	0	-	5.79	4	0	0	4.2	8	5	2	0	2.79

Brunette didn't have much success in his first experience above Double-A last year. He appears to be getting groomed as a situational lefthander. 2001 Outlook: C

Jason Christiansen (**Pos**: LHP, **Age**: 31)

	W	L	Pct.	ERA	G	GS	Sv	IP	H	BB	SO	HR	Ratio
2000	3	8	.273	5.06	65	0	1	48.0	41	27	53	3	1.42
Career	15	20	.429	4.17	299	0	10	284.2	260	146	287	21	1.43

Christiansen was a key addition when the Cardinals traded for him last July, providing lefthanded relief down the stretch. But he underwent shoulder surgery in October, and the Cardinals traded for Montreal lefty reliever Steve Kline in mid-December. 2001 Outlook: B

Will Clark (**Pos**: 1B, **Age**: 37, **Bats**: L)

	G	AB	R	H	D	T	HR	RBI	SB	BB	SO	Avg	OBP	Slg
2000	130	427	78	136	30	2	21	70	5	69	69	.319	.418	.546
Career	1976	7173	1186	2176	440	47	284	1205	67	937	1190	.303	.384	.497

Clark was a godsend for the Cardinals after they acquired him from Baltimore at the trading deadline, slugging .655 with St. Louis. That's why it was surprising when he retired after the season. 2001 Outlook: D

Shawon Dunston (**Pos**: LF/RF, **Age**: 38, **Bats**: R)

	G	AB	R	H	D	T	HR	RBI	SB	BB	SO	Avg	OBP	Slg
2000	98	216	28	54	11	2	12	43	3	6	47	.250	.278	.486
Career	1654	5594	703	1511	277	59	140	634	208	198	935	.270	.297	.416

Dunston returned to the Cardinals last spring after a two-month stint with the Mets the year before. He played at six different positions and provided a fair amount of punch for St. Louis. The Giants signed him to a one-year deal in December and he may see some time in right field as a replacement for Ellis Burks. 2001 Outlook: A

Luther Hackman (**Pos**: RHP, **Age**: 26)

	W	L	Pct.	ERA	G	GS	Sv	IP	H	BB	SO	HR	Ratio
2000	0	0	-	10.13	1	0	0	2.2	4	4	0	0	3.00
Career	1	2	.333	10.61	6	3	0	18.2	30	16	10	5	2.46

The Cardinals acquired Hackman last offseason in the same deal that netted Darryl Kile. Hackman did little to distinguish himself last year, though he's still young enough to emerge some day. 2001 Outlook: C

Thomas Howard (**Pos**: RF, **Age**: 36, **Bats**: B)

	G	AB	R	H	D	T	HR	RBI	SB	BB	SO	Avg	OBP	Slg
2000	86	133	13	28	4	1	6	28	1	7	34	.211	.255	.391
Career	1015	2483	297	655	123	22	44	264	66	165	432	.264	.311	.384

Howard returned to the Cardinals last year and had a terrific RBI-hit ratio. Problem was, he didn't have that many hits. Despite being a switch-hitter, he rarely faces lefthanders. 2001 Outlook: C

Mike Matthews (**Pos**: LHP, **Age**: 27)

	W	L	Pct.	ERA	G	GS	Sv	IP	H	BB	SO	HR	Ratio
2000	0	0	-	11.57	14	0	0	9.1	15	10	8	2	2.68
Career	0	0	-	11.57	14	0	0	9.1	15	10	8	2	2.68

When will ballplayers stop smashing walls and benches when they're upset? Matthews dislocated a bone in his hand after a poor performance sent him into battle with a bench last July. Silly, isn't it? 2001 Outlook: C

Keith McDonald (**Pos**: C, **Age**: 28, **Bats**: R)

	G	AB	R	H	D	T	HR	RBI	SB	BB	SO	Avg	OBP	Slg
2000	6	7	3	3	0	0	3	5	0	2	1	.429	.556	1.714
Career	6	7	3	3	0	0	3	5	0	2	1	.429	.556	1.714

If he never does anything else in his major league career, McDonald can at least tell his grandchildren that he homered in his first two big league at-bats. 2001 Outlook: C

Jesse Orosco (**Pos**: LHP, **Age**: 43)

	W	L	Pct.	ERA	G	GS	Sv	IP	H	BB	SO	HR	Ratio
2000	0	0	-	3.86	6	0	0	2.1	3	3	4	1	2.57
Career	84	75	.528	3.03	1096	4	141	1218.1	973	541	1107	102	1.24

The Cardinals hoped Orosco would provide situational support when they obtained him from the Mets last March. Instead, the ancient lefthander missed most of the season with a bad elbow. The Cardinals declined Orosco's option for 2001. 2001 Outlook: C

Eduardo Perez (**Pos**: 1B, **Age**: 31, **Bats**: R)

	G	AB	R	H	D	T	HR	RBI	SB	BB	SO	Avg	OBP	Slg
2000	35	91	9	27	4	0	3	10	1	5	19	.297	.350	.440
Career	383	1008	122	246	45	3	37	159	14	100	232	.244	.317	.405

Perez hit well in spring training but still couldn't crack the Cardinals' Opening Day roster last year. He might be able to help some teams as a utility player and pinch-hitter. 2001 Outlook: C

Scott Radinsky (**Pos**: LHP, **Age**: 33)

	W	L	Pct.	ERA	G	GS	Sv	IP	H	BB	SO	HR	Ratio
2000	0	0	-	-	1	0	0	0	0	1	0	0	-
Career	42	25	.627	3.34	555	0	52	479.2	457	206	355	31	1.38

The Cardinals got a terrible return on the hefty contract they gave Radinsky after the 1998 season. He managed to face only one batter last year before undergoing Tommy John surgery. The Cardinals declined Radinsky's option for 2001. 2001 Outlook: C

Jose Rodriguez (**Pos**: LHP, **Age**: 26)

	W	L	Pct.	ERA	G	GS	Sv	IP	H	BB	SO	HR	Ratio
2000	0	0	-	0.00	6	0	0	4.0	2	3	2	0	1.25
Career	0	0	-	0.00	6	0	0	4.0	2	3	2	0	1.25

The Cardinals selected Rodriguez in the 24th round of the 1997 draft. He's done nothing but relieve ever since. It isn't hard to project what his lefthanded role would be if he sticks in the majors. 2001 Outlook: C

Gene Stechschulte (**Pos**: RHP, **Age**: 27)

	W	L	Pct.	ERA	G	GS	Sv	IP	H	BB	SO	HR	Ratio
2000	1	0	1.000	6.31	20	0	0	25.2	24	17	12	6	1.60
Career	1	0	1.000	6.31	20	0	0	25.2	24	17	12	6	1.60

The Cardinals promoted Stechschulte on five separate occasions last year. Although he's saved a lot of games in the minors the past three seasons, he's probably no better than a middle relief prospect. 2001 Outlook: C

Larry Sutton (**Pos**: 1B, **Age**: 30, **Bats**: L)

	G	AB	R	H	D	T	HR	RBI	SB	BB	SO	Avg	OBP	Slg
2000	23	25	5	8	0	0	1	6	0	5	7	.320	.406	.440
Career	204	506	57	127	22	2	10	71	4	52	82	.251	.319	.362

After eight seasons in the Royals' organization, Sutton joined the Cardinals last year but spent most of the campaign in Triple-A. He might be able to hook on somewhere as a lefthanded pinch-hitter. 2001 Outlook: C

Mark Thompson (**Pos**: RHP, **Age**: 29)

	W	L	Pct.	ERA	G	GS	Sv	IP	H	BB	SO	HR	Ratio
2000	1	1	.500	5.04	20	0	0	25.0	24	15	19	4	1.56
Career	18	24	.429	5.74	94	52	0	337.0	404	161	198	55	1.68

A second-round pick of the Rockies in 1992, Thompson continues to be plagued by injuries. He was scored upon in each of his last six relief appearances with the Cardinals. He refused assignment and became a free agent. 2001 Outlook: C

Dave Wainhouse (**Pos**: RHP, **Age**: 33)

	W	L	Pct.	ERA	G	GS	Sv	IP	H	BB	SO	HR	Ratio
2000	0	1	.000	9.35	9	0	0	8.2	13	4	5	2	1.96
Career	2	3	.400	7.37	85	0	0	105.0	130	61	66	15	1.82

Wainhouse made the Cardinals last spring but couldn't get out of April before being shelved with shoulder problems. He signed a minor league deal with the Cubs in mid-December. 2001 Outlook: C

Rick Wilkins (**Pos**: C, **Age**: 33, **Bats**: L)

	G	AB	R	H	D	T	HR	RBI	SB	BB	SO	Avg	OBP	Slg
2000	4	11	3	3	0	0	0	1	0	2	2	.273	.385	.273
Career	708	2092	277	511	94	7	80	267	9	276	563	.244	.333	.411

Wilkins' 30-homer outburst in 1993 now ranks as one of the greatest fluke seasons in recent memory. The best he's hoping for now is a major league backup job. 2001 Outlook: C

St. Louis Cardinals Minor League Prospects

Organization Overview:

After Rick Ankiel made the transition from mega-prospect to bona-fide major leaguer, he left very little depth in the system. But Bud Smith and Albert Pujols emerged as legitimate prospects, and the Cardinals had enough talent to acquire Carlos Hernandez, Will Clark, Mike Timlin and Jason Christiansen to bulk up for the playoffs. The exported prospects from those deadline trades added to the dent made by the departed prospects from the Darryl Kile and Jim Edmonds' preseason deals. Acquiring a 20-game winner and an MVP-caliber center fielder certainly was worth a handful of youngsters, and GM Walt Jocketty deservedly earned *Baseball America's* Executive of the Year award for his efforts, as the Cardinals didn't falter until the NLCS.

Chance Caple

Position: P
Bats: R **Throws:** R
Ht: 6' 6" **Wt:** 215

Opening Day Age: 22
Born: 8/9/78 in Plano, TX

Recent Statistics

	W	L	ERA	G	GS	Sv	IP	H	R	BB	SO	HR
1999 A New Jersey	0	4	4.38	7	7	0	37.0	35	24	18	36	4
2000 A Potomac	7	9	4.39	22	22	0	125.0	128	68	34	97	11

A ribcage injury delayed the start of the 2000 season for Caple but didn't seem to hinder him much in the Class-A Carolina League last year. One of two Cardinals first-rounders in '99, he enticed scouts with the combination of his major league build and projectable velocity. The righthander can touch the mid-90s, but his fastball is more consistently clocked in the 89-92 MPH range. Despite his size, mechanics aren't an issue for him, although keeping the ball down in the zone is his key to remaining effective. The Cardinals believe he will air it out a little more as he gains experience. His slider already is a reliable secondary weapon, and his change has the makings of a solid third option.

Chad Hutchinson

Position: P
Bats: R **Throws:** R
Ht: 6' 5" **Wt:** 230

Opening Day Age: 24
Born: 2/21/77 in
Boulder, CO

Recent Statistics

	W	L	ERA	G	GS	Sv	IP	H	R	BB	SO	HR
1999 AA Arkansas	7	11	4.72	25	25	0	141.0	127	79	85	150	12
1999 AAA Memphis	2	0	2.19	2	2	0	12.1	4	3	8	16	2
2000 AAA Memphis	0	1	25.92	5	4	0	8.1	10	24	27	9	1
2000 AA Arkansas	2	3	3.38	11	11	0	48.0	40	21	27	54	1

Hutchinson entered the 2000 season with hopes of cracking the Cardinals' bullpen. But spring promise quickly deteriorated into concern, as his season began to unravel in Triple-A. A pure power pitcher, he inexplicably lost command of his fastball. After walking an alarming 27 in 8.1 innings, he went back to square one in Double-A.

He continued to make progress in the Arizona Fall League, showcasing an overpowering repertoire of low-to mid-90s gas, a hard 85-MPH slider and a changeup. The Cardinals awarded the 1998 second-rounder a $3.5 million major league pact to lure him away from football and still envision him making an impact in The Show.

Bill Ortega

Position: OF
Bats: R **Throws:** R
Ht: 6' 4" **Wt:** 205

Opening Day Age: 25
Born: 7/24/75 in
Havana, Cuba

Recent Statistics

	G	AB	R	H	D	T	HR	RBI	SB	BB	SO	Avg
1999 A Potomac	110	421	66	129	27	4	9	74	7	38	69	.306
1999 AA Arkansas	20	69	10	26	9	0	2	10	0	10	9	.377
2000 AA Arkansas	86	332	51	108	18	5	12	62	1	28	42	.325
2000 MLE	86	322	44	98	16	3	10	54	0	20	44	.304

Signed out of Cuba in '97, Ortega is starting to blossom as a power hitter. After leaving the yard just twice in his first 178 professional games, he has opened some eyes with his power potential in the past two years. A broken wrist interrupted his breakthrough Double-A season last year, as he was well on his way to establishing personal bests in most offensive categories. Ortega was regarded as the best defensive outfielder in the Texas League. Being a late-bloomer reduces his chances of becoming an everyday player, but he continues to improve. He is expected to be fully recovered in time for spring.

Albert Pujols

Position: 3B
Bats: R **Throws:** R
Ht: 6' 3" **Wt:** 210

Opening Day Age: 21
Born: 1/16/80 in Santo
Domingo, DR

Recent Statistics

	G	AB	R	H	D	T	HR	RBI	SB	BB	SO	Avg
2000 A Peoria	109	395	62	128	32	6	17	84	2	38	37	.324
2000 A Potomac	21	81	11	23	8	1	2	10	1	7	8	.284
2000 AAA Memphis	3	14	1	3	1	0	0	2	1	1	2	.214

Pujols exceeded expectations, emerging as the Cardinals' best position prospect just one year after coming out of a Missouri junior college as a 13th-round pick. The Dominican native didn't sign in time for a '99 debut but still managed to make a positive impression that year when he showed up to instructional league in top-notch physical shape. Pujols finished second in the Midwest League batting race with his .324 average, en route to earning the circuit's MVP honor. He's unusually selective for a young hitter and doesn't strike out often for a player with his power potential. Pujols flashed his skills at the hot corner, too, garnering recognition in the league as the best defensive third baseman with the strongest infield arm. Not intimidated easily, Pujols is only a year away from challenging for at-bats in the majors. His presence in the system may have made the decision to trade Fernando Tatis an easier one for St. Louis.

Luis Saturria

Position: OF   **Opening Day Age:** 24
Bats: R **Throws:** R   **Born:** 7/21/76 in San
Ht: 6' 2" **Wt:** 165   Pedro De Macoris, DR

Recent Statistics

	G	AB	R	H	D	T	HR	RBI	SB	BB	SO	Avg
2000 AA Arkansas	129	478	78	131	25	10	20	76	18	45	124	.274
2000 NL St. Louis	12	5	1	0	0	0	0	0	0	1	3	.000
2000 MLE	129	466	68	119	23	7	17	66	13	33	131	.255

With seven years in the organization, Saturria has been described as a scout's dream. The 24-year-old Dominican hasn't had the easiest time translating his physical gifts into baseball results, however. The Cardinals began to witness some encouraging progress from the multi-tooled prospect last season. In his second consecutive trip to Double-A, he made strides toward addressing his chief weakness: plate discipline. A raw athlete, he was rated as the fastest runner in the league. His speed, coupled with a strong throwing arm, make him an outstanding defensive center-field prospect, while also enhancing his chances as a callup.

Bud Smith

Position: P   **Opening Day Age:** 21
Bats: L **Throws:** L   **Born:** 10/23/79 in
Ht: 6' 0" **Wt:** 170   Torrance, CA

Recent Statistics

	W	L	ERA	G	GS	Sv	IP	H	R	BB	SO	HR
1999 A Peoria	4	1	2.83	9	9	0	54.0	53	20	16	59	4
1999 A Potomac	4	9	2.96	18	18	0	103.1	91	47	32	93	2
2000 AA Arkansas	12	1	2.32	18	18	0	108.2	93	32	27	102	5
2000 AAA Memphis	5	1	2.15	9	8	0	54.1	40	24	15	34	4

Smith rose from relative obscurity to register one of the most dominant seasons in baseball last year. The 1998 fourth-rounder may have been known to astute observers after a promising '99 campaign, but hurling a pair of no-hitters and winning 17 games in 2000 effectively put his name on the prospect map for all to see. He leaves hitters frustrated with his deceptive three-pitch array. His fastball will creep into the 90-91 MPH range, but it is set up by two potential plus-big league offerings: a curve and change. He displays remarkable poise considering his age, and his durability belies his stature. He adds an extra dimension with his athleticism, and he can swing the bat. At just 21 years old, he's on the verge of forcing his way onto the Redbirds' staff within a year.

Esix Snead

Position: OF   **Opening Day Age:** 24
Bats: B **Throws:** R   **Born:** 6/7/76 in Fort
Ht: 5' 10" **Wt:** 175   Myers, FL

Recent Statistics

	G	AB	R	H	D	T	HR	RBI	SB	BB	SO	Avg
1999 A Potomac	67	249	37	45	8	5	0	14	35	32	57	.181
1999 A Peoria	59	181	35	35	7	1	2	18	29	35	42	.193
2000 A Potomac	132	493	82	116	14	3	1	34	109	72	98	.235

If it were based on the time and effort Snead puts into improving, he would be a sure-fire, top-of-the-order prospect. Blessed with blinding speed, the Cardinals latest rabbit stole a Carolina League record 109 bases last year. Snead's other plus-tools are on display in center field, where he's excellent at tracking flyballs and hosing down runners with a strong arm. The switch-hitter batted just .195 righthanded, his natural side, and shows no power whatsoever from either side of the plate. He exhibited more regard for the strike zone last year. Snead also made strides in utilizing his speed by bunting and slashing the ball to the opposite field more often. While his .235 average leaves much to be desired, he improved by leaps and bounds over the .186 clip he posted two years ago. Snead could develop into a useful big league reserve.

Nick Stocks

Position: P   **Opening Day Age:** 22
Bats: R **Throws:** R   **Born:** 8/27/78 in Tampa,
Ht: 6' 2" **Wt:** 185   FL

Recent Statistics

	W	L	ERA	G	GS	Sv	IP	H	R	BB	SO	HR
2000 A Peoria	10	10	3.78	25	24	0	150.0	133	88	52	118	4

A highly-coveted 1999 first-round pick out of Florida State University, Stocks signed a $1.4 million deal and spent his 2000 debut season in the Class-A Midwest League. A Tommy John surgery survivor, he showed he's stronger than ever by amassing 150 innings. Armed with a fastball that approaches the mid-90s, Stocks also harnesses a knee-buckling curveball, which rates as one of the best breaking pitches in the system. His changeup is coming around. His command was evident, but the Cardinals also have been impressed with his intensity and heart. Stocks could speed up his timetable by honing his offspeed stuff, but St. Louis is happy with his one-step-at-a-time progress.

Others to Watch

Drafted in the first-round last year, **Shaun Boyd** (19) hit .263 in his pro debut. He was converted to second base in instructional league, where his line-drive bat and speed can help him move up the ladder. . . Righthander **B.R. Cook** (23) is a potential power pitcher with a 92-94 MPH fastball and plus-curveball, but he'll need to improve his command and consistency in Double-A. . . Righthander **Cristobal Correa** (21) was in the process of breaking out last year when the dreaded Tommy John surgery came into the picture. His lively fastball and sharp slider should return when he does in 2002. . . Righthander **Jim Journell** (23) provided a glimpse of his overpowering stuff in his pro debut. Another Tommy John success story, he blows his heat in the 94-95 MPH range with a nasty slider. . . Righthander **Blake Williams** (22) has the frame and stuff to be a big league prospect, featuring a projectable 90-92 MPH fastball, changeup and a curveball, his best pitch.

St. Louis

Qualcomm Stadium

Offense

Qualcomm Stadium is one of the best pitchers' parks in the majors. The ball doesn't carry well, and there's an above-average amount of foul territory around the infield. Below-average visibility also contributes to the suppression of home runs and batting averages.

Defense

Qualcomm's fast infield can play like artificial turf—without eliminating bad hops. The park's unique outfield configuration can be challenging for visiting outfielders. Going down the foul lines, the stands jut toward fair territory before falling back near the foul poles. This creates a situation whereby an outfielder can chase a ball into the corner and look toward home plate, only to have his view obstructed by the stands.

Who It Helps the Most

Almost all Padres pitchers enjoy the benefits of their home park. Donne Wall has the most lopsided splits; his home ERA over the last three years is in the ones. Matt Clement's extreme splits were noteworthy in 2000, and he had similar breakdowns the year before. The park hurts almost all hitters; the ones who are affected the least tend to be singles hitters such as Tony Gwynn and Eric Owens.

Who It Hurts the Most

Among power hitters, lefthanded sluggers seem to have more trouble reaching the fences. Ryan Klesko hit a disproportionate number of homers on the road in 2000, as Steve Finley often did when he was a Padre. Righthanded hitters Phil Nevin and Bret Boone were hurt last year, too, but to a lesser extent.

Rookies & Newcomers

Outfielder Mike Darr doesn't try to challenge the fences, so he shouldn't be hurt too badly. Infielder Damian Jackson seems to have altered his plate approach, which should prevent the park from hurting him as much as it used to. Catcher Ben Davis won't get any cheap homers, but this alone shouldn't stifle his growth. The park should help build the confidence and aid the development of young hurlers Matt Clement and Adam Eaton.

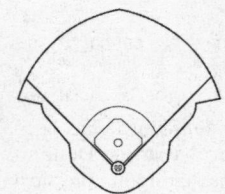

Dimensions: LF-327, LCF-370, CF-405, RCF-370, RF-330

Capacity: 46,510

Elevation: 20 feet

Surface: Grass

Foul Territory: Large

Park Factors

2000 Season

	Home Games Padres	Opp	Total	Away Games Padres	Opp	Total	Index
G	75	75	150	72	72	144	—
Avg	.252	.243	.247	.263	.277	.270	92
AB	2518	2637	5155	2526	2464	4990	99
R	328	339	667	369	405	774	83
H	635	640	1275	664	682	1346	91
2B	123	104	227	134	130	264	83
3B	12	7	19	20	14	34	54
HR	65	83	148	79	89	168	85
BB	270	264	534	268	321	589	88
SO	535	528	1063	526	438	964	107
E	80	49	129	53	49	102	121
E-Infield	72	39	111	47	43	90	118
LHB-Avg	.259	.238	.247	.280	.291	.286	86
LHB-HR	24	33	57	26	36	62	80
RHB-Avg	.249	.247	.248	.255	.266	.260	95
RHB-HR	41	50	91	53	53	106	89

1998-2000

	Home Games Padres	Opp	Total	Away Games Padres	Opp	Total	Index
G	222	222	444	221	221	442	—
Avg	.253	.240	.246	.255	.280	.267	92
AB	7326	7649	14975	7656	7482	15138	98
R	975	886	1861	1063	1162	2225	83
H	1853	1835	3688	1949	2095	4044	91
2B	341	306	647	409	385	794	82
3B	37	25	62	45	47	92	68
HR	205	219	424	242	256	498	86
BB	848	673	1521	813	829	1642	94
SO	1561	1661	3222	1542	1389	2931	111
E	179	158	337	167	153	320	105
E-Infield	159	128	287	143	130	273	105
LHB-Avg	.264	.243	.253	.272	.292	.282	90
LHB-HR	74	74	148	83	98	181	80
RHB-Avg	.245	.238	.241	.243	.271	.257	94
RHB-HR	131	145	276	159	158	317	90

2000 Rankings (National League)

- Third-highest error factor
- Lowest walk factor
- Lowest LHB batting-average factor
- Second-lowest batting-average factor
- Second-lowest run factor
- Second-lowest hit factor
- Third-lowest double factor
- Third-lowest triple factor

Bruce Bochy

2000 Season

Bruce Bochy had his share of headaches last year. With a club that already had traded away several veterans over the winter, Bochy lost steady vets Tony Gwynn, Chris Gomez and Sterling Hitchcock to serious injuries early on. That, and deadline deals that unloaded some other veterans, forced him to integrate a number of rookies and newcomers into the lineup. There were the inevitable bumps in the road, but by year's end Bochy had found roles for many players who could help for years to come. It was a difficult year, but he won respect for what he accomplished.

Offense

Bochy's most visible attribute is his patience. He takes the long view with players and won't often sour on a youngster or change a player's role until he's given the player a fair trial. He'll show uncommon patience with someone who's struggling if he believes that player has the potential to succeed with experience. He likes the running game and often gives the green light to guys such as Ryan Klesko, who might not get it from other managers.

Pitching & Defense

Bochy has had to break in a high number of young pitchers over the last few years, and he has done well with them overall. He usually takes care not to overwork or overexpose them until he feels they are ready to handle it. Bochy is unafraid to try players at new positions in order to find the best spot for them. He has a strong preference for glove men up the middle and will put up with a weak hitter if he is not error-prone. Settling on a workable situation at shortstop will be a top priority. Keeping a lefthanded hitter or two on the bench to pinch-hit is important to him.

2001 Outlook

Bochy will have several more important issues to resolve this year, including the crowded second-base situation, how much longer to go with Ruben Rivera and whether Klesko can be more than a mere platoon player. But many of the things he accomplished last year—such as assembling a solid starting rotation and bullpen—should begin to pay off in the won-lost column.

Born: 4/16/55 in Landes de Bussac, France

Playing Experience: 1978-1987, Hou, NYM, SD

Managerial Experience: 6 seasons

Manager Statistics

Year	Team, Lg	W	L	Pct	GB	Finish
2000	San Diego, NL	76	86	.469	21.0	5th West
6 Seasons		485	469	.508	—	—

2000 Starting Pitchers by Days Rest

	<=3	4	5	6+
Padres Starts	0	91	45	16
Padres ERA	—	4.57	4.79	6.07
NL Avg Starts	2	80	50	21
NL ERA	5.00	4.61	4.60	5.18

2000 Situational Stats

	Bruce Bochy	NL Average
Hit & Run Success %	31.1	33.8
Stolen Base Success %	71.2	68.8
Platoon Pct.	52.2	53.2
Defensive Subs	14	19
High-Pitch Outings	14	14
Quick/Slow Hooks	17/21	14/16
Sacrifice Attempts	52	87

2000 Rankings (National League)

- 1st in steals of home plate (2) and fewest caught stealings of third base (3)
- 2nd in starting lineups used (134) and pinch-hitters used (285)
- 3rd in steals of second base (119), double steals (5), slow hooks (21) and quick hooks (17)

Bret Boone

Position: 2B
Bats: R **Throws:** R
Ht: 5'10" **Wt:** 180

Opening Day Age: 31
Born: 4/6/69 in El Cajon, CA
ML Seasons: 9

2000 Season

How quickly things can change. In his first year in San Diego, second baseman Bret Boone enjoyed an excellent first half, ranking among team leaders in home runs and RBI. But August brought a slump and a season-ending bone bruise to his right knee. With Boone out, Damian Jackson's fine work at the keystone rendered Boone trade bait.

Hitting

Boone takes a healthy cut and has good power for a middle infielder, but he has few other offensive strengths. He's one of the few righthanded hitters who doesn't gain an advantage facing a lefthander. He's a very good breaking-ball hitter, but can have problems with high heat. He's not particularly patient and is better suited to the fifth and sixth spots, where he batted last year, than the second spot, where he hit in Atlanta. His big swing and high strikeout totals have led several teams to try to get him to focus more on making contact, but Boone has resisted such suggestions. Last year, he was hitting the ball in the air more than ever, and until August, it seemed to be working for him.

Baserunning & Defense

Boone's strong arm allows him to play deep and cover a lot of ground. With soft hands and a quick pivot, he's one of the best defensive second basemen in the game. He committed 15 errors last year, an uncharacteristically high total for him. While his straight-ahead speed is only ordinary, he runs the bases aggressively and intelligently.

2001 Outlook

It was initially expected that the Padres would pick up their option on Boone for 2001—possibly so that he could be traded—but they decided to cut their ties with him and declined their $4 million option, electing a $250,000 buyout. Regardless of where he ends up, Boone has been a very durable player in the past, so he can be expected to improve his numbers simply by staying healthy in 2001.

Overall Statistics

	G	AB	R	H	D	T	HR	RBI	SB	BB	SO	Avg	OBP	Slg
2000	127	463	61	116	18	2	19	74	8	50	97	.251	.326	.421
Career	1072	3911	503	996	215	14	125	536	47	307	758	.255	.312	.413

Where He Hits the Ball

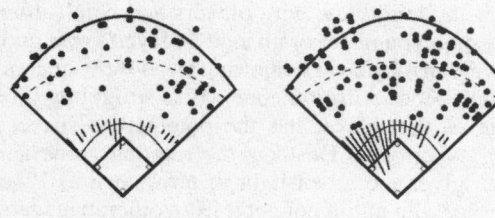

Vs. LHP   Vs. RHP

2000 Situational Stats

	AB	H	HR	RBI	Avg		AB	H	HR	RBI	Avg
Home	223	53	8	27	.238	LHP	132	31	5	18	.235
Road	240	63	11	47	.263	RHP	331	85	14	56	.257
First Half	317	81	16	62	.256	Sc Pos	125	36	10	61	.288
Scnd Half	146	35	3	12	.240	Clutch	82	26	4	10	.317

2000 Rankings (National League)

- 3rd in errors at second base (15) and lowest fielding percentage at second base (.977)
- 5th in lowest batting average on a 3-1 count (.059)
- 8th in lowest batting average vs. lefthanded pitchers
- 9th in lowest batting average
- Led the Padres in sacrifice flies (7) and lowest percentage of swings on the first pitch (20.2)
- Led NL second basemen in intentional walks (7)

Matt Clement

2000 Season

While sophomore Matt Clement hardly improved upon his rookie numbers in 2000, it was not a wasted season for him. After being babied a bit the year before, he proved he could hold up over the course of a season while pitching deep into games every fifth day. As a young groundball pitcher with control problems on a team with shoddy infield defense, he survived about as well as could have been expected.

Pitching

Clement's stuff is so nasty that it's scary to think what he might do if he harnesses it. With a sinking fastball in the low 90s and a hard slider, Clement gets tons of strikeouts and groundballs. His pitches move so much that he sometimes struggles to get them over the plate; he led the majors in wild pitches and walks allowed, and finished second with 16 hit batsmen. He's working on a changeup, a pitch that could help immensely if he masters it. Few righthanded hitters can take him out of the park. Opposing managers often load their lineups with lefthanded hitters, who still give Clement occasional trouble.

Defense & Hitting

Clement has a decent move to first but rarely uses it. Instead, he deters basestealers and keeps the double play in order by getting the ball to the plate quickly. A good athlete, Clement is quick off the mound and fields his position aggressively. He's a complete zero at the plate, good for only an occasional walk or sacrifice.

2001 Outlook

Perhaps this will be the year that Clement puts it all together. Even if it isn't, experience and an improved infield defense behind him should help him to continue moving forward. It wouldn't take much improvement from him to win 15-17 games and become the staff ace.

Position: SP
Bats: R **Throws:** R
Ht: 6' 3" **Wt:** 195

Opening Day Age: 26
Born: 8/12/74 in McCandless Township, PA
ML Seasons: 3

Overall Statistics

	W	L	Pct.	ERA	G	GS	Sv	IP	H	BB	SO	HR	Ratio
2000	13	17	.433	5.14	34	34	0	205.0	194	125	170	22	1.56
Career	25	29	.463	4.82	69	67	0	399.1	399	218	318	40	1.55

How Often He Throws Strikes

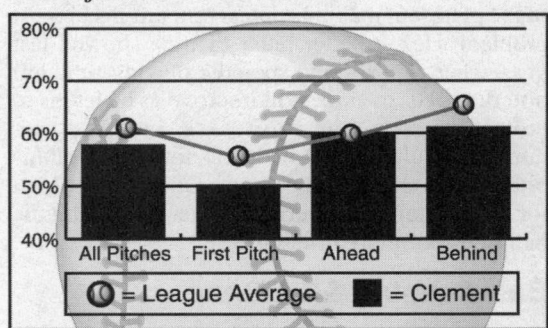

2000 Situational Stats

	W	L	ERA	Sv	IP		AB	H	HR	RBI	Avg
Home	6	8	3.86	0	105.0	LHB	412	110	14	78	.267
Road	7	9	6.48	0	100.0	RHB	370	84	8	29	.227
First Half	9	7	4.84	0	115.1	Sc Pos	220	58	10	88	.264
Scnd Half	4	10	5.52	0	89.2	Clutch	31	4	1	3	.129

2000 Rankings (National League)

- 1st in walks allowed, wild pitches (23), highest walks per nine innings (5.5) and highest ERA on the road
- 2nd in losses, hit batsmen (16) and errors at pitcher (4)
- Led the Padres in wins, losses, games started, innings pitched, hits allowed, batters faced (940), walks allowed, hit batsmen (16), strikeouts, wild pitches (23), pitches thrown (3,535), GDPs induced (19), lowest slugging percentage allowed (.384), highest groundball/flyball ratio allowed (2.1), lowest stolen-base percentage allowed (70.6), most run support per nine innings (5.1), fewest home runs allowed per nine innings (.97) and most GDPs induced per nine innings (0.8)

San Diego

Ben Davis

2000 Season

The 2000 season was something of a letdown for Ben Davis, who'd been the Padres' regular catcher over the second half of 1999. He began the season with the big club, but was demoted to Triple-A Las Vegas when Carlos Hernandez returned from a groin injury in late April. Davis was recalled in July and seemed in position to reclaim catching duties when Hernandez was dealt at the trade deadline, but a strained oblique muscle shelved him for much of August. Davis returned in September and finally got the bat going.

Hitting

Davis' power potential is evident from both sides of the plate, but making contact remains his biggest problem. He's a better hitter than he showed last year, when injuries and sporadic playing time left him rusty. His average will improve as he learns to protect the plate with two strikes, and his power numbers could jump if he learns to zone in on his pitch when ahead in the count. One positive sign for his developing power was the fact that he hit the ball in the air more often in 2000.

Baserunning & Defense

Davis already is one of the better defensive catchers in the game. His powerful throwing arm hasn't yet translated into terrific caught-stealing percentages, but it should once he refines his footwork. He must work on blocking pitches, but he has good mobility and only needs experience. His foot speed is unremarkable, though he hits the ball in the air enough to keep from grounding into too many double plays.

2001 Outlook

It's hard to knock Davis' performance thus far when you consider that he'll be only 24 years old this year. The Padres fully expect him to mature into one of the best all-around receivers in the majors, a process that could begin in earnest this season.

Position: C
Bats: B **Throws:** R
Ht: 6' 4" **Wt:** 215

Opening Day Age: 24
Born: 3/10/77 in Chester, PA
ML Seasons: 3

Overall Statistics

	G	AB	R	H	D	T	HR	RBI	SB	BB	SO	Avg	OBP	Slg
2000	43	130	12	29	6	0	3	14	1	14	35	.223	.297	.338
Career	120	397	41	94	20	1	8	44	3	39	105	.237	.303	.353

Where He Hits the Ball

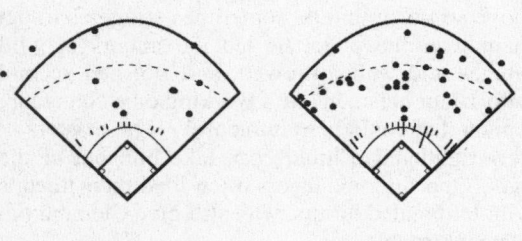

Vs. LHP   **Vs. RHP**

2000 Situational Stats

	AB	H	HR	RBI	Avg		AB	H	HR	RBI	Avg
Home	68	16	1	3	.235	LHP	36	7	2	5	.194
Road	62	13	2	11	.210	RHP	94	22	1	9	.234
First Half	21	2	0	0	.095	Sc Pos	35	8	0	9	.229
Scnd Half	109	27	3	14	.248	Clutch	29	8	0	2	.276

2000 Rankings (National League)

- Did not rank near the top or bottom in any category

Adam Eaton

2000 Season

One of the most pleasant surprises of the 2000 season for San Diego was Adam Eaton. When the Padres acquired him from the Phillies as the centerpiece of the Andy Ashby deal the previous winter, they knew he had good potential. But they didn't think he'd arrive quite so soon. He came to the majors in late May and was one of the best pitchers in the league over the next three months. Only a lack of run support prevented him from having a stellar won-lost record. His ERA was under 3.00 in late August before a tired arm led to a September slump.

Pitching

Eaton professes not to have a true out pitch. The truth is that he doesn't need one, since his arsenal includes several: a 95-MPH fastball, a moving two-seamer, a good curveball and a respectable changeup. He hits his spots and mixes his pitches with the savvy of a pitcher well beyond his 23 years. He hasn't yet developed a good approach to lefthanded hitters, but gives righthanded swingers fits. Like many young pitchers, he's at his best early in the game and tires as his pitch count approaches triple digits.

Defense & Hitting

Less significant, but equally surprising, was Eaton's hitting. He led major league pitchers who logged at least 30 plate appearances with a .289 batting average, and even contributed six walks and a pair of stolen bases. His performance in limited minor league at-bats suggests 2000 wasn't a fluke, either. He doesn't have much of a pickoff move, but gets the ball to the plate quickly and can be tough to run on. He's an alert fielder who knows what to do with the ball when he gets it.

2001 Outlook

Eaton's continuing development is one of the things the Padres are looking forward to the most in 2001. If his late-season dropoff was nothing more than a case of simple fatigue, there's no reason to think Eaton can't be a very solid middle-of-the-rotation starter this year, at the very least.

Position: SP
Bats: R **Throws:** R
Ht: 6' 2" **Wt:** 190

Opening Day Age: 23
Born: 11/23/77 in Seattle, WA
ML Seasons: 1

Overall Statistics

	W	L	Pct.	ERA	G	GS	Sv	IP	H	BB	SO	HR	Ratio
2000	7	4	.636	4.13	22	22	0	135.0	134	61	90	14	1.44
Career	7	4	.636	4.13	22	22	0	135.0	134	61	90	14	1.44

How Often He Throws Strikes

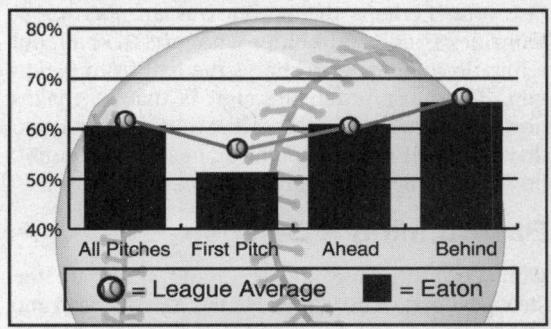

○ = League Average   ■ = Eaton

2000 Situational Stats

	W	L	ERA	Sv	IP		AB	H	HR	RBI	Avg
Home	4	3	4.04	0	78.0	LHB	269	81	8	35	.301
Road	3	1	4.26	0	57.0	RHB	247	53	6	22	.215
First Half	1	1	3.73	0	50.2	Sc Pos	134	33	2	39	.246
Scnd Half	6	3	4.38	0	84.1	Clutch	27	8	1	2	.296

2000 Rankings (National League)
- 7th in lowest batting average allowed vs. righthanded batters
- Led the Padres in pickoff throws (50)

San Diego

Wiki Gonzalez

2000 Season

Rookie catcher Wiki Gonzalez had a decent but sometimes frustrating debut season in 2000. He served as the Padres' backup catcher for the entire season, but slumps at inopportune times prevented him from expanding his role. The Padres used him full-time only in August, after Carlos Hernandez had been traded and Ben Davis had been felled by injury. Gonzalez hit well that month, but when Davis returned, Gonzalez landed back on the bench.

Hitting

Gonzalez, who hit 19 homers between the minors and majors in 1999, didn't display the same pop last year. Perhaps the power was an aberration; Gonzalez is not a pull hitter who lofts the ball, but a line-drive hitter who sprays the ball from gap to gap. The most promising sign is that he makes good contact and rarely strikes out. He needs to drive the ball more when he's ahead in the count, however, to become more of a power threat.

Baserunning & Defense

Gonzalez' throwing and receiving skills are the strongest part of his game. He has a strong arm and quick release, and if it hadn't been for an early-season game in which the Marlins stole 10 bases off pitcher Stan Spencer (who's helpless to stop basestealers), Gonzalez' caught-stealing percentage would have been quite good. He's agile behind the plate and blocks pitches well. The stocky receiver is a non-factor on the bases.

2001 Outlook

It looks like Gonzalez will remain a backup—albeit an above-average one—to young Ben Davis. He may be asked to step in if Davis is demoted once again, but it's clear that the Padres regard Davis, and not Gonzalez, as their catcher of the future.

Position: C
Bats: R **Throws:** R
Ht: 5'11" **Wt:** 203

Opening Day Age: 26
Born: 5/17/74 in Aragua, Venezuela
ML Seasons: 2

Overall Statistics

	G	AB	R	H	D	T	HR	RBI	SB	BB	SO	Avg	OBP	Slg
2000	95	284	25	66	15	1	5	30	1	30	31	.232	.311	.345
Career	125	367	32	87	17	2	8	42	1	31	39	.237	.303	.360

Where He Hits the Ball

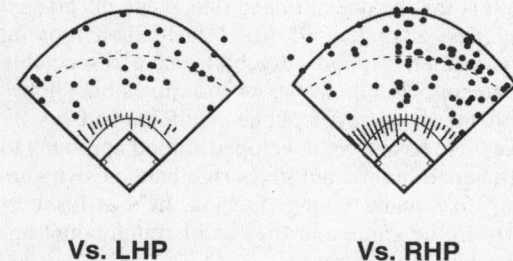

Vs. LHP   **Vs. RHP**

2000 Situational Stats

	AB	H	HR	RBI	Avg		AB	H	HR	RBI	Avg
Home	150	30	1	13	.200	LHP	83	23	1	8	.277
Road	134	36	4	17	.269	RHP	201	43	4	22	.214
First Half	129	32	3	15	.248	Sc Pos	77	13	0	20	.169
Scnd Half	155	34	2	15	.219	Clutch	54	10	3	5	.185

2000 Rankings (National League)

- Did not rank near the top or bottom in any category

Trevor Hoffman

2000 Season

In 2000, Trevor Hoffman had one of the better "off" years in recent memory. The Padres' closer started strong and finished strong, but a puzzling midsummer slump prevented him from matching his stellar numbers of the previous two campaigns. He still finished second in the National League with 43 saves and had the type of year that would be considered a major success for most closers.

Pitching

Hoffman's mid-90s fastball and drop-dead changeup form one of the deadliest combinations around. He occasionally uses a slider, as well. Hoffman makes his living on the outer half of the plate, but during his rough stretch, some thought that hitters had begun to zone in on pitches away. His effectiveness returned after he began coming inside more often. Another theory is that he was hurt by inconsistent usage, which resulted from sometimes infrequent save situations. His command was better than ever last summer, as he issued only seven unintentional walks. He's as durable as they come. Hoffman can enter a game in the eighth or work several days in a row as needed.

Defense & Hitting

Hoffman, a former minor league shortstop, has erred only once in his eight-year major league career. He isn't quick to the plate, but being able to throw a high fastball past the hitter gives his catcher a decent chance to nab any basethief. He rarely gets to bat, but hasn't entirely forgotten how to handle the stick—he's no automatic out.

2001 Outlook

Though he turned 32 last October, the Padres have Hoffman locked up through 2003, and his run as an elite closer doesn't appear to be coming to an end any time soon. Even if his slight decline last year was real, he's still plenty good enough to remain one of the best.

Position: RP
Bats: R **Throws:** R
Ht: 6' 0" **Wt:** 215

Opening Day Age: 33
Born: 10/13/67 in Bellflower, CA
ML Seasons: 8

Overall Statistics

	W	L	Pct.	ERA	G	GS	Sv	IP	H	BB	SO	HR	Ratio
2000	4	7	.364	2.99	70	0	43	72.1	61	11	85	7	1.00
Career	40	35	.533	2.72	509	0	271	581.1	426	175	665	53	1.03

How Often He Throws Strikes

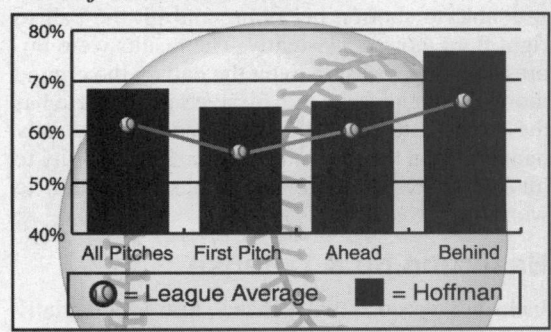

○ = League Average   ■ = Hoffman

2000 Situational Stats

	W	L	ERA	Sv	IP		AB	H	HR	RBI	Avg
Home	2	5	2.51	26	46.2	LHB	130	26	2	12	.200
Road	2	2	3.86	17	25.2	RHB	142	35	5	18	.246
First Half	1	3	3.44	22	36.2	Sc Pos	59	15	2	23	.254
Scnd Half	3	4	2.52	21	35.2	Clutch	226	50	7	30	.221

2000 Rankings (National League)

- 1st in save opportunities (50)
- 2nd in saves
- 3rd in relief losses (7), blown saves (7) and fewest baserunners allowed per nine innings in relief (9.0)
- 5th in save percentage (86.0)
- Led the Padres in games pitched, saves, games finished (59), save opportunities (50), save percentage (86.0), blown saves (7), lowest batting average allowed in relief with runners on base (.245), relief losses (7), relief innings (72.1), relief ERA (2.99), most strikeouts per nine innings in relief (10.6) and fewest baserunners allowed per nine innings in relief (9.0)

San Diego

Damian Jackson

2000 Season

Last year, Damian Jackson lost his job twice, got moved to a new position and still came out smelling like a rose. He began the year by beating out Chris Gomez for the shortstop job. A June slump—both at the plate and in the field—put him on the bench in favor of Kevin Nicholson, however. Jackson soon won the job back, only to lose it again when Desi Relaford was acquired in August. That's when Jackson was moved to second base and promoted to the leadoff spot. He simply excelled in both roles.

Hitting

Over the last two months of the season, Jackson was able to shorten his swing and hit the ball to right field more consistently. The results were impressive—he was able to hit the ball on the ground more often, and as he did, his average rose. He has the strength to reach the alleys and is especially dangerous on the first pitch. A puzzling inability to hit lefthanders is one of the things he has left to work on.

Baserunning & Defense

Jackson's speed is what makes him a potentially exciting leadoff man. In a full season atop the lineup, he could lead the league in steals. He made a smooth transition from shortstop to second base, picking up the nuances of the double-play pivot and using his strong arm to good advantage. His natural quickness translates into above-average range afield. The careless errors that plagued him at shortstop mostly disappeared at second.

2001 Outlook

The Padres are convinced that Jackson's improvement over the last two months of 2000 was real and are expecting big things from him this year. He'll begin the season as the leadoff man and starting second baseman.

Position: SS/2B/LF
Bats: R **Throws:** R
Ht: 5'11" **Wt:** 185

Opening Day Age: 27
Born: 8/16/73 in Los Angeles, CA
ML Seasons: 5

Overall Statistics

	G	AB	R	H	D	T	HR	RBI	SB	BB	SO	Avg	OBP	Slg
2000	138	470	68	120	27	6	6	37	28	62	108	.255	.345	.377
Career	309	942	138	229	56	9	16	86	66	126	229	.243	.335	.373

Where He Hits the Ball

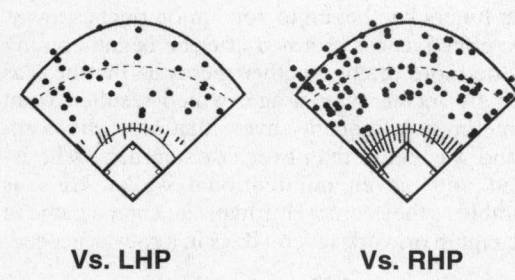

Vs. LHP   **Vs. RHP**

2000 Situational Stats

	AB	H	HR	RBI	Avg		AB	H	HR	RBI	Avg
Home	217	60	5	20	.276	LHP	121	27	1	6	.223
Road	253	60	1	17	.237	RHP	349	93	5	31	.266
First Half	240	59	3	15	.246	Sc Pos	96	20	1	25	.208
Scnd Half	230	61	3	22	.265	Clutch	68	22	0	4	.324

2000 Rankings (National League)

- 2nd in steals of third (7) and lowest slugging percentage vs. lefthanded pitchers (.298)
- 5th in lowest batting average vs. lefthanded pitchers
- 6th in errors at shortstop (19)
- 7th in lowest slugging percentage
- 8th in stolen-base percentage (82.4) and lowest batting average with runners in scoring position
- 10th in stolen bases and lowest batting average on the road
- Led the Padres in stolen-base percentage (82.4), most pitches seen per plate appearance (3.96), batting average in the clutch, bunts in play (12), highest percentage of pitches taken (58.9) and steals of third (7)

Ryan Klesko

2000 Season

The Padres traded for Ryan Klesko last winter, acquiring him from Atlanta, and it didn't take them long to decide they wanted to build around him. They signed him to a three-year contract extension through 2004 in late May that will pay him an average of $6.25 million. Klesko responded by going on a six-week tear. He tailed off over the last two months of the season, but still finished with fine numbers.

Hitting

Against righthanded pitchers, Klesko is a deadly low-fastball hitter with excellent power to all fields. His biggest problem always has been an inability to hit lefthanders. He was platooned early in the year, but faced all types of pitching in the second half; his performance against lefties improved somewhat, but remained unacceptable. His walk total was up last year, but that was as much a result of being pitched around as it was of improved patience on his part.

Baserunning & Defense

Last year, Klesko returned full-time to his less unnatural position, first base. He wasn't as great a liability there as he used to be in left field, but his glovework never will be a strength. Though his arm is strong, his hands are stiff. One of the biggest surprises of the year was his 23-for-30 performance on the basepaths. He's always had decent speed, but no one ever suspected he'd put it to such good use. He'll have a tough time repeating his success in 2001, as clubs will pay more attention to him.

2001 Outlook

The Padres may continue to play Klesko full-time, but seven years into his major league career, it seems unlikely that he'll suddenly discover the secret of hitting lefthanders. San Diego may spell him from time to time at first with Bubba Trammell, who was acquired from the Mets via trade. Despite that, Klesko should remain one of the better lefthanded power hitters in the league for years to come.

Position: 1B
Bats: L **Throws:** L
Ht: 6' 3" **Wt:** 220

Opening Day Age: 29
Born: 6/12/71 in Westminster, CA
ML Seasons: 9

Overall Statistics

	G	AB	R	H	D	T	HR	RBI	SB	BB	SO	Avg	OBP	Slg
2000	145	494	88	140	33	2	26	92	23	91	81	.283	.393	.516
Career	937	2925	462	824	173	20	165	542	49	392	604	.282	.367	.524

Where He Hits the Ball

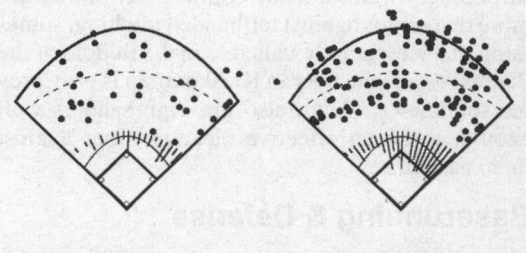

Vs. LHP	Vs. RHP

2000 Situational Stats

	AB	H	HR	RBI	Avg		AB	H	HR	RBI	Avg
Home	250	70	9	36	.280	LHP	121	31	2	16	.256
Road	244	70	17	56	.287	RHP	373	109	24	76	.292
First Half	253	80	19	56	.316	Sc Pos	140	44	7	61	.314
Scnd Half	241	60	7	36	.249	Clutch	92	20	3	15	.217

2000 Rankings (National League)

- 4th in lowest fielding percentage at first base (.992) and highest percentage of swings on the first pitch (42.6)
- 5th in errors at first base (9)
- Led the Padres in runs scored, walks, intentional walks (9), times on base (232), on-base percentage, batting average vs. righthanded pitchers, slugging percentage vs. righthanded pitchers (.560), on-base percentage vs. righthanded pitchers (.408) and games played
- Led NL first basemen in stolen bases, caught stealing (7) and stolen-base percentage (76.7)

San Diego

Phil Nevin

2000 Season

Some scoffed when the Padres signed Nevin to a multimillion-dollar contract extension in September of 1999, based only on his strong play over three months of the '99 season. Nevin proved the naysayers wrong in 2000, however, putting up numbers comparable to those of the league's elite third basemen despite missing most of September with an abdominal strain. Indeed, he proved to be a bargain.

Hitting

Nevin is deadly on pitches low in the strike zone and has over-the-fence power to all fields. His short, quick stroke allows him to protect the plate surprisingly well for a power hitter. Few hitters are more dangerous against lefthanded pitching, something that's especially valuable in the middle of the Padres' order, since Ryan Klesko often is easy prey for southpaws. Nevin also hits righthanders well enough to be an effective cleanup hitter against them as well.

Baserunning & Defense

Nevin is no basestealing threat, but middle infielders hate to see him charging toward second on a potential double play. At third base, his range is barely average and his hands aren't particularly soft, but his arm is strong and accurate. His ability to go behind the plate in a pinch is an asset, although he's become such an important part of the team's offense that they probably won't expose him to such hazardous duty very often.

2001 Outlook

Nevin has proven that his 1999 season was no fluke. Injuries are the only thing that could keep him from continuing to put up All-Star-caliber numbers. He plays hard and suffers more than his share of bumps and bruises, but to his credit, he has been tough enough to play through all but the most debilitating ones. A lingering injury, however, could diminish his production, if not his playing time.

Position: 3B
Bats: R **Throws:** R
Ht: 6' 2" **Wt:** 231

Opening Day Age: 30
Born: 1/19/71 in Fullerton, CA
ML Seasons: 6

Overall Statistics

	G	AB	R	H	D	T	HR	RBI	SB	BB	SO	Avg	OBP	Slg
2000	143	538	87	163	34	1	31	107	2	59	121	.303	.374	.543
Career	524	1685	226	442	94	4	82	286	5	178	417	.262	.336	.469

Where He Hits the Ball

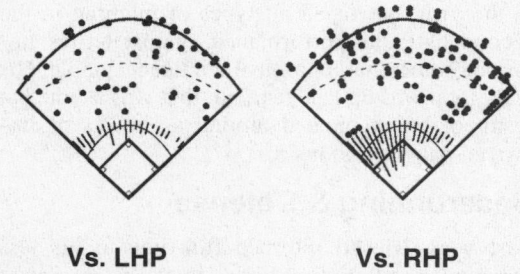

Vs. LHP   **Vs. RHP**

2000 Situational Stats

	AB	H	HR	RBI	Avg		AB	H	HR	RBI	Avg
Home	262	67	13	45	.256	LHP	146	50	13	35	.342
Road	276	96	18	62	.348	RHP	392	113	18	72	.288
First Half	324	89	18	64	.275	Sc Pos	146	41	9	72	.281
Scnd Half	214	74	13	43	.346	Clutch	98	23	5	15	.235

2000 Rankings (National League)

- 1st in errors at third base (26) and lowest fielding percentage at third base (.929)
- 4th in slugging percentage vs. lefthanded pitchers (.685)
- 5th in batting average on the road
- Led the Padres in batting average, home runs, doubles, total bases (292), RBI, intentional walks (9), GDPs (17), pitches seen (2,304), slugging percentage, HR frequency (17.4 ABs per HR), batting average with the bases loaded (.467), batting average vs. lefthanded pitchers, batting average on an 0-2 count (.244), cleanup slugging percentage (.548), slugging percentage vs. lefthanded pitchers (.685) and on-base percentage vs. lefthanded pitchers (.439)

Eric Owens

Position: RF/LF/CF
Bats: R **Throws:** R
Ht: 6' 0" **Wt:** 198

Opening Day Age: 30
Born: 2/3/71 in
Danville, VA
ML Seasons: 6

2000 Season

Eric Owens' 2000 season seemed like a replay of 1999. He started hot and took good numbers into the All-Star break, only to fade badly in the second half. He lobbied hard to be the team's leadoff man in spring training, and his hot hitting won him the job to start the season. He was a regular in the outfield, playing all three outfield positions, and remained the leadoff man until his second-half slide forced the Padres to explore other options.

Hitting

Owens doesn't have the speed or on-base prowess to be an effective leadoff man, or the power to be a regular corner outfielder. He keeps his average respectable only by hitting balls over or through the infield. Reaching the fences isn't something he does often. He bristles at the assertion that he can't maintain his strength over a full season, but has yet to disprove such a claim.

Defense & Baserunning

While he is an aggressive, hustling baserunner, Owens isn't quite fast enough to be a top-flight basestealer. He is stretched to cover center field, but has good range in left or right field. His relatively weak arm makes him best suited for left. His biggest asset is his ability to play any position except catcher and shortstop.

2001 Outlook

Owens will be 30 years old this year, and the Padres already have invested more in him than a rebuilding club might. They seem to have concluded that Owens is not to be their leadoff hitter, and since he has no other obvious role, this may spell the end for him as a full-timer. As a regular, he's overexposed, but as a reserve, he could be quite helpful. Still, the team expects that Owens will compete with Mike Darr for the starting job in center field if Ruben Rivera continues to struggle at the plate or is dealt sometime before or during the season.

Overall Statistics

	G	AB	R	H	D	T	HR	RBI	SB	BB	SO	Avg	OBP	Slg
2000	145	583	87	171	19	7	6	51	29	45	63	.293	.346	.381
Career	445	1327	181	351	49	10	16	129	81	112	168	.265	.324	.353

Where He Hits the Ball

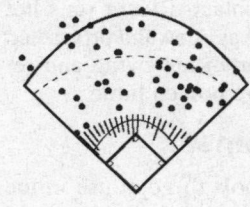 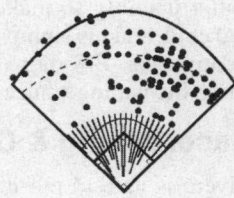

Vs. LHP **Vs. RHP**

2000 Situational Stats

	AB	H	HR	RBI	Avg		AB	H	HR	RBI	Avg
Home	288	86	4	29	.299	LHP	179	55	4	12	.307
Road	295	85	2	22	.288	RHP	404	116	2	39	.287
First Half	318	104	4	31	.327	Sc Pos	123	39	1	41	.317
Scnd Half	265	67	2	20	.253	Clutch	100	24	1	14	.240

2000 Rankings (National League)

- 2nd in singles, caught stealing (14) and highest groundball/flyball ratio (2.8)
- Led the Padres in at-bats, hits, singles, triples, stolen bases, caught stealing (14), plate appearances (636), highest groundball/flyball ratio (2.8), batting average with runners in scoring position, batting average at home, batting average with two strikes (.221), lowest percentage of swings that missed (11.7), highest percentage of swings put into play (52.6), highest percentage of extra bases taken as a runner (47.8) and games played

San Diego

Ruben Rivera

2000 Season

Ruben Rivera began the 2000 season in the same situation as the year before, needing to prove that he could hit major league pitching consistently. As he'd done in '99, he showed tantalizing flashes in the first half, but completely hit the skids in August and September. All in all, it was a wasted year in which he showed no improvement and came no closer to fulfilling his potential.

Hitting

It's no secret among pitchers that Rivera has problems timing offspeed pitches and breaking balls. He jumps at the ball and has problems staying back when he gets anything other than a fastball. His impressive power is completely negated by a profound inability to make contact. Rivera runs hot and cold, and his slumps are as deep and protracted as anyone's. Efforts to shorten his swing and revamp his batting stance have proven futile.

Baserunning & Defense

Rivera is able to put his tools to good use in the outfield, covering plenty of ground with his good speed. His range and strong, accurate arm make him one of the better all-around defensive center fielders in the league. Only one National League center fielder gunned down more runners last year, and only one started more double plays than Rivera. He hasn't been able to develop into much of a basestealing threat, due to his inability to read pitchers' moves—particularly lefthanders.

2001 Outlook

It might be a stretch to say Rivera's career is at a crossroads, since it seems he's spent his entire career there. With each passing year, the chance of him learning to hit grows slimmer. Now 27, Rivera signed a one-year, $1 million contract with the Padres in late December. San Diego gave extended looks to a few other center fielders last year, and the team still might run out of patience with him soon.

Position: CF
Bats: R **Throws:** R
Ht: 6' 3"   **Wt:** 208

Opening Day Age: 27
Born: 11/14/73 in La Chorrera, Panama
ML Seasons: 6

Overall Statistics

	G	AB	R	H	D	T	HR	RBI	SB	BB	SO	Avg	OBP	Slg
2000	135	423	62	88	18	6	17	57	8	44	137	.208	.296	.400
Career	445	1115	177	234	48	10	48	151	39	142	368	.210	.307	.400

Where He Hits the Ball

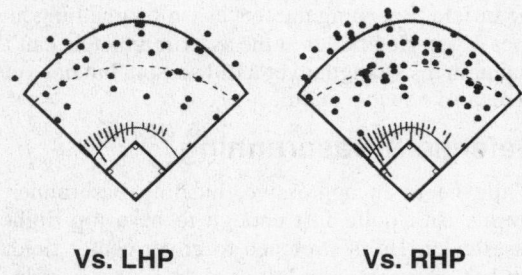

Vs. LHP   **Vs. RHP**

2000 Situational Stats

	AB	H	HR	RBI	Avg		AB	H	HR	RBI	Avg
Home	190	44	8	29	.232	LHP	149	28	5	16	.188
Road	233	44	9	28	.189	RHP	274	60	12	41	.219
First Half	200	49	10	32	.245	Sc Pos	95	20	3	36	.211
Scnd Half	223	39	7	25	.175	Clutch	73	15	4	16	.205

2000 Rankings (National League)

- 1st in lowest batting average vs. lefthanded pitchers, lowest on-base percentage vs. lefthanded pitchers (.284), lowest batting average with two strikes (.119) and lowest batting average on the road
- 2nd in errors in center field (5), highest percentage of swings that missed (33.6) and lowest percentage of swings put into play (31.9)
- 4th in lowest fielding percentage in center field (.984)
- Led the Padres in hit by pitch (10) and strikeouts

Woody Williams

2000 Season

Woody Williams had to wonder if his career had ended when an aneurysm was discovered in his armpit in May, a condition that had been causing numbness in his pitching hand. He underwent surgery and it was unclear when he would take the mound again. He returned in July, however, and to everyone's surprise, he pitched the best ball of his life for the remainder of the schedule. In addition to his performance on the field, he was lauded for his influence on the staff's younger pitchers.

Pitching

Williams lacks outstanding stuff, but makes up for it with good command and a veteran's savvy. He mixes 90-MPH fastballs with cutters, curves and changeups. First-inning troubles dogged him in 2000, but he tended to get stronger as the game went along and consistently remained effective well past the 100-pitch mark. He's vulnerable to the longball when he gets the ball up.

Defense & Hitting

Williams doesn't have a great move to first, and last year didn't get the ball to the plate quickly enough to give his catchers a decent chance. He doesn't often hurt himself with the glove. Williams was a pleasant surprise at the plate in '99, and last year he proved to be one of the best-hitting pitchers in baseball, batting .259 with four doubles, a homer and nine RBI. Bruce Bochy even considered using him as a pinch-hitter on occasion.

2001 Outlook

Williams is signed through 2001, and the Padres will look to him as an innings-eater and veteran staff leader. The only concern is that he might drop off a bit after shouldering such a heavy workload over the second half of last season.

Position: SP
Bats: R **Throws:** R
Ht: 6' 0" **Wt:** 195

Opening Day Age: 34
Born: 8/19/66 in Houston, TX
ML Seasons: 8

Overall Statistics

	W	L	Pct.	ERA	G	GS	Sv	IP	H	BB	SO	HR	Ratio
2000	10	8	.556	3.75	23	23	0	168.0	152	54	111	23	1.23
Career	50	54	.481	4.23	222	132	0	989.2	954	378	687	144	1.35

How Often He Throws Strikes

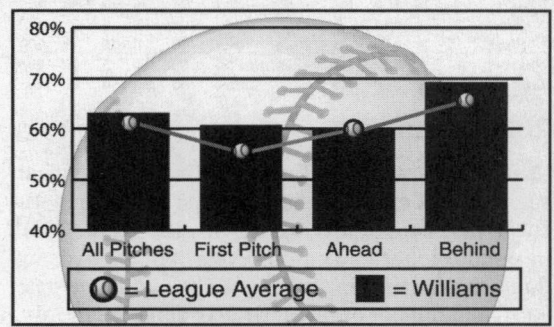

2000 Situational Stats

	W	L	ERA	Sv	IP		AB	H	HR	RBI	Avg
Home	6	5	3.71	0	106.2	LHB	289	66	4	19	.228
Road	4	3	3.82	0	61.1	RHB	347	86	19	52	.248
First Half	3	2	4.73	0	53.1	Sc Pos	120	31	8	46	.258
Scnd Half	7	6	3.30	0	114.2	Clutch	56	12	2	6	.214

2000 Rankings (National League)

- 2nd in highest stolen-base percentage allowed (81.8)
- 6th in least run support per nine innings (4.3)
- 7th in lowest on-base percentage allowed (.300)
- 8th in complete games (4)
- 10th in lowest batting average allowed (.239)
- Led the Padres in ERA, complete games (4), highest strikeout/walk ratio (2.1), lowest batting average allowed (.239), lowest on-base percentage allowed (.300), fewest pitches thrown per batter (3.70), fewest walks per nine innings (2.9), lowest ERA at home, lowest batting average allowed vs. lefthanded batters and winning percentage

San Diego

Carlos Almanzar

Position: RP
Bats: R **Throws:** R
Ht: 6' 2" **Wt:** 200

Opening Day Age: 27
Born: 11/6/73 in Santiago, Dominican Republic
ML Seasons: 4

Overall Statistics

	W	L	Pct.	ERA	G	GS	Sv	IP	H	BB	SO	HR	Ratio
2000	4	5	.444	4.39	62	0	0	69.2	73	25	56	12	1.41
Career	6	8	.429	5.37	119	0	0	139.0	156	49	110	23	1.47

2000 Situational Stats

	W	L	ERA	Sv	IP		AB	H	HR	RBI	Avg
Home	3	3	4.85	0	29.2	LHB	104	22	2	19	.212
Road	1	2	4.05	0	40.0	RHB	170	51	10	33	.300
First Half	1	3	5.27	0	42.2	Sc Pos	92	27	5	43	.293
Scnd Half	3	2	3.00	0	27.0	Clutch	80	21	4	19	.263

2000 Season

Last season was the first one Carlos Almanzar spent almost entirely in the majors, and he experienced his share of ups and downs. He pitched well in middle relief early in the year, but he gave up three-run homers in three straight outings in late April and fell out of favor. Briefly demoted in July, he pitched well in August but tired at the end of the year.

Pitching, Defense & Hitting

Almanzar throws in the low 90s and has a fairly good fastball and slider. His fastball is straight, however, and last year he toyed with a two-seamer he developed over the winter. He's also working on a changeup. He throws strikes and is homer-prone when he catches too much of the plate. A mobile fielder, Almanzar defends his position well. He has a poor move to first, and basestealers don't find him to be much of a challenge. As someone who came up through an American League organization, he's woefully inexperienced at the plate.

2001 Outlook

Almanzar has the arm to be a useful reliever, and the Padres hope that with experience he'll become a valuable setup man. He'll be given the chance to do so this year.

Mike Darr

Position: RF/CF
Bats: L **Throws:** R
Ht: 6' 3" **Wt:** 205

Opening Day Age: 25
Born: 3/21/76 in Corona, CA
ML Seasons: 2

Overall Statistics

	G	AB	R	H	D	T	HR	RBI	SB	BB	SO	Avg	OBP	Slg
2000	58	205	21	55	14	4	1	30	9	23	45	.268	.342	.390
Career	83	253	27	68	15	4	3	33	11	28	63	.269	.342	.395

2000 Situational Stats

	AB	H	HR	RBI	Avg		AB	H	HR	RBI	Avg
Home	109	29	1	18	.266	LHP	52	14	0	7	.269
Road	96	26	0	12	.271	RHP	153	41	1	23	.268
First Half	13	1	0	2	.077	Sc Pos	52	16	0	25	.308
Scnd Half	192	54	1	28	.281	Clutch	32	7	0	7	.219

2000 Season

When the Padres demoted young outfielder Mike Darr in April, he went down to Triple-A Las Vegas and tore up the Pacific Coast League for three months. He earned a July 31 callup and regular playing time over the last two months of the season. Darr took advantage of the opportunity, displaying doubles power, hustle and good defense at all three outfield spots.

Hitting, Baserunning & Defense

Darr is a line-drive hitter who uses the whole field. He doesn't have the pop to reach the fences consistently but finds the gaps often enough to collect his share of extra-base hits. A lefthanded hitter, Darr hasn't had problems with southpaws in either the minors or the majors. His above-average speed makes him both a good basestealer and a rangy defender in the outfield. He's surehanded—with zero errors in 83 major league contests—and his arm is strong and accurate enough for right field.

2001 Outlook

Darr could play an important role with the Padres next season. If the club gives up on Ruben Rivera at some point, Darr could battle with Eric Owens for starts in center field. If Tony Gwynn is bitten by the injury bug, Darr could end up in right. In any event, he should continue to play, hustle and hit.

Tony Gwynn (Hall of Famer)

Position: RF
Bats: L **Throws:** L
Ht: 5'11" **Wt:** 225

Opening Day Age: 40
Born: 5/9/60 in Los Angeles, CA
ML Seasons: 19

Overall Statistics

	G	AB	R	H	D	T	HR	RBI	SB	BB	SO	Avg	OBP	Slg
2000	36	127	17	41	12	0	1	17	0	9	4	.323	.364	.441
Career	2369	9186	1378	3108	534	84	134	1121	318	780	425	.338	.388	.459

2000 Situational Stats

	AB	H	HR	RBI	Avg		AB	H	HR	RBI	Avg
Home	56	18	1	7	.321	LHP	36	15	1	6	.417
Road	71	23	0	10	.324	RHP	91	26	0	11	.286
First Half	127	41	1	17	.323	Sc Pos	36	11	0	15	.306
Scnd Half	0	0	0	0	-	Clutch	27	8	0	5	.296

2000 Season

Thankfully, the 2000 season wasn't Tony Gwynn's last in San Diego. It would have been an awful way for the career-long Padre to go out. He was bothered for months by a sore left knee and ultimately underwent surgery in June. Though he tried to make it back before the end of the season, he wasn't able to work the knee back into shape in time. He had a career-low 127 at-bats, but continued to sting the ball when he was able.

Hitting, Baserunning & Defense

Gwynn's increasingly severe physical ailments haven't diminished his signature skill—his incredible ability to make contact. He still sprays enough line drives through the left side of the infield to keep his average well above .300 and remains one of the toughest strikeouts in the game. Last year, his immobility in the outfield rendered him a major liability. He has a decent arm.

2001 Outlook

The Padres declined a $6 million option on Gwynn for 2001, opting to eat a $2 million buyout. But after a brief test of the free-agent waters, he signed an incentive-laden $2 million deal to play his 20th season in San Diego. Unless his body tells him otherwise, expect to see him in right field almost every day.

Sterling Hitchcock

Position: SP
Bats: L **Throws:** L
Ht: 6' 0" **Wt:** 205

Opening Day Age: 29
Born: 4/29/71 in Fayetteville, NC
ML Seasons: 9

Overall Statistics

	W	L	Pct.	ERA	G	GS	Sv	IP	H	BB	SO	HR	Ratio
2000	1	6	.143	4.93	11	11	0	65.2	69	26	61	12	1.45
Career	61	62	.496	4.69	209	175	3	1067.0	1115	395	841	152	1.42

2000 Situational Stats

	W	L	ERA	Sv	IP		AB	H	HR	RBI	Avg
Home	0	2	5.40	0	18.1	LHB	50	11	3	8	.220
Road	1	4	4.75	0	47.1	RHB	208	58	9	28	.279
First Half	1	6	4.93	0	65.2	Sc Pos	65	15	1	20	.231
Scnd Half	0	0	-	0	0.0	Clutch	11	2	0	3	.182

2000 Season

It all came crashing down for lefthander Sterling Hitchcock in 2000. He'd seemingly turned the corner in '98, and was rewarded with a rich three-year contract in '99. But last year, his velocity sagged noticeably after a string of high-pitch outings in April, and his elbow blew out less than a month later. He underwent Tommy John surgery in early June.

Pitching, Defense & Hitting

Before his injury, Hitchcock had evolved into a fastball/splitter pitcher. He also throws a curve, slider and straight change, although he hadn't relied on them as heavily over the last few seasons. His reliance on the splitter rather than the breaking ball leaves him relatively vulnerable to lefthanded hitters. Though he has a good pickoff move, his high leg kick makes him fairly easy to run on. He fields his position capably, but is one of the weakest-hitting pitchers in the majors.

2001 Outlook

Hitchcock is expected to miss most, if not all, of the 2001 season as he rehabilitates his arm. He'll likely do his best to make it back to the mound by September, if at all possible, since his contract will be up at the end of the year.

San Diego

John Mabry

Position: RF/3B
Bats: L **Throws:** R
Ht: 6' 4" **Wt:** 210

Opening Day Age: 30
Born: 10/17/70 in Wilmington, DE
ML Seasons: 7
Pronunciation: MAY-bree

Overall Statistics

	G	AB	R	H	D	T	HR	RBI	SB	BB	SO	Avg	OBP	Slg
2000	95	226	35	53	13	0	8	32	0	15	69	.235	.287	.398
Career	727	2207	250	608	122	3	49	265	5	167	415	.275	.328	.400

2000 Situational Stats

	AB	H	HR	RBI	Avg		AB	H	HR	RBI	Avg
Home	106	17	3	11	.160	LHP	25	0	0	1	.000
Road	120	36	5	21	.300	RHP	201	53	8	31	.264
First Half	81	18	1	5	.222	Sc Pos	65	16	3	24	.246
Scnd Half	145	35	7	27	.241	Clutch	36	5	1	4	.139

2000 Season

John Mabry didn't do much but sit during the first four months of the 2000 season, as the Mariners failed to find a role for him. A deadline trade to the Padres proved to be a godsend for him, as he shook off the rust and began hitting again in August and September.

Hitting, Baserunning & Defense

Although he came to the majors as a contact hitter, Mabry has worked on adding power at the expense of his batting average. His strikeout rate has ballooned, but he's learned to get better loft on the ball and become more of a home-run threat. Lefthanders sap his power, and the less he's seen them, the worse he's hit them—he didn't get a single hit off a southpaw in 25 at-bats last year. His speed is not an asset, but he has decent range and a good throwing arm in right field. He's little more than an emergency third baseman.

2001 Outlook

Mabry was not offered arbitration and became a free agent over the winter. He still considers himself a full-time player and probably won't re-sign with the Padres, who can offer him little more than a part-time role with Tony Gwynn remaining in the fold.

Dave Magadan

Position: 3B
Bats: L **Throws:** R
Ht: 6' 4" **Wt:** 215

Opening Day Age: 38
Born: 9/30/62 in Tampa, FL
ML Seasons: 15

Overall Statistics

	G	AB	R	H	D	T	HR	RBI	SB	BB	SO	Avg	OBP	Slg
2000	95	132	13	36	7	0	2	21	0	32	23	.273	.410	.371
Career	1491	4031	504	1165	211	13	41	483	11	706	526	.289	.392	.378

2000 Situational Stats

	AB	H	HR	RBI	Avg		AB	H	HR	RBI	Avg
Home	63	15	1	8	.238	LHP	20	5	0	2	.250
Road	69	21	1	13	.304	RHP	112	31	2	19	.277
First Half	65	10	0	4	.154	Sc Pos	46	12	1	18	.261
Scnd Half	67	26	2	17	.388	Clutch	40	12	0	7	.300

2000 Season

The fine play of Phil Nevin limited Dave Magadan mostly to pinch-hitting in 2000. Magadan backed up third base but made more than two-thirds of his appearances coming off the bench. As always, he quietly did his job, posting a decent average and reaching base consistently.

Hitting, Baserunning & Defense

The lefthanded-hitting Magadan's line-drive bat is ideal for a pinch-hitting role. His ability to coax walks also makes him a valuable late-inning rally starter. He hasn't seen much lefthanded pitching for several years. He lacks the power to play regularly at a corner infield position. While his ability to play both first and third is useful, he's no more than adequate at either position. He has good hands and a decent arm, but little range. On the bases, he's a pure plodder.

2001 Outlook

Magadan headed into the winter as a free agent, though the Padres offered him arbitration. He likely will remain in San Diego, where he should be the team's primary lefthanded bat off the bench.

Brian Tollberg

Position: SP
Bats: R **Throws:** R
Ht: 6' 3" **Wt:** 195

Opening Day Age: 28
Born: 9/16/72 in
Tampa, FL
ML Seasons: 1

Overall Statistics

	W	L	Pct.	ERA	G	GS	Sv	IP	H	BB	SO	HR	Ratio
2000	4	5	.444	3.58	19	19	0	118.0	126	35	76	13	1.36
Career	4	5	.444	3.58	19	19	0	118.0	126	35	76	13	1.36

2000 Situational Stats

	W	L	ERA	Sv	IP		AB	H	HR	RBI	Avg
Home	0	1	3.52	0	53.2	LHB	230	65	6	26	.283
Road	4	4	3.64	0	64.1	RHB	230	61	7	23	.265
First Half	2	0	3.33	0	24.1	Sc Pos	109	22	3	31	.202
Scnd Half	2	5	3.65	0	93.2	Clutch	22	5	0	0	.227

2000 Season

When Brian Tollberg was promoted in June, he was a 27-year-old who had a checkered minor league record and had missed almost all of the previous season with right elbow problems. Though he pitched well at Triple-A in 2000, little was expected of him. Then came his debut: seven one-hit innings. He won his second start as well, and pitched creditably for the rest of the year.

Pitching, Defense & Hitting

It isn't hard to see why it's taken so long for Tollberg to reach the big leagues. He has unremarkable stuff—a 90-MPH fastball, a curve and a changeup. It's his immaculate command that sets him apart. Throwing strikes and working ahead in the count, he comes right at hitters and gets by on an economy of pitches, allowing his share of homers but very few walks. In big situations, he works more carefully. His delivery is compact, and he controls the running game well. He's a very weak hitter but is a deliberate and surehanded fielder.

2001 Outlook

Tollberg never will be a star, but he's shown he can be a useful big league pitcher. The big question is how his arm will respond to the 194.1 innings he threw last year—a career high by 40 frames. If he's sound, he'll be in San Diego's rotation in 2001.

Kevin Walker

Position: RP
Bats: L **Throws:** L
Ht: 6' 4" **Wt:** 190

Opening Day Age: 24
Born: 9/20/76 in Irving, TX
ML Seasons: 1

Overall Statistics

	W	L	Pct.	ERA	G	GS	Sv	IP	H	BB	SO	HR	Ratio
2000	7	1	.875	4.19	70	0	0	66.2	49	38	56	5	1.31
Career	7	1	.875	4.19	70	0	0	66.2	49	38	56	5	1.31

2000 Situational Stats

	W	L	ERA	Sv	IP		AB	H	HR	RBI	Avg
Home	5	0	3.07	0	29.1	LHB	105	27	1	9	.257
Road	2	1	5.06	0	37.1	RHB	133	22	4	25	.165
First Half	3	0	4.42	0	36.2	Sc Pos	68	18	3	30	.265
Scnd Half	4	1	3.90	0	30.0	Clutch	112	23	1	10	.205

2000 Season

Lefthander Kevin Walker was called up last April to cover for an injury, having pitched only a handful of games above the Class-A level. He was expected to be sent back down at the first opportunity, but the Padres immediately fell in love with his power arm; every time the club made a roster move, Walker survived the cut. Soon, he had become the Padres' primary lefthanded setup man, and he remained in that role for the rest of the year.

Pitching, Defense & Hitting

It's easy to see why the Padres love him—young lefthanders who throw in the low 90s are hard to find. His command occasionally wavers and his breaking ball is nothing special, but he's able to get by on pure heat most of the time. He's tough on both lefthanded and righthanded hitters and is especially tough from a full windup, but he has problems from the stretch. He has a good pickoff move and is difficult to run on. As a fielder, he's adequate. As a hitter, he's unproven.

2001 Outlook

Barring injury, Walker should continue to be an important member of the Padres' bullpen. If he's able to refine his command or develop a second pitch, he could come on quickly.

San Diego

Donne Wall

Traded To METS

Position: RP
Bats: R **Throws:** R
Ht: 6' 1" **Wt:** 205

Opening Day Age: 33
Born: 7/11/67 in Potosi, MO
ML Seasons: 6
Pronunciation: DONN-ee

Overall Statistics

	W	L	Pct.	ERA	G	GS	Sv	IP	H	BB	SO	HR	Ratio
2000	5	2	.714	3.35	44	0	1	53.2	36	21	29	4	1.06
Career	31	24	.564	4.01	185	37	2	410.1	400	131	278	51	1.29

2000 Situational Stats

	W	L	ERA	Sv	IP		AB	H	HR	RBI	Avg
Home	3	0	1.37	0	26.1	LHB	91	19	2	13	.209
Road	2	2	5.27	1	27.1	RHB	96	17	2	7	.177
First Half	2	2	3.58	0	32.2	Sc Pos	46	10	0	13	.217
Scnd Half	3	0	3.00	1	21.0	Clutch	134	27	2	14	.201

2000 Season

Last April, Donne Wall fielded a bunt, threw to first, and felt a twinge in his shoulder. The pain lingered for the entire season, but when he was able to take the mound, he was as good as ever. The shoulder ailment shelved him for all of June and most of September and may require arthroscopic surgery over the winter.

Pitching, Defense & Hitting

Wall's strength is his precise command. His stuff isn't all that impressive, but he's able to mix fastballs, sliders, changeups and split-finger fastballs to good effect. His ability to neutralize lefthanded hitters with a heavy overhand curve makes him uniquely valuable. His only weakness is that he needs a day off between appearances. He's quick to the plate, and few basestealers try to run on him. He won't hurt himself with the glove. Wall is a decent hitter although he rarely gets to display his skill with the bat.

2001 Outlook

Wall was traded to the Mets in mid-December for Bubba Trammell. He is expected to be ready for spring training, even if he has to undergo surgery. If he's able to get back to full strength by the start of the season, he should serve as a solid setup man for New York.

Jay Witasick

Position: SP
Bats: R **Throws:** R
Ht: 6' 4" **Wt:** 235

Opening Day Age: 28
Born: 8/28/72 in Baltimore, MD
ML Seasons: 5
Pronunciation: wih-TA-sick

Overall Statistics

	W	L	Pct.	ERA	G	GS	Sv	IP	H	BB	SO	HR	Ratio
2000	6	10	.375	5.82	33	25	0	150.0	178	73	121	24	1.67
Career	17	26	.395	5.76	92	56	0	359.1	431	182	272	63	1.71

2000 Situational Stats

	W	L	ERA	Sv	IP		AB	H	HR	RBI	Avg
Home	3	2	5.62	0	73.2	LHB	298	94	15	62	.315
Road	3	8	6.01	0	76.1	RHB	307	84	9	38	.274
First Half	2	8	6.25	0	76.1	Sc Pos	180	48	11	76	.267
Scnd Half	4	2	5.38	0	73.2	Clutch	20	3	1	3	.150

2000 Season

After his strong finish with Kansas City in 1999, Jay Witasick began the 2000 season hoping to pick up where he'd left off the year before. It didn't work out that way. A string of April shellings landed him in the Royals' bullpen, and he bounced back and forth between the pen and the rotation for the next three months. A deadline trade for Brian Meadows landed him in San Diego, where he continued to struggle.

Pitching, Defense & Hitting

Witasick is a pure power pitcher whose main weapon is a moving fastball in the low to mid-90s. His curve and changeup are nothing special, and he must keep the ball down to be effective. Command, however, is not a strength, and until he cuts down on his walks, inconsistency will plague him. He's a decent fielder, but his long delivery allows basestealers to take advantage of him. Witasick has had only a handful of pro at-bats, and it shows.

2001 Outlook

While Witasick's arm is easy to like, the Padres may not be as patient with him as the pitching-poor Royals were. San Diego did re-sign him to a one-year deal in late December, and the 2001 season will go a long way toward determining whether Witasick has what it takes to make it in the majors.

Other San Diego Padres

Gabe Alvarez (Pos: 3B, Age: 27, Bats: R)

	G	AB	R	H	D	T	HR	RBI	SB	BB	SO	Avg	OBP	Slg
2000	12	14	1	2	1	0	0	0	0	3	2	.143	.294	.214
Career	92	266	22	59	15	0	7	33	1	24	76	.222	.289	.357

The Reds claimed Alvarez in December's Rule 5 draft. He played the outfield in Triple-A last season, after years at third base. He has mid-range power. 2001 Outlook: C

Brian Boehringer (Pos: RHP, Age: 31)

	W	L	Pct.	ERA	G	GS	Sv	IP	H	BB	SO	HR	Ratio
2000	0	3	.000	5.74	7	3	0	15.2	18	10	9	4	1.79
Career	16	19	.457	4.53	152	21	0	298.1	299	165	240	39	1.56

Boehringer had shoulder troubles in 1999 and 2000. His 2000 season ended in June and he had surgery in July. He signed with the Yankees in December. 2001 Outlook: C

Buddy Carlyle (Pos: RHP, Age: 23)

	W	L	Pct.	ERA	G	GS	Sv	IP	H	BB	SO	HR	Ratio
2000	0	0	-	21.00	4	0	0	3.0	6	3	2	0	3.00
Career	1	3	.250	7.08	11	7	0	40.2	42	20	31	7	1.52

Carlyle looked like a potential fixture in the Padres' rotation when he reached San Diego in 1999 at the age of 21. But after returning to Triple-A last year, his rights were sold to play in Japan. 2001 Outlook: D

Will Cunnane (Pos: RHP, Age: 26)

	W	L	Pct.	ERA	G	GS	Sv	IP	H	BB	SO	HR	Ratio
2000	1	1	.500	4.23	27	3	0	38.1	35	21	34	2	1.46
Career	9	5	.643	5.33	108	11	0	163.2	187	83	136	22	1.65

Cunnane has been shuttling between Las Vegas and San Diego the past three seasons. He returned to the starting rotation in the minors last year, but his best big league chance is likely in the bullpen. 2001 Outlook: B

Tom Davey (Pos: RHP, Age: 27)

	W	L	Pct.	ERA	G	GS	Sv	IP	H	BB	SO	HR	Ratio
2000	2	1	.667	0.71	11	0	0	12.2	12	2	6	0	1.11
Career	4	2	.667	4.06	56	0	1	77.2	74	42	65	5	1.49

Davey was acquired from Seattle in the Al Martin deal last July. He pitched well in September and will be looking for a job in middle relief. 2001 Outlook: C

Kory DeHaan (Pos: RF, Age: 24, Bats: L)

	G	AB	R	H	D	T	HR	RBI	SB	BB	SO	Avg	OBP	Slg
2000	90	103	19	21	7	0	2	13	4	5	39	.204	.239	.330
Career	90	103	19	21	7	0	2	13	4	5	39	.204	.239	.330

DeHaan was selected as a Rule 5 draftee and averaged about four at-bats per week with the Padres. He'll likely return to the minors this season. 2001 Outlook: C

Todd Erdos (Pos: RHP, Age: 27)

	W	L	Pct.	ERA	G	GS	Sv	IP	H	BB	SO	HR	Ratio
2000	0	0	-	5.93	36	0	2	54.2	63	28	34	7	1.66
Career	2	0	1.000	5.70	53	0	2	77.1	90	37	51	10	1.64

The Padres lost Erdos in the expansion draft when Arizona selected him in 1997, but San Diego reacquired him after the Yankees waived him last July. Last year was his first full season in the majors. 2001 Outlook: C

Chris Gomez (Pos: SS, Age: 29, Bats: R)

	G	AB	R	H	D	T	HR	RBI	SB	BB	SO	Avg	OBP	Slg
2000	33	54	4	12	0	0	0	3	0	7	5	.222	.306	.222
Career	794	2570	286	644	126	10	33	270	21	278	516	.251	.328	.346

Gomez underwent knee surgery for the second straight season and was lost for the year last June. He will compete at short with Alex Arias and Santiago Perez. 2001 Outlook: B

Domingo Guzman (Pos: RHP, Age: 25)

	W	L	Pct.	ERA	G	GS	Sv	IP	H	BB	SO	HR	Ratio
2000	0	0	-	9.00	1	0	0	1.0	1	1	0	0	2.00
Career	0	1	.000	19.50	8	0	0	6.0	14	4	4	1	3.00

Guzman throws hard but isn't the most polished pitcher. He's worked his way through the Padres' system and reached Triple-A at age 25 last year. 2001 Outlook: C

Brandon Kolb (Pos: RHP, Age: 27)

	W	L	Pct.	ERA	G	GS	Sv	IP	H	BB	SO	HR	Ratio
2000	0	1	.000	4.50	11	0	0	14.0	16	11	12	0	1.93
Career	0	1	.000	4.50	11	0	0	14.0	16	11	12	0	1.93

Kolb's strikeout rate is good, and he never has been plagued by the longball. He was traded to the Brewers in early December for Santiago Perez. 2001 Outlook: C

Greg LaRocca (Pos: 3B, Age: 28, Bats: R)

	G	AB	R	H	D	T	HR	RBI	SB	BB	SO	Avg	OBP	Slg
2000	13	27	1	6	2	0	0	2	0	1	4	.222	.250	.296
Career	13	27	1	6	2	0	0	2	0	1	4	.222	.250	.296

LaRocca is a minor league journeyman who can play third base and second base as well as shortstop and the outfield in a pinch. He enjoyed a fine Triple-A season at age 27 last year. 2001 Outlook: C

Carlton Loewer (Pos: RHP, Age: 27)

	W	L	Pct.	ERA	G	GS	Sv	IP	H	BB	SO	HR	Ratio
2000					Did Not Play								
Career	9	14	.391	5.68	41	34	0	212.1	254	65	106	27	1.50

After arriving in a deal last offseason, Loewer didn't pitch an inning for San Diego, suffering from a stress fracture and a bum rotator cuff. 2001 Outlook: B

Rodrigo Lopez (Pos: RHP, Age: 25)

	W	L	Pct.	ERA	G	GS	Sv	IP	H	BB	SO	HR	Ratio
2000	0	3	.000	8.76	6	6	0	24.2	40	13	17	5	2.15
Career	0	3	.000	8.76	6	6	0	24.2	40	13	17	5	2.15

Lopez pitched parts of four seasons in Mexico in addition to his time in the Padres' organization. He allowed a .377 average in the majors. 2001 Outlook: C

Dave Maurer (Pos: LHP, Age: 26)

	W	L	Pct.	ERA	G	GS	Sv	IP	H	BB	SO	HR	Ratio
2000	1	0	1.000	3.68	14	0	0	14.2	15	5	13	2	1.36
Career	1	0	1.000	3.68	14	0	0	14.2	15	5	13	2	1.36

The Giants returned Maurer to San Diego after taking him in the Rule 5 draft after the 1999 season. He's been effective throughout his pro career. 2001 Outlook: B

San Diego

Steve Montgomery (Pos: RHP, Age: 30)

	W	L	Pct.	ERA	G	GS	Sv	IP	H	BB	SO	HR	Ratio
2000	0	2	.000	7.94	7	0	0	5.2	6	4	3	3	1.76
Career	2	8	.200	4.98	72	0	3	90.1	88	56	67	20	1.59

Montgomery went on the disabled list last spring with a shoulder sprain and eventually was shut down with a partial tear in his rotator cuff. He had pitched well for Philadelphia the year before. 2001 Outlook: C

Rodney Myers (Pos: RHP, Age: 31)

	W	L	Pct.	ERA	G	GS	Sv	IP	H	BB	SO	HR	Ratio
2000	0	0	-	4.50	3	0	0	2.0	2	0	3	0	1.00
Career	5	2	.714	4.89	111	1	0	160.0	172	76	115	20	1.55

The Padres acquired Myers from the Cubs last spring, in exchange for Gary Matthews Jr. Soon thereafter, Myers went on the DL with a torn rotator cuff. He later was lost with a torn patellar tendon. 2001 Outlook: C

Kevin Nicholson (Pos: SS, Age: 24, Bats: B)

	G	AB	R	H	D	T	HR	RBI	SB	BB	SO	Avg	OBP	Slg
2000	37	97	7	21	6	1	1	8	1	4	31	.216	.255	.330
Career	37	97	7	21	6	1	1	8	1	4	31	.216	.255	.330

Nicholson is not a prototypical shortstop and is working out at second base to increase his versatility. He has shown some punch with the bat, but being able to play various positions could keep him in the majors. 2001 Outlook: C

Vicente Palacios (Pos: RHP, Age: 37)

	W	L	Pct.	ERA	G	GS	Sv	IP	H	BB	SO	HR	Ratio
2000	0	1	.000	6.75	7	0	0	10.2	12	5	8	4	1.59
Career	17	20	.459	4.43	134	44	7	372.0	348	158	270	44	1.36

Palacios has bounced between the majors, minors and Mexican leagues since 1983. He doesn't have quite the following of Fernando Valenzuela. 2001 Outlook: D

Desi Relaford (Pos: SS, Age: 27, Bats: B)

	G	AB	R	H	D	T	HR	RBI	SB	BB	SO	Avg	OBP	Slg
2000	128	410	55	88	14	3	5	46	13	75	71	.215	.351	.300
Career	365	1193	136	274	53	10	11	120	30	135	207	.230	.317	.319

The Padres acquired Relaford from the Phillies in an August trade, then waived him in October, when he was claimed by the Mets. He's still young enough to surprise, and the Mets re-signed him for 2001. 2001 Outlook: B

Carlos Reyes (Pos: RHP, Age: 31)

	W	L	Pct.	ERA	G	GS	Sv	IP	H	BB	SO	HR	Ratio
2000	1	3	.250	5.72	22	0	1	28.1	25	13	17	7	1.34
Career	20	33	.377	4.62	283	26	4	518.1	536	215	347	76	1.45

Reyes returned to the Padres' organization last May following a spring fling with the Phillies in which he spent time on the DL with a pulled hamstring. He pitched well in the minors. 2001 Outlook: C

John Roskos (Pos: LF, Age: 26, Bats: R)

	G	AB	R	H	D	T	HR	RBI	SB	BB	SO	Avg	OBP	Slg
2000	14	27	0	1	1	0	0	1	0	3	7	.037	.133	.074
Career	37	49	1	4	3	0	0	2	0	4	19	.082	.151	.143

For someone who has mashed the ball in the minors, Roskos' struggles' in the majors are perplexing. He now mainly plays first base and the outfield. 2001 Outlook: C

Heathcliff Slocumb (Pos: RHP, Age: 34)

	W	L	Pct.	ERA	G	GS	Sv	IP	H	BB	SO	HR	Ratio
2000	2	4	.333	4.98	65	0	1	68.2	69	37	46	9	1.54
Career	28	37	.431	4.08	548	0	98	631.0	636	358	513	38	1.58

Slocumb became a Padre in a deal with St. Louis last year. He's worked at least 60 innings each of the past seven seasons. 2001 Outlook: B

Stan Spencer (Pos: RHP, Age: 31)

	W	L	Pct.	ERA	G	GS	Sv	IP	H	BB	SO	HR	Ratio
2000	2	2	.500	3.26	8	8	0	49.2	44	19	40	7	1.27
Career	3	9	.250	5.54	23	21	0	118.2	129	34	107	23	1.37

After years of injuries, Spencer finally seemed to establish himself last season with eight mostly solid starts. But the injury bug bit again, this time as a strained shoulder. He didn't pitch after June. 2001 Outlook: C

Ed Sprague (Pos: 3B/1B, Age: 33, Bats: R)

	G	AB	R	H	D	T	HR	RBI	SB	BB	SO	Avg	OBP	Slg
2000	106	268	30	65	16	0	12	36	0	25	58	.243	.312	.437
Career	1158	4001	497	982	218	12	150	542	6	347	815	.245	.317	.418

Sprague can hit the occasional home run, but he doesn't reach base much and was almost helpless against righthanders last year. He was re-signed by the Padres to a minor league deal. 2001 Outlook: B

Joe Vitiello (Pos: 1B, Age: 30, Bats: R)

	G	AB	R	H	D	T	HR	RBI	SB	BB	SO	Avg	OBP	Slg
2000	39	52	7	13	3	0	2	8	0	10	9	.250	.365	.423
Career	244	617	64	146	29	1	23	91	2	73	151	.237	.326	.399

After nine seasons in the Royals' organization, spent mostly at Triple-A, Vitiello signed with the Padres last year. About the most he can expect at this point in his career is being a bat off the bench. 2001 Outlook: C

Matt Whisenant (Pos: LHP, Age: 29)

	W	L	Pct.	ERA	G	GS	Sv	IP	H	BB	SO	HR	Ratio
2000	2	2	.500	3.80	24	0	0	21.1	16	17	12	1	1.55
Career	9	8	.529	4.96	189	0	3	158.0	146	104	114	8	1.58

After appearing in 137 games between 1998 and 1999, Whisenant's shaky control abandoned him last year, and he spent part of the season in Triple-A. He became a free agent in October and signed with LA. 2001 Outlook: C

Matt Whiteside (Pos: RHP, Age: 33)

	W	L	Pct.	ERA	G	GS	Sv	IP	H	BB	SO	HR	Ratio
2000	2	3	.400	4.14	28	0	0	37.0	32	17	27	6	1.32
Career	18	14	.563	5.01	271	1	9	386.0	426	145	244	44	1.48

Whiteside pitched great last May before turning into a pumpkin in June. He spent part of the year at Triple-A and declared for free agency after the season. He was signed by Los Angeles in December. 2001 Outlook: C

George Williams (Pos: C, Age: 31, Bats: B)

	G	AB	R	H	D	T	HR	RBI	SB	BB	SO	Avg	OBP	Slg
2000	11	16	2	3	0	0	1	2	0	0	4	.188	.235	.375
Career	172	428	62	104	19	2	10	48	0	74	103	.243	.362	.367

Williams had always been a pretty decent hitter, but his defense behind the plate had been a concern. His average suffered last year at Triple-A and he's on the wrong side of 30. 2001 Outlook: C

San Diego Padres Minor League Prospects

Organization Overview:

A lack of homegrown offensive talent in the '90s led to some major turnover within the player-development and scouting departments after the '99 season, although Kevin Towers remained on as general manager. The system's strength lies in a hopeful core of young guns, which was bolstered by brilliant trades that brought Adam Eaton and Dennis Tankersley on board last year. Sean Burroughs, who's emerging as one of the brightest young hitting stars in the game, and 2000 second-rounder Xavier Nady should help beef things up on offense, while Vince Faison, Ben Johnson and Jeremy Owens are promising young players with raw tools and high upsides.

Sean Burroughs

Position: 3B · **Opening Day Age:** 20
Bats: L **Throws:** R · **Born:** 9/12/80 in Atlanta, GA
Ht: 6' 2" **Wt:** 200

Recent Statistics

	G	AB	R	H	D	T	HR	RBI	SB	BB	SO	Avg
1999 A Fort Wayne	122	426	65	153	30	3	5	80	17	74	59	.359
1999 A Rancho Cuca	6	23	3	10	3	0	1	5	0	3	3	.435
2000 AA Mobile	108	392	46	114	29	4	2	42	6	58	45	.291
2000 MLE	108	373	36	95	23	2	1	32	4	37	48	.255

Each year, Burroughs adds a chapter to his storied baseball career. The former two-time Little League World Series Champion helped Team USA to gold last summer in Sydney after hitting .291 as a 19-year-old in Double-A. The ninth overall pick in '98, Burroughs reached base safely in 57 consecutive games, a testament to his professional approach at the plate. The pure-hitting third baseman has yet to develop any home-run power, as he mainly concentrates on staying inside the ball and driving hard liners to all fields. Physically strong with a muscular build, his power is expected to come around when he starts turning on balls and developing more lift in his swing. At the hot corner, Burroughs has improved and displays good athletic mobility, soft hands and a strong arm. Nothing should be ruled out when considering the Padres' burgeoning phenom, not even a 2001 breakthrough into the big league lineup.

Mike Bynum

Position: P · **Opening Day Age:** 23
Bats: L **Throws:** L · **Born:** 3/20/78 in Tampa, FL
Ht: 6' 4" **Wt:** 200

Recent Statistics

	W	L	ERA	G	GS	Sv	IP	H	R	BB	SO	HR
1999 R Idaho Falls	1	0	0.00	5	3	0	17.0	7	0	4	21	0
1999 A Rancho Cuca	3	1	3.29	7	7	0	38.1	35	17	8	44	1
2000 A Rancho Cuca	9	6	3.00	21	21	0	126.0	101	55	51	129	4
2000 AA Mobile	3	1	2.91	6	6	0	34.0	31	12	16	27	2

In just a year and a half, Bynum has emerged as the most advanced pitching prospect in the organization. The lefty elicits comparisons to one of the greatest southpaws of all time, Steve Carlton. While nobody is predicting Bynum to win 329 major league games, his dominant slider evokes memories of Lefty. Bynum has been posting numbers that would rival his protege, though. He logged 29 innings before permitting an earned run and then registered a sub 3.00 ERA in his first full season. In addition to his often-unhittable slider, he delivers a running 89-91 MPH fastball and changeup. By finishing last year with six promising starts in Double-A, his tenure in San Diego is not far off.

Kevin Eberwein

Position: 1B · **Opening Day Age:** 23
Bats: R **Throws:** R · **Born:** 3/30/77 in Tacoma, WA
Ht: 6' 4" **Wt:** 200

Recent Statistics

	G	AB	R	H	D	T	HR	RBI	SB	BB	SO	Avg
1999 AA Mobile	10	35	5	6	1	0	1	2	0	3	16	.171
1999 A Rancho Cuca	110	417	69	108	30	4	18	69	7	42	139	.259
2000 AA Mobile	100	372	57	98	16	2	18	71	2	45	77	.263
2000 MLE	100	357	44	83	13	1	14	55	1	29	83	.232

Drafted as a third baseman in '98, Eberwein shifted across the diamond to first to accommodate Sean Burroughs in Double-A last year. A gifted athlete, Eberwein adapted well, having already spent two years at first base at UNLV. His strong throwing arm isn't as much of an asset now, but the Padres want his powerful bat in the lineup. Given his untapped power potential, he could be prepared to flourish in Triple-A this year. The Padres feel his athleticism will allow him to play a variety of positions, including the outfield, therefore increasing his chances of breaking into the bigs by 2002.

Junior Herndon

Position: P · **Opening Day Age:** 22
Bats: R **Throws:** R · **Born:** 9/11/78 in Liberal, KS
Ht: 6' 1" **Wt:** 190

Recent Statistics

	W	L	ERA	G	GS	Sv	IP	H	R	BB	SO	HR
1999 AA Mobile	10	9	4.69	26	26	0	163.0	172	96	52	87	24
2000 AAA Las Vegas	10	11	5.13	26	26	0	135.0	151	90	65	75	13

Herndon doesn't receive a lot of attention because he doesn't mow hitters down with overpowering stuff. A ninth-round pick out of a Colorado high school in 1997, the righthander has been aggressively promoted through the system. Herndon endured a rough season in the hitter-friendly Pacific Coast League, however. His fastball has been clocked in the low 90s and he complements it with a curve and change, but it is said that he lacks a knockout punch. His poor strikeout-walk ratio attests to that theory. Herndon's bulldog mentality will bolster his chances of breaking into the majors by 2002.

San Diego

Xavier Nady

Position: 3B   **Opening Day Age:** 22
Bats: R **Throws:** R   **Born:** 11/14/78 in
Ht: 6' 2" **Wt:** 205   Carmel, CA

Recent Statistics

	G	AB	R	H	D	T	HR	RBI	SB	BB	SO	Avg
2000 R Padres	1	4	0	1	0	0	0	1	0	1	1	.250
2000 NL Padres	1	1	1	1	0	0	0	0	0	0	0	1.000

Nady's talent was evident when he won the Freshman of the Year award at Cal. He followed his standout rookie year with a pair of All-American efforts and was one of the most sought after prospects in the nation. With Scott Boras as his agent, Nady's contract demands caused him to slip into the Padres' laps in the second round. The Padres hoped to get Nady ready for his 2001 pro debut with a stint in the Arizona Fall League, but in his first game, he felt a twinge in his elbow. His quick explosive bat generates exciting raw power. With Sean Burroughs considered the future at third base in San Diego, Nady's position is uncertain, although his contract ensures a quick ascent to the show.

Jacob Peavy

Position: P   **Opening Day Age:** 19
Bats: R **Throws:** R   **Born:** 5/31/81 in Mobile,
Ht: 6' 1" **Wt:** 180   AL

Recent Statistics

	W	L	ERA	G	GS	Sv	IP	H	R	BB	SO	HR
1999 R Padres	7	1	1.34	13	11	0	73.2	52	16	23	90	4
1999 R Idaho Falls	2	0	0.00	2	2	0	11.0	5	0	1	13	0
2000 A Fort Wayne	13	8	2.90	26	25	0	133.2	107	61	53	164	6

Nobody expected much from Peavy after the Padres stole him in the 15th round of the '99 draft. But Peavy pitched his way to the Rookie-level Arizona League's Triple Crown in '99. The Alabama-native, who was expected to attend Auburn, continued his streak of dominance last year by overpowering the Midwest League. He showcased an impressive four-pitch repertoire that consists of a projectable low to mid-90s heater, a curve, slider and change. His aggressiveness and ability to change speeds helped him fan 164 batters in 133.2 innings.

Santiago Perez

Position: SS   **Opening Day Age:** 25
Bats: B **Throws:** R   **Born:** 12/30/75 in Santo
Ht: 6' 2" **Wt:** 150   Domingo, DR

Recent Statistics

	G	AB	R	H	D	T	HR	RBI	SB	BB	SO	Avg
2000 AAA Indianapols	106	408	74	112	26	7	5	34	31	44	96	.275
2000 NL Milwaukee	24	52	8	9	2	0	0	2	4	8	9	.173
2000 MLE	106	395	60	99	23	5	3	27	23	36	97	.251

The Padres acquired Perez from the Brewers for fledgling prospect Brandon Kolb in December. Originally signed by the Tigers in '93, the Padres hope to extract the potential from Perez' broad base of raw tools. After tearing up in Double-A, he has regressed in back-to-back

Triple-A campaigns, while connecting for just 15 home runs in over 900 at-bats there. A sleek athlete who runs well, Perez flashes the tools to be a big league shortstop, but he'll need to improve his consistency to cut down on lofty error totals. His lack of regard for the strike zone could hinder his chances of landing the everyday shortstop position in San Diego.

Wascar Serrano

Position: P   **Opening Day Age:** 22
Bats: R **Throws:** R   **Born:** 6/2/78 in Santo
Ht: 6' 2" **Wt:** 178   Domingo, DR

Recent Statistics

	W	L	ERA	G	GS	Sv	IP	H	R	BB	SO	HR
1999 A Rancho Cuca	9	8	3.33	21	21	0	132.1	110	58	43	129	10
1999 AA Mobile	2	3	5.53	7	7	0	42.1	48	27	17	29	5
2000 AAA Las Vegas	0	1	14.18	4	4	0	13.1	24	23	10	19	5
2000 AA Mobile	9	4	2.80	20	20	0	112.1	93	42	42	112	11

There haven't been many pitchers in the Padres' system who have achieved as much success as Serrano in the last three seasons. But for some reason he hasn't garnered much attention outside of San Diego. The results speak for themselves, as does Serrano's overpowering repertoire. The Dominican native slings a moving 92-96 MPH fastball, filthy slider and change from a tough to hit three-quarters delivery. He was a bit overwhelmed upon his promotion to Triple-A, which is nothing to be concerned about after posting a 2.80 ERA and averaging close to a strikeout per inning in Double-A.

Others to Watch

A product of the Padres '99 draft, righthander **Gerik Baxter** (21) can blow hitters away with 92-96 MPH gas from a deceptively low-effort delivery. He has the makings of good offspeed and breaking offerings. . . Another '99 first-rounder, outfielder **Vince Faison** (20) struggled in his first full-season exposure, hitting just .219 with 26 walks and 159 strikeouts in the Midwest League. The Padres remain optimistic about his high ceiling. . . Outfielder **Ben Johnson** (19) was one of the best position prospects in the Cardinals' system before coming over in a late-season trade for Carlos Hernandez. Oozing with raw tools, he hit just .230 last year in the Midwest League but previewed his intriguing speed/power combo with 17 steals and 16 homers as a teen. . . Outfielder **Jeremy Owens** (24) is in the developing stages as a hitter, which makes his 55 extra-base hits in the California League even more impressive. Electrifying on the bases and in the outfield, he struck out 183 times last year. . . Hard-throwing lefty **Mark Phillips** (19) was considered to have one of the best fastballs and curves in the draft last summer convincing the Padres to use the ninth overall pick on him. He never learned to throw a changeup in high school and needs to refine his command. . . Stolen from the Red Sox, righthander **Dennis Tankersley** (22) was thrown into the Ed Sprague deal. He's aggressive with his low to mid-90s heat, and punched out 161 in 141.2 innings between the two organizations last year.

Pacific Bell Park

Offense

When critics looked at the first plans for Pacific Bell Park, they saw the 307-foot right field fence and the 48 feet behind home plate and immediately began thinking "band box." But Pac Bell actually appears to favor the *pitcher* slightly. If anything, the deep alleys serve to reduce overall power. One early trend that will have to be backed up with a couple more years of data is that Giants hitters produced significantly lower strikeout ratios at home.

Defense

Probably the only position that Pac Bell places unusual defensive demands on is in center field, where it's deep, especially in right-center. That happens to be one position where the Giants are lacking. The better turf and more predictable weather conditions helped San Francisco commit the fewest errors of any National League team.

Who It Helps the Most

Virtually every Giants pitcher, led by lefthanders Kirk Rueter and Shawn Estes, pitched significantly better at home. The team ERA was 3.45 at home and 4.99 on the road. The Giants' own lefthanded pull hitters benefited, especially J.T. Snow. Barry Bonds set a career high with 49 homers and used the right-field wall to his advantage when it came to smacking doubles. The Giants tied for the best home record in the National League at 55-26, so you have to say the park helped the whole team.

Who It Hurts the Most

Mark Gardner, who relies on finesse and a fastball that moves into lefthanded hitters, was the only Giants pitcher hurt by Pac Bell. No player had a significantly negative home-road differential.

Rookies & Newcomers

The Giants have to be wary of finesse righthanders and acknowledge that lefthanded pitchers of any sort, whether it be finesse types like Rueter or power-sinker types like Estes, may have an advantage in the park. The 2001 roster will have few changes, so the Giants will be able to study the issue for another year.

Dimensions: LF-335, LCF-370, CF-404, RCF-420, RF-307

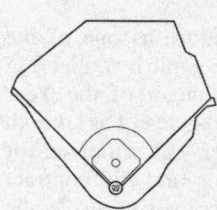

Capacity: 40,800

Elevation: 0 feet

Surface: Grass

Foul Territory: Average

Park Factors

2000 Season

	Home Games			Away Games			
	Giants	Opp	Total	Giants	Opp	Total	Index
G	72	72	144	75	75	150	—
Avg	.281	.244	.263	.270	.280	.275	95
AB	2356	2416	4772	2634	2526	5160	96
R	407	265	672	426	405	831	84
H	663	590	1253	712	707	1419	92
2B	127	107	234	142	129	271	93
3B	24	11	35	18	26	44	86
HR	99	54	153	100	81	181	91
BB	304	251	555	353	307	660	91
SO	404	475	879	539	507	1046	91
E	30	37	67	58	54	112	62
E-Infield	28	29	57	42	46	88	67
LHB-Avg	.271	.235	.255	.275	.279	.277	92
LHB-HR	39	16	55	50	28	78	77
RHB-Avg	.290	.249	.267	.267	.280	.274	98
RHB-HR	60	38	98	50	53	103	102

1998-1999 (3Com Park)

	Home Games			Away Games			
	Giants	Opp	Total	Giants	Opp	Total	Index
G	148	148	296	149	149	298	—
Avg	.273	.249	.261	.272	.274	.273	96
AB	4868	5112	9980	5342	5141	10483	96
R	747	630	1377	814	802	1616	86
H	1328	1275	2603	1455	1407	2862	92
2B	254	224	478	286	274	560	90
3B	19	21	40	22	29	51	82
HR	161	171	332	163	165	328	106
BB	626	521	1147	637	582	1219	99
SO	948	1083	2031	952	906	1858	115
E	95	105	200	94	100	194	104
E-Infield	81	93	174	82	80	162	108
LHB-Avg	.286	.255	.272	.279	.272	.276	99
LHB-HR	69	64	133	71	48	119	116
RHB-Avg	.260	.246	.252	.266	.275	.271	93
RHB-HR	92	107	199	92	117	209	101

2000 Rankings (National League)

- Lowest error factor
- Lowest infield-error factor
- Third-lowest run factor
- Third-lowest hit factor
- Third-lowest walk factor
- Third-lowest LHB batting-average factor

San Francisco

Dusty Baker

2000 Season

Dusty Baker solidified his stature as one of the most respected managers in the game by collecting his third National League Manager of the Year Award in eight years. The season wasn't as smooth as it could have been, as Baker was criticized for some of his postseason moves and his contract status was a persistent topic of conversation. But he was able to meld some strong-willed personalities and hard-nosed players into a division-winning team. He's now the fourth-longest tenured manager in baseball, trailing only Tom Kelly (14 years), Bobby Cox (11) and Felipe Alou (nine).

Offense

The Giants are a leading practitioner of the power/patience approach at the plate, which Baker has been advocating since he began managing. He likes to use platoon strategies on offense and even will sit highly paid veterans like J.T. Snow and Marvin Benard if the matchups warrant it. Baker often employs double switches and has a bench filled with players who can play multiple positions. This helped the Giants finish second to last in the National League in pinch-hitting appearances.

Pitching & Defense

Baker showed a subtly greater willingness in 2000 to let his hurlers face multiple batters instead of allowing platoon matchups to dictate his pitching changes. This might have been a function of the team's deeper and more effective bullpen. He also won't hesitate to let his starters go deep into games. Baker was especially light on closer Robb Nen, who pitched far less frequently in multiple-inning save situations. Baker also substituted for defense more often than he had previously, an adjustment likely based on having better options on his bench, such as Ramon Martinez and Calvin Murray.

2001 Outlook

The first news of the Giants' offseason, was to announce that Baker had signed a two-year, $5.3 million contract through 2002. Despite the losses of Ellis Burks and Bill Mueller, San Francisco will return virtually its entire club next year. Maybe fewer people will be surprised if Baker leads the Giants to another title.

Born: 6/15/49 in Riverside, CA

Playing Experience: 1968-1986, Atl, LA, SF, Oak

Managerial Experience: 8 seasons

Manager Statistics

Year	Team, Lg	W	L	Pct	GB	Finish
2000	San Francisco, NL	97	65	.599	—	1st West
8 Seasons		655	577	.532	—	—

2000 Starting Pitchers by Days Rest

	<=3	4	5	6+
Giants Starts	0	72	60	23
Giants ERA	—	4.01	4.26	5.24
NL Avg Starts	2	80	50	21
NL ERA	5.00	4.61	4.60	5.18

2000 Situational Stats

	Dusty Baker	NL Average
Hit & Run Success %	47.5	33.8
Stolen Base Success %	66.9	68.8
Platoon Pct.	55.8	53.2
Defensive Subs	22	19
High-Pitch Outings	25	14
Quick/Slow Hooks	8/17	14/16
Sacrifice Attempts	86	87

2000 Rankings (National League)

- 1st in sacrifice-bunt percentage (90.7), hit-and-run success percentage (47.5), starts with over 120 pitches (25), starts with over 140 pitches (1) and 2+ pitching changes in low-scoring games (31)
- 3rd in fewest caught stealings of second base (34)

Rich Aurilia

2000 Season

Rich Aurilia's 2000 season was a virtual duplicate of his 1999 campaign on offense. His 20 home runs and 79 RBI led all National League shortstops last year and were indistinguishable from his career highs the previous season. Granted, his power numbers don't match up to the Rodriguez/Tejada/Garciaparra types in the American League. But Aurilia's consistency and production have received very little recognition among his peers in the senior circuit.

Hitting

While Aurilia isn't blessed with outstanding bat speed or special strength, he makes the most of his abilities. He's learned to recognize the pitches that he can pull and loft, and aggressively attacks them. Some feel that he puts too much emphasis on reaching the 20-homer plateau and would be a better hitter using his bat control to deliver more singles and doubles. That's questionable, as the home run-oriented approach is the only one that's succeeded for Aurilia at any level.

Baserunning & Defense

Probably the most significant improvement in Aurilia's game last year was on defense. He showed better range and was more consistent with his hands on groundballs. Like teammate Jeff Kent, Aurilia doesn't have an especially strong arm. He benefits greatly from having Gold Glove first baseman J.T. Snow at the receiving end of his sometimes weak and off-target throws. Aurilia is a below-average runner who will only steal or take an extra base when the defense makes a mistake.

2001 Outlook

Aurilia is headed into his final year before he can become a free agent and the Giants already are preparing themselves for a decision. On one hand, Aurilia's offensive and defensive consistency make more seasons like 1999 and 2000 very predictable. But is that kind of production, which is unlikely to improve because of his modest physical tools, worth a long-term, big-money contract? If Ramon Martinez is getting increased looks at shortstop during the first half of 2001, the answer will be obvious.

Position: SS
Bats: R **Throws:** R
Ht: 6' 1" **Wt:** 185

Opening Day Age: 29
Born: 9/2/71 in Brooklyn, NY
ML Seasons: 6
Pronunciation: ah-REEL-yuh
Nickname: Dickie

Overall Statistics

	G	AB	R	H	D	T	HR	RBI	SB	BB	SO	Avg	OBP	Slg
2000	141	509	67	138	24	2	20	79	1	54	90	.271	.339	.444
Career	575	1919	236	518	92	6	61	257	12	162	292	.270	.327	.419

Where He Hits the Ball

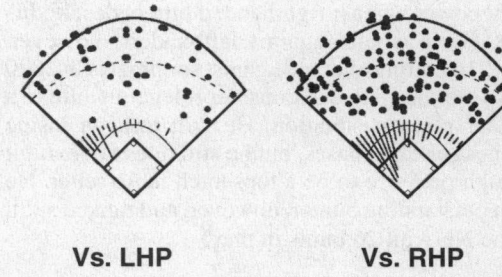

Vs. LHP   **Vs. RHP**

2000 Situational Stats

	AB	H	HR	RBI	Avg		AB	H	HR	RBI	Avg
Home	254	73	12	33	.287	LHP	119	34	7	25	.286
Road	255	65	8	46	.255	RHP	390	104	13	54	.267
First Half	261	70	8	41	.268	Sc Pos	143	43	5	56	.301
Scnd Half	248	68	12	38	.274	Clutch	65	21	5	14	.323

2000 Rankings (National League)

- 4th in errors at shortstop (21)
- 5th in lowest fielding percentage at shortstop (.967)
- Led the Giants in batting average in the clutch
- Led NL shortstops in home runs, RBI, slugging percentage, HR frequency (25.5 ABs per HR) and slugging percentage vs. righthanded pitchers (.421)

Marvin Benard

Position: CF/RF/LF
Bats: L **Throws:** L
Ht: 5' 9" **Wt:** 185

Opening Day Age: 31
Born: 1/20/70 in
Bluefields, Nicaragua
ML Seasons: 6
Pronunciation:
buh-NARD

2000 Season

The Giants rewarded Marvin Benard for productive 1998 and '99 efforts with a three-year, $11.1 million contract extension in April of 2000. But based on his performance last year, San Francisco has to be disappointed with the early return on its investment. Benard neither hit with the same power he displayed in the previous two campaigns nor reached base with the same frequency. His total of 102 runs, a career high, seems impressive on the surface. But when you play every day and have Barry Bonds and Jeff Kent hitting behind you, it's not an impressive figure.

Hitting

Benard is a slashing hitter who can generate some alley power against righthanded hitters despite his size. He is woeful against lefthanders, however. His .216 batting average against southpaws in 2000 may lead the Giants to consider relegating him to a regular platoon situation. He will turn on inside pitches for extra bases, but he still does not exhibit enough patience to be a top-notch table-setter. He is an outstanding bunter, however, and ranked sixth in the NL with 26 bunts in play.

Baserunning & Defense

The Giants could overlook Benard's subpar offensive year if he brought more to the table on defense and on the bases. While he is a gamer and hustler in both areas, he lacks good instincts. Although Benard has an accurate arm in the outfield, his routes are inconsistent and he doesn't have the raw speed to make up for his mistakes. He frequently moved to left or right field in late-inning situations where he is better suited defensively.

2001 Outlook

This season likely will bring some sort of compromise between the Benard of 1998 and 1999, who was a developing big league leadoff hitter, and the Y2K version. The best-case scenario would be to get him out of the lineup against lefthanders, which would both improve his overall performance level and make the Giants' lineup more effective. But Calvin Murray is the only other center-field option on the roster, which means the situation probably won't change much in 2001.

Overall Statistics

	G	AB	R	H	D	T	HR	RBI	SB	BB	SO	Avg	OBP	Slg
2000	149	560	102	147	27	6	12	55	22	63	97	.263	.342	.396
Career	651	2044	350	562	107	16	38	199	89	225	353	.275	.352	.399

Where He Hits the Ball

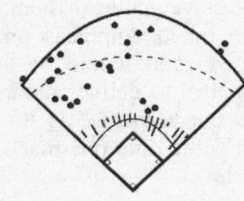 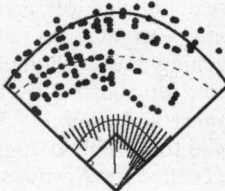

Vs. LHP   **Vs. RHP**

2000 Situational Stats

	AB	H	HR	RBI	Avg		AB	H	HR	RBI	Avg
Home	275	74	6	26	.269	LHP	102	22	1	5	.216
Road	285	73	6	29	.256	RHP	458	125	11	50	.273
First Half	297	81	7	33	.273	Sc Pos	126	30	2	39	.238
Scnd Half	263	66	5	22	.251	Clutch	61	15	1	5	.246

2000 Rankings (National League)

- 1st in fielding percentage in center field (.996)
- 6th in bunts in play (26)
- 9th in lowest on-base percentage for a leadoff hitter (.341)
- Led the Giants in stolen bases, highest ground-ball/flyball ratio (1.6), stolen-base percentage (75.9), bunts in play (26) and highest percentage of extra bases taken as a runner (57.7)

Barry Bonds

2000 Season

Despite turning 36 years of age last summer, Barry Bonds set career highs in home runs and slugging percentage and tied his career mark for runs scored. If he hadn't missed time with a hairline fracture of his right thumb in July, the MVP race with teammate Jeff Kent may have been even closer, as Bonds finished second to Kent by 113 points. Another factor pulling down Bonds' overall numbers was the substandard production of San Francisco's top two hitters in the order.

Hitting

Bonds is one of the most severe flyball hitters in baseball. He has an incredibly short and quick uppercut swing and is extremely selective. As he has grown older, his production against lefthanded pitchers has slipped to near-pedestrian levels. But Bonds dominates righthanders to the point where they should just walk him, as they frequently do. While his production at home was slightly better than on the road, the short right field fence at Pac Bell didn't benefit him as much as some think.

Baserunning & Defense

Bonds is surging towards 500 career home runs much faster than 500 stolen bases. His 11 steals last season were a career low and represented the fourth straight year that his total dropped. He's generally at the opportunist level on the bases now, taking what the opposition gives him. The eight-time Gold Glove award winner probably has gathered his last piece of that hardware, but he continues to be a fundamentally sound and competent fielder.

2001 Outlook

Bonds didn't hire agent Scott Boras last year to help him diversify his investment portfolio. Bonds' contract runs out at the end of 2001, and while his lifestyle, family life and legacy are firmly entrenched in the Bay Area, it would be out of character for him not to demand top dollar. If he can stay healthy, it wouldn't be surprising to see him produce a season similar to last. In fact, San Francisco is counting on such production, especially after watching the free-agent bat of Ellis Burks depart for Cleveland.

Position: LF
Bats: L **Throws:** L
Ht: 6' 2" **Wt:** 210

Opening Day Age: 36
Born: 7/24/64 in Riverside, CA
ML Seasons: 15
Nickname: BB

Overall Statistics

	G	AB	R	H	D	T	HR	RBI	SB	BB	SO	Avg	OBP	Slg
2000	143	480	129	147	28	4	49	106	11	117	77	.306	.440	.688
Career	2143	7456	1584	2157	451	69	494	1405	471	1547	1189	.289	.412	.567

Where He Hits the Ball

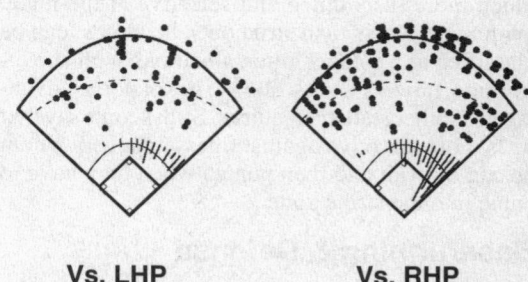

Vs. LHP   **Vs. RHP**

2000 Situational Stats

	AB	H	HR	RBI	Avg		AB	H	HR	RBI	Avg
Home	243	78	25	58	.321	LHP	148	34	12	32	.230
Road	237	69	24	48	.291	RHP	332	113	37	74	.340
First Half	246	76	28	57	.309	Sc Pos	107	31	10	56	.290
Scnd Half	234	71	21	49	.303	Clutch	68	17	8	13	.250

2000 Rankings (National League)

- 1st in walks, HR frequency (9.8 ABs per HR), slugging percentage vs. righthanded pitchers (.759), on-base percentage vs. righthanded pitchers (.487) and lowest groundball/flyball ratio (0.6)
- 2nd in home runs, intentional walks (22), slugging percentage, on-base percentage and fielding percentage in left field (.989)
- 3rd in runs scored
- Led the Giants in home runs, runs scored, walks, intentional walks (22), slugging percentage, on-base percentage, HR frequency (9.8 ABs per HR), fewest GDPs per GDP situation (4.5%), batting average vs. righthanded pitchers and highest percentage of pitches taken (60.9)

Ellis Burks

2000 Season

Although he was limited to 122 games by his aching knees, a left quadriceps muscle problem in May and Armando Rios' emergence against righthanded pitchers, Ellis Burks enjoyed one of his best seasons in 2000. His production when he did play was exceptionally high. He ranked among the elite hitters in the game when he was healthy. Perhaps most importantly, Burks was the unquestioned emotional leader of the Giants' clubhouse.

Hitting

Burks' continued maturation as a hitter, even into his mid-30s, has been remarkable. He has retained his bat speed and quick trigger. But he has become much more disciplined and selective at the plate. With more walks than strikeouts, he almost can be classified as a contact hitter, albeit one with above-average power. Burks shows no platoon advantages or other statistical quirks. Still, scouts say that he is more effective against finesse pitchers whom he can outwait and then punish when they have to come into the strike zone.

Baserunning & Defense

Although it's hard to believe with his multiple knee surgeries and advancing age, Burks was the Giants' fastest player down the first-base line last season. That's a testament to both his athletic ability and his conditioning regimen. Burks isn't as agile and quick running the bases when he has to make quick stops and starts. Defensively, he is a solid if unspectacular right fielder. He can be tentative going into the corner after balls, but he runs good routes and has an accurate throwing arm.

2001 Outlook

Burks signed a three-year, $20 million contract with Cleveland in mid-November. With the Tribe losing Manny Ramirez to the Red Sox, Burks will play right field for the Indians and also pick up some DH duties to spell his knees. Burks' signing will have significant implications for the Giants, both on the field and in the clubhouse. Some feel that his ability to direct praise to and draw responsibility away from moody superstars Barry Bonds and Jeff Kent was one of the keys to San Francisco's continuing success.

Position: RF
Bats: R **Throws:** R
Ht: 6' 2" **Wt:** 205

Opening Day Age: 36
Born: 9/11/64 in Vicksburg, MS
ML Seasons: 14

Overall Statistics

	G	AB	R	H	D	T	HR	RBI	SB	BB	SO	Avg	OBP	Slg
2000	122	393	74	135	21	5	24	96	5	56	49	.344	.419	.606
Career	1672	6044	1045	1770	334	61	285	1012	171	657	1093	.293	.364	.510

Where He Hits the Ball

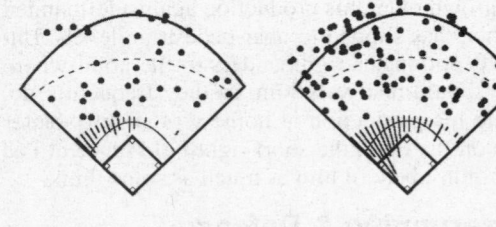

Vs. LHP   **Vs. RHP**

2000 Situational Stats

	AB	H	HR	RBI	Avg		AB	H	HR	RBI	Avg
Home	185	67	15	52	.362	LHP	100	36	4	21	.360
Road	208	68	9	44	.327	RHP	293	99	20	75	.338
First Half	193	70	10	40	.363	Sc Pos	138	48	4	70	.348
Scnd Half	200	65	14	56	.325	Clutch	50	16	1	3	.320

2000 Rankings (National League)

- 4th in batting average with two strikes (.290)
- 5th in fielding percentage in right field (.982)
- Led the Giants in batting average with runners in scoring position and batting average with two strikes (.290)
- Led NL right fielders in batting average with runners in scoring position and batting average with two strikes (.290)

Shawn Estes

2000 Season

Shawn Estes enjoyed his best season since his breakthrough 1997 campaign, although his 15-6 record last year was deceptive. He was given an average of 8.65 runs per nine innings, the highest rate among major league pitchers with at least 162 innings. He was maddeningly inconsistent, as has been his history. Estes tossed four complete games, second on the staff, but his 108 walks kept his pitch counts high and the Giants bullpen busy in the middle innings of most of his outings.

Pitching

Estes throws two fastballs, a four-seamer that tops out at around 95 MPH and a two-seamer that gets hard, heavy sink at 88-90 MPH. The two-seamer helped give him one of the highest groundball-flyball ratios in baseball and limited opposing hitters to only 11 home runs. His best pitch, however, is a big breaking curveball that completely over-matches lefthanded hitters. The curve also is the source of much of his control problems, as the size of the break makes it difficult to control. He also has a good changeup that he'll throw occasionally to righthanded hitters, but it's very much a secondary pitch.

Defense & Hitting

Estes is a good athlete, which helps him both on the mound and in the batter's box. He's quick off the mound and has a good pickoff move to first base. He hit .206 with one homer and 10 RBI last year and led all San Francisco players with 11 sacrifice bunts.

2001 Outlook

There is always the hope in San Francisco that Estes will fully harness his physical talents and become one of the best starting pitchers in baseball. Most feel that it's only a matter of mental adjustments for the cerebral young southpaw, who will be 28 this season. His multiyear contract ran out at the end of 2000, but he is a four-plus player for arbitration purposes. He still has two seasons left before he can become eligible for free agency.

Position: SP
Bats: R **Throws:** L
Ht: 6' 2" **Wt:** 195

Opening Day Age: 28
Born: 2/18/73 in San Bernardino, CA
ML Seasons: 6
Pronunciation: EST-us
Nickname: Buck

Overall Statistics

	W	L	Pct.	ERA	G	GS	Sv	IP	H	BB	SO	HR	Ratio
2000	15	6	.714	4.26	30	30	0	190.1	194	108	136	11	1.59
Career	55	42	.567	4.30	133	133	0	831.0	794	444	686	63	1.49

How Often He Throws Strikes

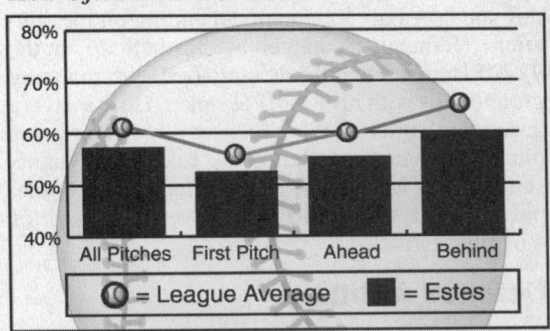

= League Average   = Estes

2000 Situational Stats

	W	L	ERA	Sv	IP		AB	H	HR	RBI	Avg
Home	9	4	3.21	0	92.2	LHB	102	22	1	13	.216
Road	6	2	5.25	0	97.2	RHB	603	172	10	62	.285
First Half	8	3	3.88	0	95.0	Sc Pos	171	41	4	66	.240
Scnd Half	7	3	4.63	0	95.1	Clutch	16	4	0	0	.250

2000 Rankings (National League)

- 1st in GDPs induced (40), most run support per nine innings (8.7) and most GDPs induced per nine innings (1.9)
- 2nd in fewest home runs allowed per nine innings (.52) and winning percentage
- 3rd in shutouts (2), most GDPs induced per GDP situation (23.3%), highest on-base percentage allowed (.371) and highest walks per nine innings (5.1)
- Led the Giants in sacrifice bunts (11), shutouts (2), wild pitches (11), GDPs induced (40), lowest slugging percentage allowed (.377), highest groundball/flyball ratio allowed (2.1), most run support per nine innings (8.7) and fewest home runs allowed per nine innings (.52)

San Francisco

Livan Hernandez

2000 Season

Livan Hernandez emerged as the Giants' ace in 2000, winning 17 games while finishing among the National League leaders in innings pitched. He was especially strong in the season's second half, going 10-4 with a 3.19 ERA after the All-Star break. With his extensive experience dating back to the 1997 World Series, it's easy to forget that Hernandez pitched all of last year at the age of 25.

Pitching

A power pitcher when he first arrived in the big leagues, Hernandez has evolved into a crafty veteran. He throws three quality pitches: a fastball, curveball and changeup. He will mix their velocities and types of movement depending on the situation. Hernandez can get his fastball up in the 92-MPH area, but he's also satisfied with inducing groundballs with his 87-MPH sinker. He is a severe groundball pitcher who focuses on keeping his pitches low in the strike zone. Like most Giants staffers, he was much more effective at home, posting a 2.98 ERA at Pac Bell versus a mark of 4.61 on the road.

Defense & Hitting

Hernandez is one of the best hitting and fielding pitchers in the game, on a level with hurlers like Greg Maddux and Mike Hampton. He is quick off the mound, a necessity for a groundball pitcher. Only four runners stole successfully against him in 2000, a phenomenal total for someone who threw 240 innings. Hernandez hit .236 with a home run and nine RBI last year and now owns a .227 career average. He also is effective at laying down sacrifice bunts.

2001 Outlook

Hernandez has run up high pitch and inning counts at a young age. But concern about those high counts seems to be misplaced. He's in better shape and is a better pitcher than ever. He will enter 2001 on the cusp of joining the short list of top pitchers in the game. Hernandez is signed through the 2003 season with a club option for 2004, so there will be no contract distractions for him.

Position: SP
Bats: R **Throws:** R
Ht: 6' 2" **Wt:** 222

Opening Day Age: 26
Born: 2/20/75 in Villa Clara, Cuba
ML Seasons: 5
Pronunciation: LEE-vahn her-NAN-dezz

Overall Statistics

	W	L	Pct.	ERA	G	GS	Sv	IP	H	BB	SO	HR	Ratio
2000	17	11	.607	3.75	33	33	0	240.0	254	73	165	22	1.36
Career	44	38	.537	4.19	114	113	0	773.1	830	293	545	87	1.45

How Often He Throws Strikes

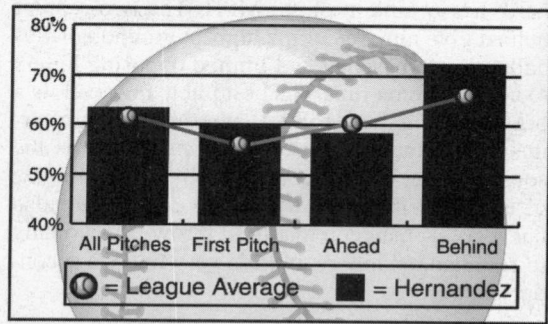

| | = League Average | ■ = Hernandez |

2000 Situational Stats

	W	L	ERA	Sv	IP		AB	H	HR	RBI	Avg
Home	12	3	2.98	0	126.2	LHB	414	112	9	46	.271
Road	5	8	4.61	0	113.1	RHB	518	142	13	54	.274
First Half	7	7	4.25	0	127.0	Sc Pos	193	54	5	71	.280
Scnd Half	10	4	3.19	0	113.0	Clutch	98	33	0	16	.337

2000 Rankings (National League)

- 1st in hits allowed
- 2nd in batters faced (1,030) and pitches thrown (3,825)
- 3rd in shutouts (2)
- 5th in complete games (5) and innings pitched
- Led the Giants in ERA, wins, games started, complete games (5), shutouts (2), innings pitched, hits allowed, batters faced (1,030), pitches thrown (3,825), pickoff throws (135), highest strikeout/walk ratio (2.3), lowest on-base percentage allowed (.325), fewest pitches thrown per batter (3.71), fewest walks per nine innings (2.7), lowest ERA at home and lowest ERA on the road

Jeff Kent

2000 Season

The 2000 campaign was a recognition year for Jeff Kent. His numbers were fairly consistent with his previous three seasons in terms of run production, though he easily set career highs in batting average and walks. The difference was his fast start—he had 85 RBI by the All-Star break—and the acclaim he finally received from the media for his exploits at the plate. The result was a National League MVP Award, as he edged out teammate Barry Bonds for the circuit's top honor.

Hitting

The biggest evolution in Kent's game has been as an overall hitter. He was formerly known as a dead-red fastball hitter who would fish for breaking balls out of the strike zone. He now is a polished all-around batsman who exhibits patience and the ability to drive all different types of pitches against both lefthanders and righthanders.

Baserunning & Defense

Kent always has posted above-average numbers according to all the various statistical methods of measuring defense. But he's still considered a marginally adequate defender by scouts. He is big and physical and lacks good quickness. Still, his arm strength bails him out on some plays and makes him solid at turning the double play. Kent possesses below-average speed on the bases but is an aggressive and astute runner who often looks for an extra base.

2001 Outlook

Even with his MVP showing, don't expect Kent to become a media star or rest on his achievements. He is a grinder who plays hard all the time and who will take the field hurt. Interestingly, he played 16 games at first base in 2000, mostly against lefthanded pitchers, after playing only two games at that position the previous two years combined. Not only does that give the Giants a stronger lineup against southpaws with J.T. Snow on the bench, it takes some wear and tear off Kent's often-bruised body. Kent is signed through the 2002 and the Giants will need another big year from him to help compensate for the loss of free agent Ellis Burks.

Position: 2B/1B
Bats: R **Throws:** R
Ht: 6' 1"   **Wt:** 205

Opening Day Age: 33
Born: 3/7/68 in Bellflower, CA
ML Seasons: 9

Overall Statistics

	G	AB	R	H	D	T	HR	RBI	SB	BB	SO	Avg	OBP	Slg
2000	159	587	114	196	41	7	33	125	12	90	107	.334	.424	.596
Career	1191	4329	680	1228	274	25	194	793	61	387	877	.284	.348	.493

Where He Hits the Ball

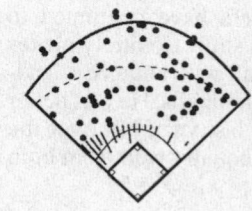
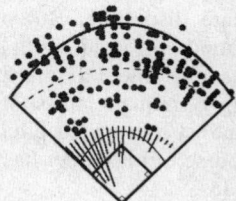

Vs. LHP   **Vs. RHP**

2000 Situational Stats

	AB	H	HR	RBI	Avg		AB	H	HR	RBI	Avg
Home	284	95	14	60	.335	LHP	145	47	5	24	.324
Road	303	101	19	65	.333	RHP	442	149	28	101	.337
First Half	324	115	23	85	.355	Sc Pos	181	62	13	94	.343
Scnd Half	263	81	10	40	.308	Clutch	82	22	2	17	.268

2000 Rankings (National League)

- 2nd in lowest stolen-base percentage (57.1)
- 4th in RBI, times on base (295) and on-base percentage vs. lefthanded pitchers (.459)
- 5th in batting average, hits and fielding percentage at second base (.986)
- Led the Giants in batting average, at-bats, hits, singles, doubles, triples, total bases (350), RBI, caught stealing (9), times on base (295), pitches seen (2,637), plate appearances (695), batting average vs. lefthanded pitchers, batting average on an 0-2 count (.179), cleanup slugging percentage (.595), on-base percentage vs. lefthanded pitchers (.459), batting average at home, batting average on the road and games played

San Francisco

Bill Mueller

2000 Season

Bill Mueller was healthy and in the everyday lineup for the first time in his career last season. The results were mixed, however. On the plus side, he established career highs for doubles, triples, home runs and runs scored. On the other hand, Mueller's batting average and on-base percentage plummeted to significant career lows. Those are poor markings for a hitter who batted in the No. 2 hole and whose primary job was to reach base for the middle of the order.

Hitting

Mueller's standard offensive talents would appear to make him ideal for the second spot in the lineup. He is a switch-hitter with good bat control and plate discipline. But pitchers have continued to pound him inside with hard stuff. He rarely makes the adjustment to pull the ball with authority, leading to frequent jam-shot groundballs. He was better against lefthanded pitchers last year, but over the course of his career has hit equally well from both sides.

Baserunning & Defense

Mueller is very surehanded at third base and his quick first step enables him to reach plenty of groundballs. He is not afraid to sacrifice his body in order to make the play on hard shots. His weakness is his arm strength, which is below average. He's probably been the biggest beneficiary of J.T. Snow's Gold Glove ability to handle throws in the dirt. Mueller's speed is below average and he isn't much of a threat on the bases, although hitting in front of Barry Bonds and Jeff Kent doesn't encourage Mueller to take many liberties.

2001 Outlook

Mueller was dealt to the Cubs in mid-November for righthanded reliever Tim Worrell and is slated to be Chicago's starting third baseman and No. 2 hitter in 2001. Mueller's slugging percentages the last three years have been .395, .362 and .388, so it's not as if last year's rise in extra-base hits constitutes a power surge. Still, the move from Pac Bell park to Wrigley Field should give him a decent boost in his overall power numbers, and should help the Cubs plug a nagging hole in their infield.

Position: 3B
Bats: B **Throws:** R
Ht: 5'10" **Wt:** 180

Opening Day Age: 30
Born: 3/17/71 in Maryland Heights, MO
ML Seasons: 5
Pronunciation: MIL-ler
Nickname: Ferris, Muley

Overall Statistics

	G	AB	R	H	D	T	HR	RBI	SB	BB	SO	Avg	OBP	Slg
2000	153	560	97	150	29	4	10	55	4	52	62	.268	.333	.388
Career	597	2098	333	607	121	8	28	213	15	268	294	.289	.370	.395

Where He Hits the Ball

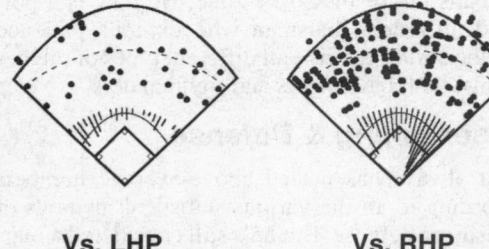

Vs. LHP   **Vs. RHP**

2000 Situational Stats

	AB	H	HR	RBI	Avg		AB	H	HR	RBI	Avg
Home	276	67	3	25	.243	LHP	108	33	3	11	.306
Road	284	83	7	30	.292	RHP	452	117	7	44	.259
First Half	307	87	6	35	.283	Sc Pos	122	26	2	40	.213
Scnd Half	253	63	4	20	.249	Clutch	76	23	3	12	.303

2000 Rankings (National League)

- 1st in fielding percentage at third base (.974)
- 4th in lowest percentage of swings that missed (8.0)
- 6th in lowest batting average at home
- 8th in highest percentage of swings put into play (51.8)
- Led the Giants in lowest percentage of swings that missed (8.0), highest percentage of swings put into play (51.8) and batting average on a 3-2 count (.308)
- Led NL third basemen in sacrifice bunts (7), lowest percentage of swings that missed (8.0) and highest percentage of swings put into play (51.8)

Robb Nen

Position: RP
Bats: R **Throws:** R
Ht: 6' 5" **Wt:** 215

Opening Day Age: 31
Born: 11/28/69 in San Pedro, CA
ML Seasons: 8

2000 Season

Fresh off the worst season of his career in 1999, Robb Nen overcame offseason elbow surgery to produce his best campaign in 2000. The Giants worked him sparingly the first two months of the season, which enabled Nen to get to full strength. He actually carried a lighter workload than ever over the course of a full season. With a fresh arm, Nen's second half was spectacular. He was perfect in 24 save opportunities, recorded a 0.85 ERA and allowed only 19 baserunners in 31.2 innings after the break.

Pitching

Nen noticeably changed his pitching approach last year. He essentially junked his split-finger pitch and went solely to his fastball and slider. Instead of mixing the two, he frequently went with one pitch or the other. He throws the fastball in the high-90s, while his slider is much improved and late breaking. Nen's power arsenal and awkward multiple-piece delivery disguises the fact that he really is a control pitcher. He has averaged fewer than three walks per nine innings the last three seasons. Righthanded hitters were helpless against Nen once again in 2000, hitting just .128 against him.

Defense & Hitting

The less said about Nen's defense and hitting the better. He isn't agile on the mound and does a poor job holding the few runners who reach base. He didn't have a plate appearance in 2000, so he didn't have a chance to record the first hit of his career.

2001 Outlook

With teammate J.T. Snow enjoying his first back-to-back good seasons in 1999 and 2000, Nen is now the most on-and-off player on the Giants' roster, if not in all of baseball. His ERAs the last six years are 3.29, 1.95, 3.89, 1.52, 3.98 and 1.50. The San Francisco closer signed a unique four-year, $32.5 million contract last year that gives him player options for the 2003 and 2004 seasons, and the club is hoping his ERA roller-coaster ride is over.

Overall Statistics

	W	L	Pct.	ERA	G	GS	Sv	IP	H	BB	SO	HR	Ratio
2000	4	3	.571	1.50	68	0	41	66.0	37	19	92	4	0.85
Career	35	35	.500	3.08	496	4	226	563.2	485	218	619	43	1.25

How Often He Throws Strikes

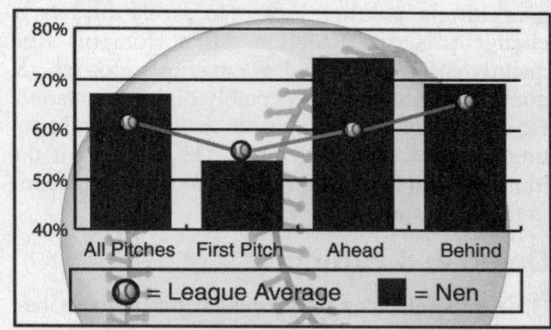

= League Average   = Nen

2000 Situational Stats

	W	L	ERA	Sv		IP		AB	H	HR	RBI	Avg
Home	3	1	1.07	21		33.2	LHB	119	23	3	11	.193
Road	1	2	1.95	20		32.1	RHB	109	14	1	5	.128
First Half	3	3	2.10	17		34.1	Sc Pos	66	6	1	13	.091
Scnd Half	1	0	0.85	24		31.2	Clutch	150	23	1	13	.153

2000 Rankings (National League)

- 1st in lowest batting average allowed in relief with runners on base (.138), lowest batting average allowed in relief with runners in scoring position (.091), relief ERA (1.50) and fewest baserunners allowed per nine innings in relief (7.9)
- 2nd in save percentage (89.1), games finished (63) and lowest batting average allowed in relief (.162)
- 3rd in save opportunities (46) and saves
- Led the Giants in saves, games finished (63), save opportunities (46), save percentage (89.1), blown saves (5), first batter efficiency (.133) and lowest batting average allowed in relief with runners in scoring position (.091)

San Francisco

Russ Ortiz

2000 Season

Russ Ortiz didn't come close last year to matching his 18-9 record or 3.81 ERA of 1999, though few expected him to. In fact, without his performance last August, Ortiz was a less-than-mediocre 8-12 with a 6.03 ERA. But during that month, he led the Giants' surge into first place with a 6-0, 1.12 mark. For his achievement, Ortiz was named the National League Pitcher of the Month.

Pitching

For a starter, Ortiz is unusually dependent on just two pitches. He pitches high in the strike zone with a riding low-90s fastball. He will then throw a hard overhand curveball from the same release point to give hitters another look. He rarely throws a changeup. Ortiz' problems stem from his frequently spotty command. He averages close to 18 pitches per inning, unacceptably high for a starter. He constantly is working from the stretch and putting pressure on his defense. He has shown no improvement in this area in his two and a half years in the big leagues.

Defense & Hitting

Ortiz generally is a good fielder, but perhaps because of the number of runners he puts on first base (239 singles plus walks), Ortiz allowed more steals than any other Giants pitcher. His total of 21 was the fourth highest in the National League. Ortiz is a good hitter for a pitcher. He shows both power and an exceptional batting eye. His eight walks were three more than the rest of the San Francisco staff combined.

2001 Outlook

Although he is signed through 2003 with a team option for 2004, this will be a key season for Ortiz. He must show signs that he is a pitcher more than just a thrower. He also needs to work ahead in counts more often and give the Giants' bullpen more of a break. If he begins this season the same way he pitched over the first few months of 2000, there might be signs of impatience among the San Francisco brass.

Position: SP
Bats: R **Throws:** R
Ht: 6' 1" **Wt:** 210
Opening Day Age: 26
Born: 6/5/74 in Encino, CA
ML Seasons: 3
Pronunciation: or-TEEZ

Overall Statistics

	W	L	Pct.	ERA	G	GS	Sv	IP	H	BB	SO	HR	Ratio
2000	14	12	.538	5.01	33	32	0	195.2	192	112	167	28	1.55
Career	36	25	.590	4.50	88	78	0	491.2	471	283	406	63	1.53

How Often He Throws Strikes

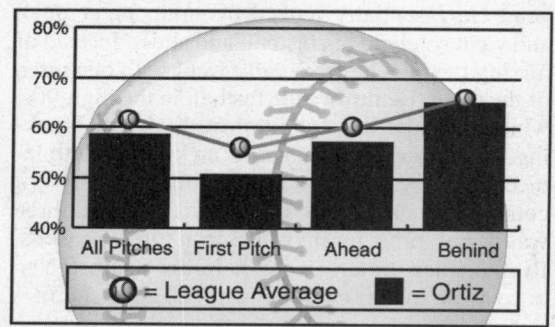

○ = League Average   ■ = Ortiz

2000 Situational Stats

	W	L	ERA	Sv	IP		AB	H	HR	RBI	Avg
Home	6	5	4.21	0	92.0	LHB	358	95	8	37	.265
Road	8	7	5.73	0	103.2	RHB	378	97	20	59	.257
First Half	4	8	6.92	0	95.0	Sc Pos	184	44	10	73	.239
Scnd Half	10	4	3.22	0	100.2	Clutch	30	10	1	6	.333

2000 Rankings (National League)

- 2nd in highest walks per nine innings (5.2)
- 3rd in walks allowed
- 4th in stolen bases allowed (21) and most pitches thrown per batter (3.99)
- 7th in highest on-base percentage allowed (.361) and highest ERA on the road
- 8th in runners caught stealing (9)
- 10th in most strikeouts per nine innings (7.7), highest ERA and lowest strikeout/walk ratio (1.5)
- Led the Giants in losses, home runs allowed, walks allowed, hit batsmen (7), strikeouts, stolen bases allowed (21), runners caught stealing (9), lowest batting average allowed (.261) and most strikeouts per nine innings (7.7)

Kirk Rueter

2000 Season

Last season was vintage Kirk Rueter. He reversed a two-year trend towards rising ERAs and finished with a 3.96 mark, his lowest since 1997. With 31 starts and 184 innings, he further established himself as one of the most consistent starters in baseball. Over the last four years, Rueter has made between 31 and 33 starts and thrown between 184 and 191 innings. You can't get more consistent than that.

Pitching

Judging by his stuff, it's hard to figure out how Rueter retires hitters. He strikes out fewer batters per nine innings than just about any pitcher in baseball and doesn't boast of a pitch that any scout would call better than average. While his fastball generally is in the mid-80s, he spots it all over the strike zone and will cut or sink it depending on the situation. Rueter's sweeping curveball is effective against lefthanders but has to be spotted carefully against righthanded hitters. While he has a reputation as a changeup pitcher, he actually threw fewer changeups in 2000 than ever before and was more aggressive establishing the inside half of the plate. As one scout noted, "Rueter pitches like a power pitcher with a finesse pitcher's stuff."

Defense & Hitting

Rueter maximizes every advantage he can get and is one of the best in the business defensively and with a bat in his hands. Baserunners have just about stopped trying to run on him, as Rueter allowed only one successful steal in six attempts last year. He is a very efficient hitter who makes consistent contact. He continues to be a proficient bunter.

2001 Outlook

Rueter signed a three-year, $15.6 million contract near the end of the 2000 season. It was widely believed that he signed for well under his open market value, but he emphatically said that his only desire was to remain in San Francisco. With Rueter's consistency, it would be foolish to predict anything other than 185 innings and 10-15 wins this season.

Position: SP
Bats: L **Throws:** L
Ht: 6' 2" **Wt:** 205

Opening Day Age: 30
Born: 12/1/70 in Centralia, IL
ML Seasons: 8
Pronunciation: REE-ter
Nickname: Woody

Overall Statistics

	W	L	Pct.	ERA	G	GS	Sv	IP	H	BB	SO	HR	Ratio
2000	11	9	.550	3.96	32	31	0	184.0	205	62	71	23	1.45
Career	81	48	.628	4.16	193	191	0	1074.1	1149	302	537	126	1.35

How Often He Throws Strikes

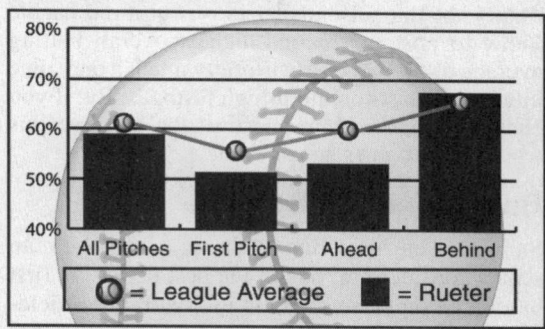

= League Average   = Rueter

2000 Situational Stats

	W	L	ERA	Sv	IP		AB	H	HR	RBI	Avg
Home	6	5	3.15	0	105.2	LHB	135	33	4	14	.244
Road	5	4	5.06	0	78.1	RHB	572	172	19	73	.301
First Half	6	4	3.87	0	95.1	Sc Pos	167	41	4	58	.246
Scnd Half	5	5	4.06	0	88.2	Clutch	23	7	0	1	.304

2000 Rankings (National League)

- 1st in fewest strikeouts per nine innings (3.5)
- 2nd in lowest stolen-base percentage allowed (16.7)
- 3rd in lowest strikeout/walk ratio (1.1)
- 6th in most GDPs induced per nine innings (1.1)
- 8th in highest batting average allowed (.290) and highest batting average allowed vs. righthanded batters
- 9th in GDPs induced (22)
- 10th in lowest ERA at home and lowest ground-ball/flyball ratio allowed (1.0)
- Led the Giants in lowest stolen-base percentage allowed (16.7)

San Francisco

J.T. Snow

Position: 1B
Bats: L **Throws:** L
Ht: 6' 2" **Wt:** 205

Opening Day Age: 33
Born: 2/26/68 in Long Beach, CA
ML Seasons: 9
Nickname: Snowball

2000 Season

While J.T. Snow didn't enjoy his best season in 2000, he did finally break out of his long established on-again, off-again pattern at the plate that had afflicted his career. The only categories where Snow set career highs were the dubious areas of strikeouts and hit by pitches, but his RBI total was on par with '99, and he increased his batting average by 10 points over the previous campaign. He also pocketed his sixth Gold Glove.

Hitting

Snow abandoned switch-hitting late in 1998 and finally started showing signs of hitting lefthanded pitching last year, batting .256 against southpaws. That's not Barry Bonds territory, but it did enable Snow to post the second-highest overall batting average of his career. He is pretty much a one-zone hitter who feasts on thigh-high fastballs. But if you change speeds on him and bust the ball over his hands, he becomes an easy out.

Baserunning & Defense

Snow makes his living with his glove. Veteran scouts consider him one of the best defensive first basemen ever because of his ability to save infielders errors on throws. None of the Giants other infielders are considered better than adequate defensively, yet San Francisco annually is among the league leaders in fielding percentage. His only defensive flaw is that he lacks good range on groundballs. Snow is neither quick nor fast on the bases and is strictly a base-to-base runner.

2001 Outlook

Snow is locked up through the 2003 season, with an option for 2004, by virtue of a four-year, $24 million contract he signed late last July. He has played between 155 and 161 games for four of the past five seasons, so durability is not a concern. One teammate who might cut into Snow's at-bats slightly in 2001 is Jeff Kent, who played far more at first base against lefthanded pitching last year than ever before. Still, Snow almost always entered the game as a defensive replacement in the later innings.

Overall Statistics

	G	AB	R	H	D	T	HR	RBI	SB	BB	SO	Avg	OBP	Slg
2000	155	536	82	152	33	2	19	96	1	66	129	.284	.365	.459
Career	1106	3847	553	1022	188	10	151	635	14	493	786	.266	.350	.437

Where He Hits the Ball

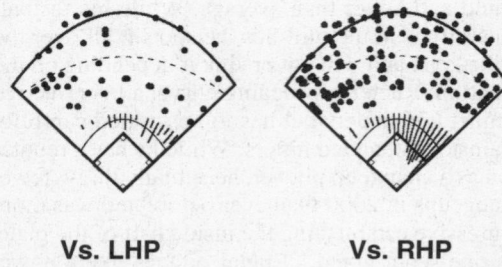

Vs. LHP   **Vs. RHP**

2000 Situational Stats

	AB	H	HR	RBI	Avg		AB	H	HR	RBI	Avg
Home	262	82	10	48	.313	LHP	129	33	4	27	.256
Road	274	70	9	48	.255	RHP	407	119	15	69	.292
First Half	297	92	10	46	.310	Sc Pos	156	44	5	79	.282
Scnd Half	239	60	9	50	.251	Clutch	70	18	2	11	.257

2000 Rankings (National League)

- 1st in sacrifice flies (14) and lowest percentage of extra bases taken as a runner (23.5)
- 2nd in GDPs (20) and fielding percentage at first base (.995)
- 7th in most pitches seen per plate appearance (4.09)
- 8th in strikeouts
- Led the Giants in sacrifice flies (14), hit by pitch (11), strikeouts, GDPs (20), most pitches seen per plate appearance (4.09) and lowest percentage of swings on the first pitch (21.3)
- Led NL first basemen in sacrifice flies (14) and GDPs (20)

Russ Davis

Position: 3B
Bats: R **Throws:** R
Ht: 6' 0" **Wt:** 195

Opening Day Age: 31
Born: 9/13/69 in Birmingham, AL
ML Seasons: 7

Overall Statistics

	G	AB	R	H	D	T	HR	RBI	SB	BB	SO	Avg	OBP	Slg
2000	80	180	27	47	5	0	9	24	0	9	29	.261	.302	.439
Career	559	1813	245	465	95	5	77	259	15	129	454	.256	.309	.442

2000 Situational Stats

	AB	H	HR	RBI	Avg		AB	H	HR	RBI	Avg
Home	80	21	5	16	.263	LHP	103	32	7	17	.311
Road	100	26	4	8	.260	RHP	77	15	2	7	.195
First Half	98	30	3	9	.306	Sc Pos	43	11	4	18	.256
Scnd Half	82	17	6	15	.207	Clutch	21	2	1	2	.095

2000 Season

The Giants signed Russ Davis for the 2000 season as an insurance policy at first and third base and as a righthanded pinch-hitter with some power off the bench. With Bill Mueller healthy all year, Davis saw sparse action. Davis' 2000 production, projected out to his 1997-99 regular duty at-bats with Seattle, almost exactly matched expectations.

Hitting, Baserunning & Defense

Davis' offensive value lies with his power against lefthanded pitchers. He always has been a marginal offensive player against righthanders and had an even worse platoon differential as a part-time player in 2000. Defensively, Davis is more sure-handed than he was in 1998 when he made 32 errors for Seattle, but he's essentially a step-and-dive fielder with limited range and hard hands. He is not a factor on the basepaths.

2001 Outlook

San Francisco re-signed Davis shortly after trading Mueller to the Cubs. Davis will enter spring training in a three-way fight with rookie Pedro Feliz and utility infielder Ramon Martinez for playing time at the hot corner. Davis should get more at-bats than he did in 2000, but if he gets too many more, it could spell trouble for the team.

Alan Embree

Position: RP
Bats: L **Throws:** L
Ht: 6' 2" **Wt:** 190

Opening Day Age: 31
Born: 1/23/70 in Vancouver, WA
ML Seasons: 7
Pronunciation: EMM-bree

Overall Statistics

	W	L	Pct.	ERA	G	GS	Sv	IP	H	BB	SO	HR	Ratio
2000	3	5	.375	4.95	63	0	2	60.0	62	25	49	4	1.45
Career	17	15	.531	4.41	303	4	4	292.0	268	139	258	33	1.39

2000 Situational Stats

	W	L	ERA	Sv	IP		AB	H	HR	RBI	Avg
Home	0	2	3.14	2	28.2	LHB	91	26	2	24	.286
Road	3	3	6.61	0	31.1	RHB	135	36	2	18	.267
First Half	1	2	6.00	1	36.0	Sc Pos	83	24	1	36	.289
Scnd Half	2	3	3.38	1	24.0	Clutch	82	27	2	17	.329

2000 Season

A series of poor outings early last season marred Alan Embree's ERA, though he was again a productive pitcher for the Giants. The presence of fellow lefty Aaron Fultz changed how manager Dusty Baker used Embree in many situations. Embree had more multi-batter outings and established a career high with 60 innings.

Pitching, Defense & Hitting

Embree is a power pitcher who depends on his mid-90s fastball to overmatch hitters. He also will mix in a hard slider on occasion. Because he throws from an overhand release point and primarily is a fastball pitcher, Embree actually is more effective against righthanded hitters. He can still get wild in streaks. Embree is not especially effective holding runners on base. He has two plate appearances in his career.

2001 Outlook

Embree is signed through 2001 with a team option for 2002. Since Baker is willing to stretch Embree out and get him out of single-batter appearances, expect Embree to match his 2000 innings total, that is if free agent Tim Worrell doesn't take too many righthanded batters away from him. Embree had minor elbow surgery in late November, but he's expected to be fully recovered by spring.

San Francisco

Bobby Estalella

Position: C
Bats: R **Throws:** R
Ht: 6' 1" **Wt:** 205

Opening Day Age: 26
Born: 8/23/74 in Hialeah, FL
ML Seasons: 5
Pronunciation: ess-tah-LAY-yah

Overall Statistics

	G	AB	R	H	D	T	HR	RBI	SB	BB	SO	Avg	OBP	Slg
2000	106	299	45	70	22	3	14	53	3	57	92	.234	.357	.468
Career	182	528	77	120	29	4	28	87	4	82	161	.227	.331	.456

2000 Situational Stats

	AB	H	HR	RBI	Avg		AB	H	HR	RBI	Avg
Home	138	36	6	25	.261	LHP	72	18	4	19	.250
Road	161	34	8	28	.211	RHP	227	52	10	34	.229
First Half	161	46	9	34	.286	Sc Pos	79	24	5	42	.304
Scnd Half	138	24	5	19	.174	Clutch	32	10	2	6	.313

2000 Season

In one sense Bobby Estalella enjoyed a breakout season in 2000, setting career highs in every offensive category. But much of his production came in the first half. When the league adjusted, Estalella struggled, hitting .174 after the All-Star break with a woeful .355 slugging percentage.

Hitting, Baserunning & Defense

Estalella is immensely strong, prompting a teammate to remark, "He sort of gets into his uniform differently than the rest of us." That strength helps when Estalella makes solid contact, but otherwise leaves him with a long, stiff swing and makes him vulnerable to hard fastballs and sliders on the inside half. The biggest concern is that he didn't show any signs of adjusting when he struggled. Estallela has a strong and on-target throwing arm but can be slow and stiff behind the plate, as evidenced by his 10 passed balls last season. He is a below-average runner though not a base clogger.

2001 Outlook

Estalella's second-half swoon will force him to make improvements to his swing early in 2001. Otherwise, he may find himself out of a job. Triple-A catcher Guiseppe Chiaramonte isn't much different from Estalella in his overall skills and tools, and will challenge Estalella during spring training.

Aaron Fultz

Position: RP
Bats: L **Throws:** L
Ht: 6' 0" **Wt:** 196

Opening Day Age: 27
Born: 9/4/73 in Memphis, TN
ML Seasons: 1

Overall Statistics

	W	L	Pct.	ERA	G	GS	Sv	IP	H	BB	SO	HR	Ratio
2000	5	2	.714	4.67	58	0	1	69.1	67	28	62	8	1.37
Career	5	2	.714	4.67	58	0	1	69.1	67	28	62	8	1.37

2000 Situational Stats

	W	L	ERA	Sv	IP		AB	H	HR	RBI	Avg
Home	2	1	3.25	1	36.0	LHB	86	19	3	14	.221
Road	3	1	6.21	0	33.1	RHB	169	48	5	30	.284
First Half	2	1	6.69	0	39.0	Sc Pos	76	20	1	32	.263
Scnd Half	3	1	2.08	1	30.1	Clutch	74	18	3	15	.243

2000 Season

Aaron Fultz made his major league debut last year after eight seasons and 915 innings in the minors. He struggled early, but manager Dusty Baker was rewarded for his patience when Fultz had a 2.08 ERA with only five walks over the second half. Scouts noticed that Fultz seemed to fear tough situations far less than most rookie pitchers.

Pitching, Defense & Hitting

Fultz relied on his two primary pitches as a reliever, a fastball and slurve, although he also has a workable changeup from his days as a minor league starter. His fastball is in the range of 88-91 MPH. It has good sink and tails at the lower velocities. With consistently good location, Fultz' slurve is especially effective against lefthanded hitters. He is a good fielder who does the best job of any Giants reliever at holding runners. He went 2-for-6 with a sacrifice bunt at the plate.

2001 Outlook

Fultz is better at retiring lefthanded hitters than San Francisco's other southpaw reliever, Alan Embree. But Fultz' background as a starting pitcher has also prepared him for stints of two to three innings. He should return as a versatile member of the bullpen.

Mark Gardner

Position: SP/RP
Bats: R **Throws:** R
Ht: 6' 1" **Wt:** 220

Opening Day Age: 39
Born: 3/1/62 in Los Angeles, CA
ML Seasons: 12
Nickname: Gardy

Overall Statistics

	W	L	Pct.	ERA	G	GS	Sv	IP	H	BB	SO	HR	Ratio
2000	11	7	.611	4.05	30	20	0	149.0	155	42	92	16	1.32
Career	94	88	.516	4.51	322	260	1	1673.0	1659	594	1203	220	1.35

2000 Situational Stats

	W	L	ERA	Sv	IP		AB	H	HR	RBI	Avg
Home	6	3	4.56	0	73.0	LHB	240	73	7	31	.304
Road	5	4	3.55	0	76.0	RHB	335	82	9	41	.245
First Half	5	4	5.28	0	59.2	Sc Pos	138	40	4	53	.290
Scnd Half	6	3	3.22	0	89.1	Clutch	34	8	0	1	.235

2000 Season

At age 38, Mark Gardner bounced back from the worst season of his career in 1999 to have one of his best in 2000. His 4.05 ERA was his lowest since 1991 and his 11-7 record is even better considering his 4.65 runs of support per nine innings. Most importantly, he solidified the rotation during the second half after Joe Nathan went on the disabled list.

Pitching, Defense & Hitting

Gardner's pitching style makes him much more effective as a starter. He nibbles off the plate with his below-average fastball early in the count and uses his big-breaking curveball to put hitters away. He doesn't have the stuff to challenge hitters. Overall, Gardner is a consummate competitor who gets by on guts and knowledge. He is a good fielder and holds runners well. He is a weak hitter.

2001 Outlook

Gardner re-signed with the Giants in early December, a one-year, $2 million deal with a team option for 2002. He had shoulder surgery shortly after the season, but he should be ready for spring training. His veteran presence and dependability make him ideal protection should one of San Francisco's younger pitchers go down with an injury, as occurred last year.

Ramon Martinez

Position: SS/2B
Bats: R **Throws:** R
Ht: 6' 1" **Wt:** 187

Opening Day Age: 28
Born: 10/10/72 in Philadelphia, PA
ML Seasons: 3

Overall Statistics

	G	AB	R	H	D	T	HR	RBI	SB	BB	SO	Avg	OBP	Slg
2000	88	189	30	57	13	2	6	25	3	15	22	.302	.354	.487
Career	168	352	55	101	20	2	11	44	4	33	41	.287	.348	.449

2000 Situational Stats

	AB	H	HR	RBI	Avg		AB	H	HR	RBI	Avg
Home	85	27	4	11	.318	LHP	64	19	2	6	.297
Road	104	30	2	14	.288	RHP	125	38	4	19	.304
First Half	103	31	5	19	.301	Sc Pos	39	13	1	19	.333
Scnd Half	86	26	1	6	.302	Clutch	26	5	0	4	.192

2000 Season

Ramon Martinez established himself as one of the best utility infielders in baseball last year. Playing primarily at shortstop and second base, he made only one error in 197 chances while hitting over .300 with good power. About the only thing he didn't do well was pinch-hit, going hitless in 12 at-bats in that role.

Hitting, Baserunning & Defense

Martinez is bigger and physically stronger than many middle infielders, and he has learned how to turn on the ball against both righthanders and lefthanders. While he doesn't possess exceptional quickness on defense, he has sure hands and the arm strength to play the left side of the infield. He is a below-average runner but doesn't run himself into many outs.

2001 Outlook

Since third baseman Bill Mueller was traded to the Cubs and shortstop Rich Aurilia enters his final year before free agency, there is a strong thought in the Giants' organization that Martinez soon could become a starter at one of those positions. He probably is better defensively than either Aurilla or Russ Davis. Look for Martinez to get more innings at third base and more at-bats in 2001.

San Francisco

Calvin Murray

Position: CF
Bats: R **Throws:** R
Ht: 5'11" **Wt:** 190

Opening Day Age: 29
Born: 7/30/71 in Dallas, TX
ML Seasons: 2

Overall Statistics

	G	AB	R	H	D	T	HR	RBI	SB	BB	SO	Avg	OBP	Slg
2000	108	194	35	47	12	1	2	22	9	29	33	.242	.348	.345
Career	123	213	36	52	14	1	2	27	10	31	37	.244	.347	.347

2000 Situational Stats

	AB	H	HR	RBI	Avg		AB	H	HR	RBI	Avg
Home	83	22	1	10	.265	LHP	115	31	2	18	.270
Road	111	25	1	12	.225	RHP	79	16	0	4	.203
First Half	116	32	1	13	.276	Sc Pos	45	13	1	18	.289
Scnd Half	78	15	1	9	.192	Clutch	25	9	0	3	.360

2000 Season

The Giants had high hopes for Calvin Murray after he was named the Pacific Coast League's Player of the Year in 1999. Murray fulfilled the Giants' expectations on defense and on the bases, appearing in 104 games in center field as San Francisco's primary late-inning defensive replacement. But his bat proved to be too soft for everyday play.

Hitting, Baserunning & Defense

While Murray shows good patience at the plate, he hits too many weak flyballs and hasn't shown the aptitude to learn how to use his speed to reach base. The Giants might consider using Murray more as a pinch-hitter, especially against lefthanded pitchers. He has piled up stolen bases in the minors, swiping as many as 52 sacks in a season in 1997 with Double-A Shreveport. Murray's primary value is in the field, where his above-average speed and solid instincts make him an ideal backup for the team's defensively challenged outfielders.

2001 Outlook

Murray fills an important role on the Giants because of his speed and defensive skills. The departure of Ellis Burks and Armando Rios' recovery from elbow surgery could open up more opportunities for Murray, but he'll have to share playing time with free-agent acquisition Shawon Dunston.

Joe Nathan

Position: SP
Bats: R **Throws:** R
Ht: 6' 4" **Wt:** 195

Opening Day Age: 26
Born: 11/22/74 in Houston, TX
ML Seasons: 2

Overall Statistics

	W	L	Pct.	ERA	G	GS	Sv	IP	H	BB	SO	HR	Ratio
2000	5	2	.714	5.21	20	15	0	93.1	89	63	61	12	1.63
Career	12	6	.667	4.70	39	29	1	183.2	173	109	115	29	1.54

2000 Situational Stats

	W	L	ERA	Sv	IP		AB	H	HR	RBI	Avg
Home	3	0	2.63	0	48.0	LHB	180	52	4	26	.289
Road	2	2	7.94	0	45.1	RHB	169	37	8	32	.219
First Half	5	2	4.92	0	78.2	Sc Pos	99	26	2	43	.263
Scnd Half	0	0	6.75	0	14.2	Clutch	21	6	1	3	.286

2000 Season

Joe Nathan was handed the fifth slot in the Giants' rotation at the beginning of last season and pitched well in stretches. He was especially effective at home, where he recorded a 2.63 ERA. But he went on the disabled list twice due to shoulder problems and threw only 14.2 innings after the All-Star break.

Pitching, Defense & Hitting

Nathan has a power pitcher's build and assortment of pitches. His fastball can touch 96 MPH, and he complements his heat with a hard curveball and workable changeup. His main problem at this point is his command. He has trouble spotting his off-speed stuff and pitches up in the zone too often with his fastball. Originally signed as a shortstop, Nathan predictably is a good-hitting pitcher and slugged two home runs last year. He is agile around the mound and has improved his ability to hold runners.

2001 Outlook

Nathan's shoulder problems did not require surgery and he should be 100 percent this spring. He will go into camp as the favorite to be the No. 5 starter, especially if the Giants don't re-sign veteran free agent Mark Gardner, who took Nathan's spot in the rotation last year.

Armando Rios

Position: RF/LF
Bats: L **Throws:** L
Ht: 5' 9" **Wt:** 185

Opening Day Age: 29
Born: 9/13/71 in
Santurce, Puerto Rico
ML Seasons: 3

Overall Statistics

	G	AB	R	H	D	T	HR	RBI	SB	BB	SO	Avg	OBP	Slg
2000	115	233	38	62	15	5	10	50	3	31	43	.266	.347	.502
Career	199	390	73	115	24	5	19	82	10	58	80	.295	.383	.528

2000 Situational Stats

	AB	H	HR	RBI	Avg		AB	H	HR	RBI	Avg
Home	109	24	2	17	.220	LHP	42	7	2	10	.167
Road	124	38	8	33	.306	RHP	191	55	8	40	.288
First Half	146	38	4	31	.260	Sc Pos	66	28	3	38	.424
Scnd Half	87	24	6	19	.276	Clutch	42	13	3	11	.310

2000 Season

Last year marked Armando Rios' first full season in the big leagues. He responded well, providing power and run production as a part-time substitute for oft-injured right fielder Ellis Burks. In fact, Rios provided virtually the same RBI per at-bat as teammates Barry Bonds, Burks and Jeff Kent.

Hitting, Baserunning & Defense

Rios is an aggressive hitter who fares much better against pitchers who challenge him with heat. Manager Dusty Baker often tried to keep Rios away from soft-tossing righthanders. He struggled against lefthanders, hitting .167 against them in 42 at-bats. His aggression also is evident in the field. He is a good defensive corner outfielder with above-average arm strength, though he's prone to occasional mistakes when he tries to make a spectacular play. His speed is below average, but he will take the extra base when given the opportunity.

2001 Outlook

With Burks moving to Cleveland, the Giants would like for Rios to become their regular right fielder. Rios underwent Tommy John surgery on his throwing elbow in late October, however, and his availability for the start of the regular season is questionable. The Giants signed Shawon Dunston in December to also handle some right-field duties.

Felix Rodriguez

Tough on Lefties

Position: RP
Bats: R **Throws:** R
Ht: 6' 1" **Wt:** 190

Opening Day Age: 28
Born: 12/5/72 in
Montecristi, Dominican
Republic
ML Seasons: 5

Overall Statistics

	W	L	Pct.	ERA	G	GS	Sv	IP	H	BB	SO	HR	Ratio
2000	4	2	.667	2.64	76	0	3	81.2	65	42	95	5	1.31
Career	7	8	.467	3.87	203	1	8	248.2	235	133	225	20	1.48

2000 Situational Stats

	W	L	ERA	Sv	IP		AB	H	HR	RBI	Avg
Home	3	0	2.75	2	39.1	LHB	133	21	0	11	.158
Road	1	2	2.55	1	42.1	RHB	163	44	5	26	.270
First Half	3	0	3.14	2	48.2	Sc Pos	89	22	2	34	.247
Scnd Half	1	2	1.91	1	33.0	Clutch	177	39	4	21	.220

2000 Season

The well-traveled Felix Rodriguez blossomed into one of the best setup men in baseball in 2000. The Dodgers, Reds and Diamondbacks had all given up on the former catcher while acknowledging that he had the arm to become a dominant reliever. He was especially effective during the second half of last season and overmatched lefthanded hitters.

Pitching, Defense & Hitting

Rodriguez is pure power on the mound. He throws his fastball consistently in the 95-98 MPH range, frequently with riding and sailing life to it. When he rarely backs off, it's with a high-80s slider that he's shown dramatic improvement in controlling. As a pitcher who records a lot of strikeouts and flyballs, Rodriguez doesn't get many chances defensively on the mound. But he recorded the incredibly low total of three assists and no putouts last year. A former catcher, he knows how to swing the bat but rarely gets an opportunity.

2001 Outlook

The Giants bought Rodriguez out from his first arbitration year with a two-year contract, and he is signed through the end of this season. Combined with Robb Nen, Rodriguez gives the Giants potentially the most dominant late-inning duo in baseball, and certainly the hardest throwing.

Felipe Crespo (**Pos**: LF/1B, **Age**: 28, **Bats**: B)

	G	AB	R	H	D	T	HR	RBI	SB	BB	SO	Avg	OBP	Slg
2000	89	131	17	38	6	1	4	29	3	10	23	.290	.351	.443
Career	189	338	37	89	18	3	6	53	8	39	67	.263	.350	.388

Crespo signed with the Giants after getting released by Toronto following the 1999 season. He filled in well as a utility player and pinch-hitter last year. 2001 Outlook: B

Miguel del Toro (**Pos**: RHP, **Age**: 28)

	W	L	Pct.	ERA	G	GS	Sv	IP	H	BB	SO	HR	Ratio
2000	2	0	1.000	5.19	9	1	0	17.1	17	6	16	3	1.33
Career	2	0	1.000	4.61	23	1	0	41.0	41	17	36	8	1.41

del Toro pitched at Class-A in the Pirates' system in 1992, before working the next six seasons in the Mexican League. He saw a lot of action as a starter at Triple-A last year. 2001 Outlook: C

Doug Henry (**Pos**: RHP, **Age**: 37)

	W	L	Pct.	ERA	G	GS	Sv	IP	H	BB	SO	HR	Ratio
2000	4	4	.500	3.79	72	0	1	78.1	57	49	62	12	1.35
Career	32	40	.444	3.95	529	0	82	590.0	536	296	484	69	1.41

The Giants acquired Doug Henry last July as they prepared for their stretch run. He compiled a 2.49 ERA over the final two months and limited opponents to a .207 batting average overall. He signed a two-year, $2.9 million deal with Kansas City in early December and he has an outside shot to close for the Royals. 2001 Outlook: A

John Johnstone (**Pos**: RHP, **Age**: 32)

	W	L	Pct.	ERA	G	GS	Sv	IP	H	BB	SO	HR	Ratio
2000	3	4	.429	6.30	47	0	0	50.0	64	13	37	11	1.54
Career	15	19	.441	4.01	234	0	3	278.1	269	115	234	38	1.38

After leading the National League with 28 holds in 1999, Johnstone saw his ERA more than double last year. He had surgery after the season to correct the back pain he experienced, which may help. 2001 Outlook: B

Terrell Lowery (**Pos**: LF, **Age**: 30, **Bats**: R)

	G	AB	R	H	D	T	HR	RBI	SB	BB	SO	Avg	OBP	Slg
2000	24	34	13	15	4	0	1	5	1	7	8	.441	.548	.647
Career	123	248	42	70	20	1	3	23	2	32	71	.282	.367	.407

Once a top prospect after playing basketball in college, Lowery has now played for five organizations. Don't get too excited by his average with the Giants last year. He hit under .200 at Triple-A and was released by San Francisco in mid-November. 2001 Outlook: C

Juan Melo (**Pos**: 2B, **Age**: 24, **Bats**: B)

	G	AB	R	H	D	T	HR	RBI	SB	BB	SO	Avg	OBP	Slg
2000	11	13	0	1	0	0	0	1	0	0	5	.077	.077	.077
Career	11	13	0	1	0	0	0	1	0	0	5	.077	.077	.077

Melo reached Triple-A at the age of 20, so you know he was once highly regarded. Since then, he's been traded three times and released twice, so you know he's not so highly regarded now. Still, the Giants re-signed him to a minor league deal in late November. 2001 Outlook: C

Doug Mirabelli (**Pos**: C, **Age**: 30, **Bats**: R)

	G	AB	R	H	D	T	HR	RBI	SB	BB	SO	Avg	OBP	Slg
2000	82	230	23	53	10	2	6	28	1	36	57	.230	.337	.370
Career	140	359	37	84	19	2	8	43	1	51	95	.234	.332	.365

Mirabelli finally got a chance to play a full season in the majors last year. He shares many of the same attributes as Bobby Estalella. Mirabelli underwent knee surgery in October. 2001 Outlook: B

Scott Servais (**Pos**: C, **Age**: 33, **Bats**: R)

	G	AB	R	H	D	T	HR	RBI	SB	BB	SO	Avg	OBP	Slg
2000	40	109	7	24	4	0	1	13	0	9	17	.220	.283	.284
Career	809	2477	242	605	130	2	63	319	3	181	404	.244	.305	.375

Servais' playing time has decreased every year since 1996. He hit .218 for Colorado last season, which is pretty hard to do. He's backup material at this point in his career, and the Giants did not offer him arbitration. 2001 Outlook: B

Chad Zerbe (**Pos**: LHP, **Age**: 28)

	W	L	Pct.	ERA	G	GS	Sv	IP	H	BB	SO	HR	Ratio
2000	0	0	-	4.50	4	0	0	6.0	6	1	5	1	1.17
Career	0	0	-	4.50	4	0	0	6.0	6	1	5	1	1.17

Zerbe had been released by two organizations and had toiled in an independent league before the Giants rescued him in 1997. You have to admire his persistence, but the odds are against him. 2001 Outlook: C

San Francisco Giants Minor League Prospects

Organization Overview:

San Francisco won a major league best 97 games before suffering a disappointing loss in the playoffs to the Mets. Rich Aurilia, Marvin Benard, Bill Mueller and Russ Ortiz were the only homegrown players to contribute regularly to the Giants' success, and the organization hasn't developed a star player in some time. Mueller was traded after the season to help make room for Triple-A home-run hitting sensation Pedro Feliz. But this year should, once again, yield no significant rookie contributions unless top pitching prospect Kurt Ainsworth overwhelms his way into the rotation. San Francisco added an affiliate in the Rookie-level Arizona League, which can only help in developing younger, higher-ceiling players.

Kurt Ainsworth

Position: P
Bats: R **Throws:** R
Ht: 6' 3" **Wt:** 185
Opening Day Age: 22
Born: 9/9/78 in Baton Rouge, LA

Recent Statistics

	W	L	ERA	G	GS	Sv	IP	H	R	BB	SO	HR
1999 A Salem-Keizr	3	3	1.61	10	10	0	44.2	34	18	18	64	1
2000 AA Shreveport	10	9	3.30	28	28	0	158.0	138	67	63	130	12

Ainsworth jumped to Double-A for his first full season, just one year after the Louisiana State product was drafted with the 24th overall pick. The collegiate All-American, and Tommy John surgery poster boy, finished fifth in the Texas League with a 3.30 ERA while allowing a tough .234 batting average. That performance, paired with his polished arsenal that is made up of a four-seam fastball that reaches 94-95 MPH, a running two-seamer, slider and changeup, helped Ainsworth earn a spot in Team USA's Olympic rotation. He won his only two starts, posting a 1.54 ERA in the process. The Giants project Ainsworth as a potential frontline starter, and he's not far from making his splash in the majors.

Pedro Feliz

Position: 3B
Bats: R **Throws:** R
Ht: 6' 1" **Wt:** 195
Opening Day Age: 23
Born: 4/27/77 in Azua, DR

Recent Statistics

	G	AB	R	H	D	THR	RBI	SB	BB	SO	Avg
2000 AAA Fresno	128	503	85	150	34	2	33	105	1	30	94	.298
2000 NL San Francisco	8	7	1	2	0	0	0	0	0	0	1	.286
2000 MLE	128	478	63	125	28	1	24	78	0	22	97	.262

After six years in the system, Feliz entered last season with an undistinguished role as a prospect. Coming off consecutive lackluster campaigns in the Double-A Texas League, he blossomed into a full-fledged power prospect in Triple-A. Extra offseason work with minor league hitting coordinator Joe Lefebvre paid off. Feliz had hit just 45 homers in his first 1,930 career at-bats before enjoying a power surge last year when he left the yard 33 times. He made minimal strides with his plate discipline, drawing 30 walks. Named the best defensive third baseman in the Pacific Coast League, Feliz is expected to compete for at-bats with Russ Davis and Ramon Martinez at the hot corner.

Sean McGowan

Position: 1B
Bats: R **Throws:** R
Ht: 6' 6" **Wt:** 240
Opening Day Age: 23
Born: 5/15/77 in Winchester, MA

Recent Statistics

	G	AB	R	H	D	THR	RBI	SB	BB	SO	Avg
1999 A Salem-Keizr	63	257	40	86	12	1	15	62	3	20	56	.335
1999 A San Jose	2	8	1	3	1	0	0	1	0	0	3	.375
2000 A San Jose	114	456	58	149	32	2	12	106	4	43	71	.327
2000 AA Shreveport	18	69	5	24	4	0	0	12	0	1	8	.348

McGowan came out of Boston College as one of the nation's most prolific power hitters after posting a .916 slugging percentage as a senior. A third-round pick in '99, he possesses the best longball potential in the system, but he needs to improve his command of the strike zone. Although his home park last year suppressed home runs, his 12 dingers were a bit disappointing for a 23-year-old at that level. The hulking first baseman finished second in the California League in hitting before earning a promotion to Double-A. With only two potential plus tools, his bat will have to carry him because his wheels and glove won't. Capable of tape-measure home runs, McGowan needs to sharpen his approach, as time is one thing that isn't on his side after four years of college.

Damon Minor

Position: 1B
Bats: L **Throws:** L
Ht: 6' 7" **Wt:** 230
Opening Day Age: 27
Born: 1/5/74 in Canton, OH

Recent Statistics

	G	AB	R	H	D	THR	RBI	SB	BB	SO	Avg
2000 AAA Fresno	133	482	84	140	27	1	30	106	0	87	97	.290
2000 NL San Francisco	10	9	3	4	0	0	3	6	0	2	1	.444
2000 MLE	133	457	62	115	22	0	21	79	0	64	100	.252

A borderline prospect because of his age, Minor has received a lot of attention due to his intriguing background. The fraternal twin brother of Baltimore's Ryan Minor, the towering Damon delivered the game-winning home run for Oklahoma in the 1996 College World Series. The former 12th-rounder has become more of a selective hitter through the years to supplement his moonshot power. Like Sean McGowan, power is Minor's calling card, although he has worked hard to improve his agility around the bag at first. He puts on a stunning show in batting practice, and turned some heads by launching three bombs in his abbreviated cup-of-coffee. He regularly could hit balls into the bay at Pac Bell, but J. T. Snow currently is occupying first base.

Lance Niekro

Position: 3B   **Opening Day Age:** 22
Bats: R **Throws:** R **Born:** 1/29/79 in Winter
Ht: 6' 3" **Wt:** 210   Haven, FL

Recent Statistics

	G	AB	R	H	D	T	HR	RBI	SB	BB	SO	Avg
2000 A Salem-Keizr	49	196	27	71	14	4	5	44	2	11	25	.362

The son of former big leaguer Joe Niekro, Lance emerged as a prominent prospect in 1999 by dominating the Cape Cod League. He made a run at the Triple Crown and was awarded the MVP of the wooden bat league. While he didn't show as much power during his final year at Florida Southern, the Giants drafted Niekro in the second round last June. It didn't take long to establish himself as a hitter, running away with the Northwest League batting title. The second-best prospect in the circuit, he impressed the Giants with his mature big league approach. At the hot corner, Niekro showed the arm strength and actions to handle the position. He's jumped into the upper tier of the organization's depth and should be able to handle a promotion to Double-A.

Tony Torcato

Position: 3B   **Opening Day Age:** 21
Bats: L **Throws:** R **Born:** 10/25/79 in
Ht: 6' 1" **Wt:** 195   Woodland, CA

Recent Statistics

	G	AB	R	H	D	T	HR	RBI	SB	BB	SO	Avg
1999 A Bakersfield	110	422	50	123	25	0	4	58	2	30	67	.291
2000 A San Jose	119	490	77	159	37	2	7	88	19	41	62	.324
2000 AA Shreveport	2	8	1	4	0	0	0	2	0	0	1	.500

Drafted with the Giants' first pick in 1998 out of high school, Torcato has compiled a .307 batting average in the minors despite playing against more experienced competition. The organization's lack of a full-season Class-A affiliate below the advanced California League forced the Giants to start Torcato at that level as a teenager in '99. He held his own offensively, hitting .291 with 25 doubles, but the pure-hitting lefty began to mature as a hitter in repeating the circuit last year. He can rip fastballs, but he's also adept at adjusting to offspeed and breaking stuff. His 37 doubles provide a glimpse of what is expected to develop into home-run power down the line. He's less advanced in the field, committing 40 errors, and with the depth at third base in the system, an eventual position change could be a perfect match.

Ryan Vogelsong

Position: P   **Opening Day Age:** 23
Bats: R **Throws:** R **Born:** 7/22/77 in
Ht: 6' 3" **Wt:** 195   Charlotte, NC

Recent Statistics

	W	L	ERA	G	GS	Sv	IP	H	R	BB	SO	HR
2000 AA Shreveport	6	10	4.23	27	27	0	155.1	153	82	69	147	15
2000 NL San Francisco	0	0	0.00	4	0	0	6.0	4	0	2	6	0

Vogelsong made a name for himself by overpowering his way to a major league debut last year. The 1998 fifth-rounder is armed with one of the best fastballs in the organization, hitting the low to mid-90s from a maximum-effort delivery. He still needs to improve the command of his slider and change, and he could be an ideal candidate to shift to the bullpen. Last year in the Double-A Texas League, Vogelsong proved to be durable, making 27 starts and fanning 147 batters in 155.1 innings. Lefties managed to hit just .213 off him. Vogelsong impressed the brass by finishing three games in September, while showcasing his lively arm.

Jerome Williams

Position: P   **Opening Day Age:** 19
Bats: R **Throws:** R **Born:** 12/4/81 in
Ht: 6' 3" **Wt:** 180   Honolulu, HI

Recent Statistics

	W	L	ERA	G	GS	Sv	IP	H	R	BB	SO	HR
1999 A Salem-Keizr	1	1	2.19	7	7	0	37.0	29	13	11	34	1
2000 A San Jose	7	6	2.94	23	19	0	125.2	89	53	48	115	6

Since signing as a nondrafted free agent in 1999, Williams quietly has made his presence felt by overmatching older competition. A native of Hawaii, he already throws smoke in the mid-90s and demonstrates poise beyond his years. As a teenager in the high Class-A California League last year, Williams allowed just 6.4 hits per nine innings and posted a promising strikeout-walk ratio. His curveball, slider and changeup are progressing as reliable complimentary pitches, and he's sound mechanically. Williams doesn't turn 20 until after the season, at which time he'll have two years of full-season competition under his belt. He hasn't been overworked, but he's on the fastest track.

Others to Watch

The Giants top pick last year was fireballing righthander **Boof Bonser** (19). At a huge 6-foot-4, 240 pounds, his conditioning has been a question, but his arm and 95-MPH heater haven't. He struggled with command in his debut, walking 29 in 33 innings. . . Outfielder **Doug Clark** (25) is an athletic prospect still making adjustments to baseball after a college football career. He batted .272 last year at Shreveport and produces line drives with a quick lefthanded bat. . . Righthander **Felix Diaz** (19) showcased a live arm in his pro debut by allowing just 56 hits in 62.2 innings in the Rookie-level Arizona League. . . Righthander **Jake Esteves** (25) was forced to undergo Tommy John surgery. With the success of that procedure, chances are good that he'll be able to regain the form that helped him win 14 games two years ago with his low-90s fastball and sharp slider. . . Outfielder **Chris Magruder** (23) spent his second straight season in Double-A, making slight improvements. His best attribute is getting on base, reflected by his 67 walks. . . It took outfielder **Carlos Valderrama** (23) parts of three seasons in the Northwest League to emerge in a full-season circuit. The speedster swiped 54 bases and showed some pop in his bat.

2000 American League Leaders

Batters

Batting Average
minimum 502 PA

Nomar Garciaparra	**.372**
Darin Erstad	.355
Manny Ramirez	.351

Home Runs

Troy Glaus	**47**
Jason Giambi	43
Frank Thomas	43

Runs Batted In

Edgar Martinez	**145**
Mike Sweeney	144
Frank Thomas	143

Games Played

Jose Cruz	**162**
Carlos Delgado	**162**
Mo Vaughn	161

At Bats

Darin Erstad	**676**
Johnny Damon	655
Garret Anderson	647

Runs Scored

Johnny Damon	**136**
Alex Rodriguez	134
2 players tied with	121

Hits

Darin Erstad	**240**
Johnny Damon	214
Mike Sweeney	206

Singles

Darin Erstad	**170**
Derek Jeter	151
Mike Sweeney	147

Doubles

Carlos Delgado	**57**
Nomar Garciaparra	51
Deivi Cruz	46

Triples

Cristian Guzman	**20**
Adam Kennedy	11
Johnny Damon	10

Stolen Bases

Johnny Damon	**46**
Roberto Alomar	39
Delino DeShields	37

Caught Stealing

Mark McLemore	**14**
Ray Durham	13
Gerald Williams	12

Walks

Jason Giambi	**137**
Carlos Delgado	123
Jim Thome	118

Intentional Walks

Nomar Garciaparra	**20**
Carlos Delgado	18
Frank Thomas	18

Hit by Pitch

Carlos Delgado	**15**
Mike Sweeney	**15**
Mo Vaughn	14

Strikeouts

Mo Vaughn	**181**
Jim Thome	171
Troy Glaus	163

GDP

Ben Grieve	**32**
Magglio Ordonez	28
2 players tied with	25

Sacrifice Hits

Alex S. Gonzalez	**16**
Carlos Febles	13
Jose Valentin	13

Sacrifice Flies

Magglio Ordonez	**15**
Mike Sweeney	13
Johnny Damon	12

Plate Appearances

Darin Erstad	**747**
Johnny Damon	741
2 players tied with	717

Times on Base

Carlos Delgado	**334**
Jason Giambi	316
Frank Thomas	308

Total Bases

Carlos Delgado	**378**
Darin Erstad	366
Frank Thomas	364

Slugging Percentage
minimum 502 PA

Manny Ramirez	**.697**
Carlos Delgado	.664
Jason Giambi	.647

Slugging vs. LHP
minimum 125 PA

Troy Glaus	**.854**
David Justice	.716
Garret Anderson	.661

Slugging vs. RHP
minimum 377 PA

Carlos Delgado	**.727**
Jason Giambi	.719
Manny Ramirez	.684

Cleanup Slugging
minimum 150 PA

Manny Ramirez	**.697**
Carlos Delgado	.664
Nomar Garciaparra	.610

On-Base Percentage
minimum 502 PA

Jason Giambi	**.476**
Carlos Delgado	.470
Manny Ramirez	.457

OBA vs. LHP
minimum 125 PA

Troy Glaus	**.500**
Derek Jeter	.461
Nomar Garciaparra	.457

OBA vs. RHP
minimum 377 PA

Jason Giambi	**.499**
Carlos Delgado	.492
Manny Ramirez	.437

Leadoff Hitters OBA
minimum 150 PA

Darin Erstad	**.409**
Trot Nixon	.398
Rich Becker	.397

AB per HR
minimum 502 PA

Manny Ramirez	**11.6**
Jason Giambi	11.9
Troy Glaus	12.0

Ground/Fly Ratio
minimum 502 PA

Rey Sanchez	**3.35**
Derek Jeter	2.10
Jacque Jones	2.07

% Extra Bases Taken
minimum 40 Opp to Advance

Darin Erstad	**70.3**
Mike Bordick	69.4
Chris Singleton	68.0

% Runs/Time on Base
minimum 502 PA

Carlos Lee	**50.2**
Chris Singleton	50.0
Jose Valentin	49.1

SB Success %
minimum 20 SB Attempts

Roberto Alomar	**90.7**
Jose Valentin	90.5
Derek Jeter	84.6

Steals of Third

Roberto Alomar	**12**
Omar Vizquel	7
Delino DeShields	6

AVG Scoring Position
minimum 100 PA

Mike Sweeney	**.385**
Carlos Delgado	.384
Frank Thomas	.377

AVG Late & Close
minimum 50 PA

Manny Ramirez	**.444**
Mike Bordick	.404
Gregg Zaun	.400

AVG Bases Loaded
minimum 10 PA

Bernie Williams	**.692**
Johnny Damon	.667
Jason Giambi	.636

GDP/GDP Opp
minimum 50 PA

Rich Becker	**0.02**
Carl Everett	0.03
Denny Hocking	0.03

AVG vs. LHP
minimum 125 PA

Derek Jeter	**.395**
Nomar Garciaparra	.383
Mike Sweeney	.374

AVG vs. RHP
minimum 377 PA

Nomar Garciaparra	**.369**
Darin Erstad	.363
Carlos Delgado	.357

AVG at Home
minimum 251 PA

Darin Erstad	**.388**
Nomar Garciaparra	.375
Johnny Damon	.361

AVG on the Road
minimum 251 PA

Nomar Garciaparra	**.370**
Mike Sweeney	.359
Alex Rodriguez	.356

Pitchers

AVG on 3-1 Count
minimum 10 PA

Troy Glaus	**.769**
Jason Giambi	.667
Manny Ramirez	.667

AVG with Two Strikes
minimum 150 PA

Orlando Palmeiro	**.340**
Nomar Garciaparra	.331
Derek Jeter	.312

AVG on 0-2 Count
minimum 20 PA

Brad Ausmus	**.333**
Orlando Palmeiro	**.333**
David Justice	.333

AVG on Full Count
minimum 40 PA

Mike Sweeney	**.439**
Gregg Zaun	.385
Orlando Palmeiro	.378

Pitches Seen

Carlos Delgado	**2938**
Jim Thome	2869
Troy Glaus	2843

Pitches per PA
minimum 502 PA

Manny Ramirez	**4.27**
Alex Rodriguez	4.23
Jim Thome	4.19

% Pitches Taken
minimum 1500 Pitches Seen

Rich Becker	**66.6**
Mark McLemore	64.6
Jason Giambi	64.5

% Swings that Missed
minimum 1500 Pitches Seen

Chuck Knoblauch	**7.6**
Omar Vizquel	9.4
Kenny Lofton	9.5

% Swings Put in Play
minimum 1500 Pitches Seen

Omar Vizquel	**54.9**
Deivi Cruz	54.1
Rey Sanchez	54.0

Bunts in Play

Alex S. Gonzalez	**26**
3 players tied with	25

Earned Run Average
minimum 162 IP

Pedro Martinez	**1.74**
Roger Clemens	3.70
Mike Mussina	3.79

Wins

Tim Hudson	**20**
David Wells	**20**
Andy Pettitte	19

Losses

Brad Radke	**16**
5 players tied with	15

Win-Loss Percentage
minimum 15 decisions

Tim Hudson	**.769**
Pedro Martinez	.750
Dave Burba	.727

Games

Kelly Wunsch	**83**
Mike Venafro	77
Bob Wells	76

Games Started

Rick Helling	**35**
David Wells	**35**
6 players tied with	34

Complete Games

David Wells	**9**
Pedro Martinez	7
2 players tied with	6

Shutouts

Pedro Martinez	**4**
Tim Hudson	2
Aaron Sele	2

Games Finished

Derek Lowe	**64**
Billy Koch	62
Mariano Rivera	61

Innings Pitched

Mike Mussina	**237.2**
David Wells	229.2
Kenny Rogers	227.1

Hits Allowed

David Wells	**266**
Brad Radke	261
Kenny Rogers	257

Batters Faced

Kenny Rogers	**998**
Mike Mussina	987
Brad Radke	978

Runs Allowed

Chris Carpenter	**130**
Kenny Rogers	126
2 players tied with	125

Earned Runs Allowed

Chris Carpenter	**122**
3 players tied with	119

Home Runs Allowed

Jeff Suppan	**36**
Eric Milton	35
2 players tied with	34

Walks Allowed

Kevin Appier	**102**
Chuck Finley	101
Rick Helling	99

Hit Batsmen

Jeff Weaver	**15**
Pedro Martinez	14
Esteban Loaiza	13

Strikeouts

Pedro Martinez	**284**
Bartolo Colon	212
Mike Mussina	210

Wild Pitches

Dan Reichert	**18**
Jason Grimsley	16
Hideo Nomo	16

Balks

Jim Parque	**5**
Ramon Ortiz	4
3 players tied with	3

Run Support per 9 IP
minimum 162 IP

Andy Pettitte	**7.61**
Tim Hudson	7.34
Pat Rapp	7.14

Baserunners per 9 IP
minimum 162 IP

Pedro Martinez	**7.2**
Mike Mussina	10.8
Orlando Hernandez	11.2

Opposition AVG
minimum 162 IP

Pedro Martinez	**.167**
Tim Hudson	.227
Bartolo Colon	.233

Opposition SLG
minimum 162 IP

Pedro Martinez	**.259**
Bartolo Colon	.371
Tim Hudson	.374

Opposition OBP
minimum 162 IP

Pedro Martinez	**.213**
Mike Mussina	.291
Orlando Hernandez	.298

Home Runs per 9 IP
minimum 162 IP

Pedro Martinez	**0.71**
Aaron Sele	0.72
Andy Pettitte	0.75

Strikeouts per 9 IP
minimum 162 IP

Pedro Martinez	**11.78**
Bartolo Colon	10.15
Hideo Nomo	8.57

Walks per 9 IP
minimum 162 IP

David Wells	**1.2**
Pedro Martinez	1.3
Mike Mussina	1.7

K/BB Ratio
minimum 162 IP

Pedro Martinez	**8.88**
David Wells	5.35
Mike Mussina	4.57

Steals Allowed

Tim Wakefield	**31**
Makoto Suzuki	27
Tim Hudson	24

Caught Stealing Off

Hideo Nomo	**14**
Ken Hill	12
Jeff Weaver	11

SB % Allowed
minimum 162 IP

Jeff Weaver	**26.7**
John Halama	35.7
Chris Carpenter	36.4

GDPs Induced

Scott Schoeneweis	**30**
Albie Lopez	29
Kenny Rogers	29

GDPs per 9 IP
minimum 162 IP

Scott Schoeneweis	**1.6**
Albie Lopez	1.4
John Halama	1.2

GDP/GDP Opp
minimum 30 BFP

Peter Munro	**0.25**
Jamie Brewington	0.22
Jaret Wright	0.22

Ground/Fly Ratio Off
minimum 162 IP

Scott Schoeneweis	**2.4**
Tim Hudson	2.0
Chuck Finley	1.8

AVG Allowed Sc Pos		Blown Saves			Fielding	

Fielding

AVG Allowed Sc Pos		Blown Saves		Errors by Pitcher	
minimum 125 BFP					
Pedro Martinez	.133	**Troy Percival**	10	**Kip Wells**	5
Frank Castillo	.195	**Bob Wells**	10	3 players tied with	4
Makoto Suzuki	.197	3 players tied with	9		

Pitches Thrown		Save Opportunities		Errors by Catcher	
Rick Helling	3791	**Derek Lowe**	47	**Ramon Hernandez**	13
Mike Mussina	3658	Todd Jones	46	3 players tied with	8
Chuck Finley	3645	John Wetteland	43		

Pitches per Batter		Save Percentage		Errors by First Base	
minimum 162 IP		minimum 20 SvOp			
David Wells	3.37	**Kazuhiro Sasaki**	92.5	**Mo Vaughn**	14
Scott Schoeneweis	3.47	Todd Jones	91.3	Carlos Delgado	13
Brian Moehler	3.49	Derek Lowe	89.4	2 players tied with	10

Pickoff Throws		Holds		Errors by Second Base	
Kenny Rogers	176	**Paul Shuey**	28	**Adam Kennedy**	19
Mike Sirotka	162	Buddy Groom	27	3 players tied with	15
Steve Trachsel	161	Kelly Wunsch	25		

ERA at Home		Relief Innings		Errors by Third Base	
minimum 81 IP					
Pedro Martinez	1.84	**S. Hasegawa**	95.2	**Troy Glaus**	33
Mike Mussina	2.90	Derek Lowe	91.1	**Mike Lamb**	33
Chuck Finley	3.20	Keith Foulke	88.0	Dean Palmer	23

ERA on the Road		Relief AVG Allowed		Errors by Shortstop	
minimum 81 IP		minimum 50 relief IP			
Pedro Martinez	1.66	**Jeff Nelson**	.183	**Jose Valentin**	36
David Wells	3.24	Kazuhiro Sasaki	.184	Derek Jeter	24
Frank Castillo	3.25	Arthur Rhodes	.205	Cristian Guzman	22

AVG vs. LHB		Relief Runners/9 IP		Errors by Left Field	
minimum 125 BFP		minimum 50 relief IP			
Pedro Martinez	.150	**Keith Foulke**	9.2	**Bobby Higginson**	7
Justin Speier	.171	Mariano Rivera	9.9	Chad Curtis	5
Bob Howry	.174	Bob Wells	10.3	Steve Cox	4

AVG vs. RHB		Relief Strikeouts/9 IP		Errors by Center Field	
minimum 225 BFP		minimum 50 relief IP			
Pedro Martinez	.184	**Kazuhiro Sasaki**	11.2	**Terrence Long**	10
Barry Zito	.195	Doug Creek	10.8	Gabe Kapler	8
Freddy Garcia	.205	Arthur Rhodes	10.0	4 players tied with	6

Relief ERA		% Inh Runners Scored		Errors by Right Field	
minimum 50 relief IP		minimum 30 inh runners			
Mike Fyhrie	2.39	**Rob Ramsay**	14.7	**Jermaine Dye**	7
Jeff Nelson	2.45	Al Levine	16.1	**Raul Mondesi**	7
Derek Lowe	2.56	Steve Reed	16.7	Tim Salmon	6

Relief Wins		1st Batter AVG		% CS by Catchers	
		minimum 40 relief first BFP		minimum 70 SB Attempts	
S. Hasegawa	10	**Jeff Nelson**	.155	**Brad Ausmus**	43.2
Jim Mecir	10	Mariano Rivera	.177	Ben Molina	32.7
2 players tied with	9	Al Levine	.179	Jorge Posada	30.0

Relief Losses	
Steve Karsay	9
Arthur Rhodes	8
3 players tied with	7

Saves	
Todd Jones	42
Derek Lowe	42
Kazuhiro Sasaki	37

2000 National League Leaders

Batters

Batting Average
minimum 502 PA

Todd Helton	.372
Moises Alou	.355
Vladimir Guerrero	.345

Home Runs

Sammy Sosa	50
Barry Bonds	49
Jeff Bagwell	47

Runs Batted In

Todd Helton	147
Sammy Sosa	138
Jeff Bagwell	132

Games Played

Luis Gonzalez	162
Shawn Green	162
Neifi Perez	162

At Bats

Andruw Jones	656
Neifi Perez	651
Doug Glanville	637

Runs Scored

Jeff Bagwell	152
Todd Helton	138
2 players tied with	129

Hits

Todd Helton	216
Jose Vidro	200
Andruw Jones	199

Singles

Luis Castillo	158
Eric Owens	139
Doug Glanville	134

Doubles

Todd Helton	59
Jeff Cirillo	53
Jose Vidro	51

Triples

Tony Womack	14
Vladimir Guerrero	11
Neifi Perez	11

Stolen Bases

Luis Castillo	62
Tom Goodwin	55
Eric Young	54

Caught Stealing

Luis Castillo	22
3 players tied with	14

Walks

Barry Bonds	117
Brian Giles	114
Jeff Bagwell	107

Intentional Walks

Vladimir Guerrero	23
Barry Bonds	22
Todd Helton	22

Hit by Pitch

Fernando Vina	28
Richard Hidalgo	21
Andres Galarraga	17

Strikeouts

Preston Wilson	187
Sammy Sosa	168
Jim Edmonds	167

GDP

Moises Alou	21
Javy Lopez	20
J.T. Snow	20

Sacrifice Hits

Ricky Gutierrez	16
5 players tied with	14

Sacrifice Flies

J.T. Snow	14
3 players tied with	12

Plate Appearances

Andruw Jones	729
Luis Gonzalez	722
Jeff Bagwell	719

Times on Base

Todd Helton	323
Jeff Bagwell	305
Brian Giles	297

Total Bases

Todd Helton	405
Sammy Sosa	383
Vladimir Guerrero	379

Slugging Percentage
minimum 502 PA

Todd Helton	.698
Barry Bonds	.688
Vladimir Guerrero	.664

Slugging vs. LHP
minimum 125 PA

Chipper Jones	.777
Vladimir Guerrero	.744
Jeff Bagwell	.688

Slugging vs. RHP
minimum 377 PA

Barry Bonds	.759
Todd Helton	.732
Gary Sheffield	.685

Cleanup Slugging
minimum 150 PA

Todd Helton	.770
Mark McGwire	.769
Lance Berkman	.696

On-Base Percentage
minimum 502 PA

Todd Helton	.463
Barry Bonds	.440
Gary Sheffield	.438

OBA vs. LHP
minimum 125 PA

Jeff Bagwell	.496
Chipper Jones	.480
Sammy Sosa	.461

OBA vs. RHP
minimum 377 PA

Barry Bonds	.487
Todd Helton	.467
Brian Giles	.446

Leadoff Hitters OBA
minimum 150 PA

Luis Castillo	.419
Craig Biggio	.413
Quilvio Veras	.404

AB per HR
minimum 502 PA

Barry Bonds	9.8
Gary Sheffield	11.7
Sammy Sosa	12.1

Ground/Fly Ratio
minimum 502 PA

Luis Castillo	4.74
Eric Owens	2.82
Rafael Furcal	2.24

% Extra Bases Taken
minimum 40 Opp to Advance

Steve Finley	73.9
Rafael Furcal	72.5
Tom Goodwin	72.3

% Runs/Time on Base
minimum 502 PA

Jeff Bagwell	49.8
Geoff Jenkins	49.3
Jim Edmonds	48.9

SB Success %
minimum 20 SB Attempts

Pokey Reese	90.6
Cliff Floyd	88.9
Eric Young	88.5

Steals of Third

Reggie Sanders	9
4 players tied with	7

AVG Scoring Position
minimum 100 PA

Todd Helton	.392
Jeff Cirillo	.391
Mitch Meluskey	.374

AVG Late & Close
minimum 50 PA

Todd Helton	.393
Scott Rolen	.384
Luis Lopez	.381

AVG Bases Loaded
minimum 10 PA

Pat Burrell	.727
Jeff Cirillo	.667
Mitch Meluskey	.625

GDP/GDP Opp
minimum 50 PA

Kevin Elster	0.00
Rafael Furcal	0.03
Jim Edmonds	0.03

AVG vs. LHP
minimum 125 PA

Chipper Jones	.415
Jeff Cirillo	.379
Vladimir Guerrero	.376

AVG vs. RHP
minimum 377 PA

Todd Helton	.387
Luis Castillo	.350
Moises Alou	.350

AVG at Home
minimum 251 PA

Jeff Cirillo	.403
Jeffrey Hammonds	.399
Todd Helton	.391

AVG on the Road
minimum 251 PA

Mike Piazza	.377
Moises Alou	.362
Todd Helton	.353

AVG on 3-1 Count
minimum 10 PA

Mark McGwire	**1.000**
Geoff Jenkins	.714
Mike Piazza	.714

AVG with Two Strikes
minimum 150 PA

Todd Helton	**.336**
Quilvio Veras	.298
Edgardo Alfonzo	.297

AVG on 0-2 Count
minimum 20 PA

Todd Helton	**.484**
Brian L. Hunter	.375
Jeffrey Hammonds	.368

AVG on Full Count
minimum 40 PA

Quilvio Veras	**.471**
Mike Lieberthal	.459
Dave Hansen	.433

Pitches Seen

Sammy Sosa	**2877**
Bobby Abreu	2833
Jeff Bagwell	2812

Pitches per PA
minimum 502 PA

Luis Castillo	**4.30**
Jim Edmonds	4.29
Todd Zeile	4.22

% Pitches Taken
minimum 1500 Pitches Seen

Todd Zeile	**65.8**
Bobby Abreu	63.7
Tom Goodwin	62.5

% Swings that Missed
minimum 1500 Pitches Seen

Mark Loretta	**6.9**
Eric Young	7.6
Luis Castillo	7.9

% Swings Put in Play
minimum 1500 Pitches Seen

Mark Grace	**59.1**
Eric Young	58.9
Fernando Vina	55.6

Bunts in Play

Rafael Furcal	**33**
Peter Bergeron	32
2 players tied with	30

Pitchers

Earned Run Average
minimum 162 IP

Kevin Brown	**2.58**
Randy Johnson	2.64
Jeff D'Amico	2.66

Wins

Tom Glavine	**21**
Darryl Kile	20
2 players tied with	19

Losses

Omar Daal	**19**
Matt Clement	17
Steve Parris	17

Win-Loss Percentage
minimum 15 decisions

Randy Johnson	**.731**
Shawn Estes	.714
Scott Elarton	.708

Games

Steve Kline	**83**
Scott Sullivan	79
Mike Myers	78

Games Started

5 players tied with	**35**

Complete Games

Randy Johnson	**8**
Curt Schilling	**8**
2 players tied with	6

Shutouts

Randy Johnson	**3**
Greg Maddux	**3**
6 players tied with	2

Games Finished

Armando Benitez	**68**
Robb Nen	63
Mike Williams	63

Innings Pitched

Jon Lieber	**251.0**
Greg Maddux	249.1
Randy Johnson	248.2

Hits Allowed

Livan Hernandez	**254**
Jose Lima	251
Jon Lieber	248

Batters Faced

Jon Lieber	**1047**
Livan Hernandez	1030
Greg Maddux	1012

Runs Allowed

Jose Lima	**152**
Matt Clement	131
Chris Holt	131

Earned Runs Allowed

Jose Lima	**145**
Chris Holt	123
Jon Lieber	123

Home Runs Allowed

Jose Lima	**48**
Brian Anderson	38
Jon Lieber	36

Walks Allowed

Matt Clement	**125**
Chan Ho Park	124
Russ Ortiz	112

Hit Batsmen

Jamey Wright	**18**
Matt Clement	16
Pedro Astacio	15

Strikeouts

Randy Johnson	**347**
Chan Ho Park	217
Kevin Brown	216

Wild Pitches

Matt Clement	**23**
Scott Williamson	21
Darren Dreifort	17

Balks

Reid Cornelius	**5**
Brian Anderson	4
Darren Dreifort	3

Run Support per 9 IP
minimum 162 IP

Shawn Estes	**8.65**
Andy Benes	7.16
Scott Elarton	7.10

Baserunners per 9 IP
minimum 162 IP

Kevin Brown	**9.3**
Greg Maddux	10.0
Randy Johnson	10.3

Opposition AVG
minimum 162 IP

Kevin Brown	**.213**
Chan Ho Park	.214
Rick Ankiel	.219

Opposition SLG
minimum 162 IP

Mike Hampton	**.325**
Kevin Brown	.337
Greg Maddux	.338

Opposition OBP
minimum 162 IP

Kevin Brown	**.261**
Greg Maddux	.276
Randy Johnson	.288

Home Runs per 9 IP
minimum 162 IP

Mike Hampton	**0.41**
Shawn Estes	0.52
Jamey Wright	0.66

Strikeouts per 9 IP
minimum 162 IP

Randy Johnson	**12.56**
Rick Ankiel	9.98
Pedro Astacio	8.85

Walks per 9 IP
minimum 162 IP

Greg Maddux	**1.5**
Brian Anderson	1.6
Rick Reed	1.7

K/BB Ratio
minimum 162 IP

Kevin Brown	**4.60**
Randy Johnson	4.57
Greg Maddux	4.52

Steals Allowed

Greg Maddux	**32**
Randy Johnson	26
Al Leiter	22

Caught Stealing Off

Pat Hentgen	**16**
Randy Johnson	**16**
Al Leiter	13

SB % Allowed
minimum 162 IP

Darryl Kile	**15.4**
Kirk Rueter	16.7
Curt Schilling	25.0

GDPs Induced

Shawn Estes	**40**
Chris Holt	31
Jimmy Haynes	29

GDPs per 9 IP
minimum 162 IP

Shawn Estes	**1.9**
Jamey Wright	1.4
Chris Holt	1.3

GDP/GDP Opp
minimum 30 BFP

Mike Fetters	**0.26**
Osvaldo Fernandez	0.24
Shawn Estes	0.23

Ground/Fly Ratio Off
minimum 162 IP

Greg Maddux	**2.7**
Mike Hampton	2.5
Jamey Wright	2.1

Fielding

AVG Allowed Sc Pos		Blown Saves		Errors by Pitcher	
minimum 125 BFP					
Chan Ho Park	.159	**Billy Wagner**	9	**Rick Ankiel**	7
Scott Williamson	.163	Rick Aguilera	8	6 players tied with	4
Robert Person	.190	4 players tied with	7		

Pitches Thrown		Save Opportunities		Errors by Catcher	
Randy Johnson	4026	**Trevor Hoffman**	50	**Todd Hundley**	13
Livan Hernandez	3825	Antonio Alfonseca	49	Mitch Meluskey	12
Tom Glavine	3706	2 players tied with	46	Jason Kendall	10

Pitches per Batter		Save Percentage		Errors by First Base	
minimum 162 IP		minimum 20 SvOp			
Greg Maddux	3.18	**Antonio Alfonseca**	91.8	**Kevin Young**	17
Andy Ashby	3.38	Armando Benitez	89.1	Andres Galarraga	14
Brian Anderson	3.42	Robb Nen	89.1	Lee Stevens	11

Pickoff Throws		Holds		Errors by Second Base	
Armando Reynoso	190	**Felix Rodriguez**	30	**Ron Belliard**	19
Al Leiter	186	Mike Remlinger	23	Mark Grudzielanek	17
John Burkett	161	2 players tied with	22	3 players tied with	15

ERA at Home		Relief Innings		Errors by Third Base	
minimum 81 IP					
Kevin Brown	1.79	**Scott Sullivan**	106.1	**Phil Nevin**	26
Mike Hampton	2.05	Danny Graves	91.1	Adrian Beltre	23
Chan Ho Park	2.34	Matt Herges	87.2	Chipper Jones	23

ERA on the Road		Relief AVG Allowed		Errors by Shortstop	
minimum 81 IP		minimum 50 relief IP			
Brian Bohanon	2.79	**Armando Benitez**	.148	**Desi Relaford**	31
Randy Johnson	2.79	Robb Nen	.162	Edgar Renteria	27
Greg Maddux	3.03	Donne Wall	.193	Rafael Furcal	23

AVG vs. LHB		Relief Runners/9 IP		Errors by Left Field	
minimum 125 BFP		minimum 50 relief IP			
Al Leiter	.119	**Robb Nen**	7.9	**Gary Sheffield**	10
Armando Benitez	.133	Gabe White	8.8	Cliff Floyd	9
Felix Rodriguez	.158	Trevor Hoffman	9.0	2 players tied with	7

AVG vs. RHB		Relief Strikeouts/9 IP		Errors by Center Field	
minimum 225 BFP		minimum 50 relief IP			
Chan Ho Park	.200	**Byung-Hyun Kim**	14.4	**Jay Payton**	6
Kevin Brown	.201	Scott Williamson	13.2	5 players tied with	5
Scott Williamson	.204	John Rocker	13.1		

Relief ERA		% Inh Runners Scored		Errors by Right Field	
minimum 50 relief IP		minimum 30 inh runners			
Robb Nen	1.50	**Curtis Leskanic**	9.7	**Vladimir Guerrero**	10
Gabe White	2.36	Mike Myers	14.1	**Sammy Sosa**	10
Tim Worrell	2.47	Turk Wendell	15.0	Dante Bichette	8

Relief Wins		1st Batter AVG		% CS by Catchers	
		minimum 40 relief first BFP		minimum 70 SB Attempts	
Matt Herges	11	**Kevin Walker**	.119	**Mike Matheny**	51.1
Gabe White	11	Turk Wendell	.119	Damian Miller	30.6
Danny Graves	10	Donne Wall	.128	Carlos Hernandez	30.0

Relief Losses	
Terry Adams	9
Jason Christiansen	8
5 players tied with	7

Saves	
Antonio Alfonseca	45
Trevor Hoffman	43
2 players tied with	41

Stars, Bums and Sleepers: Who's Who in 2001

Who will follow in the footsteps of American League Rookie of the Year Kazuhiro Sasaki, one of our sleeper picks for 2000? It will be most of a year before we know for sure, but we present our choices and more in this section of the book.

Some of our sleepers for 2000 were Rick Ankiel, Lance Berkman, Pat Burrell, Bruce Chen, Brad Fullmer, Jacque Jones, Gabe Kapler, Adam Kennedy, Derrek Lee, Mike Lowell, Mitch Meluskey and Mark Quinn. The system we use to project a future brighter than a player's past performance is the creation of Bill James, who introduced his forecasting methods in *The Bill James Baseball Abstract.* Over the years, Bill and STATS founder John Dewan have refined the system, combining advice from our scouts and staff experts.

The system is used to project more than just sleepers. The following pages also are dedicated to predicting players in decline and those we can expect consistent performance from in 2001. There are some general truths that go into these projections. Younger players are inclined to improve and older guys tend to decline. Age 27 is when we can expect peak performance and career years from major league hitters. Players who enjoy an unexpectedly good year commonly fail to repeat their success, while those who experience a dropoff in their numbers often rebound.

Each player position in this section is broken into four groups: Expect a Better Year, Look for Consistency, Production Will Drop and Sleepers. Play- ers are placed into these groups based on 2000 performance only.

We take a different approach with Sleepers. The statistics we show here combine major and minor league totals, and we factored in projected playing time for 2001 when we made our decisions late in 2000. Not all of our picks will demonstrate the budding promise of Sasaki or Fullmer, but a number of them will emerge this season.

Major leaguers are considered at their most common position in 2000, with a few adjustments for anticipated positional changes. Then we look at their career trends. Using the complex formula refined by Bill and John, forecasts are generated based on complete careers. That way an unusually good or bad 2000 season isn't the primary determinant of a projection.

When appropriate, minor league numbers also are factored into the system. Bill found that minor league performance, when properly adjusted, is just as reliable as major league performance in making big league projections.

Of course, there are factors outside of our control. While we evaluate teams' positional battles in estimating playing time, spring-training results and injuries will alter the picture for many players. We also concede that pitchers are full of surprises. For every five hitters who perform consistently, there may be just one pitcher who's as reliable.

Catcher

Expect A Better Year

	2000 Statistics			
	Avg	HR	RBI	SB
Ivan Rodriguez	.347	27	83	5
Mitch Meluskey	.300	14	69	1
Mike Lieberthal	.278	15	71	2
Jason Varitek	.248	10	65	1
Ramon Hernandez	.241	14	62	1
Eddie Taubensee	.267	6	24	0
Michael Barrett	.214	1	22	0
Henry Blanco	.236	7	31	0
Wiki Gonzalez	.232	5	30	1
Dan Wilson	.235	5	27	1
Einar Diaz	.272	4	25	4
Doug Mirabelli	.230	6	28	1
Scott Hatteberg	.265	8	36	0
Eli Marrero	.225	5	17	5
Kelly Stinnett	.217	8	33	0
Mark L. Johnson	.225	3	23	3
Mike Redmond	.252	0	15	0
Mike DiFelice	.240	6	19	0

Look for Consistency

	2000 Statistics			
	Avg	HR	RBI	SB
Mike Piazza	.324	38	113	4
Jason Kendall	.320	14	58	22
Javy Lopez	.287	24	89	0
Bobby Estalella	.234	14	53	3
Brook Fordyce	.301	14	49	0
Damian Miller	.275	10	44	2
John Flaherty	.261	10	39	0
Brad Ausmus	.266	7	51	11
Chris Widger	.233	13	35	1
Sandy Alomar Jr.	.289	7	42	2
Tony Eusebio	.280	7	33	0
Jeff Reed	.214	4	25	0
Carlos Hernandez	.256	3	35	2
Raul Casanova	.247	6	36	1
Bill Haselman	.275	6	26	0

Production Will Drop

	2000 Statistics			
	Avg	HR	RBI	SB
Jorge Posada	.287	28	86	2
Charles Johnson	.304	31	91	2
Ben Molina	.281	14	71	1
Darrin Fletcher	.320	20	58	1
Todd Hundley	.284	24	70	0
Mike Matheny	.261	6	47	0
Joe Girardi	.278	6	40	1
Brent Mayne	.301	6	64	1
Gregg Zaun	.274	7	33	7
Benito Santiago	.262	8	45	2
Chad Kreuter	.264	6	28	1

Sleepers

	2000 Statistics (includes minor leagues)			
	Avg	HR	RBI	SB
Ben Petrick	.317	12	67	8
Ramon Castro	.298	16	59	0
Ben Davis	.248	10	54	6
A.J. Pierzynski	.312	10	70	2
Jason LaRue	.249	19	60	3
Matt LeCroy	.244	20	70	0
Josh Paul	.251	5	27	7

First Base

Expect A Better Year

	2000 Statistics			
	Avg	HR	RBI	SB
Mark McGwire	.305	32	73	1
Sean Casey	.315	20	85	1
Richie Sexson	.272	30	91	2
Paul Konerko	.298	21	97	1
Tony Clark	.274	13	37	0
Travis Lee	.235	9	54	8
Kevin Millar	.259	14	42	0
Rico Brogna	.232	2	21	1

Look for Consistency

	2000 Statistics			
	Avg	HR	RBI	SB
Jeff Bagwell	.310	47	132	9
Jim Thome	.269	37	106	1
Mo Vaughn	.272	36	117	2
John Olerud	.285	14	103	0
Eric Karros	.250	31	106	4
Mark Grace	.280	11	82	1
Derrek Lee	.281	28	70	0
Tino Martinez	.258	16	91	4
Andres Galarraga	.302	28	100	3
Brian Daubach	.248	21	76	1
Kevin Young	.258	20	88	8
Lee Stevens	.265	22	75	0
Dave McCarty	.278	12	53	0
Tyler Houston	.250	18	43	2
Wally Joyner	.281	5	32	0

Production Will Drop

	2000 Statistics			
	Avg	HR	RBI	SB
Todd Helton	.372	42	147	5
Carlos Delgado	.344	41	137	0
Jason Giambi	.333	43	137	2
Rafael Palmeiro	.288	39	120	2
Mike Sweeney	.333	29	144	8
Ryan Klesko	.283	26	92	23
Fred McGriff	.277	27	106	2
Todd Zeile	.268	22	79	3
J.T. Snow	.284	19	96	1
David Segui	.334	19	103	0
Ron Coomer	.270	16	82	2
Greg Colbrunn	.313	15	57	0
Mike Stanley	.238	14	46	0

Sleepers

	2000 Statistics (includes minor leagues)			
	Avg	HR	RBI	SB
Pat Burrell	.269	22	104	1
Chris Richard	.273	30	112	16
Erubiel Durazo	.299	12	45	1
Julio Zuleta	.309	29	106	5
Fernando Seguignol	.277	18	53	1
Robert Fick	.221	4	29	3
Carlos Pena	.299	28	105	12
Jay Gibbons	.321	19	75	3

Second Base

Expect A Better Year

	2000 Statistics			
	Avg	HR	RBI	SB
Craig Biggio	.268	8	35	12
Damion Easley	.259	14	58	13
Todd Walker	.290	9	44	7
Warren Morris	.259	3	43	7
Carlos Febles	.257	2	29	17
Chuck Knoblauch	.283	5	26	15
Quilvio Veras	.309	5	37	25
Jose Offerman	.255	9	41	0
Bobby Smith	.234	6	26	2
Jay Canizaro	.269	7	40	4
Homer Bush	.215	1	18	9

Look for Consistency

	2000 Statistics			
	Avg	HR	RBI	SB
Edgardo Alfonzo	.324	25	94	3
Roberto Alomar	.310	19	89	39
Ray Durham	.280	17	75	25
Bret Boone	.251	19	74	8
Ron Belliard	.263	8	54	7
Jay Bell	.267	18	68	7
Mark Grudzielanek	.279	7	49	12
Adam Kennedy	.266	9	72	22
Pokey Reese	.255	12	46	29
Fernando Vina	.300	4	31	10
Mark McLemore	.245	3	46	30
Frank Catalanotto	.291	10	42	6
Mickey Morandini	.257	0	29	6
Miguel Cairo	.261	1	34	28
Tony Graffanino	.274	2	17	7

Production Will Drop

	2000 Statistics			
	Avg	HR	RBI	SB
Jeff Kent	.334	33	125	12
Jose Vidro	.330	24	97	5
Luis Castillo	.334	2	17	62
Eric Young	.297	6	47	54
Randy Velarde	.278	12	41	9
Delino DeShields	.296	10	86	37
Luis Alicea	.294	6	63	1
Placido Polanco	.316	5	39	4
Mike Lansing	.240	11	60	8
Denny Hocking	.298	4	47	7

Sleepers

	2000 Statistics (includes minor leagues)			
	Avg	HR	RBI	SB
Jose Ortiz	.348	24	109	22
Jerry Hairston Jr.	.278	9	44	18
Marlon Anderson	.283	9	68	26
Frank Menechino	.268	8	28	2
Luis Rivas	.276	6	71	20
Brent Abernathy	.290	5	50	23

Third Base

Expect A Better Year

	2000 Statistics			
	Avg	HR	RBI	SB
Eric Chavez	.277	26	86	2
Fernando Tatis	.253	18	64	2
Robin Ventura	.232	24	84	3
Matt Williams	.275	12	47	1
Jose Hernandez	.244	11	59	3
Vinny Castilla	.221	6	42	1
Ken Caminiti	.303	15	45	3
John Valentin	.257	2	2	0
Russ Johnson	.239	2	20	5
Shane Andrews	.229	14	39	1

Look for Consistency

	2000 Statistics			
	Avg	HR	RBI	SB
Chipper Jones	.311	36	111	14
Jeff Cirillo	.326	11	115	3
Tony Batista	.263	41	114	5
Scott Rolen	.298	26	89	8
Corey Koskie	.300	9	65	5
Adrian Beltre	.290	20	85	12
Dean Palmer	.256	29	102	4
Mike Lowell	.270	22	91	4
Aaron Boone	.285	12	43	6
Mike Lamb	.278	6	47	0
Cal Ripken Jr.	.256	15	56	0
Bill Mueller	.268	10	55	4
Scott Brosius	.230	16	64	0
Geoff Blum	.283	11	45	1
David Bell	.247	11	47	2
Carlos Guillen	.257	7	42	1
Enrique Wilson	.293	5	27	2
Willie Greene	.201	10	37	4
Kevin Jordan	.220	5	36	0

Production Will Drop

	2000 Statistics			
	Avg	HR	RBI	SB
Troy Glaus	.284	47	102	14
Travis Fryman	.321	22	106	1
Phil Nevin	.303	31	107	2
Joe Randa	.304	15	106	6
Herbert Perry	.302	12	62	4
Chris Stynes	.334	12	40	5
Jeff Conine	.284	13	46	4
Bill Spiers	.301	3	43	7
Charlie Hayes	.251	9	46	1

Sleepers

	2000 Statistics (includes minor leagues)			
	Avg	HR	RBI	SB
Aubrey Huff	.309	24	90	2
Aramis Ramirez	.295	10	61	2
Chris Truby	.272	13	89	8
Lou Merloni	.341	1	23	1
Andy Tracy	.284	21	68	3
Joe Crede	.307	21	97	3
Jose Nieves	.230	8	33	2

Shortstop

Expect A Better Year

	2000 Statistics			
	Avg	HR	RBI	SB
Mark Loretta	.281	7	40	0
Barry Larkin	.313	11	41	14
Julio Lugo	.283	10	40	22
Orlando Cabrera	.237	13	55	4
Alex Gonzalez	.200	7	42	7
Rey Ordonez	.188	0	9	0
Gary DiSarcina	.395	1	11	0
Dave Berg	.252	1	21	3

Look for Consistency

	2000 Statistics			
	Avg	HR	RBI	SB
Alex Rodriguez	.316	41	132	15
Nomar Garciaparra	.372	21	96	5
Derek Jeter	.339	15	73	22
Miguel Tejada	.275	30	115	6
Rafael Furcal	.295	4	37	40
Neifi Perez	.287	10	71	3
Edgar Renteria	.278	16	76	21
Rich Aurilia	.271	20	79	1
Damian Jackson	.255	6	37	28
Tony Womack	.271	7	57	45
Royce Clayton	.242	14	54	11
Alex S. Gonzalez	.252	15	69	4
Ramon E. Martinez	.302	6	25	3
Alex Cora	.238	4	32	4

Production Will Drop

	2000 Statistics			
	Avg	HR	RBI	SB
Jose Valentin	.273	25	92	19
Omar Vizquel	.287	7	66	22
Deivi Cruz	.302	10	82	1
Cristian Guzman	.247	8	54	28
Mike Bordick	.285	20	80	9
Ricky Gutierrez	.276	11	56	8
Rey Sanchez	.273	1	38	7
Pat Meares	.240	13	47	1
Melvin Mora	.275	8	47	12
Felix Martinez	.214	2	17	9

Sleepers

	2000 Statistics (includes minor leagues)			
	Avg	HR	RBI	SB
Jimmy Rollins	.279	12	74	27
Alfonso Soriano	.279	14	69	16

Left Field

Expect A Better Year

	2000 Statistics			
	Avg	HR	RBI	SB
Mark Quinn	.294	20	78	5
Rusty Greer	.297	8	65	4
Daryle Ward	.258	20	47	0
Jacque Jones	.285	19	76	7
Troy O'Leary	.261	13	70	0
Rondell White	.311	13	61	5
Reggie Sanders	.232	11	37	21
Shane Spencer	.282	9	40	1
Wilton Guerrero	.267	2	23	8
Felipe Crespo	.290	4	29	3

Look for Consistency

	2000 Statistics			
	Avg	HR	RBI	SB
Ben Grieve	.279	27	104	3
Carlos Lee	.301	24	92	13
Shannon Stewart	.319	21	69	20
Geoff Jenkins	.303	34	94	11
Greg Vaughn	.254	28	74	8
Cliff Floyd	.300	22	91	24
Dmitri Young	.303	18	88	0
Ray Lankford	.253	26	65	5
B.J. Surhoff	.291	14	68	10
Ron Gant	.249	26	54	6
Henry Rodriguez	.256	20	61	1
Benny Agbayani	.289	15	60	5
Wil Cordero	.276	16	68	1
Ricky Ledee	.236	13	77	13
Bruce Aven	.250	7	29	2
Randy Winn	.252	1	16	6
Bobby Bonilla	.255	5	28	0

Production Will Drop

	2000 Statistics			
	Avg	HR	RBI	SB
Barry Bonds	.306	49	106	11
Darin Erstad	.355	25	100	28
Luis Gonzalez	.311	31	114	2
Gary Sheffield	.325	43	109	4
David Justice	.286	41	118	2
Bobby Higginson	.300	30	102	15
Glenallen Hill	.293	27	58	0
Alex Ochoa	.316	13	58	9
Al Martin	.285	15	36	10
Rickey Henderson	.233	4	32	36
Stan Javier	.275	5	40	4
Terry Shumpert	.259	9	40	8
Orlando Palmeiro	.300	0	25	4
Chad Curtis	.272	8	48	3

Sleepers

	2000 Statistics (includes minor leagues)			
	Avg	HR	RBI	SB
Dee Brown	.264	23	74	20
Jason Tyner	.295	0	41	40

Center Field

Expect A Better Year

| | 2000 Statistics | | | |
	Avg	HR	RBI	SB
Ken Griffey Jr.	.271	40	118	6
Ruben Mateo	.291	7	19	6
Gabe Kapler	.302	14	66	8
Juan Encarnacion	.289	14	72	16
Carlos Beltran	.247	7	44	13
Peter Bergeron	.245	5	31	11
Doug Glanville	.275	8	52	31
Chris Singleton	.254	11	62	22
Torii Hunter	.280	5	44	4
Jeff Abbott	.274	3	29	2
Roger Cedeno	.282	6	26	25
Devon White	.266	4	13	3
Jacob Cruz	.241	0	5	1

Look for Consistency

| | 2000 Statistics | | | |
	Avg	HR	RBI	SB
Bernie Williams	.307	30	121	13
Jose Cruz	.242	31	76	15
Kenny Lofton	.278	15	73	30
Mike Cameron	.267	19	78	24
Jay Payton	.291	17	62	5
Todd Hollandsworth	.269	19	47	18
Marvin Benard	.263	12	55	22
Brady Anderson	.257	19	50	16
Marquis Grissom	.244	14	62	20

Production Will Drop

| | 2000 Statistics | | | |
	Avg	HR	RBI	SB
Brian Giles	.315	35	123	6
Andruw Jones	.303	36	104	21
Johnny Damon	.327	16	88	46
Richard Hidalgo	.314	44	122	13
Jim Edmonds	.295	42	108	10
Preston Wilson	.264	31	121	36
Carl Everett	.300	34	108	11
Steve Finley	.280	35	96	12
Garret Anderson	.286	35	117	7
Terrence Long	.288	18	80	5
Tom Goodwin	.263	6	58	55
Gerald Williams	.274	21	89	12
Ruben Rivera	.208	17	57	8
Adrian Brown	.315	4	28	13
Damon Buford	.251	15	48	4

Sleepers

| | 2000 Statistics (includes minor leagues) | | | |
	Avg	HR	RBI	SB
Corey Patterson	.253	24	84	28
Juan Pierre	.325	0	53	54
Milton Bradley	.278	8	44	12
Chad Hermansen	.214	13	46	16
Alex Escobar	.288	16	67	24
Vernon Wells	.242	16	66	23
Emil Brown	.281	8	41	29

Right Field

Expect A Better Year

| | 2000 Statistics | | | |
	Avg	HR	RBI	SB
Shawn Green	.269	24	99	24
Albert Belle	.281	23	103	0
Juan Gonzalez	.289	22	67	1
Raul Mondesi	.271	24	67	22
Larry Walker	.309	9	51	5
J.D. Drew	.295	18	57	17
Matt Stairs	.227	21	81	5
Brian Jordan	.264	17	77	10
Steve Cox	.283	11	35	1
Bubba Trammell	.265	10	45	4
Tony Gwynn	.323	1	17	0
Jose Guillen	.253	10	41	3

Look for Consistency

| | 2000 Statistics | | | |
	Avg	HR	RBI	SB
Vladimir Guerrero	.345	44	123	9
Manny Ramirez	.351	38	122	1
Bobby Abreu	.316	25	79	28
Jeromy Burnitz	.232	31	98	6
Magglio Ordonez	.315	32	126	18
Tim Salmon	.290	34	97	0
Dante Bichette	.294	23	90	5
Derek Bell	.266	18	69	8
Michael Tucker	.267	15	36	13
Mark Kotsay	.298	12	57	19
Trot Nixon	.276	12	60	8
Eric Davis	.303	6	40	1
Midre Cummings	.277	4	24	0

Production Will Drop

| | 2000 Statistics | | | |
	Avg	HR	RBI	SB
Sammy Sosa	.320	50	138	7
Jermaine Dye	.321	33	118	0
Matt Lawton	.305	13	88	23
Moises Alou	.355	30	114	3
Jeffrey Hammonds	.335	20	106	14
Ellis Burks	.344	24	96	5
Paul O'Neill	.283	18	100	14
Eric Owens	.293	6	51	29
Jay Buhner	.253	26	82	0
John Vander Wal	.299	24	94	11
Danny Bautista	.285	11	59	6
Rich Becker	.242	8	39	2
Armando Rios	.266	10	50	3
Dave Martinez	.274	5	47	8

Sleepers

| | 2000 Statistics (includes minor leagues) | | | |
	Avg	HR	RBI	SB
Adam Piatt	.290	13	65	3
Lance Berkman	.305	27	94	10
Ichiro Suzuki*	.387	12	54	21
Jeremy Giambi	.265	12	58	1
Timoniel Perez	.348	8	48	17
Mike Darr	.317	10	95	22

(* played for Orix Blue Wave in Japan's Pacific Lg)

Designated Hitter

Expect A Better Year

	2000 Statistics			
	Avg	HR	RBI	SB
Jose Canseco	.252	15	49	2
David Ortiz	.282	10	63	1
Olmedo Saenz	.313	9	33	1
John Jaha	.175	1	5	1

Production Will Drop

	2000 Statistics			
	Avg	HR	RBI	SB
Frank Thomas	.328	43	143	1
Edgar Martinez	.324	37	145	3
Brad Fullmer	.295	32	104	3
Scott Spiezio	.242	17	49	1
Luis Polonia	.276	7	30	12

Look for Consistency

	2000 Statistics			
	Avg	HR	RBI	SB
Harold Baines	.254	11	39	0
Butch Huskey	.261	9	45	1

Sleepers

	2000 Statistics (includes minor leagues)			
	Avg	HR	RBI	SB
Billy McMillon	.334	17	74	4
Russ Branyan	.242	37	98	1

Starting Pitchers

Expect A Better Year

	2000 Statistics				
	W	L	ERA	Sv	Ratio
Barry Zito	7	4	2.72	0	1.18
Kevin Millwood	10	13	4.66	0	1.29
Adam Eaton	7	4	4.13	0	1.44
Kris Benson	10	12	3.85	0	1.34
Gil Meche	4	4	3.78	0	1.34
Joey Hamilton	2	1	3.55	0	1.21
Andy Ashby	12	13	4.92	0	1.39
Pete Harnisch	8	6	4.74	0	1.37
Alex Fernandez	4	4	4.13	0	1.43
Kerry Wood	8	7	4.80	0	1.45
Jaret Wright	3	4	4.70	0	1.39
Brad Penny	8	7	4.81	0	1.50
Rob Bell	7	8	5.00	0	1.45
Shane Reynolds	7	8	5.22	0	1.49
Pete Schourek	3	10	5.11	0	1.43
Francisco Cordova	6	8	5.21	0	1.53
Seth Etherton	5	1	5.52	0	1.49
Dave Mlicki	6	11	5.58	0	1.57
Jose Rosado	2	2	5.86	0	1.37
Chris Carpenter	10	12	6.26	0	1.64
Masato Yoshii	6	15	5.86	0	1.52
Steve Woodard	4	10	5.85	0	1.53
Jason Schmidt	2	5	5.40	0	1.77
Charles Nagy	2	7	8.21	0	1.61
Scott Karl	4	5	7.42	0	1.96
Scott Erickson	5	8	7.87	0	1.89
Ismael Valdes	2	7	5.64	0	1.53
Paul Byrd	2	9	6.51	0	1.49
Omar Olivares	4	8	6.75	0	1.80
Jason Johnson	1	10	7.02	0	1.67
Hideki Irabu	2	5	7.24	0	1.66
Darren Oliver	2	9	7.42	0	1.79
Dan Serafini	2	5	5.51	0	1.64
Omar Daal	4	19	6.14	0	1.68
Jose Lima	7	16	6.65	0	1.62
John Snyder	3	10	6.17	0	1.76
Kip Wells	6	9	6.02	0	1.86
Ryan Rupe	5	6	6.92	0	1.67
Juan Guzman	0	1	43.20	0	5.40
Miguel Batista	2	7	8.54	0	1.87
Mike Thurman	4	9	6.42	0	1.79
David Cone	4	14	6.91	0	1.77
Vladimir Nunez	0	6	7.90	0	1.79
Trey Moore	1	5	6.62	0	2.15
Roy Halladay	4	7	10.64	0	2.20
Horacio Estrada	3	0	6.29	0	2.05
Mike Lincoln	0	3	10.89	0	2.37
Bill Pulsipher	0	2	12.15	0	2.70

Look for Consistency

	2000 Statistics				
	W	L	ERA	Sv	Ratio
Pedro Martinez	18	6	1.74	0	0.74
Randy Johnson	19	7	2.64	0	1.12
Kevin Brown	13	6	2.58	0	0.99
Greg Maddux	19	9	3.00	0	1.07
Tom Glavine	21	9	3.40	0	1.19
Al Leiter	16	8	3.20	0	1.21
Mike Hampton	15	10	3.14	0	1.35
Mike Mussina	11	15	3.79	0	1.19
Curt Schilling	11	12	3.81	0	1.18
Roger Clemens	13	8	3.70	0	1.31
Jeff D'Amico	12	7	2.66	0	1.16
Woody Williams	10	8	3.75	0	1.23
Mike Sirotka	15	10	3.79	0	1.38
Rick Reed	11	5	4.11	0	1.23
Brian Anderson	11	7	4.05	0	1.24
Bartolo Colon	15	8	3.88	0	1.39
Jon Lieber	12	11	4.41	0	1.20
Orlando Hernandez	12	13	4.51	0	1.21
Carl Pavano	8	4	3.06	0	1.27
Mark Gardner	11	7	4.05	0	1.32
Gil Heredia	15	11	4.12	0	1.41
Chuck Finley	16	11	4.17	0	1.43
Andy Pettitte	19	9	4.35	0	1.46
Jeff Weaver	11	15	4.32	0	1.28
Aaron Sele	17	10	4.51	0	1.39
Darren Dreifort	12	9	4.16	0	1.36
Eric Milton	13	10	4.86	0	1.25
Denny Neagle	15	9	4.52	0	1.39
Rick Helling	16	13	4.48	0	1.43
Kirk Rueter	11	9	3.96	0	1.45
Freddy Garcia	9	5	3.91	0	1.42
James Baldwin	14	7	4.65	0	1.37
Brad Radke	12	16	4.45	0	1.38
Chuck Smith	6	6	3.23	0	1.35
Paul Abbott	9	7	4.22	0	1.36
Ramiro Mendoza	7	4	4.25	0	1.31
Randy Wolf	11	9	4.36	0	1.42
Scott Elarton	17	7	4.81	0	1.46
Kenny Rogers	13	13	4.55	0	1.47
Brian Moehler	12	9	4.50	0	1.47
Kevin Appier	15	11	4.52	0	1.55
Pat Hentgen	15	12	4.72	0	1.50
Brian Bohanon	12	10	4.68	0	1.47
Jamey Wright	7	9	4.10	0	1.49
Sidney Ponson	9	13	4.82	0	1.38
Kevin Tapani	8	12	5.01	0	1.30
Tomokazu Ohka	3	6	3.12	0	1.38
Todd Ritchie	9	8	4.81	0	1.39
Andy Benes	12	9	4.88	0	1.46
Armando Reynoso	11	12	5.27	0	1.35
Todd Stottlemyre	9	6	4.91	0	1.41
Bobby J. Jones	11	6	5.06	0	1.42
Steve Parris	12	17	4.81	0	1.55

Look for Consistency (continued)

	W	L	ERA	Sv	Ratio
Jamie Moyer	13	10	5.49	0	1.47
Hideo Nomo	8	12	4.74	0	1.47
Russ Ortiz	14	12	5.01	0	1.55
Dustin Hermanson	12	14	4.77	4	1.52
Jeff Suppan	10	9	4.94	0	1.49
Brian Meadows	13	10	5.13	0	1.52
John Halama	14	9	5.08	0	1.57
Matt Clement	13	17	5.14	0	1.56
Pedro Astacio	12	9	5.27	0	1.50
Steve Trachsel	8	15	4.80	0	1.52
Jeff Fassero	8	8	4.78	0	1.56
John Burkett	10	6	4.89	0	1.59
Reid Cornelius	4	10	4.82	0	1.48
Tim Belcher	4	5	6.86	0	1.65
Jesus Sanchez	9	12	5.34	0	1.50
A.J. Burnett	3	7	4.79	0	1.50
Blake Stein	8	8	4.68	0	1.44
Makoto Suzuki	8	10	4.34	0	1.53
Ramon Ortiz	8	6	5.09	0	1.36
Wade Miller	6	6	5.14	0	1.39
Rolando Arrojo	10	11	5.63	0	1.48
Kelvim Escobar	10	15	5.35	2	1.51
Scott Schoeneweis	7	10	5.45	0	1.47
Jimmy Haynes	12	13	5.33	0	1.65
Kent Bottenfield	8	10	5.40	0	1.53
Chris Holt	8	16	5.35	0	1.56
Ron Villone	10	10	5.43	0	1.65
Jimmy Anderson	5	11	5.25	0	1.58
Joe Nathan	5	2	5.21	0	1.63
Mark Mulder	9	10	5.44	0	1.69
Carlos Perez	5	8	5.56	0	1.56
Eric Gagne	4	6	5.15	0	1.64
Brian Rose	7	10	5.79	0	1.55
Joe Mays	7	15	5.56	0	1.62
Scott Downs	4	3	5.29	0	1.67
Pat Rapp	9	12	5.90	0	1.64
Brian Powell	2	1	5.74	0	1.50
Ramon Martinez	10	8	6.13	0	1.64
Ryan Glynn	5	7	5.58	0	1.67
Jay Witasick	6	10	5.82	0	1.67
Brian Cooper	4	8	5.90	0	1.61
Jim Brower	2	3	6.24	0	1.79
J.C. Romero	2	7	7.02	0	1.77
Dave Eiland	2	3	7.24	0	1.74
Chad Durbin	2	5	8.21	0	1.85

Production Will Drop

	2000 Statistics				
	W	L	ERA	Sv	Ratio
Tim Hudson	20	6	4.14	0	1.24
David Wells	20	8	4.11	0	1.29
Darryl Kile	20	9	3.91	0	1.18
Chan Ho Park	18	10	3.27	0	1.31
Frank Castillo	10	5	3.59	0	1.22
Livan Hernandez	17	11	3.75	0	1.36

Production Will Drop (continued)

	W	L	ERA	Sv	Ratio
Rick Ankiel	11	7	3.50	0	1.30
Ryan Dempster	14	10	3.66	0	1.36
Jarrod Washburn	7	2	3.74	0	1.20
Glendon Rusch	11	11	4.01	0	1.26
Stan Spencer	2	2	3.26	0	1.27
Robert Person	9	7	3.63	0	1.38
Garrett Stephenson	16	9	4.49	0	1.36
Jose Mercedes	14	7	4.02	0	1.47
Steve W. Sparks	7	5	4.07	1	1.32
Javier Vazquez	11	9	4.05	0	1.42
Albie Lopez	11	13	4.13	2	1.45
Cliff Politte	4	3	3.66	0	1.39
Tony Armas Jr.	7	9	4.36	0	1.31
Jim Parque	13	6	4.28	0	1.49
Dave Burba	16	6	4.47	0	1.52
Shawn Estes	15	6	4.26	0	1.59
Esteban Loaiza	10	13	4.56	1	1.43
Mark Redman	12	9	4.76	0	1.41
Bryan Rekar	7	10	4.41	0	1.38
Cal Eldred	10	2	4.58	0	1.45
Dwight Gooden	6	5	4.71	2	1.55
Jason Bere	12	10	5.47	0	1.59
Kevin Jarvis	3	4	5.95	0	1.49
Ariel Prieto	1	2	5.12	0	1.74

Sleepers

	2000 Statistics (includes minor leagues)				
	W	L	ERA	Sv	Ratio
Paul Wilson	8	9	3.49	0	1.19
Britt Reames	10	6	3.42	0	1.24
Luke Prokopec	8	4	2.53	0	1.13
Osvaldo Fernandez	10	4	4.18	0	1.34
Paxton Crawford	11	8	3.79	0	1.14
Brian Tollberg	10	5	3.29	0	1.26
Travis Harper	11	7	3.89	0	1.22
Paul Rigdon	11	6	4.32	0	1.35
Geraldo Guzman	12	8	3.81	3	1.28
Matt Wise	12	9	4.12	0	1.24
Matt Kinney	13	5	3.72	0	1.32
Dave Coggin	9	7	4.31	0	1.45
Jay Spurgeon	14	4	3.53	0	1.19
Jon Garland	13	10	3.81	0	1.44
Bronson Arroyo	10	8	4.84	0	1.44
Brian Sikorski	11	12	4.40	1	1.47
Ruben Quevedo	10	12	5.98	0	1.53
John Parrish	10	11	4.66	0	1.50
Rocky Biddle	12	8	3.78	0	1.37
Pasqual Coco	12	7	3.88	0	1.35
Tim Drew	11	10	4.96	0	1.50
Jake Westbrook	5	9	5.27	0	1.58
Marcus Jones	8	5	4.45	0	1.42
Dave Borkowski	3	3	5.99	0	1.45

Relief Pitchers

Expect A Better Year

	2000 Statistics				
	W	L	ERA	Sv	Ratio
Jeff Shaw	3	4	4.24	27	1.34
Bob Howry	2	4	3.17	7	1.17
LaTroy Hawkins	2	5	3.39	14	1.33
John Rocker	1	2	2.89	24	1.70
Kerry Ligtenberg	2	3	3.61	12	1.28
Turk Wendell	8	6	3.59	1	1.22
Carlos Reyes	1	3	5.72	1	1.34
Lorenzo Barcelo	4	2	3.69	0	1.10
Ryan Kohlmeier	0	1	2.39	13	1.71
Scott Williamson	5	8	3.29	6	1.49
Ugueth Urbina	0	1	4.05	8	1.20
Matt Mantei	1	1	4.57	17	1.46
Sang-Hoon Lee	0	0	3.09	0	1.37
Doug Jones	4	2	3.93	2	1.42
Randy Choate	0	1	4.76	0	1.29
Paul Quantrill	2	5	4.52	1	1.49

Expect A Better Year (continued)

	W	L	ERA	Sv	Ratio
Jason Christiansen	3	8	5.06	1	1.42
Jason Grimsley	3	2	5.04	1	1.47
Tim Crabtree	2	7	5.15	2	1.46
Scott Sauerbeck	5	4	4.04	1	1.81
Tim Wakefield	6	10	5.48	0	1.47
Dennis Cook	6	3	5.34	2	1.59
Guillermo Mota	1	1	6.00	0	1.30
T.J. Mathews	2	3	6.03	0	1.64
Jay Powell	1	1	5.67	0	1.78
Amaury Telemaco	1	3	6.66	0	1.60
Scott Service	1	2	6.38	1	1.75
Luis Rivera	1	0	1.23	0	1.50
Russ Springer	2	4	5.08	0	1.56
Jose Mesa	4	6	5.36	1	1.61
Jeff Zimmerman	4	5	5.30	1	1.64
Kent Mercker	1	3	6.52	0	1.78
Matt Karchner	1	1	6.14	0	2.05
Gregg Olson	0	1	5.09	0	1.58

Expect A Better Year (continued)

Name	W	L	ERA	Sv	Ratio
John Frascatore	2	4	5.42	0	1.64
John Johnstone	3	4	6.30	0	1.54
Billy Wagner	2	4	6.18	6	1.66
B.J. Ryan	2	3	5.91	0	1.57
Kevin Hodges	0	0	5.19	0	1.73
Scott Aldred	1	3	5.75	0	1.62
Francisco Cordero	1	2	5.35	0	1.75
Wayne Franklin	0	0	5.48	0	1.69
Eric Cammack	0	0	6.30	0	1.70
Brian Boehringer	0	3	5.74	0	1.79
Jack Cressend	0	0	5.27	0	1.90
Kyle Farnsworth	2	9	6.43	1	1.82
Craig Dingman	0	0	6.55	0	1.91
Stan Belinda	1	3	7.71	1	1.65
Pedro Borbon	1	1	6.48	1	1.99
Scott Linebrink	0	0	6.00	0	2.17
Leo Estrella	0	0	5.79	0	1.93
Rick Croushore	2	1	7.88	0	1.88
Sean DePaula	0	0	5.94	0	2.04
Brad Clontz	0	0	5.14	0	2.57
Steve Sparks	0	0	6.75	0	2.25
Rich Rodriguez	0	1	7.78	0	2.00
Jesse Orosco	0	0	3.86	0	2.57
Allen Watson	0	0	10.23	0	2.18
Jeff M. D'Amico	0	1	9.22	0	2.49
Grant Roberts	0	0	11.57	0	2.14
Leslie Brea	0	1	11.00	0	2.44
Mike Garcia	0	2	11.12	0	2.47
Rafael Roque	0	0	10.13	0	2.63
Brad Rigby	0	0	11.85	2	2.56
Darren Holmes	0	1	13.03	1	2.38
David Lee	0	0	11.12	1	2.82
Mike Munoz	0	1	13.50	0	3.50

Look for Consistency

Name	2000 Statistics				
	W	L	ERA	Sv	Ratio
Armando Benitez	4	4	2.61	41	1.01
Trevor Hoffman	4	7	2.99	43	1.00
Mariano Rivera	7	4	2.85	36	1.10
Derek Lowe	4	4	2.56	42	1.23
Kazuhiro Sasaki	2	5	3.16	37	1.16
Dave Veres	3	5	2.85	29	1.19
Todd Jones	2	4	3.52	42	1.44
Roberto Hernandez	4	7	3.19	32	1.35
Rudy Seanez	2	4	4.29	2	1.14
Rick Aguilera	1	2	4.91	29	1.36
Steve Kline	1	5	3.50	14	1.40
Bob Wickman	3	5	3.10	30	1.32
Mike Williams	3	4	3.50	24	1.33
John Wetteland	6	5	4.20	34	1.52
Troy Percival	5	5	4.50	32	1.44
Mike Remlinger	5	3	3.47	12	1.27
Donne Wall	5	2	3.35	1	1.06
Rich Garces	8	1	3.25	1	1.17
Greg Swindell	2	6	3.20	1	1.20
Kelly Wunsch	6	3	2.93	1	1.29
Scott Sullivan	3	6	3.47	3	1.18
John Franco	5	4	3.40	4	1.29
Keith Glauber	0	0	3.68	0	0.95
Jose Paniagua	3	0	3.47	5	1.32
Paul Shuey	4	2	3.39	0	1.27
Matt Morris	3	3	3.57	4	1.32
Dave Weathers	3	5	3.07	1	1.38
Hipolito Pichardo	6	3	3.46	1	1.37
Arthur Rhodes	5	8	4.28	0	1.15
Kevin Walker	7	1	4.18	0	1.30
Dan Miceli	6	4	4.25	0	1.29
Antonio Osuna	3	6	3.74	0	1.37
Mark Petkovsek	4	2	4.33	2	1.35
Bobby Chouinard	2	2	3.86	0	1.35
Chad Zerbe	0	0	4.50	0	1.17
Doug Brocail	5	4	4.09	0	1.40
Mike Stanton	2	3	4.10	0	1.35
Mike Venafro	3	1	3.83	1	1.51
Octavio Dotel	3	7	5.40	16	1.50
Mike Magnante	1	1	4.31	0	1.74
Julio Santana	1	5	5.67	0	1.53
Onan Masaoka	1	1	4.00	0	1.41
Byung-Hyun Kim	6	6	4.46	14	1.39
Anthony Telford	5	4	3.79	3	1.26

Look for Consistency (continued)

Name	W	L	ERA	Sv	Ratio
Al Reyes	1	0	4.58	0	1.37
John Wasdin	1	6	5.38	1	1.42
Ricky Bottalico	9	6	4.83	16	1.46
Greg McMichael	0	0	4.41	0	0.98
Jose Santiago	8	6	3.91	2	1.39
Rodney Myers	0	0	4.50	0	1.00
Ricky Rincon	2	0	2.70	0	1.50
Chris Brock	7	8	4.34	1	1.35
Scott Mullen	0	0	4.35	0	1.26
Aaron Fultz	5	2	4.67	1	1.37
Brett Tomko	7	5	4.68	1	1.43
Rheal Cormier	3	3	4.61	0	1.33
Jeff Sparks	0	1	3.54	0	1.52
Matt Whisenant	2	2	3.80	0	1.55
Terry Adams	6	9	3.52	2	1.41
Bill Simas	2	3	3.46	0	1.34
Lou Pote	1	1	3.40	1	1.37
Doug Henry	4	4	3.79	1	1.35
Juan Acevedo	3	7	3.81	0	1.31
Mike Timlin	5	4	4.18	12	1.58
Mike Trombley	4	5	4.13	4	1.46
Wayne Gomes	4	6	4.40	7	1.45
Adam Bernero	0	1	4.19	0	1.34
Manny Aybar	2	2	4.31	0	1.37
Steve Reed	2	0	4.34	0	1.41
Lance Painter	2	0	4.72	0	1.37
Terry Mulholland	9	9	5.11	1	1.53
Rich Sauveur	0	0	4.35	0	1.35
Kris Wilson	0	1	4.19	0	1.43
Matt Blank	0	1	5.14	0	1.21
Will Cunnane	1	1	4.23	0	1.46
Allen Levrault	0	1	4.50	0	1.42
Tanyon Sturtze	5	2	4.74	0	1.48
Hector Mercado	0	0	4.50	0	1.43
Vicente Padilla	4	7	3.72	2	1.53
Vic Darensbourg	5	3	4.06	0	1.44
Darrell Einertson	0	0	3.55	0	1.58
Alan Embree	3	5	4.95	2	1.45
Mike Morgan	5	5	4.87	5	1.60
Chuck McElroy	3	0	4.69	0	1.48
Heathcliff Slocumb	2	4	4.98	1	1.54
Mark Guthrie	3	6	4.67	0	1.50
Miguel del Toro	2	0	5.19	0	1.33
Jerry Dipoto	0	0	3.95	0	1.54
Mike Buddie	0	0	4.50	0	1.50
Cory Lidle	4	6	5.03	0	1.48
Mark Wohlers	1	2	4.50	0	1.29
Steve Rain	3	4	4.35	0	1.47
Matt Anderson	3	2	4.72	1	1.43
Braden Looper	5	1	4.41	2	1.59
Travis Miller	2	3	3.90	1	1.72
Ricky Bones	2	3	4.54	0	1.56
Hector Carrasco	5	4	4.69	1	1.63
Kevin McGlinchy	0	0	2.16	0	2.04
Mike DeJean	4	4	4.89	0	1.58
Dan Murray	0	0	4.66	0	1.55
V. de los Santos	2	3	5.13	0	1.43
Dennys Reyes	2	1	4.53	0	1.65
Marc Wilkins	4	2	5.07	0	1.61
Jim Morris	0	0	4.35	0	1.65
Jose Silva	11	9	5.56	0	1.68
Mark Thompson	1	1	5.04	0	1.56
C.J. Nitkowski	4	9	5.25	0	1.58
Jamie Brewington	3	0	5.36	0	1.65
Sean Runyan	0	0	6.00	0	1.33
Esteban Yan	7	8	6.21	0	1.45
Armando Almanza	4	2	4.86	0	1.75
Tim Young	0	0	6.43	0	1.29
Sean Lowe	4	1	5.48	0	1.66
Rich Loiselle	2	3	5.10	0	1.72
Yorkis Perez	2	1	5.16	0	1.72
Alan Mills	4	1	5.29	2	1.84
Marc Valdes	5	5	5.08	0	1.66
Felipe Lira	5	8	5.40	0	1.62
Doug Davis	7	6	5.38	0	1.69
Jose Cabrera	2	3	5.92	2	1.53
Jesus Pena	2	1	5.13	1	1.78
Everett Stull	2	3	5.82	0	1.64
Mike Johnson	5	6	6.39	0	1.58
Scott Kamieniecki	3	4	5.59	2	1.83
Todd Erdos	0	0	5.93	2	1.66
Chris Fussell	5	3	6.30	0	1.71

Look for Consistency (continued)

	W	L	ERA	Sv	Ratio
Brett Hinchliffe	0	0	5.40	0	1.20
Ted Lilly	0	0	5.63	0	1.63
Alan Benes	2	2	5.67	0	1.67
Brandon Kolb	0	1	4.50	0	1.93
Andrew Lorraine	1	2	5.88	0	1.62
Derrick Turnbow	0	0	4.74	0	1.89
Jamie Arnold	0	3	6.18	1	1.58
Daniel Garibay	2	8	6.03	0	1.70
Paul Spoljaric	0	0	6.52	0	1.45
Allen McDill	0	0	7.20	0	1.40
Frank Rodriguez	2	1	6.27	0	1.73
Todd Belitz	0	0	2.70	0	2.40
Jay Tessmer	0	0	6.75	0	1.50
Steve Schrenk	2	3	7.33	0	1.63
Larry Luebbers	0	2	6.20	1	1.92
Jason Boyd	0	1	6.55	0	1.83
Pat Mahomes	5	3	5.46	0	1.72
Don Wengert	0	1	7.20	0	1.70
Mark Johnson	0	1	7.50	0	1.71
Peter Munro	1	1	5.96	0	2.10
Jeremy Powell	0	3	7.96	0	1.69
Mark Holzemer	0	1	7.71	0	1.71
Dan Smith	0	0	8.10	0	1.50
Brian Williams	1	1	7.23	1	1.94
Jason Ryan	0	1	7.62	0	1.81
Mark Brownson	1	0	7.20	0	2.00
Erik Hiljus	0	0	7.36	0	1.64
Jeff Wallace	2	0	7.07	0	2.13
Rob Stanifer	0	0	7.62	0	2.00
Brett Laxton	0	1	8.10	0	1.98
Calvin Maduro	0	0	9.64	0	1.93
Matt Perisho	2	7	7.37	0	1.93
Andy Larkin	0	3	7.96	1	1.96
Gabe Molina	0	0	9.00	0	2.53
Tim Byrdak	0	1	11.37	0	2.37
John Bale	0	0	14.73	0	2.18
Juan Alvarez	0	0	13.50	0	3.50

Production Will Drop

	W	L	ERA	Sv	Ratio
			2000 Statistics		
Robb Nen	4	3	1.50	41	0.85
Keith Foulke	3	1	2.97	34	1.00
Billy Koch	9	3	2.63	33	1.22
Danny Graves	10	5	2.56	30	1.35
Gabe White	11	2	2.36	5	0.94
Ray King	3	2	1.26	0	0.98
Antonio Alfonseca	5	6	4.24	45	1.51
Jose Jimenez	5	2	3.18	24	1.29
Jason Isringhausen	6	4	3.78	33	1.43
Kevin Tolar	0	0	3.00	0	0.67
Curtis Leskanic	9	3	2.56	12	1.41
Mike Myers	0	1	1.99	1	1.06
Chad Bradford	1	0	1.98	0	1.02
Scott Strickland	4	3	3.00	9	1.13
Jim Mecir	10	3	2.96	5	1.25
Steve Karsay	5	9	3.76	20	1.36
Jeff Nelson	8	4	2.45	0	1.28
Mike Fetters	6	2	3.24	5	1.20
Matt Herges	11	3	3.17	1	1.27
Bob Wells	0	7	3.65	10	1.10
Jeff Tam	3	3	2.63	3	1.27
Felix Rodriguez	4	2	2.64	3	1.31
S. Hasegawa	10	5	3.48	9	1.44
Rod Beck	3	0	3.10	0	1.13
Bruce Chen	7	4	3.29	0	1.21

Production Will Drop (continued)

	W	L	ERA	Sv	Ratio
Eddie Guardado	7	4	3.94	9	1.30
Rick White	5	9	3.52	3	1.21
Nelson Cruz	5	2	3.07	0	1.27
Mike Fyhrie	0	0	2.39	0	1.31
Mike James	2	2	3.16	2	1.25
Justin Speier	5	2	3.29	0	1.24
Bryan Ward	0	0	3.29	0	1.17
Tim Worrell	5	6	2.99	3	1.46
Chris Peters	0	1	2.86	1	1.31
Dan Plesac	5	1	3.15	0	1.50
Josias Manzanillo	2	2	3.38	0	1.40
Elmer Dessens	11	5	4.28	1	1.45
Joe Slusarski	2	7	4.21	3	1.32
Todd Van Poppel	4	5	3.75	2	1.48
Julian Tavarez	11	5	4.43	1	1.48
Matt Whiteside	2	3	4.14	0	1.32
Felix Heredia	7	3	4.76	2	1.35
Danny Patterson	5	1	3.97	0	1.46
Willie Blair	10	6	4.88	0	1.40
Buddy Groom	6	3	4.85	4	1.42
Al Levine	3	4	3.87	2	1.54
Tom Martin	1	0	4.05	0	1.41
Carlos Almanzar	4	5	4.39	0	1.41
Rob Ramsay	1	1	3.40	0	1.65
Mike Holtz	3	4	5.05	0	1.34
Jeff Brantley	2	7	5.86	23	1.68
Dan Reichert	8	10	4.70	2	1.62
Bobby M. Jones	0	1	4.15	0	1.48
Doug Creek	1	3	4.60	1	1.45
Ed Vosberg	1	1	4.13	0	1.63
Bryce Florie	0	4	4.56	1	1.54
Jerry Spradlin	4	5	6.00	7	1.48
Jonathan Johnson	1	1	6.21	0	1.83

Sleepers

	W	L	ERA	Sv	Ratio
			2000 Statistics (includes minor leagues)		
Danny Kolb	4	4	3.32	4	1.37
John Riedling	9	4	2.49	6	1.24
Dave Maurer	6	3	3.15	0	1.17
Mark Buehrle	12	5	2.86	0	1.09
Cam Cairncross	2	1	2.11	5	1.21
Jason Marquis	5	5	4.85	0	1.48
Kevin Beirne	2	5	5.42	0	1.40
Ben Weber	5	10	3.52	7	1.28
Gene Stechschulte	5	1	3.70	26	1.29
Joel Pineiro	10	2	3.73	0	1.26
Jason Green	11	4	3.14	16	1.37
Craig House	3	3	4.10	21	1.42
Danny Mota	5	3	2.67	8	1.20
Matt DeWitt	5	5	5.51	15	1.69
Tom Jacquez	5	4	3.02	5	1.35
Will Ohman	7	4	2.17	3	1.30
Darwin Cubillan	4	1	4.25	8	1.42
Trevor Enders	6	5	3.76	0	1.17
Randy Keisler	15	5	3.34	0	1.36
Kane Davis	3	5	5.17	0	1.52
Jim Mann	3	4	3.20	3	1.20
Matt Ginter	12	8	2.81	0	1.26
Ismael Villegas	2	6	5.03	4	1.58
Doug Nickle	8	3	2.81	16	1.05
Buddy Carlyle	8	6	4.62	0	1.42
Oswaldo Mairena	2	6	3.75	0	1.42
David Moraga	14	7	3.99	0	1.35

STATS' Top 50 Prospects

STATS ranks the top 50 prospects in baseball below. Only players who haven't exceeded major league rookie limits of 130 at-bats and 50 innings pitched were considered. The ages listed are as of Opening Day (April 1, 2001).

Hitters	Pos	Age	2000 Levels	G	Avg	HR	RBI	SB	OBP	SLG
1. Corey Patterson, ChC	OF	21	Majors/AA	129	.253	24	84	28	.330	.477
3. Carlos Pena, Tex	1B	22	AA	138	.299	28	105	12	.414	.533
4. Alex Escobar, NYM	OF	22	AA	122	.288	16	67	24	.375	.487
7. Vernon Wells, Tor	OF	22	Majors/AAA	130	.242	16	66	23	.312	.430
8. Josh Hamilton, TB	OF	19	A	96	.301	13	61	14	.345	.474
10. Antonio Perez, Sea	SS	19	A+	98	.276	17	63	28	.376	.527
11. Nick Johnson, NYY	1B	22		Did Not Play—Injured						
12. Jose Ortiz, Oak	2B	23	Majors/AAA	138	.348	24	109	22	.406	.567
13. Sean Burroughs, SD	3B	20	AA	108	.291	2	42	6	.383	.401
16. Dee Brown, KC	OF	23	Majors/AAA	140	.264	23	74	20	.320	.476
17. Alfonso Soriano, NYY	SS	23	Majors/AAA	133	.279	14	69	16	.314	.454
18. Joe Crede, CWS	3B	22	Majors/AA	145	.307	21	97	3	.383	.488
19. J.R. House, Pit	C	21	A	110	.348	23	90	1	.414	.586
20. Hee Seop Choi, ChC	1B	22	AA/A+	132	.298	25	95	7	.383	.557
21. Aubrey Huff, TB	3B	24	Majors/AAA	147	.309	24	90	2	.377	.538
22. D'Angelo Jimenez, NYY	SS	23	AAA/A+/R	37	.210	2	7	2	.322	.323
26. Marcus Giles, Atl	2B	22	AA	132	.290	17	62	25	.388	.472
27. Brad Wilkerson, Mon	OF	23	AAA/AA	129	.295	18	79	13	.416	.537
28. Kevin Mench, Tex	OF	23	A+	132	.334	27	121	19	.427	.615
29. Jack Cust, Hou	OF	22	AA	129	.293	20	75	12	.440	.526
30. Gookie Dawkins, Cin	SS	21	Majors/AA	109	.230	6	34	22	.305	.357
31. Austin Kearns, Cin	OF	20	A	136	.306	27	104	18	.415	.558
34. Dernell Stenson, Bos	1B	22	AAA	98	.268	23	71	0	.349	.487
35. Adam Dunn, Cin	OF	21	A	122	.281	16	79	24	.428	.469
36. Jimmy Rollins, Phi	SS	22	Majors/AAA	147	.279	12	74	27	.341	.449
37. Mike Cuddyer, Min	3B	22	AA	138	.263	6	61	5	.351	.394
39. Wilson Betemit, Atl	SS	20	A-	69	.331	5	37	3	.393	.457
41. Keith Reed, Bal	OF	22	A	135	.264	19	90	29	.332	.434
42. Jason Hart, Oak	1B	23	AAA/AA	140	.324	31	125	4	.400	.580
46. Felipe Lopez, Tor	SS	20	AA	127	.257	9	41	12	.303	.371
50. Keith Ginter, Hou	2B	24	Majors/AA	130	.332	27	95	24	.454	.581

Pitchers	Pos	Age	2000 Levels	W	L	ERA	IP	H	BB	SO
2. Ryan Anderson, Sea	LHSP	21	AAA	5	8	3.98	104.0	83	55	146
5. C.C. Sabathia, Cle	LHSP	20	AA/A+	6	9	3.57	146.1	123	72	159
6. Ben Sheets, Mil	RHSP	22	AAA/AA	8	8	2.40	153.2	132	56	119
9. Jon Rauch, CWS	RHSP	22	AA/A+	16	4	2.66	166.0	138	49	187
14. Roy Oswalt, Hous	RHSP	23	AA/A+	15	7	2.21	175.0	158	33	188
15. Josh Beckett, Fla	RHSP	20	A	2	3	2.12	59.1	45	15	61
23. Kurt Ainsworth, SF	RHSP	22	AA	10	9	3.30	158.0	138	63	130
24. Matt Ginter, CWS	RHSP	23	Majors/AA	12	8	2.81	189.0	171	67	132
25. Chris George, KC	LHSP	21	AAA/AA	11	7	3.68	142.0	139	71	107
32. Jesus Colome, TB	RHSP	20	AA	10	6	3.96	125.0	117	57	104
33. Bobby Bradley, Pit	RHSP	20	A	8	2	2.29	82.2	62	21	118
38. Chin-Hui Tsao, Col	RHSP	19	A	11	8	2.73	145.0	119	40	187
40. Matt Belisle, Atl	RHSP	20	A	12	9	2.83	181.0	151	29	168
43. Aaron Myette, Tex	RHSP	23	Majors/AAA/AA	7	5	4.16	129.2	114	68	107
44. Ben Christensen, ChC	RHSP	23	AA/A+	7	3	2.36	106.2	79	30	105
45. Danys Baez, Cle	RHSP	23	AA/A+	6	11	4.02	152.1	143	52	133
47. Luis Rivera, Bal	RHSP	22	Majors/AAA/R	1	3	5.18	41.2	47	30	23
48. Donnie Bridges, Mon	RHSP	22	AA/A+	16	12	2.68	201.1	162	69	150
49. Jerome Williams, SF	RHSP	19	A+	7	6	2.94	125.2	89	48	115

About STATS, Inc.

STATS, Inc. is the nation's leading sports information and statistical analysis company, providing detailed sports services for a wide array of commercial clients. In January 2000, STATS was purchased by News Digital Media, the digital division of News Corporation. News Digital Media engages in three primary activities: operating FOXNews.com, FOXSports.com, FOXMarketwire.com and FOX.com; developing related interactive services; and directing investment activities and strategy for News Corporation, as they relate to digital media.

As one of the fastest growing companies in sports, STATS provides the most detailed, up-to-the-minute sports information to professional teams, print and broadcast media, software developers and interactive service providers around the country. STATS recently was recognized as "one of Chicago's 100 most influential technology players" by *Crain's Chicago Business* and has been one of 16 finalists for KPMG/Peat Marwick's Illinois High Tech Award for three consecutive years. Some of our major clients include Fox Sports, the Associated Press, America Online, *The Sporting News*, ESPN, Electronic Arts, MSNBC, SONY and Topps. Much of the information we provide is available to the public via STATS On-Line. With a computer and a modem, you can follow action in the four major professional sports, as well as NCAA football and basketball and other professional and college sports.

STATS Publishing, a division of STATS, Inc., produces 12 annual books, including the *Major League Handbook*, *The Scouting Notebook*, the *Pro Football Handbook*, the *Pro Basketball Handbook* and the *Hockey Handbook*. In 1998, we introduced two baseball encyclopedias, the *All-Time Major League Handbook* and the *All-Time Baseball Sourcebook*. Together they combine for more than 5,000 pages of baseball history. Also available is *From Abba Dabba to Zorro: The World of Baseball Nicknames*, a wacky look at monikers and their origins. A new football title was launched in 1999, the *Pro Football Scoreboard*, and we added the *Pro Football Sourcebook* in 2000. All of our publications deliver STATS' expertise to fans, scouts, general managers and media around the country.

In addition, STATS Fantasy Sports is at the forefront of the booming fantasy sports industry. We develop fantasy baseball, football, basketball, hockey, golf and auto racing games for FOXSports.com. We also feature the first historical baseball simulation game created specifically for the Internet—FOX Diamond Legends. No matter what time of year, STATS Fantasy Sports has a fantasy game to keep even the most passionate sports fan satisfied.

Information technology has grown by leaps and bounds in the last decade, and STATS will continue to be at the forefront as both a vendor and supplier of the most up-to-date, in-depth sports information available. For those of you on the information superhighway, you always can catch STATS in our area on America Online or at our Internet site.

For more information on our products, or on joining our reporter network, contact us via:

America Online — Keyword: STATS

Internet — www.stats.com

Toll Free in the USA at 1-800-63-STATS (1-800-637-8287)

Outside the USA at 1-847-470-8798

Or write to:

STATS, Inc.
8130 Lehigh Ave.
Morton Grove, IL 60053

Index

706

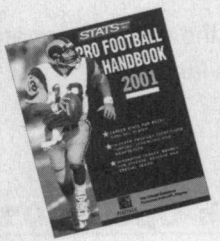

Books (Free first-class shipping for books over $10)

Qty	Product Name	Item Number	Price	Total
	STATS Major League Handbook 2001	HB01	$ 19.95	
	STATS Major League Handbook 2001 (Comb-bound)	HC01	$ 24.95	
	The Scouting Notebook 2001	SN01	$ 19.95	
	The Scouting Notebook 2001 (Comb-bound)	SC01	$ 24.95	
	STATS Minor League Handbook 2001	MH01	$ 19.95	
	STATS Minor League Handbook 2001 (Comb-bound)	MC01	$ 24.95	Sold Out!
	STATS Player Profiles 2001	PP01	$ 19.95	
	STATS Player Profiles 2001 (Comb-bound)	PC01	$ 24.95	
	STATS Minor League Scouting Notebook 2001	MN01	$ 19.95	
	STATS Batter Vs. Pitcher Match-Ups! 2001	BP01	$ 24.95	
	STATS Ballpark Sourcebook: Diamond Diagrams	BSDD	$ 24.95	
	STATS Baseball Scoreboard 2001	SB01	$ 19.95	
	STATS Pro Football Handbook 2001	FH01	$ 19.95	
	STATS Pro Football Handbook 2001 (Comb-bound)	FC01	$ 24.95	
	STATS Pro Football Sourcebook 2001	PF01	$ 19.95	
	STATS Hockey Handbook 2000-01	HH01	$ 19.95	
	STATS Pro Basketball Handbook 2000-01	BH01	$ 19.95	
	STATS All-Time Major League Handbook, 2nd Edition	ATHB	$ 79.95	

Total

Books Under $10 (Please include $2.00 S&H for each book/magazine)

	From Abba Dabba to Zorro: The World of Baseball Nicknames	ABBA	$ 9.95	
	STATS Baseball's Terrific 20	KID1	$ 9.95	
	STATS Player Projections Update 2001	PJUP	$ 9.95	

Total

Previous Editions (Please Circle appropriate years and include $2.00 S&H for each book)

	Product	Years	Price	Total
	STATS Major League Handbook	'90 '91 '92 '93 '94 '95 '96 '97 '98 '99 '00	$ 9.95	
	The Scouting Notebook/Report	'95 '96 '97 '98 '99 '00	$ 9.95	
	STATS Player Profiles	'93 '94 '95 '96 '97 '98 '99 '00	$ 9.95	
	STATS Minor League Handbook	'92 '93 '94 '95 '96 '97 '98 '99 '00	$ 9.95	
	STATS Minor League Scouting Notebook	'95 '96 '97 '98 '99 '00	$ 9.95	
	STATS Batter Vs. Pitcher Match-Ups!	'94 '95 '96 '97 '98 '99 '00	$ 9.95	
	STATS Diamond Chronicles	'97 '98 '99 '00	$ 9.95	
	STATS Baseball Scoreboard	'91 '92 '93 '94 '95 '96 '97 '98 '99 '00	$ 9.95	
	Pro Football Revealed: The 100-Yard War	'94 '95 '96 '97 '98	$ 9.95	
	STATS Pro Football Handbook	'95 '96 '97 '98 '99 '00	$ 9.95	
	STATS Pro Football Scoreboard	'99 '00	$ 9.95	
	STATS Pro Football Sourcebook	'00	$ 9.95	
	STATS Hockey Handbook	'96-97 '97-98 '98-99 '99-00	$ 9.95	
	STATS Pro Basketball Handbook	'93-94 '94-95 '95-96 '96-97 '97-98 '98-99 '99-00	$ 9.95	
	All-Time Major League Handbook (Slightly dinged)	First Edition	$ 45.00	
	All-Time Major League Sourcebook (Slightly dinged)	First Edition	$ 45.00	

Total

TOTAL

Mail:
STATS, Inc.
8130 Lehigh Avenue
Morton Grove, IL 60053

Phone:
1-800-63-STATS
(847) 677-3322

Fax:
(847) 470-9140

Bill To:
Company_____
Name_____
Address_____
City_____ State_____ Zip_____
Phone ( )_____ Ext.____ Fax ( )_____
E-mail Address_____

Ship To: *(Fill in this section if shipping address differs from billing address)*
Company_____
Name_____
Address_____
City_____ State_____ Zip_____
Phone ( )_____ Ext.____ Fax ( )_____
E-mail Address_____

Method of payment:
All prices stated
in U.S. Dollars

❏ Charge to my *(circle one)*
   Visa
   MasterCard
   American Express
   Discover

❏ Check or Money Order
   (U.S. funds only)

Please include credit card number
and expiration date with charge orders!

Exp. Date [/]
   Month Year

X_____
   Signature *(as shown on credit card)*

Totals for STATS Products:

Books	[ ]
Books Under $10 *	[ ]
Prior Book Editions *	[ ]
order 2 or more books/subtract: $1.00/book *(Does not include prior editions)*	[ ]
Illinois residents add 8.5% sales tax	[ ]
Sub Total	[ ]

Shipping Costs

Canada	**Add $4.00/book**	[ ]
* **All books under $10**	**Add $2.00/book**	[ ]
	Grand Total	[ ]
	(No other discounts apply)	

(Orders subject to availability)

Free First Class Shipping For Books Over $10